W9-CHP-062

WORK YOUR WAY AROUND THE WORLD

By Susan Griffith

Distributed in the U.S.A.
by Peterson's, a division of Thomson Learning
2000 Lenox Drive, Lawrenceville, New Jersey 08648-4764
www.petersons.com
800-338-3282

Published by Vacation Work, 9 Park End Street, Oxford
www.vacationwork.co.uk

WORK YOUR WAY AROUND THE WORLD

by Susan Griffith

First published 1983

Revised every other year

Tenth edition 2001

Copyright © 2001

ISBN 1 85458 251 8

Cover Design and Chapter Headings
Miller Craig & Cocking Design Partnership

Maps by William Swan

Typeset by Wordview Publishing Services (01865-201562)

Printed by William Clowes Ltd., Beccles, Suffolk, England

Contents

Work Your Way

Work Your Way in Europe

Work Your Way Worldwide

To our North American Readers: Your fact-finding mission and job journey abroad will differ from your British counterparts. Because the US and Canada do not belong to the European Union (Austria, Belgium, Denmark, Finland, France, Germany, Greece, Ireland, Italy, Luxembourg, the Netherlands, Portugal, Spain, Sweden and the United Kingdom), there will not be the job reciprocity in these countries or some of the special schemes which British travellers enjoy. Getting a work permit will prove difficult for American citizens – and sometimes the best jobs can be had without one. Remember, too, that certain British expressions may be unfamiliar to American ears and that wages and prices are normally stated in pounds sterling (£1=$1.49 at the time of going to press).

Preface

For this tenth edition of *Work Your Way Around the World* my network of informants has encompassed a Canadian woman who crewed a luxury yacht along the coast of Turkey, a postgraduate in computing who worked at a children's interactive museum in Bolivia, a single mother who fixed up a live-in nanny position in Spain, an Irishman who made a small fortune by working 14-hour days at a tree nursery in northern Germany, a gap year student from Cardiff who taught at a primary school in Zanzibar, a politics graduate who worked at a children's summer camp in Poland, a female welder who packed melons in Western Australia, the owner of a printing business who discovered he preferred teaching English in Brazil, an American writer (*nom de plume* the Pizza Chronicler) who did odd jobs in the Swiss Alps to fund trips around North Africa and Eastern Europe, and a one-time council worker from Merseyside who worked variously at a hostel in Auckland, a sandwich shop in a beach suburb of Sydney and at last report on a cruise ship in the Red Sea. Almost with one voice, they urge people whatever their backgrounds to give it a go and expose themselves to the unexpected friendliness and generosity of foreign residents and fellow travellers.

The correspondence which this book generates (increasingly via email) is one of my chief delights. The first edition was published in 1983 which means that some of the individuals who blazed a trail as working travellers a decade or more ago are now in a position to help the new generation of working travellers. For example a former gap year student who now runs a language school in Brazil invites students to come and conduct conversation classes in exchange for trips into Amazonia (see page 442); an American who has settled in Thailand on an organic farm welcomes volunteers (page 517); and a British pilot who used *Work Your Way Around the World* in the early days now publishes a book and runs a web-site on which pilots post details of free or heavily subsidised flights on private planes (page 57).

Anybody who occasionally feels the call of the road or the spirit of adventure flicker will enjoy reading this book and dreaming. One of the more striking images of the much-maligned Millennium Dome in Greenwich was the serried rows of hamster cages in the Work Zone followed by more cages, doors ajar, and finally doors wide open and the cages empty. I doubt that the zone designers imagined these liberated creatures queuing up for a no-frills flight but that is the choice that humans have if they are feeling caged. There is no time like the present to take stock and ask yourself whether or not you want to be swept along by the current trend that sees people in the developed world working longer hours and experiencing more stress.

My aim has been to make the information in these 544 pages as concrete and up-to-the-minute as possible, to cut all the vague generalities and waffle. Nothing is more irritating than to pick up a book or article on the subject of working abroad than to read 'you'll have to depend on word of mouth' or 'for information on the visa situation, contact the embassy'. But amongst all the specific contact addresses, web-sites and realistic practical advice, the stories of working travellers are interwoven to inspire and encourage. This book tries to renew optimism and spark the imagination of all potential travellers.

Susan Griffith
Cambridge
January 2001

Acknowledgments

This new revised edition of *Work Your Way Around the World* would not have been possible without the help of hundreds of travellers who have generously shared their information. Some have been writing to me since the early editions of this book in the mid-1980s, and their loyalty is greatly appreciated.

As well as all the people who helped with previous editions, many of whose names appear throughout these pages, we would like to thank the travellers who have made a contribution over the past two years. In one case, a contributor expended half his worldly wealth (while working on a fruit farm in France) to buy a stamp to send along his story.

Robert Abblett (whose name appears first not just because of its place in the alphabet), Steve Bastick, Roger Blake, Daniel Boothby, John Boyland, Mónica Boza, Simon Brooks, John Buckley, Sofie Buelens, Catharine Carfoot, Amelia Cook, Jennie Cox, Nicola & Peter Dickinson, Jacqueline Edwards, Dan Eldridge, Felix Fernandez, Tony Forrester, James Gillespie, Emiliano Giovannoni, Jane Harris, Emma Hoare, Jennifer Holland, Danny Jacobson, Sarah Johnson, Allan Kirkpatrick, Annette Kunigagon, Aaron Lenhart, Michelle Manion, Emma Louise Parkes, Emma Purcell, Gordon Robertson, Sara Runnalls, Caroline Scott, Bridgid Seymour-East, Adam Skuse, Darren Slevin, Wayne Stimson, Joseph Tame, Elizabeth Tenney, Murray Turner, Theo West, Juniper Wilkinson, Julee Wyld and Ben Yeomans.

INTRODUCTION

The Decision to Go

For many, deciding to get up and go is the biggest stumbling-block. Often the hardest step is fixing a departure date. Once you have bought a ticket, explained to your friends and family that you are off to see the world (they will either be envious or disapproving) and packed away your possessions, the rest seems to look after itself. Inevitably first-time travellers suffer some separation anxieties and pre-departure blues as they contemplate leaving behind the comfortable routines of home. But these are usually much worse in anticipation than in retrospect. As long as you have enough motivation, together with some money and a copy of this book, you are all set to have a great time abroad.

Either you follow your first impulse and opt for an immediate change of scenery, or you plan a job and a route in advance. On the one hand people use working as a means to an end; they work in order to fund further travelling. Other people look upon a job abroad as an end in itself, a way to explore other cultures, a means of satisfying their curiosity about whether there is any truth in the clichés about other nationalities. Often it is the best way to shake off the boredom which comes with routine. Zoe Drew felt quite liberated when she decided to drop everything – her 'cushy secretarial job, Debenhams account card, stiletto heels' – and embark on a working holiday around Europe. Bruce Lawson finally kicked over the traces of the 'Office Job from Hell' and went off to Thailand to teach English.

When you are wondering whether you are the right sort to work abroad, do not imagine you are a special case. It is not only students, school-leavers and people on the dole who enjoy the chance to travel and work, but also a large number of people with a profession, craft or trade which they were happy to abandon temporarily. We have heard from a man who left the Met Office to pick grapes in Pauillac, a sixth former teaching in Nepal, a mechanical engineer crewing on yachts in the South Pacific, an Israeli busker in Switzerland, a career civil servant who enjoyed washing dishes in a Munich restaurant, a physiotherapist who has packed cod in Iceland, a nurse who busked in Norway and another who has worked on a sheep station in Australia, an Australian teacher who became a nanny in Istanbul, a Scottish lawyer who worked as a chalet girl in a French ski resort, a German tourism trainee who planted trees in Canada, a chartered surveyor who took more than two years off from his job to work his way around the world and a journalist and tour operator couple who picked up casual jobs to fund their 'Stuff Mammon World Tour' and ended up living quite comfortably in Hong Kong. They were motivated not by a desire to earn money but by a craving for new and different experiences, and a conviction that not all events which make up one's life need to be career-furthering or 'success'-oriented.

PREPARATION

It is not the Mr. Micawbers of this world who succeed at getting jobs. If you sit around 'waiting for something to turn up' you will soon find yourself penniless with no prospects for replenishing your travel funds. If you wait in idleness at home or if you sit in your *pension* all day worrying about your dwindling pesetas or drachmas, hesitating and dithering because you are convinced the situation is hopeless or that you lack the necessary documents to work, you will get absolutely nowhere.

Every successful venture combines periodic flights of fancy with methodical planning. The majority of us lack the courage (or the recklessness) just to get up and go. And any homework you do ahead of time will benefit you later, if only because it will give you more confidence. But it is important to strike a good balance between slavishly following a predetermined itinerary which might prevent you from grasping opportunities as they arise and setting off with no idea of what you're looking for. Many travel converts regret their initial decision to buy an air ticket with a fixed return date.

For many people, a shortage of money is the main obstacle. It is the rare individual who, like Ian McArthur, specialises in 'reckless arrivals' (Istanbul with £5, Cairo with $20 between him and a friend, New York with $1). Other people wait until they have substantial savings before they dare leave home which gives them the enviable freedom to work only when they want to. Sometimes pennilessness acts as a spur to action as it did in the case of Jason Davies. His timidity had been getting the better of him until he realised in Nice he was down to his last 100 francs, whereupon he decided to stop being so fussy about the restaurants he approached for work. The next day he found a job.

Anyone embarking on an extended trip will have to have a certain amount of capital to buy tickets, visas, insurance (see below), etc. But it is amazing how a little can go a long way if you are willing to take a wide variety of casual jobs en route and willing to weather the financial doldrums. Stephen Psallidas had £40 one December and four months later (most of which was spent working as a waiter in Paris) he had £1,600 for a planned year in Australia. An even more impressive rags to riches story came from Mark Hurley who spent his last 3,000 drachmas on the ferry from Athens to the island of Santorini, and had to borrow from some new-found travelling companions for food and accommodation:

> *The next day we all tried to find work with me trying harder than the others because I was skint and going into debt. After looking for work every possible hour of the full four days, I was just about to give it all up as a bad joke, when I pulled myself together – 200 Nos in four days doesn't do a lot for your self-esteem – and had another look in a small village called Kamari. The last hotel I came to was still under construction and said they would take me on to help the tiler which was great. I started the next day for dr5,000 a day and as much as I could eat. The job lasted five weeks, by which time I had paid back my friends. Later I got a job in a winery and settled down there. I met so many great people from all over the world, and have filled two address books. After two and a half years I had £4,500.*

Money

It is of course always a good idea to have an emergency fund in reserve if possible, or at least access to money from home should you run into difficulties (see *In Extremis*). Yet a surprising number of our correspondents have written in with the advice not to bother saving money before leaving home. Adrian McCay is just one who advocates packing your bags and going even if you have only £10 (though he later confesses that he left for Australia with £300). How much you decide to set aside before leaving will depend on whether or not you have a gambling streak. But even gamblers should take only sensible risks. If you don't have much cash, it's probably advisable to have a return ticket. For example, if you decide to crew on a yacht from the Mediterranean and don't have much money, you could buy a very cheap last minute return flight to Rhodes or the Canaries. If you succeed and waste the return half of your charter, wonderful; if not, you will have had a few weeks in the sun – disappointing perhaps but not desperate.

Attitudes to saving vary too. A Malaysian student, T. P. Lye, thinks that there is no better feeling than planning travels while saving for them (assuming you realise your ambition). On the other hand, Ian McArthur finds saving over a long period depressing and starts to long for those pints of lager and late-night curries of which he has been deprived. But even Ian admits that 'living on the edge' is no fun when only a couple of hundreds of unattainable pounds stand between you and the air ticket you want to buy. When Xuela Edwards returned after two years of working her way around Europe, she tried to hang on to the travelling mentality which makes it much easier to save money:

> *My advice is to consider your home country in the same way as others. It makes you more resourceful. Try to avoid the car loans and high living that usually make up home life. I'm sure that the reason bulb workers in Holland for example save so much money is because they live in tents (which I admit would be tricky at home).*

Mike Tunnicliffe spent more on his world travels than he intended but didn't regret it:

> *Originally, I intended to finance my year with casual work and return to England having spent only the price of my ticket. In the end, I delved far*

deeper into my life's savings than I had intended to do, but I was fortunate in having savings on which to draw, and I made the conscious decision to enjoy my year while I had the chance. In other words, fun now, pay later!

Once you are resolved to travel, set a realistic target amount to save and then go for it wholeheartedly. Estimate how long it will take you to raise the desired amount and stick to the deadline as if your home country was going to sink into the ocean the day after. Don't get just any job, get one which is either highly paid (easier said than done of course) or one which offers as much overtime as you want. Dedicated working travellers consider a 70-hour week quite tolerable which will have the additional advantage of leaving you too tired to conduct an expensive social life. If you are already on the road and want to save, head for a place which allows this possibility, even if it won't be much fun. Adam Cook spent a miserable eight weeks picking peaches for an impossible French farmer but had saved £1,000 by the end of it. Murray Turner saved £4,000 in Hong Kong which soon made him forget the horrors of labouring on consecutive night shifts. If you have collected some assets before setting off, you are luckier than most. Property owners can arrange for the rental money to follow them at regular intervals.

The average budget of a travelling student is about £20 a day though many survive on half that. Whatever the size of your travelling fund, you should give some thought to how and in what form to carry your money. Travellers' cheques are much safer than cash, though they cost an extra 1% and banks for encashing them are not always near to hand. The most universally recognised brands are American Express, Thomas Cook and Visa. It is advisable also to keep a small amount of cash. Sterling is fine for most countries but US dollars are preferred in much of the world such as Latin America, Eastern Europe and Israel. The easiest way to look up the exchange rate of any world currency is to check on the internet (e.g. www.xe.net/ucc) or to look at the Monday edition of the *Financial Times*. A Currency Conversion Chart is included in the Appendices.

Credit cards are useful for many purposes, provided you will not be tempted to abuse them. Few people think of crediting their Visa, Access, etc. account before leaving and then withdrawing cash on the credit card without incurring interest charges (since the money is not being borrowed). Visa now have a TravelMoney service which works like a phone card; you credit it with cash and then access the money from cash machines worldwide with a pin number. This is probably the most efficient way of transferring funds abroad, however find out whether your credit card charges a handling fee (typically 1.5%).

Otherwise a credit card is invaluable in an emergency and handy for showing at borders where the officials frown on penniless tourists. Several round-the-world travellers have opened a bank account in their destination country before leaving home, partly as an incentive to reach the country and also to prevent having to carry the money on their persons.

If you have been slaving over a tepid sink full of washing up every day for the last few months, it would be disappointing to have your well-gotten gains stolen. From London to La Paz there are crooks lurking, ready to pounce upon the unsuspecting traveller. Theft takes many forms, from the highly trained gangs of gipsy children who artfully pick pockets all over Europe to violent attacks on the streets of American cities. Even more depressing is the theft which takes place by other travellers in youth hostels or on beaches. Risks can be reduced by carrying your wealth in several places including a comfortable money belt worn inside your clothing, steering clear of seedy or crowded areas and moderating your intake of alcohol. If you are mugged, and have an insurance policy which covers cash, you must obtain a police report (often for a fee) to stand any chance of recouping part of your loss.

While you are busy saving money to reach your desired target, you should be thinking of other ways in which to prepare yourself, including health, what to take and which contacts and skills you might cultivate.

Baggage

While aiming to travel as lightly as possible (one pair of jeans instead of two) you should consider the advantage of taking certain extra pieces of equipment. For example many working travellers consider the extra weight of a tent and sleeping bag worthwhile in view of the independence and flexibility it gives them if they are offered work by a farmer who cannot provide accommodation. A comfortable pair of shoes is essential, since a job hunt abroad often involves a lot of pavement pounding. Stephen Hands had his shoes stolen while swimming at night and found that bleeding feet were a serious impediment to finding (never mind, doing) a job. Others pack items essential to their money-making projects such as a guitar for busking, a suit for getting work as an English teacher, a pair of fingerless gloves for cold-weather fruit-picking, and so on. Leave at home anything of value (monetary or sentimental). The general rule is stick to the bare essentials (including a Swiss army knife). One travelling tip is to carry dental floss, useful not only for your teeth but as strong twine for mending backpacks, hanging up laundry, etc.

If you plan to work in one place for a long period of time, for instance on a kibbutz, you might allow yourself the odd (lightweight) luxury, such as a favourite tape, a short-wave radio or a jar of peanut butter. If you have prearranged a job, you can always post some belongings on ahead. You could even use poste restante for items you don't want to carry around for the first part of your trip (say hiking equipment) though you would have to have an itinerary fixed in cement for this to be an option.

Good maps and guides always enhance one's enjoyment of a trip. If you are going to be based in a major city, buy a map ahead of time. If you are in London, visit the famous map shop Edward Stanford Ltd. (12-14 Long Acre, Covent Garden, WC2E 9LP; 020-7836 1321/fax 020-7836 0189) and Daunt Books for Travellers (83 Marylebone High Street, W1M 4DE; 020-7224 2295). The National Map Centre (22-24 Caxton St, London SW1H 0QU) is another place for Londoners to visit. The Map Shop (15 High St, Upton-on-Severn, Worcestershire WR8 0HJ; 01684 593146/ themapshop@btinternet.com) does an extensive mail order business and will send you the relevant catalogue. Two other specialists are the Inverness-based Traveller's Companion (www.travellerscompanion.co.uk) and Maps Worldwide, PO Box 1555, Melksham, Wilts. SN12 6XJ (01225-707004/www.mapsworldwide.co.uk). A new trend is to combine a travel book shop with a travel booking desk or travel information staff and a café, for instance the Itchy Feet travel store at 4 Bartlett St, Bath (01225-337987).

There are dozens of travel specialists throughout North America, including the Complete Traveller Bookstore (199 Madison Ave, New York, NY 10016; 212-685-9007/fax 212-481-3253/completetraveller@worldnet.att.net) which also issues a free mail-order catalogue and, in Canada, Wanderlust (1929 West 4th Avenue, Kitsilano, Vancouver, BC, V6J 1M7; 604-739-2182/fax 604-733-9364/wanderlust@uniserve.com).

Health

No matter what country you are heading for, you should obtain the Department of Health leaflet T6 *Health Advice for Travellers*. This leaflet should be available from any post office or you can request a free copy on the Health Literature Line 0800 555777.

If you are a national of the European Economic Area, namely the UK, Ireland, Netherlands, Belgium, Liechtenstein, Luxembourg, Denmark, Germany, France, Italy, Spain, Portugal, Greece, Austria, Finland, Sweden, Norway and Iceland) and will be working in another EEA country, you will be covered by the European Community Social Security Regulations. Advice and the leaflet SA29 *Your Social Security Insurance, Benefits and Health Care Rights in the European Community and in Iceland, Liechtenstein and Norway* may be obtained free of charge from the Contributions Agency, International Services, Department of Social Security, LongBenton, Newcastle-upon-Tyne NE98 1ZZ (0645 154811/fax 0645 157800).

The T6 contains an application form to obtain form E111 (called the 'E-one-eleven') which is a certificate of entitlement to medical treatment in the EEA. The E-111 is not issued to EEA nationals who are going to work in another member country for less than 12 months and who continue to pay UK National Insurance contributions. Form E128 is now issued which gives entitlement to a full range of health care. This form also applies to students staying temporarily in another EEA country as part of their studies. If you will be working for a foreign employer, you should seek advice from the Contributions Agency International Services.

If you are planning to include developing countries on your itinerary, you will want to take the necessary health precautions, though this won't be cheap unless you are able to have your injections at your local NHS surgery where most injections are free or given for a minimal charge e.g. £13 for yellow fever. (If GPs charged the market rate, the yellow fever vaccine would cost £200.) A further problem is that GPs cannot be expected to keep abreast of all the complexities of malaria prophylaxis for different areas, etc. and many are downright ignorant.

Private specialist clinics abound in London but are thin on the ground elsewhere. Most charge both for information and for the jabs. For example the Hospital for Tropical Diseases (ring 020-7388 9600 for appointments or 09061-337733 for automated information costing 50p per minute) offers consultations at their clinic near Oxford Circus for £15. If you have your jabs there, the fee is waived. Most inoculations cost £15 though yellow fever costs £29. The drop-in Vaccination Clinic in Earls Court (131-135 Earls Court Road; 020-7259 2180) offers free advice and a complete range of jabs (from £7 for tetanus or polio to £48.50 for hepatitis A&B). Check their website www.vaccination-clinic.cwc.net. You can also trust the advice of the Interhealth Travel Clinic, 157 Waterloo Road, London SE1 8US (020-7902 9000), Nomad (0891 633414) and the Trailfinders Travel Clinic (194 Kensington High Street, London W8; 020-7938 3999). There are 25 British Airways Travel Clinics throughout the UK; ring the recorded message 01276 685040 for your nearest one.

Some countries have introduced HIV antibody testing for long-stay foreigners and the certificate may be required to obtain a work or residence visa. If you are going to be spending a lot of time in countries where blood screening is not reliable you should consider carrying a sterile medical kit. These are sold by MASTA (Medical Advisory Service for Travellers Abroad) at the London School of Hygiene and Tropical Medicine, Keppel St, London WC1E 7HT. MASTA (www.masta.org) maintains an up-to-date database on travellers' diseases and their prevention. You can ring their interactive Travellers' Health Line on 0891 224100 or 0906 822 4100 with your destinations (up to six countries) and they will send you a basic health brief by return, for the price of the telephone call (60p per minute).

Two excellent general guides on the subject are Richard Dawood's *Traveller's Health: How to Stay Healthy Abroad* and Ted Lankester's *The Traveller's Good Health Guide* (1999, £6.99). These books emphasise the necessity of avoiding tap water and recommend ways to purify your drinking water by filtering, boiling or chemical additives. MASTA has details of a water purifier called the 'Travel Well Trekker' for £69. Tap water throughout Western Europe is safe to drink.

Americans seeking general travel health advice should ring the Center for Disease Control & Prevention Hotline in Atlanta on 404-332-4559; www.cdc.gov. For a list of more than 100+ doctors in North America who are travel health experts, send a large self-addressed envelope and and 99 cents in stamps to Travelers Health & Immunization Services, 148 Highland Ave, Newton, MA 02465-2510. Increasingly, people are seeking advice via the internet; check, for example, www.fitfortravel. scot.nhs.uk; www.tmb.ie and www.travelhealth.co.uk.

Malaria is at present making a comeback in many parts of the world, due to the resistance of certain strains of mosquito to the pesticides and preventative medications which have been so extensively relied upon in the past. You must be particularly careful if travelling to a place where there is falciparum malaria which is potentially fatal. (Last year a record 2,500 travellers returned to the UK with malaria, 19 of whom died.) All travellers are urged to protect themselves against mosquito bites. Wearing fine silk clothes discourages bites. A company which markets mosquito repellants and nets is Oasis Nets (High St, Stoke Ferry, Norfolk PE33 9SP; 01366 500466); they will send a free fact sheet about malaria in your destination country.

There are two principal types of drug which can be obtained over the counter: Chloroquine-based and Proguanil (brand name Paludrine). Many areas of the world are reporting resistance to one of the drugs, so you may have to take both or a third line such as Maloprim or Mefloquine available only on prescription and with possible side effects. Unfortunately these prophylactic medications are not foolproof, and even those who have scrupulously swallowed their pills before and after their trip as well as during it have been known to contract the disease. It is therefore also essential to take mechanical precautions against mosquitoes. If possible, screen the windows and sleep under an insecticide-impregnated mosquito net. Marcus Scrace bought some netting intended for prams which occupied virtually no space in his luggage. If these are unavailable, cover your limbs at nightfall with light-coloured garments, apply insect repellant with the active ingredient DEET and sleep with a fan on.

It is a good idea to join the International Association for Medical Assistance to Travellers (IAMAT) whose European headquarters are at 57 Voirets, 1212 Grand-Lancy-Geneva, Switzerland and in North America at 40 Regal Road, Guelph, Ontario, Canada N1K 1B5 (519-836-0102) with other offices in the US (417 Center St, Lewiston, NY 14092) and New Zealand (PO Box 5049, Christchurch). This organisation co-ordinates doctors and clinics around the world who maintain high medical standards at reasonable cost e.g. US$55 per consultation for IAMAT members. They will send you a directory listing IAMAT centres throughout the world as well as detailed leaflets about malaria and other tropical diseases and country-by-country climate and hygiene charts. There is no set fee for joining the association, but donations are welcome; at the very least you should cover their postage and printing costs. Further information is available on their website www.sentex.net/~iamat.

Consider taking a first aid course before leaving. The St. John Ambulance offers a range of Lifesaver and Lifesaver Plus courses. The standard one-day course costs £30-£50 (depending on region).

Insurance

Given the limitations of state-provided reciprocal health cover (i.e. that it covers only emergencies), you should certainly take out comprehensive private cover which will cover extras like loss of baggage and, more importantly, emergency repatriation. Every enterprise in the travel business is delighted to sell you insurance because of the commission earned. Shopping around can save you money. Ring several insurance companies with your specifications and compare prices. If you are going abroad to work, you are expected to inform your insurer ahead of time (which is often impossible). Many policies will be invalidated if you injure yourself at work, e.g. put out your back while picking plums or cut yourself in a restaurant kitchen, though it is not clear how they would know how or where the accident took place. There is no need to ask a broker to quote for a tailor-made policy since many of the backpacker policies specifically cover casual work.

Europ-Assistance Ltd of Sussex House, Perrymount Road, Haywards Heath, W Sussex RH16 1DN (01444 442365; www.europ-assistance.co.uk) is the world's largest assistance organisation with a network of doctors, air ambulances, agents and vehicle rescue services in 208 countries worldwide offering emergency assistance abroad 24 hours a day. The Voyager Travel policy covering periods from 6 to 18 months costs £265 for 12 months in Europe and £545 worldwide. The policy is invalidated if you return home during the period insured. American readers can obtain details from Worldwide Assistance, 1133 15th St NW, Suite 400, Washington, DC 20005-2710 (1-800-821-2828/www.worldwideassistance.com).

Many companies charge less, though you will have to decide whether you are satisfied with their level of cover. Most offer a standard rate which covers medical emergencies and a premium rate which covers personal baggage, cancellation, etc. Some travel policies list as one of their exclusions: 'any claims which arise while the Insured is engaged in any manual employment'. If you are not planning to visit North America, the premiums will be much less expensive. Some companies to consider are listed here with an estimate of their premiums for 12 months of worldwide cover (including the USA). Expect to pay roughly £20-£25 per month for basic cover and £35-£40 for more extensive cover.

usit-Campus Go Banana Travel Insurance, 52 Grosvenor Gardens, London SW1W 0AG (0870-240 1010) or regional branches. £339 with baggage cover, £270 without. Must be under 35.

Club Direct, Dominican House, St John's St, Chichester, W Sussex (0800-083 2455/www.clubdirect.com). Work abroad is included provided it does not involve using heavy machinery. £179 for basic year-long cover (renewable); £249 including baggage cover.

Columbus Direct, 17 Devonshire Square, London EC2M 4SQ (020-7375

0011/08450-761030). Globetrotter policy (basic medical cover only) costs £188 for one year. More extensive cover is offered for £312 and £364.

Dove Insurance Brokers, Green Tree House, 11 St Margaret's St, Bradford-on-Avon, Wilts. BA15 1DA (01225 867571). £222 excluding baggage.

Downunder Worldwide Travel Insurance. 3 Spring St, Paddington, London W2 3RA (0800 393908; www.downunderinsurance.co.uk). Backpacker policy covers working holidays (excluding ladders and heavy machinery). £171 or £227 with baggage cover.

Endsleigh Insurance, Endsleigh House, Cheltenham, Glos GL50 3NR. Offices in most university towns. Twelve months of cover in Europe costs from £215, worldwide £338 (£299 and £485 respectively for a higher level of cover).

gosure.com, www.gosure.com offer a 5% discount for customers arranging their insurance on-line: £320. Certification and documents arrive by e-mail.

Preferential Direct, Worldtrekker policy (01702 423280; www.worldtrekker.com) for people 18-35. £175 or £264.

MRL Insurance, Lumbry Park, Selborne Road, Alton, Hants GU34 3HF (0870 845 0050; www.insure4cover.co.uk). £179.

Travel Insurance Agency, 775B High Road, North Finchley, London N12 8JY (020-8446 5414/5).

Travel Insurance Club - 01702 423398/www.travelinsuranceclub.co.uk. Backpacker policy includes working holidays. £175.

If you do have to make a claim, you may be unpleasantly surprised by the amount of the settlement eventually paid. Loss adjusters have ways of making calculations which prove that you are entitled to less than you think. For example when Caroline Langdon was mugged in Seville she suffered losses of about £100, for which her insurance company paid compensation of £22.30. The golden rule is to amass as much documentation as possible to support your application, most importantly a police report.

Americans who spend $22 on an International Student Identity Card are automatically covered by a basic accident/sickness insurance package. Contact the Council on International Educational Exchange (633 Third Ave, 20th Floor, New York, NY 10017) or any Council Travel office. Other recommended US insurers for extended stays abroad are International SOS Assistance Inc (8 Neshaminy Interplex, Suite 207, Trevose, PA 19053-6956; 1-800-523-8930; www.internationalsos.com) which is used by the Peace Corps and is designed for people working in remote areas. A firm which specialises in providing insurance for Americans living overseas is Wallach & Company (107 West Federal St, PO Box 480, Middleburg, VA 20118-0480; 1-800-237-6615/www.wallach.com).

Qualifications

These sensible precautions of purchasing maps, buying insurance, finding out about malaria, etc. are relatively straightforward and easy. Other specific ways of preparing yourself, such as studying a language, learning to sail or dive, cook, drive or type, or taking up a fitness programme, are a different kettle of fish. But the traveller who has a definite commitment may well consider embarking on a self-improvement scheme before setting off. Among the most useful qualifications you can acquire are a certificate in Teaching English as a Foreign Language (see chapter *Teaching*) and a knowledge of sailing or diving (see *Tourism* chapter for the address of a course which also offers job placement).

The person who has a definite job skill to offer increases his or her chances of success. After working his way from Paris to Cape Town via Queensland, Stephen Psallidas concluded:

> *There are several professions which are in demand anywhere in the world, and I would say that anyone who practises them would be laughing all the way to the 747. These are: secretary, cook/chef, accountant, nurse and hairdresser.*

Nursing training is very useful and, after a year of working her way through Europe doing a variety of things, Mary Hall is glad she stuck the training since she has found that medical doors opened for her in Gibraltar, Uganda and South Africa. Childcare experience is also a highly portable skill.

It is a good idea to take documentary evidence of any qualifications you have earned. Also take along a sheaf of references, both character and work-related, if possible, all on headed notepaper. It is difficult to arrange for these to be sent once you're on the road. This was obviously a good idea in Karen Heinink's case, when she approached a coastal hotel in South Africa:

> *I showed them my CV and references which I always carry round when travelling (just in case), had a quick chat with the owners and was told I could start right away.*

Language

Having even a limited knowledge of a foreign language is especially valuable for the job-seeker. Stephen Hands thinks that this can't be over-emphasised; after an unsuccessful attempt to find work in France, he returned to Britain and, even before phoning home, signed up for a language course (and received the additional perk of a student card).

Evening language classes offered by local authorities usually follow the academic year and are aimed at hobby learners. Intensive courses offered privately are much more expensive. If you are really dedicated, consider using a self-study programme with books and tapes (which start at £30), correspondence course or broadcast language course. Even if you don't make much headway with the course at home, take it with you since you will have more incentive to learn once you are immersed in a language.

There are a great many teach-yourself courses on the market from Berlitz (020-7518 8300), the BBC (020-8225 7700), Linguaphone (020-7589 2422/www. linguaphone.co.uk), Audioforum (www.audioforum.com). All of them offer deluxe courses with refinements such as interactive videos and of course these cost much more (from £150). Linguaphone recommends half an hour of study a day for three months to master the basics of a language. If you are interested in an obscure language and don't know where to study it, contact the CILT Library (020-7379 5110) which has a certain amount of documentation on courses especially in London.

A more enjoyable way of learning a language (and normally a more successful one) is by speaking it with the natives. The cheapest way to do this is to link up with a native speaker living in your local area, possibly by putting an ad in a local paper or making contact through a local English language school. Numerous organisations offer 'in-country' language courses, though these tend to be expensive. EF International Language Schools (020-7878 3550), CESA Languages Abroad (Western House, Malpas, Truro, Cornwall TR1 1SQ; 01872 225300; www.cesalanguages.com) and Euro-Academy (77a George St, Croydon CR0 1LD; 020-8681 2363) offer the chance to learn languages on location. Caledonia Languages Abroad (The Clockhouse, Bonnington Hill, 72 Newhaven Road, Edinburgh EH6 5QG; 0131-621 7721) combines language courses with voluntary placements in Peru, Costa Rica and Europe. In the USA, language learners might like to contact the National Registration Center for Study Abroad (PO Box 1393, Milwaukee, WI 53201; info@nrcsa.com) for a listing of 125 language schools in more than 25 countries. Many include options to participate in volunteer work or career-focused internships. Full-immersion courses are available at Eurocentres worldwide; ring 1-800-648-4809 for details.

Another possibility is to forgo structured lessons and simply live with a family, which has the further advantage of allowing you to become known in a community which might lead to job openings later. (See *Making Contacts* below). Several agencies arrange paying guest stays which are designed for people wishing to learn or improve language skills in the context of family life. Try En Famille Overseas (The Old Stables, 60b Maltravers St, Arundel, West Sussex BN18 9BG; 01903 883266) which specialises in France, Spain and Germany. EIL, a non-profit cultural and educational organisation, offers short-term homestay programmes in more than 30 countries; contact EIL for their fees (287 Worcester Road, Malvern, Worcestershire WR14 1AB; 01684 562577). Euroyouth (301 Westborough Road, Westcliff-on-Sea, Essex SS0 9PT; 01702 341434) and Home Language International (17 Royal Crescent, Ramsgate, Kent CT11 9PE; 01843 851116) also arrange homestays with or without a language course. In the US contact Language Liaison Inc. (4 Burnham Parkway, Morristown, NJ 07960; 1-800-284-4448).

Making Contacts

The importance of knowing people, not necessarily in high places but on the spot, is stressed by many of our contributors. Some people are lucky enough to have family and friends scattered around the world in positions to offer advice or even employment. Others must create their own contacts by exploiting less obvious connections. Dick Bird, who spent over a year travelling around South America, lightheartedly anticipates how this works:

> *In Bolivia we hope to start practising another survival technique known as 'having some addresses'. The procedure is quite simple. Before leaving one's country of origin, inform everyone you know from your immediate family to the most casual acquaintance, that you are about to leave for South America. With only a little cajoling they might volunteer the address of somebody they once met on the platform of Clapham Junction or some other tenuous connection who went out to South America to seek their fortunes. You then present your worthy self on the unsuspecting emigré's doorstep and announce that you have been in close and recent communication with their nearest and dearest. Although you won't necessarily be welcomed with open arms, the chances are they will be eager for your company and conversation. Furthermore these contacts are often useful for finding work: doing odd jobs, farming, tutoring people they know, etc.*

Paul Rowlatt accumulated a list of contacts all over Brazil just by being 'nosey and talkative'.

Everyone has ways of developing links with people abroad. Think of distant cousins and family friends, foreign students met in your home town, pen friends, people in the town twinned with yours, etc. Human rights groups in your home country might have links with your destination or even know about opportunities for doing voluntary work in their offices abroad. Jacqueline Edwards placed a small notice in European vegetarian and vegan newsletters asking for a live-in position for herself and young son. Tony Dalby of Swindon came up with an original way of forging links with Japan:

> *I wrote off to our new Honda car plant and requested some contacts in order to gain some first-hand experience of Japanese culture and language before travelling. I now have links with a Japanese family.*

School exchanges and membership in the Youth Hostels Association can also result in valuable contacts (Trevelyan House, 8 St. Stephen's Hill, St. Albans, Herts AL1 2DY; www.yha.org.uk); adult membership currently costs £12/$25.

One way of developing contacts is to join a travel club such as the Globetrotters Club (BCM/Roving, London WC1N 3XX/mail@globetrotters.co.uk) for £15/$29 a year. The Club has no office and so correspondence addressed to the above box office address is answered by volunteers. Members receive a bi-monthly travel newsletter and a list of members, many of whom are willing to extend hospitality to other globetrotters and possibly to advise them on local employment prospects.

Servas International is an organisation begun by an American Quaker, which runs a worldwide programme of free hospitality exchanges for travellers, to further world peace and understanding. Normally you don't stay with one host for more than a couple of days. To become a Servas traveller or host, contact 4 Southfield Road, Burley-in-Wharfedale, Ilkley, Yorks LS29 7PA (www.servasbritain.u-net.com) who can forward your enquiry to your Area Coordinator. Before a traveller can be given a list of hosts (which are drawn up every autumn), he or she must pay a fee of £25 (£35 for couples) and be interviewed by a coordinator. Servas US is at 11 John St, Suite 407, New York, NY 10038-4009 (212-267-0252). There is a joining fee of US$55 and a refundable deposit of $25 for host lists in up to five countries. Janet Renard from the US stayed with 21 Servas hosts during her six months in Europe:

> *We call it 'Servas Magic'. Each visit was a great experience. The houses we visited ranged from a 16th century farmhouse in Wales to a cramped apartment in Naples. While we were on an archaeological dig in France, one family hosted us for three weekends, taking us to St. Malo and even sailing in*

a regatta. For some hosts, we gardened, chopped wood or cooked; others insisted on waiting on us completely.

There are other hospitality clubs and exchanges worth investigating. Women Welcome Women World Wide (88 Easton St, High Wycombe, Bucks. HP11 1DJ; tel/fax 01494 465441/ www.womenwelcomewomen.org.uk) enables women of different countries to visit one another. There is no set subscription, but the recommended minimum donation is £20/$35, which covers the cost of the membership list and three newsletters in which members may publish announcements. There are currently 2,500 members in nearly 70 countries.

Hospitality exchange organisations crop up from time to time. One which was advertising recently was called The World for Free; send an s.a.e. to PO Box 137, Prince Street Station, New York, NY 10012 (info@worldforfree.com; fax 212-979-8167). Membership costs $25. Another possibility is Hospitality Exchange, PO Box 561, Lewistown, MT 59457 (406-538-8770) which sells directories of travellers; the price is $20 for two country directories.

On-line communications and electronic chat rooms may eventually replace corresponding with penpals but, until then, pen friend organisations in Europe and North America which charge varying fees still match up correspondents. After years of corresponding with a girl in a small East German town, Kathy Merz from South Carolina paid what she thought would be a brief visit and instead turned into a six month stay while she worked in the family's butcher shop. International Pen Friends (PO 340, Dublin 12, Ireland) is a long-established club; the average charge for a list of pen friends is £10-£16. The UK representative is Pamela Walker, IPF, PO Box 42, Berwick upon Tweed, Northumberland TD15 1RU. The long-established American representative is Eileen Bouldin, PO Box 42232, Philadelphia, Pennsylvania 19101-2232, USA; the fees in the US for an adult to be sent the addresses of 14 potential pen friends is $25. World Pen Pals (PO Box 337, Saugerties, NY 12477; tel/fax 914-246-7828) charges $3 plus s.a.e. for each penpal; all members are under 23.

Travelling Alone

Many travellers emphasise the benefits of travelling alone, such as a chance to make friends with the locals more easily. Most are surprised that loneliness is hardly an issue, since there is always congenial company to be met in travellers' hostels, kibbutzim, etc. some of whom even team up with each other for short or long spells. Of course, if you are working in a remote rural area and don't speak the language fluently, you will inevitably miss having a companion and may steer away from this kind of situation if it bothers you. If you are anxious about the trials and traumas of being on your own, try a short trip and see how you like it.

Women can travel solo just as enjoyably as men, as Woden Teachout discovered:

I'm 24, female, American and like to travel alone. I have travelled with friends on occasion which is definitely more 'fun' but it lacks the perilous sense of possibility and adventure that I love most about travelling. Whatever situations you get yourself into when you are on your own, you have to get out of. I have been terribly frightened: I spent the night of my 21st birthday huddled in a cellar hole in downtown Malmo Sweden, wet and shivering, knowing that a local rapist had claimed three victims within the fortnight. But by the same token, the glorious moments, the stick-out-your-thumb-and-be-glad-for-whatever-is-going-to-happen-next moments, the feelings of triumph and absolute freedom, are uniquely yours.

Travelling Companions

You have to be fairly lucky to have a friend who is both willing and available when you are to embark on a working trip. If you don't have a suitable companion and are convinced you need one, you can publish your request in the pages of the Globetrotters Club newsletter *Globe* (address on previous page), the Youth Hostels Association's *Triangle* magazine or the 'Travel Link' column of *Overseas Jobs Express* (in which potential job-seekers can announce their travel plans).

There are also a few agencies which try to match up compatible travel companions for an annual or a one-off fee, for example the long-established Travel Companion Exchange, PO Box 833, Amityville, NY 11701 (516-454-0880; www.whytravelalone. com). A sample copy of their travel newsletter is US$6 ($9 outside the US).

Sarah Clifford describes the easiest way of all to find companions:

I think you should warn people that Work You Way Around the World *is infectious. Even people who I would never have thought would want to go anywhere start flicking through the pages, then get more and more absorbed, become incredibly enthusiastic and demand to go with me on my travels!*

Staying in Touch

The revolution in communication technology means that you are never far from home. Internet cafés can be found in almost every corner of the world, where you can check your e-mail and link up with other travellers. Many travellers acquire a hotmail address before leaving home (www.hotmail.com) and use it to keep in touch with (and receive messages from) home and friends met on the road. Many companies sell international phone cards which simplify calling home. Lonely Planet, the travel publisher, has an easy-to-use communications card called eKno which offers low cost calls, voicemail and email (www.ekno.com).

Clearly there are advantages to such easy communication, though there are also travellers out there who spend an inordinate amount of time tracking down and inhabiting cybercafés instead of looking around the country and meeting locals in the old-fashioned, strike-up-a-conversation way. Danny Jacobson from Madison is also ambivalent about its virtues (and committed his thoughts to paper):

I've met loads of travellers using e-mail to meet people on-line, to keep in touch with people they've met travelling, to find out information about a place and to publish their own adventures. It all seems to be making the world an incredibly small place. Myself, I admit I've spent a fair share of money on e-mail and rely on it at times quite a bit. I worry that it is getting easier and easier to do everything from a sitting position.

It would be a shame if e-mail deprived long-term travellers of arriving at a poste restante address they've left behind and having the pleasure (sweeter because it has been deferred) of reading their mail.

RED TAPE

Passports and Work Visas

A ten-year UK passport costs £28 for 32 pages and £38 for 48 pages, and should be processed by the Passport Agency within ten days, though it is safer to leave one month. Queuing in person at one of the six passport offices (in Liverpool, London, Newport, Peterborough, Glasgow and Belfast) will speed things up in an emergency but will incur a surcharge; addresses are listed on passport application forms (available from main post offices). Ring the Passport Agency on 0870 521 0410.

The free reciprocity of labour within the European Union means that the red tape has been simplified (though not done away with completely). See the chapter *EU Employment.* As will become clear as you read further in this book, work permits/work visas outside the EU are not readily available to ordinary mortals. In almost all cases, you must find an employer willing to apply to the immigration authorities on your behalf months in advance of the job's starting date, while you are in your home country. This is usually a next-to-impossible feat unless you are a high ranking nuclear physicist, a foreign correspondent or are participating in an organised exchange programme where the red tape is taken care of by your sponsoring organisation. Wherever possible, we have mentioned such possibilities throughout this book. The official visa information should be requested from the Embassy or Consulate (if only to be ignored); addresses in London and Washington are listed in Appendix IV. For general information about visas, see *Travel.*

Student Cards

With an International Student Identity Card (ISIC) it is often possible to obtain reduced fares on trains, planes and buses, £1 off each night's stay at a youth hostel in the UK, discounted admission to museums and theatres, and other perks. The ISIC is available to all students in full-time education. There is no age limit though some flight carriers do not apply discounts for students over 31. To obtain a card (which is valid for 15 months from September) you will need to complete the ISIC application form, provide a passport photo, proof of full-time student status (NUS card or official letter) and the fee of £6 (£6.50 if obtained via ISIC mail order). Take these to any students' union, local student travel office or send to ISIC Mail Order, PO Box 36, Glossop, Derbyshire SK13 8HT (enquiries@nussl.co.uk). When issued with an ISIC, students also receive a handbook containing travel tips, details of national and international discounts and how to get in touch with the ISIC helpline, a special service for travelling students who need advice in an emergency.

Americans can obtain an ISIC card at Council Travel offices. An alternative card is the International Student Exchange Identity Card available from ISE Cards, 5010 East Shea Blvd, A-104, Scottsdale, AZ 85254 (1-888-473-2273/www.isecard.com) at a cost of $20.

If you are not eligible, people have been known to walk into their local college, say that they are about to start a course and request a student card. There are a great many forgeries in circulation, most of which originate in Bangkok or Cairo.

Bureaucracy at Large

Having your papers in order is a recurring problem for the working traveller. Andrew Winwood thinks that this book underestimates the difficulties:

> *I wish that you would be honest about immigration, obtaining the proper visas, etc. But having said that, I wouldn't have had the nerve to go in the first place if I'd known how hard it would be.*

It is easy to understand why every country in the world has immigration policies which are principally job protection schemes for their own nationals. Nevertheless it can be frustrating to encounter bureaucratic hassles if you merely intend to teach English for a month or so, and there is really no local candidate available with your advantages (e.g. fluency). In all the countries with which we deal, we have tried to set out as clearly as possible the official position regarding visas and work and/or residence permits for both EU and non-EU readers.

If you are cautious by nature you may be very reluctant to transgress the regulations. People in this category will feel much happier if they can arrange things through official channels, such as approved exchange organisations or agencies which arrange permits for you, or by finding an employer willing to get them a work permit, which must normally be collected outside the country of employment. Arranging things this way will require extra reserves of patience.

It seems that a great many decisions are taken at the discretion (or whim) of the individual bureaucrat. Whether or not a document is issued seems to depend more on the mood of the official than on the rulebook. Leeson Clifton from Canada followed all the rules for getting official status as a temporary employee in Norway. When she took her passport to the police for their stamp she was told it would take two weeks and she could not work in the meantime. She returned to the same office the next day and got it done on the spot. She concludes:

> *The left hand didn't know what the right hand was doing, but of course this is the same in any country. When dealing with government authorities always be patient and pleasant, but keep on asking for what you want and in most cases you'll get it (eventually). Losing your cool gets you nowhere; after all they have no obligations to you.*

Other travellers are prepared to throw caution to the winds and echo Helen Welch's view that 'government bureaucracy is the same anywhere, i.e. notoriously slow; by the time the system discovers that you are an alien you can be long gone.' This is more serious in some countries and in certain circumstances than in others, and we have tried to give some idea in this book of the enthusiasm with which the immigration laws are enforced from country to country and the probable outcome for employer and employee if the rules are broken. The authorities will usually turn a blind eye in areas where there is a labour shortage and enforce the letter of the law when there is a glut of unemployed foreign workers. If you do land an unofficial job (helping a Greek islander build a taverna, picking kiwifruit in New Zealand, doing odd jobs at an orphanage in central Africa) try to be as discreet as possible. Noisy boasting has been the downfall of many a traveller who has attracted unwelcome attention. It is always important to be as sensitive as possible to local customs and expectations.

Julian Peachey is another veteran traveller who is suspicious of the value of using official channels:

> *One of my conclusions is that going through the official channels and taking advice from officialdom is often a mistake. 'Officially' (i.e. the view of the British Council in Paris) it is very hard to get teaching work, as there are so many highly qualified English people living in Paris. The French agricultural information office warns that there is very little in the way of farm work for foreigners.*

And yet Julian had a variety of teaching and agricultural jobs throughout France. He claims that if he had believed all that he had been told by officialdom and had taken all the suggested precautions, he would never have been able to go in the first place.

GETTING A JOB BEFORE YOU GO

The subsequent chapters contain a great deal of advice and a number of useful addresses for people wishing to fix up a job before they leave home. If you have ever worked for a firm with branches abroad (e.g. Virgin Records, Alfred Marks, even McDonalds) it may be worth writing in advance to ask about prospects. There is a lot to recommend prior planning especially to people who have never travelled abroad and who feel some trepidation at the prospect. There are lots of 'easy' ways to break into the world of working travellers, for instance working on an American summer camp, joining a two-week voluntary workcamp on the Continent or going on a kibbutz, all of which can be fixed up at home with few problems. Inevitably these will introduce you to an international circle of travellers whose experiences will entertain, instruct and inspire the novice traveller.

Professional or skilled people have a chance of prearranging a job. For example nurses, plumbers, architects, motor mechanics, piano tuners, teachers, divers, secretaries and computer programmers can sometimes find work abroad within their profession by answering adverts in British newspapers and specialist journals, by writing direct to hospitals, schools and businesses abroad, and by registering with the appropriate professional association. For example the Royal College of Nursing (20 Cavendish Square, London W1M 0AB) offers its members overseas employment advice which can be accessed through RCN's International Office: 020-7409 3333. (The fact that the International Office has been handling more enquiries than before is attributed to the level of dissatisfaction in the NHS at present.)

But the majority of people who dream about working their way around the world do not have a professional or trade qualification. Many will be students who are on the way to becoming qualified, but are impatient to broaden their horizons before graduation. The main requirement seems to be perseverance. Dennis Bricault sent off 137 letters in order to fix up a summer job as a volunteer at an alpine youth hostel.

For many other jobs, it is not at all easy to fix something up in advance. In an ideal world, you could stop in at your local branch of an international employment agency, impress them with your talent and keenness and be assigned your choice of job whether entertainments manager on a Caribbean cruise or ski tow operator in New Zealand. But it just isn't like that and people who expect jobs abroad to be handed to them on a platter by some agency or other are naïve in the extreme. Very very few employers anywhere in the world are willing to hire someone they haven't met. Some cynics would maintain that an employer who cannot fill vacancies locally, and who hires foreign people sight unseen, must be suspect. John Linnemeier worked at a Norwegian hotel, 'for a guy who had such a terrible reputation that none of the locals would work for him'.

Several editions ago, a reader and traveller (Stephen Hands) expressed his longing for a miraculous network of information for working travellers:

Wouldn't it be great if someone set up a scheme, whereby people could forward correspondence to an exchange of some kind, for people to swap addresses of places they've worked abroad. For example someone planning to work in Nice could write to some agency to obtain the address of another traveller who could tell him what the manager's like or if the chef is an axe-wielding homicidal maniac or that the accommodation is a hole in the bottom of the local coal mine. This would enable working travellers to avoid the rip-off places; also it might save them turning up in places where the work potential is zero.

The scheme which Stephen thought was a pipedream just a few years ago now has a name, the internet. Somewhere on the web, you can probably find out that the axe-wielding chef has been replaced by a Quaker and that the coal mine has been tastefully refurbished.

Employment Agencies

Adverts which offer glamorous jobs and high wages abroad should be treated with scepticism. They are often placed by one-man companies who are in fact selling printed bumph about jobs on cruise ships, in the United States or whatever, which will not get you much closer to any dream job whatever their ads promise (e.g. 'Earn up to £400 a week in Japan' or 'Would you like to work on a luxury cruise ship?'). A not infrequent con is to charge people for regular job listings and contacts in their chosen destination, which may consist of adverts lifted from newspapers or addresses from the Yellow Pages long out of date.

According to the Employment Agencies Act of 1973, UK employment agencies are not permitted to charge job-seekers an upfront fee. They make their money from the company or organisation seeking staff. (The exceptions are au pair agencies and modelling or theatrical agencies.) Every so often a bogus agency will place false recruitment advertisements in the tabloid press charging a 'registration fee', say of £15 for building workers in the Middle East, and possibly an extra sum for a magazine about living and working in the Middle East. They then disappear without trace. Some operate as clubs offering members certain services such as translating and circulating CVs. Before joining any such club, try to find out what their success rate is. You could even ask to be put in touch with someone whose membership resulted in their getting a job.

There are of course reputable international recruitment agencies in Britain, the USA and elsewhere. Specialist agencies for qualified personnel can be very useful, for example the British Nursing Association (a commercial agency which can assist UK nurses to work abroad) or other agencies for financial and IT vacancies (e.g. Robert Walters Resourcing with offices in 12 cities around the world; www. robertwalters.com). Agencies with a range of specialities from disc jockeys for international hotels to English teachers for language schools abroad are mentioned in the relevant chapters which follow.

Do not neglect EURES, the state-run employment service within Europe (see chapter on *EU Employment*. A random trawl of jobs available through EURES recently included strawberry pickers for Denmark, musical entertainers for Cyprus and children's reps in Bulgaria. To obtain the addresses of private agencies, contact the Recruitment & Employment Confederation (36-38 Mortimer St, London W1N 7RB; 0800 320588; www.rec.uk.com) which publishes lists of its members according to specialisation for £3.75. These agencies are almost invariably seeking highly qualified professionals, technicians and managers. A good source of addresses for such agencies is *The Directory of Jobs & Careers Abroad* (Vacation-Work, £11.95) and the classified advertisements in the fortnightly newspaper *Overseas Jobs Express* (address below). The latter makes an honest attempt to vet agencies and invites any reader who is dissatisfied with the service offered by an advertiser or comes across one which attempts to charge a fee to complain.

International Placement Organisations

Established organisations which assist students and other young people to work abroad are invaluable for guiding people through the red tape problems and for providing a soft landing for first time travellers:

BUNAC, 16 Bowling Green Lane, London EC1R 0BD (020-7251-3472; www.bunac.org.uk) is a student club which helps UK students to work abroad. It has a choice of programmes in the United States, Canada, Australia, New Zealand, South Africa, Ghana and Argentina, and in all cases assists participants to obtain the appropriate short-term working visas.

Council Exchanges, (Council on International Educational Exchange, 52 Poland St, London W1V 4JQ (020-7479 2000/fax 020-7734 7322/www.councilexchanges. org.uk). Programmes in the USA, Canada, Australia, Japan and China.

Council Exchanges; 20th Floor, 633 Third Avenue, New York, NY10017 (1-888-COUNCIL). Runs work abroad programmes for students in the following countries, for which it charges a fee of $250-$375 and can arrange working visas: Ireland, France, Germany, Canada, Australia, New Zealand, Costa Rica, Japan and China. American students should contact their local Council Travel office or obtain a copy of the 'Work Abroad' booklet from Council.

Council Australia, University Centre, Level 8, 210 Clarence Street, Sydney 2000 (02-9373 2730). Some of the same work abroad programmes for Australian and New Zealand students.

InterExchange Inc, 161 Sixth Avenue, New York, NY 10013 (212-924-0446/www.interexchange.org). Teaching assistantships in Bulgaria, Poland, Russia and Ukraine; various work programmes including some au pair placements in the UK, France, Germany, Italy, Netherlands, Norway, Poland and Spain.

Camp Counselors & Work Experience USA, Green Dragon House, 64-70 High Street, Croydon CR0 9XN; 020-8688 9051; england@workexperienceusa.com; www.workexperienceusa.com). Work experience programmes in the US (general and summer camps) and in Australia/New Zealand. The US headquarters of CCUSA are at 2330 Marinship Way, Suite 250, Sausalito, CA 94965 (www.campcounselors. com) which run outgoing programmes to Australia, New Zealand and Russia.

Youth exchange organisations and commercial agencies offer packages which help their nationals to take advantage of the work permit rules. For example Travel CUTS in Canada sends Canadian students to work in the UK, Ireland, France, Germany, Australia, New Zealand, South Africa and Japan (45 Charles St E, Suite 100, Toronto, Ontario M4Y 1S2), Activity International does the same for Dutch and Belgian nationals (PO Box 7090, 9701 JB Groningen, Netherlands), Exis in Denmark, GIJK in Germany and so forth.

Rita Hoek is one person who decided to participate in an organised programme, i.e. Travel Active's 'Work & Travel Australia' programme (PO Box 107, 5800 AC Venray, Netherlands):

> *Though I'm not suggesting these programmes are perfect for everybody's specific plans, it's been of great help to me. You join a discount-group airfare (cheaper and easier), they help with getting a visa and most programmes provide a first week of accommodation, assistance in getting a tax file number and opening a bank account, a service to forward your mail, general information about work and travelling and heaps more. If you don't want to feel completely lost at the airport while travelling for the first time (as I was), I can surely recommend it.*

Other organisations fix up actual jobs for qualifying applicants. In fact many of the placements arranged through such organisations are tantamount to voluntary work since remuneration may consist in not much more than board and lodging. See the chapter *Voluntary Work* and also the country chapters for organisations which are active in specific countries.

The *Central Bureau for International Education and Training* (10 Spring Gardens, London SW1A 2BN; 020-7389 4004; cbresources@britishcouncil.org) is a central source of information about official work schemes and exchanges, many of them aimed at students. IAESTE is the abbreviation for the International Association for the Exchange of Students for Technical Experience. It provides international course-related vacation training for thousands of university-level students in 65 member countries. Placements are available in engineering, science, agriculture, architecture and related fields. British undergraduates should apply directly to *IAESTE UK* at the Central Bureau (020-7389 4774) in the autumn term for placements commencing the following summer. The US affiliate is the Association for International Practical Training (AIPT, 10400 Little Patuxent Parkway, Suite 250, Columbia, Maryland 21044-3510; 410-997-3068) which can consider applications from graduates and young professionals as well as college students.

In the US, several agencies offer a range of programmes for varying fees. *Alliances Abroad,* 702 West Ave, Austin, TX 78701, USA (1-888-6-ABROAD/1-888-622-7623; info@alliancesabroad.com/ www.alliancesabroad.com) arranges volunteer placements in Africa (Ghana and Senegal), China, Latin America (Ecuador, Costa Rica, Mexico and Guatemala) and Australia. Internships are arranged in Ireland, Spain, Germany and China, and work programmes in England and Austria.

International Co-operative Education (15 Spiros Way, Menlo Park, CA 94025; 415-323-4944; www.icemenlo.com) places more than 400 students each summer to work in Germany, Switzerland, Belgium, Finland, Japan, etc. Their placement fee is $600 in addition to an application fee of $200.

Useful Sources of Information

Apart from contacting specific organisations, you should consider consulting reference books on the subject, directories of jobs and specialist journals. Publications covering specific countries or specific kinds of work (e.g. *Teaching English Abroad* or *Kibbutz Volunteer*) are mentioned in the relevant chapters. Of general interest are:

The Directory of Summer Jobs Abroad (Vacation Work, 9 Park End Street, Oxford OX1 1HJ; £9.99 plus £1.50 postage). Published each November.

Working Holidays (Central Bureau for International Education & Training, 10 Spring Gardens, London SW1A 2BN; www.britishcouncil.org/cbiet). £9.99 plus £2 postage. 2000 edition is the most recent after the decision was taken not to update annually. Also publish *A Year Between* for £9.99 and other work-related titles.

Taking a Gap Year (Vacation-Work, £11.95) by me. A revised edition will be published summer 2001. Covers all the specialist placement organisations as well as extensive county-by-country advice on how to wing it on your year off.

CSU (Higher Education Careers Services Unit, Prospects House, Booth St E, Manchester M13 9EP; 0161-277 5200; www.prospects.csu.man.ac.uk). Publishes a range of careers information for graduates and students in the UK and overseas, including profiles of most areas of work and international opportunities.

Directory of International Internships (Career Development & Placement Services, Michigan State University, 113 Student Services, East Lansing, Michigan 48824-1113, USA). 1998. $25 (includes US postage).

Overseas Jobs Express (20 New Road, Brighton, East Sussex BN1 1UF; 01273 669777). Fortnightly newspaper for international job hunters. Subscription costs are £29.95 for three months, £75 for 12 months.

Transitions Abroad, (Dept. TRA, Box 3000, Denville, NJ 07834, USA). Annual subscription (six issues) costs $28 within the US. Valuable resource guide with range of work-abroad books as well. The editorial address is PO Box 1300, Amherst, MA 01004 and their excellent website is at www.transitionsabroad.com.

When researching a trip, budget some money for information-gathering. Many organisations now give out information through automated interactive premium lines, which usually cost 50p a minute but some are £1 or even £1.50. The internet opens up lots of cheaper possibilities though there is a bewildering array of resources.

Try a search engine like www.monster.com which lists over 50,000 jobs worldwide or an introduction to the range of lists available on www.job-hunt.org. A host of websites promise to provide free on-line recruitment services for travellers. These include Working Zoo, recently launched by STA Travel (www.workingzoo.com) and there are many others like www.hotrecruit.co.uk, www.summerjobs.com, Jobs Abroad Bulletin (www.payaway. co.uk), www.summerjobseeker.com, www.gapwork.com, www.anyworkanywhere.com, www.youngtravellers.com and so on. Because many are in their infancy, they often seem to offer more than they can deliver and you may find that the number and range of jobs posted are disappointing. But everywhere you look on the internet potentially useful links can be found. A surprising number of company home pages feature an icon you can click to find out about jobs. Elsewhere on the web, committed individuals around the world manage non-commercial sites on everything from kibbutzim to bar-tending. The Vacation Work website (www.vacationwork.co.uk) has a regularly updated section listing job vacancies for travellers both in Britain and abroad.

Advertisements

Some foreign newspapers can be read on-line which makes it easier to reply to job advertisements as soon as they appear which is much more satisfactory than trying to get hold of hard copies in libraries or embassy reading rooms. While you are still at home you might be in a position to advertise yourself abroad (or both). Specialist newsagents do often carry foreign papers, though in some cases bulky Saturday supplements (including classified employment ads) have been jettisoned before shipping.

Unless you have very specialised skills, it is probably not worth advertising your services and availability for work in a foreign newspaper since anyone interested in hiring you would probably want to meet you first and advertising this way is expensive. If you have set your sights on finding work in a specific region, it is possible to advertise in the classified sections of newspapers abroad either directly (check addresses in *Willings Press Guide* in any library) or through a UK-based representative (e.g. Smyth International Media Representatives, 1 Torrington Park, London N12 9GG).

Another paper which might be worth checking is *LOOT* (24-32 Kilburn High Road, London NW6 5TF; 020-7328 1771) which bills itself as 'London's noticeboard,' although the *Loot* group publishes a total of 26 weekly publications throughout the UK. Among its many categories of classified ads (which are free to private advertisers) are 'International Jobs Offered/Wanted' (which doesn't usually contain anything very exciting) and 'Au Pair Jobs Offered/Wanted.' The paper is published daily Monday to Friday and costs £1.30. It is just one of many free newspapers worldwide in the Free Ads Paper International Association, usually printed on coloured newsprint. It is possible to advertise free of charge in any of these papers (from San Diego to Sofia, Rio to Ravenna) which are listed in each issue of *LOOT* with instructions for placing ads.

If you use a foreign newspaper's box office service, there may be delays in receiving replies. In any case, you must allow plenty of time to receive replies and (with luck) negotiate a suitable position. If possible talk to your prospective employer on the telephone and ascertain as many details as possible, to prevent what happened to Eric Mackness:

> *I had an 'interesting' time in Hungary. I answered an ad in* The Lady *magazine for a house-sitter in a house mid-way between Budapest and Vienna. It was an absolute nightmare. A grubby little house, full of cats (there must have been 30) at the end of a mile-long mud track in the middle of a Hammer Horror forest, all dripping skeletal mist-enshrouded trees and howling dogs (wolves?). Quite an experience.*

Always try to obtain a written promise of work and terms of employment before making any life-changing decisions.

GETTING A JOB ON ARRIVAL

For those who leave home without something fixed up, a lot of initiative will be needed. Many travellers find it easier to locate casual work in country areas rather than cities, and outside the student holiday periods (although just before Christmas is a good time, when staff turnover is high). But it is possible in cities too, on building sites, in restaurants and in factories. If you go for the jobs which are least appealing (e.g. an orderly in a hospital for the criminally insane, a loo attendant, doing a street promotion dressed as a koala or a hamburger, a pylon painter, assistant in a battery chicken farm, salesman of encyclopaedia, dog meat factory worker, dog policemen (in Berlin, people are hired to follow dog-walkers) or just plain dogsbodies, the chances are you will be taken on sooner rather than later.

It always helps to have a neat appearance in order to dissociate yourself from the image of the hobo or hippy. You must show a keenness and persistence which may be out of character but are often essential. Even if a prospective employer turns you down at first, ask again since it is human nature to want to reward keenness and he or she may decide that an extra staff member could be useful after all. Polite pestering pays off. For example, if your requests for work down on the docks produce nothing one day, you must return the next day. After a week your face will be familiar and your eagerness and availability known to potential employers. If nothing seems to be materialising, volunteer to help mend nets (thereby adding a new skill to the ones you can offer) and if an opening does eventually arise, you will be the obvious choice. If you want a job teaching English in a school but there appear to be no openings, volunteer to assist with a class one day a week for no pay and if you prove yourself competent, you will have an excellent chance of filling any vacancy which does occur. So patience and persistence should become your watchwords, and before long you will belong to the fraternity of experienced, worldly-wise travellers who can maintain themselves on the road for extended periods.

Casual work by its very nature is changeable and unpredictable and can best be searched out on the spot. It pays to have your wits about you at all times. According to a collection of the oddest odd jobs spotted on the Lonely Planet web-site, a penniless traveller in Paris was nearly killed by a bag of tools falling from a construction site. He caught the bag, climbed the scaffolding with the tools, told the builders how they could easily arrange a pulley and was immediately hired as a mason's assistant for a month.

You may follow the advice in this book to go to Avignon France in August, for example, to pick plums or to Magnetic Island Australia to get bar work. When you arrive you may be disappointed to learn that the harvest was unusually early or the resort has already hired enough staff. But your informant may go on to say that if you wait two weeks you can pick grapes or if you travel to the next reef island, there is a shortage of dining room staff. In other words, one thing leads to another once you are on the track.

A certain amount of bravado is a good, even a necessary, thing. If you must exaggerate the amount of experience you have had or the time you intend to stay in order to get a chance to do a job, then so be it. There is little room for shyness and self-effacement in the enterprise of working your way around the world. (On the other hand, bluffing is not recommended if it might result in danger, for example if you pretend to have more sailing experience than you really do for a transatlantic crossing.) After circumnavigating the globe and working in a number of countries David Cooksley comments:

> *All the information and contacts in the world are absolutely useless unless you make a personal approach to the particular situation. You must be resourceful and never retiring. If I were the manager of a large company which needed self-motivating sales people, I'd hire all the contributors to* Work Your Way Around the World *since they have the ability to communicate with anyone anywhere in any language.*

Meeting People

The most worthwhile source of information is without question your fellow travellers. After you have hurled yourself into the fray you will soon become connected up with kindred spirits more experienced at the game than you, whose advice you should heed. Other travellers are surprisingly generous with their information and assistance. David Hewitt claims that this cannot be overemphasised; he and his Brazilian wife have been consistently helped by their compatriots from Berlin to Miami. A Mexican correspondent who arrived in Toronto cold sought out the Latino community and, after taking their advice, was soon comfortably housed and employed.

Hitch-hiking is a good means for getting leads on work, providing you pump the local people who give you lifts for any useful information. If you arrive in a new place without a prearranged contact, there are many ways of meeting the locals and other travellers to find out about job possibilities. Youth hostels are universally recommended, especially out of season, and many hostel wardens will be well versed in the local opportunities for casual jobs. Membership in the Youth Hostels Association costs £12 if you're over 18; you can join at any hostel or at their London office (14 Southampton St, WC2E 7HY; 020-7836 8541).

Private hostels outside the International Youth Hostels Federation are sometimes even better sources of information on local work opportunities. Check the website www.hostels.com for a selection worldwide. VIP Backpacker Resorts of Australia (PO Box 600, Cannon Hill, Brisbane, Qld 4170, Australia) have hundreds of hostels in Australia New Zealand and worldwide.

Universities and polytechnics are good meeting places in term-time and also during the vacations when it is often possible to arrange cheap accommodation in student residences. Seek out the overseas student club to meet interesting people who are foreigners just like you. Investigate the student or bohemian parts of town where the itinerant community tends to congregate. Go to the pubs and cafés frequented by worldly-wise travellers (often the ones serving Guinness).

If you have a particular hobby or interest, ask if there is a local club, where you will meet like-minded people; join local ramblers, cyclists, cavers, environmental activists, train spotters, jazz buffs – the more obscure the more welcome you are likely to be. Join evening language courses, frequent the English language bookshop (which may well have a useful notice board) or visit the functions of the English language church, where you are likely to meet the expatriate community or be offered free advice by the vicar. Marta Eleniak introduced herself to the local Polish club, since she has a Polish surname and a fondness for the country, to ask if she could put up a notice asking for accommodation. The kindly soul to whom she was speaking told her not to worry about it; she'd find her something she could move into the next day. She has come to the conclusion that learning to be a 'fog-horn' is an invaluable characteristic.

Not that the people you will meet in this way will necessarily be able to give you a full-time job, but it sets the wheels in motion and before too long you will be earning your way by following their advice and leads. Provided your new friends speak the local language better than you, they can make telephone calls for you, translate newspaper advertisements, write out a message for you to show possible employers and even act as interpreters. One young Englishman was dragged along to the local radio station by his Italian hosts who persuaded the station to have him co-host an afternoon programme. The manager of another traveller's hostel in Cairo wrote out an Arabic notice for him, offering private English lessons.

If your contacts can't offer you a real job they might know of a 'pseudo job' or 'non-job' which can keep you afloat: guarding their yacht, doing odd jobs around their property, babysitting, typing, teaching the children English, or just staying for free. These neatly avoid the issue of work permits, too, since they are arranged on an entirely unofficial and personal basis. Human contacts are usually stronger than red tape.

Chance

When you first set off, the possibility of being a sheep-catcher in the Australian outback or an English tutor in Turkey may never have crossed your mind. Chance is a fine thing and is one of the traveller's greatest allies. Brigitte Albrech had saved up leave from her job in the German tourist industry to go on holiday in Mexico. While there, she became friendly with some Québecois who invited her to join them as tree planters in Western Canada, and she never made it back to her job.

There will be times when you will be amazed by the lucky chain of events which led you into a certain situation. 'Being in the right place at the right time' would have made a suitable subtitle to this book, though of course there are steps you can take to put yourself in the right place, and this book tries to point out what these might be. Here are some examples of how luck, often in combination with initiative, has resulted in travellers finding paid work:

Mark Kilburn took up busking in a small Dutch town and was eventually asked to play a few nights a week in a nearby pub for a fee.

Stuart Britton was befriended by a fisherman in a dusty little town in Mexico and was soon tutoring some of the fisherman's friends and acquaintances (and living in his house).

While standing in a post office queue in the south of France, Brian Williams overheard the word *boulot* (which he knew to mean odd job) and *cerises*. He tapped the lady on the shoulder and offered his cherry picking expertise. After a protracted search for the address she had given him, he finally asked directions of someone who offered him a job in their orchard instead.

On a flight to Reykjavik, Caroline Nicholls happened to sit next to the wife of the managing director of a large fish-packing cooperative in Iceland who told her they were short of staff.

After finishing his summer stint as a camp counsellor in the US, Mark Kinder decided to try one parachute jump. He enjoyed it so much that he learned how to pack parachutes and was able to fund himself at the aerodrome for months afterwards.

While looking for work on a boat in Antibes, Tom Morton found a job as a goatherd for six weeks in the mountains near Monte Carlo.

Dominic Fitzgibbon mentioned to his landlady in Rome that he intended to leave soon for Greece since he had been unable to find a job locally in six weeks of looking. She decided he was far too nice to become a washer-up in a taverna and arranged for him to work as a hall porter at a friend's hotel.

I. A. Gowing was a little startled to wake up one evening in Frankfurt station to find a middle-aged women staring down at him. She offered him the chance of working with her travelling fun-fair.

While getting her jabs for Africa at a clinic in Gibraltar, Mary Hall (a nurse cycling across Europe) noticed a door marked 'District Nurses', barged in and the following week had moved in as a live-in private nurse for a failing old lady.

While shopping in a supermarket in Cyprus, Rhona Stannage noticed a local man with a trolley full of wine and beer, and assumed it could not be for his own consumption. She approached him, ascertained that he ran a restaurant and a day or two later was employed as a waitress.

Connie Paraskeva shared a taxi in Bangkok with an American nurse who told her about a vacancy in a refugee camp.

While sunbathing on an isolated Greek beach, Edward Peters was approached by a farmer and asked to pick his oranges.

The examples could be multiplied *ad infinitum* of how travellers, by keeping their ears open and by making their willingness to help obvious, have fallen into work. One of the keys to success is total flexibility. Within ten minutes of a chance conversation with a family sharing her breakfast table in an Amsterdam hotel, Caroline Langdon had paid her bill, packed her bags and was off to Portugal with them as their mother's help.

Of course there is always such a thing as bad luck too. You may have received all sorts of inside information about a job on a Greek island, a vineyard or in a ski resort. But if a war has decimated tourism (as the Gulf War did) or if there was a late frost which killed off the grapes or if the snowfalls have been poor, there will be far fewer jobs and your information may prove useless. Unpredictability is built into the kinds of jobs which travellers do.

Design

But you cannot rely on luck alone; you will have to create your own luck at times. You may have to apply to 20 hotels before one will accept you and you may have to inform 20 acquaintances of your general plans before one gives you the address of a useful contact. Public libraries can be helpful as proved by the traveller who found a directory of wildlife and environmental organisations in a South African library and went on to fix up a board-and-lodging job at a game reserve.

You must check notice boards and newspaper advertisements, register with agencies and most important of all use the unselective 'walk-in-and-ask' method, just like job-seekers anywhere. The most important tools for an on-the-spot job hunt are a copy of the Yellow Pages and a phone card. When Mary Hall was starting her job search in Switzerland, a friend gave her an odd piece of advice which she claims works, to smile while speaking on the phone. Some people say that all initial approaches are best made by telephone since refusals are less demoralising than in person and you need not worry about the scruffiness of your wardrobe.

One old hand Alan Corrie, describes his approach:

The town of Annecy in the French Alps looked great so I found a fairly cheap hostel and got down to getting organised. This meant I was doing the rounds of the agencies, employment office, notice boards and cafés for a few days. After a matter of minutes in a town, I begin to sprout plastic bags full of maps, plans, lists, addresses and scraps of advice from people I have met on the road.

Alan sounds unusually cheerful and optimistic about job-hunting and the result is that he worked in Europe for the better part of a decade. He concludes:

Looking for work in Annecy was an enjoyable pastime in early autumn. Making contacts and job hunting in a new place is a whole lot more fun than actually working and worrying about the bills as I've often found before.

Our working wanderers have displayed remarkable initiative and found their jobs in a great variety of ways:

Waiter in Northern Cyprus: *I arranged my job by writing direct to the restaurant after seeing a two-minute clip on a BBC travel programme. Rita wrote back and here I am.*

Farmhand on a Danish farm: *I placed an advert in* Landsbladet, *the farmers' weekly, and chose one from four replies.*

Au pair to a family in Helsinki: *I found work as a nanny in Finland simply by placing advertisement cards in a few playgroups.*

Teacher at a language school in southern Italy: *We used the Yellow Pages in a Sicilian Post Office and from our 30 speculative applications received four job offers without so much as an interview.*

Winery guide in Spain: *I composed a modest and polite letter and sent it to an address copied from one of my father's wine labels. I was astonished at their favourable reply.* Several years later the same contributor wrote to say, *I sent a copy of the page in your book where I am mentioned to prospective employers in Australia, and I was offered a job on a vineyard near Melbourne.*

Factory assistant in Ghana: *I asked the local Amnesty International representative for any leads.*

Implicit in all these stories is that you must take positive action.

REWARDS AND RISKS

The Delights

The rewards of travelling are mostly self-evident: the interesting characters and lifestyles you are sure to meet, the wealth of anecdotes you will collect with which you can regale your grandchildren and photos with which you can bore your friends, a feeling of achievement, an increased self-reliance and maturity, learning to budget, a better perspective on your own country and your own habits, a good sun tan... the list could continue. Stephen Psallidas summed up his views on travelling:

Meeting people from all over the world gives you a more tolerant attitude to other nationalities, races, etc. More importantly you learn to tolerate yourself, to learn more about your strengths and weaknesses. While we're on the clichés, you definitely 'find yourself, man'.

One traveller came back from a stint of working on the Continent feeling a part of Europe rather than just an Englishman. (Perhaps some Brussels bureaucrat should be subsidising this book.) Sometimes travels abroad change the direction of your life. After working his way around the world in many low-paid and exploitative jobs, Ken Smith decided to specialise in studying employment law. After deciding to cycle through Africa on an extended hospital, Mary Hall ended up working for aid organisations in Africa and the Middle East.

One of the best aspects of the travelling life is that you are a free and unfettered agent. Albert Schweizer might have been thinking of the working traveller instead of equatorial Africans when he wrote:

He works well under certain circumstances so long as the circumstances require it. He is not idle, but he is a free man, hence he is always a casual worker.

The Dangers

Of course things can go desperately wrong, as they did for Louise Woodward. Several other young women and men who have been travelling and looking for work abroad have been murdered. Any women who are feeling especially anxious about the risks of travelling and working abroad might be cheered by the statistic that of all the letters addressed to the editor of this book (nearly half from women), not one hinted that she was sorry she had gone. In many ways a solo woman traveller gains extra respect from the people she meets and in many cases finds it easier to get work. A worthwhile book to browse in for advice and encouragement is *Women Travel* (Rough Guides, £12.99).

A much less remote possibility is that you might be robbed or lose your luggage. You may get sick or lonely or fed up. (Always arrange to keep in e-mail contact or to receive mail from time to time via poste restante or American Express to avoid becoming completely alienated from your roots.) You might have a demoralising run of bad luck and fail to find a job, and begin to run out of money (if this is the case, consult the chapter *In Extremis*).

Many unofficial jobs carry with them an element of insecurity. You may not be protected by employment legislation and may not be in a position to negotiate with the boss. Often the work may be available to travellers like you because the conditions are unacceptable to a stable local population (or because the place is too remote to have a local population). Phil New is probably right when he says that the travellers who worry that they won't get paid or won't get hired are the very ones who do encounter problems. If you have cultivated the right attitude, you will not hesitate to drift on to a new situation if the old one should become undesirable for any reason.

Exploitative working conditions will show you how much you are prepared to tolerate. Paul Bridgland was not sorry to have worked for a tyrannical and abusive boss in Crete, since he now thinks he has developed such a thick skin that no future employer could penetrate it.

Much is now said about 'socially responsible tourism' and perhaps working travellers who put up with dreadful employers are doing both their host community and other travellers a disservice. Stephen Psallidas's advice (based on his own experience of exploitative Greek bosses) is not to put up with it:

> *My advice when you are mistreated or your employer acts unprofessionally is to shout back when they shout at you. If things don't improve threaten to walk out and then do so. You will be doing a favour to future working travellers, and you will almost certainly be able to find something else if you try hard enough.*

Charlotte Jakobson's worst employer was a hotelier in the middle of nowhere in Norway. When she discovered how underpaid she was she contacted a union official who was shocked and wanted to take action. Today she regrets that she was so keen to get away that she didn't stay to present the case and thinks of other girls who were probably subjected to the same bad experiences as a result.

Travellers have a responsibility towards future travellers in other respects. Robert Mallakee felt that he should work especially hard for a Cypriot farmer who had lent his previous English helper £200 just before the fellow absconded. The respect and sensitivity you should show to other cultures is even more important in a working context.

Some people set off with false expectations about the life of the working traveller. Armin Birrer (who has travelled long enough to have earned his right to make such pronouncements) says that some of the enthusiasm with which travel writers tend to glorify travel should be moderated a little. The travelling life is full of uncertainty and hardship. To quote the inveterate working traveller Stephen Psallidas once more, 'I would say that the bad times even outnumber the good times, but the good times are *great* and the bad times are good for you in the end.'

Even when a planned working holiday does not work out successfully, the experience will be far more memorable than just staying at home. This view is held by Stephen Hands who didn't regret his decision to go abroad to look for work (although it didn't work out) but he did regret boasting to all his friends that he was off for an indefinite period to see the world. After writing pages about her dodgy and difficult jobs in Australia, Emma Dunnage concluded with a typical paradox: 'But we did have the best time of our lives'.

Though travelling itself is never dull, a job which you find to help out your finances along the way may well be. True 'working holidays' are rare: one example is to exchange your labour for a free trip with an outback Australian camping tour operator (see *Australia* chapter) or for a cruise to the midnight sun (see *Scandinavia*). But in many cases, the expression 'working holiday' is an oxymoron (like 'cruel kindness'). Jobs are jobs wherever you do them. David Anderson, who found himself working on an isolated Danish farm where he didn't feel at home in any way, recommends taking (a) your time to decide to accept a job, (b) a copy of *War and Peace* and (c) enough money to facilitate leaving if necessary. The best policy is to leave home only after you have the reserves to be able to work when you want to.

Coming Home

Kristin Moen thinks that there should be a big warning at the beginning of *Work Your Way Around the World:* WHEN YOU FIRST START TO TRAVEL THERE IS NO WAY YOU CAN STOP! Correspondents have variously called travel an illness and an addiction. Once you set off you will probably come across a few restless souls for whom the idea of settling down is anathema and for whom the word 'vagabondage' was invented. One contributor met a 44 year old New Zealander in Sydney recently who had been travelling and working for 25 years. Undoubtedly some use it as a form of escapism, believing it to be a panacea for all their problems. But these are the exceptions.

In the majority of cases, homesickness eventually sets in, and the longing for a pint of bitter, a bacon sandwich, a baseball game, Radio 4's 'Today' programme, green fields, Marks & Spencer or Mum's home cooking will get the better of you. Or perhaps duty intervenes as in the case of Michael Tunison:

> *I had planned to go on to South America this summer, but I had to return home under emergency circumstances. Not one, but two of my best friends were getting married. What is a poor globetrotter to do with people rather inconsiderately going on with their lives when he isn't even there? But after a year it was actually quite nice to have a chance to organise my things and repack for further adventures.*

At some point your instinct will tell you that the time has come to hang up your rucksack (assuming you haven't sold it).

Settling back will be difficult especially if you have not been able to set aside some money for 'The Return'. As soon as he left Asia en route back from Australia, Riwan Hafiz began to feel depressed and when he arrived at Heathrow wanted to put a blanket over his head. It can be a wretched feeling after some glorious adventures to find yourself with nothing to start over on. One travel writer has compared the post Travel Blues to SAD (Seasonal Affective Disorder). Life at home may seem dull and routine at first, while the outlook of your friends and family can strike you as narrow and limited. If you have been round the world between school and further study, you may find it difficult to bridge the gulf between you and your stay-at-home peers who may feel a little threatened or belittled by your experiences. If you have spent time in developing countries the reverse culture shock may be acute, as Chris Miksovsky from Colorado discovered:

> *Memories of the trip already come racing back at the oddest of times. A few days after returning to the US, I went to a large grocery store with my mother. It was overwhelming. Rows and rows of colours and logos all screaming to get your attention. I wandered over to the popcorn display and stood dumbfounded by the variety: buttered, lite, generic, Redenbacker, Paul Newman's au naturel, from single serving sachet through economy family popcorn-orgy size. I counted over 25 unique offerings... of popcorn.*

But it passes. The reverse culture shock normally wears off soon enough and you will begin to feel reintegrated in your course or job. In some cases the changes which travel have brought about may be more than just psychological; for example David Hewitt set off on his travels a bachelor, married a fellow volunteer from Brazil met on his kibbutz and then had a child whom they were trying to make into a working traveller before she reached her first birthday by putting her forward for promotions in the US.

People often wonder whether a long spell of travelling or living abroad will damage their future job prospects. According to numerous surveys on graduate employment, most employers are sympathetic to people who defer entry to the labour market. The prominent Channel 4 newsreader Jon Snow was quoted in an interview about the changes that doing a stint with VSO radicalised him and transformed him from being a very sheltered Englishman into someone who had discovered resourcefulness in himself and wanted to stretch himself. And look what happened to J.K. Rowling who began writing Harry Potter while teaching English in Portugal.

In the majority of cases, travel seems to be considered an advantage, something that makes you stand out from the crowd. Marcus Scrace found that even in his profession of chartered surveying, employers looked favourably on someone who had had the get-up-and-go to work his way around the world. Jeremy Pack chose to join the computing industry upon his return and claimed that he did not meet one negative reaction to his two years off. Naturally it helps if you can present your experiences positively, if only to prevent the potential employer from imagining you out of your skull on a beach in Goa for 12 months. Your travels must be presented constructively and not as an extended doss. Stephen Psallidas, who recently returned to a more settled existence after three years on the road, is convinced that he would never have got a good job (as Projects Manager in Computer Education) before he left. Not that he gained any relevant experience on his travels but he had learned how to be persistent and pester employers for an interview.

Some hostility is probably inevitable especially when the job market is shrinking making employers more conservative. Jane Thomas knew that it would be tough finding a job when she got back to England, but she didn't know how tough. Some interviewers did express their concern and suspicion that she would want to take off again (which at that time was exactly what she did want to do). But she also found that she could adapt the short-term jobs she had done in the US and Australia to fit whatever job she was trying to get. And after a certain period of time has elapsed, your absence from the conventional working world ceases to be an issue. At last report Jane had a job making videos with the possibility of some work with the BBC.

In some cases the jobs you have found abroad are a positive boost to your 'real life' prospects, as in the case of Michael Tunison from Michigan:

> *Newspaper work was exactly what I thought I was leaving behind by globetrotting. I'd temporarily sacrificed (I believed) my career as a journalist. The last place I thought I'd be working was at a daily in Mexico. But things never work out as planned and before I knew it I was the managing editor's assistant and a month or so later the managing editor of the paper's weekend editions. How ironic. By taking a step my newspaper friends believed to be an irresponsible career move, I was soon years ahead of where I'd have been following the old safe route back home.*

Conclusion

While some identify the initial decision to go abroad as the hardest part, others find the inevitable troughs (such as finding yourself alone in a sleazy hotel room on your birthday, running out of money with no immediate prospect of work, etc.) more difficult to cope with. But if travelling requires a much greater investment of energy than staying at home, it will reward the effort many times over.

A host of travellers have mentioned how much they value their collection of memories. Since we have been guided by the experiences of ordinary travellers throughout the writing of this book, let one of their number, Steve Hendry, end the *Introduction*:

> *I left home with about £100 and no return ticket. I spent two years in Israel, three years in Thailand, one year in Japan. I have lived in the sun for years, with Arabs on the seashore and with wealthy Japanese. If I can do it, you can too. I've learned so very much. Travelling is 100% fun and educational. What are you waiting for?*

WORKING A PASSAGE

Many people setting out on their world travels assume, not unreasonably, that a large chunk of their savings must inevitably be swallowed up by airlines, railways and shipping companies. This need not be so. With a little advance planning, a fair amount of bravado and a dose of good fortune you can follow the example of thousands of travellers who have successfully voyaged around the globe for next to nothing.

Hitch-hiking is an excellent way to cross several continents (see *Travel*), but usually fails to solve the problem of sea crossings. Since it is a relatively slow means of travel, it also eats into your funds since you need to sustain yourself en route. Fortunately, if you are serious about travelling free or cheaply in ways other than hitch-hiking, there are several methods of working a passage by land, sea or air.

SEA

Commercial Shipping

Only registered seafarers are allowed to work on British-registered ships. The only realistic hope for casual employment and attendant transport lies with the more far-flung lines of Scandinavia and the Far East, or with the numerous ships sailing under flags of convenience e.g. Panama, Liberia and the great maritime nation of Liechtenstein. A high percentage of UK ships are flagged out (i.e. registered abroad) to avoid the high cost of unionised British labour. Very occasionally a medium-sized cargo ship takes on an individual with a skill such as catering or carpentry who has petitioned the captain for work, though in the vast majority of cases, merchant ships are fully staffed with low paid, non-unionised workers, many of whom are recruited from Third World countries.

We have heard of very few intrepid travellers who have succeeded with this method. After spending six months in India some years ago, one such traveller went down to the enormous bustling harbour of Bombay and asked the captain of a cargo boat from Ghana to take him on as an assistant; within an hour of asking he had set sail for Egypt. His duties were simply to run messages, keep watch and share the cooking duties. Later during his travels around Africa, Steve tried the same technique, this time in Conakry the capital of Guinea on the coast of West Africa. He started at one end of the commercial harbour and the fifth boat agreed to take him to Casablanca (a nine-day trip) in exchange for his labour and about £20 towards expenses. This was not nearly as enjoyable a voyage as the one across the Arabian Sea since he was given the most unpleasant jobs like cleaning the cargo hold and pumping out the bilge, plus he wasn't given a proper berth.

The harbour authorities can be helpful, especially in countries off the beaten track. (Be careful not to confuse them with customs officers.) They will sometimes show enquirers a list of all the ships arriving and departing, since commercial shipping is almost as carefully regulated as air traffic. Sometimes you will have to ask their permission to go on to the docks, for example in Port Sudan you need to get a permit from the wharf police before you can ask captains for a lift to Mombasa or India. It is worth getting on the right side of the harbour-master since captains may tell him about their need of extra crew. At least, they can advise you about the tides. When it is coming up to high tide (spring tide) boats leave, and so this is a good time to ask around. Harbourside bars are not a good place to introduce yourself to captains since this is their off-duty time. They are more likely to consider your offer seriously when they are aboard their vessel. It is a good idea, however to chat up the barman in the local harbour bar, buy him a drink and ask him to keep his ears open.

Cruise Liners

The luxury cruise liner business is absolutely booming. Apparently more British holidaymakers went on a cruise last year than had a skiing holiday. Over a thousand liners sail the world's oceans at present, with more being built all the time, including two from the Disney Corporation that have gone into service in the past couple of years. Every cruise ship requires a full range of staff, just as a fancy hotel does. Most recruitment takes place through agencies or 'concessionaires', all of whom say that they are looking only for qualified and experienced staff. But in many cases it is sufficient to be over 21 and have an extrovert personality and plenty of stamina for the very long hours of work on board. Job-seekers with no skills should be wary of agencies that invite them to pay a fee to circulate their CV on-line; this may well work for the highly qualified but there are probably far more people looking for work than there are employers looking for staff this way. Websites to try are: Sea Cruise Enterprises (www.seacruisent.com), Blue Seas' International Seafarers Exchange (www.jobxchange.com) and Ocean Crews Maritime Employment (www. maritimeemployment.com). The privately run site www.ucs.mun.ca/ ~rklein/ cruise.html calls itself a no frills page of cruise lines and cruise links, and it is possible to find contact details of cruise lines and concessionaires here.

According to Jane Roberts, who crossed the Atlantic from Venezuela to Estonia as a cruise line croupier, not all employees are experienced professionals:

> *I worked in the casino department of four different cruise ships and met many people doing jobs as waiters, bar tenders, stewards and stewardesses. These jobs are very easy to come by. In fact 80% of all crew members are people who have never done that particular job in their lives. The turn-over of staff is high, even when people sign year-long contracts, since few people complete them. It is difficult to live and work with the same people 24 hours a day. Crew don't get days off, perhaps just the odd breakfast or lunch off once a month. Patience levels have to be extremely high, since people who take holidays on cruise ships seem to think that they own the damn ship. Having to be sickeningly nice can take its toll very quickly.*

Contract lengths (some as short as four months) and conditions vary from ship to ship. The smaller, classier ships are your best bet. On larger ships you may have four to a cabin and communal, smelly showers/toilets. Wages are usually US$300-$400 a month but can be increased with tips.

In most cases it is essential to be hired through an agency. When Stephen Cleary was in Acapulco he decided he wanted to work on a ship. When he asked a ship owned by the British company Princess Cruises (owned by P&O) he was told that he would have to go to Los Angeles because they could not sort out the paperwork and when he enquired in LA he was told he had to apply in Southampton. On the other hand some local cruise ships may hire people on-the-spot. When Stephen Psallidas was working on the Greek island of Mykonos, he noticed that several Aegean cruise ships were looking for staff.

Some UK and European agencies that have advertised for cruise line staff in the past year include:

Crewsline UK, 0151-339 2278/fax 0151-339 8946; Crewslineuk@btinternet.com. Recently seeking food and beverage service staff for US cruise lines.

Cruise Service Center Ltd, Palme & Associates, 123 Warwick Rd, Banbury, Oxon. OX16 2AR (01295 701450; office@cruiseservicecenter.com/ www.cruiseservicecenter.com). Recruits middle and senior hotel management and service staff year round.

CTI Group London, 207/209 Regent St, London W1 (020-7734 9412; cti-uk@cti-usa.com; www.cti-usa.com). Official recruiters of catering staff for Renaissance Cruises, Carnival Cruise Line, etc. Head office is in Fort Lauderdale Florida: 1535 SE 17th St, Suite 2-06, Fort Lauderdale, FL 33316; ctigroup@cti-usa.com).

International Cruise Management Ag A/S, PO Box 95, (Jernbanetorget 4B), Sentrum, 0101 Oslo, Norway (+47 23 35 79 00; office@icma.no; www.icma.no). Recruits staff with 2-3 years experience for four luxury vessels (Norwegian Crystal Cruises). More than 1,000 people hired each year out of 10,000 applicants.

Openwide International Ltd, 7 Westmoreland House, Cumberland Park, London NW10 6RE (020-8962 3400; www.openwideinternational.com). Recruits entertainers and performers to work on cruise ships in the Mediterranean and Caribbean.

Princess Cruises Recruiting Agents, c/o P&O Cruises Ltd., Richmond House, Terminus Terrace, Southampton SO14 3PN.

Seafarers Recruitment Ltd, PO Box 34, Longue Hougue Lane, St Sampson, Guernsey GY1 3US. Recruiting mid-2000 for Sun Cruises (a division of Airtours).

Sea Sources Inc., Molckhofgasse 3 T.7, 5020 Salzburg, Austria (+43 662-849786). Recruiting for Silversea Cruises Ltd. Highly professional staff needed for expanding fleet.

Seefar Associates, 7 Berkeley Crescent, Gravesend, Kent DA12 2AH (01474 32990; seefar@globalnet.co.uk). Hire for Disney Cruise Line, Festival Cruise Line, Royal Caribbean and Celebrity Cruise Lines.

Ads for professional hotel and catering staff for cruise lines appear in the specialist press like *The Caterer* and *Hotel Keeper.* Specialist catering agencies like VIP International (17 Charing Cross Road, London WC2H 0EP; 020-7930 0541) supply experienced catering, management and other personnel for various cruise lines.

Anyone interested in working on a cruise ship should consult a specialist book listing the cruise lines and the companies that do their hiring for them. *Working on Cruise Ships* by Sandra Bow (Vacation-Work, £10.99) contains many useful addresses to follow up. Do not be misled by advertisements which read 'Cruise Ships are Hiring Now' or websites with names like shipjobs or cruiselinejobs. These are almost always placed by someone trying to sell a book about employment on cruise ships, and these are of varying quality. One of the more useful in the field is the one from Innovative Cruise Services (36 Midlothian Drive, Glasgow G41 3QU; 0141-649 8644/fax 0141-636 1016; info@cruiseservices.co.uk/ www.cruiseservices.co.uk); the fee for the 2001 edition is £25 which includes two years' access to Newsletters containing vacancy lists supplied by a partner agent in Florida (Falcon Corporate Ltd in Floral City).

One of the best books published in the US is *How to Get a Job with a Cruise Line* by Mary Fallon Miller (Ticket to Adventure Inc, PO Box 41005, St Petersburg, FL 33743-1005; 727-822-5029/1-800-929-7447); the 2000/2001 edition costs $16.95 plus $4 US postage/$9 overseas. It contains a directory of cruise line headquarters and employment agencies, most of which are in Florida.

Anyone already in Florida might be able to arrange interviews with the cruise lines or their concessionaires. But do not get too excited if you see advertisements in newspapers or universities for people (including students) to work on cruise ships. Sander Meijsen from the Netherlands paid a fee of $150 to an agency called Job Success Inc whom he'd seen advertising, but in fact never got a job on a cruise line:

> *In my case I had to call the agent every day to find out if anything new came up which meant a huge phone bill (since they put you on hold all the time to retrieve your file). So I quit calling which probably means that I will lose my fee. I chose this agency because they told me you do not need a work permit. But when no cruise companies called me, I took the liberty of calling them and most told me that they hire only people with work authorisations.*

The correct visa for working at sea is a C/1-D visa which is granted only after you have a job contract. Other cruise lines to call in Florida are Dolphin, Princess, Royal Caribbean and Renaissance.

Private Yachts

People who sail the seas for pleasure are not subject to the same restrictions as merchant or cruise ship owners. They may hire and fire a crew member whenever they like, and work permits are not a problem. If you display a reasonable level of common sense, vigour and amiability, and take the trouble to observe yachting etiquette, you should find it possible to persuade a yachtsman that you will be an asset to his crew. It should be stressed that inexperienced crew are almost never paid; in fact most skippers expect some contribution towards expenses; US$25 a day is standard for food, drink, fuel, harbour fees, etc. Safety is of paramount importance as was highlighted by the tragedy in 2000 when several Cambridge University students crewing for an experienced skipper were lost in the North Sea.

After crewing from Tonga to New Zealand and then on to Australia, Gerhard Flaig summed up the pros and cons of ocean sailing:

> *It definitely is adventurous to sail on the ocean. You usually meet dolphins, whales, fish and birds. You get in close touch with nature to see and feel the waves and to see wonderful sunsets. You learn about sailing, meteorology, navigation. But there are also drawbacks. Maybe you get seasick, that's no fun. Then you have to deal with pouring rain and heavy storms. You have to get up in the middle of the night for the watch. The boat is wobbling all the time so that makes every little job more difficult, even going to the toilet. Maybe there is no wind at all for days and then it's frustrating not to move and to be far away from land. If you are willing to deal with all that then a sailing trip can be most rewarding.*

Obviously, it is much easier to become a crew member if you have some experience. But there are opportunities for people who lack experience at sea, and it is unwise to exaggerate your skills. Once you have worked on one yacht it will be much easier to get on the next one. The yachting world is a small one. The more experience you have, the more favourable arrangements you will be able to negotiate. Also, your chances are better of having a financial contribution waived if you are prepared to crew on unpopular routes, for example crossing the Atlantic west to east is much tougher than vice versa. If you are embarking on a serious round-the-world-on-a-shoestring venture, read a yachting book such as the *RYA Competent Crew Handbook* which contains invaluable information on technical sea terms and the basics of navigation. If you demonstrate to a skipper that you take safety seriously enough to have learned a little about the procedures and if you are clean and sober, sensible and polite, you are probably well on your way to filling a crewing vacancy.

Also consider doing a short sailing course (and take your certificate with you). The first level, Competent Crew, can be reached in a five-day course at any Royal Yachting Association recognised centre for £250-£400; details from the RYA, Romsey Road, Eastleigh, Hants. SO50 9YA (023 8062 7400; www.rya.org.uk), who can also send you a leaflet 'Careers in Sailing' and a list of crew registers in Britain. Anyone who is a confident cook, carpenter, electrician, mechanic or sewing machine operator (for sail-mending) may be able to market those skills too.

Several firms specialise in preparing people for a career in sailing or watersports such as the UK Sailing Academy (West Cowes, Isle of Wight PO31 7PQ; 01983 294941; www.uk-sail.org.uk) and Flying Fish (25 Union Road, Cowes, Isle of Wight PO31 7TW; 01983 280641/fax 01983 281821); see *Tourism: Activity Holidays* for further details. If these courses are too expensive, go down to your nearest marina and offer to do some hard and tedious maintenance work, sanding, painting, varnishing or scraping barnacles from the hull, in exchange for sailing tuition. Later you can aim for an easier life looking after a boat for an absent skipper by living onboard and checking anchors and bilges. It is a good idea to buy a log book in which you can enter all relevant experience and voyages, and be sure to ask the captains of boats you have been on for a letter of reference.

As one skipper comments, 'A beginner ceases to be a passenger if he or she can tie half a dozen knots and hitches, knows how to read the lights of various kinds of ships and boats at night, and isn't permanently seasick.' Sometimes the arrangement is halfway between working and hitching a lift. There may not be much actual work to do but you could make cups of coffee, sand deck chairs, play Scrabble with the captain's wife or help look after the children of a cruising family. Women must take care in defining their role on board before they set sail, and should make sure they are not going to be exploited in any way. Adverts which read something like, 'Mature male 40 years of age looking for attractive young lady to help on board with cooking and entertaining on cruise to Med' should probably be treated with some suspicion. Some solo women sailors concentrate on job-hunting on cruisers sailed by retired couples partly for this reason and also because they are often the ones looking for a young deck hand.

Nearer destinations should be easier to reach than distant and exotic ones, both because of the larger numbers of yachts sailing short distances, and their greater willingness to take a chance on you. If you merely want to get from Tangiers to Gibraltar, from the Bahamas to the United States, from one Pacific Island to another or from Rhodes to Turkey, any small yacht harbour might provide the appropriate lift. On the other hand skippers are more likely to want extra crew on long journeys on the open seas (sometimes just to satisfy insurance requirements) rather than on the more enjoyable and leisurely coastal cruising.

If you are planning your trip a long way in advance, scour the classified columns of *Yachting Monthly, Yachting World* or *Practical Boat Owner*, though advertisers are likely to require a substantial payment or contribution towards expenses on your part. Lots of sites on the internet promise to match crew with captains, though as in the case of cruise ships, postings of jobs sought outnumber those offered. One worthwhile site is www.floatplan.com/crew.htm which carries details of actual vacancies, for example 'UK - GREECE – Delivery crew required immediately for three-masted Schooner for voyage from UK to Greece. These are paid positions. Contact Reliance Yacht Management at crew@reliance-yachts.com' or 'EL SALVADOR - PANAMA – Looking for crew for a 53' ketch leaving El Salvador for Panama. 3 months cruise to explore the Costa Rican and Panama coasts. Share expenses for food and fuels. This should be a fun leisurely cruise.' A certain number of listings contain a lonely hearts element: 'Mexico and Beyond – Attractive fit slender female crew member wanted for Mexico, South Pacific and beyond. Seeking a smart, stable woman, who loves adventure, cruising, has a sense of humor and a good heart. Romance a possibility, but as we will be short-handed most of the time, the passion for sailing and a life of adventure is the crucial element.'

Crewing agencies in Britain, France, Denmark, the West Indies, the United States and elsewhere carry out the same function of matching yacht captains and crew (see regional sections below). These are mostly of use to professional experienced sailors.

The *Cruising Association* (CA House, 1 Northey St, Limehouse Basin, London E14 8BT; 020-7537 2828/fax 020-7537 2266; www.cruising.org.uk/crewing.htm) runs a crewing service to put skippers in touch with unpaid crew. Meetings are held on the first Tuesday of the month at 6.30pm between February and July for this purpose. They claim to offer a variety of sailing (including two or three week cruises to the Mediterranean and transatlantic passages) to suit virtually every level of experience. The fee to non-members for this service is £24.

One of the best and largest crewing register in the UK is operated by *Crewseekers* (Crew Introduction Agency, Hawthorn House, Hawthorn Lane, Sarisbury Green, Southampton, Hants. SO31 7BD; tel/fax 01489 578319; info@crewseekers.co.uk). Their membership charges for UK members are £50 for six months, £65 for a year, for overseas members £55 and £70. Joint members may be added for an extra £10. Their web pages (www.crewseekers.co.uk) are updated daily showing the latest boats worldwide requiring crew. New members may also register on-line.

Alternatives are:

Aquarius Worldwide Ltd, 4 Lynher Building, Queen Anne's Battery Marina, Coxside, Plymouth, Devon PL4 0LP (tel/fax 01503 269046; info@aquariusworldwide. co.uk; www.aquariusworldwide.co.uk). International agency that specialises in providing qualified chefs, engineers and crew for yachts and island resorts. Encourages gap years students to register as well as experienced personnel. Job-seekers must pay a registration fee of £35/$50.

Crew Network Worldwide, fax 01257 450155; joe@crewnetwork.com.

Sea Gem International, Yacht Crew Agency & Yacht Brokers, 23 Rectory Road, Broadstairs, Kent CT10 1HG (01843 867960; seagem@compuserve.com). Supply stewards, deckhands, chefs, mates, etc. to yachts. Job-seekers pay no fee.

Once you're abroad, you'll have to track down your own sailing adventures. Frank Schiller split expenses with the New Zealand couple who took him (a complete sailing novice) aboard their yacht bound for Tonga and he ended up spending NZ$400 for four months of cruising. Always be sure to discuss the details of payment before setting sail. Many captains will ask you to pay a bond (say $500) for a long journey. Captains are responsible for making sure their crew can get back to their country of origin after the voyage is finished.

Whenever you end up finding a yacht to crew on, you may be letting yourself in for discomfort and danger, not to mention boredom, especially if you find yourself painting the boat in dock for the umpteenth time. Yachts require a surprising amount of maintenance. Offshore sailing is a risky business and you should be sure that the skipper to whom you have entrusted your life is a veteran sailor. A well-used but well-kept boat is a good sign.

Make sure before you leave the safety of dry land that your personality and politics do not clash with that of the captain. Quickly tiring of Gibraltar, Nicola Sarjeant and her Dutch boyfriend decided to join the hordes of people looking for a working passage on a yacht:

> *We asked around from boat to boat but most people weren't interested or wanted experienced people. We also put up a note in a shop in the harbour. This was answered by an Englishman who wanted a couple to help him crew to the Canaries and on to the West Indies. We had to contribute to food and expenses as well as do two four-hour watches per day. We also scrubbed and painted the bottom of the yacht. Because we were inexperienced we weren't paid which at the time seemed the best deal going in Gibraltar as there were many experienced people looking for crewing positions.*
>
> *I must caution anybody considering this kind of thing to think seriously about whether they can get along with the other people on the boat for a period of several weeks without throwing someone overboard. It turned out the captain had wanted a couple because he assumed a woman would cook dinner, wash dishes, etc. By the time we reached Gran Canaria (after three weeks because we made so many stops) the four of us were at each others' throats. My boyfriend and I hopped off (penniless). The trip had turned out to be quite expensive, though we saw islands I wouldn't otherwise have seen (Madeira in particular) and we got to learn a little about sailing. However the sailing is mostly quite boring (a yacht is very slow moving) and when you don't like the people, a lot of the fun goes out of the trip.*

Also try to ascertain in advance whether you will be subjected to any unfair pressures or unexpected fees. While travelling in Fiji, Melanie Grey met a man who had had a disastrous time crewing from Cairns:

> *After having paid in full for the entire sail from Cairns to New Zealand, Derek was forced to leave the vessel in Vanuatu along with several other crew members. This was due to the Hitler-style regime of the Belgian skipper and his girlfriend. After parting with large amounts of money (A$25 a day), the crew were treated like slaves, every morsel of food consumed was closely monitored, and the female members of the crew were often reduced to tears. The skipper obviously took on crew purely for the financial gain and not for the company or the pleasure of sailing. The crew members who left the trip prematurely were not reimbursed.*

It is also not unknown for crew to be thrown off a boat, perhaps on a remote island, if there is a personality clash. Never underestimate the stress of life afloat. Try to sign a contract entitling you to some compensation if you do not complete all the legs of the journey. And don't do anything which could get the captain into trouble. (Carrying drugs is the most extreme example; a boat that is found to be carrying drugs will be confiscated.)

The chartering business is booming in holiday resorts and many are owned by companies rather than individuals, which means that you will have to submit a formal application. If looking for work on a charter yacht, Paula Hurwitz suggests compiling a list of yacht brokers by impersonating a high-spending tourist and asking for brochures. This will give you a useful starting place for selling your services to charter companies.

Charming the Captain

In every marina and harbour there are people planning and preparing for long trips. There may be requests for crew posted on harbour notice boards, in yacht clubs or chandlery shops from Marina Bay in Gibraltar to Rushcutter's Bay in Sydney. Or you may have to approach skippers on spec. The most straightforward (and usually the most successful) method is to head for the nearest yacht marina and ask captains directly. To locate the yacht basin in an unfamiliar town, simply ask at your hotel or the tourist office. The harbour water supply or dinghy dock is usually a good place to meet yachties. One sailor looking for a berth in Thailand found that he had to swim out to the anchored yachts to knock on their hulls, which culminated in a free ride to Malaysia.

Since many of the yachts moored are used for local pleasure sailing only, concentrate on the yachts with foreign flags. Some travellers contend that boat-owners appreciate a straightforward approach: 'Good morning. I'd like to work for you.' Others think that this might catch captains off guard, and that it is better to approach the question in a more roundabout fashion. Many British, North American and Australian travellers are working their way around by cleaning boats and then participating as crew members as a means of alleviating travel expenses to their next destination. If you are not afraid to ask, your options can be greatly increased. Nothing can be lost by asking and much may be gained.

A yacht is a home, so an unwelcome intrusion on board is as bad as entering a house uninvited. The accepted phrase is 'permission to board?'. Once on board, behave as politely and as deferentially as you would in any stranger's home. Once you get to know both the boat and its owner, you can find ways to make yourself useful, whether washing up or scraping barnacles from the hull. You are then more likely to be offered a berth when the yacht finally sails.

Unless you are exceptionally lucky, you must expect to face a lot of competition for crewing positions and be prepared for repeated rejections and humiliations. Posting a notice on a marina notice board is usually not enough: you must visit the docks and sell yourself. This is one time when it is *not* a good idea to exaggerate your qualifications, since skippers who find out that they have been misled will be justifiably furious and, at worst, it could be life-endangering. Britons will probably do better with yachts sailing the British flag, and women often have an edge if only because of their relative novelty in a world dominated by men.

Women sailors encounter special problems and in fact are usually trying *not* to charm the captain to excess. Mirjam Koppelaars, who responded to a notice posted by a yachtsman in Gibraltar, spells out the problems:

> I must put some words of warning, especially for the female sailors. Most captains who are actively looking for crew are not really interested in finding competent crew, but in finding female company for day – and nighttime. Be aware of this and think it over before boarding a boat. Elise from Norway and I sailed with this extremely peculiar captain and a third crew member (Simon from England) over to the Canary Islands. I shouldn't complain too much about it, since we were one of the only boats which actually made this trip without any damage that year, but anyway, we were all three very glad that we could jump over to another boat in Las Palmas.

Crewing From Britain

There are many yacht basins along the south coast of Britain, from Burnham-on-Crouch in Essex to Falmouth, Cornwall, with Brighton, Chichester Harbour, Lymington, Hamble and other marinas in between. Cruising yachtsmen set sail from all these marinas to various destinations across the Channel or across the Atlantic. After finding out which bars the yachting fraternity frequents, you should make your face and your requirements known (assuming you do not use a crewing agency). The run-up to Cowes Week in early August is a good time to try since this is England's premier regatta.

Boat owners who leave in the spring are probably planning to cruise around the Mediterranean for the summer; those leaving in late October/early November may well be going to spend the winter in the Caribbean. Some are also heading to Scandinavia as Adam Cook reports:

> After a heart-stopping 11 days to windward from Gibraltar to Lymington, I stayed on as crew for the trip to Norway. Wow, the North Sea, it really is yellow sou'wester country out there. The sea is full of oil rigs, Danish fishing boats and the infamous 'stealth' tanker, the kind that only turns on its running lights when you're right up its blunt end.

Crewing in the Mediterranean

The standard pattern is for a traveller to get a job on a yacht for the summer charter season on the Mediterranean and then sail with the same yacht or power boat (the latter are generally more boring) to the Americas or (very occasionally) South Africa. Hundreds of boats descend on Gibraltar in the spring, many of which will be ready for a crew change. Hundreds more leave each autumn from the French Riviera, the Costa del Sol, the Canary Islands, etc. The annual ARC (Atlantic Rally for Cruisers) from the Canaries (departing the last Sunday in November in order to reach the West Indies for Christmas) is a convoy for the cautious more than a race, so this is an excellent time to be in Gran Canaria looking for a boat especially if you are willing to contribute $25 a day for the three week crossing. Gran Canaria is the last traditional victualling stop before the Atlantic crossing; the contemplation of thousands of miles of Atlantic Ocean often encourages owners and skippers to take on extra crew.

Asking from boat to boat is the only way of discovering who are the boat owners looking for someone to share the tiring night watches. One of the favoured routes for yachts travelling from the eastern Mediterranean towards the Atlantic includes Rhodes, Malta, Palma (Majorca), Alicante, Gibraltar, Las Palmas in the Canaries and the Azores before going on to the Caribbean, the Eastern Seaboard of the US or Brazil. The Crew Network Worldwide with its HQ in Florida (see section below on the Americas) has offices in Antibes (22 Avenue Thiers, 06600 Antibes; 04-93 34 4735; antibes@crewnetwork.com) and Palma de Mallorca (YachtHelp! C/ de la Torre de Peraires, 5-2 Porto Pi, 07015 Palma de Mallorca; 971-40 28 78; check@crewnetwork.com).

If the competition in Las Palmas is too discouraging, take a bus to some of the smaller marinas on the island such as Puerto de Mogan. The main crewing agencies in Antibes are housed in the same building, viz. La Galerie du Port, 8 boulevard d'Aguillon, 06600 Antibes. Try contacting Star Crew (info@starcrew.com/ www.starcrew.com) at the entrance to the Galerie du Port, next door to its sister company The Office where CVs can be compiled, the internet surfed and secretarial services provided. Star Crew specialise in chefs, stewards and stewardesses for the yachting industry as well as domestic staff for villas and chalets. Also in the Galerie du Port, try Peter Insull's Crew Agency (04-93 34 64 64/fax 04-93 34 21 22; crew@insull.com) or the Blue Water Yacht Crew Agency (04-93 34 34 13/fax 04-93 34 35 93; bluewater@riviera.fr). Smaller yachts and fishing boats are sometimes looking for crew in La Rochelle in southwest France; an early morning visit to the marina might pay off.

Tom Morton included a transatlantic sailing trip in his year between school and university:

> *Anyone wishing to cross the Atlantic should seriously consider investigating the ARC. It's good to get down there at least two weeks before the start and get to know the people and boats. The atmosphere is extremely friendly and most hopefuls find a passage, even if it is only two days before departure. It must be borne in mind that nearly all the boats are run by families who will want a contribution towards food.*

Crewing from the Caribbean

Yachts arrive in the Caribbean in the autumn (October to December) and leave again in April and May before the hurricane season begins (the official date is June 1st though plenty of boats stay around until July). A multitude of yachts gathers at the biggest end-of-season event, Antigua Race Week (end of April/beginning of May), which affords excellent opportunities to arrange a berth to Venezuela, Europe or the South Pacific. If you have accumulated experience during the season you should have little difficulty in finding a passage back to the Mediterranean or the UK.

The best places to look for a lift are Barbados between November and February and St Lucia at the beginning of December. Barbados is traditionally the place transatlantic vessels arrive, though vessels participating in the ARC often end up at Rodney Bay Marina on St Lucia in the first two weeks of December which makes this an ideal time and place to search for a crew position. After the long Atlantic crossing many skippers and crew are desperate to get away from each other.

Another excellent place to head is the Yacht Haven Marina in St Thomas, US Virgin Islands. Hanging around the Bridge pub and the yacht supply stores should result in contact with skippers. Pinning a note on the notice board outside the launderette should work. Also try Trinidad at Carnival time in February. This is the largest gathering of cruisers in the Caribbean and therefore offers some extraordinarily good crewing opportunities.

Kenneth Dichmann from Denmark spent a thoroughly enjoyable six months hitching lifts and working on six different sailboats in the Caribbean. His favourite crew-seeking method was the VHF radio. On several occasions he announced his intentions on the radio net (like a notice board on the airwaves) to which the majority of sailors tune in each morning. This worked for him in Trinidad and St. Martin. To gain access to the VHF Net, enquire at the marina office or bar.

His second method was the usual one of camping out at the dinghy dock and asking everyone who comes through. Take a notebook and pencil since you will be given leads to follow up later. On a few occasions Kenneth didn't wait for skippers to come to him but he went out to their yachts moored in the harbour either by swimming (as he did in Admiralty Bay on Bequia) which can be unpleasant if the harbour is polluted, or by hiring a pirogue (ocean kayak). Tireless in his searches, he made eye-catching notices for all the possible notice boards and checked them at least once a day. He talked to marina staff especially the dock master and travel lift master.

His general tips for inspiring confidence in skippers include dressing neatly, telling the skipper that you meet immigration requirements (and if you don't have an onward ticket offer to leave an equivalent deposit), showing your health insurance certificate, reassuring him that you are not carrying any illegal substances (inviting him to search your luggage if he would like), and finally if possible showing a reference from another skipper. Of the many yachts he joined, the daily fees for expenses varied from $18 to nil.

After crewing in the Caribbean for a year, Marcus Edwards-Jones summarised the experience: 'If you are keen on sun, sea and sand and do not have much money, crewing on yachts is a fantastic way of seeing the world, getting brown and enjoying yourself while being paid to do so.' See the chapter on the *Caribbean* for more information on crewing.

Crewing from the Americas

Apart from introducing yourself to boat-owners, possibly in a popular boat supply store, the primary ways to find a crewing position in the US are by registering with a crewing agency, answering an advert in the yachting press or hanging around at a yachting supply store, some of which have notice boards. Several crewing agencies are located in Fort Lauderdale, the yachting capital of Florida.

Here is a list of Fort Lauderdale crewing agencies, partly courtesy of Floyd's webpage (see reference to Floyd's Hostel below):

Crew Network Worldwide, 1053 SE 17th St, Fort Lauderdale, FL 33316 (954-467-9777/fax 954-527-4083; info@crewnetwork.com/ www.crewnetwork.com). Registration fee for crew is $25 ($40 for couples). Summer office in Rhode Island (8 Fair St, Newport, RI 02480; 401-849-9980; newport@crewnetwork.com).

Crew Unlimited, 2065 South Federal Highway (954-462-4624/fax 954-523-6712).

Crew Finders, 404-408 SE 17th St (954-522-2739/fax 854-761-7700; www.crewfinders.com). Also has summer office in Newport, Rhode Island (Casey's Marine; 401-849-0834) and in Port de Plaisance, Sint Maarten in the Netherlands Antilles (5995-43780).

Hassel Free Crew Services/D & R Woods International, 1635 South Miami Road (954-763-1841/524-0065; www.hasselfree.com).

Elite Crew International, 714 SE 17th St (954-522-4840/fax 954-522-4930).

Palm Beach Crew, 561-863-0082.

Bob Saxon & Associates, 1500 Cordova Road (954-760-5801/fax 954-467-8909).

Seven Seas Cruising Association, 954-463-2431.

The agencies normally charge job-seekers a fee of $25-$75. Experienced crew often bypass the agencies and simply ask captains directly. Chefs/cooks are especially in demand. For jobs with the Disney Cruise Line, call the Disney Jobline 407-566-SHIP (www.disney.com/DisneyCruise/jobs).

Boat supply stores are an excellent place to meet boatowners and pick up information. For example in South Florida, visit West Marine on Dixie Highway in Coconut Grove, Miami; Sailorman on State Road 87 in Fort Lauderdale or Smallwood's Yachting Supply at 1001 SE 17th St, Fort Lauderdale. A great place to stay in Fort Lauderdale is Floyd's Hostel and Crew House (954-462-0631; Floyd@floydshostel.com/ www.floydshostel.com) which accepts only international travellers and yachties who should ring or email for the address. Floyd's Hostel also acts as a crewing agency. The two marinas in Fort Lauderdale are Bahia Mar Marina and Pier 66 a mile to the west. Just south of Pier 66 on SE 17th Street is an enormous collection of yacht brokers who sell a huge number of new yachts to sailors who might be nervous enough about their maiden voyage to take on a willing crew member.

Yachts leaving the American east coast to cross the Atlantic tend to jump off from their home ports in the early autumn or spring according to the weather. Your best bet is to look in Miami or Fort Lauderdale (Florida), Newport (Rhode Island), Bridgeport (Connecticut), Martha's Vineyard (Massachusetts) or Annapolis (Maryland). You might want to check or place adverts in the relevant journals such as the glossy *Cruising World.*

Yachts sail from the west coast of North America to Hawaii, Tahiti and beyond in April/May or September/October. In October there are several organised gatherings of 'yachties' in California which provide an excellent chance to fix up a crewing position. As well as running relevant classified adverts, the monthly yachting magazine *Latitude 38* (15 Locust Ave, Mill Valley, CA 94941; 415-383-8200; www.latitude38.com) compiles a Mexico Only Crew List in October which costs just $5 for inclusion – the deadline is September 15th – and also hosts a 'Crew List Party'. Women job-seekers are advised by Latitute 38 to use a PO box number. Latitude 38's webpage has scores of useful links including a couple to crew agencies such as a Yacht Crew Register in Vancouver British Columbia (1755 Robson St, Suite 571, Vancouver, B.C. V6G 3B7; 604-990-9901; info@yachtcrew.ca/ www.yachtcrewregister.com).

Elsewhere in California try the San Francisco Yacht Club, Santa Barbara and Marina del Rey in Los Angeles. Ports along Baja California (the long Mexican peninsula) are surprisingly popular because skippers want to avoid the high mooring fees of California just to the north. It has been estimated that there are as many as 400 foreign yachts moored in La Paz at any one time, a Baja town 22 hours by bus from Tijuana.

Further south, Panama is an excellent place to find a passage especially in March but any time between January and May. Apparently there are always a few sailboats stranded there for lack of crew. Helping yachts to negotiate the locks of the Panama Canal as a 'linehandler' enables you to make the acquaintance of prospective skippers. Try also the Cristobal Yacht Club or the Balboa Yacht Clubs in Panama City. Near the Balboa Club is a small white booth where you can find out which boats are departing the next day. A motor boat shuttles out to yachts from which you can make your requirements known to captains. The vast continent of South America may afford possibilities. Between May and August, hundreds of yachts congregate in Puerto la Cruz and Cumaná in Venezuela to avoid the hurricanes in the Caribbean. Elsewhere in South America try the yacht clubs in Buenos Aires and Rio.

Crewing in the South Pacific

After several exhausting but lucrative months of fruit-picking in Australia and New Zealand, Frank Schiller from Germany was all set to fulfil one of his dreams:

> *I was hellbent on scoring a ride on an ocean-going yacht for any Pacific destination – after all I'd read alluring stories of Joseph Conrad and Jack London. In June I stood in front of a 4-Square shop window in Russell in New Zealand's Bay of Islands when by pure chance a notice was put up by the shop keeper: 'Crew wanted for Tonga.' Less than an hour later I found myself sailing across the bay back to Opua. After a week of doing odd jobs on the*

boat I was en route to Nukualofa. Pure magic. All this despite never having set foot on a yacht before, once more stressing the theme of your book that nothing's impossible!

Since the New Zealand owners had two kids, they needed someone to give them a hand. In no time I was doing night watches, taking sights with the sextant (the skipper taught me a few lessons on navigation which I was very keen on), cooking and washing up and most important of all – I became 'Uncle Frankie' to the kids. If you get along well with everyone on board, there are no worries going sailing in a matchbox. (But if there are hassles – no escape, even on a 100 footer.) Yachting, in fact, can be a very rewarding and adventurous thing to embark on.

Gerhard Flaig, also German, crewed in the opposite direction from the Vavau islands of Tonga to New Zealand. He had to pay a mere $100 for the three-week journey. The best season to ask around is July to October when most boats leave Fiji, Samoa, Tonga, etc. to sail to Hawaii or New Zealand. Suva, the capital of Fiji, and Papeete in Tahiti are hubs of much yachting activity in the South Pacific. Try the Royal Suva Yacht Club or Tradewinds Marina (Suva). Frank Schiller provides more detailed advice on crewing between South Pacific Islands:

As good as Neiafu harbour in Tonga is in July, Malolo-Lailai has got to be the best in September when the annual yacht race to Port Vilal/Vanuatu starts. There were quite a few 'crew wanted' signs in evidence, since everyone's getting the hell out of the Pacific at that time.

Other stops in the Pacific include Mauna Kea and Ala Wai (Hawaii) and Majuro in the Marshall Islands.

In New Zealand the best place by far to find crewing jobs are Opua in the Bay of Islands and Whangarei where the boats are close together and the people all know one another. Parties in the yacht club provide a good chance to meet sailors. Although the Westhaven Marina in Auckland Harbour is one of the biggest in the southern hemisphere, it can be more difficult to meet the right people because of the anonymity of a big city. You might try the Auckland office of the crewing agency Crew Network Worldwide (McKay Shipping Ltd; 09-308 0399; newzealand@crewnetwork.com).

While in Auckland some years ago, Marcus Scrace saw many ads for crew (mostly on a share-expenses basis) bound for Australia, Tonga, Fiji, and the USA. As for the timing, March and April are the months to pick up a boat leaving Westhaven or the Bay of Islands. The early departures are usually heading further east (i.e. to Tahiti) while the later ones are likely to be destined for the Tonga/Samoa/Fiji triangle. Many end up in Australia at the end of the season, i.e. late October when all South Pacific sailors head for shelter from cyclones.

To leave eastern Australia, head for Airlie Beach and the Whitsunday Islands in Queensland (especially during the Fun Race held in September), Cairns or Townsville; check adverts in the *Cairns Post* most of which specify a payment of $15-30 a day. Marcus Scrace, who was teaching at the Pacific Sailing School in Rushcutters Bay, Sydney, noticed an advert for crew on the notice board and was soon on his way to New Zealand. From Darwin boats leave for Indonesia from May; check the notice board at the Darwin Yacht Club in Fannie Bay. The Darwin-Ambon race between Australia and Indonesia in July is especially promising.

The 56ft ketch *Orka* has been sailing the waters of the South Pacific for several decades with a new intake of crew on every voyage. Write to the skipper Chris Van de Vijver for his itinerary (Yacht Orka, PO Box 7266, Wellington, New Zealand). From June 2001 he is sailing from Australia to New Caledonia, Vanuatu, the Solomon Islands, Papua New Guinea and back to Australia in November. The minimum period is four weeks and the contribution to expenses is NZ$40 a day. Kristie McComb from South Carolina spent three enjoyable months on *Orka*:

I just got off Orka last month after crewing from Vanuatu to NZ via New Caledonia (where in Nouméa I saw many announcements looking for crew who were only asked to pay for their food). Though I got a bit tired (we all did) of corned beef and bread and jam, I loved the places we went, the people we met, fresh coconuts on the aftdeck and silent anchorages. The captain is set in his ways but the adventure is worth it for those who want to learn to sail. Furthermore Chris is a very safe captain. I'd much rather be out at sea with a safe captain than a life-of-the-party one.

Crewing from Other Countries

Many yachts travelling around Africa lose their crew in Cape Town and need new crew for the onward journey. January is not a good time to look however judging from the number of notices from people looking for crewing positions which Stephen Psallidas noticed in the Cape Town Yacht Club. Yachts leave the East African coast for the Seychelles in January or February and for Madagascar and South Africa in August/September. Visit the yacht clubs in Dar es Salaam and Mombasa. Similarly private yachts heading east or west from the Indian subcontinent which stop at tropical Sri Lanka are often short of hands. Ask around the visitors' yacht basins in Colombo or Galle. Both ports are part of the popular South-East Asia yachting circuit which also takes in Bali (Port Benoa), Singapore (try the Changi Sailing Club or Sembawang Yacht Club), Penang and Phuket. Dustie Hickey noticed quite a few notices stuck to palm trees on the less-touristy islands of southern Thailand, i.e. the ones without roads, looking for crew to sail to Australia and elsewhere. The best time to try in South-East Asia is September/October. West of Sri Lanka there are crewing opportunities each spring to the Red Sea, Mauritius, the Seychelles and East Africa.

In fact the possibilities are infinite for people without a fixed timetable. For example the author of this book met by chance a charming sailor in a post office in Cochin, South India and could have crewed across the Indian Ocean to Dar es Salaam had it not been for the tyranny of publisher's deadlines (alas).

Yacht Delivery

Once you have some basic crewing experience you might go upmarket and try to get a job delivering yachts. Britain is still a major distributor and exporter of yachts and the easiest way to export a yacht is to sail it. This necessitates a crew, ideally one which considers the journey itself sufficient payment for the work, though licensed skippers often earn $1 a mile and the crew 50 cents. It is normally the purchaser's responsibility to arrange delivery and so he will want to get in touch with willing volunteers. Hence the yachting magazines carry adverts requesting crew for such journeys; again *Yachting Monthly* offers the most scope and carries a number of advertisements for delivery agencies in Britain. A typical advert might read: 'Sailing Crew required for yacht deliveries to Tahiti departing October/November. All onboard expenses paid but not airfares. Crew must be experienced.'

LAND

If you possess a heavy goods vehicle (HGV) or passenger carrying vehicle (PCV) licence, you will have a distinct advantage wherever you go. These are costly in money and time to acquire, but open opportunities throughout the world. The ten-day PCV course will cost £600-£700 plus a £60 test fee. People with enough mechanical knowledge to make running repairs to their vehicle are especially in demand.

You might still be able to work for a trucking company even if you do not have any driving qualifications, by being taken on as day labour to help load and unload international lorries. It may be worth ringing around nearby haulage companies (addresses in the *Yellow Pages* under 'Road Haulage' or 'Freight Forwarding and Warehousing'). Julian Peachey found that a local firm in Oxford merely satisfied themselves that he looked respectable before fixing him up with a ride to Italy. Like Julian, you might have to accept the first lift on an unpaid basis. But once you have established yourself as a reliable worker, you might be asked to accompany the driver to his European destination in order to help unload at the other end. Make sure that the arrangement is flexible enough to allow you to stay abroad after fulfilling your duties.

When the time comes for you to return to Britain you ring your transport company and ask if they intend to send any lorries requiring an assistant in your direction in the near (or distant) future. After James Spach became friendly with the dispatcher in one firm, he found it easy to arrange one way trips to and from Europe provided his dates were flexible enough. Or seek out the large international truck depots throughout Europe.

Overland Tours

If you do have or are willing to train for one of the specialist licences and some knowledge of mechanics, you may be eligible to work as an expedition driver. Competent expedition staff (including cooks) are greatly in demand by the many overland companies and youth travel specialists which advertise their tours and occasionally their vacancies in magazines like *TNT*. Look also in the glossy monthly magazine *Wanderlust* (01753 620426; www.wanderlust.co.uk) for independent travellers (cover price £2.80 in selected newsagents; £16 annual subscription). It carries a few ads which might be relevant in its Jobshop column.

Leaders have to contend with vehicle breakdowns, border crossings, black market money exchanges and the trip whinger (usually the one with a calculator). It is always an advantage to have been on one of the tours of the company you want to work for.

Here is a selected list of overland operators; others are listed on the Overland Expedition Resources website (www.go-overland.com). Specialist companies which operate only in Africa are mentioned in that chapter.

Dragoman Overland Expeditions, Operations Department, Camp Green, Kenton Road, Debenham, Suffolk IP14 6LA (01728 861133; www.dragoman.co.uk). Have a good reputation and look for leader drivers over 25 willing to train for the PCV licence in their workshops (if they don't already have one). Minimum commitment of two years for expeditions to Africa, Asia, South and Central America.

Encounter Overland, Training & Recruitment, Wren Park, Hitchin Rd, Shefford, Beds. SG17 5JD (www.encounter-overland.com). Full-time expedition leader/drivers in Africa, Asia and South America are expected to work for at least three years. Applicants (aged 25-35) must have or be prepared to obtain a PCV licence. Training lasts ten months including time in their workshops, learning to repair the modified Bedford trucks they use.

Exodus, 9 Weir Road, London SW12 0LT (www.exodus.co.uk). Suitable candidates (aged 25-32) can acquire the appropriate licence during the months of training. Minimum age 24. Knowledge of Italian, Spanish, French or Japanese highly valued.

Explore Worldwide Ltd, 1 Frederick St, Aldershot, Hants. GU11 1LQ (01252 760200; www.explore.co.uk). Europe's largest adventure tour operator employing more than 100 tour leaders for Europe, Africa, Asia and the Americas. Must have first aid certificate and preferably a second language. Training given.

Guerba Expeditions, Wessex House, 40 Station Road, Westbury, Wilts. BA13 3JN (01373 826611; www.guerba.co.uk). Originally an Africa specialist, runs trips to other continents.

Kumuka Expeditions, 40 Earl's Court Road, London W8 6EJ (020-7937 8855; julia@ kumuka.co.uk). Looking for qualified diesel mechanics with a PCV licence to be drivers. Tour leaders (ages 25-40) chosen according to experience and personality.

Travelbag Adventures, 15 Turk St, Alton, Hants. GU34 1AG (01420 541007; www.travelbag-adventures.com). Tour leaders 25+ with first aid qualification.

After getting past the interview stage as an adventure tour leader, you may be invited to go on a training trip of at least six weeks at your expense – at least several hundred pounds. This money is generally returned to you after you have been accepted and completed an agreed term of work. Procedures vary for choosing and training couriers. One old hand, writing in the *Traveller* magazine, claims that to be a good tour leader you have to be 'a cross between a Butlins redcoat and Scott of the Antarctic'.

The pay on your training trip will be low, say £50 per week. Incidental expenses such as visas, passports, air tickets, etc. are paid for. Your company will also pay your kitty contributions and will cover any compulsory money changes that may exist en route. Although it is hard work, it is undoubtedly an interesting or exciting job. Once you are a full expedition leader, you will be paid at least £70 and possibly over £150 per week in addition to expenses. If you do land an overland job, you may find yourself driving a converted Bedford or Mercedes truck across the Sahara.

Brett Archer from New Zealand enjoyed his stint of working for an African overland company though found it a little daunting to have 18 people dependent on him in such circumstances. After eight months, his contract was not renewed because of a drop in bookings.

Expeditions

One romantic idea for working your way around the world is to become part of an expedition venturing into the more remote and unspoiled parts of the world from Tierra del Fuego to Irian Jaya. It would be nice if you could be invited to join a party of latter-day explorers in exchange for some menial duty such as portering or cooking. However expedition organisers and leaders nowadays demand that participants have some special skills or expertise to contribute beyond mere eagerness. No one will accept you for the ride. For example an advert for people needed on an Arctic expedition included among its volunteer requirements a post-doctoral archaeologist, an electronics officer for proton magneto-meter maintenance and an antenna theorist. One suspects that they weren't inundated with applications.

The Royal Geographical Society (1 Kensington Gore, London SW7 2AR) encourages and assists many British expeditions. Occasionally there are requests from expedition leaders for specialists with either scientific or medical skills, preferably with past expedition experience, and for this a register of personnel is maintained. Those who have a particular skill to offer and wish to be included on the register should send an s.a.e. to the Expedition Advisory Centre at the RGS for the appropriate form and a copy of their booklet *Joining an Expedition* (£6.95). If you want personal advice on mounting an expedition, fundraising and budgeting for expeditions, you can make an appointment to visit the EAC (020-7591 3030; eac@rgs.org).

Another organisation worth contacting is the World Expeditionary Association or WEXAS (45-49 Brompton Road, London SW3 1DE; 020-7589 3315) who not only make awards to worthwhile expeditions but, more to the point, carry advertisements and announcements in their quarterly publication *Traveller* where you can advertise your skills (free to members) and hope that a potential expedition leader sees it. WEXAS membership costs £44 though they often invite people to join at a reduced cost.

Raleigh International is a UK-based charity which aims to develop young people aged 17-25 (most recently Prince William) by offering them the chance to undertake demanding environmental and community projects on expeditions overseas. Applicants attend an assessment weekend and if successful are asked to raise about £3,000 (see section on Gap Year Placement Organisations in the Voluntary Work chapter).

World Challenge Expeditions (Black Arrow House, 2 Chandos Road, London NW10 6NF; 020-8728 7220; www.world-challenge.co.uk) takes on about 300 expedition leaders to supervise school expeditions to developing countries. Trips take place in the summer and the minimum commitment is four weeks. Applicants must be at least 24, have a MLTB (Mountain Leader Training) and some experience of working with young people and preferably of travelling in the Third World. No wage is paid but expenses are covered.

When joining any expedition you are unlikely to escape a financial liability, for most expeditions levy a fee from each participant. Sponsorship, and the amount of it, from companies, trusts and other sources will depend upon the aims of the expedition and the benefits to the donor. And once the money and equipment are forthcoming the expedition then has obligations to its sponsors and forfeits much of its freedom. Raising sponsorship, a job with which all expedition members should help, is probably the biggest headache of all and involves endless letter-writing and the visiting, cap in hand, of dozens of commercial establishments and other possible sources of income.

AIR COURIERS

Every day international courier companies undertake to move tons of 'time sensitive documents' between countries and continents. Because of airline restrictions, some of these packages cannot travel as passenger baggage unless they are indeed accompanied by a passenger who will clear them through customs as 'excess passenger baggage'. In fact these restrictions have been liberalised over the past couple of years in many airports so that it is no longer a requirement that someone physically accompany the documents. Furthermore, the universal use of e-mail has made it unnecessary for some of the documents to be shipped. Altogether the industry has seen a sharp decline. For example, Bridges Worldwide (one of the main UK courier companies) served 30 destinations two years ago but currently serves just three, Tokyo, Seoul and Sydney.

The cost of pre-booked courier flights has been rising over the years just as the cost of discount flights has been falling, so that in some cases there is very little difference between the two. The only hope of a real bargain is if you are lucky enough to be able to take advantage of a last minute vacancy. Furthermore most courier flights are return flights, with a maximum stay of as little as two weeks, so they are of little interest to the job-seeker. But British Airways' in-house courier department still sells thousands of tickets per year and some 30,000 courier flights originate in the US, so there is scope for a while yet.

Most courier flights are now sold through 'on-board courier broker' firms which supply couriers to a specific company or airline/s. Prices vary according to the time of year, just like other air tickets: November and February are the cheapest times while Christmas and summer are most expensive. It is worth noting that once you have been a successful courier you will find it easier to arrange another flight. One traveller had a marvellous fortnight's holiday in Brazil (having taken advantage of a £300 courier return from London) and several weeks later was rung up by the courier company asking her if she would like to go again, this time for £200.

Here are the companies which will send a list of their destinations in return for a self-addressed stamped envelope. Some will be booked up months in advance. This information changes constantly.

ACP Worldwide, (Air Cargo Partners), Unit 8, Radius Park, Faggs Road, Feltham, Middlesex TW14 0NG (020-8897 5130/fax 020-8587 0123; www.acp-the-gsa.com). Courier tickets sold on behalf of Virgin Atlantic to various US cities, Tokyo, Hong Kong, Shanghai, Sydney, Melbourne, Johannesburg, Athens and a few others. Prices to New York start at £199 and to Los Angeles at £250 return. ACP offer one ways to Tokyo (from £275), Jo'burg and Sydney/Melbourne (from £399). Maximum validity of tickets varies from 2 to 3 months. Offices in the US plus Dublin, Johannesburg, Melbourne and Sydney (see website for addresses).

Bridges Worldwide Wholesale Express, Jupiter House, 3 Horton Road, Colnbrook, Slough SL3 0BB (01895 465065/fax 01753 746399). Return flights to Tokyo (£349) and Seoul (£269) on Lufthansa and to Sydney (£399) on Japan Airlines.

British Airways Travel Shops, Room E328-332, 3rd Fl, E Block, BA Cranebrook S551, Off Jubilee Way, PO Box 10, Heathrow Airport, Middlesex TW6 2JA (0870 606 1133). Maximum stay of 2 weeks in 13 destinations, viz. Budapest (from £90), Philadelphia (£180), New York, Boston, Washington, Miami (£190), Chicago, San Francisco, Seattle (£210), Buenos Aires, Bangkok (£450), Tokyo (£470) and Mauritius £550.

Once you have booked a courier flight the procedure is as follows: you turn up in plenty of time at the appointed meeting place with your passport, visa (if necessary), insurance and luggage (most companies nowadays allow their couriers the full 23kg allowance). There you will be met by the company's agent who is frequently very late, thereby causing severe anxiety to the hopeful courier. He shows the paperwork to airline staff, checks in up to a score of mail bags and sees you through customs. At the other end, another agent greets you (at least in theory), escorts you through customs and disappears with the packages.

If you're already abroad it is also worth trying for reduced flights as Marcus Scrace reports:

> *During my trip around the world I saw many ads for air couriers. The way to get a job as a courier is to look up in the Yellow Pages under 'International Couriers' and ring or visit in person the companies which are usually based*

very close to the airport. For instance there are about 20 companies in Mascot, Sydney. (I used Airpack Couriers for a return trip to New Zealand at a cost of $200 which is about half price). This company also had flights to the States, Singapore and Hong Kong. In Auckland all the courier offices are situated in the airport suburb of Mangere.

In Hong Kong, try Jupiter Air Freight Forwarding (2237 1822 or 2735 1886).

JFK Airport in New York (like Heathrow) is buzzing with air courier activity. It is harder to get a domestic courier flight within the US than an international one but both are possible. The biggest courier broker in the US is Now Voyager Freelance Couriers (74 Varick St, Suite 307, New York, NY 10013; 212-431-1616; www.nowvoyagertravel.com) which charges a $50 fee the first time you fly. Recently they have been offering $294 returns from New York or Boston to London (plus taxes), a fare which an accompanying non-courier companion can also have. Fares to Copenhagen, Brussels, Madrid and other European cities are $299-$399.

If in New York, try the following, which may have return flights to London or other international destinations like Frankfurt, Brussels and Amsterdam for from $200:

Courier Network, 5125 W 29th St, New York, NY 1001 (212-947-6336). Calls accepted 6pm-8pm (Eastern Standard Time).

Global Delivery Systems, 14705 176th St, Jamaica, NY 11434 (718-656-5000). The widest range of European destinations.

Micom America, Building 14, JFK International Airport, Jamaica, NY 11430 (718-656-6050).

World Courier, 1313 4th Ave, New Hyde Park, NY 11040 (516-354-2600).

Air Cargo Partners, 1983 Marcus Ave, Suite 108, Lake Success, NY 11042 (877-227-9700; www.acp-the-gsa.com). Other offices in Chicago, Los Angeles and worldwide listed on website.

Air-Tech, 588 Broadway, Suite 204, New York, NY 10012 (212-219-7000, ext. 206; fly@airtech.com; www.airtech.com). Offer courier flights as well as space-available flights (see Travel chapter). Courier flights at time of writing to Brazil ($350) and Hong Kong ($386).

For flights from the West Coast, try International Bonded Couriers (310-665-1760) and Jupiter Air (310-670-1197) both in Los Angeles.

The Air Courier Association (15000 West 6th Avenue, Suite 203, Golden, Colorado 80401; 1-800-822-0888 ext 2404/303-215-9000; www.aircourier.org) collates courier information worldwide and publishes it in its literature distributed to members, in its bi-monthly magazine *Air Courier Journal* ($6 for a single issue) or on its website (www.aircourier.org) which lists last minute specials (e.g. $25 to Mexico, $150 to Singapore, $100 to Rome). Ring the ACA for an enrolment kit; annual membership costs $39 which allows access to the bargains posted on the website.

Other sources of information on courier flights include the *International Association of Air Travel Couriers* (PO Box 1349, Lake Worth, Florida 33460; 561-582-8320; www.courier.org) which publishes a clearly laid out and up-to-date bi-monthly bulletin. IAATC also publishes the *Shoestring Traveler* newsletter for freelance couriers. Annual membership costs $45 in the US, $50/£32 in the UK. Membership also confers the right to access the flights mentioned on its website.

The book *Air Courier Bargains* by Kelly Monaghan provides an introduction to the subject published by Intrepid Traveler, Box 438, New York, NY 10034 ($14.95, last updated November 1998) as does *The Courier Air Travel Handbook* by Mark Field from Perpetual Press, PO Box 30414, Lansing, MI 48909-7914 (1-800-793-8010) last issued in 1999 (price $9.95).

Of course there are outfits not listed in the *Yellow Pages* which employ couriers to transport more exotic substances. Unless you want an extended holiday in one of H.M. prisons or a long vacation making licence plates in San Quentin, you should steer clear of this sort of operation.

TRAVEL

Not everyone has the time nor the stamina to work a passage. There follow some general guidelines for finding bargains in train, coach, ship and air travel. More detailed information on specific destinations can be found in travel guides from Lonely Planet and Rough Guides. The amount of information on the internet is staggering and this chapter cannot hope to tap all its resources. There are websites on everything from sleeping in airports (www3.sympatico.ca/donna.mcsherry/airports.htm) to sharing lifts across Europe or the US (www.rideseek.net). Many sites have pages of intriguing links; to name just one, try www.budgettravel.com.

General advice on minimising the risks of independent travel is contained in the book *World Wise – Your Passport to Safer Travel* published by Thomas Cook in association with the Suzy Lamplugh Trust and the Foreign Office (www.suzylamplugh.org/worldwise; £6.95 plus £1 postage). Arguably its advice is over-cautious, advising travellers never to hitch-hike, ride a motorbike or accept an invitation to a private house. Travellers will have to decide for themselves when to follow this advice and when to ignore it. In some people's books, hitch-hiking is not only the best travel bargain around, it is the most rewarding.

Hitch-hiking

Over the past generation, hitch-hiking has fallen out of fashion, possibly because young travellers and students are generally more affluent and also because of a heightened sense of paranoia (though dangers remain infinitesimal). However there are still enough people out there interested to support a number of websites; for example have a look at www.suite101.com/welcome.cfm/hitch_hiking.

In the experience of many travellers, hitching is cheap, safe and fascinating (and what else could anyone ask for?) The uncertainty of the destination is one of its great attractions to the footloose traveller. While hitching from France to Germany in pursuit of work, Kevin Boyd got a lift with a Russian truck bound for Leningrad. He was tempted to stay for the whole trip but, as the lorry averaged 35km an hour on the autoroute, he decided to stick with his original idea. Hitch-hiking has one positive virtue for job seekers: you can sound out the driver for advice on local job opportunities. Friendly drivers often go miles out of their way and may even ask in villages about work possibilities on your behalf, as happened to Andrew Winwood in Switzerland during the *vendange*. Lorry drivers often know of temporary jobs you could do.

Hitch-hiking is also good for the environment. In 1998, a UK government report was published to promote car-sharing. One of the suggested measures was to introduce hitch-hiker pick-up zones at motorway junctions which would be brightly lit and possibly equipped with closed circuit TVs. Some French roads already feature hitch-hiking zones. The popularity of hitch-hiking in the US has increased since single occupant cars were banned from the fast lanes in some American cities.

Some readers have expressed disapproval that we recommend hitch-hiking as a good way of getting around. Hitch-hiking, like any form of transport, has its dangers, but that is not a sufficient argument for a wholesale ban. The existence of road rage and air rage, of attacks on or derailment of trains, does not result in mass avoidance of these modes of travel. By following a few rules the risks of hitch-hiking can be minimised. Never accept a lift from a driver who seems drunk, drowsy or suspicious. Women should try not to hitch alone. A small dose of paranoia is not a bad thing, whether at midnight in Manchester or midday in Manila, especially in view of the murders of several hitch-hiking travellers in Australia and stories like the following from a reader of this book:

> *After my friend had decided to go back to Thailand and (by mistake) took most of my money, I continued on alone. I was offered a ride to Kuala Lumpur by*

what seemed like a very pleasant Malaysian guy. After about an hour he pulled over to the side of the road. I thought he was stopping to get a drink and something to eat. Before I knew it, he'd central-locked the doors (this truck was like Fort Knox) and pulled the curtains round, turned off the lights and undressed. For the next two hours he proceeded to tell me in graphic details how he was going to rape me and throw my dead body from the truck. Panic set in quickly, but I managed not to show it too much. I told the guy that he was frightening me and that I had people waiting for me in Singapore, and if I wasn't back by a certain time, they would not hesitate to call the police. I also started to tell him all about myself and my family. This makes the person see you as a human being and not just a lump of meat. Eventually he let me go.

Try to put the risks into perspective. It is worth mentioning that my friend Simon Calder, the author of *Hitch-hikers Manual: Britain* and *Europe: a Manual for Hitch-hikers,* has found cycling in London a far more dangerous and damaging pursuit than thumbing lifts (and has lived to become the Travel Editor of the *Independent* newspaper). Usually the worst danger is of boredom and discouragement when you have a long wait. A few readers have written to say that they cannot understand how people manage to enjoy hitching especially across Europe. It is of course a game of patience. Eventually you will get a lift, but whether you have the stamina to wait for it is another matter.

But many hitchers have been amazed at their good fortune. Isak Maseide met nothing but nice people on the 3,200km between Oban in Scotland and Copenhagen via the Bavarian Alps. He was worried just once when he noticed a shoulder holster on a driver who had stopped for him; this man turned out to be an undercover policeman on his way home. On F. Dixon from Nottingham's first trip abroad, he hitched, and was pleasantly surprised by the ease with which great distances could be covered:

I thought the odds were against me from the start. I am 6'6 tall, black and 18 stone. Who the hell is going to pick me up? Once in Denmark we got good lifts. One nice couple put me up at their home for the night and phoned her father who picked me up and took me to where I was going. I am now making my way to France getting good lifts. Can you tell other black people not to be afraid to travel?

The word hitch-hiking is of American derivation and the concept is primarily Western. In North America, Europe and Australia, a person standing by the side of the road with an outstretched thumb can expect (eventually) to be offered a free lift. It is essential to look neat and enthusiastic, and try to make eye contact with drivers. Hi-tech hitchers often use aids such as destination signs, flags (which indicate you are a genuine visitor from afar) and attention-attracting costumes such as a boiler suit or kilt. Ben Nakoneczny took up juggling by the side of the road and, if his 2,190km lift from Thessaloniki to Cologne is anything to go by, this attracts the right sort of attention. Eye-catching signs are especially recommended such as the one used by Malcolm Green in his quest for a grape-picking job in Australia; LONDON TO MILDURA PLEASE. R. J. Hill used a sign 'Moon'; eventually a vicar stopped, presumably because he had some inside information. Try to look respectable without looking too prosperous.

Elsewhere, there may be no tradition of giving free lifts and if you are picked up, a small payment will be expected. Since the local people often get lifts with private vehicles and pay for them, there is no reason why you should be driven free of charge. In some Western countries this technique has been formalised by organisations which fix drivers up with cost-sharing passengers upon payment of a small fee (see the section on Europe below).

An interesting variation is to prearrange a ride by talking to lorry drivers at local depots, lorry parks, truckers' cafés, pubs or wherever you see them. Antony Hunt describes his success in the northern suburbs of London:

The first time I tried hitching, I got a lift from the Scratchwood Services in a German lorry heading for Heidelberg. I got a free ferry crossing, a free cabin and a dinner ticket. The driver gave me his phone number and promised me a lift home when I wanted it since he did a weekly trip to Manchester.

If possible find out in which pubs lorry drivers tend to drink. For example Andrew Giles found that Rodolfo's Bar and the Pig and Whistle in Gibraltar were good places to get to know drivers. Drivers are increasingly wary of offering lifts to complete strangers, since there are several drivers in foreign prisons for having done just that.

Driving

In some countries you might decide to buy a cheap car and hope that it lasts long enough for you to see the country. This worked well for Frank Schiller, a German traveller in Australia:

How about becoming a car owner yourself if you just wanna roll along for a while? After two successful months of hitching in Tasmania (including a combined Landrover and yacht lift to Maria Island), the three of us decided to change our means of transport. We bought a Holden off a Canadian guy for $500 which included insurance, a few spare parts, a tool kit and some snorkelling equipment. (I'd suggest buying a standard model rather than an E-type Jaguar for ease of finding spares.) After ten weeks and 10,000 kilometres, we sold it to a wrecker in Alice Springs for $250. So each of us had paid $80 for the car plus about $120 for petrol – all in all a much better bargain than a bus pass.

A camper van is also an appealing idea, especially if you are interested in chasing fruit harvests around. It is possible to pick up a reliable vehicle for less than £1,000 in the UK if you're lucky. Australians like Ben Hockley are devoted van users:

My girlfriend and I were spending a lot of money looking for work in Spain so we decided we needed a campervan to help cut the accommodation costs. Vans are not very cheap in Spain and the casual relaxed attitude of the locals makes car hunting a nightmare. So we hopped a train to Amsterdam where I had learnt that vehicles were 40% cheaper. It was true and after three weeks we had an old Bedford camper for about £1,000. Life in the van was great, we could just park on any street and we had a home for the night.

The main van market in London takes place daily on York Way at Market Road, N7 near the Caledonian Road tube station. You might also check ads in *Auto Trader* and *LOOT*.

Those who own their own vehicle might consider taking it with them. Certainly a car or motorcycle on the Continent will make life easier when it comes to visiting potential employers, especially in the countryside. On the negative side, it will be an expensive luxury and a serious encumbrance if you decide to travel outside continental Europe. If you are considering taking your car, contact your local AA or RAC office for information about International Driving Permits, motor insurance, green cards, etc.

Train

The conventional wisdom is that trains are preferable to buses because they allow you to walk around or lie down on long journeys. Anyone who has experienced travelling unreserved on Indian trains or on long distance Italian trains in high summer (where theft is rife) will be aware of the limitations of this generalisation. Besides which, the traveller working his or her way around the world is more interested in financial considerations than in ones of comfort. So you will probably choose a slow, cheap bus in preference to a luxurious high-speed train. But in areas which have a dreadfully creaky and overcrowded rail service (running to a calendar rather than a timetable), it may well be the cheapest way of getting around. Even in developed nations, you may find rail fares rivalling coach ones especially if you are eligible for discounts. Rail passes are generally not much use to job-seeking travellers since they benefit people who want to do a great deal of travelling. The UK agent for rail travel in Canada, the UK, Australia, New Zealand and Japan is Leisurail, PO Box 5, Peterborough, PE3 8XP (0870 7500222).

However other youth and student discounts can be very useful; for example the Kilometic ticket valid for 3,000km of travel in two months on Italian trains for one to five people for £88 (from Rail Choice, 15 Colman House, Empire Square, High Street, Penge, London SE20 7EX; 020-8659 7300) or the 12-25 rail card for France which costs £28 to buy (from Rail Europe 0990 848848) and gives a 25%-50% discount on off-peak rail journeys in France for a year.

The Thomas Cook *Overseas Timetable* is the bible for overland travellers outside Europe; within Europe, consult the *Continental Timetable*. In the US, a once-useful resource *Eurail and Train Travel Guide to the World* published by Houghton Mifflin ($18.95) has not been updated since February 1998.

Coach

Coach travel has never enjoyed a favourable press. After buying a cheap coach ticket from London to Athens, Mark Hurley's conclusion was 'never again': even after the on-board loo packed up, there were only two rest stops every 24 hours. The last leg of the journey through Greece was done on another coach which was already full when Mark's lot turned up. On the other hand, coaches have some confirmed fans who positively relish long-distance journeys when life is reduced to its constituent pleasures of sleeping, eating, reading and socialising. The great advantage of course is the low cost.

In many areas of the world such as Nepal and Papua New Guinea, public road transport is the only way to get around the country short of flying. Fortunately this monopoly of the travel market is not generally reflected in high fares, usually because of competing companies. Such free enterprise is wonderfully apparent at the Topkapi Gate Bus Station in Istanbul where salesmen for a host of competing companies call out their destinations and prices. Bus prices are below a penny per mile in much of the Third World (possibly to compensate for the purgatory of non-stop Kung Fu videos in some parts of the world) and increase rapidly to nearly a pound for a half mile in Central London. Except where smooth air-conditioned buses provide an alternative to sub-third class rail travel, coaches are generally less expensive than trains. The Thomas Cook *Overseas Timetable* is valuable for coach as well as train travellers.

Another informative reference book for those who anticipate crossing international waters is the quarterly *ABC Cruise & Ferry Guide* which lists both domestic and international shipping companies, their routes and timings but scant information on prices. Look for it in your library.

One of the most interesting revolutions in youth travel has been the explosion of backpackers' bus services which are hop-on hop-off coach services following prescribed routes. These can be found in New Zealand, Australia, USA, Canada, Scotland, England and the continent. Generally they are not really cheap enough to serve as a job-seeker's preferred mode of transport. For example a month long coach pass on Busabout Europe (258 Vauxhall Bridge Road, London SW1V 1BS; 020-7950 1661/www.busabout.com) costs £259 for those under 26.

Air

Scheduled air fares as laid down by IATA, the airlines' cartel, are best avoided. They are primarily designed for airline accountants and businessmen on expense accounts. You should be looking at cheap charters, discounted tickets and standby flights. Air travel within individual countries and continents is not always subject to this choice, though some special deals are available.

For longhaul flights, especially to Asia, Australasia and most recently Latin America, discounted tickets are available in plenty and there should never be any need to pay the official full fare. Previously the sale of these tickets was restricted to the original 'bucket shops', often seedy discount agencies. Now high street travel agents such as Thomas Cook are openly selling discounted tickets and because of their enormous turnover and sophisticated computer systems can often offer the best deals.

But the very lowest fares are still found by doing some careful shopping around. Bucket shops advertise in London weeklies like *TNT* and *Time Out,* and also the London *Evening Standard.* Phone a few outfits and pick the best price. Those with access to the internet should start by checking relevant web-sites, for example www.cheapflights.co.uk which is the brainchild of the well-respected travel journalist John Hatt and has links to other useful sources of travel information. Alternatives are www.travelocity.com and www.lastminute.com. Viewers can log onto their destination and then see a list of prices offered by a variety of airlines and agents. Increasingly, it is possible to book tickets on the internet too.

Another tip for finding the cheapest available fares is to tap into the expat community of the country to which you would like to fly. For example the cheapest flights from the US to Hong Kong are probably for sale in Chinatown and may be advertised in Chinese language newspapers.

The cheapest flights are available from airlines like Aeroflot or Biman Bangladesh which are considered dubious by cautious and conservative types. East European carriers (like Tarom) and Asian carriers (like Garuda) are often worth investigating for low fares. Try to overcome your reluctance, since flying with them is guaranteed to be more interesting than flying on KLM, Air Canada or British Airways. You may find that your flight leaves at 7am on a Sunday morning with a 12-hour stopover in Dhaka, but these inconveniences are a small price to pay for savings of a hundred pounds or more. The agency Eastways (6 Brick Lane, London E1 6RF: 020-7247 2424/3823) has the franchise for discounting tickets for Aeroflot, the Russian airline, whose reputation for safety has been tarnished since the fall of communism.

Once you accept a price, check that the fare will not be increased between paying the deposit (typically £50 or £75) and handing over the balance in exchange for the ticket; if the agency is unable to make such a guarantee, ask for a written promise that you can reclaim the deposit in the event of a fare increase. Similarly, if the agency claims that your ticket is refundable if unused, request a letter confirming this: any legitimate agency should be happy to comply. Buying dodgy tickets is always worrying since it is impossible to grasp all the complexities of international air travel. Hand over the balance only when you are satisfied that the dates and times agree with what you anticipated. But don't expect the fare shown on the ticket to bear any relation to the price you actually paid.

The price of round-the-world tickets has been coming down over the past few years. Check www.roundtheworldflights.com for ideas. The cheapest start at £500 for under-26s in the low season and usually involve one or more gaps which you must cover overland. Most are valid for up to a year. An example of a good fare is £875 for a RTW fare from London to Sydney with six stopovers in Asia and North America on Qantas and BA. Sometimes the fare can be brought down if you are willing to cover some sectors by land.

The principal agencies specialising in longhaul travel for student and budget travellers are:

STA Travel, Priory House, 6 Wrights Lane, London W8 6TA (020-7361 6161 Europe, 020-7361 6262 Worldwide; 020-7361 6160 insurance and other travel services; www.statravel.co.uk). Leading agency for independent and youth travel with more than 300 branches worldwide including the US. They can organise flexible deals, domestic flights, overland transport, accommodation and tours.

Usit Campus, 52 Grosvenor Gardens, London SW1W 0AG (020-7730 8111/0870 240 1010; www.usitcampus.co.uk). Also 0161-200 3278 in Manchester, 0131-668 3303 in Scotland, 0117-929 2494 in Bristol. Britain's largest student and youth travel specialist with 49 branches in high streets, at universities and in YHA Adventure Shops. As well as worldwide air fares, they sell discounted rail and coach tickets for destinations around the world, budget accommodation and insurance.

Council Travel, 28A Poland St, London W1V 3DB (020-7287 3337 Europe; 020-7437 7767 worldwide). Travel division of the Council on International Educational Exchange in New York and America's largest youth, student and budget travel group with 60 branches worldwide. Council Exchanges UK (same address) organises international work exchanges.

Trailfinders Ltd, 194 Kensington High St, London W8 7RG (020-7938 3939 longhaul; 020-7937 5400 Europe and transatlantic). Also travel centres in Birmingham, Manchester, Newcastle, Bristol, Cambridge, Glasgow, Dublin, Sydney, Brisbane and Cairns Australia.

Marco Polo Travel 24A Park St, Bristol BS1 5JA (0117-929 4123). Discounted air fares worldwide.

North South Travel, Moulsham Mill Centre, Parkway, Chelmsford, Essex CM2 7PX (01245 608291). Discount travel agency which donates profits to projects in the developing world.

Travel Cuts, 295a Regent St, London W1R 7YA (020-7255 2082 longhaul and North America; 020-7255 1944 Europe; www.travelcuts.com).

Travel Bug, 597 Cheetham Hill Road, Manchester M8 5EJ (0161-721 4000; www.flynow.com). London office: 125 Gloucester Road, SW7 4SF (020-7835 2000). All of these offer a wide choice of fares including RTW. Telephone bookings are possible, though these agencies are often so busy that it can be difficult to get through. When purchasing a discounted fare, you should be aware of whether or not the ticket is refundable, whether the date can be changed and if so at what cost, whether taxes are included, and so on.

In the US, check the discount flight listings in the back of the travel sections of the *New York Times* and *Los Angeles Times.* Contact any of Council Travel or STA's many offices throughout the country. Discount online tickets are available from Air Treks (442 Post Street, Suite 400, San Francisco, CA 94102; 1-800-350 0612, www.airtreks.com) which specialises in multi-stop and round-the-world fares.

By far the cheapest air fares from the US are available to people who are flexible about departure dates and destinations, and are prepared to travel on a standby basis. The passenger chooses a block of possible dates (up to a five-day 'window') and preferred destinations. The company then tries to match these requirements with empty airline seats being released at knock-down prices. Air-Tech at 588 Broadway, Suite 204, New York, NY 10012 (212-219-7000; www.airtech.com) advertises its fares by saying 'if you can beat these prices, start your own damn airline'. The transatlantic fares being advertised at the time of writing were $169 plus tax one way from the east coast and $229 from the west coast. Discounted fares of $250 return between the US and Mexico or the Caribbean are also available. One satisfied customer is Lisa Russo who read about Air-Tech in an earlier edition of *Work Your Way Around the World,* used it to travel to Europe and went on to become Director of Marketing for a time.

Air-hitch also sells space-available vouchers which can be turned into cheap fares. Their fares to Europe are $169 from the east cost, $199 from the southeast (Florida and Atlanta), £219 from Chicago, Toronto, Denver, etc.) and $249 from the west coast. These fares do not include taxes of $16 eastbound plus $46 westbound. Contact them toll-free on 1-800-326-2009 or on the web www.airhitch.org; Airhitch has offices in New York, LA and Paris. The Air Courier Association described above in *Working a Passage* sells Airhitch tickets (303-279-3600).

Mig Urquhart was happy to take potluck with the company Airhitch and ended up in Dublin:

I'd put down Paris, Amsterdam or Athens on the registration form and got offered Zurich or Dublin. In 30 seconds I had to decide that Switzerland was too expensive and I had never been to Ireland. I'm very happy with the decision and with life in Donnybrook.

While Britain, Benelux, Switzerland, the States, Australia and other bastions of the free world have highly developed discount ticket markets, most countries do not. While hundreds of agents in Britain will sell you a cheap flight to Rio, no Brazilian is able to reciprocate. So beware of being stranded if you fly out to an exotic destination on a one-way ticket. Even nearer destinations can prove problematic as Allan Kirkpatrick from Glasgow found last year:

I had very little income while staying in Italy but managed to survive for a few weeks before booking a flight to Amsterdam. Now I know one should never attempt to track down a cheap flight out of Rome. It's like attempting to find a bullfight and matador in Venice.

You can get a friend in London to send you a discounted ticket for your homeward journey, but this is a tricky, risky and time-consuming business. On the other hand it is probably cheaper in the end and more flexible to piece together your own longhaul itinerary by buying cheap tickets en route, provided you have plenty of time wait around for the best deals.

If someone tries to sell you the unwanted half of their ticket, be warned that airline tickets are not transferable and with increased security, check-in staff will almost certainly compare the name on the passport and the boarding pass with the name on the ticket. Even for those with a thoroughly legitimate ticket, there are still a few pitfalls to avoid. Reconfirm your booking with the airline at least 72 hours before each flight and arrive at the airport by the latest time shown for check-in. Otherwise, you forfeit your rights to compensation if the flight happens to be overbooked. Also, find out whether airport tax is included in the fare or has to be paid upon departure. Air passenger duty in the UK is £10 for Europe and £20 for the rest of the world.

An unusual way of locating cheap flights is available from Adventurair (PO Box 757, Maidenhead, SL6 7XD; 01293 405777; www.rideguide.com) who produce *The Ride Guide* which gives details of companies operating cargo planes, aircraft deliveries and private planes. Any of these may have seats available for bargain prices. The book costs £13.35 in the UK, $17.99 plus postage in the US.

Bicycle

Cycling is not only healthy and free, it can simplify the business of finding work, as Adam Cook discovered in France:

> *Looking for work by bicycle is one of the very best methods as it allows you free unlimited travel far from the big towns and the competition. You can so easily visit the small villages and farms, some of which are off the beaten track.*

In addition, employers may realise that people who have been cycling for a while are at least moderately fit and may choose them for the job, ahead of the flabbier vehicle-bound competition. In many parts of the world you will also become an object of fascination, which can only aid your job-finding chances. If you do decide to travel extensively by bicycle, you might consider joining the Cyclists' Touring Club (69 Meadrow, Godalming, Surrey GU7 3HS; 01483 41721; www.ctc.org.uk) which provides free technical, legal and touring information to members; membership costs £25.

EUROPE

The European land mass is one of the most expensive areas of the world to traverse. Fortunately, hitch-hiking is at its easiest, cheapest and safest in Europe. Of course not all European countries are equally hitchable: Greece and Italy are fine – if you're blonde and female; Portugal is good, Sweden is dreadful, Germany is far easier than France, while Ireland, Denmark and Switzerland are excellent, and so on. Readers of this book have turned in some impressive times: Jason Davies hitched from Barcelona to Frederikshavn in 3¹/2 days, while in the opposite direction Tony Davies-Patrick got from Denmark to Avignon in a day. Meanwhile Kevin Vincent wonders if he might hold a world record: it took him nine days to hitch from Cadiz to Barcelona, a distance of less than 800 miles. The toll booths on French and Italian motorways are recommended by seasoned hitchers as the best place to stand.

Often lifts can be arranged informally without having to stand out in the weather. Check notice boards in hostels or youth travel bureaux. In some countries (like Spain) it is customary to ask drivers politely if they can give you a lift rather than take your chances by the side of the road. An underrated alternative is to use a lift-sharing agency of which there are dozens of outlets across Europe, especially in Germany, where there are Citynetz offices in Berlin, Düsseldorf, Freiburg, Hamburg, Munich, etc. (Cologne address below). For a varying fee (usually about £10 plus a share of the petrol) they will try to find a driver going to your chosen destination. See the website www.allostop.com.

Here are some details of European agencies:

France: Allostop Provoya, 8 rue Rochambeau, 75009 Paris (1-53 20 42 42/fax 01-53 20 42 44. Access also by internet www.ecritel.fr/allostop and Minitel: 36 15 code ALLOSTOP. Prices are set according to distance of journey: F30 for less than 200km, F45 for 200-300km, F60 for 300-500km and so on. Sample prices are Paris-Amsterdam for F167, Grenoble-Perpignan for F158 and Bordeaux-Madrid for F221.

Belgium: Taxistop/Eurostop, 28 rue Fossé-aux-Loups, 1000 Brussels (02-223 23 31/fax 02-223 22 32). Taxistop Flanders, Onderbergen 51, 9000 Gent (09-223 23 10/fax 09-224 31 44) Opening hours are 9am-6pm and the web address is www.taxistop.be. The cost to the passenger is BF1 per kilometre (minimum BF250, maximum BF800) to be paid to the driver plus BF0.3 per kilometre to be paid to Taxistop for administration.

Netherlands: International Lift Centre, NZ Voorburgwal 256, 1012 RS Amsterdam (020-622 43 42). The fee is between 17 guilders and 30 guilders plus 6 cents per kilometre to the driver.

Germany: Citynetz, Mitzfahrzentrale, Saarstr. 22, D-50677 Köln (0221-19444). Also in dozens of other cities. Prices are DM50 to Berlin, DM47 to Paris, DM76 to Vienna and DM22 to Frankfurt.

Spain: Iberstop Mitzfahrcentrale, 85 C/ Elvira, 18010 Granada (958-29 29 20).

Elsewhere try to locate Eurolift in Portugal (01-888 5002 in Lisbon), Eurostop in Budapest (01-138 2019) and Eurostop in Prague (02-204383). Nicola Hall made good use of this service when she wanted to leave Germany:

> *There is a lift-sharing place in Munich next to the main station behind one of the main hotels which is very cheap. They charge a fee and the rest depends on how many people will be in the car to share the cost of petrol. I paid DM70 for a ride to Amsterdam.*

Matches can seldom be made straightaway, so this system is of interest to those who can plan ahead.

The cheapest ferry deal is an out-of-season day return from Ramsgate, Dover or Folkestone to a French or Belgian channel port for £5-£10 (as opposed to the standard one-way fare of over £20). Andy Green recommends joining the Ferry Travel Club (Channel View Road, Dover, Kent CT17 9TP; 01304 213533; www.travel-market.co.uk) for £6 which gives members access to cheap day-returns from £4. Day return tickets are not allowed to be used as one-way tickets, so people with large rucksacks will not be allowed to buy day returns. Stephen Hands, who was refused a day-trip ticket, suggests transferring your belongings into plastic bags. Philip O'Hara was approached by a German girl at the Dover ferry terminal offering to sell him the unused portion of her return ferry ticket for £7. Alternatively you can try to sell the unused part of your own day return at the other side. If you are leaving Britain by ferry to Scandinavia, there are substantial student discounts available. If you want to cross cheaply from France, Andy Green says try to buy a cheap day-return (from F50) from a travel agent in advance rather than waiting till you get to the ferry port.

You may even be able to hitch a free ride on the ferry to France or Ireland if you strike up an acquaintance with people travelling in a vehicle. In some cases, the fare is per vehicle and covers all passengers (up to five). Through coach fares from London to Paris or Amsterdam contain a much-reduced ferry element.

On the whole the railways of Europe are expensive. Even with under-26 discounts available through Usit-Campus or specialist agents like Freedom Rail Ltd. in Surrey (01252 728506; www.freedomrail.co.uk), it is often cheaper to fly on one of the new no-frills ticketless airlines shuttling between Stansted or Luton and many European destinations. They do not take bookings via travel agents so it is necessary to contact them directly:

Buzz - 0870 240 7070; www.buzzaway.com Stansted to Berlin, Bordeaux, Geneva, Helsinki, La Rochelle, Milan, Vienna and a number of others.

Easyjet - 0870 6000000; www.easyjet.com. If you book over the internet, you can save £5 per return flight. Flies from Luton to Scotland, Nice, Barcelona, Amsterdam, Madrid, Malaga, Palma de Mallorca, Athens, Geneva and Zurich.

GO - 08456 054321; www.go-fly.com. The British Airways-linked airline flies from Stansted to Rome, Milan, Venice, Copenhagen, Lisbon, Faro, Munich, Madrid, Bilbao, etc.

Ryanair - 0870 333 1231; www.ryanair.com. To Irish airports and dozens of European cities. Amazing bargains on internet such as return fares from £10. Hard to get through to.

Virgin Express - 020-7744 0004/www.virgin-express.com. From Gatwick or Heathrow to Shannon, Brussels, Berlin, Copenhagen, Barcelona, Madrid, Malaga, Milan, Nice and Rome.

Eclipse Direct, the direct-sell travel agent, offers very cheap offers on long stay flights which depart from the UK for European resorts in the winter and return before the holiday season begins. For example a two month return from Cardiff to Tenerife or from Birmingham to Malta might cost £59. Details from 08705 329326. Other holiday companies out of peak season try to fill up seats on charter flights, by advertising or (increasingly) over the internet.

Europe's largest and best-connected scheduled coach tour operator is Eurolines serving 500 destinations in 25 countries from Killarney on the west coast of Ireland to Bucharest. Prices start at £33 return for London-Amsterdam. You can write to Eurolines (UK) head office for schedules and prices at 4 Cardiff Road, Luton, Beds LU1 1PP or call 08705 143219 for reservations or check fares and times on www.eurolines.com. Passengers under the age of 26 are eligible for a 10% discount.

For smaller independent coach operators, check advertisements in London magazines like *TNT*. For example Kingscourt Express (15 Balham High Road, London SW12 9AJ; 020-8673 7500/www.kce.cz) runs daily services between London and Prague or Brno; fares start at £64 return.

NORTH AMERICA

Incredibly, the price of flying across the Atlantic has been steadily decreasing over the past decade. Off-peak student returns to New York start at less than £200. Competition is fiercest and therefore prices lowest on the main routes between London and New York, Miami and Los Angeles. In many cases, summer fares will be twice as high as winter ones. One way fares are also available to eastern seaboard cities like Washington for £100-£150. When comparing fares, always take the taxes into consideration since they represent about £45-£50.

Outside summer and the Christmas period you should have no problems getting a seat; at peak times, a reliable alternative is to buy a discounted ticket on one of the less fashionable carriers which fly to New York, such as Air India or El Al. A one-year return London-New York on Kuwait Air might start at £250 plus taxes. Recommended specialist agencies in the UK are Major Travel (28-34 Fortess Road, London NW5 2HV; 020-7393 1060), Globespan (0990 561522) for Canada and Eclipse (08705 010203) among many others.

The USA and Canada share the longest common frontier in the world, which gives some idea of the potential problems and expense of getting around. You will want to consider Driveaway (see *United States* chapter) and also bus and air travel which are both cheaper than in Europe. In the US, consult any branch of Council Travel or STA (1-800-777-0112) and in Canada look for an office of Travel Cuts, the youth and student travel specialist. If you intend to travel widely in the States check out air passes. One working holidaymaker timed long journeys to coincide with night flights to save on accommodation and food. Hitch-hiking in the USA is often unnerving and sometimes fraught with danger, danger not only from crazy drivers but also from the law, especially where 'No Hitch-hiking' signs abound. It is a more reasonable proposition in Canada.

South of the Canadian border, bus passes (Ameripass) are a travel bargain for people who want to cover a lot of ground. Greyhound's office in the UK no longer sells the passes though they can be bought through STA, usit-Campus, Trailfinders, etc. In 2001, Greyhound (www.greyhound.com) are offering 4, 7, 10, 15, 21, 30, 45 and 60 day passes for $135, $155, $209, $235, $285, $335, $355 and $449. Once you are in the US timetable and fare information is available 24 hours a day on the toll-free number 1-800-231-2222. Discounts are normally available to anyone who purchases a ticket three weeks in advance. After taking advantage of this discount, Colin Rothwell was amazed to discover that Greyhound let him change the date. Greyhound also offer a Canada Pass (valid west of Montreal) which costs £109 for 7 days in ten, £165 for 15 days in 20, £195 for 30 days in 40 and £259 for 60 days in 80. The all-Canada pass costs an extra £14-£36; see www.greyhound.ca.

Other forms of transport in the USA are probably more expensive but may have their own attractions, such as the trips run by Green Tortoise (494 Broadway, San

Francisco, California 94133; 800-867-8647; www.greentortoise.com) which use vehicles converted to sleep about 35 people and which make interesting detours and stopovers. There may even be an option to swap your labour for a free ride.

The deregulation of US domestic airlines has resulted in lunatic discounting. South-West Airlines based in Dallas (www.southwest.com) is one of the better known discount companies offering cheap fares and no-frills service. Normally the cheapest advance purchase coast-to-coast fares are about $200 though you might get cheaper ones with discount domestic airlines like Reno Air (1-800-736-6247; information@renoair.com). Canada 3000 offers standby fares, e.g. $215 Vancouver to Los Angeles. The best advice within the USA is to study local newspapers, as fare wars are usually fought using full page advertisements.

Attempts to revive long-distance train travel in the US have had some beneficial effects resulting in some good value rail passes, though trains are still largely the domain of tourists. Leisure Rail in the UK (0870 7500222) specialises in booking rail travel in North America (and elsewhere). The basic three-and-a-half day train trip from Toronto to Vancouver costs about C$550 in the summer, $400 off-season with further discounts for advance booking. The ViaRail info line in Canada is 800-681-2561 (www.viarail.ca).

In both Canada and the USA there is an alternative way to ride the rails, as Marcel Staats found (some years ago now):

An absolutely great way to see North America is by train. However, if you don't have that much money on you, do it the illegal way and 'hobo'. I left most of my luggage in a cloakroom and hoboed my way across the States. To hobo' (also known as freight-hopping' – Ed) *means that you jump on goods trains (called freight trains) and stay there as long as possible. Hoboing is not what it was in the 40s and 50s. There's much tighter security, including frequent checks and padlocked doors. However there are possibilities.*

For accommodation in North America (mainly Canada), get hold of the list of hostels from Backpackers Hostels Canada (Longhouse Village, RR 13, Thunder Bay, Ontario P7B 5E4; www.backpackers.ca). The list can be viewed on the net for free or sent by post in exchange for $5 or four IRCs.

LATIN AMERICA

In the low seasons of January to May and October-November, you can get from London to South America for under £200 one way, though this is rarely the best way to do it because international tickets bought out there are very expensive. Having a return ticket makes it much easier to cross borders. Open-dated returns are available as are open jaw tickets (where you fly into one point and back from another). It might be possible to extend these even if you decide to stay longer than a year; Nick Branch had an Alitalia ticket which he extended more than once for a $100 fee.

A fully-bonded agency which specialises in travel to and around this area of the world is Journey Latin America (12-13 Heathfield Terrace, Chiswick, London W4 4JE; 020-8747 3108; www.journeylatinamerica.co.uk) who consistently offer the lowest fares and the most expertise. Another advantage is that they deal exclusively with Latin America and hence are the best source of up-to-date travel information. One of the best deals at the time of writing was on Delta who were offering a six-month return to Lima for £478 plus £45 tax.

Taxes are levied on international flights within South America: the cheapest way to fly from one capital to another (assuming you have plenty of time) is to take a domestic flight (within, say, Brazil), cross the border by land and then buy another domestic ticket (within, say, Peru). There is also a plethora of airpasses available which are cheaper if bought at the same time as your transatlantic ticket; Journey Latin America publish a guide to these *(Papagaio)*. The alternatives include the remnants of a British-built railway system and the ubiquitous bus, both of which are extremely cheap and interesting. A rough estimate of the price of bus travel in South America is US$1.50 for every hour of travel. Hitch-hiking is highly unpredictable, and usually the cost depends upon your bargaining ability. The degree of safety depends upon sheer good fortune. Not that taking public transport guarantees a safe journey. Dick Bird describes the bus system of Rio de Janeiro:

> *Bus drivers are paid on a piece rate basis, so understandably they drive like speed-crazed lunatics. The first problem is to flag down one of these monsters as it hurtles along six inches from the kerb sucking old ladies, debris and small dogs into its slipstream. Just as you are meekly offering your cruzeiros to the conductor at the rear of the bus, you are suddenly slammed back against the emergency exit as the bus takes off in a flurry of G-forces worthy of a medium-sized moon rocket. On your second attempt to pay, you find yourself jack-knifed and doubled up over the turnstile. At last you manage to flop into the upholstery like a landed fish and find yourself in a position of uncomfortable intimacy with the inevitable fat lady in the window seat. You sit quivering, vowing to go by DC-10 next time.*

Rio newspapers regularly lead with headlines like *Onibus no Canal* (bus in the canal) or *Onibus Mergulho da Ponte – 50 Mortos* (bus dives off bridge killing 50).

For information on travel in Latin America join South American Explorers (formerly the South American Explorers' Club). They maintain two clubhouses: Av. Portugal 146, Brena, Postal Casilla 3714, Lima 100, Peru (1-425 0142) and Jorge Washington 311 y L. Plaza, Postal Apartado 21-431, Quito, Ecuador (tel/fax 2-225 228). The US office is at 126 Indian Creek Rd, Ithaca, NY 14850 (607-277-6122; www.samexplo.org) and membership costs $40. In addition to travel information they are also developing extensive databases of voluntary and teaching jobs for members to access.

AFRICA

Flights to Cairo are advertised from £150 single, £200 return, while the special offers to Nairobi start as low as £280 single, £395 return. A specialist agency for Southern Africa is Melhart Travel (020-8953 4222; info@melharttravel.com). A 12-month return to Johannesburg on Virgin in the low season (April-July) was costing about £550 before tax at the time of writing. Another agency to try is the Africa Travel Centre (21 Leigh St, London WC1H 9QX; 020-7387 1211). Note that there is no regular ferry service between Greece and Alexandria, Egypt.

The overland routes are fraught with difficulties, and careful research must be done before setting off via the Sahara (the route through the Sudan is impossible at present). Jennifer McKibben, who spent some time in East Africa, recommends trying to negotiate a cheap seat in one of the overland expedition vehicles which are so much in evidence in that part of the world, assuming 'half their number have stormed off the bus or truck, unable to bear each other any longer'.

ASIA

The famous hippy overland route to Nepal has been problematical for many years though not impossible. Although Afghanistan is still off-limits, it is possible to cross Iran into Pakistan (a very rigorous but very cheap trip, assuming you can get a transit visa for Iran). Once you're in Pakistan, you might assume that the freedom of the sub-continent was before you, but due to the problems in the Punjab, the Indo-Pakistan border cannot be relied upon to be open. An alternative is to make the journey with an established overland company which charge between £100 and £150 a week not including the food kitty. Most travellers simply take advantage of the competitive discount flight market from London to Asian destinations. For example the cheapest quoted return price London to Delhi is £300. The cheapest carrier to Bangkok is Tarom the Romanian airline which has a one-year return for £330 with a stopover in Bucharest. The price of flights to Japan has dropped significantly in the past few years, especially if you are willing to fly on Aeroflot. In London a wide range of travel agents advertise cheap fares to Asia. In the US, try Chisholm Travel (500 N. Clark Ave, Chicago, IL 60610; 1-8090-631-2824; www.chisholmair.net).

Once you're installed in Asia, travel is highly affordable. The railways of the Indian sub-continent are a fascinating social phenomenon and also dirt cheap. Throughout Asia, air fares are not expensive, particularly around the discount triangle of Bangkok, Hong Kong and Singapore. Lifts with trucks or private vehicles are likely to cost a nominal sum, so usually it's preferable to rely on public transport. The notable exception to the generalisation about cheap public transport in Asia is Japan, where the possibility of hitching marginally compensates for the high cost of living and travelling.

Travel within the People's Republic of China can initially be exasperating as you struggle with the inscrutable bureaucracy and the utterly incomprehensible nature of stations and airports (where no allowance is made for those who do not understand Chinese characters). But like most things in the East, once you come to terms with the people and their way of life, travelling once more becomes a pleasurable experience. With upheavals in Russia, the Trans-Siberian rail journey is not as cheap as it used to be.

AUSTRALASIA

The Australian Tourist Commission's *Traveller's Guide* contains quite a bit of hard information and useful telephone numbers as well as all the advertising; request a copy by ringing 0906 863 3235. An excellent free guide for backpackers is the free *Australia & New Zealand Independent Travel Guide* from TNT (14-15 Child's Place, London SW5 9RX; 020-7373 3377); send an A5 s.a.e. with a 70p stamp..

Per mile, the flight to the Antipodes is cheaper than most. The Indonesian carrier Garuda has traditionally been the cheapest; for example a 12-month return on Garuda might be £150-200 cheaper than the dominant airlines. The cheapest advertised fares are on charter flights (from £469 return with Austravel 020-7584 0202/0870 055 0215) but for these you must normally return within eight weeks. One-way fares to Sydney, Perth or Brisbane start at £200.

Your transport problems are by no means over when you land in Perth or Sydney. The distances in Australia may be much greater than you are accustomed to and so you will have to give some thought to how you intend to get around. Even with increased airline competition, flying is costly, though you should look into the new no frills Spirit Airlines (www.spiritairlines.com) which is promising walk-on fares of A$95 Melbourne to Sydney, $220 Melbourne to Perth, etc. and Richard Branson's Virgin Blue (www.virginblue.com.au) which is launching daily flights from Sydney/Melbourne/ Adelaide to Brisbane. Substantial discounts are offered by the major domestic airlines to overseas visitors who buy a certain number of domestic flights. There are also other discounts for booking at the last minute, and for travelling at unsocial hours or standby.

If you plan a major tour of the country you might consider purchasing a Greyhound Pioneer coach pass along a pre-set route. Prices start at $110 for a mini-pass (Sydney to Brisbane) and go up to an all-Australia pass costing $1,640 (less a YHA discount of 15%). If you just want to get from one coast to another as quickly as possible and qualify for the very cheapest deals, you will pay around A$350 one way on the coach or train (excluding berth and meals). A multiplicity of private operators has sprung up to serve the backpacking market including one or two which fix their routes to suit job-seeking fruit-pickers. Writing from New South Wales, Geertje Korf passed on the following warning:

> *A guy I met from Canada arrived here on a bus whose driver had promised him guaranteed work for up to $100 a day. He paid $70 for transport from Sydney and had the impression that he would be taken to an orchard, shown where to pitch his tent, etc. But instead the driver simply dropped him off at the job centre. He could have saved money by just catching the ordinary bus and walking.*

Having your own transport is a great advantage when job-hunting in Australia. Some places have second-hand cars and camper vans for sale which they will buy back at the end of your stay. Also in Sydney check the car market in Kings Cross (corner of Ward Avenue and Elizabeth Bay Road; 02-9358 5000/www.carmarket.com.au). The price of camper vans starts at $2,000 though this would not necessarily be a reliable vehicle. Car hire is expensive, but occasionally 'relocations' are advertised, i.e. hire cars which need to be returned to their depots. Bridgid Seymour-East noticed a Melbourne company offering relocation cars (07-3252 5752/fax 07-3257 3952) and also says that Britz Campervans (03-9483 1888/www.britz.com) frequently advertise for people to 'reposition' vehicles sometimes charging drivers as little as $10 a day.

If you can't afford the luxury of organised transport or buying your own vehicle, you might be drawn to the idea of hitch-hiking. A coast to coast journey won't take you much less than a week, so it's a major undertaking. Be careful about being dropped on isolated stretches of the road across the Nullarbor Plain where, without water, you might just expire before the next vehicle comes along. On the other hand, you might be lucky and get one of those not uncommon lifts which covers 3200km in 96 hours.

Many women travellers have expressed their reluctance to travel alone with a long-distance lorry driver in remote areas, especially after the well-publicised backpacker murders a couple of years ago. According to a policeman Lucy Slater spoke to, drivers are less inclined to pick up hitchers in view of the trouble. (Nevertheless, Lucy and her boyfriend hitched from Perth to Kalgoorlie and found that the people who gave them lifts were mines of information about job possibilities.) The Queensland coastal road is notoriously dangerous. Violence is rare, but if you are unlucky you might be evicted from the truck unless you comply with the driver's wishes. All backpackers' hostels are a good bet for finding drivers going your way, provided you are able to wait for a suitable ride.

You need not confine yourself to cars and lorries for hitching. Adrian McCay hitched a lift on a private plane from remote Kununurra to Mildura. While working at a remote property in Western Australia, David Irvine hitched a couple of lifts with the flying doctor service. Earlier in his travels he got stranded in Norseman after a truck ride across the Nullarbor. Here he met an aboriginal swagman who advised him to hop a freight which he did, which turned out to be a coal train. Suddenly there was a very rare rainstorm which turned the coal dust on which he was sitting in his open hopper to disgusting sludge.

Unfortunately the flight from Australia to New Zealand is not particularly cheap unless bought in conjunction with a longhaul flight. The standard return fare of A$800 can usually be halved by canny shopping; check out www.travel.com.au for leads, or the no-frills New Zealand Air (www.freedomair.co.nz). But once in New Zealand it is difficult to imagine a country more favourable to hitch-hikers. Travellers regularly cover the whole country, using youth hostels and hitching, and spend about £200 a month.

A day return on the ferry between North and South Island costs the same as the single, so it is worth trying to sell the return half when you reach the other side. It also provides a good opportunity for finding drivers heading in your direction.

FORMALITIES AT BORDERS

Whichever mode of transport you choose, there are a number of formalities, which must be tackled before you set off, to ensure that your journey is not fraught with an unexpected range of disasters.

Visas

With over 150 nations crammed onto this minor planet, you can't continue in one direction for very long before you are impeded by border guards demanding to see your papers. EU nationals who confine their travels to Europe have little to worry about. Everyone else should do their homework. Always check with the Consulate or (second best) a travel agent who will have a *Travel Information Manual (TIM)* which contains all visa, customs and other information. Alternatively consult Thomas Cook's timetables or the quarterly *Guide to International Travel* in local libraries. You will then be in a position to bore your friends and fellow travellers with your knowledge of the documentation required by North Korean visitors to the United Arab Emirates. Getting visas is a headache anywhere, but is usually easier in your home country. Fees are rising.

If you are short of time or live a long way from the Embassies in London, there are private visa agencies such as the VisaService, 2 Northdown St, London N1 9BG (020-7833 2709/fax 020-7833 1857/www.visaservice.co.uk) which will obtain the relevant visa for fees from £20 plus VAT per visa. An alternative is Global Visas, 181 Oxford

St, London W1D 2JT (020-7734 5900). The World Travel Document Services in the US provides visa, passport and travel information via fax (202-785-3256) or try Travel Document Systems also in Washington (www.traveldocs.com). Details of work permit regulations and so on can be found in the country chapters in this book. See also the introductory section *Red Tape*. The Health consultancy MASTA now operates a Visa and Passport line charged at £1 a minute (0897 501100)

The Foreign and Commonwealth Office has reviewed its list of incompatible countries and the United Kingdom Passport Agency (Clive House, 70-78 Petty France, London SW1H 9HD) has tightened up on issuing a second passport to people who intend to travel both to Israel and hostile Arab countries. For up-to-date information on this subject, ring the Passport Office's Enquiry line: 0870 521 0410 (www.ukpa.gov.uk).

The Foreign Office has a Travel Advice Unit which can be contacted on 020-7008 0232/fax 020-7238 4545/www.fco.gov.uk/travel. If you have access to BBC Ceefax look at pages 470 and following. North Americans may wish to obtain the relevant consular information sheet from the US State Department. Reports cover entry requirements, crime, terrorist activities, medical facilities, etc. Travel warnings are still issued for dangerous countries. Ring 202-647-5225 for automated information (which may err on the side of caution).

If you intend to cross a great many borders, especially on an overland trip through Africa, ensure that you have all the relevant documentation and that your passport contains as many blank pages as frontiers which you intend to cross. Travellers have been turned back purely because the border guard refused to use a page with another stamp on it.

Money

On arrival at a border, you may be asked to prove that a) you have enough to support yourself for the duration of your proposed stay, and b) that you have the means to leave the country without undermining the economy by engaging in unauthorised activities (e.g. working, changing money on the black market, smuggling, etc.). The authorities are more likely to take an interest in a scruffy impecunious looking backpacker. Sometimes border personnel wish to see proof of absurdly large sums such as $500 before you can board the boat between Greece and Israel or $1,000 for each month of your proposed stay in New Zealand. Remember that well-dressed travellers who carry suitcases rather than rucksacks will be challenged less often. Because Michel Falardeau was travelling on one-way tickets without all that much money, he wore a business suit whenever he was due to meet an immigration official, and this worked for him on his round-the-world trip. You can get away with having less money if you have an onward ticket, and the names and addresses of residents whom you intend to visit.

There are several ways round the problem. Some travellers have gone so far as to declare the loss of their travellers cheques, in order to use the duplicate set as 'flash money'. As soon as the duplicates have done their duty at the border, the supposedly lost originals can then be burned. A less dramatic technique is to show off your range of credit cards. Or take a IATA miscellaneous charges order. This is effectively a voucher for a specified amount (say £100) worth of air travel. It may be bought from any IATA airline, and has several advantages: it is usually accepted as proof of your intention to leave the country in lieu of a straight airline ticket and may be used as such across virtually any border, plus it adds an extra £100 to your worth, i.e. the money you're supposed to be injecting into the country's flagging economy. When you get home you may cash it in at face value. The only difficulty is that officials in off-the-beaten track countries may not recognise the document.

After reconfirming your booking with your airline 72 hours before a flight; find out whether there is a departure tax. For example to fly out of Kenya you must pay US$20, Ecuador $25, Hong Kong HK$100, Nepal Rs700, Korea 9,000 won, Tanzania $45, India Rs300 and so on. This can be an unexpected nuisance or a total disaster. Information about transferring emergency funds from home is given in the chapter *In Extremis* at the end of this book.

ENTERPRISE

You don't have to spend eight hours a day washing dishes in order to earn money abroad. Many travellers have found or made opportunities to go into business for themselves, exchanging steady wage packets for less predictable sources of income. The people who have succeeded in this type of work tend to have a large degree of initiative, determination and often creativity; they have identified some local need and exploited it.

Often they find themselves on the borderline of the law. If you paint the sun setting over a harbour you are an artist; sell the painting to someone who stops to admire it and you may, in law, become a street trader requiring a permit. If you wash motorists' windscreens at traffic lights, you might be doing them a service, but the police might consider you an obstruction. At worst you will find yourself being moved on, though a few exceptions have been noted in the country chapters.

The chapter will first deal with importing and exporting: the ways in which you can make money by buying cheaply in one country and selling in another. The second part of the chapter will deal with the kinds of marketing opportunities which you should watch out for within the country you're visiting, many of which involve pandering to the desires of homesick tourists. The final two sections deal with odd-jobbing and gambling.

IMPORT/EXPORT

With experience, travellers come to know what items can be bought cheaply in one country and profitably sold in another. Wherever something is exorbitantly priced, it is possible to sell informally to local people or fellow tourists at a profit. But as the world shrinks and trade barriers dissolve, the possibilities are becoming fewer. After his extensive travels in Turkey and Asia, the American Tim Leffel concluded:

> *The enterprise opportunities seem to be vanishing faster than you can say 'free trade'. There weren't many things in high demand that you could buy cheaper in the US or across a neighbouring border, at least where we were, unless you were dealing in big-ticket electronics. Bringing things back, of course, is a different story.*

On the other hand niches can always be found. For example, a Derbyshire man realised that Germans in the town twinned with his loved British goods including the obvious like tea and marmalade. He went over with a supply of Union Jack beach towels and sold them at the local market in a very short time. Or a Scottish woman had T-shirts printed up with Gaelic motifs and sold them at the Canadian Highland Games. Another traveller found that condoms were in great demand in Malawi and traded them to advantage.

One of the most portable and profitable items that readers have recommended carrying around is cigarette papers which are expensive in Scandinavia for example, and unobtainable in Greece, Brazil, etc. Ian McArthur planned to take about 500 packets to Goa where he'd heard that the selling price was five times higher than in Britain. Travellers in the Far East (Bangkok, Hong Kong and Japan) have been known to stock up on the newest play station games (which are often a third the price they are in the UK) with a view to selling them discreetly at home, possibly outside video shops. Only a buff would be able to make this work, since only certain UK computers are 'chipped up' (adapted) to cope with import games.

Some travellers think it's worthwhile to load up on bronze trinkets, alpaca sweaters, jade jewellery, rosewood boxes, sisal baskets from Kenya, Tibetan woollens, Turkish carpets or anything else which they know are more expensive or unobtainable elsewhere. Before engaging in this sort of activity you'll have to master the art of haggling, which involves patience and good humour. Usually it is difficult to make much of a profit on one-off trips abroad. Also, you should be thoroughly acquainted with customs regulations. Americans should acquire a copy of *A Basic Guide to Exporting* (S/N 003-009-00604-0) from the US Department of Commerce & Federal Express ($15 from the Superintendent of Documents, US Government Printing Office, Washington, DC 20402).

Do not believe every foreign trader who promises you vast profits in your home country, for example selling Tahitian pearls or Sri Lankan gems, or who assures you that you will have no difficulty at customs. In fact do not believe any of them. Almost invariably they are inventing a story in order to make a bulk sale. No consumer protection is available to their gulls. Bangkok seems to be the capital of smooth-talking swindlers. A warning notice in a Bangkok hostel, which reads 'These people are vicious and evil and all they say is lies' was written by a German who parted with US$1,100 for '$3,000 plus' of sapphires, only to be told by his 'guaranteed buyer' (an unwitting jeweller in Sydney) that their true value was $250.

Yet there is a host of travellers successfully selling exotica as Kristen Moen reports:

> *I was in Corfu selling jewellery I had bought in India, Nepal, Thailand and China. Quite a lot of my friends do similar things. When they come home from Asia and South America they sell jewellery and other things and they make almost enough money to finance their trip. Of course you have to be careful when you buy so you don't get cheated but you learn along the way.*

You don't have to wait until you get home to sell. Many travellers successfully sell jewellery and knicknacks from Thailand and India in Taiwan and Hong Kong. Westerners can be seen selling leather goods and other items brought from India in European markets.

Duty-Free

Selling your duty-free tobacco, alcohol and consumer durables is probably the most obvious and simple way of earning money. In some Asian countries, Scotch whisky (Johnny Walker Red Label seems to be the preferred brand) and European cigarettes are widely coveted. In other countries, these products are available in the shops but for a colossal price. In the past, people have made as much as four times their outlay, for example, after bringing back a box of high quality cigars from Cuba to Europe.

Be very cautious about taking alcohol into strict Islamic countries where it is forbidden. There is a good market in 'softer' Islamic countries; for example touts and guides in Tangiers are willing buyers. Beware of highly organised local competition, for example along international trading routes where drivers and overland couriers will know all the tricks. Exploiting price differentials across international borders can be lucrative if you are well situated. For example people who live in Spain and work in Gibraltar can make a sizeable profit on cartons of Winston cigarettes bought in Gibraltar and sold in bars in La Linea. (Officially you are entitled to carry one carton a month across the border.)

Within Europe, duty-free differentials have been abolished, though this doesn't mean that cigarettes and wine aren't a lot cheaper in France than England. Tobacco and alcohol bought abroad must be for personal consumption, a law that is widely flouted. So many operators within Europe have been importing goods to sell at a profit that this illegal trade has seriously dinted profits in the drinks trade of Southeast England and customs checks at British ports have become much tougher.

Currency Exchange

In countries where there is a soft currency, i.e. one that cannot officially be used to buy dollars or sterling, or where the government attaches an unjustifiably high value to its currency, a black market often develops. Tempting as the rewards might be, you should be aware of the pitfalls (in addition to the fact that it might be unethical to deprive banks of hard currency which helps poor economies to keep ticking over). The black market attracts all sorts of shady characters who very regularly cheat even the canniest travellers, making them regret their greed. Favourite ploys include handing the tourist an envelope full of shredded newspaper or one large denomination bill wrapped cleverly around a wad of lower bills, or pretending to spot a policeman and then vanishing after taking your dollars but before giving you your pesos, rupees, shillings, etc.

Even more worrying situations can arise if you realise that the black marketeer is an *agent provocateur* who is in cahoots with the police. The law will appear instantly either to arrest you (unlikely) or to demand some baksheesh. To guard against such an outcome, always avoid trading on the street. By asking around at budget hotels, you'll soon learn where to find legitimate traders, often in shops or travel agencies. Familiarise yourself with the appearance of all denominations of currency and take along a friend to assist you.

Second-hand Gear

Outside the consumer societies of the West, there is a fluctuating demand for gadgets and gewgaws, and various items we take for granted can be sold or traded. T-shirts with Western slogans have had spells of popularity in different places, though in most cases a local entrepreneur will have latched on to this market. Even if you don't get cash, you might trade for goods and services or an interesting souvenir.

If you are a frequent visitor to a country, you might try to learn what kinds of used items are in demand at markets. Foreigners in Britain could reserve a table at a car boot sale (for about £5-10) to try to sell any items of interest from their country. Elfed Guyatt from Wales thinks that Sweden is a particularly promising destination for any would-be entrepreneurs:

> In the weekend market stalls people just set up their own table and sell off all sorts of odds and ends. The prices are incredibly high compared to Britain for certain things. You should make 500% profit on selling things like medals, caps, British and American books in subjects that interest the Swedes, in fact anything that looks different and not easily available in their country. They do like showing off possessions here. Souvenirs of London or Shakespeare go well. I saw a very cheap, small brass Big Ben table bell sell for £12.50 and an old battered cricket bat went for £25.

SPOTTING LOCAL OPPORTUNITIES

The opportunities for finding eager customers on whatever doorstep you find yourself are endless and we can only give some idea of the remarkable range of ways to earn money by using your initiative and your imagination. If you see a gap in the market, try to fill it. For example Stephen Psallidas toyed seriously with the idea of buying a bicycle in the tomato-growing capital of Queensland in order to hire it out to job-seeking tomato pickers since at the time Bowen was, if not a one-horse town, a one-bicycle town. After getting to know the Greek island of Levkas fairly well, Camilla Lambert hired a jeep at weekends for £35 a day and took three paying passengers out for a day's excursion. One Englishman acquired a chain saw in Spain and made a killing by hiring himself out to farmers to prune their olive trees. A Canadian who was having trouble being hired by a language school in a provincial city in Taiwan set up his own English immersion social club which easily covered his costs in the two months he ran it. You just need to exploit any manual or artistic or public relations skill you already have or which you have cultivated for the purpose.

Homemade Handicrafts

A number of people have successfully supported themselves abroad by selling home-made jewellery and other items on the street. Careful preparations can pay dividends; for example Jennifer Tong picked up shells from a beach near Eilat and invested £5 in a pair of pliers and some wire, clips and beads when she was in Israel. With these materials she made simple earrings which were bought for £2 a pair on the Greek Islands. Even more simply Amy Ignatow collected smooth pebbles at her moshav, decorated them with a permanent pen and sold them on the street in Jerusalem for £3 each. Steve Pringle sold earrings in Madrid which he had made from a stock of cheap imitation diamonds he had brought over from London. Braided or knotted friendship bracelets are popular in travellers' resorts and can usually be sold for £2 or £3 and take 15 minutes to make. You have to find something that doesn't require too much time, which Emma Hoare failed to do while on her gap year:

In the south of France I met up with a girl I had been previously travelling with, and decided to make money by selling bags that we'd sewn. We went on to Spain and quickly discovered that sitting in little pensione rooms stitching minuscule beads onto cheap, flimsy fabric was a recipe for mental deterioration and, at times, uncontrollable hysteria. Then I decided that I had put too much effort into my bags to sell them. They were my little works of art and I was damned if I was going to let some horrible young tourist have it for a fiver and then leave it on the floor in a club somewhere (see what I mean about mental deterioration?)

It is worth looking out for cheap and unusual raw materials such as beads from Morocco, shells from Papua New Guinea or bamboo from Crete. Grimly Corridor taught himself how to make pan pipes from the local bamboo and sold them for about £5 (which included a recitation of the Pan legend which American tourists found difficult to resist). One natural resource to avoid exploiting is coral. Corals are vulnerable living creatures and should not be removed from their habitat.

If you can draw, knit, sew, sculpt or work with wood or leather then you may be able to produce something that people want to buy in holiday resorts. The skill of braiding hair with beads or 'hair wraps' can make a lot of money. All you need is the expertise, some cheap multi-coloured beads and thread with which to tie off the ends. One contributor met a girl making the equivalent of £35 a day in a Cape Town market doing this. While on holiday on the island of Formentera off the coast of Spain, Georgina Bayliss-Duffield found that braiding people's hair was a lucrative pastime, especially with a companion on whom to demonstrate. Eventually she was able to complete a head whether male or female in about 20 minutes (depending on the hair) for which she charged the equivalent of £8.

Beaches and Mobs

You should learn to look on any crowd of people as a potential market for what you have to sell. People emerging from a disco are often grateful for a hotdog or a sandwich or skiers queuing for a lift might appreciate some chocolate. If you loiter in a place where people regularly emerge from a remote place, as at the end of treks in Nepal or New Zealand, you could probably sell some interesting food and drink of which they have been deprived. Stephen Psallidas decided to become a portable off-licence with a view to selling wine to the devotees who flock to see Jim Morrison's grave in Paris. Unfortunately this was not a popular idea with the local cannabis sellers and he ended up drinking the wine himself.

Sunbathers on a wide unspoilt beach may be longing for a cold bottle of beer, sun tan lotion, a donut, or a few pre-stamped postcards and a ballpoint pen, and won't mind paying over the odds for them (especially if you have printed up your own postcards from your travel photos). Choose your beach carefully: if a beach is already swarming with cold drinks salesmen (as is the case along much of the French and Spanish Mediterranean), you're unlikely to be welcomed by potential customers. If a beach has none, selling may well be forbidden, as one reader discovered at Sydney's Bondi Beach, when the beach inspector chased them off after a few minutes.

If a crowd is scheduled to gather for a special occasion, think of the things they will want to buy. For example you could buy a few dozen roses in Niagara Falls, 'honeymoon capital of the world', and sell them individually to the happy couples at a high mark-up. The award for the most original salesman should go to the person who spotted an unruly crowd waiting for the arrival of the then Canadian Prime Minister in Sudbury, Ontario. He got hold of some eggs and sold them for use as missiles. Another situation which could be exploited is the refusal to allow scantily clad tourists into some European churches: renting out a pair of trousers would be a valuable service.

If you have the right product, you can sell to a wider market. One traveller earned his way in South America by selling peanut butter he'd made himself from local peanuts to American tourists outside the archaeological sites of Colombia. Ski bums regularly make pocket-money by delivering croissants from the local bakery to self-catering holiday-makers. Meanwhile another traveller sold popcorn to fishermen in Crete. If you are a fisherman yourself, you can try to sell your catch door to door in residential areas. Tessa Shaw picked snails at night by the River Ardèche in southern France and then set up a stall in the market at Carpentras. She found that Fridays were particularly profitable, since restaurateurs and shopkeepers drove down from Paris to buy stock for the weekend.

Anyone who owns and can use a pack of Tarot cards can sell his or her expertise. Leda Meredith had noticed people doing this in Florence and Avignon (where the going rate for a reading was F30) and set herself up on the Greece-Italy ferry with a table, two chairs and a sign in English.

Selling tickets to popular sporting or entertainment events is probably best left to locals in the know like Floyd Creamer Jr. from Wisconsin. He made $867 by spending less than two hours before seven college football and hockey games buying unwanted tickets for a pittance and selling them at (or almost at) face value, even for games which were not sold out. He found that it was even possible to buy a single day vendor's permit for $10 which made his activities perfectly legal.

Julian Peachey landed a job as warden in a youth hostel in Marseille, and soon began supplementing his income by selling wine at the hostel. The local supermarket delivered supplies at 40p per bottle, which he sold to the hostellers for 80p. Even though they realised he was selling at a substantial profit, the hostellers were happy to patronise his store when their own supplies had run out late at night. More recently, Roger Blake in South Africa was taken on by a backpackers hostel to run the bar and help with the nightly ostrich barbecues. He also took the opportunity to serve breakfast too which was like being self-employed. He was responsible for buying all the ingredients and was allowed to keep the profit, earning him after six weeks a 'small but worthwhile fortune'.

People staying in hostels often leave behind belongings (intentionally or otherwise) which could perhaps be sold, as Dustie Hickey did at an Avignon flea market earning herself £30 in an hour. Meanwhile Brett Archer was working as an assistant warden at the youth hostel in Bruges (Belgium) and began hiring out abandoned bicycles on a daily basis.

Writing and the Media

A few lucky people manage to subsidise their journeys abroad by selling articles or photographs based on their travels. There are two main markets for your creative work: local English language publications abroad, and newspapers and magazines in your home country. A trip to Northern Queensland might not seem newsworthy to you when you're there, but Frank Schiller sold an account of his trip to a German magazine for several hundred dollars. You can find out about local publications by studying news-stands when you are abroad.

For contacts in Britain, consult *The Writers' and Artists' Yearbook* (published by A&C Black, 35 Bedford Row, London WC1R 4JH) and consider getting hold of a book by Guy Marks called *Travel Writing and Photography* (£9.95 plus £1.20 postage from Traveller's Press, Box 6, 1 & 2 Cobbolds Row, Earl Soham, Suffolk IP13 7RL). In the US consult the *Travel Writer's Handbook* by Louise Purwin Zobel or *Writer's Market* ($23.99) and *Photographer's Market* ($19.99) published by Writer's Digest Books, 1507 Dana Ave, Cincinnati, Ohio 45207. In-flight magazines of foreign airlines sometimes buy freelance pieces. Enterprising journalists have also set up sites on the worldwide web and have funded it or made a profit through sponsorship.

If you have already published take along a cuttings book. Before you go abroad, it is a good idea to study the market, to get an idea of what editors are looking for. Many magazines issue editorial guidelines. One such is *Lookout* published in Malaga which describes the kind of travel article which it (like many others) is looking for:

> *We try to achieve a fresh view, a new angle, on travel destinations. Feel free to use the first person singular in a travel article. Describe those interesting or curious little incidents which, while not being of earth-shaking significance,*

help to brighten up the story. Quote the people you met on the trip: the innkeeper, the museum guard... Of course, you must also give practical information on how to get there, what to see, where to stay and where to eat, but this information should be delivered in a light, readable manner.

According to one experienced freelancer, sex really does sell abroad as at home, as do accounts of people coming through tragedies.

If at all possible, persuade an editor to give you a commission before you leave, as Tim Leffel did:

I had a few assignments set up before I left New Jersey as a travel writer and have started to sell a few other things from the trip now that I'm back. I've already made over $1,400 from various pieces, though none of the cheques were in hand until after my return. It's not something to do for quick money: 'quick' in an editor's mind means 'less than a year'.

I've met lots of would-be writers and photographers who hit me up for advice on financing their travels, having not done the most basic research steps it takes to even get started. In my opinion, you must be someone who has something to say and be good at marketing it to even cover your costs, much less make a profit. I do make a profit now and then, but that's because of a trade publication I've written for for a few years (they pay my good money to review swank hotels).

Illustrated travel articles are best of all. Black and white prints are best for this purpose, or colour transparencies. Remember that editors are less interested in arty effects than in photos which tell a story.

English language newspapers around the world are a real source of potential casual work from Japan to Eastern Europe, Mexico City to Bangkok. The website http://worldnewspapers.about.com has links to a number of them from the *Phnom Penh Post* to the *St Petersburg Times*. There is an entire sub-culture of bright young travellers working their way around these papers. Some are using it as a short-cut in a journalism career; others are merely adventurers. Many of the people working on these papers had never been inside a newsroom before. Business experience might well be appreciated in this context. Anyone who can get a job as a proofreader and show themselves competent will quickly advance to copy-editor or even reporter. Editors may not want to hire globetrotters, but staff turnover is often so high that they don't have any choice.

International firms with branches abroad are less glamorous employers of writing skills, but they may need someone to edit their newsletter or brochures. An army of foreigners is employed in Beijing to polish the prose of journals and documents which have been translated into English. If you notice a badly written company report or piece of publicity it might be worth introducing yourself (especially in Japan), though make your point as tactfully as possible. Even such a long-established English language publication as the *Athens News* was so full of mistakes that a traveller from Los Angeles was taken on as a proofreader after circling and correcting all the errors in a randomly chosen issue and presenting it to the editor. You can always offer to correct the English of museum labels, menus or travel brochures. You might get a free meal in exchange for your grammatical expertise, though you may unwittingly be depriving future travellers of a source of amusement. If you have a knack for penning catchy phrases, you might get hired as Helen Welch did by a Taiwanese businessman, to invent slogans for badges.

You do not necessarily have to be sensational; the local paper in Windsor, Ontario may like to print the opinions of a visitor from Windsor, Berkshire about its fair city. Research can pay off. For example, Tony Davies-Patrick established from local libraries and bookshops that there was a shortage of material on the subject of freshwater angling abroad. So he spent a year travelling around Europe and the Middle East taking photographs and assembling information to sell to freshwater angling magazines. Andrew Vincent intended to concentrate on radio journalism in which he had some local experience. At last report he had been promised £20 a week by his local BBC station to send weekly telephone pieces from North America.

One of the most remarkable literary coups was reported in the papers a few years ago. A student called Daniel Wilson sent his CV and an example of his verse to the president of Kiribati asking if he would like him to become the poet-in-residence. To his astonishment, he had a reply inviting him to occupy a beach hut and become their national poet for a time.

All you readers who imagine that the ideal job would be to write a travel guide should pay attention to the following description by Woden Teachout who spent one summer researching Ireland for the well-known *Let's Go* series:

> *I got lucky and was hired by Harvard Student Agency (which hires only students) to update their chapter on Ireland. They gave me $600 for air travel and $40 a day for expenses and profit. It was a mixed blessing. I spent most of each day visiting local historical societies and talking to all the Mrs. O'Learys who run B&Bs, checking their bathrooms for cleanliness and trying to figure out how to vary descriptions of fluffy white bedrooms. At night I would run around to three or four pubs, trying to encapsulate each atmosphere in a good one-liner and then back to the hostel to write up the day's work. When you're writing a guidebook you can never quite relax, since you are always evaluating in your head. And since you have a fixed itinerary, you are not as free to follow the whims of chance and circumstance. It was definitely nice to get paid to travel, and go to places I otherwise would have missed, but on the whole it felt like indentured servitude.*

Photography

A number of photo libraries in the UK accept high quality travel photographs. The photos are lent or leased to the agencies which in turn rent them to clients such as publishers and advertising agencies. Most photo libraries offer a 50-50 split of the earnings from the photographs. They also usually demand a minimum initial submission of at least 50 photos, a minimum period of time for keeping your photos with the agency and at least a year's notice of withdrawal. They also prefer a contributor to send photos regularly. The bible of freelance photographers which lists all the libraries in the UK is the *Picture Researcher's Handbook* published by Blueprint (Chapman and Hall) available in most public libraries.

Stephen Psallidas decided to give it a go after he returned from spending time in Greece, Africa and Australia:

> *I'm not going to pretend that I'm a great photographer but out of 2,000 35mm slides, there were about 50 which I thought were quite good. I sent off a selection of my photos to a couple of well known photo libraries. However, both libraries returned my slides saying that they were too 'arty' and not commercially oriented enough. I would advise against having too high expectations, as the market is difficult in these days of cost-cutting and digital technology. At the same time, if you don't try you never get anywhere and readers of your book are unlikely to be daunted by poor odds!*

Stephen concluded that it would have been better to contact some photo libraries before setting off to establish what kind of thing they are looking for. Many will offer useful technical advice. When sending in photos, make sure that they are presented well, e.g. in transparent sleeves with detailed captions, and it is a courtesy to include return postage. Many travel photo libraries accept only colour images which should be on slide film no faster than ISO 100 (Stephen recommends Fuji Velvia ISO 50). The larger the format, the better, though the standard 35mm is usually acceptable. Don't send in any poor shots just to make up the numbers since these will reflect badly on the overall submission. If a photo is used by a library it will generate between £50 and £150 every time it is used, so if you have 20 or 30 photos accepted, it could be quite lucrative. Stephen's story has a happy ending since he persevered and had some photos accepted by a third photo library, and has made £160 in six months.

Even if you have no particular skill with a camera or pen you may be able to profit from being in the right place at the right time. Earl Young has strong opinions on the subject:

Anyone who fails to carry a camera in foreign countries is a fool. What if an international incident happens to take place in the street in front of you one day and you don't happen to be carrying your camera?

If you do get a photo of an assassination attempt or any newsworthy event, don't waste a second contacting the news wire services; Reuters, Agence France Presse and Associated Press have offices or representatives in most capital cities. If your photograph is the one that's syndicated in newspapers worldwide, you need not work your way any further.

An easier way of setting yourself up as a photographer would be to take portraits with a Polaroid instant camera in cafés, on beaches near monuments, etc. Nudist beaches are reported to provide willing customers for these but check with your subjects before you snap them or they may snap back. Michael Jenkins had the bright idea of taking photos of tourists on their first parascending ride in Corfu. Most who expressed mild interest beforehand were so pleased with the photos (which Michael had developed in town) that they were delighted to spend 1200 drachmas for three.

Another place to set yourself up as a freelance photographer is at a place that specialises in hosting weddings of holidaying couples. Certain places (and not just Las Vegas) become popular with couples looking for something different from the village church. Long-time working travellers Nicola and Peter Dickinson found just such a place on Rhodes where they tied the knot themselves and dream of returning as a freelance photographer and painter:

> *There is a little church on St Paul's Bay in Lindos where many people get married throughout the season. With 80 or 90 weddings a season somebody could set themselves up as a photographer. Obviously they would have to be good before offering their services to people getting married so you'd probably need to take a course on photography beforehand. With so many people getting married in Lindos and spending their honeymoons there, people would want photographs of the happy occasion. You'd need to have a decent camera, though a polaroid would suffice for the pubs, clubs and restaurants.*

You don't have to have a camera to make money from photographs. We have heard of two gap year students trying to raise money for a trip who travelled round car boot sales and junk shops buying old post cards and photos which they framed attractively and sold at a decent profit at antique markets.

Busking

If you can play an instrument, sing, tap dance, juggle, conjure, draw cartoons or act, you may be able to earn money on the streets. Most successful buskers say that musical talent is less important than the spot you choose and the way you collect. Two Americans busking in Morocco decided that the local man they employed to collect money for them was more entertaining than they were so gave him the money.

To busk, you need the tools of your trade, perhaps an accomplice to collect money and an audience. A favourable climate helps, though some of the most successful buskers we have heard from have played in Northern Europe in mid-winter. One of the keys to success (in addition to talent) is originality. We have had reports from opposite ends of the world (Sweden and Northern Queensland) that kilted bagpipe-playing buskers are always a hit. (We're assuming that it wasn't the same busking Scot.) Mary Hall is one busker who is convinced that talent is not essential, as she discovered in Bergen, Norway:

> *I finally plucked up the courage to do a bit of busking on my pennywhistle. I'd only just bought it so was only able to play two songs 'Amazing Grace' and 'The Sounds of Silence'. Still I made £15 in 15 minutes. With a couple of extra songs I could well be on the way to my first million. It helped that my audience were pretty drunk.*

Most international buskers say that people abroad (especially Scandinavia, Germany, Switzerland, Spain) are more generous than in Britain, that there is less trouble with being moved on and it is not too difficult to keep yourself by busking around the cafés of Europe. Helen Chenery was very sorry that she had not taken her accordian with her to Greece, since she soon saw that she could have elevated her diet of bread and jam if she'd had her instrument with her. Some advise that if you have to choose between carting around an instrument or your luggage, leave your luggage at home. You need a great deal of confidence in your abilities, to go abroad specifically to busk; it may be better to regard performing as a possible way of subsidising a holiday.

Festivals and other large gatherings of merry-makers are potentially lucrative; bear in mind that the more potential a position has, the greater the competition is liable to be for it. Armin Birrer made his living by busking around Norway, Wales, Ireland and New Zealand (including a 15-hour stint in an Invercargill hair salon); in fact he even saved enough in Europe for his air fare to New Zealand. (One assumes he has more musical talent than most.) He generally found busking best in small towns where buskers were seldom seen. Your main enemies are the weather and the police. David Hughes who busked with a borrowed guitar in Taipei encountered a more mysterious obstacle in the form of red graffiti appearing near his spot in the subway and veiled threats from people he could only guess were local gangsters or traders. He didn't hang around to find out.

Regulations about street performing vary from country to country, but in general you will be tolerated if you are causing no obstruction or other harm. There are a few places where it is positively encouraged if you meet a high enough standard: buskers in the Covent Garden precinct in London and the Centre Georges Pompidou in Paris have to be judged worthy before they can perform. In contrast, you may be prosecuted if you perform in the London Underground (but are more likely to be moved on). You may even find that busking leads to better things: Mark Kilburn was offered a job playing guitar in a night club in Holland on the basis of his street performances, Armin Birrer was encouraged by a film writer who heard him to try for a job as a film extra in Melbourne, and Kev Vincent was invited to leave the streets of San Tropez behind to entertain on a millionaire's gin palace. If you can perform, there is no harm in offering your talents, particularly to pubs in Ireland and bars and cafés in Turkish resorts frequented by what Ian McArthur calls the 'Marlboro, Levis and Coca Cola generation'.

Artists

An artist who paints local scenes or copies local post cards can do well in holiday resorts. Nicola Dickinson mentioned above would gladly have bought a painting of the church in Lindos where she and so many others got married, but none was for sale, so she has now taken an oil painting class in the hope of one day going back and making a profit.

If you can draw a reasonable likeness you could set yourself up as a street portraitist. Two friends Belinda and Pandora found it fairly easy to make money both in Britain and the Continent especially among holiday-makers. Belinda used unlined brown paper bought in an industrial roll and oil pastels or children's crayons. You can also use driftwood or smooth pebbles. It is awkward to carry around two chairs with you so she relied on borrowing them from an adjacent café or church hall. Artistically you shouldn't be overscrupulous; when a disappointed subject asked 'Do I really look that old?' Belinda didn't hesitate to erase a few wrinkles. Once you become known, you may get more lucrative portrait commissions in people's houses.

Apparently boat owners are a particularly vain bunch and will often jump at the chance to have their vessel immortalised on canvas, so loiter around yacht marinas with your sketchbook. Wealthy home owners might also be interested in commissioning a sketch of their homes and a professionally produced leaflet might unearth some customers. Stephen Psallidas noticed a trend in Mykonos for tavernas, banks and other public buildings to display paintings of themselves. John Kilmartin's decorations of buildings on his kibbutz were so highly valued they were praised in an Israeli newspaper which prompted people to pay him to draw their portraits.

Face painting is a portable skill and there is money to be made from organising children's parties wherever there is an expat community. Even if you can't make any money from your artistic endeavours, you may bring pleasure to the locals. While in Ching Kong in northern Thailand, Dustie Hickey sat outside a hut painting Winnie the Pooh and blowing up balloons for the children. When the local English teacher noticed how spellbound the children were, she asked Dustie if she would like to teach at the school on a voluntary basis. She did the same at a children's hospital in Calcutta which so impressed both the children and nuns that she was invited back as a longer term volunteer.

Film Extras

If you like the idea of mingling with the stars in Hollywood for a few days and being well paid for it – forget it. In most international film studios even extras belong to trade unions which exclude outsiders. When a film is being shot on location you may have the opportunity of helping to fill out a crowd scene – in fact the accepted term is 'crowd artist' – but it is a matter of luck coming across these, though your chances are better in some places than others. The picturesque streets of old Budapest together with the relatively lower shooting costs make it a favourite location (in fact the author spotted Ben Kingsley in a restaurant in Pest).

In the massive Asian film industry, film-makers actively seek out Caucasian faces, especially to be villains, dupes or dissolutes. Agents for film companies usually look for their supernumerary staff among the budget hotels of Bombay, Hong Kong, Cairo, etc. knowing that they will find plenty of travellers only too willing to spend one or two days hanging around a film set in exchange for a few rupees or dollars. In fact by local standards the wage is generous. (See the chapter on *Asia* for further details.) Japanese advertising companies are often on the lookout for European faces and pay extremely well, e.g. £130 for a half day's 'work'.

Armin Birrer followed up the tip to visit film studios in Melbourne and was paid $80 after tax for a day's work, which mostly consisted of hanging around:

> *In Melbourne there are always films and movies being made. If you are interested you should make the rounds of the studios. They take a photo of you and put you in their file, which usually means wait. But you might be the character they've been looking for and get work straight away.*

Another traveller phoned up several Melbourne advertising agencies and was told that they did need some extras on location in the Northern Territory. Although jobs are normally found by word of mouth there are agencies in some places which will register you as potential extras. Apparently there are at least three agencies in Bangkok, one of which was successfully used by Vaughan Temby. Be wary of an agency which charges a fee. David Hughes found one in Vancouver which charged $50 and 'guaranteed' work. It turned out that if you didn't get hired by a film company, you didn't get a refund, your period of registration was simply extended.

Whether you work as an extra in the East or West you are unlikely to be given a part that will stretch your acting talents. But the work can still be demanding: hours can be erratic (for example in Hong Kong filming normally begins at midnight), and you may have to undergo a lengthy session in the make-up and costume departments. Make sure you take along a good book to fill in the idle hours.

If you hear rumours of a film being shot, try to find the crew and ask whom you should see about work. Dave Bamford asked at the police station in Geneva but their directions came to nothing. By chance the next day he found the film vans, talked to someone in charge and was paid £40 to appear in the background of *The Unbearable Lightness of Being*. He was also invited to a hotel meal where he made lots of contacts for future work.

ODD JOBS

If you can't or don't want to get a steady job you could consider offering your services as an odd job person. By all accounts there is a world shortage of emergency plumbers, car and bike mechanics and piano tuners, so someone with these special skills who puts up notices locally should have no trouble finding paying customers. Brian Williams from North Wales, travelling with his partner Adrienne Robinson and their three year old son, found his skills as a mechanic in demand wherever he went, including Fiji, New Zealand and Australia, as Adrienne recounts:

> *Not only did we encounter fewer problems buying and selling cheap vehicles for us to tour around in but in some places Brian's skills as a mechanic could be used as leverage to get better prices or even in exchange for accommodation. In Fiji we negotiated a better price on the assumption that Brian would look at the 'new transport' which he did. Of course once he did this, the villagers wanted him to look at other things too. An orchard we stayed at in New Zealand only took us on when Bri said he was a mechanic – the tractor was broken.*

If your sphere of expertise is domestic, you can often find a market for housework and ironing. Hand deliver a little printed notice in the neighbourhood where you're based and see what happens. When I was staying in Sydney last year, I was rather tempted by the leaflet that appeared in the mailbox 'Do you need a break?! Call Cathy's Home Help for housework and ironing now'.

Another skill which has proved popular is tattooing. One world traveller carried his tattooing gun with him to Australia and earned extra pocket money with it between fruit harvests. However there are plenty of jobs for the unskilled too: you don't have to study art to paint a garden fence. You may not earn a lot, but you should at least be promptly paid in cash, with no questions asked. There should be no problems about work permits unless you knock on the door of an immigration officer. Another odd job craze which started in New York is to offer to wash windscreens while motorists sit at red lights. Prize venues have been known to earn some lucky windscreen operatives £70 a day. (See description at end of chapter on Germany).

It is a good policy to suggest a specific job when you are on the doorstep, rather than just to ask vaguely if there is anything to be done. Householders are more likely to respond favourably if you tactfully suggest that their garden is not devoid of weeds, or that the hinges on the gate could be brought into the twenty-first century. You should never underestimate the laziness of other people: in summer lawns need mowing, garages need cleaning, cars need washing, and in winter snow needs clearing. If you propose to specialise in something like window cleaning you should invest in some basic equipment: people prefer to hire a window cleaner who has his own bucket, shammy and ladder. Some people have adopted a gimmick to attract custom, for example they offer their window-washing services while wearing roller skates. Dean Fisher had none of these when he had a brainwave in the south of France:

> *I was running out of money in Aix-en-Provence and got talking to an English guy who was working as a petrol attendant. I started washing windscreens for the people coming into the garage and ended up earning more money in tips than the petrol attendants' wages. Once a guy in a jeep gave me a 100 franc tip which was amazing. I was my own boss (and didn't tell the guys how much I was getting).*

The best areas to look for odd jobs and household maintenance jobs are in expatriate enclaves abroad (especially on the Mediterranean or in Mexico). Richard Adams did best in the semi-rural areas of Germany, where he found the population were less hasty to turn you away than fast-living city dwellers. You should consider your appearance carefully. An old age pensioner in Munich may not trust someone who looks as if has arrived on foot from Morocco. On the other hand, a housewife in Los Angeles has every right to be suspicious of someone wearing a three-piece suit who offers to clean her swimming pool.

It is also possible to fix up a low-level maintenance job before leaving home. Writing in *Overseas Jobs Express* Richard Ginger describes how he got hold of a brochure of holiday properties in France owned by expats (from a company called Chez Nous) and simply wrote to 20 of the most likely sounding ones. On the strength of a polite request for work, he was invited to stay in a chateau in the Pyrenees by a retired professor who turned out to be a first rate cook. Soon the professor's neighbours were asking him to do odd jobs for cash.

Susan and Eric Beney took a break from travelling with their daughters overland to Australia to spend a while on the small Greek island of Halki. They arrived in April, before the tourist rush, and there was no evidence of any work around. But they successfully created a job from scratch:

> *The beach was a terrible mess with rubbish washed up in the winter storms, so we set ourselves the task of cleaning it up and asked the Mayor for rubbish bags. After we had been here for five weeks and our funds were sadly depleted, Eric was asked if he would like the job of 'port cleaner'. This job entailed sweeping the harbour and cleaning the streets three days a week and cleaning the loos daily. The job hadn't been done for a month so was quite a task in the beginning but I helped Eric get the loos to a reasonable standard and after that the job was quite a nice little number with plenty of time off. The pay was more than £100 a month and of course it has endeared Eric to the locals, none of whom would do such a job. Apparently a council allowance is made for this job so it could be worthwhile searching out the local Mayor and offering your services. Even the police are happy about it or turn a blind eye. Because we have now been here a while Eric has also done lots of other odd jobs for people as there is very little spare labour on the Island (or the locals are too lazy!)*

Apparently Halki's beaches are in good shape these days but, according to Tom Hawthorne, Gibraltar would benefit if some future traveller could talk the council into funding a clean-up operation.

Collecting bottles and cans for their deposits is mentioned in the chapter *In Extremis* but in some countries it is lucrative enough to count as an odd job, for instance in Scandinavia. One unusual 'odd job' is to participate in medical trials, which is discussed in the chapters on the UK and USA. If you are accepted (a major if) it is possible to earn £100 a day.

GAMBLING

Many countries run state lotteries but the chance of winning a prize are mostly too remote for this to be a useful way of supplementing diminished funds. Casinos and gambling on horse racing may be slightly better bets but again the percentages are always against the punter.

If you must play roulette, bet with the wheel and never against it; it is always possible that there is a slight mechanical fault which favours certain players or numbers. If there are some really big players at the table, bet last and bet against them. Crooked wheels are not unknown and if the casino plans to wipe out the high rollers you stand to profit if you keep your chips well clear of theirs.

Well used by a practised operator, a pack of cards, a backgammon board or set of poker dice are a much more promising source of extra income. When Peter Stonemann was living in Copenhagen he noticed people gathered at the wall of Hallands Kirke where they offered to play fast games of chess for bets of 20 kroner. Poker, bridge and backgammon, but particularly poker, are widely played for money throughout the world; if you become proficient there is every reason to use your skills for profit. The great thing about poker and backgammon is that they are comparatively simple games in which at every stage there is a mathematically correct play. The vast majority of players in amateur schools never take the trouble to learn the percentages. If you do, and so long as you keep out of the professional games, you will win. If interested, get a copy of *The Education of a Poker Player* by Herbert O. Yardley, published by Sphere Books in paperback. Clearly if you learn to deal 'seconds' or off the bottom of the pack, you will increase your chance of winning though you may well diminish your prospects of longevity.

Another gambit is to become adept at less well known games that pack neatly into your luggage like cribbage, bezique or shut-the-box and then entice your unsuspecting pals to play with you. Lose the board when they look like catching up on your expertise.

The 'Three Card Trick' or 'Spot the Lady' requires a definite element of dexterity but with regular practice you will become competent in a few weeks and can confidently invite customers to place their money on the Lady which hopefully is never the card they choose. As if you were cutting the pack, you hold one card face down lengthwise between thumb and middle finger of the left hand and two cards in a similar manner with your right hand. When releasing the cards from the right hand the top card (i.e. nearer the palm) is released first thus reversing the apparent positions of the two right hand cards when placed on the table. Keep your elbows up and let your wrist hang loose. After a while your audience will start to get wise to the game which is the time to make your apologies and leave. If you are playing with only one person, give them the three cards and you double your previous winnings as they attempt what you have been practising for weeks.

Rolling two dice for someone and getting them to bet on what number will come up is also a possible ruse. The possible numbers are 2 to 12 so the odds about any one number appear to be 10/1. In fact they range from 35/1 for a 2 or 12 to 5/1 for a 7. Actually it is better to get the pigeon to roll the dice and let you bet on 6's 7's and 8's (6/1, 5/1, 6/1) and keep him paying out at 10/1 until he can stand it no longer.

Another ploy which can be used to advantage is to fleece a con-man. It never fails but has its dangerous side and it works like this. All over the world you will find pool halls, pubs or arcades where sharks try to induce mugs to play pool, darts or some other game for money. You put on your best clothes and go into one of these alone and quietly play by yourself – obviously you are not very good and the con-artist soon spots you as a possible touch.' He invites you to play. But con-men, like the rest of us, are greedy; they don't want just to take $1 off you; they want the lot and they aim to do this by letting you think you are a match for them and even raise your hopes that you may win some money. To do this they will always lose the first and probably the second game. You take the money and leave – and make sure you know where the exit is.

Amazingly the big operators in Las Vegas and Atlantic City in the US and the Gold Coast in Australia can also be taken for a few dollars on the same principle. Always looking to get new punters into their gaming palaces they subsidise day tours or return trips to their gleaming portals in the desert or by the sea. The fare (subsidised) may be $5 and when you get there they give you free food and possibly even some chips, say $20 worth, to play the tables or the machines. Cash these in and you are a day older with all expenses paid.

EU EMPLOYMENT AND TAX

Legislation has existed for many years guaranteeing the rights of all nationals of the European Union to compete for jobs in any member country. According to Article 8a of the Maastricht Treaty, every citizen of the European Union has the right to travel, reside and work in any member state. The only reason for refusing entry is on grounds of public security and public health. But this does not mean that all the red tape and attendant hassles have been done away with. Talk of the Single Europe should not lull Euro-jobseekers into thinking that they need not worry about the formalities.

EU rulings notwithstanding, barriers to the free movement of labour do remain which are only gradually being dismantled. The very idea of unimpeded movement of goods, services, capital and persons is utopian. The minute you have immigration laws of any kind, freedom is curtailed, especially when unemployment is a problem. But unemployment has been declining of late and in fact labour shortages are predicted in coming years, good news for the job-seeker in Europe. Not so good news is that the European Commission is calling (November 2000) for a radical new common immigration policy that would permit the controlled admission of workers from outside Europe. The influx of economic migrants from Eastern and Central Europe throughout the 1990s has had a huge impact on the number of jobs available for EU travelling workers; a perfect illustration of this is that most of the fruit picked in Greece these days is picked by Albanians and Romanians, not by young travellers.

The EU consists of 15 member states: Austria, Belgium, Denmark, Finland, France, Germany, Greece, Ireland, Italy, Luxembourg, the Netherlands, Portugal, Spain, Sweden and the United Kingdom. Outside the EU, legislation varies from country to country. The free reciprocity extends to countries of the European Economic Area (EEA), i.e. EU countries plus Iceland, Liechtenstein and Norway. (Switzerland is a special case; see chapter.) In the wake of the Nice Treaty (December 2000), it seems that expansion of the European will go ahead eventually; the countries that are in negotiation to join the EU are Poland, Czech Republic, Hungary, Slovenia, Cyprus and Estonia.

The standard situation among all EU countries (and EEA countries, though the denotation EU is used throughout this book) is that nationals of any EU state have the right to look for work for up to three months. At the end of that period they should apply to the police or the local authority for a residence permit, showing their passport and job contract. The residence permit will be valid for five years if the job is permanent or for the duration of the job if it is for less than one year.

But there is no guarantee that this will be easy. Bureaucracies sometimes get in the way of progressive legislation. Many readers have written to say that it has taken, say, eight months for their *carte de séjour* in France to come through or that their Greek residence permit arrived on the last day of a nine-month contract. On his year out from university, Matt from Manchester worked in both France and Germany. In theory he should have had no problem regularising his status. In practice, he encountered many difficulties. The social security number for which he applied in France took 12 months to come through. In Germany he fared even worse, trapped in a vicious circle of 'no job – no papers – no accommodation'. Without papers he was turned away by the federal employment service, which all EU nationals are entitled to use. But resistance was useless.

Similar problems have been encountered by travellers attempting to claim unemployment benefit (now known as job-seeker's allowance in the UK) abroad (procedures detailed below). Again in Germany, I. A. Gowing attempted to claim unemployment benefit at the *arbeitsamt* in Frankfurt, having followed the correct procedure and armed himself with his form E303. He was told that this was not possible unless he could produce a residence permit, and to get this permit he would need letters proving that he had accommodation there – and a job, which resulted in a classic Catch-22 situation; he was not allowed to collect unemployment benefit (to which he was entitled) because he was unemployed. David Ramsdale compared his attempts to get benefit from the Danish *Komune* (municipality) to trying to get blood out of a stone. Unfortunately, it requires time and energy to appeal against such decisions, which may simply be the result of bureaucratic prejudice. The DSS (now grandly called the Benefits Directorate) in Britain has no control over its counterparts abroad when such problems arise and can only put forward a claimant's side of the argument, with no guarantee of success. But in light of the success of a few, it is certainly worth a try.

Another Catch-22 affects self-employed workers, particularly self-employed building workers. Although there is a demand for bricklayers, plasterers, plumbers, etc. especially in Germany, the Netherlands and Belgium, employers are reluctant to hire anyone who does not have form E101 from the relevant office of the Benefits Agency (address below) which proves that you are paying self-employed contributions in the UK and are therefore exempt from local tax and social security contributions for up to 24 months. However the Benefits Agency will issue the form only to people who have been registered self-employed in the UK for six months making it difficult for people in paid employment at home to conduct a speculative job search abroad. A further problem is that some unscrupulous employers make sizeable deductions even though an E101 should mean that the worker is exempt.

But despite the fact that the system does not always work perfectly, a lot of labour does move freely over national borders. In fact approximately three-quarters of a million European Union nationals are employed outside their country of citizenship. This chapter is aimed exclusively at nationals of European Union member states. (Schemes and exchanges relevant to other nationalities are mentioned throughout the rest of the book.) Nancy Mitford made the U and non-U distinction famous (upper class and not upper class) but for the purposes of this book EU and non-EU has replaced it as an individual's defining characteristic. Some Americans may have access to the EU if they are fortunate enough to be of Irish or Italian descent and can prove that they have a grandparent of either nationality, in which case they can obtain an Irish or Italian passport. An increasing number of Americans are taking up this option for employment reasons and have been dubbed 'paper Europeans'. Americans of Greek extraction may be eligible for EU nationality, however they should first find out whether this will carry with it an obligation to do national service. (The United States allows its citizens to hold more than one passport, but does not recognise dual citizenship.)

From the European traveller's point of view there are many bureaucratic advantages to the EU. For instance France was proposing at the end of 2000 to introduce a Europe-wide minimum wage of £4.50 which would be higher than many working travellers are now paid. However, the push for European harmonisation has the potential for undermining long-standing agreements between the UK and the Commonwealth. For example some commentators have suggested that eventually Brussels will try to ban the working holiday arrangements between the UK and Australia, New Zealand, Canada and South Africa.

NATIONAL EMPLOYMENT SERVICES IN THE EU

Every EU country possesses a network of employment offices similar to British Jobcentres, details of which are given in the individual country chapters. Although EU legislation requires national employment services to treat applicants from other member states in exactly the same way as their own citizens, it is impossible to prevent a certain amount of bias from entering the system. An employer is allowed to turn down an applicant who does not speak enough of the language to perform his job adequately for obvious reasons.

Average unemployment across Europe has been falling over the past couple of years and now stands at 9.2% (compared to 10.9% two years ago). But it is still high in some countries (e.g. 8.4% in Germany, 9.5% in France, 14.3% in Spain) and no amount of positive legislation will change the attitude of the official of the Amsterdam employment office who said 'How can we help the English to find work? We do not have enough jobs for our own people' or of the French ANPE (Jobcentre) employee who told Noel Kirkpatrick that he would prefer to give a job to any Moroccan or Algerian before someone from Britain. If there are two equally qualified job applicants of different nationalities, most employers will choose their fellow countryman/woman. In the words of experienced Euroworker Paul Winter:

Please make it clear to your readers that all this talk of one Europe and a Europe without borders doesn't mean that jobs are easy and simple to get abroad. It's not easy. Plan ahead, try to learn a language and take as much money as you can. That being said, the chances of working around Europe are still there to be enjoyed, just use a little common sense.

Many developed nations welcome migrant workers who are prepared to take jobs that no local would consider. For example the bulb-packing factories of Holland and hotel kitchens in Germany have traditionally taken on large numbers of British and Irish workers during their busiest times of year. But throughout Europe there has been a noticeable increase in the number of nationals (especially students) willing to take such jobs. And when they are not, East European migrant workers certainly are.

A Europe-wide employment service called EURES (EURopean Employment Service) operates as a network of more than 400 EuroAdvisers who can access a database of jobs within Europe. These vacancies are usually for six months or longer, and for skilled, semi-skilled and (increasingly) managerial jobs. Language skills are almost always a requirement. A random sample of job vacancies might include a nursery nurse for Finland, welders and chefs for Germany, a loom turner for Ireland and (surprisingly) bar staff for Sicily. On average, 500 new posts are registered with EURES each month though if you have a specific destination in mind, they are unlikely to be able to offer much choice of vacancy. Rather than settle for consulting your local EuroAdviser at home, you might get a more complete picture by telephoning the EURES office in your destination. The staff should be able to communicate in English and should be well-informed about such matters as transferring your job-seeker's allowance. Ask at your local Jobcentre how to contact your nearest EuroAdviser. In the UK most of the expertise is based in the headquarters of the national Employment Service. The Overseas Placing Unit, Rockingham House, 123 West St, Sheffield S1 4ER (0114-259 6051/fax 0114-259 6040) co-ordinates all dealings with overseas/EU vacancies. The websites http://europa.eu.int/jobs/eures and http://eu.int/europedirect have extensive information for Euro-jobseekers.

EURES also publishes a series of country-by-country factsheets called 'Working in...' which are free from Jobcentres or from the OPU. Although they do not contain much job-finding information not included in this book, they do provide some useful background information on taxation, health benefits, etc. for the job-seeker and are worth obtaining.

Information Centres for European Careers are being set up in all EU member states to provide information on training, education and employment in Europe, mostly to help careers services and their clients. Careers Europe (Fourth Floor, Midland House, 14 Cheapside, Bradford BD1 4JA; 01274 829600/fax 01274 829610; www.careerseurope.co.uk) produce the Eurofacts and Globalfacts series of International Careers Information, and Exodus, the Careers Europe database of international careers information, all of which can be consulted at local careers offices. Another source of information on European programmes is Eurodesk (Community Learning Scotland, Rosebery House, 9 Haymarket Terrace, Edinburgh EH12 5EZ; 0131-313 2488) which has an on-line database (www.eurodesk.org).

Language training and privately run trainee placement organisations are mentioned throughout this book, for example Interspeak (Stretton Lower Hall, Stretton, Cheshire SY14 7HS; 01829 250641/ www.interspeak.co.uk) can arrange short and longer term traineeships (internships or *stages*) in France, Spain, Italy and Germany in the fields of marketing, international trade, computing, tourism, etc. Successful candidates live with host families. Interspeak's booking fee is £500 for 8-24 week placements; accommodation and board are normally included in the programme.

Other (less expensive) training placements have been made available through other agencies, though the battle for funding is annual and several have stopped. Most recently, Direct Training Services in Devon, which once arranged fully-funded work placements in Europe under the auspices of the Leonardo Programme (see next section), have suspended this programme due to lack of support from Leonardo. Similarly, the pilot project TICCITS (The International Careers Contacts Information & Training Service) run from Richard Huish College in Taunton came to the end of its funding by the National Lottery at the end of 1999. It was hoping to be able to continue matching young people (especially those from disadvantaged backgrounds) with employers for structured work experience in Europe, but this depends on whether it can achieve charitable trust status and further funding; updates on the situation can be obtained by phoning 01823 251250 or on the web at www.ticcits.co.uk. In the other direction, Trident Transnational (Saffron Court, 14b St Cross Street, London EC1N 8XA; 020-7242 1515; ttn@trid-demon.co.uk) arranges internships in Britain for students from the EEA.

Jobs with EU Organisations

To find out about vocational training exchanges within the EU, such as the Leonardo programme, contact the Central Bureau for International Education & Training (10 Spring Gardens, London SW1A 2BN; 020-7973 1985). Participants gain experience and training through a work placement or training scheme.

The representation of the European Commission in the UK (8 Storey's Gate, London SW1P 3AT; 020-7463 8177/fax 020-8694 0099) issues several free publications of interest including the general leaflet 'Europe Direct: Routemap for Jobseekers in the EU', which has a list of factsheets you can order on individual countries and topics (e.g. Taxes in the Netherlands or Right of Residence in Portugal). The European Commission's literature can be requested on Europe Direct (freephone 0800 581591) or check the web-site on http://europa.eu.int/citizens and www.cec.org.uk.

The European Commission is based in Brussels but has small representation offices in Cardiff, Edinburgh and Belfast as well. High flyers who would like to work for the European Commission as administrators, translators, secretaries, etc. must compete in recruitment procedures known as open competitions; the London office above can provide information (www.cec.org.uk). The Commission does not offer any work placements or summer jobs other than the five-month *stagiaire* programme for graduates in Brussels. Applications must be postmarked not later than 30th September for positions starting in March (and 31st March for positions starting in October). Details and application forms can be obtained from the website http://europa.eu.int/ comm/stages or from the Traineeships Office, European Commission, 200 Rue de la Loi, 1049 Brussels, Belgium (02-295 39 93).

Short-term white-collar contracts may be available on the spot for people who are bilingual and/or have secretarial skills. Michael Jordan, an American who spent a few months in Strasbourg, met a number of people (including Americans) who were employed by the Council of Europe on temporary contracts continuously renewed. Special rules govern the red tape of employees of international organisations.

CLAIMING JOB SEEKER'S ALLOWANCE IN THE EU

It may come as a pleasant surprise to discover that it is possible to claim Job-Seeker's Allowance in other EU countries. The two ways in which this can be done are covered in detail below: to understand them it is necessary to understand the principle behind what used to be known as unemployment benefit.

Payments are not paid automatically to people who are out of work. It is an entitlement that has to be 'bought' by paying a certain number of contributions into a country's unemployment insurance organisation. In Britain these contributions are represented by Class 1 National Insurance contributions. Class 1 contributions are paid only by people who are employees earning at least £62 per week. Other groups of people may pay either Class 2 and 4 contributions (for the self-employed) or Class 3 contributions (a voluntary payment for those who would otherwise not be covered by

National Insurance) which entitle them to some social security benefits, but not job-seeker's allowance.

Other EU countries have similar systems, and contributions paid in one country can be taken into account when building up an entitlement to unemployment benefit in another. Whichever of the two means of claiming benefit is relevant to you depends on where you last paid contributions, as you will be covered under that country's unemployment insurance scheme.

In Britain people who are not eligible to claim the job-seeker's allowance may claim income support if they have no other means of support. The amount paid depends on the needs of the applicant - whether there are any relatives to support, how much is needed to pay for rent, etc. - and it is intended to cover only the essentials of life. All EU countries except Greece and Portugal have equivalents, but the right to claim these is not transferable between countries in the same way as unemployment benefit. Normally it is handled by municipal authorities who stipulate that eligibility depends on a claimant having been resident in the district for several years. Applications for income support abroad are very unlikely to succeed. Deportation is a more likely outcome.

Claiming UK Job-seeker's Allowance in Europe

Any EU national who has been registered unemployed for at least four weeks in the UK and is entitled to receive the UK allowance can arrange to receive it for up to three months, paid at the UK rate, while looking for work elsewhere in the EU. The applicant should inform his local Employment Service Jobcentre in Britain of his or her intention to look for work elsewhere well before departure, usually at least six weeks. It is helpful if you have a precise departure date and a definite destination, preferably with an address. Note that if you go abroad on holiday and decide to stay on to work, the benefit cannot be transferred. Your local Jobcentre should have a leaflet (ref. JSAL 22) for people going abroad or coming from abroad plus an application form for transferring benefit. Alternatively, ring the number in the next paragraph to request it and Factsheet No. 1 'UK contribution-based JSA abroad'.

Within seven days of arriving, you must register for work at the national employment office and apply for UK benefit from the following:

Austria: Arbeitsamt
Belgium: Office National de l'Emploi/Rijksdienst voor Arbeidsvoorziening
Denmark: Arbeidsformidlingskontor
Finland: Työvoimatoimistot (and then claim separately at the local office for social security)
France: Agence Nationale pour l'Emploi/ANPE
Germany: Arbeitsamt
Gibraltar: Department of Labour & Social Security (23 John Mackintosh Square)
Greece: Organismos Apascholiseos Ergatikou Dynamikou/OAED
Iceland: Atvinnuleysistryggingasjodur in Reykjavik
Ireland: FAS
Italy: Sezione circoscrizionale per l'impiego
Liechtensten: Amt für Volkswirtschaft in Vaduz
Luxembourg: Administration de l'Emploi
Netherlands: Gewestelijk Arbeidsbureau and the Gemeenschappelijk Administratiekantoor
Norway: Arbeidsformidlingen or Arbeidskontoret
Portugal: Centro de Emprego
Spain: Instituto Nacional de Empleo (INEM)
Sweden: Arbetsfönmedlingen
United Kingdom: Jobcentre.

When you have told your local Jobcentre your plans, they will supply a letter in English and that of your destination country explaining that you are eligible to claim benefit. This introductory letter (called DLJA 402/403) will be useful when you register with the appropriate authorities in your destination country, which must be done within seven days. Your local Jobcentre will inform the Pension &

Overseas Benefit Directorate of the Department of Social Security (on form DLJA 401) who will then decide whether or not to issue a E303 which authorises the Employment Services in the other EU/EEA country to pay UK contribution-based JSA for up to three months. In the case of Denmark, Gibraltar, Ireland, Luxembourg and the Netherlands, the E303 is sent by the DSS directly to a counterpart organisation. If you are heading for any other country, the E303 will be sent directly to you. The DSS Jobseekers & Benefit Enhancement Section of the Pensions & Overseas Benefit Directorate (Tyneview Park, Benton, Newcastle upon Tyne NE98 1BA; 0191-218 7652/fax 0191-218 7147) can send you a fact sheet (if your local employment office hasn't been able to supply one) and should be able to answer any specific questions you have.

If someone tries to claim unemployment benefit abroad without making these preparations there may be delays of several months while the application is cleared. Be warned that even if the correct procedure is followed there may still be delays because of the time necessary to forward and translate correspondence. Literature published by the Youth Information organisation Use It in Copenhagen sums it up:

Transferring benefits can be a good way of tiding you over whilst you settle in, but it is essential that you are aware of the realities of the situation. Although it is your right and in theory a great way of encouraging young unemployed people to try their luck abroad, you should not expect to be handed a cheque on the day of arrival. The process can be long and painful so it is very important that you have plenty of money to get you started. It can take months before you see any of your benefits in hard cash.

In theory, people looking for work in more than one EU country can continue to receive unemployment benefit under this system in each country visited, as long as they register for work in each new country promptly on arrival and have given adequate notice to the relevant office in the country from which they wish the benefit to be transferred. Overall however payment of unemployment benefit will not exceed the three month maximum. In fact complications and delays are bound to ensue if you country-hop.

Inside the United Kingdom employed persons who have paid the appropriate UK contributions can normally receive the job-seeker's allowance for up to six months. It is important to note that this maximum can be affected by the length of time you claim unemployment benefit abroad; if you claim benefit abroad for the maximum period of three months and then remain abroad for a further period of time, your right to claim job-seeker's allowance on your return to Britain lapses, according to EU regulations. But the Benefits Agency has discretion to allow those who would still be allowed to claim if they had not left the country to do so on their return.

These arrangements are standard within the EU: thus, a German wishing to look for work in Britain must obtain a letter of authorisation and E303 from his or her local Arbeitsamt, and so on. The EU principle of equality of treatment means that an EU citizen claiming unemployment benefit under a foreign social security scheme who moves to another country including his own, can arrange to collect unemployment benefit at the rate set by the foreign unemployment insurance fund for up to three months. In the case of Britons who have worked abroad, the foreign rate might be higher or lower than the standard United Kingdom job-seeker's allowance. If after three months the applicant has still not found employment, he is no longer eligible for foreign unemployment benefit but may then apply for income support.

The UK is more suspicious of EU nationals claiming benefit than they used to be, but Greece and Belgium are reputed to be relatively easy countries in which to claim. Rob Jefferson had no trouble in the Netherlands and wrote to tell us that he received his UK benefit with no problem because he had arranged everything in England, just as *Work Your Way Around the World* advised.

Anyone who is planning to quit work (to travel), go on the dole for the requisite four weeks and then head off to Europe to collect their benefit will be disappointed. Anyone who quits work voluntarily in the UK must wait 26 weeks before they are eligible to claim job-seeker's allowance.

Eligibility Requirements for Unemployment Benefit in EEA Countries

Country	Name of Unemployment Benefit	Qualifying Conditions
Austria	Arbeitslosengeld	At least 52 weeks (or 26 weeks if under the age of 25) in preceding 104 weeks
Belgium	Allocations de chômage	Between 75 days employment in last 10 months and 600 days employment in last 36 months, depending on age
Denmark	Dagpenge	Membership of an unemployment fund during the last 12 months and in employment for at least 6 of these months
Finland	Työttömyysavustus	At least 26 weeks in preceding 24 months
France	Allocation d'assurance chômage (also known as ASSEDIC)	Must be out of work or legitimately dismissed; must be capable of work and less than 60 years old, plus must have paid 3 months UB insurance in the last 12 months
Germany	Arbeitslosengeld	At least 480 days of insurable employment during the last 3 years
Gibraltar	Unemployment benefit	At least 30 paid contributions in the last 52 weeks
Greece	Epidoma anergias	At least 125 days of work during the 14 months preceding job loss
Iceland	Tryggingastofnun	425 hours in preceding 12 months
Ireland	Unemployment benefit	39 weeks paid insurance plus 48 contributions paid/credited in the year preceding the benefit year
Italy	Indennita ordinaria	One year during the previous 2 years; must also have been registered for at least 2 years with an unemployment insurance scheme
Luxembourg	Allocations de chômage	At least 26 weeks in the previous 12 months
Netherlands	Werkloosheidswet (also known as WW)	26 weeks in the previous 39 weeks
Norway	Arbeidsledighetstrygd	Must have earned approx. 22,000 Kroner in previous year
Spain	Prestación por Desempleo	At least 12 months employment within previous 6 years
Sweden	Dagpenning	At least 80 days spread over 5 months in preceding 12 months
United Kingdom	Job-seeker's allowance (flat rate)	Contributions must have been paid in one of the 2 tax years on which the claim is based amounting to at least 25 times the minimum contribution (i.e. 25 x £85)

You should request a copy of leaflet SA29 *Your Social Security Insurance, Benefits and Health Care Rights in the European Community* (dated August 1998) from your local DSS or from the International Services Department of the Contributions Agency in Newcastle (DSS, Longbenton, Newcastle upon Tyne NE98 1ZZ); the International Services Helpline on 0645 154811/fax 0645 157800 should be able to answer any specific questions you have. The booklet *Community Provisions on Social Security* might also prove useful.

Claiming Unemployment Benefit from Another EU Country

In order to claim unemployment benefit from another EU country you must have worked there and paid contributions into its unemployment insurance fund. The length of time for which you must have worked varies from country to country: the details are listed below. It cannot be emphasised too much that contributions paid in one country can be taken into account in another, and so for some people a very short period of work abroad may be sufficient to allow them to claim unemployment benefit there. Your history of paying contributions should be itemised on form E301 from the Overseas Benefit Directorate and sent to the corresponding office abroad. For the purposes of clarity the chart omits some of the complications, and mentions only the unemployment benefit that is normally paid to people who have just lost their jobs.

In many cases, it will be necessary to join the relevant union who may be responsible for distributing benefit.

How Much?

Great Britain and Ireland differ from most other EU countries in paying a flat rate of job-seeker's allowance (approximately £50 per week for a single person in the UK). Other member countries base their rates of unemployment benefit on a percentage of the wage most recently earned by the applicant, varying from 30.3% (plus a small daily allowance) in France to 90% in Denmark. In the Netherlands, claimants receive 70% of the minimum wage for up to six months. In Spain they receive 70% for the first 180 days and after that 60%. There are, of course, upper and lower limits on the amount paid to make sure that low earners do not suffer and the highly paid do not benefit excessively. Some Scandinavian countries pay a basic daily allowance to people who have not qualified for membership in an unemployment fund but who can prove that they are unemployed (approximately 125 markka per day in Finland, 245 kroner in Sweden).

How to Claim Unemployment Benefit

The same principles apply when claiming unemployment benefit in all member states of the EU, although the names and procedures may vary from one country to another. In order to claim you must:
- have become unemployed in that country through no fault of your own
- be both fit and available to work
- possess documentary proof of your last job and (normally) a residence permit
- be registered as unemployed with the employment office
- be aged under 65
- have paid sufficient contributions into unemployment insurance organisations in the EU

Unemployment insurance funds are not always administered by a country's national employment service. A country by country guide is listed below:

Austria: Local office of the national employment service *(arbeitsamt)*.

Belgium: Trade union members claim from the union's unemployment insurance division. Non-union members should go to CAPAC (the *Caisse auxiliaire de paiement des allocations de chômage*).

Denmark: Unemployment insurance is distributed by trade unions though non-union members may join an unemployment fund *(arbedjsløshedskammer)*.

Finland: Social Insurance Institution

France: Local office of the national employment service *(Agence Nationale pour l'Emploi)* or the local town hall if there is no *agence* nearby.

Germany: Local office of the national employment service *(arbeitsamt)*.

Greece: OAED (Labour Office).

Iceland: Unemployment Insurance Fund *(Atvinnuleysistryggingasjodur)* (Sudurlandsbraut 24, 150 Reykjavik; 588 2500).

Ireland: Local employment exchange or employment office.

Italy: Local employment office or the local office of the *Istituto della previdenza sociale* (national social welfare institution).

Luxembourg: National labour office *(Office National du Travail)* or the secretariat of the commune where you are living.

Netherlands: Previous employer's professional or trade association.

Norway: Local employment office *(Arbeidformidling)*

Portugal: Local office of the national employment service *(Centro de Emprego) and Centro Regional de Segurança* (CRSS).

Spain: Local office of the national employment service *(Oficina de Empleo)* or *Instituto Nacional de Seguridad Social* (INSS).

Sweden: Local employment office *(Arbetsfönmedlingen)*

United Kingdom: Local Jobcentre.

In all countries it is essential to register as unemployed with the national employment service before claiming from the unemployment insurance fund. Unemployment benefit (see chart for appropriate name in different countries) is only paid from three days after the date when you first register as unemployed, so it is important to register as soon as you lose your job. You will also be required to continue to register as unemployed with the insurance fund at regular intervals.

If you need to have a period of work in another EU country taken into account to make you eligible for unemployment benefit you will need to provide proof of the contributions you paid there on form E301 which you should obtain from the unemployment insurance organisation of the country where you paid the contributions. If you do not have this form to hand when you apply for unemployment benefit the office at which you are claiming can obtain it for you, but this may lead to a delay in processing your application.

TAX

Calculating your liability to tax when working outside your home country is notoriously complicated so, if possible, check your position with an accountant, preferably one who specialises in expatriate matters.

There really isn't any such thing as legal tax-free income whatever an agency or employer promises. The only people who are not liable to pay any tax are those who earn less than the personal allowance (whatever that may be). However there are ways to minimise tax. Although the details of income tax systems vary from country to country, there are some common characteristics. In theory EU students working in the EU for less than six months are not liable for tax, so students should always show their employers documents to prove their status. The traveller who works for less than the full tax year will generally find himself paying too much in tax: this section outlines the circumstances when it may be possible to reclaim some of it. Individual cases should be discussed with the local tax authority.

If you are working on a longer term basis abroad, your UK tax liability depends on several factors, the principal one being whether you are classed as 'resident', 'ordinarily resident' or 'domiciled' in the UK. Working travellers are normally considered domiciled in the UK even if they are away for more than a year. Formerly it was possible to claim a 'foreign earnings deduction' (i.e. pay no tax) if you were out of the country for a full 365 days. However two years ago, the legislation changed so that you are eligible for this only if you have been out of the country for a complete tax year (6 April to 5 April) though you are allowed to spend up to 62 days (i.e. one-sixth) of the tax-year back in England without it affecting your tax postion. Anyone who is present in the UK for more than 182 days during a particular tax year will be treated as resident with no exceptions.

Inland Revenue leaflets which might be of assistance are IR20 'Residents and

Non-Residents: Liability to Tax in the UK' and IR139 'Income from Abroad? A guide to UK tax on overseas income'. The Inland Revenue also has a good website if you have the patience to look for the information you need (www.inlandrevenue.gov.uk); it lists the relevant contact offices that deal with specific issues. General enquiries may be directed to 020-7438 6420. If they can't help they will refer you to the appropriate section. General tax enquiries may be addressed to the Inland Revenue Financial Intermediaries and Claims Office (Non-Residents), St. John's House, Merton Road, Bootle, Merseyside L69 9BB (0151-472 6214/5/6). A possible source of further information on tax is the annually revised book *Working Abroad* published by Kogan Page in conjunction with the *Daily Telegraph*.

If US citizens can establish that they are resident abroad, the first $80,000 (from the year 2000) of overseas earnings are tax-exempt in the US.

Why you can Reclaim Tax

Countries do not charge income tax on a person's income up to a certain figure, which is known as a personal allowance or a basic deduction. The exact size of this figure varies from country to country, but it is generally at least 20% of the national average wage. For example in Germany anyone who earns less than DM530 per month (DM390 in the former East Germany) should not have to pay income tax. In theory, you won't have to pay any tax if your total earnings are below this figure.

In practice, however, most countries deduct tax under a withholding system or 'pay as you earn', which assumes that your weekly wage is typical of your annual earnings. Thus, if you work in Britain for two weeks for a weekly wage of £100, you will be taxed as if you were earning £5,200 a year. Sometimes you have the right to reclaim any tax you have paid on income up to the value of your personal allowance when you have finished work and are about to leave the country or at the end of that country's tax year. Unfortunately there are residential and other requirements in some countries which make this impossible.

This may seem to imply that you could escape from tax altogether by getting a series of short term jobs around the world and never exceeding your personal allowance in any one country. Unfortunately, there are a number of 'double taxation' agreements between most western countries which prevent this. Among other things, they ensure that the taxman can ultimately track you down in your 'country of permanent residence', where you will be liable to pay tax on all your earnings abroad at the local rate. Hence the popularity among tax exiles of countries with very low rates of tax.

How to Minimise Tax

Keep all pay slips, receipts and financial documents in case you need to plead your case at a later date. If your tax status abroad is not completely legitimate, you will be taxed in the UK as Jamie Masters found to his cost after nine months of English teaching in Crete:

> I didn't know that if you are working abroad for less than a year, you are liable to be taxed in Britain, and had cheerfully let the tax people know that I was working in Greece. The rules state that the tax you pay in Greece can be transferred to England to offset the tax you owe at home. But I didn't pay any tax in Greece (just bribes). Stupid, stupid. I should have just told the IR that I was travelling. Rule number one: if you're working illegally, deny everything.

In many countries where you can work legitimately (e.g. EU countries) your employer will expect you to clarify your tax position with the local tax office at the beginning of your work period. This can be to your advantage, for example in Denmark where, unless you obtain a tax card *(skattekort)*, you will be put on the Danish equivalent of an emergency code and 60% of your earnings will be automatically deducted at source. Glyn Evans who picked apples in Denmark returned several times to the local Radhus to complain about the excessive tax, and finally obtained a *skattekort* entitling him to a taxation rate of 31%. Germany is another country where it is customary for foreign workers to register at the tax office *(Finanzamt)*. Be sure to get a tax code in Gibraltar since this, together with a tax return filled in before departure, will allow you to reclaim income tax once you're back in Britain.

France has an unusual tax system, and the general advice given in this section does not apply there. Instead of deducting tax on the 'pay as you earn' system, the French authorities charge tax retrospectively: in other words, with every pay packet French workers are paying off in instalments their tax bill from the previous year. So the working traveller in France will escape any deductions for tax unless he or she is unlucky enough to be working over the end of the tax year, which is from January 1st to December 31st. However he or she will have to pay social security contributions which are high in France at 23.6%.

How to Reclaim Tax

When you have finished a job your employer should give you a form which will state the amount of tax he has taken from your wages. If he can't do this for any reason you should collect your pay slips. Even a scruffy piece of paper may be sufficient proof of your having paid tax if it states the dates you worked and the amount of tax deducted, and is signed by your employer. If your employer won't give you any written proof at all, the odds are that he has been pocketing the money he has deducted, in which case there is no point in trying to reclaim it from the tax office!

You then take this evidence to the local tax office and fill in a tax rebate form. On this form you will have to state that you will not be working in that country again during the tax year, and give the date of your departure. You may be asked to surrender your residence and/or work permit to prevent you from simply moving to another town and getting a new job or you may have to show your return ticket to prove that you are leaving. Bureaucratic delays often mean that your refund will have to be posted to you abroad. It can take weeks, and frequently months, for your claim to be processed. You therefore need to be sure that you will be at the address you give them for some length of time; if you are not sure of your future movements, give the address of a relative or friend.

Some countries, e.g. Germany, Denmark and the US, stipulate that you are not allowed to reclaim any tax until the end of the tax year. The rule in Germany as in Britain is that you must have resided in Germany for at least six months of the tax year in order to qualify for a rebate. In Denmark tax refunds can be issued only six months after the year in which the tax was paid.

It is not essential that you reclaim tax directly from the authorities of the country where you have been working, since double taxation agreements state that any tax you have paid on earnings abroad can be credited as if it had been paid in your own country. So, in principle, if you have paid too much tax you can reclaim it from your own national tax authority. In practice, however, this can turn into a long drawn out process as the bureaucracies of two countries attempt to communicate with each other: it took Tessa Shaw two years to obtain a refund of tax she had overpaid in Denmark through the British Inland Revenue. You are therefore strongly advised to deal directly with the tax offices of the countries in which you have worked whenever possible.

Work Your Way

TOURISM

The long-term prospects for the tourist industry are rosy. A staggering 19 million jobs in the European Union are travel and tourism-related which represents nearly 13% of the workforce. According to an estimate submitted to the European Commission, tourism could create between 2.2 and 3.3 million new jobs in the EU by 2010. The tourist industry, like agriculture, is a mainstay of the traveller-cum-worker. The seasonal nature of hotel and restaurant work discourages a stable working population, and so hotel proprietors often rely on foreign labour during the busy season. Also, many tourist destinations are in remote places where there is no local pool of labour. Travellers have ended up working in hotels in some of the most beautiful corners of the world from the South Island of New Zealand to Lapland.

Agencies

People with a background in hotels and catering may be able to fix up overseas contracts while still in the UK. The Overseas Placing Unit of the Employment Service registers quite a few foreign vacancies in the tourist industry (particularly in France and Italy) with Jobcentres. Specialist agencies will be of interest to qualified hotel staff including chefs, hotel receptionists and restaurant staff, such as Towngate Personnel Ltd (65 Seamoor Road, Westbourne, Bournemouth BN4 9AE; 01202 752955) which specialise in the Channel Isles and UK but occasionally have vacancies further afield; and Transcontinental (18 High St, Beckenham, Kent BR3 1BL; 020-8650 2344). Quest Elite (4-6 High St, Eastleigh, Hants. SO5 5LA; 023-8064 4933; www.quest-elite.co.uk) recruits qualified and experienced hotel and catering staff for hotels and resorts worldwide. The Recruitment and Employment Confederation (020-7323 4300; www.rec.org.uk) can send a list of specialist agencies at a cost of £3.75.

The agency Jobs in the Alps (17 High St, Gretton, Northants. NN17 3DE; 01536 771150; alan@jobs-in-the-alps.com) places young Britons in French, German and Swiss hotels for at least three months during the summer season, for which the application deadline is April 15th. (See section below on Ski Resorts for further information.)

For people who are pursuing a career in travel and tourism, it would be worth looking at another Vacation-Work Publications title *Working in Tourism* (£11.95). Further information is available from the Travel Tourism, Services and Events National Training Organisation (01932 345835; www.tttc.co.uk). Several specialist employment agencies such as T & T Travel Recruitment (www.ttrecruitment.demon.co.uk) place candidates in travel agencies, administrative positions, ground-handling firms, etc. The internet is a valuable source of leads. For example try www.worktheworld.com.au for overseas vacancies in the hospitality industry.

If you have extensive experience of travelling on at least two continents (other than Europe and North America), you might be interested in working for one of the youth travel agencies like STA (Travel Recruitment, 6 Wrights Lane, London W8 6TA; 020-7361 6220; recruitment@statravel.co.uk).

The independent travellers' monthly magazine *Wanderlust* has a Job Shop column which advertises vacancies with adventure travel companies, e.g. as cycle or hill-walking tour leaders.

HOTELS AND RESTAURANTS

If you secure a hotel job without speaking the language of the country and lacking relevant experience, you will probably be placed at the bottom of the pecking order, e.g. in the laundry or washing dishes. Some hotels might confuse you by using fancy terms for menial jobs, for example 'valet runner' for collector-of-dirty-laundry or 'kitchen porter' for pot-washer. Reception and bar jobs are usually the most sought after and highly paid. However the lowly jobs have their saving graces. The usual hours of chamber staff (7am-2pm) allow plenty of free time. Some people prefer not to deal with guests (particularly if they are shaky in the language) and are happy to get on at their own speed with the job of room cleaning or laundering or vegetable chopping. The job of night porter can be excellently suited to an avid reader since there is often very little to do except let in the occasional late arrival.

Even the job of dish-washer, stereotyped as the most lowly of all jobs with visions of the down and out George Orwell as a *plongeur* washing dishes in a Paris café, should not be dismissed too easily. Nick Langley enjoyed life far more as a dish-washer in Munich than as a civil servant in Britain. Simon Canning saved enough money in five months of working as a dish-washer in an Amsterdam office block to fund a trip across Asia. Benjamin Fry spent a highly enjoyable two weeks washing dishes at the Land's End Hotel in Alaska and earned more per hour than he ever had in Britain. And Sean Macnamara was delighted with his job as dish-washer in a French hotel near Chamonix:

> *After a brief interview I was given the job of dish-washer. The conditions were excellent: F3,000 per month (£300) plus private accommodation and first class meals, including as much wine as I could drink. I earned my keep, though, working six days a week from 8am to 10pm with three hours off each afternoon. I was the only foreigner and was treated kindly by everyone. Indeed I can honestly say I enjoyed myself, but then I was permanently high on the thought of all that money.*

If your only experience of hotels is as a guest, you may be in for a surprise when you go backstage. Even the most luxurious hotels have been known to have dirty, disorganised kitchens, inadequate laundering facilities and lousy (literally) staff quarters. It is quite possible that the waitress who smilingly emerges from the kitchen bearing your food has just been threatened and abused by the chef for not working quickly enough. It may have something to do with the heat generated by the ovens in large kitchens, the pride they take in their creations, or the pressures under which they work, but chefs have a terrible reputation for having fiery tempers. S. C. Firn describes the working atmosphere in a 'rather classy restaurant and bar' in Oberstdorf in Southern Germany near the Austrian border:

> *I had to peel vegetables, wash dishes, prepare food, clean the kitchen and sometimes serve food. Everything was done at a very fast pace, and was expected to be very professional. One German cook, aged 16, who didn't come up to standard, was punched in the face three times by the owner. On another occasion the assistant chef had a container of hot carrots tipped over his head for having food sent back. During my three months there, all the other British workers left, apart from the chef, but were always replaced by more.*

So if you consider yourself to be the sensitive fragile type, perhaps you should avoid hotel kitchens altogether.

On the other hand many people thrive on the animated atmosphere and on kitchen conviviality. Nick Langley, who also worked in a German kitchen, loved the atmosphere. He maintains that once you're established you'll gain more respect by shouting back if unreasonable demands are made, but adds the proviso, 'but not at the powerful head cook, please!'. Heated tempers usually cool down after a couple of beers at the end of a shift.

Applications

The earlier you decide to apply for seasonal hotel work the better are your chances. Hotels in a country such as Switzerland recruit months before the summer season, and it is advisable to write to as many hotel addresses as possible by March, preferably in their own language. A knowledge of more than one language is an immense asset for work in Europe. If you have an interest in working in a particular country, get a list of hotels from their tourist office in London and write to the largest ones (e.g. the ones with over 100 rooms). If you know someone going to your chosen country, ask them to bring back local newspapers and check adverts. Enclose international reply coupons and try to write in the language of the country. Amanda Smallwood wrote to 20 hotels in a German resort and received seven job offers out of 15 replies.

On the other hand you might not be able to plan so far ahead, or you may have no luck with written applications, so it will be necessary to look for hotel work once you've arrived in a foreign country. All but the most desperate hoteliers are far more willing to consider a candidate who is standing there in the flesh than one who writes a letter out of the blue. One job-seeker recommends showing up bright and early (about 8am) to impress prospective employers. Perseverance is necessary when you're asking door to door at hotels. One of our contributors was repeatedly rejected by hotels in Amsterdam on the grounds that she was too late in the summer (i.e. August). Her last hope was the Hilton Hotel and she thought she might as well give it a try since it might be her only chance to see the inside of a Hilton. She was amazed when she was hired instantly as a chambermaid. It also might be necessary to return to the same hotel several times if you think there's a glimmer of hope. Kathryn Halliwell described her job hunt in Les Gets in the Haute Savoie of France:

I had to ask from hotel to hotel for three days before finding the job, and experienced what I have come to know through experience and others' reports is the normal way to hire a casual worker. The boss told me blankly that he had no work. As I was leaving he said, what sort of work? I told him anything. He said I could come back the next day in case something came up. I did and was told he was out, come again tomorrow. I eventually did get the job and realised he had just been testing my attitude as he had every other employee when they first applied.

When going door to door, you should start with the biggest hotels. Try to get past the receptionist to ask the manager personally. If you are offered a position (either in person or in writing) try to get a signed contract setting out clearly the hours, salary and conditions of work. If this is not possible, you should at least discuss these issues with the boss.

Another way to get a foothold in a resort is to cultivate the acquaintance of the reps from the big travel firms. Not only will they know of immediate openings, but they can establish your position with local hoteliers who normally know and respect the reps. This is a job-finding ploy which has to be used with care since reps are constantly being asked for favours. You might volunteer to help them, meeting a group or standing in for someone who is ill. Lisa Brophy met a local tour representative in an Austrian ski resort and was soon introduced to a restaurant manager with a staff vacancy.

Only in a handful of cases can agencies and leisure groups place people without any expertise in foreign hotels; however wages in these cases are normally negligible. For example Eurotoques, the *Communauté Européenne des Cuisiniers,* places kitchen and waiting assistants in hotels throughout Germany; staff earn no wage but are given free board and lodging (see German chapter). Travelbound (Olivier House, 18 Marine Parade, Brighton, East Sussex BN2 1TL; 0840 900 3200) send about 250 summer staff and 750 winter staff to clubhotels and chalets in Austria and France; staff must have EU nationality but need not have relevant experience.

Advantages and Disadvantages

The same complaints crop up again and again among people who have worked in hotels: long and unsociable hours (often 8am-10pm with a few hours off in the afternoon plus lots of weekend work), exploitative wages, inadequate accommodation and food, and unbearably hot working conditions exacerbated by having to wear a nylon uniform. A great deal depends on whether or not you are the type to rough it. The working atmosphere can vary a lot from hotel to hotel. If you are lucky enough to get a job in a small friendly family hotel, you will probably enjoy the work more than if you are just one in a large anonymous group of workers in a sterile and impersonal institution where you have no job security.

It can be very aggravating to be asked to do extra duties beyond the ones specified in your contract. It seems to be a common occurrence, especially in French and German hotels, that the proprietor takes for granted that you will do unpaid overtime, without time off in lieu at a later date. If a contract is being breached in this way, you should try your best to sort it out with the employer. If this fails don't hesitate to go to the appropriate employment authorities to lodge an official complaint. This has far more chance of success if you have a written contract to show the authorities.

Not all hotels are like this and many people emphasise the benefits which they have found in the experience of working in a hotel: excellent camaraderie and team spirit, the opportunity to learn a foreign language, and the ease with which wages can be saved, including the possibility of an end-of-season bonus. Although Kathryn Halliwell was forced to share a windowless room which had an intermittently working light and water streaming down the roof beams into constantly overflowing buckets, she still enjoyed her time working at a hotel in Corsica, simply because of the conviviality of her 'fellow sufferers'.

Other Catering

Hotels represent just one aspect of the tourist trade, and there are many more interesting venues for cooking and serving, including luxury yachts, prawn trawlers, holiday ranches, safari camps and ski chalets. People with some training in catering will find it much easier to work their way around the world than the rest of us. The serious traveller might even consider enrolling in a catering course before embarking on his or her journey.

Of course, there are opportunities for the unskilled. You might find a job cooking hamburgers in a chain such as McDonalds or Burger King, which can be found from Tel Aviv to Toronto. (Bear in mind that the Oxford English Dictionary now includes the coinage 'Mcjob' to refer to any form of dead-end, low-paid employment.) Anyone who is not confident communicating in the language of the country can still hope for employment in a fast food kitchen. Pay is low, hours unreliable or inconvenient and the attitude to discipline more worthy of school children, however it is a good way of earning while you familiarise yourself with a new place. When you are applying for jobs like this, which are not seasonal, you should stress that you intend to work for an indefinite period, make a career of fast food catering, etc. In fact staff turnover is usually very high. This will also aid your case when you are obliged to badger them to give you extra hours.

A good way of gaining initial experience is to get a kitchen job with a large organisation in Britain such as Butlins Family Entertainment Resorts in Bognor Regis (Job hotline 01243 841190), Minehead (01643 709638) and Skegness (01754 761502) which offer a variety of jobs, including kitchen, restaurant, administration, bar and shop work. Alternatively, consider PGL Adventure (Alton Court, Penyard Lane, Ross-on-Wye, Herefordshire HR9 5NR; 01989 767833). Since they have so many vacancies (most of which pay only pocket money), the chances of being hired for a first season are reasonably good. PGL also have holiday centres abroad (mostly in France) which are staffed on the same principle.

You may also find catering jobs which have nothing to do with tourism, for example in canteens, on industrial sites, mining camps or army bases. These settings are not among the most congenial in the world, though they often have the advantage of offering more social hours than restaurants. Railway stations and airports have catering divisions which employ casual staff. Schiphol airport in Amsterdam is especially well known for hiring foreign young people.

OTHER OPPORTUNITIES

Your average big-spending pampered tourist, so often ridiculed by budget travellers, indirectly provides a great number of employment opportunities. He wants to eat ice cream on the beach or croissants in his ski chalet, so you might be the one there to sell it to him. He would be most distressed if he got dripped on in his hotel bed, so you may get hired to tar the roof before the season begins. He doesn't want to be pestered by his children, so you spend the day teaching them how to swim or draw at a holiday camp. He is not happy unless he goes home with a genuine sachet of Ardeche lavender or a Texan 10-gallon hat sold to him by a charming souvenir shop assistant, who will be you. He needs to be entertained so you get a job in an amusement arcade, the local disco or windsurfing school. His wife wants to keep up appearances so a freelance hairdresser's services are very welcome. And so it could continue. The point is that casual jobs proliferate in tourist centres.

Of course there are also many opportunities at the budget end of tourism, in travellers' hostels and so on. Dustie Hickey describes the way she went about getting a job in the Avignon Youth Hostel:

I checked out all the hostels in Avignon through the Minitel system. I had help to write a letter in French. Then I telephoned because I did not get a reply. The hostel could not promise me any work till they met me. Before I left the farm in Brittany where I was working, I telephoned again to remind them I was on my way. When I arrived the hostel was very busy. For free B & B, I just had to keep the dormitory clean, but I pitched in and helped with cleaning, laundry, breakfast, etc. The manager was pleased and gave me a little money. At the end of July the paid assistant left so I was given her job, and eventually I had a room to myself.

Many private travellers' hostels worldwide employ long-stay residents to act as PR reps at railway and bus stations, trying to persuade new arrivals to patronise their hostel. A free bed is always given and usually a small fee per successful 'convert'.

Pubs and Clubs

Bars and nightclubs should not be omitted from your list of likely employers. Caroline Scott bought the club magazine *Mixmag* in the winter and contacted a number of Ibiza clubs, one of which hired her for the summer season (see *Spain* chapter). If you want to look for work after arrival, you might consider carrying a set of 'black and whites' (black trousers/skirt and white shirt) in case you pick up a job as a bartender or waiter. If you have no experience, it can be worthwhile volunteering to work at your local pub before you leave home for a week and then ask for a reference. Once you are abroad, ask at English-style pubs which are found from the Costa del Sol to the Zamalek district of Cairo, from Santa Monica California to Austrian ski resorts and try to exploit the British connection. Irish people are at an even greater advantage since there are Irish bars and pubs around the world from Molly Malone's in Paris to Fibber Magee's in Dubai. In ordinary bars on the Continent you may be expected to be proficient in the prevailing language, although exceptions are made, particularly in the case of glamorous-looking applicants. Women (especially blonde ones) can find jobs from Amsterdam to Hong Kong, but should be sure that they can distinguish between bars and brothels.

Places like the Canaries, Ibiza, Corfu and the Caribbean islands are bursting at the seams with 'nite spots' of one kind or another. Not only is there a high turn-over of staff but there is a rapid turn-over of clubs too, and you may not have much job security. As long as you investigate the establishments in the place you want to work before accepting a job, you should not encounter too many unpleasant surprises. Handing out promotional leaflets for bars and discos is a job which travellers frequently do, especially in Spain.

The idea that Britons know their way round the music scene better than other nationalities is fairly widespread, and anyone who knows how to use a turntable might get occasional work, not only in the obvious resorts but in farflung places like Bangkok (as Laurence Koe did). Experienced DJs who want to work abroad should request details from a specialist agency like Juliana's Leisure Services (15-17 Broadway, West Ealing, London W13 9DA; 020-8567 6765) which offers wages of £760-£960 per month for working in Europe or the Middle East where they have an office. They supply entertainment packages to 5-star hotels and other clients. Another agency which supplies people to entertain in a different way is Openwide International Ltd (7 Westmoreland House, Cumberland Park, London NW10 6RE; 020-8962 3400; www.openwideinternational.com) who send about 100 entertainers and entertainment programme organisers to work in holiday hotels in Spain, Cyprus, Greece and Turkey.

The show business newspaper *The Stage* published every week sometimes carries adverts for dancers both respectable and otherwise for resorts abroad as well as in the UK.

Special Events
Great bursts of tourist activity take place around major events. For example armies of volunteers were hired primarily through the Adecco Agency for the Sydney Olympics. No wage is paid and perks are few in many of these world events since the organisers know that there will be no shortage of eager participants.

On a smaller scale, annual festivals and sporting events, trade fairs and World Fairs are all useful providers of casual employment possibilities, both during and before and after when facilities are set up and then dismantled. It is not possible for an event such as Okterberfest in Munich (held every year in late September) to host over 6 million visitors without a great deal of extra labour being enlisted to prepare the 560,000 barbecued chickens, 346,000 pairs of sausages and to dispense the 1,000,000 gallons of beer consumed. Enterprising mechanics might consider taking their tools and some spare parts and setting up in the car park to fix and adjust the thousands of travel-weary vans and cars which assemble there. The main problem is finding affordable accommodation.

TOUR OPERATORS
Acting as a tour guide, rep or courier for a tour operator is one way of combining work with travel. Two-month jobs are rare in this field since in most cases employers want staff who will stay at least for the whole summer season April to October inclusive. The peak recruitment time is the preceding September, though strong candidates can be interviewed as late as February. Knowledge of a European language is always requested, though it is unusual for reps in Greece or Portugal to speak those languages. Otherwise, personality and maturity are what count most and a commitment to the company, and possibly also to tourism as a career. By all accounts interviews can be fairly gruelling as they try to weed out the candidates who will crack under the pressure of holidaymakers' complaints and problems. It is estimated that only one in forty applicants gets a job.

In the first instance, pick up a range of brochures from your local travel agent and see which company's style suits you. Then send a large s.a.e. to the head office requesting their recruitment procedures. Here are some of the biggest UK tour operators:

Airtours Holidays Ltd, Wavell House, Holcombe Road, Helmshore, Rossendale, Lancs. BB4 4NB (24-hour recruitment line: 0870 241 2642/fax 01706 232328; www.airtours.co.uk). Hire customer services reps, children's club leaders, administrative and many other kinds of staff between March and October in wide range of resorts.

Club Med, Kennedy House, 115 Hammersmith Road, London W14 0QH; 020-7348 3333). Range of staff (who must be able to speak French) for their upmarket holiday villages in Europe and North Africa. As well as general hotel and catering staff, they require sports instructors, children's reps, hostesses, shop staff and tour guides. In the US ring Club Med's Employment Hotline: 407-337-6660 (www.clubmed.com).

Cosmos Holidays, Human Resources, Tourama House, 17 Homesdale Rd, Bromley, Kent BR2 9LX (020-8464 0802; www.cosmos-holidays.co.uk). Reps, admin staff, children's reps, etc. can apply on-line if they choose.

First Choice Ski Lakes & Mountains, Olivier House, 18 Marine Parade, Brighton, East Sussex BN2 1TL (0840 900320/fax 01273 600486; jobs@fcski.co.uk). 500 staff needed for 25 clubhotels and 55 chalets in alpine resorts (mainly France and Austria).

Mark Warner Ltd, George House, First Floor, 61/65 Kensington Church St, London W8 4BA; 020-7761 7300; www.markwarner.co.uk) runs beachclub hotels in Corsica, Italy, Sardinia, Greece and Turkey for which it hires club managers, receptionists, chefs, bar and waiting staff, watersports and tennis instructors, pool attendants, laundry staff, handymen, drivers, gardeners, night watchmen and nannies (but not couriers or resort representatives). All staff must be over 19 and available from mid-April to mid-November, though there is a continuous need for replacements throughout the season. The wages run from £50-£250 per week;

benefits include use of watersports facilities, travel, medical insurance and the potential for winter work at their ski chalet hotels in Europe.

Saga Holidays, ring 01303 774903 for application form (www.saga.co.uk). Holidays for an older clientele.

Thomson Holidays Ltd, Human Resources Overseas, Greater London House, Hampstead Road, London NW1 7SD (020-7387 9321; www.thomsonholidays. com/jobs). Employ so many people to service their estimated four million customers that they publish a large-format leaflet about their recruitment requirements. As is the case with most of the major companies, Thomson employ reps (minimum age 21), children's reps (minimum age 19) and entertainment reps (from age 20) for the summer season (June to mid-September). All the usual qualities required: flexibility, diplomacy, etc. A knowledge of French, Spanish, Italian, Greek, Portuguese or German would be an advantage.

Considering the rigours and pressures of the job of package tour company representative, wages are low, though of course accommodation is provided. Often wages (from £60 or £70 a week) are paid into a bank account at home. Meagre wages can usually be supplemented with commissions from restaurant, shops and car hire.

A number of travellers who have done some casual hotel work abroad go on to take up jobs as reps with British tour companies. On her return from her extensive travels and numerous casual jobs en route, Xuela Edwards applied for various rep jobs in February:

> *They all told me that September is the best time to apply. But I managed to get a few interviews on the strength of my work abroad and ended up being sent to the Greek island of Paxos. I loved Paxos but I found I was too restless and used to independent travel to settle for seven months.*

Camping tour operators employ thousands of site representatives (see section below).

There are several kinds of holiday company looking for different kinds of courier and rep. Couriers are needed to escort groups on tours within Europe by companies like Top Deck Travel, 131-135 Earls Court Road, London SW5 9RH (020-7244 8641) who are also looking for coach drivers and cooks. Jayne Nash described her season with Top Deck as 'an amazing if exhausting experience':

> *It enabled me to visit nearly every part of Europe, get involved in some really exciting events and meet some wonderful people, namely the South Africans (non-whites I might add) whom I later went to visit.*

Applications should be sent in writing by the end of November.

Often these companies charge a training bond of £200-400 which may be non-refundable if you are considered unsuitable. Drivers need to have a Passenger Carrying Vehicle (PCV) licence which costs several hundred pounds to obtain. Working in Africa, Asia and Latin America as an adventure tour leader is discussed in the chapter *Working a Passage: Overland Tours.*

A list of special interest and activity tour operators (to whom people with specialist skills can apply) is available from AITO, the Association of Independent Tour Operators (33A St Margaret's Road, Twickenham TW1 1RG). In the US, consult the *Specialty Travel Index* (305 San Anselmo Ave, San Anselmo, CA 94960; www.specialtytravel.com); the directory is issued twice a year at a cost of $10 in the US, $22 abroad.

A number of companies specialise in tours for school children, both British and American. For example the London office of the American Council for International Studies (AIFS UK, 38 Queen's Gate, London SW7 5HR; 020-7590 7474; tmdepartment@acis.com) is looking for 100 clever linguists to accompany groups of American high school students around Europe. Casterbridge Tours (Bowden Road, Templecombe, Somerset BA8 0LB; 01963 370753; tourops@casterbridge-tours.co.uk) employ guides to escort groups between March and July. Successful applicants must attend one of their weekend training courses for tour guides in the winter.

Contiki Holidays (Wells House, 15 Elmfield Road, Bromley, Kent BR1 1LS; 020-8290 6777) specialise in coach tours for clients aged 18-35 and hire EU nationals aged 23-30 as site representatives, tour managers and coach drivers. Applicants for the position of tour manager must have independent travel experience and an interest in European history and current affairs. Two other youth-oriented European tour operators are Busabout (www.busabout.com/employment) and Tracks Travel (The Flots, Brookland, Romney Marsh, Kent TN29 9TG; 01797 344164; www.tracks-travel.com) which advertise for road crew in the autumn. Busabout hold interviews in London and Australia in November and December and offer a full training course in March.

You need not confine your aspirations to Europe. While travelling in South-East Asia or South America several contributors have been invited to shepherd tourists around (e.g. the island resorts of Thailand and Venezuela) by a ground handling tour agency. You would have to be on hand to find out about this sort of opportunity. You can even set yourself up in business as a guide or courier, as Jennifer McKibben noticed long-stay travellers doing in East Africa.

Campsite Couriers

A different kind of courier is needed by the large camping holiday operators. British camping holiday firms (addresses below) hire large numbers of people to remain on one campsite on the Continent for several months. The Eurocamp Group alone recruits up to 1,500 campsite couriers and children's couriers. The courier's job is to clean the tents and caravans between visitors, greet clients and deal with difficulties (particularly illness or car breakdowns) and introduce clients to the attractions of the area or even arrange and host social functions and amuse the children. All of this will be rewarded with on average £90-£100 a week in addition to free tent accommodation. Many companies offer half-season contracts April to mid-July and mid-July to the end of September. Setting up and dismantling the campsites in March/April and September (known as *montage* and *démontage*) is often done by a separate team (sometimes called 'squaddies'). The work is hard but the language requirements are nil.

Some camping holiday and tour operators based in Britain are as follows (with the European countries in which they are active):

Canvas Holidays, 12 Abbey Park Place, Dunfermline, Fife KY12 7PD (01383 644018; www.canvas.com). France, Germany, Austria, Switzerland, Italy, Luxembourg and Spain.

Club Cantabrica Holidays Ltd, 146/148 London Road, St. Albans, Herts. AL1 1PQ (01727 843766). France (including Corfu), Italy and Spain (including Majorca).

Eurocamp plc, Overseas Recruitment Department (Ref WW) - 01606 787522. Austria, Belgium, Luxembourg, France, Germany, Italy, Spain, Switzerland, Netherlands and Denmark. Telephone applications from October. Interviews held in Hartford, Cheshire over the winter. Also trade under Holidaybreak, Hartford Manor, Greenbank Lane, Northwich, Cheshire CW8 1HW (same telephone number).

Eurosites Recruitment/Airtours plc, Wavell House, Holcombe Road, Helmshore, Lancs. BB4 4NB (01254 300622/3/4). France, Spain and Italy.

Haven Europe, 1 Park Lane, Hemel Hempstead, Herts. HP2 4YL (01442 203287/fax 01442 260779). Courier and children's courier staff for France, Spain and Italy.

Holidaybreak, see Eurocamp. On-line applications accepted on www.holidaybreakjobs.com.

Keycamp Holidays, Overseas Recruitment Department, Hartford Manor, Greenbank Lane, Northwich, CV8 1HW (01606 787522/e-mail: recruit@keycamp.co.uk). France, Italy, Spain, Germany.

Solaire Holidays, 1158 Stratford Road, Hall Green, Birmingham B28 8AF (0121-778 5061; www.solaire.co.uk). France, Spain.

Successful couriers make the job look easy, but it does demand a lot of hard work and patience. Occasionally it is very hard to keep up the happy, smiling, never-ruffled courier look, but most seem to end up enjoying the job. Alison Cooper described her job with Eurocamp on a site in Corsica as immensely enjoyable, though it was not as easy as the clients thought:

> *Living on a campsite in high season had one or two drawbacks: the toilets and showers were dirty, with constant queues, the water was freezing cold, the campsite was very very noisy and if you're unfortunate enough to have your tent in sunlight, it turns into a tropical greenhouse. Of course we did get*

difficult customers who complained for a variety of reasons: they wanted to be nearer to the beach, off the main road, in a cooler tent with more grass around it, etc. etc. But mostly our customers were friendly and we soon discovered that the friendlier we were to them, the cleaner they left their tents.

I found it difficult at first to get used to living, eating, working and socialising with the other two couriers 24 hours a day. But we all got on quite well and had a good time, unlike at a neighbouring campsite where the couriers hated each other. Our campsite had a swimming pool and direct beach access, though nightlife was limited. The one disco did get very repetitive.

Despite all this, she sums up by highly recommending that others who have never travelled or worked abroad work for a company like Eurocamp which provides accommodation, a guaranteed weekly wage and the chance to work with like-minded people.

Caroline Nicholls' problems at a campsite in Brittany included frequent power failures, blocked loos and leaking tents:

Every time there was a steady downpour, one of the tents developed an indoor lake, due to the unfortunate angle at which we had pitched it. I would appear, mop in hand, with cries of 'I don't understand. This has never happened before.' Working as a courier would be a good grounding for an acting career.

She goes on to say that despite enjoying the company of the client families, she was glad to have the use of a company bicycle to escape the insular life on the campsite every so often. Some companies guarantee one day off-site which is considered essential for maintaining sanity. The companies do vary in the conditions of work and some offer much better support than others. For example a company for which Hannah Start worked ignored her pleas for advice and assistance when one of her clients had appendicitis.

The big companies advertise in the *Sunday Times,* etc. and many are listed in the *Directory of Summer Jobs Abroad.* They interview hundreds of candidates and have filled most posts by the end of January. But there is a very high dropout rate (over 50%) and vacancies are filled from a reserve list, so it is worth ringing around the companies as late as April for cancellations. Despite keen competition, anyone who has studied a European language and has an outgoing personality stands a good chance if he or she applies early and widely enough. According to Carla Mitchell, not having too posh an accent helps when applying to companies based in the North; with her Surrey accent, she was given a job without too much 'client profile'.

Activity Holidays

Many specialist tour companies employ leaders for their clients (children and/or adults) who want a walking, cycling, watersports holiday, etc. Companies which operate in only one country are included in the country chapters.

3D Education & Adventure Ltd, Business Support, Osmington Bay, Weymouth, Dorset DT33 6EG (01305 836226; darren@3d-education.co.uk). 500 activity instructors for Center Parcs holiday parks in Holland, Germany and Belgium as well as the UK and Ireland.

Acorn Adventure Ltd, 22 Worcester St, Stourbridge, W. Midlands DY8 1AN (01384 446057; topstaff@acornadventure.co.uk). Require qualified canoeing, climbing, hillwalking, kayaking, sailing and windsurfing instructors to work in centres in the UK, France (Ardeche), Italy and Spain.

PGL Travel, Alton Court, Penyard Lane (874), Ross-on-Wye, Herefordshire HR9 5GL (01989 767833; www.pgl.co.uk/personnel). Recruit for about 2,500 seasonal vacancies at their holiday centres throughout Britain and France. They publish a detailed brochure of their requirements for activity instructors, group leaders, catering and support staff. The norm is to pay pocket money of £50-£80 per week and to provide training opportunities and a fun lifestyle.

Ramblers' Holidays Ltd, PO Box 43, Welwyn Garden City, Herts. AL8 6PQ (01707 331133/fax 01707 333276; mandy@ramblersholidays.co.uk). Tour leaders for programme of walking holidays worldwide. From £440 per month.

Sunsail International, The Port House, Port Solent, Portsmouth, Hants. PO6 4TH (01705 214330). Employs over 600 staff for their flotilla and bareboat sailing holidays and watersports hotels in Greece and Turkey. From March to October, positions are available as flotilla skippers, hostesses, diesel engineers, qualified dinghy, yacht and windsurfing instructors, receptionists, chefs, bar staff and qualified nannies. Wages vary from £180 to £500 a month plus return flights. A knowledge of French or (especially) German is an advantage.

Tall Stories, 67A High St, Walton-on-Thames, Surrey KT12 1DJ (01932 252002/fax 01932 225145; www.tallstories.co.uk). Sports reps (minimum age 22) for adventure holidays in Austria, Spain, France and Corsica.

Village Camps, Dept 820, 14 rue de la Morache, 1260 Nyon, Switzerland (022-990 94 05/fax 022-990 94 94; personnel@villagecamps.ch/ www.villagecamps. com). Recruit 300 staff for their multi activity and language camps for international children during the spring, summer and autumn in Switzerland, Austria, England, France and the Netherlands. Jobs are available for foreign language teachers, sports instructors, general counsellors, nurses, administration staff, domestic and kitchen staff. They also hire 100 ski counsellors and other staff for the winter season in the Swiss Alps. Room and board, accident and liability insurance are provided (plus a ski pass in the winter) as well as an allowance. Staff must be English-speaking, over 21 and have experience working with children.

Any competent sailor, canoeist, diver, climber, rider, etc. should have no difficulty marketing their skills abroad. If you would like to do a watersports course with a view to working abroad, you might be interested in courses offered by Flying Fish (25 Union Road, Cowes, Isle of Wight PO31 7TW; 01983 280641; www. flyingfishonline.com). They offer training as instructors in windsurfing, diving, dinghy sailing and yachting. A typical ten-week course involves three or four weeks of sports training in North Wales or Poole England, followed by a placement (eight weeks on average) in Australia or Greece. Prices vary but a ten-week course would cost about £4,000.

WINTER RESORTS

Ski resort work is by no means confined to the Alps. There are skiing centres from Geilo in Central Norway to Mount Hermon on the Lebanon/Israel border, from the Caucasus to the Cairngorms of Scotland, from the dormant volcanoes of North America to the active ones of New Zealand. If you are such an avid skier that it always depresses you to see the winter snows melt from the European Alps in April, you should consider going to seek work in the Australian and New Zealand Alps or even the Chilean Andes, where the ski season lasts from late June until early October. And there are many ski resorts in North America, in addition to the most famous ones such as Banff in the Canadian Rockies, or Aspen in Colorado.

Winter tourism offers some variations on the usual theme of hotels and catering. Staff are needed to operate the ski tows and lifts, to be in charge of chalets, to patrol the slopes, to file, wax and mend hired skis, to groom and shovel snow, and of course to instruct would-be skiers. The season in the European Alps lasts from about Christmas until late April/early May. Between Christmas and the New Year is a terrifically busy time as is the middle two weeks of February during half-term. If you are lucky you might get a kitchen or dining room job in an establishment which does not serve lunch (since all the guests are out on the slopes). This means that you might have up to six hours free in the middle of the day for skiing, though three to four hours is more usual. However the hours in some large ski resort hotels are the same as in any hotel, i.e. eight to ten hours split up inconveniently throughout the day, and you should be prepared to have only one day off per week for skiing. Because jobs in ski resorts are so popular among the travelling community, wages can be low, though you should get the statutory minimum in Switzerland. Many employees are (or become) avid skiers and in their view it is recompense enough to have easy access to the slopes during their time off.

Either you can try to fix up a job with a British-based ski tour company before you leave (which has more security but lower wages and tends to isolate you in an English-speaking ghetto), or you can look for work on the spot.

Ski Holiday Companies

In the spring preceding the winter season in which you want to work, ask the ski tour companies listed below for an application form. Their literature will describe the range of positions they wish to fill. These may vary slightly from company to company but will probably include resort representatives (who may need language skills), chalet girls (described below), cleaners, qualified cooks, odd jobbers and ski guides/instructors. An increasing number of companies are offering nanny and creche facilities, so this is a further possibility for women and men with a childcare background. Most staff have been hired by mid-June, though there are always a few last minute cancellations.

Here are some of the major UK companies. Some have a limited number of vacancies which they can fill from a list of people who have worked for them during the summer season or have been personally recommended by former employees. So you should not be too disappointed if you are initially unsuccessful.

Inghams Travel, 10-18 Putney Hill, London SW15 6AX (020-8780 8829/fax 020-8780 8805). Hire reps, chalet staff, hostess/cleaners, *plongeurs* and maintenance staff for resorts in France, Italy, Austria, Switzerland, Slovenia and Andorra. Perks include free ski pass, ski and boot hire, meals, accommodation and return travel from the UK.

Crystal Holidays, King's Place, Wood St, Kingston-upon-Thames KT1 1JY (0870 888 0028; recruitment@crystalholidays.co.uk). Jobs in ski resorts in Europe and North America (visa required). Resort reps, chalet staff and qualified nannies for France, Austria and Italy.

Ski Esprit, Oaklands, Reading Road North, Fleet, Hants. GU13 8AA (01252 618318; www.esprit-holidays.co.uk). Resort reps, chalet hosts and nannies for France and Switzerland.

First Choice/Skibound, Olivier House, 18 Marine Parade, Brighton, East Sussex BN2 1TL (0840 900320/fax 01273 600486; jobs@fcski.co.uk). 750 winter staff employed in France, Italy, Austria and Canada.

Handmade Holidays Ltd, The Old Barn, Yew Tree Farm, Thrupp, Nr. Stroud, Glos. GL5 2EF (01453 885599; www.handmade-holidays.co.uk). For resorts in the French and Italian Alps, plus USA and Canada.

Neilson, 29/31 Elmfield Road, Bromley, Kent BR1 1LT (0870 241 2901; skijobs@neilson.co.uk/ www.neilson.co.uk/winter/skiing). Andorra, Austria, Bulgaria, Canada, France and Italy. Website has a section on Recruitment.

PGL Travel Ltd, Ski Department, Alton Court, Penyard Lane, Ross-on-Wye, Herefordshire HR9 5GL (01989 768168). School group operator with rep and snowboard instructor vacancies for 1-3 weeks during peak school holidays. Must be reasonable skier with knowledge of French, Italian or German.

Powder Byrne, 250 Upper Richmond Road, London SW15 6TG (020-8246 5310; www.powderbyrne.com). Upmarket company operating in Switzerland, France, Italy.

Simply Ski, Kings House, Wood St, Kingston upon Thames KT1 1SG (020-8541 2227; personnel@simply-travel.co.uk). Chalet and other staff needed in Austria, France and Switzerland.

Ski Gower, 2 High St, Studley, Warks. B80 7HJ (01527 851420/fax 01527 857236). Reps and evening programme organisers for school trips to Switzerland and Poland.

Ski Total, 3 The Square, Richmond, Surrey TW9 1DY (020-8948 6922; www.skitotal.com). France, Austria, Switzerland and Canada.

Skiworld, 41 North End Road, London W14 8SZ (020-7565 7945; www.skiworld.ltd.uk). Chalet holidays in all the major European and North American resorts.

A couple of specialist recruitment agencies may be of interest: Ski Personnel, Morton House, 29 Throgmorton Rd, Yateley, Hants. GU46 6FA (01252 673707;

www.skistaff.co.uk) and Free Radicals (www.freeradicals.co.uk) which calls itself a one-stop shop for recruitment of winter staff for Europe and North America. A new agency in the field is Ski Recruit (185 Battersea Bridge Road, London SW11 3AS; 020-7924 6292; www.skirecruit.com). Natives.co.uk declares itself to be the 'Season Workers' website where many ski jobs as well as summer jobs are posted before the season (020-8400 3827; www.natives.co.uk). Ski resort staff are needed by many companies so it does no harm to send or e-mail your CV to some such as jobs@skistaff.co.uk or ring 01252 673707 for more information. Meanwhile www.fresh-tracks.com offers tips on how to get a job in a ski resort (www.fresh-tracks.com).

The book *Working in Ski Resorts* (Vacation Work £10.99) contains many addresses of ski companies and details of the job hunt in individual European and North American resorts. In response to the thousands of enquiries about alpine jobs which the Ski Club of Great Britain receives, it distributes *The Alpine Employment Fact Sheet*; send £2 and an s.a.e. to the SCGB, 57-63 Church Rd, Wimbledon SW19 5SB; 020-8410 2000/9; www.skiclub.co.uk). The Club also takes on intermediate skiers over 22 with experience of off-piste skiing to work as ski reps in 33 European resorts. Ski reps work for between one and three months after doing a two-week training course in Tignes (which costs £1,000).

You can find other ski company addresses by consulting ski guide books, magazines and travel agents. Another good idea is to attend the *Daily Mail* Ski Show held each November at Earl's Court in London where some ski companies hand out job descriptions and applications.

Rhona Stannage, a Scottish solicitor, and her husband Stuart applied to all the companies they could find addresses for and ended up working for Skibound:

> *Only one company gave us an interview. No one else would touch us because we were too old (i.e. 28), married and had no experience in the catering trade. Skibound gave us both jobs as chalet girls (yes, Stuart signed a 'chalet girl' contract) working in a four-person chalet with a manageress and a qualified chef. The wages were dire (as expected) but we got free ski passes, accommodation in our own apartment and food. Stuart was a bit worried about the uniform but it was only a purple T-shirt.*

Another way of fixing up a job in advance is to go through the agency Jobs in the Alps (17 High St, Gretton, Northants. NN17 3DE). They recruit a variety of staff for Swiss ski resorts, for which good German or French is usually required. You must arrange to be interviewed by the end of September and be prepared to sign a contract for the whole season, four months in the winter December-April. Wages are £500 a month net for a five-day week. Under the name Alpotels, the agency carries out aptitude tests on behalf of German and French hotels for the winter season; candidates must have EU nationality. There is an agency fee of £30 plus £20 per month of the contract up to a maximum of £110. Enquirers must send an s.a.e.

Applying on the Spot

The best time to look is at the end of the preceding winter season though this has the disadvantage of committing you a long way in advance. The next best time is the first fortnight in September when the summer season is finishing and there are still plenty of foreign workers around who will have helpful advice. The final possibility is to turn up in the month before the season begins when you will be faced with many refusals. In November you will be told you're too early because everything's closed, in December you're too late because all the jobs are spoken for. Some disappointed job-seekers reckon there must be a 24-hour window between these two, and if you miss it, you're out of luck.

Assuming you can afford to finance yourself for several weeks, arrive as early as you can (say early November) so that you can get to know people and let them get to know your face. Weekends are better than weekdays since more shops and other tourist establishments will be open. Apply directly to hotels, equipment rental agencies, tourist offices, etc. It is also an idea to travel to the ski resorts out of season to look for work repairing or redecorating ski chalets, for instance, and then move on to a ski tow or bar job once the season begins. If you miss out on landing a job before the season, it could be worth trying again in early January, since workers tend to disappear after the holidays.

The people who do succeed on the spot claim that it is easy and the people who fail claim that it is an impossibility. Every negative experience (see chapter on Switzerland for example) is counter-balanced by others like Mary Jelliffe's account of opportunities in the French resort of Méribel:

> At the beginning of the season there were many 'ski bums' looking for work in Méribel. Many found something. People earned money by clearing snow, cleaning, babysitting, etc. for which they were paid about F30 an hour. You do need some money to support yourself while looking for work but if you are determined enough, I'm sure you'll get something eventually. One group of ski bums organised a weekly slalom race from which they were able to make a living. Another set up a video service; another made and sold boxer shorts for F100 a pair.

Andy Winwood asked in over 200 places in Crans Montana, Verbier and Haute-Nendaz and came up with 10 or 12 possibilities. When he finally heard the magic words, 'You can start on December 15th', he rushed outside, let out a whoop of delight and headed for the nearest bar.

Chalet Staff

The number of chalets in the Alps has hugely increased over the past decade with the biggest areas of expansion being Méribel, Courchevel and Val d'Isère in France, Verbier in Switzerland and St Anton in Austria. Chalet clients in chalets are looked after by a chalet girl or (increasingly) chalet boy. The chalet host does everything (sometimes with an assistant) from cooking first-class meals for the ten or so guests to clearing the snow from the footpath (or delegating that job). She is responsible for keeping the chalet clean, preparing breakfast, packed lunches, tea and dinner, providing ice and advice, and generally keeping everybody happy. Fifteen-hour days are standard.

Although this sounds an impossible regimen, many chalet girls manage to fit in several hours of skiing in the middle of each day. The standards of cookery skills required vary from company to company depending on the degree of luxury (i.e. the price) of the holidays. Whereas some advertise good homecooking, others offer cordon bleu cookery every night of the week (except the one night which the chalet girl has off). In most cases, you will have to cook a trial meal for the tour company before being accepted for the job or at least submit detailed menu plans.

Pandora Balchin, who got a job as a chalet maid on the strength of her catering degree, described her job this way:

> It was a fantastic experience though it was very hard work. Although I had never skied before I went to Méribel, I have to admit that I am now completely hooked, as are all the others who worked there. The spirit of comradeship in the resort was amazing, and also typical of other resorts I'm told.

Average pay starts at about £75 a week, plus perks. Obviously your accommodation and food are free. Also you should get a season's ticket to the slopes and lifts (called an *abonnement* and worth several hundred pounds), free ski hire and free travel from the UK. Recruitment of the 1,000+ chalet staff needed in Europe gets underway in May so early application is essential.

Ski Instructors

To become a fully-fledged ski instructor, qualified to work in foreign ski schools, costs a great deal of money (at least £2,000) and then competition is extremely stiff for jobs in recognised alpine ski schools. In France and to a lesser extent Italy there has been a great deal of resistance to foreign instructors, though banning them from the slopes has repeatedly been ruled illegal by the EU. Freelance or 'black' instructors – those who tout in bars offering a few hours of instruction in return for pocket money – are persecuted by the authorities in most alpine resorts. The main legitimate opportunities for British skiers without paper qualifications are as instructors for school parties or as ski guides/ski rangers.

David Robinson got an instructor's job over Easter with a company that sends 4,000 school children to Swiss and Italian resorts each winter. He found the responsibility rather nerve-racking at first since, on his first run, a beginner broke his leg and had to be rescued by helicopter. Soon after that he led a group of intermediate skiers down a hill he hadn't had a chance to explore himself and it was considerably harder than the standard they had achieved; but as it happened there was no mishap and they all found it very exhilarating. Being a ski instructor is not all swooping down slopes past pretty girls and eager students. Groups of children can be tiresome to instruct, emergencies can arise and the job can be exhausting. But it still remains one of the most enjoyable and rewarding seasonal jobs you can hope to get abroad.

If you are interested in qualifying as an instructor, contact the British Association of Snowsport Instructors or BASI (Glenmore, Aviemore, Inverness-shire PH22 1QU; 01479 861717; www.basi.org.uk). BASI runs training and grading courses throughout the year and also publishes a Newsletter in which job adverts appear. The most junior instructor's qualification is a Grade III which is awarded by BASI after a five-day foundation course following a two-week training course on the Continent or in Scotland. Courses take place throughout the season and also on the glacier in the summer. BASI also run courses in five disciplines: alpine skiing, snowboarding (which is gaining enormous popularity), Telemark, Nordic and Adaptive. Most instructors teach from two to six hours a day depending on demand. Pay can start from as little as £150 a week, though this often includes accommodation. Some participation in the evening entertainments is expected. It is of course much easier for Ski Teachers (Grade II) and National Ski Teachers (Grade I) to find lucrative work in Europe or beyond.

Ski Resorts Worldwide

In conclusion, there are plenty of jobs in ski resorts au pairing, cooking, guiding, selling, cleaning and so on. If you do end up in a resort looking for a job, try the ski equipment hire shops which may offer you very short term work on change-over days when lots of skis need prompt attention, or the ski-lift offices preferably in the autumn. You might even find that the tourist office in the big resorts like Zermatt and Val d'Isère may be able to help. Outside the EU you will encounter work permit difficulties (details in individual country chapters), though when there is a labour shortage, there is usually a way round the difficulties. Unfortunately labour shortages these days are becoming rarer and the drifting population looking for jobs in ski resorts can be much greater in one area than the number of jobs available. You should therefore try as hard as you can to sign a contract ahead of time, or failing this, be prepared to move around to less popular areas to find work.

For a thorough list of ski resorts in Europe, consult the annually revised *Good Skiing & Snowboarding Guide*. Some major ski resorts are listed below.

Ski resorts around the world

France	*Switzerland*	*Austria*	*Italy*
Chamonix	Davos	Kitzbühel	Cortina d'Ampezzo
Les Contamines	St. Moritz	Söll	Courmayeur
Val d'Isère	Zermatt	Lech	Sestriere
Courchevel	Gstaad	Badgastein	Bormio
Méribel	Champery	St.Anton	Campitello
St. Christoph	Saas Grund	Mayrhofen	Canazei
Flaine	Wengen & Mürren	Lermoos	Livigno
Avoriaz	Crans-Montana	Alpbach	Abetone
Les Arcs	Kandersteg	Brand	Folgarida
La Plagne	Adelboden	Kirchberg	Forni di Sopra
Tignes	Verbier	St. Johann	Sauze d'Oulx
Montgenèvre	Grindelwald	Solden	Asiago
	Arosa	Obergurgl	S. Stefano di Cadore
	Saas Fee	Zell am See	Alleghi

Spain	*Germany*	*Norway*	*Scotland*
Sol y Nieve	Garmisch-	Voss	Aviemore
Formigal	Partenkirchen	Geilo	Glenshee (Glenisla)
Cerler	Oberstdorf	Telemark	Carrbridge
	Berchtesgaden	Lillehammer	Glencoe
Andorra		Gausdal	
Arinsal		Synnfjell	
Soldeu			

New Zealand	*Australia*	*Canada*	*USA*
Queenstown	FallsCreek (VIC)	Banff	Aspen, Colorado
Coronet Peak	Mount Hotham	Lake Louise	Copper Mountain
Mount Hutt	Mount Buffalo	Waterton	Steamboat Springs
Mount Ruapehu	Baw Baw	Ottawa	Vail
	Mount Buller	Huntsville	Winter Park
	Thredbo (NSW)	Collingwood	Alpine Meadows, Calif.
	Perisher	Barrie	Lake Tahoe
	Mount Field (Tas)		Mount Batchelor,
	Ben Lomond		Oregon
			Mount Hood
			Timberline
			Park City, Utah
			Sun Valley, Idaho
			Jackson Hole, Wyoming
			Sugar Mt. Resort, NC
			Waterville Valley, NH
			Stowe, Vermont
			Sugarbush Valley
			Dore Mountain, NY

AGRICULTURE

HARVESTING

Historically, agricultural harvests have employed the greatest number of casual workers. Itinerant workers have traditionally travelled hundreds of miles to gather in the fruits of the land, from the tiny blueberry to the mighty watermelon. It might even be possible to pick your way around the world, by following the seasons and the ripening crops. The old-style gypsies, who roamed over Europe picking fruit as they went, have been joined both by nomadic young people and large numbers of East Europeans looking to earn western wages.

The well organised picker in Europe might find himself starting the year in Britain, picking mundane vegetables like cabbages and potatoes. He then moves on to strawberries and gooseberries in June, cherries, currants and raspberries in July, apples and plums in August and then on to choosing between the Kentish hop harvest in September or grape-picking in France. He could follow the *vendange* (grape harvest) north and then into Germany where grapes are picked into November, back to France for the chestnut harvest in late November and December. Tiring at last of the cold northern climate, our itinerant picker could flee south to pick oranges on the Greek Peloponnese.

Furthermore, living and working in rural areas is a more authentic way of experiencing an alien culture compared to working in tourism. It is easy to see why farms, vineyards and orchards play such a large part in the chapters which follow, since harvests provide so much scope for people working their way around the world. No serious self-funding traveller can afford to ignore the employment opportunities available at harvest time. When Gerhard Flaig was in New Zealand, he dedicated himself to the task of building up his travelling fund by accepting the hardest picking job of the three he was offered:

I chose the squash packing job because it offered the highest wages, but it was bloody tough. Almost every day I had to move about 15,000 squash, which is about 25 tons of squash. After my season, which lasted about 14 weeks, I had moved more than one million single squash. I suffered from cuts and muscle strain. Very often I thought of giving up but the good wages kept me going. Now I am very proud that I could manage this tough job. And it was mainly this job that covered more than half of all the costs of my journey around the world.

Although the problem of work permits does dog the footsteps of fruit pickers abroad, there is always a good chance that the urgency of the farmers' needs will overrule the impulse to follow the regulations. But if you do end up picking fruit without a permit, it is best to keep a low profile in the village pub. Even locals who would not consider doing this kind of work might feel jealous of the imagined fortune you're earning while they are unemployed.

The availability of harvesting work in Europe has been greatly reduced by the large numbers of Slovaks, Poles, Albanians, etc. now roaming every corner of Europe trying to earn the money their own struggling economies cannot provide. Often a certain amount of hostility exists between these economic migrants and working travellers, primarily because farmers have been dropping wages as a result of the new competition for jobs, and because impoverished Easterners will accept below-par wages.

Where to look for work

Once you have arrived in the right area at the right time of year, the next step is to find out which farmers are short of help. Asking in the youth hostel or campsite and in the local pub is often successful, though not always; Jon Loop says this is great for people who are good at meeting prospective employers in pubs, unlike him who just gets drunk and falls over. The great advantage of job-hunting in rural areas rather then in cities is that people are more likely to know their neighbours' labour requirements and often are more sympathetic and helpful in their attitudes. Adam Cook interrupted a cycling tour of the South of France to look for fruit-picking work:

> *Faced with having to decide between hurrying north to catch up with the cherries and going south to meet the first peaches, I decided to go south. It took ten good days of asking everywhere, cafés, bars, post offices, grocery shops – one of the best places I found to look as the owners very often know who is picking what and where.*

If the word of mouth technique does not work at first, you will have to visit farmers personally. Since they will be generally working out of doors it is not difficult to approach them. Farm hands and people already picking in the fields will be able to offer advice as well. If farms are widely scattered, you may have to consider hiring or borrowing a bicycle, moped or car for a day of concentrated job-hunting.

Alternatively you might be able to get a list of farms and ring around. Farm co-operatives can be useful sources of this kind of information. Local newspapers may carry advertisements for pick-your-own farms or roadside fruit stands which may provide a job or at least a lead. If there is a weekly market or co-operative at which local farmers sell their produce, this is an ideal venue for job-hunting. Even if you don't find a farmer looking for pickers, they may need people to unload the lorries or man the market stall. They may also hold an auction and it may be possible to broadcast your request for work over the public address system, auctioning yourself off to the highest bidder as it were. If you are with several friends, you may find that it is difficult to find a farmer willing to offer work to all of you. You may then be able to work out a job-sharing arrangement, although this is more likely to be acceptable to the farmer if accommodation is not his responsibility.

It may not be necessary to approach farmers directly if you can fix up a harvesting job through the district employment office. In some countries, there is a special branch of the national employment service which deals exclusively with agricultural vacancies, such as the Agricultural Employment Services of Canada and the cantonal offices of Landdienst (agricultural service) in Switzerland.

One of the job-seeker's best allies is a very detailed map. Helpful locals can then point out their suggestions on a map rather than give verbal instructions (possibly in a language you barely know). An excellent reference book for prospective grape-pickers is Hugh Johnson's *World Atlas of Wine* (published by Mitchell Beazley) which includes splendidly detailed maps of wine-producing regions from Corsica to California. It is of course much too heavy and expensive (£30) to carry around, though you could perhaps take a few good photocopies of the regions you plan to try. Alternatively, get a list of vineyards from the regional tourist offices and write to (or visit) the proprietors, asking for work.

Mechanisation

Although harvesting techniques have become increasingly mechanised, human toil continues to play a large part. The recent mechanisation of the hop harvest for example has made a dramatic difference and yet a large number of helpers are still needed for various ancillary jobs. Although more and more vineyards are employing mechanical harvesters, often the rows of vines are too close together or on too steep a gradient for the machines to be of use. There are cherry-picking machines which work by shaking the fruit off the trees; these not only leave the fruit damaged but also loosen the roots and in the long run destroy the trees. Despite advances in agricultural technology, there is no immediate danger of humans being replaced altogether. That being said, it certainly can't hurt to go abroad with some tractor-driving experience.

One job which can't be done by machinery is selective picking. There are not many fruits and vegetables which ripen all at once. Pickers soon develop the ability to spot the lettuces, cauliflowers or strawberries that are ready and leave the rest for a later onslaught. Sometimes the process of selection becomes quite complicated if you are expected to sort the size and quality of the produce as you proceed; for example pickers must sometimes drop apples through a wire loop to determine the size.

Technique

Picking fruit may not be as easy as it sounds. For many people, their only experience of fruit picking may have been on family outings to an orchard where most of the time was spent in tree-climbing or sibling-bombardment exploits. Picking fruit for your living will not be so idyllic. If you are part of a large team you may be expected to work at the same speed as the most experienced picker, which can be both exhausting and discouraging.

Having a little experience can make the whole business more enjoyable, not to mention more financially worthwhile if you are being paid piece work rates. The vast majority of picking jobs are paid piece work (with the notable exception of grape harvests in Europe), though a minimum level of productivity will be expected, particularly if you are being given room and board.

Try not to feel too discouraged at the end of the first day or even the first week of working in an orchard when you see that some old hands have picked three times as much as you. When Andrew Walford was tempted to feel envious of the people who could fill seven or eight bins of apples a day in Shepparton Australia, he consoled himself that, even if his record was only five, at least he wasn't as eccentric as they were. Rather than succumb to feelings of inferiority, watch their technique closely. Ask their advice about where to place the ladder, since moving a ladder can be time-consuming. (Note that this is not a job for anyone who suffers from vertigo.) After a week or two your confidence and your earnings will certainly have increased. Once you learn how to snap strawberries off with a quick twist of the wrist (leaving the floret intact) you will be surprised at how your speed improves. In the case of other fruits, shaking trees to dislodge fruit is almost always frowned upon by employers, though this does not prevent some pickers from resorting to it. There may even be scouts in large orchards patrolling in order to prevent this practice.

It is not merely technique which separates the professionals from the amateurs, but fitness as well. Richard Walford interrupted a cycling trip along the Rhine to pick grapes for a few weeks, and assumed that all his cycling would have prepared him for the work. He soon learned however that grape-picking uses different muscles entirely and he found the first few days gruelling. It would be taking things too far to recommend back-strengthening exercises before setting off on your world travels, but at least you should be warned that the first few days of picking can be an unwelcome reminder of your physical limitations.

There are often external limitations to the amount you can earn. Sometimes picking is called off in bad weather. Sometimes you are forced to take some days off while the next crop ripens fully or because the price on the market has dropped. Be prepared to amuse (and finance) yourself on idle days.

Some farmers prefer to hire men if the work is particularly taxing or if a lot of lifting is involved. But there are few actual picking jobs which women can't do equally well. Agility is often more important than strength and for some soft fruits, female pickers are preferred because they are assumed to have a gentler touch. If the fruit is very delicate, beginners are sometimes paid an hourly rate to discourage careless and damaging picking.

Informal competitions can enliven the tedium. Alan Corrie describes his fellow tomato-picker on a farm near Auch in the Gascony region of southern France, with undisguised admiration:

In August I was taken on by a farmer to join his contracted Moroccan worker picking tomatoes. This is paid by the crate, and iron discipline and single-minded determination are needed to breach the fifty crates barrier per ten-hour day, and get in amongst the good earnings. When my first half century had been verified, I was punching the air in triumphant salute. The next day, toying with extremis, fifty-three was achieved, and I had the distinct feeling while unloading at the depot that the workers there nudging one another and confiding 'c'est lui, mon dieu, comme une tempête dans les tomates!'

Ahmed, meanwhile, was touching seventy crates a day. Any day now, I reasoned, we'd be on a par, sending the boss off to buy a calculator and to order extra crates. This was not to be however. I had peaked. Desperation set in; the crates were becoming bigger, tomatoes always lying awkwardly, the heat blistering; I began to flounder, drained and dejected in the low forties. My colleague when I last asked him was turning in a cool eighty a day, which if you knew anything about tomato picking I would not ask you to believe. You would have to see it for yourself. I'm thinking of giving guided tours of the scene of his campaign for knowing seasonal workers and afficionados: 'Yup,' I'll nod my head – greyhaired as it now is after the experience – in the direction of a little altar-like structure, 'I was there, seen it wi' m'own eyes. I swear it, them little rascals wuz up'n jumpin' in that thaar bucket of his.' Anyway, good luck to him. It was with some relief that I was transferred to the shady plum groves across the road.

Equipment

During August in the South of France the only equipment you'll need is a sun hat. But if you are planning to pick apples in British Columbia or olives in the Greek winter, you will need warm clothing, waterproofs and possibly also rubber boots for muddy fields. When packing for your intercontinental fruit picking holiday, it might be an idea to pack a sturdy pair of gardening gloves for frosty mornings. Gloves can also be useful if you are picking fruit which has been sprayed with an insecticide that irritates cuts or stains your hands an unsightly colour. If it is too awkward to pick wearing gloves, you can tape up your hands with surgical tape to prevent blistering.

In each country chapter, we have dealt with the possibilities for willing and well-prepared pickers. Wherever possible we have included tables of crop locations and harvesting dates, so that you will know which specific areas to head for. This information can be more easily assimilated by examining the symbols on the sketch maps which should be used in conjunction with detailed country and regional maps.

FARMING

Not all casual work in rural areas revolves around fruit and vegetable harvests. There are a lot of miscellaneous seasonal jobs created by the agricultural industry, from castrating maize to crutching sheep, from scaring birds away from cherry orchards to herding goats (something which seems to reduce most novices to tears), from weeding olive groves to spraying banana plantations. There is always the chance of work if you knock on farmers' doors. Every working traveller ought to be able to turn his hand to the basic tasks of pruning, planting and harvesting.

Many farms, especially in Europe, are relatively small family-run businesses, and the farmer may not need to look any further than his own family for labour. But often farmers are looking for one able-bodied assistant over the summer months, and if you are fortunate to be that one, you will probably be treated as a member of the family, sharing their meals and their outings. It is more important to be able to communicate with the farmer than if you are hired as a fruit picker, since the instructions given to farm hands are more complicated. It also helps to have some tractor-driving or other farm experience or at least an aptitude for machinery.

Whereas picking a given crop can quickly become tedious, working as a general assistant provides much more variety as Ed Peters describes, based on his experience of working in mainland Greece:

The work ranged from langorous to arduous – scattering chemical fertiliser, picking up wood, digging shallow ditches for water pipes, supervising irrigation (a sinecure if ever there was one) and spraying weed killer from ten litre containers on your back (murderous!).

But even if the work you are given is tedious, this might be exactly what you want, as was the case with Joseph Tame who spent a few weeks working on an organic farm in Switzerland in spring 2000 while waiting for his visa to come through for a summer job in a Swiss hotel:

> *The type of work can at times be tremendously repetitive (such as the four hours a day every day spent scraping cow shit from the yard!). Yet in this repetitiveness you have a freedom, a freedom of the mind that enables you to mull over any thoughts or feelings that in England would be swept aside by the stress of everyday life. Here I have all the time in the world; and in this world, time is not money.*

Advertising

Placing an advert in the national farmers' journal is especially worthwhile for people who have had some relevant experience. Gary Tennant placed the following advert in the Danish farmers' weekly *Landsbladet*:

> *23 year old Englishman now in Denmark would like farm work. Have been working on a kibbutz (4 months) in the fields and tractor work. Just finished gardening work in England and want to try different farming. Telephone 06191679, ask for Gary.*

Although he started his job hunt in the autumn (the worst time of year), he received four offers. An Englishwoman he met who had experience of dairy farming received 11 offers from such an advert.

Targeting small rural newspapers can also pay dividends partly because it will almost certainly be a novelty. Ken Smith noticed a small ad in the *Oamaru Mail* in New Zealand: 'Young German man seeks farm work. Has tractor experience and good work habits.'

Range of Opportunities

Many long-term itinerant workers meet up with people who are interested in alternative lifestyles which may include organic farming or goat cheese production as a way of earning a living. In rural areas, a polite request for room and board in exchange for half a day's work often succeeds. The 'small is beautiful' philosophy may mean that smallholders will not be able to pay wages, but this can be a congenial way to pass some time, as Rob Abblett has done all over the world from Mexico to Malawi, Sweden to Salt Spring Island, Canada. He simply gathers lists of contacts from organisations like the ones listed in this section and gets in touch with the ones that sound appealing:

> *I've visited, worked and had many varied experiences on over 30 communes around the world. I like them because they are so varied and full of interesting people, usually with alternative ideas, beliefs, but also because I almost always find someone that I can really connect with, for sometimes I need to be with like-minded folk.*

Other jobs in agriculture require experience and skill. Although shearing itself is a skilled job, there are lots of other associated jobs, from skirting the fleece to baling the wool to cooking for the extra hands. Commercial flower production often provides opportunities in the greenhouses, transplanting, picking and packing. For the seasonal worker, the most famous is the bulb and flower industry of Holland. But we have heard of jobs in flower nurseries in Helsinki, Israel, Crete, South Island of New Zealand and Vancouver Island as well.

Occasionally the specialist press (like *Farmers Weekly* published Fridays) contains advertisements for jobs abroad. Tree nurseries are often a good source of casual work and in some countries (especially Canada) tree planting is a job often done by nomadic types. A few specialist agencies in agricultural or forestry work exist (like FTS in Dublin, mentioned in the chapters on the Netherlands and Germany). If you do find a job through an agency do not rely exclusively on the agency's information. It is better (if possible) to talk to your future employer direct to avoid the fate which befell Lee Morton when he was placed as a trainee groom in California: the employer was so demanding that he left the day after he arrived.

Equestrian Work
Experienced grooms, riding instructors and stable staff may consider registering with A World of Experience Equestrian Employment Agency (52 Kingston Deverill, Warminster, Wilts. BA12 7HF; 01985 844102). For people with relevant experience, they have vacancies in 20 countries in Europe and worldwide which pay between £100 and £200 a week plus free accommodation for an 8-12 hour day. All employers are English-speaking.

Other agencies advertise in the specialist press, for example *Horse & Hound*. Stable staff and lightweight riders are needed for work on studs and in racing establishments around the world. Check the situations vacant columns in *The Sporting Life* and *Racing Post*. An equestrian centre in Scotland (Hayfield International, Hazlehead Park, Aberdeen AB15 8BB) has set up a web-site called EquiWorld (www.equiworld.net) which is linked to 6,000 other equestrian websites worldwide and provides a way for people looking for equestrian work to locate potential employers. A search for employment listings will turn up a few vacancies and agencies. One is the White Horse Agency (9 Chapel St, Stonebroom, Nr. Alfreton, Derbyshire DE55 6JX; 01773 873299; www.equusuk.co.uk) which claims to have international jobs, though mainly features UK vacancies.

For further leads, have a look at the book *Working with Animals: UK, Europe & Worldwide* by Victoria Pybus (Vacation-Work, £11.95).

Gaining Experience
Without any formal training in agriculture, it is possible to get some preliminary experience. Many European countries have programmes whereby young people spend a month or two assisting on a farm, e.g. Norway and Switzerland. A farming background is not necessary for participating in these schemes, though of course it always helps. Israeli kibbutzim often give their volunteers exposure to a range of farming jobs. You might like to get an initial taste of farm life by having a 'farm holiday'. Rural tourism is gaining popularity and the tourist organisations of countries like Italy and New Zealand encourage tourists to take a holiday on a working farm and participate in the daily round of activities to whatever extent they like. You then have the chance not only of having a relatively inexpensive and interesting holiday, but also of learning a little about hay-baling, cheese-making and so on.

It is not impossible to find work on farms and ranches which have diversified to accept paying visitors. This has been particularly popular in the United States (where guest ranches are called 'dude ranches') and Australia. These establishments need both domestic and outdoor assistants to lead guests on trail rides, show them places or events of local interest, etc. Tourist organisations can provide lists of guest ranches.

Organic Farms
With growing fears of genetically modified foods, the organic farming movement is attracting more and more of a following around the world, from Tonbridge to Togo. A headline in the *Independent* last year read 'One in six farms to go organic within decade'. Organic farms everywhere take on volunteers to help them minimise or abolish the use of chemicals and heavy machinery. There are various co-ordinating bodies, many of which go under the name of WWOOF (Willing Workers on Organic Farms). WWOOF has a global website www.wwoof.org with links to the national offices in the countries that have a WWOOF co-ordinator (known as WWOOF Independents) and individual farm listings in countries with no national organisation. It is necessary to join WWOOF before you can obtain addresses of these properties.

National WWOOF co-ordinators compile and sell a worklist of their member farmers willing to provide free room and board to volunteers who help out and who are genuinely interested in furthering the aims of the organic movement. Each national group has its own aims, system, fees and rules but most expect applicants to have gained some experience on an organic farm in their own country first. WWOOF is an exchange: in return for your help on organic farms, gardens and homesteads, you receive meals, a place to sleep and a practical insight into organic growing. (If the topic arises at immigration, avoid the word 'working'; it is preferable to present yourself as a student of organic farming organising an educational farm visit or a cultural exchange.)

Mike Tunnicliffe joined the long-established WWOOF New Zealand to avoid work permit hassles and his experience is typical of WWOOFers' in other countries:

My second choice of farm was a marvellous experience. For 15 days I earned no money but neither did I spend any, and I enjoyed life on the farm as part of the family. There is a wide variety of WWOOF farms and I thoroughly recommend the scheme to anyone who isn't desperate to earn money.

If you are starting in Britain, send an s.a.e. to the UK branch of WWOOF (PO Box 2675, Lewes, Sussex BN7 1RB) who will send you a membership application form. Membership costs £15 per year and includes a subscription to their bi-monthly newsletter which contains small adverts for opportunities both in Britain and abroad.

The active Australian branch of WWOOF publishes its own *Worldwide List* of farms and volunteer work opportunities in those countries with no national WWOOF group. This is a marvellous resource which can be obtained by sending A\$22/£10/US\$20 to WWOOF, Mt Murrindal Co-operative, Buchan, Vic 3885, Australia; +61-3-5155 0218/fax 3-5155 0342; wwoof@net-tech.com.au/ www.wwoof.com.au. Organic farm organisations are mentioned in the following chapters of this book: UK, Ireland, Denmark, Finland, Norway, Germany, Italy, Japan, Sweden, Switzerland, Austria, Hungary, Australia, New Zealand, USA, Canada, Ghana and Togo.

Many communities (what used to be called communes) welcome foreign visitors and willingly exchange hospitality for work. Although not all the work is agricultural, much of it is. The details and possible fees must be established on a case-by-case basis. The following resources are relevant:

Diggers and Dreamers: The Guide to Co-operative Living published by Edge of Time, BCM Edge, London WC1N 3XX (0800 083 0451; www.edgeoftime.co.uk). Primarily a book about UK communities but contains details of about 140 contacts abroad. A new edition is published every other autumn: the 2000/2001 edition costs £10 plus £1.50 UK postage.

Communities, 138 Twin Oaks Road, Louisa, VA 23093, USA (540-894-5798; order@ic.org/ www.ic.org). In 2000, a new edition of the *Communities Directory: A Guide to Co-operative Living* was published; price US\$34 (\$38 overseas by surface post). It lists about 600 communities in the US and about 100 abroad including 'ecovillages, rural land trusts, co-housing groups, kibbutzim, student co-ops, organic farms, monasteries, urban artist collectives, rural communes and Catholic Worker houses'. Annual updates are sold as supplements for \$5 (\$8 overseas). Some country-by-country listings are posted on their website.

Global Ecovillage Network, European office, Via Torri Superiore 5, 18039 Ventimiglia (+39 0184-215504/fax 0184-215914; info@gen-europe.org/ www.gaia.org). Setting up the Network for Eco-worker Travellers (NEWT), similar to the WWOOF exchange. Contact organisers Peter and Chrystina Bemment for details (PO Box 2043, Bellingham, WA 98227; ChrysD@aol.com).

TERN (Travellers Earth Repair Network), Friends of the Trees Society, PO Box 4469, Bellingham, WA 98227, USA (360-724-0503/fax 360-671-9668; www.geocities.com/RainForest/4663/tern.html). Lists of potential hosts (total on database is 3,500 in 100 countries) for travellers interested in sustainable agriculture and forestry. Write for application. Fee of \$50 (\$35 for students) entitles you to request maximum of ten country or regional lists.

Before arranging a longish stay on an organic farm, consider whether or not you will find such an environment congenial. Many organic farmers are non-smoking vegetarians and living conditions may be primitive by some people's standards. Although positive experiences are typical, Craig Ashworth expressed reservations about WWOOF, based on his experiences in New Zealand, and claims that a proportion of WWOOF hosts are 'quite wacky'. (See Danish chapter for a first-hand account of total incompatibility in this context.) Bear in mind that the work you are given to do may not always be very salubrious: for example Armin Birrer, who has spent time on organic farms in many countries, claims that the weirdest job he ever did was to spend a day in New Zealand picking worms out of a pile of rabbit dung to be used to soften the soil around some melon plants.

Agricultural Exchanges

There are opportunities worldwide for young people aged between 18 and 30 who have good practical farming experience. Agriventure (run by the International Agricultural Exchange Association) arranges placements for British and European participants in the USA, Canada, Australia, New Zealand and Japan. Placements in the USA and Canada begin in February, March and April and last for seven or nine months. Placements for Australia and New Zealand begin in April, May, July, August and September and last for six to nine months. Placements in Japan begin in April and last four to twelve months. There are also several round-the-world itineraries which depart in the autumn to the southern hemisphere for six to seven months followed by another six to seven months in the northern hemisphere.

These programmes cost participants between £1,725 and £4,100 but trainees are then paid a realistic wage. Included in the cost is a pre-departure information meeting, airline tickets, visas, insurance, stopover (if applicable), orientation seminar and board and lodging throughout with a host family. UK and Eire participants should contact Agriventure, IAEA, YFC Centre, National Agricultural Centre, Stoneleigh Park, Kenilworth, Warwickshire CV8 2LG; freephone 0800 783 2186 or 02476 696578/fax 02476 696684; uk@agriventure.com for a brochure; or check the website www.agriventure.com). Mainland European applicants should contact: Agriventure, IAEA, Lerchenbörg Gods, 4400 Kalundborg, Denmark (+45 59 51 15 25; europe@agriventure.com).

North American agriculturalists are also eligible for the programmes in Europe (excluding the UK), Japan, New Zealand and Australia. US applicants should contact IAEA at 1000 1st Avenue South, Great Falls, Montana 59401 (1-800-272-4996; usa@agriventure.com); and Canadian applicants can write to Agriventure, IAEA, No. 105, 7710-5 Street SE, Calgary, Alberta T2H 2L9 (canada@agriventure.com). Another organisation that arranges agricultural exchanges for Americans is Communicating for Agriculture (112 East Lincoln Ave, Fergus Falls, MN 56537; 218-739-3241; http://ca.cainc.org) which makes placements in agriculture, horticulture, equine or oenology in 23 countries from the Baltics to Argentina. Future Farmers of America runs a World Experience in Agriculture Programme (National FFA Center, 6060 FFA Drive, PO Box 68960, Indianapolis, IN 46268-0999; 317-802-6060; www.ffa.org/international/index.html) for which candidates must be aged 18-24 for Europe and 19-24 for Australia/New Zealand, with previous experience in dairy, livestock, crops, horticulture, greenhouses, soils or fruit/vegetables.

The International Farm Experience Programme, YFC Centre, Stoneleigh Park, Kenilworth, Warwickshire CV8 2LG (02476 857211/fax 02476 857229; ifep@nfyfc.org.uk) is administered by the National Federation of Young Farmers Clubs. The programme offers a wide range of practical training placements in agriculture, horticulture, equine studies and agri-tourism in Europe, USA, Canada, Australia, New Zealand and South Africa. Applicants must be between 18 and 30 with experience relevant to the type of placement requested, normally two years in the industry. Assistance is given with travel, health, visa requirements, insurance and orientation. Placements last 3-6 months in Europe, 6-12 months in the rest of the world. Board and lodging and a basic wage are provided. The programme includes language study options for Europe or university study in the USA. IFEP has a partner office in 25 countries providing support throughout your stay.

TEACHING ENGLISH

This chapter used to begin with a quotation from a traveller-turned-professional-EFL-teacher, Dick Bird:

It is extremely difficult for anyone whose mother tongue is English to starve in an inhabited place, since there are always people who will pay good money to watch you display a talent as basic as talking. Throughout the world, native speakers of English are at a premium.

But this rosy view of the traveller's prospects must now be moderated somewhat. Although the English language is still the language which literally millions of people around the world want to learn, finding work as an English teacher is not as easy as many people assume. Furthermore there is a worrying trend even for people with a qualification to have difficulty. The number of both public and private institutes turning out certified TEFL teachers has greatly increased in the past five years, creating a glut of teachers all chasing the same jobs, especially in the major cities of Europe.

Having sounded that warning note, it must be said that there are still areas of the world where the boom in English language learning seems to know no bounds, from Ecuador to China, the Ukraine to Vietnam. In cowboy schools and back-street agencies, being a native speaker and dressing neatly are sometimes sufficient qualifications to get a job. But for more stable teaching jobs in recognised language schools, you will have to sign a contract (minimum three months, usually nine) and have some kind of qualification which ranges from a university degree to a certificate in education with a specialisation in Teaching English as a Foreign Language (known as TEFL, pronounced 'teffle'). This chapter covers both possibilities.

One of the best sources of information about the whole topic of English teaching (if I may be permitted to say so) is the 2001 edition of *Teaching English Abroad* by Susan Griffith (Vacation-Work, £12.95). This chapter can only provide the most general introduction to such topics as TEFL training and commercial recruitment agencies; for specific information about individual countries, see the country chapters.

TEFL Training

The only way to outrival the competition and make the job-hunt (not to mention the job itself) easier is to do a TEFL course. If interested, write to the English Information Centre of the British Council (Bridgewater House, 58 Whitworth St, Mancheser M1 6BB; 0161-957 7755) for an information sheet 'How to Become a Teacher of EFL' and a list of approved Certificate centres.

There are two standard recognised qualifications that will improve your range of job options by an order of magnitude. The best known is the Cambridge Certificate in English Language Teaching to Adults (CELTA) administered and awarded by the University of Cambridge Local Examinations Syndicate (UCLES TEFL Unit, 1 Hills Road, Cambridge CB1 2EU; 01223 553355; efl@ucles.org.uk/ www.cambridge-efl.org.uk). The other is the Certificate in TESOL (Teaching English to Speakers of Other Languages) offered by Trinity College London, 89 Albert Embankment, London SE1 7TP (020-7820 6100/fax 020-7820 6161; tesol@trinitycollege.co.uk/ www.trinitycollege.co.uk). Both are very intensive and expensive, averaging £850-£950. These courses involve at least 100 hours of rigorous training with a practical emphasis (full-time for four weeks or part-time over several months). Although there are no fixed pre-requisites apart from a suitable level of language awareness, not everyone who applies is accepted.

A list of the several hundred centres both in the UK and abroad offering the Cambridge Certificate course in Britain and abroad is available from UCLES in exchange for a large s.a.e. Here is a small selection:
Basil Paterson Edinburgh Language Foundation, Dugdale-McAdam House, 22/23

Abercromby Place, Edinburgh EH3 6QE (0131-556 7696; www.basilpaterson.co.uk). 8 courses per year; £999.

Frances King Teacher Training, 5 Grosvenor Gardens, Victoria, London SW1W 0BD (020-7630 8055; www.francesking.co.uk/teachertraining). £799. Jobs noticeboard and contact with a range of employers/agencies.

Hammersmith & West London College, Gliddon Road, London W14 9BL (020-8563 0063; www.hwlc.ac.uk. £695.

International House, 106 Piccadilly, London W1V 9FL (020-7491 2598). Has several sister centres in Hastings and Newcastle. Certificate course run monthly.

Pilgrims Language Courses, Pilgrims House, Orchard St, Canterbury, Kent CT2 2BF (01227 762111; clientservices@pilgrims.co.uk). Courses held on University campus 5 times a year.

St Giles College Highgate, 51 Shepherd's Hill, Highgate, London N6 5QP (020-8340 0828; www.tefl-stgiles.com). £895.

Stanton Teacher Training, Stanton House, 167 Queensway, London W2 4SB (020-7221 7259; www.stanton-school.co.uk). £682.

Centres offering the Trinity College Certificate include:

Coventry TESOL Centre, Coventry Technical College, Butts, Coventry CV1 3QD (01203 526742; language@covcollege.ac.uk). £695. Also offer the course in Czech Republic, Poland, Hungary, Spain and Turkey for £300 extra to cover accommodation.

EF English First Teacher Training, 1-3 Farman Street, Hove, East Sussex BN1 3AL (01273 747308; www.ef.com). Optional fifth week focusing on teaching abroad, business English and teaching young learners. £850. EF aims to recruit successful trainees from the course to work for EF schools worldwide.

Grove House Language Centre, Carlton Avenue, Greenhithe, Kent DA9 9DR (01322 386826). £875.

Language Link Training, 181 Earl's Court Road, London SW5 9RB (020-7370 4755/ www.languagelink.co.uk). £723 plus moderation fee of £77. Can help place successful candidates in posts in Central and Eastern Europe.

The Language Project, 78-80 Colston Street, Bristol BS1 5BB (0117-927 3993; www.languagewise.com). £900. Also offer Introduction to TEFL/TESL.

Oxford House College, 28 Market Place, Oxford Circus, London W1W 8AW (020-7580 9785; www.oxford-house-college.ac.uk). Large Trinity College validated centre. 4-week course offered in London, Barcelona and Tuscany.

A number of centres offer short introductory courses in TEFL, which vary enormously in quality and price. Although they are mainly intended to act as preparatory programmes for more serious courses, many people who hold just a short certificate go on to teach. Among the best known are:

i-to-i, One Cottage Road, Headingley, Leeds LS6 4DD (0870-333 2332; www.i-to-i.com). Intensive 20-hour weekend TEFL courses at venues in 13 UK cities. Fees are £195 for waged applicants, £175 for unwaged and students. On-line TEFL course also available from any location worldwide. Courses include on-line tutor back-up and CD Rom. Price £270/US$400. Internet address: www.onlinetefl.com.

INTESOL, 19 Lower Oakfield, Pitlochry, Perthshire PH16 5DS (tel/fax 01796 474199; www.intesoltesoltraining.com). Distance Learning Preliminary Certificate in TESOL: £195 UK, £210-£230 overseas. Also offer combined programme with residential fortnight following 2 weeks home study (£795) including accommodation and meals.

Language Link Training (address as above). One-week pre-TESOL introductory courses according to demand.

Saxoncourt Teacher Training, 59 South Molton Street, London W1Y 1HH (020-7499 8533; www.saxoncourt.com). Introductory TEFL course throughout the year.

Sussex Language Institute, University of Sussex, Falmer, Brighton, E. Sussex, BN1 9QN (01273 877715; www.sussex.ac.uk/langc). 1-week Introduction to TEFL course held several times a year. £140. Also offers the Trinity CertTESOL course.

Cambridge CELTA courses are offered at nearly 100 overseas centres from the Middle East to Queensland, including several in the US:

ELC@Language Exchange, 1 East Broward Blvd, Suite 303W, Fort Lauderdale, FL 33301 (954-525-9100; www.tefltraining.com). $2,100.

Embassy CES, 330 Seventh Avenue, New York, NY 10001 (212-629-7300; www.studygroupintl.com). $2,325.

International House USA, 200 SW Market St, Suite 111, Portland, OR 97201 (503-224-1960; www.ih-usa.com). Also offers courses in San Francisco. $2,150.

St Giles Language Teaching Center, One Hallidie Plaza, Suite 350, San Francisco, CA 94102 (415-788-3552; www.stgiles-usa.com). $2,695.

Other centres for American readers to consider are Transworld Schools, 701 Sutter St, 2nd Floor, San Francisco, CA 94109 (1-888-588-8335/415-928-2835; www.transworldschools.com) and New World Teachers, 605 Market St, Suite 800, San Francisco, CA 94105 (1-800-644-5424; www.goteach.com) which offer their own four-week Certificate courses in Mexico, Hungary and Thailand as well as the US. Both have excellent contacts with language schools worldwide and can assist with the job hunt.

What English Teaching Involves

It is difficult to generalise about what work you will actually be required to do. At one extreme you have David Cooksley whose job it was to listen to Korean businessmen reading English novels aloud for him to correct their pronunciation. At the other extreme Gillian Forsyth, who taught for a private language school in the industrial north of Germany, had a gruelling schedule of 30 hours of teaching including evening classes, translation work and extensive preparation. Whatever the teaching you find, things probably won't go as smoothly as you would wish. After a year of teaching English in Italy, Andrew Spence had this sensible advice:

> *Teaching is perhaps the best way there is of experiencing another country but you must be prepared for periods when not all is as it should be. The work is sometimes arduous and frustrating, or it can be very exhilarating. Be prepared to take the very rough with the fairly smooth.*

Native speaker teachers are nearly always employed to stimulate conversation rather than to teach grammar. Yet a basic knowledge of English grammar is a great asset when pupils come to ask awkward questions. The book *English Grammar in Use* by Raymond Murphy has been highly recommended for its clear explanations and accompanying student exercises (2000 edition, £8.95 from CUP).

Each level and age group brings its own rewards and difficulties. Beginners of all ages usually delight in their progress which will be much more rapid than it is later on. Not everyone, however, enjoys teaching young children (a booming area of TEFL from Portugal to Japan) which usually involves sing-songs, puzzles and games. Intermediate learners (especially if they are adolescents) can be difficult, since they will have reached a plateau and may be discouraged. Adults are usually well-motivated though may be inhibited about speaking. Teaching professionals and business people is almost always well paid. Discipline is seldom a problem at least outside Western Europe. In fact you may find your pupils disconcertingly docile and possibly also overly exam-oriented.

Most schools practise the direct method (total immersion in English) so knowing the language shouldn't prevent you from getting a job. Some employers may provide nothing more than a scratched blackboard and will expect you to dive in using the 'chalk and talk' method. If you are very alarmed at this prospect you could ask a sympathetic colleague if you could sit in on a few classes to give you some ideas. Brochures picked up from tourist offices or airlines can be a useful peg on which to hang a lesson. If you're stranded without any ideas, write the lyrics of a pop song on the board and discuss; favourites include 'Here Comes the Sun' and 'When I'm 64'.

The wages paid to English teachers are usually reasonable, and in developing countries are quite often well in excess of the average local wage. In return you will be asked to teach some fairly unsociable hours since most private English classes take place after working hours, and so schedules split between early morning and evening are not at all uncommon. There may also be extracurricular duties and you should be prepared to do anything from making sausage rolls for an international food day to revising course materials. Even without these, hours will be very long, when you take into account class preparation time. Teaching of any kind is a demanding job and those who are doing it merely as a means of supporting their travelling habit may find it a disillusioning experience.

FINDING A JOB

Teaching jobs are either fixed up from home or sought out on location. Obviously it is less nerve-racking to have everything sorted out before you leave home, but this option is usually available only to the qualified. It also has the disadvantage that you don't know what you're letting yourself in for.

In Advance

Check the adverts in the Education section of the *Guardian* every Tuesday and in the weekly *Times Educational Supplement (TES)* published on Fridays. The best time of year is between Easter and July. In some cases, a carefully crafted CV and enthusiastic personality are as important as EFL training and experience.

Recruitment agencies maintain a database of teachers' CVs which they then try to match with suitable vacancies in their client schools. In order to be registered with such an agency it is normally essential to have at least the Cambridge or Trinity Certificate and usually some experience. The major language school chains hire substantial numbers of teachers, many of whom will have graduated from in-house training courses. These are some of the major employers of EFL teachers:

Benedict Schools, 3 Place Chauderon, P.O. Box 270, 1000 Lausanne 9, Switzerland (+41 21-323 66 55; www.benedict-schools.com). 80 franchised business and language schools in Europe, Africa, South and North America.

Berlitz UK, 9-13 Grosvenor Street, London W1A 3BZ (020-7915 0909) or in the USA: 400 Alexander Park, Princeton, NJ 08540-6306 (609-514-9650); www.berlitz.com. One of the largest language training organisations in the world with about 400 centres in 40 countries.

EF English First, Teacher Recruitment Section, 1-3 Farman Street, Hove, East Sussex BN3 1AL (01273 747308/fax 01273 746742; e1recruitment@ef.com). Recruitment of up to 400 EFL teachers takes place year round for EF's schools in Indonesia, Russia, Poland, China, Mexico, Morocco, Ecuador, Lithuania, Azerbaijan, Kazakhstan, Slovenia, Singapore and Thailand. In the US contact: EF Education (Human Resources, EF Education, One Education Street, Cambridge, MA 02141; 617-619-1955/fax 617-619-1001; Careers@ef.com).

ELT Banbury, 49 Oxford Road, Banbury, Oxon. OX16 9AH (01295 263480; www.elt-banbury.com). Maintains Teacher Directory for worldwide recruitment.

inlingua Recruitment, Rodney Lodge, Rodney Road, Cheltenham, Glos. GL50 1HX (01242 253171; recruitment@inlingua-cheltenham.co.uk). Recruits 200+ teachers for its 300 centres worldwide (especially Spain, Italy, Germany, Russia, Poland, Turkey and Singapore).

International House, 106 Piccadilly, London W1V 7NL (020-7518 6970; hr@ihlondon.co.uk). Human Resources Department can advise on teaching posts in the IH network.

Language Link, 21 Harrington Road, London SW7 3EU (020-7225 1065; www.languagelink.co.uk). Places Certificate holders in its network of affiliated schools in Eastern and Central Europe, Germany, Vietnam and China.

Linguarama, Group Personnel Department, Oceanic House, 89 High St, Alton, Hampshire GU34 1LG (01420 80899; www.linguarama.com). Specialises in providing language training for business in France, Finland, Italy, Germany and Spain.

Nord Anglia International Language Academies, 10 Eden Place, Cheadle, Cheshire SK8 1AT (0161-491 4191; www.language-academies.com). Operates over 80 summer schools in the UK plus schools abroad including Ukraine, Spain, Poland, Portugal and Taiwan. Teachers are invited to send their CVs to International Recruitment, Nord Anglia Education Personnel, 9 Swinsens Yard, Stony Stratford, Milton Keynes MK11 1SY.

Opening English School, Via Augusta 238, 08021 Barcelona, Spain (+34 93-241 89 00; awesterman@openingschool.com). Recruits 450 teachers for Spain and also for schools in France, Greece, Brazil and Portugal.

Saxoncourt and English Worldwide 124 New Bond Street, London W1Y 9AE (0207-491 1911; recruit@saxoncourt.com). One of the largest UK-based recruiters of EFL teachers, placing over 600 teachers per year in schools in 30 countries (e.g. Japan, Taiwan, Poland, China, Italy, Spain, Russia, Thailand, France, Peru and Brazil).

Wall Street Institute International, Rambla de Catalunya 2-4, Planta Baixa, 08007 Barcelona, Spain (+34 93-412 00 14/301 00 29; www.wallstreetinstitute.com). Chain of commercial language institutes for adults which employs approximately 750 full-time EFL teachers in Europe (Spain, Switzerland, Portugal, Italy, France and Germany) and Latin America (Mexico, Chile, Venezuela).

More than 100 websites are devoted to EFL/ESL jobs, many with links to Dave Sperling's ESL Café (www.eslcafe.com) which dominates the field. It provides a job list updated daily and a mind-boggling but well-organised amount of material for the future or current teacher including accounts of people's experiences of teaching abroad. Others worth trying are www.edunet.com; www.eslworldwide.com; www.eflweb.com; www.englishexpert.com and www.tefl.net.

There is also scope for untrained but eager volunteers willing to pay an agency to place them in a language teaching situation abroad. In addition to those included here, see the chapter on *Eastern Europe.*

Council Exchanges, Council UK, 52 Poland St, London W1V 4JQ (020-7478 2000; www.councilexchanges.org). Administers the Japan Exchange & Teaching (JET) and Teach in China Programmes (see Asia chapter).

i-to-i (address above). Voluntary English teaching placements in Latin America, Africa, Russia and Asia.

Teaching & Projects Abroad, Gerrard House, Rustington, West Sussex BN16 1AW (01903 859911; info@teaching-abroad.co.uk/ www.teaching-abroad.co.uk). About 1,000 people are recruited mainly as volunteer English language teaching assistants in the Ukraine, Russia, India, Ghana, Mexico, China, Peru, Togo, Nepal, Thailand and South Africa. No TEFL background required. Self-funded packages cost from £795-£1,595 (excluding airfares).

Travellers, 7 Mulberry Close, Ferring, West Sussex BN12 5HY (tel/fax 01903 502595; www.travellersworldwide.com). Volunteers teach conversational English (and/or other subjects like music, maths and sport) in India, Nepal, Sri Lanka, Russia, Cuba, South Africa, Ukraine and Malaysia, for short or longer periods. Sample charge of £925 for 2-3 months in India/Sri Lanka and £775 in Ukraine (excluding airfares).

The *Central Bureau for International Education & Training,* (10 Spring Gardens, London SW1A 2BN; 020-7389 4004; centralbureau@britishcouncil.org) administers language assistant placements to help local teachers of English in many countries from France to Venezuela. Applicants for assistant posts must be aged 20-30, native English speakers, with at least two years of university-level education, normally in the language of the destination country. In some countries (especially in Latin America and Eastern Europe) posts are of particular interest to graduates interested in a career in TEFL. Application forms are available from October; the deadline is December of the preceding academic year.

The important organisations in the US are:

Amity Volunteer Teachers Abroad (AVTA), Amity Institute, 10671 Roselle St, Suite 101, San Diego, CA 92121-1525 (858-455-6364/fax 858-455-6597; mail@amity.org/ www.amity.org). Provides voluntary teaching opportunities in Latin America (Argentina, Peru, Mexico, the Dominican Republic), Africa (Senegal and Ghana) and France. Participants must be at least 21, stay for eight or nine months from January/February or August/September and have a knowledge of Spanish (for Latin America).

ELS Language Centers, International Division, 400 Alexander Park, Princeton NJ 08540 609-750-3512; smatson@els.com/ www.els.com). 50 franchised English language schools overseas many of which recruit separately (all addresses listed on their admirably clear website).

ELTAP (English Language Teaching Assistant Program), University of Minnesota-Morris, Minnesota 56267 (320-589-6464; jkuechle@mrs.umn.edu; www.mrs.umn.edu/cerp/eltap). Placement of university students for a minimum of 11 weeks at various times of year in huge range of countries from Belarus to Cameroon. $300 placement fee plus travel and living expenses.

TESOL (Teachers of English to Speakers of Other Languages, Inc.), 700 S Washington St, Suite 200, Alexandria, VA 22314 (703-836-0774/fax 703-836-6447; tesol@tesol.org/ www.tesol.org). Basic membership is $50 ($36 for students). Members can receive a listing of job vacancies worldwide, or search jobs online.

WorldTeach Inc., Center for International Development, Harvard University, 79 John F Kennedy Street, Cambridge, MA 02138 (617-495-5527/800-4-TEACH-0; info@worldteach.org/ www.worldteach.org). Non-profit organisation that places several hundred volunteers as teachers of EFL or ESL in countries which request assistance. Currently, WorldTeach provides college graduates for 6 or 12 months to Costa Rica, Ecuador, China, Namibia and South Africa.

On the Spot

Jobs in any field are difficult to get without an interview and English teaching is no different. In almost all cases it is more effective to go to your preferred destination, CV in hand, and call on language schools and companies. The director of the Mainz branch of a chain of language schools is just one language school director who has emphasised the importance of applying locally:

Schools like ours cannot under normal operating circumstances hire someone unseen merely on the basis of his/her resumé and photo. Moreover, when the need for a teacher arises, usually that vacancy must be filled within a matter of days which, for people applying from abroad, is a physical impossibility. I would suggest that an applicant should arrange for a face-to-face interview and make him/herself available at a moment's notice. Of course, I do appreciate the compromising situation to which anyone in need of employment would thus be exposed. Regrettably, I know of no other method.

When looking for work at private language schools, it is helpful if you can claim some qualifications, though you will seldom be asked to provide proof of same. If you happen to have a BA, take along the certificate. Steven Hendry, who taught English in Japan with no qualifications, stresses the importance of dressing smartly, having a respectable briefcase and a typed CV which exaggerates (if necessary) your experience. However these days it is rare for that to be enough.

There are many means by which you might fix up the odd spot of teaching during your travels. The names of specific language schools and methods of securing a job are mentioned in the various country chapters.

Accents can be important, especially in Latin America and the Far East where American English is favoured (though never to the exclusion of British). But many foreign language speakers cannot distinguish, and Geordies and Australians are as welcome as people who speak with a BBC accent. The important factor is whether or not you speak slowly and clearly. In a few cases, Americans may have an advantage, since some groups (e.g. Japanese and Middle Eastern businessmen) who hope to do business in the US, prefer to learn the language from an American speaker. In other countries (like Spain and Italy) an English accent is preferred.

Consult the British Council in your destination and the *Yellow Pages* in order to gather together a list of addresses where you can ask for work. Business schools often need teachers of commercial English. Read the adverts in the English language papers.

Visit centres where foreigners study the local language and check the notice board or befriend the secretary. Several factors will affect the length of time it will take before you find something: for example at what point of the term you begin your search (e.g. late August/September is usually best followed by Christmas-time; summers are usually hopeless), whether you know the vernacular language (especially an advantage in Spanish-speaking countries) and how convincing you look carrying a briefcase. If you have no luck in the major cities, consider trying resorts popular with English speaking tourists. Here you will find plenty of locals very eager to learn enough English to secure them a job in the local tourist industry.

An alternative to working for a language school is to set yourself up as a freelance private tutor. While undercutting the fees charged by the big schools, you can still earn more than as a contract teacher. Normally you will have to be fairly well established in a place before you can attempt to support yourself by private teaching, preferably with some decent premises in which to give lessons (either private or group) and with a telephone. Laurence Koe gave after-hours conversation classes in northern Italy and charged each child 50 pence. Michel Falardeau opened his own English immersion social club in Taiwan. You should bear in mind the disadvantages of working for yourself, viz. frequent last-minute cancellations by clients, unpaid travelling time (if you teach in clients' homes or offices), no social security and an absence of professional support and teaching materials.

If you do decide to try this, you will have to promote yourself unashamedly. Try posting eye-catching bilingual notices all around town (especially the prosperous areas) or even leafletting door to door. You can be more selective, and concentrate on relevant notice boards. To find school-age pupils you could visit ordinary state schools, introduce yourself to the head teacher and ask him/her to announce your willingness to offer extra English tuition. If you are less interested in making money than integrating with a culture, exchanging conversation for board and lodging may be an appealing possibility, which usually relies on having a network of contacts. But not always. According to our contributors, invitations to participate in such an arrangement have come while chatting to a Parisian businesswoman, lying on a Turkish beach or sitting by the side of a road in Thailand.

CHILDCARE

The terms au pair, mother's help and nanny are often applied rather loosely, since all are primarily live-in jobs concerned with looking after children. Nannies may have some formal training and take full charge of the children. Mother's helps work full-time and undertake general housework and/or cooking as well as childcare. Au pairs are supposed to work for no more than 30 hours a week and are expected to learn a foreign language while living with a family.

One of the great advantages of these live-in positions generally is that they are relatively easy to get (at least for women). After proving to an agency or a family that you are reasonably sensible, you will in the majority of cases be able to find a placement, though it is much easier and quicker in some countries than others, e.g. easy in France, Austria, Italy and Israel, but more difficult in Scandinavia and Portugal. Furthermore au pairs can often benefit from legislation which exempts them from work permit requirements.

Usually the reasons for wanting to be an au pair are that you want to improve your knowledge of the country's language and culture, that you want to take a break from the routine of studies, work or unemployment, or that you wish to get some experience of catering and children before pursuing a career along those lines. Occasionally, young men can find live-in jobs, and slowly the number of families and therefore agencies willing to entertain the possibility of having a male au pair is increasing.

The standard length of stay is for one academic year, typically September to June. Summer stays can also be arranged to coincide with the school holidays. The advantage of a summer placement is that the au pair will accompany the family to their holiday destination at the seaside or in the mountains; the disadvantage is that the children will be your responsibility for more hours than they would be if they were at school, and also most language classes will close for the summer. Make enquiries as early as possible, since there is a shortage of summer-only positions.

Anyone interested in finding out about all aspects of live-in childcare should consult *The Au Pair & Nanny's Guide to Working Abroad* (Vacation-Work, £10.99).

PROS AND CONS

The relationship of au pair to family is not like the usual employer/employee relationship; in fact the term au pair means 'on equal terms'. The Home Office leaflet on au pairs in Britain uses the terminology 'hostess' and 'hospitality'. Therefore the success of the arrangement depends more than usual on whether individuals hit it off, so there is always an element of risk when living in a family of strangers. The Council of Europe guidelines stipulate that au pairs should be aged 18-27 (though these limits are flexible), should be expected to work about five hours a day, five days per week plus a couple of evenings of babysitting, must be given a private room and full board, health insurance, opportunities to learn the language and pocket money.

Once you have arrived in the family, it is important to clarify immediately what your hours and duties will be, which day you will be paid, whether you can expect a rise and how much notice either party must give if they wish to terminate the arrangement. This gets everyone off to a business-like start. But no matter how well-defined your duties are, there are bound to be occasions when your extra services will be taken for granted. It may seem that your time is not your own. Kathryn Halliwell worked for a family in Vancouver, Canada for a year and describes this problem:

> *A live-in job is a very committed one. It is extremely difficult to say no when the employers ring at 6pm to say they can't be home for another two hours. Children don't consider a nanny as an employee and tension develops if a child can't understand why you won't take him swimming on your day off.*

So the standard working hours can soon turn into an unofficial string of 14 hour days. Whether you can tolerate this depends entirely on your disposition and on the compensating benefits of the job, e.g. free use of car and telephone, nice kids, good food, lots of sunshine, etc.

No matter how carefully you try to determine your duties and privileges, there is still plenty of scope for different interpretations of how the arrangement should work. At one extreme you have the family (with one well-behaved child) who invites you along on skiing trips with them and asks you to do a mere 24 hours of child-minding and light housework a week. On the other hand you might be treated like a kitchen skivvy by the mother, and like a concubine by the father, while at the same time trying to look after their four spoiled brats. So it is advisable to find out as much as possible about the family before accepting the job. If you do not like the sound of the family at the beginning you should insist that the agency offer any available alternatives.

Even though an au pair does have her own room, there may be a definite lack of privacy. This can be the logical extension of being treated like a member of the family. For example Claire Robson, who spent a summer working as an au pair in Greece, described how the mother accused her of being unsociable because she wouldn't come and watch television (all in Greek!) when invited. Such unreasonable expectations are often the result of different national temperaments as well as simple personality clashes. In conservative countries (e.g. Turkey, Spain, southern Italy), it is unacceptable for young women to go out alone at night, so your social life may be very restricted.

On the other hand, Gillian Forsyth's experience when she au paired in Bavaria was a great success:

> *I had no official day off or free time but was treated as a member of the family. Wherever they went I went too. I found this much more interesting than being treated as an employee as I really got to know the country and the people. In the evenings I did not have to sit in my room, but chatted with the family. Three years later we still keep in close contact and I have been skiing with them twice since, on an au pair/friend basis.*

If you do not have such a friendly arrangement with your family, you may feel lonely and cut off in a foreign country. Many au pairs make friends at their language classes. Some agencies issue lists of other au pairs in the vicinity. For those wanting to meet other au pairs in a similar situation, Leeson Clifton, who came from Canada to be a mother's help in Britain, recommends placing an advertisement in the local paper for an au pair get-together. Despite all the possible problems, au pairing does provide an easy and often enjoyable introduction to living and travelling abroad. A family placement is a safe and stable environment for young, underconfident and impecunious people who want to work abroad.

Pay

You may enjoy being an au pair but you are unlikely to get rich quick. Mind you, things have improved since pre-war days when, according to one of our older contributors, you were liable not to be paid a penny until you had completed your six-month contract, and even then it would barely cover your train fare home from Switzerland. The standard pocket money paid to au pairs in Britain nowadays is £35-£40 per week and untrained mother's helps £55+ per week. The amount of pocket money paid abroad differs somewhat with the USA and Switzerland paying the most pocket money of £65-£75.

One reason that au pairing is exempt from the usual governmental restrictions requiring work permits (with exceptions such as Switzerland, Canada and the USA) is because it is not a salaried job and normally not subject to taxation.

Of course there are more lucrative opportunities for people with childcare or catering experience. For example a nanny will be paid from £100 per week in the Home Counties and over C$1,000 (before deductions) per month in Canada. Having some nursery training or childcare experience can open other doors. Most large tour and campsite holiday operators (addresses in *Tourism* chapter) employ nannies to look after the children of holidaymakers. This can be an excellent passport to spending a season in a summer or winter resort.

Duties

Before accepting a position which involves cooking you should establish what standard your employer has in mind. Unless you do this you may end up like Sally Collins, who wrote about her experiences in the *New Zealand News*:

> *I soon began to understand that simple cooking – which I had rashly said I could do, imagining boiled eggs and toast – in fact involved a certain amount of cordon bleu knowledge. I had no idea what to do with the pheasant which was presented to me.*

Perhaps it would be a good idea to ask for a *Delia Smith's Complete Cookery Course* for your birthday (£9.99 in paperback).

Most au pairs' duties revolve around the children. For some, taking sole responsibility for a child can be even more alarming than cooking pheasant for the first time. You should be prepared to handle a few emergencies (for example sick or lost children) as well as the usual excursions to the park or collecting them from school. The agency questionnaire will ask you in detail what experience you have had with children and whether you are willing to look after newborn infants, etc., so your preferences should be made known early. You must also be prepared to hurt the children's feelings when you leave. Nicky Parker left a family in Majorca after just nine weeks and reported, 'I could only feel guilty and sad at the distress caused to the children by yet another in a long line of people whom they had learned to love, leaving them forever.'

APPLYING

It simplifies matters to use the services of an au pair or domestic agency (European and North American agencies are listed at the end of this chapter). The most established agencies in the UK belong to the Recruitment and Employment Confederation (36-38 Mortimer St, London W1N 7RB; www.rec.org.uk). If you dial their Jobseekers' line on freephone 0800 320588, you can order a specialist list of Childcare agencies for £3.75.

In the first instance send an s.a.e. to several agencies to compare terms and conditions. If your requirements are very specific as regards location or family circumstances, ring around some agencies and ask them to be blunt about their chances of being able to fix you up with what you want. Some provide a follow-up and travel service as well as placement. In the UK agencies are permitted to charge a fee of up to £40 plus VAT only after a placement has been verified. Unfortunately this means that many prospective au pairs register with a number of agencies and simply choose the best sounding job. This high level of backing out means that UK agencies do not take the trouble over individual applications which their European counterparts do who are allowed to charge substantial registration fees.

Some people have complained that if you go through an agency, you are taking potluck, though this can be minimised by making an effort to communicate with the family by phone or letter before the job begins. Nevertheless you may prefer to arrange something on your own. The best way of doing this is to answer or place advertisements in *The Lady* (39/40 Bedford St, London WC2E 9ER) published each Tuesday. Advertisements usually evoke responses from all over the world, since this magazine has a virtual monopoly in this field. For example, Julie Richards, who had had no luck with the agencies because of her lack of childcare experience, placed an advert in *The Lady* and received 30 job offers. There is a special classification of au pair jobs in the fortnightly newspaper *Overseas Jobs Express*.

On the Spot

If you are already abroad, check in the local English language newspaper such as the *Athens News* or the *Anglo Portuguese News* in Lisbon, or visit an au pair agency office in the country where you are (addresses provided in country chapters). Other ways of hearing about openings are to check the notice boards at the local English-speaking churches, ask the headmistress of a junior school if she knows of any families wanting an au pair or visit a school at the end of the school day and chat with the mothers and au pairs who are there to collect their charges. One tip for finding babysitting jobs in resorts is to introduce yourself to the *portière* or receptionist on the desk of good hotels and ask them to refer guests looking for a babysitter to you, possibly offering 10-15% commission.

Agencies

Last year the UK government legislated to create a register of approved nanny agencies, though this will regulate agencies providing live-in child-carers to British families, not those sending them abroad. There is very little regulation in the world of au pair agencies, though in view of the fact that Louise Woodward was participating in one of the most tightly controlled programmes, this may not in the end make too much difference. Many leading au pair agencies and youth exchange organisations in Europe belong to IAPA, the International Au Pair Association (c/o FIYTO, Bredgade 25H, 1260 Copenhagen K, Denmark; www.iapa.org), an international body trying to regulate the industry.

Agencies that specialise in one country are mentioned in the country chapters. The following UK au pair and/or nanny agencies all deal with a number of European countries. Agencies abroad which both place foreign au pairs/nannies in their country and place their nationals abroad are mentioned in the country chapters:

1st for Au Pairs & Nannies, Highfield House, 1562 Stratford Road, Hall Green, Birmingham B28 9HA (0121-733 2433; nannies@waverider.co.uk). Placements in Belgium, France, Germany, Italy, Spain and Turkey. Nannies needed in holiday resorts in Turkey, Corsica, Sardinia, etc.

Abacus Au Pair Agency, 1A Ruskin Road, Hove, E. Sussex BN3 5HA (info@abacusaupairagency.co.uk).

Academy Au Pair & Nanny Agency, 42 Cedarhurst Drive, Eltham, London SE9 5LP (020-8294 1191; www.academyagency.co.uk). Place nannies in Australia as well as Europe.

Anderson Au Pairs, 164 Seabrook Road, Hythe, Kent CT21 5RA (01303 260971; www.childcare-europe.com).

Anglo Continental Nanny & Au Pair Placement Agency, 21 Amesbury Crescent, Hove, E. Sussex BN3 5RD (tel/fax 01273 705959; anglocont@applied-tech.com). Wide range of European countries including Scandinavia.

A-One Au Pairs & Nannies, Suite 216, The Commercial Centre, Picket Piece, Andover, Hants. SP11 6RU (01264 332500; www.aupairsetc.co.uk).

The Au Pair Agency, 231 Hale Lane, Edgware, Middlesex HA8 9QF (020-8958 1750; elaine@aupairagency.com). Mainly France, Spain, Italy and Germany.

Au Pair and Nanny Bureau, 91 Havelock Road, Brighton, BN1 6GL (01273 562764/fax 01273 883954; aupair@mistral.co.uk). Usual countries plus Netherlands and USA.

Au Pair Connections, 39 Tamarisk Road, Wildern Gate, Hedge End, Southampton SO30 4TN (tel/fax 01489 780438; Aupairconnect@aol.com).

Au Pair International, 115 High St, Uckfield, E. Sussex TN22 1RN (01825 761420; www.aupairinternational.co.uk).

Au Pair Network International, 118 Cromwell Road, London SW7 4ET (020-7370 3798; www.apni.co.uk).

Au Pairs by Avalon, 7 Highway, Edgcumbe Park, Crowthorne, Berks. RG45 6HE (tel/fax 01344 778246; www.aupairsbyavalon.com).

Au Pairs Online Employment Agency, 56 Mansfield Road, London NW3 2HT (020-7419 9972; www.aupairsonline.com). Actual vacancies posted on website.

Bunters Au Pair Agency, The Old Malt House, 6 Church St, Towester, Northants. NN12 8NB (01327 831144/fax 01327 831155; www.buntersaupairs.co.uk).

Castle Au Pairs, Pen-y-Parc, Red Lane, Powis Castle, Welshpool, Powys SY21 8RI (tel/fax 01938 850389; squibbt@aol.com).

Childcare Europe/Childcare America, Trafalgar House, Grenville Place, London NW7 3SA (020-8959 3611/906 3116; www.childint.co.uk).

Edgware Agency, 1565 Stratford Road, Hall Green, Birmingham, W. Midlands B28 9JA (0121-745 6777; www.100s-aupairs.co.uk). Solihull Au Pair Agency is part of the same organisation and operates from the same address (0121-733 6444; solihull@100s-aupairs.co.uk).

EIL, 287 Worcester Road, Malvern, Worcs. WR14 1AB (01684 562577/fax 01684 562212; www.eiluk.org). USA, Australia, France, Spain and Norway.

Janet White Agency, 67 Jackson Avenue, Leeds LS8 1NS (0113-266 6507/fax 0113 268 3077/e-mail: janet@janetwhite.com).

Jolaine Agency, 18 Escot Way, Barnet, Herts. EN5 3AN (020-8449 1334; aupair@jolaine.prestel.co.uk).

Lucy Locketts & Vanessa Bancroft Nanny Agency, 400 Beacon Road, Wibsey, Bradford, BD6 3DJ (tel/fax 01274 402822). Also fill vacancies in hotels for chamber, waiting and kitchen staff, mainly in UK but some abroad.

*Mondial Agency,*The Old Barn, Shoreham Lane, Halstead, Sevenoaks, Kent TN14 7BY (01959 533664; www.mondialaupairs.co.uk).

Problems Unlimited Agency, '177a Cricklewood, Broadway, London NW2 3HT (02-8438 9938; info@krsa.prinex.co.uk).

Quick Help Agency, 307A Finchley Road, London NW3 6EH (020-7794 8666; www.quickhelp.co.uk).

Solihull Agency, 1565 Stratford Road, Hall Green, Birmingham, W. Midlands B28 9JA (0121-733 6444; solihull@100s-aupairs.co.uk). Amalgamated with Edgware Agency.

South Eastern Au Pair Bureau, 39 Rutland Avenue, Thorpe Bay, Essex SS1 2XJ (tel/fax 01702 601911).

Worldnet UK, Avondale House, 63 Sydney Road, Haywards Heath, W Sussex RH16 1QD (01444 457676).

Agencies Abroad

Americans and Canadians interested in an au pair placement in Europe should contact the following agencies:

Accord Cultural Exchange, 750 La Playa, San Francisco, CA 94121 (415-386 6203/fax 415-386-0240). Family placements in France, Germany, Spain, Austria and Italy. $1,200 placement fee ($750 for summer positions).

Au Pair Canada, 15 Goodacre Close, Red Deer, Alberta, Canada T4P 3A3 (tel/fax 403-343-1418; aupaircanada@home.com). France, Holland, Switzerland, Germany and Iceland.

Au Pair in Europe, PO Box 68056, Blakely Postal Outlet, Hamilton, Ontario, Canada L8M 3M7 (905-545-6305/fax 905-544-4121; aupair@princeent.com; www.princeent.com). Au pairs placed in Austria, Australia, Belgium, Bermuda, Denmark, England, Finland, France, Germany, Greece, Holland, Iceland, Italy, Japan, New Zealand, Norway, Russia, Spain, Sweden and Switzerland. Registration fee is charged. Enquiries to the Directors, Corinne and John Prince.

InterExchange Inc, 161 Sixth Avenue, New York, NY 10013 (212-924-0446/fax 212-924-0575; infor@interexchange.org/ www.interexchange.org). Contact Mr. Paul Christianson.

Scotia Personnel Ltd. Au Pair Section, Cherry St, Halifax, NS B3H 2K4 (902-422-1455; www.scotia-personnel-ltd.com). Places au pairs in Holland, Italy, Germany, France and the US.

Au pairing is very popular in South Africa. One of the main sending agencies is Youth Discovery Programmes, PO Box 2821, Parklands, 2121 Johannesburg (011-326 2796; www.ydp.co.za) with offices in Cape Town, Pretoria, Jo'burg and Durban. Similarly various agencies in Australia and New Zealand recruit live-in child-care staff for Britain and Europe such as Affordable Au-Pairs & Nannies, 19/43 Jeffcott St, West Melbourne, VIC 3206 (www.nanny.net.au).

BUSINESS & INDUSTRY

Although work in offices, mines, shops and factories is not seasonal in the way that work in orchards and hotels is, there are plenty of casual opportunities. You might be needed in a shop during the pre-Christmas rush, or in a swimming pool firm before the summer, or on an Easter-egg production line in February/March. You may be needed to do general labouring while a new motorway is being built or to type reports after an annual conference. Temporary openings are often created during the summer months when regular staff are away on holiday, especially in large department stores and supermarkets.

In fact during a recession, the demand for temporary staff actually increases. Firms which once would not have hesitated to take on extra permanent members of staff become more cautious and prefer to hire people on a short-term basis for peak periods. In some countries the law encourages this practice; for example in Belgium employers are legally required to provide a whole range of benefits after an employee has worked for a certain length of time; to avoid this, they tend to hire people for short periods often through temporary employment agencies.

Shops

It is not only during the Christmas rush that temporary sales staff are recruited, but also for the stock-clearing sales of January and July. Many large shops take an inventory once or twice a year and you can get two days of work counting sheet music or items of women's lingerie. Large stores often advertise in local papers for extra help, whereas smaller shops are more likely to carry a card in their window. It is worth registering with the personnel departments of large stores even before they advertise. The most important qualification for shop work is a presentable appearance. Not having an extensive wardrobe can be a hindrance in some shops; for example if you have been living out of your rucksack for a while, you are unlikely to make the right sort of impression at Saks of Fifth Avenue. Since people who serve in shops have a high public profile, you will normally be expected to have your papers in order. Marcel Staats from the Netherlands has worked in shops around the world from a corner store in Manhattan to Woolworths in Sydney. According to Marcel, references are very important in the retail business. So always ask for one, no matter how short a time you have been employed.

Even monolingual people may find shop work outside the English-speaking world by approaching shopkeepers who sell primarily to tourists. You could present yourself to a carpet merchant in a coastal Turkish town or to an electronics shop in a Japanese shopping precinct favoured by American tourists and offer to sell (initially) on commission. Not only will your fluency in English be an asset but your enthusiasm about the product for sale may inspire confidence in your compatriots. Make sure the percentage you are given is worthwhile; the range will be 2%-20% depending on the value of the goods (lower for video recorders and higher for cheap souvenirs). If you have a working knowledge of the language of the country, you might try to get work in the English language bookstore in a foreign city.

Selling

Readers with well-developed business instincts should read the chapter on *Enterprise* which suggests many ways to market a product independently. But if you can't make earrings or find snails to peddle, you might consider becoming a salesperson for a company. Although technically you would be working for an employer, in practice it can be close to self-employment, since the income you earn will be geared to your own efforts.

If you examine the small ads of any newspaper in the world, you'll find offers of untold riches for little effort. Often they will employ euphemisms such as 'manager's assistant' for salesperson. Employers will rarely be troubled by your lack of a work permit; as long as you sell their product, many are quite happy to pay your commission in cash with no questions asked. Even in times of high local unemployment, there is usually scope for foreign sales staff; this may be either because their accent and nationality match up with the product (e.g. selling English language courses in Italy) or, more generally, because there is a lot of in-built resistance to selling on commission, especially on account of the insecurity involved.

Commissioned selling usually takes place door to door. Whether it is encyclopaedia or frozen steaks which you are flogging, you will be given some training which normally includes a set spiel to learn by heart. Even sceptics have been surprised by the effectiveness of this method, and after the spiel works for you once, you can repeat it with more feeling the next time.

The two qualifications you must have to be a successful salesperson are an outgoing, confident personality and a lack of squeamishness about twisting the truth. Many products sold door to door are of dubious value, for example travellers have written from Ireland to South Africa about their employment as salesmen of 'genuine original paintings' which they soon discover are actually made in Taiwanese factories. Depending on your scruples, you might want to conduct your own little investigation into both the quality of the product and the business practices of the company before committing yourself. At least find out how long they have been in business and try to dig up a bank reference if possible, especially if they are trying to recruit from abroad.

Although there may be nothing dubious about the quality of the encyclopaedia being sold, some of the sales tactics may make you feel uncomfortable, such as accusing parents from lower income brackets that they will be harming their children's future if they don't sign on the dotted line.

Selling every day objects like brushes or fire extinguishers is less lucrative but your success rate may be higher than if you're selling something as expensive as encyclopaedia or property. Make sure you are not expected to buy the goods first, even on an alleged sale or return basis. Lodge a deposit with your wholesalers if necessary, but make clear that this is a precaution against your potential dishonesty rather than against your possible failure as a salesman.

Although some salesmen must depend solely on commission, others are paid a minimal salary before commission. Others are given quite generous perks, such as a vehicle and hotel vouchers. Working holidaymakers in Australia are regularly hired to sell pens on behalf of a Sydney charity and may even be given a caravan in which to travel and live. When people detect that you are not a career salesman but somebody funding a holiday in their country they may show hospitality (without any intention of buying your product) which will compensate for the hostility you encounter elsewhere.

Not all commissioned selling takes place door to door, and you may feel happier if you don't run the risk of being mistaken for a Mormon or a Jehovah's Witness and having doors slammed in your face. For example 'telesales' are gaining in popularity in Europe after being commonplace in North America for some time. Chris Daniels found an evening job in Minneapolis trying to persuade past members of a dinner club to rejoin:

There were lots of advertisements for people to sell door to door or by phone, and these firms seemed keen to hire people with an English accent. First it was necessary to learn a sales pitch which would be repeated continuously for four hours each evening to a surprisingly tolerant if somewhat uninterested audience. We were paid a fairly low wage (which suited me better than commission) and there was a very high turnover of employees. I recommend that people look into this kind of work which will provide a modest income while looking for something better. You never know, perhaps you'll discover that with the help of your foreign charm, you are a born salesman.

Ben Nakoneczny did this job for a London newspaper but gave up after a couple of weeks when he noticed that 'the most successful salespeople were the most obnoxious and least genuine.'

There are other ways of avoiding the possibility of slammed doors. For example you might get a job selling ice cream by driving a van around suburban Detroit or by roaming the beaches of the Côte d'Azur. You might be hired as a demonstrator in a department store whose main task is merely to give away as many samples of shampoo or cheese as possible. You might get a job (though these are usually badly paid) distributing advertising leaflets around a neighbourhood, which means you don't have to confront your 'victims'. Sometimes companies hire people to 'warm up' potential customers so that the hard saleman can take over. This may consist of door to door visits or of accosting people in the street to collect their names and telephone numbers in order that others may phone them up later to sell, say, life insurance; payment is for each genuine name and number. You can always explain this system to sympathetic passers-by who may be persuaded to disclose their particulars just so you can collect your 50p.

Another variation especially in the US involves canvassing for a charity such as Greenpeace or collecting for charities on commission (see Australia chapter).

Market Research

Collecting information from strangers is quite distinct from selling them something. Surprisingly, fluency in the language of the country is not always a prerequisite since there are firms in major European cities which operate on a pan-European scale and hire English-speakers to telephone from a list of English-speakers and so on. Of course your chances of being hired are better if you are bilingual. The Market Research Society (15 Northburgh St, London EC1V 0JR; 020-7490 4911/ www.marketresearch.org.uk) may be able to advise on companies with an international profile.

Market research can be done door to door, on the street or by telephone and the latter medium can be especially pleasant. Mike Tunnicliffe scoured the local *Yellow Pages* while he was in New Zealand and secured a market research job:

The work proved interesting, doing door to door interviews, but there really wasn't sufficient work to sustain one. It would have been useful as a second job.

Commercial and Secretarial

Students and recent graduates in business, management science, marketing, accounting, finance, computer applications or economics may be interested in an organisation run by a global student network based in 87 countries. AIESEC – a French acronym for the International Association for Students of Economics and Management – has its UK headquarters at 29-31 Cowper St, 2nd Floor, London EC2A 4AP (www.workabroad.org.uk). It can organise placements in any of its 84 member countries, aimed at giving participants an insight into living and working in another culture.

Interspeak (Stretton Lower Hall, Stretton, Cheshire SY14 7HS; 01829 250641/ www.interspeak.co.uk) can arrange short and longer term traineeships (internships or *stages*) in France, Spain, Italy, Germany and the US in the fields of marketing, international trade, computing, tourism, etc. Successful candidates live with host families. Their booking fee is £500 for 8-24 week placements; accommodation and board are normally included in the programme.

The Foreign and Commonwealth Office (Recruitment Team; 020-7238 4283/ pmd.fco@gtnet.gov.uk) offers 50 British university students in their penultimate year unpaid summer work experience placements in consulates worldwide. Work in the Overseas Undergraduate Attachment Scheme is normally in the commercial or information sections of the embassy or high commission. Participants must cover their own costs, though help may be given with finding accommodation. For information about traineeships with the European Commission, see the section on 'Jobs with EU Organisations' in the chapter *EU Employment.*

English is the commercial language of the world, so English speaking people with office skills and a knowledge of the country's language are often in demand. Trained secretaries who are fluent in a European language should be able to arrange work within the EU (see chapter on EU Employment for information about the recruitment procedures of the Commission of the European Communities). At one time suitable candidates could fix up work through a UK agency such as the long-established

International Secretaries; however with the single market individuals are better placed going to interim agencies in their destination countries. Agencies such as Merrow Employment Agency Language Recruitment Specialists (23 Bentick St, London W1U 2EZ; 020-7935 5050) and Appointments Bi-Language (020-7355 1975) deal with senior bilingual and multilingual secretarial positions in Europe. Agency posts tend to be long term, and for highly experienced secretaries. The Recruitment and Employment Confederation (36-38 Mortimer St, London W1N 7RB; www.rec.org.uk) produces a list of agencies that specialise in overseas work; it can be ordered by ringing 0800 320588 and paying £3.75.

If you pore over the classified ads in English language dailies abroad, you may eventually secure a job for which fluent English is needed, for example to write explanations of delays in shipment or in payment to British agents.

Secretarial and employment agencies from Brussels to Brisbane can be especially useful to travellers who are qualified to work as office temps. You will have to sit for a typing test and in some cases a spelling test. Be warned that temp agencies abroad (Australia in particular) often administer these tests more rigorously than they do in Britain. You should register with more than one agency. If you work for such an agency before travelling abroad, ask if they have any overseas branches. For example Manpower has 3,500 branch offices in 54 countries; most addresses are posted on the internet (www.manpower.co.uk in the UK and www.manpower.com in the US). Other multinationals like Drake (www.drakeintl.com) and Western Staff Services can provide a list of offices and, assuming you have performed satisfactorily, a letter of introduction. Drake International promises anyone who works successfully for them for at least three months a Career Passport which will be recognised by their agencies in ten countries worldwide; visit any of their branches, such as 43 Maiden Lane, Covent Garden WC2 (020-7481 0117). No matter how briefly you have worked for an agency, request a letter of reference which may allow you to bypass the typing and other tests if you work for the same company elsewhere.

Other Opportunities in Business

There is a worldwide shortage of information technology workers. According to a report published in 2,000, the number of unfilled IT vacancies is predicted to rise to 1.7 million across Europe in the coming years. Governments including the British and American are relaxing work permit regulations in order to attract IT specialists from abroad to fill these vacancies. Web design is becoming an increasingly portable skill.

Accountancy skills are similarly in demand in many countries and international agencies based in London may be able to assist with placement. For example Robert Walters has a dedicated international department located in each of its offices including London, Dublin, Melbourne, Sydney, Wellington, Auckland and Johannesburg. Through this international network, interviews are pre-arranged for candidates at their city of arrival and in the case of high calibre candidates, teleconference links are set up. Australia, New Zealand and South Africa are currently experiencing a real shortage, and candidates with banking, telecommunications, secretarial and IT experience are in great demand. Further information can be obtained from Robert Walters (25 Bedford St, London WC2E 9HE; 020-7379 3333; marlo.sullivan@robertwalters.com).

Another kind of job which requires an advanced skill is that of translator. If you are literate in two languages, you should register with translation agencies which can be found in most big cities abroad. You can also enquire at universities where there is a fluctuating demand for people able to translate technical and academic papers (rather than racy novels). After a year of living in Germany, James Spach had achieved the required proficiency in German and could earn about DM300 in a weekend translating a paper.

Finding a job as a delivery person is usually quite easy. Contact take-out pizza or Chinese restaurants in North America, mail order houses, stationers, Interflora, etc. If you are settled in one place and are an early riser, you can usually find a job as a newspaper boy/girl or (in countries where milk is still delivered to the doorstep) a milkman. If you run out of money on a Thursday or Friday, presenting yourself at the offices of the local newspaper as a delivery person might see you through the weekend. People are also needed by the telephone company to deliver new directories once every year or two. If you have a vehicle, even if just a bicycle, contact a courier firm or set yourself up as a messenger in the financial centre of a big city.

One enterprising business idea is to become a taxi driver. You can approach the largest taxi companies and ask if they recruit trainees. This is something you have to stick at to make a worthwhile income, since your technique will improve substantially with practice. If you already have a portable skill such as experience as a mechanic, you'll probably have no trouble finding casual opportunities wherever you go.

Labouring

Labouring jobs have traditionally been a source of instant money for men. The ease with which you can find manual industrial work depends on the local labour supply and these days a shortage is a rare thing. Anyone with some building experience and a set of tools and some steel-capped boots stands a good chance of finding work abroad. *Overseas Jobs Express* published some statistics in 2000: construction output is set to soar by 11.4% across Europe and the countries predicted to experience the biggest growth in 2001 and 2002 are Portugal, Spain, Ireland, Norway and Sweden. The same newspaper carries adverts for building contractors, especially for work in Germany, which plumbers, carpenters, etc. may want to follow up. Within the EU it is also a great advantage to have an E101, documentary proof that you are self-employed (see chapter on *EU Employment*).

The best idea is to concentrate on areas of sudden expansion, such as world exhibitions or major sporting events like the Olympics, but preferably in remote or otherwise undesirable places, for example land bases for oil and gas exploration, new mining developments, motorway construction, etc. Another possibility is to offer your services in a ski resort out of season when chalets and hotels are being remodelled and expanded. Something that has worked in the past couple of years in the US is to show up after major disasters like the hurricane which flattened some Florida communities and the Los Angeles earthquake. In times of crisis the authorities might not be too bothered about working visas. Check the *Yellow Pages* for furniture removal firms. Wherever you are and especially in areas where holiday homes are being built or renovated, it is worth keeping your eyes open for buildings under construction and making enquiries.

If you are making local enquiries, make contact with the British labourers already employed by frequenting the same pubs that they do (where much of the hiring takes place). Without an industrial skill you're more likely to get taken on by cowboy firms which tend to pay higher wages to foreign workers than to locals but provide no job protection or welfare benefits. Horror stories persist of unpaid or radically reduced wages and disappearing agents.

Sometimes there is an early morning meeting place for hopeful labour, perhaps outside the casual employment office in big cities or in the town square of smaller communities. As a working holidaymaker you may be rather conspicuous among the desperados, winos, and illegal immigrants waiting to be picked up by an employer. Or pay an early morning call on likely businesses such as haulage contractors. This system is of course highly erratic, and it might be less depressing to advertise yourself locally as 'Instant Labour' which could lead to something more stable.

There are lots of industrial activities apart from construction which require labourers. In large ports like Rotterdam, Hamburg, Goteborg or Seattle there is work to be had cleaning out tankers or doing general wharf work; freelance stevedores are in an ideal position to earn good money in short bursts. Unfortunately dockers in most countries belong to powerful and exclusive unions. If possible get to know a union member and ask them to contact you whenever there is a need for extra casuals.

Unskilled labourers are often needed by landscape contractors and related businesses. Writing from Florida, Floyd Creamer has a suggestion for enterprising individuals:

In any city there are tree trimming companies which will take you on temporarily if you bring customers with you. That is, if you tell a company that you know several people who want tree service, they will hire you as 'ground crew', even women and undocumented aliens. Go to a flea market or similar place with lots of pedestrians and talk to as many people as possible. Offer tree trimming/pruning, tree removal, stump grinding, hedge trimming and brush hauling. Offer a free estimate and get their name, address and phone number. After you get some leads (I got 20 in one morning at a busy Fort Lauderdale flea market), call some tree services and explain the situation. There is lots of money in trees, enough for me to start my own company.

Factory Work

Production lines impose a terrible tyranny: if you fall behind packing those Mars bars or calibrating those petrol pumps, you will cause chaos, just as falling off a ski tow causes everything to grind to a halt. But if you are willing to tackle this sort of work (and it is possible to do anything for a short period) you can save a handy sum. Factories in which the pressures are less, where your bunglings are tolerated and you are permitted to switch jobs, tend to pay lower wages but are more fun. In a factory where high standards are set you will have to expect a certain amount of abuse (usually good-natured) on account of your being a 'sloppy British workman only interested in tea and striking' or a 'naïve and dreamy student'.

Some of our contributors have thoroughly enjoyed the work they have done in factories abroad: Richard Adams who worked for a shock absorber factory in the industrial Ruhr Valley of Germany was delighted to participate in the racing department and to attend weekend rallies since these were both exciting and very well paid; Chris Daniels found interesting and rewarding work in a Minnesota factory which provided employment for handicapped people; Steve Smith, who worked in a crate-making factory in Ghana, enjoyed the challenge of seeing everything run smoothly. Another possible perk is that you may be entitled to take home free samples of whatever the factory produces, so try to get a job with Carlsberg in Copenhagen or Rowntrees in York rather than Fisons or Dulux. Even those travellers who have found little job satisfaction in their factory jobs have been pleased with the pay packets.

Canning and food processing factories are a good bet because of their highly seasonal nature. Check the brand names on tinned or frozen foods (e.g. Lockwoods, Smedleys, Bird's Eye, Green Giant) and contact them for casual work. Advertising promises such as 'Only two hours from the field to the freezer' indicate the urgency of the labour requirements in this industry.

The Manpower Agency can be a worthwhile source of employment wherever you are, since it operates in over 30 countries. In addition to factory work, it is also strong on temporary warehouse packing and clerical jobs. You can locate Manpower in the telephone directories of many big cities.

VOLUNTARY WORK

The year 2001 is the International Year of the Volunteer and vast amounts of government money are being poured into the field to encourage volunteer exchanges. Voluntary work can provide a unique stepping stone to further adventures abroad and is often an adventure in itself. Many schemes are open to all nationalities and avoid work permit hassles. By participating in a project such as digging wells in a Turkish village, looking after orphaned refugee children or just helping out at a youth hostel, you have the unique opportunity to live and work in a remote community, and the chance to meet up with young people from many countries who can point you towards new job prospects. You may be able to improve or acquire a language skill and to learn something of the customs of the society in which you are volunteering. You will also gain practical experience, for instance in the fields of construction, archaeology, or social welfare which will stand you in good stead when applying for paid jobs elsewhere.

It should be pointed out that the majority of voluntary jobs undertaken abroad leave the volunteer out-of-pocket. Many organisations, especially in the US, charge volunteers large sums to cover the cost of recruiting, screening, interviewing, pre-departure orientation, insurance, etc. on top of travel, food and lodging, which can be disillusioning for anyone who thinks that a desire to help the world is enough. After participating in several prearranged voluntary projects in the United States, Catherine Brewin did not resent the fee she had paid to Involvement Volunteers (whose activities are described below):

The whole business of paying to do voluntary work is a bit hard to swallow. But having looked into the matter quite a bit, it does seem to be the norm. While it may be a bit unfair (who knows how much profit or loss these voluntary organisations make or how worthy their projects?), most people I've met did seem to feel good about the experience. The group I was with did raise the odd comment about it all, but did not seem unduly concerned. However I should mention that most were around 18 years old and their parents were paying some if not all the costs.

Sources of Information

If you are interested in short or long term voluntary projects you might like to start by browsing in the *International Directory of Voluntary Work* (Vacation-Work, £10.99; Peterson's $15.95). The 2000 edition describes the voluntary requirements of 700+ organisations. Another excellent compendium is *Worldwide Volunteering for Young People* compiled by Youth for Britain and published by How To Books (£15.95). The World Service Enquiry of the respected charity Christians Abroad, Bon Marché Centre, Suite 233, 241-251 Ferndale Road, London SW9 8BJ (020-7346 5950; wse@cabroad.org.uk/ www.wse.org.uk) provides information and advice to people of any faith or none who are thinking of working overseas, whether short or long term, voluntary or paid. A free booklet *The Millennium Guide* contains a useful listing of organisations in the UK and overseas, and details how and where to begin a search for work abroad. For qualified people, *Opportunities Abroad*, a monthly listing of vacancies through around 60 agencies, is available on subscription (£5 for a single issue, £20 for ten via e-mail). A database of skilled personnel is kept and searched on behalf of agencies looking for staff (£15 admin fee).

The revolution in information technology has made it easier for the individual to become acquainted with the amazing range of possibilities. There are some superb websites with a multitude of links to organisations big and small that can make use of volunteers. For example www.idealist.org (from Action Without Borders) is an easily searchable site that will take you to the great monolithic charities like the Peace Corps as well as to small grassroots organisations in Armenia, Tenerife or anywhere else. It lists 20,000 organisations in 150 countries. Another impressive site is one from AVSO, the Association of Voluntary Services Organisations, in Belgium (174 rue Joseph II, 2000 Brussels; www.avso.org) which is supported by the European Commission. The British-based oneworld.net lists vacancies primarily of interest to aid professionals. The Voluntary Work Information Service (PO Box 2759, Lewes, Sussex BN7 1WU; tel/fax 01273 470015) can be found on www.workingabroad.com; access to its networking service costs £32.

Christian Vocations (St James House, Trinity Road, Dudley, West Midlands DY1 1JB; 01384 233511; www.christianvocations.org) publishes a directory listing short-term opportunities with Christian agencies. The *STS Directory* (Short-Term Service) is available for £7 including postage. They also publish a book on longer term openings called *Mission Matters* as well.

For a very general outline of possibilities, request a one-page information sheet called 'Voluntary Work Overseas' from Oxfam, which starts with the rather surprising sentence 'Oxfam does not send volunteers overseas' (Oxfam Supporter Services, 274 Banbury Road, Oxford OX2 7DZ). Anyone who wants to become better informed about volunteering before beginning the application process might consider sending an s.a.e. to ICA UK, PO Box 171, Manchester M15 5BE or checking their website www.ica-uk.org.uk. They run Volunteer Orientation Weekends which cost £65 (£45 unwaged).

Pros and Cons

Bear in mind that voluntary work, especially in the developing world, can be not only tough and character-building but also disillusioning (see Mary Hall's description of her year at a Uganda clinic in the *Africa* chapter). And just as the working traveller must be alert to exploitation in paid jobs, so he or she should be careful in voluntary situations as well. Misunderstandings can arise, and promises can be broken just as easily in the context of unpaid work. Occasionally eager young volunteers are forced to conclude that the people in charge of the organisation charge volunteers well in excess of essential running costs. Fortunately the experiences of one volunteer in Africa are rare: he claims to have discovered that the community development projects described in the literature from an organisation in Sierra Leone did not exist and furthermore the director had previously jumped bail from Freetown CID. If you are in any doubt about an organisation you are considering working for, ask for the names of one or two past volunteers whom you can contact for an informal reference. Any worthy organisation should be happy to oblige.

Disillusionment can be a problem for even the most privileged volunteers working for the most respectable charities. When Danny Jacobson visited Bulgaria in 2000, he found the country stuffed full of Peace Corps volunteers:

I had always envisioned Peace Corps volunteers to be off in Third World countries living in huts, repairing trees and teaching English to tribal children. In fact, in Bulgaria they all had sly apartments, decent salaries and an average of about 20 hours a week to commit to the cause. Everything from toothpaste to toilet paper was provided and twice a year they were all carted out to some fancy hotel to practise the language and bond. Pretty much everyone we met had a similar story: they joined to try to make a difference and were now left disenchanted and feeling useless. Since the Peace Corps is pretty relaxed about assigning duties – basically you are dropped off in a town and left to your own resources with no supervision – Chris had to start teaching English and later worked with a couple of guys to help build mountain huts and maintain hiking trails. Everyone was pessimistic because it seemed to take forever to get anything done.

Morale might well be higher in other countries.

Carina Strutt's experiences in Central America are uncommon, but worth bearing in mind when considering joining a privately-run project sight unseen. In good faith she went to work for an environmental project and spent most of her time there painting T-shirts for the owners who wanted the task done in time for their holiday in

Australia. Worse, they treated the local people with scant respect. (Needless to say, this project is not included in this book.)

Gap Year Placements

Far more students take a year out between school and university than used to be the case. Both STA and usit Campus, the two biggest youth travel agencies in the UK, produce free gap year listings (see www.statravel.co.uk/explore.gaplinks.htm). In 2001, the number of deferred entry applicants rose to over 22,000. Many organisations attempt to make it possible for school-leavers (normally in their gap year) to undertake useful voluntary work for part of their year between school and higher education. Selection often takes place after a weekend assessment. All volunteers are asked to fundraise substantial sums, normally £2,000-£3,000. This is a brief listing of the major specialist organisations; for more information see my book *Taking a Gap Year* (new edition due to be published in 2001) or *Taking a Year Out* by Polly Bird (Hodder & Stoughton).

A number of UK organisations make it possible for school-leavers in their gap year to work for 6-12 months abroad. Most of the organisations listed here are founder members of the Year Out Group (PO Box 29925, London SW6 6FQ; 07980 395789/ www.yearoutgroup.org) formed to promote well-structured gap year programmes:

GAP Activity Projects, 44 Queen's Road, Reading, Berks. RG1 4BB (0118-959 4914; www.gap.org.uk). Posts are for between four and eleven months (six is average) and cost the volunteer £685 plus airfares and insurance, while board, lodging and (sometimes) pocket money are provided.

Gap Challenge, Black Arrow House, 2 Chandos Road, London NW10 6NF (020-8537 7980; www.world-challenge.co.uk). Teaching and other placements in India, Nepal, Tanzania, Malawi, Malaysia, Belize and Peru. Fees £1,600-£2,700 including airfares.

Africa & Asia Venture, 10 Market Place, Devizes, Wilts. SH10 1HT (01380 729009; www.aventure.co.uk). Voluntary teaching and other projects for year-out students.

Changing Worlds, 11 Doctors Lane, Chaldon, Surrey CR3 5AE (01883 340960; www.changingworlds.co.uk). Placements in Zimbabwe, Tanzania, Nepal, India, Australia and New Zealand.

i-to-i, One Cottage Road, Headingley, Leeds LS6 4DD (0870-333 2332; www.i-to-i.com). TEFL and conservation placements in Latin America, Africa, Russia and Asia.

The Project Trust, The Hebridean Centre, Ballyhough, Isle of Coll, Argyll PA78 6TE (01879 230444; projecttrust@compuserve.com). Educational charity which sends British school-leavers aged 17-19 overseas for a year to a great many countries. Fund-raising target for 2001 is £3,250.

Quest Overseas, 32 Clapham Mansions, Nightingale Lane, London SW4 9AQ (020-8673 3313; www.questoverseas.com). Run gap year projects and expeditions in South America, Central America and South Africa.

Raleigh International, 27 Parsons Green Lane, London SW6 4HZ (020-7371 8585; www.raleigh.org.uk). Offers young people aged 17-25 the chance to undertake demanding environmental and community projects overseas. Destinations include Chile, Belize, Namibia, Ghana and Mongolia. The fundraising target is about £3,000.

Students Partnership Worldwide (SPW), 17 Dean's Yard, London SW1P 3PB (020-7222 0138; www.spw.org). Educational and environmental programmes lasting 4-10 months in Africa and Asia for 18-28 year olds.

Teaching & Projects Abroad, Gerrard House, Rustington, West Sussex BN16 1AW (01903 859911; www.teaching-abroad.co.uk). About 1,000 people are recruited annually as English language teaching assistants and in other fields. Volunteers work in Ukraine, Russia, (Moscow, St. Petersburg and Siberia), India, Ghana, Mexico and China, Peru, Togo, Nepal, Thailand and South Africa.

Travellers, 7 Mulberry Close, Ferring, West Sussex BN12 5HY (tel/fax 01903 502595; www.travellersworldwide.com). Volunteers teach conversational English (and/or other subjects) in India, Nepal, Sri Lanka, Russia, Cuba, South Africa, Ukraine and Malaysia.

Venture Co Worldwide, Pleck House, Middletown, Moreton Morrell, Warwick, CV35 9AU (01926 651071; www.ventureco-worldwide.com). Gap year programmes in the Indian subcontinent and South America.

Workcamps and Other Placement Organisations

Voluntary work in developed countries often takes the form of workcamps which accept unskilled short-term labour. As part of an established international network of voluntary organisations they are not subject to the irregularities of some privately run projects. As well as providing volunteers with the means to live cheaply for two to four weeks in a foreign country, workcamps enable volunteers to become involved in what is usually useful work for the community, to meet people from many different backgrounds and to 'increase their awareness of other lifestyles, social problems and their responsibility to society' as one volunteer has described it. According to one of the leading organisers, workcamps are a 70-year-old programme of conflict resolution and community development and an inexpensive and personal way to travel, live and work in an international setting.

Andrew Boyle, who has done a variety of jobs abroad subsequently, got off to an excellent start by joining several European workcamps:

> *I participated in three voluntary workcamps: two in West Germany and one in the French Alps. The former, particularly, were excellent value, both in the nature of the work (Umweltschutz or environmental protection) and in that the group of about 20 became part of the local community – meeting the locals in the kneipen or socialising with the 'Ziwis' (conscientious objectors doing community service instead of military service). These camps are an excellent introduction to travelling for 16 to 20 year olds, say, sixth formers who have never been away from a family type social structure. I suspect that their value would be more limited to an experienced traveller.*

The European Voluntary Service is an initiative of the European Commission to encourage young Europeans (aged 18-25) to join short and long term projects in social care, youth work, outdoor recreation and rural development. The largest provider of EVS volunteers from Britain is EIL, 287 Worcester Rd, Malvern, Worcs. WR14 1AB (0800 018 4015; www.eiluk.org) which also sends volunteers to Ecuador, Mexico and Ghana for between one and six months. Another agency involved is Connect Youth at the British Council (10 Spring Gardens, London SW1A 2BN; 020-7389 4030; www.britcoun.org/education/connectyouth). The European Commission helps to fund the programme and in some cases subsidises costs.

Within Europe, and to a lesser extent further afield, there is a massive effort to co-ordinate workcamp programmes. This normally means that the prospective volunteer should apply in the first instance to the appropriate organisation in his or her own country, or to a centralised international headquarters. The vast majority of camps take place in the summer months, and camp details are normally published in March/April. Understandably, these organisations charge £4-£6 for a copy of their international programmes. It is necessary to pay a registration fee (usually £70-£120 for overseas camps) to join a workcamp, which includes board and lodging but not of course travel. In developing countries, there may be an extra charge to help finance future projects or to pay for specialised training. The vast majority of placements are made between mid-April and mid-May.

The largest workcamp organisation is Service Civil International with branches in 25 countries. The UK branch is International Voluntary Service (IVS) (addresses below). Occasionally in the pages of this book, we have included foreign addresses of workcamp organisations for the benefit of long-term travellers who are already in the country in which they want to join a workcamp or for readers who do not know the address of their national partner organisation.

When requesting information from the workcamp organisations listed below always send a stamped self-addressed envelope or international reply coupon, since these organisations are charities which need to keep costs to a minimum and in most cases cannot reply to letters without a stamp. They all now have websites with camp listings accessible free to anyone with access to the internet.

International Voluntary Service (IVS Field Office), Old Hall, East Bergholt, Colchester, Essex CO7 6TQ (01206 298215/fax 01206 299043; ivsgbn@ivsgbn.demon.co.uk/ www.ivsgbn.demon.co.uk). IVS North: Castlehill House, 21 Otley Road, Headingley, Leeds LS6 3AA (0113-230 4600/0113-230 4610) and IVS Scotland: 7 Upper Bow, Edinburgh EH1 2JN (0131-226 6722/fax 0131-226 6723). Programme of camps published in April for £4. In 2001 the cost of registration on workcamps outside the UK is £120 (£95 for students and low-waged) which includes £25 membership in IVS.

Concordia Youth Service Volunteers Ltd, Heversham House, 20-22 Boundary Road, Hove, East Sussex BN3 4ET (tel/fax 01273 422218; info@concordia-iye.org.uk/ www.concordia-iye.org.uk). Programme of workcamps costs £3. Registration costs £85.

Quaker Voluntary Action, Friends Meeting House, 6 Mount St, Manchester M2 5NS (0161-819 1634; qva@quakervolaction.freeserve.co.uk). Registration fee of £80 (£60 students/low-waged; £45 unwaged).

UNA Exchange, United Nations Association, Temple of Peace, Cathays Park, Cardiff CF10 3AP (029-2022 3088; unaiys@btinternet.com). Majority of camps cost £90-£125 to join. Run a separate North/South Exchange Programme for selected volunteers to work in sub-Saharan Africa and Southern Asia after a six-month application procedure involving a training weekend in Cardiff.

Youth Action for Peace/YAP, 8 Golden Ridge, Freshwater, Isle of Wight PO40 9LE; 01983 752577/fax 01983 756900; yapuk@ukonline.co.uk/ www.yap-uk.org). Formerly the Christian Movement for Peace. Workcamps held in many countries in Western and Eastern Europe, plus Mexico, the Middle East and Bangladesh. Registration fee £50 plus £25 for some camps.

You are not normally expected to have workcamp experience in your home country before being placed abroad, though this is not a fixed rule. However camps in developing countries rarely take inexperienced volunteers. It should be noted that for workcamps in developing nations and sometimes for Eastern Europe, British volunteers may have to be interviewed before being placed, or attend orientation meetings. European organisations have traditionally accepted volunteers of all nationalities; however it has become more difficult for nationals outside the European Union and North America to be accepted. This is due to the fact that some people have been abusing the system by applying for a workcamp, using the letter of invitation at immigration control and then not showing up.

American volunteers should apply to one of the major workcamp organisations in the US:

Council (Council Exchanges), International Volunteer Projects, 20th Floor, 633 Third Ave, New York, NY 10017 (1-888-COUNCIL; www.councilexchanges.com/vol). 600 International Volunteer Projects in 30 countries. Their directory of opportunities is available from April and costs $12 or can be viewed on their web page. Placement fee is $200 for most overseas workcamps.

SCI-USA (Service Civil International), 814 NE 40th St, Seattle, WA 98105; scitalk@sci-ivs.org/ www.sci-ivs.org).

Volunteers for Peace, 1034 Tiffany Road, Belmont, Vermont 05730 (802-259-2759; vfp@vfp.org/ www.vfp.org). Annual membership $20. VFP publish an up-to-date *International Workcamp Directory* with over 1,200 listings in 70 countries, available from mid-April. Registration for most programmes is $200 ($225 if under 18).

The majority of projects are environmental or social. They may involve the conversion/reconstruction of historic buildings and building community facilities. Some of the more interesting projects recently include building adventure playgrounds for children, renovating an open-air museum in Latvia, organising youth concerts in Armenia, constructing boats for sea-cleaning in Japan, looking after a farm-school in Slovakia during the holidays, helping peasant farmers in central France to stay on their land, excavating a Roman villa in Germany, forest fire spotting in Italy, plus a whole range of schemes with the disabled and elderly, conservation work and the study of social and political issues. It is sometimes possible to move from project to project throughout the summer, particularly in countries such as France or Morocco where the workcamp movement is highly developed.

Living conditions (and the quality of food in particular) vary greatly. The working week is 30 hours though it can stretch to a maximum of 40 hours, spread over five or six days. On the whole, camps are under the direction of one or two leaders but participants often help in the decision making. Social events and excursions are invariably included in the programme and some organisations arrange study sessions. Although English is the language of many international camps, some of them do require knowledge of a foreign language.

Holiday Schemes

An interesting possibility for working your way as a volunteer is to offer to assist people with special needs to take 'independent' holidays. The Royal Association for Disability and Rehabilitation (12 City Forum, 250 City Road, London EC1V 8AF; 020-7250 3223; radar@radar.org.uk) publishes an information sheet *Voluntary and Paid Opportunities* which includes holiday projects, a few of which are outside the UK. Send an A4 s.a.e. to receive a copy.

The Disaway Trust (65 Shaftesbury Road, Carshalton, Surrey SM5 1HJ; tel/fax 020-8640 0712) arranges for able-bodied volunteers to accompany disabled holidaymakers abroad for 8-10 days. Volunteers pay about half the cost of the holiday (between £200 and £400). The Guide Dogs for the Blind Association (0118-983 5555) has a holidays department which pairs sighted with visually impaired holidaymakers and offers subsidies on holidays such as trekking in Nepal. Mencap Holiday Services also looks for volunteers to accompany their groups of children and adults with learning disabilities; Optimum House, Clippers Quay, Salford Quays, Manchester M5 2XP (0161-888 1200).

Archaeology

Taking part in archaeological excavations is another popular form of voluntary work, but volunteers are usually expected to make a contribution towards their board and lodging. Also, you may be asked to bring your own trowel, work clothes, tent, etc. Archaeology Abroad (31-34 Gordon Square, London WC1H 0PY; fax 020-7383 2527; www.britarch.ac.uk/archabroad) is an excellent source of information, as they publish bulletins in March, May and October with details of excavations needing volunteers; in the past year between 700 and 1,000 definite places on sites were offered to subscribers. They do stress however that applications from people with a definite interest in the subject are preferred. An annual subscription costs £10 ($30/£12 overseas).

Another valuable list of over 200 digs worldwide needing volunteers is the *Archaeological Fieldwork Opportunities Bulletin* published by the Archaeological Institute of America in Boston (fax 617-353-6550; www.archaeological.org) and available from Kendall/Hunt Publishing, 4050 Westmark Drive, PO Box 1840, Dubuque, Iowa 52002 (1-800-228-0810). It is published every January and costs $15 plus postage of $4 (US), $7 (surface abroad). It includes details of digs from Kentucky to Sri Lanka.

For those who are not students of archaeology, the chances of finding a place on an overseas dig will be greatly enhanced by having some digging experience nearer to home. Details of British excavations looking for volunteers are published in *British Archaeology* magazine from the British Council for Archaeology (see *UK: Voluntary Work*).

Anthony Blake joined a dig sponsored by the University of Reims and warns that 'archaeology is hard work, and applicants must be aware of what working for eight hours in the baking heat means!' Nevertheless Anthony found the company excellent and the opportunity to improve his French welcome.

Israel is a country particularly rich in archaeological opportunities, many of them organised through the universities. Digs provide an excellent means of seeing remote parts of the country through Israeli digs tend to be more expensive than most.

Conditions vary, but can be fairly primitive. Jennifer McKibben found 'washing (apart from hands and face) was allowed only one day in four, when one enjoyed the luxury of a communal hose-pipe shower to remove all of the sand and grime that easily accumulates after four days of digging in the desert.'

Conservation

People interested in protecting the environment can often slot into conservation organisations abroad. One enterprising traveller in South Africa looked up the 'green directory' in a local library, contacted a few of the projects listed in the local area and was invited to work at a cheetah reserve near Johannesburg in exchange for accommodation and food.

For a directory of opportunities in this specialised area, consult the book *Green Volunteers: The World Guide to Voluntary Work in Nature Conservation* published in Italy and distributed by Vacation Work Publications in Europe (£10.99 plus £1.50 postage). Related titles from the same publisher are *Working with the Environment* and *Working with Animals*.

To fix up a short-term project ahead of time, contact the British Trust for Conservation Volunteers (BTCV) which runs a programme of International Conservation Holidays in Iceland, France, Portugal, Greece, Turkey, Hungary and most other European countries, as well as North America, Senegal, Japan and Thailand; further details are available from the BTCV, 36 St. Mary's St, Wallingford, Oxfordshire OX10 0EU (01491 821600/fax 01491 839646; www.btcv.org). Prices start at £190 excluding travel from the UK.

The international system of working-for-keep on organic farms is another good way of visiting unexplored corners of the world cheaply. A description of the organisation WWOOF (Willing Workers on Organic Farms) may be found in the *Agriculture* chapter. Also, staying on communes, peace centres and the like may be of interest, as discussed in the same chapter.

Involvement Volunteers Association Inc (PO Box 218, Port Melbourne, Victoria 3207, Australia; +61-3-9646 9392; www.volunteering.org.au) arranges short-term individual, group and team voluntary placements in many countries including Australia, New Zealand, California, Hawaii, Fiji, Papua New Guinea, Thailand, India, Lebanon and Germany. Most projects are concerned with conservation, though some are with community-based social service organisations assisting disadvantaged people as teachers, specialists or general helpers. The combined programme fees are about A$450 covering any number of placements lasting 2-12 weeks within one year. The European office is at Naturbadstr. 50, D-91056 Erlangen (tel/fax 091 358075; ivgermany@volunteering.org.au).   Catherine Brewin from St. Albans joined two IV projects in the US. Her reaction is typical of many people who undertake voluntary work of any kind in exotic locations:

> *After a fortnight of doing general maintenance at a Conference Centre in southern California, I flew to Hawaii to work at a centre for mentally handicapped people. This was a considerably more restrictive environment than LA and involved us living with the handicapped residents ('clients') in a fenced off complex some distance from the nearest town. Again we did some physical work such as tree planting and weeding, and also took the clients on day trips and organised a disco. It was not an easy place to be and could hardly have been more of an antithesis to what the mind conjures up when you think of Hawaii, but it's amazing how your sense of humour and the people around you can pull you through, and I think we all learned from the experience.*
>
> *Both the projects demanded quite a bit of flexibility. Things were seldom apparent or well organised, and there were times when we were unsure as to what we were supposed to do, or felt that we were expected to work on tasks totally outside our brief. I think anyone considering joining a voluntary work project should be aware that this may be the case. I must admit that for me, two fortnight-long projects was enough and I was happy to move on, leave a group situation and start travelling and doing what I wanted to do.*

There are several organisations whose function it is to help and staff scientific expeditions by supplying fee-paying volunteers. These are in effect specialist tour operators, and it seems that there is a booming market for this sort of working holiday. Scientific expedition organisations that use self-financing volunteers include the following, some of whose expeditions are mentioned in the country chapters:

Coral Cay Conservation Ltd, 154 Clapham Park Road, London SW4 7DE (020-7498 6248; www.coralcay.org). Recruits paying volunteers to assist with tropical forest and coral reef conservation expeditions in Honduras and the Philippines.

Discovery Initiatives, 51 Castle Street, Cirencester, Glos. GL7 1QD (01285 643333; www.discoveryinitiatives.com). Glossy brochure details expensive conservation holidays worldwide.

Earthwatch Europe, 57 Woodstock Road, Oxford OX2 6HJ (01865 318838; www.earthwatch.org/europe). International non-profit organisation that recruits over 4,000 volunteers a year for 50 countries to assist professional, scientific field research expeditions around the world. Prices range from less than £100 for a short local project to £2,450 for helping to study the echidna in Australia. The average duration is two weeks though some are one week and others last a month. Prices do not include air travel to location.

Ecovolunteer Program, c/o 59 St Martins Lane, Covent Garden, London WC2N 4JS. UK branch of the international programme to co-ordinate placement of volunteers. Headquarters are at Meyersweg 29, 7553 AX Hengelo, Netherlands; +31-6-519 27677; info@ecovolunteer.org/ www.ecovolunteer.org. About 600 volunteers for 1-4 week projects. The organisation Proyecto Ambientale is at the same UK address (www.interbook.net/personal/delfinc). See Spain chapter for details of their research projects in Tenerife.

Frontier, 77 Leonard St, London EC2A 4QS (020-7613 2422; www.frontierprojects.ac.uk). Conservation projects and surveys carried out on land and sea in Vietnam, Tanzania and Madagascar. Volunteers must fund-raise £2,450 for ten-week expeditions or £3,750 for 20 weeks.

Greenforce, 11-15 Betterton St, London WC2H 9BP (020-7470 8888; www.greenforce.org). Environmental projects in Africa and the Amazon, and marine project in the South Pacific. Aimed at those who want to make a career of conservation.

Trekforce Expeditions, 34 Buckingham Palace Road, London SW1W 0RE (020-7828 2275; www.trekforce.org.uk). Projects in Belize, Indonesia and Kenya concentrating on endangered rainforests.

In the US, try:

Earthwatch, 680 Mt. Auburn Street, PO Box 403, Watertown, Massachusetts 02272-9924, USA (www.earthwatch.org).

Explorations in Travel, 1922 River Road, Guildford, VT 05301 (802-257 0152; www.volunteertravel.com). Rainforest conservation, wildlife projects, etc. in Ecuador, Costa Rica, Belize, Puerto Rico, Mexico, Nepal, Australia and New Zealand. Other placements in animal shelters, on small farms and in schools. Placement fees $750-$950.

Institute of Cultural Ecology, 758 Kapahula Avenue, 150, Honolulu, HI 96816; 808-782-6166; www.islandtime.org). Internships on several Hawaiian islands, Fiji and Thailand. Sample placements cost $1,900 for four weeks, $3,850 for 12 weeks at a gibbon reserve in northeast Thailand.

Wildlands Studies, 3 Mosswood Circle, Cazadero, CA 95421 (707-621-5665; www.gonetropo.com/ws). 27 projects in the US (including Alaska and Hawaii), Belize, Thailand or Nepal.

Developing Countries

Commitment, no matter how fervent, is not enough to work in an aid project in the developing world. You must normally be able to offer some kind of useful training or skill unless you are prepared to fund yourself and don't mind that your effort to help will be more a token than of lasting benefit. Many organisations offer ordinary people the chance to experience life in the developing world by working alongside local people for a brief period and these are mentioned throughout the chapters on Africa, Asia and Latin America later in this book.

Among the main voluntary and aid organisations in the UK and Europe are:

VSO (Voluntary Service Overseas), Enquiries Unit, 317 Putney Bridge Rd, London SW15 2PN (020-8780 7500; enquiry@vso.org.uk/ www.vso.org.uk). Recruits volunteers in the fields of education, health, natural resources, technical trades and engineering, business and social work for two-year assignments. VSO pays a modest local wage, various grants, national insurance, provides accommodation, health insurance and return flights. Volunteers need to be aged 20-68, and qualified and experienced. A shortage of volunteers has prompted VSO to investigate shorter periods with companies keeping open the volunteer's job. They also run the Overseas Training Programme which provides 10-12 months of work experience for UK university students.

International Co-operation for Development, Unit 3, Canonbury Yard, 190a New North Rd, Islington, London N1 7BJ (020-7354 0883). Overseas technical assistance programme of CIIR (Catholic Institute for International Relations) employs professionals.

AFS, Leeming House, Vicar Lane, Leeds LS2 7JF; 0113-242 6136; www.afsuk.org). Voluntary work opportunities for students and others aged 18-29 in Latin America and South Africa. Placements last 6 or 12 months and involve living with a local family.

Inter-Cultural Youth Exchange, Latin American House, Kingsgate Place, London NW6 4TA (tel/fax 020-7681 0983; info@icye.co.uk). Students and others aged 18-25 spend a year abroad with a host family and undertake voluntary work placements, for example in drug rehabilitation, protection of street children and ecological projects, in Bolivia, Brazil, Costa Rica, Honduras, Colombia, Mexico, Uruguay, India, Ghana, Nigeria, South Korea, Taiwan, Japan, New Zealand, Kenya, Switzerland or Poland. 8-month stays in Eastern Europe may be fully funded by the European Commission.

World Exchange is a church-sponsored volunteer abroad programme based at St Colm's International House, 23 Inverleith Terrace, Edinburgh EH3 5NS (0131-315 4444; we@stcolms.org) which sends people worldwide to work with community organisations for 10-12 months or on some two-month workcamps. The minimum contribution a volunteer must make to their one-year placement is £2,000.

Peace Brigades International (1a Waterlow Road, London N19 5NJ; 020-7281 5370; www.igc.apc.org) is an international non-governmental organisation working on non-violent resolution of conflicts. PBI provides physical and moral support to peace and justice activists whose lives and work are threatened by violence. The work is carried out by sending teams of international volunteers to work on projects in Mexico (the Chiapas region), Colombia, Haiti and the Balkans.

NORTH AMERICAN OPPORTUNITIES

Three books that prospective volunteers might want to consult for ideas are:

Volunteer Vacations (Chicago Review Press/Independent Publishers Group, 814 N Franklin St, Chicago, IL 60610; 800-888-4741/www.ipgbook.com). Updated every other year; last edition published September 1999.

Working for Global Justice: A Directory of Progressive Organizations Offering Volunteer, Internship, Educational Travel and Career Opportunities in the US or Abroad (JustAct - Youth Action for Global Justice, 333 Valencia St, Suite 101, San Francisco, CA 94103; 415-431-4204; info@justact.org/ www.justact.org). Strong listings for Latin America. Donation of $10 requested.

Invest Yourself: The Catalogue of Voluntary Opportunities (Commission on Voluntary Service and Action, c/o Susan Angus, PO Box 117, New York, NY 10009; 1-718-638 8487). $11 including US postage. New edition 2000. 200 organisations.

In the US, the website of the International Volunteer Programmes Association has links to all the mainstream organisations (www.volunteerinternational.org).

ImpactOnline in Palo Alto California runs a website that tries to link volunteers with projects via www.volunteermatch.org. InterAction based in Washington DC posts vacancies in international relief and development agencies; a one-month subscription costs $10 (www.interaction.org/jobs).

Companies that maintain databases of opportunities (mostly unpaid) and offer personalised consultations to fee-paying clients (often young people aged 16-25) attempt to match them with a suitable work, volunteer or study placement abroad. Many of the placement organisations to which candidates will be referred offer what are basically volunteer vacations, i.e. two or three week service programmes in developing countries for a substantial fee:

Taking Off, PO Box 104, Newton Highlands, MA 02161 (617-630-1606/fax 617-630-1605; Tkingoff@aol.com). Gives clients access to a database with 2,500 options worldwide. The owner (Gail Reardon) charges $500 for short-term consultation and $1,500 for ongoing personalised assistance. New office opened in New York in 2000.

Center for Interim Programs, PO Box 2347, Cambridge, MA 02238 plus offices in Princeton and Boulder.

Horizon Cosmopolite, 3011 Notre Dame Ouest, Montreal, Quebec, Canada H4C 1N9 (tel 514-935-8436; www.horizon.cosmpolite.com). Database of 1,500 opportunities. Consultation fee C$345.

World Wide Volunteer Services (WWVS), PO Box 3242, West End, NJ 07740 (732-571-3210; http://welcome.to/volunteer_services). Individually arranged multi-cultural experiences and internships in a variety of settings around the world. Application fee $50; placement fee $100.

The Quaker Information Center (1501 Cherry St, Philadelphia, PA 19102; 215-241-7024) can send a packet of information on short and long term volunteer and service opportunities worldwide. The information, which is updated sporadically, covers what they aptly call a 'smorgasbord' of opportunities ranging from weekend workcamps through to two-year internships with aid agencies. The packet can be ordered by sending $10 ($12 outside the USA) to the above address. This information is freely available on their website www.afsc.org/qic.htm where the data is organised into 16 lists of voluntary and service opportunities.

The first organisation that American volunteers think of is the *Peace Corps* (1111 20th St NW, Washington, DC 20526; 1-800-424 8580/202-692-1800; www.peacecorps.gov) which sends skilled and experienced volunteers on two-year assignments to 77 countries. Others included:

Global Volunteers, 375 E Little Canada Road, Little Canada, Minnesota 55117, USA (651-407-6100/toll-free 1-800-487-1074; www.globalvolunteers.org). Non-profit voluntary organisation that sends 1,500 paying volunteers a year to scores of projects lasting from one to three weeks in Africa, Asia, the Caribbean, the Americas and Europe. Service programmes cost between $450 (for projects in the US) and $2,395 excluding airfares. Details are available from Global Volunteers.

Global Service Corps, 300 Broadway, Suite 28, San Francisco, CA 94133 (www.globalservicecorps.org). Co-operates with grass-roots organisations in Kenya, Thailand and Costa Rica and sends volunteers and interns for two or three weeks or longer (fee from $1,700).

Global Citizens Network, 130 N Howell St, St Paul, Minnesota 55104 (651-644-0960; www.globalcitizens.org). Sends volunteers to projects in Kenya, New Mexico (USA), Nepal and South and Central America. Programme fee is $550-$1,600.

Go Global, International Volunteer Programme, International YMCA, 71 West 23rd St, Suite 1904, New York, NY 10010 (212-727-8800; www.ymcanyc.org). Outbound programmes to YMCAs around the world. Work normally consists of camping, childcare, sports instruction or English teaching. Separate Volunteer-in-Africa programme lasting 6 weeks to 6 months.

Habitat for Humanity, 121 Habitat St, Americus, GA 31709 (912-924-6935 ext 2489; www.habitat.org). Christian housing ministry with positions for people to help build simple decent houses in over 100 countries. They prefer a long-term commitment though opportunities may be available locally in the countries where Habitat works.

In the course of your travels, you may come across wildlife projects, children's homes, special schools, etc. in which it will be possible to work voluntarily for a short or longer time. You may simply want to join your new Tongan, Bangladeshi or Guatemalan friends in the fields or wherever they are working. You may get the chance to trade your assistance for a straw mat and simple meals but more likely the only rewards will be the experience and the camaraderie.

Some travellers who find themselves in the vicinity of a major disaster think that their assistance will be welcomed. But with no practical skills, they often become a nuisance and a burden to professional aid workers.

People who work in the Third World often experience just as much culture shock on their return home as they did when they first had to adapt to difficult conditions abroad. For a graphic and amusing description of this process see *The Innocent Anthropologist* by Nigel Barley (Penguin).

Work Your Way in Europe

United Kingdom

Many readers of this book will begin to plan their world travels in Britain, and it is in Britain that they will want to save up an initial travelling fund. The amount of savings will vary from a few pounds to more than a thousand, depending on the ambitiousness of the travel plans and on the individual's willingness to live rough and take risks once he or she sets out. Some people are lucky enough to have a reasonably well paid and stable job as a nurse, postman or computer programmer before they set out on their adventures and will be in a good position to save. Others will have to gather together as many funds as possible from doing casual work at home before pursuing the same activities abroad.

Readers in other countries will also be interested in the information contained in this chapter if they are planning a working holiday in Britain. Armies of young people, particularly Antipodeans, arrive year round and quickly plug into the network of like-minded travellers looking for work in London and beyond. Everyone knows that London is an expensive city and not a pleasant place for people with few funds. Joe Warnick from Washington arrived with $500 and within three weeks was down to a measly $30. But the good news is that the unemployment figures at the beginning of 2001 are the lowest they have been since 1975, i.e. 3.7% and work is easy to come by.

RED TAPE

Nationals of the European Union are not subject to immigration controls and are therefore entitled to enter Britain to look for work. For non-EU citizens, most of whom enter on six-month tourist visas (which can normally be renewed on re-entering the country after an absence), it is difficult to find legal work. In general the Department of Employment does not issue work permits to unskilled and semi-skilled workers. Until recently, employers seldom asked to see proof of status (though they would ask for your National Insurance number). However a law has been introduced to curb illegal employment by requiring employers to see documentary proof of status and not rely solely on verbal assurances. Employers found employing people illegally will be liable to fines of up to £5,000 per employee.

The high levels of employment in southern England mean that seasonal employers are having a very hard time filling vacancies. Whereas fruit farmers could a few years ago count on a ready supply of local people willing to earn a few bob during the harvest season, those same people are likely now to have a year-round (and indoor) job stacking supermarket shelves or similar. In more skilled areas of employment (primarily information technology, especially in the London area), labour shortages are increasing to the point that the government has introduced a new fast-track work permit for seasonal and temporary workers. Immigration are being relaxed on a number of fronts, for example in some cases it is no longer necessary to leave the country to apply for a work permit.

Commonwealth nationals who can produce documentary evidence that a parent or grandparent was born in the UK can gain permission to stay and work. After completing four continuous years of work they can apply for permanent residency.

Working Holiday Visas

Working holiday-maker status may be obtained by members of Commonwealth countries between the ages of 17 and 27 inclusive with no dependants over the age of five. Last year 45,800 people with working holiday visas entered the UK. The working holiday permit entitles the holder to work in Britain with the primary intention of funding a holiday, for up to two years. It does not allow the holder to work for more than 25 hours a week, nor to work for more than a half of the total stay. It is essential to apply in the country of origin rather than at the point of entry. Immigration officials will want to be reassured that the employment you will be seeking is incidental to your travels and that it is your firm intention to leave the UK after no more than a total of two years which must be continuous from the date of entry to Britain. You may be asked to prove that you have enough money to support yourself and fund a return airfare.

Other Visas

The Training & Work Experience Scheme (TWES) is a special arrangement within the Work Permit scheme which allows foreign nationals to do work-based training for a professional or specialist qualification, a graduate training programme or work experience. TWES permits are issued on the understanding that the individual will return overseas at the end of the agreed period and put the skills learned to use for at least two years. Normally, they will not be allowed to transfer to work permit employment. Applications for permits can only be made by employers based in the UK on behalf of the person they wish to employ. Details are available from the Overseas Labour Service of the Department for Education and Employment (W5, Moorfoot, Sheffield S1 4PQ). Printed information is available by phoning 0990 210224 or downloaded from the internet (www.dfee.gov.uk/ols).

Students who are not nationals of a European Economic Area (EEA) country who are studying in the UK, and who have in their passports a stamp stating that they cannot work 'without the consent of the Secretary of State' are no longer required to obtain permission to take spare time and vacation work, or to undertake work or internship placements. Only students on courses lasting more than six months are eligible. They are allowed to work up to 20 hours a week during term-time and they should not fill a permanent full-time vacancy in pursuit of their career.

Anyone entering the country as a visitor or tourist who intends to stay longer than a few weeks should have a water-tight story, something Woden Teachout from Vermont had not prepared:

> *Coming into the UK I had a horribly distressing immigration experience. On the advice of my travel agent, I had bought a six-month return ticket rather than an open return and expected no problems. Everything went awry. I think it was when I wavered over how long I meant to be in the country that the immigration official became suspicious. The lady-turned-ogre forced me to produce my passport, ticket, money, address book and wrote down my entire life's history in cramped cursive on the back of my entrance card. I portrayed myself as a spoilt and privileged child, funded by Mummy and Daddy in her*

GREAT BRITAIN

Thurso
Ullapool
Inverness
Aviemore • Aberdeen
SCOTLAND
Ben Nevis Pitlochry Forfar
Blairgowrie Firth of Tay
North Sea
GLASGOW EDINBURGH
Belfast
LAKE DISTRICT
Isle of Man
DUBLIN
Leixlip
IRELAND
Llandudno
Cheshire
BIRMINGHAM
THE FENS King's Lynn
Wisbech
Stourport
Worcester
Pershore
Hereford Evesham
Cambridge
Lowestoft
Saxmundham
Tiptree
WALES
Pembroke
Cardiff
BRISTOL Oxford
Abingdon
Henley
Chelmsford
LONDON
Westward Ho!
Bridgwater
Guildford
Tonbridge
Ramsgate
Maidstone Sandwich
Kent
WEST COUNTRY
Sidmouth
Southampton
Bournemouth
Cornwall
Torquay
Plymouth
Brighton
Bognor
Isle of Wight
English Channel

WILLIAM SWAN

aimless intercontinental wanderings. When she at last grudgingly stamped me into the country, she called after me in a voice thick with derision, 'Do you think you'll ever work for a living?'

A few weeks later Woden had five different jobs.

SPECIAL SCHEMES & EXCHANGE ORGANISATIONS

This chapter describes a number of special schemes for young people from the United States, Canada, Australia, New Zealand, Central and Eastern Europe, etc. which allow them to work legally in Britain. For example the Seasonal Agricultural Workers Scheme or SAWS (see section on Harvests) and BUNAC's reciprocal work exchanges are open to large numbers of young people from various countries. The Home Office is the body which governs these schemes: Immigration & Nationality Directorate, Block C, Whitgift Centre, Croydon CR9 1AT (enquiry line 0870 606 7766; www.homeoffice.gov.uk/ind).

Students and others from EU and non-EU countries may be able to participate in work exchange programmes, many of which charge a substantial placement fee. Careers advisers in universities and colleges should be the best source of information. To take a few specific examples, a reciprocal Swiss/UK trainee exchange agreement allows for a special annual quota of 400 Swiss trainees to gain work experience for up to 18 months with a TWES permit. Details are available from the Swiss Federal Aliens Office (Bundesamt für Ausländerfragen/BFA, Auswanderung und Stagiaires, Quellenweg 15, 3003 Bern; 31-322 42 02/swiss.emigration@bfa.admin.ch) or from the Overseas Labour Service in Sheffield (address above).

Students from Central and Eastern Europe interested in temporary work in the UK should find out about the Harvesting Opportunity Permit Scheme (HOPS) which recruits a limited number of Central and East European full-time students aged 20 to 25 to pick fruit, vegetables or hops on HOPS (GB) registered farms for three months between May and November. The scheme is so over-subscribed that the co-ordinator asked not to have the contact address published in this book. (See the section below on the Seasonal Agricultural Workers Scheme.)

Interspeak based in the north of England undertakes to find traineeships *(stages)* for students mainly in the fields of commerce, marketing, engineering, hotel work and computers. A fee of £250 is payable for placements which last from two to six months. Accommodation is arranged with host families which helps participants to improve their English, though a knowledge of English is necessary before acceptance. Details will be sent on receipt of an s.a.e (A5) from Interspeak, Stretton Lower Hall, Stretton, S. Cheshire SY14 7HS (01829 250641; www.interspeak.co.uk). They also organise *mini-stages* in the UK whereby students aged 16-18 are found short work placements for one or two weeks (for a fee of £330 or £530).

Similarly Trident Transnational (Saffron Court, 14b St. Cross Street, London EC1N 8XA; 020-7242 1515; www.trident-transnational.org) arranges internships for students from the EEA and USA. In exchange for a fee of between £140 and £420, they will send CVs around relevant companies on behalf of people who want to work for between four weeks and six months. Occasionally they also help non-European students to be placed and to obtain a TWES permit, as described above.

The problem of work permits does not normally arise in the case of voluntary work, though participants will have to have a valid visa to be in Britain (where applicable). Conservation camps and other voluntary projects generally offer an enthusiastic welcome to foreign participants (see section on voluntary work at the end of this chapter). For example Community Service Volunteers (237 Pentonville Road, London N1 9NJ; 0800 374991/020-7278 6601) run an overseas programme in which people of all nationalities aged 18-35 are placed alongside British volunteers in projects with people who need extra help with daily living. During the projects which last from between four and 12 months, food, accommodation, pocket money and travel expenses from the point of entry are paid. The placement fee for those applying from outside the European Union is £512. It is possible to apply through a cultural exchange organisation in the US like People to People International (501 E Armour Boulevard, Kansas City, MO 64109-2200; 816-531-4701; www.ptpi.org).

Many recruitment agencies specialise in bringing EEA nationals to the UK (and to Jersey, the Isle of Man and the Republic of Ireland) to work in hotels (see *Tourism* section below).

Lots of commercial agencies on the continent sell packaged working holidays to young people. Caution should be exercised when paying over large sums to a mediating agency since some offer a very poor service as Emiliano Giovannoni from Italy explains:

> *Every year there are hundreds of Italian, French, German and Spanish guys and girls who get to London, 'thanks' to the service of some unscrupulous agencies which operate in these countries and have the monopoly on 'advising' youngsters. These agencies charge enormous fees, promising jobs, accommodation and English lessons which they don't always deliver. I have met very many people in London who, after having paid a lot of money, had to live with rats and, after weeks, still haven't been given the chance of attending one interview for a job which they usually ended up finding themselves or thanks to the local Jobcentre. All this just because they did not have access to some genuine information.*

Established youth and student exchange organisations in European capitals like EXIS in Denmark and Travel Active Programmes in the Netherlands (addresses in relevant country chapters) are more reliable.

A number of English language schools in the UK run work placement schemes alongside language courses. Some are listed in the Student Pages of the *English Now* website (www.english.now.co.uk) such as Twin School of English, 24 Clarendon Rise, London SE13 5EY (020-8297 1132; info@twinschool.co.uk) which claims to have links with 700 companies and 1,000 hotels.

Working Holidays for Americans

The programme for American students wishing to work in Britain is called the Work in Britain Program, which allows about 3,750 full-time college students over the age of 18 to look for work after arriving in Britain or pre-arranged. They must obtain a Blue Card (work permit) for a fee of about $240, which is authorised by the British Home Office. Participants may arrive at any time of the year and work for up to six months. Candidates must be US citizens enrolled at an accredited US or Canadian university or college or no more than one semester away from the most recent full-time semester. They must prove that they have access to at least $800. For further information contact BUNAC USA, PO Box 430, Southbury, CT 06488 (1-800-GO-BUNAC or 203-264-0901; wib@bunacusa.org). The *Work in Britain Participants' Handbook* contains the addresses of scores of potential employers. The BUNAC offices in London (16 Bowling Green Lane, EC1R 0QH) and Edinburgh have files of possible UK employers as well as current vacancy lists of cheap accommodation and job offers. The Work in Britain programme is the counterpart of BUNAC's Work America Programme for British students (see chapter *United States*).

According to statistics compiled on the Work in Britain programme, about a fifth of participants arrange their jobs before leaving the States, and almost all of these are in career-related jobs, often fixed up through campus contacts. The remaining students wait until they arrive, and spend an average of four to five days job-hunting before finding work. The majority work in offices, hotels, restaurants, pubs and shops. It is not only American style establishments which hire them, but also bastions of English tradition like Harrods. The average wage for participants is £180-200 per week, though secretarial jobs pay up to £250. A single room in London will cost from £75 per week while a shared room will cost £50.

US citizens who have been offered a full-time position in their field of study or experience in the UK may apply for a work permit through the Association for International Practical Training (Career Development Exchanges, 10400 Little Patuxent Pkwy, Suite 250, Columbia, MD 21044-3510; www.aipt.org).

The cultural exchange organisation Alliances Abroad can place American full-time students in temporary jobs in British hotels and restaurants for between one and six months; details are available from Alliances Abroad (702 West Ave, Austin, TX 78701; www.alliancesabroad.com). Fees range from $511 for one month to $983 for six months. A number of educational and commercial organisations in the US fix up internships for students in the UK, mainly London. Try for example the College Division of the American Institute for Foreign Study (AIFS, River Plaza, 9 West Broad St, Stamford, CT 06902-3788).

US citizens who wish to spend seven weeks from mid-June volunteering in a social service programme in Great Britain (e.g. working in youth clubs, with the homeless, HIV/AIDS sufferers and in psychiatric rehabilitation) and then travel independently for two weeks should request an application from the Winant & Clayton Volunteers (109 E 50th St, New York, NY 10022; 212-378-0271); the application deadline is January 31st. Free room and board is provided, and the volunteer pays all travel expenses (approximately $2,500-$3,000).

Working Holidays for Commonwealth Nationals

As mentioned, Canadian students can apply for a working holiday visa independently or, if they want the security of a package arrangement, they may participate in the Student Work Abroad Programme (SWAP) which is comparable to the Work in Britain programme. It is administered by the Canadian Universities Travel Service (Travel CUTS) with many local offices across Canada.

Before prospective working holidaymakers leave home, a general starting place might be *The Big O.E. Pack* produced by the British Tourist Authority (www.uktheguide.com). Various backpacker agencies in Australia, South Africa, etc. have links with London agencies and sell packages that make arrival and the initial job hunt much easier. Many also distribute *South2North* magazine published in October by Commonwealth Publishing (New Zealand House, 80 Haymarket, London SW1Y 4TE) and aimed at the working holiday market. In Australia, a good source of preliminary information is Travellers Contact Point with offices in several Australian cities plus London (2-6 Inverness Terrace, London W2 3HX; www.travellers.com.au). The 1st Contact Club at 68 North End Road, London W14 9EP; 07020 921 414; www.1st-contact.co.uk) acts as a support office for people on working holidays; membership costs A$75 or A$115 depending on level of service required. New Zealanders should find out about the services offered by Usit Beyond in NZ's university towns (www.usitbeyond.co.nz) or the agency Overseas Working Holidays (www.owh.co.nz). South Africans might like to look into what the Overseas Visitors Club can offer (230 Long St, Cape Town 8001; 021-423 4477/ www.ovc.co.za). Clients can make use of usitCampus's Work the World Lounge in London (2b Lower Belgrave St; 020-7730 5809/ usitlounge@usitworld.com) which fields requests for casual workers from employers and agencies.

Tax

One clear advantage of obtaining legal working holiday status is that you are entitled to apply for a National Insurance number which you should promptly do, from the local Contributions Agency (formerly the Department of Social Security or DSS) which can be found in any telephone directory. Most new employees are put onto the emergency tax code (denoted by 'X' at the end of your tax code) and immediately begin to forfeit a quarter of their wages. Since single people are entitled to a personal allowance of £4,385 per year (2001), it is likely that the maximum tax deducted under the PAYE system (Pay As You Earn) will be in excess of what you owe. The rate is 10% on the first £1,520 of taxable income and 22% after that. If you work for less than 12 months you are entitled to claim the full allowance. Some foreign workers have found it advantageous to set themselves up as a limited company (normally with the help of a tax advisory service as the rules have become stricter) and thereby avoid PAYE. PAYE is compulsorily deducted from the pay packets of all employees whose weekly earnings are in excess of £76.

Both UK residents and Commonwealth nationals can claim personal allowances. Foreign nationals can claim personal allowances if they have been in the UK for at least 183 days in any tax year. If the total is less than 183 days, they may be able to claim as a foreign national and/or resident of a country with which the UK has a double taxation agreement. Inland Revenue operates a telephone information service for the public on 020-7667 4000/1. But in the world of taxation, rules are subject to discretionary interpretation, so even if you don't think you're eligible, it does no harm to put in a claim. Always keep tax documents such as the P60 (end-of-year tax certificate). When you finish work, send both parts of the P45 which your employer has to give you to your employer's tax office. When you are ready to leave Britain, complete and submit form P85, a leaving certificate which asks your intentions with respect to returning to the UK to work.

Always take the precaution of making photocopies of any forms you send to Inland Revenue for the purposes of chasing later, and be prepared to wait at least six weeks. If you leave Britain before the refund is processed, it may be better to nominate someone locally to forward the money to you. If you have worked briefly, then travelled for a while and started work again, your next employer may be able to arrange a tax rebate for you provided you can hand over the P45 from your previous job.

You can make things easier for yourself by using an accountancy firm that specialises in tax rebates. They normally keep a percentage (about 18%) of whatever they get back for you. Try for example one of the following London firms: 1st Contact (19/20 Garlick Hill, London EC4V 2AL; 020-7236 7583; www.1st-contact.co.uk), Taxback (167 Earls Court Road, London SW5 9RF; 020-7244 6666), Tax Return Ltd. (213 Piccadilly, London W1V 9LD; 020-7437 9182) and Travellers Tax Ltd (020-8993 9132).

Foreign students are treated the same as UK students and can be exempted from tax. They should ask their employer for a P38(S) form which exempts students from paying tax on vacation earnings.

In addition to income tax, you must also pay National Insurance Contributions of 10% on taxable earnings above £87 a week (up to a maximum of £575 in 2001). Foreign students of English or agriculture (who can present a certificate in English from their institution proving that they are studying these subjects) can apply for an exemption.

Claimants

It is estimated that the rate of unemployment among people under 21 is more than double the national average. If you are claiming benefit and then find a temporary job, you will have to sign off, your rent-allowance will be stopped and your file closed. If you know in advance where your employment is going to be, you should ask for form A7 from your local benefit office which allows you to claim rent, etc. at your job destination. You may even be entitled to travel expenses to your new job (e.g. a Welsh hotel or fenland farm). Enquire at your local Jobcentre.

Voluntary or part-time work may affect certain benefits. Further information on this subject is contained in leaflet FB26 *Voluntary and Part-time Workers,* but in general you are allowed to earn no more than £2 a day in addition to out-of-pocket expenses and you cannot be away from home doing voluntary work for more than a fortnight a year. If you are doing voluntary work but are available for work at short notice, you may need to fill in form UB672V.

In an effort to crack down on so-called 'benefit tourism', the government introduced a test that must be passed before social security benefit will be paid. Anyone applying for benefit must prove that they are 'habitually resident' in the UK, though the definition seems to be discretionary. This has been catching out not only newly arrived foreign job-seekers but also British nationals returning from abroad.

EMPLOYMENT PROSPECTS

Although British manufacturing is in decline, many other sectors of the economy are booming. In some part of southern England there is close to full employment. But even in areas where unemployment is higher, seasonal and temporary work opportunities can usually be found. There are, for example, a multitude of harvests from the daffodils of Cornwall to periwinkles on the Isle of Mull for which the local work force is not sufficient. The tourist industry provides many opportunities for bar, catering and hotel staff in London, coastal resorts, the Lake District, Scotland and Wales. The increasing demand for childcare frequently outstrips the availability of willing candidates. In the South lots of office jobs can be seen advertised in the windows of employment agencies specialising in temporary work or in the 'Sits Vac' pages of local newspapers. Part-time and casual jobs are often advertised on cards posted in the windows or newsagents and sub-post offices. The National Minimum Wage introduced in April 1999 has improved the lot of many seasonal workers. The rate is £3.70 an hour for those over 21 and £3.30 for workers aged 18-20. For details contact the NMW information line 0845 845 0360 or 0845 600 0678. Unless you are very lucky in finding cheap accommodation, it will still be very difficult to save on these wages especially in Southeast England where the cost of living is higher than elsewhere.

Agencies

One estimate claims that there are 6,000 employment agencies in the UK, though a large number of these are for specific professions. You should not be content to register with just one, since the degree of enthusiasm with which these numerous agencies try to find suitable work for their temps varies enormously, especially if the temps can't type 60 words a minute. Manpower and Alfred Marks are among the biggest general agencies; the latter has dozens of branches in London alone and many more nationwide. Blue Arrow has an industrial division which willingly signs up students and others to carry out casual cleaning, packing and warehouse work. Colin Rothwell from South Africa found industrial agency work a very satisfactory way to save for his future travels, though he couldn't stomach all his assignments:

> *In England I found the easiest way to find work was through temping agencies. However, it was also the most inconvenient way as they liked you to have an address and a phone number. They were also the biggest sharks around and you got paid half the going wage as they took a very healthy cut from your hard-earned blood, sweat and tears. It did have its advantages though; you worked when and where it suited you, and some agencies sent you all over the place to do all kinds of weird jobs. For example, the worst job I did on my whole trip was at a dog meat factory. You arrived at the crack of dawn and were sent into a massive fridge where you were met with tons of semi-defrosting offal, with blood everywhere, and a stench like you wouldn't believe. So, as desperate for money as I was, I only lasted two days.*

If you are a trained nurse, nanny, chef, tractor driver, accountant, financial analyst, teacher, etc. there are specialist agencies eager to sign you up, especially in London and the Home Counties. Catering agencies abound and anyone with a background as a chef will probably be in demand. (See section below *Tourism & Catering*). Temping allows a great deal of flexibility, though most agencies you approach will want to be reassured that you are not about to flit off somewhere. Most will ask foreign temps for evidence of permission to work.

Despite the agency fees, wages for labouring and warehouse jobs should be in excess of the minimum wage, and up to £5-£6 on a night shift. When you get a temp job through an agency, the agency generally becomes your employer and pays your wages. People who perform well on typing or shorthand tests will find that they are placed much more promptly than those who lack any office skills and will be paid accordingly. Skilled secretarial wages start at about £8 an hour, while unskilled clerical work pays £4-£6 an hour.

One recommended agency for people with working holiday visas or EU nationality is the Australian-linked temp agency Bligh Appointments (70 North End Road, West Kensington, London W14 9EP; 020-7603 6123; bligh.appointments@btinternet.com) which has vacancies for nannies, secretaries, etc. as well as an agricultural section to place people on farms throughout Britain.

Anglo-Continental Placements Agency (Dial Post House, West Sussex RH13 8NQ; 01403 713344; www.anglocontinentalplacements.com) place staff in hotels, as nannies and on farms in England. They will register anyone with an appropriate visa or Europeans with a reasonable knowledge of English.

Temping at any kind of job is a good way of exposing your skills to potential employers. It is a good idea to ask for an application form at those workplaces to which you are temporarily assigned which you enjoy, assuming you are looking for longer term work. The principal disadvantage of temping is the uncertainty of hours. Working for an agency can also be a good way to meet fellow travellers, since lots of people signed up with agencies are there to save money for an upcoming trip.

Ian Mitselburg from Sydney got so tired of the London scene that he repaired to Edinburgh where he found it was even easier to find work and that the lower wages were counterbalanced by the lower cost of living:

I put my name down at almost every agency that would take it and had all sorts of temporary jobs including washing dishes, stuffing envelopes, transferring stocks and shares, labouring and unpacking delivery bags of foreign currency.

Another foreign visitor to Scotland, Cindy Roberts, was pleased that the agency she approached did not ask to see a work permit, nor did the dowager duchess for whom she worked on the west coast of Scotland, cooking, light housekeeping and errand-running.

Newspapers and Books

In addition to private agencies, you should make use of newspapers, where up to half of all job vacancies are advertised. There are several free weekly newspapers and magazines in London aimed at the ex-pat communities, mainly Australians, New Zealanders and South Africans. Yet these can prove to be excellent sources of casual jobs for anyone. You will find distribution boxes for *TNT* (14-15 Child's Place, Earls Court, SW5 9RX; 020-7373 3377; www.tntmag.co.uk), *New Zealand News UK* (3rd Floor, New Zealand House, 80 Haymarket, SW1Y 4TE) and *LAM* (Living Abroad Magazine, 191 Marsh Wall, London E14 9RS; 020-7005 3500/www.lam-online.com) in selected locations throughout London, e.g. outside travel agencies, tube stations, favoured pubs, etc. *TNT* and *LAM* are published every Monday. The majority of unskilled and semi-skilled jobs advertised are for mother's helps, sales people, in bars and farm workers. Recruitment agencies advertise for nurses and professionals in accountancy, banking, IT, law, etc.. TNT's sister publication *Southern Cross* published Wednesdays is also worth checking, as is their *Great Britain & Ireland Travel Planner*. The latter booklet is published twice a year and can be obtained by sending a large s.a.e with a 64p stamp to TNT.

Every October Commonwealth Publishing (publisher of the *New Zealand News*) produces *South2North* magazine mentioned earlier with articles and advertising relevant to travellers and job-seekers, particularly those from South Africa, Australia and New Zealand (enquiries to 020-7747 9200/7747 9223; www.nznewsuk.co.uk). Job-seekers in London can visit the South2north Travellers Info Centre at 25 Royal Opera Arcade, just behind New Zealand House on Haymarket where job and accommodation advertisements are updated on the shop noticeboard and advice is available.

The Yellow Pages is much easier to use now that it is searchable on-line. For example a search for 'Fruit & Vegetable Growers' on www.yell.co.uk would turn up a long list of contact addresses. If you are looking for a summer job anywhere in Britain you should have a look at an annual publication which gives many addresses to which you can apply: *The Directory of Summer Jobs in Britain* (Vacation-Work, £9.99). The majority of jobs listed in *Summer Jobs in Britain* are in hotels or holiday camps, with a further emphasis on seasonal farm work. However there are also lots of unusual and interesting jobs like market researchers, travel reservation clerks, swimming pool life guards, English teachers and monitors, marquee erectors, conservation wardens and information officers for company libraries.

When answering adverts by phone, make sure you have a phone card, since otherwise you'll constantly be worrying about running out of change. It is also very helpful to have a contact telephone number.

Jobcentres

Finally, in your job search, you should not omit the obvious step of visiting your local Jobcentre. Jobcentres are notified of an estimated one-third of the job vacancies in Britain. Details of available jobs are posted on display boards so centres are primarily self-service. If things look grim one week, they might improve the next, especially in areas where there is a concentration of seasonal farm work.

HARVESTS
The principal fruit growing areas of Britain are: the Vale of Evesham over to the Wye and Usk Valleys; most of Kent; Lincolnshire and East Anglia, especially the Fens around Wisbech; and north of the Tay Estuary (Blairgowrie, Forfar). But there is intensive agricultural activity in most parts of Britain so always check with the Jobcentre or Farmers' Union in the area(s) where you are interested in finding farm work. Again *The Directory of Summer Jobs in Britain* lists many fruitgrowers, some of whom need over 100 pickers. Harvest dates are not standard throughout the country, since the raspberries of Inverness-shire ripen at least two or three weeks later than the raspberries on the Isle of Wight; nor are the starting dates the same from one year to the next.

Seasonal Agricultural Workers Scheme
SAWS is administered by seven approved operators under the oversight of the Home Office. The total number of seasonal workers recruited each year is restricted, currently to 10,000. Because of acute labour shortages in the summer of 2000 and the subsequent loss of thousands of tonnes of unpicked crops, the National Farmers Union has been lobbying the government to increase or even double the quota.

New SAWS participants must be students in full-time education abroad and aged 18-25 inclusive. Applicants are required to provide proof of age and status to the scheme operator. However participating operators may issue Home Office work cards to workers who have proved reliable in the past. The work card records the period for which the worker is required and at which farm and which operator issued the card. Although this period may vary, workers can remain in the UK only until 30th November. If no work is available at the original farm the worker may be transferred to another farm within the scheme. The Immigration Officer needs to be satisfied that the worker does not intend to take any other employment and that he or she intends to leave the country on completion of the period of work.

The seven approved operators of the SAWS scheme are:

Concordia Ltd, Heversham House, 20-22 Boundary Road, Hove, Sussex BN3 4ET (01273 422293/fax 01273 422443).

Friday Bridge International Farm Camp, March Road, Friday Bridge, Wisbech, Cambridgeshire PE14 0LR (01945 860255).

G's Marketing Ltd, Hainey Farm, Barway, Ely, Cambs. CB7 5TZ (01353 720427).

HOPS (GB), YFC Centre, Stoneleigh Park, NAC Kenilworth, Warks. CV8 2LG (01203 857206/7).

International Farm Camp, Hall Road, Tiptree, Colchester, Essex CO5 0QS (01621 815496).

Leroch Farm, Alyth, Blairgowrie, Perthshire PH11 9NZ (01828 640280).

R. & J.M. Place, International Farm Camp, Church Farm, Tunstead, Norwich, Norfolk NR12 8RQ (01692 536225).

Fruit Farms
Although the work is hard at the beginning (and also unreliable in bad weather), the international atmosphere can be enjoyable. Some farmers even organise a social and sporting programme. You are likely to meet some veteran travellers who can offer useful advice about job-hunting in their countries or whose names you can add to your address book.

Here are a few farm camps in addition to the ones listed above which hire at least 50 fruit pickers during the season, so it may be worthwhile for British and EU people to approach them directly:

Boxford (Suffolk) Farms Ltd., Hill Farm, Boxford, Sudbury, Suffolk CO10 5NY (01787 210348). Up to 800 pickers required.

C. de Angelis & Son, 333 London Road, Wyberton, Boston, Lincs. PE21 7AU (tel/fax 01205 722891). 200 fruit pickers for soft fruit, plums and apples.

Gaskain's Ltd., Norham Farm, Selling, Faversham, Kent ME13 9RL (01227 752239; Gaskains@farmline.com). Minimum of three weeks between May and October. Campsite provided.

W. Brice & Son Ltd., Mockbeggar Farm, Higham, Rochester, Kent ME3 8EU (01634 717425). Up to 400 fruit pickers and packers.

Langdon Manor Farm, Seasalter Road, Goodnestone, Faversham, Kent ME13 9DA (01795 530035). Soft fruit farm.

Hugh Lowe Farms Ltd, Barons Place, Mereworth, Maidstone, Kent ME18 5NF (01622 812721).

Edward Vinson Ltd, Graveney Road, Faversham, Kent ME13 8UP (01795 539452).

Heaton & Hunt Soft Fruit Growers, Boundary Farm, Maidstone Road, Hadlow, Tonbridge, Kent TN11 0JH (01732 851184; ianskelton@aol.com). Raspberry pickers and packers.

Clock House Farm, Coxheath, Near Maidstone, Kent ME17 4PG (01622 743955; clockhousefarm@farmline.com/ www.members.farmline.com/manda).

Kent Salads, The Drove, Northbourne, Deal, Kent CT14 0LW (01304 382437). 100 salad packers.

Hill Farm Orchards, Droxford Road, Swanmore, Hants. SO32 2PY (01489 878616; hifol@farmline.com). 30 soft fruit pickers and up to 50 apple pickers.

A.P. & S.M. Parris, Cutliffe Farm, Sherford, Taunton, Somerset TA1 3RQ (01823 253808). 30+ pickers.

Haygrove Fruit, Redbank Farm, Ledbury, Herefordshire HR8 2JL (01531 633659; fruit@haygrove.co.uk). 100+ soft fruit pickers and packers.

Lubstree Park Farm, The Humbers, Donnington, Telford, Shropshire TF2 8LW (01952 604320/fax 01952 670307; www.e.trade.btinternet.co.uk/strawberry). Non-EU nationals should apply between January and March so that work permits can be arranged.

Auchrennie Farm, Muirdrum, Carnousite, Angus (01241 852800; j-gray@bigfoot.com). Strawberry pickers needed 6th July to 6th September. Accommodation provided.

W. Henderson, Seggat, Auchterless, Turiff, Aberdeenshire AB5 8DL (01888 511223). Strawberry pickers and packers.

D & B Grant, Wester Essendy, Blairgowrie, Perthshire PH10 6RA (01250 884389). Berry picking and processing.

Thomas Thomson (Blairgowrie) Ltd., Bramblebank Works, Blairgowrie, Perthshire PH10 7HY (01250 872266; www.strawberry.fsnet.co.uk). 100 strawberry and raspberry pickers.

The raspberry harvest in Scotland usually begins in July, but can vary by as much as three weeks. About 3,000 pickers are at work throughout Perthshire and Angus at the peak of the harvest. On an exceptionally good day a picker might gather more than 150lb of fruit and earn £40. Even in the furthest corners of Scotland, there may be opportunities on farms. Heather McCulloch from Australia asked the owners of the hostel where she was staying on the Orkney island of South Ronaldsay if they had any work on their farm and, although she confessed to having no farm experience, was hired to join other travellers for various jobs including 'the sometimes farcical task of rounding up cattle and sheep' and cooking ('opening tins of beans and rice pudding'). For this she was paid a fair wage with food and accommodation thrown in.

One of the latest harvests is of apples which should be more lucrative than many others since the weather can be cold and wet between mid-September and mid-October. Unfortunately this is not what Paul and Tracey Foulkes from New Zealand found at an apple farm in Hampshire:

We worked for £2.76 per hour with no overtime rate which made it hard to believe that £150 was the average weekly net wage as promised by the management before we arrived. The campsite resembled an overgrown backyard surrounded by stinging nettles. The cooking area consisted of three small sinks, two of which were blocked and no plugs. Rats as big as cats were in and out all the time. After travelling round the world and visiting nearly 20 countries, these were the most unhygienic conditions we have come across. After enduring eight days work we left, and intend to call the health department.

Advertised earnings are often only what a dedicated and experienced worker can achieve, as Lanka Dianova from Slovakia discovered when she abandoned the London rat race for life in rural Norfolk:

Together with an Aussie I met in a hostel, I found an advert in TNT magazine for strawberry pickers in Norfolk. It said you could make £35-55 a day, but when we got there, they sent us to a factory where we were folding boxes and packing tins for about £25 a day, working 12 hours. After one day, we said we wanted to leave, but they told us we gotta stay at least a week, otherwise we wouldn't get paid. So we stayed packing fresh salads (approximately £25 for an 8-hour day).

Canning and food processing plants go into high gear in fruit growing regions during the harvests and employ large numbers of seasonal workers. Lucrative overtime is often available. Among the largest in the country is Salvesen Food Services with freezing works in several Lincolnshire towns (Bourne, Easton and Spalding), plus Lowestoft, Peterborough, Grimsby, Hull, Edinburgh, Dundee and Inverness. Ask at local Jobcentres or check the papers in market towns like Wisbech and Kings Lynn.

Pay and Conditions

The two methods of payment used by farmers are piece rates (dependent on the quantity picked) or by the hour. In some cases farmers operate a combination of these two methods, paying an hourly rate plus a bonus for each bin of top quality fruit (which the supermarkets demand). If you are employed on a piece rate basis you must earn at least the minimum rates stipulated by the Agricultural Wages Board (which are in line with the minimum wage). The minimum rate for casual workers over 19 is £3.73 and £5.60 overtime (for work above 39 hours a week or 8 a day or on Sundays and public holidays). The casual rates for 17 and 18 year olds are £2.61 and £3.20 respectively. Where an employer provides accommodation for workers (over the age of 19), up to £19.95 can be deducted per week (a much lower figure than was the case a couple of years ago). Further details are available from the AWB, Nobel House, 17 Smith Square, London SW1P 3JR (020-7238 6862 or the Agricultural Wages helpline on 0845 0000134). Another useful source of information is the Ministry of Agriculture, Fisheries & Food brochure *Planting, Picking or Packing Agricultural Produce? Your Rights Explained* (0645 556000; maff@sr-comms.co.uk).

Pickers being paid piecework sometimes overestimate their likely earnings. Legally they can't earn less than the minimum wage though in practice, pickers who are not picking enough (say 10 kilos of strawberries an hour) to reach that amount are summarily fired. Novices invariably find the work discouraging, especially if rain curtails picking and therefore earning potential. Piecework rates may not be standard in one fruit-picking area so it can be worth doing some comparison shopping before promising a farmer that you will work for him, preferably a month or so before the harvest is due to begin. Some crops pay more than others, usually because they're more difficult or painful to pick. Blackcurrants grow low on the ground and require hours of stooping at an uncomfortable height. Gooseberries share this characteristic and in addition must be picked individually from among vicious thorns. Inexperienced pickers often leave after their first long gruelling day when they find they have not even earned enough to cover living expenses.

You cannot count on accommodation being provided on fruit farms. Even fruit growers who take on large numbers of pickers may provide nothing more than a field, which may or may not be properly levelled, well-drained or cleared of nettles. Sometimes you need to work a minimum number of hours per week, e.g. 15, to be allowed to use the campsite. Others provide completely equipped caravans or bunkhouses, but may make a deduction from your wages for this luxury.

If you do not independently enjoy camping, you are not likely to enjoy life on a Farm Camp. Mark Stephenson grew very fond of the 'wet sloping field' where he was directed to pitch his tent at a farm camp in Perthshire:

After surveying the field which was to be my home for the next few weeks, I turned and noticed the terrific view; the sky may have been all grey clouds but this didn't diminish the magnificence. Social life thrived in and around this temporary community on the Scottish hillsides. Visits to the pub were usually musical events since traditional folk music was frequently played and often we visitors were invited to contribute a southern favourite like 'Maybe it's because I'm a Londoner.' Fruit-picking in Scotland may not leave you much richer in pocket but it gives you several weeks of camping surrounded by open fields and sky, combined with the chance to meet young people not only from Scotland but from all over the world.

Agricultural Agencies

Farm staff agencies like Fletcher Relief Services in Aylesbury (Fieldside Farm, Quainton Nr. Aylesbury, Bucks. HP22 4DQ; 01296 655777) are normally interested only in qualified agriculturalists, milkers and tractor drivers, though others like Bligh Appointments (70 North End Rd, London W14 9EP; 020-7603 6123) regularly deal with unskilled picking and packing as well as skilled work.

Outback International Work Hostels (Jark House, Beechhurst, 8 Commercial Road, Dereham, Norfolk NR19 1AE; 01362 691608/fax 01362 691593) run several hostels in Norfolk for casual workers on farms and in food processing. Work is available year round. For £70-£80 a week, you get a dorm bed, breakfast, packed lunch and dinner and transport to work. A young man from Spain spent six months working for this company and describes conditions:

Outback hostels have a bar with subsidised beer and Sky TV. The lowest pay I earned was £2.97 at a broccoli factory in Ely while the highest was £5.25 for flower planting in Spalding. The hostels provided transport to the workplace, but £3 per day was deducted. At one of the hostels (in Attleborough near Norwich), all the work was in chicken factories.

Another agricultural agency which specialises in placing working holiday makers is called Working Wonders, Waspbourne Manor Farm, Sheffield Park, Uckfield, East Sussex TN22 3QT (01825 723414; recruitment@wowo.co.uk). Plenty of overtime is available. Caravan accommodation can be arranged. For other leads, check adverts in *TNT* or *New Zealand News*; for example adverts have been spotted lately providing just phone numbers (01728 832918, 01772 516744 and 01884 266206).

Caution is always required when accepting a picking job since conditions are notoriously rough and earnings can be disappointing if you are inexperienced.

The organisation WWOOF (Willing Workers on Organic Farms) can put members in touch with more than 200 organic farmers throughout the UK who offer free room and board in exchange for help. Membership costs £15; details from WWOOF UK, PO Box 2675, Lewes, Sussex BN7 1RB.

Hop-Picking

Traditionally the hop fields of Kent and to a much smaller extent Herefordshire employed large numbers of pickers in the month of September. However the industry is in serious decline due to the inability of English producers to compete with cheap continental hops, prompting quite a few farmers to switch to other crops, especially in Kent. Yet enough hop-growers are optimistic that the demand will revive that there are still jobs left for pickers in the hop industry. Take-home pay is often in excess of £150 per week. Tom Morton fixed up a job well in advance:

I wrote to hop farms in April and fixed up a job at Spelmonden Estate. Work started at 7am and finished at 6pm. Accommodation (£8 per week) was in 'portakabins' with a large common room and kitchen for about 15 people. Take leather gloves and bandages for your wrists or they will be lacerated by the hops in no time. Although the work was hard there was a great atmosphere.

Here are some addresses of hop producers:

Adrian Scripps Ltd., Moat Farm, Five Oak Green, Paddock Green, Tonbridge, Kent TN12 6RR (01892 832406).

S.C. and J.H. Berry Ltd., Gushmere Court Farm, Selling, Faversham, Kent (01227 752205).

Spelmonden Estate, Spelmonden Farm, Goudhurst, Kent TN17 1HE.
L. Wheeler & Sons, Bullen Farm, East Peckham, Tonbridge, Kent TN12 5LX (01622 871225).
Stocks Farm, Suckley, Worcestershire WR6 5EH (01886 884202).

TOURISM & CATERING

Despite its infamous weather and cuisine, Britain attracts millions of tourists from abroad. It has been estimated that one in ten of the employed labour force of Britain is involved in the tourist industry and that by the turn of the century the industry will be the biggest employer in the country.

Somebody has to look after the needs of all those pleasure-seekers, whether selling rock candy or playing the guitar to provide entertainment. (Many buskers have found holiday resorts during the season to be far more profitable than large urban areas.) Seaside hotels normally provide staff accommodation and food, though the standard will be considerably lower than that enjoyed by the paying guests at the hotel. There is also plenty of hotel work in London from the international hotels on Park Lane to the budget hotels of Earls Court, though it is the norm in London for staff to live out.

Wages in the hotel trade are notoriously low, and exploitation is common, though the introduction of the minimum wage has alleviated the situation for the lowest paid. Hotel staff with silver service or other specialist experience can expect to earn a decent wage as can restaurant staff in London who should earn at least £4.50 an hour plus free food. Waiting staff can supplement their wages with tips, however chamber and bar staff will generally have to be content with their hourly wage.

People who are available for the whole season, say April to October will find it much easier to land a job than those available only for the peak months of July and August. Most hotels prefer to receive a formal written application in the early part of the year, complete with photos and references; however it can never hurt to telephone (especially later in the spring) to find out what the situation is. You may work from the selective list of hotels in the *Directory of Summer Jobs in Britain* mentioned above or work systematically through a hotel guide such as those published by the Automobile Association, the Royal Automobile Club or the English Tourist Board. The more bedrooms listed in the hotel's entry, the better the chances of a vacancy.

It is worth contacting large hotel chains for up-to-date vacancy information, particularly if you have relevant experience. For example Hilton UK (Maple Court, Central Park, Reeds Crescent, Watford WD1 1HZ; 01923 246464) can give advice on which of their 41 UK hotels have current vacancies, although these should be applied to individually for employment. Similarly Choice Hotels Europe offer numerous opportunities in the UK and Ireland on a short-term (minimum four months) or long term basis to suitable applicants, qualified and/or experienced in the hotel business. A good working knowledge of English is essential. CVs and covering letter in English should be sent to the Human Resources Department, 112-114 Station Road, Edgware, Middlesex HA8 7BJ (hr@choicehotelseurope.com/ www.choicehotelseurope.com). Thistle Hotels Plc (2 The Calls, Leeds LS2 7JU; 0113-243 9111) have more than 50 hotels in the UK. Live-in accommodation is provided in some hotels but not all. The minimum period of work is three months and non-European nationals must possess a work permit before applying.

Fast food restaurants around the world have many vacancies. If you are prepared to work overtime, you should be able to earn a living from McDonalds, Pizza Hut, etc. working as a 'crew member', though usually you have to be content with part-time work until you prove yourself reliable. A good bet over the next few years will be KFC who at the end of 2000 announced that they intend to create 10,000 new jobs in the UK over the next five years. A large percentage of workers is foreign. Having a reference from one of these chains can be useful if you want to move to another branch.

Anyone who can acquaint themselves with EU hygiene regulations before any interview would have the edge. Many employment agencies specialise in placing seasonal staff in the hospitality industry, for example:
Aspire Recruitment, 6 Cathedral Lane, Truro, Cornwall TR1 2QS (01872 241486; info@aspirerecruitment.co.uk). Chefs, managers, reception, bar, waiting, and

other staff mainly for Southwest England and the Channel Islands.

EuroCom, Suite 8, Surbiton Business Centre, 46 Victoria Road, Surbiton, Surrey KT6 4JL (020-8390 4512; post@europeancommunications.com). Provide staff to 4 and 5 star hotels; minimum contract 6 months year round.

European Work Experience Programme – 020-8572 2993; www.ewep.com.

Helping Hand Agency, 24 Stourvale Gardens, Chandlers Ford, Hants. SO53 3NE (02380) 254287; helphand@tcp.co.uk). Live-in hotel and catering staff for minimum of six months. Can be arranged in conjunction with English classes.

Highland Hospitality, 4 South Crescent, Garlieston, Wigtownshire, Scotland DG8 8BQ (01988 600782; www.hotel-recruit.com). Hospitality recruiters who specialise in finding seasonal and vacation work for students, backpackers and travellers throughout the UK.

Lucy Locketts & Vanessa Bancroft Agency, 400 Beacon Road, Wibsey, Bradford, Yorks. BD6 3DJ. Placement of European waiters, porters, chambermaids, etc.

Montpelier Employment, 34 Montpelier Road, Brighton, Sussex BN1 2LQ (01273 778686/ www.themontpelieremploymentagency.co.uk)

North-South Hotel Recruitment Agency, 1 Turnpike Close, Darlington DL1 3SH (tel/fax 01325 467431).

Southern Work Experience, 12 Eversfield Road, Eastbourne, Sussex BN21 2AS (01323 638523). Hotel and industry work experience placements for 2-3 months.

Pubs

Live-in pub work is not hard to come by. You usually have to work throughout pub opening hours six days a week, but you should be rewarded with about £4-£5 an hour. The introduction of the minimum wage affected many pubs which traditionally offered live-in work, since they are now allowed to deduct only £20 a week for accommodation, which is good news especially for the army of foreign working holidaymakers but has increased costs for the brewery chains like Fullers and Youngs. Many people work some evenings in a pub in addition to their day job to boost their finances for future travelling. This is one job in which there is a good demand for working couples and (at least in London) for Australians and New Zealanders. In fact STA Travel in association with The Original London Pub Company based in Brisbane (www.londonpubau.com) distribute a dedicated leaflet in Australia and New Zealand: 'Live and Work in a London Pub'. Women with bar experience normally find it easier to find a job than barmen, and can often negotiate a better package.

Waiting for an ad to appear is usually less productive than going pub to pub. An American traveller found himself nearly penniless in the popular tourist town of Pitlochry in Perthshire and made the rounds of the pubs asking for work. In each case the management were either fully staffed or were too concerned about his lack of a work permit. He claims that in the 34th and final pub, they asked him if he were free to start work that minute, and he gleefully stepped behind the bar and began work, without knowing shandy from Guinness. Americans may need to be reminded that you do not get tips in a British pub though you may be bought a drink now and then. Americans often have trouble with the different accents they will encounter as Woden Teachout found:

I had a hard time deciphering the orders over the music; 'Bakes' does not sound remotely like 'Becks' to the American ear.

Pub jobs vary a great deal and it is better if you can find one which you find compatible. Ken Smith from New Zealand has extensive experience:

I worked in four pubs while in England, three of which were really good. I was regularly invited into the customers' homes for meals or tea and in one pub there was a retired gentleman who would drive me around historic country pubs. The six months I spent working in a pub near Russell Square were absolutely fantastic; the money was great (£130 a week cash-in-hand of which I could comfortably save £100), excellent food, great boss and brilliant customers. On the other hand I spent two months in a Surrey pub which was terrible in every conceivable way, but I was short on money and jobs were scarce. The final straw was when they started working on the roof in November and the freezing cold wind blew right into my bedroom. The job was only ever a roof over our heads and they even took that away.

Scotland

Although unemployment is higher in Scotland than England, plenty of tourist-related jobs are available. Charlotte Jakobsen from Denmark (who 'fell in love with this country, its people and lifestyle' on arrival) travelled to Edinburgh for interviews with the Hilton and Sheraton Hotels, among others, and was soon working evenings in a hotel bar. Her employer did not provide accommodation but she was able to stay longterm at the Frances Kinnaird Christian Hostel for women (14 Coates Crescent) which now charges £55 a week, and concluded that although it is next to impossible to find a bar or hotel job with a decent wage, it is a very enjoyable way to pass a few months.

Many foreign job-seekers in Britain tire of the London scene or are attracted to the peace and quiet of Scotland as Isak Maseide from Norway was:

We were originally going to Edinburgh to work at the Festival, but after Athens we preferred somewhere quieter, so went to the resort of Oban on the west coast of Scotland. Even though we arrived in the middle of the season (which lasts from mid-May to the end of September) we soon found work. Apparently McTavish's Kitchens is the place to go first since it is the biggest employer and has live-in facilities, pays well and employs quite a number of young people. My New Zealand girlfriend and I preferred to have a wee feeling of freedom so we rented a bedsit for £65 a week.

McTavish's has a restaurant in Oban (8 Argyll Square, PA4 4BA) and another in Fort William (High Street, PH33 6AD).

Agents sometimes advertise in London for live-in hotel work in Scotland. Keith Flynn answered such an ad and ended up working in an isolated place ten miles from the nearest town and with no public transport, which made it an ideal place to save money:

I saw Dee Cooper's advert and decided to ring up. Basically you just call and say what job you do, e.g. kitchen porter, bar, waiter/waitress and she gives you a list of vacancies around Scotland at no cost to you.

Dee Cooper works for more than 1000 hotels in Scotland, England and Wales supplying live-in staff; phone 01764 670001 or 01764 679765 or fax 01764 679728 (dee@livein-jobs.demon.co.uk/www.livein-jobs.co.uk).

Paul Binfield from Kent travelled further north in Scotland and was rewarded with a healthy choice of casual work in the Orkney Islands:

Unemployment here is about 5% and from March to September there is an absolute abundance of summer jobs. We worked in one of the several youth hostels on the islands, have done voluntary work for the Orkney Seal Rescue and I am currently earning a very nice wage working at the historical site Skara Brae on a three-month contract. There is loads of seasonal work available in hotels and bars, cutting grass for the Council and other garden contracts, etc.

European Waterways (35 Wharf Road, Wraysbury, Staines, Middlesex TW19 5JQ; fax 01784 483072; ewbarging@aol.com/ www.gobarging.com) hire hostesses and crew for barge holidays in Scotland (as well as England and France). The basic weekly wage of £110 is usually supplemented with tips.

The Aviemore Highlands Hotel (Aviemore Mountain Resort Ltd, Aviemore, Inverness-shire PH22 1PJ; 01479 810771; personnel@aviehighlands.demon.co.uk) offers temporary live-in positions as receptionists, bar, waiting, housekeeping and kitchen staff to fit in with school and college vacations.

A surprising range of jobs can be found in Scotland from being a distillery guide (for example at the Glenfiddich Distillery, Dufftown, Banffshire AB55 4DH) to pushing tourists around in rickshaws in Edinburgh. For the distillery job it is necessary to attend an interview at your own expense before the end of April and to be available to work from at least the end of June till the end of August. Whelk and periwinkle collecting can apparently be done on the islands of Skye, Mull or elsewhere along the west coast. Conditions are best at low tide around the full and new moons. Agents provide bags, tide tables and a collection service (see Yellow Pages). Most people can earn up to £30 in one tide, double at Christmas when wellies and warm gloves must be worn.

The Channel Islands

In general, the Channel Islands are a favourite destination for seasonal workers in the hotel/hospitality industry. For a list of 100+ establishments, many offering accommodation in Guernsey, write to the States Tourist Board, PO Box 23, North Esplanade, St. Peter Port, Guernsey GY1 3AN (enquiries@tourism.guernsey.net). Several agencies specialise in recruiting catering and other staff for the Channel Islands, e.g. Connectus on Guernsey (01481 729309) and Towngate Personnel (65 Seamoor Road, Westbourne, Bournemouth BH4 9AE; 01202 752955; enquiries@towngate-personnel.co.uk). Towngate supply staff for permanent live-in vacancies in the Channel Islands and in the UK. Jersey Recruitment (La Rue le Masurier, St Helier, Jersey JE2 4YE; 01534 617373) cannot really process applications from students since their season finishes in October.

The tax status of the Channel Islands works to the advantage of seasonal workers (just as it does to offshore millionaires). The exemption limit for a single person is £10,750 per calendar year; further details are available from the CI Tax Department (01534 603000). The lovely island of Sark is also a magnet for itinerant workers.

Niamh Cordon is one of the many people who regularly returns to Jersey to work the season:

> *After returning home to Ireland from working on the Greek islands, I still had itchy feet. I had heard from friends that Jersey was a great place to go to pick up work easily. There is a job centre but more importantly a recruitment agency that deals with the catering trade and also has jobs for bar staff, waiting staff and receptionists. Accommodation is very expensive in Jersey but most hotels have live-in positions. You need to get over in early May before the hordes of students arrive. I spent two summer seasons as a receptionist and then signed up with the temping agencies and began clearing £300 working as a typist.*

Holiday Camps and Activity Centres

Anyone with a qualification in canoeing, yachting, climbing, etc. should be able to find summer work as an instructor. Since the Lyme Bay canoeing tragedy of 1993 in which several young people were drowned at an activity centre on the south coast, directors have been looking for higher standards of training and experience. Centres which belong to the British Activity Holidays Association (01932 252994) submit to regular safety inspections. To find out whether a centre is licensed, contact the Adventure Activities Licensing Authority (17 Lambourne Crescent, Cardiff Business Park, Llanishen, Cardiff CF14 5GF; 029 20 755715; www.aala.org).

Foreign equivalents of the British Canoe Union, Royal Yachting Association, etc. should suffice. There are also plenty of jobs as general assistants for sports-minded young people, especially at children's multi activity centres. Suzanne Phillips, who worked at an adventure centre in North Devon, claims that 'a person's character and personality are far more important than their qualifications.' The trouble is that the pay is not usually very much for this kind of work, perhaps about £40-50 per week in addition to food and accommodation, though this may be supplemented by an end-of-season bonus at some centres. Quite often foreign applicants will be asked to provide police clearance forms if the job involves working with children.

One of the largest employers is PGL Travel, with a staggering 2,500 vacancies during the season which extends from February to October. PGL's Seasonal Personnel Department can be contacted at: Alton Court, Penyard Lane (874), Ross-on-Wye, Herefordshire HR9 5NR (01989 767833/fax 01989 768769/recruitment@pgl.co.uk).

Here are some other activity centres which may require domestic as well as leadership staff:

Ardmore Adventures, Berkshire College, Burchetts Green, Maidenhead, Berkshire SL6 6QR (01628 826699). Residential multi activity and English language camps for overseas children throughout the UK.

Barracudas Summer Activity Camps, Graphic House, Ferrars Road, Huntingdon, Cambs. PE18 6EE (01480 435090). Various residential and day camps in southern England.

EF Language Travel, EF House 1-3 Farman St, Hove, Sussex BN3 1AL (01273 723651). Residential courses for European students throughout Britain. 1,000 group leaders and EFL teachers are hired.

Kids Klub, The Lodge, The Hall, Great Finborough, Stowmarket, Suffolk IP14 3EF (01449 742700).

Kingswood Group, Old Bembridge School, Hillway Road, Bembridge, Isle of Wight PO35 5PH (01983 875353; jobs@kingswood.co.uk). Employment opportunities in Staffordshire, Isle of Wight and north Norfolk coast. Parent company of Camp Beaumont and Freetime Summer Camps.

Prime Leisure, 56 Sparecacre Lane, Eynsham, Oxford OX8 1NP (01865 884200). Various multi activity centres for children aged 4-14 in Oxfordshire, Berkshire and Hertfordshire.

For catering, domestic and other work at family holiday centres contact the following:

Butlins Holiday Worlds Ltd., Bognor Regis, Sussex PO21 1JJ (Jobs Hotline 01243 224206). Their five centres are Somerwest World (Minehead, Somerset TA24 5SH), Southcoast World (Bognor Regis, Sussex PO21 1JJ), Starcoast World (Pwllheli, Gwynedd LL53 6HX; 01758 612112), Funcoast World (Skegness, Lincolnshire PE25 1NJ; 01754 762311) and Wonderwest World (Heads of Ayr, Scotland KA7 4LB). Applications should be sent to the preferred centre.

HF Holidays, Recruitment & Training Department, Redhills, Penrith, Cumbria CA11 0DT (01768 899988). Operate 20 country house hotels throughout the UK for people on walking and special interest holidays. Need children's activity leaders, walking leaders and domestic staff.

Pontin's, Sagar House, Eccleston, Nr. Chorley, Lancs. PR7 5PH. Hiring takes place for eight family holiday centres.

Prestatyn Sands Holiday Park, Shore Road, Gronant, Prestatyn, Flintshire, Wales LL19 (01745 856471). 250 staff.

American-style theme parks, which are fast gaining popularity in Britain, have large seasonal staff requirements. As well as the usual scivvying jobs, they may also require ride operators, entertainers for both children and adults, lifeguards, DJs, shop assistants, etc. The main disadvantage is that accommodation is generally not provided. Among the largest are:

Alton Towers, Alton, North Staffordshire ST10 4DB (01538 703344). Approximately 1,000 vacancies between March and November.

American Adventure Theme Park, Pit Lane, Ilkeston, Derby DE7 5SX (01773 531521). 150 ride operators, 70 retail staff, 120 catering assistants, etc.

Bourne Leisure Group, Normandy Court, 1 Wolsey Road, Hemel Hempstead, Herts. HP2 4TU (01442 241658). 500 staff needed at 20 holiday parks throughout Britain.

Chessington World of Adventures, Leatherhead Road, Chessington, Surrey KT9 2NE (01372 729560). Employs between 500 and 1,000 people each year.

First Leisure plc, Empress Buildings, 97 Church St, Blackpool, Lancs (01253 293002). Owners of Blackpool Tower, Llandudno Pier, Eastbourne Pier and various other resort attractions.

Frontierland Western Theme Park, The Promenade, Morecambe, Lancs. LA4 4DG (01524 410024). 100+ ride operators and general assistants in all departments.

Legoland Windsor, Winkfield Road, Windsor, Berks. SL4 4AY (01753 626150). 700 seasonal workers needed in total.

Pleasureland Amusement Park, Marine Drive, Southport, Lancs. PR8 1RX (01704 532717).

Thorpe Park, Staines Road, Chertsey, Surrey KT16 8PN (01932 577120). Limited accommodation provided for the 400+ ancillary staff.

Youth Hostels

Up to 200 seasonal assistant wardens are employed by the Youth Hostels Association (England and Wales) from March to October each year to help in the running of YHA's 240 youth hostels in the UK. The job involves cooking for large numbers, general cleaning, cash handling and some clerical work. Accommodation and food are provided along with a basic salary from £370 per month. For an application form, apply in writing to the National Recruitment Department (Hostel Staff), YHA, PO Box 11, Matlock, Derbyshire DE4 2XA (01426 939216; www.yha.org.uk), after which an interview may be scheduled, often at short notice.

There are also a number of independent hostels and budget accommodation around the country. Three hundred of these are listed in the pocket-sized *Independent Hostel Guide* from the Backpackers Press, 2 Rockview Cottages, Temple Walk, Matlock Bath, Derbyshire DE4 3PG (tel/fax 01629 580427; DaveDalley@aol.com), at a cost of £5 (plus £1 postage, £2 overseas). Independent hostels are a good source of temporary work, often providing a few hours a day of work in return for bed and board. The Backpackers Press is able to circulate staff vacancy information to the hostels in its occasional newsletter.

Special Events

Events such as the Henley Regatta in June, Test Matches at Headingley in Leeds, the Edinburgh Festival in August/September and a host of golf tournaments and county shows need temporary staff to work as car park attendants, ticket sellers and in catering. Sporting events like the British Open and Wimbledon employ a myriad of casual workers. Ask the local tourist office for a list of upcoming events and contact the organisers. Outside catering and other companies which hold the contracts for staffing special events include:

Afar Exhibition Services, Suite 4, Craven Hall, Sackville St, Skipton, Yorks. BD23 2PB (01756 797877; afarex@btinternet.com).

Events Staff, 25 York Road, Northampton NN3 6QB (01604 627775). 1000+ stewards, programme sellers, car park and security staff for racing fixtures, etc.

FMC, All England Lawn Tennis and Croquet Club, Church Road, Wimbledon, London SW19 5AE (020-8947 7430; resourcing@fmcatering.co.uk). One of the largest outdoor caterers in Europe.

Leapfrog International, Riding Court Farm, Datchet, Berks. SL3 9JU (01753 580880; eng@leapfrog-int.co.uk). Up to 100 event crew for family fun days, etc.

Adrian Little enjoyed the atmosphere of the British Open when it took place at the famous golf club in St. Andrews in Scotland. Jobs can be found as scoreboard operators, course scorers, radio operators, etc. In addition to earning £90 for the one-week event, he got an excellent (free) view of the action. Look also for work during the Ryder Cup (when the tournament takes place in Britain).

Colin Rothwell from South Africa spent a few months in Nottingham trying to scrape together enough money to move on and recommends looking for work at fairs, horse races and rock concerts.

> *It's long hard work but the pay is usually not bad and there are sometimes good perks that go along with the job. I worked at a chicken and chips stand in Newcastle while Joe Cocker, Status Quo and Rod Stewart played away. During my short breaks I was allowed in to enjoy the concert. When it was all finished, there was a lot of roast chicken to take home (or sell). Then it was back to Nottingham in the early hours of the next morning with £40 in my back pocket.*

CHILDCARE & DOMESTIC

Au Pairs

One of the easiest ways for European citizens between the ages of 17 and 27 to arrange to work in the United Kingdom is to become au pairs. There are an estimated 25,000 foreign au pairs in this country, mainly from eastern Europe. The list of permitted nationalities includes all European Economic Area countries plus Switzerland, Cyprus, Malta, Turkey, Hungary, Czech Republic, Slovakia and the former Yugoslavia (but not

Poland or any Russian Federation states). Anyone from outside the EEA seeking entry as an au pair has to show documents at entry proving that an arrangement has been made; changing status after entry as a visitor is not permitted. The maximum stay is two years, though it is possible to change families in this time.

Several years ago the Home Office issued new guidelines reducing the number of working days from six to five and the weekly number of hours from 30 to 25, not counting some evening babysitting. The work of an au pair consists of childcare and light housework duties. These guidelines cannot be enforced and many families ignore them, in which case the au pair should bring the Home Office directives to the attention of the host family.

The pocket money for au pairs is currently £35-£45 a week; this category of work was declared exempt from minimum wage regulations. Details about working in Britain as an au pair are given in the *Au Pair & Nanny's Guide to Working Abroad* from Vacation Work (£10.99 or look in libraries). See the list in the introductory chapter *Childcare* for addresses of UK agencies, though normally foreign young people contact an agency in their own country in the first instance. In some areas it is easy to find live-in positions after arrival, but not in all areas, where there are far more notices posted by foreign au pairs looking for jobs than families looking for au pairs.

Nannies

Young women (and very occasionally men) wishing to become mother's helps have a good chance of succeeding since the market in this field is also booming, especially in the Home Counties. A television news programme in 1999 claimed that there are 100,000 nannies in the UK. An untrained, unqualified young woman can expect to be paid from £70 a week in addition to room and board. Mothers' helps with some experience often earn twice this amount and nannies even more.

Nannying in the UK is the option that many young women from Australia and New Zealand choose, partly because it takes care of accommodation and pays a good wage. Those with the working holiday visa can make use of agencies; others will have to answer private ads.

A less binding variation is to babysit, for which you should receive a standard hourly rate of at least £2.50 or £3. Check notice boards, student broadsheets, etc. for such opportunities. A Malaysian student in London followed up a notice she spotted on the board next to Earls Court tube station and arranged free room and board in exchange for taking a child to and from school.

Many childcare agencies advertise in the weekly *Lady* magazine as well as in the free papers like *TNT* and *New Zealand News UK*. The government introduced a register of approved nanny agencies which have been inspected for the benefit of parents looking for quality control which has hitherto been lacking. If you decide to register with one of the approved agencies, your references will be verified and a police check will be carried out on you. A good website to use with links to established nanny and au pair agencies is www.bestbear.co.uk.

If you want a live-in position but not looking after children, there are agencies which specialise in providing carers for the elderly and disabled, for example Cura Domi-Care at Home (8 North St, Guildford, Surrey GU1 4AF; 01483 302275) pays £215-£310 a week to residential care workers. Oxford Aunts is another venerable agency in this field (3 Cornmarket St, Oxford OX1 3EX; 01865 791017). Also look for opportunities to house-sit. Obviously London is the best place for such an activity, though other provincial agencies offer this service. Agencies such as Home & Pet Care Ltd. (Nether Row Hall, Hestket-Newmarket, Wigton, Cumbria CA7 8LA; 016974 78515; sue@homeandpetcare.co.uk) and Housewatch (01279 777412) do not take on people for one-off jobs but are looking for mature people with a fixed address (preferably resident in the UK for at least two years) and impeccable references to house-sit for clients throughout the UK.

TEACHING

Although there is a veritable epidemic of English language schools along the south coast and in places like Oxford and Cambridge, you may find it more difficult to get a job as a language tutor in Torquay than in Taipei, harder in Ramsgate than in Rio. It takes more than a tidy appearance to get one of the well-paid summer jobs at one of the 600-800 summer language schools operating in Britain. And the situation has not been improved with the strong pound which has seen a falling off of numbers at many language schools. It is not uncommon for summer staff to be offered jobs which are contingent on student numbers, which makes it difficult to plan anything with certainty.

The majority of language schools in Britain insist that their teachers have a formal qualification in TEFL (Teaching English as a Foreign Language) or at the very least a university degree, teacher's certificate or fluency in a foreign language. If you satisfy any or all of these requirements you should apply to a number of language schools several months prior to the summer holiday period. The average starting salary for EFL teachers is £170-£200 per week, though Certificate-qualified teachers should earn £250-£300. Many employers provide staff accommodation for which there will be a deduction from wages.

If you lack the necessary qualifications to teach, you might still consider blitzing the language schools, since many of them also run a programme of outings and entertainments for their foreign students and they may need non-teaching supervisors and sports instructors. Working at one of these language summer schools is an excellent way of making contact with Italian, French and Spanish young people who might offer advice or even hospitality once you set off on your travels.

A list of 200+ English language schools and colleges accredited by the British Council may be obtained from the Association of Recognised English Language Services (ARELS) at 56 Buckingham Gate, London SW1E 6AG (020-7802 9200; www.arels.org.uk). These schools employ only qualified or experienced teaching staff. Also check the Tuesday *Guardian* throughout the spring. Schools are located throughout the UK, but are concentrated in the South-East, London, Oxford and Cambridge. For further addresses, check in the following *Yellow Pages* under 'Language Schools' or 'Schools – Language': Bournemouth, Brighton, Cambridge, Canterbury, Exeter, Oxford and Tunbridge Wells. Two useful websites which list English language schools in Britain are www.EnglishinBritain.co.uk (accredited by the British Council) and www.tlcuk.com

Here is a short list of major language course organisations which normally offer a large number of summer vacancies:

Alexanders International School, Bawdsey Manor, Bawdsey, Woodbridge, Suffolk IP12 3AZ (tel: 01394-411633; fax: 01394 411257. E-mail: english@alexandersint.demon.co.uk. Employ about 24 teachers for an international summer school for 11-18 year-olds mid-June to late August. Minimum 2 weeks. Activity staff also employed.

Anglo Continental Educational Group, 33 Wimborne Road, Bournemouth BH2 6NA 901202 557414/fax 01202 556156). Up to 100 EFL teachers for adult summer courses and 20 for adolescents.

Anglo-European Study Tours, 8 Celbridge Mews, Porchester Road, London W2 6EU (020-7229 4435/fax 020-7792 8717; e-mail: c.morris@aest.co.uk. Website: www.aest.co.uk). 200+ at centres throughout the UK for 2-6 weeks. £190-£235 per week. No accommodation.

Anglophiles Academic, 34 North End Road, London W14 OSH. Fax 020-7603 2441. E-mail: sutton@anglophiles.demon.co.uk. Teachers/supervisors for French teenagers at Easter, and summer (July and August) in Basingstoke, Boston, Bristol, Bury, Chelmsford, Kings Lynn, Nottingham, Peterborough, Plymouth and Skegness. Some residential.

Concorde International Summer Schools, Arnett House, Hawks Lane, Canterbury, Kent CT1 2NU (01227 765537/fax 01227 762760; e-mail: info@concorde.ltd.uk; website: www.concorde.ltd.uk). 120 teachers. £210 a week depending on the course. Average 15 hours teaching and 20 supervising activities. Full board residential accommodation is provided. Experience and TEFL qualification required. Contact Beth Stavely.

EF Language Travel, Cherwell House, 3rd Floor, Cherwell House, London Place, Oxford OX4 1BD. Tel: 01865-200720. Fax: 01865-243196. E-mail: lt.oxford@ef.com. Website: www.ef.com. 25-30 teachers needed per year and hundreds of group leaders for centres in Hastings, Brighton, London, Cambridge and Oxford. All teachers must be native speakers with TEFL or substantial experience. 3 weeks from 9am-midday or 1.30-4.30pm. £23 per 3-hour session. B&B accommodation can be found with host families. Contact Aneli Oakes.

Elizabeth Johnson Organisation, West House, 19/21 West St, Haslemere, Surrey GU27 2AE. With 35 centres around the UK. 85-90 teachers needed at peak time (July). Two weeks to a month minimum. £185-£270 per week. Three schools are residential.

Embassy CES, Head Office: Lorna House, 103 Lorna Road, Hove, East Sussex BN3 3EL. Tel 01273-322353. Fax 01273-322381. E-mail emb_recruit@bsg.ac.uk. Summer schools from end of June to end of August at 40 centres around the UK. Employs 400 teachers throughout UK and Ireland. Minimum requirement is a TEFL Cert. Accommodation can be provided.

Embassy CES, Highcliffe House, Clifton Gardens, Folkestone, Kent CT20 2EF (01303 258536/fax 01303 851455). One of their many centres (see above). 20+ teachers.

English Language & Cultural Organisation, Lowlands, Chorleywood Road, Rickmansworth, Herts. WD3 4ES (01923 776731/fax 01923 774678). 20-30 EFL teachers to work at several locations in the south of England during the summer.

International Quest Centres, 9 Stradbroke Road, Southwold, Suffolk IP18 6LL; tel 01502-722648 and 50 Oxford Street, Southampton SO14 3DP. Tel: 023 803338858. Fax: 023 80338848. E-mail: english@internationalquest.co.uk. Website: www.internationalquest.co.uk). 300-400 EFL teachers for 3-6 weeks. 17 hours per week. Wage of £10 per hour. Accommodation is not normally provided except in Oxford and Kent where recruitment is difficult. Contact A. McCarthy.

International Study Programmes, The Manor, Hazleton, Nr. Cheltenham, Glos. GL54 4EB (01451 860379).

Kent School of English, 3,5,10,12 Granville Road, Broadstairs, Kent CT10 1QD (tel 01843-874870); fax 01843-860418; e-mail: enquiries@kentschool.co.uk). Hires 25 teachers at Easter and from late June to August in summer. Must be graduates with either CELTA or TESOL. £210-£270 per week. Supplement for outstanding staff. No accommodation.

Kingswood Group, Linton House, 164-180 Union St, London SE1 0LH (020-7922 1234). Summer camps in southern England needing 40-45 EFL teachers.

Nord-Anglia, 10 Eden Place, Cheadle, Stockport, Cheshire SK8 1AT (0161-491 8477/491 8415/fax 0161-491 4409). 300+ EFL teachers for more than 80 centres around Britain, especially the North. Apply March-June for UK summer work. Also runs TEFL courses in various centres abroad including in Australia and the Czech Republic.

OISE Youth Language Centres, OISE House, Binsey Lane, Oxford OX2 0EY (01865 258350/fax 01865 792706). 500 summer and Easter vacancies in dozens of locations. OISE offer their own training course to tutors.

Passport Language Schools, 37 Park Road, Bromley, Kent BR1 3HJ (020-8466 5925). Employ about 150 teachers for schools in 30 towns in England and South Wales.

SUL Language Schools, Beech Holm, 7 Woodland Avenue, Tywardreath, Par, Cornwall PL24 2PL (01726 814227/fax 01726 813135). E-mail: claire@sul-schools.com. Website: www.sul-schools.com. Employ 200-300 a year with degree and TEFL Cert. Minimum 2 weeks. Mornings only. £22.90-£34 per morning. Residential.

TASIS England American School, Coldharbour Lane, Thorpe, Surrey TW20 8TE. Of special interest to American EFL teachers who want to teach in Britain from late June to late August; only suitably qualified Americans are eligible for work permits.

Thames Valley Cultural Centres, 15 Park St, Windsor, Berks. SL4 1LU (01753 852001/fax 01753 831165). Up to 60 teachers around England.

Torbay Language Centre, Conway Road, Paignton, Devon T04 5LH; tel 01803-558555; fax 01803-559606; e-mail tlc@lalschool.org). Employs about 40 teachers from the last week of June to the third week of August for a minimum of two weeks. Pay is £8.50 per hour; average 22 and a half hours per week. Also runs a small residential centre in North Devon.

YES Education Centres, 12 Eversfield Road, Eastbourne, East Sussex BN21 2AS

(01323 644830/fax 01323 726260). EFL teachers for summer courses in Abingdon, Brighton, Hastings, Oxford and Seaford.

The shortage of qualified teachers for primary and secondary schools in deprived areas is still acute, both in London and elsewhere. Many local Education Authorities, mainly in inner and outer London, are constantly in need of supply or temporary short-term teachers who are paid a daily rate ranging from £80 to £126, though usually in the £90-£100 range. For example inner city areas like Tower Hamlets depend very largely on Antipodean teachers who currently account for about half the supply teachers working in that borough. Wandsworth is another borough in which there are a great many teacher vacancies.

The alternative to applying direct to the relevant local boroughs is signing on with a specialist agency, to which most boroughs now turn for their supply staff. Agencies place thousands of teachers in state schools:

Capita Education – 020-8600 1300. Offices in London, Bristol, Reading, Wales, Manchester, Newcastle and Sheffield.

Capstan Teachers – 0800 731 6871. Have offices in five boroughs of London plus Leeds, Birmingham, Sheffield, etc.

Spring Education – education@spring.com

Teachers Pet – Clocktower House, 287-289 Cranbrook Road, Ilford, Essex IG1 4UA (0800 068 1117; www.teachers-uk.co.uk)

TimePlan Teachers – 0800 358 8040; www.timeplan.com.

In order to obtain 'Qualified Teacher Status' (QTS), trained teachers from outside the EU must successfully complete a training period as a graduate or registered teacher. Details of the programme can be obtained from Bench Marque Ltd., 5 Euston Place, Leamington Spa, Warks. CV32 4LN (01926 330006).

APPLYING LOCALLY

British readers may decide that it is easiest to save money by working close to home. If you have had no luck through the Jobcentre, by answering newspaper adverts or by registering with private employment agencies, you may want to spread your net even wider. The *Yellow Pages* are an invaluable source of potential employers in anything from market gardening to market research. Personal visits are also a good idea, for example to the Personnel Managers of large department stores, supermarkets, the Body Shop, fast food restaurants or canneries in your area, especially as summer approaches. Staff turnover is high at DIY chain stores. Or you could approach the local council, most of which hire temporary staff during the summer or at Christmas. Look for small notices advertising for house cleaners.

Market research agencies often require interviewers, though jobs in this industry are tighter than they were at the beginning of the decade. Since a few days of training are normally given, you should be available to work for at least three months, though the work is almost invariably part-time. A telephone is normally essential, a car useful. Telephone interviewers are paid slightly less than personal interviewers. An Australian, Ian Mitselburg, got work in Edinburgh with a town planning consultancy (Halcrow, Fox & Associates, 16 Abercrombie Place, Edinburgh EH3 6LB; 0131-272 3300) interviewing people in Linlithgow on why, when and how they used their cars.

This was done in the evening and I have never been sooo cold in my life. Knocking on doors seemed to crack my frozen fingers but the Oz accent helped a lot as it seemed to arouse curiosity and thus got me invited inside where it was warm. The same firm sent me to Oban to interview ferry passengers. Apart from the initial bout of sea-sickness, this was an excellent job as I got to see the outer Hebrides for free.

Investigate every avenue for boosting your travel fund. Brendan Barker says the oddest odd job he had in England was in police identity parades. He got £3 for 15 minutes 'work' while Thames Valley Police pay £10 per appearance. You have more chance of being called back if you are male and look fairly scruffy, though the Cambridge Constabulary have been known to flag down dons cycling to the library to fill a last-minute vacancy in a parade. Ian Mitselburg several times replied to the police request received at his Edinburgh hostel but thought that the system was unfair to the suspect since the Australasians, North Americans and Germans invariably had a healthier appearance than the Scots.

After job-seekers from abroad have been based in one place for a time, they can normally find some work. Although Woden Teachout, a young travelling American woman, did not have the benefit of a work permit, she pieced together several jobs in Cambridge within a couple of weeks:

> *In my terror at my shrinking funds, I accumulated five jobs: two cleaning, one nannying, one behind the bar at a red plush Turkish nightclub and one (which has stood me well) as a personal assistant to a professor.*

The latter job, which was advertised on a notice board at the Graduate Student Centre, was by far the most interesting and also lucrative at £4 an hour. Similar notices for research assistants are posted in universities around the world, mostly in department offices and teaching buildings rather than in student unions.

Medical Experiments

There are an estimated 55 clinical research units in the UK according to the Association of Independent Clinical Research Contractors, many of which rely on testing their drugs on human guinea pigs. The demand for willing volunteers is so great that some of the larger pharmaceutical companies like SmithKline Beecham advertise in the mainstream media. Drug testing is overseen by ethical committees, but many people fear that the long-term consequences of taking unlicensed drugs cannot be safely predicted. The companies all give assurances that their tests are safe, but not everyone accepts this.

Nevertheless many people rely on drug testing as a regular source of income, earning as much as £100 a day. Most company literature states that expenses will be reimbursed, but payment is normally more generous than this. If interested, it is worth checking notice boards and making enquiries at any teaching hospital or asking any medical student you happen to meet. To obtain details from SmithKline Beecham of their programme of experiments in Cambridge, ring the Volunteer Recruitment Line on 0800 328 4195. They needs volunteers in other locations as well. Other clinics to try include:

Chiltern Research Unit, Freepost SL2543, Slough SL2 4BL (0800 783 0976/01753 642222).

Glaxo Wellcome Pharmacology Unit, Level 7, Northwick Park Hospital - 020-8864 3322

Hammersmith Medicines Research, Central Middlesex Hospital, Park Royal, Acton, London NW10 7NS (020-8963 4531; jcruikshank@hmr-pharmacology.co.uk).

International Clinical Trials, 99 New Cavendish St, London W1M 7FQ (0808 100 1177).

Kingshill Research Centre, Victoria Hospital, Okus Road, Swindon SN1 4JU (01793 481182; info@kingshill-research.org).

Royal Free Hospital, Pharmacology Dept, Hampstead - 020-7830 2405.

Kent & Canterbury Hospital - 0800 515267

Leicester Clinical Research - 0116 273 3553

Another pharmaceutical company operates in several locations:

Bray House, 101 New London Road, Chelmsford, Essex CM2 0PP (01245 266900).

Globecrown House, 32 High St, Maldon, Essex CM9 5PN (telephone as above).

Unit 1, Plymouth Court Business Park, 164/166 Plymouth Grove, Manchester M13 0AF (0161-274 3230).

In some cases, volunteer subjects must produce a medical certificate from their own doctor attesting to their good health, and in most cases foreign volunteers must prove that they are in the country legally. If you are not thoroughly screened, it may be that the research company does not comply with the rigorous standards set out by the Association of Independent Clinical Research Contractors and should be avoided.

Reluctantly Rob Abblett signed up for a study of hay fever tablets in his home town (Leicester) to revive his flagging fortunes between world trips:

> *Lots of blood samples and lots of TV. Thankfully, my veins are too fine so I won't be making a career out of this. I'll get about £950 if I last the distance from 16th June to 11th July. This includes two nights residential and two return visits each week.*

The majority of opportunities are in London. One of the well-regulated clinics which carries out tests on healthy volunteers is the Charterhouse Clinical Research Unit located at the Stamford Hospital, Ravenscourt Park, W6 0TN (020-8741 7170). If you qualify and they have places available on any experiment you will be asked to attend for screening by the Volunteer Recruitment Officer. After passing the screening (you must have taken no medications or drugs in the previous fortnight), you must undertake to abstain faithfully from nicotine, alcohol, tea, coffee, cola and chocolate for 48 hours on either side of the test. Between swallowing the experimental medications and having tests (e.g. blood tests, blood pressure, etc.), you will be given meals and entertained with videos (possibly *Zombie Flesheater, Coma* or *Love at First Bite*).

Guys Hospital also has a Drug Research Unit (6 Newcomen St, London SE1; 020-7403 3756) which is always looking for healthy volunteers and which pays £80-£120 a day. On first arriving in London after a protracted round-the-world working trip, Jimmy Henderson signed up at Guys and did a 20-day experience at £100 a day which set him and his girlfriend Bridgid up in London. The best time to ring is between 10am and noon during the week when you will be told when male volunteers should contact them and when female volunteers.

If the thought of subjecting your body to unknown drugs upsets you, then psychological experiments provide an easier (if less lucrative) alternative. Psychology researchers constantly need large numbers of volunteers and often receive grants specifically to pay subjects. It is worth enquiring at any university's psychology department about this opportunity.

New regulations governing sperm donation have made it more difficult for men to make £10 by donating sperm. One clinic was seen advertising in 2000 for donors aged 18-40 (020-7935 1840).

Job Creation

If you can't find anyone to hire you, you can set yourself up in a small odd-jobbing business. Karen Weaving and Chris Blakeley, who claim to have no particular skills, set themselves up in Basingstoke as 'Spare Hands – Household & Domestic Services' and managed to save £4,000 in seven months, enough to fund a round-the-world trip. Within two months they were both working over 80 hours a week and earning an average of £2.50 an hour having found that gardening, decorating and catering were the most lucrative areas. After delivering and posting some publicity leaflets, they got a few customers, and word spread quickly that they were reliable and cheap. According to Karen and Chris, the question is not 'can I make a sandwich?' but 'can I sell a sandwich?'. Notice boards in newsagents' windows, colleges and unions sometimes give leads to potential dog-walkers, flat-cleaners, shirt-ironers, etc.

Anyone thinking of starting a new business should approach his or her local Business Link (formerly the Training & Enterprise Council/TEC) which can offer advice and in some cases financial support. Instant Muscle Ltd. (Springside House, 84 North End Road, London W14 9ES; 020-7603 2604) is a charity that helps unemployed people in London, Wales and the Midlands to set up in business or find employment generally. Another organisation, Shell LiveWIRE, specialises in helping young people aged 16-30 to start their own business (Hawthorn House, Forth Banks, Newcastle-upon-Tyne NE1 3SG; 0191-261 5584 or 0845 757 3252/ www.shell-livewire.org).

Building and Other Seasonal Work

The building trade has emerged from recession, and there is plenty of work around. Ask around at new building sites to speak to the foreman (or gaffer) who may have powers of hiring or will at least be able to advise you on possibilities. There is more work for unskilled labourers as the foundations are being laid, though you might get hired at a later stage as a hodman carting the bricks and mortar up a ladder to the mason or bricklayer. Iain Kemble has financed several trips abroad after a spell as a self-employed hod carrier. Wages, even for the unskilled, are above average. When you are asking for work, don't admit either to being a student or having no experience.

You may prefer to build temporary rather than permanent structures. The work of erecting marquees is strenuous and pays fairly well, especially since time spent travelling to the destination is also paid, and there is usually plenty of overtime. Try, for example, Field and Lawn (Marquees) Ltd who operate throughout the north of England (Southlands, Leeds Road, Thorpe Willoughby, Yorks. YO8 9PZ; 01757 210444/ www.fieldandlawn.com). Check the local *Yellow Pages* for other firms to contact. Keith Larner recommends a variation on this:

> *Now I can tell you about another good avenue for casual work. I've just completed a job erecting temporary grandstands for sporting events such as golf, racing and tennis. It is very physical work, extremely heavy-going, but financially rewarding: £30-40 per day, 7 days per week but only between April and October.*

Certain agricultural jobs are very seasonal in nature, such as turkey plucking in December. Eric Mackness braved the gruelling job of working on a Christmas tree plantation near Abingdon in Oxfordshire for one month from November 10th:

> *I was recruited at the end of the summer tourist season on Sark by an Irish company which has outlets in Ireland, Scotland and Kent as well as Abingdon near Oxford where I worked. The job consists of sorting, pricing and loading Christmas trees. It's not that well paid at £5 (now £5.50) an hour but because of the potential for working a hideous number of hours (80-90 a week with no days off) it is possible to earn a tidy sum. Accommodation is provided and the food is excellent. The work was the hardest I have ever done (and I have done some hard jobs). Working on top of a trailer loaded with frozen trees in a snowstorm is not for the faint-hearted.*

Apparently many of the workers return from one year to the next in order to earn up to £1,500 in five weeks, but new vacancies do crop up with the Emerald Group; applications to Temple House, Templeshannon, Enniscorthy, Co. Wexford (davidbarrett@emeraldgroup.ie). Another Christmas tree distributor who takes on casual workers from October to December is Worcestershire Woodlands at Leigh Sinton Farm, Near Malvern, Worcs. WR14 1UU (01506 870033; nicola@harburnhouse.com).

Some of the best-paid jobs are the least desirable such as painting electricity pylons for which Mark Wilson was paid £200 a week. He can't recommend this to anyone who can't handle heights, but he certainly preferred it to chicken-catching.

> *I've done unpleasant jobs before (including four years down a coal mine) but this job really was the pits. You are expected to catch six chickens in each hand at a rate of 600 an hour. You then carry them outside (the only time the chickens ever see daylight) and load them onto lorries. While they are pecking and clawing your arms, you can often feel their legs breaking. This together with the screams and cries of the chickens and the stench in the sheds meant that I didn't keep this job up very long and have since given up eating factory-farmed products.*

Finally, don't overlook the obvious. The Post Office employs 100,000 temporary workers between the end of November and Christmas. The pay is well above the minimum wage.

LONDON

Most new arrivals in the capital report that there is no shortage of work. The problem is finding affordable accommodation which allows you to save from what is seldom a startlingly good wage. Ian Mitselburg from Sydney went through the usual processes:

> *The first job I got was through a hostel notice board: labouring for a shifty hotel owner, who was restoring his hotel in the Paddington/Bayswater area (where else?) for a few weeks, paid cash-in-hand. After that I worked through the Everyman Agency in Earls Court which is run by a couple of Kiwis who clearly favoured Australasians.*

With over 2,000 employment agencies, London is the best place to look for temporary work. The advertising pages of free magazines aimed at the ex-pat community (e.g. *TNT, LAM, New Zealand News*) all carry scores of ads for agencies specialising in everything from banquet catering to landscape gardening. It is normally pointless to write to agencies before arrival in the capital, especially foreign applicants who have no chance of obtaining a work permit and who do not speak fluent English. You can expect to earn £3.70-£4.70 as a kitchen porter (the most lowly job) and up to twice that as an assistant chef. Ask your agency about obtaining hygiene certificate training. Among the many agencies active in this field are Drake International (Hirst Hall, East Lane Business Park, East Lane, Wembley, Middlesex HA9 7PX; 020-8426 5266) and Mayday Staff Services. Mayday has several offices including 2 Shoreditch High St, E1 6PG (020-7377 1352/ maydaytemporary@maydaygroup.co.uk); 21 Great Chapel St, W1V 3AQ (020-7439 3009) for bar work and 35 Goldhawk St, W12 8QQ (020-8749 3139).

Also check out cleaning and security work, for which there seems to be an insatiable demand in London. An active agency in the field of gardening and landscape labouring is Target Appointments, 5th Floor, Sicilian House, Sicilian Avenue, WC1A 2QH (020-7242 1183; targettemp@aol.com). Jimmy Henderson from Glasgow recommends a building agency in Lewisham, South London called Site Masters, who gave him very regular work. For security work, you will need a checkable work history going as far back as ten years. Raymond Oliver, who spent several years travelling the world, showed potential employers travel diaries, photos and letters home to prove his case, but was still not hired.

Anyone who can speak a foreign language has an excellent chance of finding work at a tourist attraction. Young Europeans based in London should give this a go as Brigitte Albrech did:

> *With basic English and a lot of courage, I applied for a job at Madame Tussauds Museum and was surprised they accepted me without a lot of questions. They are always in need of people speaking a foreign language to work as guides and are looking for people who appear clean and patient. There is an opportunity of being trained as a cashier or planetarium operator, which would mean more money. It can be hard work but getting a work reference from Madame Tussauds is not bad at all.*

Apply to the Human Resources Officer, The Tussauds Group, Marylebone Road, NW1 5LR (020-7487 0200; www.madame-tussauds.com).

There is a very high turn-over of staff at pubs (see section on pub work above), shops, wine bars, station buffets, etc. Check the classified adverts in the *London Evening Standard* (which comes out at about 11am), the free weekly *TNT* and *LOOT*. As mentioned earlier in this chapter, the office of *New Zealand News* in the Haymarket has a useful notice board for job-seekers,

Modelling is a traditional way of earning cash; try the Chelsea School of Art, the St Martin's School of Art or the London College of Printing for nude or clothed jobs (£5+ per hour). Aspiring film or television extras can register with the agency Allsorts (020-8491 7000) for about £15 and hope to be deployed at rates of between £30 and £90 a day (extra if you are required to have a haircut). Equity has a list of other agencies (0207 379 6000) or you could make enquiries of the agency Saffron ID (26 Pancras Road, London NW1 2TB; 020-7278 2110; http://website.lineone.net/~saffron). Beware of rogue agencies that take your money but fix up nothing. Agencies will ask for at least one recent professional quality photo, probably black and white (8 X 10).

Americans and others lacking working papers may find that agencies will not be prepared to help them. After watching his travel fund dwindle from $500 to $30 in just three weeks, American Joe Warnick was reduced to doing one of the sleaziest jobs around: he went to work for a prostitute posting her business cards in London phone booths. Just two days into the job, he managed to upset his plump, middle-aged, heavily made-up employer and told her to find someone else, using somewhat colourful language, whereupon she threatened to send round her pimp to teach him a lesson. Fortunately the thug never materialised and within a short while Joe had landed a job with a family-run window cleaning business which he thoroughly enjoyed for four months.

> *I was treated extremely well by this wonderful family. Cleaning windows above the bustling streets of London was a real buzz. It afforded me countless opportunities to visit with Londoners in their flats and meet many of them at their places of work.*

Pubs
Anyone who has been on a pub crawl in London will know that a huge percentage of the people working behind the bar are Australian. Although there are employment agencies specialising in bar work, they aren't usually very helpful to people looking for casual bar work.

Kristen Moen from Norway describes her job in a London pub:

> *I loved it: the atmosphere was great, I had so much fun and met so much nice people at work. The only thing I can complain about is that the money is not very good – or maybe the rents for flats in London are too high. If I had had a work permit, I would have gotten a job immediately, but it took me two weeks. First I went around asking in pubs and restaurants. Everybody was really helpful. They would always suggest another place I could go to or tell me to come back in a few weeks. At the same time I was also reading the job ads in the Evening Standard. 70% turned me down because of my missing work permit, but finally I got something and worked happily there for four months.*

Now that EEA citizens are allowed to work in Britain, Norwegians like Kristen will find the job hunt much easier.

Couriers
Driving is a standard stop-gap job, for example of vans and mini-cabs or as a courier. Motorcycle owners might be tempted by the money which can be earned by despatch riders. For those who don't own their own bikes, they can be leased from the firm for about £60 a week. According to Ben Nakoneczny, despatch riders can earn between £200 and £500 a week:

> *Earnings are commission-only; they increase dramatically according to number of hours worked, knowledge of London streets and relationship with your controller. There is also a very high risk of serious injury, hence insurance premiums will be very high if you choose to declare your occupation for insurance and tax purposes, which many don't.*

The north London firm Moves (141 Acton Lane, London NW10; 08700 104310) is always looking for drivers, couriers and porters, and seems sympathetic to the erratic habits of people working for relatively short periods to fund their travels. The nearest tube station is Harlesden plus it has offices in other UK towns and cities including Manchester, Birmingham and Coventry. Another company to try is KLR Personnel, 2nd Floor, 42-43 Lower Marsh, London SE1 6EY (020-7928 5111) provided you have your own bicycle or motorcycle and work references.

Although cycle couriers don't earn as much as despatch riders, it appeals to some brave souls like T. P. Lye from Malaysia who claimed that you do it for love not money:

> *After the first few weeks of courier cycling (which is the best job I've ever had) it should be possible to earn £80-150 per week. Anyone who is reasonably fit, can endure from 20 to 30 miles of cycling in a day, knows London pretty well, can read a map and loves the thrill of dodging in and out of the London traffic should try it. It can be quite scary cycling in the rain when your brakes don't work and you have to cope with cretinous pedestrians who can't see beyond their brollies, but after a while that sort of experience is part of the whole fun of courier cycling.*
>
> *The company I worked for was Arrow Express. They were always looking for new people since there is a high turnover especially during the winter months. The pay is always cash-in-hand and by the week. In my experience the most boring days have been fine, sunny ones when everyone wants to work and there aren't enough jobs to go round. One of the worst problems is punctured tyres.*

Sales
People working in shops are often paid a commission in addition to the average weekly wage of £200+. Harrods is constantly looking for temporary staff to cover their busy sale periods (July and January) and the run-up to Christmas; contact the Recruitment

Centre, 11 Brompton Place, SW3 1QE (020-7893 8793) for details.

Jobs in 'telesales' are also plentiful in London. Telesales involve telephoning complete strangers and persuading them to buy a product. Advertisements for this type of work frequently appear in the free local newspapers in the London area, although they may not always mention the nature of the job in the advert. The ones to look out for say things like: 'Do you want to earn up to £X/week in your spare time?'.

Accommodation in London

If you are worried that you won't be able to afford to stay in London (short of sleeping in Victoria Station), you might choose to stay at Tent City where the overnight charge is £5. This hostel-under-canvas operates from early June to September and is staffed by volunteers who commit themselves to stay for six weeks. They receive £33 a week out-of-pocket expenses plus bed and food. Contact the administrator at Tent City (Old Oak Common Lane, East Acton, W3; 020-8743 5708). All postal enquiries must be accompanied by an SAE or IRC. Another place to go for a cheap bed (£10 a night) is Eurotower (Courland Grove, Larkhall Lane, Clapham SW8 2PX; 020-7720 5191) where weekly and monthly discounts are available.

It might be worth bearing in mind that London's casinos serve free food to members; membership is free but must take place 48 hours before turning up.

Free food and accommodation in exchange for some duties is a great bonus in London. For example the charity SHAD recruits full-time volunteers to assist people with severe physical disabilities to live independently in the community. Volunteers are required to stay for a minimum of three or four months, and receive a place to live and an allowance of at least £56 a week plus expenses. A shift system is worked by volunteers allowing plenty of free time to explore London. There are several borough offices in London including SHAD Haringey, Winkfield Resource Centre, 33 Winkfield Road, Haringey N22 5RP (020-8365 8528) and SHAD Wandsworth, 5 Bedford Hill, Balham, SW12 9ET (020-8675 6095; www.shadwand.org.uk). Similarly Independent Living Alternatives (Trafalgar House, Grenville Place, NW7 3SA; tel/fax 020-8906 9265; www.ILA.mcmail. com) pays its full-time volunteers £63.50 a week in addition to free accommodation.

VOLUNTARY WORK

Community Service Volunteers mentioned at the beginning of this chapter guarantee a voluntary placement to anyone aged 16-35 who commits him/herself to work in hostels or day centres for at least four months. Volunteers receive £25.50 a week in addition to accommodation and meals; freephone the Volunteers' Hotline on 0800 374991 or consult the CSV homepage www.csv.org.uk. Another organisation which provides board, lodging and pocket money to volunteers willing to work at centres for the homeless is the Simon Community (PO Box 1187, London NW5 4HW; 020-4785 6639) whose minimum stay is three months.

There are many shorter term opportunities for volunteers, especially during the summer months when organisations such as the Winged Fellowship Trust (Angel House, 20-32 Pentonville Road, London N1 9XD; 020-7833 2594), Break (7a Church St, Sheringham, Norfolk NR26 8QR; 01263 822161) and Mencap's Holiday Service (Optimum House, Clippers Quay, Salford Quays M5 2XP; 0161-888 1200) recruit volunteers to help at their holiday centres for people with disabilities. Winged Fellowship, with centres in Southampton, Southport, Redhill, Nottingham and Chigwell, needs volunteers (British or otherwise) from February to November and pays all board, lodging and travel to the centres from within the UK. If interested in this kind of work, send an s.a.e. to RADAR, the Royal Association for Disability and Rehabilitation, requesting their information sheet 'Voluntary and Paid Opportunities for People Looking for Work with and for Disabled People and Disability Issues' (12 City Forum, 250 City Road, London EC1V 8AF; www.radar.org.uk).

If you are more interested in conservation work, there are several national bodies which arrange one to three week working holidays where volunteers repair dry stone walls, clear overgrown ponds, undertake botanical surveys, archaeological digs or maintain traditional woodland. You will be housed in comfortable volunteer basecamps with about a dozen other volunteers. For a free brochure listing projects organised by the National Trust, ring 020-8315 1111 or send a postal request to PO Box 39, Bromley, Kent BR1 3XL (www.nationaltrust.org.uk/volunteers). Projects take place year round. Most summer projects cost £60 to join whereas out-of-season working holidays cost £45.

The British Trust for Conservation Volunteers (36 St. Mary's St, Wallingford, Oxfordshire OX10 0EU) can also send a calendar of their projects on request (01491 824602/www.btcv.org.uk). BTCV organise 600 working holidays from the Anglesey coast to the Scottish highlands. The Scottish counterpart is the Scottish Conservation Projects Trust (Balallan House, 24 Allan Park, Stirling FK8 2QG; 01786 479697) which organises residential Action Breaks throughout Scotland between March and November. For volunteers interested in the routine maintenance and conservation of old buildings, contact Cathedral Camps at 16 Glebe Avenue, Flitwick, Beds. MK45 1HS. These organisations charge a modest fee to cover expenses, e.g. £50 a week. Bird-lovers can become volunteer wardens for up to four weeks with the Royal Society for the Protection of Birds (RSPB, The Lodge, Sandy, Beds. SG19 2DL; 01767 680551; www.rspb.org.uk). Accommodation is provided free but the volunteers must provide their own food. The Waterway Recovery Group Ltd (PO Box 114, Rickmansworth, Herts. WD3 1ZY; 01923 711114; enquiries@wrg.org.uk) run week-long voluntary Canal Camps.

A number of organisations in Britain which require volunteers for limited periods are listed in the *International Directory of Voluntary Work* £10.99). Anyone who wants to participate on an archaeological dig should subscribe to *British Archaeology* for £23, available from the Council for British Archaeology, Bowes Morrell House, 111 Walmgate, York YO1 9WA (01904 671417; www.britarch.ac.uk). The magazine is produced six times a year and lists archaeological digs to which volunteers can apply.

Volunteering is an excellent solution for anyone who has work permit problems. Americans, and indeed anyone, can fix up voluntary jobs independently as well as through the programmes mentioned at the beginning of this chapter. Janet Renard and Luke Olivieri are two particularly enterprising American travellers who arranged several voluntary positions before they left home. One of the most unusual was working for the Festiniog Railway Company (Harbour Station, Porthmadog, Gwynedd LL49 9NF; www.festrail.co.uk) which operates a famous narrow gauge railway and provides hostel accommodation to volunteers.

> *Many of the volunteers are railroad/steam engine fanatics, but accepted us even though we didn't know the first thing about it. We elected to work in the Parks & Gardens section and spent a week weeding, planting, clearing, etc. The work was hard and the evenings were busy too. We were taken to a pub one night, asked to dinner another, visited a Welsh male voice choir and went climbing in the area. Festiniog Railway depends completely on volunteers who come from all over, all ages, all professions. But they can always use more help, so we may just go back.*

Other historic railways looking for volunteers, both in beautiful parts of the country, are the Strathspey Railway Co in Aviemore (01479 810725) and the Welshpool & Llanfair Railway (01938 810441).

Communes (which are now properly called communities) may provide a good opportunity for people sympathetic to a back-to-basics lifestyle. The Centre for Alternative Technology in Wales (Machynlleth, Powys SY20 9AZ; 01654 702400; www.cat.org.uk) takes on volunteers between March and September, many on a short-term basis, paying £5.50 a day for food. Advance booking is essential. A directory called *Diggers & Dreamers* with details of communities both in Britain and abroad is available for £10 plus £1.50 UK postage from Edge of Time, BCM Edge, London WC1N 3XX (0800 083 0451; www.edgeoftime.co.uk).

Buddhist communities throughout Britain run retreats either for a modest fee or on a work-for-keep arrangement. For example the Losang Dragpa Centre in the Pennines (Dobroyd Castle, Pexwood Road, Todmorden, W. Yorks. OL14 7JJ; 01706 812247) requires volunteers to assist with various projects maintaining the Victorian castle in which it is housed. Also in Yorkshire is the Madhyamaka Centre (Kilnwick Percy Hall, Pocklington, Yorks. YO42 1UF; 01759 304832; www.madhyamaka.org) where Shona Williamson enjoyed a working holiday so much she decided to make it her home for an extended period. In exchange for 35 hours of work per week she got free dormitory accommodation, vegetarian meals and the chance to attend evening meditations and teachings.

Laura Hitchcock from New York state managed to fix up two three-month positions in the field of her career interest by agreeing to pay her own expenses if they would take her on and help her find accommodation in local homes. Her jobs were in the publicity departments of the Ironbridge Gorge Museum (Ironbridge, Telford, Shropshire TF8 7AW) and then in a theatre-arts centre in East Anglia (The Quay at Sudbury, Quay Lane, Sudbury, Suffolk CO10 6AN):

> *I learned when writing not to ask for 'internships' but rather for 'unpaid work experience'; otherwise the British will ask you what hospital you are with!*
> *The particularly good feature of my jobs was that the people were so friendly. If you were willing to help yourself they'd do all they could for you.*

If you intend to become involved in the workcamps or organic farm movements abroad, it is advisable to get local experience first (see *Voluntary* chapter for addresses of internationally-active organisations and *Agriculture* for a description of the activities of WWOOF: Willing Workers on Organic Farms).

Ireland

The rise in Ireland's fortunes over the last decade have been astonishing and the employment situation is far more promising than it has been for generations. (Ten years ago Ireland's rate of unemployment was the worst in Europe.) No longer is the traffic of migrant labour one-way; nowadays lots of Europeans are flocking to Ireland for work; and recruitment agencies actively assist the process. The phenomenal amount of building work going on in Dublin is a reliable indicator of the vigour of the economy and justifies the description 'Celtic tiger'. Taxes and the cost of living are still high but wages are beginning to catch up.

Few working travellers find it difficult to adjust to 'Irish time'. While sometimes being frustrated by it, Mig Urquhart hopes that it will never disappear because it certainly beats the uptight stressed-out life in other countries where she has worked like the United States. She goes on to point out one important exception: 'pubs have some of the best trained and fastest barmen in the world, who take great pride in their profession'.

The Republic of Ireland is a member of the EU and so no work permit is needed by EU nationals. British citizens do not even require a passport. Generally, Irish employers are as little constrained by bureaucracy as any working holidaymaker could wish.

The Irish government introduced a new visa system in 2000 for certain categories of employees from non-EEA countries, mainly IT, construction and nursing. Further details are available from the Department of Foreign Affairs, 80 St. Stephen's Green, Dublin 2 (01-478 0822).

Working Holiday Schemes

US nationals who can prove Irish ancestry may be eligible for unrestricted entry to Ireland and even Irish nationality (which would confer all EU rights). Enquiries should be directed to the relevant Irish Embassy.

Full-time North American students in tertiary education or recent graduates are eligible to apply for an 'Exchange Visitor Programme Work Permit'. For American students the permit is valid for up to four months at any time of the year and for Canadians the limit is 12 months. Council Exchanges in New York (633 Third Ave, New York, NY 10017) administer the programme in the US; and SWAP/Travelcuts (45 Charles Street East, Suite 100, Toronto, Ontario M4Y 1S2) administer it in Canada.

Once in Ireland, the student travel service Usit Now (19-21 Aston Quay, O'Connell Bridge, Dublin 2; 01-602 1777; www.usitnow.ie) will advise on job opportunities. Earnings up to a threshold of £5,700 are tax-free. Usit Now does not currently administer the working holiday scheme for Australians and New Zealanders who should apply for exchange visitor permits from the Irish embassy in their own country.

If you visit their office on the south side of the River Liffey, you can inspect a large notice board with many Jobs Available notices, including many for au pairs.

THE JOB HUNT

The employment service of Ireland is FAS (Foras Aiscanna Saothair) with about 70 offices throughout the country which EU nationals may consult. The best office for foreign enquiries is the EURES office in the FAS at 27-33 Upper Baggot Street, Dublin 4 (01-607 0500; www.fasjobs-ireland.com). There are a number of private employment agencies listed in the 'Irish Golden Pages' with whom you may register. The Irish Department of Enterprise, Trade & Employment (Davitt House, Adelaide Road, Dublin 2) can issue on request a list of licensed employment agencies in Ireland (01-661 4444; www.entemp.ie/lfd/working.pdf).

Mig Urquhart from Glasgow ended up in Dublin by chance rather than choice since that was the cheapest flight she could get out of New York. She ended up staying for two years and says that the FAS is very useful for jobs if only because you can use their phones to follow up leads. The main newspapers are worth checking: the *Evening Herald* for more casual jobs and the *Irish Independent* (Thursdays and Sundays; www.loadza.com) and the *Irish Times* (Fridays; www.ireland.com) for more professional appointments. She also found that the Dublin Corporation Community & Youth Information Centre in Sackville Place off O'Connell St (01-878 6844; ycinfo@iol.ie) offers information on employment and training, welfare rights, study at home and abroad, travel and accommodation. They offer a free legal service and free internet access. Finally, she took advantage of the cheap CV service for the unemployed offered by the Trade Union Trust (Solidarity Trust Resource Centre, 48 Fleet St, Dublin 2).

Tourism

The tourist industry is the main source of seasonal work in Ireland. Outside Dublin, the largest demand is in the southwestern counties of Cork and Kerry, especially the towns of Killarney (with well over 100 pubs) and Tralee. Vacancies are sometimes registered through EURES, for example hotel jobs paying IR£180 a week plus accommodation were on offer at the time of writing to waiting staff with at least one year's experience. Write to the addresses in any guide to hotels in Ireland. When applying, you should mention any musical talent you have, since pubs and hotels may be glad to have a barman who can occasionally entertain at the piano. Directly approaching cafés, campsites, amusement arcades and travelling circuses is usually more effective than writing. Two hundred thousand people a year visit the Aillwee Caves in County Clare; the company which manages the attraction recruits seasonal guides and support staff (Aillwee Cave Co. Ltd., Ballyvaughan, Co. Clare; 065-707 7036; www.aillweecave.ie).

The Anglo-Continental Placements Agency in England (Dial Post House, West Sussex RH13 8NQ; 01403 713344; www.anglocontinentalplacements.com) places staff, from experienced chefs to inexperienced kitchen porters, in Irish hotels. They will register anyone with an appropriate visa or Europeans with a reasonable knowledge of English. Similarly, North-South Hotel Recruitment Agency (1 Turnpike Close, Darlington DL1 3SH; tel/fax 01325 467431) and the Transcontinental Agency in outer London (020-8658 4059) fill vacancies in Ireland. The website www.irishjobsearch.com is a free up-to-date register of people looking for work in Ireland's hospitality and leisure industry. Kitchen staff, housekeepers, waiters, receptionists, office staff and gardeners are all needed for a minimum of two months.

Experienced assistants and instructors may be needed by riding stables and watersports centres throughout Ireland. The horse industry is still very strong in Ireland; experienced individuals looking for stable work should contact the National Stud Company (Tully, Co. Kildare; 045-521251). Anyone with experience of horses might have success by contacting stables and riding holiday centres. For example monitors and instructors are needed mainly for children at Errislannan Manor Connemara Pony Stud, Clifden, Co. Galway 095-21134; www.connemara.net/Errislannan-Manor) where pony trek leaders are needed for the summer; the minimum stay is three months and applications must be made before March).

There are innumerable festivals throughout Ireland, mostly during the summer. Big-name bands often perform at concerts near Dublin. A small fortune can be made by amateur entrepreneurs (with or without a permit) who find a niche in the market. Heather McCulloch had two friends who sold filled rolls and sandwiches at a major concert and made a clear profit of over £1,000 in just a few hours.

'The Rose of Tralee', a large regional festival held in Tralee, Co. Kerry in the first week of September, provides various kinds of employment for enterprising workers, as Tracie Sheehan reports:

As 50,000 people attend this festival each year, guest houses, hotels, restaurants and cafés all take on extra staff. Buskers make great money, as do mime artists, jugglers and artists. Pubs do a roaring business, so singing or performing in a pub can be very profitable.

Dublin

According to Mig Urquhart, 'crappy jobs are very easy to get in Dublin, whereas real jobs are scarce'. Mig has variously worked in a Dublin hostel, bed and breakfast, Irish-owned fast food company Supermacs, canteen of a government department and for the boat taxi on the River Liffey patronised by tourists, school groups and commuters. Check the notice boards in the main travellers' hostels like the Dublin International Youth Hostel at 61 Mountjoy Street.

Try the trendy spots in Temple Bar in the city centre. Writing from Dublin in June 2000, the American Dan Eldridge found the city to be a land of opportunity:

Restaurant and pub work is still exploding in Dublin especially in Temple Bar but also north of the river on and around Grafton Street, basically anywhere you see people. My experience has been that when your would-be employer asks if you have working papers (and they all do) your best bet is to say that you're in the process of getting them together, and they'll surely get the drift. For travellers who can't stand the idea of working in a pub, try the youth hostel in Temple Bar. The manager actually offered to sponsor me for a year.

Even a few years ago Heather McCulloch had great success with agency work in Dublin:

It took two weeks of enlisting with every agency I could find in Dublin before one called with work in their offices. My hourly rate was £4 with plenty of overtime (though tax and PRSI are extortionate).

Heather also did a stint of door to door selling and reports that the Irish are more welcoming than most nations especially to someone with a foreign accent. Although she was enjoying this job, she soon quit, not only because it was on a commission-only basis but because she felt uncomfortable passing off mass-produced Taiwanese pictures as 'original oil paintings'.

Grafton Street in Dublin is *the* place for buskers and street traders. The Irish are a generous nation and appreciate musical talent. It is also Dublin's equivalent of Regent Street in London, yet in the run-up to Christmas 2000 the stores were finding it difficult to recruit Father Christmases, apparently because the usual candidates had all found lucrative casual work elsewhere.

Au Pairing

Foreign women may wish to consider au pairing in Ireland via one of a number of agencies for example Langtrain International (Torquay Rd, Foxrock, Dublin 18; 01-289 3876) which is both an English teaching centre and an au pair agency, and the Job Options Bureau (Tourist House, 40-41 Grand Parade, Cork; 021-275369; also has Dublin office) which is the Irish representative of the International Au Pair Association. The recommended pocket money for au pairs is IR£40 a week for 30-35 hours of duties. One important difference between Irish and English agencies is that the ones in Dublin charge a placement fee to incoming au pairs, normally IR£40.

Ireland is a popular destination for students of English from the Continent, so anyone with a background in TEFL might apply to one of the many language schools and camps for a summer job as an English teacher or monitor. Many language schools arrange work placements as well as courses for instance the Centre of English Studies, 31 Dame St, Dublin 2 (01-671 4233) and Pace Language Institute (01-276 0922; pace@indigo.ie).

Agriculture

There is not much chance of finding paid work on farms because of high rural unemployment. Even if the occasional vacancy does arise, the farms are small, widely dispersed and have no co-ordinating body to facilitate recruitment. However there is a good network of farms and smallholdings which allow people to work in exchange for keep. One source of farms where you can stay for a weekend, week, month or longer is WWOOF Ireland, Harpoonstown, Drinagh, Co. Wexford. For a membership fee of IR£10 (US$15) they will (eventually) send the current listing of about 90 farm members.

Joe Warnick from the US was very grateful for the WWOOF arrangement after the tribulations of trying to find work in London:

> *Your information on the WWOOF organisation was tremendously helpful. It was a superb way to experience rural Ireland, and make friends with so many good people. I stayed on a traditional farm one hour from Galway where I picked potatoes and herded dairy cows down an old lane surrounded by stone fences. My carpentry skills were handy when repairing the attic floor as well. At night the old farmer Tom would play his accordian and sing Irish songs. We'd take shots of moonshine and exchange tales. Tom's wife Maureen was a wonderful cook. Her homemade bread was out of this world. It was great to eat such healthy food and fresh vegetables after the excesses of London's nightlife.*

Another American, David Stamboulis, writing in the magazine *Transitions Abroad*, also found the opportunities in rural Ireland to offer plenty of non-financial rewards:

> *I discovered farmers, three nursery owners and small communities with plenty of work to be done. Just politely asking was usually all it took to get four hours of work per day in exchange for room and board. Always, the work was fun, challenging and unpressured, because I was not doing it for money. The food was usually self-produced and self-prepared; and the accommodations were always interesting, ranging from small crofts to large farms.*

Ken Smith from New Zealand worked as a farmhand for several stretches of a couple of months:

> *For me it has proved invaluable as a way to plan my next move while in a family environment. I enjoy the work which involves cleaning out the cattle houses, cutting silage, fencing and a thousand and one other odd jobs which need doing on a farm. The work is for board and lodging only and I'm very happy with the arrangement. It's great to be outside in the fresh air and at the ground level of Irish rural life. I am now a familiar face in the local community. When the work's done the Irish like to enjoy themselves, and the atmosphere in country pubs is great, with story-telling and music.*

Outdoor work can be found in the Christmas tree industry. Having failed to secure work on the apple harvest in England due to early frosts, Robert Abblett contacted Emerald Trees (Temple House, Templeshannon, Enniscorthy, Co. Wexford; davidbarrett@emeraldgroup.ie). By arriving in September, Rob was assured a place on the harvest in December. Working conditions were just as tough as those described in the UK chapter (see section on Seasonal Work) but he managed to save £750 including a tax rebate. Those who prove themselves on the harvest might then be taken on for pruning and planting which is fairly lucrative and much more civilized.

Fishing

Robert Abblett gave a lift to an Irish fisherman who passed on some tips on finding work in the fishing industry:

> *He mentioned three places to try. I visited Rossaveal fish factory west of Galway and could have got a job easily extracting the roe from herrings. The work was paid piece work and the boss told me that the average experienced worker earns £50 a day, and the fastest worker double that, for a maximum of*

five days a week (weather permitting). Most people only last a few days as the work is dirty, smelly and boring. The season here lasts from mid-October till February only. I then visited Dingle and enquired at the fish factory, where the wages were £3 plus bonus. I didn't bother checking Castletownbere on the Beara peninsula which is a large whitefish port. Work on the fishing boats and factories is apparently available most of the year.

Robert showed admirable enterprise in tracking down these opportunities. He picked out likely looking village names from the Michelin map, and dialled Directory Enquiries (1190) to phone the local post office. They were usually able to give the telephone numbers of the local fish factories. To make things easier for readers, the Rossaveal factory can be contacted at Iasc Mara Teoranta, Rossaveal, Co. Galway (091-572136/fax 572271). Their 30 vacancies as general operatives were posted on the EURES website (http://europa.eu.int/eures) in the summer of 2000. The advertised wage was IR£5 an hour.

Work on the fishing boats can be very well paid but it is normally necessary to have experience. Rumours of wages topping £500 a week are commonplace.

Voluntary Opportunities

The Volunteer Resource Centre aims to match individuals who wish to volunteer with organisations that offer suitable volunteering opportunities. They are located in Carmichael Centre for Voluntary Groups, Coleraine House, Coleraine St, Dublin 7 (01-872 2622; www.volunteeringireland.com).

A range of 2-3 week voluntary workcamps are held all over Ireland from June to October. Projects include for example playschemes for inner city, refugee and traveller children, environmental work and holiday schemes for wheelchair users. Projects in Ireland are organised by Voluntary Service International (30 Mountjoy Square, Dublin 1; 01-855 1011; vsi@iol.ie). Applicants in Britain should contact IVS in Colchester, Leeds or Edinburgh. Volunteers can expect to pay roughly £100 which covers full board, insurance and administration.

The Simon Community of Ireland (St. Andrew's House, 28-30 Exchequer St, Dublin 2; 01-671 1606; simonnat@indigo.ie) takes on committed volunteers with an excellent standard of spoken English for a minimum of six months to live and work with long-term homeless people at their shelters and residential houses in four Irish cities. Volunteers work and live on-site for three days and then get two days off where they stay in a separate flat. The remuneration is IR£40 per week.

The Corrymeela Community (Ballycastle, Co. Antrim BT54 6QU; www.corrymeela. org) is an ecumenical Christian organisation committed to reconciliation in Ireland. Approximately 25 volunteers per week are needed in the summer to work in arts and crafts, recreation, housekeeping, etc. as well as some longer term volunteers from March or September. All volunteers receive free board and lodging plus a stipend of £25 a week if they stay for six months or more. The deadline for summer applications is April 1st.

An Oige, the Irish Youth Hostels Association (61 Mountjoy St, Dublin 7; 01-830 4555) has 36 hostels throughout the country and relies to a large extent on voluntary help. Many assistant wardens are needed June to September and general assistants to help with maintenance, office work, conservation, etc. year round. As throughout the world, you can always approach busy hostels to see if they need an assistant. The hostel just outside Killarney often employs foreign travellers.

Members of the long-established Atlantis community (Burtonport, Co. Donegal) which is related to the parent community in Colombia (see *Latin America* chapter) are restoring their 50-ft wooden sailboat. Volunteers with skills are always welcome and will be given bed and board (075-42304; afan69@hotmail.com).

Conservation Volunteers Ireland (The Green, Griffith College, South Circular Road, Dublin 8; 01-454 7185; www.cvi.ie) aims to protect and enhance Ireland's natural and cultural heritage through practical conservation projects. These are operated year-round throughout the country and include nature trail construction, pond restoration and tree planting. Membership costs £15 (£10 unwaged) and volunteers must pay a nominal charge for food, accommodation and transport (e.g. £16 for a weekend, £56 for a week).

Netherlands

British and Irish young people continue to pour off ferries, check into hostels and begin looking for the highly paid jobs and liberal attitudes (e.g. to drugs and prostitution) they've heard about. Some draw benefit while they look and in some cases Dutch tolerance has been tested. Yet the market for unskilled non-Dutch-speaking workers is far from saturated since unemployment stands at just 2.5%, the lowest for 20 years.

The job search should not be confined to Amsterdam, since there are temporary employment agencies aplenty and many opportunities in Rotterdam, The Hague, Haarlem, Leiden and Utrecht. Unemployment is highest in the south and north-west, so these areas should probably be avoided. Competition for work is much less outside the summer season.

REGULATIONS

Contrary to what one might have expected in the new harmonised Europe, the Dutch have been tightening up the regulations in an attempt to clamp down on squatters, drug abusers and other undesirables. All new employees can be asked by their employers to show suitable proof of identification such as a passport. They should carry ID around at work in case of spot checks by tax, social security or immigration inspectors.

EU Nationals

All job-seeking EU nationals must follow the bureaucratic procedures which are strictly followed by agencies and employers in all but a handful of cases. If you intend to stay for more than three months, the first step is to acquire a sticker in your passport from the local aliens police (*Vreemdelingenpolitie*) or Town Hall, normally over-the-counter. They will expect you to provide a local address – hostel addresses will normally suffice – and it is best to use this same address throughout your stay. The passport should then be taken to the local tax office to apply for a *sofinummer* or *'sofi'* (social/fiscal number). It is also possible to apply for a *sofi* from outside the Netherlands, though this will take at least six weeks; send a copy of your passport details to Belastingdienst Particulieren/Ondernemingen buitenland, Postbus 2865, 6401 DJ Heerlen; 045-573 5761.

Normally you will have to complete both these steps before being allowed to register with employment bureaux or take up a job, though in some cases the *sofi* will suffice. To turn the initial sticker into a residence permit *(Verblijfsvergunning* or *verblijfskaart)* after three months (which can be extended for a further three months if you can prove you are still searching for work), you will have to show a genuine work contract or letter of employment from an employer (not an agency) and pay a fee of 35 guilders. The contract will have to show that the legal minimum wage and holiday pay are being paid and the proper tax and deductions are being made. The registration office for foreigners in Amsterdam *(Dienst Vreemdelingenpolitie)* is at Johan Huizingalaan 757, 1066 VH Amsterdam (020-559 62 14), while the tax office *(Belastingdienst)* is at Kingsfordweg 1, 1043 GN Amsterdam (020-687 77 77). In rural parts of Holland, satisfying the bureaucrats may take several days and use up lots of petrol.

A further complicating factor is that job agencies may not be willing to sign you up unless you have a bank account and banks in areas frequented by short-stay workers have become reluctant to open accounts. In some cases a returnable deposit of 100 guilders has been charged. Look for the V.S.B. Bank which has been recommended.

Non-EU Nationals

The situation for non-EU nationals is predictably more difficult. North Americans, Antipodeans and others who require no visa to travel to the Netherlands are allowed to work for less than three months, provided they report to the Aliens Police within three days of arrival and their employer has obtained a *tewerkstellingsvergunning* (employment permit) for them. Non-EU nationals wishing to work for longer than three months must in the first instance obtain an authorisation for temporary stay or *machtiging tot voorlopig verblijf* (MVV) before their employer can apply for an employment permit from the CBA (Centraal Bestuur Arbeidsvoorziening). The MVV can be applied for through the Dutch Embassy in your country. In practice, the *tewerkstellingsvergunning* is unlikely to be issued for casual work. Jill Weseman, an American who worked as an au pair in Groningen, regretted her decision to follow the letter of the law:

> *The amount of paperwork I was required to present to the police was ridiculous. It took six visits plus several phone calls before I was 'official', at which point my passport was filled with meaningless but huge stamps.*

Chris Miksovsky is one of those rare Americans who has found a European employer willing to back an application for a work permit:

> *I've been here in Holland the past two months doing marketing work for a company that makes radio-controlled model racing cars, a long-time hobby of mine. It was pure luck that they were looking for someone just like me when I faxed them out of the blue (from Auckland). It's been two months already and the company is still paying me in cash while all the red tape is processed. The company has really had to back me up with lots of explaining as to why the position can only be filled by me and not a native citizen. It can be done, but you need to be damn lucky, damn qualified or (preferably) both.*

A leaflet in English called 'Working in the Netherlands: New Rules for Aliens' and a booklet 'Working in the Netherlands' dated April 1998 are available from Dutch Embassies including the one in London (38 Hyde Park Gate, SW7 5DP; www.netherlands-embassy.org.uk). For detailed information, contact the Dutch immigration service, Immigratie-en Naturalisatiedienst, Stafafdeling In- en Externe Betrekkingen, Postbus 30125, 2500 GC Den Haag (070-370 31 24).

Red Tape

The Dutch have some of the most progressive laws in the world to minimise exploitation of workers, though the minimum wage no longer seems much higher than the rest of Europe as it did in the 1990s. Because the minimum wage is lower for younger workers, employers often prefer to hire younger people whenever possible, often Dutch school children. Compulsory holiday pay of at least 8% of your gross

BENELUX

North Sea

Groningen

De Koog

Friesland

Emmeloord

Andijk

Zwolle

Alkmaar

Haarlem · AMSTERDAM

NETHERLANDS

Enschede

Heemstede

Hillegom

Hoofddorp

Apeldoorn

Lisse

Sassenheim

Nieuwveen

Katuijk a/Zee

Ter Aar

Arnhem

Leiden

Utrecht

Wageningen

The Hague

Naaldwijk

Delft

Nijmegen

Hook of Holland

Rotterdam

Gorinchem

Tiel

Breda

Vlissingen

Baarland

Knokke-Heist

Antwerp

GERMANY

Bruges

Hasselt

Ostend

Ghent

Vilvoorde

BRUSSELS

Rixensart

BELGIUM

Liege

Namur

Charleroi

FRANCE

Wiltz

Diekirch

LUXEMBOURG

Bouillon

LUXEMBOURG

Esch

Remich

The symbol for flowers
refers to packing and processing bulbs
as well as picking flowers.

WILLIAM SWAN

salary should also be paid on all but the most temporary casual jobs. Do not count on receiving the holiday pay immediately after finishing a job. Although one of Ian Govan's friends received his holiday pay two weeks after the vegetable harvest in Westland, Ian and another friend were told that it would be sent to their UK bank account several months later. Sure enough £250 arrived in time for Christmas. Similarly tax rebates may be owing at the end of the tax year, and so employees should save all pay slips showing income and deductions.

Several travellers have recommended the *Arbeidsbureau* (Dutch equivalent of a Jobcentre) as a useful source of work. For example the one in Leiden treated Xuela Edwards and her travelling companion Nicky Brown better than any English Jobcentre they had ever visited. The helpful staff checked their computer, fixed up an interview and Xuela started work the following day. To find the local address, look up *Gewestelijk Arbeids Bureau* in the local telephone directory. Dutch Euroadvisers might also be helpful since they would have an overview of the range of temporary and permanent possibilities for EEA nationals.

The process for EU nationals of registering at the town hall should be straightforward, but it had unforeseen consequences for Lowenna Bartlett from Cornwall and her boyfriend:

> *After registering with the town hall to receive our six-month residency cards, we were held at gun point by our landlord, later to find out that it was loaded and the safety catch removed. It seems that he had been claiming sick pay and housing benefit from the council. When we registered his address, the council caught up with him for not declaring our rent money and issued him with a back-dated fine, which obviously outraged him. To all those seeking accommodation in the Netherlands, I advise a quick telephone call to the local aliens police before renting any flat or room.*

If you feel that you are not being treated fairly by an employer or landlord, you can get free legal advice from any branch of YIPs (Youth Information Points) or you can make enquiries at any Arbeidsbureau.

Private Employment Agencies

The majority of employers turn to private employment agencies (*uitzendburos* – pronounced 'outzend') for temporary workers, partly to avoid the complicated paperwork of hiring a foreigner directly. Therefore they can be a very useful source of temporary work in Holland. They proliferate in large towns, for example there are over 125 in Amsterdam alone.

Look up *Uitzendburo* in the telephone directory or the *Gouden Gids* (Yellow Pages) and register with as many as you can in your area. Not all will accept non-Dutch-speaking applicants. Unless you have a telephone you must visit the office daily at opening time and perhaps twice a day since often the allocation of jobs is not systematic and once the phone is put down the agency forgets about you. Do not expect to be offered a job instantly, for the competition is stiff, especially in Amsterdam and especially during school holidays in August.

While looking for dock work north of Haarlem, Murray Turner concluded that the *uitzendburos* were in the habit of promising more than they could deliver. He had just five days of work out of three weeks, and those were found by asking around at the docks, while the agencies produced nothing. By contrast, Martyn Rutter was pleased with the service he received:

> *It's still quite easy to find work with the agencies. It took me two days of trying at the Manpower agency before they gave me a job in a warehouse. Most people get a job within three or four days. In fact I must have met 25 English and Irish people in the two months I was in Amsterdam, all of whom had found work through agencies. The only must is to be clean and tidy when applying.*

Uitzendburos deal only with jobs lasting less than six months. Most of the work on their books will be unskilled work such as stocking warehouse shelves, production line work in factories, washing dishes in canteens, cleaning, hotel work or fixing roofs in the snow. Most agencies are accustomed to foreign job-seekers and even in the so-called 'boondocks' will have an English-speaking member of staff.

Like all employment agencies *uitzendburos* gain their income by charging the employer a percentage of the wage, which in some cases is 100% or more. Allan Kirkpatrick, who worked for a company in Arnhem as an 'order picker,' is just one of the many clients who is puzzled by the economics of the system:

I tried to understand the whole uitzendburo thing. I was paid 10 guilders an hour while the agency got 26 guilders. So why doesn't the company (and it was a very good company) pay me 18 guilders and save themselves some money, and cut out the crazy uitzendburo altogether? Insurance purposes I think was the problem. I made this point to the very nice but hard-working boss and he said 'That's a good idea' and no more was said about the matter until I reminded him again, and again, and again. I gave up in the end and got a cheap coach to London.

Allan was less critical of the system a few months later when his *uitzendburo* (Olympia in Arnhem) sent on a cheque for £200, his entitlement to holiday pay.

Among the largest *uitzendburos* are Randstad (with about 300 branches), Unique, Manpower, Creyf's Interim, BBB and ASB. The agency ASA (Algemene Studenten Arbeidsverlening) specialises in finding jobs for students. The Amsterdam branch receives many enquiries from English-speaking job-seekers and can place only a handful.

BULB INDUSTRY

Traditionally, the horticultural sector has had difficulty in finding enough seasonal labour for the processing of flower bulbs for export and related activities. Hordes of young travellers descend on the area between Leiden and Haarlem in the summer and there aren't enough jobs to go around. Still, large numbers of unskilled workers are employed in fields and factories to dig, peel, sort, count and pack bulbs, especially in the early spring and through the autumn.

Finding the Work

Increasingly, farmers use agents or middle men to recruit casual labour. Links are especially strong between Holland and Ireland as Garrett Mohan from County Monaghan discovered. Garrett's first agricultural job in the Netherlands resulted from answering an advert in the Irish *Sunday Independent* placed by an agency in Breda (see next section) whereas his job in the bulb industry was connected with the well-known Irish agency Fitzwilliam Technical Services (24 Upper Fitzwilliam St, Dublin 2; 01-676 4125):

After receiving a phone call from a friend who was working in the bulbs around Venhuizen (40km northwest of Amsterdam), I phoned the farmer directly but he put me onto the agent that he uses, Nick Nicholson, and I was offered the job as long as I could get there the next day. Because we are working through an agent, we're only getting paid 10 guilders per hour which is quite bad money for bulb work and 20% of our wages are held back as a deposit against the house which is provided free of charge. I think that most of the farmers around here are using agents so it may be hard to find a well-paid job. Our farmer pays FTS in Dublin 22 guilders an hour for us and we only get 10.

Darren Slevin also worked through FTS for a bulb factory 3km from Leiden, Colijns of Voorhout. He did not appreciate the way the Irish workers were treated as thieves and drug-users (which they weren't) nor did he enjoy the mind-numbing work which caused pain in back, legs and feet. His boss's favourite word was 'snell, snell' (faster, faster). But he did enjoy the international camaraderie. Darren has come across two similar agencies offering work in bulb factories and glasshouses but has no first-hand experience of them: Atlanco Ltd (221/223 Lower Rathmines Road, Rathmines, Dublin 6; 01-491 0555) and IPS (Inter-Ocean Personnel Services) in England.

A couple of years ago Rob Abblett travelled to Holland after the *vendange* in Switzerland, just because he'd never been before. He headed for Andijk near Enkhuizen north of Amsterdam:

By great luck and effort I managed to find a job on foot, but later discovered that I had to go through a job agency anyway, unless I had worked there the year before. The job agencies helped me and, now that I have their telephone numbers, I can even phone them from England, say, to check on work availability.

The agency Rob found was Zaankracht Uitzendburo, De Tuin 27, 1611 KR Bovenkarpsel (0228-511370; zaankracht@multiweb.nl). Work in the Andijk factories is available mid-July to September and mid-October till February/March. He returned to Hillegom in September 2000, armed with an address bestowed on him by a fellow traveller, and this connection made it much easier to land a job. Eighty caravans were parked behind the factory, full of Polish workers with German passports (a new phenomenon). His job was to sprinkle glitter on waxed pine cones for the Christmas market, for which we was paid 12.5 guilders after tax (though no one received any wage slips) which is about equivalent to the UK minimum wage. After a month, he couldn't face it any more and returned home.

The busy times differ among employers according to their markets. For example mail-order companies (like P. Bakker mentioned below) need employees to pick and pack customers' orders from February until the end of April and again from September to December. The busy time for bulb peeling is the second half of June. Ask at the local *Arbeidsbureau* or look for signs *(Bollenpellers Gevraagd)* in Hillegom, Lisse, Noordwijk, etc. This work is paid piece work, between 4 and 6 guilders per crate and it takes most people well over an hour to fill one. Because you are paid only according to how much you do, many workers take time off to visit the bulb factories in the neighbourhood to put their names on various waiting lists, in an attempt to secure a more lucrative job as a bulb packer. This doesn't start until the end of July or even early August and lasts to October, when many factories and associated campsites close down.

Anyone who shows up in high summer will probably find that the full-time jobs have already been allocated to the people who have been around for the peeling and to those who return every year for the opportunities to work and drink hard. The only possibility is to follow Xuela Edwards' advice which is to 'be prepared to knock on doors every day, not to be put off by the No Work signs and keep going back to factories and agencies'. At least you may find a few days work. For example one correspondent went to the Werknet Uitzendburo in Hillegom and got three 10-hour days of work filling and stacking boxes of bulbs, which paid a satisfying 500 guilders net, including overtime and holiday pay.

The best towns to head for are Hillegom, Lisse, Sassenheim and Bennebroek. An agency in Hillegom (now closed) got Iona Taylor and many others work with J. Onderwater & Co. Export B.V., Heereweg 352, 2161 CC Lisse. New arrivals will have no trouble locating the properties of the bulb barons once they arrive. In Hillegom head for Pastoorslaan or Leidsestraat where many of the factories are concentrated and in Lisse, look along Heereweg.

The majority of bulb exporters consider only candidates who are around when there are vacancies. Two large employers to which it can be worthwhile sending written enquiries in March/April are: Van Waveren B.V. Pastoorslaan 30, PO Box 10, 2180 AA Hillegom (0252-516141/fax 523112), and Peter Keur BV, Noorder Leidsevaart 26 (Postbox 129), 2182 NB Hillegom (0252-516608/fax 0252-521790). It is always worth trying the famous bulb exporters P. Bakker B.V., Postbus 600, 2160 AP Lisse (0252-438438/fax 438440) which employs up to 2,000 people at busy times doing shift work (3.30pm-11.30pm and 6.30am-2.30pm). Unauthorised days off are grounds for instant dismissal. Other potential employers are Flora Direct in Lisse (Achterweg Zuid 33-C, 2161 DX Lisse; 0252-418999) for whom Shelly Harris worked a season and M.G.M. van Haaster, Lissedk 490a, 2165 AH Lissebroek. The long established firm Frylink & Zonen B.V. in Noordwijkerhout receives plenty of applications via word of mouth as do Baartman & Koning BV (PO Box 27, 2170 AA Sassenheim; also Teylingerlaan 7, 22156 Voorhout) and JH de Groot BV (Blumenzwiebeln 2211, Leidsevaart 151, Noordwijkerhout WD) both recommended by a friend of Emiliano Giovanni's who stayed at them.

It should be noted that like all employers the bulb companies can accept applications only from European Union nationals; people from outside the EU who write are wasting their time and money. Even if you do receive a job offer in advance, you cannot be sure that the company will honour its promise. It costs them nothing to promise jobs to enquirers, to cover themselves in case of a worker shortage, as happened to Gordon Robertson from Glasgow in 2000:

The bulb exporter sent some details of the work during the flower bulb season which appeared to be quite interesting. I then confirmed my interest in the position and within a couple of weeks received my start date and was invited to go over and work for them. I also telephoned them a couple of times to enquire about a few minor details and they were quite helpful. I then saved up some money to pay for the flight and a week's spending money and travelled on the start date. I settled down and prepared for the next day's work but was told I would start work a day later. Then on that day, I was told in no uncertain terms that there was no employment for me. I was then instructed to find work elsewhere and later informed to leave their premises. These events totally ruined my working holiday and I don't understand how they could let me go all that way and let me pay all that money to go to Holland just to be told to go away.

Traditionally seasonal workers congregate on big campsites, and will normally be willing to advise newcomers. The job hunt will be easier if you're carrying a tent. A couple of years ago, campsites in the area banned bulb workers after the latter staged an 'uprising', but the situation seems to have improved. The need for workers is so urgent that employers have to find some way round the problem of accommodation. Martin and Shirine from Crawley worked for a farmer who risked trouble from the police by letting them camp in a disused field. Renting a flat is even more problematical since foreign workers have such a bad reputation for rowdiness and irresponsibility that few landlords will risk it. In the words of regular bulb worker Steve Dwyer:

A lot of undesirable modern hippies are going over to Holland just it seems to party, and this is bad news for the 'real travellers' like myself.

Again this claim is borne out by Robert Abblett's experiences:

Lots of the workers smoke dope from waking up, at work (if they can) and the rest of the day. Coming back to my house and finding my three co-habitants totally stoned is quite normal. But I can't blame them, for the work requires a positive mental attitude to withstand the boredom and if you haven't got it, then you must choose insanity, oblivion or just leave.

Obviously if the competition is like this, it is not too surprising that his boss at De Jongs Lily Factory made him supervisor of the night shift line.

Yet competition for jobs remains acute, though less so at the more far-flung factories. Mark Wilson recommends having some transport:

Along with a tent, a necessity when looking for bulb work is a bicycle. While out exploring on my bike I came across an area full of factories just outside Noordwijkerhout, a village west of Lisse.

Second-hand bicycles can be picked up for between 50 and 100 guilders.

Pay and Conditions

The bulb industry is better regulated than it once was which means that there is much less black work around. The hiring of non-EU nationals has virtually ceased and exploitation is less common than it was, though membership in the bulb workers' union (Voedingsbond FNV) is not generally available to foreigners.

Excellent earnings are possible: Iona and Steve Dwyer return every year because in their opinion they can earn twice or three times more than they could in an equivalent time anywhere else. Shelley and her boyfriend Terry were making 20 guilders an hour in late 1998. Overtime paid at a premium rate is what makes the big savings possible. Like most agricultural work, earnings fluctuate according to the weather; on a rainy day when the flowers don't open people are lucky to get four hours work.

The most commonly heard complaint about packing is how boring it is, 'worse for your head than boxing' according to one veteran. But most workers receive enough breaks throughout the long day to make it bearable. Naturally there are good employers and bad employers and Garrett Mohan felt himself lucky to be working for one of the former:

Our boss is quite easy-going but, like the rest of the Dutch, very big on punctuality. He has provided us with a TV and VCR and regularly records English films for us. We have heard of another local farmer who separates the Irish so they can't talk to each other, won't allow music to be played in the factory and acutally stands on the conveyor belts as they move to ensure everyone is working.

Bulb-peeling is a much more unpleasant job as Martin and Shirine recall:

The work was hard on our hands and we soon resorted to wearing rubber gloves or plasters. The hours of work were 8am-5pm with an hour's lunch break and the choice to work until 10pm. That was a long time to spend crouched over a table, sitting on an old wobbly stool that was the wrong height for you.

Mark Wilson had an even more miserable experience as a bulb peeler:

The first job I had was peeling the skin off the bulbs which was the most mind-numbingly boring job I have ever done. Later I was condemned to two weeks in the hyacinth shed which is kept away from the main factory. While working on a sorting machine in a loose T-shirt I found to my horror and my Dutch workmates' amusement that bulb dust is a very powerful irritant, so after a couple of hours of itching like a madman, I resigned on the spot, ran back to the campsite and dived into the shower to relieve my tormented skin.

AGRICULTURE

According to information from the European Employment Service EURES, there are plenty of opportunities for seasonal agricultural workers:

From mid-April to October jobs might be available picking asparagus, strawberries, gherkins, apples and pears. During the same period of time there are also jobs in greenhouses and mushrooms, though these jobs are popular with locals and usually can be filled with local job-seekers.

Many harvests take place in fertile pockets of southern Holland for example in the Baarland in the extreme south-west and in Limburg to the east along the Belgian border (see section below). Garrett Mohan travelled to the tiny village of Kwadendamme near Goes in the Baarland in early September (after local school children had returned to school) to join the apple and pear harvest which ends in early November. Two agencies which may be able to assist are Eurocom recommended by Garrett Mohan (Hoboken 213, 4826 EC Breda; 76-711468) and Creyf's Interim (Piet Heinstraat 8, 4461 GL Goes; 113-211223/fax 113-216911).

Although Garrett Mohan's boss was a 'Jekyll and Hyde' type (laughing and joking one minute and shouting 'pick, pick, quickly and with two hands' the next), he grew to like Dutch people and rural life in Holland enough to want to move from the hard fruit harvest to bulb work. In seven weeks of hard work, he had saved 1,500 guilders, after buying a rucksack and a camera out of his earnings.

Another area where hard fruits are harvested in the autumn is the area south of Utrecht called Betuwe (which means 'Good Land') around the towns of Culemborg and Buren.

Limburg

The 'deep south' of Holland is known among working travellers as more than the place where the Maastricht Treaty was signed. The area around Roermond (about 50km southeast of Eindhoven and north of Maastrict in the province of Limburg) is populated by asparagus growers and other farmers who need people to harvest their crops of strawberries, potatoes and other vegetables, especially in the spring. You can travel south from Roermond (on the N271) to villages such as Linne, St. Odilienberg, Montfort, Posterholt and as far as Susteren to find work. Going north, head for Venlo, Helden and nearby Panningen. If possible find someone to translate ads in the local paper *De Limburger*. The agencies around here are less accustomed to dealing with non-Dutch applicants but can be all the more helpful for that. Joanne Patrick and Steve Conneely recommend an agency which deals exclusively with agricultural work: Limburgse Land-en Tuinbouwbond (LLTB), Wilhelminasingel 25, Postbus 960, 6040 AZ Roermond (04750-33243). Independently they found work picking potatoes and earned 1,600 guilders between them in two weeks in late February and early March. They were so taken aback to earn so much money that they spent it all on good times across the German border. Asparagus picking starts just after the middle of April and lasts through to mid-June. Expect to start on the minimum of 8 or 9 guilders an hour but wages of more than double that are possible. A tent is a great advantage here. Murray Turner paid 7.5 guilders a night at a family-run campsite in Helden north of Roermond. The *uitzendburo* he recommends is Adia Keser in the same town. According to Murray one of the biggest asparagus farms around Venlo is Teeuvan (04760-71444). Despite initial hopes that earnings would be high in the peak season, he ended up earning the standard 9 guilders an hour (or 1.20 guilders per kilo). He moved on to the strawberry harvest where earnings from piece work (2 guilders per 3-4kg crate) were very unreliable because of the weather. The asparagus harvest is similarly affected by weather; if it's hot you can work as long as you are able.

Westland

The area between Rotterdam, the Hook of Holland and Den Haag is known as the Westland. K. ('Moondog') McCausland recommends tomato picking here as another good alternative to bulb packing. The principal villages in the area are Naaldwijk, Westerlee, De Lier and Maasdijk, but the whole region is a honeycomb of greenhouses.

The tomato harvest begins in early to mid-April and this is the best time to arrive, although work is generally available all year round if you are prepared to work for at least one month. Although the work was boring and dirty with long hours – it was normal to start work at 5am and finish at 7pm or 8pm – conditions were usually good and accommodation was provided in a barn.

Once again a lot of the work in the area is registered with *uitzendburos*. Ian Govan recommends trying the ones in Naaldwijk, 's-Gravenzande and Poeldijk for work picking cucumbers, peppers, flowers, etc. Also try the flower and vegetable auctions *(bloemenveiling/groenteveiling)* in Westerlee/de Lier and Honselersdijk which need people to load the stock for auction buyers, etc. Ian Govan's overtime pay of up to 200 guilders was paid in cash on top of the 300-350 guilders he netted for a 38-hour week.

Work in tree and other nurseries abounds in and around Boskoop, 11km from Gouda north of Rotterdam. Anyone with any relevant experience should aim to arrive in the area between February and April. Nurseries are concentrated along Reijerskoop and Laag Boskoop. Job agencies will help, such as Creyf's Interim at Bootstraat 7, 2771 DL Boskoop (0172 212424/fax 0172-216401), one of 38 branches of Creyf's throughout the Netherlands. It could also be worth advertising in the free local paper, as Dermot Campbell recommends:

I think it would be worthwhile putting an advert in the Boomkwekerij section of the 'Gouwe Kourier' even if one hasn't any experience. Nobody ever really asked if I had any experience whatsoever. Only if you appear to be enthusiastic.

Food Processing

Onion pickling in Baarland, near Vlissingen in Southern Holland, sounds fairly grim, so you might follow James Pollock's advice and work in apple, cherry and green bean factories instead:

There were many advantages. We did not reek of onions; we were paid fairly and directly by the factory owners rather than being ripped off by an agency; plus there were perks like the 'dead animal reward', a sum of £5 for any animal (from slugs to rabbits) found dead or alive amongst the green beans. As you can imagine many of the unfortunate creatures (often picked off roads on the way to work) completed many rounds on the conveyor belt. Some of us managed to double our wages so it was no mean perk.

There are several food canning factories in Zuid Holland (between Amsterdam and Rotterdam); make enquiries in Nieuwveen, Ter Aar and Roelofarendsveen. In the latter town try the Koelans pickle factory on De Lasso.

TOURISM

Dutch hotels and other tourist establishments often employ foreigners, especially those with a knowledge of more than one European language. A few tour operators like Holidaybreak and Village Camps (see *Tourism* chapter) employ British young people as staff at their camps for the summer season. Centerparcs started in Holland and their recruitment of activity instructors is carried out by 3D Education & Adventure Ltd (Business Support, Osmington Bay, Weymouth, Dorset DT3 6EG; 01305 836226).

In Adam Skuse's year off before university, he almost succeeded in finding hotel work but not quite:

> *One very useful resource I found was the web-site www.visitholland.com, where I got a list of hotels and then systematically emailed them all asking for a job. Most had no vacancies, a couple told me to call them when I was in Amsterdam, and one actually arranged an interview with me. But even the knockbacks were pleasant. Quite a few offered to buy me a drink anyway. Alas, I never managed to find the hotel in time, ran out of funds and am now back in Blighty. I had plans for my gap year, but just ended up sitting around on the dole.*

According to Simon Whitehead, foreigners are the last to be hired and the first to be fired, so do not expect job security in a hotel job. Although you may be lucky enough to obtain a hotel job through an *uitzendburo,* your chances will normally be better if you visit hotels and ask if any work is available, or keep your ears open in pubs frequented by working travellers.

While visiting a friend in the seaside resort of Zaandvoort south of Haarlem, Martin and Shirine tried to find work washing dishes for one of the many bars which line the beach. They knew that without speaking Dutch this was the only job they could reasonably expect to get. Unfortunately the poor weather that June meant that business was bad and the bars were not willing to take on extra staff. (As an aside, tradesmen looking for work should ask around at the Shamrock Bar in Zandvoort.) Holiday parks and campsites are always worth trying.

Working on Boats

A little known opportunity for people who can communicate in German or Dutch is to work on one of the 250 *Platbodems,* traditional sailing boats that cruise the waters of Ijsselmeer and Waddensea off the north coast of the Netherlands in spring, summer and autumn. They cater mainly to school groups and are staffed by a skipper and one mate *(maat)* one of whose jobs is to offer simple instruction to the guests though he or she must also help the skipper on watch, carry out repairs and so on. Even without any background in sailing, Felix Fernandez was offered ten jobs after adding his CV to the databank *(vacature bank)* of job-seekers and ended up working the 1999 summer season on the two-masted ship *Citore*:

> *Skippers who are looking for maats can get the data about interested people from the data bank. I didn't have sailing experience before. The first week of sailing was a nightmare because of my lack of experience but I got through and now there is no problem. It is normal to work seven days a week with one day off a month. You have to be prepared to work around 70 hours a week. Having little privacy is also something one has to get used to. Nevertheless there are many advantages of the job and I met a lot of people who have returned for several seasons.*

The address he supplied for the agency BBZ (Belangenvereniging Beroeps Zeilende) in Enkhuisen is no longer valid but could possibly be traced on the spot. The company that owns *Citore* is Hanzestad Compagnie, Postbus 5, 8260 AA Kampen, Netherlands.

OTHER WORK

Labouring work may be available in some of the massive docks of Rotterdam and Ijmuiden north of Haarlem. According to Shelly Harris's partner Terry, who got work straightaway unloading fishing boats, it's just a case of turning up at the offices on the docks early (about 5.30am) and asking for work. The money is good, about 300 guilders a week, but the work is hard, cold and irregular. It used to take Terry two hours to thaw out in front of a fire after knocking off work about 3.30pm. Domestic cleaning is a more promising area of work. Although the job hunt in Leiden took Paul Bridgland four weeks, he finally found cleaning work (no thanks to any *uitzendburos*) which gave him 50 hours of not particularly strenuous work a week at 10 guilders an hour after tax. Nicola Sarjeant had a shorter wait before the Effect 2000 Uitzendburo in Haarlem found her work cleaning banks for the same wage.

Urban Dutch people have such a high degree of competence in English after they finish their schooling that there is not much of a market for EFL teaching. What language schools there are tend to provide business English, and people with extensive commercial or government experience as well as a teaching qualification might find an opening, for example at Feedback (Lassusstraat 9a, 1075 GV Amsterdam; 020-671 67 09; feedback @wxs.nl) and Pimental Communications International (Bachlaan 43, 1817 GH Alkmaar; 072-512 11 90; www.pcitalen.nl) where experience in technical writing would be useful.

The agency Franglais Taalbureau, Molenstraat 15, 2585 VW The Hague (070-36 1703; learn@franglais.nl) claims that it is often looking for native English speakers to edit texts by e-mail written in English by non-native speakers. The pay is 10 cents per word of the original text.

Opportunities in Amsterdam

As throughout the world hostels employ people to clean, cook, do maintenance and night porter duties. An average wage for this kind of work would be 9 guilders an hour on top of room and board, which Carolyn Edwards describes as pretty good considering that's what she was getting temping in London with no food and accommodation.

As in Athens some Amsterdam hotels and hostelries hire 'runners' to meet the morning and afternoon international trains to persuade travellers to patronise the hostel. Enquire at budget hotels and hostels near the station. There are a number of Christian hostels in Amsterdam which allow residents who do some cleaning to stay free. Ian Mitselburg from Australia did this until he 'got sick of the niceness of the rest of the staff, especially the '"whitebreds" from Ohio and Idaho.'

Advertising on notice boards is a popular way to draw attention to the service you can offer such as teaching English, typing, house cleaning, window washing and babysitting. Two of the best notice boards are at the Public Library (Prinsengracht 587, just north of Leidsegracht) and the University (the library is near the flower market at Singel 425 and the Literature Faculty is at 183 Singel behind the post office). It is worth taking some trouble over the presentation of your advert, and if you are wanting to teach English, type manuscripts, etc. it might even be worth getting a notice printed (which is quite cheap). Most people employ the technique of tear-off strips to save potential clients the trouble of copying down their name and particulars. Apparently people who can teach Spanish or creative dance are in great demand, whereas English tutors are ten a penny.

You might want to contact office cleaning services directly (see 'Schoonmaakbedrijf' in the *Gouden Gids* which are kept in public libraries but not in phone boxes), or ask cafés, of which there is no shortage in Amsterdam, if they would like you to clean their windows on a weekly or regular basis. (The Dutch are very particular about the cleanliness of their windows.)

The European Data Collection Center is an international market research agency that advertises for native-speaking personnel, especially Germans and Scandinavians. From the call centre in Amsterdam they conduct surveys in 17 European countries. They are looking for people with computer experience and a polite voice who are willing to work for a minimum of 12 hours a week for three months. The working hours are divided into three shifts: morning, afternoon and evening, Monday to Saturday. The EDCC is located close to the centre of Amsterdam (Overtoom 519-521, 1054 LH Amsterdam; 020-589 6676).

Busking is an ever-popular way to earn some money and the tolerance for which the Dutch are famous extends to street entertainers. The best venues are in the Vondelpark (where many Amsterdammers stroll on a Sunday) and in the city squares like Stadsplein and Leidseplein. Some pitches (like the one outside the 'smoking' coffee shop the Bulldog) are in such demand that you may have to wait your turn.

Au Pairs

Since Dutch is not a language which attracts a large number of students, au pairing in the Netherlands is not well known; however there is an established programme for those interested. Working conditions are favourable (e.g. pocket money of 500 guilders per month and insurance costs are met by host family) but you must stay at least six months with the family. The main agencies are reputed to offer solid back-up, guidance on contacting fellow au pairs and advice on local courses. The agency with the largest incoming au pair programme is Au Pair Discover Holland (C. Barendregtlaan 9-F, 3161 HA Rhoon) which runs a series of excursions and activities for au pairs which are either free or reasonably priced.

The international exchange organisation Travel Active (PO Box 107, 5800 Venray; 0478-551900; info@travelactive.nl) has an incoming programme for foreign au pairs aged 18 to 30 though its main function is to send Dutch young people abroad on various work exchanges. Application must be made through one of Travel Active's partner agencies. In the UK this is Au Pair Network International (118 Cromwell Road, London SW7 4ET; 020-7370 3798/ www.apni.co.uk) and in the US, *InterExchange* (161 Sixth Avenue, New York, NY 10013; www.interexchange.org).

Another important agency is Activity International, Steentilstraat 25, 9711 GK Groningen, or PO Box 7097, 9701 JB Groningen (050-31 30 666/fax 051-31 31 633; www.activity.aupair.nl) which annually places between 300 and 500 au pairs in the Netherlands as well as running an outgoing programme for Dutch young people. The agency organises meetings and trips for au pairs while the families pay for insurance, travel costs to and from the Netherlands and a language course. Jill Weseman from the States was very pleased with the service Activity International provided and also with her experiences as an au pair in a village of just 500 people 30km from Groningen:

After graduation I accepted an au pairing position in Holland, mainly because there is no prior language requirement here. I really lucked out and ended up with a family who has been great to me. Though the situation sounds difficult at best – four children aged 1¹/2, 3, 5 and 7, one day off a week and a rather remote location in the very north of Holland – I have benefitted a great deal. The social life is surprisingly good for such a rural area.

The newest agency is Au Pair Agency Know-How established in 2000 (Kweldergrasveld 3, 1313 CA Almere; 036-530 5631; toiny@braam-de-wildt.myweb.nl). Two other agencies that belong to IAPA (International Au Pair Association) are Juno Au Pairs (Weide 37, 3121 XV Schiedam; juno@worldonline.nl) and World Wide Au Pair & Nanny (Burg. Hogguerstraat 785, 1064 EB Amsterdam).

Voluntary Work

Although the Netherlands is in so many ways a progressive country, there are still undeveloped corners as Joan Regan found when she joined a farm-based project not far from Rotterdam which was affiliated to IVS. In fact all the major workcamp organisations arrange camps in Holland over the summer. If you are in the Netherlands you might also make enquiries of SIW Internationale Vrijwilligersprojekten whose office is a five-minute walk from the Utrecht station but keeps limited opening hours (Willemstraat 7, 3511 RJ Utrecht; 030-231 7721; www.siw.nl); otherwise apply through affiliated workcamp organisations at home, e.g. IVS, Quaker Voluntary Action and UNA in Britain. The registration fee for most Dutch workcamps is about 100 guilders.

Archaeological and building restoration camps are arranged by NJBG (Nederlandse Jeugdbond voor Geschiedenis, Prins Willem Alexanderhof 5, 2595 BE Den Haag; fax 070-335 2536; www.njbg.nl) who do not yet publish their brochure in English though there is a small section in English on their website. The worldwide charity International Building Companions is particularly active in the Netherlands and has its headquarters in Nijmegen: St Annastraat 172, 6524 GT Nijmegen (080-226074; www.bouworde.nl).

The website www.markt.nl describes (in English) voluntary openings in the Netherlands ranging from hospital radio to a multicultural home for the elderly.

Belgium

Belgium is a country which is often ignored. Sandwiched between France and the Netherlands, its population of just over 10 million can be broadly divided between the French-speaking people of Wallonia in the south (about 42% of the total population) and those who speak Flemish (which is almost identical to Dutch) in the north. The wages in Belgium fall somewhere between the high wages of Holland and those of France.

Belgium has no large agricultural industry comparable to those of its neighbours: it needs neither the extra fruit pickers that France does, nor the unskilled processors of Dutch bulbs. Furthermore the unemployment rate in Belgium is considerably higher than in the UK.

As in neighbouring Holland, employment legislation is strictly enforced in Belgium with favourable minimum wages, compulsory bonuses, sickness and holiday pay for all legal workers. The demand for temporary workers is especially strong in Belgium because of the generous redundancy regulations which discourage employers from hiring permanent staff. Of course the large number of multinational companies, attracted by the headquarters of the European Union in Brussels, have a constant and fluctuating demand for bilingual office workers.

Regulations

The usual rules apply to EU nationals coming to work or live in Belgium: EU nationals arriving in Belgium to look for work and who intend to stay for a period of three months or more should register within eight days at the local Town Hall where the *administration communale* will issue either a temporary *certificat d'immatriculation* valid for three months or the one year certificate of registration (*certificat d'inscription au registre des étrangers* – CIRE).

Non-EU citizens will have to find an employer willing to apply for a work permit on their behalf from the Office National de l'Emploi. They must be in possession of a residence entry visa and a work permit before arrival, when they can then apply for an authorisation of provisional sojourn. The Belgian Embassy in London (fax 020-7259

6213) will send information in exchange for a large self-addressed stamped envelope. Brett Archer from New Zealand reported that a rising number of labour checks designed mainly to catch Belgian nationals working black have made employers much more reluctant to hire people from outside the EU. Brett was caught but was lucky enough not to be penalised.

Seasonal Work

Although Belgium's seaside resorts like Knokke-Heist, Blankenberge and De Panne, and other holiday centres like Bouillon in the Ardennes are hardly household names, there is a sizeable tourist industry in Belgium where seasonal work is available. The more mainstream tourist centre of Bruges is very busy in the summer. Travellers are often given free accommodation in exchange for some duties at one of the city's four or five private hostels. According to Brett Archer, who worked several seasons at the Bauhaus International Youth Hostel at Langestraat 35 (fax 031-50 33 41 80), there are never enough people around to work in restaurants and bars during the summer. Expect to earn at least BF200 an hour. Look also for opportunities as a seasonal guide with one of the coach tour companies which run tours of scenic and historic Belgium. Venture Abroad (1 Coal Hill Lane, Farsley, Leeds LS28 5NA; www.ventureabroad.co.uk) employs reps, including students with a background in scouting or guiding, for its programme in Belgium.

One harvest which has a substantial need for seasonal labour is the hop harvest centred on the town of Poperinge in Flanders close to the French border. Every September Belgian students, Polish migrant labourers and a handful of other nationalities gather for three weeks to bring in the harvest which services Belgium's renowned brewing industry. Most farmers are well set up to welcome foreign pickers and offer comfortable accommodation and a good atmosphere.

The best way of finding short-term general work, apart from contacting possible employers directly, is to visit a branch of the Belgian employment service in any town. A special division called T-Interim specialises in placing people in temporary jobs. Most jobs obtained through the T-Interim service will be unskilled manual ones such as stocking supermarket shelves. They may also be able to help skilled secretaries who can function in French to find temporary office positions.

The employment services in Belgium are divided into three regional branches: Greater Brussels (ORBEM for French speakers, BGDA for Flemish), French-speaking Belgium (Office Wallon de la Formation Professionnelle et de l'Emploi) and Flemish-speaking Belgium (VDAB), with addresses as follows:

ORBEM (Office Régional Bruxellois de l'Emploi) and BGDA (Brusselse Gewestelijke Dienst voor Arbeidsbemiddeling), Boulevard Anspach 65, 1000 Brussels (02-505 14 11; www.orbem.be or www.bgda.be). The EURES adviser can be reached here on 02-505 14 20/1 (http://europa.eu.int/jobs/eures). The T-Interim office is next door at number 69 (02-511 23 85).

Office Wallon de la Formation Professionnelle et de l'Emploi, Boulevard J. Tirou 104, 6000 Charleroi (071-20 61 74; communic@forem.be/ www.hotjob.be). There are 33 T-Interim offices in Wallonia (0800 20525; info@interim.com/ www.tinterim.com).

VDAB, Keizerslaan 11, 1000 Brussels (02-506 15 11/ www.vdab.be).

T-Interim branches include:
Sint Jacobsmarkt 66, 2000 Antwerp (03-232 98 60).
Rue Général Molitz 24, 6700 Arlon (063-22 66 45/fax 063-21 96 48; mh.pivetta@tinterim.com).
Eckhoutstraat 29, 8000 Bruges (050-44 20 44).
Keizerslaan 11, 1000 Brussels (02-514 57 00/070-345000/www.t-interim.vdab.be).
Lemonnierlaan 129-131, 1000 Brussels (02-514 57 00).
Avenue des Arts 46, 1040 Brussels (02-513 77 39).
Place de Tramways 9/3, 6000 Charleroi (071-20 20 80/20 50 56).
Burgstraat 49, 9000 Ghent (091-224 09 20).
Thonissenlaan 18, bus 1, 3500 Hasselt (011-26 49 90).
Kloosterstraat 2, 2200 Herentals (014-23 39 43).

Reepkai 3, bus 19, 8500 Kortrijk (056-25 36 90).
Bd de la Sauvernière 60, 4000 Liège (04-230 30 80/fax 04-232 03 71; l.dechany@tinterim.com).
De Merodelei 86, 2300 Turnhout (014-42 27 31).
Witherenstraat 19, 1800 Vilvoorde (02-253 98 63).
rue Haute 20, 1300 Wavre (010-23 78 00).

People who live in the south-east of England should make use of EURES Crossborder HNFK (Shakespeare Centre, 145-147 Sandgate Road, Folkestone, Kent CT20 2DA; 01303 226184; fax 01303 249445) which assists people looking for jobs in Belgium, especially in West-Vlaanderen and Hainaut (western Belgium). The trilingual Euro-Adviser can put job-seekers in touch with network partners on the continent and can also give advice and information about living and working conditions.

Agencies

Private employment agencies in Belgium are licensed either to make temporary or permanent placements but not both. Contracts through temp agencies are normally for a maximum of six months. They are required to become the employer and to provide the same benefits to temps as those to which full-time employees are entitled. Unlike Dutch *uitzendburos*, they are normally equipped primarily to find jobs for qualified and experienced workers. For example the agency Select Interim (Avenue de la Joyeuse Entrée 1-5, bte. 14, 1040 Brussels; 02-231 03 33) places secretaries and personal assistants in positions lasting at least three months. About half of these temporary assignments turn into permanent ones. Other agencies with offices throughout Belgium include Randstad Interim and GREGG Interim which specialises in placing temporary personnel in the European Commission. Randstad has 30 branches and operates an English-speaking personnel department at its office in central Brussels (Hoofdkantoor, Muntplein, Prinsenstraat 8-10; 02-209 12 11). It is particularly strong on catering personnel.

As in the UK, candidates do not pay a fee to employment agencies. A complete list of personnel agencies can be found in the *Yellow Pages* (Volume B, Section 7485) and in the *Pink Pages* (Volume 1B, Section 9000).

Au Pairs

Anyone who wishes to be an au pair in Belgium has a very good chance of success since the demand far exceeds the supply and is increasing all the time. Belgian agencies which can help find au pair families are Stufam (Vierwindenlaan 7, 1780 Wemmel; 02-460 33 95; aupair.stufam@pi.be) and the Catholic organisation Services de la Jeunesse Feminine (29 rue Faider, 1050 Brussels; 02-539 35 14/081-30 91 35). Stufam no longer charges au pairs who apply directly a registration fee of BF1,000. The current monthly pocket money for au pairs is BF10,000-14,000 whereas mother's helps should receive up to BF18,000.

The free weekly newspaper *Vlan* is an effective advertising medium for prospective au pairs under the heading *Gens de Maison*. Au pairs from outside the EU must apply to the employment service in the region where they plan to work for a one year 'B' permit (see addresses of Office Wallon de la Formation Professionelle et de l'Emploi, ORBEB/BGDA and VDAB above). Further details can be obtained by writing to the Belgian Embassy in your country.

Teaching

The casual EFL teacher will probably have trouble finding work in Belgium where there is a great deal of competition from highly qualified expatriates. A number of language schools advertise in *The Bulletin* (see next section); the magazine publishes an annual 'Schools Guide' in April containing a section on language schools, though there is not much point in applying to the kind of school which teaches senior EU bureaucrats unless you have professional qualifications. Almost all foreign teachers who begin to work for an institute do so on a freelance basis and will have to deal with their own tax and social security. The starting pay at most schools is BF600-BF650 an hour.

Berlitz have several schools in Belgium which employ up to 50 native English speakers with a university degree after they have done the compulsory 12-day pre-service training course in the Berlitz Method; contact Berlitz at Avenue de Tervueren 265, 1150 Brussels (02-763 08 30). They pay BF321 for a 40-minute lesson. Linguarama Belgium are constantly recruiting freelance teachers with a TEFL qualification and one year's experience (rue Lincoln 64, 1180 Brussels; 2-343 14 56; brussels@linguarama.com).

Other schools to try if you have a TEFL background include Brussels Language Studies (rue du Marteau 8, 1210 Brussels; www.kiddyclasses.net), Ceran Lingua International (Av. du Chateau 16, 4900 Spa; www.ceran.be), Euro Business Languages (Leuvensesteenweg 325, 1932 Zaventem), Call International (Boulevard de la Cense 41, 1410 Waterloo & Avenue des Drapiers 25, 1050 Brussels) and Phone Languages (rue des Echevins 65, 1050 Brussels; www.phonelanguages.com). The latter employs people with American or British accents to teach over the phone and pays about £10 an hour.

Prolinguis runs summer language courses for teenagers (67 Place de l'Eglise, 6717 Thiaumont; 063-22 04 62; www.prolinguis.be). Philip Dray, an EFL teacher from Ireland, worked for them one summer:

> *I am employed in a freelance capacity to work 90 days between April 5th and September 15th. The salary is the equivalent of £60 a day and I have a sort of hotel room in a building that houses the students' dorms. For my keep I have to check the dorms twice a week, which is not too bad since most of the kids have been co-operative. The work is grammar-based but with some emphasis on games and role play.*

Contacts

The Federation Infor Jeunes Wallonie-Bruxelles is a non-profit making organisation which co-ordinates 12 youth information offices in French-speaking Belgium. These can give advice on work as well as leisure, youth rights, accommodation, etc. A leaflet listing the addresses is available from the Federation at rue Henri Lemaitre 25, 5000 Namur (070-233444/081-22 08 72) or it can be read on the internet (www.inforjeunes.be). Among Infor Jeune's services, they operate holiday job placement offices (Service Job Vacances) between March and September.

Belgium's English language weekly publication *The Bulletin* carries job adverts such as live-in positions and language tuition. Its address is 1038 Chaussée de Waterloo, 1180 Brussels (02-373 99 09); the magazine is published on Thursdays and can be bought from newsstands for BF90. *Newcomer* is a free bi-annual publication (available from the above address) which is aimed at new arrivals in Belgium and carries useful sections called 'Getting to Grips with the Red Tape' and 'Job-Seekers' Guide'. Jobs and other classified ads are carried on the website www.xPATS.com. The daily *Le Soir* (rue Royale 120, 1000 Brussels; www.lesoir.be) is also worth consulting for employment and au pair work.

Voluntary Work

The Flemish association of young environmentalists called Natuur 2000 (Bervoetstraat 33, 2000 Antwerp; 03-231 26 04; http://home.planetinternet.be/~n2000) organises summer conservation workcamps open to all nationalities. The registration fee of BF1,500 covers accommodation, food, insurance and local transport. They also need volunteers for their environmental information centres in Antwerp and Ostend (for which facility with computer programmes would be essential). Other possibilities exist in their bat reserve-cum-nature education centre situated in an old WWI fortress near Antwerp (May till September).

Those interested in participating in residential archaeological digs for three weeks in July should contact Archeolo-j (Avenue Paul Terlinden 23, 1330 Rixensart; 02-653 8268/fax 02-673 40 85; www.skene.be). There is a charge for membership in the Society and for camp expenses. The excavation and restoration of an 11th century abbey church in eastern Belgium requires paying volunteers between the end of June and end of July; the fee for participation is BFr1,000. Contact the Centre Stavelotain d'Archéologie, Abbaye, B-4970 Stavelot (tel/fax: 080-86 41 13). Alternatively, you can join a dig at a mediaeval castle in Flanders through Jeugd en Kultureel Erfgoed (Heidestraat 118, 3590 Diepenbeek) where two-week camps cost up to BF1,000.

Toc H (1 Forest Close, Wendover, Aylesbury, Bucks. HP22 6BT) runs occasional short-term residential projects in Belgium lasting for two to seven days only. The Flemish branch of IVS/SCI is at Draakstraat 37, 2018 Antwerp (03-235 94 19/fax 03-235 29 73).

The organic movement is flourishing in Belgium though the system of volunteering to work on organic farms is still in its infancy. Nature et Progrès (Rue de Dave 520, 5100 Jambes; 081-30 36 90) publishes a list of organic producers in the French-speaking part, primarily for the benefit of consumers rather than volunteers. The Flemish counterpart is Velt (Uitbreidingstraat 392c, 2600 Berchem; 03-281 74 75; http://gallery.uunet.be/velt). Their bi-monthly newsletter *Seizoenen* contains adverts for organic farms with which individuals could make contact asking for work.

Luxembourg

If Belgium is sometimes neglected, Luxembourg is completely by-passed. Yet it is an independent country with an unemployment rate of less than 3%, the lowest in the EU, and a number of useful facilities for foreigners. The national employment service (Administration de l'Emploi or ADEM) at 10 rue Bender, L-1229 Luxembourg (352-478 53 00; www.etat.lu/ADEM/adem.htm) operates a *Service Vacances* for students looking for summer jobs in warehouses, restaurants, etc. To find out about possibilities, you must visit this office in person, although EU nationals looking for long-term jobs may receive some assistance from EURES counsellors. Other branches of the employment service are located in Esch-sur-Alzette (54 10 54), Diekirch (80 29 29) and Wiltz (95 83 84), but the headquarters is the only one to have a *Service Vacances* section. Paul Newcombe found the service very helpful and was delighted to be given details of a job vacancy at an American bar in the capital.

While cycling through the country, Mary Hall was struck by the number of travellers working on campsites and in restaurants in Luxembourg City. More recently Danny Jacobson was hitch-hiking through Luxembourg and stayed at the main hostel, a big affair full of groups of kids during the summer. He noticed a sign at the desk for dishwashers so he enquired and worked three hours on several mornings. In return he received a free bed and meals, a definite deal since the place is not cheap. He hinted that he might be prepared to stay on if there was any chance of a small wage being paid, but his hint was not taken up, so the arrangement is strictly work-for-keep.

Anyone who wants to reside in Luxembourg must register with the authorities and prove that they have sufficient means to live. No work permit is needed by EU nationals. Non-EU nationals must obtain a work permit *(Déclaration Patronale)* from an employer which has been approved by the Administration de l'Emploi and by the Ministère de la Justice, Police des Etrangers, 16 Bd. Royal, L-1333 Luxembourg.

The Range of Jobs

With a population of less than 400,000, job opportunities are understandably limited, but they do exist especially in the tourist industry. Even the Embassy in London at 27 Wilton Crescent, London SW1X 8SD (020-7235 6961) maintains that 'seasonal jobs are often to be found in the hotels of the Grand Duchy of Luxembourg' and will send a list of the 250+ hotels in exchange for an A4 envelope and a 50p stamp. Wages are fairly good in this sector, often about £500 per month after room and board. (The franc is equivalent to the Belgian franc.)

The main language is Luxembourgish (variously called Luxembourgeois and Letzeburgesch) but both German and French are spoken and understood by virtually everyone. Casual workers will normally need a reasonable knowledge of at least one of these. Temporary office work abounds since many multinational companies are based in Luxembourg, some of whom may regard a knowledge of fluent English in addition to a local language as an advantage. Addresses of potential employers can be obtained from the Luxembourg Embassy who on receipt of an s.a.e. will send a list of British firms, as well as of the largest local companies. Several agencies specialise in temporary work. Manpower-Aide Temporaire, 42 rue Glesener, L-1630 Luxembourg (48 23 23/fax 40 35 52; cmathenot@manpower.lu) handles all types of temporary work.

Other Helpful Organisations

The Centre Information Jeunes (CIJ), 26 Place de la Gare, Geleria Kons, 1616 Luxembourg (26 29 3-200/fax 26 29 3-203) runs a holiday job service between January and August for students from the EU. They can also inform you what the national minimum wage is for someone of your age and background.

Luxembourg Accueil Information (10 Bisserwee, L-1238 Luxembourg-Grund; 24 17 17) is a centre for new arrivals and residents. They put on courses and workshops and may have resources available which will help newcomers to conduct their own job search. Requests for information about au pairing will be passed on to the Europair agency (31 93 14). Legislation requires au pairs to submit an 'Accord Placement Au Pair' to the *Administration de l'Emploi* setting out the conditions of work signed by both employer and au pair.

If you want to check newspaper adverts, buy the *Luxemburger Wort* (especially on Saturdays or check job listings on http://job.wort.lu), *Tageblatt* (44 rue du Canal, L-4050 Esch-Alzette; www.tageblatt.lu) or the English language *Luxembourg News* (25 rue Philippe II, L-2340 Luxembourg; 46 11 22-1) which costs 90 francs and is published on Thursdays. *Le Jeudi* which appears every Thursday contains a section of job ads (32 rue du Curé, 1368 Luxembourg). One final place to check is the internet: the sites www.carrieres.lu and www.monsite.lu post actual vacancies of interest mainly to French speakers.

Grape-Picking

Luxembourgeois wine producers need help in the vineyards along the Moselle in the southeast of the country around the town of Remich. The harvest normally begins around the middle of September and continues for two or more weeks. The Institut Viti-Vinicole, B.P. 50, 5501 Remich (699288/fax 699590) does not arrange jobs, though it may be able to estimate the starting date of the harvest and give more precise dates closer to the time. Starting dates fluctuate from about the 13th to the 25th of September though the average is usually the 16th. Its website (www.meridian.lu/vin) has a wine route showing the location of most of the vineyards.

The only way of finding out about harvest jobs, as Ian Black discovered, is to go straight to the region and ask the farmers directly. Kristof Szymczak picked grapes in Luxembourg for a number of seasons in a row:

> It was very easy to find work just walking along the Moselle valley from the villages of Schengen and Wasserbillig. People are really wonderful. I always received board, lodging and about £25 per day.

France

Although you may occasionally encounter the legendary hostility of the French towards the English, more often you will be treated with warmth and helpfulness especially in the countryside. There are so many English-speaking people resident in France that expatriate grapevines are an invaluable source of job information. Unemployment is high but falling: 9.5% in the autumn of 2000 compared to 11.8% two years earlier, though the rate among the young remains high. It would be a mistake to expect to walk into a job just because you have a GCSE in French and enjoy eating *pains au chocolat*.

Although the French tourist industry offers many seasonal jobs, there are even more in agriculture: approximately 100,000 foreign workers are employed on the grape harvest alone. Most of these foreign workers are from Eastern Europe, North Africa, Spain and Portugal, but plenty of other nationalities can be found picking fruit too. You may find yourself working in the fields next to an office worker from Basingstoke and a student from Harvard or a young Dane or Scot who is touring Europe as a nomadic worker. It is possible to support yourself throughout the year in France by combining work in the various fruit harvests with either conventional jobs such as tutoring in English, or more unusual occupations from busking to gathering snails.

One important feature of working in France is that you should be paid at least the *SMIC (salaire minimum interprofessionel de croissance)* or national minimum wage. There are slightly different rates for seasonal agricultural work and full-time employees; at present the standard rate is F42 per hour, which is adjusted annually to take account of inflation. The French are proposing an EU-wide minimum wage of nearly F48 (£4.50) though this is not popular with many countries and of course not with Britain.

REGULATIONS

A powerful political lobby wants to clamp down on black work, and the authorities are committed to enforcing French employment legislation. Tax inspectors and immigration officers carry out spot checks in tourist resorts, and employers in even the most out-of-the-way places have refused to hire anyone who lacks the right documents, whether or not they are EU nationals. Wine-makers in Bordeaux have been told that if they are caught employing people without papers, they will not be allowed to bring in their harvest the following year.

French workers enjoy some of the most generous employment legislation in Europe. At the beginning of 2000, the government cut the length of the working week from 39 to 35 for anyone working in a firm with more than 20 employees. Naturally this frightened the large number of UK tour operators who do not offer their campsite couriers, chalet girls, etc. an equivalent of the SMIC nor statutory perks. It has now been decided that because of the short-term nature of the contracts, they are exempt. Their workers are paid in sterling into British bank accounts.

For European Union Nationals

As in all member states, EU nationals are permitted to stay in France for up to three months without obtaining a residence permit *(carte de séjour)*. Once you have a job and know you are going to stay longer than three months, you should apply for a *carte de séjour* at the local police station *(préfecture)* or town hall *(mairie)*. Take your passport, four photos, some proof of your local address (e.g. rental contract, receipt for rent) and a job contract or, failing that, proof of funds (F1,000 should be enough) and credit cards (with recent receipts to prove their validity). The list of requested documents differs from place to place and in some cases you will be asked to show an officially translated and authenticated copy of your birth certificate, which must show your parents' names. Geoff Halstead followed the instructions given by the French Consulate in London and ended up spending more than £25 turning his birth certificate into an acceptably 'legalised' document. If in France, ask at any of the six British Consulates.

The *carte de séjour* itself is free, and should be granted automatically once you have the right documents. This can take some time to come through – eight months to be precise in Stephen Psallidas's case – but in the meantime a *récépissé* for a *carte de séjour* should satisfy most employers. If you are planning to stay in France for no more than three months, you shouldn't have to bother with any of this, though employers are often unaware of the regulations, in which case you should suggest that they contact the *préfecture* to confirm it. But having a residence permit improves your chances of being hired; for example Vicky Nakis is fairly sure that she missed out on a short-term cleaning job at Disneyland Paris the first time round because she lacked one.

Confusingly, some employers and job centres have insisted that prospective employees obtain a *fiche d'état civil* from the *mairie* (town hall). For this you will need the same documents as for the *carte de séjour* apart from the job contract. Brendan Barker describes his struggle to obtain one in Bordeaux:

We met the patron *who was looking for plum pickers, but he said that we needed a* fiche d'état. *So we went to the* mairie *to get one. We were asked if we had our birth certificates and we said no (my girlfriend's was lost and mine was locked up in storage in England). We were told 'no birth certificate, no* fiche d'état'. *Back to the* patron *who said 'no* fiche d'état, *no work.' We went back to the guest house depressed. That evening I read* Work Your Way Around the World *and was sparked by some of your contributors' determination in trying again. So the next day we marched down to the* mairie *and this time we explained our situation to the mayor. As she was looking us up and down, we both gave desperate smiles and the mayor said it was OK for us to be given the FDC. We breathed a great sigh of relief and got the work picking plums.*

You also need a social security number, usually referred to as a *sécu*. Some employers may claim that they cannot hire you without one, but this is not the case. You should explain that as soon as you are given a contract of employment, you can take this immediately to the Caisse Sociale and obtain an emergency sécu straightaway which can be used while you are waiting for the proper one to come through which your employer should apply for. Employment agencies may not be willing to register you without one. Several travellers have suggested inventing one according to the following formula: 1 for men, 2 for women, followed by your year of birth, followed by your month of birth, followed by 99 if you're not French, followed by any three digits, so for example the number for a female foreigner born in May 68 could be 2-68-05-99-222.

Legal employers will deduct as much as 18% for social security payments, even before you have a number. These can be counted towards National Insurance in Britain, if you subsequently need to claim benefit. You may also lose a further 5% in tax. It is worth pointing out that anyone with a *carte de séjour* may be able to reduce their rent bill significantly, provided their earnings two years prior to applying were low. The benefit is administered by the Caisse d'Allocations Familiales (CAF), as Andrew Sykes discovered when he spent a year teaching English at a language school in Tours:

> *If your income two years before applying was low (e.g. if you worked as a campsite courier as I did), a substantial part of your rent (anything up to 65-70%) may be paid by the French government. At first glance, getting hold of all the paperwork may seem a drag (and expensive in the case of official translations of documents) but it is financially beneficial if they decide you are eligible. As an indication of how much they pay out, the rent that I pay for a large town centre studio is F2,300 per month and the benefit I receive is F1,341 (just under 60%).*

In order to apply, it is necessary to furnish the CAF with a signed/stamped declaration from your landlord, a declaration of income for the calendar year preceding the year of benefit, a *Fiche Individual d'Etat Civile* and various other bits and pieces.

A problem for some legal workers crops up when they try to cash pay cheques. After the plum harvest finished, Brendan Barker was told that he would have to wait eight days to be paid and that the cheque could be cashed only at the local village Credit Agricole. Stephen Psallidas reports that it is so difficult for foreigners to open a bank account, that you'll have to eat your pay cheques before you can cash them. His solution was to open an account at the Post Office for which it is necessary to show an *attestation de domicile* (letter from your landlord saying that you really do live there) plus a photocopy of a recent gas or electricity bill.

A useful source of information is the leaflet published by the CIDJ (address and description below) called *Séjour et emploi des ressortissants de l'Union Européenne* (*fiche* no. 5.5702) which costs F20 by post.

Non-EU Formalities

Non-EU nationals must obtain work documents before they leave their home country in order to work legally and this is fiendishly difficult since it depends on finding an employer who can argue that no French or EU national could do the job. A more manageable approach is to turn yourself into a student. After an initial year of study, people on a student visa are permitted to work 10-20 hours a week in term-time and up to 39 hours in vacations. In order to obtain a student visa, you will have to have good French language skills, two years of higher education (which may be waived if attending art college) and proof of financial support in the form of a notarised statement from a bank or benefactor that you can access at least $500 a month. With a student visa and stable accommodation, you can apply for a *carte de séjour* and after that for jobs, preferably jobs that French people can't do like teaching English, guiding groups of foreign students, etc.

For further details consult the leaflets *Séjour et emploi des étrangers* (*fiche* no. 5.5701) from the CIDJ or *Séjour et emploi des étudiants étrangers* (*fiche* 5.574).

Special Schemes for Americans

There is a special scheme by which American students with a working knowledge of French (normally a minimum of two years' study at university) are allowed to look for a job in France at any time of the year and work for up to three months with an *authorisation provisoire de travail*. This scheme is organised by the Council on International Educational Exchange (633 Third Avenue, 20th Floor, New York, NY 10017-6706; 1-888-COUNCIL). Eligible Americans already in France may apply to the Council office in Paris (1 Place de l'Odéon, Paris 75006; 01-44 41 74 69; info@councilexchanges-fr.org/ www.councilexchanges-fr.org) which provides a lot of support to programme participants. For example it produces a list of potential

The symbol for flowers refers to the castration of maize flowers

WILLIAM SWAN

employers which have hired American students in the past. According to Council's most recent statistics, 95% of participants work in Paris and suburbs.

French Cultural Services section of the French Embassy collates information of use to Americans who wish to study or intern in France (972 Fifth Ave, New York, NY 10021; 212-439-1400; www.info-france-usa.org/culture) with links to *Stages en Entreprise* and teaching assistantships. Americans who are interested in arranging an internship in France should contact AIPT (see *Introduction*) or the French American Chamber of Commerce which oversees an Exchange Visitor Program (6th Floor, 1350 Avenue of the Americas, New York, NY 10019; 212-765-4460). Most internships are in business and are open to graduates with relevant professional experience. The six-month visa can be renewed twice.

US volunteers are placed in a variety of social projects in France by the Société Bienfaisance Mutuelle, 210 Post St, Suite 502, San Francisco, CA (www.frenchfoundation.com). The programme lasts eight weeks from early July; dates and details of costs are available from the International Volunteer Program organiser.

THE JOB HUNT

French speakers should be aware of the widely used French Telecom subscriber service *Minitel*. Minitel is a computerised information system which operates via a small screen which plugs into an ordinary telephone. Minitel screens may be available at information centres and main post offices. With it, ordinary people can access a variety of databases including one for job vacancies or even to advertise their own availability for work. CIDJ's query number is 3615 CIDJ and you can also try 3615 TOPJOBS. Other relevant numbers include 3614 Alpes for vacancies in winter resorts and 3617 for the magazine *L'Etudiant* which lists internships and other jobs for students.

Not all hitch-hikers rank France very highly but once you get into the countryside, the French can be remarkably generous not only in offering lifts but in helping their passengers to find work. As usual the *Pages Jaunes* (Yellow Pages) can be a great help when drawing up a list of relevant places to ask for work. If you are offered seasonal work ahead of the job starting date and plan to leave the area in the meantime, stay in constant touch with the employer; not only can starting dates vary but farmers and hotel managers don't always keep their promises.

ANPE

The *Agence National pour l'Emploi* or ANPE is the national employment service of France, with dozens of offices in Paris and almost 600 others throughout the country. The headquarters are at 4 rue Galilée, 93198 Noisy-le-Grand (01-49 31 74 00/49 31 77 11) and their website lists all the branches by region or postcode (www.anpe.fr), providing addresses, telephone and fax numbers. Although EU nationals are supposed to have equal access to the employment facilities in other member states, this is not always the case in France unless the job-seeker speaks good French and has a stable local address. If possible foreign job-seekers should work with a EURES Advisor.

EURES in Sheffield always knows of vacancies for EU nationals in France, most of them in the tourist industry. It has a regional branch in south-eastern England (EURES Crossborder H.N.F.K., South Kent College, Shakespeare Centre, 145-147 Sandgate Road, Folkestone, Kent CT20 2DA; 01303 226184) which can provide information and assistance on employment in the northern French region of Nord-Pas-de-Calais.

But for all the ANPEs which are unsympathetic, there are exceptions. Phil New was lucky enough to find an ANPE employee in Lyon who claimed to like the English and who gave him the address of a farmer near Belleville with an opening, and Vicky Nakis heard about a promising-sounding housekeeping job through a Paris ANPE. So if you speak French you should visit the ANPE, while being prepared for a disappointing reception. Most ANPEs display cards with potential employers to whom you can apply directly.

Seasonal offices are set up in key regions to deal with seasonal demands like the *Service Vendanges* for the grape harvest and the *Antennes Saisonnières* set up in ski resorts. These may be more likely to assist working travellers than the permanent offices which deal primarily in full-time jobs for French citizens. The addresses of ANPE offices recommended as offering seasonal work are listed in the relevant sections later in this chapter.

CIJ

There are 32 regional *Centres d'Information Jeunesse* (CIJ) and 1,500 smaller youth information points in France which may be of use to the working traveller. Helping people to find jobs is only one of their activities: they can also advise on cheap accommodation, the legal rights of temporary workers, etc. The main Paris branch is CIDJ *(Centre d'Information et de Documentation Jeunesse)* whose foyer notice board is a useful starting place for the job-seeker in Paris. It can also provide leaflets on such subjects as seasonal agricultural work, possibilities for work in the summer or winter, and the regulations that affect foreign students in France. To obtain their catalogue of *fiches* or leaflets by post, send four international reply coupons to CIDJ at 101 Quai Branly, 75740 Paris Cedex 15 (01-44 49 12 00/www.cidj.asso.fr). Most *fiches* cost F10 if picked up in person or F20/six IRCs if requested by post. Note that their website does not broadcast job offers.

In order to find out about actual vacancies you must visit the offices in person, preferably first thing in the morning. Employers notify centres of their temporary vacancies; some offices just display the details on notice boards, while others operate a more formal system in co-operation with the local ANPE. You will find *Centres d'Information Jeunesse* in the following towns: Amiens, Bastia (Corsica), Besancon, Bordeaux, Caen, Cergy Pontoise, Clermont-Ferrand, Dijon, Evry, Grenoble, Lille, Limoges, Lyon, Marseille, Melun, Montpellier, Nancy, Nantes, Nice, Orleans, Poitiers, Reims, Rennes, Rouen, Strasbourg, Toulouse and Versailles. Julian Peachey found the Marseille CIJ helpful for agricultural jobs (including on the *vendange*), though at that time they mainly held details of jobs at holiday centres, especially as *animateurs*.

Some CIJs publish free lists of potential employers. For example Stuart Bellworthy made good use of a list given out by the CIJ in Angers (now closed) which gave all the *producteurs* in the area with estimated harvest dates. About a third of the vacancies with which the CIJs deal are for mothers' helps, for which good French is not a prerequisite.

A similar range of jobs is notified to the Centres Régional des Oeuvres Universitaires et Scolaires (CROUS) in all university towns. Although they primarily assist registered students to find part-time and holiday jobs, they have been known to help foreign travellers who approach them in the right way.

Private Employment Agencies

Private employment agencies in France are prohibited from dealing with permanant jobs and so all are *agences de travail temporaire* (temporary work bureaux) or *agences intérimaire*. Among the largest are Manpower, Bis and Select France; others can be found in the Yellow Pages under the heading *Travail Intérimaire*. Many specialise in a field such as industrial, medical or office work, and vacancies for unskilled jobs are few and far between. To find a job through an agency you first need to register, which is not as easy as it sounds. The law requires that you have a French social security number to give them, which you will only have if you have already had a legal job in France – another of those classic working travellers' catch-22s: you can't get work in France unless you've worked in France.

Yet some travellers have made good use of agencies. On his year abroad during his degree course, Matthew Binns went to a job agency in Paris without high hopes of success:

I foolishly said I was prepared to do anything. The bloke in the agency looked astonished and gave me, I think, the most unpopular job on his books – plongeur in a factory canteen in the suburbs. George Orwell's account in Down and Out in Paris and London *about his time as a plongeur should be required reading for all would-be dishwashers in Paris. I did three weeks in this job until the regular plongeur came back, poor sod. The worst bit is arriving at work with a hangover and putting on yesterday's wet clothes. But the pay was excellent.*

TOURISM

The best areas to look for work in the tourist industry of France are the Alps for the winter season, December-April, and the Côte d'Azur for the summer season, June-September, though jobs exist throughout the country. The least stressful course is to fix up work ahead of time with a UK campsite or barge holiday company in summer or ski company in winter. For example Travelbound (Olivier House, 18 Marine Parade, Brighton, East Sussex BN2 1TL; 0870 900 3200/fax 01273 600486) hires people, not necessarily with qualifications, to work in hotels in the Alps and Normandy. Sun Esprit hire resort managers, chalet hosts and childcare staff for their summer programme in the Alps; contact them at Oaklands, Reading Road North, Fleet, Hants. GU13 8AA (01252 618318; recruitment@esprit-holidays.co.uk).

Horizon HPL (Signet House, 49/51 Farringdon Road, London EC1M 3JP; 020-7404 9192/fax 020-7404 9194) is an Anglo-French training organisation which offers packages lasting between two and 12 months combining language tuition and live-in hotel work placements and company placements all over France. The wages are on a trainee scale, from £50 per week plus accommodation, while the package fee is £240. Horizon's office in France is at 22-26 rue du Sergent Bauchat, 75012 Paris (01-40 01 07 07/fax 1-40 01 07 28) while the Dublin office is at 3 Lower Abbey St, Dublin 1 (01-8745 002).

If you set off without anything pre-arranged, one of the easiest places to find work is at fast food establishments like Pizza Hut France or France Quick. Americana is very trendy in France and English-speaking staff fit well with the image. The hardest place to find work, except at the lowest level (e.g. dishwasher) is with reputable French-owned hotels and restaurants, where high standards are maintained. Your best chances will be in small family-run hotels where the hours and conditions vary according to the temperament of the *patron*. One reader met an English couple hitch-hiking through the rain to take up jobs as silver service waiting staff at a hotel in the Médoc, despite not speaking French or having had any relevant experience. The jobs had been pre-arranged through the ANPE in Pauillac.

Hotels and Restaurants

People with enough time to make long term plans can write directly to the hotels in the region which interests them, listed in any tourist hotel guide. Remember that the vast majority of restaurants are staffed by waiters rather than waitresses. Newspapers in holiday towns may carry adverts, e.g. *Nice Matin*.

But most people succeed by turning up at a resort and asking door to door, and in the opinion of veteran British traveller Jason Davies, 'door-to-door' should be just that:

> *Before I was down to my last F100 I had been choosy about which establishments to ask at. 'That doesn't look very nice' or 'that's too posh' or 'that's probably closed' were all thoughts which ensured that I walked past at least three in five. But in Nice I discovered that the only way to do it is to pick a main street (like the pedestrianised area in Nice with its high density of restaurants) and ask at EVERY SINGLE place. I visited 30-40 one morning and I would say that at least 20 of those needed more employees. But only one was satisfied with my standard of French, and I got the job of commis waiter.*

Speaking French to a reasonable standard greatly improves chances of finding a job, though fluency is by no means a requirement. Kimberly Ladone from the American east coast spent a summer working as a receptionist/chambermaid, also in Nice, though her job hunt did not require the same dogged determination as Jason Davies did:

> *I found the job in April, at the first hotel I approached, and promised to return at the start of the season in June. While there, I met many English-speaking working travellers employed in various hotels. No one seemed bothered by work permit regulations as most jobs paid cash in hand. (A friend who had a work permit from CIEE in New York spent weeks looking for a job and once he found one, his boss paid him under the table anyway.) My advice to anyone seeking a job on the French Riviera would be to go as early in the season as possible and ask at hotels featured in English guidebooks such as* Let's Go: France, *since these tend to need English-speaking staff. My boss hired me primarily because I*

could handle the summer influx of clueless tourists who need help with everything from making a phone call to reading a train schedule.

Beach restaurants are another hopeful possibility. Julian Peachey put on his one white shirt and pair of smart trousers and began visiting the restaurants along the beach by Avenue Montredon in the eastern part of Marseille. After the third request for work he was handed a tea towel, and proceeded to work 14-16 hours a day, seven days a week. Only the thought of the money kept him sane. The wage was severely cut on days when it rained or the mistral blew and no one came to the beach.

It must be said that not everyone finds work so easily as Alison Cooper found:

Last summer I tried to find work along the French Riviera, but was unsuccessful. I met many people at campsites who were in the same position as myself. From my experience most employers wanted people who could speak fluent French, and German as well. Otherwise you have to be very very lucky.

In the opinion of Andrew Giles the best time to look for work on the Côte d'Azur is the end of February when campsites well known to working travellers, such as Prairies de la Mer and La Plage at Port Grimaud near St Tropez host representatives from camping holiday companies trying to get organised in time for Easter. If you are on the spot you can often wangle free accommodation in exchange for three or four hours of work a day. If you can't be there then, try the middle of May at the beginning of the peak season. Bars recommended by Andrew where you can meet local workers and residents include Marilyns (Prairies de la Mer), Mulligans (Holiday Marina), Finnigans (Port Grimaud) and L'Utopée (Marines Cogolin). Also, try to listen to the English station Radio Riviera based in Nice which at 9.30am and 4.30pm broadcasts job vacancies along the coast and will also announce your request for a job free of charge. When Peter Goldman couldn't find work on boats as he had hoped (because of rainy September weather) he tuned in to Radio Riviera and got a job stripping wallpaper from luxury apartments in Monte Carlo for F400 a day.

Campsite Holidays

There are an estimated 7,000 campsites in France, some of them small family-run operations which need one or two assistants, others on an industrial scale. You can write directly to the individual campsite addresses listed in any guide to French campsites (e.g. the Michelin *Camping and Caravanning Guide*), or you can simply show up. Robert Mallakee and a friend easily found campsite jobs as they hitched along the Mediterranean coast in August which is the month when almost everyone in France takes their annual holiday. There is a point in the summer at which workers who have been there since the beginning of the season are getting bored and restless, which creates a demand for emergency substitution to cover the last two months of the season. Jobs included cleaning the loos, manning the bar or snack bar, doing some maintenance, etc. Some will be especially interested in people with musical ability. Even if there are no actual jobs, you may be given the use of a tent in exchange for minimal duties.

A number of British-based travel companies offer holidaymakers a complete package providing pre-assembled tents and a campsite courier to look after any problems which arise. Since this kind of holiday appeals to families, people who can organise children's activities are especially in demand. In addition to the Europe-wide companies like Eurocamp (addresses in *Tourism* chapter), the following all take on campsite reps/couriers and other seasonal staff:

Canvas Holidays Ltd, 12 Abbey Park Place, Dunfermline, Fife KY12 7PD (01383 644018; www.canvas.com).

Carisma Holidays, Bethel House, Heronsgate, Chorleywood, Herts. WD3 5BB (01923 284235; personnel@carisma.co.uk).

Fleur Holidays, 4 All Hallows Road, Bispham, Blackpool FY2 0AS (01253 593333; employment@fleurholidays.co.uk).

French Life Holidays, Kerry House, Kerry St, Leeds LS18 4AW (0113 281 9998).

Haven Europe, 1 Park Lane, Hemel Hempstead, Herts. HP2 4YL (01442 203287).

Ian Mearns Holidays, Tannery Yard, Witney St, Burford, Oxon. OX18 4DP (01993 822655; karen@ianmearnsholidays.co.uk). People able to start work in March especially in demand.

Keycamp Holidays, Hartford Manor, Greenback Lane, Northwich, CW8 1HW (01606 787522).

Select France, Fiveacres, Murcott, Kidlington, Oxford OX5 2RE (01865 331350; selectfrance@sol.co.uk).

Solaire Holidays, 1158 Stratford Road, Hall Green, Birmingham B28 8AF (0121-778 5061; www.solaire.co.uk).

The best time to start looking for summer season jobs from England is between November and February. In most cases candidates are expected to have at least 'A' level standard French, though some companies claim that a knowledge of French is merely 'preferred'. It is amazing how far a good dictionary and a knack for making polite noises in French can get you. Many impose a minimum age of 21.

The massive camping holiday industry generates winter work as well. Brad Blanchisserie is a French-registered company in Sautron, Nantes which cleans and repairs tents and bedding on behalf of many of the major companies. Staff (who need not speak French though it is an advantage) are needed between September and May. A wage of F350 a day plus gite accommodation is provided (so having your own transport is an advantage). Their UK office is at Abbey Lakes Hall, Orrell Road, Wigan WN5 8QZ (01695 632797; info@bradint.co.uk) or in France email bradblanch@oceanet.fr.

Short bursts of work are available in the spring (about three weeks in May) and autumn (three weeks in September) to teams of people who put up and take down the tents at campsites, known as montage and démontage. Sometimes the camping tour operators contract out this work to specialist firms like Mark Hammerton Travel (6-8 Garden St, Tunbridge Wells, Kent TN1 2TB; 01892 525456; enquiries@markhammerton.co.uk) who pay their crews nearly £100 a week in addition to all expenses. Rob Abblett found a job with Holidaybreak (01606 787522) at the end of summer 2000:

> *I got the job after a telephone interview and met the group in London to travel to Bordeaux where we were split up and sent to different campsites. I was to work with about 12 teenagers and young adults, cleaning the tents before dismantling and packing. Now I love France and it could have been a great time, but I couldn't stand the incessant loud music and how every evening seemed to revolve around drinking games and drunken behaviour. So I hit the road after one week. I really must be getting old.*

Holiday Centres

Outdoor activity centres are another major employer of summer staff, both general domestic staff and sports instructors. Try the companies mentioned in the chapter *Tourism* such as PGL and Acorn Adventure (01384 446057; topstaff@acornadventure.co.uk). Keen cyclists could try to get a job with a cycling holiday company active in France such as Belle France (15 East St, Rye, East Sussex TN31 7JY) and Susi Madron's Cycling for Softies (2-4 Birch Polygon, Rusholme, Manchester M14 5HX; www.cycling-for-softies.co.uk). Headwater Holidays looks to hire French-speaking reps (minimum age 21) and British Canoe Union qualified canoe instructors (01606 813306; mike@headwater.com).

For work in a more unusual activity holiday, contact Bombard Balloon Adventures, Chateau de Laborde, Laborde au Chateau, 21200 Beaune (03-80 26 63 30) who hire hot-air balloon ground crew for their summer season May to October; Americans should contact the US head office, 33 Pershing Way, West Palm Beach, FL 33401 (240-384-7107; www.bombardsociety.com/jobs). The job requires excellent physical fitness and strength, a cheerful personality, clean-cut appearance and year-old clean driving licence.

The Youth Hostels Association of France (FUAJ) employs hostellers for short periods at various hostels to work in the kitchen, reception and as sports leaders. The headquarters of the Fédération Unie des Auberges de Jeunesse (27 rue Pajol, 75018 Paris; www.fuaj.org) distributes a guide to the 185 French hostels to which interested workers must apply directly.

Ski Resorts

France is the best of all countries in Europe for British and Irish people to find jobs in ski resorts, mainly because it is the number one country for British skiers, 200,000 of whom go there every year. Most of the resorts are high enough to create reliable snow conditions throughout the season. The main problem is the shortage of worker accommodation; unless you find a live-in job you will have to pay nearly holiday prices or find a friend willing to rent out his or her sofa. Since many top French resorts are purpose-built, a high proportion of the holiday accommodation is in self-catering flats or designed for chalet parties. This means that not only is there a shortage of rental accommodation, but there are fewer jobs as waiters, bar and chamber staff for those who arrive in the resorts to look for work. There is an increasing number of English and Irish style pubs which are good places to find out about work.

If trying to fix up a job from Britain, there are one or two agencies that arrange for young people with a very good knowledge of French to work in ski resorts. Alpotels (17 High St, Gretton, Northants. NN17 3DE) carry out aptitude tests on behalf of various resort employers and liaise between suitable candidates and prospective employers who pay a net salary of approximately £500. Enquirers (EU nationality only) must send an s.a.e.

Another agency is UK Overseas Handling (UKOH, PO Box 2791, London W1A 5JU; 020-7629 3064; personnel@nbvltduk.freeserve.co.uk) which provides seasonal and annual staff to hotel and restaurant chains and chalet operators in ski resorts (as well as beach resorts) in France (and Europe). Applicants must be EU-passport holders. A UK agency that interviews and places all levels of chalet and hotel staff, au pairs and nannies with British ski companies in the French Alps can be reached by ringing 01252 673707 or via e-mail on jobs@skistaff.co.uk. Similarly Free Radicals places qualified/experienced nannies in a range of alpine resorts; nannies are paid £65 a week plus given transport to and from the resort, ski pass, equipment and lessons plus of course board and lodging (0117-924 4606; info@freeradicals.co.uk).

Between 20 and 30 British tour companies are present in Méribel alone, so this is one of the best resorts in which to conduct a job hunt. It may even be worth calling into the tourist office to ask about seasonal employment, though it is more promising to ask for work in person at hotels, bars, etc. The company Brown Rock (Taverneroc@aol.com) runs a number of outlets (Hotel le Roc, Dick's Tea Bar, Pizza Express, Les Castors and la Taverne). The manager may let you stay very cheaply out-of-season while you suss out job possibilities in the resorts. Looking for work out-of-season in October and November has the added advantage that well-placed youth hostels (like the one in Séez les Arcs where Matthew Binns stayed) are empty and relatively cheap. Matthew also recommends the free Red Cross hostel in Bourg-St Maurice.

Resorts like Méribel are flooded with British workers just before the season and eventually by British guests, many of them school groups. The functioning language of many establishments is English. Since the infrastructure work was done for the Olympics, British chalet operators have established a strong presence in Courchevel; Neilson and Simply Ski have their main French offices in the picturesque village of Le Praz, one of the five villages that comprise the resort of Courchevel.

Most jobs with British companies pay low wages but allow workers to ski between 10am and 4pm. Five of the many UK operators which recruit staff for France are Scott Dunn (Fovant Mews, 12 Noyna Road, London SW17 7PH; ski@scottdunn.com), Bien Ski based in Meribel (Southbank House, Black Prince Road, London SE1 7SJ; personnel@bienski.com), Meriski (The Old School, Great Barrington, Oxon. OX18 4UR; 01451 843125 or apply on-line www.meriski.co.uk), Ski Esprit (address above under Sun Esprit) and Ski Beat (Metro House, Northgate, Chichester, Sussex PO19 1BE; www.skibeat.co.uk). The latter has jobs in La Plagne, Tignes, Val d'Isère and La Tania. Lotus Supertravel (Sandpiper House, 39 Queen Elizabeth St, London SE1 2BT; 020-7962 1369) takes on winter staff for France, primarily chalet hosts with excellent cooking skills, reps fluent in French, qualified masseurs, nannies and handymen. All applicants must hold an EU passport and be over 21.

Another promising area of employment is nannying. Matt Tomlinson, who spent a year near Paris as an au pair, spent the winter season in Courchevel:

I'm not sure if I just luck out getting work or whether it is a question of having done most jobs, being presentable and enthusiastic. There certainly doesn't seem to be any shortage of employment opportunities in Courchevel and Le Praz during the busy periods. My first job was as a private nanny: easy work, F1,000 for the week plus another F700 for extra babysitting. I moved on to doing Children's Club with Simply Ski and then Snow Club with Ski Esprit. Not everyone was NNEB qualified though all had substantial childcare experience and most were hired in England. I would recommend anyone thinking of doing a nanny job in the Alps to think seriously before taking it on. The days were very long and tiring, especially when you have to keep track of 18 sets of ski gear.

Another promising resort is Chamonix, where Sean Macnamara obtained a series of manual jobs as a dishwasher and handyman through the local ANPE office. In fact the ANPE mount a concerted campaign every winter called A3 (ANPE Alpes Action) to attract qualified resort staff. Temporary job centres *(Antennes A3 ANPE Saisonnières)* are set up in most resorts and are co-ordinated by the permanent ANPE offices in Albertville, Annecy, Cluses and so on. For example the Albertville ANPE in the Savoie (45 ave Jean Jaurès, BP96, 73203 Albertville Cedex; 04-79 32 20 03) has a centralised placement service for vacancies in a range of resorts including Tignes, Val d'Isère and Méribel.

Some other relevant offices open year-round include:

Annecy ANPE, 8 bis Rue de Rumilly, 74000 Annecy (04-50 51 00 42).

Cluses ANPE, Immeuble l'Armorial, 14 rue du 8 Mai 1945, 74300 Cluses (04-50 98 92 88).

St Jean-de-Maurienne ANPE, 100 rue du Grand Coin, 73301 St Jean de Maurienne (04-79 64 17 88).

Chambery ANPE, 32 rue Paulette Besson, 73000 Chambery (04-79 60 24 70).

Thonon les Bains ANPE, 5 place de la Gare, 74207 Thonon les Bain Cedex (04-50 71 31 73).

Success is far from guaranteed in any ski resort job hunt and competition for work is increasing. Val d'Isère attracts as many as 500 ski bums every November/December, many of whom hang around bars like G-Jays or the ANPE for days in the vain hope that work will come their way. With such an inexhaustible supply of ski bums, some employers are ready to hire people for Christmas, work them non-stop over the high season, pay them far less than the *SMIC* and fire them if they complain. If looking for work in Val, try Radio Val which broadcasts from next door to the tourist office. Job vacancies are announced in the morning (mostly babysitting and kitchen portering) and then posted in French outside the studio. The earlier you try for these, the better your chances.

One problem which recurs every winter is the dispute between British tour operators and French ski schools. The rules state that only qualified instructors and guides can accompany holidaymakers which means that English-speaking ski guides or ski-hosts (part rep, part guide) hired by UK tour companies face arrest on the slopes. But since 1999, the French (under pressure from the European Commission) have accepted that BASI-qualified British ski instructors have an equal right to work in the Alps.

Selling to Tourists

A well known job in the south of France consists of selling refreshments on beaches. You may find foreigners doing this on beaches in and around Port Grimaud, San Tropez, Fréjus, Pampelonne and indeed all along the Mediterranean coast. Buy one of them a drink and he or she will direct you to their boss. Many bosses allow sellers to camp on their land. Sellers are paid on commission and earnings differ enormously. It helps if you are a raging extrovert with the gift of the gab. Nigel Baker who worked on the beaches along the Côte d'Azur for three seasons found that, for him, the positive aspects of the job outweighed the negative ones and wrote about his experiences in *TNT* magazine:

Beach selling is not for wimps. It is hard work, competitive and sometimes risky. However, if you find a good beach (the good ones change from year to year) you can spend a great couple of months living in a beautiful place... it's a great way to make a living!

The alternative to working for a boss is to go into business for yourself, by stocking up on fizzy drinks and beer from the local hypermarket, buying blocks of ice and heading for a beach crowded with thirsty holiday-makers. To do this legally you should have a licence (which costs thousands of francs). Otherwise you must be constantly vigilant and impersonate a tourist if you see the police coming. If caught, you will lose your stock at best and be arrested and fined at worst. The advantage is that you get to keep all the profits: sellers with experience and stamina can make up to £50 a day.

Stephen Hands travelled to Marseillan Plage near Montpellier. He thought he had prepared himself well with a cool bag, but discovered that a cool box was what was required since no one would believe the drinks in his bag were cool. He sold three cans in one hour before giving up while his friend managed eight cans in five hours.

Such entrepreneurial activities often meet with opposition from those who have already staked a claim, as Stephen Psallidas found in Père Lachaise cemetery in Paris:

I really was penniless so I thought up a scheme to make (I thought) vast profits. I would sell wine to all the hippies and camera-wielding tourists around Jim Morrison's grave. Macabre huh? So I bought a few bottles of el cheapo vin rouge and set up shop, complete with a sign in six languages. Unfortunately I was very quickly moved on by the established operators, who were mostly selling more exotic substances. So I drank the wine myself and had a very jolly time for the rest of the day.

Selling treats to tourists in ski resorts has also proved a lucrative sideline for some travellers-cum-ski bums. Simon Isdell-Carpenter started in Courchevel selling chocolates to the ski queues. Other entrepreneurs have made money by delivering croissants to chalets and inns either as an independent business or as an employee of the local bakery. Chalet staff often spend an extra half-hour in the mornings making sandwiches for clients and sell them for F25 which is quite a lot less than they cost on the mountain. They can also try to sell cans of drink at a mark-up.

As usual you might be able to sell your talent to tourists as a busker. Leda Meredith made about F300 an hour as a dancer/mime in Avignon before and during the festival in August. Dustie Hickey also found work during the festival doing promotions (i.e. selling tickets and T-shirts) for an American theatre group. After the festival is over, however, street performers need a permit, and will be moved on by the police otherwise.

Yachts

Kevin Gorringe headed for the south of France in June two years ago with the intention of finding work on a private yacht. His destination was Antibes, where so many British congregate, and began frequenting likely meeting places like the Gaffe Bar and the Irish bar as well as the agencies like Adrian Fisher and Blue Water. He recommends using the services of The Office (La Galerie du Port, 8 Blvd d'Aguillon, 06600 Antibes; 04-93 34 09 96; theoffice@wanadoo.fr) which for a small fee can be used as a contact point for potential employers. The two women who run The Office have recently opened a crew agency (info@starcrew.com) joining several other crewing agencies housed in the same building (see *Working a Passage*).

Kevin recommends staying at one of the cheap campsites at Biot on the other side of Antibes, which is easily reached by public transport, though Stella's and the usual crew houses are also possibilities. He and his girlfriend went round the quays asking for work but soon tired of begging for scrubbing jobs and decided to move on. They concluded that to find work in Antibes you have to be 'persistent, focused and able to get into the click'. Bill Garfield is one traveller who stuck at it. After a week of failure, Bill began asking at every single boat including the ones already swarming with workers and also all the boats big and small in the 'graveyard' (refitting area). Two weeks after leaving Solihull this tactic paid off and he was hired for a nine-week period to help refit a yacht in preparation for the summer charter season.

You might also pick up some job tips by listening to Radio Riviera mentioned above. Smaller places like St Tropez are reputed to be not nearly as good, though other people have recommended Beaulieu-sur-Mer, Villeneuve-Loubet-Plage and Cros-de-Cagnes. It is essential to start early, preferably the beginning of March, since by late April most of the jobs have been filled. Boats frequently take on people as day workers first and then employ them as crew for the charter season if they like them.

Look tidy and neat, be polite and when you get a job work hard. The first job is the hardest to get, but once you get in with this integrated community, captains will help you find other jobs after the refitting is finished. Of course many continue through the summer as deckhands on charter yachts and are paid £100 a week plus tips (which sometimes match the wage). The charter season ends in late September when many yachts begin organising their crew for the trip to the West Indies.

A British tour company which hires instructors and reps for its sailing holidays in Southwest France is Sail France, Rockley Watersports, Poole, Dorset BH15 4LZ. They operate out of two of the largest RYA recognised watersports centres in Europe.

Barges

Holiday barges which ply the rivers and canals of France hire cooks, hostesses, deckhands and captains. It is better to apply to the companies in the new year; addresses may be found in the travel advertisement sections of English Sunday papers. All will want to employ only people who feel comfortable functioning in French.

One employer is European Waterways. If you land a job before the season begins, you may be flown to Amsterdam to join the barge on which you will spend April to October as a hostess earning more than £110 a week (which can sometimes be tripled in tips). The UK address is European Waterways Ltd, 35 Wharf Road, Wraysbury, Staines, Middlesex TW19 5JQ; fax 01784 483072; ewbarging@aol.com/ www.gobarging.com). Vacancies also exist throughout the year for chefs, housekeepers, deck hands, tour guides and barge pilots for the luxury barge fleet. Applicants must have an EU passport (or have the right to work in the UK), be at least 21 and possess a current driving licence. A knowledge of French is useful.

French Country Waterways (Croisières Touristiques Francaises, 2 Route de Semur, 21150 Venarey-les-Laumes; 03-80 96 17 10; ctf.bateau@wanadoo.fr) take on seasonal chefs, driver/guides, stewardesses and deckhands in five regions of France. Long hours are rewarded with from £600 a month. Interviews of EU nationals are held in London in January. Continental Waterways with headquarters in Dijon employ many seasonal staff including chefs, bar staff, stewardesses, and deckhands on their fleet of luxury floating hotels; recruitment is carried out in the UK by Diana Mathisen, PO Box 31, Godalming, Surrey GU8 6JH; 01252 703577; crews@continentalwaterways.co.uk.

GRAPE-PICKING

Every year the lure of the *vendange* seems to be irresistible. Past participants agree about the negative aspects of the job: the eight or nine hours a day of back-breaking work, often for seven days a week, and the weather, which is too cold and damp in the early autumn mornings and too hot at mid-day. Waterproofs are essential because you will be expected to continue picking in the pouring rain. The accommodation may consist of a space in a barn for a sleeping bag, and the sanitation arrangements of a cold water tap. But despite all this, every year the grape-growing regions of France are flooded with hopeful *vendangeurs*, some of them drawn by a romantic notion which usually evaporates by the end of the first day, though not always, as Peggy Carter from Pennsylvania describes:

> *We asked some people we met at a bar in Nantes (Brittany) how feasible it was for Americans to find work picking grapes. They asked if we had any connections which we did not and they said it would be very hard. Well, it was our luck that one of them was from a family who owned vineyards in the area and we ended up in a field in St Fiacre at 8am the following Monday. The first four days were backbreaking, and also a little awkward since no one spoke English and no one made an effort to find out how much we understood. But eventually we became the centre of talk and everyone tried to make us feel comfortable. It was an unparalleled view into French small town culture, plus we received an insider's view of winemaking, we were able to practise our French and we overall just had a wonderful time. They've given us an open invitation to return for pleasure or for work.*

Part of the attraction is the wage. Although it is not usually much higher than *le SMIC* of F42 (porters sometimes earn more especially when the vineyards are located on steep hills), there is little opportunity to spend your earnings on an isolated farm and most people save several hundred pounds during a typical fortnight-long harvest. Martin and Shirine from Crawley earned £1,550 between them during the ten-day harvest of white grapes followed a week later by the red harvest in the first half of October. More typically, Rob Abblett walked away from the *vendange* in Chateauneuf de Pape a couple of years ago with cut fingers, an aching back and £250. If you work for the same *patron* for seven consecutive days, you should be paid an overtime rate. Be prepared for at least 15% to be deducted for social security.

The major threat to jobs at present comes from mechanisation. A great many farmers are clubbing together to invest in the great noisy juggernauts harvesting day and night, which have almost completely replaced human beings in some areas like Cognac and south of Bordeaux. However predictions that hand-picking will completely disappear are unlikely to come to pass. Prestige chateaux which produce Grand Cru wines and Champagne are sticking with hand-picking. The *Independent on Sunday* reported in June 2000 that the chairman of Moet & Chandon feared for the future of Champagne partly because of a shortage of grape-pickers (and also because of competition from Spanish and Australian wines).

Jon Loop describes the relationship with machines at the chateau where he picked grapes:

> *They had started using machines at Pontet Canet in the 1980s, but returned to using grape-pickers in the 1990s. The reasons they gave were purely economic: the machines lie idle over much of the year; they pick up stones, small animals, dirt and destroy the vines. They must be very certain of this because they have completely refurbished the dormitories and cooking facilities for 150 pickers.*

Work and Conditions

The working and living conditions can vary greatly from farm to farm. Often the size of the farm has a bearing on this: obviously it is easier for the owner of a small vineyard with a handful of workers to provide decent accommodation than for the owner of a chateau who may have over a 100 workers to consider. Farmers almost always provide some sort of accommodation, but this can vary from a rough and ready dormitory to a comfortable room in his own house. Food is normally provided, but again this can vary from the barely adequate to the sublime: one picker can write that 'the food was better than that in a 5-star hotel, so we bought flowers for the cook at the end of the harvest', while another may complain of instant mashed potatoes or of having to depend on whatever he or she can manage to buy and prepare. When both food and accommodation are provided there is normally a deduction of one or two hours' pay from each day's wage.

Free wine is a frequent feature of the job, though Martin and Shirine looked in vain for it at their chateau. In addition to her wage of F220 per day, Dustie Hickey was allowed a seemingly endless supply of wine which 'lifted up the workers' spirits but often left me falling into the bushes.' (When she was offered the same perk during the olive harvest later in the autumn, she wisely sold her daily two litres of wine.)

Hours also vary. Whereas one traveller (who chooses to call himself Rizla Plus) found the structuring of the working day ridiculous, with a $1^1/2$ hour lunch break and no other breaks between 7.45am and 6pm, others have found themselves finishing the day's picking at lunchtime, especially in the far south near the Spanish border, where the sun is unbearably hot in the afternoon.

The work itself will consist either of picking or portering. Picking involves bending to get the grapes from a vine that may be only three and a half feet tall, and filling a pannier that you drag along behind you. New regulations have resulted in the use of new secateurs which make it much less hard to cut yourself than with the old *vendangettes* but also make it harder to pick the grapes. Plastic gloves are useful if you don't want your hands stained by grape juice (white grapes are the worst). The panniers full of grapes are emptied into an *hotte* a large basket weighing up to 100lb which the porters carry to a trailer.

The first few days as a *cueilleur/cueilleuse* or *coupeur* (picker) are the worst, as you adjust to the stooping posture and begin to use muscles you never knew you had. The job of porter is sought after, since it does not require the constant bending and is less boring because you move around the vineyard.

The further south you go the more likely you are to find yourself competing with migrant workers from Spain, Portugal, Morocco and Algeria, though East Europeans have also found their way to most grape-growing corners of France. Large and famous chateaux (like Lafite) often use a contracted team of pickers who return every season and who can stand the fast and furious pace. These immigrant workers tend to return to the same large vineyards year after year, where they work in highly efficient teams which are normally preferred to individual travellers. Xuela Edwards noticed many Eastern Bloc nationals being picked up by farmers at railway stations in the south of France and suspected that they were paid considerably less than the SMIC.

Another source of competition comes from gypsies who organise crews. When Phil New was traipsing between unhelpful ANPEs in Champagne he was approached by several gypsy crew leaders. He decided to ignore the warnings he'd heard and joined a crew. He can't understand what the fuss is about: he reckons that he earned only slightly less than if he'd worked for the farmer directly and, contrary to what he'd been told, he was paid promptly and fairly at the end of the fortnight's harvest. Others have not had such happy experiences. If you are offered either far too much money or far too little, it is sensible to be suspicious.

How to Find Work

ANPEs are not always the best informed source of temporary job information. Jason Davies describes his experiences with them:

> *At the end of August I phoned the ANPE at Bordeaux and was informed that the vendange was going to start early, about September 4th or 5th. So I worked a week's notice at my restaurant in Nice and set off for Bordeaux. When I arrived I went to the ANPE for addresses to contact. 'Oh no, not yet,' said the pretty girl behind the desk (whom I would have liked to put through the window). 'The vendange won't be starting until the 25th at the earliest. It's a bit late this year,' she added. In Avignon the ANPE was just as unhelpful. 'We are no longer concerned with the vendange here'. Altogether I was amazed at the incompetence and uselessness of the ANPEs. If I ever use them again, I will be very cautious with the advice they offer.*

Provided you are prepared to disregard their negative advice, there is no harm in visiting the local ANPE in a wine-growing region on the off-chance that they will be able (and willing) to tell you which farmers need workers. Rizla Plus was told by the ANPE in Saumur, as well as the tourist office, a *maison de vin* and a private employment agency 'C'est complet.' Undaunted he headed east along the Loire and, after a ten-mile walk though the vineyards, found a job.

When Michael Jordan (not the basketball legend) was looking for grape-picking work in Alsace, he noticed that every *mairie* had a poster up advising job-seekers to present themselves to the ANPE in Colmar. That office sets up a special *Service Vendanges* in a courtyard where addresses are given out at the discretion of ANPE staff. They wouldn't give Michael any addresses, not because he is American but because he confessed that he didn't have a car and there were no more vacancies at farms with accommodation. David Loveless was told by the ANPE in Sélestat (16A pl. Marche aux Choux) also in the Alsace region that 50 people searching for *vendange* jobs were being turned away daily. David happened to meet some travellers in Riquewihr (near the main Alsatian town of Colmar) who advised him to try the local wine-grower. He was promptly hired for three weeks and was even offered F200 to come back the next season. Because of its more northerly location, Alsace can be very cold during the harvest, which puts some potential competition off.

Typically, the first-time grape-picker cannot step into a very desirable situation. After chucking his job at the Met Office in Britain, Jon Loop hitched until he hit good weather and started looking. For the first week in the Médoc he had no luck but eventually came across one possibility in Pauillac. It wasn't very satisfactory, since it was 15km from the nearest campsite and the vineyard didn't provide food or accommodation, but it was bearable for two weeks and started him off on his grape-picking career.

The ANPE in Pauillac is very helpful during the *vendange* when they operate a *Ligne Directe Vendange* and circulate employer details (one of which seen recently was for Chateau St. Fort in St. Estephe which has a campsite for *vendangeurs*).

Below are listed the addresses of major ANPEs in the wine-producing regions, with rough guidelines as to the starting dates of the harvest. It should be stressed that these dates can vary by days or even weeks from year to year. Even vineyards a few miles apart may start picking up to a week apart.

Alsace – October 15th
ANPE, rue Georges Wodli, 67081 Strasbourg Cedex (03-88 21 42 70).
ANPE, 54 ave de la République, BP 508, 68021 Colmar Cedex (03-89 20 80 70)
Beaujolais – September 10th
ANPE, 169 rue Paul Bert, 69665 Villefranche-sur-Saone Cedex (04-74 60 30 03).
Bordeaux – September 25th
ANPE, 1 Terrasse du Front du Médoc, 33076 Bordeaux (05-56 90 85 20).
ANPE, 19 rue A. Chauvet, BP 108, 33250 Pauillac (05-56 73 20 50/fax 5-56 59 62 49).
Burgundy – October 6th
ANPE, 71 rue Jean Mace, BP 20, 71031 Macon Cedex (03-85 21 93 20).
ANPE, 7 rue des Corroyeurs, BP 1504, 21034 Dijon (03-80 59 68 10).
Champagne – October 1st
ANPE, 40 rue de Talleyrand, 51057 Reims Cedex (03-26 89 52 60).
Languedoc-Roussillon – September 15th
ANPE, 10 rue Léon Paul Fargue, BP 4055, 66042 Perpignan Cedex (04-68 08 10 30).
ANPE, 90 avenue Pierre Sémard, BP 586, 11009 Carcassonne Iéna Cedex (04-68 10 30 00).
ANPE, 79 rue Christian Martinez, BP 7023, 30910 Nimes Cedex (04-66 04 90 90).
ANPE, rue du 19 Mars 1962, 30205 Bagnols sur Cèze (04-66 90 59 80).
ANPE, 31 quai du Port Neuf, CS 641, 34536 Beziers Cedex (04-67 11 80 60).
Loire – October 6th
ANPE, 9 rue du Docteur Herpin, BP 709, 37027 Tours Cedex (02-47 60 58 58).
ANPE, 6 Square Lafayette, 49000 Angers (02-41 24 17 20).

These are the most famous wine-making regions but there are many others. K. McCausland recommends the Savoie as being off the beaten track of job-seekers. The villages of Apremont, Montmélian and Les Marches near Chambery are recommended. The harvest here begins approximately October 1st. He also recommends trying to get a job picking table grapes in the département of Lot. It is harder work (because you have to be careful not to damage the fruit) but the wages are higher and the work lasts longer than for the *vendange*.

The demand for pickers in all regions is highly unpredictable. Whereas there is usually a glut of pickers looking for work at the beginning of the harvest (early to mid-September), there is sometimes a shortage later on in the month. Harvests differ dramatically from year to year; a late spring frost can wreak havoc. The element of uncertainty makes it very difficult for individuals (let alone agents) to arrange jobs for people who are not on the spot.

Experienced grape-pickers recommend visiting or phoning farms well before the harvest starts and asking the farmer to keep a job open. According to Jon Loop the key to success is serial phoning:

The best time to phone is July. Then phone in August to ask when to phone for starting dates. Then phone in September to say you are coming, to ask when it starts. You may also have to phone a week before the start to confirm.

If you are hunting in person, it is advisable to visit farmers in small villages far from the big towns where there is a superfluity of job seekers once the harvest starts. Also check the CIJ and university notice boards, for example the one in the cafeteria at the University of Dijon. As usual, a village bar is often the hub of activity during the *vendange* as Keith Flynn found to be the case in Chateauneuf de Pape (which incidentally is where the famous system of *appellation controlée* was invented):

One of the easiest ways of finding work is to go to the one and only bar in town across from the tourist office. All the workers go there in the evening and a lot of the bosses so just ask everybody. There were at least 30 or 40 pickers in town in the middle of September and more arriving; yet everybody seemed to have plenty of work.

Written applications are probably not worthwhile though some of our contributors have succeeded this way. Brian Williams obtained the addresses of ten large vineyards from a travel article in the *Sunday Times:* he wrote to them early in the year, and received five job offers in a week. Even more simply, copy the names of chateaux from wine bottles. Equally useful addresses can be found in Hugh Johnson's *World Atlas of Wine* which contains some superbly detailed maps of wine regions. Since it costs £30 to buy, try to find it in a library and photocopy maps of the areas you plan to visit. The publisher Mitchell Beazley also produce a series of useful guides to wine regions (Alsace, Bordeaux, Provence, Rhone and Loire) under the title *Touring in Wine Country* which cost £12.99 each.

While some job-seekers do succeed by trudging from vineyard to vineyard on foot to ask for work, there are alternatives. After badly blistering his feet on the country roads near Montpellier, Stephen Hands recommends borrowing or hiring a bicycle. More recently Rob Abblett spent a very discouraging few days hunting in several regions, including near Nimes: 'on foot without a tent I had no luck at all as no one had accommodation'. He did eventually find work in Chateauneuf du Pape but had to live in a big shed with no facilities. He later learned from some regular *vendangeurs* that he might have found it easier to find work in Beaujolais.

Phoning is a more leisurely option for French speakers though it too can be discouraging, as one working traveller found:

I had nothing fixed up in advance and the ANPE in Bordeaux was no help. So I got a Yellow Pages from the main post office, picked the famous appellation controlée of Margaux and started phoning. I got about 25 chateaux down the list, which was pretty disheartening, when Chateau Prieure-Lachine told me I could start on Monday.

Look up *viticulteurs* or *producteurs négociants*.

Jon Loop found the Syndicat d'Initiative (tourist office) in Cursac Fort Médoc very helpful in obtaining vineyard addresses. Always enquire at the *départementale* office rather than the city one. Many rural towns have a *chambre d'agriculture, maison d'agriculture*, a *syndicat général des vignerons* or a *conseil inter-professionel du vin*, all of which may have leads.

You should also look out for the offices of wine producers' co-operatives, whose staff are often friendly and helpful to prospective pickers. Keith Flynn from Dublin describes how this worked to his advantage in Nyons:

The great thing about Nyons and the surrounding town is that they are all co-op based and the farmers bring their grapes each evening between 6pm and 7pm. This means that there is no need to walk to all the domains. The four of us stood outside the co-op in Nyons for about three hours with signs in French saying 'we want to pick grapes' before we all got a job on a family-owned vineyard.

Alison Cooper was not so immediately successful when she doggedly tried to find a job through the Co-op in Limoux (between Perpignan and Toulouse). Success came in the end not through the Co-op but by a stroke of good fortune:

Fate intervened when a Portuguese and a Frenchman turned up at the Co-op in a car, with an address of a vineyard which might need five workers. I got into that car immediately with two Spaniards and we all ended up with jobs. First class French cuisine and a bed were provided (for a deduction of £10 a day) and I earned £250 tax free in ten days.

OTHER HARVESTS

Although the *vendange* may produce the highest concentration of seasonal work, there are tremendous opportunities for participating in other harvests and with far less competition for the available work. While increasing mechanisation threatens the future of grape-picking by hand, there are not yet any machines which can cope with apples, plums, peaches and olives.

One longstanding source of seasonal work which has all but disappeared is maize castrating or maize topping *(l'écimage)*, which consisted of picking off the flowers of the male maize plants. According to the ANPE in Riom in the Auvergne (4 allée des Tilleuls, BP 5, 63201 Riom Cedex; 04-73 38 09 58) the working period lasts only three to seven days, no accommodation is provided and the starting date is not known until the very last minute, making it impractical for people from outside the region to look for work with maize farmers. Furthermore there is a new kind of maize which is sterile.

France is an overwhelmingly rural country. The *départements* of Hérault, Drôme and Gers are among the most prolific fruit and vegetable producers, especially of plums, cherries, strawberries and apples. Crops ripen first in the south of the country, and first at lower altitudes, so it is difficult to generalise about starting dates. For example the strawberry harvest on the coastal plain around Beziers normally takes place between mid-May and late June, whereas 60km inland in the Haut Languedoc near Sauclieres, it starts in mid-July. Cherries and strawberries are the first harvests, normally taking place between May and July. Blueberries are picked throughout July and August. Peaches are picked from June after the trees have been pruned, while pears are picked throughout the summer but especially (like apples) from mid-September to mid-October. Apples are grown throughout France, including in the Hautes-Alpes south of Grenoble. The Belgian traveller Vincent Crombez wrote from the village of Monetier-Allemont (between Gap and Sisteron) to recommend the area:

Apple picking starts about the 1st of September and lasts until the end of October. I was paid the SMIC and worked 9 or 10 hours a day every day except Sunday. It's no problem to save F4,000 a month if you don't go to the only pub in this wonderful village every day. Now I'm back here for the apple thinning. I'm working 9 hours a day, but it's easy, always sunny and I will save F8,000 for the two months.

As well as the usual places to ask about harvesting work referred to on earlier pages, try the large fruit co-operatives and *ventrés directes* stalls on main roads including the *Route Nationale*. Not that asking shopkeepers always works, as Jon Loop found when he hitched round the Périgeux region hoping to find the chance to pick apples:

After four or five days looking we'd had no luck at all. Sure enough there were apples to be picked since all the shops had signs saying 'New apples', but as soon as we asked the shop owners, they were struck by premature senility: they didn't know where the apples came from, who to ask, even if they were new apples or apples from last year. Apparently a lot of the work is under the table, in the family and so they obviously don't want nosy foreigners asking stupid questions. On the other hand it seems an ideal situation for someone who is good at meeting prospective\employers in bars. I'm not. I just get drunk and fall over.

Sarit Moas from Israel found it very worthwhile asking a fruit weigher at one of the open markets in Paris about harvesting work:

The owner of the market stand answered, 'Why do you want to do tedious backbreaking picking?' In the end he offered me a job working with him selling from 6am to 2pm. I'd assemble the fruit stands with him five days a week and receive F250 daily.

Harvest work is paid either hourly (normally the SMIC) or by piece rates. If you are floundering with piece work, you may be transferred to a different job where you can earn an hourly wage as happened to Brendan Barker when he was picking plums in the Bordeaux area:

For the first two days we were on picking duty as part of a team, though we were marked down individually for each crate we filled. The rate was F10 a crate and some of the people were doing 30-35 even 40 crates a day. My girlfriend and I were hitting a measly 15 crates – inexperienced and unfit. So on the third day we were put on the factory line where the incoming wounded plums were sorted out and put onto wooden trays for the three giant furnaces that would shrivel them into prunes. For this work we were put on the SMIC which was better for us financially though we had the patron (an ex-military man) barking down our necks 'Allez vite, quick, rapido' for the benefit of the French, the Portuguese and us.

It is normally up to workers to provide their own food and accommodation, and so a tent and camping equipment are essential. If a farmer does provide board and lodging he will normally deduct the equivalent of two hours' wages from your daily pay packet. If you are planning to leave as soon as the harvest is over, bear in mind that agricultural wages are often not paid until seven to ten days after the harvest finishes (to ensure workers do not leave prematurely). Furthermore the wages may have to be cashed at a local bank, so be prepared to hang around.

In addition to fruit picking there are many other kinds of work which travellers end up doing, from cheese making to haymaking. There may be late autumn work pruning vines and orchards. Poultry farms (especially in the Anjou area) are often looking for chicken-catchers-cum-lorry-loaders who are (not surprisingly) paid fairly well.

The Avignon Region

All manner of fruit is grown in the Rhône Valley in the vicinity of Avignon. Working travellers have achieved long spells of continuous employment in the *départements* of Vaucluse and Ardèche by following the different harvests. In late July go to the Ile de Barthelasse, which is a 16km-long island in the River Rhône near Avignon which is entirely given over to fruit and vegetable growing. The village of Aubignan has several sheds where melons, courgettes, peppers and apricots are packed in September. Grape-picking could follow in nearby Vacqueyras and carries on till mid-November on the high slopes of Mont Ventoux. Those with stamina could head north to Privas in the Ardèche where chestnuts are picked in the frost.

Stuart Bellworthy looked for work in this area. Having started in Lyon, it wasn't until he got to Avignon with its massive fruit distribution centres and the Ile de Barthelasse with its promising sounding street names (Chemin des Vignes, Chemins des Raisins) that he became optimistic:

I spent a whole (very hot!) day wandering around the Ile de Barthelasse, without any luck (though I have never eaten so much fruit in my life free of charge). Just up the road from Camping Etoile (a very cheap campsite near Avignon just on the island) there is a map of the island and a list of all the producteurs. *It is worth starting at the north of the island since the farmers nearest Avignon probably get asked for jobs about every ten minutes.*

After I was convinced there were no jobs, I travelled 10km south to Chateaurenard and found a pear-picking job. All the roads to the north of Chateaurenard are lined with farms. The villages of St Remy, Barbentane and Rognons are also good. The pear season lasts from mid-July to early August.

Stuart goes on to recommend visiting the nearby Marché d'International (preferably at about 5am) and asking the farmers for work either on their farms or helping with their market stalls.

The theme of struggle is taken up by Bridgid Seymour-East who was further hindered by her inability to speak French and her New Zealand passport:

Neither of us can speak even school book French, so going around asking for jobs was quite difficult. We stayed on the Ile de Barthelasse at the Camping Bagatelle which was brilliant. We walked and walked around the Ile with no success. Finally on the afternoon of the second day we were heading back feeling fed up and exhausted. We passed a boarding hostel for young men and a group sitting outside asked us to join them for a coffee. As it turned out, one of them happened to work on a nearby orchard and immediately got us a job with his boss (M. Bernard has several farms on the Island) which looked all set to last for a couple of months. But the farmer wanted to see our passports and couldn't afford to take the risk of employing me. He did give us work for ten days, though, and was rather annoyed that he couldn't keep us on longer, as a lot of local labour was not so reliable.

Through meeting people at the Koala Bar in Avignon Dustie Hickey fixed up a job picking olives between early November and late December in St Remy. She says that she would happily do this work again since it was so peaceful, and furthermore you can earn money at it:

We worked at Mas de la Dame, a place where Van Gogh painted. The job involved climbing ladders but as I'm light I would climb right into the trees (best view!) and comb, comb, comb the branches so the olives would fall into the net below. When the tree is cleared, you have to pick out all the twigs and leaves and roll the olives into the crates. It's very satisfying to fill a few crates from one tree (but not at all satisfying when the net turns out to be too small). I was paid F2 a kilo plus two litres of wine a day. It is easy to rent cheap accommodation in St Remy at this time of year. The only problem was transport: although there is a bus to Avignon there is no off-season service south to Les Baux de Provence.

The Loire Valley

Strawberries, apples, pears and many other crops can be found along the River Loire: the towns of Segré, Angers and Saumur are especially recommended. Stephen Febers spent an enjoyable five weeks in the late spring in this area picking strawberries in Varennes-sur-Loire. The harvest here lasts six to eight weeks from early/mid April.

Two unusual crops are grown round Saumur, both of which are picked from the beginning of July, mushrooms and blueberries. While working on a farm in Kent, Andrew Pattinson-Hughes found out that the farm secretary owned a blueberry farm in Brain-sur-Allonnes, a few kilometres north of Saumur:

After hounding her to write us a letter of recommendation, she gave in. I borrowed £50 from my dad for the coach fare to Tours, then caught a train to Saumur and an over-priced taxi to the farm, Anjou Myrtilles (myrtille is French for blueberry). *The farmer speaks fluent English and agreed to hire us. It's easy to earn £40 a day. We stayed on a campsite in Brain-sur Allonnes (F20 a night) about a 40 minute walk away, as the farm is in the middle of the sticks.*

They continued picking until the end of August and then moved on to the apple harvest in the nearby village of Parcay les Pins where Andy was expecting to earn F5,500 per month for up to two months.

Organic Farms

Although the organic movement is powerful in France, there is no independent WWOOF organisation that maintains an up-to-date list of organic farmers looking for volunteers. However the International List from WWOOF Australia (see *Agriculture*) lists pages of farms, many of them run by expatriates or by exiles from the big city; descriptions without addresses can be seen on the web page wwoof.org/frdepart.html. The atmosphere on this kind of farm is often different from that on purely commercial farms, though you will still be expected to work hard. Most temporary workers hear of farms like this by word of mouth *(de bouche à l'oreille)*, but it is always polite to ring or write ahead rather than show up unannounced. The kind of information they are interested in includes your background, age, experience, whether or not you are vegetarian, mode of travel (preferably a bicycle) and of course dates of intended visit.

If you can arrange to swap your labour for room and board you shouldn't have to worry about the red tape. Two Americans staying in Strasbourg, Cindy Roberts and Michael Jordan, phoned the number of a Brittany farmer mentioned in an old edition of *Work Your Way Around the World* and were offered work immediately. They stayed seven weeks and were treated as members of the family and even given the best room in the house.

This experience was in complete contrast to the next farmer they visited, a woman notorious for exploiting volunteers and making them work ludicrously long hours for virtually no money. That employer (in the village of Narcy) was in fact prosecuted on a number of counts and so is unlikely to be in a position to hire unwitting travellers in future.

TEACHING

There are so many expatriates living in Paris and throughout France that being a native speaker of English does not cut much ice with prospective employers of English teachers. Without a TEFL qualification, BA or commercial flair (preferably all three) it is very difficult to get a teaching contract. Of course if you can make yourself look ultra-presentable and have an impressive CV, you should ring to make appointments and then tramp round all the possible schools to leave your CV. (As is usual in Europe, there is virtually no hope of success in July and August.)

The technique of making a personal approach to schools in the months preceding the one in which you would like to teach is often successful. On the strength of her Cambridge Certificate from International House, Fiona Paton had been hoping to find teaching work in the south of France in the summer but quickly discovered that there are very few opportunities outside the academic year. On her way back to England, she disembarked from the train in the picturesque town of Vichy in the Auvergne just long enough to distribute a few self-promotional leaflets to three language schools. She was very surprised to receive a favourable reply from one of them once she was home, and so returned a few weeks later for a happy year of teaching.

In Paris many schools advertise in the *métro*, or you can look up addresses in the Yellow Pages under *Enseignements Privé de Langues* or *Ecoles de Langues*. A great many of these cater for the business market, so anything relevant in your background should be emphasised. Typical wages are F100-F140 per hour (gross). As is increasingly common, schools are reluctant to take on contract teachers for whom they would be obliged to pay taxes and social security, and so there is a bustling market in freelance teachers who work for themselves and are prepared to teach just a few hours a week for one employer.

Partly because of France's proximity to a seemingly inexhaustible supply of willing English teachers, working conditions in France are seldom brilliant. Although Andrew Boyle enjoyed his year teaching English in Lyon and the chance to become integrated into an otherwise impenetrable community, he concluded that even respectable schools treated teachers as their most expendable commodity, a view corroborated by the veteran traveller Jayne Nash who lasted only three months in Le Havre:

> *Thirty plus hour weeks (not including preparation time), irregular hours at any time between 8am and 8pm with last-minute classes to cover for absent colleagues, and classes of mixed ability, soon took their toll. The money wasn't that good either. I felt my employer cared little for his employees. After three months I found myself under so much stress that I was obliged to leave, although I am normally not someone to shun a challenge or responsibility.*

A more realistic possibility is to offset the high cost of living in Paris by doing some tutoring which sometimes shades into au pairing. Language exchanges for room and board are commonplace in Paris and are usually arranged through advertisements (in the places described below in the section on Paris) or by word of mouth. Kathryn Kleypas studied the notice board at the American Church to good effect:

> *I contacted a family from the notice board and was invited to come over to their home for an interview and to meet the three children to whom I would be teaching English every day. I was not asked if I had any teaching experience, yet was offered the position which involved 18 hours of English teaching/conversation in exchange for room, board and F1,400 per month. My family took me with them to the seaside near Bordeaux in July and to their castle near Limoges during August.*

This is a good way for Americans and others to circumvent red tape difficulties as

Beth Mayer from New York found in Paris:

I tried to get a job at a school teaching, but they asked for working papers which I didn't have. I checked with several schools who told me that working papers and a university degree were more important than TEFL qualifications. So I placed an ad to teach English and offer editing services (I was an editor in New York City before moving here) and received many responses. I charged F80 per hour but found that after I had spent time going and coming, I earned only F40. It would be better to have the lessons at your apartment if centrally located. I not only 'taught' English but offered English conversation to French people who wanted practice. I met a lot of nice people this way and earned money to boot.

This is most commonly done in Paris though it can work just as easily in other French cities. The usual methods of advertising in newspapers, sticking up photocopied ads in libraries and stores such as Prisunic supermarkets could work. A telephone and answering machine are great assets in the initial stages. Conversation classes with adults are easier than teaching children but tend to pay less well. Employers often expect their teachers to have their own transport.

University language students who would like to spend a year as an English language *assistant* in a French school should contact the Language Assistants Team of the Central Bureau for International Education & Training (British Council, 10 Spring Gardens, London SW1A 2BN; 020-7389 4764). They send hundreds of undergraduates studying French at British universities and recent graduates aged 20-35 to spend an academic year in primary or secondary schools throughout France. Assistants only work 12 hours a week and are paid F5,734 (gross) a month. Similar posts are also available in other francophone countries, i.e. Belgium, Quebec (Canada) and Switzerland. As mentioned earlier, Americans can also become *assistants* for seven months between October and April through the French Consulate in New York.

CHILDCARE

Au pairing has always been a favoured way for young women to learn French and, increasingly, for young men too. The pocket money for au pairs in France is linked to the *SMIC* and is currently F1,700-F1,750 per month plus a city transport pass. Au pairs plus should earn F2,200 per month and nannies F4,000. There are dozens of agencies both in Britain (see list in *Childcare* chapter) and in France which arrange placements. Most agencies make enrolling in a French course a necessary condition.

CIJ offices and even ANPEs may have a list of families looking for live-in help, and this is the one category of work for which fluent French is unlikely to be a necessity. In Paris, the notice boards described below are always crammed with announcements of live-in positions and so there is little chance of being left jobless if you wait until arrival to look.

Quite a few foreigners are too hasty in arranging what seems at the outset a cushy number and only gradually realise how little they enjoy the company of children and how isolated they are if their family lives in the suburbs (as most do). Unless you actively like small children, it might be better to look for a free room in exchange for minimal babysitting (e.g. 12 hours a week). Matt Tomlinson went into his au pair job with his eyes open:

I'd heard too many horror stories from overworked and underpaid au pair friends to be careless, so chose quite carefully from the people who replied to my notice on the upstairs notice board of the British Church (just off the rue de Faubourg St Honoré). My employers were really laid back, in their mid-20s so more like living with an older brother and sister. The little boy was just over two whilst the little girl was three months old, and they were both completely adorable. On the whole it was great fun. Baking chocolate brownies, playing football and finger-painting may not be everybody's idea of a good time but there are certainly worse ways to earn a living (and learn French at the same time).

Although it is still more difficult for men than women to find au pair placements, France seems to be streets ahead of Britain in this respect, as Iain Croker reports:

I have had a thoroughly rewarding and enjoyable year as an au pair in France – so much so that I'm going back again in September for another year. Certainly in France there are quite a few male au pairs – four in my village near Fontainebleau alone. In my experience the boys tend to get placed in families with a lot of energetic children or families that have traditionally had a large turn-over of au pairs. After a year in the sticks with four kids I feel I have proved myself and my agency have offered me one of their best placements in Paris, one child and my own apartment. By the way, my agency (Soames International) is great.

Applying directly through a French agency is commonplace. The most established agencies are members of UFAAP, the Union Francaise des Associations Au Pair, an umbrella group set up in 1999, based at present at Butterfly et Papillon listed below. Their literature in English can also be requested by e-mail (ufa-aupair@egroups.com). The Union secretary says that member agencies place foreign students in French families free of charge, though several do state that they make a charge. Registration fees charged by other agencies, especially those attached to language schools, can be steep, e.g. over F1,000 even for short-term summer placements. Members of UFAAP include:

Alliance Francaise, 55 rue Paradie, 13006 Marseille (04-91 33 28 19; info@alliancefrmarseille.org).

Association Families Jeunesse, 4 rue Massena, 06000 Nice (04-93 82 28 22; domenge@webstore.fr).

Association Mary Poppins, 4 place de la Fontaine, 38120 la Fontanil (04-76 75 57 33; Mary.Poppins@wanadoo.fr).

Au Pair Contact International, 42 rue Monge, 75005 Paris (01-43 54 40 82; aupair.contact@mail.com).

Butterfly et Papillon, 5 avenue de Genève, 74000 Annecy (04-50 46 08 33; aupair.france@wanadoo.fr).

Europair Services, 13 rue Vavin, 75006 Paris (01-43 29 80 01; europairservices@wanadoo.fr).

France Au Pair - Eurojobs, 6 Allée des Saules, BP 29, 17420 Saint Palais sur Mer (05-46 23 99 88; contact@eurojob.fr/ www.eurojob.fr).

Institut Euro-Provence, 69 rue de Rome, 13001 Marseille (04-91 33 90 60; euro.provence@infonie.fr). Largest au pair agency in southern France. Registration fee is F1,100.

MCB Langues, B.P. 176, Caudéran, 188 av. Louis Barthou, 33020 Bordeaux (05-56 48 56 00; mcb.langues.bx@wanadoo.fr).

Oliver Twist Association Aquitaine Au Pair, 50 avenue de la California, 33600 Pessac (05-57 26 93 26; oliver.twist@wanadoo.fr).

Soames Paris Nannies, 6 route de Marlotte, 77690 Montigny sur Loing (01-64 78 37 98/fax 01-64 45 91 75; Soames.Parisnannies@wanadoo.fr).

Other established agencies include the following:

Accueil Familial des Jeunes Etrangers, 23 rue de Cherche-Midi, 75006 Paris (01-42 22 50 34/fax 01-45 44 60 48; afjeparis@aol.com). Registration fees F710 for summer stay, F680 for longer stay; higher for non-EU students.

Au-Pair Europea, B.P. 5050, 20 rue Victor Michelet, 83091 Toulon Cedex (04-94 62 83 83). Placements on the French Riviera and Corsica.

Inter-Séjours, 179 rue de Courcelles, 75017 Paris (01-47 63 06 81/fax 01-40 54 89 41; intersejours@europost.org). Incoming registration fee F880.

Laurence Cherifat Programmes Au Pair, 95 avenue Général Leclerc, Bat. B, 94700 Maisons Alfort (tel/fax 01-43 76 48 61; laurencecherifat@minitel.net).

Séjours Internationaux Linguistiques et Culturels, 32 Rempart de l'Est, 16022 Angouleme Cedex (05-45 97 41 45; www.silc.fr). Au pair and work placements throughout France.

By law, families are supposed to make social security payments to the local URSSAF office on the au pair's behalf, though not all do and you might want to enquire about this when applying. Au pairs in or near Paris should receive the *carte orange* (travel pass) which normally costs about £35 a month.

North Americans can fix up au pair placements directly with a French agency, bearing in mind that the high placement fees must be paid in advance and that in some cases very little information about the family is available at the time the fee must be paid.

BUSINESS & INDUSTRY

You will normally need impeccable French in order to work in a French office which eliminates the sort of temping jobs you may have had back home. If you are lucky enough to get a job in a French office – as Ben Nakoneczny did through a family connection – you may find yourself benefitting from such perks as a subsidised canteen serving French food and wine. With no contacts, Michael Jordan from St Louis Missouri had no luck when he mounted a job search in his field in Strasbourg which involved cycling round all the bakeries at 2am.

Fee-paying training and exchange programmes can provide an opening to employment in French business and industry. Andy Green participated in a scheme run by Interspeak (see introductory chapter *Business & Industry*) and spent two months in an office in Limoges. Since his role was mainly to observe rather than to work, he was unpaid by the firm to which he was attached, and by the time he had paid the agency fee and for food and accommodation, he was £1,000 out-of-pocket, yet still considered it all worthwhile for the experience. Interspeak now also offer 'mini-stages' which last just one or two weeks. These appeal mostly to 16-18 year olds with £500 at their disposal.

A cheaper way to find a base in France from which to improve your knowledge of the language is to participate in the work exchange programme offered by the Centre International d'Antibes, a French language school on the Côte d'Azur. Volunteers with the right to work in Europe do administrative or domestic work in exchange for board and lodging and/or French tuition. Details of the scheme are available from CIA, 38 boulevard d'Aguillon, 06600 Antibes (04-92 90 71 70; cia@imcn.com).

Anyone with secretarial skills and a knowledge of French has a chance of finding office work, particularly in Paris. The Syndicat des Entreprises de Travail Temporaire (SETT, 54-56 rue Laffitte, 75009 Paris) should be able to provide a list of temporary agencies specialising in bilingual secretarial staff. The Sheila Burgess Agency in Paris specialises in placing bilingual secretaries (62 rue St Lazare, 75009 Paris; 01-44 63 02 59).

A number of British-run building firms (not all of them licensed) are active in areas like the Dordogne where many English people build homes. You are more likely to come across building work informally as the American Peter Goldman did:

I was hitching south from Paris when a kind woman stopped near Tours. She was heading to her farm house near Bordeaux where a Dutchman was putting a new roof on the house. I explained that I had some experience in construction and I was hired on the spot. I worked for ten days, received F1,000 plus tons of food, beer and wine and a bed. The Dutchman was happy with my work and took me to Biddary near Bayonne to help him renovate another house. There I earned a small wage on top of all living expenses, learned a lot about European building methods, rural France and met some great people.

It can be profitable to let your fingers do the walking when you are in France: the telephone directory can be an invaluable ally when you are looking for new addresses to contact. Here are a few headings to look under: *Publicité direct* and *Distributeurs en publicité* for jobs handing out leaflets, *Déménagement* for house removals, *Entreprises de nettoyage* for domestic work cleaning houses and *Surveillance* for security work.

VOLUNTARY WORK

France has as wide a range of opportunities for voluntary work as any European country, and anyone who is prepared to exchange work for subsidised board and lodging should consider joining a voluntary project. Projects normally last two or three weeks during the summer and cost between F50 and F120 a day. Many foreign young people join one of these to learn basic French and make French contacts as well as to have fun.

Archaeology

A great many archaeological digs and building restoration projects are carried out each year. Every May the Ministry of Culture (Direction de l'Architecture et du Patrimoine, Sous-Direction de l'Archéologie, 4 rue d'Aboukir, 75002 Paris; 01-40 15 77 81) publishes a national list of excavations throughout France requiring up to 5,000 volunteers which can be consulted on its website (www.culture.fr/fouilles). Most *départements* have *Services Archéologiques* which organise digs. Without relevant experience you will probably be given only menial jobs but many like to share in the satisfaction of seeing progress made.

Anthony Blake describes the dig he joined which the History Department of the University of Le Mans runs every summer:

> *Archaeology is hard work. Applicants must be aware of what working 8.30am-noon and 2-6.30pm in baking heat means! That said, I thoroughly enjoyed the working holiday: excellent company (75% French so fine opportunity to practise French), weekends free after noon on Saturday, good lunches in SNCF canteen, evening meals more haphazard as prepared by fellow diggers. Accommodation simple but adequate.*

Here is a selection of other digs. Bear in mind that most digs will charge unskilled volunteers for board and lodging, perhaps F40 per day.

Laboratoire d'Anthropologie, UMR 6566 du CNRS, Université de Rennes I, Campus de Beaulieu, 35042 Rennes Cedex (02-99 28 16 30; Jean-Laurent.Monnier@univ.rennes1.fr). Summer digs in Brittany.

Muséum National d'Histoire Naturelle, Lab. de Préhistoire, IPH, 1 rue René Panhard, 75013 Paris (att: Professor Henry de Lumley). Human palaeontology, pre-history and archaeology students/specialists preferred who can stay for at least a month in the summer. Excavations of pre-historic sites carry on July, August and September each year in Southeast France.

Arkeos, Musée de la Chartreuse, Service Archéologique, 191 rue St-Albin, 59500 Douai (03-27 71 38 90/fax 3-27 71 38 93; arkeos@wanadoo.fr/ http://arkeos.org). Summer dig on a Mèrovingian abbey and mediaeval town.

Louis Roussel, 52 rue des Forges, 21000 Dijon (louisroussel@hotmail.com). Annual July dig near Dijon. Project includes sketching, model-making and restoration of finds. Volunteers contribute F100 per week.

Conservation

France takes the preservation of its heritage *(patrimoine)* very seriously and there are numerous groups both local and national engaged in restoring churches, windmills, forts and other historic monuments. Many are set up to accept foreign volunteers, though they tend to charge more than archaeological digs.

APARE, Association pour la Participation et l'Action Régionale, 41 cours Jean Jaurès, 84000 Avignon (04-90 85 51 15; www.apare-gec.org). An umbrella organisation which runs a total of 20 work sites in southern France. Cost of F750 for adults, F2,000 for teenagers for three weeks.

Chantiers d'Etudes Medievales, 4 rue du Tonnelet Rouge, 67000 Strasbourg (tel/fax 03-88 37 17 20). F500 for 15 days of restoring mediaeval monuments.

Club du Vieux Manoir, Ancienne Abbaye du Moncel, 60700 Pontpoint (03-44 72 33 98). Board and lodging cost F80 per day.

REMPART, 1 rue des Guillemites, 75004 Paris (01-42 71 96 55/fax 01-42 71 73 00; Minitel 3616 REMPART; www.rempart.com). Similar to the National Trust in Britain, in charge of 140 endangered monuments around France. Most projects charge F40-50 per day plus F220 for membership and insurance. Registration must be done by post.

La Sabranenque, Centre International, rue de la Tour de l'Oume, 30290 Saint Victor la Coste (04-66 50 05 05; www.sabranenque.com). Approximately F1,300 per fortnight. US applicants should contact Jacqueline Simon, 217 High Park Blvd, Buffalo, NY 14226 (716-836-8698).

UNAREC (Etudes et Chantiers), 33 Rue Compagne, Premiere, 75014 Paris (01-45 38

96 26; www.unarec.org). Environmental workcamps. Registration F600 plus F100 membership and F50 insurance.

Try to be patient if the project you choose turns out to have its drawbacks, since these organisations depend on voluntary leaders as well as participants. Judy Greene volunteered to work with a conservation organisation and felt herself to be 'personally victimised by the lack of organisation and leadership' or more specifically by one unpleasantly racist individual on her project. Tolerance may be called for, especially if your fellow volunteers lack it.

PARIS

Like all major cities in the developed world, Paris presents thousands of ways to earn your keep, while being difficult to afford from day to day. Unless you are very lucky, you will have to arrive with some money with which to support yourself while you look around. Check notice boards, the weekly property paper *Particular à Particulier* published on Thursdays or (if you can afford it) use an agency which will cost you at least a month's rent but will help to ensure that you get your deposit of two months' rent back.

The Grapevine

There are expatriate grapevines all over Paris, very helpful for finding work and accommodation. Most people find their jobs as well as accommodation through one of the city's many notice boards *(panneaux)*. The one in the foyer of the CIDJ at 101 Quai Branly *(métro* Bir-Hakeim) is good for occasional studenty-type jobs such as extras in movies, but sometimes there are adverts for full-time jobs or *soutien scolaire en Anglais* (English tutor). It is worth arriving early to check for new notices (the hours for most CIDJ services are Monday-Friday 9.30am-6pm and Saturday 9.30am-1pm). Another job which is increasingly advertised at the CIDJ is that of *coursier* or courier. Unlike their counterparts in London, Parisian couriers do not have to take their lives into their hands since they travel by *métro* to the various offices where packages and documents have to be delivered. The pay is quite reasonable and cash-in-hand.

The other mecca for job and flat-hunters is the American Church at 65 Quai d'Orsay (01-40 62 05 00; *métro* Invalides). Official notices are posted on various notice boards inside and out; the cork board in the basement is a free board where anybody can stick up a notice. You will bump into lots of other people studying the board here, and so it is a good place to make contacts. Obviously it is necessary to consult the notices in person; they are not available by phoning the church or on the internet.

The American Cathedral in Paris at 23 avenue George V (www.us.net/amcathedral-paris; *métro* Alma Marceau or George V) has a notice board featuring employment opportunities and housing listings. The Cathedral also offers volunteering opportunities as well as career forums for job-seekers. Also check the two British churches where there are few employment or language exchange notices: St Georges Anglican at 7 rue Auguste-Vacquerie in the 16th *arrondissement* and its sister church St Michael's at 5 rue d'Aguesseau in the 8th *(métro* Madeleine). These churches are happy to provide notice boards as a way of helping people get settled in Paris but they are not employment agencies.

The British Institute at 11 rue de Constantine has a notice board with some live-in tutoring and au pair jobs. Although the notice board at the Alliance Francaise (101 Boulevard Raspail; *métro* Notre Dame des Champs) is for the use of registered students of French, you may be able to persuade a student to look at the adverts for you, many of which are exchanges of room for some babysitting and/or teaching. The notice board is in the annex around the corner at 34 rue de Fleurus.

The book and website *Paris-Anglophone* by David Applefield is a good source of all kinds of information about Paris including some information for people who want to work in the city. For example it lists companies and employment agencies on-line which might want to hire English speakers ($14.95 plus postage from 32 rue Edouard-Vaillant, 93100 Montreuil; www.paris-anglo.com).

Arguably the most eccentric bookshop in Europe is Shakespeare and Company at 37 rue de la Bûcherie in the fifth *arrondissement* (on the south side of the Seine). It has a small notice board, but is more useful as a place to chat up other expats about work and accommodation. The shop operates as a writer's guest house. If you are prepared to write a short account of yourself, you can stay free for up to a week, assuming there is space. The elderly American expat owner George Whitman (grandson of Walt) still hosts weekly Sunday open house for aspiring *literati* and also hires English-speaking staff to clean, run errands and work behind the till. When Claire Judge was just 17, she was given a room overlooking Notre Dame in exchange for two hours of work a day.

Most expat places like WH Smith's Bookshop near the Place de la Concorde and the Virgin Megastore on the Champs Elysées distribute the free bilingual English newsletter *France-USA Contacts* or *FUSAC* (www.fusac.com) which comes out every other Wednesday. It comprises mainly classified adverts which are best followed up on the day the paper appears. It is possible to place an ad before your arrival in France. An advert in *FUSAC* costs US$20 for 20 words, and can be e-mailed to franceusa@aol.com or sent in the US to France Contacts at PO Box 115, Coopers Station, New York, NY 10276; 212-777-5553/fax 212-777-5554). Ask to place your ad under the heading 'Work wanted in France'. Alternatively you can pay $15 to have a notice posted at the magazine's Paris office for ten days. Other possible sources of job and accommodation leads are the weekly free ads paper *J'Annonce* and *Paris Voice*.

As usual pubs are a good place to pick up job tips. Try any of Paris's growing number of Irish pubs including Tigh Johnny's (55 rue Montmartre), Molly Malone's (21 rue de Godot de Maure in the 9th arrondissement) or Kitty O'Shea's at 10 rue des Capucines on the right bank.

Disneyland Paris

The enormous complex of Disneyland Paris, 30km east of Paris at Marne-la-Vallée, has 5,800 hotel rooms and an entertainment centre as well as the theme park, employing about 12,000 people in high season both on long-term and seasonal contracts. Seasonal positions are from March or May to September. The minimum period covers the high season from 15th June to 31st August.

'Cast members' (Disneyspeak for employees) must all have a conversational level of French and preferably a third European language. The majority of jobs are in food and beverage, housekeeping, merchandising and custodial departments, though one of the best jobs is as a character like Micky Mouse. The French standard working week is 35 hours long for which staff are paid F6,982 a month (gross); social security deductions will be about F1,000. Travel expenses are reimbursed on completion of a contract and assistance is given in finding accommodation. Further details are available from Service du Recruitement-Casting, Disneyland Paris, BP 110, 77777 Marne-la-Vallée Cedex 4 (01-49 31 19 99). Specific vacancies at Disneyland Paris are often registered with EURES, the European Employment Service which can be accessed through any Jobcentre. For all jobs the well-scrubbed look is required (though the no facial hair rule has recently been dropped), and of course they are looking for the usual friendly, cheerful and outgoing personalities.

Whether you will be impressed by the fringe benefits is a matter of individual taste; they consist of discounts on merchandise and in the hotels, some free entrances to the theme park itself and the possibility of 'meeting' the occasional superstar.

Specific Jobs

The job hunt in Paris is probably somewhat easier these days than the one Mark Davies described:

> *Although it has taken me five and a half weeks to find paid employment (plongeur in a creperie) I console myself with the fact that there is high unemployment here at the moment. To give you an example, I turned up as stated on the job notice at 5pm for a dishwashing job, and there were eight other people doing the same, and they were by no means all poor-looking immigrants. The pay for the job I'm doing now is lousy but it pays the rent while I look for something better. But as long as I'm in the Jardin du Luxembourg and the sun is shining I can't complain.*

Stephen Psallidas describes the outcome of pounding the pavements in his job-hunt:

Faced with the prospect of sleeping under the Eiffel Tower to save the few pounds I had left, I went around all the Greek restaurants in the Quartier Huchette in the Latin Quarter (métro St Michel) and found a job in half an hour. I started straightaway, and worked there for five weeks. I wish I could say it was good, but it was a terrible job. I worked 12 or 13 hours every day doing the bar, preparing food, serving, etc. I was paid very poorly – around F180 cash in hand... The only reason I stayed so long was because I was getting two free meals a day and, what with working all day, I didn't spend a centime on my social life since I was continually shattered. So I saved F100 a day (after spending F80 at the youth hostel) but I was going slowly mad.

Sarit Moas from Israel doggedly enquired at all the restaurants and street food stalls until she got a job selling crepes and taffy in the Tuilleries amusement parks. Since that time Haagen-Dasz ice cream outlets have sprung up in various locations and are always hiring staff.

Although many restaurants insist on work papers and social security numbers, other do not. Pay is usually *SMIC* plus tips and one or two meals a day, although an experienced waiter with excellent French could make over F500 per night. There are many American-style fast food restaurants which employ a majority of non-French staff. Among the best known employers are the Quick chain (with outlets in high profile places like the Boulevard St. Michel, Boulevard Poissonniere and Place de la République) and the Chicago Pizza Pie Factory (5 rue de Berri, 75008 Paris; *métro* George V; 01-45 62 50 23). The related Chicago Meatpackers at 8 rue Coquillière (01-40 28 02 33; métro Les Halles) also has a high staff turnover. If you write in advance, the most that will happen is that they will write to assure you that you will be offered an interview after arrival in Paris. If you show up, you will be asked to fill out an application form before seeing the manager on duty. If there is a vacancy (as there often is) you could be offered a 45-hour-a-week job at SMIC rates plus tips and one meal a day.

Survival

Talented musicians should consider joining the buskers on the Left Bank on a Friday or Saturday night and graduating to the highly competitive métro. Transit authorities issue licences (free of charge) which allow you to perform in prescribed locations. Playing on the trains themselves is not allowed, though many ignore the regulations.

It has been mentioned elsewhere in this book that English churches are often helpful sources of contacts. Jonathan Poulton found himself very short of money in Menton (near Monte Carlo) after discovering that the starting date of his job in a patisserie had been postponed. He wandered into the English church which happened to be next door, explained his situation to the vicar and within five minutes had secured a job as a gardener for one of the congregation. Religious foundations also run many emergency shelters and free hostels throughout France. The only catch according to Dustie Hickey's is that they are almost all for men only, which she considers grossly unfair.

Julian Peachey made use of the Night Shelter in Marseille when he arrived to look for work:

I looked around for likely helpful characters and asked a young man, obviously penniless, where to stay. He told me to go to the Accueil de Nuit in rue Plumier near Vieilleport. This was run by a Catholic order and the routine was very strict: entry between 7.00 and 7.10pm, in bed by 9pm, up at 5am, and out by 6.30am. This did however allow me to recover from my long hitch-hiking journey, without having to spend my emergency fund.

Look up *Foyers/Asiles de Nuit* in the telephone directory or ask a *gendarme* on the beat. According to a BBC 1 documentary shown in 2000, 'Brits Abroad', begging is legal in France and people are generous. One British beggar being interviewed on the Cote d'Azur was raking in £300 per week while his accommodation and meals were paid for by the council.

See the section on Regulations earlier in this chapter on how to claim housing benefit. Alternatively, you could try to make ends meet by house-sitting; check adverts in the *Lady* magazine.

If you would like to survive in rural France, communal living is a possibility. Roberta Wedge enjoyed several months at the 'bleakly beautiful' Le Cun de Larzac Peace Centre (Route de Saint-Martin, 12100 Millau; 05-65 60 62 33) and says that they need work-for-keep volunteers in the summer to look after visitors, tend the gardens, preserve the fruit, etc.

Dozens of French communes are listed in *Diggers and Dreamers* (see the introductory chapter *Agriculture*) and in the Australian WWOOF list. Several Gandhian Communities of the Ark accept volunteers, including La Borie Noble (34650 Roqueredonde; 04-67 44 09 89) and La Flayssière (34650 Joncels; 04-67 44 40 90). Robert Abblett moved from one community to another with mixed results:

From the Australian WWOOF list, I found the address of Les Courmettes. This was my favourite WWOOF for it was situated on an 800 metre plateau above the Côte d'Azur. I spent a wonderful $3^1/2$ weeks here in August 1998 in a most peaceful place camping and swinging in my hammock, contemplating life and exploring the top of the mountain nearby naked. On my days off I would go swimming in some of the most beautiful rivers and swimming holes with the other volunteers. I would work four days washing up followed by three days off. My French really helped me enjoy the experience.

Then I hitched down to an anarchist commune called Longo Mai near Forcalquier with its own radio station and met some of the most unfriendly people, who openly criticised my lifestyle and goals. This was hard, but I stuck it out and did find a few gentle souls amongst them.

If you are more into private enterprise, you may wish to follow Tessa Shaw's example. She learned that there were many edible snails to be found along the canal and river banks in the *département* of Vaucluse which she could sell in the market. The snails move about only on still, dank nights: so Tessa would be found between the hours of 2am and 7am scouring the waterside with the help of a torch. She would then keep them in a sack or bin for four or five days until they exuded all the poison in their systems, and then sell them in the market of Carpentras. There is a closed season for snail collecting between April 1st and June 30th.

While you're waiting for something to turn up, it is possible to sleep in parks, railway stations or on beaches, though this is unlikely to be trouble-free. Do not consider spending the night at the Gare de Lyons unless you can produce a current ticket since the patrolling police will not be over-gentle when evicting you. T. J. Coles recommends the pebble beach at Nice, though the police regularly arrive at 2.30am shouting *'Debout Debout'*.

Lee Merrick found the UCRIF Etapes Jeunes (27 rue de Turbigo, BP 6407, 75064 Paris Cedex 02; 01-40 26 57 64; www.ucrif.asso.fr) very helpful for accommodation both in Paris and beyond. They have 54 residential centres throughout France, including nine in Paris, which are about the cheapest hostel accommodation available and largely frequented by young people from overseas.

CORSICA

Although the island of Corsica is officially a French *département,* the inhabitants have more in common with Sardinians than with the mainland French. There is a large proportion of Arabs from North Africa who are willing to work hard for low wages, so there will always be competition for casual work. Corsica is a poor and undeveloped region, but its warm climate does create a few opportunities in farming and tourism for the working traveller.

K. McCausland found the ANPE in Porto Vecchio on Route D'Arca (04-95 70 21 65) to be surprisingly helpful, given that there is quite a measure of local animosity to incomers. In the end, he was so put off by the frequent spectacle of road signs riddled with bullet holes that he didn't pursue the idea of working in Corsica. The Corsican separatist movement is active, so caution is advised.

Tourism

The tourist industry is concentrated in a small number of towns: Ajaccio the capital, Bastia, Bonifacio, Calvi, Ile Rousse and Propriano. Unfortunately these have been the occasional targets of separatists' bombs. Anyone with a knowledge of German would be at an advantage since the level of German tourism in Corsica is very high. Kathryn Halliwell found her job in the hotel Sofitel at Portticio, a resort about 12km down the coast from Ajaccio, by the time-honoured method of asking from door to door. She worked as a chambermaid on a hotel staff of 150, and mentioned that the worst problem faced by the female members of staff was the level of unwelcome attention from local Arab men.

Alison Cooper found the heat to be a more serious impediment to her enjoyment of her summer as a Eurocamp courier in Corsica, but managed to have a great season:

I enjoyed this job immensely even if it did get unbearably hot when it's 40°C and you're trying to clean a tent in direct sunlight with a hangover. We had one and a half days off a week on average with a fantastic beach to go and chill out on, or a quick dip in the campsite pool after cleaning. On the whole it was a good summer.

The British tour company Simply Travel (King's House, Wood St, Kingston-upon-Thames, Surrey KT1 1SG; 020-8541 2227; personnel@simply-travel.com) employs resort reps (fluent in French and over 24) and more junior staff in resorts throughout the island. The latter receive only pocket money in addition to living expenses. Try also VFB Holidays, Normandy House, High St, Cheltenham, Glos. GL50 3FB (01242 57644; www.vfb.co.uk) which employs French-speaking reps for the whole season from late April to early October.

Farm Work

Although Corsica is not as far south as Greece, many sub-tropical fruits such as kiwifruit, clementines and avocados thrive. Most of this fruit ripens in mid-November and is picked through December. There is also an important grape harvest which takes place in September/early October.

The best region to try for fruit-picking work is the fertile area on the east coast especially around Bastia and half-way down around Aleria. Vineyards are concentrated along the coast to the north of Calvi, around Ajaccio and Sartene. Grapes are picked around Pianottoli Caldarello, a town between Sartene and Bonifacio. Ask at the local farming co-operative, though be prepared for stiff competition, as Sian Gronow encountered:

Although the Moroccans cannot write, they seemed to have addresses of vineyards and clementine farmers. The co-operatives we asked had a pre-arranged work force. I also had the impression that as girls, we would have problems working with the single Moroccan men.

If you haven't got a job to go to and you can't speak French, it will be very difficult to get someone to accommodate and employ you when there are dozens of North African migrant workers to do the job.

Perseverance paid off for Rob Abblett who had the address of a farmer in northern Corsica to whom he had written three times over the years, enclosing French references and s.a.e. Finally, in autumn 2000 the phone call came and Rob took a no-frills flight to Sardinia (£80 on Ryanair) and on to Corsica by ferry:

I arrived at the orchard and am now living in a little simple one-bed building with kitchen, loo and shower on the property. It's really quiet and peaceful (no TV, radio or people), only the third time in my life that I have experienced this solitude. A time to shore up my 'battered timbers' from years of travel. My days are spent quietly snipping away at the clementines with the pungent aroma of oranges in the air and the cool sunshine on my head. I work hard and long and my boss seems to have taken a shine to me and lets me have the accommodation rent-free. I started in mid-November and have signed a contract to stay until the end of the harvest about 10th January although I have been offered the chance of staying until May doing the pruning. It's a hell of a long time to live so quietly with only the sound of a fire to occupy me. But I hope at some point to get some time off to go exploring this beautiful (though expensive) island with its history of violence and rebellion.

Germany

Ever since the reunification of Germany in 1990, foreign workers have been flocking to Germany especially from Poland, the former Yugoslavia and other eastern European countries but also from Portugal, Vietnam, Ireland and Britain to join the millions of Turkish *gastarbeiter* (guest workers) who have been in Germany for more than a generation. Good job prospects and high wages attracted them both before and since recession loomed in 1999. The unemployment rate is falling sharply at present and the number of unfilled vacancies steadily climbing (534,600 in October 2000 compared to 474,000 the previous year). Unemployment is still higher in the former East Germany but the tide of movement from east to west in search of jobs and prosperity has diminished over the past decade.

Job opportunities abound for foreigners and students, especially in certain regions such as Bavaria and in fields of employment such as hotels and fast food, nursing and skilled building trades. Anyone who has a reasonable command of German can expect to find decently paid work at some level in Germany.

The Regulations

If you are an EU national you are free to travel to Germany to look for work. However if you want to stay more than three months, you will be subject to the labyrinthine bureaucracy, as David Hughes from the UK discovered when he went to Frankfurt to take up a job as a nurse:

I believe (hope) we've finished our dealings with those German bureaucrats. Cumbersome is the exact adjective. I'm not sure about why or what we were doing some of the time. After establishing myself here as a legal worker, I fully understand the writings of Franz Kafka!

The first step is to obtain the *Anmeldebestätigung* (the registration document required by Germans as well as foreigners) from the local authority *(Einwohnermeldeamt)* or *Meldenstelle.* Go to your local town hall *(Ortsamt* or *Rathaus)* to pick up the right form *(Anmeldung)* which will have to be signed by your landlord as proof that you have a German address and are therefore entitled to an ID card. People who are not in rented or owned accommodation will have problems. One young job-seeker staying at a youth hostel in Berlin described it, 'I was trapped for a week in a vicious circle of no job – no papers – no accommodation; without one of these it is very difficult to get the others.'

If you do have a job and accommodation, the application for a residence permit should be straightforward. Go to the aliens' authority *(Ausländerbehorde* or *Ausländeramt)* to apply for an *Aufenthaltserlaubnis* (residence permit) or *Aufenthaltsgenehmigung* (valid up to three years). Take all your processed documents, your passport and three photos. David Hughes offers a word of advice:

> On the opening times of offices: absurd, ridiculous, inconvenient and too bloody early are thoughts that spring to mind. For example the aliens office in Frankfurt is open Monday, Wednesday and Friday from 7.30am to 1pm; tough if you're already working. Be prepared for hordes of other hopefuls. We arrived at 6.20am, queued till 8am and were finished by 8.30am. On a curiosity note, we had to sign a form saying that if at the end of five years, we can't speak German, we must leave, which must surely go against the European constitution.

Apparently the situation is far worse in Berlin where queues form at 4am in order to be processed the same day.

Raids on hotels, restaurants, building sites, etc. are becoming more frequent to clamp down on people working black *(Schwartzarbeiter)*, including illegal workers from Eastern Europe and elsewhere. Employers can now be fined up to £10,000 for employing illegal workers. For many jobs (e.g. childcare, food service, etc.) you must also acquire a *Gesundheitszeugnis* (health certificate) from the local *Gesundheitsamt* (health department). Again, restaurants will be heavily fined if they are caught employing anyone without it. When you go for the medical examination, you will have to produce the proper form *(Anmeldung)* which you have purchased earlier as well as a hefty fee (from DM80). You return a week later, and then your *Gesundheitszeugnis* will be posted. Whereas this works smoothly for some, Ann Barkett was given the run-around in Munich:

> It took three weeks to complete the medical exam and receive the results, because the doctor required me to meet with her personally for the results. Her office failed to inform me that the results had not arrived, therefore causing me to make several unnecessary trips (for which I was billed!)

Non-EU Regulations

The most important document for Americans and other non-Europeans to obtain is the *Aufenthaltserlaubnis* or residence permit. For this, applicants will require a notarised certificate of good conduct, evidence of health insurance as well as a *Gesundheitszeugnis* (as above), proof of accommodation and means of support. The permit must specify that employment is permitted before the bearer has any chance of going on to obtain an *Arbeitslaubnis* (work permit) from the *Arbeitsamt* (Employment Office, described below).

Maree Lakey from Australia fixed up a position as an au pair with a family in Frankfurt and was determined to do things by the book:

> I applied for a visa at the German Consulate in Melbourne which I was told was essential before I left the country. Despite applying three months in advance, it didn't come through until a few days before I was due to fly, and only then because I had phoned my host-mother in Germany and asked her to enquire personally from her end. The initial visa needed to be extended after three months which involved an enormous amount of paper work and leg work on my part.

Special Schemes

Council Exchanges administer two programmes in Germany. American students who have studied some German at college can work for up to three months between mid-

May and mid-October or students who can fix up a career-related internship can work for up to six months at any time of year. In the US details may be requested by phoning 1-888-COUNCIL (www.councilexchanges.org). Council's office in Germany can be found at Oranienburger Str. 13-14, 10178 Berlin (030-28 48 59-0; InfoGermany@ councilexchanges.de/ www.council.de).

InterExchange in New York can place full-time students in German resorts during the summer provided they have intermediate German. Applications must be in by the middle of February.

Similar six-month internships for American students or recent graduates in business, engineering or technical fields are available through CDS International Inc. (871 United Nations Plaza, 15th Floor, New York, NY 10017-1814; 212-497-3500/ www.cdsintl.org). If needed, the first month can be spent at an intensive language course in Cologne, after which participants undertake a paid internship which they have secured previously with the help of the Carl Duisberg Gesellschaft e.V. (CDG), the partner organisation of CDS International. Longer placements of 12-18 months are also available.

The IJAB (International Youth Exchange) in Bonn has a EuroDesk which administers various student and employment exchanges (Hochkreuzallee 20, 53170 Bonn; 0228-95 06 208/ www.ijab.de). The Happy Hands working holiday scheme places gap year students from the UK and other students from Europe who know some German in the field of rural tourism. Participants are given monthly pocket money of DM300 and full board and lodging with families on farms or in country hotels. In return they look after children and/or horses, farm animals. The preferred stay is three to six months though a six-week commitment is also allowed; details available from Happy Hands, Roemerberg 8, 60311 Frankfurt; 069-293733; Anne.Gleichen@t-online.de/ www.workingholidays.de. The registration fee is a steep DM450. Note that the scheme is also open to unemployed people on benefit.

Interspeak is a UK-based work experience placement agency that can place young people who have studied German in hotels, coffee shops and on farms in Germany especially Westphalia; details from Interspeak, Stretton Lower Hall, Stretton, Cheshire SY14 7HS (01829 250641/ www.interspeak.co.uk/german.htm). Placements last 8-24 weeks year round and include full board accommodation plus pocket money of DM300 a month; the placement fee starts at £500.

Alliances Abroad (702 West Avenue, Austin, TX 78701; info@alliancesabroad. com) places interns in unpaid company positions in their field of interest in or near major German cities. Internships can be fixed up for one to three months for a substantial fee.

The AGABUR Foundation Inc (9 Eastwood Road, Storrs, CT 06268; 860-429-1279; austin@uconnvm.uconn.edu/ www.mannheim-program.necaweb.com) runs a professional programme in Germany consisting of language training, university study and optional paid internships. The summer programme costs $2,900 plus $500 for an internship in a German firm.

Tax

You can use the *Anmeldebestätigung* (residence permit) to obtain a *Lohnsteuerkarte* (tax card) or a *steuernummer* (tax number). Legal workers can expect to lose between 33% and 40% of their gross wages in tax and social security contributions unless they earn less than the personal allowance (about DM12,500). One of the taxes included in the tax bill is a church tax *(Kirchensteuer)* which accounts for 8-9% of income tax, unless you claim an exemption due to atheism (and thereby forego the possibility of ever being married or buried in a German church).

Emma Forster visited the tax office *(Finanzamt)* in Hamburg after working for two months and was told that she was entitled to all her tax back. When you finish work in Germany, take your *Lohnsteuerkarte* to the tax office and complete a declaration of earnings *(Steuerklärung)* and hope that you are eligible to receive a rebate, which will be transferred to your home bank account.

Students taking up a short-term job in the Federal Republic of Germany during their university vacations for not longer than 183 days should be exempt from German income tax, provided they can prove to their German employer that they are enrolled

North Sea

NETHERLANDS

Fehmarn

Heiligenhafen

Burg

Baltic Sea

Timmendorf

Travemunde

Rostock

Stade

HAMBURG

Altland

Verden

Munster

Minden

Hannover

BERLIN

Paderborn

GERMANY

Iserlohn

Göttingen

Dusseldorf

Cologne

Bonn

Eschwege

Giessen

Rhine

B

Koblenz

Mosel

Piesport

Rheingau

Bernkastel

Ruwer

Trier

Nahe

L

Saarburg

Saar

Rudesheim

Mainz

Nierstein

FRANKFURT

Darmstadt

Rheinhessen

Alzey

Bergstrasse

Franconia

Wurzburg

Bamberg

Neustadt

Deidesheim

Heidelberg

Nürnberg

Zirndorf

Bohmer Wald

FRANCE

Baden-Baden

Stuttgart

Baden

Wurttemberg

Black Forest

Neckar Valley

Neu-Ulm

CZECHOSLOVAKIA

Freiburg

Augsburg

Bavaria

Passau

Ravensburg

MUNICH

Friedrichshafen

Lake Constance

Fussen

Bavarian Alps

Chiemsee

Garmisch Partenkirchen

SWITZERLAND

Oberstdorf

Mittenwald

AUSTRIA

WILLIAM SWAN

in higher education. Students who are eligible should go the local German tax office before completing their summer contracts and file a claim. They should also make their student status known to prospective employers, for whom student employees are cheaper than non-students. Other categories which are exempted from tax (but not social security contributions of about 13%) are teachers and professors (from the EU) who work in Germany for less than two years.

You will need your processed *Anmeldung* to open a bank account. Anyone who can show a student card will be exempt from bank charges.

German National Employment Service

The *Bundesanstalt für Arbeit* (Regenburgerstr. 104, 90237 Nürnberg; www. arbeitsamt.de) is the Federal Employment Institute. Although private employment agencies now operate, these are still strictly controlled and the state agency still dominates employment in Germany. The whole of Germany is covered by the Bundesanstalt's network. There are 181 principal *Arbeitsamter* (employment offices) and a further 660 branch offices. These are all connected by a number of co-ordinating offices which handle both applications and vacancies that cannot be filled locally.

Arbeitsamter are entitled to refuse to help you if you do not have residence papers though the self-service system (SIS) means that anyone can inspect job vacancy information updated daily on SIS computer terminals. Even before this computerised system was introduced, many praised the efficiency of the *Arbeitsamt*, among them Nick Langley who used the one in Munich near the U-bahn station Goetheplatz:

> *Germany has one of the most efficient National Employment Services in the world. In Munich there is a massive modern complex which is organised on the basis of different departments handling job vacancies for different work categories such as building and construction, engineering, restaurant work, hotel work, etc. It may be necessary to visit several departments to maximise your chances of a job. Each department has counsellors to handle enquiries, tell you what's on offer and arrange interviews. There is also a microfiche reader listing hundreds of vacancies in the area. I was immediately offered a job at a new Burger King restaurant about to open in the main station.*

The full address is Kapuzinerstrasse 26, 80337 Munich (Muenchen@arbeitsamt.de; www.arbeitsamt.de/muenchen).

Not all *Arbeitsamter* are as co-operative as the Munich one. Emma Forster doesn't mince words:

> *Firstly don't waste your time going to the employment offices. You have to wait hours in order to be laughed out of the place. Our reception was cooler than cool.*

However, if you speak German and aren't in a hurry, it's probably worth registering. Look for their weekly publication *Markt und Chance* which lists job vacancies.

It is possible to use the Federal Employment Service from outside Germany. The Zentralstelle für Arbeitsvermittlung (Central Placement Office) has an international department *(Auslandsabteilung)* for dealing with applications from German-speaking people abroad. Details and application forms are available from ZAV, Villemombler Str. 76, 53123 Bonn (0228-713-0; fax 0228-713 1111; www.arbeitsamt.de). All applications from abroad are handled by this office. Although people of any nationality can apply through the Zentralstelle, only citizens of EU countries who have German language skills are entitled to expect the same treatment as a German. People of other nationalities are accepted only within the framework of special exchange programmes and government-approved schemes such as the one administered by CDS International mentioned above.

There is one exception to this rule. The Zentralstelle has a special department which finds summer jobs for students of any nationality, because this is felt to be mutually beneficial to employers and employees alike. Students who wish to participate in this scheme should contact the Zentralstelle before March. Students must be at least 18 years old, have a good command of German and be available to work for at least two months. ZAV places students in all kinds of jobs, but mainly in hotels and restaurants, in industry and agriculture. The Zentralstelle assigns jobs centrally, according to employers' demands and the level of the candidate's spoken German. For example those with fluent German may be found service jobs while those without will be given jobs such as chambermaiding and dishwashing. If you decline the first job offered by the Zentralstelle, you may not be offered another.

The Bundesanstalt also operates mobile temporary employment offices, called *Service-Vermittlung* in addition to permanent *Arbeitsamter.* These are set up as an emergency measure where employers need extra workers immediately for short periods of time. It is, however, worth looking for them at any of the trade exhibitions and wine or beer festivals in which the Germans take such delight.

Other Sources of Work

Anyone with office experience and a knowledge of German should look for branches of private employment agencies such as Adia, Manpower and Interim in the big cities; these will be listed in the *Gelbe Seiten* (Yellow Pages) under *Personalberatung* or *Stellenvermittlungsburo.* A German reader Brigitte Blanka noticed agency advertisements in Bonn and recommends looking out for Persona Service in major German cities.

To avoid bureaucracy completely, EU nationals with a student card should try the *studentische arbeitsvermittlung* in all German universities. Casual jobs like babysitting and cleaning are registered with the student job service attached to the ASTA students' council. One traveller from Glasgow visited the Student *Arbeitsamt* in Munich (with a forged student card) and within an hour was working on a building site.

Most of the main dailies like *Frankfurter Allgemeine Zeitung* carry their job supplements on Saturdays which go on sale on Friday evening. *BZ* in Berlin has a good selection of vacancies for unskilled people.

The Irish agency mentioned in the chapter on the Netherlands recruits workers for Germany too, as described in 2000 by Darren Slevin from County Westmeath:

> *I am working in a baumschule (tree nursery) in the village of Rostrop near Oldenburg in northern Germany. I got the job through an agency FTS, 24 Upper Fitzwilliam St, Dublin 2 (+353-1-676 54125). Accommodation, transport to and from work and insurance are provided. Our boss pays FTS 26 marks per hour but we only receive 11 marks which is very unfair. But the working conditions are quite good. Before I came to Germany, I assumed the people would be cold and aloof but I've found them to be very friendly and generous people. On cold mornings, my supervisor gives us brandy or rum to warm us up. Even those with only a few words of English make the effort to talk and on St. Patrick's Day, our boss came with us to an Irish pub in Oldenburg.*

Darren describes the various jobs at Bruns – the largest tree nursery company in Europe – including tree-planting, removing the trees with a mechanised digger, wrapping the trees in netting (very hard on the back) and the cushiest job working on the trailer, guiding the netted trees into position. Long hours meant that Darren was clearing £200+ a week.

If you are looking for labouring or other casual work after arriving in Germany, seek out the local Irish bar or British pub. There are dozens of these from the Oscar Wilde in Berlin to the English Shop in Stuttgart. All tend to be staffed by British and Irish people and are often meeting places for expat workers.

Accommodation

Flats and apartments are not as scarce as they were but accommodation is still expensive. Many find it necessary to go through an agency. *Mitwohnzentralen* are helpful and charge less than many other agencies (some charge two months' rent); in Emma Forster's case the fee charged by the *Mitwohnzentral* in Hamburg was a quarter of a month's rent. There is even a facility for people who are looking for flat-mates. Even here you may not be free of German bureaucracy since some agencies will not take you onto their books without a *Burgschaft*, the name and address of a local referee. If you are chasing a flat through the classifieds of a local paper, be warned that the competition will probably buy the first edition in the wee small hours and not wait until morning to ring potential landlords. Free listings newspapers are useful for those seeking accommodation, for instance the *Zypresse* in Freiburg.

TOURISM AND CATERING

The German tourist industry depends heavily on immigrants and students during the busy summer months. Despite the huge number of (illegal) immigrants from the former Yugoslavia who are often willing to work for exploitative wages, many other nationalities do find jobs in hotels and restaurants, especially those which have been raided and are reluctant to break the law.

If you are conducting a door-to-door search of hotels and restaurants in the cities, you will be at an enormous advantage if you speak decent German. For example every time Danny Jacobson turned around in Freiburg (after a fruitless search for harvesting work in the countryside), he met young people from around the world working at campsites and in bars. You may be lucky and find a manager who speaks English and who needs someone behind the scenes to wash dishes, etc. When Robert Lofts worked in a hotel kitchen, he had to phone up his German-speaking brother who was living nearby every time he received a new instruction ('He wants you to peel the cucumbers'). Robin Gray was not so lucky as to have a linguistically talented sibling and he accepted a job in a kitchen without really understanding what he was meant to do:

> *The manageress told me she was looking for a salad chef and I said I was a chef. The waitresses were coming in with the orders, but I didn't know there were about seven different salads. I was just putting a couple of slices of lettuce, tomatoes, bit of cucumber, etc. on all the plates and they were going off their heads because there wasn't enough watercress or no tomatoes with that certain salad. I started at 10am and got the sack at 2pm, but I got paid for it so I wasn't too bothered.*

As well as trying the Zentralstelle beforehand, you can try to fix up a summer job ahead of time by sending off speculative applications. This worked for Dean Fisher, an unemployed engineering apprentice, who went to wash dishes in Berchtesgaden on the Austrian border:

> *I spent 2¹/2 months working in a very orderly and efficient kitchen on the top of a mountain in the Kehlsteinhaus (Eagle's Nest) with the most amazing view I've ever seen. I actually enjoyed the work even though it was hard going. I met loads of good people and learned a lot of German.*

Get hotel addresses from tourist office brochures or, if you know anyone going to Germany on holiday in the spring, ask them to bring back local newspapers.

If your German is shaky and you are finding a door-to-door search isn't producing results, take Emma Forster's advice and concentrate on fast food outlets as she did in Hamburg:

> *Go in person to any McDonalds or Burger King. We had no trouble getting job offers on the spot, without speaking a word of German. The wages by British standards are high. I got DM11.50 per hour and 20% extra if I did the night shift. We aimed to save DM2,000 after two months work.*

Since then the wage range for general catering work has risen to DM12-18. So if you want to save money quickly, selling hamburgers in Hamburg and frankfurters in Frankfurt would seem to be the answer, not to mention clearing tables and washing dishes in Berlin (where the job boom continues) or other major German cities.

Munich is estimated to have 2,000 pubs and restaurants (concentrated in the fashionable suburb of Schwabing) and Berlin is similarly well endowed with eateries (try the American style places on Kurfürstendamm). The Munich beer gardens, especially the massive Chinese Tower Biergarten, pay glass collectors and washers-up (most of whom have lined their jobs up at the beginning of the season) DM100 a day tax free at the height of the season, when people work 14-hour days. Look for adverts in the local press, especially *Abendzeitung* in Munich. Key words to look for on notices and in adverts are *Notkoch und Küchelhilfe gesucht* (relief and kitchen assistant required), *Spüler* (dishwasher), *Kellner, Bedienigung* (waiters/waitresses), *Schenkekellner* (pub type barman); *Büffetier* (barman in a restaurant), *Büffetkrafte* (fast food server), or simply *Services.*

Be prepared for hard work. In hotels, it is not unusual to work 10 or 12 hours a day and to have only a day or two off a month. Those whose only experience of hotels and catering has been in Britain are usually taken aback by German discipline. Waitresses are normally expected to keep all customers' payments until the end of a shift, when the total is calculated and handed over as a lump sum. Those who lose track while being shouted at in German will not last long.

The punitive hygiene laws do not help matters. Once you realise that restaurants and hotels are frequently visited by the health department you will appreciate why it is that the head cook orders you to scrub the floors, clean the fat filters regularly, etc. But the high wages make it worthwhile.

Paul Winter has worked several seasons on the lakes near Munich:

I found that it is best to apply around April/May in person if possible. What they usually do is to tell you to come back at the beginning of June and work for a couple of days to see how you get on. As long as you are not a complete idiot they always keep you on until September. Even as late as July I knew of places looking for extra staff but as a rule most places are full by the end of May. I worked for the summer as a barman/waiter earning DM1,600 per month, net. With the tips I got I generally managed to double this. The guy who worked in the kitchens pulled in DM1,200 after his room and board were taken off.

Both Amersee and Starnbergersee can be reached by S-Bahn from Munich. These two lakes are ringed by towns and villages which all have hotels and restaurants, popular mainly with German tourists. Be warned that competition for work from students from the old East Germany has decreased the range of possibilities.

Other recommended areas to try for a summer job are the Bavarian Alps (along the border with Austria), the shores of Lake Constance, the Bohmer Wald (along the Czech border), the Black Forest (in south-west Germany), and the seaside resorts along the Baltic and North Seas. One employer on the Baltic coast hires a number of general assistants, food and beverage staff, child carers and sports instructors at a coastal campsite/golf and holiday park. The hours are long and you must be able to speak German but the wages are good. Apply in the spring to Camping Wulfener Hals, Riechey Freizeitanlagan GmbH, 23769 Wulfen/Fehmarn (04371 8628-0/ www.wulfenerhals.de).

The UK agency Alpotels carries out aptitude tests on behalf of German hoteliers looking for about 50 English-speaking staff (with EU nationality) for the summer and winter seasons. If interested in this scheme, send an s.a.e. to Alpotels, 17 High St, Gretton, Northants. NN17 3DE (www.jobs-in-the-alps.com). The Bloomsbury Bureau (PO Box 12749, 37 Store St, London WC1E 7BH; 020-7813 4061/fax 020-7813 4038; bloomsburo@aol.com) recruits up to 40 general assistants for hotels mainly in Bavaria. Applicants must be EU citizens and have a knowledge of German. A net wage of DM1,300 on top of free room and board is promised in exchange for working a 45-hour week.

The organisation Eurotoques (Europäische Union der Köche Office Deutschland) is based at a hotel in the Black Forest (Schassbergers Kur- und Sporthotel, Winnender Str. 10, 73667 Ebnisee, Schwäbischer Wald; 07184-292102/fax 07184-91053; office@eurotoques.de/ www.Eurotoques.de). Eurotoques finds jobs for German-speaking people as kitchen assistants and waiting staff throughout Germany. The catch is that no wage is paid for working nine hours a day, five days a week, for a minimum of three months (at any time of the year); board and lodging are provided.

The Warner Bros. Movie World employs between 400 and 500 staff for food concessions (restaurants, bakeries, ice cream stalls, fast food, etc.). Applicants should be able to converse in German and preferably Dutch as well as English. Accommodation is not provided. Applications to Warner Allee 1, 46244 Bottrop-Kirchellen (02045-899540; info@freizeitsparks.de).

Not as many travellers work for hostels as in some other countries. In Berlin try the Circus (www.circus-berlin.de) or the Clubhouse (www.clubhouse-berlin.de).

Winter Resorts

Germany is reported to be a good place to pick up jobs in ski resorts although few British tour companies operate there. Alpotels mentioned above helps in the recruitment of chambermaids and kitchen staff for the winter season in Germany; fluent German is not always required. The two main skiing areas are Garmisch-Partenkirchen (which also has hotels and services for the American Army) on the Austrian border 50 miles southeast of Munich, and the spa resort of Oberstdorf in the mountains south of Kempten. Seasonal vacancies are mostly in the kitchen or housekeeping departments where the net pay starts at DM1,300 after deductions for tax, social insurance and accommodation.

In addition to the jobs generated by the American Forces Recreational Center (AFRC) in Garmisch (described in the next section), some work is available in German-owned establishments such as the Wittelsbacher Hof (Prinzenstrasse 24, 87561 Oberstdorf; info@wittelsbacherhof.de) which hires people for the Christmas period as well as for the whole season; and the Ramada Sporthotel (Am Riess 5, 82467 Garmisch-Partenkirchen).

As always, timing is crucial. One highly qualified job-seeker (with experience in hotels and restaurants, a knowledge of German, French and English, and a good skier) went on the old 'hotel-trot' in Garmisch and was repeatedly told that they wouldn't be hiring until the beginning of the season (circa December 15th).

Work on Military Bases

Cutbacks in military spending and the perceived decrease in risk from hostile powers has meant the withdrawal of both American and British troops and resources from military bases in Germany. Many large US bases such as the ones in Munich and Berlin have closed. Yet there are still jobs around for Americans and Britons on the relevant bases.

Any employer that falls within the Status of Forces Agreement (SOFA) is restricted as to nationality and visa status of employees. Strict labour laws which protect German employees (and by extension EU nationals) mean that US bases have a strong preference for hiring US citizens since they are so much cheaper. After completing the summer season in Scotland, Isak Maseide from Norway hitched the 2,000km from Oban to Garmisch only to be told that Americans were preferred for casual jobs, since employers are exempt from having to pay the high level of social security on their behalf.

The US Army runs two Armed Forces Recreation Centers or AFRCs in Bavaria. The Chiemsee resort sits on the shore of Lake Chiemsee and the Garmisch AFRC sits at the foot of Germany's highest peak, the Zugspitze. Anyone wishing to get employment information about AFRC Europe can contact the Civilian Personnel Office (CPO) at Lazarettstr. 7, 82467 Garmisch-Partenkirchen (08821-729112/fax 729213; www.afrceurope.com/cpo/empl.htm).

Americans do not require work permits to work on US bases. Joe Warnick from Washington state hitched to Garmisch and arrived with just $30, which is rather risky, especially since there are no hostels in Garmisch. But before long, he was earning good wages:

I would say that if you're an American in Garmisch and show a little patience, you'll get a job. After enduring a few nights out in the cold, I found a job as a housekeeper with the Von Steuben Hotel. Because AFRC caters to US military families, a conservative appearance is a must. I had to cut off my ponytail and shave my goatee for the job, but it was a small price to pay for food in my belly and a warm place to live. Also, AFRC runs a very tight ship and unwelcome antics and drugs will find you out the door in a big hurry. I found this out first hand after a New Year's Eve party during which I was unable to subdue the impulse to climb on the 35ft rafters above the dance floor. I soon found myself being escorted home by the military police and a day later I was fired and my name was added to a long list of names banned from AFRC forever. I took it in my stride and found a job outside AFRC's control, at Woody's Barbeque Chicken Shop at the PX (run by AAFIES). There's always a way.

Although AFRCs offer a wide range of job vacancies, ordinary military bases are also a possible source of employment for travelling Americans. US bases are normally self-contained, providing servicemen with all the catering facilities, shops, entertainment and other services they need. Employees are mostly American and are paid in US dollars, though very occasionally a local national (German or EU citizen) is hired.

Every base in Europe and Asia has a food court in the commissary area where you will find a Burger King, KFC, Baskin-Robbins, Pizza Hut and other fast food outlets. The largest base in Germany is Heidelberg with other facilities in Mannheim, Kaiserslautern and Hanau where the largest commissaries are located. Each base also has an officers' club and hotel facilities for Armed Forces personnel where they need waiters and chamber staff. Since Heidelberg is the headquarters for the US Army in Europe, there is also a need for secretaries, clerks, etc. A bulletin board inside the front door at the headquarters building for the European Division of the University of Maryland (30 Im Bosseldorn, 69126 Heidelberg) posts job notices.

The *Stars and Stripes* is the US Army newspaper and is worth checking for jobs, especially as nannies or au pairs. Ana Güemes from Mexico answered an advert and was hired over the phone by a service family in Beibesheim near Darmstadt. The low pay (US$400 per month) and loss of freedom meant that Ana did not stay long, but it would be easy to move to a better family once you were on a base.

Work on British bases along the Rhine such as Verden, Minden, Münster and Paderborn is now very scarce though British nationals are occasionally still hired at the Berlin base for waitressing, bar work, cleaning and administration. The programme whereby young people were funded by the Army Welfare Service (BFPO 140) to work in youth clubs during the summer has been dropped.

Special Events

Oktoberfest starts each year on the last Saturday in September and lasts a fortnight. They begin to erect the giant tents for the festival about three months ahead so you can begin your enquiries any time in the summer. Some of the hiring is done directly by the breweries, so it is worth contacting the Hofbräuhaus and Löwenbräu for work, as well as pubs, restaurants and hotels. There is also work after it finishes as Brad Allemand from Australia discovered:

> *On the Monday after Oktoberfest finished I went around to all of the Beer Halls which were being taken down asking for some work. The first one I went to was Spatenbräu and the boss obliged. Even though my German was almost non-existent, I managed to understand what was needed of me. Many other foreigners were also on the site – English, Australian, Yugoslav, etc.*

Brad enjoyed the work, which lasted about six weeks. He worked 7am-5pm five days a week for an hourly rate of DM12.

Here are some other special events that need large numbers of people to set up stands and deal with the maintenance, catering, etc. Some of the major ones are listed below:

March	Frankfurt Trade Fair
April	Hannover Trade Fair
August	International Frankfurt Trade Fair
August	Mainz Wine Festival
August	Wiesbaden Wine Week
August	Rüdesheim Wine Festival
late Sept/early Oct	German Wine Harvest Festival (Neustadt)
late Sept/early Oct	Wiesbaden-Rheingau Wine Festival
late Sept/early Oct	Cannstadt Folk and Beer Festival (Stuttgart)
late Sept/early Oct	October Beer Festival (Munich)
mid October	Frankfurt Book Fair

Armin Birrer reported from Hamburg that they hold a fair ('Dom') three times a year, for a month after Christmas, Easter and late summer. He helped to dismantle the place at the end of the Easter fair after seeing a 'Worker Wanted' sign on some of the stalls. Opportunities for casual work also exist before the fairs open.

Many high-profile trade fairs are held at the huge Frankfurt Exhibition Hall *(Messe)*, such as the Frankfurt Book Fair in mid-October. Applications for work at one of the numerous fairs held in Frankfurt can be addressed to Messe Frankfurt GmbH, Ludwig-Erhard-Anlage 1, 60327 Frankfurt; 06975750). Only people with a stable base in Frankfurt and a good command of languages (for example for running messages) can be considered.'

BUSINESS AND INDUSTRY

Germany is once again becoming a mecca for foreigners looking for work in the manufacturing industries though, as in Britain, some of the traditional heavy industry of the Ruhr Valley has been struggling to survive. Very high wages are no longer universal, though most production line work pays about DM16-22 an hour.

You generally need to be on the spot to find this sort of job or have contacts. The best advice is simply to head for large industrial towns, such as Stuttgart, Cologne, Düsseldorf, Munich and Hannover, and start asking for work in *Arbeitsamter* and at factory gates. You should also check the sits vac columns, for example in the *Rheinische Post* in Düsseldorf and *Süddeutche Zeitung* and *Munchner Merkur* in Munich (particularly the Wednesday and Saturday editions which can be bought the previous evening in stations).

In Munich Robin Gray found a better job quite by chance:

I went in to a factory next to the building site (where I'd worked for a couple of days) for a drink of water since there was none on site. The owner of this factory which made mirrors warned me that the guy I was working for was disreputable and offered me a job. I got paid DM12 an hour and stayed for a month. There is a lot of work in Munich. I met people from all over the world doing everything from labouring to welding, tree surgeons to bar work.

Building Work

In the wake of reunification the German building industry boomed, as half a million new houses, plus hotels, roads and public buildings were commissioned, mostly in East Berlin and the former GDR. A huge number of British and Irish building workers, most of them skilled bricklayers, carpenters, tilers and plasterers, rushed off to Germany. They answered ads in the UK popular press or heard of jobs through the grapevine. The reason that German bosses were eager to hire so many foreigners was to avoid having to pay the statutory high wages which German builders demanded and steep national insurance contributions and taxes. But German building workers were not happy to see their jobs filled by foreigners and staged mass demonstrations against the deregulation which allowed tens of thousands of foreigners to compete for jobs in Potsdamer Platz, the huge building site in Berlin.

That boom is now over and the German construction industry is shrinking. The British and Irish workers who remain tend to be in more stable employment earning the same wages as German building workers. Inspectors regularly visit building sites and issue on-the-spot fines to employers breaking the rules. This has gone a considerable way in clamping down on the dodgy agents or sub-contractors who for many years recruited men from Britain and Ireland on behalf of German construction companies.

Technically it is illegal to work as a self-employed person on German construction sites without being registered at the Chamber of Handicrafts *(Handwerkskammer)* which requires you to show proof that you are properly trained and experienced for the job, preferably by showing a European Union Certificate of Experience (EC2/GN) obtainable from the Department of Trade and Industry.

TEACHING

If you enquire at an *Arbeitsamt* about teaching, translation or secretarial work in the major cities, you will probably be told (truthfully) that there is a surplus of people offering those services. However you may find that they are more helpful in smaller cities like Ravensburg in southern Germany where Nick Barton (writing in *Overseas Jobs Express*) found teaching work within days. He was surprised that the staff were so helpful considering how much trouble he was having with the local dialect Schwabisch. After working for a local language institute, he began to acquire a number of private clients and ended up staying for nearly two years.

Graduates with a background in economics or business who can speak German have a better chance of finding teaching work in a German city than arts graduates, since most of the demand comes from companies. Private language schools have multiplied in the eastern *Lander*, many with an American bias, though it seems that demand peaked in the late 1990s. Try for example Deutschland GmbH (Petersstrasse 39-41, 04109 Leipzig; 0341-211 4817); Sprache und Wirtschaft (Sternwartenstr. 4-6, 04103 Leipzig; 0341-257 7127/ sprache.wirtschaft@t-online.de) which employs about 40 teachers; and Lingua Franca (Pfalzburger Strasse 51, 10717 Berlin; 030-863 98 080/ www.lingua-franca.de).

A TEFL Certificate has less clout than relevant experience, as Kevin Boyd found when he arrived in Munich in September, clutching his brand new Cambridge Certificate:

> *I was persuaded by a teaching friend to go to Munich with him to try to get highly paid jobs together. As he spoke some German and had about a year's teaching experience, he got a job straightaway. Every school I went to in Munich just didn't want to know as I couldn't speak German and only had four weeks teaching experience.*

If you do intend to look for a teaching job take evidence of any qualifications and some good references *(zeugnisse)* which are essential in Germany. You can always try to arrange private English lessons to augment your income, though you are unlikely to be able to make a living this way. During the four winter months Ann Barkett spent in Munich, she put up flyers for private and group lessons but received no response. She finally answered an ad for a private student whom she taught for a few weeks.

Many secondary schools in Germany (including the former East) employ native English-speaking *Helferen* (assistants), posts normally reserved for students of German who apply through the Assistants Department of the Central Bureau for International Education & Training (10 Spring Gardens, London SW1A 2BN; 020-7389 4764). Americans may request information about teaching assistant programmes in Germany from the Pädaggogischer Austauschdienst, Nassestr. 8, Postfach 22 40, 53012 Bonn (0228-501-0; pad.eitze-schuetz@kmk.org/ www.kmk.org/pad/home.htm) or via the Institute of International Education, 809 UN Plaza, New York, NY 10017-3580.

Language teaching organisations whose addresses are included in the introductory chapter *Teaching English* have a sizeable presence in Germany: Berlitz (fax 06169-400506/ imke.finke@berlitz.de), Bénédict with 37 branches, Language Link, inlingua with 50 branches (e.g. Kaiserstrasse 37, 60329 Frankfurt; 069-242 92 03/ inlingua-schwarz@t-online.de) and Linguarama which specialises in language training for business. Linguarama Spracheninstitut Deutschland (Rindermarkt 16, 80331 Munich; 89-260 70 40; munich@linguarama.com) employs between 25 and 70 teachers at each of its eight centres in Germany. An indigenous organisation to try is the Academy of Business Communication or ABC (Marienstr. 41, 70178 Stuttgart; info@abc-stuttgart.de) which has been expanding.

Many commercial institutes employ teachers on a freelance basis, often resident expatriates willing to work just a few hours a week. In Munich, check the Jobmarket section of the English language magazine *Munich Found* which carries regular TEFL vacancies and is also on-line at www.munichfound.com.

Working freelance can make the red tape easier for non-EU teachers. This was what Ann Barkett from Georgia hoped to do in Munich, but didn't succeed in the end due to an unaccountable change of heart on the part of her employer:

When I sent my resumé around I received a quick response from Berlitz. During my interview, the Director expressed a desperate need for English teachers and enrolled me into the training course which I successfully passed.

After several weeks of tackling German bureaucracy re work permits, Ann phoned Berlitz to say that all was in order. Ann was mystified to be given the cold shoulder with a muttered excuse about troubles with the union. Her fellow trainees (all EU nationals) were all teaching up to 40 hours a week. She was never able to ascertain why one week they were practically begging her to work and then rejected her later.

Anyone with a higher degree (minimum MA) may wish to consider applying for a teaching position at one of the US universities with a German campus on US military bases (e.g. Maryland, Central Texas, Oklahoma, City College of Chicago). Full-time staff tend to be Americans hired through the home institution but term appointments are made on the spot. Some come with base privileges, others with none. Eugene Tate, PhD, describes possibilities:

I worked for the University of Maryland in Europe for four years. Courses are offered in the social sciences, sciences, business, humanities, mathematics and computer science. There is always a need for instructors in the latter two areas. Salaries vary from university to university and according to whether or not housing is included. Generally these jobs will be offered on a term by term basis (terms are eight weeks long). My advice for a person wanting to teach in Europe is to get a copy of the University Bulletin for the European Division *and note the address of each area director. An alternative approach is to contact the local college representative on the base for an application to teach.*

Childcare and Domestic

Most UK au pair agencies have partner organisations in Germany who make family placements. Some, like the Bloomsbury Bureau (address given above in the section on jobs in tourism), specialise in Germany. Helvian Services, 52 Coolhurst Road, London N8 8EU (tel/fax 020-8347 7388; helvians@aol.com) is a reasonably new agency with strong contacts in Germany.

Au pairs must be aged 18-24, have some knowledge of German and experience of childcare. Authorised agencies in Germany are:

IN VIA Germany, Ludwigstr. 36, Postfach 420, 79004 Freiburg (0761-200208; invia@caritas.de). Affiliated to the Roman Catholic network of au pair agencies, ACISJF, In Via has 43 branches in German cities all keen to attract au pairs.

Verein für Internationale Jugendarbeit, Goetheallee 10, 53225 Bonn (0228-698952/fax 0228-694166; au-pair.vij@netcologne.de/ www.vij-Deutschland.de). The German YWCA has more than 20 offices in Germany and places both male and female au pairs for a preferred minimum stay of one year. Pocket money of DM420 net per month.

Au Pair e.V., Staufenstr. 17, 86899 Landsberg (08191-941378/fax 941379; www.sta-net.de/au-pair). Places 300 au pairs a year.

Au Pair in Deutschland, Baunscheidtstr. 11, 53113 Bonn (0228-957300/ www.gijk.de). Part of GIJK, a cultural exchange organisation, which is also involved in holiday job and internship placements for German young people. Has an informative brochure in English. Applications must be made through a partner agency in your home country.

Au Pair Network International, Augustastr.1, 53173 Bonn (0228-956950; www.step-in.de). Place American au pairs via InterExchange in New York (212-924-0446).

Perfect Partners Au Pair Agency, Schlesierstrasse 13, 97450 Arnstein (09363-994291; www.perfect-partners.de).

The monthly pocket money for an au pair in Germany is in the range DM380-DM500 (average DM400). Some families offer to pay for a monthly travel pass or even your fare home if you have stayed for the promised period of nine months. In return they will expect hard work which usually involves more housework than au pairs normally do, as Maree Lakey found during her year as an au pair in Frankfurt:

I found that Germans do indeed seem to be obsessed with cleanliness, something which made my duties as an au pair often very hard. I also found that from first impressions Germans seem to be unfriendly and arrogant, however once you get to know them and are a guest in their home, they can be the most wonderful and generous people. The Germans I met were sincerely impressed by my willingness to learn their language and at the same time genuinely curious about life in Australia, my home country.

It is possible for non-EU citizens to become au pairs through one of the above organisations provided they are not older than 24. A special au pair visa must be obtained before leaving the home country, a process which requires you to show an *Annahmebestätigung* or official confirmation of placement. (US au pairs are exempt from this requirement.) The major North American au pair agencies listed in the introductory *Childcare* chapter can make placements in Germany.

If you consider your standards of hygiene to be sufficiently high, you might try to find work as a cleaner. The demand for this sort of work is reported to be high in cities such as Mainz, Stuttgart and Munich, and the pay is DM13-20 an hour. The advantage of office cleaning is that the early morning and early evening hours leave plenty of time for other activities including the possibility of a second job. Johannes Sempert, a Munich resident, suggests contacting cleaning firms listed in the *Yellow Pages,* especially in the summer months. Also check notices in supermarkets.

FARM WORK

Farms in Germany tend to be small and highly mechanised: most farm work is done by the owner and his family, with perhaps the help of some locals at busy times. Only on rare occasions are harvesting vacancies registered with the local *Arbeitsamt.* Alan Corrie was treated as quite a novelty by the locals when he worked on a Rhineland farm:

The old girls on the farm were unused to having gallivanting seasonal workers pass their way and share their toils. They were a bit wary the first morning, but soon accepted me as a new and curious diversion.

Grape production is the only branch of agriculture which employs casual workers in any great number. The harvest, which takes place mostly in the west of the country, is usually later than the one in France, taking place throughout the month of October. The vast majority of harvesting jobs are taken by East Europeans. While hitching through the Rhine Valley recently, Danny Jacobson asked repeatedly about grape-picking and every response included a reference to Polish migrant workers who appear to have a monopoly on the harvest work. Philip O'Hara was not prepared for the competition when he set off by bicycle to look for grapes to pick along the River Mosel a couple of years ago:

I had to travel 20km from Trier before I found a Weingut that hadn't already finished its harvest. When I finally caught the harvest up, I found the place littered with Polish cars and vans. There were hundreds of little Polski Fiat 126s with muscle-bound Poles crammed inside. Believe me when I say that finding work is hard. I was told by many vineyard owners that they had plenty of workers and there was no advantage in employing an Englishman in preference to a Pole. Poles were viewed as being honest, tolerant of poor pay and conditions, strong, friendly, hard-working – it is hard work – and hard-drinking. Strangely enough it seems that Irishmen are viewed the same way here. Since I had an Irish passport, I began to boast of my Irishness. That and the bicycle were enough. I worked only with Polish people on the grape harvest at Leiwen/Mosel.

Wages on the steep slopes of the Rhine and Mosel have not risen in the last couple of years and in some cases have even declined because of the availability of East European workers. This situation partially accounts for the difficulty some farmers have been having in recruiting labour. According to an article in the *Daily Telegraph* in summer 2000:

More and more family growers are being defeated by a combination of geography and commercial pressure from producers of inferior, cheaper products. Families who have made wine for centuries on the Rhine banks can no longer find workers prepared to slog up and down the sheer slopes to tend to the vines and pick the grapes for the wages on offer. 'You cannot work these slopes with machinery' said the president of the Rhineland-Palatinate farmers and winemakers association, 'It has to be done by hand, but the young people do not want this work any more. I fear that in the next 20 years 40%-50% of the vineyards that are left will be gone.

So this might provide a chance for travellers not only to earn a crust but to help save a centuries-old industry.

As usual your chances are better if you can visit the vineyards a month or two before the harvest to fix up work. Ask any German tourist office for a free leaflet about wine festivals since it includes some sketch maps of all the grape-growing regions of Germany. The main concentration of vineyards is along the Rivers Saar, Ruwer, Mosel and Nahe, centred on places familiar from wine labels like Bernkastel, Bingen, Piesport and Kasel. There are ten other areas, principally the Rheingau (around Rüdesheim and Eltville), Rheinpfalz (around Deidesheim, Wachenheim and Bad Dürkheim) and Rheinhessen (around Oppenheim and Nierstein).

Because the harvest is late, be prepared for cold weather, as Alan Corrie explains:

The lateness of the harvest means that the weather can be bad for workers out in the fields all day. The weather was cold and damp, but the people warm and friendly and the three half-hour breaks for hot wine, soup and sandwiches always pleasant. Everyone would be gathered around the wagon which brought us up into the high fields. At these moments, the clouds parted, the glinting river with its long ships, the vivid autumnal winefields, the forested hills and the constant changes in light made the atmosphere idyllic.

Apart from grapes, the most important area for fruit picking is the Altland, which lies between Stade and Hamburg to the south of the River Elbe and includes the towns of Steinkirchen, Jork and Horneburg. The main crops are cherries, which are picked in July and August, and apples in September and October. Apples and other fruit are grown in an area between Heidelberg and Darmstadt called the Bergstrasse, and also in the very south of the country, around Friederichshafen and Ravensburg near Lake Constance. Peter Radomski recommends the Bodensee area for apple picking: small villages such as Oberdorf, Eriskirch and Leimau sometimes employ migrant workers.

An account of the strawberry harvest near Wilhelmshaven in northern Germany from Kristof Szymczak goes some way to explaining why so few travellers work on German fruit harvests:

I was strawberry-picking in June/July, and I don't recommend this kind of work to anybody who isn't desperately short of money. Strawberry picking for me is really hard work, almost all day under the sun or rain. Of course it's piece work. The pickers are only from Vietnam and Turkey (already resident in Germany) and of course Poles like me. During 20 days of work from 20th June to 10th July I earned about DM800. For travel and living costs, I spent about a third, so not much left.

More recently an illegal Ukrainian migrant called Yuli earned DM150 a day in the May/June strawberry harvest.

Those who wish to volunteer to work on organic farms should contact the German branch of WWOOF (Willing Workers on Organic Farms), Postfach 210 259, 01263 Dresden (info@wwoof.de). Membership costs DM30 which gives access to about 160 farm addresses.

VOLUNTARY WORK

Most of the international organisations mentioned in the introductory chapter *Voluntary Work* operate schemes of one sort or another in Germany. Justin Robinson joined a workcamp to restore an old fortress used by the Nazis as a concentration camp. The green movement in Germany is very strong and many organisations concentrate their efforts on arranging projects to protect the environment or preserve old buildings. For example Internationale Jugendgemeinschaftsdienste (IJGD) organise summer 'eco-camps' and assist with city fringe recreational activities. This organisation was highly praised by a former volunteer Andrew Boyle who wrote:

The camp was excellent value both in the nature of the work and in that the group became part of the local community. These camps are an excellent introduction to travelling for 16 to 26 year olds.

Contact IJGD at Kaiserstrasse 43, 53113 Bonn (0228-22 80 00-11; www.ijgd.de) for details, or Concordia or UNA Exchange in Britain. An initial fee of DM170 is charged for projects in west Germany, and DM130 in east Germany.

Other German workcamp organisations to try are:

Arbeitskreis Denkmapflege, Goetheplatz 9B, 99423 Weimar (0643-502390; akdenkmalpflege@t-online.de/ www.ak-denkmalpflege.de). Building projects to restore historic monuments in rural areas. Skilled volunteers like carpenters and bricklayers preferred.

Internationale Begegnung in Gemeinschaftsdiensten (IBG), Schlosserstrasse 28, 70180 Stuttgart (0711-649 11 28/ www.workcamps.com). Publish a booklet in English of their projects in both eastern and western Germany. Application fee for most camps is DM150.

Mountain Forest Project (Bergwald Projekt e.V.), Sophienstr. 19, 70178 Stuttgart (0711-607 55 09; oekonsult@t-online,de/ www.bergwaldprojekt.ch). One-week forest conservation projects in the alpine regions of southern Germany. Basic knowledge of German is useful since the foresters conduct the camps in German.

Norddeutsche Jugend im Internationalen Gemeinschaftsdient (NIG), Am Wendländer Schilde 5, 18055 Rostock (381-492 2914/ www.campline.de). Range of projects in northeastern Germany.

Nothelfergemeinschaft der Freunde e.V., Fuggerstr. 3, 52351 Düren (02421-76569; ndf-dn@t-online.de). Building, gardening or social projects for one month in spring and summer.

Pro International, Bahnhofstr. 26A, 35037 Marburg/Lahn (06421-65277/ www.pro-international.de). Social projects published in English (booklet and website). Application fee DM100.

Vereinigung Junger Freiwilliger (VJF), Hans-Otto-Str. 7, 10407 Berlin (030-428 506 03; office@vjf.de). Most camps are in the former East Germany. Registration fee for applicants who apply directly is DM220.

There are some longer term possibilities as well. Internationaler Bund (IB), Freier Träger der Jugend-, Sozial- und Bildungsarbeit e.V. (Postfach 600460, 60334 Frankfurt am Main; www.Internationaler-Bund.de) takes on young people for a period of six or twelve months in various social institutions such as hospitals, kindergartens, homes for the elderly or disabled people. In some German states, young people may also work on ecological projects. Volunteers are paid pocket money plus full board and accommodation. Their literature is published in English but their website is only in German.

An international conference centre in the Harz Mountains employs young Europeans both short term (for the duration of a conference) or longer (up to one year) as domestic staff, looking after children and as conference assistants. Contact Internationales Haus Sonnenberg, Clausthalerstr. 11, 37444 St Andreasberg (Sonnenberg@tu-clausthal.de).

The Australian voluntary organisation Involvement Volunteers has an office in Germany: IV Deutschland: Naturbadstr. 50, 91056 Erlangen (tel/fax 09135-8075; ivde2@t-online.de).

Survival

Living close to the edge is probably less fun in Germany than in most other countries. Joe Warnick was reduced to sleeping in a doorway for a few nights in the ski resort of Garmisch-Partenkirchen since there was no cheap accommodation at all. Fortunately he found a job in a hotel before he froze to death.

After his motorbike broke down, Robin Gray and a friend hitched to Munich leaving them with just DM10:

We bought a bucket, a scraper, squeezed some washing-up liquid from a shelf into the bucket, filled it up at a fountain, went to a set of traffic lights and began what was to become our trade for the next two months. When the traffic stopped we quickly washed the car windscreen then asked the drivers if they had any change. The first car gave us DM5. We worked for about half an hour and got about DM40, then went for something to eat.

This was a novelty in Germany at that time, and six or seven cars out of ten gave us something. We could have earned a lot of money doing it but the German police didn't approve and stopped us. From then on we would hitch to other German towns, do the windows until we got stopped by the police, then get the bus or train back to Munich. Sometimes we would make DM100-200 for a few hours work.

Medical clinics in Germany such as the Iphar Clinic in Munich and LAB in Neu-Ulm are reputed to pay volunteers on medical trials very high fees, but it is increasingly difficult for foreigners to be accepted on to these lucrative pharmacological experiments. Most insist that you speak and read fluent German, so they can be sure you understand and legally agree to any risks involved. But the American Rod Fricker reported that he had spent several weeks in various medical testing centres in Germany, thanks to this book, but didn't specify how long ago. Blood donor clinics pay about DM50 and you are allowed to donate every six weeks.

If you do happen to speak German watch out for media market researchers who are sometimes on the lookout for guinea pigs, as Isak Maseide discovered:

The different agencies working for TV and movie companies were picking people at random off the streets of Munich when we were there to show them a cut of an episode of a TV series or new film before release. They then interview you to find out what the public thinks. We were accosted by an interviewer just near the Toy Museum and were paid DM10 each for a nice hour in a warm room with plenty of coffee and tea and a rotten German TV series. According to the interviewer, you can make quite a lot of money going from agency to agency. Some pay as much as DM25.

Finding affordable accommodation in Germany is a challenge and travellers solve this problem in various ways. Dave Hewitt managed to find a room in a *Studentenheim* (university residence) in Berlin. International youth camp Kapuzinerhölzl (in den Kirschen 30, 80992 Munich; 089-1414 300; www.the-tent.de) is the German equivalent of Tent City in London which costs DM15 to stay on the floor or DM19 per night in a bed, both including breakfast. If this is beyond your means, you can follow the example of Robin Gray who camped next to the River Isar about half a kilometre from the city centre, favoured by German tramps as well as travellers from Poland, Ireland, the former Yugoslavia, etc.

If you are really in straitened circumstances, you might like to investigate the Bahnhofsmissions (Travellers' Aid) which can be found at most mainline stations. But even these cannot be relied upon as Nicola Hall discovered one cold and hungry night in Munich when she found the Bahnhofmission closed. Station waiting rooms are not recommended either, at least not by Philip O'Hara:

I personally don't recommend Berlin Hauptbahnhof as a jolly sleeping experience unless you get your kicks from watching baton-wielding policemen removing the drunks every hour or so through the night, interspersed with said drunks returning to wake you to offer you a drink or try to cadge a fag.

German people do not generally enjoy a reputation for friendliness to poor travellers, though Joe Warnick from the US had no complaints. After an unsuccessful few hours of hitching on a ramp to the autobahn, he approached a nearby home to ask for water. They not only offered him a drink but also a place to pitch his tent, a delicious dinner and, the next morning, a lift to a truck stop.

Greece

Greece has countless attractions: beautiful scenery and climate, friendly and carefree people, memorable wine and food, a much lower cost of living than in the UK. It is no wonder that 11,000 Brits have settled in Greece and that so many travellers join the general drift to Greece from Northern Europe in the autumn, and the second migration from Israel and elsewhere after Easter. Many decide to extend their stay in Greece by picking up casual work, such as orange picking, dish-washing or building. Once you become a confirmed Graecophile, working will seem infinitely preferable to spending your remaining travel fund on a ticket home. Greece seems to be the country where travellers are most willing to gamble their last few thousand drachmas on getting a job.

The complicating factor in the last few years has been the influx of Albanians, Serbs, Romanians, Bulgarians and Georgians. At first most of these people were working in Greece illegally and would regularly be rounded up and sent back over the border. But from 1998 (when there were a reported 450,000 illegal immigrants in the country), migrant workers from Eastern Europe became eligible to apply for a white card that allows them to work legally. They have monopolised the vast bulk of casual work on farms, building sites, etc. since they are willing to work for half of the standard daily wage and are very hard workers. In many cases, it is impossible for other travellers to compete with them, and this often results in friction between the two groups of job-seekers, although some travellers have managed to get on the 'Albanian grapevine' and have found work alongside them.

The casual work that remains is mainly for young women in bars and tavernas all over Greece, and also in English language schools and private households looking after children. Outside Athens the hiring of itinerant workers to pick fruit, build houses, unload lorries, etc., often on a day-to-day basis, generally takes place in the main café of square of the town or village, where all the locals congregate to find out what's going on and possibly offer a day's work to willing new arrivals. You need to strike a balance here: if there are too many eager job-seekers your chances of success will obviously be diminished. Word of mouth and the direct approach are the only effective ways to find work in Greece, though be prepared for the 'cult of *avrio*', i.e. a tendency to put off making decisions until tomorrow.

REGULATIONS

When EU nationals stay in any member country longer than three months, they are supposed to apply for a residence permit at least three weeks before that period expires. To get a residence permit in Greece, take your passport and a letter from your employer to the local police station or, in Athens, to an office of the Aliens Department *(Grafeio Tmimatos Allodapon)*.

EU nationals in employment should make sure that their employer registers them with the Greek social security scheme (IKA). Contributions will be about 16% of earnings. After two months of paying contributions, you must go with your employer to apply for an IKA book; thereafter you are entitled to free medical treatment and reduced cost prescriptions. The IKA office (in Athens the address is 8 Agiou Constantinou St, 10241 Athens; 01-520 0555-64/ www.ika.gr) will give you a list of participating doctors who treat IKA patients free of charge.

Because of the expense, employers are sometimes in no hurry to regularise the status of their foreign workers. For example Julian Richards, a British graduate who went to teach English in the town of Veria, went to the trouble and expense of getting certified and translated copies of his degree certificate in order to obtain a teacher's licence and hence a residence permit; however by the end of his nine-month contract his school had still not got the documents nor had a drachma of his IKA contributions been paid, which all employers are obliged to do.

The official literature states that even EU nationals who intend to work for periods of less than three months are supposed to report to the police within eight days of arrival in the country. But work in Greece is normally undertaken so sporadically that many decide that it is not worthwhile changing their status from that of tourist. Many working travellers who want an extended stay find it easier to pop over a border and re-enter on another three-month tourist visa. Although most casual jobs are illegal because employers aren't paying contributions, the police mostly turn a blind eye, at least to EU citizens. On the other hand, officials do sometimes visit places known to pay their staff under-the-counter and it is common for a taverna to close for the evening when they hear the 'control' is coming to visit or they ask their illegal staff to pretend to be customers or run out the back door when the police arrive.

Detailed information sheets on the procedures for EU nationals intending to work in Greece and on the social security system can be requested from the Counsellor's Office for Economic & Commercial Affairs, Greek Embassy, 1a Holland Park, London W11 3TP (020-7727 8860; UK@dos.gr).

The Greek government employment office is OAED (Ethnikis Antistasis 8 str., 16610 Ano Glyfada; 01-998 9000; www.oaed.gr) through which EURES counsellors can be contacted.

Non-EU Nationals

Non-EU nationals who find employment are supposed to have a 'letter of hire' sent to them in their home countries. Fines are steep on employees working without a permit and even stiffer on employers. Yet so much of the work undertaken in Greece (including by Greeks) is done 'black', many casual workers from abroad have been hired, in many cases with the full knowledge of the local police. (Of course they will not hesitate to invoke the law if they want to get rid of you as happened to some aggressive Antipodeans in Santorini who were hassling tourists. They were jailed overnight and deported the next day.)

The immigration police seem to target some places and not others. For example an Australian woman worked quite happily for an Athens hostel but was not allowed to work in the café next door (under the same management) since it was often raided by the tourist police. Harvesting areas are sometimes the target of immigration raids, mounted to catch large numbers of illegal East Europeans rather than working holidaymakers. For more high profile and longer-term jobs like English teaching, it

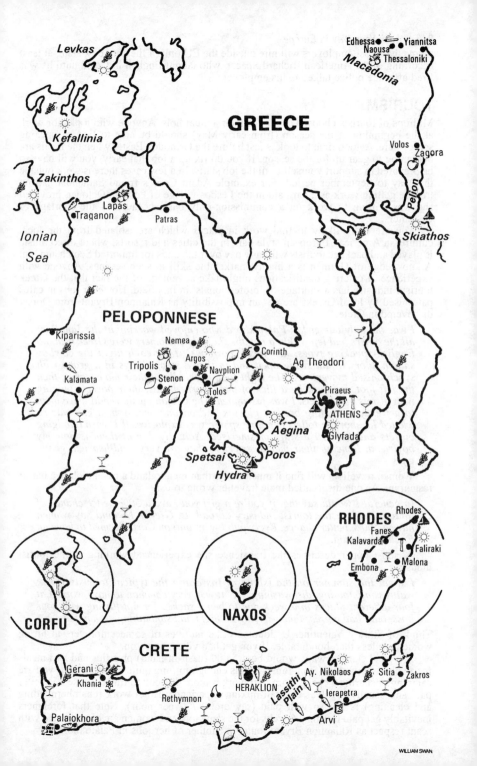

WILLIAM SWAN

seems that most employers will hire outside the EU only if they are desperate, at least according to the American Richard Spacer, who taught English in Corfu until he was fired after the police talked to his employer.

TOURISM

Millions of tourists choose Greece for their annual hols. Anyone who looks for work at the beginning of the season (from early May) should be able to find an opening somewhere. A good time to look is just before the Orthodox Easter when the locals are beginning to gear up for the season. If you do fix up a job that early, you will have to be prepared to support yourself until the job starts. In a few cases there is work outside the May to September period. For example Adam Cook's friend Samantha had no trouble getting work as a barmaid in the Lesbos village of Petra in October, provided she was willing to work on a commission-only basis because of the shortage of customers.

You are more likely to find work in places which are isolated from the local culture, in American/European style bars in the cities and resorts, where disco music is played and package tourists willingly pay over the odds for imported Scotch and gin. A knowledge of German is a highly marketable skill in such settings. Anyone with experience or catering qualifications might take advantage of the fact that the Greek tourism industry has a shortage of 'professionals' in this field. However jobs in cafés patronised by local Greeks are not an impossibility as Rhiannon Bryant from Dorset discovered in Crete:

> *I was the only bar girl in Palaiokhora who enjoyed working at the Jam Bar; all the others had left within a month. The only customers were Greek men, no English-speaking types, just local 'cowboys'. Late each night the cowboy saloon doors would swing open and in they'd step, always in a group with synchronised movements. The right foot, a twiddle of their moustaches, then the left foot, followed by a flick of their worry beads, their pockets bulging with pistols and bullets. I was fascinated. The Cretan music would drive them to a frenzy, smashing bottles, glasses and on one occasion, a guy was so excited he shot the toilet. The atmosphere was explosive. If I wasn't dodging bullets and glass, I'd stare mesmerised. Actually one of them is now my boyfriend. Beneath their macho exteriors they are very kind-hearted, gentle guys.*

Women travellers will find it much easier than men to land a casual job in a bar or restaurant. As one disgruntled male traveller wrote to us:

> *In general I would say that if you're a girl you have a 50% better chance of finding work in the tourist industry abroad. In Greece I would say women have a 500% better chance. Every pub I went into on Corfu seemed to have an English barmaid.*

Alison Cooper describes the transience she experienced working in the tourist industry:

> *I spent the summer on the island of Ios doing the typical touristy work: waitressing, touting, dishwashing, etc. It was very common to have worked at four different places in a week due to being sacked for not flirting with your boss, but I had a great time partying all night and sunbathing all day long.*

Think of Shirley Valentine. Undoubtedly the motives of some employers in hiring women are less than honourable. If you get bad vibes, move on.

A typical starting wage would be dr5,000 (cash-in-hand) plus tips and two meals for an eight-hour shift (5pm-1am). This is enough to fund quite a good time if you are camping or sharing a cheap room. Bar work is more difficult to find because it is better paid and usually involves cocktail-mixing experience. Hotel work (chambermaiding and cleaning) is not so well paid (say dr600-700 per hour). Note that foreigners inevitably get paid less than Greeks for the same job, and women are often treated with scant respect as Rhiannon Bryant found in another of her jobs in Palaiokhora:

The men patronise you, put you down and think you're just a bimbo. As the weeks went on, I had more and more responsibilities in the restaurant but was still treated like dirt (though I think I made the best wages of any holiday worker in town, the equivalent of £18 a day). In the end I told my boss what I thought and walked out.

What I will never get used to is the Greek men flirting with the tourists. They call it kamaki *which means 'harpooning'. If an attractive girl came in, the restaurant stopped and the victims never realised it.*

(Perhaps another reason she was keen to quit was to get away from a distasteful aspect of her job which was to stand beside the food display outside the front door squeezing the lobsters' eyes to make them move to prove how fresh they were.)

Some women find the legendary attention paid by prowling male Greeks intolerable; others have said this unwanted admiration is not unduly difficult to handle. Once you have established your reputation (one way or the other) you will be treated accordingly, at least by the regulars. On her gap year, Emma Hoare lasted precisely 20 days in a job as receptionist in a hotel on Mykonos before realising that (a) she was being totally ripped off and (b) her boss was a big fat disgusting immoral bully, whom another disgruntled ex-employee described as 'feral'. When Nicola Sarjeant's bar at Perissa Beach on Santorini was quiet, she was expected to liven things up by dancing, to which she said 'No thanks'.

Always insist on getting paid at the end of each day's work, so no misunderstandings can arise, at least until you feel you can trust your employer. Laura O'Connor describes the difficulty she had with her employer on Mykonos (history does not relate whether it was the same as Emma Hoare's above):

I would not recommend this job to a fellow traveller. We worked in the laundry room from 11am-7pm, and had all our meals (which were hearty) and accommodation provided. The only problem was in getting our money. It's like blood out of a stone. We were told dr4,000 per day but when you go for your money there's no one around, or you wait ages then they say 'tomorrow, tomorrow'. Well, we finally got our money but only dr3,000. You haven't a leg to stand on. They'll pay if you stand up to them, especially if you are a woman since they are so shocked.

Even people who love Greece and have enjoyed working there offer warnings about Greek employers. Stephen Psallidas (who speaks Greek) describes his life as a waiter on Mykonos as idyllic but goes on to describe the 'down side' and how to cope with it:

Greek employers are the worst I've ever known! You should be very careful since they will always try to rip you off when you first arrive. You must stand up for yourself, since any weakness will be exploited. Greek restaurant bosses are also often very unprofessional, for example requiring you to present 'fiddled' bills to customers or, even worse, pinching your tips.

He recommends threatening to leave and carrying out the threat if things don't improve, as much for the sake of travellers coming after you as for your own.

Corfu, Ios and Paros seem to offer the most job openings in tourism, though Rhodes, Naxos, Santorini and Mykonos, and to a lesser extent Aegina, Spetsai and Skiathos have been recommended. A job-seeker from Yorkshire who posted a notice on Lonely Planet's Thorn Tree website thinks that Kos would be a good bet:

I was in Kardamena (Kos) briefly in early May 2000 and in that time I must have passed a dozen bars/restaurants with 'Staff Wanted' blackboards outside.

The standard daily wage is dr5,000-dr6,000 (about £10). The Ionian island of Zakynthos is particularly recommended. In fact a new employment agency called Zak Recruitment, Argassi, Zakynthos 29100 (tel/fax 0695-44250; zak_recruit@hotmail.com) has been set up by two expatriate Englishwomen married to Greeks. Barbara Clother Ambelas describes the job market:

Our husbands have separate businesses as do many of our friends here and it became clear to us that there is a desperate need for reliable quality workers during the tourist season (May to October inclusive). So Zak Recruitment was born. The meteoric growth of tourism here has put pressure on employers and the number of good workers has not matched the employment opportunities. We aim to provide responsible and reliable staff to employers across the spectrum which means not only the seasonal work like waitressing, guiding, cheffing, shop assistants, entertainers (badly needed for next year) and so on but the permanent jobs too: hairdressing and teaching for example. We are the only organisation of this kind in Zakynthos.

An accommodation and flight advisory service is also included in the registration fee of dr10,000 or £22 which remains valid for a year. Note that the childcare agencies Au Pair Activities in Greece and Worldnet UK sometimes have vacancies in hotels as well as families (addresses below).

Working in very heavily touristed areas can leave you feeling jaded. Scott Corcoran describes Kavos in the south of Corfu as a 'nightmare resort town full of northerners drinking Newcastle brown ale and eating chip butties' but since it has 200 bars and restaurants there is plenty of employment. (Scott got work as a 'PR' persuading tourists into 'his' restaurant which paid dr2,000 a day and which he found a 'real doss'.) Jill Weseman describes the 1,000-bedded Pink Palace on Corfu (066-53103) as a cross between a Club Med for backpackers and an American summer camp. It employs an army of foreign workers as bartenders, cooks, receptionists, etc. but the pay and conditions are reputed to be below average. Try also the Club Barbati on Corfu. On Paros, there are jobs in the main town of Parikia and also in the quieter town of Naoussa where the season is shorter, accommodation less expensive and wages higher. The Sani Beach Holiday Resort in Thessaloniki (www.saniresort.gr) employs a large number of hospitality industry trainees for a minimum of five months on what they describe as a 'training wage'.

Safra Wightman was delighted at how easily she found work on Naxos:

Finally I cashed my last travellers cheque and headed for the largest of the Cycladic islands, Naxos, to find a job. The numerous bars, cafés and tavernas seemed quite daunting at first. I decided to be choosy and approach only the places which appealed to me. I strolled the paralia and a café caught my eye. I marched up to a Greek guy standing in the doorway and asked him if he had a job for me. He simply said yes and I started work that evening. The Greeks appreciate a direct approach. They are kind, welcoming, generous people.

Safra went on to recommend going to the favourite haunts of working travellers on Naxos to find out about openings, viz. the Ocean Club, Musique Café, Mike's Bar and Ecstasis.

Foreigners (especially women) may also be hired in tourist resorts to deliver cars for car rental firms or to act as transfer couriers. Xuela Edwards and her companion Nicky Brown went to the package resort of Lindos on Rhodes in April and were offered several jobs on the first day. They worked as 'escorts' on day-trips from the village (which paid £12 per excursion) and also did airport transfers for British tour companies which paid about £15 (whether or not an arriving flight was delayed). They found this work by asking around at those local travel agencies which acted as the headquarters for overseas reps. About 1,000 Brits live on Rhodes so it should be easy to find someone to offer advice. According to Xuela this work requires that you be 'presentable, reliable, able to work all night and get up very early in the morning'.

Another long-time contributor Camilla Lambert was based on the Ionian island of Levkas for five months working for Sunsail (see section *Boats* below) and acted as an occasional freelance guide on the side:

I also earned money driving tourists round the island in a hired jeep, as many had forgotten their driving licences and I knew which roads were passable and where the cheapest tavernas were. It cost me about £30 a day to rent a 4-wheel drive vehicle so if you take three passengers and they pay £15 each you make a profit while getting away from base.

If men are finding it difficult to find a service job, they may find taverna-owners willing to hire them as washers-up or roof menders. Some men are needed to build, paint or clean villas and hotels. In populous resorts, men are hired to unload trucks of supplies (crates of soft drinks, Retsina, etc.) for the cafés.

Seasonal jobs can be arranged from the UK. Mark Warner (George House, First Floor, 61/65 Kensington Church St, London W8 4BA; 020-7761 7300) have several beachclub hotels in Greece which require British staff who are paid between £50 and £250 per week depending on the position, in addition to full board and accommodation, use of watersport facilities and flights. Three other possibilities are Pavilion Tours (Lynnem House, 1 Victoria Way, Burgess Hill, West Sussex RH15 9NF; www.paviliontours.co.uk) which need children's instructors; Sailing Holidays Ltd (105 Mount Pleasant Road, London NW10 3EH; 020-8459 8787; www.sailingholidays.com) which are looking to hire flotilla skippers and hostesses, boat builders and marine engineers for their holiday programme in the Greek and Dalmatian islands; and, finally, Golden Sun Holidays (150 Kentish Town Road, London NW5 2AG; www.goldensun.co.uk) advertising for 150 overseas representatives to work in Greece or Cyprus for three months or more between April 1st and October 31st.

Hostels

The competition for business among hostels and cheap pensions is so intense that many hostel owners employ travellers to entice/bully new arrivals into staying at their hostel. In exchange for meeting the relevant boat, train or bus, 'runners' (otherwise known as couriers, touts or hawkers) receive a bed, a small amount of cash-in-hand (normally dr3,000) and a small commission for every 'catch.' The system of hustling or touting is well established in Athens (especially among the hostels around Omonia Square) and to some extent on the islands, but is not necessarily to be recommended. Kathy Hood from New Zealand describes her experience on Naxos:

On a recent stay in Greece, my boyfriend and I unfortunately became enlightened as to the illegality of 'hawking' people for hotels. It is illegal to hawk on boats or on the port past a certain line which is usually made clear by hordes of screaming hotel owners. Having spent a night in the port police offices sand an afternoon in court, I would storngly recommend that travellers don't take up such an opportunity should it arise. We were, however, let off on the grounds of traveller's naiveté.

The situation in Athens is cut-throat. There will be as many as 30 hostels vying for custom at Athens station, not to mention further competition and much animosity from taxi drivers (who want to earn a commission from hotels). Working conditions vary among the hostels and you soon learn which are the bad ones. If you are looking for this work, it is easier making enquiries at the station where the runners congregate rather than going from hostel to hostel. During Isak Maseide's stint as a runner, several hotels tried to bribe him to defect. According to Isak, 'if you vaguely resemble the conscientious hard-working type, you have a job, since so many runners have to be replaced every week due to the sheer uselessness and proneness to alcoholic binges so often seen in northern Europeans visiting Mediterranean countries.'

Many enjoy the hostel atmosphere and the camaraderie among hostel workers (at least the ones who do not take the job too seriously), and they regard the job as a useful stop-gap while travel plans are formulated, often based on the advice of fellow travellers. Anyone who sticks at it for any length of time may find themselves 'promoted' to reception; in this business a fortnight might qualify you for the honour of being a long-term employee.

A great many hostels offer the same wage and perks to people who will spend a few hours a day cleaning. This work is easy-come, easy-go, and is seldom secure even when you want it to be. The popular and cheap Hotel Festos near Syntagma Square in Athens (18 Fillelinon St, 10557 Athens; 01-323 2455) has a notice for staff posted permanently. The owner Mr Theodore Consolas also advertises in the UK, inviting applicants to write to him for details at Consolas Travel, 100 Eolou St, 10559 Athens

(01-325 4931/consolas@hol.gr/www.consolas.gr). As well as working in the upstairs bar, Heather McCulloch worked in the Consolas travel agency, dodging traffic in the stifling heat to deliver and collect tickets and generally acting as an office skivvy. However she was pleased with the wage (paid after an unpaid trial week) plus board and lodging which has since gone up to dr15,000 a day. Mr. Consolas also owns another youth hostel on the island of Paros (0284-21635) where employment might be possible. He may also be able to arrange bar and restaurant work and agricultural jobs on the island of Gavdos, two hours south of Crete (www.gavdostudios.gr).

Selling & Enterprise

When taking advantage of the opportunities afforded by tourism, you need not confine yourself to hotels, restaurants and cafés. Mandy Blumenthal funded her island-hopping by selling 500 pairs of sunglasses brought from England. If you have any handicraft skills like making jewellery, the tourist areas of Greece could provide a lucrative market for your wares. Safra Wightman was very glad she had remembered to take her scissors to Naxos where she was able to market her training as a hairdresser. If you are arriving from Asia, you can stock up on cheap Eastern jewellery as Kristen Moen did. She found Corfu a very successful market for Indian, Nepali, Thai and Chinese jewellery.

You may try to sell your product to souvenir shops, set up an independent market stall or sell on the streets. If you choose the latter, make sure that it is allowed, since the police in busy resorts have been cracking down on this as Nicola Hall (now Dickinson) reported from Crete several years ago:

> We came across a young lad who had been making friendship bangles and hair pieces and street trading in Hersonisos (on the coast east of Heraklion). It is now illegal to sell on the street here, as it is in Malia, the next town along. The police give you three warnings and then fine you dr60,000 and if you can't pay they put you in jail for 22 days where all you are given is bread and water. He was paid to look out for the cops and, if they came, to clear up the stuff and run with it.

Anyone who can paint portraits may be in for a bonanza. Street artists in the main resorts charge £10 for a 15-minute portrait and can expect to do four in an evening. You can also try to sell paintings of restaurants, banks, etc. to the establishment concerned. There is often work to be had painting signs and notice boards (primarily at the beginning of the season) or decorating the walls and doors of tourist places themselves. This can be quite well paid if you are good at it and get a good reputation. Nicola saw so many misspelled signs on Zakynthos (her favourite advertised 'daft Cider') she was sure someone with both artistic and orthographic talents could persuade Greek bar owners to pay for a sign.

Another way of exploiting a market was found by Michael Jenkins, also on Corfu. With a friend he would chat up holidaymakers about to try parascending, take photographs of any who seemed at all interested and arrange to meet them again in the evening at no obligation. Michael and his partner took turns going into Corfu town on their rented motorbike to get the pictures developed at a commercial developer. Most people bought the pictures for dr1,200 which meant Michael earned a fair bit that summer.

On her most recent trip to Greece, Nicola Hall became Nicola Dickinson in a picturesque little church on St. Paul's Bay, Rhodes:

> Many people get married here throughout the season including us. We noticed that of all the oil paintings there was none of St. Paul's Bay and the church, which was a shame because it is so lovely and we would gladly have bought a picture of it. So I've taken up oil painting classes in the hope of one day going back there and providing a service for newly weds.

Not to be outdone, her husband Peter Dickinson recommends photography on Lindos where there are plenty of tourists in all the restaurants, pubs and clubs but nobody with a polaroid camera which he reckons could be the key to a lucrative stay. More serious photographers might take advantage of the fact that 80-90 couples get married and many more spend their honeymoons in Lindos. The plan is that next time they go to the Cyclades, they will go as a freelance team.

Boating

Yachting holiday companies are a possible source of jobs, which can be fixed up either ahead of time or on the spot. Camilla Lambert greatly enjoyed her season with the sailing holiday operator Sunsail (see *Tourism* chapter) which started in April with a two-week refit of the clubhouse and scrubbing and painting the boats. In the past people have found work by visiting skippering brokers and yacht agencies around Piraeus. English companies such as Camper & Nicholson prefer to hire English speakers, as do many local firms.

On islands where there is a lot of yachting traffic, you might find a job living on a boat. Mary Falls frequented a popular bar in Rhodes Town and soon found a half day's work polishing the brass of a boat. Someone who happened to notice how industriously she worked invited her to stay on his boat, working in exchange for her keep. After that she was taken on as the cook while the boat cruised the Turkish coast. The numerous cruise ships which ply the Aegean Sea are occasionally looking for personnel to replace people who have left their jobs in the ship's restaurants, bars or in the entertainment programme. Phone numbers of the relevant companies can be obtained from travel agents or found in the Yellow Pages under *Krouazieres*.

AGRICULTURE

Working in the English-speaking environment of tourism is not for everyone and certainly does not conform to Ben Nakoneczny's philosophy of travel:

> *If you are to work abroad it is preferable to be employed in a capacity which allows an insight into the people of the country you are visiting. To serve English tourists bottled beer in a western-style bar is merely to experience the company of those travellers who cling to what they know, unprepared to risk the unfamiliarity of an alien culture. I believe that the best way of breaking cultural boundaries is to work outside the tourist areas, probably in agriculture.*

Unfortunately these days you might end up deserting an English-speaking environment only to find yourself in an Albanian or Romanian one. Most of the feedback received over the past couple of editions of this book has read more like an epitaph than a how-to guide. Tony Forrester's account is typical:

> *I recently returned to Nafplion for a vacation. Aristotle (affectionately known as 'Arry') still runs the kafeneion on Amalias. He told me all about orange picking, as it is now. I was there in the 'good old days' (his words) of 1988 and again in 89. The pickers now are all Slavs and Albanians who never use Arry's. He's going broke and says he's going to sell up in two years time. So if you want to see this legend, this father to the orange pickers, go soon. We spent a few afternoons reminiscing about the old days when the entire world seemed to come to Naf for the oranges. It's sad.*

But he holds out one scrap of hope when he says that a few jobs still go to travellers who earn Dr7,000 a day.

Likewise Siôn from Wales revisited the Peloponnese on a sentimental journey, recalling his experiences as a fruitpicker and casual worker in the early 1980s (when he was a contributor to this book in its infancy):

> *The citrus pickers I watched in the Sparta region seemed to be Romanians and Greeks. I didn't notice any of the sort of seasonal workers in Kalamata, Mystras and Sparta that I knew in the early eighties in Greece. I remembered my time on the mainland when I and others had been offered seasonal work by drivers merely by walking along roads.*

Inevitably, travellers will continue to meet farmers in cafés and be asked to lend a hand here and there in the harvesting of oranges, olives, grapes and other crops. But the employment of young international travellers does not take place on the massive scale it once did and so the lengthy sections in previous editions on fruit harvesting in Greece have been reduced.

Truck drivers in rural areas are a useful source of tips on job openings, as Peter Radomski from Poland found during his stint of apricot picking and general maintenance work near Corinth. Assuming you have had no luck at the café or youth hostel, you can go into the countryside as Tim Gunn recommends:

The best way to get work is to approach a farmer when his fruit looks ripe and use sign language to find out if he will employ you. Ascertain wages and accommodation in the same way because there is very little chance of his speaking anything other than Greek.

Jane McNally suggests mastering the following few words: *kopse* (cut), *sheera* (drill/row), *ilea* (olives), *thermo keepio* (greenhouse), *kafasi* (crate), none of which will be found in a conventional phrase book (which is more likely to translate for you 'Excuse me, does Yorkshire pudding come with my roast beef?' or 'I'm going to be sick' rather than 'Do you need help in your fields?') Make very sure of your instructions before tackling the task. Rhiannon Bryant's Greek was not very advanced but she did decipher the word *kopse* when she went to the Cretan village of Kondouras to help in one of the many tomato greenhouses. She proceeded to hack her way through the plants, but was never paid for her stint since in five hours she had managed to destroy an entire crop.

Orange groves abound between Corinth and Argos and south to Tolo. Picking oranges can be heavy and tiring, but is generally thought to be easier than other picking jobs. The season runs from late November or early December to late February, with the crop at its peak between mid-December and mid-January. The harvest can be badly hit by rain, frost and other calamities. The centre of orange picking on the Peloponnese is Drepano which is where Shelly Harris and her boyfriend headed in the late 1990s:

We camped at the Argolic Strand Campsite which is open all year. It was costing us dr21,000 a week, so we soon moved to an apartment where the rent was dr40,000 a month. The oranges were late that year but finally the harvest started a week or two later. When we arrived there were about 15 or 20 people (most of them Albanians) waiting in the square for work in the morning. In my first day's work I earned dr6,000 and finished at 1.30pm but this turned out not to be typical; mostly you earn dr5,000 and have to work till 4pm. It is good if you can find local people with oranges to pick and avoid the big contractors as they pay by the kilo and you have to count how many boxes you do which always leads to disputes. Also, for much of the time there was no work because only a few boxes (or none at all) were released. More people were arriving by the day so that by the first week of February there were up to 50 people waiting for work. So we left, having had some good experiences and having made some friends. I think Greece is a lovely country but I would never go back to work because the competition is far too great.

Also try the villages of Tolo, Assini and Inaxos near Argos. The orange harvest begins to drop off at the end of February, though in good years picking carries on as late as May in good years.

The Mani peninsula on mainland Greece is famed for its olives. Visitors may be welcomed to help with the December harvest more for local colour than for money. A journalist writing in the *Times* (September 1999) described how she fulfilled her romantic ambition to 'commune with the olive groves' by staying in Areopoli and helping an expatriate Austrian olive farmer in Pyrgos Dirou to harvest his organic olive crop. Apparently he and his wife are happy to help foreign travellers looking for holiday work in the November-March harvest time on a hospitality basis, i.e. free room and board but no wage; the contact given is Fritz Blauel, Pyrgos 24024 (0721-77492/fax 77590).

A few years ago Jane McNally earned dr5,000 a day doing back-breaking melon weeding around Kiparissia alongside a gang of Romanians. She claims that work in the melon harvest in June is available in this area only for men. In addition to

Kiparissia, Lapas west of Patras is another place to try for watermelon picking and greenhouse work, and Tragano for the tomato harvest.

Crete and the Islands

Crete, the largest of the Greek islands, was once able to provide a huge amount of work to travellers, from the bananas in Arvi on the south coast (the most northerly commercial banana plantations in the world) to the potato harvest around Ayios Georgios in the Lassithi Plain in August but mainly involving the grape and olive crops. The olive harvest normally begins in late November but can be delayed if the rains are late. In the old days, the villagers waited for the ripe olives to fall by themselves into nets beneath but nowadays the trees are beaten with sticks and branches are shaken to dislodge the olives. A pair of pickers can strip about five trees in a day.

Men may be able to find jobs in olive processing plants as Scott Corcoran did one December:

> *I eventually got a job at an olive oil processing shed in the village of Kallithea (5km southwest of Heraklion). This involved working 16 hours a day (8am till midnight) carrying sacks of olives and processing them in the factory. I was paid dr8,000 a day and was given free room and board. By Christmas I had had enough and moved on.*

Most villages operate a co-operative olive press so it is worth asking in any village café, particularly along the south coast.

The two areas which absorb the most pickers are around the two largest cities: a few kilometres south of Heraklion you will hit valley after valley of grapes which are picked from mid-August and just west of Khania, crops are grown around Platanias and Gerani. The village of Voukolies south-west of Khania is recommended by Andrea Militello, a long-time wandering fruit picker from Italy, both for olives (from late November to mid-February) and oranges (January to April):

> *My Cretan experience has been interesting. On the bad side, there are difficulties with Cretan people (few speak foreign languages, they don't have open minds, some are cold to foreigners) and it has also been difficult to save money. Picking olives is very hard, believe me, especially if you don't work with the special machine. In most cases, Greek bosses don't seem to respect you and your job, so the relationship with them is not easy.*

Tomatoes are grown in hothouses around Palaiokhora and in the village of Stomio on the south coast; the picking mainly takes place from April to June. Try also the area around Sitia and Ayios Nikolaos and the remote village of Zakros in the extreme east. You may stumble across opportunities on other islands. Siôn was recently in Samos and noticed olives being harvested around Manolates and oranges and tangerines around Milli, but on such a small scale that families were carrying out the work themselves and selling their meagre harvest in the market at Pithagorion. According to a local who stopped to offer him a lift on a country road, Samos offers so little employment outside the tourist industry that locals were grateful to work during the harvest.

Fruit (e.g. strawberries) is grown on Naxos, for example, and grapes are grown throughout the country, especially on the Ionian Islands (Zakynthos, Levkas, etc.) and on Rhodes.

Northern Greece

Although much of northern Greece is rugged and forbidding, some of it is very fertile. It is also closer to the Yugoslav, Albanian and Bulgarian borders. The area west of Thessaloniki, encompassing the market towns of Veria and Yiannitsa, is a major peach growing area, centred on the villages of Makrohoria, Diavato, Kavasila, Kasmena and Stavros all near Veria. The harvest gets started in mid-July but peaks after August 1st. Tomatoes are picked in the village of Kavasila. A good worker who can stand the sun can make a lot as piece work rates are paid. Yiannitsa 50km northwest of Thessaloniki is the centre of a rich agricultural area, especially known for its tobacco crop. Further west there is apple and pear picking in September/October around the towns of Skedra and Edhessa. Another region to try is the Pelion peninsula south of Volos. This area is very fertile and green with apple trees, pears, walnuts and blackberries fruiting in September. Most of the apple picking is centred on Zagora, though work can be found in the much smaller town of Makrirakhi.

OTHER WORK

It is sometimes worth checking the Situations Vacant column of the English daily *Athens News* (3 Christou Lada, 10237 Athens; 01-333 3404). You can check the classified ads on the internet (http://athensnews.dolnet.gr). Adverts range from the distinctly dodgy ('Smart-looking girls required for co-operation in luxury bar') to the legitimate ('English girl wanted for babysitting'). Most are for au pair jobs in private households. Obviously these jobs may not be the most desirable in the world as Vaughan Temby discovered: he left his 'hideous valet/houseboy job' after just two days. You could also try placing your own advertisement in the column 'Lessons' or 'Situations Wanted'. The minimum rate for advertising is dr2,500 for 15 words.

Childcare

Au Pair Activities accepts postal applications from young Europeans and American women for au pair positions and can also place candidates after arrival in Athens. Contact the agency at PO Box 76080, 17110 Nea Smyrni, Athens; tel/fax: 01-93 26 016; porae@iname.com). The owner Kalliope Raekou prides herself on her after-placement service, meeting regularly with au pairs at coffee afternoons. There is no fee to au pairs.

The Athenian Nanny & Domestics Agency (PO Box 51181, T.K. 145.10 Kifissia, Athens; tel/fax: 301-808 1005; mskiniti@groovy.gr) keeps detailed dossiers on vacancies, most of which are for a year, providing information about the children and the household, e.g. 'single ship-owning mother travels a lot' or 'summer on islands and yacht'. Among employers in this category, all speak fluent English and most have domestic staff, so nannies and au pairs mostly deal only with childcare duties. The going rate for full-time au pairs in Athens is dr180,000 a month, while full-charge nannies can earn twice that. All employers offer free outgoing flights and health insurance to long-term au pairs/nannies. There is a limited number of summer positions available for which application should be made in April. The Athenian Agency charges no fee.

Au pair and mother's help positions may of course be booked through agencies in Britain. Worldnet UK fills not only live-in childcare vacancies in Greece but also domestic positions in hotels (Avondale House, 63 Sydney Road, Haywards Heath, W. Sussex RH16 1QD; 01444 453566). Lucy Locketts & Vanessa Bancroft Nanny Agency (400 Beacon Road, Wibsey, Bradford, BD6 3DJ; tel/fax 01274 402822) has summer vacancies for mothers' helps in the Greek islands and mainland.

Julie Richards tried using several UK agencies but was disappointed that they expected nannying experience. She decided to go to Athens in any case and was offered five jobs in the first few days. The main advantage of waiting until you get to Greece is that you can meet your prospective family first. It is far better for both parties if you can chat over a cup of coffee and bargain in a leisurely fashion for wages, time off, duties, etc. Adverts appear in the *Athens News* placed by well-off families in the wealthy suburbs of Athens like Kifissia, Politia, Pangrati and Kolonaki as well as in Thessaloniki, Patras and the islands. The Greek attitude to privacy differs from the British one, but in most cases the au pair is given a private room except on summer holidays where she might be expected to share with the children.

Mig Urquhart arrived in Athens on a Friday, got the *Athens News* on Saturday, had an interview on Sunday and started a live-in job a week later, even though she had hoped to avoid that option. She would have preferred an English teaching job but hadn't done a training course and lacked the confidence to bluff. At that time of year (September) few jobs seemed to be around that didn't require a knowledge of Greek. Live-in jobs of course cut out the hassle and cost of finding accommodation. Although

Mig liked the children and the father well enough, she didn't enjoy being treated more like a servant than a member of the family by the mother. The last straw was being told she was hanging up socks on the washing line the wrong way and being faced with piles and piles of ironing so she quit.

Teaching English

There are an estimated 5,000-6,000 private language schools called *frontisteria* throughout Greece, which create a huge demand for native English speaker teachers. This is one job for which there will be no competition from Albanians, though it should be noted that Australians, South Africans and North Americans of Greek ancestry are often given teaching jobs in preference to people with non-Greek surnames.

Standards at *frontisteria* vary from indifferent to excellent, but the run-of-the-mill variety is usually a reasonable place to work for nine months. By no means all of the foreign teachers hired by *frontisteria* hold a TEFL qualification, though all but the most dodgy schools will expect to see a university degree (which is a government requirement for a teacher's licence) and EU nationality.

The majority of jobs are in towns and cities in mainland Greece. Athens has such a large expatriate community that most of the large central schools are able to hire well-qualified staff locally. But this is not the case in Edessa, Larisa, Preveza or any of numerous towns of which the tourist to Greece is unlikely to have heard. The basic gross hourly wage is currently dr2,000 (dr1,650 net); anyone with some training or experience should be able to ask for at least dr2,200. Earnings can be increased substantially by compulsory bonuses at Christmas and Easter and holiday pay at the end of the contract. Be prepared for long hours by normal English teaching standards, often 30 or more hours per week.

Chains of schools are always worth approaching with your CV. Try for example:

Strategakis Schools of Foreign Languages & Computing, 24 Proxenou Koromila St, 546 22 Thessaloniki (031-264276; stratkey@compulink.gr). 25 teachers for 100 schools all over northern Greece.

Omiros Association, 52 Academias St, 106 79 Athens (01-36 22 887/fax 01-36 21 833; omiros@omiros.gr/ www.omiros.gr). 120 branches throughout Greece.

Several teacher recruitment agencies actively seek teachers to work for one academic year. Interviews are carried out in Greece and the UK during the summer for contracts starting in September. These agencies are looking for people with at least a BA and normally a TEFL certificate (depending on the client *frontisterion's* requirements). The following undertake to match EU teachers with *frontisteria* and do not charge teachers a fee:

Anglo-Hellenic Recruitment, PO Box 263, 201 00 Corinth (tel/fax 0741-53511; jobs@anglo-hellenic.com/ www.anglo-hellenic.com). Dozens of posts in wide choice of locations for university graduates from the UK, preferably with a CELTA or Trinity TESOL. Interviews conducted in London, Corinth or Athens during the summer.

Cambridge Teachers Recruitment, 33A Makryanni St, New Halkidona, 143 43 Athens (tel/fax 01-218 5155; macleod_smith_andrew@hotmail.com). One of the largest agencies, placing 80-100 teachers per year in vetted schools. Applicants must have a degree and in most cases a TEFL Certificate, a friendly personality and conscientious attitude.

Native English Teachers (NET), 72 Windsor Road, Worthing, West Sussex BN11 2LY (01903 218638). Interviews British teachers for up to 20 vacancies.

The Greek-run teacher agency ESAC (English Studies Advisory Centre, Cosmos Center, 125-127 Kifisias Ave, 115 24 Athens; 01-69 97 017/fax 01-69 94 618) did not confirm its activities for this edition but may still be active.

After travelling and working in Greece for a couple of years, Jane McNally wrote from a school in Macedonia with some advice:

> *Most English speakers find work in private English schools. It can be difficult to find work by just knocking on school doors. Most school owners recruit their staff through agents two or three months in advance of the new term. If you want to bring a partner check first with your employer in case you are*

expected to share a flat or even a room with another teacher. All my colleagues and myself have had discipline problems in the classroom. Be prepared for employers that range from nutty to demented!

By the time Jamie Masters decided to go to Crete to teach English, it was too late to register with the agencies. He arrived in Heraklion in October:

I advertised (in Greek) in the Cretan newspapers, no joy. I lowered my sights and started knocking on doors of frontisteria. I was put onto some guy called Saridakis who ran an English-language bookshop and went to see him. Turned out he was some kind of lynch-pin in the frontisterion business and in fact I got my first job through him. Simultaneously I went to something which roughly translates as the 'Council for owners of frontisteria' and was given a list of schools which were looking for people. The list, it turned out, was pretty much out of date. But I had insisted on leaving my name with the Council (they certainly didn't offer) and that's how I found my second job.

Private lessons, at least in the provinces, are easy to find. The going rate is dr2,500-3,000 an hour for First Certificate teaching, dr5,000 for the more advanced Cambridge Proficiency. Athenian rates are higher. Most employed teachers do at least three or four hours a week of private undeclared teaching – more than enough to cover their Retsina bill.

Voluntary Work

Conservation Volunteers in Greece (15 Omirou St, 145 62 Kifissia, Athens; fax 01-801 1429; cvgpeep@otenet.gr/ www.cvgpeep.org) is a non-profit organisation promoting intercultural exchanges and nature and heritage conservation. Projects include work in protected landscapes, conservation of traditional buildings and work on archaeological sites. Applications can be sent directly or via UNA Wales.

Organisations involved in the protection of sea turtles actively use volunteer helpers. Archelon is the Sea Turtle Protection Society of Greece (Solomou 57, 104 32 Athens; tel/fax 01-523 1342; stps@archelon.gr/ www.archelon.gr) which carries out research and conservation on the loggerhead turtle on Zakynthos, Crete and the Peloponnese. A free campsite is provided for those who stay at least a month; volunteers will need at least dr2,500 a day for food plus pay a registration fee of dr20,000. The Italian research organisation CHELON is active on Rhodes taking a census of loggerhead nests, helping to tag turtles and doing observation studies; details from CHELON, Viale Val Padana 134B, 00141 Rome (+39 06-812 5301; chelon@tin.it). Volunteers must fund themselves. Conservation Koroni (Poste Restante, Koroni 240 04, Messinias; fax 0725-22779) has in the past taken on volunteers in phases between mid-May and mid-October to spend a couple of hours each day working to clean up the beach and surrounding habitats of the loggerhead turtle near Koroni in the Peloponnese. No wage is paid and the cost of accommodation for one month is £100. Bears are even more threatened than marine turtles. Arcturos accepts short-term volunteers at its bear protection centre (Victor Hugo 3, 546 25 Thessaloniki; 031-55 46 23/ www.forthnet.gr/arcturos).

Another interesting possibility for people with specific skills willing to work for pocket money for at least three months (May to July or August to October) is at the holistic holiday centre on the island of Skyros in the northern Aegean. A number of 'work scholars' help with cleaning, bar work and domestic and maintenance duties in exchange for full board and accommodation and £40 a week. Only English-speaking nurses, head chefs, maintenance/handypersons and fluent Greek speakers are hired. The main perk is that they are welcome to join one or more of the 250 courses on offer from abseiling to windsurfing. Details are available from Skyros, 92 Prince of Wales Road, London NW5 3NE (020-7267 4424; connect@skyros.com).

In past summers, volunteers have been recruited to row a 170-oared trireme, a reconstruction of a ship used by the ancient Greeks now berthed at Poros. Unfortunately the hull of the *Olympias* was badly damaged by Mediterranean shipworm a few years ago and repairs have been slow. Interested people can check the web-page of the Trireme Trust (www.atm.ox.ac.uk/rowing/trireme.html) to find out whether sea-trials will be resumed in time for the Athens Olympics.

Cyprus

Although the Cypriot economy like the Greek relies heavily on tourism (2.6 million tourists visited the island last year) and agriculture which can normally be counted on to provide work for travellers, the very strict immigration regulations make it difficult. At the end of the last century Cyprus commenced negotiations for accession to the European Union, though this seems a remote possibility at present in view of the partition of the island.

A visitor to Greek Cyprus will be struck by the similarities with Greece (cuisine, architecture, landscapes and culture) but then surprised by the relative prominence of English and the widespread British influence. Because of the longstanding relationship between Cyprus and the UK, the English language has a much higher profile in the Cypriot educational system than the Greek, which means that there is less demand for native speaker English teachers in private institutes. However the tourist industry requires a huge influx of seasonal labour.

Regulations

Citizens of the EU may be granted an employment permit whilst in Cyprus, provided all requirements are met. Their prospective employer must prove that no one among the local population is qualified to do the job and then obtain the necessary permission from the Migration Officer at the Ministry of the Interior in Nicosia (D. Severis Avenue, 1457 Nicosia; 02-804410/fax 676944). The Cyprus High Commission in London (93 Park St, W1Y 4ET; 020-7299 8272) issues an information sheet (dated October 1992) 'Employment in the Republic of Cyprus' which sets out the rules briefly and lists five employment agencies in Nicosia and Limassol.

Work permits are required for both paid and unpaid work. They are rarely issued in the case of jobs in the tourist industry but very occasionally an application is granted. Karen Holman from Nottingham wrote a few years ago to say that she had been working legally as a barmaid in Cyprus for two years. Her work permit was granted for an initial three months and then renewed after she had provided a police clearance certificate and HIV test. But most people working in the Cypriot tourist industry do not have work permits. It was recently reported in the British press that restaurateurs in resorts like Ayia Napa and Protaras were threatening to close down if the government did not reverse its policy on refusing work permits to foreigners. They claimed that without foreign staff, these resorts could not operate.

Employers who want to hire English-speaking staff are likely to tell you that you don't need a work permit for temporary work and many foreigners accept work on this basis. However it should be stressed that large fines and bans from returning to the country are real possibilities for those caught. Cyprus is one country where the regulations are enforced. The Immigration Police have very sharp eyes and ears and frequently visit cafés and bars likely to employ foreigners. Two of Tom Parker's friends working at back street bars in the old town of Limassol had to impersonate a customer whenever the police visited. A Briton called Dave who was helping to renovate a yacht in Larnaca boatyard was discovered by immigration after three days and was forced to leave town. Yet the same man went on to work a season as a drinks waiter in Protaras (he had had the foresight to bring a pair of black trousers and white shirt) and was not troubled by immigration once. It seems that the authorities concentrate their efforts at the beginning of the season and are less inclined to bother you once the season gets busy.

Even entering the country as a tourist can be tricky if an immigration officer asks you to prove that you can support yourself by showing $1,000 in cash. Tourist visas expire after three months but may be renewed if you can show enough money to support yourself. It might be easier to cross the border (to Greece or Israel) and return to Cyprus when your tourist visa will be renewed. You cannot cross between Greek and Turkish Cyprus for longer than one day.

Surprisingly, there have been several reports from working travellers in the self-styled Turkish Republic of Northern Cyprus (see separate section below). The red tape here is much less tricky, though the morality of the situation may give you pause. Before working in the TRNC, you will first have to overcome your qualms about working in a place whose regime was responsible for the forcible eviction of so many Cypriots and destruction of property and artefacts following the invasion of 1974.

The Tourist Industry

As in Greece, women are at a great advantage when looking for work in cafés, bars and restaurants, but they should exercise caution according to Karen Holman:

In my two years there I heard stories about Cypriot employers expecting more of their barmaids than just bar work. I worked in two pubs and I would say that both bosses employed me with an ulterior motive. I was lucky – both of them were shy. By the time they realised I wasn't going to be their girlfriend, they had found me to be a good worker and were used to me being around. Many employers will sack the girls, or threaten to report them for stealing. If you're legal, your work permit is valid for that job only, so if you leave the job, you have to leave the country.

Just such a serious case of exploitation and harassment was reported in the British press. A 23 year old trainee lawyer who had met her employer on a previous holiday found herself working 15 hours a day without a day off in temperatures of over 100°. The final straw came when the manager hit her after she rebuffed his advances. She instantly quit and was paid C£40 for 15 days work. She had no recourse because she had no work permit.

Rhona Stannage was much luckier: her boss (whom she met in a novel way) was gay. In the supermarket in Protaras she and her husband Stuart introduced themselves to a man whose trolley was so full of bottles, they reckoned he must run a restaurant. He practically offered Rhona a job on the spot as waitress and cleaner, and offered Stuart a cooking job two days later.

Tom Parker had little success with a job search along the seafront in Limassol in April:

We headed for the tourist area and were soon told that we would stand a better chance if we bought a drink for the manager before asking about jobs. The only concrete result was that we got very drunk. No job opportunities (they told us we were too early). The next day we concentrated on the small cafés in the back streets of the old town. Here my two companions (both girls) were offered jobs in separate cafés. The kitchen job paid £13 a day and the waiting job £16, both plus tips. They both also worked in a bar in the evening, sitting round talking to the mainly local customers and being bought drinks for which the customer was charged £6.50 whether it was water or vodka and they earned a commission of £1 per drink, in addition to the evening fee of £13.

Outdoor Work

Because he was male, Tom Parker did not find a restaurant job. But on the advice of his guest house landlady he found two weeks of (backbreaking) weeding work with a landscape gardener, which paid £20 a day.

There is a lot of casual day work in the Larnaca boatyard mentioned above. However security is strict, and you are obliged to leave your passport with a guard at the gate of the harbour (this is how immigration caught Dave mentioned above). Apparently if you have been promised a position as a crew member you are exempt from the work permit requirements. Try putting up a notice in the Globe Bar or asking a member to put up a notice for you in the private Marina Bar.

Moving away from the tourist resorts, grape-picking takes place between August and October. Olives are also picked in the autumn. There are two strawberry harvests a year, one in May/June and another in November/December. Oranges are picked for up to three months around Limassol. Women's wages are lower than men's. Men interested in labouring work should look for new tourist developments in resorts like

Ayia Napa on the south-east coast. Arrange to be paid daily or weekly rather than monthly, since it can be difficult to extract earned money.

The cost of living in Cyprus is high. For example it took Rhona and Stuart a long time to find a cheaper alternative to their £13-a-day apartment.

TURKISH REPUBLIC OF NORTHERN CYPRUS

As is well known, Cyprus is a divided island. The southern part is the Republic of Cyprus, a member of the British Commonwealth. The north, occupied by Turkey since the intervention of 1974, is called the Turkish Republic of Northern Cyprus (Kibris). It is not recognised by any country except Turkey. Surprisingly, there is a sizeable expat community here and a slowly expanding tourist industry, hampered by the lack of direct flights (incoming tourists must travel via Turkey). Because it is off the beaten track, the pool of potential seasonal or casual labour is much smaller than it is elsewhere on the Mediterranean.

Eric Mackness, a correspondent of long standing, reiterates his enthusiasm for Northern Cyprus as a destination for job-seekers:

> *I think that Turkish Cyprus is quite a unique location work-wise. I don't want to make light of my undoubted charm and my ability to chop a tomato into four pieces, but I think anyone with a little common sense can always find a job here. I hear of job vacancies literally every day. Of course it is early in the year and as the season progresses the vacancies won't be quite so numerous. But if you work hard, prove yourself to be honest and reliable, there are always vacancies here in the North. Quite a few new restaurants have opened since I was last here, all looking for chefs and bar and waiting staff.*

Turkish Cyprus is a very small place (population 170,000) and job vacancies become known as soon as they exist. For every one advertised in the English language paper *Cyprus Today* there are six heard of on the grapevine. The notice board outside the Post Office in the main town of Kyrenia is a very good source of information on jobs, accommodation, etc. Most opportunities lie in the catering trade and are open to men and women. Many are in restaurants, etc. owned or managed by expats. The wages are poor by British standards, say between £100 and £200 per month. But this is on top of food and accommodation (which is offered in 99% of cases) and tips. The official minimum wage is equivalent approximately to £150 per month. But this must be offset by non-financial compensations including the relaxed pace of life (some say like the Turkish coast was 20 or 30 years ago), unspoiled scenery and cheap pleasures.

Eric fixed up his first job in an amazing way: he simply wrote directly to a restaurant called Rita-on-the-Rocks in the village of Lapta 10km from the capital Kyrenia (Girne in Turkish) which he had heard mentioned briefly on a BBC travel programme. Even without any catering experience apart from some part-time dish-washing when he was a mature student, he was offered a job. (Since then, Rita has retired home to England with her Cypriot husband.) The highest concentration of restaurants and bars is along the picturesque harbour of Kyrenia, with a further concentration in Lapta, Karaman and Alsancak to the west.

The pre-season spruce-up normally takes place in February to prepare for an opening date in early March. So this is a good time to make enquiries. The season doesn't get very busy until June but by then most of the vacancies will be filled. Independent accommodation is available; two-bedroomed houses can be rented for £200 a month out-of-season, while Eric Mackness was offered a number of chances to house-sit.

Tour Companies

Pat Kennard is another reader who found work in Northern Cyprus. While her husband found a technical job at the Acapulco Casino (5 miles west of Kyrenia), she landed a job with Kibris Travel Service, the ground handling agent for ten UK tour operators. She enjoyed a fantastic season as a holiday rep even though, as she admits, it is a very demanding job having to do early morning and late night airport runs, sort out clients' problems with their accommodation and conduct tours of the island. Kibris Travel

Services Ltd (PO Box 358, Girne, Mersin 10, Turkey; 90-392 815 7555/fax 90-392 815 7730) placed prominent ads in *Cyprus Today* for seasonal reps who are fluent in English, holders of a full driving licence and ready to commence employment immediately after being trained by KTS. The Anglo-Cypriot Association has a noticeboard in front of the Girne post office where it might be worth posting your interest in finding work.

Northern Cyprus is not a cheap package holiday destination and tends to attract a more discerning clientele, who are interested in visiting the sites as well as enjoying the marvellous scenery and climate. It is a popular destination for Germans, so some knowledge of German would be an advantage. After making friends with several residents, Theresa Thomas (a trained teacher) accepted a job with a local tour operator. Typically, the interview took place in a café:

> *My job was to take out daily coach tours (the clients were mostly professionals from the UK) six days a week, explain the history of the island and liaise with bus drivers, restaurateurs, etc. The good features were that I was able to see so much of this beautiful island and mix with interesting people. The bad features were poor pay for long working hours (sometimes in extreme heat), having no workers' rights and always having to deal with sexual harassment.*

Other jobs can be found on boats such as the one run by Bicen Tours which employs about six English people on the boat as well as on land (leading tours, bike hire, etc.).

Red Tape

In contrast to Greek Cyprus, the authorities are refreshingly unconcerned about the red tape, whatever your nationality. The only requirement is that you have to leave Cyprus every three months to renew your tourist visa; this entails a two-hour catamaran trip to mainland Turkey at a cost of about £20. Note that a stamp from TRNC (the Turkish Republic of Northern Cyprus) could make future visits to Greece difficult. At entry you can request that the stamp be put on a separate form.

Long-stay travellers may be able to persuade an employer to obtain a work permit on their behalf. Fees are roughly £40 for a 6-month residence permit, £75 for 12 months and £100 for a 6-month work permit.

Italy

Italy is a remarkably welcoming country. Once Italians accept you, they will go out of their way to find you a place in their communities, without any emphasis on the barriers of nationality. Once you get a toehold, you will find that a friendly network of contacts and possible employers will quickly develop. Without contacts, if only a sympathetic landlady at your pension, it is virtually impossible to find work.

Some travellers mistakenly expect Italy to be poor and backward in some respects. They are surprised, especially in the north, to discover that the cost of living is considerably higher than in other Mediterranean countries. They find the best-dressed and most sophisticated people in the world. Image counts for a great deal in Italy, and it has to be said that good-looking smartly dressed people have far more chance of success than their dowdy counterparts. With an unemployment rate of about 12%, it is going to take time to find a job no matter what your dress sense. The situation for casual job-seekers has been made more difficult by the arrival of Albanians and refugees from the old Yugoslavia.

The Regulations

Unfortunately there are more red tape hassles in Italy than there are in other EU countries. Matters have been made worse by legislation intended to prevent an influx of refugees from eastern Europe. Many job-seekers have found employers reluctant to consider hiring them because of the bureaucratic hurdles which must be jumped. The 'Notes for British Citizens Wishing to Visit Italy' available from the Consular Section of the British Embassy in Rome (Via XX Settembre 80a, 00187 Rome) do not go into much detail about the red tape, and the leaflet 'General Information Regarding Living and Working in Italy' issued by the Italian Consulate in London contains even fewer hard facts. Procedures vary from place to place, and possibly even from official to official. Persistence and patience will be needed in all cases. If you decide you are being treated unreasonably and given the run-around, try standing your ground and insisting that you be dealt with on the spot rather than passed on to another department.

If you arrive with the intention of working, you must first apply to the police *(questura)* for a *Ricevuta di Segnalazione di Soggiorno* which allows you to stay for up to three months looking for work. Upon production of this document and a letter from an employer, you must go back to the police to obtain a residence permit – *Permesso di Soggiorno*. Then in some cases you will be asked to apply for a *Libretto di Lavoro* (work registration card) from the town hall or *Municipio* (although, in theory, this should not be necessary for EU nationals). If you want to open a bank account for example, you need to register at the registry office *(Ufficio Anagrafe)*; in Rome the address is Via Luigi Petroselli 50.

Even farmers eager to hire people for a very temporary period will ask to see your papers for fear of being caught and fined, as Xuela Edwards found when she looked for grape-picking work in the Chianti region:

Several vineyard owners were keen to take us on but insisted we get the correct papers. As EU citizens we were entitled to work and so set out to get our papers. We were told to apply for a Libretto di Lavoro *from the Town Hall on the Piazza del Campo in Siena. When we found the right office they said we needed a first and directed us to another part of Siena. On application we were told that it would take 60 days to come through, by which time of course the grape harvest would be over. We did hear that it was possible to get a* Permesso *by queuing all day in Rome; arrive very early, take a couple of passport photos and a packed lunch.*

Once the paperwork has been dealt with, your employer will have to pay contributions on your behalf which can be very substantial in Italy. As usual, all of this should be more straightforward for EU nationals than in fact it is. When Ian McArthur tried to get a *libretto di lavoro* he was treated little better than an illegal immigrant (but nevertheless has embarked on a 'lifelong love affair with Italy'). Roberta Wedge who taught English for a year in Bari recalls the red tape:

I had to visit three different government offices about eight times in total. Not exactly the free movement of labour! My health card arrived six months after the wheels were set in motion.

Work visas for non-EU nationals *(extracomunitari)* will be issued only by Italian Embassies or Consulates in the applicant's home country. According to the Italian Embassy in Washington, the requirements for a *lavoro subordinato* are an authorisation to work *(Autorizzazione al Lavoro)* obtained from the Ministry of Labour or from a local *Servizio politiche del lavoro* (provincial labour office) and an authorisation from the local police. The book *Living, Studying and Working in Italy* by Travis Neighbor and Monica Larner (published by Owl Books in 1998) is aimed specifically at Americans and contains much practical advice about coping with the bureaucracy. Note that from Easter 2000, non-EU nationals travelling to Italy were being asked to show sufficient funds, at least £150, reportedly to stem the tide of backpackers.

Do not be too discouraged by the regulations and the red tape since there is a great deal of unofficial, cash-in-hand work or *lavoro al nero* available in Italy. One young working holidaymaker from Berkshire who spent part of the winter season working in a ski resort bar kept a drink strategically placed at the end of the bar so she could vault over and pose as a punter should the *carabinieri* come in. She decided that this was preferable to making four separate train journeys down from the mountains to get the appropriate *bolli* (stamps). Even reputable au pair agencies encourage their non-European au pairs to tell the authorities that they are in Italy as house guests or on a cultural exchange rather than face the bureaucracy. (Other agencies like Amicizia listed below simply won't accept non-Europeans onto their books.)

Before Dominic Fitzgibbon left his home in Australia he decided he wanted to live in Italy for a year and arrived in Rome in the spring. He spent six weeks unsuccessfully looking for a job which used up a large proportion of his travel fund. But the landlady of the flat he was renting off the magnificent Piazza Navona took a shine to him, and arranged for him to work for one of her friends who owned a 3-star hotel as a night porter, although he had 'no work permit and practically no Italian'.

Remember that medical expenses can be crippling if you're not covered by the Italian Medical Health Scheme (USL or *Unita Sanitaria Locale*). If your employer is

SWITZERLAND

FRANCE

AUSTRIA

Courmayeur

L. Maggiore Valtellina

Cannero
Stresa   Chiesa   Livigno

Sestriere

Claviere   Como   Bormio
Sauze d'Oulx   TURIN   Cles   Bressanone
   Aprica   Canazei

Asti   Lombardy   Alto
   MILAN   Adige   Dolomites   Cortina
San Remo   Albenga   Cremona

   Brescia
Italian Riviera   Portofino   Verona   VENICE

   Vignola   Bologna   Trieste

   Emilia Romagna
   Abetone
Pisa   FLORENCE   Rimini

   Siena   Arezzo
Corsica   Elba   Chianti   Pescara   Adriatic
   Perugia   Sea

   ITALY

Sardinia   ROME

   Campobasso

Cagliari   Caserta

   NAPLES
   Sorrento
   Capri   Bari
   Amalfi

Calabria

Sicily

WILLIAM SWAN

not paying contributions, you might want to take out your own insurance at an office of SAI, one of the major Italian insurance companies.

In some areas, anyone who gets a job in the food and beverage sector must obtain a *Tessere Sanitaria* (hygiene certificate) even if they are not handling food themselves. Even the most laid-back employers insist on it since they can be in serious trouble if found employing people without it. Emma Purdy describes the process she underwent in Rome:

> *After a couple of weeks, we had received several offers of bar work, all on condition that we could present a Tessere Sanitaria. To get our certificates we had to visit the USL office nearest where we were staying (an Italian friend rang up for us to find out where it was). All the people we dealt with were friendly but by the end of it we felt as though we had visited every office in Italy. One office said that we first needed our permesso whereas another never mentioned it. We did need passport photos and a receipt from the local post office to prove that we had paid L24,000 into the proper USL account. The examination itself was very quick, just checking under fingernails and a couple of injections (requiring several visits to the USL). I wish we had known all this before we arrived in Italy.*

Again rules differ from place to place. In some places, a more thorough medical examination will be necessary and a different sum of money due.

FINDING WORK

If you can't speak a word of Italian, you will be at a distinct disadvantage. Provided you can afford it and are sufficiently interested, you should consider studying a little Italian before you set off on your travels or enrolling in one of the many short Italian language courses offered in most Italian cities. Italian is one of the easiest languages to learn, especially if you already have some knowledge of a Latin-based language.

However your inability to speak Italian need not be an absolute barrier, as Ian Moody found when he got a job as a door-to-door salesman of English books and language courses, without himself knowing any Italian. His technique was more amusing in retrospect than it was successful:

> *I was given the spiel in phonetic Italian and told to learn it off by heart before knocking on the doors of middle class, professional Italians in various northern Italian towns. Reeling off the sales pitch parrot-fashion was okay until they asked a question which I couldn't make head nor tail of. I found it was often easier to run away. So it was extremely difficult to make many sales. For those who persevered at the door, sales were often promised just to get rid of the rep. Still the working conditions were good, mainly because it was permanently sunny. And you were able to meet people (even if you couldn't actually understand a word they were saying).*

This sort of work crops up from time to time. After graduation Mr. P. G. Penn wanted to work abroad and learn a language for six months and landed a job as a travelling book salesman:

> *Having submitted my CV I was accepted for a one-month trial period. I flew to Rome and immediately received bad vibes when I learned that of the 17 English-speaking people hired in the previous six months only two remained. The other two guys in my group had become very stressed and seemed permanently tired, a fate which did not escape me. The work was 8am-9pm Monday to Friday with a half-day on Saturday. We had no time to learn the language, since the sales talk had pre-programmed answers to questions. This was what ultimately led me to leave. Sales work is difficult but this was demanding too much, whilst denying personal freedom and time.*

Although you should not neglect scouring the newspapers for job adverts, you may be disappointed. Ian Abbott noticed in Roman newspapers that there were more adverts placed by *stranieri* (foreigners) asking for work than there were situations vacant. The following publications might be of use to Italian-speaking job-seekers:

Il Sole 24 Ore, Via Lomazzo 52, 20154 Milan (fax 02-310 3426/341062). Newspaper with a careers supplement in October.

Corriere della Sera – the Friday edition of this major Italian daily has the employment adverts.

Campus, Tuttolavoro, Trovalavoro and *Bollettino del lavoro* are all monthly employment magazines.

The first free-ads papers in Europe were published in Italy in 1977. *Secondamano* (meaning Second Hand) is published in ten regional editions covering the industrialised north of the country.

Some foreigners have topped up their travel funds by doing life modelling for which there is a great demand in Florence and other cities. Simply visit art schools and ask to sit in on a life drawing class to make sure that the situation is one you can cope with. Expect to be paid between L18,000 and L30,000 per hour.

In Vacanza Lavorando (Via Albertazzi 31/2, 40137 Bologna; tel/fax 051-397816) maintains a databank of information on working holidays, voluntary work and traineeships in Italy and abroad used by youth information centres in Italy. Their literature includes the addresses of the Centro per l'impiego in several northern cities, which is the regional office for seasonal work in agriculture and hotels:

Agenzia del Lavoro – Centro per l'impiego di Trento, Via Maccani 76, 38100 Trento (0461-496189/496190; www.agenzialavoro.tn.it).

Centro per l'impiego di Fiera di Primiero, Via Fiume 10, 38054 Fiera di Primiero (Trento) (0439-762232). Hotel work in the Alps.

Centro per l'impiego di Riva del Garda, Via Vannetti 2, 38066 Riva del Garda (0464-552130). For hotel work on Lake Garda.

Centro per l'impiego di Cavalese, Via Bronzetti, 38033 Cavalese (TN) (0462-340204). Hotel and agricultural working holidays in the Alps.

Centro per l'impiego di Tione, Via Damiano Chiesa 1, 38079 Tione (Trento) (0465-321113). Hotel and agricultural working holidays in the Alps.

The Employment Service

Officially, all foreign job-seekers are obliged to register with the government employment service. (As in several other European countries, private employment agencies are prohibited.) Unless you are fluent in Italian, the state employment service *(Ufficio di Collocamento)* is unlikely to be much use to you. It is normally necessary to visit them regularly (preferably every day) to make your presence felt. The employment offices in the smaller towns might be more helpful than the ones in the main cities being less accustomed to foreign job-seekers. For example before the summer season, the ones in seaside resorts often have lists of hotel and restaurant jobs. The website www.agenzialavoro.tn.it has links to the addresses of regional Agenzia del Lavoro.

Contacts

Contacts are even more important in Italy than in other countries. Many of the people we have heard from who have worked in Italy (apart from TEFL teachers, au pairs, etc.) have got their work through friends. They may not necessarily have had the friends or contacts when they arrived, but they formed friendships while they were there as visitors. Louise Rollett, for example, first went out as a paying guest to a town near Bologna (an arrangement made through the Experiment in International Living, mentioned in the *Introduction*) and then extended her stay on a work-for-keep basis as an English tutor. Dustie Hickey went for treatment to a doctor in Milan who immediately offered to pay her L20,000 an hour to tutor his children in English.

You can't expect preferment over the locals' own friends and relatives however as Allan Kirkpatrick found last year:

> *I took a flight to Rome to visit an old Italian friend who lives in Anzio near Rome. I stayed in her house and found some bar work for only ten days out of my total stay of two months, due to the fact that my Italian wasn't too good. The school holidays must have been a big factor too in my lack of success; friends, relatives and next door neighbours come first before a young backpacking, English-speaking Scot.*

In Rome try the notice boards in the following locations: the English language Lion Bookshop at Via dei Greci 33/36, the Church of England on nearby Via del Babuino and the student travel agency CTS (Centro Turistico Studentesco e Giovanile) at Via Genova 16, 00184 Rome (06-462 0431; www.cts.it); the nearest underground station is Repubblica on the A line. Language school notice boards are always worth checking; at the *Centro di Lingua & Cultura Italiana per Stranieri* where Dustie Hickie took cheap Italian lessons in Milan, there was a good notice board with adverts for au pairs, dog-walkers, etc. Dustie got a cleaning job this way. Every region has a Youth Information Office *(Centro Informazione Giovani)* which is in a position to advise on holiday work, for example in Bologna try Informagiovani, Via Pier de Crescenzi 14, Bologna (051-525842; informagiovani@comune.bologna.it).

Laurence Koe had collected the addresses of many of his pupils at a summer school where he had worked on the south coast of England. The first one he looked up was in Como and the family promptly invited him to stay until he found work (an invitation which made him marvel at the contrast with English habits of hospitality). One of the daughters had the idea of asking the local radio station to employ Laurence, mainly for novelty value. She accompanied Laurence to the station and stood in for him at the interview, inventing freely about his past history as a DJ. They put him on a jointly presented afternoon music programme and his task seemed to be to adjudicate the correct English pronunciation of song titles. No wage was paid, but it was good experience and good fun. Also he became very well known in the town, a kind of celebrity, and felt that he was giving something to the community instead of just taking. He would let it slip on the radio that he was there to teach English and opportunities began to present themselves.

Even with contacts you are not guaranteed of finding work, as Edward Peters found one summer:

> *After travelling through Eastern Europe and Austria, we had hoped to find something in Italy; but three sets of contacts were unable to find us anything – perhaps because it was August (national holidays) or perhaps because we were too busy enjoying ourselves in Milan, Rome and Ischia.*

TOURISM

Italy's tourist industry employs between 6% and 7% of the Italian workforce and does not seem to have many openings for unskilled non-Italians. It is also difficult to find work with a UK tour company, since there are severe legal restrictions on the hiring of non-Italian staff.

Of course some readers have succeeded. As mentioned above, a Scot found occasional work in a bar in Anzio where he was paid L18,000 an hour to collect dishes, clean tables and also wash dishes. The Australian Dominic Gibbon also mentioned earlier found a job in a hotel in Rome:

> *After six weeks of no luck I told my landlady that perhaps I would head off to Greece. She said I was far too nice to look for dishwashing work and told me about a friend who needed help running his seasonal hotel off Piazza Barberini. Within 20 minutes I was behind the counter having the telephone system explained to me and was told I would be paid L1,100,000 a month for six nights a week as a night porter. After praying the telephone wouldn't ring for the first few weeks, everything settled down. It's quiet, a little boring, but allows me to read and study Italian, more than the few key words related to the hotel trade I knew before. My boss is even going to lend me a TV to help me improve my Italian. I now know how lucky I was to find my place and this job.*

As throughout the world, backpackers' haunts often employ travellers for short periods. Jill Weseman recommends trying the Fawlty Towers hostel at Via Magenta 39, 00184 Rome; 06-445 0374; fulang@flashnet.it) near the Termini Station in Rome where she noticed several Antipodeans working in reception, maintenance and cleaning. (Bruce Fawlty doesn't have quite the same ring as Basil.) While planning her escape route from a less-than-satisfactory summer au pairing job in Naples, Jacqueline

Edwards asked in the Sorrento youth hostel about job possibilities and a few weeks later moved in to take over breakfast duties in exchange for free bed and breakfast.

One reader who thoroughly enjoyed a season working in an Italian city is Carolyn Edwards who was hired by the tour operator Contiki (Wells House, 15 Elmfield Road, Bromley, Kent BR1 1LS) as a general cleaning assistant at their stopover site in Florence for clients on 18-35 tours of Europe. The company operates as an 'art and cultural association' to get round the Italian regulations, and this suited Carolyn who found that she loved standing in front of 53 people talking about the local sites. When the season with Contiki finished in October she got a job in an American-style bar in Florence called the Red Garter where she worked for four months with barely enough Italian to get by. As usual, try British and Irish-style pubs first.

Although less well known than the seaside resorts of other Mediterranean countries, there may be seaside possibilities for foreign job-seekers, especially in the resorts near Venice, as an Italian reader Lara Giavi confirms. She is familiar with two holiday regions: the Lake Garda resorts like Desenzano, Malcesine, Sirmione and Riva del Garda; and the seaside resorts near Venice like Lido di Jesolo (which she says is a great resort for young people), Bibione, Lignano, Caorle and Chioggiaa, all of which are more popular with German and Austrian tourists than Britons so a knowledge of German would be a good selling point. Lara disagrees that there are few opportunities for foreigners in catering, bars and hotels in Italy, though she admits that a knowledge of Italian is necessary in most cases, apart from the job of *donna ai piani* (chambermaid).

The seaside resorts are full of people (including Italians) working black and not being paid the going wage, overtime or holiday pay, but earning plenty of tips. It is difficult enough for an Italian never mind a foreigner to find an employer who pays by the book. In Lara's opinion, travellers looking for a 'working holiday experience' who don't mind about the money should certainly pursue this possibility. Try to track down local hotel associations or hotel chains, for example the following along the Adriatic:

Alberghi Consorziatai, 61032 Fano (0721-827376)
Associazione Albergatori di Rimini, Viale Baldini 14, 47037 Rimini (fax 0541-56519)
Associazione Pesarese Albergatori, 61100 Pesaro (0721-67959)
Associazione Balneare Azienda Turismo – 0733-811600
Associazione Bagnini di Numana e Sirolo, 60026 Numana Ancona (0721-827376).

The Blu Hotels chain has hotels in Lake Garda, Sardinia, Umbria, Abruzzo, Tuscany, Rome, Palinuro and Calabria (as well as Austria); the head office is at Via Porto Portese 22, 25010 San Felice di Benaco (Brescia; 0365-559900; www.bluhotels.it).

The relatively low rate of unemployment in the Veneto region makes it a better bet than some of the other tourist regions of Italy such as the Adriatic coastal resorts of Rimini and Pescara and the Italian Riviera between Nice and Genoa (Portofino, San Remo, etc.), though it may be worth trying resorts in Italy's lake region, like Stresa and Cannero on Lake Maggiore. Michael Cullen worked in three hotels around Como and Bellagio and found 'a nice friendly and warm atmosphere, despite the heat and long hours'. Even in flourishing resorts like Rimini, there seems to be nearly enough locals and Italian students to fill the jobs in hotels, bars and on the beach. As Stephen Venner observed, 'Although prospects appeared to be good in Rimini, café and hotel owners were unwilling to take on foreigners because of the paperwork,' which reinforces the points about red tape made above. Assistance may be available from the temporary employment office Sinterim (Via Bruno 20, 47037 Rimini; 0541-53274) which has branches in ten other offices in northern Italian cities. High unemployment in the south of Italy together with a huge population of migrant workers from poor countries means that it is probably not worth trying the resorts south of Naples, viz. Capri, Sorrento and Amalfi.

If you don't get a job in a hotel, you might get work servicing holiday flats or gardening. If you plan far enough in advance (and speak some Italian) you might get a job as a campsite courier with one of the major British camping holiday organisers such as Canvas Holidays (see the chapter on *Tourism*). The smaller Venue Holidays (1

Norwood Road, Ashford, Kent TN23 1QU; www.venueholidays.co.uk) employs summer season reps at campsites on the Venetian Riviera, Lake Garda and in Tuscany. Catherine Dawes enjoyed her campsite job near Albenga on the Italian Riviera – 'a fairly uninspiring part of Italy' – even more than she did her previous summer's work on a French campsite. She reports that the Italians seemed to be more relaxed than the French, especially under high season pressure, and would always go out of their way to help her when she was trying to translate tourists' problems to the mechanic or the doctor.

You can also try Italian-run campsites which have a large staff to man the on-site restaurants, bars and shops. Stephen Venner noticed that the two main campsites in Rome including the Flaminio take on English help before the season begins (i.e. March). With the help of some Argentinian friends, Andrea Militello rounded up a job at a campsite Santa Teresa di Gallura in northern Sardinia for the summer season.

The agency Romana Musicisti (Via La Spezia 100, 00055 Ladispoli, Roma; tel/fax 06-9922 1766; www.caerenet.it/romus) recruits musicians, singers, DJs and entertainers for summer jobs around Italy. It would not be worth paying the registration fee unless you spoke good Italian.

Winter Resorts

On-the-spot opportunities are probably more numerous in the winter resorts of the Alps, Dolomites and Apennines. Many of the jobs are part-time and not very well paid, but provide time for skiing and in many cases a free pass to the ski-lifts for the season. Sauze d'Oulx and Courmayeur are the best resorts for job hunting, particularly the former according to Jaime Burnell who, while in her gap year, left an exploitative job with a British ski tour operator near Trento to job-hunt in Sauze d'Oulx:

> *I cannot recommend enough winter work in Sauze d'Oulx. I arrived on the 14th of January. Everyone tells you that the turnover is high but that is an understatement. Going out every night you couldn't be sure who would be behind the bar that day.*

Jaime goes on to offer one more nugget of information which proves once and for all that blondes really do have more fun:

> *The best investment you can make in Italy is a bottle of blonde hair dye. My tips tripled.*

Cathy Salt describes her success in Sauze d'Oulx:

> *Upon arrival at Sauze d'Oulx on 14th November, we found we were much too early for on-the-spot jobs. The place was practically dead. Only a few bars were open. Fortunately an English guy working in a bar informed us that the carpenter was looking for help. My partner Jon was able to get four weeks work with him, sanding down and varnishing, also enabling him to be on the spot for other work that would come up. The same day I found a babysitting job for a shop owner's son, but I wouldn't start until 5th December. We were both fortunate in finding this since we came up on a Thursday and have since found out that the weekend is a much better time to look because the ski shops and restaurants are open.*

Such stories are counterbalanced by the inevitable failures: Susanna Macmillan gave up her job hunt in the Italian Alps after two weeks when she had to admit that her non-existent Italian and just passable French were not getting her anywhere. Perhaps she was looking in the wrong resorts like Cortina which is sophisticated and expensive and has a high percentage of year-round workers.

Crystal Holidays Ltd (King's Place, Wood St, Kingston-upon-Thames, Surrey KT1 1JY; 0870 888 0028) hire resort reps and chalet staff for work in the Italian Alps as well as staff for summer holidays. The Ski Department of PGL Travel Ltd (Alton Court, Penyard Lane, Ross-on-Wye, Herefordshire HR9 5GL) offer some jobs as ski reps, leaders and ski/snowboard instructors (to BASI-qualified skiers), especially for short periods during half-term and Easter holidays.

As in other alpine resorts there are also jobs for chalet girls, though not as many as in neighbouring countries due to the very strict regulations which govern chalets in

Italy. You are more likely to find a job in a small family run bar or hotel than in one of the big concerns. The large hotels usually recruit their staff in southern Italy and then move them en masse from the sea to the mountains in the autumn.

AU PAIRS

The majority of European au pair agencies deal with Italy, so you should have no trouble arranging a job or, rather, a placement for 'cultural reasons' (to satisfy the bureaucracy). Au pairs coming from outside Europe (e.g. the USA, Canada, Australia) must be aged 18-25. If they intend to stay for longer than three months they must obtain a student visa.

Angie Copley was delighted with the situation to which her British agency sent her:

After finding the address of agencies in your book, I wrote to one and before I knew it they had found me a family in Sardinia. I couldn't believe it was so easy. All I had to do was pay for a flight out there and that was that. When I arrived, the family met me and took me to their house. Some house. It wasn't just a house but a castle where the Italian royal family used to spend their holidays. What was even better was that the family had turned it into a hotel, the best possible place for meeting people. I ended up having the best summer of my life in Sardinia. Once I picked up the language I went out, met lots of people, had beach parties. My work involved not much more than playing with their two-year old boy all day and speaking English to him. Basically it was one big holiday.

Summer-only positions are readily available. Most Italian families in the class that can afford live-in childcare go to holiday homes by the sea or in the mountains during the summer and at other holiday times which did not prove as idyllic as it sounds for Jacqueline Edwards:

My first job as an au pair in Italy was with a family who were staying in the middle of nowhere with their extended family. It was a total nightmare for me. I could just about say hello in Italian and couldn't understand a word of what was going on. After three weeks I was fed up, homesick and ready to jump on the next plane to England. But a few days later we moved back to town (Modena) and from then on things improved dramatically. I was able to go out and meet other au pairs and nannies at the park, etc. and we all socialised together. I ended up learning Italian quite well, making lots of friends (partly through my language school, which was free by the way) and visiting most of the Italian cities. The only part that I didn't like in that job was going away with the family to their holiday houses for skiing, etc. You end up working twice your usual hours for the same pay, have no social life as you don't have any friends there, can't go skiing as you are minding the baby and then they tell you to cheer up because you're on holiday.

The average monthly wage for au pairs is in the range L400,000-L600,000, for mother's helps L600,000-L1,000,000, and for junior nannies up to L1,400,000. Wages are slightly higher in the north of Italy than central and southern parts of the country because the cost of living is higher. The demand for nannies and mothers' helps able to work 40+ hours is especially strong since a high percentage of families in Italy have two working parents.

With the demise of the Kent-based agency Au Pairs in Italy after nearly 25 years, no British agency specialises only in Italy. However most of the Italian agencies speak English and welcome applications from British au pairs. Make sure first that you won't be liable to pay a hefty registration fee. Try any of the following:

Amicizia, Via G.T. Invrea 3/7, 16129 Genoa (010-553 1096/fax 010-553 1152; terminisimona@hotmail.com). Booking fee of L50,000.

L'Aquilone, Via Giovanni Pascoli 15, 20129 Milan (02-29 52 96 39/fax 02-29 52 21 75; aquilone@azienda.com; www.s.snf.it/aquilone). Registration fee of L100,000 covers assistance for 12 months.

ARCE, Via XX Settembre 20/124 16121 Genoa (010-583020/fax 010-583092; arceita@tin.it). Long established agency which makes placements free of charge throughout the country.

Au Pair International, Via S. Stefano 32, 40125 Bologna (051-267575/238320; aupair@tin.it). Member of IAPA. No placement fee.

Aupairitaly.com, Via Demetrio Martinelli 11/d, 40133 Bologna (051-383466; info@aupairitaly.com/ www.aupairitaly.com).

The English Agency, Via Pigafetta 48, 10129 Turin (tel/fax 011-597458; www.theenglishagency.com). No placement fee is charged.

Euro-Placements, Res. Trefili M 12, 20090 Segrate, Milan (02-264 11 275/fax 02-264 17 986; euro@posta2000.com).

Intermediate SNC, Vioa Bramante 13, 00153 Rome (06-5730 0683; www.intermediateonline.com). Member of IAPA.

Mix Culture Au Pair Agency, c/o The British Institute of Rome, Via Nazionale 204, 00184 Rome (06-4788 2289; mixculture@tiscalinet.it).

Au Pairs Recruitment, Via Gaeta 22, 10133 Torino (011-660 2076; annaparavia@paravia.it).

Roma Au Pair Agency, Via di Frino 1, 40136 Bologna (051-345882; www.nuovomondo.com/romaaupair).

TEACHING

Hundreds of language schools around Italy employ native English speakers. Unfortunately for the ordinary traveller, the vast majority of the jobs require a degree, TEFL qualifications and knowledge of Italian. Xuela Edwards arrived with a friend who was a qualified English teacher at the right time (September) and reported that the language schools were flooded with teachers and just being able to speak English was not enough. This view has to be set against P.G. Penn's experience. After he left his selling job, he went to Turin to find TEFL work and after putting in some effort he succeeded without any experience whatsoever.

Doing an introductory TEFL course at home simplifies the job search, especially since many of the training organisations feed their 'graduates' to Italian schools. But not everyone who does a TEFL course is handed a job on a platter. After doing a short TEFL course in England, Bruce Nairne and Sue Ratcliffe set off to find work:

> *Rather unimaginatively we packed our bags and made for Italy in the middle of the summer holidays when there was no teaching work at all. Nevertheless we utilised the Yellow Pages in the SIP office (the equivalent of British Telecom) in Syracuse, Sicily and proceeded to make 30 speculative applications, specifying our status as graduates who had completed a short course in TEFL. By the end of September we had received four job offers without so much as an interview.*

Unfortunately the jobs in Bari which they chose to accept fell through at the last moment. This is not so unusual since many schools wait until their enrolment figures are finalised before signing teachers' contracts. So Bruce and Sue once again resorted to looking up *Scuole di Lingue* in the Yellow Pages, this time in Milan railway station where they managed to secure the interest of three or four establishments for part-time work. This is the normal way to get started as a teacher if you wait until you arrive in Italy, and may involve dashing between institutes to scrape together enough hours to live on. Mr. Penn recommends Turin over the more glamorous cities of Milan and Rome where there are just as many language schools but fewer aspiring teachers.

Without any TEFL training whatsoever, the job hunt will be an uphill struggle as Laurence Koe discovered in both Como and Lecco. He visited all the language schools, some of them three times, and was always told he needed a TEFL qualification or that he was there at the wrong time (October). After three weeks of making the rounds he was asked to stand in for an absent teacher on one occasion, and this was enough to secure him further part-time work. After a few more weeks he found work teaching an evening class of adults. He began to attend the weekly English club (a good source of contacts and leads) and was offered a few thousand lire to answer questions on the plot after English film shows.

Similarly Natalia de Cuba could not persuade any of the language schools in the northern town of Rovereto where she was based to hire her without qualifications. So she decided to enrol in the Cambridge Certificate course run by International House in Rome (Viale Manzoni 22, 00185 Rome). She found the month-long course strenuous but not terribly difficult, and worth the fee (which now stands at L2,460,000). Job offers come into IH from all over Italy and no one seems to have a problem getting a job immediately after the course. Natalia went back to a teaching job in Rovereto where she was well paid for 18 hours of fairly enjoyable teaching a week. A standard teaching wage in 1999 was L1,500,000 (net) per month, while freelancers are paid L18,000-L25,000 per hour. Teachers in Italy should not expect their accommodation to be paid for, but schools generally help their staff to find something reasonably priced.

There are several Italian-based chains of language schools which you might try. Recruitment is normally carried out by the individual schools, but the administrative offices should be able to provide a list of addresses. For example. The British Institutes (Via Leopardi, 8, 20123 Milan; 02-439 0041; www.britishinstitutes.org) group has nearly 200 member schools; email addresses can be searched on their website or you can pick up a leaflet listing them from the youth travel bureau CTS (also represented in most cities). Oxford Schools hire up to 30 teachers for their 15 schools in northeast Italy (Via S. Pertini 14, Mirano 30035 Mirano, Venice; tel/fax 041-570 23 55; www.oxforditalia.it); whereas the quite separate Oxford Institute (10/12 Via Adriatica 10/12, 73100 Lecce; tel/fax 0832-390312; sponsiello@tiscalinet.it) hires about half that many (qualified) teachers on nine-month contracts October to June. Wall Street Institutes is also a major employer of certificate-qualified EFL teachers (Corso Buenos Aires 79, 20124 Milan; 02-670 3108; wsi@wsi.it).

Another possibility is to set up as a freelance tutor, though a knowledge of Italian is even more of an asset here than it is for jobs in schools. You can post notices in supermarkets, tobacconists, primary and secondary schools, etc. It may be worth advertising in a free paper which cost Dustie Hickey (for example) less than £15 for four editions of the local free paper in Rimini. Soon she had several private pupils who paid her about £10 per hour to be taught in her idle afternoons as an au pair. As long as you have access to some premises, you can try to arrange both individual and group lessons, and undercut the language institutes significantly. The ever-enterprising Laurence Koe presented himself to a classroom teacher who asked her class of 12 and 13 years olds if they would like to learn English from a native. They all said Yes and paid Laurence the equivalent of 50p each for a class after school. With no TEFL background, Dustie Hickey ended up tutoring a Milanese doctor who had treated her for a head wound. Whereas she charged him L20,000 an hour, she charged a younger less prosperous woman who wanted conversation practice L15,000, which seemed fair in view of the fact that the woman invited her to stay and eat a meal after the lesson.

As in other European countries, summer camps for unaccompanied young people usually offer English as well as a range of sports. The organisation called A.C.L.E. Summer Camps (Via Roma 54, 18038 San Remo, Liguria; tel/fax 0184-506070; www.acle.org) advertises in the UK for more than 80 young people with a genuine interest in children who must be 'fun-loving, energetic and have high moral standards' to teach English and organise activities including drama for one, two or three months. The promised wage is £400 per month plus board, lodging, insurance, bonus and travel between camps within Italy. However summer staff must enrol in a compulsory three-day introductory TEFL course for which a deduction of £120 is made from earned wages.

Two other organisations which hire native English speakers to work at summer language camps are WorldNet UK (Avondale House, 63 Sydney Road, Haywards Heath, W Sussex RH16 1QD (01444 457676) and Smile (Via Vigmolese 454, 41100 Modena; tel/fax 059-363868).

AGRICULTURE

In most Italian harvests, there is no tradition of hiring large numbers of foreign young people. With the arrival of so many Albanians and East Europeans joining the traditional Moroccan workers, the situation has become even less promising. Seasonal jobs in the grape and olive harvests are reserved and carefully regulated among locals and other Italian unemployed. However if you have local friends and contacts or if you speak some Italian it is worth trying to participate in one of the autumn harvests which by most accounts are thoroughly enjoyable. Wages are also good.

Although they would be a long shot, the *Centro per l'impiego* agencies listed above (under the heading *Finding Work*) might be helpful.

Val di Non Apple Harvest

The main exception to the shortage of harvest jobs for foreign travellers is the apple harvest in the Val di Non around the town of Cles in the valley of the River Adige north of Trento. It is one of those famous destinations for migrant workers which a number of readers have praised, most recently Marisa Wharton from Argentina who met the Englishman there who became her husband a year or two later. Andrea Militello (from another part of Italy) has participated in harvests from Spain to Tasmania, but his favourite is the apple harvest in Revo near Cles where he has picked fruit for many years:

> *This year I had a great time with the other pickers. The harvest starts about the 20th-25th September and last until 25th October, but it's better to arrive at least ten days early. In the beginning it's best to go to Cles and talk with Padre Tiziano, one of the best people I have ever met. He helps everybody. This harvest unites people from everywhere, South America, Spanish, black people... so there's a meeting of many cultures.*

Without waxing quite so lyrical, Amanda Bridle from Hampshire also enjoyed the 'short sharp shock of physical labour with a large pay packet at the end of it' in the Val di Non. Women normally sort the apples (for an hourly wage of L9,000) which the men have picked (for a slightly higher wage). To get the crop picked as quickly as possible, the farmers expect workers to pick ten hours a day with no days off (nine hours after the clocks go back). The standard arrangement is for L1,000 per hour to be deducted if the farmer provides lunch and accommodation, though this varies. According to Amanda, it is becoming increasingly difficult to find work without a *libretto di lavoro* though in her experience some farmers afraid of a clampdown by the *Guardia di Finance* are willing to traipse around with people they have hired to the various offices chasing the necessary documents (see introductory section on *Regulations*).

Of course not everyone is successful at finding a job. Kristof Szymczak from Poland described the area as a tower of babel and couldn't find an orchard owner willing to hire him. But if you do manage to break in, it sounds one of the most enjoyable harvests in this book, at least as described by the American Natalia de Cuba:

> *Apple picking is great on the ground. The ladders require much more concentration (beware of drinking too much wine!) and are considered a man's job. Lunch with the family was included – pasta, salad, wine and a shot of grappa. It was delicious and friendly, as all the pickers – many of them family members – ate together and gossiped and joked. There is always plenty of opportunity to chat while working, especially if you are assigned the job of sorting the fruit. The Italian pickers really do sing opera in the orchards.*

Grape-Picking

Several people have succeeded in finding a place on the grape harvest *(vendemmia)*. Italy was called *Oenotria* by the ancient Greeks meaning 'the land of wine' and it remains the biggest producer of wine in the world. Today there are no regions of Italy which are without vineyards. Xuela Edwards and Nicky Brown made enquiries at vineyards in the Chianti region and met several growers who were keen to pay them the equivalent of £30 a day for the three weeks of the harvest. Although there seemed to be no prejudice against women pickers, the employers did insist that they obtain the proper papers which, as reported earlier in this chapter, turned out to be impracticable.

Once you are in a fruit-growing area, a good place to look for work is the warehouse run by the local cooperative where all the local farmers sell their produce to the public. There may even be a list of farmers who are looking for pickers. Natalia de Cuba found her job picking grapes (and also apples) this way, by going to the *Societá Agricultura Vallagarina* in Rovereto in the region of Trentino, a major agricultural area.

The style of grape-picking is reputed to be easier than in France since the plants are trained upwards onto wire frames, rather than allowed to droop to the ground, so that pickers reach up with a clipper and catch the bunch of grapes in a funnel-type object, which is less strenuous than having to bend double for hours at a stretch. The worst problems that Natalia de Cuba encountered were stained hands (which could be avoided by wearing rubber gloves) and bee stings (which apparently can be soothed with grated potato, bound in place and left as long as possible). Accommodation can also be a problem since it is not normally provided by farmers.

Tomatoes are supposed to be a well-paid picking crop in Italy. Also there may be seasonal agricultural work in the strawberry harvests of Emilia Romagna. Cherries are grown around Vignola (just west of Bologna) and are also picked in June. The Valtellina area, near the Swiss border, is another area with a multitude of orchards. Olives are almost never picked by foreigners. Andrea Militello investigated possibilities for olive pickers in Tuscany (around San Miniato) but the wages were so low he didn't pursue the idea.

The contact for Willing Workers on Organic Farms (WWOOF) in Italy is Bridget Matthews, 109 Via Casavecchia, 57022 Castegneto Carducci (LI); 0565-765001; wwoofitalia@oliveoil.net. At the beginning of 2001 they became a legal organisation which means that all WWOOF volunteers in Italy must join the national association (at a cost of L45,000/£14/$20) for insurance purposes.

VOLUNTARY WORK

Many Italian organisations arrange summer work projects which are as disparate as selling recyclable materials to finance development projects in the Third World to restoring old convents or preventing forest fires. Here is a selection of voluntary organisations that run working holidays. In some cases, it will be necessary to apply through a partner organisation in your home country:

Abruzzo National Park, Viale Tito Livio 12, 00136 Rome (06-3540 3331/fax 06-3540 3253). Volunteers carry out research and protection of flora and fauna in remote location. Further details are available by contacting the local park office in Pescasseroli (0863-1955) or Villetta Barrea (0864-9102/fax 0864-9132).

AGAPE, Centro Ecumenico, 10060 Prali (Torino) (0121-807514; agape@perosa.alpcom.it). Manual workcamps in remote location.

CHELON Marine Turtle Conservation, Viale val Padana 134B, 00141 Rome (06-812 5301; chelon@tin.it). Conservation projects to protect loggerhead turtles last two weeks (minimum) and cost about £380.

Emmaus Italia, Via Castelnuovo 21/B, 50047 Prato (0574 541104). Social and community workcamps.

International Building Companions (Soci Costruttori), Via Smeraldina 35, 44044 Cassana, Ferrara (0532-730079/fax 0532-734049; www.nettuno.it/fiera.ibo). Renovation projects in deprived communities.

LIPU, Lega Italiana Protezione Uccelli, Via Trento 49, 43100 Parma (0521-273034/fax 0521-273419; www.lipu.it). Italian equivalent of the RSPB which publishes a list of their working holidays, that mostly take place in summer. Camps last one or two weeks and cost from L250,000 per week. LIPU's literature is in Italian though a short summary in English can be supplied on request.

Mani Tese, P. le Gambara 7/9, 20146 Milan (02-407 5165; manitese@manitese.it). International workcamps to raise funds for projects in developing countries include study and discussion of development issues for which a basic knowledge of Italian is needed.

OIKOS, Via Paolo Renzi 55, 00128 Rome (06-508 0280; www.oikos.org/ecology/volunteer.htm). Environmental projects.

La Sabranenque, Centre International, rue de la Tour de l'Oume, 30290 Saint Victor la Coste, France (04-66 50 05 05; www.sabranenque.com). French-based organisation uses voluntary labour to restore villages and monuments in Altamura (inland from Bari in Southern Italy) and Gnallo (Northern Italy). The cost of participation is £180 for three weeks.

Servizio Civile Internazionale, Via Cardano 135, 00146 Rome (06-558 0661; info@sci-italia.org).

WWF Italia, Servizio Campi, Via Donatello 5/B, 20133 Milan (02-295 13 742). Publishes an annual list of ecological workcamps in Italian only.

There are also archaeological camps which volunteers can join. The national organisation Gruppi Archeologici d'Italia is hard to track down but was last heard of at Via Degli Scipioni 30/A, 00100 Rome (06-397 34 449/fax 06-372 1935/ www.gruppiarcheologici.org). Another possible source of information is Archeoclub d'Italia, Via Sicilia 235, 00100 Rome (06-488 1821/fax 428 81 810). The fee for participation is likely to be about £150 per week.

Malta

Although small in area (30km by 15km), Malta has much of interest for the traveller. Malta has undergone an EFL boom over the past decade and a number of private language schools cater to groups of language learners from around the Mediterranean. Their interests are represented by FELTOM, the Federation of English Language Teaching Organisations Malta (Foundation for International Studies, Old University Building, St. Paul St, Valletta VLT 07; website: www.go-ed.com/feltom).

The problem with working in Malta has always been the difficulty of obtaining a work permit. The procedure of obtaining an employment licence is to obtain a signed form from your prospective employer, who must prove that the position cannot be filled by a local, and send it to the Department for Citizenship and Expatriate Affairs (3 Castille Place, Valletta CMR 02; 356-250868/fax 356-237513; citizenship@ magnet.mt). The Department is at its busiest between May and October when many English teaching institutes submit applications to employ EFL teachers. Preparatory information can be obtained from the Malta High Commission in London Malta House, 36-38 Piccadilly, London W1V 0PQ (020-7292 4800; tony.bonnici@magnet.mt).

The student and youth travel organisation NSTS (220 St Paul St, Valletta VLT 07; 246628/fax 230330; www.nsts.org) markets English courses in conjunction with sports holidays for young tourists to Malta. NSTS run weekly vacation courses from June to August, and it might be worth approaching them for a job, particularly if you are a water sports enthusiast. NSTS was keen to hire Robert Mizzi from Canada, especially when they learned he was half-Maltese:

I was offered a job quite casually when NSTS found out I was volunteering conversational English in the main youth hostel in Valletta. Perhaps one reason they wanted to hire me was they knew the visa would not be a problem. However I was surprised by how relaxed the offer was. It was just mentioned in passing rather than at an actual interview. I guess it is the Maltese way; once you are one of them, then everything is gravy.

Tourism plays such a large part in the island's economy that it may be possible to get a job on the spot. Try cafés, bars, hotels and shops in Sliema, Bugibba and beach resorts in the south. Although Robin Gray was in Malta to enjoy a holiday rather than to work, he met a number of people who were working in tourist establishments, some of whom had set up their jobs ahead of time by writing to prospective employers. Wages are far from high.

The Malta Youth Hostels Association (17 Triq Tal-Borg, Pawla PLA 06; tel/fax 356-693957; myha@keyworld.net) can put volunteers aged between 16 and 30 to work for a minimum of 21 hours a week in exchange for free accommodation and breakfast. Jobs to be done include administration, decorating, building, etc. The minimum period of work is a fortnight and the maximum is three months. A good faith deposit and application fee must be paid; the deposit will be forfeit if the volunteer works less than the prescribed number of hours. MYHA obtains work permits for participants, a process that takes up to three months. Send three IRCs for details.

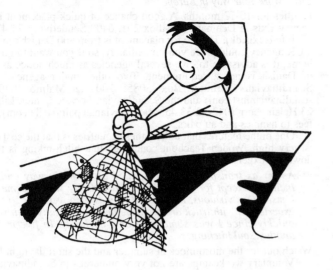

Scandinavia

Denmark, Sweden and Finland are full members of the European Union, whereas Norway and Iceland have decided to stay outside the Union but are part of the European Economic Area (EEA) which permits the free movement of goods, services and people from the EU. European citizens are entitled to enter any Scandinavian country for up to three months to look for work. When they find a job and get a 'Confirmation of Employment' from their employer, they can then apply to the police for a residence permit which, in the case of open-ended (i.e. permanent) jobs, will be for five years; otherwise it will be for the duration of the job. At least in principle, the only prohibition in the two non-EU countries is that foreign workers are not entitled to claim social security.

This has made the employment prospects of non-EEA nationals even gloomier than they were. In order to work legally, North Americans and others will have to obtain work permits before leaving home, which is well-nigh impossible. The American-Scandinavian Foundation (Exchange Division, 58 Park Avenue, New York, NY 10016; 212-879-9779/fax 212-249-3444; trainscan@amscan.org/ www.amscan.org) places about 30 American trainees aged 21-30 each summer in the fields of engineering, chemistry, computer science and business in Scandinavia, primarily Finland and Sweden. It also has a year-long English teaching TEFOL programme in Finland (see below). Summer assignments usually last 8 to 12 weeks, though longer placements are also possible. The deadline for applications is January 1st and there is a non-refundable application fee of $50. Trainees are paid the going wage but accommodation is not paid for. The ASF can also help 'self-placed trainees', i.e. those who have fixed up their own job or traineeship in a Scandinavian country, to obtain a work permit.

A knowledge of a Scandinavian language is not essential since English is so widely used throughout Scandinavia. One contributor humorously points to the few areas where English will not cut any ice (literally): 'Lapland, among migratory Lapp shepherds, among polar Eskimo hunters in North Greenland and among Russian coal miners in Spitzbergen'.

The demand for English-speaking au pairs has been increasing in Scandinavia, especially Denmark, so that many young women over 18 are being placed with families for 10-12 months. A good chance of quick placement is through the au pair agency Exis in Denmark (Postbox 291, 6400 Sønderborg; 74 42 97 49/fax 74 42 97 47; info@exis.dk). The fee for placement is from 800 Danish crowns. It is unlikely that a UK agency could place you immediately, so if you want to go through an agency at home, it is advisable to give several agencies as much notice as possible. Knowledge of Danish is not a requirement. Two other major agencies are in Sweden: the Scandinavian Institute, Box 3085, 200 22 Malmö (040-93 94 40; www.scandinavianinst.com) and the Scandinavian Service Center, Lilla Strandgatan 2, 252 23 Helsingborg (042-12 33 45; scandinavian.aupair@telia.com); the latter charges no fees to nannies and au pairs.

One of the features that unifies these countries is that the cost of living and of travel is very high. Woden Teachout concluded that hitch-hiking is the only way to keep down the expense:

As far as transport goes, I hitched all over Norway and Sweden without incident, except for one ominous truck driver who told me leeringly that he himself was virtuous, but he had friends who were not so reliable. My other experiences with truck drivers have been universally positive. I got rides very quickly since I was something of a curiosity. In five months I didn't see another soul hitching.

Watch out for the mosquitoes in summer and the short daylight hours in winter.

Voluntary workcamps are not very numerous in Scandinavia but a few voluntary organisations are mentioned in the country sections. If you see adverts for an international organisation that goes under the names Humana People to People, Tvind or One World, check the website www.tvindalert.org.uk.

Busking, begging and street-selling are illegal in many places, however prosecutions are rare. As long as you are not causing a nuisance or blocking traffic you should be left alone by the authorities but will attract the attention of many passers-by for whom busking is a novelty. Scandinavians have the reputation of being both rich and generous.

Denmark

Denmark has the highest average wage of any EU country and a fast diminishing rate of unemployment (4.7% in 2000) though the rate is higher among people aged 16-24 in Copenhagen. Denmark is an undeniably rich country and there are many opportunities for casual work. Employers are obliged to pay legal workers an extra 12.5% holiday pay *(feriepenge)*.

Work exists on farms and in factories, offices and hotels: the main problem is persuading an employer to take you on in preference to a Danish speaker. May Grant from Glasgow corroborated that the attitude in the job centres seemed to be 'Denmark for the Danes' and to find work it was necessary to explore other avenues.

Any job-seeker in Copenhagen should take advantage of the youth information centre Use It, Rädhusstraede 13, 1466 Copenhagen K (33 73 06 20/fax 33 73 06 49; www.useit.dk). Their primary function is to help newcomers find affordable accommodation but they also distribute an excellent free booklet *Working in Denmark* in almost faultless English which has information about red tape procedures and some realistic tips for those trying to find a job or study Danish. It covers everything from the hours and locations where busking is permitted to how to register for a social security number. If requesting the booklet before arrival, send two IRCs and an s.a.e. Newly arrived job-seekers can visit Use It to consult their files, newspapers and *fagboden* (Yellow Pages) and to check their notice board for lift-shares (there is no jobs board). The helpful staff will even translate ads on request, though Use It is a tourist information centre for budget travellers, not an employment agency, and cannot offer or arrange employment. They offer a Poste Restante service (not parcels) but can't accept incoming phone calls on your behalf.

Peter Anthony Stonemann is one foreigner who made good use of Use It's facilities during his long stay in Copenhagen. Although initial impressions are that non-Danish

ICELAND

Höfn
Isafjordur
Pingeyri
REYKJAVIK
Hafnarfjordur
Vestmannaeyjar
Vopnafjordur
Akureyri
Seydisfjordur
Djupivogur
Skaftafell

SCANDINAVIA

Vardo
Hammerfest
Finnmark
Karasjok
Tromso
Lapland

FINLAND

SWEDEN

Are
Trondheim
Geiranger
Romsdal Fjord
Nordfjord
Vaga
Hovringen
Loen
NORWAY
Lillehammer
Bergen
Geilo
Gol
Hardanger
OSLO
Ski
Tonsberg
Stavanger
Kristiansand

Ostersund

Savonlinna
Hameenlinna
Lahti
Turku
HELSINKI
Saimaa Lakes

STOCKHOLM
Orebro

Gotland

Oland

Skagen
Hirtshals
Mors
Logstrup
DENMARK
Esbjerg
Ørbaek
Fejö
Goteborg
Frederikshavn
Jutland
COPENHAGEN
Roskilde
Dragør
Skane
Malmo

North Sea

WILLIAM SWAN

speakers have little chance of finding work, Mr. Stonemann claims that the reality is not so bad, provided you speak English. Partly because benefits are so generous in Denmark, many unemployed people are reluctant to move to find work, to take on unpleasant jobs or work at unsocial hours, which leaves plenty of opportunities for the energetic foreigner.

It is possible to place a free advertisement in English or Danish in the twice-weekly Copenhagen paper *Den Bla Avis* (meaning The Blue Paper), a member of the Free Ads Paper International Association; it comes out on Monday and Thursday. The free Copenhagen paper *Sondagsavisen* carries a good number of ads for casual work and is distributed on Sundays. If you know a Danish speaker, check adverts in the job *(erhvervs)* section of the Sunday and Wednesday editions of *Berlingske Tidende* and *Politiken* newspapers, though these are mostly for qualified people. Advertisements in English are accepted by these papers.

The Regulations

EU nationals who intend to stay longer than three months should apply for a residence permit *(Opholdsbevis)* from the Copenhagen Overpraesidium (Hammerensgade 1, 1267 Copenhagen K; 33 12 23 80). Although the office stays open until 3pm most days, it is better to go as close to opening time at 10am as possible. Take the approved form (which you can request by post ahead of time), two photos, passport and, if possible, a contract of employment or, alternatively, proof of means of support. The contract should show that you are employed for a minimum of 20 hours a week and that your wages are at least kr7,200 per month before taxes. If your application is straightforward, you should be sent the permit within a week.

Non-EU nationals will find it much more difficult, though certain categories may be eligible (such as au pairs). As usual, work and residence permits must be applied for at a Danish consular representative in the applicant's home country. Details of the procedures are posted in English on the Danish Immigration Service website (www.udlst.dk). The office of the Immigration Service, recently renamed *Udlaendingestyrelsen,* is at Ryesgade 53, 2100 Copenhagen Ø; 35 36 66 00.

Another essential document you will need if you will be staying in Denmark for more than three months is a *personnummer* (or CPR) which is simply a personal registration number which you are supposed to apply for within five days of finding a place to live (other than a hostel or hotel). In Copenhagen this can be obtained from the Folkeregistret, Dahlerupsgade 6, 1640 Copenhagen V (33 66 33 66). This will entitle you to open a bank account (essential for some jobs and for accepting the return of rent deposits), to register for tax purposes and eventually to use the Danish health service.

The minute you find employment, even if it is going to be very temporary, apply for a tax card *(skattekort)* in the municipality where you are working (or where your employer has his head office). In Copenhagen, the *Skatteforvaltning* (tax office) is at Gyldenløvesgade 15, 1639 Copenhagen V; 33 66 33 66). You will need a *personnummer* in order to apply. Give your tax card to your employer the day you get it. Without one, you will be taxed at a punitive 60% on all earnings. The tax card entitles you to a monthly personal allowance of about kr2,600 (and then a tax rate of 40%-45%). If you do end up overpaying, you won't have a chance of getting a rebate until six months after the calendar year in which you worked. The office is open 9.30am-2.30pm Monday to Wednesday, 9.30am-5.30pm Thursday and 9.30am-1pm Friday.

Copenhagen

Copenhagen, the commercial and industrial centre of the country, is by far the best place to look for work. It is also the centre of the tourist industry, so in summer it is worth looking for jobs door to door in hotels, restaurants and the Tivoli Amusement Park. The highest concentration of restaurants is located from Vesterbros Torv to Amalienborg Slot and from Sø Torvet to Christiansborg Slot. Many of the large hotels have personnel offices at the rear of the hotel which should be visited frequently until a vacancy comes up. The Mercur Hotel has a high turnover of staff and pays from kr80 per hour before tax. Also try the English Pub, the Scottish Pub and Rosie McGee's near Tivoli Gardens.

Some job-seekers may have no trouble finding hotel work, as in the case of the Dutch traveller Mirjam Koppelaars:

My Norwegian friend Elise and I rather liked Copenhagen but realised that money was going quick again and decided to try to find some work. After filling in an application form and having a very brief interview at the Sheraton, we both got offered jobs as chambermaids starting the next day. To get a permit, we only needed an address. The next five weeks I cleaned 16 rooms and 16 bathrooms a day in a very funny uniform. Although I had to pay over half in tax, I was able to save for more travels.

Fast food restaurants, such as Burger King and McDonalds are also recommended, though they will expect you to fill out an application form in Danish and not all consider people who don't speak the language.

Au pairing opportunities abound especially looking after young babies since they are not accepted into nursery before they are ten months (see agencies mentioned at beginning of this chapter).

The Jobcenter in Copenhagen at Kultorvet 17 (33 55 17 14/33 55 10 20) should be able to assist EU nationals with a sought-after skill and a knowledge of Danish. They can do nothing for people who send their CVs. The casual work centre *(Løsarbejderformidling)* is at Tøndergade 14, Vesterbro, next door to the *Studenterformidlingen* (Student Job Centre). People gather inside the main entrance on Vesterbro early in the morning (between 6am and 8.30am) Monday to Friday to be assigned casual work such as cleaning and furniture removal; however a knowledge of Danish is a pre-requisite.

Private employment agencies *(vikarbureauer)* will also expect clients to speak Danish. It may still be worth registering with a number of those listed in the Yellow Pages, such as Adia Interim (which May Grant found helpful for hotel jobs) and Manpower. Mr. Stonemann recommends the following:

Alterna Group – 38 34 85 00. Client companies include those looking for film extras as well as special events companies wanting to hire catering, cleaning and security staff for festivals (of which there are many in Denmark), concerts, etc.

Attention (part of the Olsten Corporation), Falkoner Alle 1, 2000 Frederiksberg (38 88 94 00; www.attentionservice.dk and www.jobbanken.dk). Temp agency. Part-time wages of kr95.

Vikar Denmark, Norre Voldgade 9, 1358 Copenhagen (33 13 05 11). Temp agency.

Among the largest employers of casual staff in Denmark are newspaper distribution companies. More than 100,000 Danes subscribe to a daily or weekly newspaper and an army of 3,000 workers is needed to deliver them. This job is not done by school children as in Britain and North America because most of the deliveries are done at night. Typically, papers must be collected from a local depot at midnight and delivered by 7am. The job is much easier if you have invested in a second-hand bicycle (from kr200) or a wagon.

Bear in mind that the reason for the chronic shortage of workers is that the work is no doddle. Mr. Stonemann describes what is involved:

Few buildings in Denmark have private mail boxes at the entrance, so deliverers must go up to the fourth or fifth floor to put the paper through the right slots. Hence this is physically demanding work, especially in winter. Payment is according to quantity of work done. New workers take only one or two routes, whereas some veteran workers can do six or seven by themselves. After the first week of practice, a new worker can usually earn kr400 or kr500 per night (before losing half in taxes). So in less than two nights he has financed his bicycle, especially if he chooses to work on Sundays and holidays. In winter the payment is 10% more. Payment is made every 14 days by bank transfer, so the worker needs to open a bank account before beginning a contract.

To get a job as an *omdeler* or 'paper boy/girl', contact A/S Bladkompagniet, Dag Hammarskjölds Allé 13, 2100 Copenhagen Ø (35 27 71 06; bladkompagniet@ bladkompagniet.dk) or check the *Yellow Pages* under the heading 'Aviser

Distriktsblade' for other companies. Another big hiring company is the morning paper *Morgenavisen Jyllands-Posten*. They employ 4,000 people on weekdays and 5,000 on Sundays to deliver all their papers before 6.30am (8am on weekends). In Jutland/Fyn ring 80 81 80 82 and in Sjaelland 33 30 80 33 or email avisbud@jp.dk for details; their website www.jp.dk/avisbud/dk is in English.

A number of agencies specialise in cleaning work which is well paid in Denmark; look up *Rengøring* in the Yellow Pages. Non-Danish speakers are invariably the last to be hired and first to be fired. Royal Service Appointments at 28B Nørregade, 1165 Copenhagen (33 13 30 99) has been mentioned by various contributors over the years, most recently by May Grant who was offered work as a chambermaid. Obviously they prefer to hire unionised workers and are not really oriented to helping casual workers.

Agriculture

Farming plays an important part in the Danish economy and farm work is arguably the easiest door by which to enter the working life of Denmark. The main crops are tomatoes (picked throughout the summer), strawberries (picked in June and July), cherries (picked in July and August) and apples (picked in September and October). Despite competition from cheap East European exports, the Danish fruit industry continues to thrive and worker shortages are a problem. Several schemes have been set up to address the problem, for example the British company Earth Work Ltd (8 Beauchamp Meadow, Redruth, Cornwall TR15 2DG; 01209 219934) hires 200 strawberry pickers for its holdings on Samsø. Applications are invited from EU nationals before June 1st ready for a 12th or 26th June start date. The youth travel and exchange organisation Exis mentioned above in the context of au pairs now recruits EU nationals to pick strawberries on the same island. Pickers earn on average kr250 net per day for working between 6am and noon or 1pm.

The island of Fyn has often been recommended for fruit-picking work, especially the area around Faaborg, for example by a Polish traveller, Kristof Szymczak:

> *Yes it's true that Fyn is the best fruit-picking part of Denmark. I started seeking work in July. I tried so many places, and always received the same answer, 'I am sorry, We don't need a helper.' Finally I met the most friendly family in the world and they helped me find a job. I picked flowers for about two weeks.*

No doubt most of Kristof's difficulty in finding a job was due to the fact that he did not have the good fortune to be born in an EU country. All the farmers stress that they can accept only EU nationals with an E-111 form which incidentally will reduce the rate of tax. Here are a couple of strawberry farms to try:

Alstrup Frugtplantage, Alstrupvej 1, Alstrup, 8305 Samsø (86 59 13 38/fax 86 59 31 38; elicc@samso.com/ www.alstrupfrugt.subnet.dk). Carl Jensen's standard letter names 15th June as the starting date. Picking continues six days a week for between four and six weeks. Camping is free and the piece work rate is approximately kr6 per kilo picked. Minimum age 19.

Birkholm Frugt & Baer ApS, Hornelandeveg 2D, 5600 Faaborg (tel 62 60 22 62/fax 62 60 22 63; birkholm@post11.tele.dk/ http://home11.inet.tele.dk/birkholm). Season lasts from 5th June to 20th July. Piecework rate is kr5.30 per kilo picked. Minimum period of work is two weeks. Picking starts at 5am. Free campsite available.

Gordon Robertson from Glasgow wrote to these two addresses but received an enthusiastic reply from a different farmer, Sten Andersen, Honeballevej 24, Langemark, 8305 Samsø. Two others for which recent confirmation was not received are Anders Ploug-Sorensen (Broholm, Tastebjerggyden 13, Horne, 5600 Faaborg; 09 60 10 28) and Graevlerupgaard Frugtplantage (Egsgyden 38, Horne, 5600 Faaborg; 62 60 22 31). The farmers know one another and can direct you to one of their colleagues with vacancies.

Starting dates and picking hours are unpredictable so do not count on making a quick fortune.Anyone with a farming background and time to plan ahead could place an advertisement in the main farming journal *Lands Bladet* or one of its four sister publications, all published by De Danske Landbo Foreninger at Vester Farimagsgade 6, 1606 Copenhagen V. Gary Tennant's was immediately successful (see introductory chapter *Farming*). He was paid about £400 a month after tax, living expenses and Danish lessons since the latter were provided free by the commune.

Another possibility is to contact VHH (the Danish WWOOF) to obtain a list of their 25-30 member farmers, most of whom speak English. In return for three or four hours of work per day, you get free food and lodging. Always phone or write before arriving. The list can be obtained only after sending £5/US$10/kr50 to Inga Nielsen, Asenvej 35, 9881 Bindslev. May Grant and her boyfriend Ian visited two VHH places, one very relaxed where they only had to weed the garden, the other more strenuous. Rob Abblett had a very positive experience working briefly for a friendly farmer who took him to Copenhagen to visit the Botanical Gardens and other sites.

If communal living appeals, you may want to visit the Svanholm Community which consists of 75 adults and 40 children. Numbers are swelled in the summer when more volunteers arrive to help with the harvest of the organic produce. This possibility is open only to EU nationals. Guests work 30-40 hours a week for food, lodging and (if no other income is available) pocket money. If interested, write to the Visitors Group, Svanholm Community, Svanholm Allé 2, 4050 Skibby (www.svanholm.dk).

As usual it is best to find out as much as you can about what you're letting yourself in for. David Anderson made private arrangements to work on an organic farm on Mors in the north of Jutland. He regretted his haste in deciding to take the job:

I arrived at the doorstep with the equivalent of £10. The owner was a strict vegetarian (all home-grown) and expected me to be the same. And there was no hot water. I was the only staff to pick the fruit and vegetables plus I had to help him build a greenhouse in the shape of a pyramid since he was convinced pyramids have some special power. When I received my pay for the first three weeks, I left and headed straight for the McDonald's in Esbjerg.

Unlike most organic farms, this one paid a wage of about £50 a week, but this was not nearly enough to make up for the culture shock David was experiencing in the 'back of beyond,' as he no doubt described it to his fellow diners at McDonald's.

Voluntary Work

You can arrange to spend a few weeks during the summer on a voluntary workcamp in Denmark by applying through the organisations mentioned in the chapter on *Voluntary Work* (IVS and UNA) or, only if you are already in Denmark, Mellemfolkeligt Samvirke, Studsgade 20, 8000 Aarhus C (info@msdan.dk). MS organise summer workcamps in Denmark which last two or three weeks. The main objective of these camps, which carry out projects such as building playgrounds, conservation work, etc., is to bring participants into contact with the social problems found in every society. After paying the participation fee of kr885 for Denmark, everything is provided except travel expenses. MS also organise a few month-long camps in Greenland; the fee of approximately kr6,000 includes travel expenses from Denmark and a compulsory two-day training event in Copenhagen. Among recent tasks in Greenland was the renovation of a Viking village.

Survival

Two contributors, Peter Stonemann and May Grant, have independently suggested various ways to survive. Both recommend bottle-collecting from bins early in the morning or from annual festivals like the Roskilde Festival. The pickings are rich along certain Copenhagen streets especially on Sunday morning when only a few supermarkets are open to accept returns; try for example the one at Rantzausgade.

After he had had an HIV blood test and been in the country for three months, May's boyfriend Ian earned £20 (tax-free) by donating sperm at Cryos. You are allowed to donate three times a week but are asked to stop after conceiving 30 children. (Unfortunately Ian's sperm did not freeze well so he never got this far.) If women are excluded from this money-making wheeze, men are not in demand to hand out promotional leaflets outside the Museum Erotica. Doing a similar job for the Little Mermaid English Theatre would be more wholesome.

Buskers head for the pedestrian streets of Central Copenhagen like Købmagergade and Strøget where, on a busy summer's day, it is not unusual for a talented musician, juggler or acrobat to earn 200kr in an hour. Buskers much not use amplifiers and must not perform in groups of more than three. Hours are restricted in some places, though Radhuspladsen and Kogens Nytorv by Krinsen are open to buskers between 7am and 10pm. Musicians need not apply to the police for a licence but street performers like magicians and jugglers do.

Few buskers brave the winter conditions but instead might find work removing snow for shopkeepers and individuals. If your circumstances become desperate, there is a travellers aid' office beside the Central Railway Station (Bernstorffsgade) where they will not let you starve and will direct you to two hostels for homeless people. Alternatively you can try to persuade the Hare Krishna to let you eat their vegetarian buffet in exchange for some work (Govindas, Nørre Farimagsgade 82).

Finland

Finland offers short-term paid training opportunities. The International Trainee Exchange programme in Finland is administered by CIMO, the Centre for International Mobility (PO Box 343, 00531 Helsinki, Finland; 09-7747 7033/fax 09-7747 7064; cimoinfo@cimo.fi/ www.cimo.fi or http://finland.cimo.fi); their website is in English. British students and graduates who want on-the-job training in their field (agriculture, tourism, teaching, etc.) lasting between one and 18 months should apply directly to CIMO. Short-term training takes place between May and September, while long-term training is available year round. Applications for summer positions must be in to CIMO by the end of January.

Note that the longstanding Finnish Family Programme organised through CIMO whereby young people spent some months living with a family, helping with the children and speaking English came to an end in 2000. It is now open only to foreign students studying the Finnish language at foreign universities. The programme's cancellation might in the future increase the demand for foreign au pairs.

Readers in other countries should write to CIMO about possibilities for non-EU nationals and Americans can contact the American-Scandinavian Foundation mentioned above. If an individual does succeed in fixing up a traineeship, work and residence permits are granted for the specific training period offered by a named Finnish employer. Immigration queries can probably be answered by looking at the English language website of the Directorate of Immigration (UVI), PL 92, 00531 Helsinki (09-476 5500; www.uvi.fi).

To qualify to become a trainee, you must have studied for at least one year, preferably with a year's related experience as well, in a subject such as commerce, economics, forestry, tourism or teaching. Despite the designation 'trainee', wages are on a par with local Finnish wages for the same work.

Teaching

One of the programmes offered by the American-Scandinavian Foundation (58 Park Avenue, New York, NY 10016; 212-879-9779/fax 212-249-3444; trainscan@amscan.org/ www.amscan.org) is a TEFOL programme in Finland (Teachers of English as a Foreign Language). Participants teach in a variety of educational establishments including state schools, institutes and private organisations for a period of between three months and one academic year, and are paid US$900-$1550 monthly. Accommodation is arranged, but must be paid for by the teacher at $180-$270 per month. Flights, insurance and internal travel are also at the teacher's expense. The application deadline is February 1st for placement the following autumn.

The academic year lasts from the end of August or beginning of September until the end of May. Of course most schools prefer their native speaker teachers to stay for the whole year though one-term positions are possible. Salaries average about FIM6,500 per month to offset a high cost of living. Teachers paid by the lesson can expect to earn between FIM100 and FIM130 for 45 minutes.

Anyone with experience of the business world might persuade Richard Lewis Communications (Länsituulentie 10, 02100 Espoo, Helsinki; 09-4157 4700; www. crossculture.com) to hire them to teach English to corporate clients. RLC has offices in many other Finnish cities and one in the UK at Riversdown House, Warnford, Southampton, Hants. SO32 3LH (01962 771111).

Casual Work

Those who do not qualify as international trainees will find it more difficult to find work, however there are areas of employment which have occasional labour shortages, such as the flower nurseries around Helsinki, language tutoring and the 500 hotels included in the Tourist Board's list of hotels, especially in resorts like Hämeenlinna and Lahti.

Some time ago, Natasha Fox fixed up her own work with private families:

I found work as a nanny in Finland simply by placing advertisement cards in a few playgroups. The best area to place them if you are in Helsinki, is Westend Espoo, the most affluent area of the capital. My job paid £110 a week for working Monday to Friday 8am-4pm.

If you have Finnish friends, ask them to translate newspaper advertisements for you. Helsingin Sanomat, Finland's daily newspaper, has several vacancies for domestic positions each day. It's certainly worth ringing up and asking if they would like an English speaker for the children's benefit. (Since so many Finnish parents want their children to learn English, this often works.) If you advertise yourself, try to write in Finnish; it shows you aren't an arrogant foreigner. You probably won't have to speak a word of it in the job.

Here is the advert I put up:

Haluaisitko vaihtaa vapaale', lasten hoidon lomassa? Iloinen, vastuullinen Englandtilais-tytto antaa sinulle mahdollisuuden! Olen vapaa useimpina päivinä/iltoina.

This translates as, 'How would you like a break from the kids? Responsible cheerful English girl will give you the chance! I am free most days and evenings.'

There is no reason why male readers could not advertise themselves likewise. In fact anyone could try this technique for any kind of job, especially teaching English.

On a more frivolous note, busking might be one way of stretching your travel fund, especially outside Helsinki. According to a correspondent in Finland, buskers are an unfamiliar sight which means that they attract crowds and a lot of money can be made. As in Denmark, collecting empty bottles, both alcoholic and non-alcoholic, can be profitable.

Voluntary Work

To join WWOOF Finland, send US$10 or FIM50 plus two IRCs and an s.a.e. to Anne Konsti, Partala Information Services for Organic Agriculture, Huttulantie 1, 51900 Juva (15-321 2380; anne.konsti@mtt.fi).

The co-ordinating workcamp organisation in Helsinki is called KVT, the Finnish branch of Service Civil International (Rauhanasema, Veturitori, 00520 Helsinki; www.kaapeli.fi). They organise about 15 summer camps each year. Allianssi (Olymdiastadion, Eteläkaarre, 00250 Helsinki; 9-34824 312; vaihto@alli.fi) co-operates with the members of the Alliance of European Voluntary Service Organisations placing volunteers sent by their counterparts in other countries in workcamps in Finland.

Iceland

Iceland has a tiny population of about 250,000 and a very low rate of unemployment of less than 3%. Demand is greatest within the fish, construction, metal and tourist industries and often during the summer season only. There is also a demand for skilled labour in certain service industries, health care and IT. But the greatest number of vacancies open for those who do not speak Icelandic are in the fish industry, agriculture and unskilled hotel jobs. Generally employers wish to hire people for at least three months but preferably 6-12.

There are eight regional Employment Offices in Iceland, the largest in Reykjavik (Vinnumidlun Hofudborgarsvaedisins/VMH, Engjateigur 11, 105 Reykjavik; 588-2580/fax 588 2587). The e-mail address of the Euroadviser is jon.s.karlsson@svm.is and the phone number is 552 7600. Job vacancies can be accessed through the EURES website (http://europa.eu.int/comm/dg05/elm/eures). Obviously these jobs are open only to EU citizens. One employer posted his vacancies in summer 2000 for room attendants and kitchen and laundry assistants for a small chain of hotels/motels with restaurants operating in four locations in Iceland; the promised monthly wage was 80,000 kroner (£650+) with free accommodation; details from Lykilhotel, Borgartun 32, 105 Reykjavik (fax 511 6031; booking@keyhotel.is).

Efforts are concentrated on recruiting workers from other Scandinavian countries primarily through the Nordjobb scheme which arranges summer jobs for Nordic citizens aged 18-25 in other Nordic countries for at least four weeks (www.nordjobb.norden.no).

If you are planning to take advantage of the freedom of all EEA nationals to go to Iceland to look for work, take plenty of money to cover the notoriously high cost of living, e.g. £7 for a bottle of wine and £2-£3 for a cup of coffee or a loaf of bread. (One reasonably priced place to eat in Reykjavik is Kattisetric at 103 Laugavegur near the bus station where an all-you-can-eat bueffet costs kr790, about £7.) Accommodation is of course also very expensive. One way of solving the problem is to arrange to live with a family in exchange for minimal duties (housekeeping, English conversation, etc.) Check the adverts in the main national daily *Morgunbladid*.

Queries about work permits can be addressed to the Immigration Office (Utlendigaeftirlitid), Hverfisgata 115, 150 Reykjavik (fax 624440).

THE FISHING INDUSTRY

The fishing industry is fairly labour intensive, employing 14% of the working population directly and many more indirectly. Fish products account for three-quarters of the country's exports. It is a seasonal industry and the busiest season coincides with the long dark winter. The demarcation of jobs seems to be strictly adhered to according to sex: men go to sea or do the heavy lifting and loading in the factories and women do the processing.

Work on fishing trawlers was available a generation ago, but not any more as Tim Wetherall described after a fruitless search for work:

I was in Reykjavik for three weeks in October/November and failed to find work of any kind. Maybe I was unlucky but I don't think so. I'm normally pretty good at finding work when I need it but couldn't manage to pull it off in Iceland. I was ideally looking for work aboard a trawler but then realised that experienced Icelandic trawlermen were unemployed. Years ago casual labour was available to many foreigners aboard trawlers but now Icelandic people are very keen to get taken on because of the excellent money to be earned (around £3,000 per month). A resident Englishman told me that in order to get work on a trawler these days you need to marry the skipper's daughter. I couldn't get a job in a fish factory either. One consolation is that the people of Iceland are very friendly.

Fish Processing

Processing work is not popular or particularly well paid so there are still opportunities for foreigners at fish processing plants in the regions of Reykjavik and Akureyri. The factories are always located by the seaport. Work is pressurised because the fish must be processed quickly to maintain freshness. Shifts of 12 or 14 hours with few breaks are the rule. The peak season is February and April/May and again in September/October.

There are various tasks to be done in a fish-processing plant including sorting, cleaning, filleting, weighing, deworming and packaging. The worst job is in the *Klevi* or freezer where the temperature is around -43°C (-45°F). The work of packing and shifting boxes of fish would not be too bad were it not for the intense cold. Without proper gear including fur-lined boots and gloves, a balaclava and layers of sheepskin, this work is unendurable. In the rest of the factory the temperature is 10°C-16°C (50°F-62°F).

It takes weeks of practice before you can fillet and pack fish expertly. Standards are usually very high and if the supervisor finds more than two bones or worms, the whole case will be returned to you to be checked again. Since pay is normally according to performance, your earnings will increase as your technique improves, but the wages will not be wonderful in view of the high cost of living. Debbie Mathieson described her work at a small factory in Hnfisdal as 'not really difficult, but mind-blowingly boring'. One of the compensating features of the job for Debbie was that she was eligible for a tax rebate at the end of her contract which amounted to several hundred pounds.

There is little conventional social life in the fishing villages of northern Iceland, though many are so prosperous that they offer facilities that would be unheard of in a village of similar size elsewhere. The five dark months of winter, when villages are cut off from their neighbours, can be depressing. Vicki Matchett signed a six-month contract with a factory in the village of Vopnafjörd in north-east Iceland and describes the life:

Fishing villages usually have about 800 inhabitants with almost no social life, no pubs, not even any wildlife, and the weather between December and May made sightseeing risky. For the sake of saving £1,000 I'm not sure it's worth vegetating for six months. I must admit I spent most of my spare time reading travel journals to remind myself that civilisation still existed.

Other

Agriculture is a major enterprise in Iceland. Hay-making is an important summer job; much of the grass is cut by scythe as tractors cannot work the steep slopes, particularly in the narrow valleys where many of the farms are located. However this work is mainly done by school children. The private employment agency Ninukot (Skeggjastadir, 461 Hvolsvöller; tel/fax 487 8576) specialises in agricultural and horticultural jobs throughout Iceland. Another (unconfirmed) possibility for farm work is Baendahöllinni, 107 Reykjavik (563 0300).

Janet Bridgeport was staying as a tourist at a guest house in Hvollsvollur which happened to be next door to a horse trekking centre:

Because I'd worked with horses and wasn't in any rush to get home, I knocked on the door of the trekking centre and asked if they needed any casual help for the summer. I was really amazed when they said they'd take me on (for board and lodging only). A lot of the riding guests spoke English so I suppose that weighed in my favour.~

The Icelandic Nature Conservation Council runs a summer programme of projects at eight locations throughout Iceland lasting from between one and ten days, which are open to everyone. Transport from Reykjavik is usually provided free (including to the remote Vestmannaeyjar Islands), as is the food and accommodation in huts or (weather permitting) tents. Recent projects have been mainly involved with building paths and steps in national parks such as Jökulsárgljúfur National Park. You can fix up some of these ahead of time through the International Development Unit of the British Trust for Conservation Volunteers (36 St. Mary's St, Wallingford, Oxfordshire OX10 0EU), which arranges two to three week volunteer tours of Iceland 'not for the faint-hearted'. The cost is about £500 including flights.

Norway

After years of escalating intolerance of foreigners working in their country, the Norwegian authorities are having to face the fact that citizens of any EEA country may enter Norway for up to three months to look for work. Robert Abblett is not convinced that equality of opportunities is being taken seriously enough in employment offices in Norway:

Before I flew out to Norway, I thought I would test the water a bit by phoning the Oslo Jobcentre and a private employment agency. I think I was a bit naïve, really, wasted loads of money on phone calls and got a bit wound up about it. I even wrote to the Norwegian Embassy in London pointing out that their booklet 'Looking for Work in Norway' is misleading. When I phoned Oslo I was passed on to three different people each of whom flatly refused to give me any information because I could not speak Norwegian. The same happened when I phoned Manpower in Bergen. In perfect English we argued over the point that this was a racist barrier against foreign workers from Europe from claiming their legal right to work in Norway.

The EURES department of the *Arbeidsmarkedsetaten* (Employment Service) may be more willing to assist job-seekers in person; contact the Euroadviser, Øvre Slottsgate 11, Postboks 420 Sentrum, 0103 Oslo; 22 42 41 41/fax 22 42 44 38). A temporary work unit *(Vikartjenesten)* operates from the same address (22 42 60 00/fax 22 42 10 08) and the ordinary job centre is nearby at Akersgate 1-5. The main employment service website www.aetat.no is only in Norwegian.

To make contact with private temp agencies, look up *Vikarutleie* in the Yellow Pages or look for names like Manpower, Top Temp and Norsk Personnel in city centres. Rob Abblett tried the Manpower agency in Bergen (55 30 31 00). Also check ads in the main daily paper *Aften Posten* or try placing one yourself. (As in Denmark, the delivery departments of the main newspapers employ lots of people; ring the Green Line 800 33 166 for particulars). Once EU nationals find a job, they must apply to the police for a residence permit *(oppholdstillatelse)* on a specified form.

As throughout Scandinavia, wages are high, though the high cost of living makes it difficult to save. Almost no jobs pay less than 68 Norwegian kroner (about £5) per hour. Travellers have commented on how friendly and generous Norwegian people are. Because buskers are a relative novelty, earnings can be remarkably high. Mary Hall plucked up the courage to do some busking in Bergen on her newly acquired penny whistle. Although she knew only two songs, she made £15 in 15 minutes, mostly due to the fact that her audience was drunk.

Oslo also has a Use It office (Ungdomsinformasjonen) one of whose aims is to find work and accommodation for young visitors while offering a range of services, as in Copenhagen. Use It is located at Møllergata 3, 0179 Oslo (22 41 51 32/fax 22 42 63 71; Post@unginfo.oslo.no) and is open year round from 11am to 5pm with longer opening hours during the summer. Their website www.unginfo.oslo.no/streetwise in English has lots of concrete tips for living and working in Oslo.

Tourism

A reasonable number of English-speaking tourists visit Norway each summer, so there are some openings for English-speaking staff. You can also try winter resorts like Geilo, Hemsedal, Lillehammer, Nordseter, Susjoen, Gausdal and Voss. For either season, you can try to get something fixed up ahead of time by writing to hotels listed in the accommodation brochure available each February from the Norwegian Tourist Office, Charles House, 5-11 Lower Regent St, London SW1Y 4LR (send a 9X6 envelope and 53p in stamps), in which hundreds of hotels are listed. There is a greater density of hotels in the south of Norway including beach resorts along the south coast around Kristiansand, and inland from the fjords north of Bergen (Geilo, Gol, Vaga, Lillehammer, and in the Hardanger region generally). Remember that even in the height of summer, the mountainous areas can be very chilly.

The Norwegian Hotels Association sets wages and deductions for board and lodging, which are revised annually. The starting net monthly wage of an unskilled hotel worker is kr7,800-8,500 with a deduction of between kr500 and kr1,000 for board and lodging. Wages are lower outside the big cities, but the work may be more pleasant.

Norwegian youth hostels have a steady demand for unskilled domestic staff but pay little more than a living wage. You can try approaching the Youth Hostels central office as Dennis Bricault did:

I wrote to several IYHF national offices to offer my services as a volunteer and specified some of my talents (kitchen, maintenance, painting, cleaning, etc.). The Norwegian and the German organisations were the most accommodating.

The Norwegian Hiking Association take on some people to be caretakers at their network of mountain huts, though the only foreigner we have heard of who did this job was studying at the University of Oslo and therefore was on the spot.

The ski holiday market is much smaller in Norway than in the Alps and almost no British tour operators hire staff for holidays in Norway. Neil Tallantyre, who spent several winter seasons in Lillehammer, found that there is quite a demand for British workers. He was amazed at the resourcefulness of travellers who have extended their time in ski resorts (primarily to ski), by doing odd jobs like snow clearing and car-cleaning, waitressing, DJing (especially common since the British are thought to know their way around the music scene), au pairing and English teaching. One traveller who happened upon a short-term opportunity for teaching is David Moor:

I saw an advert in a supermarket in Lillehammer for a native English speaker to teach for a month and jumped at the chance, although I had gone there for a skiing holiday. I'd intended to stay in the hostel or a cheap hotel but was finding Norway expensive, and was lucky that another teacher was able to put me up and feed me. I was just working for keep, but only teaching three days a week, so I had lots of spare time.

Woden Teachout describes one intriguing avenue you might pursue:

The other opportunity I know of is something I nearly did. There is a very posh cruise during the summer months that sails up the coast past the Arctic Circle, touring the fjords under the midnight sun. Because it is such a luxury liner they need a lot of staff to pander to the passengers. I called the offices and asked if they needed help; they said to meet the boat in Bergen at the docks and ask the captain. I did this on three successive days and none of the captains wanted help. But they didn't laugh at me (as I'd expected) and in fact were quite encouraging, saying that chances were I'd get something within the week. I imagine the trick is to catch them quite early in the season. I don't know what the wages were but the trip is supposed to be so spectacular that it would be worth doing one 14-day run for nothing. Ask as early in the season as possible.

you can find out more about the Norwegian Coastal Voyage on the internet at www.norwegiancoastalvoyage.com.

Norwegian Working Guest Programme

Atlantis Youth Exchange at Kirkegata 32, 0153 Oslo (tel/fax 22 47 71 79; post@atlantis-u.no/ www.atlantis-u.no) runs an excellent 'Working Guest Programme' which allows people aged between 18 and 30 of any nationality to spend two to six months in rural Norway (Americans and other non-Europeans may stay for no more than three months). The only requirement is that they speak English. In addition to the farming programme open to all volunteers, placements in family-run tourist accommodation are available to European nationals.

Farm guests receive full board and lodging plus pocket money of at least kr700 a week (£57) for a maximum of 35 hours of work. The idea is that you participate in the daily life, both work and leisure, of the family: haymaking, weeding, milking, animal-tending, berry-picking, painting, house-cleaning, babysitting, etc. A wardrobe of old rugged clothes and wellington boots is recommended.

After receiving the official application form you must send off a reference, two smiling photos, a medical certificate confirming that you are in good health and a registration fee of kr1,300 (£100) for stays of up to three months and kr2,500 (£200) for longer stays. British applicants can apply through Concordia and Americans through InterExchange (161 6th Avenue, New York, NY 10013; 212-924 0446; www.interexchange.org).

Atlantis will try to take into account individual preferences and preferred part of the country. There are about 400 places (for all nationalities), so try to apply at least three months before your desired date of arrival. If they are unable to place you, all but kr250 will be refunded. Applying through Concordia/InterExchange increases the applicant's chances of acceptance.

Robert Olsen enjoyed his farm stay so much that he went back to the same family another summer:

The work consisted of picking fruit and weeds (the fruit tasted better). The working day started at 8am and continued till 4pm, when we stopped for the main meal of the day. After that we were free to swim in the sea, borrow a bike to go into town or whatever. I was made to feel very much at home in somebody else's home. The farmer and his daughter were members of a folk dance music band, which was great to listen to. Now and then they entrusted me to look after the house while they went off to play at festivals. Such holidays as these are perhaps the most economical and most memorable possible.

Outdoor Work

One of the best areas to head for is the strawberry growing area around Lier, accessible by bus from Drammen. Wages are notoriously bad in this area, and as a result the majority of harvesters are foreign. Kristin Moen and her Italian friend Maurizio were given jobs at the first farm phoned, but earned only kr120 between them after $2^1/2$ hours, and then quit. The strawberry season here reaches its peak in early July.

Further north the harvest is a little later. For example in Steinkjer (north of Trondheim), it goes from mid-July to August. Wages are a little higher here since the fruit is smaller, and accommodation may be available, unlike in the south where you normally have to provide a tent. Nordfjord, south of Romsdal, is also a possibility. The raspberry harvest starts at the beginning of August at Andebu near Tansberg. Potatoes and other vegetables are harvested in early September; try the village of Loen, in the Romsdal area and inland around Hamar.

The steep hillsides on either side of the many fjords support abundant wild blueberries. It is possible to freelance as a berry picker and then sell the fruit to the local produce and jam co-operatives. In Lapland it is not permitted to pick certain berries in certain seasons, since only native Lapps have the right, so make local enquiries first. Autumn brings wild mushrooms – Norway has about 2,500 varieties. In some of the larger towns, there are weekend mushroom controls where you can have what you have picked checked.

The Norwegian organic farm organisation APØG (c/o Nøll, Langeveien 18, 5003 Bergen; 55 32 02 45; organic@online.no/ www.home.online/organic) distributes a list of about 50 ecological farms that need help. Whereas some farms are looking for trainees who can stay for a year, others are seeking help for only a couple of weeks in the summer. Send £15/$20/kr125 for the list which is in Norwegian, though most of the organic farmers listed will be able to correspond in English.

The harvest season is not the only time when extra help is needed. Jill Weseman and seven others found themselves having to help round up some sheep for slaughter:

Sheep-herding was one of the most difficult things I have every attempted. Armed with walkie-talkies, binoculars and backpacks stuffed with energy-giving chocolate and coffee, we banded together and hit the hills. We strategically chased the stupid animals down from the mountain and into the valley where they marched back to the farm and towards their deaths.

The major industry in the far north of Norway is fishing. Not enough locals are prepared to work in the fish processing plants, as Rob Abblett had confirmed when he rang a fish factory (PO Box 51, 9951 Vardø) this year:

I spoke to a manager called Leis who had picked up an American accent somewhere and he told me almost everyone at the factory was Finnish because the local people don't want to do the work. Speaking Norwegian was not a pre-requisite here (hurray) but he did say that he would only consider long-term applicants, minimum one year, as it takes up to six months to train someone the finer arts of fish processing, which sounded a little incredible to me. He was probably gently trying to put me off wasting my money on the effort of making the huge journey only to be disappointed with the work and leave. But I was sorely tempted to send my CV which he said he'd consider. I like the idea of experiencing the aurora borealis and weeks of nighttime/daytime, wild coastline and very very nippy weather for most of the year.

Accommodation is provided cheaply and the wage is kr90 an hour.

Au Pairs

The situation is promising for au pairs of all nationalities (provided they speak some English), though the red tape is still considerable for non-Europeans. Atlantis runs a programme for 100-150 incoming au pairs who must be aged 18-30 and willing to stay at least six months but preferably 8-12 months. The first step is to write to Atlantis or one of its partner organisations for an information sheet on their Au Pair in Norway programme and application forms. The information is readily available on their website www.atlantis-u.no as well. Atlantis charges a sizeable registration fee of kr1,000, a quarter of which is non-refundable if the placement doesn't go ahead. Au pairs from an EEA country can obtain the residence permit after arrival.

When a family has been found for someone from outside Western Europe, the co-operating agency in Norway obtains an agreement of which four copies are forwarded to the au pair, together with an invitation letter. These must be presented to the Norwegian Embassy in the applicant's home country, together with an original birth certificate. At least three months should be allowed for these procedures. Upon arrival in Norway you must register with the local police within a week.

The pocket money in Norway is at least kr2,800 per month which sounds generous until you realise that it could be taxed at 25%-30% (depending on the region), leaving a net amount of kr1,800-2,200. Atlantis can advise on possibilities for minimising tax by obtaining a *frikort* which entitles you to a personal allowance of kr22,599.

The majority of families are in and around Oslo, Bergen or the other cities in southern Norway, although applicants are invited to indicate a preference of north, south, east or west on their initial application. Virtually all employers will be able to communicate in English. Au pairs are given a travel card worth kr400 a month.

The Oslo *Yellow Pages* contain several au pair agency addresses, though these are primarily for Norwegians wanting to go abroad as au pairs. One possible alternative to Atlantis is Inter Au Pair, Astubben 68,0381 Oslo (22 52 15 60), the partner agency of several well-known European au pair agencies.

Voluntary Work

The workcamp organisation in Norway is called Internasjonal Dugnad at Nordahl Brunsgate 22, 0165 Oslo. If you're in Norway and want to spend two or three weeks as a volunteer, for example at a peace centre or an experimental farm, contact them; otherwise you must apply through the Service Civil International/IVS branch in your own country.

Sweden

EU/EEA nationals may enter Sweden to look for work as in any other member state. Non-Europeans must submit to their local Swedish Embassy a written offer of work on form AMS PF 101704, at least two months before their proposed arrival. Immigration queries should be addressed to Migrationsverket, the Swedish Migration Board (601 70 Norrköping; 11-15 60 00; www.migrationsverket.se). Full details are posted in English on their web pages or you can request printed leaflets.

The addresses of employment offices *(Länsarbetsnämnden)* around Sweden can be found on the website of the Swedish Employment Service (www.ams.se). The job centre in Stockholm might be worth visiting at 24-26 Svaevagen. If you find work, you will have to obtain a tax card which is straightforward.

Casual Work

State handouts are so generous in Sweden that many natives are unwilling to undertake jobs like dishwashing and fruit picking for a few kroner an hour. Even without the benefit of having the right stamp in your passport, there are possibilities, as the American Woden Teachout discovered:

> *In southern Sweden I did the cleaning lady's tour of Swedish mansions. I found the first job through a couple who picked me up hitch-hiking and who contacted a friend of theirs. There are a great number of large country houses*

in Skane, and the Swedes who live in them find it no luxury to pay for household help. All the families I worked for were the acme of respectability, and a neat appearance in probably very important. So I had several weeks of sweeping out from behind stoves, washing windows, and generally helping with the spring clean. Housework has never been my great speciality, but the living was easy since the relics of Swedish gentry are both rich and hospitable. I had my own room, four-course meals under the evening sun and they took me merrily along to celebrate midsummer, or on outings to the beach or theatre. Plus I was paid the equivalent of $4 an hour.

A rather more elevated casual job has been found by well-educated foreigners as proof-readers and polishers. So many documents in Sweden are translated into English that it is worthwhile phoning publishing companies for freelance work which should pay about kr250 (£20) an hour.

Some years ago Elfed Guyatt from Wales chanced his luck by looking for work after arrival in Sweden and soon found work as a barman in both Malmö and Lund. In Malmö he worked as a barman in a sports club where the pay was negligible but he was given all the beer and food he wanted plus accommodation shared with one of the club members. Lund was also a good place to look for work and shared accommodation through the student grapevine.

It may be worth trying to find work in hotels, usually in the kitchen. Your best bets are the large hotels in Stockholm and Göteborg. Elsewhere you might try areas where tourism is well established. Try the Sunshine Coast of western Sweden including the seaside resorts between Malmö and Göteborg, especially Hölsingborg, Varberg and Falkenberg. Other popular holiday centres with a large number of hotels include Orebro, Västeras, Are, Ostersund, Jönköping and Linköping. The chances of fixing up a hotel job in advance are remote. After writing to dozens of Scandinavian hotels, Dennis Bricault's conclusion was 'Forget Sweden!'.

If you are interested in outdoor work, try the southern counties, especially Skane, where a wide variety of crop is grown. Woden Teachout found morning work at a strawberry farm near Skane:

Strawberry picking jobs are incredibly easy to come by. Our motley crew consisted of six spindly Swedish teenagers, most of whom quit over the course of the harvest, myself and a carload of Polish students. We worked from 7am till lunch and could make up to $3.50 an hour if we worked fast.

With wages like that, it is obvious why few Swedes would want to accept such jobs.

Vacancies also exist in the market gardening sector. Peas, cucumbers, spinach and many other vegetables are grown under contract to canneries and if you can't find work in the fields, you might find it in the processing plants. In the eastern part of Skane there is specialised fruit growing: apples, pears, plums, cherries, strawberries and raspberries. The islands of Oland and Gotland are also very fertile and you might find a farming family short of a helper.

If you can't find an employer willing to take you on, you could consider freelancing as a berry picker. Wild strawberries, blueberries and raspberries can be found in the forests of Sweden from June till September and might be successfully sold at weekend street markets, in youth hostels, etc. In the late summer there are mushrooms and loganberries to pick, though you should be knowledgeable about which mushrooms are edible before trying to market them and also be sensitive about local laws which protect the livelihood of Laplanders. Be warned that forested areas in Sweden are commonly mosquito-ridden, so be prepared. Either remain fully clothed at all times (despite the summer heat) or apply liberal lashings of a powerful repellant.

Check ads in the free paper *Platsjournalen*; jobs (in Swedish only) are posted on its website http://jobb.amv.se.

Au Pairs

Au pairs are subject to the same regulations as all other foreign employees so non-EU nationals must obtain a work permit before leaving their home country.

The Scandinavian Institute in Malmö (Box 3085; 040-93 94 40/fax 040-93 93 07;

info@scandinavianinst.com) makes au pair placements in Swedish families and throughout Scandinavia. Another possibility is Au Pair World Agency, Kaflegatan 6, 461 40 Trollhättan (520 138 13/fax 520 311 89; InterTeam THN@swipnet.se). Once you arrive, it is worth checking university notice boards for baby-sitting openings. The same social class which employed Woden Teachout as a cleaner is often willing to hire live-in childcare. In fact the last family for whom Woden cleaned gave her free room and board in exchange for acting as a companion to their ten year old daughter.

Teaching

Casual work teaching English is rarely available. The Folk University of Sweden runs an adult English language programme in many towns throughout the country in which native speaker teachers are placed for one academic year (nine months). There are five trusts closely linked to the universities of Stockholm, Gothenburg, Lund, Uppsala and Umeå, with branches in many smaller towns. Anyone interested in teaching in Sweden on this scheme should contact the programme co-ordinator, Peter Baston, Folkuniversitetet, Box 2116, S-22002 Lund; 46-19 77 00/fax 46-19 77 80; peter.baston@folkuniversitetet.se; www.folkuniversitetet.se. Interviews can be held in the UK at the Salisbury School of English (36 Fowler's Road, Salisbury, Wilts. SP1 2QU; 01722 331011). They look for candidates with a first degree or recognised teaching qualification or initial TEFL certificate and two years experience. Classroom experience is essential and experience in other fields is an advantage.

Voluntary Work

The main workcamps organiser in Sweden is Internationella Arbetslag (IAL), Barnangsgatan 23, 11641 Stockholm, which is the Swedish branch of SCI. It is essential to apply for one of their camps (which are mostly on an ecological theme) through your local branch of Service Civil International (IVS in Britain).

WWOOF is now represented in Sweden: Andreas Hedren, Hunna, Palstorp, 340 30 Vislandia (0470-75 43 75) which so far has about 20 host farms. Robert Abblett enjoyed rural Sweden in summer 2000:

> My WWOOF host lived on a farm in the countryside and looked a bit like a Swedish 'Steptoes dad.' But he was very kind and sympathetic and I enjoyed my time working with him, repairing his barn. I went off cycling or kite-flying on my days off. Money was getting a bit low which was a shame because I would like to have visited a commune or two.

Stifelsen Stjärnsund (77071 Stjärnsund; 0225-80001/fax 80301; info@frid.nu) is located amongst the forests, lakes and hills of central Sweden. Founded in 1984, the community aims to encourage personal, social and spiritual development in an ecologically sustainable environment. It operates an international working guest programme throughout the year, but is at its busiest between May and September when most of the community's courses are offered. Carpenters, builders, trained gardeners and cooks are especially welcome. A contribution to lodging is normally expected though is negotiable according to means and length of stay. Those who are prepared to work 30 hours a week are normally given free food and lodging. Enquiries should be made well in advance of a proposed summer visit.

A Camphill-community for mentally disabled adults in Delsbo needs volunteers to stay for at least six and preferably twelve months. A small wage is paid in addition to living expenses. Details are available from Staffansgarden, PO Box 66, Furugatan 1, 82060 Delsbo (fax 653-10968).

Survival

Collecting discarded bottles and cans can be a fairly profitable way to earn some money anywhere in the country. The carnivals which take place in July and August are recommended as prime targets for bottle-collecting; Elfed Guyatt earned around £50 a day during three days in Norrköping. British and American souvenirs are trendy, so you can make up to 500% profit by selling such things at local weekend markets. Medals, caps, books, etc. are worth stocking up on at home for possible sale in Sweden.

Spain & Portugal

Although unemployment remains the highest in the EU (touching 20%), the demand for foreign labour, particularly in English language teaching, persists. Spain's tourist industry continues to absorb thousands of foreign young people in a temporary and part-time capacity. Otherwise there is not much job mobility, due to a legal requirement that anyone (employer or employee) who signs a contract must pay compensation if he or she breaks the contract.

Do not imagine that it will be easy to find work in Spain nor that the living will be cheap while you look. After hitching successfully around Europe, Martin and Shirine found that the lifts dried up as soon as they crossed the Spanish border, and everything was more expensive. For example campsites were the same price as youth hostels and all food items in supermarkets seemed to cost the equivalent of one pound, whether it was a tin of tuna or a bag of carrots.

The Regulations

The procedures for regularising your status are similar to those in other EU countries. Those who intend to stay more than three months must apply for a residence card (Tarjeta de Residencia) within 30 days of arrival. Application should be made to the local police headquarters (Comisaría de Policia) or to a Foreigners' Registration Office (Oficina de Extranjería) which in Madrid is at C/ Madrazo 9; this office now gives out appointment times for presenting applications; ring 900 610 620. The documents necessary for the residencia are a contract of employment, three photos, a passport and (sometimes) a medical certificate. This information can be confirmed with the Labour & Social Affairs Counsellor's Office of the Spanish Embassy (20 Peel St, London W8 7PD; 020-7221 0098; spanlabo@globalnet.co.uk) and with the British Consulate-General in Spain (c/ Marqués de la Ensenada 16-2°, 28004 Madrid; 91-308 5201). Their notes Settling in Spain (last updated in 2000) include detailed advice on sorting out red tape as well as the addresses of all 14 British Consulates in Spain. The bureaucracy involved in staying in Spain long-term is so convoluted that it is worth paying for the expertise of a gestoria, an expert in Spanish documentation.

The immigration situation for non-EU citizens has become increasingly difficult. Employers who want to hire an American teacher or New Zealand tour manager will have to go through an expensive, complex and very lengthy rigamarole. Non-EU nationals must first obtain a *visado especial* from the Spanish Embassy in their country of residence after submitting a copy of their contract, medical certificate in duplicate and authenticated copies of qualifications. In some cases a further document is needed, an *antecedente penale* (certificate proving that they have no criminal record). Invariably the Spanish authorities take months to process this and then quite often reject the application if they think that a Spanish or EU national could do the job. If a visa is issued (normally Type A which is for one specific job), it must be collected from a Spanish consulate in the applicant's home country. Excellent detailed information on the legal processes can be seen on the website of *The Broadsheet,* an English-language monthly magazine in Madrid (www.thebroadsheet.com). The American organisation, InterExchange (161 Sixth Avenue, New York, NY 10013; 212-924-0446 ext. 109; www.interexchange.org) arranges language assistant programmes in Spain for a placement fee of $400-$600.

The strict rules make it almost impossible for people from outside Western Europe to pick up casual work legally as Ana Güemes from Mexico found:

> *Although we Latin Americans speak Spanish, I insist on saying that Spain is one of the hardest countries to find a job in. Everywhere you go they ask to see your identity card because of the problems they have with Moroccans.*

That being said, Ana did make friends with the daughters of a vineyard owner and picked grapes in exchange for free food, wine and tours of the area.

Americans, Canadians, Australians, etc. do sometimes find paid work as monitors in children's camps, tutors at language schools and in private households, touts for bars and discos, etc. When their tourist visas are about to expire, they usually follow the example of those who simply cross into France or Portugal to extend their tourist visa for a further three months on their return to Spain.

TEEMING TOURISM

Spain hosts a staggering 40 million visitors a year, including 12 million Britons, making Spain the most popular destination for British tourists by far. Of the top ten package holiday destinations for Britons, five are Spanish: Majorca, Tenerife, Ibiza, Menorca and the Costa Blanca. Spain's coastal resorts continue to draw hordes of tourists, especially Lloret de Mar, Calella (Costa Brava), Benidorm (Costa Blanca), Torremolinos, Benalmadena, Fuengirola (Costa del Sol), Mojacar (Costa de Almeria) and Ibiza and Palma (Majorca). The proverbial British tourist in Spain is not looking for undiscovered villages but wants to have the familiar comforts of home along with the Mediterranean sunshine. The Spanish tourist industry has recognised this preference for a long time and has employed large numbers of English-speaking young people to make the tourists feel at home. A. Fuller from Lincolnshire so enjoyed his four months of working behind a bar in Benidorm and sharing a flat in Albir just outside the resort that he wants to write a book about it.

It is always worth checking the English language press for the sits vac columns which sometimes carry adverts for cleaners, live-in babysitters, chefs, bar staff, etc. Look for *SUR in English* (www.surinenglish.com) which has a large employment section and is used by foreign and local residents throughout southern Spain. It is published free on Fridays and distributed through supermarkets, bars, travel agencies, etc. If you want to place your own ad, contact the publisher Prensa Malaguena, Avda. de Maranon 48, 29009 Malaga.

If you can arrange to visit the Spanish coast in March before most of the budget travellers arrive, you should have a good chance of fixing up a job for the season. The resorts then go dead until late May when the season gets properly underway and there may be jobs available. If you are heading for the Canary Islands, the high season for British package tourists is November to March. Bear in mind that while working in these environments you will barely get a glimpse of genuine Spanish culture.

Year-round resorts like Tenerife, Gran Canaria, Lanzarote and Ibiza afford a range of casual work as bar staff, DJs, beach party ticket sellers, timeshare salesmen, etc. Caroline Scott, who has written a dissertation on youth culture in Ibiza, describes the employment scene she found during the summers of 1999 and 2000:

Bar work was the highest paid, then waitressing and worst touting which is what I did for the club Godskitchen, where wages were enough to get by. Most of the clubs in Ibiza are British like Ministry of Sound, Cream, Renaissance, Gatecrasher and Miss Money Penny's. Accommodation becomes harder to find in July, so it's recommended to go May/June when the better jobs are also available. This year I went back for a second season working for a different club, which I obtained by sending my CV to British clubs in January. (I got the addresses from Mixmag, a club magazine.) Arriving early in the season, there is a short supply of work, so it's a matter of finding the balance between finding a job and a place to stay. Wages are low, lower than last year, £40-£50 a week, though this picks up in the high season. Postering jobs are very well paid, £120 for five days work.

Caroline believes that Ibiza does not deserve its reputation as a cesspit of vice with nothing but sex, drugs and hooliganism (which a couple of years ago prompted the British Vice Consul to Ibiza to resign in disgust). According to her, most of the clubs are outside San Antonio and the atmosphere is usually happy and calm. If you prefer pubs to clubs, check out Langley S.L. in San Augustin (971-342815) which employs a large number of seasonal staff for its seven pubs in Ibiza including an Irish Theme Bar.

The website www.gapwork.com has information about working in Ibiza and provides the web addresses for some of the clubs mentioned above and others like www.manumission.com and www.slinky.co.uk. They claim that about 6,000 Britons try to find work on Ibiza each year so it is important to offer a relevant skill.

People have successfully found (or created) jobs in highly imaginative ways. One of the most striking examples is a 19-year-old Finnish student who wrote to the address on a Spanish wine label and was astonished to be invited to act as a guide around their winery for the summer. Tommy Karske returned home 'knowing a lot about wine and believing that anything is possible'. Tradespeople, mechanics, handymen and gardeners can usually find work inside the expatriate community in any resort.

The major cities also create many jobs for travellers. One of Jon Loop's colleagues teaching English in Madrid decided to supplement his income from teaching by washing dishes at weekends:

He found the job in mid-October after picking a street and going to every restaurant. He walked into the restaurant and asked the barman or waiter to direct him to the manager because he wanted a job. He only had to visit six before he was offered a job washing dishes from 9pm-4am on Friday and Saturday. This despite his complete lack of Spanish, apart from a few phrases. He says there are always lots of jobs available.

A more conventional form of employment is with a British tour company such as Canvas Holidays, Eurocamp, Keycamp Holidays, etc. (see *Tourism* chapter). Haven Europe and Solaire Holidays (1158 Stratford Road, Hall Green, Birmingham B28 8AF; 0121-778 5061/ www.solaire.co.uk) need Spanish-speaking couriers and children's staff to work at mobile home and tent parks from early May to the end of September. Clubs Abroad Ltd (Guildbourne Centre, Worthing, W. Sussex BN11 1LZ; 01903 201225) specialises in Balearic resorts in Menorca and Majorca. And don't ignore the possibility of winter work with a British tour company in a Pyreneen ski resort either in the Spanish province of Huesca or in the principality of Andorra.

Odd Jobs and Touting

There is a job which is peculiar to the Spanish resorts and which allows a great many working travellers to earn their keep for the season. The job is known variously as 'PRing', 'propping,' 'blagging' or touting, that is to entice/bully tourists to patronise a certain bar or disco. Many readers have found it a good way to spend the season, among them Ian Govan from Glasgow in Lloret de Mar:

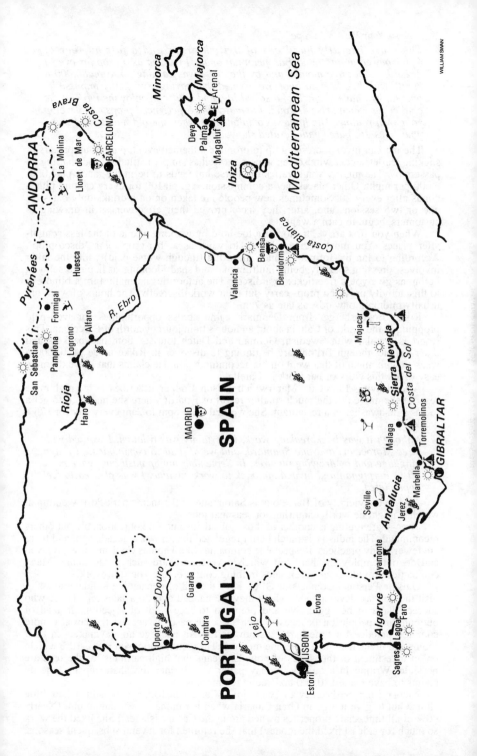

WILLIAM SWAN

There are literally hundreds of British props and a fair number of Commonwealth and other European nationals. I worked as a prop for over a dozen bars in three months and by the end I was earning up to pta80,000 a month with free beer to boot. Be warned that saving is virtually impossible, but you will have one hell of a social life, and will soon enjoy the job and the challenges which arise as you try to match the experienced props and develop your own routine. The highest compliment is when the old hands start using your lines. It's pure unadulterated showbiz.

The job can involve dressing up to promote a themed event, putting up posters or sticking leaflets under windscreen wipers, as well as simply leafletting and chatting up passers-by. The nightly wage varies of course but tends to be in the range pta4,000-6,000 per night. Other places pay a commission, e.g. pta100 for every capture plus a bonus after every 20. Sometimes new people are taken on on a drinks-only basis for one or two sessions and, after they have proved their effectiveness in drawing in customers, begin to earn a wage.

When you first arrive, try to get a toe-hold by working at one of the less sought-after places. You must decide whether to work as a 'bar-prop' or a 'disco-prop'. According to Ian the former is much more fun (though worse paid) while the latter involves 'dressing snazzily, being multilingual and shady-looking, as liable to sell you heroin as give you a free ticket to a disco'. The authorities normally turn a blind eye to this activity provided props carry out their work discreetly. The hours of work are usually midnight onwards, as late as 7am.

Rikke Bogensberger from Denmark came across opportunities for well-paid propping in the resort of Calella about an hour's train journey north of Barcelona. This resort is popular with Swedish, German and Dutch tourists, both backpackers and older people, though Britons are beginning to discover it. Rikke made pta10,000 a week though much of that went on his accommodation. He claims that it is extremely easy to get this work or bar work in Calella.

After leaving Lloret de Mar (which Alison Cooper describes as a 'nightmare resort') she moved to the much smaller resort of Estartit where she managed to get a job as a dishwasher in a restaurant. She worked from 6pm to 2am every day for £75 a week:

Although it was backbreaking work, it certainly was a laugh. I worked with three Moroccans and one Spaniard, and we all had to communicate by sign language and by drawing pictures. In September my Spanish boss gave me a lift to Perpignan and invited me back to work anytime. I was pleased to feel appreciated.

Also in the vicinity of Barcelona is Salou, site of the theme park Port Aventura at which it might be worth enquiring for seasonal jobs.

Time-share touting is another of those jobs that some find objectionable but others recommend. The industry is much better regulated than it was a decade ago, and there are fewer shady practices. Respectable companies like Thomas Cook are now involved and do not employ the hard-sell which gave time share such a bad name. Many companies provide a one-week sales training course before you start work.

Outside Personal Contacts or OPCs have the job of persuading holidaymakers to visit the holiday development, where they are handed over to a sales rep. Those who succeed have to be aggressive and prepared to face a lot of rejection. Instead of buttonholing people on beaches (which in some cases is against the law), a more common practice for timeshare reps now is to visit package holidaymakers in their rooms and invite them to a welcome meeting. The commission paid is 8%-10% which, on an investment of thousands of pounds, means that high earnings for the reps are possible. Writing in a quality Sunday paper, one former timeshare rep in Tenerife claims to have made £20,000 tax-free in ten months.

Nicola from Saskatchewan (with joint Canadian/British nationality) had little choice but to give it a go in Gran Canaria when her money was running out. (Nearly 40% of all time-share properties owned are in the Canary Islands.) She liked the work so much (or at least liked the money) that she returned for several subsequent seasons, most recently in Alcudia on the north side of Mallorca and Cala D'Or in the south-east of the island. She reported that in Gran Canaria, it is now necessary for OPCs to wear identification and stand in one approved spot, which makes it much more difficult to engage with tourists.

It is possible to get a job as an OPC or sales rep simply by showing up in the island resorts in the winter and asking around. Alternatively some companies advertise ('Fun in the Sun') in the British press and the fortnightly *Overseas Jobs Express*. Most companies will pay for your accommodation for the first two to four weeks or even reimburse your flight after they've seen whether you're any good. No one should expect to make a lot of money at the beginning, nor should they be too cavalier about the police *(guardia civil)* who can come down very hard on anyone openly working the beaches or streets.

Exploiting the Tourist Market

As in all areas of heavy tourism, selling your handicrafts and busking should prove to be profitable. Martin and Shirine's money-making schemes in Benalmadena are typical: while she made money on the promenade making hairwraps each evening, he plied the English bars with a bag of rune stones and some well-placed rhetoric.

If your skills are literary, rather than manual or musical, you should try to sell an article to one of the many English language magazines and newspapers which thrive on tourism and resident expatriates. Get hold of, for example, the *Costa Blanca News* in Alicante, *Lookout*, the *Majorca Daily Bulletin* or the *Island Sun* in Gran Canaria, and see what type of article would suit (probably articles about hitch-hiking would go over less well in this market than articles about yacht cruising).

Barcelona is especially popular among buskers. Although there will be plenty of foreign buskers already installed, the majority of tourists and locals will pay to be serenaded as they sip their drinks in one of the hidden squares in the Old Town, provided the quality is sufficiently high.

Sailing

Many yachts are moored along the Costa del Sol and all along the south coast. It might be possible to get work cleaning, painting or even guarding these luxury craft. There are also crewing possibilities as Peter Goldman discovered:

> *In Alicante I was taking a day off from hitching and was engrossed in the sunset when I noticed some folks coming off a sailboat. I asked them if they needed crew and they said they did. I hinted that I had little experience (really none) but they said that was no problem and I was on. We sailed around Spain including Ibiza and settled in Palma de Majorca. There were five of us and we decided we would look for work in Palma and live on the boat, but we soon discovered that Palma is a terrible place to look for work in January/February.*

Acorn Adventure (22 Worcester St, Stourbridge, West Midlands DY8 1AN; 01384 446057/topstaff@acornadventure.co.uk) need seasonal staff for their watersports and multi activity centre near the resort of Tossa de Mar on the Costa Brava. RYA qualified windsurfing and sailing instructors, BCU qualified kayak instructors and SPSA qualified climbing instructors are especially in demand, for the season April/May to September.

TEACHING ENGLISH

The boom in English language teaching has subsided somewhat, apart from in the area of teaching children as young as pre-school (for which a knowledge of Spanish is virtually essential, not to mention songs and games). However there are of course thousands of foreigners still teaching English in language institutes from the Basque north (where there is a surprisingly high concentration) to the Balearic and Canary Islands. The entries for language schools occupy 18 pages of the Madrid Yellow Pages. But the days are gone when any native speaker of English without a TEFL background could reasonably expect to be hired by a language academy.

Job Hunting on-the-Spot
Most teaching jobs in Spain are found on the spot and, with increasing competition, it is necessary to exert yourself to land a decent job. Most people simply use the usual method of consulting the Yellow Pages *(Las Paginas Amarillas)* and pounding the pavements of the place where they are staying. The best time to look is at the beginning of September, after the summer holidays are ended and before most terms begin on October 1st. Spanish students sign up for English classes during September and into early October. Consequently the academies do not know how many classes they will offer nor how many teachers they will need until quite late. It can become a war of nerves; anyone who is willing and can afford to stay on has an increasingly good chance of becoming established.

Kevin Boyd didn't decide to go to Spain until mid-October. Although he had previously failed to get work in Munich and Bologna, even with a Cambridge Certificate, he landed a job with a good school in Valencia at that unpromising time of year. Ben Hockley from Australia recommends trying Wall Street Institutes, whose head office in Spain is at Rambla de Catalunya 2-4, 08007 Barcelona (93-412 0014/412 5736/fax 93-412 3803; www.wsi.es). With 140 academies in Spain, this chain is reputed to have a high staff turnover, partly because the pay is at the lower end of the spectrum. Ben had no trouble fixing up a job with them on his second visit to Madrid; the first time he had no luck job-hunting because he had no TEFL qualification and no Spanish. Try also Berlitz, whose six Madrid branches including the main one at Gran Via 80 4°, 28013 Madrid (91-542 3586) recruit EFL teachers with a degree but not necessarily any teaching experience or qualifications. They also offer summer-only positions as does the Vigvatten Natur Klubb (Apartado 3253, 01002 Vitoria Gasteiz; 945-28 17 94) which runs sports camps in the Basque country, Pyrenees and Sierra de Urbion (near the town of Soria), which pay pta40,000 (£145) for a fortnight. Other summer camps looking for monitors and teachers are The Farm, C/ Santa Lucia 1, 01129 Leorza-Maeztu, Alava (easy@iponet.es) and one in the Basque region run by ABC English (Calle Solde Abajo 3, Antonana, 01128 Alava).

Other sources of job vacancy information include the Madrid daily *El Pais* which usually has a few relevant classifieds under the heading *Trabajo – Idiomas*. Also try *The Broadsheet* for Madrid's English-speaking community and *Segundamano,* Madrid's free ads paper which comes out Monday, Wednesday and Friday. The English and Irish pubs that advertise in the English language press are usually good places in which to make contact with like-minded job-seekers, for example Kitty O'Shea's, the Shamrock and the Scottish Pub Haddock Café in Barcelona and Finbar's, Finnegans and O'Connors in Mardrid. Another way to make contacts with the local community is to attend (or organise) an *intercambio* in which Spanish speakers and English speakers exchange conversation in both languages.

In Advance
Anyone with an EFL component on their CV might try to fix up work ahead of time. The best place to start for a list of language schools is the Education Department of the Spanish Labour Office (20 Peel St, London W8 7PD; 020-7243 8535/020-7727 2462; asesores@dial.pipex.com/ www.cec-spain.org.uk) which can send a list of the 350 members of FECEI, the national federation of English language schools, together with an outline of Spanish immigration regulations and a one-page handout 'Teaching English as a Foreign Language.' The book *Teaching English Abroad* (published in 2001 by Vacation-Work) has about 140 addresses of language schools which hire native speaker teachers.

Qualified EU applicants might want to make use of a recruitment agency, whether a general one or one which specialises in Spain, such as English Educational Services (Alcalá 20-2°, 28014 Madrid; 91-532 9734/531 4783; fax 91-531 5298; movingparts@excite.com). The owner Richard Harrison recommends that candidates with just a degree and Cambridge Certificate come to Spain in early September and contact his agency on arrival.

For voluntary work as an English assistant on summer language/sports camps, try Relaciones Culturales, the youth exchange organisation at Calle Ferraz 82, 28008

Madrid (91-541 71 03/fax 559 1181), which also places native speakers with Spanish families who want to practise their English in exchange for providing room and board. Two other agencies involved in making this sort of live-in placements are GIC, Pintor Sorolla 29, Apdo. 1080, 46901 Monte Vedat (Valencia) and Castrum, Ctra. Ruedas 33, 47008 Valladolid (983-222213/ www.terra.es/personal2/castrumspain). The latter makes placements in Castille and Leon whereby participants undertake to spend three or four hours a day teaching English to members of the family and to enrol in a Spanish course (minimum five hours a week). The placement fee is pta25,000.

Michelle Manion from the US was happy with the language exchange arranged for her by Elena Garcia Perez of Castrum:

I would recommend the programme to anyone in my situation, i.e. anyone who wants to live in Spain but not as an au pair and is not entitled to a work permit. I was placed with a family with two boys aged 11 and 14. In the morning I went off for my Spanish lesson and then gave a lesson to the boys in turn. Spanish boys are notorious for being spoilt and impossible to control, but also for possessing wonderful personalities and great senses of humour. Carlos and César were typically Spanish and always managed to be both delightful and infuriating. Anyone interested in undertaking this venture should try to ascertain the children's level of English before arriving in Spain and to bring textbooks, magazines and children's books to work with, since English books are difficult to find in Spain. Also, when you arrive in Spain try to make as many friends and take up every opportunity you're given as this is the best way to learn Spanish.

One option which makes the job hunt easier is to do a TEFL training course in Spain. In addition to the several Cambridge CELTA course providers (e.g. International House in Madrid and Barcelona), an independent training organisation whose courses are patronised mainly by Americans is the International Career Center (ICC) in Barcelona; in the US ring 888-256-2519 or look at www.teflbarcelona.com for details of their monthly courses which come with on-going job assistance and advice on obtaining work visas.

Conditions of Work

Salaries for English teachers are not high in Spain. The standard negotiated wage is about pta150,000 per month for a full-time teacher. Compulsory social security *(seguridad social)* payments of 4%-7% will be deducted. Tax deductions are paid in arrears and do not normally affect teachers on nine-month contracts. A full-time contract normally consists of 25 contact hours or in some cases 30, which can feel gruelling, especially if the teacher teaches in off-site locations and has to travel around a big city like Madrid.

One of the worst problems in the classroom is the difficulty in motivating students. Many are children or teenagers whose parents enrol them in classes in order to improve their performance in school exams. David Bourne echoes this complaint after completing a nine-month contract in Gijón:

I have found it very hard work trying to inject life into a class of bored ten year olds, particularly when the course books provided are equally uninteresting. The children themselves would much rather be outside playing football. So you spend most of the lesson trying (unsuccessfully in my case) to keep them quiet.

Despite this he still sums up his job in Spain as exhilarating.

A reluctance to learn is not confined to the youth of Spain as Jon Loop found when he spent a year teaching at a Madrid language academy:

A lot of my groups were civil servants. They were excruciating because they didn't want to be there. The government has to spend its language training budget and picks people at random. I taught other classes including some university students who were very enthusiastic and great to work with, and also a group of technicians from the meteorological office who were keen because it was linked to their work.

Jon recommends taking advantage of the friendliness and helpfulness of students who may be in a position to lend you an unoccupied holiday house or put you in touch with their friends who want private tuition in English. In Jon's case, one of his students arranged for him to spend the harvest at a family vineyard and another helped him fix up work editing technical papers.

Private Tutoring

As usual, private tutoring pays much better than contract teaching because there is no middle man. The going rate for teaching individuals is pta2,000 per hour. Freelance rates in Madrid are higher to take account of travelling time.

It is difficult to start up without contacts and a good knowledge of Spanish; and when you do get started it is difficult to earn a stable income due to the frequency with which pupils cancel. Getting private lessons is a marketing exercise and you will have to explore all the avenues which seem appropriate to your circumstances. Obviously you can advertise on relevant notice boards e.g. at universities, corner shops and wherever else you think there is a market. Send neat notices to local state schools asking them to pin it up broadcasting your willingness to ensure the children's linguistic future.

AU PAIRS

Gone are the days when all the live-in positions in Spain were taken by Irish girls because of their Catholicism (so that it is said that the aristocracy of Spain regularly used such expressions as 'Begorra', according to Maura Laverty's amusing book about being a governess in Spain in the 1920s and 30s called *No More Than Human*).

The pocket money for au pairs at present is pta7,000-8,500 a week. Au pair links between Spanish agencies and those in the rest of Europe have been increasing. As mentioned in the section above on teaching, people can also arrange to stay with Spanish families without having to do much domestic or childcare duties. If you deal directly with a Spanish agency, you may have to pay a placement fee:

ABB Au Pair Family Service, Via Alemania 2, 5°A, 07003 Palma de Mallorca (971-752027/fax 971-298001).

A.P. Euro, Avda. Barón de Cárcer 48, 8°-P, 46001 Valencia (tel/fax 96-352 6395; a.p.euro@wanadoo.es).

Centros Europeos Galve, Calle Principe 12-6°A, 28012 Madrid (91-532 7230; ccprincipe@inicia.es). Mainly places au pairs in the Madrid, Valencia and Alicante areas. Registration fee of pta15,000.

GIC, Pintor Sorolla, Apt. 1080, 46901 Monte Vedat-Valencia (tel/fax 96-156 5837). Founding member of the International Au Pair Association.

Intercambio 66/Experiment, Fernández de los Rios 108, 28015 Madrid (91-549 3368/fax 91-544 7962/e-mail: experiment-inter66@mad.servicom.es).

Relaciones Culturales, Calle Ferraz 82, 28008 Madrid (91-541 71 03/fax 559 1181).

S & C Asociados, Avda. Eduardo Dato 46, 2°B, 41005 Seville (tel/fax 95-464 2447; s_c@mundivia.es). Long-term au pairs pay no registration fee (only four IRCs); short-term au pairs pay pta3,000. Most positions in southern Spain.

If you want to make informal contacts and meet expatriate families who might be looking for live-in childcare, you could visit the Mothers and Toddlers Group at the English-speaking Church at C/ Nunez de Balboa 43 (91-639 35 68).

Non-EU nationals who wish to work as au pairs should apply for a student visa before leaving their country of residence. Officially the Embassy requires both an offer of employment from the family and a letter from the school where the au pair is enrolled to study Spanish but in fact only the former is required, since the authorities recognise that it is usually impracticable for au pairs to enrol in classes before arrival in Spain.

AGRICULTURE

Reports of people finding harvesting work in Spain are far less common than in Greece, but they do filter through every so often. Traditionally there is an excess of exploited immigrant labour from North Africa and landless Spanish workers especially from Andalucia to pick the massive amounts of oranges, olives, grapes, and latterly avocadoes and winter strawberries. In places where migrant pickers congregate like Almeria, the Caritas charity often sets up a temporary food stall or even arranges basic accommodation. During the 2000 autumn harvest, the army of migrant labourers who gather in Almeria to work in the myriad greenhouses and who are paid about pta5,000 a day (half the average rural wage) decided to organise and go on strike. Andrea Militello from Italy went to the Valencia area at the beginning of November and did succeed in arranging work on an orange farm. But because of the many problems created by competition from Moroccans and low market prices for oranges, he left after a few days.

A not uncommon arrangement is to work in a semi-freelance capacity and earn on a percentage basis; for example you get 40% of the price at market of the fruit or almonds that you have picked, while the patron gets 60%.

Brendan Barker hitched to an organic farm near Granada (whose address he had noticed on a card displayed in a health food shop in Brixton!) and worked happily there on a work-for-keep arrangement for six months, while picking olives at a neighbouring farm in his free time. He describes the job as 'not particularly hard work but a little boring' and was told of a local superstition which claimed that having olive trees on your land means that you have been cursed by God.

Another reader who enjoyed an informal spell of work in the country was Ana Güemes from Mexico. She made friends in a local bar with a vineyard's family and arranged to help with the harvest in the village of Villasandino near Burgos (200km north of Madrid) just for the food and drink and fun of it.

The strawberry harvest lasts from Easter to June around Huelva on the southwest coast of Spain. Dozens of strawberry farms are located around the village of Moguer (from which half of Columbus's sailors came), plus Cartaya and Lepe. The usual struggle to find work pertains; newcomers must go to the hiring café at 6am each morning until a farmer picks them up. Then there is the usual struggle to earn decent money. It is possible to earn £50 a day in the latter part of the season, though £30 would be the average for a practised picker and £10 for a beginner who is not yet used to bending double in the broiling sun.

When the strawberry harvest finishes in June, the apricots in the area are ready for harvesting. Elsewhere try the Lorca area for pepper picking in early November followed by artichoke picking. You might also try the famous wine-making region of Spain, the Rioja Alta which is centred on Logrono, Haro, Cenicero and Fuenmayor. The local councils in some of these towns along the River Ebro have been known to allow migrant grape-pickers to camp free of charge in a public space.

Tomatoes and many other crops are grown on Tenerife. The Canaries are normally valued by working travellers only for their potential in the tourist industry, but there is a thriving agricultural life outside the resorts. Just a bus ride away from Los Cristianos, the farms around Granadilla, Buzanada, San Isidro and San Lorenzo may take on extra help between September and June. Most pickers camp (for example at the Nauta Campsite in southern Tenerife) and work on three-month contracts. The hourly wage probably won't top £2 but most of this can be saved. Although a few foreigners have discovered these harvests, most of the locals will consider it a novelty to employ a traveller and will help you to improve your Spanish.

The organic farming movement *(Coordinadora d'Agricultura Ecològica)* in Spain has ceased its involvement in helping prospective volunteers. A list of farms which accept people to work in exchange for board and lodging (at present there are 18 addresses on it) can be obtained by e-mail only from AEAM (Amics de l'Escola Agrària de Manresa): aeam@agrariamanresa.org. They stress that member farmers want to hear only from people whose main interest is organic farming, not learning Spanish. WWOOF Australia's *Worldwide List* contains 56 addresses in Spain.

Jon Loop is one contributor who succeeded in linking up with an organic farmer in southern Spain where he soon got down to some serious work weeding, building a pig enclosure, searching for water when the mountain stream dried up, etc. with no days off. But the surroundings were stunning, and the desolate beauty and harshness of the semi-desert made his stay very enjoyable. He even managed to enjoy goat-herding, that most challenging of rural activities:

> *This could be quite difficult since their range was 10km by 5km, and they could get through dense undergrowth while I had to follow dried-up rivers and footpaths. Also they had a habit of disappearing, even though they wore bells. The family were quite friendly, the food good was exquisite, the accommodation adequate but the temperatures were unbearable. Walking out of the house at 5pm for the evening stint was like walking into a Swedish sauna without the steam. After three weeks I decided to call it a day, and headed up north in search of rain.*

The Sunseed Trust, an arid land recovery trust, has a remote research centre in southeast Spain where new ways are explored of reclaiming deserts. The centre is run by both full-time volunteers (minimum five weeks) and working visitors (minimum one week) who spend half the day working. Weekly charges vary from £45 to £96. Typical work for volunteers might involve germination procedures, forestry trials, hydroponic growing, organic gardening, designing and building solar ovens and stills, and building and maintenance. Living conditions are basic and the cooking is vegetarian. Occasionally workers with a relevant qualification in appropriate technology, etc. are needed who are paid a small stipend. The address of the centre is Apdo. 9, 04270 Sorbas, Almeria (tel/fax 950-552770/ www.sunseed.org.net) or send £1 or 3 IRCs to PO Box 2000, Cambridge CB4 3UJ.

VOLUNTARY WORK

International workcamp organisations recruit for environmental and other projects in Spain for programmes as various as carrying out an archaeological dig of a Roman settlement in Tarragona to traditional stone quarrying in Menorca. The co-ordinating workcamp organisation in Spain is the Instituto de la Juventud (José Ortega y Gasset 71, 28006 Madrid; fax 91-309 30 66) which oversees 150 camps every year. You can approach them independently as well as through a partner organisation in your own country. Note that many camps are restricted to volunteers aged 18-26 with a few accepting volunteers up to the age of 30.

Proyecto Ambiental Tenerife runs hands-on whale and dolphin conservation projects in Tenerife which accept about 150 volunteers from the UK who join the project for 2-6 weeks from a number of start dates between June and October. A contribution of £95 a week must be made towards expenses. For details send a 31p s.a.e. to Proyecto at 59 St Martins Lane, Covent Garden, London WC2 (www.interbook.net/personal/delfinc). The project's Tenerife office is at Calle Jose Antonio 13, Arafo, Tenerife (tel/fax 922-510535). A German programme also working in cetacean research in the Canaries (on the island of Gomera) accepts volunteers year round: send 3 IRCs to MEER, Wiechselstr. 20, 10247 Berlin, Germany (meer@infocanarias.com) for details.

Jacqueline Edwards wanted a live-in position but her status as the single mother of a two-year old boy made her quest more complicated. She used her initiative and contacted vegetarian/vegan societies around Europe, asking them to put her details in their newsletter. Several of the replies she received were from Spain including from a natural therapies retreat centre in Zamora and from a German woman who needed an assistant.

Gibraltar

Gibraltar is an anomaly, an accident of history. It is a tiny British dependent territory on the Spanish coast, less than three miles square and with a working population of just 14,000. Until the 1980s, Gibraltar was inaccessible from Spain and is still separated by a wire fence and border guards. It has the same currency, the same institutions, etc. as the UK. Although Gibraltarians do not necessarily want to be a British colony, they have little choice. Under the 1713 Treaty of Utrecht Gibraltar must revert to Spain if Britain ever gives up sovereignty, a claim Spain would be unlikely to give up.

Not much recent feedback from travellers working in Gibraltar has been received which is surprising in a place where there is close to zero unemployment. The most recent account is from Allan Griffith and Paula Kershaw who found work easily between the new year and July:

We both got work in Gib. Paula was working as a chef and getting in 12 hours a day, six days a week. Hard work but she saved £3,000 in five months. I got a job on one of the tug boats working alongside the world's biggest cargo ships. Funny hours but a great job. Both jobs paid cash in hand.

But not everyone has been finding it so easy. Pat and Martin Kennard went to Gib with the intention of finding crewing positions on a transatlantic yacht (see *Working a Passage*). But when they arrived in September, the boat owners they talked to already had their crew. So they changed their tactics and tried to find land jobs. Not only was it the end of the season so bar work and related employment was scarce, they felt themselves to be discriminated against for being British. They were amazed to find job-seekers from Morocco being given a warmer welcome than they were. Furthermore the wage of £1.50 did not inspire enthusiasm for persisting in the struggle (though they liked Gibraltar and wanted to stay over the winter). In the end they were forced to purchase expensive one-way tickets home to England, declaring Gibraltar a disaster.

The restriction on British nationals working in Gibraltar was lifted in 1996 and EU nationals are free to take up any offer of employment made to them in Gibraltar. Non-EU nationals will have far more difficulty and will have to find an employer willing to help them apply for a work permit from the Employment Service, Unit 76-77 Harbour's Walk, New Harbours (40408/fax 73981) after first obtaining a Terms of Engagement form. To have an application for a work permit approved, the prospective employer must prove that no Gibraltarian or EU national is available to fill the vacancy, undertake to repatriate the worker if necessary and show that suitable accommodation has been found.

But tourism continues to flourish (partly because of Gibraltar's tax-free status) and there are hundreds of bars and restaurants in Gib, many with job vacancies during the busy summer season that can't be filled by locals. Mark Hurley's advice to the job-seeker is to start at one end of Gibraltar and work through, asking at all the bars and restaurants, which should take about two or three days. You will have a chance of work if you look tidy and sell yourself. Since the last edition, a number of international casinos and internet betting operations have opened or expanded, creating 700 new jobs. (Bilingual Chinese speakers are in high demand to deal with telephone clients in the Far East.)

Out of the scores of drinking holes, Andrew Giles recommends Charlie's Tavern on Admiral's Walk as a good source of job information. Charlie's is one of those favoured by the owners and crews of boats moored in Marina Bay. Also try another Marina Bay recommendation, the Admiral Collingwood pub opposite Safeways. Look also around the new marina Queensway Quay with moorings for 120 boats.

Even Adam Cook, who complained of the shortage of work in 'that litter-strewn blob of all that's undesirably British', managed to find a little yacht-varnishing work, and then was taken on to help redecorate a restaurant, before his big break came and he was taken on as paid crew back to England.

One possible source of work is Burger King which employed Andrew Giles, though he doesn't wax lyrical about it:

Burger King always seem to be advertising for staff. It's not the best job in the world, and you'll more than likely get treated as an imbecile but, as I kept saying to myself, you earn money and you get local contacts. Actually, working there led me to finding out about my present job as chef in the Admiral Collingwood pub.

Accommodation

There are neither campsites nor youth hostels on the Rock and free camping is completely prohibited on the beaches. Camper vans are not even permitted in after midnight. A property boom in the wake of the expanding gambling businesses means that rental property is almost non-existent. The cheapest accommodation we have heard of is at a hostel run by the charity TOC H. Most non-resident workers are therefore forced to commute from La Linea, the port town in Spain just across the border, which has been described by many as a cesspool of seediness and crime. Many travellers used to stay on a yacht or barge moored in Scotts Yard nicknamed the Graveyard since none of the boats ever left. But the authorities had it closed. All the boats were towed out and the travellers and others living on them had to move on. Even the boats that had sunk were all raised and removed, so it really is a graveyard now.

If you can prove to a boat owner that you are trustworthy, you may be able to fix up some boat-sitting. Sheppards Marina is where most of the yacht work is carried out, whereas Marina Bay is where the long distance yachts are moored. A good source of information on jobs and lodgings in the marinas is the newsagents next door to Bianca's Bistro in Marina Bay and to a lesser extent the Star Bar on Parliament Lane or Aragon Pub on Bell Lane in central Gibraltar. A notice board worth using is located in Sheppards Marina equipment shop at the Old Marina.

Opportunities for fixing up a crewing position on a yacht exist, though normally on a shared-expenses basis; see the chapter *Working a Passage.* If you want to arrange a free lift by land, frequent the Pig & Whistle and Rodolfo's Bar where long-distance lorry drivers congregate. According to Andrew Giles, however, it is necessary to get to know them a little before they are likely to offer a lift.

Portugal

At the turn of the 21st century, Portugal had one of the fastest growing economies in Europe and one of the lowest rates of unemployment, just 3.8% in mid-2000. Chances of finding work are best with tour operators or in hotels/restaurants along the Algarve coast.

There is a long and vigorous tradition of British people settling in Portugal, and the links between the two countries are strong. There are large numbers of expatriates around Lisbon and on the Algarve, many of whom are retired. English-speaking travellers might expect to find odd jobs in this community, but the friendly relations between foreigners and locals mean that the former are quite happy to employ the latter for many such jobs.

Ask expatriates for help and advice. Probably the best idea is to scan the advertisements in the English language press or place an ad yourself. The long-established English-language weekly *Anglo-Portuguese News* (Apartado 113, 2766-902 Estoril; 21-466 1551; apn@mail.telepac.pt) carries job adverts as does the Algarve-based weekly paper *The News* (PO Box 13, 8400 Portimao; fax 282-341201); the latter will print adverts up to 10 words free of charge. One of the Lisbon papers is *Expresso* (Rua Duque de Palmera 37-2, 1296 Lisbon; 21-526141).

The Regulations

Portugal has always had comparatively liberal immigration policies, possibly because it has never been rich enough to attract a lot of foreign job-seekers. As throughout the EU, citizens of the European Union must apply for a residence permit if they intend to stay for more than three months. The usual documents will be needed: proof of accommodation and means of support plus adequate health insurance or proof of paying social security contributions. Wage earners must prove that they are being paid at least the Portuguese minimum wage of 61,300 escudos per month. The permit should be obtained from the nearest immigration office (*Serviço de Estrangeiros e Fronteiras*). The address of the headquarters of the *Serviço de Estrangeiros* is Rua Conselheiro José Silvestre Ribeiro 4, 1600007 Lisbon (21-711 5000), while the regional Lisbon office is at Avenida António Augusto Aguiar 20 (21-315 9681).

The Consular Section of the British Embassy in Portugal (Rua de S. Bernardo 33, 1249-082 Lisbon; 21-392 40 00/fax 392 41 88) distributes information on taking up residence in Portugal which goes into more detail than the information from the Portuguese Consulate-General in London.

Non-EU nationals must provide the usual battery of documents before they can be granted a residence visa, including a residence visa obtained from the Portuguese Consulate in their home country, a document showing that the Ministry of Labour (*Ministerio do Trabhalho*) has approved the job and a medical certificate in Portuguese. The final stage is to take a letter of good conduct provided by the applicant's own embassy to the police for the work and residence permit. There are stories of non-Europeans arranging a residence permit after finding a job on arrival, but this is difficult.

Tourism

Thousands of Britons and other Europeans take their holidays on the Algarve creating many job opportunities in bars and restaurants. According to many travellers like Emma-Louise Parkes, the Albufeira area is the place to head:

> *I arrived at Faro Airport in June last year, and went straight to the Montechoro area of Albufeira. A job hunter here will be like a kid in a sweet shop. By 12.15pm I was in the resort, by 12.30pm I had found somewhere to stay and had been offered at least four jobs by the evening, one of which I started at 6pm. All the English workers were really friendly individuals and were a goldmine of information. Jobs-wise, I was offered bar work, touting, waitressing, cleaning, packing ice cubes into bags, karaoke singing, nannying for an English bar owner, timeshare tout, nightclub dancer...I'm sure there were more. Touts can earn £16 a night with all the drink they can stomach while waitresses can expect a little less for working 10am-1pm and 6pm-10pm. Attractive females (like myself!) will be head-hunted by lively bars, whereas British men are seen by the locals as trouble and are usually kept behind bars (serving bars that is) and in cellars.*

Emma-Louise recommends visiting the following places to make contacts: Linekars Bar, Something Else T-Shirt Shop, the Cottage, Banana's, Waikikis, Tom & Jerry's Diner and Erin's Isle Irish Bar (all situated on Av. De Carneiro, known as the Strip).

Kevin Gorringe agrees that Albufeira holds limitless possibilities for a working holiday. He met with nothing but a friendly warm response and there was no sign of red tape anywhere:

> *I left home in June as an engineer and now I am cooking English food in a place called Fat Frank's Fryer, just one of the many places to find work and friends. Other places are Casa da Fonte, Simply Delicious, Ludo's, Fernandos, the Rock Bar, Vegas Bar, Twist bar, etc. etc.*

Opportunities are not confined to Brits. Dutch and French job-seekers also succeed, though a range of nationalities is catered for in Albufeira, from the Deutsches Haus to the Koala Garden Restaurant. Very occasionally Algarve employers publicise vacancies such as the poolside snack bar at the Mayer Luz Beach Apartments at Praia da Luz in Lagos (282-789313).

Finding somewhere to stay can be more difficult than finding employment in some cases. Not surprisingly, accommodation is quite expensive during the high season. Ask around so you can avoid the dodgy landlords and expect to pay about £30 a week in a shared flat in Albufeira. It would be cheaper to do what Kevin Gorringe and his girlfriend did which was to stay at Campismo Albufeira (289-587629). Discounts may be available to long-stay campers.

The bullring does not offer much scope to working travellers, but it is has been known for an English person to work in it. Virginia Montesol (her ring name) went to

Spain, made contacts, moved on to Portugal and for two years fought as a *Rejoneador* in the Portuguese bullrings. In Portugal the bullfighter is usually on a horse and the bull is not killed. Virginia was an amateur and therefore unpaid but stayed free with a country family; the qualifications are to be an excellent rider with nerves of steel.

Teaching

The market for English tuition is fairly buoyant, especially in the teaching of young children and especially in northern Portugal. Apart from in the main cities of Lisbon and Oporto, both of which have British Council offices, jobs crop up in historic provincial centres such as Coimbra (where there is also a British Council) and Braga and in small seaside towns like Aveiro and Póvoa do Varzim. The Cambridge Certificate is widely requested by schools, but a number (especially those advertising vacancies in June, July and August) seem willing to consider candidates with a BA plus a promising CV and photo.

One of the most well-established groups of schools is the Cambridge School group (Avenida da Liberdade 173, 1250-141 Lisbon; 21-312 4600/ cambridge@ mail.telepac.pt) which every year imports about 100 British teachers. Other chains of language schools to try are Linguacultura, Apartado 37, 2001 Santarém Codex (243-309140; Linguacultura@Linguacultura.pt) which employs about 50 teachers in several locations; the Bristol School Group, Instituto de Linguas da Maia & Ermesinde, Trav. Dr. Carlos Pires Felgueiras 12-3°, 4470 Maia (22-948 8803); Encounter English, Av. Fernao de Magalhaes 604, 4350-150 Oporto (225-367916) and New Institute of Languages in Lisbon (Rua Cordeiro Ferreira, 19C 1°Dto, 1750-071 Lisbon; tel/fax 217-590 770) and Sacavém (nilportugal@mail.telepac.pt) which is one of the few schools willing to accept eager graduates with minimal training.

The consensus seems to be that wages are low, but have been improving at a favourable rate in view of the cost of living. On the positive side, working conditions are generally relaxed. The normal salary range is 145,000-185,000 escudos per month gross, and higher in Lisbon. Some schools pay lower salaries but subsidise or pay for flights and accommodation. Teachers being paid on an hourly basis should expect to earn between 1,700 and 2,000 escudos an hour.

Business

If you know some Portuguese, you might find an opening in an office; without a knowledge of the language, chances are remote. For agencies specialising in temporary work, look up the Yellow Pages *(Paginas Amarelas)* under the heading *Pessoal Temporário*. For temporary office or manual vacancies, try Manpower in Lisbon at Praça José Fontana 9c (21-313 4000; sede@manpower.pt) and also in Oporto (22-200 2426), Braga (25-321 4374), Albufeira on the Algarve (289-588113) and in the Azores (296-636341). See also www.manpower.pt. Three other Lisbon employment agencies are:

José Joaquim Calvo, Rua Marques da Silva, 46-1°, 1100 Lisbon (21-355 4665).

SELGEC, Rua Alexandre Herculano 39-1°, 1200 Lisbon (21-54 3505).

SELMARK Marketing, Rua do Salitre, 175-3°, 1200 Lisbon (21-387 7100).

The British-Portuguese Chamber of Commerce *(Camara de Comércio Luso-Britanica)* in Lisbon (Rua da Estrela 8, 1200-669 Lisbon; 21-394 2020). CVs may be sent by e-mail to bpcc@mail.telepac.pt though the Chamber cannot respond unless they have already been notified of a relevant opportunity. They plan to set up a facility whereby people can post CV details on their website (www.bpcc.pt) which would be accessible to Chamber members. They envision a system whereby the job-seeker's name and address would be divulged to prospective employers after consent had been granted and upon payment of a fee by the company. Trials are expected to begin in early 2001.

Agriculture

Although it is the fifth largest wine producer in the world, we have never heard of any traveller picking grapes. The farms are generally so small that hiring extra help is simply not done. In the words of the General Director of the Ministry of Agriculture some years ago, 'Due to the heterogeneity of the specie's distribution whose maturation is since May to November and due the small dimension of the farms, we employ the local handwork'.

Your best chance of success is to follow up leads passed on by the army of Portuguese migrant workers you might come across elsewhere in Europe, though even this is no guarantee as described by Jon Loop, who had become friendly with Portuguese workers during the French *vendange*:

> *Two friends and I decided to try our luck with the chestnut harvest in northern Portugal. We had been assured that there was lots of work picking chestnuts near Bragança near a place called (I think) Carrazedo. We got a lift in one of the Portuguese workers' coaches and eventually made it to the chestnut area. Sure enough there were lots of chestnuts just waiting to jump into our baskets.*
>
> *However we never managed to get a job. First we had trouble with the local policeman who took an immediate dislike to us. All the people we'd got to know at the grape harvest would meet us, then disappear, promising to return but they never did. Our last hope for work was a guy who had been very friendly when we'd bought him drinks during the grape harvest. He turned out to be the local thug and petty criminal who had just come out of jail after five years for (we think) drug smuggling. Not a good reference! ('Hey, we're looking for work. We're good friends with Pedro,' at which the prospective employer's eyes would narrow and he'd be thinking about calling the police.)*

The WWOOF Independents website (www.wwoof.org) includes 17 properties in Portugal including romantic sounding olive plantations and cork tree woodlands.

Voluntary and Au Pair

There isn't a strong voluntary movement in Portugal and what organisations there are seem loath to send details. The state-supported Instituto Portugues da Juventude (IPJ), Av. da Liberdade No. 194, 1269-051 Lisbon (21-317 92 00/fax 317 9216; ipj.infor@mail.telepac.pt) oversees a programme of heritage protection and other short-term voluntary projects. Applications should normally be sent through a partner organisation in the applicant's own country, for example Concordia and UNA Exchange in the UK which may also have links with other Portuguese voluntary agencies.

Au pairing is not at all common in Portugal, and very few placements are made by UK agencies to Portugal. A few positions may be advertised in *The Lady* with expat families. Summer openings are most likely to occur in the school holidays between the end of July and end of September. The international peace organisation International Friendship League (R. Ruy de Sousa Vinagre 2, 2890 Alcochete; fax 21-234 1082; ifl.por@mail.telepac.pt) may be able to arrange English tutoring placements in families. According to the director of information at the Instituto Portugues da Juventude, several other organisations can help people looking for vacation au pair placements:

Entreculturas, Rua Pereira e Sousa 76 R/C, 1300 Lisbon (21-387 0509).

Intercultura, Rua de Santo António da Glória 6 A, 1250 Lisbon (21-346 4126).

Tagus, Rua Camilo Castelo Branco 20, 1250 Lisbon (21-352 55 009).

Switzerland

With a low level of unemployment and a high proportion of foreign workers (estimated at 18% of the population), Switzerland would seem to be the working traveller's nirvana. But one of the reasons Switzerland is able to preserve its high levels of employment is that the state imposes strict work permit requirements on all foreigners. This together with the very high cost of living while you are job-hunting and the (deserved) Swiss reputation for hard work discourage many travellers. But people who have spent time working in Switzerland and have come to know the Swiss have nothing but compliments. According to Tony Mason who picked grapes four seasons running and worked as a builder:

> The Swiss are a genuinely friendly and hospitable people and we are often invited to local homes for meals and on outings to the mountains. Hitching here is excellent and also a valuable source of potential employers. I can't say enough good things about the Swiss.

The Regulations

On the other hand, the Swiss have often been accused of xenophobia (fear and loathing of foreigners) and their immigration policies are designed to make life difficult for foreign workers, although they depend on them in large measure to keep their economy flourishing. Switzerland is not a member of the EU or EEA. A bilateral treaty on free movement of persons has been concluded with the EU which should come into force in the course of 2001. The main obstacles to free movement will be abolished in 2003. A free booklet *Living and Working in Switzerland* can be obtained from the Swiss Embassy (also available via its website), but do not expect too many concrete facts and tips (16 Montagu Place, London W1H 2BQ; 020-7616 6000; telephone enquiries accepted between 3pm and 4pm; vertretung@Lon.rep.admin.ch/ www.swissembassy.org.uk). The book *Living and Working in Switzerland* by David Hampshire (Survival Books 1999, £12.95) has more detailed information about visa classes and is endorsed by the Swiss Embassy (though elsewhere it contains some startlingly outdated information).

In Switzerland, there is no separate document for working. A residence permit *(Aufenthaltsbewilligung* or *autorisation de séjour)* covers both the right of abode and employment. Employers are entitled to a certain number of *Saisonbewilligung* which are valid for four to six months at the moment, though the authorities are threatening to do away with this. The *Permis A* allows residence of up to nine months in one year and is only granted to EU passport holders. It is becoming increasingly difficult for Americans and Canadians to get permits. Rules and quotas vary from canton to canton. In some cantons (e.g. Interlaken) the minimum working period for employees applying for a permit is six months. Official regulations require that the permit be posted to an address outside the country. If you have obtained a job, your prospective employer will apply for a work and residence permit. If you can arrange to be back in your country of origin, the permit can be sent to the Swiss Embassy where you will have to pick it up, after a processing period of 6-8 weeks. However some people manage to avoid this laborious delay. Writing from Switzerland at Easter 2000, one contributor described how it worked for him:

> *The hotel has offered me a contract until October and I am now waiting on my work permit. Of course in order to obtain a permit I should be in the UK. But the hotel manager (who has supplied the Swiss authorities with my home address) has told me to advise my family in England that if they check up on my whereabouts, simply to tell them I am out at that moment, but most definitely in the UK. An alternative if you have a mobile phone bought in the UK would be to give that number, as it will always be a UK number wherever you are.*

Obviously the employer prefers to have his future staff nearer than a village in Herefordshire. The manager of an Interlaken hostel explained that the work period of four to six months is extended by the waiting period for the work permit to be processed. During this time the prospective employee should be more or less available to start work at short notice, should the permit be granted.

Approximately 30,000 *saisonniers* or *Permis A* holders worked in Switzerland last year (far fewer than three years ago), the majority of whom are from southern Europe, particularly Spain, Portugal, Italy and Turkey. *Permis B* and *C* are for more permanent work and are very difficult to get. One way of acquiring a longer term permit (*Permis G*) without being subject to the strict quotas is to become a cross-border commuter *(frontalier/Grenzgänger)*, people who work in Switzerland but live in France or Germany within 10km of the Swiss border.

Unfortunately Australians and New Zealanders are not eligible for permits and, with reports of four or five policemen posted in ski resorts simply to check visas and occasional purges elsewhere, the chances of working black are minimal, at least in the tourist industry. According to Joseph Tame from Herefordshire who spent eight months working at a hotel near Grindelwald, everyone has a permit, something that is just taken for granted. But he found the famous Swiss efficiency curiously missing from this branch of administration:

> *The visa system here seems rather haphazard. The local police who process them are overworked, and have now lost my passport. Anyway, my employers applied for my permit. I got one despite the fact that I was already in the country only because I managed to persuade them that I had relations here (very distant ones, so get out your family trees!) Whether you get a 9-month or a 4-month permit seems to be the luck of the draw. The prices vary too. For example some people paid SFr87 for their Permis A, whereas mine cost me SFr104, which I didn't have to pay until after five weeks, as the police forgot to get in touch with me. It took a month for my permit to be processed, during which time I couldn't work. So it was lucky that I had relatives to fall back on. Otherwise I would have built up huge debts.*

With a residence permit you become eligible for the state insurance scheme, for the minimum wage (approximately £850 a month) and the excellent legal tribunal for foreign workers which arbitrates in disputes over working conditions, pay and dismissals. Accident insurance is compulsory for all foreign workers and the employer pays the bulk of the premium, though foreign workers should take out their own health insurance. One advantage of having a residence permit is that in certain resort areas it entitles the holder to a *Carte d'Indigène* or 'red card' available from the *Controle de l'Habitant/Fremdenpolizei* (Aliens Police). The card may allow you to travel on public transport at a subsidised local rate, and also to buy a cheap seasonal ski pass.

Trainee exchanges have been negotiated between Switzerland and a number of other countries including the UK and US. Permits for temporary trainee placements *(stagiaires)* can be obtained from the Swiss Federal Aliens Office (BFA), Sektion Auswanderung und Stagiaires, Quellenweg 15, 3003 Bern (031-322 42 02; swiss.emigration@bfa.admin.ch). This office can also send addresses of co-operating partner organisations. The trainee position arranged must be in the vocational field of the applicant, who must be aged 18-30. The UK exchange agreement allows up to 400 young Britons to gain work experience in Switzerland for up to 18 months after completing their studies. Information in the first instance should be requested from the Overseas Labour Service of the Department of Employment, W5, Moorfoot, Sheffield S1 4PQ.

Students from outside Western Europe who wish to apply for short-term voluntary work may have a chance if they can obtain a letter of confirmation from their university stating that the work is important for their course of study. The chances for other non-Europeans are diminishing fast as Switzerland forms closer ties with Europe. Danny Jacobson went to Murren to visit a couple of North American friends working there in 2000; they told him that the law had changed and that no more permits would be issued in that canton to non-EU workers. Yet when Danny went on to Interlaken he noticed a lot of North Americans and Antipodeans working in cafés and hostels.

Casual Work

Particularly in the building trade and for agricultural work, the local supply of labour is so clearly inadequate that people without a residence permit do find jobs. Danny Jacobson from Wisconsin has spent several successful seasons piecing together odd jobs in the town of Bulle:

> *I still feel Switzerland is a working traveller's best friend in Europe. If you're willing to get dirty, there's tons of work around. If you can speak French or German, head into the more rural parts or the less touristy towns. I've based myself in Bulle, an over-sized village in the Préalpes. The word on the street is that in the off-the-beaten-track parts of Switzerland, the authorities look the other way because the hotels and restaurants are usually desperate for workers. The hotel owner has offered me a full-time position cleaning the staircases and washing dishes five days a week for SFr2,000 a month cash in hand plus food. If I choose to stay here for a bit, I shouldn't need to work again for a long long time when I hit the road again.*

He clearly preferred this boss to a previous one, a 'drunken mad man with 800 ways to mop a floor, of which a new one would be demonstrated each day because I was too inept to realise I was using yesterday's'.

Although Switzerland doesn't go so far as to demand that buskers get a work permit, Leda Meredith was surprised to find that the city of Bern (a 'goldmine for buskers') publishes a leaflet about when and where busking is permitted. Merchants keep a supply and will not hesitate to give you one if you transgress. Assaf de Hazan from Israel also found Switzerland a goldmine for buskers:

> *If you have a guitar (and can play it) here in Geneva, you are a king. If you have a bit of impudence and are willing to go around cafés and bars (not too fancy) and ask to play three songs, you are more than a king. I was getting about SFr500 for a day's playing around the train station part of the lake. You just go and ask and they always say yes. After playing just three songs, you go around with an ash-tray and get money, and lots of it.*

TOURISM

It has been said that the Swiss invented tourism. Certainly their hotels and tourism courses are still the training ground and model for hoteliers worldwide. For the hotels

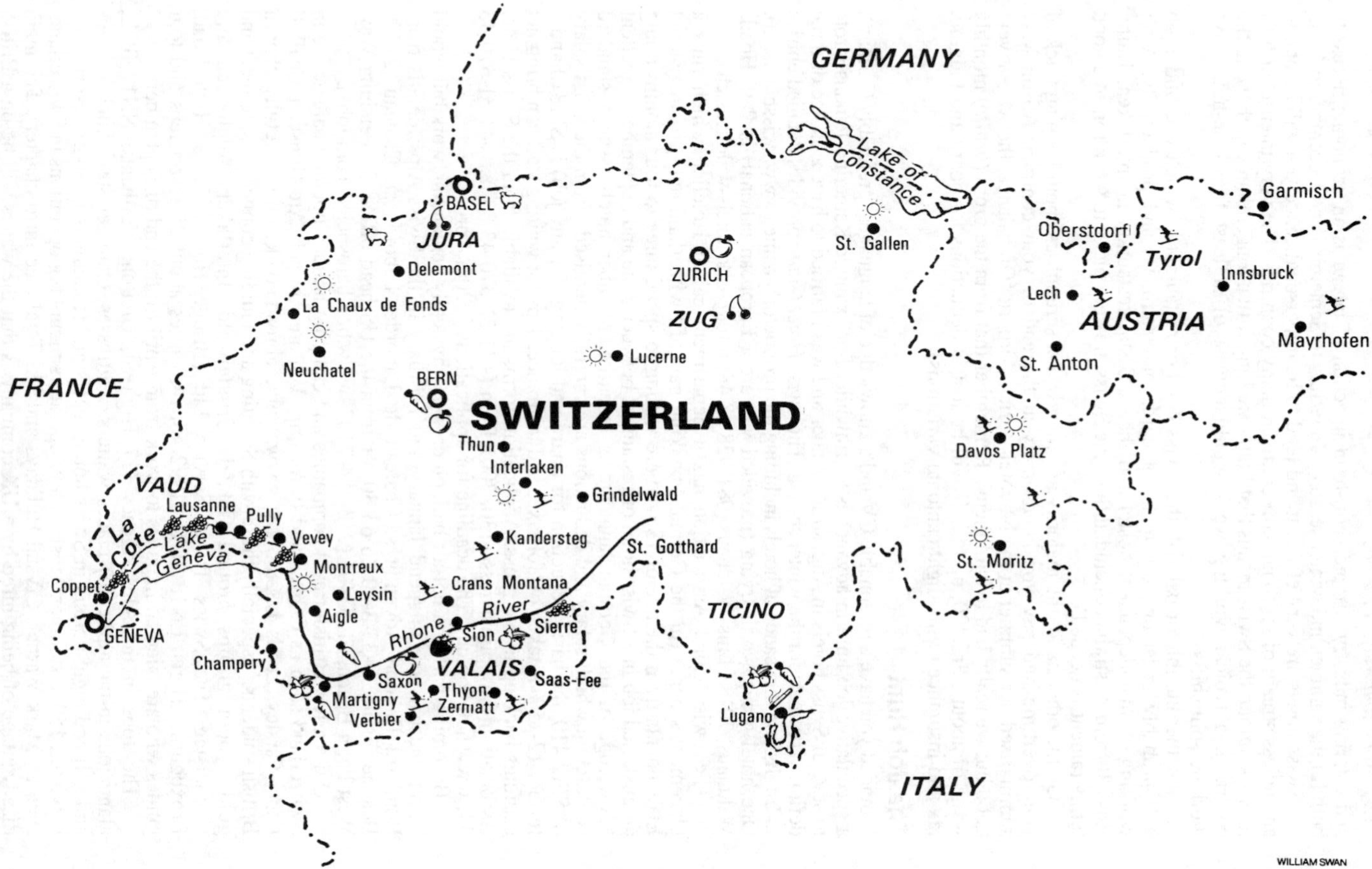

WILLIAM SWAN

GERMANY

AUSTRIA

ITALY

FRANCE

SWITZERLAND

Garmisch
Innsbruck
Mayrhofen
Tyrol
Oberstdorf
Lech
St. Anton
Davos Platz
St. Moritz

Lake of Constance
St. Gallen

Lugano
TICINO

ZURICH
ZUG
Lucerne
Grindelwald
St. Gotthard

Interlaken
Thun
Kandersteg
Crans Montana
Sierre
Saas-Fee
VALAIS
Zermatt
Sion
Thyon
Saxon
Martigny
Verbier
Rhone River

BASEL
JURA
Delemont
La Chaux de Fonds
Neuchatel
BERN

Montreux
Leysin
Aigle
Vevey
Pully
Lausanne
Champery
VAUD
Cote
Lake Geneva
Coppet
GENEVA

and catering industry, a rapid short-term injection of labour is an economic necessity both for the summer and winter season – June/July to September and December to April.

Swiss hotels are very efficient and tend to be impersonal, since you will be one in an endless stream of seasonal workers from many countries. The very intense attitude to work among the Swiss means that hours are long (often longer than stipulated in the contract): a typical working week would consist of at least five nine-hour days working split shifts.

Whether humble or palatial, the Swiss hotel or restaurant in which you find a job will probably insist on very high standards of cleanliness and productivity. After working at an independent hostel and then a 3-star restaurant in Interlaken, Kathy Russell from Australia concluded that 'the Swiss are very picky to work for, so a good temperament is needed'.

On the other hand, the majority are *korrekt*, i.e. scrupulous about keeping track of your overtime and pay you handsomely at the end of your contract. Alison May summarised her summer at the Novotel-Zürich-Airport: 'On balance, the wages were good but we really had to earn them'. Remember that from the gross *(brutto)* monthly wage of about SFr2,400, up to half will be lost in deductions for board and lodging, tax and insurance (with slight cantonal variations).

The Job Hunt

Provided you have a reasonable CV and a knowledge of languages (preferably German), a speculative job hunt in advance is worthwhile. For example Katherine Jenkins wrote to several Swiss hotels in August/September and was gratified to have a choice of three definite contracts for the winter season. The *Swiss Hotel Guide* provides detailed entries in English on thousands of hotels including the proprietor's name (www.swisshotels.ch). One hotel group worth trying (provided you are a European national) is Park Hotels Waldhaus, 7018 Flims-Waldhaus (081-928 48 48; info@park-hotels-waldhaus.ch).

The Swiss Hotel Association has a department called Hoteljob which runs a placement scheme (in the German-speaking part of Switzerland only) for registered EU students from the age of 18 who are willing to spend three to four months doing an unskilled job in a Swiss hotel or restaurant between June and September. Excellent knowledge of the German language is essential. Member hotels issue a standard contract on which salary and deductions are carefully itemised. From the gross salary of SFr2,410, the basic deduction for board and lodging (for any job) is SFr810 and a further 12-15% is taken off for taxes and insurance. Tips for waiting staff can bring net earnings back up to the gross. Application forms are available from the Swiss Hotel Association, Monbijoustrasse 130, 3001 Bern (+41-31-370 43 33/fax +41-31-370 43 34; www.hoteljob.ch). The deadline for applications is 20th April.

Becoming part of a hot-air balloon crew is physically demanding work but would be an unusual way to spend January and February in the Swiss Alps; details from Bombard Balloon Adventures, Chateau de Laborde, Laborde au Chateau, 21200 Beaune, France (+33-3-80 26 63 30) or from the US head office, 33 Pershing Way, West Palm Beach, FL 33401 (240-384-7107; www.bombardsociety.com/jobs).

Quite a few British travel companies and camping holiday operators are active in Switzerland such as Canvas and Eurocamp. Venture Abroad (Arc House, 1 Coalhill Lane, Farsley, Leeds LS28 5NA; www.ventureabroad.co.uk) hire 'carefully chosen British students,' especially those with Scouting and Guiding connections, to meet and guide youth groups around Gstaad, Grindelwald, Interlaken, Adelboden and Kandersteg. The Swiss Travel Service Ltd (Bridge House, 55-59 High Road, Broxbourne, Herts. EN10 7DT; 01992 456143) hires about 25 resort reps and tour guides who are talented linguists to work from April till the end of September.

The Jobs in the Alps Agency (17 High St, Gretton, Northants. NN17 3DE; alan@jobs-in-the-alps.com) places waiters, waitresses, chamber staff, kitchen helps and hall and night porters in Swiss hotels, cafés and restaurants in Swiss resorts, 200 in winter, 150 in summer. Most ski tour operators mount big operations in Switzerland, such as Mark Warner, Crystal Holidays and Ski Total (see intro chapter). The main disadvantage of being hired by a UK company is that the wages will be on a British scale rather than on the much more lucrative Swiss one.

The Swiss organisation Village Camps advertises widely its desire to recruit staff over 21 in their multi-activity language camps for children in Anzere, Leysin, Morgins, etc. They also hire up to 100 ski counsellors and other staff for the winter season. Jobs are available for EFL teachers, sports instructors, nurses and general domestic staff. For jobs with Village Camps, room and board are provided as well as accident and liability insurance and an allowance which amounts to pocket money. An application pack is available from Village Camps, rue de la Morache, 1260 Nyon (022-990 9405/fax 022-990 9494; personnel@villagecamps.ch/ www.villagecamps.com/staff/staff1.htm).

Another possible employer is the Haut-Lac International Centre (1669 Les Sciernes; 026-928 4200; info@haut-lac.ch/ www.haut-lac.ch) who hire teacher/ monitors of any nationality for both their summer and winter camps for teenagers.

On-the-Spot

Most people go out and fix up their jobs in person, as recommended in the introductory section on *Winter Resorts*. Steve Rout, a resort expert, has always found this to be the most satisfactory way to find work. He recommends looking in Les Portes de Soleil at Champery, Les Crosets as well as the major resorts of Leysin, Verbier, Thyon and Crans Montana. This valley is a major road and rail route and is ideal for concentrated job hunting. Another area which has been recommended is the Jura between La Chaux-de-Fonds and Delémont.

Surprisingly, tourist offices may be of use. Naturally their lists of local accommodation are a useful starting point, but tourist information staff may be of more specific assistance. Joseph Tame found that it was possible to register your name and details with the tourist office in Grindelwald for a fee of SFr10. These would then be circulated to all the hotels in town on a weekly basis (this was in September). It is useful to have a reference or two to show. Also check notice boards and adverts in local papers like *L'Est Vaudois* for the Montreux region or *Le Nouvelliste* in the Rhone Valley. The *Hotel & Tourismus Revue* carries top jobs for experienced people in the tourist industry.

Like most people, Andrew Winwood found the job hunt tough going:

All in all I asked in over 200 places for ski-season work, but eventually could have counted 10-12 possibilities. Going on that rate, it would be possible to get work after asking at 50 or 60 places, but of course the 'Grand Law of Sod' would prevail. As far as I can see, it's a simple case of ask, ask, ask and ask again until you get work. It was costing me about £80 a week to live in Switzerland, so I couldn't let up until I definitely had a way of getting the money back.

The most promising time to introduce yourself to potential employers is about a week before the end of the previous season, so late April/early May for the summer season and September for the winter. November is a bad time to arrive since most of the hotels are closed, the owners away on holiday and most have already promised winter season jobs to people they know from previous seasons or ones who approached them at the end of the summer season. When David Loveless arrived in Verbier in mid-November, he declined an invitation to add his name to the bottom of eight sheets of people waiting for jobs. After moving on to Crans Montana, David soon found work at the Hotel de l'Etrier as a *chasseur* (messenger/odd jobs man).

Rob Jefferson had no luck whatsoever and describes his discouraging experiences job-hunting in Swiss resorts:

We arrived in Grindelwald in mid-December, and stayed in the youth hostel (along with 11 others all looking for work). After ten days, only one of the hostellers had found work, and so we left for Saas Fee with half-promises of work from seven hotels of the many we'd phoned. We were flatly refused by six but the seventh promised Sonja my girlfriend a job as a waitress if the pre-contracted waiter did not show up the next day. Sonja is very attractive, speaks near perfect English and good German. We had been around about 70 hotels in all and it took a late arrival for her to get a job. If this was the case for her, what about me? No chance.

Danny Jacobson's tip is to bypass the large ski stations in favour of the less tourist-filled ones. Head for the smaller stations and the surrounding villages where your presence will be more of a novelty. Joseph Tame's surprising tip is to go up as high as possible in the mountains. After being told by virtually every hotel in Grindelwald in mid-September that they had already hired their winter season staff, he despaired and decided to waste his last SFr40 on a trip up the rack railway. At the top he approached the only hotel and couldn't believe it when they asked him when he could start. Although he had never worked in a hotel before, they were willing to take him on as a trainee waiter, give him full bed and board plus £850 a month. At first he found the job a little boring since there were few guests apart from Japanese groups on whirlwind European tours. But things changed at Christmas:

Christmas and New Year was an absolute nightmare. Three shifts a day for everyone with very little sleep and no time off. When a promised pay rise didn't materialise, I decided I had had enough and handed in my notice. But by January 5th, business had slumped and we had at least two hours off daily to ski. When my overdue pay rise came through I withdrew my notice. If you can stick the Christmas rush, things do get better. Switzerland was definitely the best thing that ever happened to me.

So good that at the time of writing he is back at the Hotel Bellevue in Kleine Scheidegg for the 2000/01 winter season (his last he says). He encourages others to apply (3801 Kleine Scheidegg; fax 033-855 1294).

The intriguingly named Hiking Sheep Guesthouse (Villa La Joux, 1854 Leysin; tel/fax 024-494 35 35; hikingsheep@leysin.net) hires general staff who speak French and English (and preferably German) to work on reception for at least a month.

Another recommended meeting place is Balmer's Herberge in Interlaken (Hauptstrasse 23-25, 3800 Interlaken; 033-822 19 61; balmers@tcnet.ch). They take on English-speaking staff for a minimum of six months and only after interviewing them in person. The owner is pleased to pass on information about other job openings in the area, as the hostel is often contacted by local hotels asking for workers.

At one time foreign travellers could sometimes pick up temporary jobs as drivers, odd job men, etc. for one of the many adventure rafting operators but after the tragedy in which 18 young holidaymakers were drowned in 1999, the industry has come under close scrutiny and that option is closed.

AGRICULTURE

Official Schemes

One report estimated that nearly one-third of farm hands employed during the summer are foreigners (mainly Portuguese). Young people who are more interested in rural experiences than in money may wish to do a stint on a Swiss farm. The Landdienst located at Mühlegasse 13 (Postfach 728), 8025 Zürich (01-261 44 88/fax 01-261 44 32; admin@landdienst.ch) fixes up farm placements for a minimum of three weeks for young people from Western Europe who know some German or French. Last year about 500 foreign young people and 3,000 Swiss were placed through the Landdienst. The scheme is open to European nationals only. Workers are called 'volunteers' and can work for up to two months without a work permit. They must pay a registration fee of SFr60.

In addition to the good farm food and comfortable bed, you will be paid at least SFr20 per day worked. Necessary qualifications for participating in this scheme are that you be between 18 and 25 and that you have a basic grounding in French or German. On these small Swiss farms, English is rarely spoken and many farmers speak a dialect which some find incomprehensible.

Most places in German-speaking Switzerland are available from the beginning of March to the end of October and in the French part from March to June and mid-August to the end of October, though there are a few places in the winter too. Each canton has a farm placement representative who liaises with the Zürich headquarters. It is also possible for Britons to apply through Concordia, preferably at least a month before you wish to work, and for other nationalities to apply through co-operating student exchange organisations in their country such as Exis in Denmark, Travel Active Programmes in the Netherlands and so on.

Despite Switzerland's reputation as an advanced nation, there are still thousands of small family farms, especially in the German-speaking cantons, where traditional farming methods are practised. Part of the reason for this is that not many mechanical threshers or harvesters can function on near vertical slopes (neither can every human harvester for that matter).

The hours are long, the work is hard and much depends on the volunteer's relationship with the family. Most people who have worked on a Swiss farm report that they are treated like one of the family, which means both that they are up by 6am or 7am and working till 9pm alongside the farmer and that they are invited to accompany the family on any excursions, such as the weekly visit to the market to sell the farm-produced cheeses. The arrangement is similar in many way to the au pair arrangement; in fact young women who get placed on a Swiss farm may be asked to do more chores inside the house than out. Gillian Forsyth found the life lonely on her isolated farm and she had few chances to improve her French since she was often alone in the house with the baby or in the fields with the goats.

Ruth McCarthy gives an idea of the range of tasks to do on the farm, and a taste of village life, which sounds like something out of *Heidi*:

The work on my farm in the Jura included cleaning out cow stalls, hay making, grass cutting, poultry feeding, manure spreading, vegetable and fruit-picking, wood cutting, earth moving, corn threshing and also housework, cooking and looking after the children. The food was very wholesome and all produced on the farm: cheeses, fresh milk, home-made jam, fresh fruit, etc. The church bells struck throughout the day and peeled at 6am and 9pm to open and close each day. As well as church bells the sound of cow bells was also present so that it was quite noisy at times. There was little night life unless you went to a gasthof bar in the village. Anyway it's probably better to get a good night's sleep.

Paul Barton arranged to work for the same farmer he'd worked for through the Landdienst the previous year. He was given a work permit and paid nearly three times his previous summer's wage. He was also expected to do twice as much work, which was impossible when he'd already been working 16 hours a day. For his own amusement he kept track of the number of hours worked and counted up to a staggering 1,250 in ten weeks before returning home for some essential rest and relaxation.

The Swiss Farmers' Union runs a programme for trainees in agriculture from Europe, North America, Brazil, the Antipodes, South Africa and Japan. Participants who want to work for 3, 4, 6 or 12-18 months must have at least two years' practical experience or relevant training and be able to speak some English, French or German. Further details are available from Agroimpuls, c/o Farmers' Union, Laustrasse 10, 5201 Brugg Switzerland (056-462 51 44; www.agroimpuls.ch).

WWOOF Switzerland (Postfach 59, 8124 Maur) keeps a constantly updated list of farmers around the country, currently 45. To obtain the list you must join WWOOF at a cost of SFr20/$15/DM30/F90 in cash. Details are available on WWOOF's web-site www.welcome.to/wwoof. Joseph Tame made use of this website to fix up a place on a farm in spring 2000:

I can honestly say that it has been an absolutely fantastic experience. The hours could be thought fairly long by some (perhaps 35 per week) considering there is no money involved, but I absolutely love the chance to work outside in this land that reminds me so much of the final setting in 'The Hobbit.' From our farm your eyes take you down the hillside, over the meadows covered in flowers, down to the vast Lake Luzern below and over to the huge snow-capped mountain Pilatus. It really is paradise here. The family have been so kind, and as I put my heart into learning all that I can about the farm they are only too happy to treat me with generosity. I really feel a part of the family.

Organic farming (known as 'Bio') is big business in Switzerland and the Soil Association (Bioterra) is better known than WWOOF. Bioterra regularly publish a book (in German only) containing details of 300 farms where volunteers can be accommodated, *Arbeit auf dem Biohof*; SFr10 from Bioterra, Dubsstrasse 33, 8003 Zurich (01-463 55 14; bioterra@swissonline.ch/ www.bioterra.ch).

The charity Caritas Schweiz (Freiwilligeneinsatz, Löwenstrasse 3, Postfach, 6002 Lucerne; caritas@caritas.ch) confirmed in October 2000 that they accept volunteers who want to help mountain farmers with renovating their farms or to support them in agriculture.

Unofficial Work

The area along the River Rhone between Martigny and Saxon in Valais has been recommended for agricultural work. Visit the local markets and make enquiries. Farmers around Martigny growing tomatoes, carrots and other crops may require casual workers.

Although Glen Mitchell was discouraged to find that New Zealanders cannot get work permits for Switzerland, he decided to try his luck in the tobacco-growing region around Bern:

> *I headed into the countryside between the towns of Murten and Kerzers at the end of July. The very first farmer I asked sent me up the road to his neighbour who offered me six weeks work picking tobacco leaves and told me I could start the next day. I was given a room in the farmer's house and excellent food. I enjoyed the company of a very nice Swiss family, was able to add a lot to my extremely limited German vocabulary and learn all about the work attitudes of the Swiss (the hours were from 7am to 7pm). The pay was SFr1,200. I was lucky to arrive at the start of the tobacco season (1st August) and to find work within half an hour.*

Grape-Picking

Like every country in Europe south of Scotland, Switzerland produces wine. The main area is in the Vaud north of Lake Geneva, but also in Valais around Sion and Sierre, where the harvest begins on October 6th, give or take a day or two, with surprising regularity. Every year scores of hopeful *vendangeurs* begin pouring into the region. Robert Abblett calculated that if he had arrived in time to catch the beginning of the harvest, he could have saved £350 from 11 days of work:

> *From Chateauneuf du Pape we headed north to find later grape work, but it took us three days of searching before we ended up at a place called Aigle in Switzerland. By sheer luck we found three days work at the end of the harvest and lived (free) with 100 other workers in some army barracks. They were an international collection of seasonal travellers who liked to party till 2am every night, so I ended up sleeping in the front of the van to get some sleep.*
>
> *The grapes were so much easier to pick here than in France and I had to stop myself from racing along the lines and leaving the others behind. It was a really pretty place to work, and the owners of the smaller vineyards were very generous with tea, coffee, wine and food. On one family vineyard we would all be swigging wine while we worked to keep the boss happy.*

Almost everyone who has written about the Swiss harvest writes in similarly glowing terms. In Salgesh, the third farm which Robin Gray tried told him to come back at 8am the next morning:

> *I worked there for two weeks and had a fantastic time. When I told the boss I was camping, he offered me his garage which was like a comfortable house. I ended up being given free food and accommodation and the equivalent of £5 an hour. What a job. The family were unbelievably nice. Every night we had a different traditional Swiss meal. The boss's mother did my washing for me and it would come back not only ironed but with the rips sewed up. Of all the places I've been, Switzerland has been the friendliest of them all. I earned about £400 in two weeks.*

Vineyards are found along the north shores of Lake Geneva on either side of Lausanne. One district is known as La Cote, between Coppet and Morges west of

Lausanne, and the other is the Lavaux, a remarkably beautiful region of vineyards, rising up the hillside along the 25km between Pully on the outskirts of Lausanne and the tourist city of Montreux. The vineyards, enclosed within low stone walls, slope so steeply that all the work must be done by hand, and the job of portering is recommended only for the very fit. The harvest here is later than in France (early to mid-October) when the weather is beginning to get cold and rainy (the latter curtails work). Also the harvest is shorter (a week to ten days), because of the lower density of grapes per hectare.

One suggestion is to visit the tourist office outside the railway station in Biel on the Lake of Biel (Bielersee) and obtain the leaflet about wine in the region, which gives the names, addresses and phone numbers of nearly 50 vineyard owners *(weinbauern)*. It is worth writing to the farmers (in French) well in advance to give them a chance to get you a seasonal permit. September can be a good time to ask, since you might be taken on early to help with netting the grapes, to minimise bird damage. Try also the northern shores of the two adjoining lakes Murtensee and Lac de Neuchatel.

Although the harvest is the time of year when there are the most vacancies, grape farmers also need people to help prune, something which Andrea Militello found very lucrative in June around Aigle. He claims that the technique is easy enough for anyone to master, though it is hard physical labour and even harder to land the job in the face of a lot of competition. He earned SFr2,880 on top of bed and board for working six days a week for four weeks.

BUILDING

There are far fewer Swiss nationals than foreigners working as building labourers. In addition to building improvement in residential areas, resorts have a continual demand for painters and builders out of season. Much of the construction work is done by Portuguese, Spanish and Italian workers. Ask them for advice or visit timber yards or estate agents *(agences immobilieres)*.

In winter you may be able to find occasional work chopping firewood or mending roofs. Danny Jacobson found out just how much wood is needed to keep a farming family warm through the Swiss winter when he spent a few weeks chopping and carting enough wood to give him a lifetime's phobia of trees. (But he was paid a handsome SFr100 per day for his trouble as well as free room and board.) A special opportunity for odd jobbers is afforded by the Swiss law that prohibits snow on roofs from reaching more than two metres depth. Apparently casual labourers are needed at the giant vegetable market in Zürich (near the football stadium). The wage for shifting heavy sacks of produce is £8 an hour. It will probably be necessary to sleep at the market since farmers start arriving long before dawn breaks.

AU PAIRS

For those interested in a domestic position with a Swiss family there are rules laid down by each Swiss canton, so there are variations. You must be a female between the ages of 17 and 29 (18 in Geneva) from Western Europe, North America and Australia/New Zealand, stay for a minimum of one year and a maximum of 18 months, be in possession of a *Permis* B (for which the family applies) and attend a minimum of three hours a week of language classes in Zürich, four in Geneva. Families in most places are required to pay half the language school fees of SFr360-SFr1,000 for six months. The agencies are at pains to remind potential au pairs that Swiss German is very different from the German learned in school which often causes disappointment and difficulties.

Au pairs in Switzerland work for a maximum of 30 hours per week, plus babysitting once or twice a week. The monthly salary varies among cantons but the normal range is SFr600-700. Rates may be slightly higher for older girls and are generally higher in Geneva than Zürich. In addition, the au pair gets a four or five week paid holiday plus SFr18 for days off (to cover food). Au pairs are liable to pay tax and contributions. In Zürich canton this amounts to a monthly deduction of SFr40 for tax, plus SFr50-75 for health insurance and SFr90 for social security.

There are two major au pair agencies. The first is Compagna whose incoming programme is co-ordinated by the Sektion Innerschweiz, Reckenbühlstrasse 21, 6005 Luzern. Compagna Zurich, Unterer Graben 29, 8400 Winterthur (tel/fax 052-212 55 30) charges a registration fee of SFr70 plus a further SFr120-180 when a family has been found. For the French part of Switzerland (Geneva and Lausanne), contact Compagna Lausanne (Rue du Simplon 2, 1006 Lausanne; 021-616 29 88/fax 021-616 29 94). The other main agency is Pro Filia which has 15 branches including 241G, Rte d'Hermance, 1246 Corsier/Geneva (022-751 02 95) for the French-speaking part, and Beckenhofstr. 16, 8035 Zürich (01-363 55 01/fax 01-363 50 88) for the German part. The registration fee of SFr35 plus the standard agency fee of SFr100 is due in the first month of your placement.

Independent agencies which place au pairs are Heli Grandjean's Placements Au Pair (Chemin de Relion 1E, 1245 Collonge-Bellerive; 022-752 38 23; grandjean@geneva-link.ch) which is active in the Geneva area, Sunshine Au Pair Agency, 128 route du Moulin-de-la Ratte, 1236 Cartigny/Geneva (022-756 82 03) and Perfect Way, Mandacherstrasse 1, 5234 Villigen (056-284 28 86; perfectway@pop.agri.ch).

VOLUNTARY WORK

Several of the international workcamp organisations operate in Switzerland mainly to carry out conservation work. For example Gruppo Volontari dalla Svizzera Italiana (C.P. 12, 6517 Arbedo; 079-354 01 61) organises camps on which groups of volunteers (who can speak one of Switzerland's official languages) help mountain communities in Maggia, Fusio and Borgogne. Volunteers pay about SFr15 per day for living expenses. Swiss WWOOF provides the addresses of four voluntary projects, though one of these (i.e. World Wide Fund for Nature) says that it has almost no opportunities for non-Swiss. By contrast the Mountain Forest Project (Bergwald Projekt) publishes its literature (and soon its website) in English and is very welcoming to foreign volunteers who know some German:

> *People from overseas travelling in Europe will surely enjoy a week's workcamp with MFP in Switzerland, Germany or Austria. You will learn a lot about alpine forests and nature in general. We do not, however, consider it reasonable to fly to Europe just for one week to work with us. We all know that airplanes pollute the air and endanger our atmosphere, climate and forests. For these reasons we offer our workcamps only to people who are in Europe anyway.*

For details send two IRCs to MFP, Hauptstr.24, 7014 Trin (081-630 41 45; www.bergwaldprojekt.ch).

In addition to the Swiss branch of SCI (Gerberngasse 21a, 3000 Bern 13), the other contact given by WWOOF Switzerland is Pro Natura (Natur Aktiv, Postfach, 4020 Basel) which has a volunteer programme at holiday camps.

Austria

For many years Austria has offered seasonal employment in its summer and winter tourist industries. Prospects for finding work are helped by the fact that unemployment in Austria at around 3.2% is well below the EU average. A good knowledge of German will be necessary for most jobs apart from those with UK tour operators. The Austrian Embassy in Britain (18 Belgrave Mews West, London SW1X 8HU (www.austria.org.uk) produces a general booklet *Living and Working in Austria* which gives information about immigration and social security.

Once you are in Austria, you could try the state-run regional employment office AMS *(Arbeitmarktservice)* though it would be virtually essential to speak German before they could assist. The AMS homepage might assist German speakers (www.ams.or.at). Some offices have a special department for seasonal work in the hospitality industry *(Sonderteil: Saisonstellen im Hotel und Gastewerbe)* which are notified of winter vacancies in November for the start of the season at the end of November. For hotel and catering vacancies in the South Tyrol try AMS Euro Biz/JobCenter International, Südtiroler Platz 14-16, 6020 Innsbruck (512-58 63 00/fax 512-58 63 00-20). The Ufficio di Lavoro is responsible for job information in the Italian-speaking region of South Tyrol. Euroadvisers are on hand to advise European job-seekers at the EuroJobCentre, Reschgasse 20-22, 1120 Vienna (1-817 45 44-113/fax 1-817 45 44-110).

Private employment agencies exist in Austria, mostly registering professional vacancies. Oscar's Job Guide may be of assistance to international jobseekers: PO Box 588, Bahnbrückenweg 6, 6800 Feldkirch (05522-76563; oscars@cble.vol.at/ www.oscars.at).

Nationals of non-European countries must obtain a work permit before departing from their home country which, as usual, is virtually impossible for casual and seasonal work. Au pairs from outside the EU must obtain both a work and residence permit *(Beschäftigungsbewilligung)* though this can be applied for inside Austria for a fee. At present there is a quota of foreign workers from outside Europe, and when the annual quota is filled, no more permits are granted that year. Politicians have been arguing that au pairs should not be included in the total since they do not take jobs from Austrians, but no change in the regulations has been reported yet.

If working legally, you can expect to have up to 16% of your gross wage deducted for contributions to the compulsory Health and Social Security Scheme (except for au pairs).

THE JOB HUNT

The thousands of East Europeans who have flooded into Austria in recent years will be keen competitors for any unskilled jobs around. Immigrants from former Yugoslavia, Croatia and Slovenia are often hired in preference to ski bums, and hotels and bars draw their staff from the pool of employees willing to work extremely hard to maintain their relatives at home.

In the 1990s Ian McArthur encountered this competition in Vienna where he worked as a cleaner in a bar:

I worked 25 hours a week and was paid £4 an hour cash-in-hand. I had the opportunity, had I stayed longer, to work as a bartender which required a basic knowledge of German. I was paid every day, which permitted me a carefree disregard for financial prudence. This is common practice among illegal workers in Vienna, many of whom are Czechs and Yugoslavs (who are notoriously badly paid). I heard of openings for life models at art colleges, restaurant work and English teaching.

Tourism

There is no shortage of hotels to which you can apply either for the summer or the winter season. Get a list from the local tourist office. The largest concentration is in the Tyrol though there are also many in the Vorarlberg region in western Austria. Wages in hotels and restaurants are low compared to Switzerland, starting at AS9,000 a month (£400) plus free room and board. A good wage before deductions is about AS13,500.

If you want to improve your chances of finding work in a ski resort, you could consider joining the annual trip to Club Habitat in Kirchberg in the Austrian Tyrol (Kohlgrub 9, 6365 Kirchberg; 05357 2254; clubhab@kirchberg.netwing.at) for the first three weeks of December. During the trip, participants are given German lessons and lectures on job opportunities and red tape at a cost of nearly £400 which includes travel and half-board accommodation. It is organised in conjunction with Top Deck Travel (131-135 Earls Court Road, London SW5 9RH; 020-7244 8641).

The main winter resorts to try are St Anton, Kitzbühel, Mayrhofen, St. Johann-im-Pongau which is a popular destination for British holidaymakers creating a demand for English-speaking staff, St. Johann in Tyrol, Lech and Söll. Once you are in a resort like St Anton or Brand which, during the season, has to accommodate and service thousands of holidaymakers, it should be easy to find an opening. Try putting an ad in the *Tiroler Tageszeitung* newspaper.

As usual, it will be necessary to enquire everywhere for jobs in hotels, shops, as an au pair, in specialist areas like the 'skiverleih' (ski hire) as a technician or just working on the drag-lifts. It is probably best to target one or two villages where there are a lot of guesthouses and hotels. The Tourist Information office and the bus drivers who convey skiers from hotels to slopes are both good sources of information. Needless to say, there are more jobs when the resorts are busy, which in turn depends on snow conditions. The ski season in the Innsbruck region is fairly reliable since the Stubai Glacier normally ensures snow from early December until the end of April.

Pubs, clubs and discos should not be overlooked since many of them regularly hire foreigners. Karin Huber, a native of Zell am See, reckons there are plenty of openings for foreigners, especially in the winter, since she found herself the only Austrian working in a club. The best time to arrive is late November.

To avoid all this you could try to fix up a job with a British tour operator beforehand. Because Austria is a very popular destination for British skiers, there is a large choice, for example Crystal Holidays, Equity Total Ski, Inghams and Ski Total (see introductory chapter *Tourism: Ski Resorts* for addresses). Lotus Supertravel (Sandpiper House, 39 Queen Elizabeth St, London SE1 2BT; 020-7962 1369) takes on winter staff for Austria, primarily chalet hosts with excellent cooking skills, reps fluent in German, qualified masseurs, nannies and handymen. All applicants must hold an EU passport and be over 21. PGL Ski Europe hires a small number of ski staff for winter as well as sports instructors for their summer programme and Tall Stories (67A High St, Walton on Thames, Surrey KT12 1DJ; 01932 252002) require resort staff in Austria. Another possibility for both seasons is First Choice/Skibound (Olivier House, 18 Marine Parade, Brighton, East Sussex BN2 1TL; 0840 900 3200/ jpbs@fcski.co.uk) which hires hundreds of people to work in hotel and resort staff for Austria; no qualifications are required because staff are given in-house training, but you must be available to stay for the whole season from May to September.

One of the more unusual casual jobs in Austria was described on a post card from Fionna Rutledge:

> *I thought you might be interested in my summer job in Vienna. I spent two months working for a classical music concert company (Strauss). There are loads of these in Vienna and most of them employ students without working permits. I was paid on commission and spent the day dressed up in Mozart costume in the main Vienna tourist spots. Hard work, but a great opportunity to meet people. You have to sell the concert to complete strangers. And I earned about £1,300 in six weeks. All you need to do is approach the 'Mozarts' on the street and ask them to introduce you to their boss.*

English Teaching

As in Germany, the market for EFL in Austrian cities is primarily for business English, particularly in-company. Most private language institutes such as SPIDI (Mariahilferstr. 32, 1070 Vienna; 01-524 17 17/40) and Talk Partners (Fischerstiege 10/16, 1010 Vienna; 01-535 9695) depend on freelance part-time teachers drawn from the sizeable resident international community. The hourly rate at reputable institutes starts at AS250, which is none-too-generous when the high cost of living in Vienna is taken into account.

Berlitz is well represented with four separate premises in Vienna alone, including the one at Graben 13, 1010 Vienna (01-512 82 86). In fact the Instructional Supervision department at the regional head office (Mariahilferstrasse 27, 1060 Vienna) recruits new English teachers for Berlitz centres in Austria, Slovakia and Slovenia. The rate of pay is AS185 for a 40-minute lesson. They are looking for people with British, Irish, American or Australian nationality who are at least 23 and with a good degree.

Inlingua also has operations in Vienna and Linz. According to an American teacher-traveller, Richard Spacer, who taught privately in Vienna for two months, the manager of inlingua in Vienna was very welcoming and informed him that the two-week methods course was offered to promising teachers free of charge. Richard earned his hourly wage cash-in-hand. Linguarama Spracheninstitut (Concordiaplatz 2, 1010 Vienna; vienna@linguarama.com) employ up to 70 native speaker English teachers.

Summer language and sport camps provide more scope for EFL teachers and others. Village Camps (14 rue de la Morache, 1260 Nyon, Switzerland) run a language summer camp at Zell-am-See. Language monitors over 21 and teachers over 23 are needed from the end of June to mid-August. Some experience of teaching children and a knowledge of a second European language are the basic requirements. Room and board, insurance and a weekly allowance of £175 are offered.

Two other organisations active in this field are the similarly named English for Children (Kanalstrasse 44, Postfach 160, 1220 Vienna; 1-282 77 177) and English for Kids (A. Baumgartnerstr. 44/A 7042, 1230 Vienna; 1-667 45 79) both of whom are looking for young monitors and English teachers with experience of working with children and preferably some TEFL background.

The organisation Young Austria Summercamps (Osterreichisches Ferienwerk, Alpenstrasse 108a, A-5020 Salzburg; 662-625 758-0/fax 625 758-2; office@camps.at/ www.camps.at) recruit about 30 teachers and monitors over the age of 20 to work at summer language and sports camps near Salzburg. For about three or four hours of each day of the two-week camp, 9 to 18 year old children receive English tuition from teachers (who must have teaching experience). Monitors organise the outdoor programme and help the teachers with the social programme as well as with the lessons. Teachers receive about AS4,420 for the two-week camp and monitors receive AS3,120 in their first year along with board and lodging and a lump sum payment of AS2,000 for travel expenses. Applications should be in by the end of February.

Au Pairs

Austria, together with Switzerland, was one of the first countries to host au pairs so there is a well-developed tradition and several well-established and respectable agencies which place hundreds of au pairs in Austria each year. Most of the families live in Vienna and Salzburg.

The two main agencies are Okista (Garnisongasse 7, 1090 Vienna; 1-401 480; www.oekista.co.at) and Auslands-Sozialdienst (Johannesgasse 16, 1010 Vienna; 1-512 7941; aupair-asd@kath-jugend.at), both of whom are accustomed to dealing with direct applications from abroad. Personal callers to Ökista should go to Türkenstr. 8/11, 1090 Vienna. Both agencies charge an upfront registration fee in the region of about AS800. A private agent, Irmhild Spitzer (Sparkassenplatz 1, 7th Floor, 4040 Linz; tel/fax 732-73 78 14) has a good choice of families throughout Austria both in towns and countryside. The weekly pocket money is AS700-1,000. Another possibility is Au Pair Service, Weidlingbachstr. 5, 3013 Tullnerbach (2233-54495; isabellasamstag@telecom.at).

Maree Lakey from Australia, who went from Germany to Austria to au pair, was told by her Austrian au pair agency that she had no chance of obtaining the permit, probably because the quota had been filled by the time she arrived in September. She did what most other non-European au pairs seemed to do which was to register as a guest in the country and then before three months were up, de-register and cross the border. Provided you complete the paperwork on time, there seemed to be no trouble as long as you left the country every three months.

It should be possible to find babysitting work if you are based in a resort. Ask for permission in the big hotels to put up a notice. The going rate is about AS80 an hour.

Voluntary Work

Service Civil International is an international peace organisation which, as a part of its work, organises two to three week workcamps mostly in summer. Work can take place indoors or out, for example working with children, old or disabled people, helping at peace or other festivals, farm work, renovation work, etc. SCI also offers the possibility of longer periods of voluntary work, e.g. three to six months in which case pocket money is paid. Contact IVS/SCI in your own country or if in Austria, SCI at Schottengasse 3a/1/59, 1010 Vienna (53 59 108).

For information about WWOOF Austria, contact Hildegard Gottlieb, Langegg 155, 8511 St Stefan ob Stainz (tel/fax 3463-82270; wwoof.welcome@telering.at). Membership costs AS250/$25 per year plus two IRCs which entitles you to the list of 90 Austrian organic farmers looking for work-for-keep volunteer helpers. For an extra AS100/$10 you can receive both Swiss and Austrian lists.

Russia & Eastern Europe

Political change in Eastern and Central Europe provoked revolutions in many spheres. One of the most important was the enthusiasm with which the governments and citizens of those countries embraced the English language giving rise to an enormous demand for native speakers to teach English. The vast majority of working opportunities in the region are in the field of English language teaching.

While Russia has been wrestling with its political and economic demons, the more stable Central European states of Hungary, Poland, the Czech Republic and Slovakia have gained an increasing level of autonomy from the West. There has been a mild backlash in some quarters against what has been seen as a selling out to the West, especially in the major capitals which are now swarming with foreigners. School directors are now perfectly aware of the English-speaking foreigner who masquerades as a teacher but really intends to indulge in cheap beer and all-night discos. They are suspicious of anyone projecting this image, disliking the fact that so many foreigners used the region as an extended party venue early on.

Yet despite having moved past making 'Western' synonymous with 'desirable,' they are still remarkably welcoming to British and American English language teachers. On most street corners, private language schools employ native speaker teachers. Working in Central and Eastern Europe may not seem as sexy as it did just after the 'revolution', but thousands of foreigners continue to fall under the spell of Prague, Budapest and Kraków. Even those who find themselves in the less prepossessing industrial cities normally come away beguiled by Central European charm.

The English language teaching industry in those countries has grown up, and is now much more likely to hire teachers with proven experience or an appropriate qualification. Massive amounts of money have been invested in Poland, Hungary and the former Czechoslovakia in retraining local teachers for the teaching of English in state schools and these programmes have been largely successful. Yet, demand continues for native speakers in state schools, private language schools and universities, often for native speakers with a sophisticated understanding of linguistic methodology. There is no question now of walking straight into a job in these countries merely because you were born an English-speaker. Yet outside the major centres, the need remains great.

As schools and language training organisations have become more choosy, so too the governments have made visas more difficult to obtain. Even in countries where English native speakers are sought after, the red tape can be offputting. For example in Russia, visas and residence permits are specific to a given employer. When a pre-arranged job turns out to be less satisfactory than expected, foreign teachers who find a much better job encounter difficulties in switching employers.

In Russia, the Baltic states of Latvia, Lithuania and Estonia and the other (not-so-newly) independent states of the old Soviet Union, the English teaching situation is more fluid. Almost any native speaker can arrange some kind of teaching, often on a private basis, but with no guarantee of earning a living wage from it.

While opportunities vary from place to place and while the future is uncertain due to the speed of change, it is true to say that there will be a great demand for native EFL teachers for many years ahead. And though these may not be the best paid EFL jobs in the world, Eastern Europe can offer historic and beautiful cities, genuinely friendly people and a unique chance to experience life in the 'other Europe' before it turns into just another group of free-market democracies.

Although the availability of resources has greatly improved, there may still be a shortage of teaching materials and of supervision. If you intend to teach outside the main centres, it is a good idea to carry your own supply of teaching aids and supplementary material, for example illustrated magazines, old comic books, travel brochures and photos of your home and neighbourhood. While tutoring adolescent girls in Russia, Hannah Start decided against using glossy fashion magazines since the pupils were so dazzled by the pictures that they didn't bother with the text; Hannah recommends using *The Big Issue* instead.

FINDING A TEACHING JOB

Many foreigners teach in state schools where there is a guaranteed salary, access to state health insurance, a long-term contract (which makes it easier to obtain a work permit) and a light teaching load after exams are over in late May. Schools and institutes in the private sector offer less financial and job security though they usually pay better.

A range of vacancies in Central and Eastern Europe, particularly in Poland, continues to be advertised in the educational press (i.e. the Tuesday *Guardian* and *Times Educational Supplement*). A certain number of commercial recruitment agencies are involved with filling vacancies in Eastern Europe with certificate-holding EFL teachers, and educational charities or gap year placement organisations send untrained volunteer teachers who normally pay a placement fee. Here are the main organisations based in the UK which continue to recruit teachers for more than one country in the region:

Central Bureau for International Education & Training, Assistants Department, 10 Spring Gardens, London SW1A 2BN (020-7389 4767). Posts for graduates are available in Hungary, Slovenia, Bulgaria, Romania and Russia, and are at primary, secondary, vocational or tertiary level.

Language Link, 21 Harrington Road, London SW7 3EU (020-7225 1065/fax 020-7584 3518; languagelink@compuserve.com). Mainly active in Russia and Slovakia but also have occasional positions elsewhere for newly qualified teachers as well as experienced ones.

Services for Open Learning (SOL), North Devon Professional Centre, Vicarage St, Barnstaple, Devon EX32 7HB (01271 327319/fax 01271 376650; sol@enterprise.net/ www.sol.org.uk). Non-profit-making organisation which annually recruits about 60 graduates (with degree in languages or education or with recognised TEFL Certificate) to teach in schools in the state sector in most Eastern and Central European countries (Belarus, Croatia, Czech Republic, Hungary, Romania and Slovakia). The SOL programme is open to all native speakers of English, though interviews take place only in Britain (March and June) and in Eastern & Central Europe. Contracts are with each school and are for a complete academic year (September to June), though a handful of posts may arise in January. All posts include free independent housing.

Teachers for Central & Eastern Europe, 21 V 5 Rackovski Blvd, Dimitrovgrad 6400, Bulgaria (tel/fax 391-24787; tfcee_klim@skat.spnet.net (attention: Stoitcho Tritchkov, Director). US contact: Interexchange in New York or telephone 707-276-4571. TFCEE Inc. appoints about 80 native speakers of English a year to teach mainly at English medium secondary schools in Bulgaria, Czech Republic, Hungary, Poland and Slovakia. University students, preferably with a TEFL background, accepted from the US, UK, Canada and Australia. Most appointments are for an academic year, though one semester placements are possible (i.e. mid-September to mid-January, or February to mid-June).

Teaching & Projects Abroad, Gerrard House, Rustington, West Sussex BN16 1AW (01903 859911; www.teaching-abroad.co.uk). Recruits volunteers to work as English language teaching assistants for the summer or during the academic year in Russia (Moscow, St. Petersburg and Siberia) and the Ukraine. No TEFL background required. Packages cost from £795 for Ukraine (excluding travel) to £1,585 for Siberia (including travel from UK). Prices include placement, accommodation and back-up. Flexible starting dates for stays lasting up to three months; extensions can be arranged for a further fee.

Travellers, 7 Mulberry Close, Ferring, West Sussex BN12 5HY (tel/fax 01903 502595; www.travellersworldwide.com). Paying volunteers teach conversational English in Russia (Moscow, St. Petersburg and Siberia) and the Ukraine (Kiev and Crimea). Sample prices for 2-3 months: Ukraine £775 and Russia £895 including food and accommodation.

Travel Teach, St James's Building, 79 Oxford St, Manchester M1 6FR (0870 789 8100; www.travelteach.com). Working holiday opportunities, teaching conversational and comprehensive English in two former republics of the Soviet Union: Lithuania and Moldova. Flexible periods of teaching from 2 weeks in Moldova/7 weeks in Lithuania to 12 months, including the summer vacation. Open to graduates, undergraduates or gap year students. Programme fee of £445 for Moldova and £495 for Lithuania includes return air travel, visas, and board and lodging with a host family.

US Organisations

Several US organisations are actively involved in teacher recruitment for the region:

Bridges for Education, 94 Lamarck Drive, Buffalo, NY 14226, USA (716-839-0180/fax 716-839-9493; jbc@buffalo.edu/ www.bridges4edu.org). Organise international summer peace camps which involve 180 volunteers teaching English for three weeks in July followed by one week of travel in Belarus, Hungary, Poland and Romania. Volunteers are given basic ESL training before departure. Participants pay their airfare and programme administration fee.

Central European Teaching Program/CETP, Beloit College, 700 College St, Beloit, WI 53511, USA (608-363-2619/fax 608-363-2449; www.beloit.edu/~cetp). 90 native speakers placed in state schools in Hungary, Romania, Poland and Lithuania. Must have university degree, overseas teaching, travel or study experience and/or TEFL/TESL experience. 10 month contracts from September. Monthly salary of $200. Placement fee of $2,000 (excluding airfares).

English for Everybody, c/o International TEFL Certificate, ITC, Kaprova 14, 110 00 Prague (02-248 4791/fax 02-248 7530; EFE@itc-training.com). Strong representation in the Czech Republic but operate throughout the region.

Interexchange, 161 Sixth Avenue, New York, NY 10013 (212-924-0446 ext. 109; info@interexchange.org). Arrange teaching assistantships in Russia, Ukraine, Bulgaria and Poland. Placement fee of $450-$600.

Once you have a work base, the supply of private teaching is usually plentiful. The pay for private lessons can be excellent compared to wages offered by schools. A small notice placed on a prominent university notice board or in a daily newspaper would have a good chance of producing results. Sometimes notices are posted in less likely places: Hannah Start reported that when she was teaching in the Russian city of Yaroslavl, locals pinned notices to trees.

CZECH & SLOVAK REPUBLICS

There seems to be an equal demand for English in both the Czech and Slovak

Republics, though the majority of TEFL teachers gravitate to the former, particularly Prague.

Teaching in the Czech Republic

The centralised contact for recruitment of teachers for state primary and secondary schools is the *Academic Information Agency (AIA)* in Prague (Dum zahranicních sluzeb MSMT, Senovázné nám. 26, 111 21 Prague 1 or PO Box 8, 110 06 Prague; 02-24 22 96 98/fax 02-24 22 96 97; aia@dzs.cz). AIA is part of the Ministry of Education and acts as a go-between, circulating CVs and applications (due by the end of April) among state schools which have requested a teacher. Schools then contact applicants directly to discuss contractual details. They place university graduates, preferably with TEFL training or experience, in schools from September 1st to June 30th. The net salary per month is 7,000-10,000 crowns plus free or subsidised accommodation. Kathy Panton is just one of the AIA's satisfied customers: 'I really recommend the AIA; they helped me out of a bad hole when I moved from Liberec to Prague and tried harder than I had any right to expect to get me out of another one, when I was assigned flea-ridden and expensive accommodation.'

Brian Farrelly was equally satisfied with the arrangement made for him by Services for Open Learning (address above):

I taught in two state schools in the Czech Republic. I had a really great time in both those schools and I felt really privileged to teach the students there. SOL placed me in a 'gymnazium' secondary school in the small town of Sedicany 60km south of Prague where I taught English conversation and regular English classes. Both the staff and the students made me tremdendously welcome. I also greatly enjoyed the freedom I had to teach as I saw fit, although initially I felt very daunted by the lack of guidance regarding what I should be doing.

But most people wait until they arrive in Prague before trying to find teaching work, which is what Linda Harrison:

The best time to apply is before June (I arrived in September which was too late) but if you persevere there are jobs around. A lot of teaching work here seems to be in companies. Schools employ you to go into offices, etc. to teach English (though not usually business English). After a short job hunt, I have been hired by Languages at Work.

Languages at Work is at Na Florenci 35, 110 00 Prague 1 (tel/fax 02-248 11 379; atwork@login.cz).

Most private language schools can count on receiving plenty of CVs on spec from which to fill any vacancies which arise. Anyone who is well qualified or experienced should have few difficulties in finding a job on the spot and obtaining a work permit. The Yellow Pages *(Zlaty Stranky)* are an excellent source of addresses under the heading *Jazykove skoly.* Among the schools with the largest demand for teachers are:

Akcent Language School, Bitovská 3, 140 00 Prague 4 (02-6126 16 38; brian@akcent.cz).

Akademie J.A. Komenskeho, Trziste 20, Mala Strana, 118 43 Prague 1 (02-5753 1476; akademie@login.cz/ www.akademie.cz). Many posts in 50 adult education centres and schools throughout the Czech Republic where British native speakers (including gap year students) are employed. Monthly net wage is 8,000 crowns.

Anglictina Expres, Korunní 2, 12000 Prague 2 (tel/fax 02-2251 3040; kelly@anexpres.cz/ www.anexpres.cz). 15-20 graduates employed for morning and evening freelance work.

Caledonian School, Vltavská 24, 150 00 Prague 5 (tel/fax 02-573 13 650; jobs@caledonianschool.com). Employ 80 teachers who must have a BA plus Cambridge Certificate or equivalent. 15,000 crowns per month for qualified teachers.

SPUSA Education Center, Rytirská 10, 110 00 Prague 1 (02-421 0813; spusa@mbox.vol.cz). 25 EFL teachers, mainly American. From 15,000 crowns per month.

Compared to the starting monthly wage in state schools of 7,000 crowns, private sector wages are normally more like 8,500-10,500 (also net). But this does not include accommodation which will account for between a quarter and a third of a teaching salary. Hourly fees start at 170 crowns less 20%-25% for tax and deductions. A full-time salary should be adequate to live on by local standards but will not allow you to save anything, unless you take on lots of private tutoring.

Czech Regulations

A new Residency Law came into force on January 1st 2000 making it necessary to apply for a long-stay Czech visa before arrival in the country. Full details are available from the Czech Embassy in London (020-7243 1115/fax 020-7243 7988) or Washington (www.czech.cz/washington). Anyone who intends to work or for any other reason stay in the Czech Republic for longer than 90 days must obtain the visa in advance. This requires gathering a raft of documents including a work permit issued by the employer, proof of accommodation, etc. all presented in the original or a notarised copy.

The work permit must be obtained by your future employer from the local employment office *(Urad práce)*. They will need a signed form from you plus a photocopy of your passport and the originals or notarised copies of your education certificates. All of this is quite a palaver and (realistically) takes at least three months, discouraging many Czech language schools from attempting to hire people who are not already on-the-spot.

Teaching in Slovakia

As the poor cousin in the former Czechoslovakia, the republic of the Slovaks has been somewhat neglected not only by tourists but by teachers as well. As one language school director put it:

> *Many teachers are heading for Prague, which is why Slovakia stands aside of the main flow of the teachers. That's a pity as Prague is crowded with British and Americans while there's a lack of the teachers here in Slovakia.*

The density of private language schools in the capital Bratislava and in the other main cities like Banska Bystrika makes an on-the-ground job hunt promising.

A few agencies in the UK actively recruit up to 100 teachers for Slovakia, notably the training and recruitment agency Language Link (21 Harrington Road, London SW7 3EU; 020-7225 1065) which is affiliated with the largest semi-private language school in Slovakia, the Akadémia Vzdelávania, Gorkého 10, 815 17 Bratislava (07-5441 0040; hviscova@aveducation.sk). It offers approximately 65 posts in adult education centres and schools throughout Slovakia, with a wage of 9,500 crowns per month in the first year in Bratislava, 9,000 crowns outside the capital.

American EFL teachers should contact the City University Slovakia (Language Assistance Programs, 919 SW Grady Way, Renton, WA 98055; jflaherty@cityu.edu) which employs 30 teachers with a BA or MA in TEFL and international living experience at their campuses in Bratislava and Trencin.

The Slovakian Embassy (www.slovakembassy.co.uk) can send details of how to apply for a Long-term Stay Permit, valid for one year but renewable. It warns that the entire process takes between three and four months. The procedures are similar to those for the Czech Republic, including a requirement that all documents be officially translated, and that the applicant submit a medical certificate, evidence of accommodation, police clearance and so on. A blood test must be carried out within a couple of weeks of arriving as a pre-requisite for a residence permit. Many employers guide their teachers through the process and pay the fee (currently about £100).

HUNGARY

English is compulsory for all Hungarian students who wish to apply for college or university entrance, and university students in both the Arts and Sciences must take courses in English, creating a huge market for English teachers. But because of the high calibre of Hungary's home-grown teachers, native speakers do not have the cachet they have in other central European countries.

Yet native speakers continue to find teaching opportunities in Hungary, especially in the business market. The invasion of foreigners in Budapest was never as overwhelming as it was (and is) in Prague, but still Budapest has a glut of teachers. The opportunities that do exist now are mostly in the provinces. The American Steve Anderson was the first foreigner to work at his school in the 1000-strong village of Vaja in northeastern Hungary close to the Ukrainian border. It became obvious to him that this region was most in need of energetic and dedicated teachers, and he found teaching there more rewarding than he had in a well-resourced school in Western Hungary the year before. Writing in *Transitions Abroad* magazine, he reiterates this preference for teaching off the beaten track:

> *Though I initially rode the wave of native English speakers who rolled in to teach in Budapest, I am glad that I jumped ship to work in the poorer provinces. Activities like preparing spicy fish soup over an open fire and swaying to folk songs fiddled by the village gypsy don't happen in urban centres... The students of Vaja, lacking the luxuries of computers and up-to-date text books, had less developed English skills than those I had encountered the year before. I rewound all the way to the ABCs with my younger class and was forced to develop creative teaching methods which I hadn't needed in my advanced school, where audio and visual materials did the work for me.*

Teachers are poorly paid in Hungary, aside from in the top-notch private schools and the British Council. Although the wage in forints has risen over the past two years, the exchange rate has dropped by more than a third. Rents in Budapest are high and take a major proportion of a teacher's salary; some schools help by subsidising accommodation, or it may be possible to arrange accommodation in return for English lessons.

Money is not the point for everybody. Trudie Darch spent her gap year teaching in Hungary through GAP Activity Projects (see *Voluntary Work: Gap Year Placements*):

> *I had been there three weeks and with very little notice I was told that I'd be teaching on my own for one whole week. This was the scariest thing that had happened so far. Virtually unprepared, I walked into a classroom full of 18 year olds (I was 19) and had to teach. The first lesson was not very good and I had some difficulties getting them to listen to me. It was hard to get over the fact that these were my students not people who were supposed to be my friends. However I overcame this and learnt that to be a more professional teacher, I had to distance myself from trying to be their friend. The school was basic, the food was interesting (pasta and icing sugar was one I hated) and my accommodation left a lot to be desired. But even the bad things I wouldn't swap because they taught me a lot.*

In the US, the Central European Teaching Program at Beloit College (description in introduction to this chapter) has its strongest base in Hungary. CETP liaises with the relevant government department in Hungary to place teachers in state schools throughout the country. It was through CETP that Steve Anderson arranged his year of teaching in Hungary, and he was impressed:

> *CETP is a professional yet personal organisation. They maintain in-country contacts for the duration of the contracts and will kindly hammer out any kinks in a teacher's experience (whether it be work-related or otherwise). They purposely keep the directorship in the hands of a young, returning teacher in order to keep administration close to what the organisation actually does.*

Steve goes on to lament the need to introduce such a substantial fee, but recommends it to anyone who can afford it.

The Regulations

Permits must be arranged before leaving your country of residence which makes the task of finding a teaching job considerably harder. Deportation is said to be a real possibility for those who continue to teach for more than 90 days without a labour permit. A foreign employee cannot be legally paid until she or he has a labour permit.

A foreigner who wishes to enter Hungary to work must possess a special working visa issued by a Hungarian Embassy or Consulate in the applicant's country of residence. General information for Britons is available on the Embassy website http://dspace.dial.pipex.com/huemblon/front.htm or by ringing 09001 171204. To apply for the working visa, the applicant must have a labour permit, obtained by the Hungarian employer from the appropriate Hungarian labour office *(Munkaugyi Kozpont).*

POLAND

Prospects for English teachers in Poland, western Poland in particular, remain more promising than almost anywhere else in the world. Even the major cities of Warsaw, Wroclaw, Kraków, Poznan and Gdansk are worthwhile destinations, though the job hunt is of course easier in the many lesser known towns and cities of Poland. As in the Czech and Slovak Republics there are numerous possibilities in both state and private schools. Any number of school directors are delighted to interview native English speakers who present themselves in a professional manner. The reverence for 'native speakerhood' still runs very high in Poland.

The Anglo-Polish Universities Association (APASS) is a non-profit fraternity of students, graduates, teachers and others willing to teach EFL in Poland. Contact details are APASS, UK North, 93 Victoria Road, Leeds LS6 1DR; telephone for emergencies only (8am-10am and 4pm-6pm) 0113-275 8121 or 0113-2744363; they have no fax or website. There are two schemes which are run in the summer only and require about 320-350 volunteers. One is for English language instructors and assistants (minimum age 16 years with parental permission) who must be English native speakers. Applicants can be young people but older teachers and mature students from British universities are also welcome to spend one month (end of July to end August) in Poland. ELT experience is of course welcomed but not essential. Furnished accommodation and food are provided for three weeks 'teaching' and there is one week allocated for a tour of Poland. All expenses and pocket money of up to £18 a week in zloties are paid by the Polish host.

APASS produces a detailed information pack, available from mid-March onwards at a cost of £3 plus 9in X 6in s.a.e. (40p stamped) which will indicate the current placement fee. Reports have been received that details of these summer placements are finalised not long before departure, so be prepared to endure some suspense. Wayne Stimson feels that this excellent scheme is not widely enough known:

> *I had often wanted to teach English and, as a politics student, I also had an interest in the history and politics of the former Eastern Bloc states. I got the opportunity last summer to combine these two when APASS arranged for me to spend seven weeks in a village near the Czech border called Dusniki Zdroj. Here I worked on two camps that gave children an activity-based holiday alongside English teaching. The children were mainly from middle class, professional backgrounds and their English skills were often quite developed so teaching and general communication was not difficult. I tried to teach a little about the customs, culture and politics of the UK. I was treated very graciously by my hosts and found Polish people to be very warm and friendly.*

Private language teaching organisations run short-term holiday courses which require native speakers, including the English School of Communication Skills (ul. Bernardynska 15, 13 100 Tarnów (tel/fax 014-621 3769; personnel@escs.pl). Will Gardner was full of praise for this organisation when he worked for them one summer, having fixed up the position from England in the spring:

> *I spent one month working for ESCS at their summer camp on Poland's Baltic Coast. The camps were well organised and great fun. As an experienced teacher who has worked in several different countries for a range of schools, I would just like to say what a pleasure it was to work with such a well organised group of people and for a school that completely lived up to its promises. The school supplied a wide range of resources to assist teachers,*

although a lot of emphasis was placed on originality. The focus was always on communication and fun. The camp facilities were perfect for the situation. Food and accommodation were supplied and the weather was beautiful. Although the students were attending lessons daily, a holiday atmosphere prevailed over all activities.

A private language school in southwest Poland runs a short scheme outside the summer holidays (which is unusual). Sixth formers and gap year students are invited to travel to the Espero School in Kedzierzyn-Kozle for 2, 3 or 4 weeks between January and July to teach English to Polish teenagers. All expenses are covered except half the coach fare from London (£35-£40). Details may be obtained by phone (077-382 1424) or e-mail (espero@espero.kk.pl).

On the Spot

Semesters begin on October 1st and February 15th, and the best time to arrive is a month or two beforehand. After arrival, try to establish some contacts, possibly by visiting the English department at the university. Although some school directors state a preference for British or American accents, many are neutral.

Private language schools catering for all kinds of English teaching sprang up everywhere as soon as private enterprise was legally possible. After obtaining some addresses, would-be teachers should dutifully 'do the rounds' of the *Dyrektors*. Some of the bigger schools include:

Albion Language Services, ul Noakowskiego 26/26, 00-668 Warsaw. (tel/fax 022-628 8992; languages@albion.com.pl). 30 native speaker teachers with friendly manners. US$10 per 45 minutes.

American English School, 3/5 Foksal, Warsaw 00-366 (022-827 26 54; ames@polbox.com.pl/ www.americanenglishschool.com.pl). 15 graduates to teach October to June.

Berlitz, Waly Piatowskie 24, 80-885 Gdansk (058-305 1613). 8 Berlitz schools in Poland.

Cambridge School of English, ul. Komwiktorska 7, 00-216 Warsaw (022-635 24 66).

EF English First, ul. Smolna 8,, 00-375 Warsaw (022-826 8206). Teachers for Warsaw and schools in Wroclaw, Lodz, Bydgoszcz, etc.

Greenwich School of English, ul. Gdanska 2/3, 01-633 Warsaw (022-833 2431; www.greenwich.edu.pl).

YES School of Language, ul. Reformacka 8, 35-026 Rzeszów (tel/fax 017-852 0720; www.yes.pl). 10 full-time experienced teachers plus 14 positions at a summer programme in the mountains.

If you base yourself in Warsaw and wish to advertise your availability for private English tuition, try placing a notice just to the right of the main gate of Warsaw University or in one of the main dailies, *Gazeta Wyborcza* or *Zycie Warszawy.*

The Regulations

A work visa (Visa 06) must be applied for in your country of origin (as for the Czech Republic, Hungary and Slovakia). Ring the Polish Embassy for details (020-7580 0475; www.polishworld.com/polemb). Original or notarised copies of your degree diploma and TEFL Certificate (if applicable) must be presented along with a promisory work permit from your future employer to the Polish Consulate in your country of residence. The Consulate then issues a residence visa. After arrival the residence visa and interim work permit are taken to the regional employment office *(Wojewódzki Urzad Pracy)* to obtain a proper work permit. The handout from the Polish Consulate entitled 'Visas for Teachers' sets out the procedures and states that the current cost of the multi-entry residence visa is £104.

Generally speaking, private language schools in Poland offer reasonable working conditions, with fewer reports of profit-mongers and sharks than in other countries experiencing a TEFL boom. Wages are reasonably high and the terms of service are seldom exploitative. It is not uncommon for overtime to be paid to teachers for hours worked in excess of the contracted number (typically 24).

Once you are working either in the public or private sector, you may be approached with various proposals, from 'verifying' English translations of scientific research papers or restaurant menus, to coaching actors and singers preparing for English performances and doing dubbing or voice-overs for films and TV.

RUSSIA & the Independent States

Two years ago, Russia was undergoing its worst political and economic crisis since 1991. The rouble was in free fall, banks and businesses were failing, unemployment was increasing, the price of real estate was dropping and confidence was at yet another all time low. Most companies, including language schools, were forced to restructure and cut costs. A year later, fear of a second financial crisis loomed on the horizon, forcing the business community to undergo a period of economic soul-searching. This was especially true for those language schools that hired native English-speaking teaching staff. Two years of uncertainty and a flagging economy gave many of these schools the impetus to use local English teachers (much cheaper than expats). As a result the number of full-time job opportunities for native English-speaking teachers decreased. Similarly, those teachers who were offered full-time employment were also offered smaller salary and benefit packages.

Yet there are still ample English teaching opportunities for those wishing to experience the real Russia. The average benefit package may have shrunk but it is still more than sufficient to live on and to enjoy the best of what Russia has to offer. There are even signs under President Putin that the rouble is stabilising.

Apart from the qualified teachers working for the major foreign-owned language chains like Benedict, Language Link and EF English First (see below), the majority of English teachers in Russia and the former Soviet Republics, including the Baltics, the Central Asian Republics and Ukraine, have come through voluntary placement organisations or are students of Russian with an interest in the language and culture.

The unregulated housing market makes it very difficult for foreign teachers to find independent accommodation. Employers normally arrange accommodation for their teachers in small shared flats, with host families or in student hostels where conditions are very basic. Many teachers lodge with landladies, of whom there is no shortage considering how many widows there are trying to make ends meet on vanishingly small pensions.

Finding a Job

Few schools can afford to advertise and recruit teachers abroad. But anyone with contacts anywhere in the region or who is prepared to go there to make contacts should be able to arrange a teaching niche on an individual basis, always assuming money is no object. Most educational institutes are suffering such serious financial hardships that they can't attract local teachers let alone Western ones.

Private lessons will be less easy to fix up than they were a few years ago when 'New Russians', those who were made relatively rich by the change to a free market, were willing and able to pay up to an outrageous US$30 an hour for one-on-one tuition, sometimes even in hard currency. While spending six months as a student of Russian in the beautiful and historic town of Yaroslavl, Hannah Start found private pupils very easily. She decided to accept only high school students to diminish the risk of crime; apparently if you are teaching in your own accommodation, it is wise to refrain from displaying any expensive Western items.

A thriving English language press has established itself in Moscow and St. Petersburg. Check adverts in the *Moscow Times, Moscow Tribune* and the weekly *St. Petersburg Press*. Look out also for the free ads paper *Iz Ruk v Ruki* in about 15 towns in Russia.

Among the major language teaching organisations, the following employ substantial numbers of native speaking teachers with a TEFL qualification:
Benedict Schools, 23 ul. Pskovskaya, St. Petersburg 190008 (812-113 85 68/114 10 90/fax 812-114 44 45; benedict@infopro.spb.su). Employ 40-60 teachers including 18-20 for St. Petersburg (main franchise holder) and others in Novosibirsk, Tomsk, Murmansk and Kemerovo. Run a Work-Study Programme

for which no TEFL background is required. UK intermediary International Educational Centre Ltd (74 Baxter Court, Norwich NR3 2ST; tel/fax 01603 763378; emma@griffin.fsbusiness.co.uk) may be able to assist UK applicants.

English First, 125 Brestskaya 1st Street, 5th Floor, 125047 Moscow (095-937 3886/fax 095-937 3889). 25 teachers for 14 schools in Moscow, St. Petersburg, Nizhny Novgorod, Ekaterinburg and Vladivostok.

Language Link Russia, Novoslobodskaya ul. 5, bld. 2, 103030 Moscow (tel/fax 095-250 8935/251 4889; jobs@language.ru). 400 teachers throughout Russia (Moscow, St. Petersburg, Volgograd, Siberia, Urals, etc.) As of 2001 BUNAC have started a Russian programme in partnership with Language Link Russia whereby freshly certified EFL teachers are placed in Russia; details from BUNAC on 020-7251 3472 (www.bunac.org).

Several organisations in the USA offer volunteers the chance to teach English at any level from university to businesses to summer camps:

Project Harmony, 6 Irasville Common, Waitsfield, VT 05673 (802-496-4545/fax 802-496-4548; www.projectharmony.org). Teaching Intern Program for recent college graduates and experienced teachers to work in host schools and institutions in Russia and Odessa in the Ukraine for six months or a year. The placement fee of $2,250 includes airfares from the US.

Petro-Teach Program, c/o Professor Wallace J Sherlock, Dept. of Curriculum and Instruction, University of Wisconsin, Whitewater, WI 53190 (sherlocw@mail.uww.edu/ www.semlab2.sbs.sunysb.edu/Users/jbailyn/ Petro.html). Cultural exchange organisation which runs a voluntary teaching scheme in St. Petersburg; year-long placements begin on September 1st. Intensive pre-teaching Russian language course is part of the programme.

CCUSA, 2330 Marinship Way, Suite 250, Sausalito, CA 94965 (1-800-999-CAMP; outbound@campcounselors.com). The Russia Program sends US volunteers to work in a Russian summer youth camp for 4 or 8 weeks between mid-June and mid-August. Participants must be between the ages of 18-35, have experience working with children and/or abroad, and have an interest in learning about the Russian language and culture. Programme fee $1600 includes round-trip travel from New York to Moscow, visa, travel insurance, orientations in New York and Moscow and room and board.

Regulations

For people participating in established international exchanges, the red tape is usually straightforward. Russia at the moment is a place where the rules change weekly. In the commercial sector, work permits are more problematic, mainly because so few Russian companies have put their tax affairs in order, which is a prerequisite for obtaining permission. Teachers should be wary of language teaching companies which refuse to give contracts bearing an official stamp.

Only after an employer receives permission to invite foreigners is he or she allowed to become a sponsor of work visas. After a telex has been sent to the Ministry of Foreign Affairs, an invitation can be sent to the applicant to present at the Russian Consulate together with the application for a Multiple Entry Visa, the required fee of £100 and proof of an HIV test (for all visitors intending to stay for more than three months). Foreigners are then given a three-month visa which can later be turned into a work permit, provided the employer posts a sizeable bond. A number of visa agencies are able to obtain one-year multiple entry visas for clients, but these cannot necessarily be turned into work permits unless the employing company on the visa form has prior permission to employ foreigners.

Numerous foreigners do work without proper authorisation, but run a constant risk of being fined or even deported. Rhys Sage became suspicious of an employer who sent him the wrong visa:

After a fiasco in Latvia, it has become apparent to me that if a company is not willing to obtain the proper visa then they must be up to something dodgy. When I negotiated my contract with a school in Novosibirsk, they accepted some pretty excessive demands on my part which made me suspicious that the contract was worthless. This, combined with the fact that they sent me a visa form for a transit visa claiming it was a work visa, resulted in my complete loss of interest in them. A transit visa means nothing. It just means that you have permission to cross Russia, and therefore you have no redress if the employer decides to withhold your wages.

The Baltic States

Arguably the most westernised part of the old Russian Empire, the Baltic countries of Lithuania, Latvia and Estonia are looking towards a future as part of Western Europe. Even if there are few private language institutes there are voluntary opportunities.

The International Exchange Center, 2 Republic Square, 1010 Riga, Latvia (fax 02-783 0257; iec@mail.eunet.lv) invites volunteers of any nationality to work as counsellors on summer camps for children in Latvia (and also in Russia). There is a registration fee of $150. Details should be available in the UK from the International Student Exchange Centre, 35 Ivor Place, London NW1 6EA (020-7724 4493; isecworld.co.uk).

Rhys Sage worked at a summer camp through the IEC one summer and, despite finding the food and working conditions barely tolerable, returned to the same camp several summers later after receiving a faxed invitation from the camp director:

I spent two months as an English teacher. Well, that's what they called it. I was merely a token English speaker and was not allowed to do any actual teaching or any real assisting. It was a typically Soviet experience where people were not expected to do anything but were paid and criticised for anything they actually did.

There is more scope for teachers in Lithuania, to which several of the major organisations send candidates including Travel Teach. Be aware that you are not likely to be given much choice about what kind of teaching you end up doing. One volunteer, who had no TEFL background and was expecting to work with children, was alarmed when he was sent off to teach business people who had high expectations of their teachers. According to a list distributed by the Lithuanian Embassy in Washington, the key organisation in the US is the American Partnership for Lithuanian Education (APPLE), PO Box 617, Durham, CT 06422 (203-347-7095).

For several years the Department of Foreign Relations at the Ministry of Education and Science (Volano Gatve 2/7, 2691 Vilnius; 02-622483/fax 612077) has been prepared to set up interviews with schools. The pay is negligible (e.g. $20 a week) though this can usually be supplemented with private teaching. However, the situation is becoming tighter, as John Morgan from Dorset reported at the beginning of 1999:

I have just been back to Lithuania and can report that it is much more difficult to get a placement in Vilnius than it was when I taught there. I called 20 schools and nobody knew or needed an English teacher. I ended up teaching privately (which pays a lot better) by placing an advert in the main daily newspaper. It is better to place the advert in English; if you have it translated, people who reply will expect you to speak Lithuanian.

The most promising time to make contact with schools is just before the summer holidays in June. There are more opportunities for teachers in Kaunas, the second city of Lithuania, and the surrounding areas than in the capital.

A letter from the Ministry or a school in Lithuania makes it possible to acquire a special visa which in the case of teachers and aid workers is free of charge.

Ukraine

The vast republic of the Ukraine has a serious shortage of English teachers and many other things besides. In addition to the British organisations mentioned at the beginning of this chapter which send volunteers to Ukraine, several emigré organisations in the US recruit volunteers, warning that teachers must be prepared to accept a modest standard of living. The main one is the Ukrainian National Association (2200 Route 10, PO Box 280, Parsippany, NJ 07054; 973-292-9800) which sponsors an English-teaching programme for qualified teachers who stay for at least four weeks between May and August.

THE REST OF EASTERN EUROPE

Romania

English was little taught before the downfall of Ceaucescu in 1989 and the collapse of communism, but now there is a growing demand as the country seeks to attract foreign investment and to modernise antiquated industries. Anyone seriously intent on teaching in Romania regardless of remuneration should be able to find an opening. Paul Converse from Oregon travelled in the country one summer a few years ago:

I doubt that anyone could make any money teaching English but they would certainly get a free place to live and food and appreciation. When I was in Felenc, the entire village wanted me to stay and teach English.

There are very few private language schools in Romania at present. The association of language schools (QUEST Romania, Prosper-ASE Language Centre, Calea Grivitei 2-2A et 2s, Bucharest; prosper1@prosper.ro; www.quest.ro) has only seven members at present.

Wages on one of the volunteer placement schemes like SOL or CETP (see beginning of chapter) will be equivalent to those earned by Romanian teachers, as little as £50 a month. Pupils are lively and curious about life in the West, and children are often up-to-date with the latest Western fashions and music from MTV. Photocopiers are scarce and paper is in short supply, if available at all. Teachers would be advised to take as many teaching materials as possible, e.g. magazine articles, postcards, language games, photos, pictures. Information about the teacher's home town always goes down well.

Slovenia

The former Yugoslav republic of Slovenia remained uninvolved in the Balkan conflict throughout, which allowed its economy to flourish. It is in the group of countries at the head of the queue to join the European Union. As in Croatia, there are a good many private schools and many opportunities can be created by energetic native speakers both as freelance teachers for institutes or as private tutors.

The English Studies Resource Centre at the British Council in Ljubljana has a long list of private language schools throughout the country which it updates constantly; see their web page (www.britishcouncil.org/slovenia.infoexch). The Council remains closely in touch with language schools and will refer qualified candidates to possible employers. The average hourly wage is 2,000 tolars (£5.70) net.

After answering an advert in the *Guardian*, Adam Cook spent a year working at a *Gimnazija* in the town of Ajdovscina. He was hired with a BA plus an introductory one-week TEFL course:

The work is great and Slovenia is a fabulous country: good standard of living, good wages. My contract stipulates 20 hours a week but I work more, to save myself from boredom if nothing else. I'm paid by the Slovene Ministry of Education but am answerable to the British Council who recruited me in the first place. Slovene students are great and I have no discipline problems.

Some private language schools which hire native speaker teachers are:
Berlitz Language Center, Gosposvetska 2,1000 Ljubljana (061-133 13 25).
Glotta Nova, Poljanska 95, 1000 Ljubljana (061-52 00 675; glotta-nova@siol.net).
Panteon College, Vojkova 1, 1000 Ljubljana (061-43 61 828).
Nista Language School, Smarska C.5D, 6000 Koper (562 50400; nista@siol.net).

VOLUNTARY WORK

The main workcamp organisations in Britain (IVS, Quaker Voluntary Action, Concordia, Youth Action for Peace, and UNA Exchange) and in the US (SCI-USA, VFP and Council) can provide up-to-date details of projects and camps in all the countries of the region including some of the (not-so-newly) independent states of the old USSR. In many cases the projects are a pretext for bringing together young people from East and West in an effort to dismantle prejudice on both sides. Often discussion sessions and excursions are a major part of the three or four week workcamps and some volunteers have been surprised to find that their experiences are more like a holiday, with very little work expected. The people of Eastern Europe are repeatedly praised for their generosity and hospitality.

Some preparation is recommended by all the recruiting organisations and participants are encouraged to get some workcamp experience closer to home first and to attend orientations. The registration fee is normally higher than for Western Europe, say £140. The national workcamp partners normally handle the travel and insurance arrangements once you arrive in their country. The language in which camps are conducted is usually English. Projects vary from excavating the ancient capital of Bulgaria to organising sport for gypsy children in Slovenia. Many projects, especially in the former satellite states of Russia, concern themselves with the reconstruction of ancient churches and other buildings which fell into ruin under Communism. There is also a high proportion of much-needed environmental workcamps.

Applications for workcamps should be sent through the partner organisation in the applicant's own country (see introductory chapter on Voluntary Work). A search of the internet will produce national representatives (e.g. www.avso.org or www.eastlinks.net). Of the national co-ordinating offices written to for this edition, only the following confirmed details:

Czech Republic – INEX, Senovázne námesti 24, 116 47 Prague 1 (fax 02-2410 2390; inex@czn.cz or bluehouse@iol.cz). Approximately 45 voluntary workcamps in the Czech Republic. Co-operate with European Voluntary Service (EVS) scheme described in Voluntary chapter.

Slovakia – INEX Slovakia, Prazská 11, 81413 Bratislava (fax 07-394707; www.inex.sk).

Slovenia – MOST, Breg 12, 1000 Ljubljana (61-142 58 067/fax 61-217 208; www.drustvo-most.si). Majority of MOST's 20 international workcamps are ecological though some are with Croatian and Bosnian refugees.

Ukraine – Union Forum, Lychakivska Str, PO Box 5327, Lviv 10 (ukrforum@ipm.lviv.ua). Organises 2-3 week international social projects in summer. Participation fee for direct applicants is DM60.

While Russia is experiencing such disastrous socio-economic and organisational problems, anyone interested in volunteering there would be advised to keep abreast of developments through a local workcamp organisation. For example the annual *Workcamp Directory* from VFP in the US provides detailed advice on obtaining a visa for Russia, explaining that workcamp volunteers should obtain a business visa through an invitation from the Russian camp organisers, a process which takes several months. The alternative is to buy a tourist visa (for $100+) through a visa agency such as Unisel Network; the visa must then be stamped after arrival at your accommodation. Detailed information on visas for Americans is available from the website www.russia.net/travel/visas.htm. The Russian Youth Hostels Association might be able to arrange the appropriate visa for people who want to have an extended stay (www.ryh.ru or www.sindbad.ru). Britons should make enquiries of Visa-to-Russia Direct (12 Chepstow Road, London W2 5BD; 020-7229 0116; www.visa-to-russia.co.uk).

To participate in summer camps on Lake Baikal in Siberia, contact the Baikal Institute for Environment & Natural Resources Use, Lermontov St 104, Irkutsk 664074 (03952-430417; bienru@irk.ru). Volunteers live for 2-5 weeks with the children in wooden cabins, and lead sports and arts and crafts, teach English and so on. Knowledge of Russian is not needed; the participation fee is $100.

Organisations in the individual Russian Republics may organise workcamps independently, such as the Association for Educational, Work and Cultural Exchange of Armenia (42 Yeznik Coghbatsi St, Apt. 22, Yerevan 375002; 02-584733; aiep@arminco.com). Camps are organised to restore and maintain mediaeval buildings in Armenia; food and accommodation are included in the participation fee.

The organic movement is gaining ground (so to speak) in Central Europe. One possibility for finding addresses of farms which might welcome working visitors is to obtain one of the guides from ECEAT (European Centre for Eco-Agro Tourism, Postbox 10899, 1001 EW Amsterdam, Netherlands; www.pz.nl/eceat). They publish separate English-language Green Holiday Guides for the Czech Republic, Hungary/Bulgaria/Romania/Slovenia, Poland and Estonia/Latvia (the latter is sold out at present) for £5/$11 each.

About a year ago, a nascent WWOOF organisation in Russia had the e-mail address bibl@mail.ur.ru in Ekaterinburg, though it doesn't seem to have survived. The only East European country to be listed in WWOOF's literature is Hungary which has about eight addresses. The present contact is Andrea Bódi of the Biokultúra Egyesület (Kitaibel, P. u. 4, 1024 Budapest; 1-316 2138/fax 1-316 2139). Rob Abblett had a short but very enjoyable stay in Hungary:

I had a great ten days living and working in a small self-sufficient village in Felsonyék (Béke u. 15, 7099 Felsonyék; 74-478 345). The only problem I found with Hungary was that hardly anyone speaks English. The organic farm experience was great. I had a house all to myself and I enjoyed the work, going to the market and being treated so well by the family and my workmates. The whole village was virtually self-sufficient, vegetable patches, ducks, geese, chickens, rabbits, vines. How I wish my mother had taught me Hungarian. I moved on to an eco-village at Gyürüfü where I spent five hard days helping to construct a rammed earth house; shovelling earth into a wooden framework in 35°C was a somewhat sweaty affair. It is mainly professional-type folk wanting to live here, and many spoke English. Great if you want to get hands-on experience of alternative building, though I preferred the traditional village lifestyle.

Gyürüfü is the only contact in Hungary provided in the most recent edition of *Diggers & Dreamers* (mentioned in the introductory chapter *Agriculture*): Gyürüfü Alapítvany, Arany János u. 16, 7935 Ibafa; bela@gyurufu.zpok.hu.

Another WWOOF listing, the Ormánság Foundation (Arany János u. 4, H-7967 Drávafok; tel/fax 073-352333), cannot offer paid employment at its farm dedicated to sustainable development located 60km southwest of Pécs. But it does offer accommodation and some voluntary work gardening, tending an orchard, etc. to suitable candidates for a minimum of a week and preferably two. It can also put volunteers in touch with neighbouring sustainable farms looking for helpers.

Students interested in innovative agricultural methods are welcomed to ETO Farm which carries out research conducted by academics of the University of Gödölló University of Agricultural Sciences. Their literature mentions that EU students can participate in training activities during the summer; contact ETO Farm, H-2687 Bercel-Jákotpuszta (035-384715) or the Department of Applied Ethology, Pater Karoly u. 1, H-2103 Gödölló (028-410131; matine@nt.ktg.gau.hu).

Summer projects in Hungary for which the British Trust for Conservation Volunteers recruit UK volunteers are also concerned with organic agriculture. The ten day projects cost about £220 to join. BTCV include other Central European countries in their list (see *Voluntary* chapter) including tracking wolves in Europe's last primaeval forest in Poland, protecting bird reserves in Bulgaria, and building footpaths in a botanical garden in Lithuania.

Of the many charities which were formed to help the children of Romania, the Nightingales Children's Project operates a full-time volunteer programme. Volunteers spend from one to six months (average three) working at an orphanage in Cernavoda, 80km from the Black Sea resort of Constanta. Volunteers work with approximately 160 children, some of whom are disabled and have special needs, some with the HIV virus. Accommodation is shared with eight volunteers in a flat; volunteers contribute £2.50 a day to cover their rent and food. For further information send an s.a.e. to Nightingales Children's Project, 11 Colin Road, Preston, Paignton, Devon TQ3 2NR (fax 01803 527233).

Recently a new organisation has been set up primarily to run an English club in Piatra-Neamt. New graduates (and others) should obtain details from British-Romanian Connections, PO Box 86, Birkenhead, Merseyside L41 8FU (0151-645 8555/512 3355). The ecumenical charity Jacob's Well (2 Ladygate, Beverley, East Yorkshire HU17 8HU; 01482 881162) sends more than 50 volunteers to a psychiatric hospital in the Romanian town of Siret and also to hospitals and care centres in Bulgaria, Poland and the Ukraine.

Voluntary organisations working with displaced persons inside the former Yugoslavia sometimes take on foreign volunteers. A Croatian organisation provides services not only to refugees in Croatia but to the returnees and local communities. During the summer and winter school holidays, they accept volunteers for four weeks and also long-term volunteers. In the UK, volunteers are recruited by IVS Scotland, 7 Upper Bow, Edinburgh EH1 2JN (0131-226 6722). All volunteers are expected to pay DM250-300 for food and bed upon arrival.

OTHER OPPORTUNITIES

Many people based in the cities of Eastern Europe over the past decade have taken advantage of the new entrepreneurial spirit by engaging in conventional employment. Companies and recruitment agencies advertise in the English language papers and occasionally in *Overseas Jobs Express* for computer programmers, administrators, etc.

The westernising democracies of Eastern Europe are all targeting tourism as a means of aiding their economies and are encouraging foreign tour operators to develop resorts, etc. that in time may have large staff requirements. Ski tour operators like Balkan Holidays (19 Conduit St, London W1R 9TD; www.balkanholidays.co.uk) recruit a few reps outside the countries, but mostly try to hire locals. Ski Gower (2 High St, Studley, Warks. B80 7HJ) specialise in organising school ski trips in Poland (as well as Switzerland) whereas one or two companies are trying to put Sarajevo back on the list of desirable ski resorts.

Young people in east European capitals are so eager to embrace western culture that American-style restaurants and Irish pubs have sprung up everywhere, some of which hire English speakers, as attested by Bruce Collier whose British wife Sharon was hired by a restaurant near Red Square a few years ago. Such jobs will be heard about by word-of-mouth or possibly advertised in the English-language press. Turn-over of foreign students is high so if you are staying for a while your chances are reasonable. The trendy area of Moscow is on New Arbat.

Travellers' hostels may have openings. After a massive European hitch-hiking trip through Europe, Jon Loop finished up at the youth hostel in Budapest where he worked five hours a day cleaning, painting and maintaining the place in exchange for a bed and three meals. He also did touting for the hostel, but didn't make a success of the job since the opposition were much better organised and even went to the lengths of meeting buses at a service station outside Budapest to distribute their hostels' literature.

If you are looking for some casual work, ask discreetly around the universities or among expatriates teaching English. Your services as anything from a disc jockey to a freelance business consultant may be in demand. English-language papers may carry relevant adverts. For example the classified section of the *The Prague Post* (Stepanska 20, 110 00 Prague 1; 2-9633 4411/4400) can be read on-line at www.praguepost.cz. It is very cheap to place your own advert; if you send 25 words or less to classifieds@praguepost.cz you will pay just $1 a day for a minimum of ten days. Other places to look for odd jobs in the Czech capital are the notice boards at Radost FX, Laundry Kings and the Meduza Café. The internet site www.jobs.cz is aimed primarily at Czech job-seekers though it has a section in English with occasional vacancies.

Marta Eleniak started as a volunteer in Warsaw teaching English in a primary school and within a year listed her various paid activities as assistant to the Vice-President of a consulting firm, translator and teacher at a real estate agency, UK representative of a Polish musician and exporter of paragliders. She concludes that 'England seems so sleepy in comparison'. Obviously there are many niches which keen foreigners willing to stay for a while can fill.

Work Your Way Worldwide

Australia

In some ways this chapter is superfluous. Australia has developed a magnificent industry to cater specifically for backpackers and working holidaymakers. Most hostels both in the cities and the countryside are well informed about local jobs available to travellers; some act as informal employment agencies. Bus companies have routes that shuttle between fruit-picking regions for the benefit of working travellers. Outback properties offer training in the skills necessary to work on a station and then double as a placement agency. Recruitment agencies and employers with seasonal requirements target the backpacking community by advertising in the places they stay or frequent. Free newspapers and magazines are targeted specifically at backpackers, carrying employment advertisements. Employers even co-operate with regional tourist offices to find seasonal staff, as in the South Australian fruit-growing region of the Riverina. So there is no shortage of information and assistance available for the newly arrived working holiday maker.

The amount of temporary work which the 2000 Olympic Games created was unprecedented. In order to cope with a labour shortage, the government increased the quota of working holiday visas from 65,000 in 1999 to 78,000 in 2000 (compared to 33,000 in 1995) and raised the upper age limit to 30, demonstrating the strength of the Australian economy. This high level may drop slightly over the next few years, but the scheme continues in a very healthy state. On the negative side, there is a lobby in Australia which argues that the working holiday scheme deprives Australian nationals of jobs. However with a decreasing rate of unemployment (currently 6.8%), this lobby is not very powerful and prospects for working travellers are bright. Britons account for about half of all the working holiday visas issued.

Even in times of recession, there tend to be plenty of travellers' jobs around. The vast majority of unemployed Australians do not want to pick fruit, collect for charity, work on a sheep station, or do any of the other kinds of work visitors to Australia do. This is the conclusion to which a longstanding contributor to *Work Your Way Around the World*, Armin Birrer, came when he worked as recruiting officer at a vineyard in northern Victoria:

Local unemployment was very high, and yet I had severe problems getting pickers. Most of the unemployed didn't want to pick grapes because it is too hard for them. Plus lots of them don't think it's worthwhile to go off the dole for three to four weeks and then wait to go back on again. I came to the conclusion in Mildura that I can always find some work even if unemployment rises to 20%, if I go to where the work is. People who can work hard and don't make trouble are always in demand.

Those same people are probably the ones who arrive with just a few pounds after having travelled across Asia or the States and earn enough in a few months to fund further months of travel. This is not too difficult in a country where unskilled workers are generally paid $10-$12 an hour and fast word-processors (for example) can earn $15-$20 an hour in the big cities.

First-time visitors to Australia are often surprised by the degree to which that far-off continent is an imitation of Britain. Despite their reputation as 'pommy-bashers', most Australians take for granted a strong link with Britain, and this may be one reason why British travellers are so often welcomed as prospective employees. Being Scottish is even better, according to Melanie Grey from Edinburgh, especially in tele-sales since 'you always end up speaking to someone who has a granny in Dundee'.

The kinds of job you are likely to get in the rural areas are of a very different nature from city jobs. To discover Australia's more exotic features, you will have to penetrate into the countryside. While some experienced travellers declare that the big cities are the only places you can work on a steady basis at reasonably good wages, others advise heading out of Sydney as soon as you've seen the harbour. Chris Miksovsky from Connecticut found computer work in both Sydney and Melbourne offices with ease and earned $15 an hour. However after a few months he realised that the reason he had left home was to get away from spending his days in an office, so he headed north to look for station work. Work in the country or the outback often comes with accommodation whereas city rents (a minimum of $100 a week for two sharing a small flat) can eat into your wages, as can the social life.

Working Holiday Visas

Australia has reciprocal working holiday arrangements with Britain, Ireland, Canada, Netherlands, Germany, Italy, Japan, Korea and Malta. Discussions are taking place in Canberra to introduce a special temporary harvest working visa and to extend the scheme to other nationalities, i.e. the US, France, Spain, Greece, Hong Kong, Malaysia, Singapore and Cyprus. In the meantime applications from other nationalities will be considered on their merits.

The visa is for people intending to use any money they earn in Australia to supplement their holiday funds. Working full-time for more than three months for the same employer is not permitted. Full-time study used to be prohibited but from mid-2000, you can engage in up to three months of studies/training. You are eligible for a working holiday visa only once. Applicants must be between the ages of 18 and 30 and without children. Until 2000, applications from people aged 26-29 were scrutinised more closely than those of younger applicants, and they were expected to prove that their stay in Australia would be of benefit not only to themselves but to Australia. It was not known whether it will revert to this system now that the millennial year is over.

The working holiday visa will be valid for 12 months after entry, which must be within 12 months of issue. The visa is not renewable either in Australia or at home. Britons should apply to the High Commission in London (Australia House, Strand, London WC2B 4LA; 020-7379 4334) or in the north to the Australian Consulate in Manchester (Chatsworth House, Lever St, Manchester M1 2DL; 0161-228 1344). At the busiest times, applications have taken up to ten weeks to process, and personal applications were suspended. British people (and Irish, Dutch and Canadians) can also apply at Australian Consulates outside the UK. From July 1, 2000 all WHM visa-holders are permitted to leave and re-enter Australia, though the maximum duration of the visa remains 12 months from first entry into Australia.

The allocation of the annual quota of visas starts in July; once the total has run out, applications are not considered until the start of the next round, so the best time to apply is in the northern summer.

The first step is to get the working holiday information sheet and form 1150 Application for a Working Holiday Makers (WHM) visa from a specialist travel agent or from Consyl Publishing which sends out forms on behalf of the High Commission: 3 Buckhurst Road, Bexhill-on-Sea, East Sussex TN40 1QF (01424 223111); you must enclose an A4 stamped addressed envelope (66p stamp). The non-refundable visa processing fee in the UK is currently £65; this can be checked by ringing the Australian Immigration and Citizenship Information line 0891 600333 (charged at 60p per minute). The second step is to get as much money in the bank as possible. Each application is assessed on its own merits, but the most important requirement is a healthy bank balance. You must have enough money for your airfare to Australia (approximately £500) plus you must show evidence of having saved a minimum of £2,000. If your bank statements do not show steady saving, you must submit documents showing where the money came from (e.g. sale of a car, gift from a relative).

Anyone intending to work in catering and hospitality, health care, education or the pharmaceutical industry must provide a recent medical report assuring the authorities that they are fit enough to travel to Australia and back again at the end of the proposed stay. (Some GPs charge for this service.)

The granting of the WHM visa to other nationalities, who must apply at the Australian Consulate in their country of citizenship, is discretionary. Applicants must prove that a working holiday would benefit Australia as well as themselves. The numbers are small, but Americans, Spaniards and so on are sometimes granted a working holiday visa. Chris Miksovsky decided to chance his hand at the Australian Consulate in New York:

> I needed to explain what benefit my time in Australia would be to me and (more importantly) to Australia. I spent some time preparing a well worded response. Basically the model toy company I'd been working for sold products to several retailers in Australia. My argument was that in my year in Australia I would visit with each of these businesses, try to get to know their operations a bit and find out what they thought of our company's services. After the visits I said I'd fax back a report of my findings (a promise I kept). The beauty of this is that it could apply to almost anything ('I work in a convenience store/sewage factory/adult toy store...'). The only slight mistruth on my application was that I would return to my company in New York at the end of my year's travels. Anyway, I threw in an itinerary, proof of funds, etc. and got the visa with no problem. Once you have the visa you can do what you want.

Some people worry that if their application for a working holiday visa is turned down for some reason, they won't be granted a tourist visa. But the High Commission maintains that this is an unfounded anxiety. If you overstay your visa and they notice on the way out, you will be automatically barred from returning to Australia for a minimum of three years.

Other relevant information is available on the website of the Department of Immigration & Multicultural Affairs (www.immi.gov.au) or in Australia by ringing DIMA on 131881 for all visa information. The busy office in Sydney is at 88 Cumberland St in the Rocks.

Pre-Departure Schemes

A number of UK and North American travel and youth exchange agencies can assist those who want some back-up on a working holiday. They offer various packages which may be of special interest to first-time travellers. Some are all-inclusive (especially the gap year placement organisations listed below); others simply give back-up on arrival. Given how easy it is to orient yourself and find work, you should weigh up the pros and cons carefully before paying a substantial fee. Typically, the fee will include airport pick-up, hostel accommodation for the first few nights and a post-arrival orientation which advises on how to obtain a tax-file card, suggestions of employers and so on. Some even guarantee a job. Various perks may be thrown in like a telephone calling card and free maps.

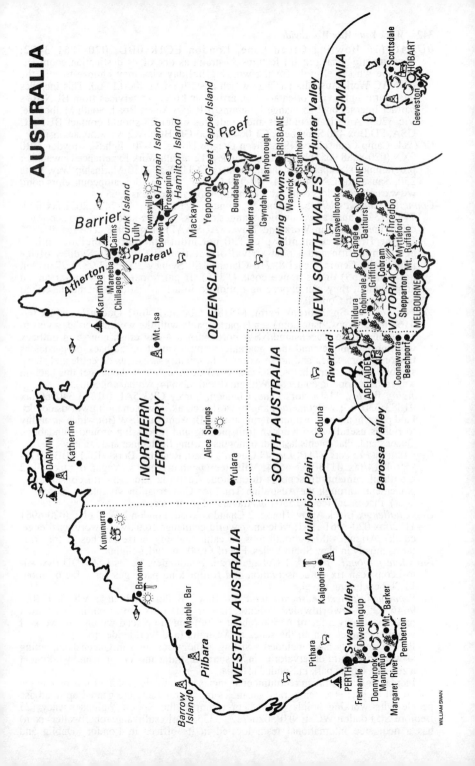

AUSTRALIA

BUNAC (16 Bowling Green Lane, London EC1R 0BD; 020-7251 3472; downunder@bunac.org.uk) features Australia as one of its destination countries. Anyone who is eligible for the working holiday visa may choose to join the BUNAC Work Australia package which costs from £1,400-£1,700. This includes the return flight, visa, orientation on arrival and back-up services from BUNAC's partner International Exchange Programs/IEP, 196 Albert Road, South Melbourne, Vic 3205. American students and graduates under 25 should contact BUNAC USA, PO Box 430 Southbury, CT 06488 (800-GO BUNAC; www.bunac.org).

CCUSA, Camp Counsellors USA, Green Dragon House, 64-70 High St, Croydon CR0 9XN (020-8688 9051) has introduced a new 12-month Work Experience Downunder programme. US applicants should contact CCUSA at 2330 Marinship Way, Suite 250, Sausalito, CA 94965 (1-800-999-CAMP; outbound@campcounselors.com/ www.campcounselors.com/australia.html). Programme fee is $365.

Council Exchanges UK, 52 Poland St, London W1V 4JQ (020-7478 2022/fax 020-7734 7322; auswat@councilexchanges.org.uk/ www.councilexchanges.org.uk) offers the Australian Work and Travel (AUSWAT) programme. The fee of £395 for the first three months plus £30 per month thereafter includes initial accommodation and a post-arrival orientation at Council's Sydney office (University Centre, Level 8, 210 Clarence St, Sydney 2000; 02-9373 2730) but not visa (£65) or insurance costs (£315). If participants want pre-arranged employment they can choose an option to join the Visitoz Scheme described below through Council.

Visit Oz Scheme, Springbrook Farm, MS188, Goomeri, 4601 Queensland (fax 07-4168 6155; www.visitoz.org) sends participants with the working holiday visa to a station on the Queensland/NSW border for a 4-day crash course in outback working techniques and then guarantees employment on outback properties as tractor drivers, stock and horse workers, hospitality assistants on cattle and sheep stations and mothers' helps. The cost is £395, though you should get this back in wages. The London contact is William (0966 528644; wdtb@aol.com).

Changing Worlds, 11 Doctors Lane, Chaldon, Surrey CR3 5AE (01883 340960/fax 01883 330783; welcome@changingworlds.co.uk/ www.changingworlds.co.uk). Paid placements on Australian farms around Broken Hill NSW (for which an ability to ride is useful). Also work in fruit picking and processing around Bundaberg, Queensland. Placements last 3 or 6 months starting September and January.

Gap Activity Projects (GAP) Ltd, 44 Queen's Road, Reading, Berks. RG1 4BB (0118-959 4914/fax 0118-957 6634; Volunteer@gap.org.uk/ www.gap.org.uk). 5-12 month placements in schools throughout Australia and 5-month conservation placements through the Australian Trust for Conservation Volunteers (described later). Placement fee of £550 plus travel and insurance.

Gap Challenge, Black Arrow House, 2 Chandos Road, London NW10 6NF (020-8961 1122/fax 020-8961 1551; welcome@world-challenge.co.uk/www.world-challenge. co.uk). Arranges three-month jobs on cattle stations, horse ranches or trail ride farms mostly in New South Wales. Fee of £1,900 includes flights.

i-to-i International Projects, 1 Cottage Road, Headingley, Leeds LS6 4DD (www.i-to-i.com) can fix up conservation and fruitpicking packages for a fee of about £1,200 excluding travel.

Involvement Volunteers Association Inc, PO Box 218, Port Melbourne, VIC 3207 (03-9646 9392; ivworldwide@volunteering.org.au) runs a programme by which participants pay a fee of A$500 (about £200) and are placed within a network of voluntary projects in all the states of Australia (and worldwide) for up to a year. Past placements have included assisting zoology research in Queensland, acting as wardens at bird observatories in Western Australia and Victoria, and working at a zoo and reptile park in South Australia.

Increasingly, Australian recruitment agencies are actively looking for people in the UK to fill their clients' temporary vacancies in Australia and are geared up to advise people with working holiday visas. For example, the Robert Walters agency (25 Bedford St, London WC2E 9HP; 020-7379 3333; marlo.sullivan@robertwalters.com) has a dedicated international team located in its offices in London, Dublin and

Johannesburg who can arrange interviews for candidates at their city of arrival. Not only does Select Connect invite backpackers with secretarial and administrative experience to register with them before leaving the UK, they will advise on initial accommodation and orientation; details on their 'Travelling Lifeline' service are available from Select Connect, 78 Old Broad St, London EC2M 1QP (020-7588 4216; connect@select.co.uk). Other agencies advertise in the backpacker press (see section on Advertisements below).

Backpacker Agencies

Specialist backpacker travel agencies and hostel groups can also assist with job-finding. Travellers Contact Point (2-6 Inverness Terrace, Bayswater, London W2 3HX; 020-7243 7887; www.travellers-contact.com.au) operate a free job search centre in connection with recruitment agencies in six offices around Australia and New Zealand. Membership for £25 includes services such as mail forwarding, e-mail and word processing access. They can also book hostel accommodation with an airport pickup for your arrival into any gateway city in Australia or New Zealand. In Sydney the TCP office is at Level 7, Dymocks Building, 428 George St, Sydney 2000 (02-9221 8744/fax 9221 3746).

The Backpacker's Resource Centre will help people with the working holiday visa to set up work as well as providing a range of other back-up services for a fee of US$250. Send for an information pack from the BRC, 167 Franklin St, Melbourne, Vic 3000 (03-9329 7525/fax 9329 7667/ brc@btg.net.au) or any of their other offices in Sydney (02-9232 7656) or Brisbane. Allied to BRC, Worldwide Workers has offices in Sydney (02-9223 7500), Byron Bay, Melbourne and Cairns (www. worldwideworkers.com). They issue a Work Card that brings with it various perks and access to their job-finding assistance which mainly consists of disseminating your details to a range of employment agencies so you don't have to register with them individually.

The Adelaide-based hostel group Nomads (288 North Terrace, SA 5000; 1800 819 883; www.nomads-backpackers.com) sells their Adventure Card in the UK for £15 through specialist travel agents like STA. Nomads concentrate on helping people with working holiday visas to find casual work. Details of their Job Package is available from any branch of STA or ring 020-7361 6150.

Permanent Migration

Many working holidaymakers entertain the possibility of staying on. The regulations have recently been loosened so that people with a skill in short supply (often in the field of information technology) and an employer who wants to employ them for longer than the three months allowed under the working holiday visa can apply for a four year business visa while still in the country. Law firms like Parish Patience in Sydney (02-9283 2255) specialise in assisting clients with visa applications.

Obtaining a resident's visa (for permanent migration) is, predictably, much more difficult, though not impossible if you have a skill in short supply and/or a close relative in Australia. Form 1126 is the initial migration form, available from Consyl Publishing mentioned above which includes notes on how to obtain one or more migration application packs (which cost £6). Rhona Stannage was very surprised to learn that three states in Australia recognise a Scottish law degree and she considered the seven-month wait and the fee of £250 for a resident's visa worthwhile, although she and her husband were really interested only in a working holiday.

Unofficial Work

Those who don't qualify for a working visa should not despair, since many Australian bosses do not take paperwork very seriously. Employers seldom ask to see the stamp in your passport and a 'no worries' attitude prevails in many areas. After meeting a number of people in Perth (both potential bosses and people working at job centres) who had never heard of the working holiday scheme, Glen Thompson began to wonder if he had wasted his time and money in obtaining the visa.

This may be set to change, however, since the Australian Minister for Immigration announced that a crackdown on illegal cash workers was on the cards for after the Olympics. (An estimated 51,000 foreigners live and work in Australia without the appropriate visa.) For the first time from November 2000, employers caught hiring illegal workers are to be fined and fined heavily (up to $66,000 and two years in prison for persistent offenders). What remains to be seen is how rigorously this new law will be enforced as one of the hostel staff in Mildura explained:

> *It's great for someone to sit in their office and make these decisions, but we have such a shortage of workers quite often during the year, that I do not believe they could police it. There is no way our harvest (January to April) could operate without taking people who do not have work visas.*

The same situation pertains in Queensland. If the new punitive fines on employers of illegal harvesters are handed out, Queensland farmers will experience a crisis, according to the Queensland Fruit & Vegetable Growers Association (www.qfvg.org.au) who in December 2000 estimated that failure to recruit enough pickers and packers already results in losses amounting to $30,000-$50,000 per farm, about a tenth of the total value of production.

There is now a Department of Immigration helpline for employers to ring to check workers' visa status. Rumours of $1,000 rewards for 'dobbing in' an illegal worker (Australian expression meaning informing on) mean that discretion is essential.

This together with compulsory tax file numbers (see below) has meant that fewer employers are as blasé about the rules as hitherto. Furthermore the Immigration authorities do show up in places where there has been widespread disregard of visa requirements. In one week of high-profile summer raids in Victoria and Queensland, the authorities uncovered 70 illegal workers. The procedure is to extract a bond of $2,000 to $5,000 from people with expired visas, and give a week to leave the country. Jane Harris thinks it should be stressed that anyone working without a visa alongside others in a similar position should be very careful, and suspicious of anyone nosing around. She describes what happened at the campsite she was staying on in Stanthorpe Queensland:

> *I got back to our campsite to discover that Immigration had raided farms throughout the area. Apparently, a local man had been running an illegal bus service to all the local farms from the three campsites in town. Someone from Immigration started checking the visas of everyone on the bus, and found seven people with tourist visas. They were told to leave the country within two weeks. That evening, four car loads of Immigration officials turned up at the campsite. They had lists of local farm employees and were matching these with people's passports, so it seems best to work under a false name (especially as the local pubs will cash salary cheques without seeing any ID). Meanwhile we stayed inside our campervan and hid all signs we'd been working (e.g. gloves, boots, pay slips).*

It seems that they do not have to see you physically working but can act on circumstantial evidence.

Similar stories have emerged from other crop-growing areas in Queensland (around Bowen and Munduberra), Shepparton and Mildura in Victoria (where raids are an annual event resulting in a large number of deportations), and from Donnybrook, Carnarvon, Kununurra and Broome in Western Australia.

Without a working holiday visa you might decide to steer clear of farms where you are relatively exposed, and find work inside the relatively safe and anonymous walls of the urban jungle or on smaller family farms where the immigration people are unlikely to bother you. Stephen Psallidas urges discretion after an Australian guy working with him in Bowen 'dobbed in' two English girls who had foolishly let it be known that they had no work visas. Immigration officials arrived and deported them.

One old hand American who has worked his way around Australia recommends changing one letter in your last name every place you go which is guaranteed to confuse the bureaucracy. Real ID can be used to cash cheques (if that is necessary) and a clerical error blamed if the teller notices the discrepancy.

Tax

All people in employment in Australia must either provide their employer with a 9-

digit tax file number or be taxed at a punitive 47% for non-residents. Therefore it is greatly to your advantage to obtain one. We have heard of several cases of people being deported for inventing tax file numbers (but giving their real names). You may come across people selling on the tax file numbers of people who have left the country for about $100.

Foreigners must apply at a tax office, for example at 100 Market St in Sydney, where queues are long, or 140 Creek St, Brisbane (national telephone number 132861; www.ato.gov.au). Processing normally takes between four and six weeks. You must submit a passport with appropriate visa plus one of a number of documents such as an original or certified copy of your birth certificate, Australian driving licence, bank statement at an Australian address, etc. Paul Edwards strongly recommends opening a bank account so that you have documentary proof of a local address, omitting the hostel name if you are living in a hostel. When applying for his tax file number, he applied for resident tax status, making sure that the address on his bank statement remained his address for correspondence with the authorities. He even went so far as to get his proof of identity and address stamped by a justice of the peace. When employers asked him if he was a resident, he replied with an indignant 'of course'. There are so many exiled Poms, especially in Perth, that Brits are not nearly as conspicuous as they would be, say, in America.

The ultimate tax liability for non-residents of Australia is 29% of all earnings (up to $397 per week) whereas residents are taxed at 20% of earnings. Non-residents are not eligible for the tax-free threshold of $5,400 nor for concessional rebates (for example residents who work in a 'remote zone' and those who work in the fruit and vegetable industries pay only 15% tax). There is some confusion about the definition of 'resident'. Although the length of the visit does not in itself determine residency status, as a general rule, a person whose intended visit to Australia is less than six months cannot be regarded as a resident. A person who is in Australia on a working holiday will be treated as a non-resident unless they can demonstrate that they are residing in Australia during their stay.

On the basis that temporary visits can turn into longer-term ones, many working holidaymakers tick the box for 'resident' on their tax file application and on all employment declaration forms, which allows them the possibility of applying for a tax rebate should they decide to leave the country at an unspecified future date. Assuming you have claimed resident's status, you should obtain a Group Certificate (statement of earnings and tax deducted, equivalent to a P45) after you leave each job, arranging to have it posted on to you if necessary. If you have earned less than your tax-free threshold during the tax year (starting July 1st), you could be eligible for a refund. On the other hand, applying for a refund brings your case to the attention of the tax authorities who may decide that you were not eligible for residency in the first place and are therefore subject to an even higher rate of tax than you have already paid and potentially for heavy penalities for giving false or misleaing information. Dawn Smith was billed over $1,000 after returning home to Worcester. The compulsory deduction of 6% for superannuation (retirement) cannot normally be reclaimed, though if this is an issue that concerns you, you could look at relevant discussions on Lonely Planet's website (www.lonelyplanet.com/letters/aus).

All earners must submit a tax return by October 31st. Pick up a free Taxpack from a tax office or pay a tax agent to make the application for you, preferably in July when the tax office is over-stretched. If you have problems or queries about your tax position in Sydney, personal callers may visit the Tax Office at 100 Market St (02-9224 0990).

If your status remains non-resident, you might be eligible for a reduction of your tax burden by claiming LAFHA (Living Away From Home Allowance) which could mean that you could set some of your living expenses against tax. Anyone who can show that they will be resident in a certain place for more than three months is eligible for a Medicare card which allows you refunds on doctors' fees and prescriptions.

THE JOB HUNT

Although everybody finds some kind of job in the end, it isn't always easy. You are likely to encounter a surprising degree of competition from others on working holidays, many of whom are chasing the same kinds of job. For example a company which operates tours of Sydney Harbour received 50 replies to an advertisement for waiting staff and a receptionist, 42 of which were from Poms. The glut of travelling workers is especially bad in Sydney and in Queensland resorts before Christmas. In addition to asking potential employers directly (which is the method used by about one third of successful job-seekers in Australia), there are four main ways of finding work: Employment National (Jobcentres), private employment agencies, newspaper advertisements and notice boards (especially at travellers' hostels).

Employment National

Three years ago the Australian government employment service was privatised. The old Commonwealth Employment Service or CES became Employment National, a network of agencies linked by computer. EN (sometimes called Centrelink) has not fared well in the marketplace while private employment agencies have become much more numerous. There was some speculation in Canberra recently that the government might opt out of the job market altogether, though they do remain active in some fields, particularly seasonal harvest work. The head office is on Level 10, 140 Sussex St, Sydney 2000; 02-9200 6800 (www.employmentnational.com.au).

Like job centres anywhere the EN has details of jobs that have been registered with them. You can walk into an EN and use a touch screen computer to check on vacancies and locate seasonal work. In some cases you will have access to a free telephone for arranging job interviews and you can also collect a copy of the *Harvest Table*. Foreign visitors without working visas are probably best advised not to register with the EN, though in some cases a passport is not asked for. But Jane Harris and her boyfriend Pete paid frequent visits to the offices and were never asked about their visas. As at Jobcentres in the UK, the range of jobs can be less than thrilling, e.g. unloading kangaroo carcasses, working in a funeral parlour and singing in a Polynesian language at a coastal resort, along with the usual bar, office and shop vacancies.

Some ENs have separate departments or even separate addresses which specialise in casual work or office temping or jobs in the hospitality industry. Competition for casual jobs such as an afternoon in a warehouse or a few days of making sandwiches varies from place to place, but there will always be a hard core of travellers attracted by the prospect of instant cash. In general, suburban offices especially in well-heeled suburbs may prove more useful than the over-used central city office.

Private Employment Agencies

As in Britain, private employment agencies are very widespread and are an excellent potential source of jobs for travellers, especially those with office skills, computer, data processing or financial experience. A surprising number positively encourage UK people on working holidays, often by circulating their details to hostel managers. The offered wages are good too: from $12 an hour for clerical work, $14 for secretarial and $15 for computer work.

An ability to type 50 words per minute is a great advantage and, at least in Stephen Psallidas's experience, virtually essential:

> *I went round the temping offices, but alas. Despite my extensive experience with computers, well-prepared CV, shirt and tie, etc. I had no luck. All of them required at least 60 words a minute typing for any office work. I would recommend anyone to take a short typing course before coming over since there is plenty of work.*

Major agencies include Drake, Bligh, Adecco, Challenge (1800 656171), Adia and ACOM. Most agencies do not occupy the equivalent of high street premises, and you will often find yourself in some obscure office block. You should make an appointment to register and allow up to an hour for each one to have your skills assessed. Your chances of being accepted will be increased if you can produce some good references from previous employment at home or elsewhere in Australia. Even when you do get an assignment, there is no guarantee that work will be continuous and you should be prepared for a certain amount of hanging around between jobs.

Look for the monthly magazine *TNT* (published in different editions for the different states) and backpacker giveaways like *Travel Maps Australia/TMA* or *The Aussie Backpacker* which can be picked up in hostels and backpacker pubs. They carry a number of ads for temp agencies. Here are three agencies in Sydney out of many more: *Bligh Appointments,* Level 7, Dymocks Building, 428 George St, Sydney 2000 (02-9235 3699; www.employment.com.au/bligh). They work closely with overseas travellers' clubs and the YHA to assist job-seekers from overseas. London office: 020-7603 6123.

Goldstein & Martens Recruitment Consultants, Level 4, 285 George St; 02-9262 3088; www.goldsteinmartens.com.au) which pays $2-$3 above the average hourly wage.

Metro Personnel, Level 6, Thakral House, 301 George St, Sydney 2000 (02-9299 5477; www.metropersonnel.com.au).

In-Store Consulting Services, 0417 672 0241/02-9679 0406. Range of casual work in stores.

There is a major shortage of temp secretaries, so if you've got decent skills, you're practically guaranteed work. Drake International/Drake Overload has been recommended by several readers; the company has offices in all the major cities including Sydney (02-9241 4488), Melbourne (03-9245 0245) and Brisbane (07-3221 6099). Because they have offices all over the world, it can be useful having one of their Career Passports which will serve as a letter of introduction to other branches.

In Sydney and Melbourne, the agencies almost always ask about your visa status. Carolyn Edwards side-stepped the issue with one agency by saying she had just moved into a flat and couldn't locate her passport and another time claiming that she had left it in a safety deposit box in Queensland and was arranging for it to be sent. After she had proved herself a reliable worker and was getting called back by companies, the agency seemed conveniently to forget about it. The two temp agencies in Kalgoorlie for whom Lucy Slater worked didn't even ask to see her passport. They were more interested in whether or not she could drive since most secretarial work there is with the mines and involves driving a company car between sites.

Some agencies specialise in certain kinds of work for example work on stations and farms, in tourist resorts or as nannies and au pairs (see relevant sections).

Advertisements

Either before you leave Britain or once you are in one of the major cities, get hold of the free booklet *Australia & New Zealand Independent Travellers Guide* published by the London-based travel magazine *TNT* (14-15 Child's Place, London SW5 9RX). It includes a section on work and some relevant advertisements as well as travel advice. The same company publishes specific monthly magazines for Sydney/NSW, Queensland, Victoria/Tasmania and the Outback, available free at airports, bus and train stations as well as from the TNT office, Level 4, 46-48 York St, Sydney (02-9299 4811/fax 9299 4861). They carry a certain number of classified ads for job-seekers and a section called 'Finding Work'.

The main daily newspapers have job supplements once or twice a week, for example on Wednesday and Saturday in the *Sydney Morning Herald* (www.smh.com.au), the *West Australian* (Perth), *Adelaide Advertiser* or the *Courier-Mail* (Brisbane). The Monday Job Market in the Melbourne *Age* is particularly worthwhile. Remember that these wide-circulation papers generate a lot of competition for jobs. Try to buy the paper the preceding evening so you can start your job at the crack of dawn. For example the *Herald* in Sydney goes on sale about 2am from outlets in Taylor Square (Darlinghurst) and near Kings Cross Station.

Ken Smith was so dismayed by the level of competition that he decided to check out the more local papers:

Any jobs that are advertised in the 'Sydney Morning Herald' are normally so flooded with replies that your chances are minimal. I replied to a bar vacancy along with 119 other people and was very honoured to make it to the final selection stages. I then started looking through the smaller papers and replied to an advertisement for labourer/factory cleaner. In this case, four people *applied for two jobs and I soon was working from 7am to 3.30pm with the prospect of daily overtime and Saturday work if I proved myself a good worker. Soon I was taking home just under $500 a week. The work (which was often very physical) was for an engineering firm in Botany Bay which designed and manufactured abattoirs.*

The range of jobs advertised in the newspaper can be discouraging. Sarah Snell describes the choice in the Darwin paper:

Jobs that were advertised included cooking on prawn trawlers (and I gathered through various accounts that this may have included rather more demanding activities than merely preparing meals for the hardy crew), jillarooing (the female counterpart of the jackaroo, who is a kind of cowboy on sheep and cattle stations in the outback), training as a croupier for a new casino, and nude modelling for aspiring life artists at the local college.

Meanwhile the 'Casual Work Available' columns in other cities can carry an equally unpromising range of opportunities including 'promoting art' (i.e. selling prints door-to-door), delivering junk mail for a pittance, telephone sales and working as a film extra (where you will be required to pay a registration fee with little immediate prospect of work). Furthermore all these jobs are gone by 6am.

However it is worth persevering since there will also be adverts for bar and restaurant jobs (especially under the specific heading 'Positions Vacant – Hospitality Industry'), for work on guest ranches, for factory jobs and so on. Posts for live-in child-carers are sometimes advertised in daily papers; check under the 'Situations Vacant – Domestic and Rural' column (though almost all the jobs are urban not rural).

If you think you might be a successful door-to-door salesman, the newspaper is the place to look. Unless you're prepared to exaggerate the virtues of your product you might last no longer than Simon Whalley from Hull did after answering an advert in the *West Australian,* for salesmen of paintings, i.e. two hours. Adam Jones found this work more congenial and managed to make about $400 a week by selling an average of seven paintings an evening. The ex-girlfriend of an American reader told him she was earning a cool $1,000 a week as a rep for a cleaning company in Brisbane. One company that was advertising heavily in 2000 was ABC (A Better Chance) which distributes Time Life books in Australia. They send sales teams (called 'Interview Teams') all around Australia (expenses paid) to sell on commission for a minimum of 6-8 weeks; in Sydney ring 02-9233 6522 and in Brisbane 07-3221 6522 (www.abetterchance.com.au).

Some charities are perennial advertisers for paid fund-raisers. For example in Sydney the Australian Quadriplegic Association (Suite 204, 2nd Floor, 64-76 Kippax St, Surry Hills, NSW 2010; 02-9281 8214) pays collectors between a quarter and a third of donations collected, which should work out to be $50-$100 a day. Another charity worth investigating is the not-for-profit environmental organisation the Wilderness Society. The Sydney branch is in Suite 203 of the same building as the AQA (02-9282 9553; www.wilderness.org.au); hourly earnings average $15-$20. A good reference from the Wilderness Society might someday come in handy in impressing a personnel officer at Disneyland. The Wilderness Society has started a door-to-door canvas which is suitable for English-speaking backpackers with some knowledge of environmental issues. The job pays a base salary of $55 per four-hour shift plus canvassers can keep a quarter of takings above a set target.

Chris Miksovsky is amusing on the subject of dressing up as a koala in Brisbane:

My year in Australia ended with a rather fitting and hilarious job, collecting for the Wilderness Society, a sort of Australian Greenpeace, wearing a koala costume. After a brief interview with the Koala Co-ordinator ('So, Chris, do you have any experience walking around as a big furry animal?'), I found myself in a busy square wearing a full-body fluffy grey koala suit complete with fake felt claws and droopy oversize ears. Actually it works. Takings per hour were about $25 on average. For me, probably the best thing was that you learned to not take yourself so seriously. I have an Ivy League degree in

Political Science but there I was dancing around a city centre dressed as a koala.

Some of the most unpleasant jobs are never advertised. One working traveller was paid $40 an hour to clean out booths at a Sydney peep show. He hosed down the booth then scrubbed the walls for three hours a day.

Hostels and Notice Boards

Youth hostels and backpackers' lodges everywhere are a goldmine of information for people working their way around the world. And nowhere are they better than in Australia. A growing number of hostel managers, especially in the major fruit and vegetable growing areas of Queensland, run their own informal job-finding service and try to put backpackers in touch with local employers. The disadvantage of basing yourself in a big city hostel is that it is always a struggle to get messages from possible employers. The group Hostelling in Homes (Gabba Guesthouse, 18 Withington St, East Brisbane, Queensland 4169; 1800 333244; www.homehostel.com) primarily arranges accommodation for paying clients with host families, though it can also arrange fruit-picking in some areas.

You may find employment in the hostels themselves of course. Stephen Psallidas describes the proliferation of work, especially on the 'Route' between Sydney and Cairns:

I've met loads of people working in backpackers' hostels. Typically you work two hours a day in exchange for your bed and a meal. Work may be cleaning, driving the minibus, reception, etc. and is always on an informal basis so there are no worries about visas, etc. I will be jumping on the bandwagon myself soon. I'll be completely shattered from picking tomatoes so I'm going to 'work' in a hostel in Mission Beach, where the owners invited me to work when I stayed there earlier. I'm going to rest up in a beautiful place before continuing my travels, and not spend any of my hard-earned dollars.

There might be night work, especially at the big city hostels, for those who are up to the job of keeping non-residents out and rounding up residents swilling beer in the garden at 4am.

Australia has 140 YHA hostels, many of which distribute details about employment available within their region. A listing of all hostels and state offices is widely available (www.yha.org.au).

One of the most successful groups of non-YHA hostels is VIP Backpackers Resorts of Australia which is especially strong in New South Wales and Queensland. A booklet listing their 115 Australian hostels is distributed far and wide or can be obtained from overseas by purchasing their VIP kit for A$30 which gives $1 off each hostel stay among other discounts; contact VIP Backpackers Resorts, PO Box 600, Cannon Hill, Brisbane, Qld 4170 (07-3395 6111; www.backpackers.com.au). Almost all VIP hostels have notice boards advertising jobs, flats, car shares, etc. and most charge $16-$20 a night for a dorm bed. It is possible to join through selected agents outside Australia including Travellers Contact Point in London (address above).

The Nomad's Backpacker chain has already been mentioned, with about 50 hostels, many of them renovated pubs. Their membership card ('Adventure Card') costs £15/A$25 per year and entitles users to access a job advice line.

The disadvantage of using hostels as your main source of jobs is that they are full of your main competition for available work. Andrew Owen was discouraged to find that every backpackers' hostel seemed to be populated almost entirely with Brits on working holidays. Also be a little suspicious of claims such as 'Plenty of farm work available for guests' since this may just be a marketing ploy on the part of the hostel (see section on Queensland Harvests).

Most Sydney hostels are well clued up on the local job scene, especially in the three main backpackers' areas, sleazy Kings Cross, trendy Glebe and Coogee Beach. See the free *TNT* guides mentioned earlier for hostel listings. The 532-bed YHA hostel opposite the Central Railway Station (corner of Pitt and Rawson Sts) features an employment bureau among a range of state-of-the-art facilities. In Kings Cross, the

Pink House at 6-8 Barncleuth Square (02-9358 1689) has good work contacts as does Carole Knight at Carole's Accommodation (209 Bridge Road, Glebe, NSW 2037; 02-9660 0998). She rents out bed-sits and flats for $240-$350 a month. In the beach suburb of Coogee (pronounced Coodjee) try the Wizard of Oz at 172 Coogee Bay Road (02-9315 7876) and Sydney Beachside next door. Both are regularly contacted for casual workers. People looking for day labour regularly come in early (7.30am). Apparently it helps if you are built like a barn, especially if they are looking for someone to move grand pianos. It is also worth sticking close to reception in the evenings when employers ring with their requirements for the next day. When working like this, insist on being paid daily.

Rizwan Hafiz was amazed by the speed with which work came his way through his hostel:

You can't help but meet people in Oz. I arranged for a Coogee hostel to pick me up from Sydney Airport and they said 'if you go to your left you'll meet another bloke from Britain who's just phoned us'. I found work in two days. The warden asked 'what are you doing in 10 minutes?' There's a job in a café down the road washing dishes'. I did nine hours of backbreaking work but received $14 in tips and a huge burger for lunch. Great way to offset the jetlag.

In Melbourne, Enfield House Backpackers in St Kilda (03-9534 8159) was once a good place to find out about work but now is more a party hostel. The Hotel Bakpak in downtown Melbourne is attached to the Backpacker's Resource Centre which can assist people with a working holiday visa as well as provide a range of other back-up services for a fee. In Adelaide, try Rucksackers International at 257 Gilles Street (08-8232 0823) or any of the others along the same road, which try to direct travellers to relevant agencies and seasonal fruit picking as well as to jobs at show time. Another recommended Adelaide hostel is Sunny's at 139 Franklin St (08-8231 2430). In Perth, try Redbackpackers, 496 Newcastle St, West Perth (08-9227 9969; www.redbackpackers.com.au) which has strong links with local employers.

In fruit-picking areas, certain hostels and campsites are populated almost exclusively by workers; see the relevant sections below.

The Internet

Searching the web for employment leads is especially productive in Australia. There are dozens of routes in to finding out about job vacancies. Before leaving home, you might like to register (free) with www.gapwork.com which is updated regularly and lists employers who hire working holidaymakers. As mentioned earlier the government employment service posts vacancies on www.employmentnational.com.au with links to EN offices in the main harvest areas. The relatively new www.jobsearch.gov.au is another government source of information with details of the National Harvest Trail. One of the best sites is a free service by the Wayward Bus Company (www.waywardbus.com.au/seaswork.htm) which has an index of actual employers, hostels and pubs recommended for job-seekers and agents. The search engine Matilda has a long list of employment related sites: www.aaa.com.au/matilda.employment including a fruit picking calendar.

The *Aussie Backpacker* magazine mentioned earlier supports a job site www.jobs-in-oz.com, though more complete information about the job hunt can be found in print. Finally some of these may be useful: http://backpackingaround.com (for Western Australia); www.travellersclub.com.au; or www.backpackerjobs.com (for jobs in the tourist industry). Plenty of other sites cater for more corporate job-seekers, such as www.seek.com.au.

RURAL AUSTRALIA and the OUTBACK

Most of Australia's area is sparsely populated, scorched land which is known loosely as the outback. Beyond the rich farming and grazing land surrounding the largest cities, there are immense properties supporting thousands of animals and acres of crops. Many of these stations (farms) are so remote that flying is the only practical means of access, though having a vehicle can be a great help in an outback job search.

Sandra Gray describes the drawbacks of spending time on a station:

> *Be warned! Station life can be severely boring after a while. I managed to land myself on one in the Northern Territory with very little else to do but watch the grass grow. If you have to save a lot of money quickly station work is the way to do it since there's nothing to spend it on. But make sure the place is within reasonable distance of a town or at least a roadhouse, so you have somewhere to go to let off steam occasionally.*

Despite the large flocks and herds, it is usually possible for one or two experienced stockmen to take care of the animals unaided. Your chances of getting a job as a station assistant (a jackaroo or jillaroo) will be improved if you have had experience with sheep, riding or any farming or mechanical experience. Several farmers are in the business of giving you that experience before helping you to find outback work, like the one mentioned above in the Visitoz Scheme. Shaun Armstrong thoroughly enjoyed a similar five day Jackaroo/Jillaroo course in Queensland:

> *Should any traveller wish to discover an introduction to authentic rural Australia, no better window of opportunity exists than Pat and Pete Worsley's Rocky Creek Experience. I braved the five-day jackaroo course with three other travellers (all Dutch). Horse riding, cattle mustering, ute driving, trail biking (the 'ings' were numerous) and other tasks occupied our days: wonderful hospitality ended each evening. Memorable days. Station placement was arranged afterwards as was transport if needed. I was sorry to leave really. I'd say the course did prepare me for most experiences encountered in the job. For example I was able to muster cattle on horseback with four experienced riders having spent only 15 hours in the saddle. It wasn't easy, but I did it.*

The course fee is $440 including job placement afterwards with one of more than 300 employers, plus ongoing back-up; alternatively you can pay $330 for the course and no job. Rocky Creek is located inland from Bundaberg (Isis Highway MS 698, Biggenden, Qld 4621; 07-4127 1377; www.isisol.com.au/rockycrkfarmstay).

Shearing is out of the question for the uninitiated. Although the post of roustabout is open to the inexperienced, jobs are generally scarce on sheep stations at present because of the decline in the wool industry due to changes in fashion and the collapse of the Asian market. Roustabouts fetch, carry, sweep and trim stained bits from the fleeces. Check adverts under the heading 'Stock and Land' for shearing team recruitment in agricultural journals like *Queensland Country Life* or *Land*. Many of the jobs on a sheep station verge on the stomach-churning, as the Dutch woman Geertje Korf vividly describes, after spending a short time on a 10,000 acre sheep farm owned by the friend of her former employer:

> *My main tasks were bringing the rubbish to the tip (including dead sheep and the waste from the killing shed, sheep guts, skins, heads, etc.) and branding the sheep after shearing which included a lot of running up and down the race trying to get those frustratingly stupid sheep where I wanted them to be. At the end of the day I was covered with sweat, dust, branding paint, sheep grease, sweat and blood. You shouldn't be too faint-hearted since often you see the bone glistening between the blood where the shearers had accidentally cut the skin off the legs. I didn't often get the chance to help with mustering (rounding up the sheep on motorbikes, which is quite fun) and I did not learn to ride a horse as I had hoped. Nevertheless, I enjoyed doing something completely different. I wouldn't have minded the hard work if I had been paid decently for it (I was working 11 hours a day for $100 a week.)*

Chris Miksovsky was not impressed with the assistance he received from two outback placement services in Alice Springs so resorted to cold-calling stations after looking them up in the phone book for northern Western Australia. After making more than 40 calls (and spending as many dollars on phone cards) he found a cattle station willing (or desperate enough) to take him on. He advises against exaggerating your experience: if you say you can ride a horse, the station manager will probably put you on

'Satan the Psycho-mare' your first day. Chris describes station life as he experienced it:

The days were long (breakfast sometimes at 3am), never-ending (I worked 32 days straight once), often painful and sometimes gruesome. But then again, where else can you gallop across the outback chasing (or being chased by) a Brahman bull and sleep out under the stars listening to other jackaroos spinning yarns around a campfire, all while getting paid? Three months on the station earned me $2,700 net. It was the best thing I've done since I started travelling.

Some city-based employment agencies deal with jobs in country and outback areas, primarily farming, station, hotel/motel and roadhouse work. In Western Australia try Pollitt's (251 Adelaide Terrace, 13th Floor, Perth 6000; 08-9325 2544) who say that experienced farmworkers and tractor drivers are paid $12-$14 an hour for 10-12 hour days, seven days a week at seeding time (April to June) and harvest time (October to December). Housekeeping, nannying and cooking positions are available for two or three months at a time throughout the year. The standard wage is $300 a week after board, most of which can be saved. For work in outback roadhouses and hotels, previous experience is essential to earn $400 a week after lodging. The three-month commitment enables travellers to experience the regional country towns, and save $4,000-$5,000 during their stay.

While travelling back from Ayers Rock Sara Runnalls popped into the CentreLink office in the Northern Territory town of Katherine to ask about local jobs. That day she was driven 80km to a property at Scott Creek:

Here I found 15 hungry workers and a disgustingly dirty, dusty, insect haven for a kitchen. I had few fresh ingredients, ample beef, plenty of salt and tomato ketchup. My mission was to feed them five times a day with a variety of beef dishes and homemade cakes. I came up with some typically English cuisine and no complaints. I saw plenty of wildlife and enjoyed my two weeks on the cattle station. They asked me to stay the whole season but I'm here to travel.

Other agricultural employment agencies in Perth are Rural Enterprises Personnel Consultants, Suite 18, 326 Hay St, Perth, WA 6000 (9325 8411; ruralent@iinet.au) and Progressive Growers Association, (division of the Pastoralists & Graziers Association of WA Inc), 9479 4544; www.pgaofwa.org.au.

Outback Staff (PO Box 8042, Allenstown, Queensland 4700; 07-4927 4300; www.rocknet.net.au/~outstaff) is an Australia-wide rural employment agency which places tractor drivers, cotton workers, cooks and seasonal staff. The minimum period of work is only two weeks.

Anyone with experience of the horse industry should contact the Stablemate Staff Agency in the UK (The Old Rectory, Belton-in-Rutland, Oakham, Rutland LE15 9LE; ep@stablemate.demon.co.uk), whose Australian partner is Stablemate, 1 Bullridge Road, East Kurrajong, NSW 2758 (02-4576 4444/STABLEMATE@bigpond.com). They deal exclusively with placing equestrian and thoroughbred staff but are sometimes able to assist people with limited experience with horses if they want to work as a nanny or general farm assistant. People over 18 with a year's practical experience should enquire of the UK office about the International Exchange Programme in Australia for which the fee is about £1,800 including airfares.

Although you may not be forced to eat witchetty grubs for tea, there are some obvious disadvantages to life in the outback, viz. the isolation, the heat and to some extent the dangers. Even if you have had experience of living in the rural areas of Europe, it may be hard to adjust to life in the outback. Lots of towns have nothing more than a post office and small shop combined, a hotel (pub) and petrol pump. The sun's heat must not be underestimated. It is important to cover your head with a cowboy hat or a towel and to carry a large water bottle with you. Droughts are not uncommon in the outback. On Tricia Clancy's guest ranch near Sofala NSW, where it hadn't rained for a year and a half, both guests and staff were permitted to have one shower a week (in spite of the terrible heat and dust) and this water had to be recycled for laundry.

Finally there is the ever-present hazard of spiders and snakes which Tricia describes:

The hay barn attracted mice and the mice attracted snakes, so whenever we entered the barn we had to make a loud rumpus to frighten them away. Huntsmen spiders proliferated. These great tarantula-like creatures were not poisonous, however it was still frightening when they emerged from behind the picture frames in the evenings.

Once you get into the habit of checking inside your boots and behind logs for snakes, and under the loo seat for redback spiders, the dangers are minimised. The outback is often a rough male-dominated world, and not suited to fragile personalities.

Conservation Volunteers

Several organisations give visitors a chance to experience the Australian countryside or bush. The main conservation organisation in Australia, the Australian Trust for Conservation Volunteers, places volunteers from overseas, though the charges are quite steep. The ATCV is a non-profit organisation which undertakes conservation projects such as tree planting, erosion and salinity control, seed collection from indigenous plants, building and maintaining bush walking tracks, etc. Overseas volunteers are welcome to become involved in these 'conservation tasks' by booking a six-week package which includes transport within Australia, food and accommodation at a cost of A\$840 (which works out at \$20 a day for accommodation, food and transport). Further details are available from the ATCV National Head Office, Box 423, Ballarat, Vic 3353 (03-5333 1483; www.atcv.com.au). There are volunteer offices in all the states.

The Willing Workers on Organic Farms organisation is very active in Australia. WWOOF headquarters are at Mt Murrindal Co-operative, Buchan, Vic 3885 (03-5155 0218; www.wwoof.com.au) though their publicity is distributed at many hostels. They publish an 'Organic Farm & Cultural Experience List' of 1,300 addresses throughout Australia of organic farmers looking for short or long term voluntary help. The list is sold with accident insurance at a cost of A\$45 within Australia, A\$50 outside.

Before becoming a Long Term volunteer with ATCV, Susan Gray joined WWOOF Australia and worked on several farms on a work-for-keep basis.

They are all growing food organically and usually in beautiful countryside. Most are very keen to show you around and show off their home region to you. The work was as hard as you wanted it to be, but about four hours of work were expected. I usually did more as I enjoyed it, and I learned a lot from those experiences.

Interesting research projects take place throughout Australia and some may be willing to include unpaid staff looking for work experience. For example a research station in northern Queensland operated by the Australian Tropical Research Foundation (PMB 5, Cape Tribulation, Qld 4873; 07-4098 0063; www.austrop.org.au) welcomes 50 volunteers a year to carry out all sorts of tasks to conserve the rainforest. Volunteers are asked to pay \$70 a week to cover their food and accommodation. It might be worth trying the *Heron Island Research Station* (Great Barrier Reef, via Gladstone, Qld 4680; www.uq.edu.au/hirs/home.htm) which has been known to offer free accommodation in exchange for about four hours of work a day.

The Australian Institute of Marine Science (AIMS) at Cape Ferguson near Townsville (07-4753 4409; visitor_coord@aims.gov.au/ www.aims.gov.au) runs a Prospective Visitors Scheme which encompasses volunteers; applicants with their own research projects or a scuba diving certificate are especially welcome. Application must be done on-line. If successful, a letter of invitation from AIMS can be used to apply for the appropriate visa.

Often the state conservation organisation organises a voluntary programme, as is the case in Western Australia with the Conservation & Land Management Department of CALM (www.calm.wa.gov.au). The programme is open to anyone though it can't provide accommodation in remote places; write to the Volunteer Co-ordinator at CALM for details (Locked Bag 104, Bentley Delivery Centre, WA 6893; 08-9334 0251). For people with a conservation background or relevant skills, CALM also runs an Educational Work Experience Programme, though none of the positions involves working with wildlife.

FRUIT PICKING

In the rich agricultural land between the coastal ribbon of urban development and the outback, a multitude of crops is grown: grapes around Adelaide and in the Hunter Valley of New South Wales, tropical fruit on the Queensland coast and north of Perth, apples in the southwest part of Western Australia and in Tasmania, etc. Although fruit farms may be more fertile than the outback, the same considerations as to isolation, heat and dangers from the fauna hold true. The standard hours for a fruit picker working in the heat are approximately 6am-6pm with two or three hours off in the middle of the day.

During certain harvests, the farmers are desperate for labour and put out appeals over the radio and on the notice boards of backpackers' hostels. On one Queensland farm where Mary Anne Mackle from Northern Ireland worked, the farmer had to bring in a team of prisoners to finish off the cucumber harvest since there was such a shortage of pickers. Just as in Europe and North America, there are professional pickers who follow the harvests around the continent, though it may be possible to spend seven or eight months in one region such as the valley of the Murray River. So if you find yourself falling behind your fellow-workers during the first few days of the harvest, you should console yourself that you are competing with years of experience.

Anyone who is serious about earning their way over a long period by fruit picking should consider obtaining the small format specialist booklet *Fruit Picking around Australia* which is available for £6 from Pickpack, 114 Hazelton Way, Waterlooville, Hants. PO8 9DW (cheques payable to R. Wedd), or in Australia for A$10 from Pickpack (11 Coral St, Saunders Beach, Queensland 4818; payable to L. Hutchinson) or from campsites and bookshops in the relevant areas. Details can be found on www.cix.co.uk/~yama.fruit.

Employment National publishes a useful little 'Harvest Table' which is free, though it is by no means comprehensive. These lists are posted on the internet (http://matilda.aaa.com.au/Fruit_Picking). Employment National encourage working holidaymakers to contact their specialist fruit and crop-picking department on 1300 720126 or of course to call in at any employment office.

Harvest seasons are often diverse: crops ripen first in Queensland and finish in Tasmania as you move further away from the equator. Even the two major grape harvests take place consecutively rather than simultaneously. For easy reference, we have included tables showing crops, regions and times of harvest (omitting grapes which appear on a separate chart) for the most important fruit-growing states of New South Wales, Victoria, South Australia, Western Australia and Queensland.

Quite often farmers will offer a shack or caravan for little or no money. Not all fruit farmers can supply accommodation, however, so serious job-seekers carry a tent. You should be able to buy a decent two-man tent for less than $100. On the other hand backpackers' hostels are never far away and in the main picking districts organise minibus transport between hostels and farms. Campervans are of course very versatile and comfortable but expensive to buy (a reliable second-hand van costs about $3,000 at the active secondhand markets in Cairns and Darwin for example) and expensive to run. One of the hop-on hop-off bus routes operated by the Adelaide-based Wayward Bus Co is called the Fruit Bowl, travelling between Sydney and Adelaide via vineyards and orchards for the benefit of fruit-pickers; schedules and fares from Wayward Bus (08-8232 6646/1800 882823; www.waywardbus.com.au).

Women on their own tend to encounter resistance among farmers (known as 'blockies'). Many of the growers are of Italian or Greek descent and the old Mediterranean sexism creeps in. Certain jobs such as cutting apricots and work in the shed generally are considered 'women's work' and with these jobs it is usually impossible to earn the big money. Louisa Fitzgerald was disgusted by the blatant discrimination:

> *I was all ready to go and pick fruit down in Victoria, but when I phoned the farm to check if work was still available and they discovered I was a girl intending to go alone, they said unless I was accompanied by a male, I couldn't pick fruit! It seems that under union rules, females are not allowed to*

lift over a certain weight which means that for fruit picking a man has to be with you to lift weights – typically chauvinist I'd say!

Mary Anne Mackle participated in a number of harvests during her working holiday and offers these tips to unsuspecting fruit pickers:
1. Although a car is not essential, it is often necessary in looking for work, and then getting to town to shop.
2. Be prepared for extremes of temperature. Although it may be in the 80s during the day, the nights are often very cold.
3. Don't expect any nightlife. A typical evening for us involved showering, washing dishes, making dinner, reading, writing and chatting with fellow fruit pickers.
4. Forget about vanity. You will stink at all times even after a shower. Your socks will never be the same again and your skin won't like the sunblock and build-up of dirt either.
5. Forget about modesty. Don't expect to have the use of toilet facilities out in the fields.
6. On an optimistic note, you will be a fitter person and, if things go well, a wealthier one too. You can then go off and take a dive course on the Great Barrier Reef, snorkel in Coral Bay, canoe down Katherine Gorge, get drunk in Darwin, hike in national parks, swim in waterfalls, until your money runs out and you start all over again.
Mary Anne's conclusion is that harvesting is certainly preferable to packing videos in a warehouse in Sydney or selling hotdogs for $8 an hour.

The Grape Harvest

Australian wines have made a startling impact on the rest of the world as the volume, quality and consumption increases each year. Regardless of their quality, the important fact for itinerant workers is that there is a large quantity of grapes to be picked (by women as well as men).

The main centres for grape-picking are the Mildura region of Victoria, the Riverland of South Australia (between Renmark and Waikerie) and the Hunter Valley of New South Wales (around Pokolbin and Muswellbrook), though they are grown in every state including Tasmania. Detailed tables are set out below. The harvests usually get under way some time in February and last through March or into April. Earnings can be impressive: Raymond Oliver from Co. Durham made $2,200 during the five or six week harvest near Mildura.

Many grape varieties are grown in Australia and all demand different styles of picking which (like any fruit-picking) take some time to master before you can earn the big money. The amount you can earn depends on the condition of the vines, the type of grape, whether you have tough enough hands to pull the grapes off (which is much faster than cutting with a knife or snips), whether you have a hard-working partner (which is faster and less demoralising than picking on your own), how fit you are and of course how competitive (or desperate for money) you are.

Normally they start with sultanas and currants moving through different grape types as the wineries demand. Picking for a winery is easiest; it doesn't matter too much if the grapes are squashed or there are a few leaves left in (a blockie would have a fit if he read that). Picking for drying means the grapes shouldn't be squashed and picking for market (i.e. table grapes) demands extreme care and is usually paid as wages or at a higher rate per box.

You will be paid by tin, by bucket (25% more) or by weight. The fairest way to pick is by weight. The idea that you can pick as long as you want or take a break in the afternoon is a misconception. The only time you are likely to get a break in the afternoon is when it is too hot to leave the grapes out in the sun. Around Perth it might be $36^{\circ}C$ ($97^{\circ}F$) which can be a determining factor when you are deciding whether or not to persevere with the work. Pickers often resort to hosing each other down before they can face the afternoon.

Certainly the demand for pickers is intense in many regions. After deciding that the Sydney employment scene was unremittingly grim, Henry Pearce phoned some job centres in mid-February and decided that Griffith in New South Wales was the best bet. When he arrived, he was delighted to see that the job board was full of grape-picking jobs. He was hustled into the harvest office, allocated to a farmer and driven to a farm in the region, where he began work the next morning. It paid the going rate of 60-70 cents a bucket and by working ten hours a day, he could manage 90 buckets.

Grape Harvests

South Australia	Dates of Harvest
Clare-Watervale	Feb-Apr
Barossa Valley	Feb-Apr
Adelaide and Southern Vales	Feb-Mar
Coonawarra	Feb-Apr
Langhorne Creek	Feb-Apr
Riverland (Waikerie, Berri, Loxton, Renmark)	Feb-Apr
New South Wales	
Orchard Hills	late Jan-mid March
Camden	early Feb-mid March
Wedderburn	mid Feb-mid March
Nolong	late Feb-April
Orange	March-April
Mudgee	late Feb-April
Hunter Valley (Pokolbin, Bulga, Denman, Broke, Muswellbrook)	early Feb-March
Murrumbidgee Irrigation area (Griffith, Leeton)	mid Feb-Mar
Dareton	Jan-April
Curlwaa	Mar-April
Buronga	Feb-June
Mid-Murray (Koraleigh, Goodnight)	late Feb-April
Corowa	Feb-Mar
Victoria	
Goulburn Valley	Feb-Mar
Swan Hill	Feb-Mar
Lilydale	Feb-Mar
Mildura/Robinvale	Feb-Mar
Great Western-Avoca	Feb-Mar
Drumborg	Feb-Mar
Glenrowan-Milawa	Feb-Mar
Rutherglen	Feb-Mar
Western Australia	
Swan Valley (near Perth)	Feb-Apr
Margaret River	Feb-Apr
Mount Barker	Feb-Apr

Across the River Murray the situation is the same around Mildura in Victoria, the grape capital of the area. Armin Birrer reported from the town of Cardross that, despite high local unemployment, 300 picking jobs were advertised in the local papers and on roadside signs. This is the area to which the EN in Melbourne is most likely to send you if you arrive in January/February. Although Caroline Perry had to wait for a month, she was eventually sent to work for an Italian grape-grower:

The owner met us at the bus station as promised and took us to our accommodation on the farm. We were dumbfounded when we saw where we had to live: it was worse than a shed with rats and cockroaches. The dunny was a tin shed with no lights and so we worried about redback spiders.

It was very tough work, which killed your back and arms before you got used to it. We could work whatever hours we liked, but because we needed the money we worked from 7am-7pm, seven days a week. We usually managed 150-200 buckets a day which isn't bad since the crop was poor that year and we were inexperienced. We were paid a very low 38 cents a bucket.

After describing all these privations Caroline goes on to say that they had a good time and that the employer (Joe Blefari) treated them well. If you plan to be in the area looking for summer work, contact Mr. Blefari (PO Box 152, Nichol's Point, Vic 3501; 03-5021 2671). He is well connected with local farmers and so if he is full will know who may need pickers.

Grape-picking isn't for everyone but most seem to enjoy the experience. Usually a degree of camaraderie develops between pickers and blockies and hassles about weights, buckets, etc. are more in the nature of a game. If you are lucky enough to find a friendly employer, there may even be an end-of-harvest party or barbecue.

Related employment includes grape trimming and grape packing, both of which were done by Alison Cooper in Robinvale southeast of Mildura:

The exciting job of grape trimming involves standing at a conveyor belt all day, trimming the bad grapes off bunches. I soon got 'promoted' to grape packing whereby I had to stand at the end of the conveyor belt being bombarded by thousands of grapes which I then had to pack nicely into boxes. At first I thought there was no way I could do this job as I'd die from boredom first, but I managed to stick it out for the season and saved $2,500.

The Apple Harvest

Although apple-picking is notoriously slow going for the beginner, you can usually pick up enough speed within a few days to make it rewarding. In harvests where the conditions seem at the outset to be unattractive, it is not hard to get work especially when it is the time of year (normally February to May) when students return to college and the weather is getting colder.

Many travellers flock to the Western Australian harvest that takes place around Donnybrook, Manjimup and Pemberton. Hourly wages are generally reasonable. The manager of Brook Lodge Backpacker Accommodation (PO Box 75, Donnybrook, WA 6239; 08-9731 1520; brooklodge@iinet.net.au) operates a list system which farmers in the area contact for seasonal pickers, throughout the year but especially between November and May, with the peak of the apple harvest falling in the summer. It can take between a couple of hours and seven to ten days to find work locally, depending on the time of year. The season starts in November with thinning out the immature apples and plums and progresses to stone fruit picking December to March, though apple picking carries on until July. Other crops are grown in the vicinity such as tomatoes (picked January to March) and pears (February to April). During the picking season, a contract rate is the norm, ranging from $300 to $500 for a six-day week. Otherwise a straight hourly wage is paid of $10-$12. Transport to work is arranged by Brook Lodge.

A number of hostels in the area help guests to find seasonal fruit-picking work at most times of the year like the YHA in Pemberton and the Tobacco Park Hostel in Manjimup. Immigration raids take place at least once a year in this area, but farmers continue to employ foreign holidaymakers who have a tax file number. The hostel-cum-caravan park is the most popular place for apple pickers to stay between March and June (08-9771 1575).

Climatic conditions will determine what else you take in addition to a long novel to keep you amused until work materialises. High summer temperatures mean that you will need to take water, sunblock and a brimmed hat into the orchards. Later on warm clothes will come in handy as Armin Birrer discovered one chilly autumn:

The only problem with the south of WA is that the wet season starts in May which lasts till August. And as the season progresses it gets colder and colder and more and more miserable. It's very hard work when you get wet and cold every day, and the trees give you a nice shower when they're wet. I had to buy a heater for my van mostly for drying wet clothes.

Mary Anne Mackle spent six weeks picking in Manjimup and found that being paid by the bin was a great motivator to work long hard hours. She and her companion started on a meagre three bins a day but by the end they were filling 16 a day, which shows what a difference some practice can make. By the time she finished, her clothes were in shreds and her body not far behind but she had saved $2,000.

Tasmania is not known as the 'Apple Island' for its shape alone. The harvest takes place between February and early May, though other fruit harvests start at the beginning of the summer. The work is available in the Huon region around Cygnet and Geeveston not far south of Hobart. Fruit pickers can find out about possibilities from the EN in Hobart at 175 Collins St (03-6220 5774) and obtain their tax file number there before going out to the rural areas. Like many before him, Robert Abblett recommends the YHA hostel 'Balfes Hill,' Main Road & Sandhill Road, Cradoc 7109 (03-6295 1551):

As the main accommodation in the area, the hostel finds work for guests and provides transport too. I spent two months working hard for several different orchards, as the crop was intermittent. With previous experience, I saved £1,000. I was put with 20 other strange people for the whole season. The owners (bless 'em) thought I would have a calming influence on them because of my age. No chance.

With years of experience of picking fruit throughout Europe and in other states of Australia, Andrea Militello was as enthusiastic about Tasmania as any place. He spent the month of March picking apples in Cygnet: 'wonderful place, great boss, small trees and big apples so you can get good good money.' The area also offers work picking berry fruit and cherries from November to April.

In February/March 2000 Rob Abblett was the only foreigner picking apples at his orchard on the Mornington Peninsula in Victoria. He was delighted to be earning a good hourly wage ($11.95 gross) and not piece work rates plus having free accommodation and the use of a ute for shopping.

Apple orchards also need to be thinned and pruned from mid-December before the picking starts. One of the most famous places for this work is Batlow NSW, near the Snowy Mountains where there are about 80 orchards. After thinning, there is about a month's gap before the picking starts in March. Ken Smith is just one traveller to have contacted the employment office in nearby Tumut to secure a job before travelling to the area. Pay and conditions are good in Batlow, better than in Griffith and Young (see section below on New South Wales Harvests). Many working travellers stay at the Batlow Caravan Park, Kurrajong Avenue, Batlow, NSW; 02-6949 1444. Bridgid Seymour-East provided the following list of potential employers:

Springfield Orchard – 02-6949 1021
Mouats Farm – 02-6949 1519
Wilgro Orchard – 02-6949 1224
Mayday View Orchard – 02-6949 1144

Other possibilities include working in the packing sheds and cannery which operate all year round. Mountain Maid Cannery (02-6949 1300) and Batlow Fruit Co-op Ltd (02-6949 1408) normally hire locals, but might be worth trying.

OTHER HARVESTS

From asparagus to zucchini there is an abundance of crops to be picked from one end of Australia to the other, and the energetic itinerant picker can do very nicely. Australia has such an enormous agricultural economy that there will always be jobs. Gordon Mitchell from Aberdeen is just one Briton who has worked out a profitable route:

I've been picking fruit in Australia for a few years. I make the best money between November and April/May, starting at Young NSW picking cherries. When they finish I do the smaller cherry harvest in Orange NSW, then on to

Shepparton Victoria in early January for the pear picking. When the sultanas start in Mildura in early February I do them, though most people stay in Shepparton to finish the pears and apples. This takes me to early or mid-March when the apples start in Orange and finish in late April or early May. Sometimes it's very hectic but that's when the picking is good.

Tobacco and Hops

There are two major areas of tobacco growing: the Atherton Tablelands in northern Queensland and around Myrtleford in the interior of Victoria. The 20 degrees in latitude which separate these two harvests mean that they take place at completely different times. The Queensland harvest goes from late September/early October till Christmas, while the Victorian harvest lasts from late January to March.

The places to head for in Queensland for tobacco work are Mareeba, Dimbulah and Chillagoe. Emma Dunnage from Cardiff worked in Mareeba for six weeks and was paid an hour wage. She warns that tobacco picking is only for the thick-skinned, literally as well as figuratively:

Beware. The tobacco plant and the chemicals they put on them are not at all good for your health. The nicotine eats your skin especially your cuticles. I'd like to warn any would-be female tobacco pickers: you have really got to be tough. After the farmer told us we had the job he asked us for sex for more pay. We made it completely clear that if he was going to harass us, we would leave right there and then. He said sorry, but he thought all 'pommie sheilas' would do it.

A less serious problem was the irregularity of the work. The tobacco does not ripen evenly and the harvesting machinery often breaks down.

Despite the enormous quantities of beer consumed in Australia, most of the hops are produced in a few areas of Tasmania, around New Norfolk inland from Hobart, around Scottsdale and in the Devonport area. Jayne Nash helped with the hop harvest near Scottsdale in northeast Tasmania from mid-March to early April, which is as long as the harvest lasts. She worked in the shed on a hop stripping machine (where most of the women were employed) while others worked on tractors. Most of their co-workers were locals of all ages who seemed to get by just working on the hops followed by the apples each year.

Queensland

As you travel north the produce, like the weather, gets more tropical so that citrus, pineapples, bananas and mangoes grow in profusion in the north, while stone fruits, apples and potatoes grow in the Darling Downs, 220km inland from Brisbane. In the tropics there are not always definite harvest seasons since crops grow year round. A good clue to the available work can be deduced from the excessively large artificial fruits by the roadside, for example the big pineapple near Nambour.

The prying eyes of immigration are everywhere along the Queensland coast and anyone whose papers are not in order must be careful. From time to time the Immigration Department co-ordinates early morning raids on farms from Bundaberg in the south to Tully in the north, which catch and deport illegal fruit pickers.

Work in the Queensland harvests is strongly monopolised by the hostels. Farmers for the most part rely on hostel wardens to supply them with a workforce, making it hard to fix up a job directly with a farmer and accommodation on farms is rare. Shuttle transport between hostel and farms is often laid on. Make sure you get paid a decent wage and pay a fair price for your transport and accommodation.

About 400km north of Brisbane, the agricultural and rum-producing centre of Bundaberg absorbs a great many travelling workers. All the hostels in town advertise help with employment including Federal Backpackers (07-4153 3711) and City Centre Backpackers (07-4151 3501) both on Bourbong St. The Nomads hostel at 64 Barolin St (0741 516097) calls itself a Workers & Diving Hostel. Bundaberg is such a magnet for working travellers that it is often bursting at the seams. Bridgid Seymour-East was not impressed with the scene:

There are too many hostels and too few jobs to go around. Hostels take about 100 people each so lots of desperate people all together. Most people get only one or two days of work a week, just enough to pay for their hostel bed and food. You cannot choose your jobs and if you quit or get fired they might not give you a job for another week.

The town of Childers is the centre of a harvesting area, though since the tragic fire in June 2000 that killed 15 backpackers at the Childer's Palace Backpackers (a hostel that was used almost exclusively by workers), it has lost much of its appeal. The best paying job in the area is sugarcane planting at $12 an hour; the two main employers are named Vella and Russo. Bridgid Seymour-East and her boyfriend managed to save $3,500 in six weeks.

The town of Bowen, centre of a fruit and vegetable-growing region (especially tomatoes) 600km south of Cairns, is another very well known destination for aspiring pickers. Julian Graham spent part of his working holiday in Australia as manager of Barnacles Backpackers in Bowen, which sounds an excellent place to find out about work:

Part of my duties consisted of finding work for travellers at the many local farms. All sorts of picking and packing is available and Bowen is a superb place to recover considerable funds. My girlfriend and I arrived broke and left with enough money to fly to Tasmania for the Sydney-Hobart race and finance a month's travelling in Tas. Anyone arriving in Bowen should do themselves a favour and go straight to Barnacles where they will find you work (May-December) and make you more welcome than anywhere else in the town by a large margin.

More recently, Alison Cooper's preferred working hostel in Bowen was Trinity's which kept her busy for three weeks working for local farmers. In fact all the hostels in Bowen cater for working travellers.

Picking and packing work is normally paid hourly – $11-$12 for men and (in sexist Queensland) $10 or $11 for women. It is possible to make more with contract picking especially if you are experienced. At a rate of $1 a bucket, a professional tomato picker can earn up to $350 a day, but even inexperienced pickers can hit $100. A good time to arrive is the end of August. If the backpackers' hostels in Bowen are full, accommodation is limited so having a tent is an advantage.

The farmers usually provide a minibus once the picking really gets going, which costs a couple of dollars from Bowen. Otherwise a bicycle would be handy. If you're job-hunting farm-to-farm, go out on the Bootooloo or Collinsville Roads or to the Delta or Euri Creek areas. Some names provided by Stephen Psallidas (who saved $5,000 in less than six months) are Wright, Price, Fisher, Morgan, Todd, Collyer and Eatough. Apparently the tail end of the harvest in November can be a good time to show up, when lots of seasonal workers are beginning to drift south. If the farmers are desperate enough, they pay premium rates, sometimes even double.

Caroline Perry got off the harvest-workers' minibus at the last stop called Climate Capital Packers (Collinsville Road, Bowen, Qld 4805; or PO Box 908, Bowen 4805; 07-4785 2622). This is a packing and freezing shed for four of the largest farms in the area, mainly capsicum and rock melons. While they do not guarantee work to backpackers, they do regularly employ them (with working holiday visas). Caroline's job earned her $3,274 net in two and a half months. In the busy season (between May and November packers can earn $500 a week. At other times, hours are shorter and therefore earnings are less. Weekly pay cheques are paid directly into a bank account (Caroline recommends the ANZ Bank.)

Heading north, vegetables are picked around Ayr south of Townsville between June and September. Mary Anne Mackle recommends staying at the Silverlink Caravan Park in Ayr, whose owners gave her a list of farmers and where all new arrivals looking for work found it within a couple of days, picking squash, zucchini, cucumbers, peppers, pumpkins and rock melons. Apparently locals prefer to work on the better paid sugar cane harvest which takes place over the same period. Frank Schiller saved a cool $1,400 after four weeks of capsicum-picking near Ayr. Among their recreations, the pickers went dancing in Ayr 'where they've got both kinds of music – Country and Western.'

Further north, Cardwell, Innisfail and Tully offer work in banana and sometimes sugar plantations. Farmers around Tully (the wettest place in Australia) organise transport between town and the properties. Try asking in the Bilyana hostel just south of Tully or at Banana Barracks at 21 Richardson St (07-4068 0455). Henry Pearce describes his gruelling job as a banana cutter in October:

The bananas all grew together on a single stem which could weigh up to 60kg. The farmer cut into the trunk to weaken it and, once I had pulled the fruit down onto my shoulder, he cut the stem and I staggered off to place them on a 'nearby' trailer. The work was physically shattering and the presence of large frogs and rats inside the bunch (thankfully no snakes) jumping out at the last minute didn't do anything to increase my enjoyment. We were paid $8 an hour and worked an eight hour day, five days a week which was standard for the area.

Working with Queensland fruits seems to be an activity fraught with danger. If you decide to pick pineapples, you have to wear long-sleeved shirts and jeans (despite the sizzling heat between January and April) as protection from the prickles and spines. Caroline Perry advises anyone who packs rock melons to wear gloves; otherwise the abrasive skin rips your hands to shreds. Worst of all apparently is that lovely fruit, the mango, as Julian Graham explains:

One in three pickers is allergic to the sap contained in mangoes, and in some cases contact with the fruit produces an extreme reaction. Having sent pickers out to the fields and seen at first hand the state they come back in I feel duty-bound to warn people that they may be that unfortunate one in three. One girl's face and limbs became so swollen she had to fly home where it took several injections of steroids to cure her. Remarkably, the hospital at Bowen proved completely incompetent in dealing with this problem and offered no remedy at all. Having spoken to many farmers, it became evident that if the sap squirts into your eyes, serious damage can occur.

Still, if you don't react badly, mango picking can be less strenuous than other harvests since the mangoes are picked off the ground after the trees have been shaken. Whereas the four-week mango harvest around Bowen starts in November, the harvest in the Atherton Tablelands (around Mareeba) starts in early to mid-December.

Southern Queensland is also a good destination. Head for Stanthorpe almost on the NSW border in November for peach and pear picking and January/February for tomato picking. Summit Lodge Backpackers (07-4683 5157) and Stanthorpe Backpackers (07-4681 8888) are good sources of job information and transport. Just after the new year Jane Harris and her friend Pete drove to Stanthorpe. During their first day of driving farm to farm and asking for work, they were hired as tomato pickers:

We spent the hardest day of our lives picking egg tomatoes. By the end of the day neither of us could stand up straight without feeling pain. So, we decided picking wasn't for us and left. Short of money, we later decided to give the place another go, knowing that the employment office was about to open for harvest work. This time was a lot more successful, sorting tomatoes for me and 'bucketing' for Pete. Bucketing means carrying empty buckets to the pickers and taking the full ones away to be sorted. When Pete told the farmer he wasn't sure he could keep it up, as the farmer employed the fastest tomato picker in Australia who was picking well over 350 buckets a day, surprise surprise, the farmer said he'd give him some easier work.

Everything was going well until the immigration raid described by Jane earlier in this chapter.

Potatoes and onions are harvested in the Lockyer Valley in the Darling Downs. The harvest around Gatton lasts from August to November, although problems caused by the increasing saltiness of the soil have been cutting yields. Head for the Tenthill Caravan Park (M.S. 149, Mount Sylvia Road, Tenthill, Qld 4343; 07-5462 7200) near Gatton where it costs $35-$40 per week to pitch a tent or $80 (plus a bond) for a caravan, and where the owner knows about local opportunities. In most cases you will have to have your own transport. Potato and onion picking is paid piece work, from $18 a bin. If you start at sunrise it is possible for a dedicated novice to pick six bins by noon, though many travellers find this work too hard to tolerate. Contract jobs with local growers of lettuce, etc. are also available but will probably pay no more than $10 an hour.

New South Wales

The southern part of the state around Wagga Wagga is known is the Riverina. The Riverina Regional Tourist Board produces a very handy little booklet called 'Working Holidays' which you can pick up from hostels or request by phone (02-6921 6422/6993 2190). (It will not be reprinted now that the information is available on the internet.) The chart of seasonal work opportunities covers the towns mentioned here (Batlow, Jugiong, Leeton. Young) as well as others (Darlington Point, Gundagai, Hay, etc.). Employment National offices in Griffith, Leeton, Wagga Wagga and Young can all assist.

The asparagus harvest at Jugiong on the Hume Highway northwest of Canberra attracts many seasonal pickers, as does the cherry harvest around Young half an hour north of Jugiong which starts as the asparagus finishes. Try for example Powers Asparagus Packing Shed, 2726 Jugiong (02-6945 4239; www.wirrilla.com.au). The packing season is a long one from about late September to at least mid-November. The work is notoriously back-breaking but can be lucrative, as much as $500 a week net.

Conflicting accounts of the cherry harvest near Young between mid-November and Christmas have been received. Whereas some recommend its money-making potential and good camp atmosphere, others advise steering clear and say that the magic figure of $100 a day in earnings is exaggerated. The unpredictable weather and piece work pay rates make it difficult to make good money. Mary Anne Mackle thought it the worst job she did in Australia (while admitting that it was her first harvesting job). She had her hands cut to ribbons trying to avoid picking the buds along with the fruit and was terrorised by bull ants which swarmed in the branches; for all this she earned $300 a week. No wonder work is so easy to obtain here. When Geertje Korf turned up at the employment office in Young, not only did a helpful member of staff find her a friendly orchard with cooking facilities, but drove her to the farm personally.

The cotton harvest in the extreme north of New South Wales needs workers from the first week of November and advertises in Sydney to attract them. The Tandarra Caravan Park in Trangie (02-6888 7176) advertises job vacancies in the area November to May. Richard Edwards discovered that the possibilities for cotton workers around Wee Waa were extensive year-round but especially in October/November which is the cotton-chipping season. Richard earned $600 a week.

Of all the many picking jobs that Henry Pearce found, the best money was earned working on onions around Griffith, where he and his girlfriend saved an impressive $5,000 in ten weeks between early January and March. For a short time Henry was paid $11 a bin and could manage 17 bins a day, alongside a clan of Turks who return every year. However, mostly he was paid the agreed daily rate (however many hours he worked) but the reliability of work made up for the low pay. You have to be lucky to find work in this harvest particularly if you don't have your own transport. Ask at all the onion-packing sheds in Griffith.

Leeton near Griffith is the centre of a citrus-growing area where Vince Crombez from Belgium headed as soon as he arrived in Australia in December. He earned $14 per bin of oranges but could pick only one every two hours because the harvest was a poor one. Ask at the campsite (where an on-site van will cost a pair of people about $100 a week).

Victoria

The summer fruit harvests in northern Victoria annually attract many participants on working holidays. The best time to arrive is mid to late January and work should continue until the end of March. On arrival in Australia contact should be made with the Northern Victoria Fruitgrowers' Association Ltd, PO Box 394, Shepparton 3632 (21 Nixon St, Shepparton; 03-5821 5844; nvfa@mcmedia.com.au), with the Victorian

Peach and Apricot Growers' Association, PO Box 39, Cobram 3644 (30A Bank St, Cobram; 03-5872 1729/fax 5871 1612) or Employment National (361 Wyndham St, Shepparton; 03-5832 0300). Send an IRC for the information leaflet 'Guide to your Working Holiday'. Victorian farmers are noted for providing accommodation more often than elsewhere, though anyone with camping gear will be placed more easily. Once again, some people make a killing while others complain of pathetic earnings. Whereas Vince Crombez earned $80 in six hours picking pears, Alison Cooper made $25 in nine hours.

Mooroopna is just outside Shepparton and is a good place to look for work. Ask in the pub about tomato-picking possibilities in February and March. You might want to buy a second-hand bicycle from the shop on the main street of Shepparton to get around the area. M'camish Bros. in Mooroopna are big growers of apricots, peaches and pears which are picked between January and April.

In the northwestern corner of the state, Mildura (mentioned above as a centre for grape-growing) is a major agricultural district and Cardross across the river is also a promising destination. Work is available virtually year-round (May is the slowest month) due to the sunny climate and epic irrigation schemes. Contact the employment agency MADEC (03-5021 3359). A high proportion of the travellers staying in Mildura's hostels take advantage of the job-finding and transport-providing services of places like the Riverboat Bungalow (27 Chaffey Avenue; 03-5021 5315) or Mildura International Backpackers (95 Cedar Ave; tel/fax 5021 0133; mildrabp@ vic.ozland.net.au) where the majority of guests are working or looking for work. Jane Inckle took advantage of the job-finding and transport-providing services of Mildura Backpackers where 90% of the guests were there because they were working:

> *The managers arrange work for everyone; consequently you're less likely to get dodgy deals, which is especially good for female travellers who, incidentally, are preferred for packing, sorting and grafting work. At the moment (spring) we've been planting vines, picking citrus fruit, packing asparagus. Rock melons start soon for good money, so I'm told. The place is a magnet for international working holidaymakers, with Poms a little thinn on the ground, which makes a pleasant change.*

Work is also available nearer Melbourne for example at the nurseries in the Dandenong Ranges (all year round) and fruit picking in November/December. Emerald Backpackers Hostel (PO Box 183, Lake View Court, Emerald, Vic 3782; 03-5968 4086) one hour east of Melbourne is renowned for finding work year-round in local nurseries. Robert Abblett stayed here while working for a cut flower grower in the winter (July/August). He spent each day bent double collecting bunches of hyacinths and tulips but was well rewarded, saving £800 in six weeks. Most of the other people in the hostel (including, for obvious reasons, many Dutch people) were also working in nurseries and factories, and using the transport provided to the farms.

Although harvesting work is often not hard to *get*, some find it hard to make any money. The pear crates may look quite small at the outset but will soon seem unfillable with mysterious false bottoms. Many eager first-timers do not realise how hard the work will be physically, and give up before their bodies acclimatise. But you should have faith that your speed will increase fairly rapidly.

South Australia

The Riverland region of South Australia (not to be confused with the Riverina in NSW) consists of Renmark, Loxton and Waikerie but is centred on Berri where most of the backpacker accommodation and job agencies like Select and Rivskills are located. The last five years have seen work available all year round due to the expansion of the wine and citrus industries. Berri Backpackers (Box 203, Berri, SA 5343; 08-8582 3144) gets rave reviews from Bridgid Seymour-East:

> *What can we say except amazing. It is the best hostel we have ever had the pleasure of staying in, let alone using as our work base. The Norwegian owner Wiggo Hernes runs the hostel on an honesty policy. The Saturday night BBQ is a highlight for $5 and worth triple that. As far as work is concerned*

it's a bit of a free for all. Whoever answers the phone first gets a job first, which can seem a bit daunting at first (survival of the fittest). We started on citrus picking for a big company Yandilla Park. Whilst the contract rate is high, you don't get that many hours in the long run because you can't pick citrus until the fruit is dry on the tree. Often you can't start picking until 11am or 12 noon which can be very frustrating. But it gives you enough money to survive until the vine work begins. At the end of June I got a job cutting canes which involves taking a cutting from the grape vines, trimming it to size and bundling it in bunches of 100. Whilst extremely boring, I never made less than $120 a day after tax and on good days $200, so I was getting pay cheques of $800-$900 a week.

The much-praised Wiggo wrote to reiterate the easy availability of work in the area. The average stay at Berri Backpackers is four months. The biggest employers in the area are:

Angas Park – Apricots and peaches are picked December to April. Men only. 7 days a week, 10 hours a day. Extra money paid at weekends. No days off (or you're fired).

Simarloo – Apricots and plums picked December to March. Contract work (i.e. per bin).

Solora – Citrus work winter and early summer. Untrained pickers take at least a week to get the hang of it.

In addition to these big companies, there are at least 1,000 small family blocks which need helpers. Other accommodation for pickers is available on campsites.

Western Australia

The area around Donnybrook is not just good for apple-picking as described earlier. Sara Runnalls picked grapes in January 2000 for $2.50 a bin before moving on to work in a nursery for five weeks planting gum seedlings. Vegetables are extensively grown in this area creating jobs in the fields and packing sheds. Armin Birrer packed onions around Manjimup just long enough to remind himself how much he dislikes indoor work, especially in dusty and smelly conditions. Cauliflower picking work is available in winter to those who can stand the freezing conditions. More appealing because warmer is the orange harvest around Harvey (north of Bunbury) which starts in June. Leads on work in this area might be available before you leave Perth from Travelworks, Suite 26, 158 William St (08-9226 2404) opposite the railway station. The $15 registration fee gives you a phone card and internet time for tracking down a job.

There are over 100 vegetable and banana plantations around the cities of Geraldton and Carnarvon north of Perth, many of which are very short of pickers in the winter when they are busy supplying the markets of Perth. The tomato harvest lasts from early August until mid-November, with the month of September being the easiest time to find work. The banana harvest starts in October, but there is casual work available anytime between April and November, most of which pays $8-9 an hour. This is such a well known area for casual workers that immigration raids are not unknown. One way of meeting farmers is to go to the warehouses or packing depots where growers come to drop off their produce.

Agricultural development around Kununurra in the extreme north of the state is extensive, and every traveller passing through seems to stop to consider the possibility of working in the banana, melon or vegetable harvests. Travellers are regularly hired during the first part of 'The Dry' (the dry season lasts from May to July). If you can't fix up work through the Youth Hostel or the Backpackers Resort hostel, contact Ord River Bananas (212 Riverfarm Rd; 08-9168 1481), Bonza Bananas (Packsaddle Plains Road; 018 938 231) and Oasis Bananas (Lot 386, 1 Packsaddle Road; 08-9168 2068).

There is a lot more work for men in Kununurra than for women, especially picking melons and bananas. Packing jobs are usually in shorter supply and are therefore quickly snapped up. You can also try to find work 'topping' or detassling corn, which may take place in temperatures of 35°C. To exacerbate the suffering of an 11 hour day, the corn gives pickers a rash on their arms and legs.

Crop	New South Wales	Dates of Harvest
Strawberries	Glenorie & Campbelltown	Sep-Dec
Cherries	Orange	Nov-Jan
	Young	Oct-Dec
Peaches &	Glenorie	Oct-Jan
Nectarines	Campbelltown	Nov-Jan
	Orange	Feb-Mar
	Bathurst	Jan-Mar
	Leeton & Griffith, Forbes	Feb-Apr
	Young	Feb-Mar
Plums	Glenorie	Nov-Jan
	Orange	Jan-Mar
	Young	Jan-Mar
Apricots	Leeton & Griffith	Dec-Jan
	Kurrajong	Nov
Apples & Pears	Oakland, Glenorie &	Jan-Apr
	Bilpin	
	Armidale	Feb-May
	Orange	Feb-May
	Bathurst	Mar-May
	Forbes	Feb-Apr
	Batlow	Feb-May
	Griffith & Leeton	Jan-Apr
	Young	Mar-Apr
Oranges (Valencia)	Outer Sydney	Sep-Feb
	Riverina, Mid-Murray	Sep-Mar
	Narromine	Sep-Feb
	Leeton	Dec-Jan
Lemons	Outer Sydney, Riverina,	
	Mid-Murray, Coomealla	Jul-Oct
Grapefruits	Mid-Murray	Nov-Apr
	Curlwaa	Jun-Feb
Asparagus	Dubbo, Bathurst, Cowra, Jugiong	Sep-Dec
Wheat	Narrabri, Walgett	Nov-Dec
Cotton	Warren & Nevertire, Wee Waa	Nov-Mar
Onions	Griffith	Nov-Mar

Crop	Queensland	Dates of Harvest
Bananas	Tully	October
Tomatoes	Bowen	Aug-Nov
Peaches & Plums	Stanthorpe	Dec-Mar
Watermelons	Bundaberg	Nov-Dec
Potatoes	Lockyer Valley	Oct-Dec
Onions	Lockyer Valley	Sep-Oct
Pineapples	Nambour, Maryborough,	Jan-Apr
	Bundaberg, Yeppoon	
Apples	Stanthorpe	Feb-Mar
Citrus	Gayndah, Mundubbera	May-Sep
Strawberries	Redlands	Jul-Nov
Mangoes	Bowen	Nov-Dec
	Mareeba	Dec-Jan
Cucumbers, etc.	Ayr	May-Nov
Courgettes	Mackay	Aug-Sep

Crop	South Australia	Dates of Harvest
Apricots	Riverland (Waikerie, Barmera, Berri, Loxton, Renmark)	Dec-Jan
Peaches	Riverland	Jan-Feb
Pumpkins &	Riverland	May-Jul
Oranges	Riverland	Jun-Apr

Crop	Victoria	Dates of Harvest
Pears & Peaches	Shepparton, Ardmona, Mooroopna Kyabram Invergordon, Cobram	Jan-Mar
Tomatoes	Shepparton/Mooroopna, Tatura Kyabram Echuca, Tongala Rochester Swan Hill Elmore	Jan-Apr
Tobacco	Ovens & Kiewa Valley	Feb-Apr
Potatoes	Warragul, Neerim	Feb-May
Cherries	Silvan, Lilydale, Warburton, Lilydale	Nov-Dec
Berries	Silvan, Wandin, Monbulk, Macclesfield, Hoddles Creek, Daylesford	Nov-Feb
Apples & Pears	Myrtleford	Mar-May
	Goulburn Valley	Jan-Apr
	Mornington Peninsula	Mar-May
Flowers & Bulbs	Emerald	Jan-Dec

Crop	Western Australia	Dates of Harvest
Apples & Pears	Donnybrook, Manjimup, Balingup, Pemberton	Mar-Jun
Oranges	Bindoon, Lower Chittering Harvey	Aug-Sept Jun-Jul
Lemons & Grapefruit	Bindoon, Lower Chittering Harvey	Nov-Feb
Apricots, Peaches & Plums	Kalamunda, Walliston, Pickering Brook	Dec-Mar
Tomatoes, vegetables	Carnarvon, Geraldton	Aug-Nov
Bananas	Carnarvon	Oct
Melons, Bananas, etc.	Kununurra/Lake Argyle	May-Oct

INDUSTRY

Factory and cannery jobs are occasionally advertised in newspapers or you may hear about openings from other working travellers. City employment agencies like Drake Industrial are a good bet. Ken Smith took the unusual step of visiting factories in Sydney door-to-door:

> *There are huge industrial estates all over Sydney and really some of them have staff turnovers that are almost daily. My advice would be to get a 336 bus from Circular Quay, get off at Matraville or Botany Bay and just walk around the factories asking if they have any vacancies. Overall Sydney is a wonderfully cosmopolitan place. Of the 23 people who worked for the engineering firm I worked for, only three were Anglo-Australians. The rest were Indians, Fijians, Indians and Chinese.*

The wages can be very good for tedious jobs and even when they're not, the basic wage is often augmented with awards (compulsory bonuses), for example a 20% award for being a casual worker.

Mining

The mining industry of Australia does offer some opportunities to travellers, particularly to those with a background in catering. Whereas some people take a chance on fronting up in the mining towns of Western Australia (e.g. Dampier, Karratha, Port Hedland, Kalgoorlie) to look for work, others approach the head offices in Perth. Melanie Grey reported that she earned $600 a week working as a breakfast chef for a catering company on a nickel mine. She recommends tracking down the head office of catering companies in Perth, 'armed with references from home and a big cheesy smile'. The wages paid on mines are very high and in some cases are augmented by 'tropical loading' (if above the 26th parallel) or by 'remote zone allowance'. Most of the offices of sub-contracting companies are located in or near Newman House at 200 St George's Terrace.

Gold mining continues to flourish, and union membership is seldom a pre-requisite of employment. The gold mining town of Kalgoorlie in Western Australia is a place which past contributors have recommended for year-round employment, among them Lucy Slater:

> *I know everyone tells you not to hitch but we found that people who gave us lifts between Perth and Kalgoorlie were mines of information with ideas of companies to try, people to ask for, etc. Through a hitching contact my boyfriend got a job in the gold mines which paid $12 an hour. The work was hard going but the hours were long and so there was a lot of money to be made. There seemed to be quite a lot of work going, which did not surprise me since the place is a hellhole. The red dust gets everywhere, it's hot, loads of flies and is quite dead.*

Employment in survey and drilling is available, provided you make certain preparations. You must undergo a drugs test, a criminal record check with the police and take a half-day safety induction course which costs $120 from Marcsta (PO Box 4599, Kalgoorlie; 08-9091 9348). Once you have completed these steps, the accepted way of finding work in Kalgoorlie is to go around or phone all the relevant companies listed in the *Yellow Pages* or on the Access list of mines, drilling, surveying and lab companies. Exploration companies occasionally hire unskilled assistants (known as 'fieldies', 'TAs' or 'offsiders') who are sometimes sent into remote areas (like Norseman and Leonora at the end of the sealed road heading north) where pay is $500 per week in the hand plus free caravan or motel accommodation. Most people work nearer town and earn about $10 an hour, with weekend work being particularly lucrative. Some offsider work requires a truck driving licence, which is very easy to get, assuming you can afford the $200 fee for about three lessons and the test (see *Driving* below). Jeremy Pack describes his job:

> *As an offsider, I have been going off into the bush with a walkie talkie, axe, tape measure and stakes, while the boss stays behind his instrument making sure my pegs are in straight. Sometimes we camp out in the really nowhere bush.*

It is possible to find opals by 'noodling', i.e. sifting through the slag heaps around Coober Pedy. Anne Wakeford had a go and found seven opals in two days of careful searching, one of which was worth $100. Other recommended places are Mintabie and Andamooka, which are on Aboriginal land in remote South Australia, but can be visited after purchasing a permit for $5 from the police in Marla.

You might also find a job in areas related to mining. For example there is a firm called Analabs whose headquarters are at 50 Murray Road, Welshpool, WA 6106 (a suburb of Perth) which occasionally takes on temporary staff (08-9458 7999). The work involves the preparation of rock samples for chemical analysis, a job which is reported to be dirty and monotonous. Some laboratory work is occasionally available too. The pay is about $13 an hour. It is also worth trying others in this chain of laboratories, in Kalgoorlie, Adelaide, Townsville and Burnie (Tas).

Construction and Labouring

Darwin has always been a mecca for drifters, deportees and drop-outs looking for labouring work, though there are fewer job adverts in the Territory's papers than there once were. As the rains recede in May, the human deluge begins and competition for jobs is intense. It is better to be around at the end of the Wet (April) to fix something up beforehand.

If you do happen to get a building job in Australia, you may benefit from some of the interesting perks which the strong unions have negotiated. Workers on buildings over eight storeys high earn a height allowance, even if their work keeps them firmly on the ground. Try ringing furniture removal firms from the Sydney Yellow Pages, e.g. United and TransCity.

Tradesmen of all descriptions usually find it easy to get work in Australia, especially if they bring their papers and tools. Plumbers, electricians and carpenters have been having a field day, particularly of course in Sydney. A pair of steel-capped boots would also be a useful accessory.

Mechanics are in great demand as Brian Williams from Wales found when he toured the country. Potential employers in Sydney were not too bothered that he lacked a working holiday visa but they did want to have his British qualifications verified (which would have necessitated showing a work visa). So he and his partner and their three year old son headed up to Darwin where, through meeting someone in a pub, he was soon working in a bodyshop.

Driving and Vehicles

Several travellers have found it possible to get driving jobs after they have gone to the trouble of acquiring an Australian licence especially the 'B' class licence which permits you to drive trucks. Dan Ould wasn't worried about failing the test:

> *The test mainly involves driving a truck around the block while the examiner gazes out of the window. If you don't crash you've passed. But the process of taking a few lessons and the test will cost several hundred dollars, worth it in my view since it opens up lots of job opportunities.*

Dan liked Broome so much that he was tempted to investigate driving a taxi for Chinatown Taxis who seemed to have a chronic shortage of drivers. Later, in the South Australian town of Ceduna on the Nullarbor highway, he heard of more driving jobs, mainly because so many locals had lost their licences for drunk driving.

An ability to drive can be a handy asset in the cities too, since papers like the Melbourne *Age* are full of adverts for furniture removers, drivers and cab mates (called 'jockeys' in Victoria). Stephen Psallidas observed that there seemed to be more bicycle and motorcycle couriers in Sydney than cars, so you might investigate possibilities.

Buying and selling vehicles can also be profitable for anyone who understands engines. Mechanic Brian Williams and Adrienne Robinson bought three vehicles for touring the country and sold two at a profit:

> *We bought one van for $950 to sell but decided to keep it and moved on. It saw us good for 12,000km and we sold it for $1,500 to a dealer.*

Private enterprise does not always pay off like this, as Chris Miksovsky found in Brisbane. He tried his hand at being an intersection windscreen washer but was bluntly made to stop by the police after his second windscreen.

Another vehicle-related job is 'detailing cars.' Rhona Stannage met two English women in Darwin who had both found this job by asking at car garages and sales offices.

TOURISM AND CATERING

This category of employment might include anything from cooking on prawn trawlers out of Darwin (read the fine print), to acting as a temporary warden in a Tasmanian youth hostel. You might find yourself serving beer at a roadhouse along the nearly uninhabited road through the Australian north-west or serving at an eat-as-much-as-you-can Sizzlers salad bar in the big cities. Casual employees make up 60% of the

140,000 workforce employed in the hospitality industry.

Casual catering wages both in the cities and in remote areas are higher than the equivalent British wage. The casual rate for waiting staff is about $10 an hour, with weekend loadings of time and a half on Saturdays and time and three-quarters on Sundays and holidays. People being paid cash-in-hand may be offered $8 an hour, as Jane Harris was last year in Sydney. Although tipping was never practised in Australia, it is gradually becoming more common and waiting staff in trendy city establishments can expect to augment their basic wage to some extent.

Standards tend to be fairly high especially in popular tourist haunts. A common practice among restaurant bosses in popular places from Bondi Beach to the Sunshine Coast is to give a job-seeker an hour's trial or a trial shift and decide at the end whether or not to employ them. Stephen Psallidas was taken aback at when he approached a hospitality employment agency in Cairns:

> *I was in Cairns in April and thought I'd have little trouble getting work. But though I had a visa and experience I had no references, having worked as a waiter in Greece, where they wouldn't know a reference if one walked up and said 'Hi, I'm a reference', so I was doomed from the start. The agency told me that if I'd had references they could have given me work immediately. Curses.*

This year Sara Runnalls, a qualified chef, was more successful with her agency in Cairns who sent her to four and five star hotels in Cairns and Port Douglas. She enjoyed this, but not half as much as working as a chef at the Olympics where she served afternoon tea to Princess Anne.

Anyone with experience as a cook or chef will probably find themselves in demand all over Australia. One tourist area which is not normally inundated with backpacking job-seekers is the stretch of Victorian coast between Dromana and Portsea on the Mornington Peninsula near Melbourne. Although most jobs don't start until after Christmas, the best time to look is late November/early December.

If exploring Australia is your target rather than earning high wages, it is worth trying to exchange your labour for the chance to join an otherwise unaffordable tour. For example camping tour operators in Kakadu and Litchfield Park have been known to do this; try Northern Explorer or Billy Can Tours.

Australia has a number of external island territories including Christmas Island, the Coral Sea Islands and Cocos Islands all of which have a tourist industry. According to an article in the newspaper *Overseas Jobs Express*, employment possibilities exist on tiny Christmas Island (population 3,214) south of Java. Bars, restaurants and discos cater to the well-heeled tourists who come, mainly for the gambling. Trained croupiers and chefs are always in demand especially if they convince the resort company that they will stay for a reasonable length of time.

Queensland

Because of Queensland's attractions for all visitors to Australia, the competition for jobs comes mostly from travellers, who are more interested in having a good time than in earning a high wage. The pay is generally so low in seasonal jobs in the Queensland tourist industry that the work does not appeal to many Australians, since they can earn nearly as much on the dole. When employers need to fill a vacancy, they tend to hire whomever is handy that day, rather than sift through applications. For example if you phone from Sydney to enquire about possibilities, the advice will normally be to come and see.

If you want a live-in position, you should try the coastal resorts such as Surfers Paradise and Noosa Heads and islands all along the Queensland coast where the season lasts from March, after the cyclones, until Christmas. If Cairns is choc-a-bloc with job-seekers try the huge resort of Palm Cove just north of the city. Many of the small islands along the Barrier Reef are completely given over to tourist complexes. You might make initial enquiries at EN offices on the mainland for example in Proserpine, Cannonvale, Mackay or Townsville, though normally you will have to visit an island in person (and therefore pay for the ferry). Among the many possibilities are the Kingfisher Bay Resort on Fraser Island and the Heron Island Tourist Resort. Anyone with relevant experience in hospitality might try to fix up something in advance through P&O Australian Resorts (Level 7, 120 Sussex St, Sydney 2000; 02-9364 8900) which run the resorts on Heron Island, Bedarra, Brampton and Dunk Islands plus Silky Oaks Lodge in the Daintree Rainforest of North Queensland. You could also try in advance Rydges Capricorn International Resort (Farnborough Road, PO Box 350, Yeppoon, Qld 4703).

Be warned that Queensland employers are notorious for laying off their staff at a moment's notice without compensation, holiday pay, etc. Emma Dunnage was disillusioned with one of the six backpackers hostels on Magnetic Island where she worked for ten weeks as a catamaran instructor-cum-general dogsbody. She was paid $100 a week, half of what most of the other staff were getting. In fact there is an 'Offshore Islands Award' for workers in isolated places which is a minimum of $350 a week in addition to board and lodging, though it seems that it is often ignored.

Tourist development along the Queensland coast is progressing at an alarming rate, especially with an eye to the Japanese market. Anyone who has travelled in Japan or who has a smattering of Japanese might have the edge over the competition (unless the competition happens to be a Japanese working holiday maker of whom there are many in Cairns and elsewhere). James Blackman, who hadn't studied any Oriental languages, describes how he got his job at a resort in the Whitsunday Islands:

I had no luck finding work in Airlie Beach, partly because I bumped into two other people looking for work in this small resort town. The next day I went to Hamilton Island to search for work. I went to practically every establishment and was turned away. However I persevered and the second last place gave me a job as a kitchen hand in a restaurant which was on the beach front. Lots of different people staffed the resort and most were quite friendly, always asking, 'How're ya going?' I spent ten weeks there earning about $150-200 per five-day week.

James also noticed that working holiday visas were expected on these resort islands. One of the larger employers is the dive industry. Although not many visitors would have the qualifications which got Ian Mudge a job as Dive Master on *Nimrod III* operating out of Cookstown (i.e. qualified mechanical engineer, diver and student of Japanese), his assessment of opportunities for mere mortals is heartening:

Anyone wishing to try their luck as a hostess could do no worse than to approach all the dive operators with live-aboard boats such as Mike Ball Water Sports in Townsville, Down Under Dive, etc. 'Hosties' make beds, clean cabins and generally tidy up. Culinary skills and an ability to speak Japanese would be definite pluses. A non-diver would almost certainly be able to fix up some free dive lessons and thus obtain their basic Open Water Diver qualification while being paid to do so. Normally females only are considered for hostie jobs.

Caroline Perry was fairly confident that a commercial resort like Surfers Paradise would offer opportunities to work but didn't have much luck filling in forms and waiting for the phone to ring. Eventually she and a friend got work in Movie World, 21km from Surfers Paradise on the Pacific Highway. Employment enquiries should be addressed to the Human Resources Department, Oxenford, Qld 4210 (07-5573 3999) who keep your details on file for up to three months. It offers good opportunities for casual work during holiday periods, mainly in food and beverage and retail service. It will be difficult to save any money since wages are not high and you will have to pay for transport between a hostel in town.

Similar attractions to try along the Gold Coast are Sea World (Sea World Drive, Main Beach, PO Box 190, Surfers Paradise 4217; 07-5588 2222; micheleb@ seaworld.com.au), and Conrad Jupiters, Broadbeach Island, Broadbeach, Qld 4218 (recruitment line: 07-5592 8614; cjhrd@conrad.com.au). Try other theme and amusement parks like Wet 'n' Wild and Dreamworld.

Ski Resorts

Another holiday area to consider is the Australian Alps where ski resorts are expanding and gaining in popularity. Jindabyne (NSW) on the edge of Kosciuszko National Park and Thredbo are the ski job capitals, though Mount Buller, Falls Creek, Baw Baw and Hotham in the state of Victoria are relatively developed ski centres too. The best time to look is a couple of weeks before the season opens which in Jindabyne is usually around the 11th of June. The employment offices in Wangaratta and Cooma can advise, though most successful job-seekers use the walk-in-and-ask method. In 'Jindy' try the Brumby Bar, Aspen Hotel, Kookaburra Lodge or any of the dozens of other hotels and pubs.

Denise Crofts went straight from a waitressing job in Kings Cross Sydney to the large Hotel Arlberg in Mount Hotham, where she had a terrific season, since that year the resort had the best snow it had had in a decade. She recommends trying for work at all of the tourist establishments like the Jack Frost Restaurant, the General Store & Bistro Tavern, BJs, Herbies, etc. There is considerable staff turn-over mid-season, though obviously May/June is a better time to look.

Henry Pearce's experiences looking for work were not so positive, despite heavy radio advertising by the employment office:

> *When we hitched to Cooma on June 2nd, we enquired about the progress of the applications we had sent in April. We were told that there had been 4,000 applications and two vacancies for bar staff to date. We carried on up to Thredbo and half-heartedly asked around a few chalets and hotels and it seemed most of them had already fixed up their basic requirements. We were told of several definite posts available once the snow fell. In Jindabyne we were hired to work at the 'highest restaurant in Australia' (at the top of the ski lift) for $12 an hour. But accommodation was uniformly expensive in Jindabyne ($100+ a week) as was the cost of lift passes and ski hire.*

Anyone qualified as a ski instructor should attend the hiring clinics held in the big resorts before the season gets underway. The Kosciuszko Thredbo Co at the Alpine Ski Village Thredbo (PO Box 92, Thredbo 2625; 02-6459 4100; recruitment@thredbo.com.au) hire the full range of ski resort staff in three categories: on-the-mountain, hotel and instruction. Their website www.thredbo.com.au provides detailed information about recruitment procedures; 2001 applications must be in by 20th April and the names of short-listed candidates will be listed on the website on April 26th; interviews take place in Sydney, Brisbane and Thredbo in early May.

Nannies can also find openings as Matt Tomlinson recounts:

> *I arrived in Mount Buller hopelessly late and found it very difficult to get work. In the end my resourcefulness called upon my experience a few years back as a nanny and I got some work with the resort's nanny agency looking after the under fours. The pay averaged $10 per hour. I was about the only person to stick with the job for the whole season. Despite the lack of a lift pass or accommodation, I stayed because it suited me to go out snowboarding when I had no work. I also enjoyed the irony of being paid to build snow people, read stories and go tobogganning.*

Cities

Now that the Olympics are over, Melbourne is once again better for work than Sydney, partly because it is so much less full of working travellers and also the cost of living is lower. Apart from restaurants and cafés, pubs and clubs, catering jobs crop up in cricket grounds, theatres, yacht clubs and (in Sydney) on harbour cruises. Function work is usually easy to come by via specialist agencies provided you can claim to have silver service experience. It is worth applying to catering companies as Fiona Cox did in Sydney, though she was not impressed with the weekly take-home pay of $200.

Easy success at job hunting in Perth is far from automatic, particularly without a working visa. Since the last edition three contributors have given up on the city and moved on. Nothing much turned up last January, even for Sara Runnalls, a qualified chef. Jenni and Eric Holland spent six weeks in Perth before they gave up, moved north and immediately found work on a melon farm. Jenni, a qualified welder met with a discouragingly sexist response when applying for welding work, 'If you want to visit your husband here, just f***ing call first'.

The best opportunities for bar and waiting staff in Perth are in the city centre, Fremantle and Northbridge, the area around William and James Streets. Rhona Stannage and her husband Stuart Blackwell arrived in Perth in November, and having had chalet experience in the French Alps and restaurant experience in Cyprus en route, were in a strong position to find hospitality work:

Since there were lots of adverts in the newspapers for bar/restaurant staff we didn't go door-knocking, but we did meet a Canadian guy who had been in Perth one week and who had immediately found work in Northbridge just by asking around in the restaurants, bars and nightclubs. We both got jobs fairly quickly – me within a week and Stuart a couple of weeks later. (I put my relative success down to the usual sexism in the hospitality trade since we have virtually the same experience.) I'm working in an Irish pub called Rosie O'Gradys (they prefer Irish accents but stretched a point when it came to my Scottish one). I would also recommend the 'traditional British pub' the Moon and Sixpence in the City, since they seem to have only Poms and no Aussies working there.

Rhona was also offered a job at the Burswood Resort Casino which often needs staff willing to work shifts (it is open 24 hours). To attract 'permanent' staff, they pay twice the going wage and offer their staff lots of perks such as free meals and a staff gym. One contributor describes how he took advantage of these same perks at the Crown Casino in Melbourne without going to the trouble of being hired. He claims that penniless starving backpackers should tell security at the staff entrance that they are from 'Pinnacle' or 'Hoban', the two catering agencies which supply staff to the casino, proceed to the uniform issuer up the escalator, claiming to be a new waiter/chef/kitchen staff working in the King's Bistro/George's, and make the trek to the staff canteen. The more honest among this book's readers might prefer to try actually being hired by the catering agencies mentioned. Alternatively they might like to have a slap-up meal at a bargain price; for example many RSL (Returned Services League) clubs offer cheap eats, perhaps a Sunday roast for $7 or an affordable mid-week all-you-can-eat Chinese buffet.

The preference for females is strong in places like Kalgoorlie where waitresses are sometimes known by the offensive name 'skimpies' (after their uniforms). Partly because Darwin has such a small population (81,000), tourist bars and restaurants rely heavily on transients for their staff. As well as being easier to find work than in Sydney or Melbourne, the cost of accommodation is substantially less.

Bridgid Seymour-East thinks that new arrivals should be warned of the dangers which Sydney poses to the traveller:

You may plan to stay a week or two and set off to travel or find work. However one or two months later, after a lot of fun, you find yourself still there and your funds severely depleted. Sydney traps you because you do have so much fun. Jimmy and I met in a youth hostel in Glebe and love blossomed.

Holiday Language Courses

Travellers with a TEFL certificate can take advantage of the seasonal demand for English tuition created by 'study tours,' popular among Japanese, Indonesian and other Asian students during their autumn and winter holidays. Demand for these holiday English courses increased dramatically as soon as the Australian immigration authorities relaxed the restrictions on visas, allowing foreign students to undertake short courses on a tourist visa. With a working holiday visa and a dash of luck, Simon Brooks fixed up several short contracts for February/March and July/August with no difficulty at all:

It's just a question of timing really and getting an interview two or three weeks before a new course starts. It took me two weeks to get work in Sydney but only five days in Perth where I had five offers on the same day. Even if you don't get a three-month contract straightaway, get yourself on the relief list and get a mobile phone (or at least stay in a backpackers' hostel with a reliable receptionist) and persist. Talking to one Director of Studies in Sydney whom I met by chance socially, there's no doubt that effort counts a lot with them and tells them something about you.

In Sydney Simon worked for Universal English College (Level 12, 222 Pitt St, Sydney 2000; 2-9283 1088/ www.uec.edu.au) and Sydney English Language Centre (Level 2, 19-23 Hollywood Avenue, Bondi Junction, NSW 2022; 2-9383 3300/ www.ics.com.au/selc) while in Perth he happily worked for Milner International College (379 Hay Street, Perth, WA 6009; 08-9325 5444; www.milner.wa.edu.au).

Special Events

Special events like test matches and race meetings can be seen as possible sources of employment. If you happen to be in Melbourne in late October or early November for the Melbourne Cup (held on the first Tuesday of November which is a public holiday in Victoria) or for the Grand Prix, your chances of finding casual work escalate remarkably. An army of sweepers and cleaners is recruited to go through the whole course clearing the huge piles of debris left by 15,000 race-goers. Hotels, restaurants and bars become frantically busy in the period leading up to the Cup, and private catering firms are also often desperate for staff. All the major cities have important horse races. Rowena Caverly was hired for the Darwin Cup Races 'mainly to check that none of the Lady Members had passed out in the loos'.

Travelling fairs are very popular and have frequent vacancies. Richard Davies joined the Melbourne Show in September and was paid $100 a day tax-free (to work 12-14 hours). It travels from Adelaide to Melbourne, Sydney and on up the Gold Coast staying a week or ten days. Ask at the local tourist office. Geertje Korf was at first thrilled to land a job with a travelling fair but it wasn't all as exciting as she had hoped:

> *The work itself was good enough, helping to build up the stalls and working on the Laughing Clowns game. But the family I got to work for were not extremely sociable company. As a result, when we left a place and headed for the next I would spend time (about a week) until the next show day wandering lonely around incredibly hot and dusty little country towns where there was absolutely nothing to do while the showmen sat in a little circle drinking beer and not even talking to me. Also, the public toilets on the showgrounds were not usually open until showday, never cleaned since the last showday and usually provided some company (at last!) such as frogs, flies and redback spiders. I got paid $200 a week plus the use of a little caravan and evening meals which was not bad. Apparently a Dutch guy had spent six months with them the year before and had a great time, so I suppose it all depends on your personality.*

The Interior

Uluru or Ayers Rock is a place of pilgrimage for 360,000 visitors a year. The nearest facilities are in the Ayers Rock Resort village about 20km north of the Rock. Ayers Rock Resort (formerly known as Yulara) is the fourth largest settlement in the Northern Territory and a good place to look for a job. Although the resort has a waiting list of job-seekers, many people have moved on before they reach the top of the list. The resort employs about 1,000 people in catering and cleaning and many other departments. Staff accommodation is available. It would be worth sending your CV if you have a catering qualification or two years experience in a four-star hotel (Human Resources Department, Ayers Rock Resort, PO Box 46, Ayers Rock Resort, NT 0872; www.voyages.com.au).

Alice Springs is a very popular tourist destination because of Ayers Rock. One traveller who stayed at one of the many backpackers' lodges reported that 8 out of the 12 women staying there were working as waitresses or bar staff. Occasional vacancies occur for hostesses to work on upmarket special interest tours. Personality and presentation are more important than qualifications and experience for jobs as hostesses and cooks.

Tourist towns like Alice also have plenty of openings for shop assistants and many stores are regularly forced to hire transients. Ally Green and Martin Spiers put in an appearance at the weekly hiring session at the K-Mart Store and had no trouble fixing up work in the housewares and gardening departments, since it was coming up to Christmas. The casual rates they were paid were higher than the regular wages.

Similarly Andrew Walford found occasional work at Lucas Supermarket in Coober Pedy (opal capital of Australia in the South Australian outback). Kununurra and Broome are other places worth trying for tourist work in the Dry (May to October). Broome hosts a big festival in early September just prior to the monsoon (when travel becomes hazardous and uncomfortable) which is a good time to try.

As a general rule the lower the wage the higher the staff turnover. However low wages are not the only reason for people staying a short time at any one job. Working at a road station can be a very lonely business. A typical station consists of a shop, a petrol pump and a bar, and they occur every couple of hundred miles along the seemingly endless straight highways through the Australian desert. The more remote the place (and these are often the ones that are unbearably hot) the more likely there will be a vacancy. If you see a job going in Marble Bar, for example, remind yourself that it is arguably the world's hottest inhabited town with summer temperatures of $50°C-52°C$ ($122°F-126°F$).

The Australian Pub

Until the early 1970s, pubs were licensed only from 5pm to 6pm, which resulted in some fairly barbaric drinking habits known as the 'six o'clock swill.' Now that the licensing hours are more civilised (from about 10am-10pm on weekdays and until midnight on Friday and Saturday) many Australian pubs or 'hotels' are now quite genteel establishments where the staff are treated courteously. An increasing number are becoming trendy and yuppified. But there still is a strong preference for hiring women rather than men. The tradition in male-dominated pubs of heavy drinking and barmaid-taunting continues, so you should be prepared for this sometimes irritating (though almost always good-natured) treatment. You may get especially tired of hearing sporting comparisons between Australia and Britain.

Standards of service are high and many hotel managers will be looking for some experience or training. Only those desperate for staff will be willing to train. Even if you have had experience of working in a British pub, it may take you some time to master the technique of pouring Australian lager properly. There is a bewildering array of beer glasses ranging from the 115ml small beer of Tasmania to the 575ml pint of New South Wales with middies, schooners, pots and butchers falling in between. Names and measures vary from state to state.

The local pub is always a good place to find out about local opportunities, from the 'Animal Bar' where fishermen drink in Karumba Queensland to the 'Snake Pit' where fruit pickers congregate on a Friday night in Waikerie SA.

CHILDCARE

The demand for live-in and live-out childcare is enormous in Australia and a few agencies in Britain cater to the demand, such as Childcare International (Trafalgar House, Grenville Place, London NW7 3SA; www.childint.co.uk). But it is easy to conduct the job hunt on arrival. Applicants are often interviewed a day or two after registering with an agency and start work immediately. Nanny and au pair agencies are very interested in hearing from young women and men with working holiday visas. Geertje Korf's experience in Tasmania illustrates the ease with which childcare work can be found:

> *I decided to go to Tasmania for a cycling holiday. At the second place I stopped I got offered a job as a nanny to four children, just by mentioning I had been nannying in Sydney. The place had beautiful surroundings, restaurants, etc. so I decided to accept. It was a good job and I left quite a bit richer.*

A number of au pair agencies place European and Asian women with working holiday visas in live-in positions, normally for a minimum of three months. Not all placements require childcare experience. Try any of the following:

Affordable Au Pairs & Nannies, 3/62A Trafalgar St, Annandale, NSW 2038 (02-9557 6644; aapn@nanny.net.au/ www.nanny.net.au). Offices in Melbourne and

Brisbane. Average wage of $150 for 30 hours a week plus two evenings babysitting.

Au Pair Around the World, PO Box 157, Sanctuary Cove, Brisbane 4212 (tel/fax 07-5530 1123); Level 1, 789 Botany Road, Roseberry, Sydney (02-9557 6644/ www.nanny.net.au). Network of offices throughout Australia.

Australian Nanny & Au Pair Connection, 404 Glenferrie Road, Kooyong, Melbourne, Vic 3144 (tel 03-9822 5296; www.nannyconnection.com.au).

Au Pair & Nanny World Service, 28 Merriman St, Kyle Bay, NSW 2221 (02-9547 3713; one@cia.com.au).

Dial-an-Angel, Suite 21, Edgecliff Mews, 201 New South Head Road, Edgecliff, NSW 2027 (02-9362 4225/fax 9362 4001; www.dial-an-angel.com.au). Long established agency with branches throughout Australia. Wages offered of $14-$18 for daytime childcare, $17-$20 for domestic cleaning and housekeeping.

Family Match Sydney, PO Box 431, North Sydney, NSW 2060 (tel/fax 02-9328 2553; www.familymatch.com.au). Place people on working holiday visas. 20-30 hours per week for salary of $125-$180 plus all live-in expenses.

People for People, PO Box W271, Warringah Mall, Brookvale, NSW 2100 (02-9972 0488; nanny@peopleforpeople.com.au/ www.peopleforpeople.com.au).

Most agencies will expect to interview applicants and check their references before placement. As in America, a driving licence is a valuable asset. As well as long term posts, holiday positions for the summer (December-February) and for the ski season (July-September) are available. As mentioned earlier Matt Tomlinson worked as a nanny in a ski resort, on the strength of the year he'd spent as an au pair in Paris:

Being a male nanny in Australia was an interesting experience. I got used to being asked if I was a child molester. On the upside, I was also offered a number of live-in jobs in Melbourne. And in case you're wondering, yes, I did get a lot of ribbing from the guy when I told them what job I was doing.

Anyone considering a childcare position may be interested in Rowena Caverly's experiences:

I looked after a 15-month old boy at a permaculture farm set in a rainforest. The job taught me new skills daily, such as how to persuade a baby that the Huntsman Spider on the wall really does not want to play. My task in summer was to teach him to toddle heavily to scare off snakes. Otherwise a nasty situation might have developed (and my money would not necessarily be on the baby as the victim).

FISHING & BOATING

It is sometimes possible to get work on prawn fishing vessels out of Broome, Darwin, Cairns, Townsville, Bowen or even Karumba on the Gulf of Carpentaria. Stephen Psallidas noticed lots of trawler and yachting jobs in the *Cairns Post* (especially on Wednesday and Saturday) and in the job centre. You can either try to get work with one of the big companies like Raptis or Toros in Queensland, or on smaller privately-owned boats. Fishing trips from Queensland tend to be day trips.

The main jobs assigned to male deckhands are net-mending and prawn-sorting. Work is especially demanding during the banana prawn season of March/April, since banana prawns travel in huge schools which are caught in one fell swoop, requiring immediate attention. Women are taken on as cooks. They should make it quite clear before leaving harbour whether or not they wish to be counted among the recreational facilities of the boat, since numerous stories are told of the unfair pressures placed on women crew members at sea, though Anne Wakeford encountered no problems of this kind when she went out on a small fishing boat from Darwin. The most that some women have had to complain about is that they were expected not only to cook but to help sort out sea snakes and jelly fish from the catch. Men are not immune to problems, of course: if the skipper takes a dislike to any of his crew, he can simply leave them stranded on an island or beach.

Ian Mudge, who worked on a diving boat in northern Queensland, heard terrible things about prawn trawler work and thinks that it would be safer for a woman to work in a Kings Cross brothel than to sign up on one. He also thinks that the general working conditions are very unsafe, though he does admit that the money can be excellent. The backpacker press sometimes carries a rather alarming ad placed by the Queensland Transport and Whitsunday Charter Boat Industry Association, headed 'At sea, no one can hear you scream.' The ad goes on to warn backpackers to be wary of predatory boat owners who chat them up at pubs and clubs and entice them on to their unseaworthy boats.

The prawn fishing season in Darwin starts on April 15th and continues through till Christmas. Any traveller who goes down to the docks at the beginning of the season has a good chance of being taken on for a one or two week trip, even without experience. Catches are much less than they used to be and most deckhands these days prefer to take a wage of a couple of hundred dollars a week as opposed to taking a share of the profits. The work of sorting and loading prawns is tedious but not too unpleasant except when the spines stick into your hands. Alternatively you may find work on the quayside unloading prawn trawlers or other vessels. The *Northern Territory News* gives details of ships in port or expected, which could provide clues.

If you don't manage to join a crew, try for work in the fish-processing plants. For example the Bundaberg fishing fleet keeps three processing plants supplied, especially with scallops while Carnarvon also has a prawn and scallop industry. The season lasts from March to October and accommodation is available in caravan parks. The rock lobster season around Geraldton WA also starts in March but lasts only three months. Sometimes you see advertisements for oyster openers, a skill worth cultivating if only for your own consumption. Scallop-splitting is another favourite among casual workers, e.g. around Bicheno on the east coast of Tasmania, though the quantities have been drastically curtailed recently by overfishing.

Dickon Young has heard that it might be possible to participate in the pearling industry on the coast of Western Australia. He suggests visiting the farms where pearls are cultivated to ask for work and, if refused, returning regularly with the same question.

Conclusion

Ian Fleming sums up what many working travellers have observed about Australians:

> *The opinion that we formed regarding Australian employers is that they are hard but fair. They demand a good day's work for a fair day's pay, and if you do not measure up to their expectations they will have no hesitation in telling you so. But generally we found that the British worker is held in quite high esteem in Australia. I also found the Aussies to be much more friendly and helpful than anticipated and very easy to socialise with (in spite of the fact that I was nicknamed 'P.B.' for Pommy Bastard).*

Most people are struck by what a good standard of living can be enjoyed for not very much money. As Gawain Paling put it so graphically, 'If you're poor in Britain it's the pits; if you're poor in Australia you can have a nice comfortable life'. There is a marvellous range of jobs even if you are unlikely to repeat Sandra Grey's coup of being paid $50 for three hours 'work' testing a sunscreen on her lily-white back, or Jane Thomas's bizarre jobs, one in a sex change clinic, the other in a morgue typing up the labels for dismembered parts of bodies.

Even after several setbacks with bosses and jobs, Louise Fitzgerald concludes:

> *To anybody not sure about going, I'd say, go, you'd be stupid not to. Australia is a wonderful country and the Australians are great people, even if the males do have a tendency to be chauvinists. If you prove to them you're as good as they are, they tend to like you for it!*

New Zealand

New Zealand is a charmingly rural country where 3.8 million human beings are substantially outnumbered by sheep. Travellers have found hitch-hiking easy, the youth hostels congenial, camping idyllic (when it's dry) and the natives very hospitable. The minimum wage in 2000 was increased to NZ$7.55, equivalent (at the time of writing) to a paltry £2.10. But the NZ cost of living is correspondingly low and therefore you should aim to spend any money you make before leaving the shores of New Zealand.

Supplementing your travel fund with cash-in-hand work, odd jobs or work-for-keep arrangements is usually good fun. Camping on beaches, fields and in woodlands is generally permitted. In addition to official youth hostels, there is a wealth of budget accommodation, where you can often learn of local opportunities for casual work, particularly the ubiquitous fruit-picking.

The Regulations

New Zealand deserves its national reputation for friendliness to visitors. Tourists from the UK need no visa to stay for up to six months, while Americans, Canadians and Europeans can stay for three visa-free months. Tourists entering the country may be asked to show an onward ticket and about NZ$1,000 per month of their proposed stay (unless they have pre-paid accommodation or a New Zealand backer who has pledged support in a crisis). In practice, respectable-looking travellers are most unlikely to be quizzed at entry.

The UK Citizens' Working Holiday Scheme allows Britons aged 18-30 to do temporary jobs in New Zealand for up to 12 months. When the scheme was introduced in 1993, the quota was 500. That number has now risen to an encouraging 8,000 working holiday visas which are granted annually on a first come first served basis starting September 1st. Although the literature says the quota fills quickly, you do not have to apply in the summer to be successful. For example in recent years there have been 800-1,000 working holiday visas left about Easter. Information can be obtained from the New Zealand Immigration Service, Mezzanine Floor, New Zealand House, 80 Haymarket, London SW1Y 4TE (fax 020-7973 0370) in person, by phone on 09069

100100 (charged at £1 per minute) or via the internet at www.immigration.govt.nz.
To apply you need the right Application for Work Visa form, your UK passport, the fee of £30, evidence of a return ticket and evidence of NZ$4,200 (about £1,200). Sponsorship from a New Zealand citizen is not considered an acceptable substitute for proof of funds. Applications for the working holiday visa must be lodged in the UK or (from April 2001) in Australia. Other working holiday schemes are open to Irish, Canadian, Japanese and Malaysian nationals who must apply in their country of nationality.

BUNAC has a Work New Zealand programme that provides the usual range of services (flights, stopovers, initial hostel accommodation and ongoing support for up to 12 months from their partner International Exchange Programs (IEP) in New Zealand; the inclusive fee is £1,600-£1,750. The new Work Experience Downunder programme from Camp Counsellors & Work Experience (Green Dragon House, 64-70 High St, Croydon CR0 9XN; 020-8688 9051) includes New Zealand as well as Australia. Prices start at £45 registration fee, £140 for extendable three-month insurance cover and from £460 for a one-way flight, £700 return. A relatively new gap year placement company Changing Worlds (11 Doctors Lane, Chaldon, Surrey CR3 5AE; 01883 340960; www.changingworlds.co.uk) offers a choice of programme in New Zealand including volunteering to work on tall ships based in the Bay of Islands as well as fruit picking, work on sheep farms (for which a clean driving licence is usually needed) or in the tourist industry.

American students are eligible to apply for a six-month work permit from Council or BUNAC USA to work between April 1st and October 21st. CCUSA at 2330 Marinship Way, Suite 250, Sausalito, CA 94965 (1-800-999-CAMP; outbound@ campcounselors.com/ www.campcounselors.com/australia.html) runs a three-month work experience programme (June to September). Also Travel CUTS in Canada administer a similar work abroad scheme for Canadian students also expiring in late October. The point of allowing foreigners to work only during the New Zealand winter is in order to prevent competition with New Zealand students seeking holiday jobs during the summer. Most students find work in catering, retailing, farming, etc. using advice from the co-operating organisation STA in Auckland.

A possible alternative for those who have contacts in New Zealand or special skills and can obtain a firm offer of employment before leaving the UK is to apply for a temporary work visa (the same non-refundable fee of £30 applies). Your New Zealand sponsor must be prepared to prove to the Immigration Service that it is necessary to hire a foreigner rather than an unemployed New Zealander. The work visa does not in itself entitle you to work, but does make it easier to obtain a work permit after arrival. If you are granted a work visa before departure it will allow you to stay for up to three years.

Changes to immigration rules came into force in March 2000 making it possible for people on working holidays to apply to extend their stay or even for residence without having to leave the country. Applicants with skills in demand may apply for a new work permit option that will be valid for up to six months at one of the seven Immigration Service offices in New Zealand. To be considered for a work permit you must have a written job offer from a prospective employer confirming that the position offered is temporary, a full description of the position, salary, evidence that you are suitably qualified (originals or certified copies of work references, qualification certificates, etc.) and evidence that the employer has made every effort to recruit local people (proof of advertising, vacancy lodged with Employment Service, etc.) If granted it will be valid for six months from the date of your entry to New Zealand. As usual there are no hard and fast rules and no guarantee of success, as Ken Smith (a native New Zealander) found when he worked alongside foreigners at Franz Josef resort;

There was a northern Irish girl working there who had been granted a work permit to work as a waitress. She was assured of the job over the phone having told them that her application for a work permit was being processed (which it wasn't) and when assured of the job she promptly set about applying for a work permit before arriving at the hotel. The work permit was granted three months later, a week or so before she was due to move on, so she was

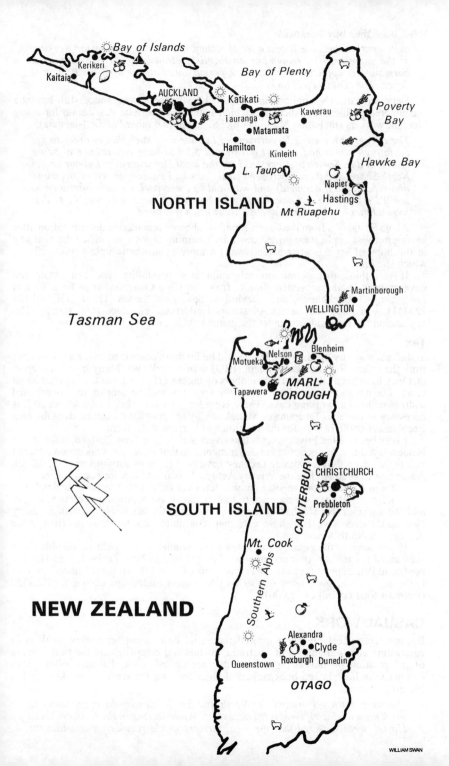

Bay of Islands
Kerikeri
Kaitaia
Bay of Plenty
AUCKLAND
Katikati
Tauranga
Kawerau
Poverty Bay
Matamata
Hamilton
Kinleith
Hawke Bay
L. Taupo
Napier
NORTH ISLAND
Hastings
Mt Ruapehu

Martinborough
Tasman Sea
WELLINGTON

Blenheim
Nelson
Motueka
MARL-BOROUGH
Tapawera

CHRISTCHURCH
Prebbleton
SOUTH ISLAND
CANTERBURY

Mt. Cook
Southern Alps

NEW ZEALAND

Alexandra
Clyde
Roxburgh
Dunedin
Queenstown
OTAGO

WILLIAM SWAN

*quite annoyed because it cost a lot of money. On a previous occasion working
at the same resort I remember an English fellow who was working as a
barman. His application for a work permit was flatly refused, so I guess it
depends on 'Do you feel lucky?'*

Deborah Porter's application with a US passport was successful but she
encountered problems in Auckland, which is the most popular destination for many
itinerant workers (including Maori people, Samoans and other Pacific Islanders):

*The queues at the city's Department of Labour were such that in order to get
an interview you had to start queuing at 5am to have any chance of being
seen that day. Someone suggested I try the local Department of Labour on the
North Shore, and there I was seen straightaway. I paid my fee (very steep and
non-refundable if declined) and was told to come back the next afternoon to
see if I'd been granted one. Luckily for me, it had, but it was specific to that
job and that employer and stated clearly when it expired.*

Alena Sestakova from the Czech Republic showed remarkable determination after
having her visa application turned down by returning to the same office the next day
in the hope of seeing (after a long wait) a more sympathetic immigration officer,
which she did.

If you think that permanent migration is a possibility, you can obtain the
government's 'Self-Assessment Guide' from the High Commission or from Consyl
Publishing, 3 Buckhurst Road, Bexhill-on-Sea, East Sussex TN40 1QF (01424
223111); you must enclose an A4 stamped addressed envelope (66p stamp). The
application fee for residence under the general skills category is NZ$700.

Tax

In the vast majority of cases employers will be far more concerned to see a tax number
from the Inland Revenue Department (IRD) than a work visa. Many travellers report
that they have been allocated IRD numbers by the tax office without being asked about
visas. The number is not allocated on the spot, but will be sent on to a nominated
address within ten working days. There is no longer a tax office in Auckland, so it is
necessary to travel to Takapuna or Manukau City to apply for a number. Ring the toll-
free number 0800 227774 for information and to request the form.

Partly because the Privacy Act is taken very seriously in New Zealand, information
is not relayed to other government departments, so that travellers working on a tourist
visa often succeed in reclaiming tax they have paid (27% of earnings up to $30,000).
According to Brett Archer, the Privacy Act is a 'wonderful law for backpackers'.

Carolyn Edwards had an IRD number left over from a visit to New Zealand four
years before, and when she returned to look for work as a temporary secretary, simply
told the agencies that she had dual nationality, and this was never queried. So many
New Zealanders have British accents that it is quite easy to blend in. (It is more
difficult for North Americans.)

If you stay in the country for at least six months, you should be eligible for a
substantial tax rebate. After six months of casual jobs in New Zealand, Jane Harris's
boyfriend Pete applied for a tax rebate just before leaving the country. Almost one year
to the day later, he got a letter sent to his UK address enclosing a cheque for NZ$330
(from his total tax bill of $2,000).

CASUAL WORK

Because New Zealand has a limited industrial base, most temporary work is in
agriculture and tourism. As in Australia, hostels and campsites are the best sources
of information on harvesting jobs and other casual work. Farmers often make
contact with hostels and backpackers' lodges looking for seasonal workers as Ian
Fleming observed:

*During our travels around the North and South Islands, the opportunity to
work presented itself on several occasions. While staying in the Kerikeri Youth
Hostel, we discovered that the local farmers would regularly come into the*

hostel to seek employees for the day or longer. (This was in July, which is out-of-season.) My advice to any person looking for farm work would be to get up early as the farmers are often in the hostel by 8.30am.

Alternatively local farmers co-operate with hostel wardens who collate information about job vacancies or they may circulate notices around youth hostels, for example, 'Orchard Work Available January to March; apply Tauranga Hostel' so always check the hostel board.

In some cases hostel wardens collate information about job vacancies and post it on the notice board. Auckland Central Travel (16 Shortland St; 09-358 4847; jobs@acb.co.nz) operate a Job Search service for backpackers; applicants for work in construction or tourism are matched with vacancies which employers have made known to the scheme's manager. Not many working holidaymakers seem to use the government job agency WINZ (Work & Income New Zealand; www.winz.govt.nz) though it may prove useful to contact the relevant office in promising places like Queenstown.

Hostels themselves employ travellers for short periods, either part-time in exchange for free accommodation or full-time for a wage as well. After crewing on a yacht from Vanuatu to New Zealand, Kristie McComb from California was very pleased to be taken on by her backpackers' hostel in Auckland.

Matt Tomlinson recommends buying a vehicle to travel and job hunt in New Zealand. He bought one for a few hundred pounds at the Sunday morning car market in the Auckland suburb of Manukau City. Look for one with a couple of months of WOF remaining (equivalent to MOT). Hitching has already been extolled. Bicycling is another attractive alternative. The Belgian world traveller Vince Crombez, who had no trouble finding work around New Zealand, is sure that the fact that he presented himself to possible employers on his loaded bicycle convinced them that he would not be a lazy worker.

Rural & Conservation Volunteering

Willing Workers on Organic Farms (WWOOF) NZ is active and popular, with nearly 600 farms and smallholdings on its fix-it-yourself list which welcome volunteers in exchange for food and accommodation. The list can be obtained from Jane and Andrew Strange, PO Box 1172, Nelson (tel/fax 03-544 9890; a&j@wwoof.co.nz/ www.wwoof.co.nz) for a fee of £13/US$20/NZ$40. WWOOF hosts often have leads for paid work in market gardens, nurseries and other farms.

A newer organisation matches working visitors with about 175 farmers throughout New Zealand. Farmstays can last from three days to several months. Farm Helpers in New Zealand (FHiNZ, 50 Bright St, Eketahuna 5480; tel/fax 06-375 8955; www.fhinz.co.uk) charges NZ$25 for their membership booklet containing all the addresses. The list is updated monthly. No experience is necessary and roughly four hours of work a day are requested. The co-ordinator (Warwick Grady) advises that hosts in the Auckland area tend to be oversubscribed, so that it is best to head into the countryside.

Craig Ashworth describes the pros and cons of exchanging your labour for food and lodging:

I met some marvellous characters and stayed in some wonderful isolated places. A great way to see places and folk off the beaten track. But beware of being used as cheap labour in some unscrupulous places. Also a lot of the WWOOF farmers are quite wacky.

Craig found that his WWOOF hosts often had leads for paid work and through WWOOF contacts he was able to fix up a job on a market garden in Kerikeri and another on an angora goat farm in Whangarei. Two unusual WWOOF hosts are a bicycle shop in central Auckland, Adventure Cycles in Auckland (1 Fort Lane; tel/fax 09-309 5566; www.adventure-auckland.co.nz), which actively promotes eco-tourism; and Flying Kiwi Wilderness Expeditions (Freeths Road, Koromiko, R.D.3, Blenheim; 03-573 8126; http://webnz.com/flying_kiwi) which maintains an organic farm near Picton as well as running alternative coach tours of New Zealand.

Adrienne Robinson and her partner and young son joined FHiNZ and arranged two enjoyable farmstays. Because they were looking for farms at the height of the summer and at Christmas, they found that many of the listed farms were already booked up for that period. They found that the general picking, weeding and mulching work they were asked to do was fairly easy to manage alongside three year old Jordan.

The New Zealand Department of Conservation (DOC) carries out habitat and wildlife management projects throughout New Zealand and publishes a detailed Calendar of Volunteer Opportunities (see their website www.doc. govt.nz/commu/involv/consvol.htm) with all sorts of interesting sounding projects from counting bats to cleaning up remote beaches. Most require a good level of fitness and a contribution to expenses, often quite small. The DOC also needs volunteer hut wardens at a variety of locations. Details are available from any office of the Department of Conservation (all addresses are listed on website).

Paul Bagshaw from Kent and his girlfriend spent a thoroughly enjoyable week on an uninhabited island in Marlborough Sound monitoring kiwis, the flightless bird whose numbers have been seriously depleted. An ongoing programme removes them from the mainland to small islands where there are no predators:

The object of the exercise was to estimate the number of kiwis on Long Island north of Picton. As the kiwi is nocturnal, we had to work in the small hours. As it's dark, it's impossible to count them so we had to spread out and walk up a long slope listening for their high-pitched whistling call. During the day they hide in burrows and foliage so it is very rare to see one. One night, when we heard one rustling around our camp, my girlfriend went outside with a torch and actually managed to see it. She was so excited that she couldn't speak and resorted to wild gesticulations to describe its big feet and long beak. The island has no water source except rainwater which collects in tanks, all very basic. We lived in tents and prepared our own meals from supplies brought over from the mainland. Our one luxury was a portaloo.

Details of other projects in the Marlborough Sounds are available from any office of the Department of Conservation. The DOC in Picton is located at 14 Auckland St (emacdonald@doc.govt.nz).

The Earthwise Living Foundation (PO Box 108, Thames 2815; 025-994204; www.elfnz.com) places international visitors in a variety of settings including a wilderness ecology and conservation programme lasting 4-14 weeks or a personalised work experience/internship programme in a career field of your choice. The fee for finding a tailor-made internship or three-month work experience programme is usually about US$500 plus variable living expenses. Many of the placements involve living with a local family. Participants must arrange their own visas as appropriate.

FRUIT PICKING

The climate of New Zealand lends itself to fruit and vegetable growing of many kinds including not only the apples and kiwifruit well known from every British supermarket but carrots, citrus fruit and other produce. The industry now seems to be recovering from the recession of the 1990s when some travellers were hired not to pick kiwifruit but to dispose of it for pig feed.

Just turning up in towns and asking around is a safe bet for work while the season is on. Below are some general guidelines as to what areas to head for in the appropriate seasons. Motueka/Nelson, Tauranga/Katikati, Hawke Bay and Kerikeri seem to be favourites among travellers. A specialist book *Seasonal Work in New Zealand* written and published by twins Gary and Heidi Andrews is widely sold in New Zealand (and Australian) bookshops (ISBN 0-473-03221-X) for $30.

Most farmers are able to provide some kind of shack or cottage accommodation (known as a 'bach' in the North Island, a 'crib' in the South), though the spring and summer weather is suitable for camping provided you have a good waterproof tent. Farmers often provide fresh fruit and vegetables, milk and sometimes lamb.

Place	Crop	Season
Nelson/Blenheim/Motueka	apples (also pears & peaches)	Feb/Mar/Apr
Motueka	apple thinning	mid-Nov/Dec
Blenheim	cherries	late Dec/Jan
Motueka	apple thinning	Feb/Mar/Apr
Wairau Valley (Marlborough area)	cherries, grapes	Dec
Nelson/Tapawera	raspberries	Dec
Kerikeri (Bay of Islands)	peaches, apricots	Dec/Jan
	citrus packing	Oct/Nov
	kiwifruit	late Apr
Northland (peninsula north of Auckland	kiwifruit	May
	strawberries	mid-Oct
Paiumhhue (just south of Auckland)	kiwifruit	May
Poverty Bay (Gisborne)	kiwifruit	May
Poverty Bay Flats	grapes	from Feb
Tauranga/Te Puke (Bay of Plenty)	citrus	Oct/Nov
	kiwifruit	May-Jul
Clive/Napier (Hawke Bay)	apples, pears & grapes	late Feb/Apr
	pruning work	Jun
Hastings	tomatoes	
	apples	late Feb/Apr
Ohakune	carrots	June
Martinborough (north of Wellington in the Wairarapa area)	grapes	Mar
Central Otago (Alexandra & Roxburgh)	plums, apricots	Jan/Feb
	apples & pears	Mar/Apr
Christchurch area	peaches	Mar
	apples, berries & mixed fruit	Jan-May
	potatoes	Jan-Mar
Invercargill	tulips	early Dec

Bay of Plenty

The Bay of Plenty is where the majority of New Zealand's kiwifruit is grown. The tiny community of Te Puke swells in number from 6,000 to 10,000 for the harvest which traditionally starts on May 1st (though it is best to arrive a week or two early to line up a job). Picking lasts four or five weeks and the packing season extends to August. Workaholics can work an evening shift packing after a day in the orchards. An hourly wage is paid for this boring work (5pm-11pm).

Just as quickly as Vince Crombez got a job in the Te Puke harvest, he quit, after deciding that the rate he was paid ($8.50 a bin) was a rip off. So he cycled on to Katikati (65km to the north) and visited the very helpful tourist information office who phoned two or three farmers for him and found him a job the same day. He stayed until the season ended (6th June) and cleared an average of $350 a week working in a gang which was not particularly dedicated. Unlike most picking jobs, this one allows leisurely morning starts, since the fruit must be dry before it can be picked, starting about 10am. Rates of pay are either by the bucket ('contract') or by the hour (called 'award rate,' as in Australia).

Hawke Bay

Local students are not available for autumn harvests such as apples and pears in the Hawke Bay area, so you may be able to pick up casual work in the apple orchards around Napier. This is one area in which it is wise to keep an eye out for immigration officials. Craig Ashworth arrived in late February and found that there was lots of no-questions-asked apple picking work around. He found it tough at first but was eventually earning about $500 for five days of work. There is also pruning work in the area in June.

Vince Crombez did well in Hastings in April:

> *Except for Granny Smiths, it is always picking according to colour which pays more. I got between $22 and $25 a bin for picking Braeburns, Fujis and other varieties. A ganger checked every hour to see if the apples were coloured enough, though usually it's 'no worries, mate', especially if you are the only traveller amongst Polynesians and Maoris. I could fill five bins between 8am and 2pm working non-stop (I was on muesli bars and energetic drinks).*

Last year the free magazine *TNT New Zealand* carried ads for boysenberry pickers in Hastings on Hawke Bay. The harvest takes place between early December and mid-January. The fruit cannot be picked in the heat of the day so working holidaymakers are invited to swim and fish in the Ngaruroro River during the day; contact Norm Brown, 1389 Matapiro Rd, Hastings (tel/fax 06-874 3705).

Poverty Bay is the large bay north of Hawke Bay where more kiwifruit plantations can be found. In early 1999, the wine giant Montana Wines was employing a phalanx of casual workers to establish new vineyards on the Poverty Bay Flats. In future years, it might be worth trying the area for grape-picking.

Travelling east, the largest carrot-producing region in the southern hemisphere is around Ohakune. Work is reputed to be available for up to nine months of the year here. While waiting for the ski season to begin, Matt Tomlinson rang some farmers out of the Yellow Pages and was soon hired to pack carrots. High staff turnover means that hiring goes on continuously. The work is boring and hard and pays $8.50-$9 an hour.

Northland

The tropical far north of the country, which specialises in citrus growing, is another favourite. In addition to the fruit picking work, there are several major packing sheds that employ a large number of casual workers in November/December. Contract pruning can be more lucrative than picking. Kiwifruit pickers normally work in gangs of ten and are paid piece work, while kiwifruit packers and citrus pickers are paid by the hour. The six weeks between early April and mid-May is a busy kiwifruit season. Any of the hostels in Kaitaia and Kerikeri will be able to advise. Especially recommended is the Aranga Holiday Park in Kerikeri (opposite the BP Service Station; 09-407-9426) which posts fruit-picking information on the internet (www.kerikeri.net/work). It provides transport to the kiwifruit and mandarin orchards for $1 a day and has tent sites which cost just $45 a week (£12.50).

Armin Birrer picked fruit from October to January and reports:

> *There is work in Kerikeri almost year round. The best way is to hire a bicycle and ask from orchard to orchard. Usually you have to work for various orchards at the same time since farmers can't afford to put too much fruit on the market at once.*

Fiona Cox found that it was difficult in this area to earn much though the work was certainly hard:

> *Our first day's work in Kerikeri was strawberry picking, backbreaking work in the hot sun which took days to recover from. For 7¹/₂ hours we got $30 and came away hot, sweaty and very pissed off.*

Nelson/Motueka/Blenheim

The Nelson/Motueka area is a great area for travellers for its jobs as well as its beaches. Many foreign travellers are hired for the apple harvest, and also at the apple packing and processing works in Stoke, just outside Nelson. The union has succeeded in making it obligatory for farmers to provide accommodation other than just a campsite; some charge will be made though often the deduction is negligible. Orchard workers must join the union. The negotiated rate is from $30 per bin; the average picker fills three to four bins a day, though star pickers like Frank Schiller manage 6-8¹/2 bins a day.

In Blenheim, make enquiries at Blenheim Backpackers (29 Park Terrace; rob.diana@xtra.co.nz) about local picking, packing and pruning work in local vineyards. Rob Abblett spent several months earning money in the south island. Apple thinning between mid-November and Christmas was fairly lucrative though more recently he fared less well with contract cherry picking around Blenheim for six weeks from late November or early December:

The season starts with select picking (on November 20th) on which nobody made any wages worth bothering about. Things picked up after the first two or three weeks but unfortunately many backpackers were paid by the kilo throughout the season, even on select picking. I was aghast to earn about £40 in the first week, £60 in the second. Way too fickle a fruit. Yeah, in an excellent year with good pollination, ideal weather and a good orchard, it might be possible to earn $800 a week (the figure used by the orchard owners to motivate the thoroughly disillusioned backpackers). But in a bad or average year, I would stick with apple thinning.

Cherries are picked around Queenstown in December. It is also worth travelling to the far south of the South Island in early December for the tulip harvest (for example at Van Eeden Tulips, West Plains, R.D.4, Invercargill). Another Otago farm which extends a welcome to overseas working holidaymakers is Schist Mountain Orchards Ltd (PO Box 302, Alexandra; tel/fax 03-449 2063) where the cherry harvest begins in mid-December followed by soft fruit harvests through the autumn. It was recently reported that massive investment in cherry production around Cromwell (not far from Alexandra) could create 400 additional seasonal jobs for the area in the early years of the 21st century.

Other Farm Work

To state the obvious, there is a great deal of sheep and dairy farming in New Zealand. Wages on sheep stations are not likely to be high, perhaps $250 a week in addition to room and board. The International Agricultural Exchange Association offers seven or eight month placements in New Zealand to trained agriculturalists from the UK or Ireland, which will cost about £2,500.

Gerhard Flaig from Germany followed up a lead from another traveller and was invited to stay on the farm, which is a very typical New Zealand scenario:

Very soon we all liked each other and I ended up staying five weeks on the sheep farm. I helped muster the sheep, sort the wool, repair fences, make firewood, do some construction work and gardening, mow the lawn, do some washing and cleaning. I didn't get money but got free board and lodging and in addition I had a wonderful time in rural countryside. We went for day trips to visit sights, we rode horses, we hunted wild pigs... There are many farmers in New Zealand willing to have travellers for some time to help them in their daily work.

The Saturday edition of the *New Zealand Herald* and the *Waikato Times* in Hamilton are recommended for people looking for work on the land. Philippa Andrews noticed that there were almost daily adverts for milkers in the latter paper between July and Christmas. Usually experience is required. Small town New Zealanders would be intrigued by an advert placed by a young traveller in their local paper. Ken Smith was impressed with the initiative of the traveller who placed an ad in the *Oamaru Mail:* 'Young German man seeks farm work. Has tractor experience and good work habits;' Ken is sure that the novelty value of this approach would almost certainly bring success.

Gina Farmer (possibly a pseudonym?) describes her reasonably well paid job as a 'rousie':

Some of the jobs I have done in New Zealand have not been at all easy. For example, as a rousie, you get up at 4am, are working by 5am and don't stop until 5pm, with no guarantee of a day off until it rains so much that the sheep get wet. If you work with a slow gang where the average number of sheep shorn is about 250 a day per shearer then life can be quite fun. However if you land with a gang where the average is 350 and you have to look after two shearers, then life get decidedly tough. So anybody considering this sort of job would be wise to make some enquiries first. Whatever the case this is not a job for the faint-hearted.

TOURISM

Openings in New Zealand's flourishing tourist industry continue to proliferate. Waiters and waitresses are usually paid $8-$9 an hour. Remember that tips in New Zealand are virtually non-existent. On the plus side, restaurant kitchens tend to be more relaxed places than they are in Europe. Hotels in Paihia in the far north are reputed to be often short-staffed. The proliferation of cafés, bars and boat trip companies means that someone determined to find an alternative to fruit-picking in this area would be likely to succeed, especially if they could conduct a job hunt in October.

Although Wellington is not the first city you think of in the context of New Zealand tourism, it has a remarkably high ratio of cafés to citizen and a booming job market. Catharine Carfoot showed up there in November 2000 with a working holiday visa (though she wasn't always asked to show it) and easily found work first and accommodation second:

I am currently working weekends driving for Wellington Cable Cars which has its ups and downs (cable car joke). And I'm doing various things during the week, mostly temping through Select Appointments and Opus International, and life modelling at the Inverlochy Art School and Vincents Art workshop ($80 cash for five hours). In fact tomorrow will be my 21st day of work without a full day off (not quite my record but nearly). Bizarrely, I seem to be practising my French conversation skills more than I have done for years, both at the Cable Car and with people met on the street asking for directions. It seems very odd that even the bigger hotels here don't always have a francophone on duty.

There are many adventurous forms of the tourist industry. You might get taken on by a camping tour operator as a cook; perhaps you could find a job on a yacht or in a ski resort (see below). Adventure Cycles mentioned above offers paid positions to experienced bicycle mechanics with cycle touring experience, especially between September and November.

Queenstown & the South Island

The lakeside resort of Queenstown is particularly brimming with opportunities. It is a town whose economy is booming due to tourism and whose population is largely young and transient. It is now almost as common to hear foreign accents among seasonal workers as New Zealand ones, though bear in mind that for this reason Queenstown has become a target for immigration investigations. It is one of the few places in which restaurants and bars (especially those that have been burned in the past) may ask to see your passport.

The central town notice board in the pedestrian mall and the notice board in supermarkets often carry adverts for waitresses, kitchen help, etc., as do the boards in the Queenstown Youth Hostel and backpacker haunts. One of the perks of being a worker in Queenstown and therefore an honorary resident (instead of a 'loopy', the local term for tourist), is that often workers can get discounts on local activities like rafting or 'zorbing' (rolling down a hill in a plastic ball). On the other hand, the town's popularity means that there are often more people (including New Zealanders) looking for work than there are jobs, so it might be advisable to try more remote tourist areas, like sparsely populated but heavily visited Milford Sound. It is accepted practice to phone the resort hotels and ask if they have any immediate vacancies. Good resorts to phone in addition to Milford Sound are Fox Glacier, Franz Josef and Mount Cook.

Ski Resorts

The ski season lasts roughly from July to October. The main ski resorts on the South Island are Coronet Peak and the Remarkables (serviced by Queenstown), Mount Hutt and Treble Cone (with access from Wanaka). On the North Island, Mount Ruapehu is the main ski area, at least when its volcanic activity is dormant. The ski field at Turoa is serviced by the resort of Ohakune and the ski area of Whakapapa by the settlement called National Park. Catering and related jobs are widely available in these resort towns. In addition to the hourly wage of $8-$9 you may be given a lift pass and subsidised food and drink. Matt Tomlinson enjoyed his two jobs in Ohakune as a barman in the ski resort bar and a waiter in a restaurant, though he came to the conclusion that New Zealand bosses like to get their money's worth. When there weren't many customers, he was put to work building shelves, chopping wood and cleaning drains. He found the jobs by checking notice boards (by the library in Ohakune and in the supermarket), reading the local newspapers and asking around. You will also have to keep your ears open if you are to find affordable accommodation. Matt Tomlinson suggests asking about the accommodation service in the Ski Country office in Ohakune. Turoa Cafeterias have some staff accommodation but you have to be early.

If you have a specific skill, e.g. ski instructor, ski patroller, ski hire technician, snowcat/plough driver, then it is worth applying to the resort in advance. Resort addresses are listed in the *Travel Survival Kit New Zealand* from Lonely Planet. Opportunities also exist for carpenters and painters in the months before the season begins; ask around in the pubs.

To get a job as an instructor, request a place on one of the hiring clinics held at the beginning of July in most resorts, for which you will have to pay (but not much). A BASI certificate or equivalent (see introductory chapter *Tourism*) is essential to get full-time instructing work. Part-timers or rookie instructors usually get a lift pass plus instructor training sessions and loggable hours of practice. Snowboard instructors are in heavy demand and may not need advanced qualifications to be hired.

Fishing

Fishing is a profitable business for New Zealand and fishermen can be found in most coastal towns. Nelson is one of the important centres for fishing and fish processing, and one of the largest processing operations is called Sealords where you might get a job (though it's a long shot) filleting, freezing and packing fish in the block freezer. If you can, try to get taken on instead as a 'wharfie,' transferring the fish from the boats to the chiller, since the pay will be better. Go down to the docks before 6am to see if any casual work is available.

The oyster season runs from April to December and oyster shelling work is available especially in Whangarei on the North Island, Orongo Bay near Russell and in Kerikeri. Fiona Cox enjoyed this work far more than fruit picking:

We found work the day after we arrived in Whangarei in December and worked for the three weeks of the Christmas rush. We phoned about four fisheries, none of which asked about visas. We even got a gumboot allowance! Loads of overtime and in terms of perks and fairness to the workers, it was one of the best places I've worked in, even if we did work in a bloody cold disco. Managed to save enough money to do some touring in the North Island.

Of course recreational fishing creates work, as the American Chris Miksovsky describes:

Queenstown was such a nice place that I decided to stay for a while. I happened upon a job with a chartered fishing boat business. We'd take small groups of angler-wanna-be's out in a motorboat and try to help them catch some rainbow trout or lake salmon. I got to go on several outings but mostly I sat at a small desk by our dock in the town harbour giving information to people about the trips and getting a commission on the trips I booked. The money was excellent some days ($150 was my record) and nil others, all paid cash-in-hand. It was probably the most relaxing and scenic job I've ever had, *right on the water, surrounded by mountains, watching the tourists of the world go by. The only downside was that I often had to listen to die-hard fishermen go on and on about all the fish they'd caught around the world. The Americans were the worst: 'Now y'all see that there Barracuuuuda?' (pointing to photo) 'I caught that big ol' boy in Faayjaay. Tuk me fowr hours to brang that there sucker in.'*

BUSINESS & INDUSTRY

Experienced secretaries are in constant demand in Auckland and Wellington, though temp agencies like Alfred Marks will want to be reassured that you have a legal right to work in the country. A mobile phone makes it much easier to stay in touch with employment agencies. Temps in Auckland earn between $15 and $18 an hour, data entry pays $13-$14. Holiday pay of 6% is also accrued. Agencies in Auckland to try are Alpha Personnel (Suite 1, Level 3, 27 Gillies Ave, Newmarket, Auckland; 09-524 2336; info@alphajobs.co.nz); Kelly Services (Level 5, Lufthansa House, 36 Kitchener St; 09-303 3122) and Robert Walters plc (PO Box 91080; 09-377 9778). The latter two have branches in Wellington too.

Without secretarial skills, try market research and labouring agencies, which sometimes require only an IRD number. Building work abounds in Auckland and in other areas of the North Island. Labouring agencies can be a good bet such as Allied Workforce in Mount Wellington. Check the Saturday and Wednesday editions of the *New Zealand Herald* and the *Dominion Press* which carry adverts for labourers, clerks, waiters, drivers, receptionists, etc.

Scouring the ads paid off for Jane Harris who hadn't been having much luck doing the rounds of the cafés and sandwich shops in Auckland. She answered an ad placed by a direct marketing company in the *Herald* and was soon selling charity pens and key rings door-to-door:

The pay for my job was commission only, but it was easy to earn $90-$100 per day. People were much more welcoming than I expected. And I enjoyed working out of doors. I did that job for two months before getting fed up with it. So I went after a job as manager of another backpackers hostel (Lantana Lodge) which I got and was given free accommodation with my boyfriend Pete. I also managed to get a second part-time job (which paid $11.33 an hour) as a telephone interviewer for a market research company. Easy work. In all cases, I told them I have a work permit (though I'm 34 and therefore ineligible); all they wanted was my IRD number and bank account details.

The shortage of teachers in New Zealand has been somewhat reduced over the past two years but there is still demand, particularly for pre-school and primary teachers. The NZ government has been providing incentives such as a $3,000 relocation grant in order to attract teachers from overseas, many from Britain, on two-year visas; details on www.teachnz.govt.nz/overseas.html. Most of the schools experiencing a shortage are rural schools off the beaten track which would afford an excellent opportunity to experience country life.

Useful websites which list actual job vacancies (most of them permanent) and dates of posting are www.nzjobs.co.nz, www.netcheck.co.nz and www.workingin.com. The latter company produces a glossy recruitment magazine (Working In Ltd, PO Box 3394, Shortland St, Auckland; 09-425 9540).

If you want to top up your travel fund before leaving New Zealand by selling used camping, tramping, biking or surf gear, go to the large sports and outdoor recreation store R & R Sport (538 Karangahape Road, Corner Gundry St, Auckland; 09-309-6444).

ANTARCTICA

As well as the highly trained scientists and others needed to run an Antarctic research station such as McMurdo Station, a certain number of dogsbodies are needed. The

Raytheon Technical Services company is subcontracted by the US government's National Science Foundation to hire between 800 and 1,000 Americans to run the station, a third of whom are women. Of these, a certain number are general assistants (GAs) who, among many tasks, do quite a lot of snow shovelling. Openings also exist for chefs, electricians, computer programmers, typists, construction workers and so on. Contracts are for four, six or twelve months.

Raytheon begin considering applications in April though may not choose their summer season personnel (to work October to mid-February) until the last moment. Even though the work schedule is nine hours a day, six days a week, these jobs are massively oversubscribed, so perseverance will be needed, plus excellent health (physical, mental and dental) and a willingness to travel at short notice. The contact address is Human Resources Department, Raytheon Technical Services (Polar Services), 61 Inverness Drive East, Suite 300, Englewood, CO 80112 (303-790-8606/800-688-8000; www.rpsc.raytheon.com).

Britain's five research stations and two research vessels in Antarctica are overseen by the British Antarctic Survey (Highcross, Madingley Road, Cambridge CB3 0ET; 01223 221508; employment@bas.ac.uk/ www.antarctica.ac.uk/Employment/index.html). All support staff hired by BAS must be suitably qualified or experienced and willing to sign an eight-month or a 33-month contract.

United States

The great American Dream has beckoned countless people who have left their homelands in eager pursuit of the economic miracle. Whether Latin Americans fleeing poverty at home or East Europeans seeking a brave new world, generations of foreigners have become part of the American population which is often described as a 'melting pot'. But the tide has changed to a trickle. Although the unemployment rate has steadily fallen to less than 4% and 10,000 new jobs are being created each day, the authorities do all in their power to keep out people who come to their country to look for work.

Despite the wide open spaces and warm hospitality so often associated with America, their official policies are discouraging for the traveller who plans to pick up some casual work along the way. The choice of the word 'alien' in official use to describe foreigners may not be intentionally symbolic, however it does convey the suspicion with which non-Americans are treated by the authorities. It is very difficult to get permission to work. Even applications for tourist visas should contain proof of means of support and documentary evidence that the applicant will be returning home. On the face of it, it is all or nothing: either your status is as a tourist who is categorically forbidden to work, or you are an immigrant who must offer a whole range of advanced qualifications and connections. But as we have found in so many other countries, there are some special provisions and exceptions to the rule.

The most important exception to the gloomy generalisation is the special work visa available through work and travel programmes like the ones run by BUNAC, the British Universities North America Club (16 Bowling Green Lane, London EC1R 0QH; 020-7251 3472; www.bunac.org.uk) and UsitNow, the Irish student travel service (19-21 Aston Quay, Dublin 2; www.usitNow.ie). All of these programmes including the summer camp agencies are described in detail since they arrange for large numbers of people to work legitimately in the USA. This is because they are authorised by the US Information Agency to give out J-1 exchange visas. Other possibilities include joining the one-year Au Pair in America Programme (see section on Childcare below) or joining one of the internship programmes, which require you to find your own position in your field of study. For a brief list of approved exchanges and internship programmes in the US, send an s.a.e. to the Educational Advisory Service of the Fulbright Commission, 62 Doughty St, London WC1N 2JZ (0120-7404 6994; education@fulbright.co.uk) or check their web-site www.fulbright.co.uk.

The other side of the coin is the possibility of working without permission, which carries a number of risks and penalties to be carefully considered beforehand. As described below, the laws are always changing in order to tighten up on black work. For example a controversial law (Proposition 187) in California prohibits undocumented aliens (of whom it is estimated there are 3.4 million in the US) from education, health care, etc. The missing link between you and a whole world of employment prospects is a social security number to which you will not be legally entitled unless you have a recognised work visa.

VISAS

Most British citizens and those of 28 other countries do not need to apply for a tourist visa in advance. Tourists can wait until arrival to obtain a visa-waiver which is valid for one entry to the US for a maximum of 90 days. Those planning trips of more than 90 days must obtain a tourist visa in advance from the Embassy. The holder of a tourist visa may be granted a stay of up to six months at the discretion of the immigration officer at the port of entry. Individuals entering visa-free under the Visa-Waiver Programme or with a visitor visa for business or tourism are prohibited from engaging in paid or unpaid employment in the US. There is an application fee for a non-immigrant visas of $45 (currently £28). For further information visit the Embassy's website at www.usembassy.org.uk or call their automated information message service or their operator-assisted visa information service on 09061-500590 (8am-8pm weekdays); calls are charged at £1.50 per minute.

The Visa Branch of the US Embassy (5 Upper Grosvenor St, London W1A 2JB) can send a brief outline of the non-immigrant visas available or it is spelled out on the website. The visa of most interest to the readers of this book is the J-1 which is available to participants of government-authorised programmes, known as Exchange Visitor Programmes (EVP). The J-1 visa is a valuable and coveted addition to any passport since it entitles the holder to take legal paid employment. You cannot apply for the J-1 without form IAP-66 and you cannot get form IAP-66 without going through a recognised Exchange Visitor Programme (like BUNAC and Camp America) which have sponsoring organisations in the US.

The programmes are allowed to exist because of their educational value. These exchanges and their quotas are reviewed regularly by the government, though with constant lobbying and proof from employers of staff shortages, the quotas have been increasing. Still it is important that the arrangement not be abused (e.g. participants breaking the terms of the programme, or even worse, breaking the law) since this will damage the reputation of the entire programme.

Other Visas

Apart from the J-1 visa available to people on approved EVPs, there are three possible visa categories to consider. The Q visa is the 'International Cultural Exchange Visa' (affectionately dubbed the 'Disney' visa, since it was introduced partly in response to their lobbying). After working at Disney World on a Q visa, Paul Binfield concluded that the main difference between the J-1 and the Q-1 was that the latter obliges you to pay more tax. If you find a job in which it can be argued that you will be providing practical training or sharing the history, culture and traditions of your country with Americans (e.g. Morris dancing teacher), you might be eligible to work legally for up to 15 months. This must be applied for by the prospective employer in the US and approved in advance by an office of the Immigration and Naturalization Service (INS).

Another possibility is the B-1 'Voluntary Service' visa. Applications must be sponsored by a charitable or religious organisation which undertakes not to pay you but may reimburse you for incidental expenses. Applicants must do work of a traditional charitable nature. In addition, the H category covers non-immigrant work visas. The H-1B 'Temporary Worker' visa for professionals with a degree is available for 'prearranged professional or highly skilled jobs' for which there are no suitably qualified Americans. In 2000, the US government proposed raising the allocation of H1-B visas from 115,000 to 195,000 over the next two years, partly to alleviate the shortage of IT specialists. The H-1B visa might be upgraded to green card status. A university degree is a pre-requisite and all the paperwork must be carried out by the American employer who must pay a training fee.

The H1-A is available only to nurses and physiotherapists. The H-3 'Industrial Trainee' visa is the other possibility. Applicants must indicate in detail the breakdown between classroom and on-the-job time, and why equivalent training is not available in their own country. H-visas are rarely relevant to the average traveller. The category EP-3 visa is available to skilled workers with at least two years relevant experience or training, but they need not have a university degree; computer programmers might qualify for example. Foreign students on an I-20 visa are allowed to work up to 20 hours a week.

It is exceedingly difficult to get an immigrant visa or 'green card' (actually it's off-white) which allows foreigners to live and work in the US as 'resident aliens'. Nearly all the permanent resident visas which are issued each year are given to close relations of American citizens. Money and love are not the only reasons to marry, though this course of action is too drastic for most. More than a few foreigners have in the past been tempted to obtain a counterfeit green card. However the Immigration & Naturalization Service (INS) has spent millions to develop a green card which they believe to be proof against forgery; it features microscopic portraits of all the presidents, a hologram of the Statue of Liberty and other hi-tech wizardry.

Every autumn, the US government holds a Green Card Lottery or 'Diversity Immigrant Visa Program' whereby applications are drawn from a hat. Strict quotas operate for different nationalities and, in recent years, Britons have been barred from entering (apart from people from Northern Ireland).

Arrival

If you have a visa, a return ticket and look tidy and confident, chances are you will whizz through immigration. But American immigration is so notoriously tough and unpleasant that it is worth describing some of the techniques used by readers to avoid possible catastrophe. If you are sure that you will not want to stay longer than 90 days, you can sign the visa waiver form at entry. One reader wrote to say that she had trouble crossing back from Mexico with a visa waiver; however the official word is that you can cross borders as long as the crossing takes place within 90 days of your return ticket from North America to Europe.

Whichever method you choose, be prepared for a gruelling inquisition when you first arrive. It is probably better to ask for a relatively short stay since the authorities are bound to be suspicious of someone who says he or she plans to be a tourist for five months. Whatever you do, don't confess that you hope to find work. Dress neatly but remember to look like a tourist, not an aspiring professional. Sander Meijsen was pulled out of the immigration queue probably because he was carrying a smart laptop computer.

If you are taken away to be interviewed, expect to have your luggage minutely examined. Be prepared to explain anything in your luggage which an average sightseeing tourist would be unlikely to have, such as smart clothes (for possible interviews). Better still, don't pack anything which could be incriminating such as letters of reference, letters from an American referring to jobs or interviews, or even a copy of this book. Having written proof that you have a full-time job to return to, property ties or a guaranteed place in higher education in the UK are also an asset. It can be helpful to provide them with a travel itinerary, a list of places and people you want to see in your capacity of tourist.

Although having a return or onward ticket is no guarantee that you will not be hassled, it helps your case. Many travellers recommend entering the US on a short-term return ticket which can be extended after arrival, for instance with Kuwait Airways or Virgin Atlantic. (If you do choose this option, make sure before you buy a

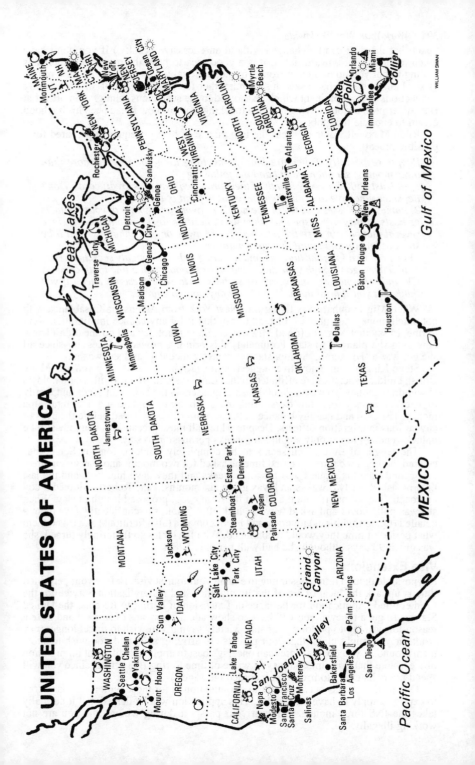

UNITED STATES OF AMERICA

WILLIAM SWAN

ticket that the date can be changed without an excessive penalty.) If you don't have much money or an onward ticket, it is a good idea to have the names of Americans willing to put you up or a letter from a friend, undertaking to support you for a month or so. Laurence Koe had asked his grandmother to type up a list of all their family connections on the continent which he showed to the suspicious immigration officer at Hawaii Airport, accompanying it with a touching story of how it had been his boyhood dream to encircle the globe.

Rilda Maxwell wants to stress the importance of being adequately prepared for a possible ordeal:

> *People (especially if they are black, travelling alone or staying more than three months) should have at hand the following:*
> *1) at least $500 for every month of their proposed stay plus credit cards. Don't lie, since you have to count the money out in front of them.*
> *2) names, addresses and telephone numbers (work and home) of your contacts or hosts. If they are suspicious, they won't hesitate to ring the numbers. Have several numbers in case the first people are away or out. Otherwise you'll be stuck at Immigration until they get an answer.*
> *3) be prepared for your luggage and handbag to be thoroughly searched. They read letters, go through your diary and address book with a fine tooth comb. A CV and reference are a give-away, so be sure to send these on ahead if you think that you'll need them. Don't leave anything to chance.*

When Mig Urquhart was flying into New York from Athens via Casablanca with not much money, she phoned a friend to say that if by any chance immigration were to ring, to say that, yes, her friend Mig was coming on holiday and no she didn't know how long she planned to stay. Fortunately this priming proved unnecessary since all she got was a 'Hi there'... Stamp, stamp... 'Have a nice day' and she was in.

Steve King has an innovative suggestion for proving how wealthy you are. Many British building societies are affiliated to the 'Link' system, which entitles card holders to withdraw money from over 20,000 cash dispensers in the US. Get friends and family to lend you money for a few days, bring the passbook up to date and then return the money. The card and healthy balance in the account can be paraded before the eyes of any curious immigration officers. Despite taking all these precautions you may still be unlucky enough to get only a couple of weeks permission to stay.

The length of time given seems to be completely random. Marcus Scrace has entered the US three times: the first time he asked for two months and was given three; the second time his request was for three weeks and they gave him two; and the last time he asked for two weeks and was given six months! Jane Roberts adopted a coy approach. She did not fill out the part of the form about proposed length of stay. When she was pulled over and asked why she had left it blank, she confidently gave them a detailed (though fictitious) itinerary and list of contacts (also fictitious) and asked them what period of time they would recommend. With the tables so flatteringly turned, she was given 90 days although she had with her only $280.

Visa Extensions

It is possible though time-consuming to extend your tourist visa. Before your permitted time is up, ask the local office of the Immigration and Naturalization Service for the form entitled 'Application for Issuance or Extension of Permit to Re-enter the United States.' To get a renewal you will have to show adequate means of support and have a reason for wishing to prolong your stay. Merely saying you wish to travel longer may work, or you might claim that your parents are arriving soon and you wish to show them around. If you do this more than once, it's best to apply to a different immigration office. (Note that it is almost always a waste of time to ring INS offices since you will spend hours listening to irrelevant recorded messages.)

One tactic that has been brought to our attention is for those with a J-1 visa about to expire to apply to have it extended. This application will be denied, but it normally takes the INS three months to return your passport during which time you are not working illegally.

Alternatively you can slip over the Canadian or Mexican border and recross the border and hope that the immigration officer on your return will automatically extend your stay. Paul Donut recommends one border crossing in particular:

The border crossing at Point Roberts near Vancouver is a good one. It is on a peninsula and once crossed you can't go anywhere except back into Canada. The US Immigration officials accept that people cross purely to visit the bars and seem to give everyone a six-month visa without asking too many questions. The last time I crossed I actually had to ask for the stamp and card (as a souvenir) as they just weren't interested. By contrast the Canadian crossing on the Pacific Highway is very strict. The officer I encountered checked everything in great detail: money, plane ticket, where I had been, where I was going, etc. I believe strongly that being polite and friendly to the border guards pays dividends.

If you overstay, you can 'lose' the immigration card showing your date of entry from your passport. In most cases it is only the airline which looks at your passport on your way out and they don't care. The best plan is to exit by land to Mexico or Canada where there is no US immigration control. If trying to re-enter the States without a valid visa, try to arrive in a car full of Americans. US citizens do not normally show any documentation at these borders, so if you have overstayed put on your all-American clean cut look, get some chewing gum, smile confidently and hope the word passport does not crop up.

WORK AND TRAVEL PROGRAMMES

Obviously it is preferable to avoid all this anxiety about visas by participating in an approved exchange programme. *BUNAC* (16 Bowling Green Lane, London EC1R 0QH; 020-7251 3472; www.bunac.org.uk) administers three basic programmes in the US: one is the 'Work America Programme' which allows full-time university students to do any summer job they are able to find; the second is 'Summer Camp USA' which is open to anyone over 18 interested in working on a summer camp as a counsellor; the third is 'KAMP' (Kitchen & Maintenance Programme) which is open to students who want to work at a summer camp in a catering and maintenance capacity. (The camp programmes are described below under the heading 'Summer Camps'. All participants must join the BUNAC Club (£4), travel on BUNAC flights between June and October and purchase compulsory insurance (about £100). BUNAC runs its own loan scheme.

If you are considering a summer job in America, it is worth contacting BUNAC headquarters or your local club branch (in most universities) as early as possible for their detailed brochure setting out the various and potentially confusing procedures. There is no easy way of circumventing the red tape and accompanying uncertainty though BUNAC are very experienced at guiding applicants as gently as possible through the process.

BUNAC's *Work America* programme (workamerica@bunac.org.uk) offers about 4,000 places to students who may take virtually any job anywhere in the US over the summer. To assist applicants in finding work, BUNAC publishes an annual Job Directory with thousands of job listings in the US from hundreds of employers, many of whom have taken on BUNAC participants in the past. The Directory is available to all potential applicants and is free of charge. Accommodation may be provided by the employer, particularly if a British student takes a job in the hospitality industry.

In addition to the registration fee of £84 for first-time applicants and the flight package of £419, you must submit a letter from your principal, registrar or tutor on college headed paper showing that you are a full-time student in the year of travel. Gap year students should submit evidence of an unconditional offer for the September/October after they have returned from the US. You are also required to take at least $400 in travellers cheques. If you are going over with a commission sales job, however, you must take at least $800 although BUNAC recommends that you take more.

In addition to BUNAC, the principal work and travel programmes (as distinct from career-oriented internship programmes described in the next section) are broadly comparable. These programmes provide full-time or deferred place students aged 19 to 30 with the opportunity to live and work in the US for a maximum of four months.

Council Exchanges, 52 Poland St, London W1V 4JQ (020-7478 2000/freephone 0800 731 9076; watusa@councilexchanges.org.uk/www.councilexchanges.org.uk) offer a Work and Travel in the USA programme in addition to their Internship USA programme described later. Participants are free to find their own summer jobs before departure (and must show back-up funds of $400) or on arrival in the US (with $800 in support funds). The fee for Work and Travel USA ranges from £638 to £745. This includes a flight to New York, San Francisco or Chicago, insurance and first night's accommodation. Council has a jobs database on its website of 20,000 jobs and internships in the USA.

Council Exchanges in Sydney (University Centre, Level 8, 210 Clarence St, Sydney, NSW 2000; 02-9373 2730; www.councilexchanges.org.au) organises Work and Travel USA for Australian students, while New Zealanders should contact STA Travel in Auckland (10 High St; 09-309 9723). Antipodeans are permitted to work in the US between November 1st and March 19th only (which makes it tricky for people working in ski resorts) but participants can stay on for an extra month on a tourist visa.

Camp Counselors & Work Experience USA, Green Dragon House, 64-70 High Street, Croydon CR0 9XN; 020-8688 9051; england@workexperienceusa.com; www.workexperienceusa.com). In addition to its summer camp programme (described below), CCUSA has a sizeable Work Experience programme whereby participants can work on a J-1 visa in any job for up to four months between June 1st and October 19th. Candidates choose whether to find their own job before or after arrival or to have CCUSA find a job for them. CCUSA works with a number of employers in resort and vacation centres throughout the United States to find placements for participants so that a job offer is guaranteed to those who are accepted onto the programme. The total package cost of £695 (deposit £95) includes a Directory of Employers, return airfare from London to New York, four months insurance, meeting on arrival and two-day orientation in New York with accommodation. Without the job-finding option, the price is £595. Interested individuals in Scotland and the north of England should contact the CCUSA office at 27 Woodside Gardens, Musselburgh, Scotland EH21 7LJ (tel/fax 0131-665 5843; scotland@workexperienceusa.com). Most recruitment takes place before April 1st. The company has a network of interviewers around the UK and organises various open houses and recruitment fairs. The US headquarters of CCUSA are at 2330 Marinship Way, Suite 250, Sausalito, CA 94965 (www.campcounselors.com) who run several outgoing programmes for American students.

EIL, 287 Worcester Road, Malvern, Worcs. WR14 1AB (01684 562577/fax 01684 562212; www.eiluk.org) now offer a Work & Travel USA programme for full-time students aged 18-30 to work for two to four months over the summer.

Internships

Internship is the American term for traineeship, providing a chance to get some experience in your career interest as part of your academic course. In many cases, internships are unpaid. The book *Internships* published by Peterson's Guides (address below) lists intern positions which are paid or unpaid, can last for the summer, for a semester or for a year. The book offers general advice (including a section called 'Foreign Applicants for US Internships') and specific listings organised according to field of interest, e.g. Advertising, Museums, Radio, Social Services, Law, etc. This annually revised book is available in the UK from Vacation-Work for £17.95 plus £3 postage.

Several organisations in the UK arrange for students and in some cases graduates to arrange work placements in the USA each year. The most important is Council Exchanges, 52 Poland St, London W1V 4JQ (020-7478 2020) which helps 1,000 full-time students and recent graduates to arrange course-related placements in the US lasting from a few weeks to 18 months. The placement can take place at any time during your studies, during the summer, as a sandwich year or up to 12 months after graduating. Although you are responsible for finding your own course-related position, Council supplies practical advice on applying for work in their 'Internships USA' information pack and with a searchable database of internships/work placements. Those who qualify get a J-1 visa. The programme fees are £250 for a stay of up to two months, plus an extra £30 per month thereafter. Applicants in France should apply to Council, 1 place de l'Odéon, 75006 Paris (1-44 41 74 74) and in Germany to Council, Oranienburger Str. 13-14, 10178 Berlin.

Council also administer the UK/US Career Development Programme in conjunction with the Association for International Practical Training (AIPT) in Maryland. (Other nationalities should apply through the partner organisation in their own countries.) This programme is for people aged 18-35 with relevant qualifications and/or at least one year of work experience in their career field. A separate section of the programme is for full-time students in Hospitality & Tourism or Equine Studies. A placement assistance service is also available for some Career Development participants. A good starting place is AIPT's on-line placement system (www.pinpointtraining.org).

BUNAC operates an internship programme dubbed OPT USA (Overseas Practical Training) sponsored by International Program Services of the American YMCA. The programme is open to non-students as well as students but must be integrated into between three and 18 months of on-the-job training (and not just work experience). Programme fees vary from £190 for a student staying up to six months to £399 for a non-student staying up to 18 months.

Challenge Educational Services (101 Lorna Road, Hove, East Sussex BN3 3EL; 01273 220261; enquiries@challengeuk.com/ www.challengeuk.com) have a USA Work Placement Programme whereby fee-paying interns aged 18-25 are placed in business and industry for one to four months. The majority of placements are in the San Francisco Bay area. Note that from 2001 all internships will be unpaid. Fees vary from £980 for one month if you find your own accommodation to about £2,600 for three months if you are placed with a host family.

Other internship sponsors include InterExchange (161 Sixth Avenue, New York, NY 10013) and Alliances Abroad (702 West Ave, Austin, TX 78701; www.alliancesabroad.com) in conjunction with an organisation called Cultural Latitudes, both of which are accredited to grant J-1 visas to European candidates. Alliances Abroad arrange internships in Denver, San Francisco and Washington DC. A smaller scale internship programme is operated by Hostelling International (733 15th St NW, Suite 840, Washington, DC 20005) which relies on interns from around the world who stay for at least ten weeks. Interns receive free accommodation at the hostel in downtown Washington plus $100 a week for BAs (students or graduates) or $150 for people working towards or finished a graduate degree. Available internships are listed at www.hiayh.org. Deadlines fall on the 1st of February, May, August and December.

The Mountbatten Internship Programme (Abbey House, 74-76 St John St, 5th Floor, London EC1M 4DZ; www.mountbatten.org) provides work experience in New York City for people aged 20-26 with business training. Placements last one year and provide free accommodation as well as a monthly wage of $940. Interns pay a participation fee of £1,175.

SUMMER CAMPS

Summer camps are uniquely American in atmosphere, even if the idea has spread to Europe. An estimated 8 million American children are sent to 10,000 summer camps each year for a week or more to participate in outdoor activities and sports, arts and crafts and generally have a wholesome experience. The type of camp varies from plush sports camps for the very rich to more or less charitable camps for the handicapped or underprivileged.

It is estimated that summer camps employ nearly a third of a million people. Thousands of 'counsellors' are needed each summer to be in charge of a cabinful of youngsters and to instruct or supervise some activity, from the ordinary (swimming and boating) to the esoteric (puppet-making and ham radio). Several summer camp organisations are authorised to issue J-1 visas, primarily Camp America and BUNAC, but some smaller ones are also mentioned below.

After camp finishes, counsellors have up to six weeks' free time and normally return on organised flights between late August and the end of September. Camp counselling regularly wins enthusiastic fans and is worth considering if you enjoy children (even the rambunctious American variety who might sue you if you shout at them) and don't mind hard work. As Hannah Start concluded after a summer at an expensive camp in upstate New York, primarily for Jewish kids, 'If you can survive the bugs and the kids, camp counselling is a healthy, rewarding way to spend the summer.' Some camps are staffed almost entirely by young people from overseas, which can be useful if you are looking for a post-camp travelling companion. Others have a reasonable proportion of American employees, in which case there is a good chance that you will be invited to visit their homes when camp finishes. In Hannah's view, whatever happens at camp is compensated by the amazing travel opportunities afterwards.

If the idea of working at a remote lakeside or mountain location appeals to you but the 24-hour-a-day responsibility for keeping children entertained and well-behaved does not, you might be interested in a behind-the-scenes job in the kitchen or maintenance. Camp directors often find it difficult to attract Americans to do these jobs, partly because the wages are low, and both BUNAC and Camp America can arrange this for British and European students.

Bear in mind that your enjoyment of a summer camp job will be largely determined by the style of the camp, the standard of facilities and its proximity to interesting places to visit on your days off. (Note that a day off is often 24 hours, so can be from 5pm one day to 5pm the next.) Signing up with one of the big organisations like BUNACAMP or Camp America is a lottery. If you happen to have had a camp recommended, you are free to contact them independently, fix up a job and then ask one of the exchange visitor programmes to expedite the paperwork. Another way of making an informed choice is to attend one of the recruitment fairs held in the new year by Camp America where you can meet camp directors. This might have helped Amy Jones, a student at Nottingham University, to avert her disastrous experience:

> *On arrival we were launched into a 75 hour week, looking after the children and the 37 horses. This increased to 85 when the only American counsellor quit after just two weeks. Apart from the exhaustion, this might have been tolerable. But the couple who ran the camp were intimidating. They seemed worried we might run away (which we did often think about). One of the new rules they imposed was that we were not allowed to speak to each other unless it concerned camp organisation. There was no privacy and no freedom. The atmosphere was filled with tension.*

Amy's conclusion was that, seen from one point of view, the recruitment agencies supply cheap labour who are not at liberty to leave because they then forfeit their free flight.

Camps have to impose rules and in many cases these are quite strict, such as no alcohol (apparently Irish and Australian counsellors, true to their reputations, are the most likely to be fined for drinking at camp.)

BUNAC

With its *Summer Camp USA* programme, BUNAC is one of the two biggest counsellor placement organisations in the field, sending between 3,000 and 4,000 people aged between 19 (occasionally 18 year olds are accepted) and 35 as counsellors at children's camps. The registration fee of £59 includes camp placement, return flight and land transport to camp and pocket money of $540-$600 (depending on age) for the whole nine-week period. The fact that you do not have to raise the money for the flight is a great attraction for many; the camp which decides to hire you advances the amount from your wages to BUNAC who in turn put it towards your flight. Interviews, which are compulsory, are held in university towns throughout Britain between November and May.

Summer camps provide more scope for employment than looking after the kids. BUNAC's Kitchen and Maintenance Programme, otherwise known as *KAMP*, is open only to students including those at the end of their gap year who are given ancillary jobs in the kitchen, laundry or maintenance department, for which they will be advanced their airfare and in some cases paid more than the counsellors, i.e. a guaranteed minimum of $675 for the nine-week period of work. The registration fee is £59.

Camp America

Camp America (37a Queen's Gate, Dept. WW, London SW7 5HR; 020-7581 7333; brochure@campamerica.co.uk/ www.campamerica.co.uk) is another major recruitment organisation in Britain, which arranges for over 9,000 people aged 18 or over, from around the world, to work on children's summer camps in the USA. The work is for nine weeks between June and August where you could be teaching activities such as tennis, swimming and arts and crafts. Camp America provides a free return flight from London to New York and guidance on applying for a J-1 visa. The camp provides free board and lodging plus pocket money.

At the end of your contract, you will be given a lump sum of pocket money which will range for $360 to $810 depending on your age, experience, qualifications and whether you've been on Camp America before. Upfront charges include the registration fee of £128, compulsory medical insurance of £117 and some extra charges for airport tax (£12) and visa administration (£34).

Despite some initial anxiety, Mark Welfare enjoyed his counselling job arranged through Camp America:

> *Although I applied in January I didn't hear that I was definitely going until three weeks before departure, when I was just about to start my A-level exams. But it all worked out and I spent a very enjoyable summer working with handicapped and problem children at a camp in the Appalachian mountains of Pennsylvania. For me the Camp America scheme was ideal. I had never been away from home and it was a very easy introduction to travelling since flight, insurance, visa and job are all arranged for you.*

One way to secure a placement early and avoid last-minute uncertainty is to attend one of Camp America's recruitment fairs in London, Birmingham, Manchester, Edinburgh or Belfast in February and March, which is what Colin Rothwell did:

> *At the recruitment fair at Manchester Poly, you could actually meet the camp directors from all over the States and find out more about particular camps. If you are lucky, like me and a thousand others, you can sign a contract on the spot. Then you leave all the 'dirty work' to Camp America and wait until they call you to the airport in June sometime.*

Camp America also offers two other summer programmes: Campower for students who would like to work in the kitchen/maintenance areas at camp and the Resort America programme (www.resortamerica.co.uk) whereby people work in holiday resorts and are paid $1,100 for the minimum 12-week period.

During Darren Slevin's second summer with Camp America, he had reason to be grateful for the compulsory insurance. Persistent stomach cramps were diagnosed as a burst appendix which necessitated surgery and a hospital stay of over a week. The bill came to $15,000 which was all covered by insurance.

Other Summer Camp Organisations

Camp Counselors USA (CCUSA) works with 850 camps in 48 states and since 1986 has placed more than 40,000 young people aged 18-30 from over 60 countries. CCUSA's programme includes return flight to the US, one night's accommodation in New York City, visas and insurance, full board and lodging during placement as well as the chance to earn up to $600 as a first year counsellor. CCUSA tries to place counsellors at camps which suit their skills and personality. Enquiries should be made as early as possible to Camp Counselors (CCUSA), Green Dragon House, 64-70 High Street, Croydon CR0 9XN (020-8688 9051; england@workexperienceusa.com; www.workexperienceusa.com). Early applicants pay a lower registration fee than later ones. The deadline for applications is April 1st.

The pocket money for first year participants is $600 for the nine-week programme. CCUSA is reputed to offer a good service, as reported by Joseph Tame:

CCUSA were very good to me. They visited us during the summer and were very efficient when it came to my flight home. All I did was call their freefone number with the date I wanted to return; there and then they said yes. The overall impression I got was that CCUSA offered a good service, being relatively small and friendly.

Worldnet UK, (Avondale House, 63 Sydney Road, Haywards Heath, Sussex RH16 1QD (01444 453566) places 200 counsellors through its CAMP USA programme with US partner InterExchange. Similarly Solihull Au Pair & Nanny Agency (1565 Stratford Road, Hall Green, Birmingham B28 9JA; 0121-733 6444; www.aupairs4u.com) has a CampUSA programme. Another possibility is the camp programme run by the YMCA; contact YMCA/Go Global, 71 W. 23rd St, Suite 1904, New York, NY 10010 (212-727-8000; www.ymcanyc.org).

Many organisations in the rest of Europe send young people to the USA as camp counsellors; for example Travel Active Programmes in the Netherlands (PO Box 107, 5800 AC Venray) have up to 1,000 places for counsellors. Readers on the Continent should enquire of their national youth exchange organisation for details.

CASUAL WORK

A law stipulates that all employers must physically examine documents of prospective employees within three working days, proving that they are either a US citizen or an authorised alien (see *Documents* below). All US employers are obliged to complete an I-9 form which verifies the employee's right to work. Employers who are discovered by the Immigration and Naturalization Service to be hiring illegal aliens are subject to huge fines. Yet it is estimated that there are up to 200,000 British workers living and working illegally in California alone.

The law is unenforceable in seasonal industries such as fruit growing and resort tourism where it is still not uncommon for more than half of all employees to be illegal. Farmers and restaurateurs have claimed that they can barely stay in business without hiring casual workers without permits. Yet those who are caught working illegally run the risk of being deported, prohibited from travelling to the US for five years and in some cases for good. If your place of work is raided and you are caught, you will be detained while your case is being 'processed', which can take up to three weeks. If you are 'in-status' (which means your tourist visa has not expired) you are given the option of departing voluntarily. If not, you will be automatically deported.

The law seems to be more strictly enforced in areas which are traditional strongholds for 'wetbacks', illegal workers from Mexico and the rest of Latin America, such as California, Texas and Florida. Several years ago, Iain Kemble spent 11 lucrative weeks packing oranges in southern Florida. When he returned at the end of the year hoping to be hired again by the boss who had promised him a job, he was turned away, because the INS had visited the farms in the area putting a stop to cash-in-hand work.

On the other hand, when the authorities are targeting illegal hispanic workers, they may not notice others, as Jan Christensen from Denmark found when he worked in southern Florida on and off for two years, in which time he had no run-ins with the INS:

I arrived in southern Florida very low on cash. So I was very pleased to be offered a job on the second farm I went to and started the same day. No one seemed to care about my status. After about two weeks I was asked by the manager to fill out an employment form which had me worried for a while. I managed to avoid the question about the form for three more weeks until the manager finally cornered me. So I laid down the cards. Apparently he couldn't care less about permits. He was only bothered that I had tried to take him for a ride, and not told him the truth right away. I ended up working there for *about six months, without paying tax and earning an average of $500 a week cash-in-hand.*

In areas less accustomed to migrant workers, immigration checks are scarcely an issue. Matt Tomlinson from Sheffield found this to be the case in Philadelphia:

I got a great job canvassing for an environmental group. I had no hassle over my lack of documentation. I said it was in the post and they forgot to check. Another staple is restaurant work. I'm now working in a pizzeria which pays the minimum wage cash-in-hand no questions asked. Most other restaurants are the same in terms of laxity, especially take-aways. My friends and I have never had to spend more than a day looking for a job.

In major cities, it might be worthwhile approaching the charity concerned with water purity called PIRG (Public Interest Research Group) for work as a collector. Another useful standby in big cities is removal firms. The best time (for men) to look for work is just before the end of the month when many leases expire and more people tend to move house. Pay is often very good, i.e. $10-15 per hour.

Eamon Nolan tells a similar story about New Orleans:

New Orleans employers accept your invented social security number and show less than a passing interest in seeing your green card. You simply say you haven't got it with you today or you had it stolen.

Always act as though you have a perfect right to work. In many cases it is prudent to keep up this pretence with your fellow workers as well as your employer, at least until you know them better. Even menial jobs are taken seriously and harmless jokes or confidences to your work mates often result in your speedy departure.

Documents

Every American can reel off his social security number by heart. J-1 visa holders normally receive theirs within three weeks. Others have managed to get a number for the purposes of banking but it will normally be stamped 'Not Valid for Employment'. This is reputed to work in some states and not others, for example in Florida but not New York.

Some travellers have managed to get away with inventing a nine digit number (3-2-4) with the first three digits taken from the holder's home town zip code. Others have 'borrowed' an American friend's number, especially if they're out of the country, or out of work, since if social security payments are deducted, they will benefit someone. If the false number is traced, the friend can claim that he lost his card and never suspected that some miscreant would find and use it. But this is risky: any foreigner caught by the authorities will be deported.

According to Maria Perez from Peru, show your passport, take a driving test and obtain a US driving licence as ID. (A driving licence is an advantage for many jobs anyway). False social security cards circulate for about $150 especially in certain places like South Beach where so many Latino people congregate.

One of the easiest ways for the authorities to realise you are working illegally is when the Internal Revenue Service processes your W-4 form which all employees must fill out when they start work. Some wily travellers recommend using a false name on the W-4 in case the INS and Internal Revenue compare notes. The danger of being caught out is greatest at the end of the tax year (December 31st). Although students should be exempt from state and city income taxes (but not normally federal tax which is 15%), these are normally withheld at source. If you think you might have overpaid, ask your employer to send a W-2 form (statement of earnings, equivalent to a P45) to your home address. This will not arrive until the end of the tax year. In January request a non-resident tax form (104ONR) and a *Tax Guide for Aliens* from a US Embassy or Consulate and file your claim accordingly.

Hostels

The first step that many travellers take in the job hunt in America is to find a hostel which will trade food and a bed for some work. This provides an excellent base from which to look for paid work elsewhere. Occasionally notices of casual jobs appear on the bulletin boards of youth hostels and backpackers' haunts, such as the Hostelling International hostel in New Orleans, Marquette House, 2253 Carondelet St, New Orleans (504-523-3014; HINewOrlns@aol.com). The owner/manager wrote in summer 2000 to say that many people make it their base while they look for a job or an apartment and Marquette House has furnished apartments as well as dormitory accommodation for longer stay visitors. The Green Tortoise Hostel at 494 Broadway in San Francisco always has strange odd jobs for pleasant and persistent travellers. Other popular hostels worth considering are the Washington DC YHA Hostel on the corner of 11th and K Streets, and Boston International YHA Hostel, 12 Hemenway St, 02115 Boston (www.bostonhostel.org). In New York, Hostelling International have a hostel at 891 Amsterdam Ave at 103rd St (212-932-2300) which is affiliated to Council and is a good place to make contacts. These big city hostels do hire foreigners but only those with legal working papers. According to Maria Perez, you can exchange four hours of work for free (shared) lodging after staying a week at the Banana Club Hostel in Miami.

Carolyn Edwards had a discouraging time looking for work in Hawaii, but came across plenty of travellers spending four hours a day cleaning in hostels in exchange for bed and board. Richard Davies was given free accommodation and paid $10 an hour to clean toilets at his Los Angeles hostel which allowed him time to look for other work. Gerhard Flaig found that the Hollywood Hills Hostel in LA took on people to work as 'runners', to visit the airport daily to meet newly arriving backpackers and persuade them to stay at his hostel. The target was seven a week in order to get a small cash bonus in addition to free room and board, but it was early in the season and Gerhard only rounded up five.

Employment in your hostel is always worth asking about since many operate an informal work-for-keep system. After giving up a depressing job hunt in California, Jane Roberts phoned some hostels on her proposed route and was not only offered a job by one in Flagstaff, Arizona, she was even advanced her flight. Ask at privately owned travellers' lodges in the Grand Canyon area; according to Iona and Steve Dwyer they pay $4-6 per hour in addition to allowing you to stay free in beautiful surroundings. The most often-recommended accommodation in the congenial university town of Flagstaff is the Hotel du Beau Hostel at 19 W Phoenix behind the station.

Mark Horobin patronised a different sort of hostel when he found himself skint in California:

Males who line up in the early afternoon outside the San Diego Rescue Mission on 12th and Market Streets have a good chance of being given a bed and meals for three days. If you need a longer stay you may consider signing up as a helper as I did, but to do this you'll have to explain your reason (claiming to be an ex-alcoholic goes over well) and attend a compulsory daily Bible study session. If you are accepted you work about four hours a day. Later I stayed at the Prince of Peace Monastery in Oceanside.

San Diego seems well supplied with such places. Steve Bastick wrote last year describing how to arrange to stay at the St Vincent de Paul homeless shelter at 1501 Imperial Ave:

Single men and women receive an initial four-month stay at the Center. It sometimes takes up to ten days for a person to get in. Every day at 10am a person should call the Info-line (619-230-0997) to ask for a referral to the PMC and must be ready to be there by noon if the referral comes through. The requirements for acceptance are an on-site TB test, a one-hour orientation and five hours of chores (usually an hour a day for five days each week). A 9.30pm curfew exists and residents who miss this will lose their bed. Residents do not have to leave the facility at any time except for the monthly field day. Laundry service, 24 hour showers, telephone message service, health care assistance and three meals a day are all available free. All in all a good deal for a layover or to recuperate.

Drive-Aways

The term 'drive-away' applies to the widespread practice of delivering private cars within North America. Prosperous Americans and Canadians and also companies are prepared to pay several hundred dollars to delivery firms who agree to arrange delivery of private vehicles to a different city, usually because the car-owner wants his or her car available at their holiday destination but doesn't want to drive it personally. The companies find drivers (an estimated three-quarters of whom are not American), arrange insurance and arbitrate in the event of mishaps. You get free use of a car (subject to mileage and time restrictions) and pay for all gas after the first tankful and tolls on the interstates. Usually a deadline and mileage limit are fixed (e.g. 400 miles or 650km a day), though these are often flexible and checks lax. When there is a shortage of drivers you may even get a fee; Michael McDonnell was paid $150 on his first of many deliveries which was from Orlando to Ottawa. A good time to be travelling east to west or north to south (e.g. Chicago to Phoenix) is September/October when a lot of older people head to a warmer climate. On the other hand, when there is a shortage of vehicles (e.g. leaving New York in the summer), you will be lucky to get a car on any terms.

The only requirements are that you be over 21 (25 in some cases), have a driving licence, preferably an International Driving Permit, and able to pay a deposit (generally $300) which will be refunded on successful delivery. Look up 'Automobile Transporters and Driveaway Companies' in the *Yellow Pages* of any big city. Companies to try are:

Auto Driveaway Company, 310 South Michigan Ave, Chicago, IL 60604; 312-341-1900 or toll-free 800-346-2277 for their Central Services Office; national100@autodriveaway.com/ www.autodriveaway.com. Available cars are listed on the website and it is possible to sign up on-line.

National Auto Transporters Inc. – www.3000.com/nati; 800-423-3266; California 818-988-9000, Chicago 312-489-3500, Miami 305-945-4104.

National Driveaway Company – 904-396-4554. Based in Jacksonville, Florida.

An alternative to the *Yellow Pages* is to ask at a travel information centre for car rental agencies which arrange delivery of rental cars to the places where there is a seasonal demand, for example to Florida or to ski resorts in the winter. The colloquial expression for these cars is 'deadheads'.

If no company has what you want, then try to leave a number where they can reach you, or arrange to phone the most promising ones daily. If you actually call in to register with the company, they are more likely to take you seriously. When establishing your criteria, try not to be too fussy. The greater your flexibility of destination, the quicker you'll be out of town. Bridgid Seymour-East and Jimmy Henderson enjoyed a wonderful 'potluck' trip around the USA, picking up a car in Los Angeles and driving to a town in Minnesota. If you want to go coast to coast, it's probably worth waiting for a through vehicle; but if you have plenty of time and people and places to visit en route, you can piece together shorter runs which will eventually bring you to your destination. Carl Griffiths' company (Auto Driveaway) offered to photocopy the forms so that he could present them to subsequent offices.

If you are travelling with one or more people, you can save money by splitting the cost of the gas. The company allows you to take co-drivers and/or passengers provided they register for insurance purposes. This precludes the picking-up of hitch-hikers, so if you start alone, you should stay that way.

The type of vehicle you are assigned to drive can make a significant difference to the overall cost. Since you are paying for gas, the more fuel-efficient the car, the cheaper your trip will be. Fuel-efficient cars are much less prevalent than gas guzzlers, especially among the kind of people who pay to have their cars moved for them.

Eventually a company will have something going in the right direction and summon you to their office where you are told the details of pick-up, drop-off, time and distance restrictions. You may have to produce two passport size photos, a returnable cash deposit ($200-$350) and your thumb prints. You will be given two copies of the way-bill, an insurance claim form and a notice informing you of the FBI's penalties for delay, diversion and other atrocities. Make sure the company is ICC bonded. You will be expected to nominate a final destination where your deposit can be returned to you. But if you change your mind, you may have to make alternative arrangements; in Carl Griffiths' case, his $350 deposit was sent to his home address in Bristol.

Few agencies store cars themselves so you will need to get a bus to the car's home. When you are introduced to the vehicle, check through a list of existing damage with the owner (or agent) and fill out a 'Condition Report'. Be very thorough, since otherwise you may be held liable for existing damage or faults. If you do have mechanical problems on the road, you pay for any repairs costing less than a specified sum (perhaps $75), which you reclaim from the recipient of the vehicle. For more expensive work you should call the owner (collect) and discuss how he will arrange payment for the repairs. Ten minutes spent checking and going for a short test ride can save an awful lot later. Even if you know nothing about cars, you should be able to check the lights, oil, battery, brakes, and seat belts and also look for rust. If you do know some elementary mechanics, look for a worn fan belt and a leaky radiator which can cause serious problems during your trip. You should point out to the owner/agent anything you are unhappy about. Also check that there is a full tank of petrol, pointing out this requirement on the way-bill if necessary.

This system is ideal for travellers who can't face the prospect of a three-day bus ride and yet are short of both money and the courage to hitch-hike. Michael McDonnell and his son enjoyed drive-aways so much that they did nothing else for their month's holiday. Mig Urquhart thought it was an excellent system:

> *One day somebody in Fort Lauderdale was talking about fishing in Alaska and about a week later three of us had a driveaway to Seattle. It was the most outstanding car to do the journey in – a Mitsubishi Montero, one of those big jeep-type 4X4s. Only two of us could drive. We did 4,700 miles in nine days which included a birthday party for me in Tampa, lunch in New Orleans, the Grand Canyon, Las Vegas, a weekend with a friend in San Francisco and finally the glorious drive from SF to Seattle. The trip cost each of us $200 including food, gas, the motel in Vegas and a really nice meal in SF. It can be tough going driving all the time and there can be personality clashes if you go with people you've just met up with. I know that my very slow, cautious driving annoyed the other driver and we didn't become best buddies, but overall I thoroughly enjoyed the expedition.*

THE JOB HUNT

Working holidaymakers from Britain and other countries can capitalise on current employee shortages during the summer season. A headline in the *Sunday Telegraph* (June 2000) revealed the extent of the problem for employers: 'US Students Say No to Summer Jobs,' with the article claiming that nearly a third of America's 16 million teenagers are choosing not to take up a summer job. This has resulted in BUNAC being besieged with calls from employers eager to hire foreign students and offering perks like subsidised accommodation, transport and free food. The majority of seasonal jobs will pay the minimum wage of $5.15, though some states have legislated a higher wage, e.g. California where the 2001 minimum wage of $6.25 will rise to $6.75 from January 2002. Connecticut, Washington DC, Massachusetts, Oregon and Washington state all stipulate a minimum of between $6.15 and $6.75. However workers aged under 20 may be paid the youth minimum of $4.35 for the first 90 days of their employment. These can be checked on the Department of Labor's website (www.dol.gov/esa/public/minwage/america.htm).

Time can productively be spent searching the internet. Dozens of sites may prove useful, though www.coolworks.com is especially recommended for seasonal jobs in the tourist industry. You might also look at the annually revised book *Summer Jobs USA* published each November in the States by Peterson's Guides (PO Box 67005, Lawrenceville, NJ 08648-4764; www.petersons.com) and distributed in Britain by Vacation Work at £12.95. Each employer's entry indicates whether applications from foreign students are encouraged. The categories for each state cover specific job listings in business and industry, summer camps and summer theatres, resorts, ranches, restaurants and lodgings, commercial attractions, as well as in government for which only American citizens are eligible.

If you wait until you arrive in the States to look for a job, bear in mind that it is more difficult to lead a hand-to-mouth existence in North America than elsewhere. Whereas in Europe it is possible to pick up a little work here and there, live on a pittance and get by okay, in North America such a lifestyle puts you at risk of going on the streets where you are vulnerable to what one reader describes as 'the geeks and weirdos of this cutthroat society'. Finding suitable accommodation should be a priority especially in a place where you can't stay long-term at the youth hostel. It may be worth investigating university residences; apparently you can stay at Columbia or NYU in New York for about $250 for the whole summer. Adda Macchich was driven out of Boston because she found it was difficult to rent a room without undergoing a credit check and proving that she had a job (and concluded that this explains why there are large numbers of homeless people begging everywhere). Peter Stonemann recommends sticking to rural areas where you can camp, while admitting that a lack of public transport outside cities makes this difficult.

You should try to avoid arriving in the States without enough money to support yourself for several months and preferably enough for an old car (normally available for about $1,000). Even in cities, a car is a great asset from the start when you may be house-hunting and job-hunting. Another invaluable acquisition is a telephone. There is no quicker way to develop a lifelong phobia for public telephones than having to conduct a job search from one. A pager or bleeper is a useful variation.

As in any place, job-seekers will rely on newspaper adverts for leads. However this tends to be less productive than walking in and asking. Similarly, placing your own advert in order to prearrange a job is not recommended since the chances of attracting undesirables are high. Kev Vincent flew all the way to Hawaii supposedly to work on the farm of the woman who had answered his advert, only to find that she had two fruit trees and was proposing to charge him $150 a month for a cupboard off the garage. Pre-arranging a job from so far away is always a danger as Lee Morton found when he arranged a position as a trainee groom in California through an agency in England. Although the house and setting were beautiful, he lasted only a couple of days because the woman for whom he was working was so unreasonably demanding.

Word of mouth and personal contact are particularly important in the States. Again and again we have heard from travellers who have been offered some casual work while hitching or chatting to local residents. Many of these jobs have been in building, landscape gardening, furniture removal, etc.

Other jobs are less conventional. Paul Donut didn't have to look too hard for work in the capital of Louisiana, but the opportunities that presented themselves were distinctly unappealing:

When I arrived in Baton Rouge I looked up a friend of a friend who I was told might be able to help me find work. She did. She found me a job escorting customers from a bar called the Chimes at the gates of Louisiana State University to their cars, as many of them had been mugged on this short but perilous journey. After considering this job for about 30 seconds, I declined it. (The murder rate in Baton Rouge is second only to that of Washington DC.) The only other job opportunity to arise was helping out on an alligator farm which I wasn't sure would be any safer than protecting people from mugging.

TOURISM AND CATERING

Labour demands in summer resorts and national parks sometimes reach crisis proportions especially along the eastern seaboard. Because tipping is so generous, employers sometimes get away with offering derisory wages, e.g. $10 for an evening shift. An average weekly take in tips for a full-time waiter/waitress might be $120 with possibilities of earning twice that. Bar staff earn much more in tips, as much as $200 a night (but note that bar staff have to be above the legal drinking age of 21). Apparently a British accent helps, except in the case of Jane Thomas who was accused of putting it on to attract a higher tip! Even if you don't get a job as a barman or 'waitperson', busboys (table clearers) are usually given a proportion of tips by the waiter whom they are helping, typically 10%. Jobs which do not earn tips (like dishwashing) usually earn a reasonable hourly wage, as much as $6.50 when restaurants are desperate.

The recruitment needs of national and state parks can often be found on the internet, for example Glacier Park on the Canadian border on www.gpiht.com and Denali Park in Alaska (hrcarolm@mtaonline.net); the latter hires nearly 1,000 people each summer (early May to mid-September). Many big parks contract out their seasonal hiring, for example Aramark manages Mesa Verde in Colorado, Shenandoah in Virginia and Denali in Alaska. The famous national parks in Utah (Bryce Canyon, Zion Canyon and the Grand Canyon North Rim) hire staff through Amfac Recreational Services, Zion Lodge, Springdale, UT 84767; 435-772-3213; www.coolworks. com/utahparks). Amfac also recruit for the even more famous Yellowstone National Park in Wyoming which offers 2,500 seasonal jobs (PO Box 165, YNP, Wyoming 82109; 307-344-5323; www.yellowstonejobs.com). The Concession Services Corporation at Yosemite National Park in California can be contacted at PO Box 578, CA 95389 (209-372-1236; ycshr@dncinc.com); they hire about 600 seasonal and permanent staff.

The majority of food-related jobs are in fast food establishments where labour is not unionised. It is always worth enquiring at the local Kentucky Fried Chicken, McDonalds or Pizza Hut for jobs, since there is a very high turnover of staff. These major chains will invariably ask to see your social security card but, if they are pushed for staff, may not insist on more than reassurance. Try to carry out your search before local college students finish their term, usually in May. The two main disadvantages of working in this kind of job are the lack of accommodation (some are even stingy about the food) and the unreliability of working hours, making it difficult to save. If you want more hours, keep pestering the manager to give you some. One British traveller says:

Fast food restaurants offer a great chance to settle into a place. You won't make great money but they're always looking for people, and you'll get to find out what's happening in a place.

At the other end of the tourism spectrum, the hotel trade is not easy to get into because of the number of people intending to make 'hospitality vending' their career. Liam Lynch tried six or seven plush hotels in downtown Seattle and got the definite impression that the management were not looking for bearded round-the-world latter-day hippies. Europeans aged 19 to 35 beginning a career in the hotel and food service industry or students studying a hotel/catering course with relevant work experience who want to train for up to 18 months in the US should write to AIPT (10400 Little Patuxent Parkway, Suite 250, Columbia, Maryland 21044-3510; info@aipt.org; www.aipt.org) for information about the Hospitality and Tourism Exchange. AIPT will advertise your specifications in a newsletter distributed to relevant organisations in the US. In the UK details are available from Council Exchanges.

Plenty of Brits and other foreigners find work in Los Angeles, in the restaurants, bistros and cafes of North Beach, San Francisco and also in the cafés of Greenwich Village New York, though you'll have to serve a great many generous tippers before you'll be able to afford accommodation in Manhattan. As an aside, Jane Thomas solved this problem by getting on a house-sitting circuit via contacts. Through a friend she met various people who were only too glad to have a nice reliable English girl live in their houses while they were away on holiday, to discourage burglars, water the plants, etc. One of the places she stayed in was a luxury apartment overlooking Central Park. The incongruity of passing the commissionaire every morning arrayed in the tacky orange uniform of Burger Heaven (where she had finally got a job after much searching and exaggeration of her experience) struck her as highly amusing. The more people she got to know, the more offers of accommodation came her way, including some of pure hospitality.

Live-in jobs are probably preferable, and are often available to British students whose term-times allow them to stay beyond Labor Day, the first Monday in

September, when American students must resume their studies. After working a season at a large resort in Wisconsin, Timothy Payne concluded:

Without doubt the best jobs in the USA are to be found in the resorts, simply because they pay a reasonable wage as well as providing free food and accommodation. Since many resorts are located in remote spots, it is possible to save most of your wages and tips, and also enjoy free use of the resort's facilities. Whatever job you end up with you should have a good time due to the large number of students working there.

New Orleans is repeatedly described as a casual workers' paradise. Any of the cheap travellers' hotels (for example along Charles St or Prytania St) should be able to recommend places to try or offer work themselves. After fleeing from a boring job in Arizona, Jane Roberts headed for New Orleans in time for the Jazz Festival at the end of April:

After 15 minutes of desperate job-hunting I landed a job in a restaurant in the French Quarter. The following day I moved my pack into the apartment above and began work over the Festival. When it ended, business dropped. I was told I could carry on working, but only for tips. No customers meant no tips, so I left.

In most cases the minimum wage is paid in addition to free accommodation. After having a hard time looking for work in Florida, Steve and Iona Dwyer moved on to New Orleans:

Our luck changed for the better when we decided to stay in the Prytania Inn about a mile outside the French Quarter. Our German boss likes to employ travellers since he thinks that they are able to turn their hand to varied tasks. While Iona went from serving breakfast to sanding and painting, I was a general dogsbody and did such diverse jobs as unblocking toilets and making beds. There are five separate buildings and the work never stops.

The address off St Charles Ave is 1415 Prytania St, New Orleans, LA 70130 (504-566-1515/fax 504-566-1518; PeterSchreiber@compuserve.com/ www.PrytaniaInns.com).

Seaside Resorts

Popular resorts are often a sure bet, especially if you arrive in mid-August (when American students begin to leave jobs), or in April/May (before they arrive). Katherine Smith, who got her J-1 visa through BUNAC, describes the range of jobs she found in Ocean City, a popular seaside resort in Maryland which absorbs a large number of Britons:

I decided to spend my summer in Ocean Beach because I knew the job scene would be favourable. I found a job as a waitress in a steak restaurant and another full-time job as a reservations clerk in a hotel by approaching employers on an informal basis and enquiring about possible job vacancies. In my case this was very fruitful and I found two relatively well-paid jobs which I enjoyed very much. Other jobs available included fairground attendant, fast food sales assistant, lifeguard, kitchen assistant, chambermaid and every other possible type of work associated with a busy oceanside town. Ocean City was packed with foreign workers. As far as I know, none had any trouble finding work; anyone could have obtained half a dozen jobs. Obviously the employers are used to a high turnover of workers, especially if the job is boring. So it's not difficult to walk out of a job on a day's notice and into another one. It really was a great place to spend the summer. I would recommend a holiday resort to anyone wishing to work hard but to have a really wild time.

According to Andrew Boyle, there seemed to be more BUNACers in Ocean City than natives and in fact he noticed considerable tension and a 'clash of ideologies' between the party-loving young workers and the older year-round residents. In fact a lot of young foreigners go to resorts like this simply to party and anyone who is willing to work really hard stands out and is usually treated better.

In Atlantic City, the only gambling town in the US outside Nevada, a number of travellers (who must be fit) earn up to $400 a week by pushing punters in rolling chairs along the Boardwalk. Nearby, Wildwood New Jersey (four hours south of New York City) is another mecca for holiday job-seekers. A very high percentage of the people working in the fast-food outlets, ice cream parlours, slot machine arcades and fun piers are UK and Irish students especially from Scotland and Northern Ireland. As long as you arrive by the Memorial Day weekend (the last one in May) there is every chance of finding work. The New Zealander Ken Smith heard about Wildwood when he was working on a farm in Northern Ireland and found it just as easy to find a job as he had been told:

I was just strolling along the boardwalk when I stopped for an ice cream at a store and was offered a job by its owner. The pay is just $5 an hour but by working 80+ hours a week, it soon adds up. The most hours I worked in a day was 19, and then was told to be back the next day at 8.30am. The other workers told me the boss ripped them off but I must say he always paid me in full.

Apparently the Harbour Bar is the place to go to find out about job possibilities and also cheap accommodation (which is easy to find in Wildwood). Ken Smith shared an apartment for $50 a week. On days when the boardwalk is rained out, you can eat cheap buffet meals at the casinos in Atlantic City. While admitting that he was exploited and maltreated to some extent, Ken made enough that season to pay for nearly two months of 'quality travelling' throughout New England as well as paying for his airfares and insurance. (He has subsequently studied law, specialising in employment law.)

The tourism and catering business is not known for its generous treatment of its employees and America is no exception. Adda Maccich described working conditions at a 4-star hotel on Cape Cod as terrible:

I found a waitressing job despite my non-existent work visa and made-up social security number. Off-duty staff were not allowed anywhere within the hotel grounds (including the beach). The accommodation turned out to be some three miles away without any public transport. I had to hitch a ride with my fellow workers every morning for the 6am start. A lot of the staff were Jamaicans brought over for the season. Staff were expected to walk long distances with a huge tray piled up with dishes held in one hand. Afraid of injury, I reduced the load as much as possible, but soon my colleagues complained and I was fired without notice and asked to move out of the housing unit the following morning.

Other resorts to try are Virginia Beach (Virginia), Myrtle Beach (South Carolina) and Atlantic Beach (North Carolina). David Hewitt found work at a specialised kind of restaurant largely on the strength of his knowledge of kosher food gained while working on a kibbutz. He worked in Jewish hotels in Miami Beach and later in the Catskill Mountains north of New York. Earnings over Passover were spectacular.

Boats

For a yachting job, Florida is the best place to look. Innumerable pleasure craft and also fishing boats depart from the Florida Keys (at the southern tip of the state) bound for the Caribbean, especially between Christmas and Easter. You might also try for work on a cruise ship (see section on the Caribbean). There is usually plenty of bar and kitchen work in the Keys, the second largest gay centre in North America and, according to Kev Vincent, many of the jobs had certain conditions attached. The area is swamped by tens of thousands of students during their spring breaks, so accommodation is almost impossible to find in March and early April.

Fort Lauderdale creates plenty of casual work on yachts year round which regularly pays $10 an hour. A good place to hear about day work on yachts, as well as opportunities in landscaping and restaurants, is Floyd's Hostel and Crew House in the southeast section of town, which accepts only international travellers. Floyd Creamer, the owner/manager (who contributed himself to an earlier edition of this book), invites people to ring 954-462-0631 for a free pick-up from bus or train station.

Tim Pask describes his experiences in Huntingdon Beach, California:

My first job was in a boat broker's yard. I found this job after days of walking around the area asking in every shop, garage, restaurant and marina. My work involved cleaning all the boats which were on display as well as any minor maintenance jobs. I held this job for a period of two months earning $5 an hour which was the going rate. The job suited me perfectly as I was able to stay in the local hostel cheaply. The boat yard was situated next to the beach, so I was able to earn whilst developing an enviable tan. From then on I accepted work which came my way even though I was not actually looking for it. I would pick up odd day jobs which included roofing, cleaning, and kitchen work, often heard about at my hostel.

Ski Resorts

There is plenty of winter work in ski resorts, especially in Colorado, between December and the 'Mud Season' in May. Aspen, Vail and Steamboat Springs Colorado have all been recommended. The best time to arrive is October/November when the big resorts hold job fairs. Jobs are available as lift operators, restaurant workers, ticket clerks, basket check (like left luggage for skiers) assistants, etc. The main problem in big resorts (especially Vail) is a lack of employee accommodation. Unless you arrive in August/September, you will have to be very lucky to find a room of any kind. Check adverts in the local papers for example in *Steamboat Today* and *Steamboat Pilot*. The former carries nearly 100 help wanted ads in the winter months (and even more in the summer). Also check the resorts' websites which have links from the employment website www.coolworks.com mentioned earlier. You should also be aware that immigration raids are frequent, which makes employers reluctant to hire people without papers even when desperate for staff. This danger is less likely at small out-of-the-way resorts like Purgatory or Crested Butte in Colorado but then of course there will be fewer jobs.

The Steamboat Springs Chamber Resort Association (PO Box 774408, Steamboat Springs, CO 80477; 970-879-0880/fax 970-879-2543; www.steamboat-chamber.com) is helpful to job-seekers. It publishes a free leaflet 'Live, Work & Play in Ski Town USA' which includes an Employment Resource List. Job Fairs are held around the first weekend of November where employers can meet job-seekers. The Colorado Workforce Center in Sundance Plaza (PO Box 881419, Steamboat Springs, CO 80488; 907-879-3075; http://workforcecenters.state.co.us/nw) assists documented job-seekers to find employment full-time, part-time and seasonal.

Condominiums or 'condos' are sometimes a good bet for casual employment. Hotels aren't a big feature of American resorts (though the two principal ones at Steamboat, the Sheraton and the Ptarmigan Inn, hire large numbers of non-local workers). Resort companies like Mountain Resorts and the Steamboat Ski and Resort Corporation hire chambermaids, maintenance men, drivers, etc. It is common for one company to own all the facilities and control all employment in one resort, and in some cases provide accommodation to all staff. In Vail try Vail Resorts Inc. PO Box 7, Vail, CO 81658 (970-845-2460) which also has a dedicated freephone jobs line 1-888-Ski-Job-1 and a website www.snow.com. If you're just looking for occasional work, chopping wood in late autumn is a simple way of making a quick profit and contracts for clearing snow from roofs are sometimes available.

Neil Hibberd worked a season as a ski lift operator for the Steamboat Corporation on a J-1 visa fixed up through Council's Internship Programme (described at the beginning of the chapter). According to Neil the Corporation offers subsidised rental accommodation to its employees who pay about $200 a month in rent.

Aspen is one of the wealthiest resorts and supports a large transient working population. When you arrive, visit the Cooper Street Pier bar and listen for foreign accents. Unfortunately wages are very low in this setting; one worker reported that he saved less than $100 a month after room and board, ski pass and equipment rental. This figure would have more than doubled if he had been able to stay until the end of the season and had been able to collect his share of the season's tips. For a list of major

American ski resorts see the end of the section on Winter Resorts in the introductory chapter *Tourism*.

Theme Parks

Although British people are acquainted with fun fairs and theme parks, they will be amazed at the grand scale on which many American amusement parks and carnivals operate, sometimes employing up to 3,000 summer assistants to work on the rides and games, food service, parking lot and maintenance, warehouse, wardrobe and security. One chain of parks is Six Flags Theme Parks which have huge operations in a few states, including New Jersey and Illinois near Chicago. Some of the biggest employers of this kind co-operate with the work and travel programme organisers described earlier. For example representatives from Six Flags attend an employment show hosted by Council Exchanges in London each winter, along with big amusement parks like Cedar Point Amusement Park (PO Box 5006, Sandusky, Ohio 44871-5006 (worldjobs@cedarpoint.com/ www.cedarpoint.com). The opportunities afforded to young people looking for summer work by just one of these enormous commercial complexes are enormous and dwarf Butlins and Alton Towers entirely. The present shortage of student labour has forced some Florida theme parks to offer generous bonuses of up to $1,000.

On a smaller scale, travelling carnivals and fun fairs may need a few assistants to set up, operate and dismantle game stands and rides. Since the keynote of American business is to encourage competition and provide incentives, many of these carnival operators let you take home a cut of the profits on your particular stall, and these can be high. The trouble is that a lot depends on the type of concession you are allotted in the first place, as well as on your personality. Whether you get rich or not, you will certainly experience a uniquely American way of life and meet some authentic American characters. Chris Daniels got a job through the BUNAC job directory with a small travelling fair in the mid-West:

> *The convoy of trucks made an impressive sight, taking 'all the fun of the fair' from one sleepy town to another linked by miles of straight, often deserted roads. The romance of this nomadic lifestyle could not unfortunately offset the harsh realities of working 18 solid hours whenever we moved on to the next town, permanently dirty truck accommodation and a low fixed wage. The other employees were a strange mixture: the fellow who ran a ride called the 'Tilt & Whirl' was called 'Rosebud' and was something out of the days of the Wild West (or at least out of a Saturday night TV Western); he chewed tobacco incessantly and spoke with an almost unintelligible drawl. The fair was owned by one man, an elderly gentleman, patriot and entrepreneur with the frontier spirit which had built it up from scratch.*

More recently, Peter Stonemann found temporary work on county fairs in the small towns of Shelby and Ashville in North Carolina. Outside the fair's office a sign stated simply 'Help Wanted. To Travel. Must be over 18'. Assuming you can handle the rough life, Peter describes it as 'one of the most picturesque and original' jobs you can do.

The International Recruiting Department of Walt Disney's EPCOT Center (PO Box 10090, Lake Buena Vista, Florida 32830-0090) prefer to rely on the word of mouth network rather than have their six month or one year vacancies for young people to work as 'cultural representatives' widely publicised. People aged 18-28 from Britain and ten other countries are hired to represent the culture and customs of their countries; in the case of the UK this means olde worlde pubs, Scotch eggs and Royal Doulton china. Anyone applying will probably have to wait months until there is space at one of the two annual recruiting presentations which Disney organises in Britain in March and October. Any job which involves tips is usually more lucrative than others; wages can be swelled by more than $100 in a five-hour shift. The staff facilities are attractive with pools, jacuzzis, tennis courts and subsidised rent.

Paul Binfield from Kent describes the process of being hired by Disney as 'a long and patient' one:

I initially wrote to Disney in October and started my contract in January, 15 months later. It was the most enjoyable year of my life, experiencing so many excellent things and making the best friends from all over the world. The pros far outweigh the cons, though some people did hate the work. Disney are a strict company with many rules which are vigorously enforced. The work in merchandising or the pub/restauarant is taken extremely seriously and sometimes it can be hard to manufacture a big cheesy Disney smile. There are dress codes, and verbal and written warnings for matters which would be considered very trivial in Britain, and indeed terminations (which is a very nasty word for being fired). If you go with the right attitude it can be great fun.

OTHER POPULAR JOBS

Selling

By reputation, anyway, American salesmen are a hardbitten lot. Some travellers have found that their foreign charm makes selling surprisingly effortless. ('Are you really English? I just love that accent.') Americans are not as suspicious of salesmen as other nationalities and you may be pleasantly surprised by the tolerance with which you are received on the doorstep and, even more, by the high earnings which are possible. The BUNAC Job Directory contains details of a number of selling jobs but you must have at least $800 in personal funds to tide you over the low periods.

Advertisements for sales positions proliferate. You may find telesales less off-putting than door-to-door salesmanship, but it will also be less lucrative. On the other hand, some working holiday makers and gap year students do not shy away from the hard edge of selling and tackle commission-only jobs. The Southwestern Company with its headquarters in Nashville markets educational books and software door-to-door throughout the US and has a recruitment office in the UK (Goldsmiths House, Broad Plain, Bristol BS2 0JR; 0117-930 4274) which targets gap year students. Its website (www.southwestern.com) contains glowing reports from past students whose earnings have been impressive. Their statistics possibly exclude all the students who give up in disgust after a few weeks of failure.

Advertisements for salesmen, especially of magazine subscriptions and cleaning products, proliferate in local papers. Many employers will not be too concerned if your visa is not in order as long as you inspire them with faith in your selling ability. Another travellers' standby is selling ice cream though nowadays the work is available only to men because of the danger of urban crime. An International Driving Permit is an asset when looking for this work.

For general comments on the pros and cons (sic) of selling, see the chapter *Business and Industry*. It can be tough if you have to rely solely on commission. Grimly Corridor (who is arguably a born salesman) answered a newspaper advert in Kansas and was soon selling cleaning products during the day and being housed in Holiday Inn-style hotels at night. After a couple of weeks in Kansas, the team of salesmen was moved on (at the company's expense of course) to Chicago. Grimly thinks that at least some of his success was due to the Cockney accent and manner which he assumed. Also he had gained some experience of American salesmanship in Portland Maine where he had worked as a telephone canvasser selling subscriptions to the local newspaper; he managed about six or eight leads at $5 each per evening.

If training is promised, be prepared to be subjected to a quasi-religious indoctrination.

Fishing and Hunting

Fishing off the coast of Alaska and fish-processing are classic money-spinning summer jobs in the US, still widely advertised in west coast newspapers, though the possible earnings are often exaggerated. The salmon industry has suffered in recent years with the change in taste away from tinned salmon. Think carefully before heading off blindly to Alaska where the cost of living is very high and the competition for work intense, particularly from American students. Ads that promise monthly wages of more than $2,000 should be treated with scepticism.

Still a few people do succeed in joining the fishing fleet. The first halibut are caught over a 24-hour period in early May and this opens the fishing season. It is easier to pin down job openings then than later at the peak salmon season of July/August. Some novices frequent the docks in places like Kodiak, Ketchikan, Homer and Petersburg in Alaska, Astoria and Newport in Oregon, etc. and try to volunteer to work in exchange for their keep on their first fishing trip. After that they will have earned a place on the boat and will be able to share in the profits. Without lots of stamina and some mechanical aptitude, it will be very difficult to persuade a skipper to take on inexperienced crew.

Not only is the job extremely gruelling and often dangerous, but the redneck society of the rest of the crew may not be to your taste. Shooting birds and even whales for fun is commonplace and fishing methods which destroy all manner of marine life are regularly used even if forbidden by law. It has forced more than one hardened traveller to leave before the end of the season and turned others into vegetarians. No doubt all join Greenpeace the minute they get home.

Finding work in an Alaskan fish processing plant is much easier but it offers low wages relative to the unpleasant working conditions. Major seafood companies have their headquarters in Seattle where much of the seasonal hiring takes place. Most companies pay the Alaska minimum wage of $5.65 per hour and about $8.50 for overtime. Perks can include free housing, food, gear, laundry and transport costs from the point of hire to the job site which means you get a free cruise up the Inside Passage. But first-timers may get few of these benefits and end up camping. The companies hire a range of ancillary staff, as well, for the laundry, mail room, kitchens, etc. and there is some movement between departments.

The internet is a valuable source of names and addresses; for example www.alaskanjobs.com lists the members of the Pacific Seafood Processors Association which includes the following:

Alaska General Seafoods, 6425 NE 175th St, Kenmore, Seattle, WA 98028 (425-485-7755; employment@akgen.com). 700 jobs, especially June 16-July 22 in Bristol Bay and July 1-September 5th in Ketchikan.

Alyeska Seafoods, Inc. PO Box 31359, 303 NE Northlake Way, Seattle, WA 98103 (206-547-2100; alyjob@jps.net).

Kodiak Salmon Packers, Inc. 20520 Brown Road, Monroe, WA 98272 (425-486-9872).

UniSea Inc., PO Box 97109, 15400 NW 90th St, Redmond, WA 98073-9719 (UniSea Jobline 800-535-8509; www.unisea.com/jobs/opportunities).

Wards Cove Packing Company, PO Box C 5030, Seattle, WA 98105-0030 (206-323-3200).

Westward Seafoods Inc. 1111 Third Avenue, Suite 2250, Seattle, WA 98101 (206-682-5949).

Processing takes place on shore or on special processing ships. Work shifts can vary from 16 hours on with 8 hours off to 6 hours on with 6 hours off. This schedule continues day after day until the end of the season leading to fatigue and (occasionally) accidents. Some processing vessels travel to link up with trawlers, possibly as far as Russia or Japan. Stephen Bastick from San Diego did not go so far afield but was not discontent:

I have worked in some pristine locations in Alaska. My processor vessel pulled into some small remote Alaska towns where I was able to hike around. I go to enjoy wilderness, and the paycheck is a necessary benefit. Often processors can volunteer to stay on between seasons and get paid work assisting the engineers or carpenters. I averaged $1,000 for every nine-day period of 16-hour shifts. Many processors belong to and are despatched out of the Inland Boatmans Union (IBU) in Seattle. Once a member, a person can anticipate continuous seasonal employment.

If you go to Alaska on spec, you should go to each cannery and put in an application (before the salmon run begins in the beginning of July for the Kenai area). After that, it is a question of waiting, preferably outside the canneries every day, to see if they are hiring. Kenai south of Anchorage has a large number of processing factories which hire hundreds of workers during the latter half of June. The big hiring days are when the fishermen come in. When there are openings, the right number of people will be picked from the waiting crowd, more or less at random, which can be very frustrating. A lot of people give up and leave, so the longer you wait the better your chances. The salmon run at different times during the summer, depending on the area of Alaska. The farther west you go in Alaska, the earlier the run is; for instance it takes place in August on the Panhandle.

Aaron Rabinovitz spent $190 on the ferry from Bellingham to Petersburg at the beginning of June to look for a job to pay for his university education. Although it didn't quite work out that way, he concluded that everybody passing through the States should try to get to Alaska:

> *The ferry is an interesting place to meet fellow travellers. There is no youth hostel in town but rather a place known as tent city (reminiscent of the squalor found in moshav housing). Tent city is a series of wooden platforms covered with tarpaulins, inhabited by a mass of strange people: travellers, hippies, vagrants, migrant workers. But it is unusually cheap at $100 a month.*
>
> *Unfortunately I arrived in town a month too early. The fishing season starts on July 5th this year. In the meantime I've been supporting myself with odd jobs around town. Several places worth checking are Harbor Lights Pizza, the Homestead Cafe and the Hammer & Wikan grocery store. The standard rate of pay is $7 an hour. By asking around and becoming friendly with the natives, I've gotten day jobs washing cars and mowing lawns: at least it's money for beer. Alaska is truly a beautiful place. Everywhere in this quaint town you can see mountains, eagles and an occasional bear. The rivers are relatively clean and if you are low on funds you can catch your dinner out of the water. Visas may be a problem. Every application form without exception asks for ID.*

A number of years ago David Irvine caught a standby flight to Anchorage in mid-July hoping to get a fishing job. After looking into the situation, he decided against fishing and tried hunting lodges instead. He got a list of recognised guides from the Alaska Department of Fish & Game and began phoning. Partly because of the difficulty of talking to the hunters (who are often out in the bush) this method did not work. Although the tourist season was already underway, a job was advertised in the *Anchorage Times* for a lodge assistant which David had the good fortune to get. He worked at a fly-in fly-out lodge in the Alaskan interior for two months, landscaping and doing maintenance work for the benefit of the JR clones and German millionaires who patronised the lodge. He had the impression that women cooks were in considerable demand at other lodges.

David also gained experience of 'moose-packing' which means lugging the shot game (often weighing over 100lbs) out of the bush. Because the carcasses attract bears, it is dangerous to do this job unarmed. By the end of September it had started to snow so David collected his meagre wages and left.

Soccer Coaching

Soccer is fast gaining popularity in North America, and demand is strong for young British coaches to work on summer coaching schemes. A number of companies recruit players to work all over the States including Hawaii:

Britannia Soccer Ltd, PO Box 2173, Centreville, VA 20122, USA (703-330-2532; www.britanniasoccer.com).

Goal-Line Soccer Inc, 1933 NW Sunview Drive, Corvallis, OR 97330 (541-753-5833; rowneyt@goal-line.com). Minimum age 21. Mostly in American Northwest.

Major League Soccer Camps, 5 Connecticut Avenue, Norwich, CT 06360, USA. The largest and best known.

Soccer Academy Inc, PO Box 3046, Manassas, VA 20108, USA (703-385-0150).

Others advertise in the specialist press. BUNAC knows about these companies, since they normally process the necessary J-1 visa. It is more important to be good at working with kids than to be a great football player, though of course it is easier to command the respect of the kids if you can show them good skills and a few tricks.

Theo West spent part of his gap year before going to Liverpool University, as a soccer coach and describes the application process and the job itself:

> *The procedure involved in getting a place is time-consuming and difficult but well worth the effort. It includes an interview to see if you have the right personality and experience in coaching followed by a couple of coaching days where you are evaluated at close quarters by senior coaches (which proved a slight problem for me since my home is in Inverness and the nearest coaching day was in Newcastle). Finally you accept a contract, list preferred working locations, pay a membership (which covers flights to the US), apply for a J-1 visa through BUNAC and attend an induction.*
>
> *On arrival in America we were briefed on where our first week-long assignment was to be and given our coaching equipment. The next day we headed off in hire cars for Monroe Woodbury, a rich area in upstate New York where we were introduced to the families that were to put us up for a week. The pay as a first year coach is around $140 a week for a three hour session each day and occasional adult coaching clinics. In terms of pay it was not great but the benefits generally come from the families that house you, feed you and entertain you. The benefits of an English accent in America are still many. I spent five weeks coaching in New York, Connecticut and finally worked with under-privileged kids in New Jersey. It was an amazing and draining experience as I got to meet many great people, saw some wonderful sights and negotiated myself with some difficulty into a number of bars (the strictness of the adherence to the 21 age limit for drinking proved annoying).*

Manual Work

Cash-in-hand work can be found, especially as a loader with removal firms (wages of up to $15 an hour), as security guards and in construction (especially for those with skills). Dan Eldridge worked at a hostel in San Francisco for a year and so knows the working scene well:

> *An interesting option is to open up the phone book to 'Movers' and personally visit them, especially any with Irish names. They all employ foreigners at $10 an hour cash-in-hand. It's tough work but $10 an hour is incredible if you're just starting out. I sent many people to the moving companies and most quit after a couple of weeks, but were happy to have the cash.*

Since houses throughout the States are wood-framed, carpenters can do well, even those without much experience. It is common practice to pay employees as 'contract labour', which leaves them with the responsibility of paying taxes, social security, etc.; this is a definite advantage if your papers are not in order. Even if you can't find work building new houses, you can offer your painting or maintenance skills to any householder, preferably one whose house is looking the worse for wear.

The USA has more than its fair share of natural disasters which always create a lot of urgent work. Paul Donut found work in Florida clearing up after a hurricane; the authorities were so desperate for workers that no questions were asked about permits. This tactic doesn't always succeed however. After the forest fires which swept through Santa Monica California a few years ago, rumours spread (like wildfire!) that there was a huge demand for building workers which attracted a large number of unemployed British builders. They all congregated in the expat pub in Santa Monica (the Old King's Head) only to be told that there was no work to speak of, since builders from other states had already arrived and the work was spoken for.

A more definite but offbeat suggestion has been proffered by Mark Kinder who wrote from rural Maryland:

After spending the summer on the Camp America programme, a friend and I decided to do a parachute jump. Once you have made about ten jumps, the instructors expect you to learn how to pack parachutes, which takes about five hours to learn. Once you have learnt how to pack you get paid $5 per chute cash and with a bit of practice can pack three or four chutes an hour which is good money. I would say that 90% of parachute centres in the US pay people cash for packing the chutes but you generally have to be a skydiver to do the job. It is definitely a fun way of earning money. Skydivers are very friendly people and are thrilled to meet foreigners, so they will often offer a place to stay. If not, you can always camp at the parachute centre.

A list of the 275 parachute centres in the US can be obtained from the national association USPA, 1440 Duke St, Alexandria, VA 22314.

Private labouring agencies can be a useful source of instant money to anyone with a legitimate visa and a social security number. It is normally essential to be at the agency office by 6am to offer yourself as day labour. Nineteen-year-old Nicola Smith worked through an agency in Dallas called Industrial Force which was desperate for workers (including ones with invented social security numbers) to work as cleaners and in fast food restaurants. Staffmasters USA in Charlotte North Carolina has been recommended as offering light and medium manufacturing employment and office work which pays $7-$10 an hour. Maria Perez enjoyed earning $9 an hour working in Customer Services for the telecommunications company MCI in Denver, a city with excellent job prospects. Check the classified columns of the Sunday papers.

Medical

Nurse shortages are chronic in the US and qualified nurses might like to investigate possibilities through a specialist UK agency. For people with a more casual interest in medicine, there is the possibility of testing new drugs as well as donating blood.

While filling in the time until her flight out of Seattle, Mig Urquhart sold plasma at the Plasma Center. She was turned down on her first visit since there was too much protein in her urine (she reckoned it was because she had been living on peanut butter sandwiches). But it was fine the next time and she earned $10, $15 or $20 depending on how often she went in a week.

When Lindsay Watt arrived in the US, he intended to sustain himself with conventional kinds of employment. But almost immediately he discovered that the longish-stay male travellers staying at his hostel in New York were all earning money solely through medical studies. Invariably, a social security number is needed though it can bear the stamp 'Not Valid for Work'. Most studies pay at least $100 a day and provide all food, accommodation and entertainment. On the three studies in which Lindsay participated, he earned $300 in five days in New York, $475 for four days in Philadelphia and $3,000 for a month in West Palm Beach (Florida). Together these funded a tour of South America. The best he ever heard of was a three-day study in Baltimore which paid $800. (It must have involved some fairly unpleasant tests, such as a spinal tap.) There are Drug Research Centers in many American cities especially Massachusetts, New York, New Jersey, Pennsylvania, Maryland and Florida. Women are seldom accepted unless they are sterile.

An excellent source of information on drug testing centres is the website www.centerwatch.com, a listing service for clinical trials. In some cases details of ongoing trials are given, though in all cases contact details for many clinical research centres are given. For example SmithKline Beecham in Philadelphia (800-661-9540; www.phillytrials.com) pay $175-$300 for every day of a trial.

Here is a brief list of possible contacts, going from east to west. Note that this list has not been verified since the last edition:

Boston University Medical Center, Massachusetts - 617-735-3351
Clinical Research Association, New York - 212-685-8788
Cornell Medical Centre, New York - 914-997-7300
Health & Science Research, Inglewood, New Jersey - 201-567-8380
Riverview Clinical Studies, Eatontown, New Jersey - 1-800-533 4852
Pharmakinetics, Baltimore, Maryland - 410-385-4500

Johns Hopkins University Hospital, Baltimore, Maryland - 410-955-3422/955-0053; was recently offering $400 to participants in a trial in Guatemala to test an anti-diarrhoeal vaccine.

Thomas Jefferson University, Philadelphia, Pennsylvania - 215-955-6086
Bio Clen, Richmond, Virginia - 804-788-6766
Deerfield Beach Clinic, Deerfield Beach, Florida - 305-421-8212
Ohio State University Hospital, Columbus, Ohio - 614-292-6908
Vanderbilt University Medical Center - Nashville, Tennessee - 615-322-2312
Biomedical Research, Kansas City, Missouri - 816-341-3322
University of Texas Medical Center, Dallas, Texas - 214-688-2373
Pharmaco, Austin, Texas - 512-462-0492
University of Utah Medical Center, Salt Lake City - 801-581-5036
California Clinical Trials Los Angeles, California - 310-854-4949
Drug Studies Unit, Berkeley, California - 510-732-4455
University of Washington, Seattle, Washington - 206-543-2317

CHILDCARE & DOMESTIC WORK

The United States Department administers the au pair placement programme which allows thousands of young Europeans with childcare experience to work for American families for exactly one year on a J-1 visa. They apply through a small number of sponsoring organisations (currently there are six) who must follow the guidelines which govern the programme, so there is not much difference between them. The Louise Woodward case has had a very damaging impact on the programme and numbers have declined significantly since 1997.

The basic requirements are that you be between 18 and 26, speak English, show at least 200 hours of recent childcare experience, have a full clean driving licence and provide a criminal record check. The childcare experience can consist of regular babysitting, helping at a local creche or school, etc. In the wake of the Louise Woodward case, anyone wanting to care for a child under two must have 200 hours of experience looking after children under two and must expect the programme interviewers to delve more deeply into the experience you claim to have than they used to. The majority of candidates are young women though men with relevant experience (e.g. sole care of children under five) may be placed. (It is still not unusual to have just a handful of blokes out of hundreds of au pairs.)

The job entails working a maximum of 45 hours a week (including babysitting) with at least one and a half days off per week plus one complete weekend off a month. Successful applicants receive free return flights from one of many cities, four-day orientation in New York and support from a community counsellor. The time lag between applying and flying is usually at least two months. The counsellor's role is to advise on any problems and organise meetings with other au pairs in your area. Applicants are required to pay a good faith deposit of $400 which is returned to them at the end of 12 months but which is forfeit if the terms of the programme are broken.

The fixed amount of pocket money for au pairs is $139.05 a week, which is a reasonable wage on top of room, board and perks. On arrival participants must receive a four-day orientation which covers child safety and development. New legislation has made first aid a compulsory component. An additional $500 is paid by the host family to cover the cost of educational courses (three hours a week during term-time) which must be attended as a condition of the visa. Au pairs are at liberty to travel for a month after their contract is over but no visa extension is available beyond that.

A separate programme exists for qualified child carers/nannies, called by Au Pair in America the 'Au Pair Extraordinaire' programme. Candidates with the appropriate NNEB, BTEC, Diploma in Nursing or NVQ3 qualification are eligible to earn $190 a week plus a $1,000 completion bonus (including the return of the $400 deposit).

The massive publicity given to the Louise Woodward murder trial damaged the reputation of the au pair programmes. It is worth bearing in mind that the vast majority of placements (more than 75,000 since 1985) have been successful. At any one time 12,000 American families are hosting a foreign au pair. This is not to say that problems do not occur, because it is not at all unusual for au pairs to chafe against rules, curfews and unreasonable expectations in housework, etc. When speaking to your family on the telephone during the application period, ask as many day-to-day questions as possible, and try to establish exactly what will be expected of you, how many nights babysitting at weekends, restrictions on social life, use of the car, how private are the living arrangements, etc. The counsellors and advisers provided by the sending organisations should be able to sort out problems and in some cases can find alternative families. Consider carefully the pros and cons of the city you will be going to. Emma Purcell was not altogether happy to be sent to Memphis Tennessee which she describes as the 'most backward and redneck city in the USA':

I was a very naïve 18 year old applying to be an au pair for a deferred year before university, during the hype of Louise Woodward (and with the same agency). During my eight months so far, I have experienced highs and lows. I have been very lucky with my host family who have made me feel one of the family. I have travelled the USA and Mexico frequently staying in suites and being treated as royalty since my host dad is president of Holiday Inn. On the bad side, I have lost numerous friends who have not had such good luck. One was working 60 hours a week (for no extra pay) with the brattiest children, so she left. Another girl from Australia lasted six months with her neurotic family who yelled at her for not cleaning the toaster daily and for folding the socks wrong. Finally she plucked up the courage to talk to her host parents and their immediate response was to throw her out. A very strong personality is required to be an au pair for a year in the States.

About half a dozen agencies in the UK send au pairs to the US, and it is worth comparing their literature. Au Pair in America is the largest organisation placing in excess of 4,500 young people in au pair and nanny placements throughout the country. Brochures and application forms can be requested on 07002 287247 or browse on www.aupairamerica.co.uk. The programme operates under the auspices of the American Institute for Foreign Study or AIFS (37 Queens Gate, London SW7 5HR) though selection has been devolved to regional offices. Contact WorldNet UK at Avondale House, 63 Sydney Road, Haywards Heath, West Sussex RH16 1QD (01444 453566/fax 01444 440445) or Emberton House, 26 Shakespeare Road, Bedford MK40 2ED (01234 352688/fax 01234 351070); info@worldnetuk.com/ www.worldnetuk.com. Northern applicants should contact the Janet White Agency, 67 Jackson Avenue, Leeds, West Yorkshire LS8 1NS (0113 266 6507/fax 0113 268 3077; janet@janetwhite.com). Au Pair in America also has representatives in 45 countries and agent/interviewers throughout the UK.

Other active au pair Exchange Visitor Programmes are smaller but may be able to offer a more personal service and more choice in the destination and family you work for:

Childcare America, Trafalgar House, Grenville Place, London NW7 3SA (020-8906 3116/fax 020-8906 3461; office@childint.co.uk/ www.childint.co.uk). The UK representative of the Au Pair Programme USA, 6965 South Union Park Center, Suite 100, Salt Lake City, Utah 84047 (801-255-7722).

AuPairCare Cultural Exchange, One Post Street, Suite 700, San Francisco, CA 94104; 415-434-8788; UK representative is Lorraine Bushell, Solihull Au Pair & Nanny Agency, 1565 Stratford Road, Hall Green, Birmingham B28 9JA (0121-733 6444/fax 0121-733 6555; www.aupairs4u.com). Also offer Au Pair Elite Programme for qualified nannies.

EF Au Pair Direct USA, 1-3 Farman Street, Hove, East Sussex BN1 3AL (020-8691 4460). Division of EF Educational which may be planning to wind down its au pair programme.

EurAupair, 250 North Coast Highway, Dana Point, CA 92629, USA (949-494 5500; www.euraupair.com). UK partner is EurAupair UK, 17 Wheatfield Drive, Shifnal, Shropshire TF11 8HL (01952 460733/maureen@asseuk.freeserve.co.uk).

Many British women who want to work for families may not qualify for or wish to join one of the approved programmes. In recent decades thousands of young Europeans have gone to the States to work as nannies or au pairs, virtually all of them on tourist visas. They should tread carefully, especially in view of all the publicity surrounding high-profile Washington politicians who have been caught employing illegal house staff as nannies, cleaners, etc.

It should be possible to fix up a job working with a family after arrival in the States, though the penalties for working illegally described earlier in this chapter apply equally. There are many job notices for au pairs and nannies on hostel notice boards (especially in San Francisco) and in big city dailies. After finding it impossible to get a job without a social security card in Houston, Ana Maria Güemes from Mexico started reading the ads and soon had a live-in job as a babysitter.

After having been in California for a while, Paul Young decided to try to market himself as an informal butler, willing to drive and cook in a household. After advertising in the rich county of San Anselmo, he received a disappointing response, mostly from disabled people offering $100 a week. He chose the most lucrative position paying $320 a week cash-in-hand, but was far from thrilled with his choice. His employer sounds the worst kind of snobbish spoiled American; even the dog was horrible and, in Paul's view, needed (and probably got!) a psychiatrist. He concludes that a sane wealthy American is a contradiction in terms, and recommends checking out the situation carefully before committing yourself.

Gerhard Flaig found a much more congenial employer by the simple expedient of pestering a contact he had (organist in the church next to his hostel in Los Angeles who had kindly let him play the organ) until he finally introduced him to the church secretary who did have an idea:

> *The secretary arranged a meeting with an old man who wanted someone to organise his files and house, to do some transcriptions and other odd jobs. He gave me my own room and free food plus paid me $5 an hour. I was overjoyed and left the hostel at once. After I'd done the transcribing, he wanted me to paint his rooms. His landlady was so satisfied with the job I did that she asked me to paint her house and then a friend of his asked me as well. I got one job after the other and was very busy working as a painter. I had a wonderful time in Hollywood and earned quite a lot of money to travel on. And I still keep in touch with the man.*

AGRICULTURE

Students of agriculture may find various schemes which allow them to receive further training in the US (see information on the International Agricultural Exchange Association and the International Farm Experience Programme in the introductory chapter on *Agriculture*).

The British agency Stablemate Staff places equine trainees in the US. Details of the exchange programme, which costs $1,100 plus travel and other expenses, are available from Stablemate, The Old Rectory, Belton-in-Rutland, Oakham, Rutland LE15 9LE (01572 717383; ep@stablemate.demon.co.uk).

Like everything else in America, many farms (often agribusinesses rather than farms) tend to be on the grand scale, especially in California and the Midwest. This means that the phenomenon of cycling along a country road, finding the farmer in his field and being asked to start work in an adjoining field is virtually unknown in the US. Furthermore it could be dangerous, since anyone wandering up a farmer's driveway would be suspected of being a trespasser and liable to be threatened with a vicious dog or a gun.

In many important agricultural areas, much of the fruit and vegetable harvesting has been traditionally done by gangs of illegal Mexicans or legal Chicanos (naturalised Americans of Spanish descent) for notoriously low wages. It is very common for an agent to contract a whole gang, so that there may be no room for individuals and pairs of travellers.

A gentler form of agriculture is practised on organic farms which flourish in many corners of the USA. Unfortunately working for keep on a farm counts as employment for the purposes of Immigration. The Program Manager of the WWOOF-style group North East Workers on Organic Farms (Box 608, Belchertown, Massachusetts 01007; www.smallfarm.org) says that NEWOOF cannot encourage international workers because their farmers find too much red tape involved in work visas, so their apprentice placement service is for US citizens only. The same is true of Southeast Workers on Organic Farms (Janus Farms Institute, 1287 Stage Coach Road, Silver City, NC 27344; 919-742-4672).

The long-established organisation Travellers Earth Repair Network (PO Box 4469, Bellingham, WA 98227; 360-738-4972) provides a networking service for international travellers, for a membership fee of $50 ($35 students). It claims to have 3,500 addresses in its database with 250 hosts who offer board and lodging in exchange for help. The WWOOF International Handbook published by WWOOF Australia and the *Intentional Communities* (details in introductory chapter on Agriculture) list a number of communes and alternative farms which accept working guests. Rob Abblett used the latter book to fix up two 'very cheap and very interesting stays' on communes in Washington and New York.

Andy's Organic Farm formerly known as the Hawaii Institute of Tropical Agriculture (PO Box 1729, Pahoa, HI 96778; 808-965-0069; natec@interpac.net) accepts apprentices and student agriculturalists who work in exchange for their keep for a minimum of four months. Inexperienced volunteers must pay $250 a month for their room and board. WWOOF Canada (see chapter) sells a list of 17 addresses throughout mainland USA plus 21 in Hawaii; the 2000 edition costs $10 plus an IRC. People who visit a rural hostel in California, Bill's Home Hostel (1040 Cielo Lane, Nipomo, CA 93444-9039; bdenneen@slonet.org) can work for two hours a day in lieu of payment for accommodation.

In the world of conventional agriculture, there is scope for finding work. While working at parachute centres in rural Delaware and Maryland, Mark Kinder from Blackpool found that farm work was easy to come by on an intermittent basis with free caravan accommodation. In every state in the Union (except perhaps Nevada, Montana and Alaska) there is some fruit or vegetable being picked throughout the summer months.

Both in large-scale harvests and on small family farms there is a chance that no one will be concerned about your legal status. This is what Jan Christensen from Denmark found when he looked for summer farm work in Minnesota:

> *The farmers seemed to have a very relaxed attitude towards permits. The best places to look are along route 210 just off Interstate 94 at Fergus Falls which is a rich farm area with good employment prospects from April/May till mid-October. But it's best to have some experience in tractor driving and combine harvester work. If you try to bluff, you will find yourself on the road PDQ. I found that my farmer expected me to know just about everything about farming and had no time to train me.*

Labour shortages in the Midwest have been so acute in the past couple of years that teams of skilled harvesters have been recruited from overseas, for example 150 New Zealanders were brought in for the 1999 wheat harvest. They worked from 7am to midnight seven days a week from June to September, travelling from Texas up to North Dakota and were paid nearly $1,400 a month plus $7 an hour on top of free food and accommodation. The team was contracted on behalf of the US Custom Harvesters Institute who post harvest schedules on their website www.customharvesters.com.

Fruit pickers congregate in the counties of Yakima, Chelan, Douglas and Okanogan in Washington State. Another example of a large-scale harvest is the peach harvest in Western Colorado around Palisade. A few thousand pickers are suddenly needed for the second fortnight in August. Similarly the three-week cherry harvest around Traverse City Michigan in late June/early July employs large numbers of non-locals.

California and Florida are the leading states for agricultural production, especially citrus, plums, avocados, apricots and grapes. Most of these are grown along the Central Valley particularly the San Joaquin Valley around Fresno. The work is notoriously poorly paid. Kev Vincent fared better in the Salinas Valley on the California coast, which is a huge vegetable growing area, again predominantly Spanish-speaking. The Farm Labor Office in Greenfield directed him to a job cutting broccoli which is extremely fast, hard and well paid, then on to the pepper harvest which was easier work but less lucrative.

Florida Harvests

Because all citrus fruit in Florida is picked by hand massive numbers of itinerant pickers or local casuals must be enlisted over the winter and spring, when the Florida climate is at its most pleasant. Citrus production is greatest in the central counties of Lake and Polk, inland from Tampa and north past Orlando, where more than 25 million boxes of fruit are picked annually. The surrounding counties of Marion, Volusia, Orange, Hillsborough, Hardee, De Soto, Highlands, Indian River and St. Lucie are also major producers. Another good area is around Arcadia in Desoto County.

The harvest season for all citrus crops broadly lasts from mid-October until early July, exactly opposite from the usual summer harvesting season. As far as individual crops are concerned, oranges normally start up in November and peak in January, February and March with another peak in May with the late Valencia orange crop.

Buses drive into large local towns at around 6am and anybody who wants to pick fruit that day can get on and be driven to that contractor's grove. Ask around in bars what the form is as regards buses, rates of pay and good groves. To them you are nothing more than a box number in a given row and so, with luck, visas won't be a problem, unless there are rumours of an impending immigration raid.

Wages are based on piece rates, the basic unit being a bin or box. You determine your own work level and nobody rushes you. Pay is given out by the day or by the week if you want, and it is cash in hand. Steve and Iona Dwyer were distinctly unimpressed with the earning potential of picking oranges in Florida:

> *We got ourselves a car in Florida which became very necessary during our jaunt. I would say that unless you are almost broke, don't bother with the orange harvest. The Hispanics have kept the wages very low. When we were there the rate was $7 per half-ton bin. For one and half days we toiled in sweltering heat to earn $60 between us.*

The speed at which you can fill boxes is heavily dependent upon your ability to place your ladder cleverly. A lot of time is wasted moving around ladders from branch to branch and this means fewer boxes filled and hence less money earned. A good picker can clear half a tree from one position – as a novice you will not be able to do so. So the best thing to do is to buy a bottle of wine and a packet of cigarettes and offer them to one of the 'winos', probably lying underneath a tree, in exchange for a lesson in placing ladders. These guys know more about picking than anybody.

An alternative method operates in the groves which supply juice factories. In this case you knock the fruit from five or six trees onto the ground, pick them up and fill a big sack which is dumped into a giant bin. Picking is organised by the foreman assigning each picker or pair of pickers a row of trees to clear. Once he realises a particular picker is keen, he or she should be given the better rows.

The picking season is divided into early, middle and late. Early picking means selecting the ripe fruit which is slow and hence badly paid. Much the same applies to late picking when one takes what is left on the trees. Middle picking starts up when the fruit demand is high and involves virtual stripping of the fruit. This is the best paid part of the season. The price being paid per box varies per week, per grove and per fruit type. The only way to make the most of the grove variation in price is to have your own car and drive around a few groves and offer yourself for work at the best paid grove or the one that looks fullest in fruit. Sometimes you may have to drive 30 miles to work. Many people do this, though the majority rely on the labour buses.

Iain Kemble headed for a small town 15 miles inland from Boynton Beach which is so far south it is a little out of the way of migrant gangs. All the picking was done by an extended family of local blacks, but foreigners were employed in the packing shed at slightly more than minimum wage.

Although citrus is the most important crop in Florida, the state also produces a whole range of vegetables. Southern Florida is the only place in the nation where vegetables can be grown between December and March (e.g. tomatoes, peppers, cucumbers). The best areas are Collier County centred around Naples on the Gulf of Mexico and the area around Homestead south of Miami. The September cucumber harvest is reputed to be the best paid work in the area ($100 a day) but the work is

	May	June	July	August	September	October
Alabama	potatoes, tomatoes					
Arizona	carrots, lettuce		cotton			
Arkansas			peaches			
California	cherries		peaches, broccoli, peppers		grapes, apples	
Colorado			cherries	apricots, peaches	peas, apples	
Florida	(winter: citrus and most vegetables)				cucumbers	
Georgia		peaches		peanuts		
Idaho			cherries	onions	apples, potatoes, sugar beets	
Illinois	asparagus (April) corn detassling					
Indiana	corn detassling			tomatoes, corn		
Iowa	asparagus corn detassling beans					
Kentucky	strawberries			tobacco		
Louisiana	strawberries				sugar cane	
Maine	asparagus (April)			blueberry-raking	apples	
Maryland	strawberries, cabbages					
Michigan		strawberries	cherries	haying	peaches	apples
Minnesota					beetroot, potatoes	
Missouri				peaches	apples	
Montana			cherries		sugar beets,	potatoes
New Hampshire					apples	
New Jersey		strawberries	cranberries	blueberries	apples	
New York	strawberries, peas, cherries				apples	
North Carolina			tobacco			
North Dakota		sugar beets				
Pennsylvania					peaches, apples, grapes	
Ohio			field vegetables			
Oklahoma	wheat cutting			corn detassling		
Oregon	strawberries, cherries		peaches		apples, nuts, hops	
South Carolina	peaches					
South Dakota			wheat	hay, potatoes		
Utah		cherries		apricots	apples, sugar beets,	potatoes
Vermont					apples	
Virginia			tobacco	apples, peaches		
Washington		cherries	berries, hops		apples	
Wisconsin			lettuce, onions, peppers			
Wyoming					sugar beets	

incredibly hard and most travellers barely survive their first day. Apparently cabbages and watermelons are none too easy either.

A lot of the produce is designed for markets outside Florida and there are dozens of packing houses in these two areas which employ thousands of seasonal workers. Contact the Southwest Florida Growers Association in Immokalee Florida for more details of times and locations of harvests and job availability in the packing factories. Try growers in and around Route 31 near Arcadia, such as McBee Ltd., Chastiens Farms, Singletary Farms and Hatton Desoto Farms.

In Jan Christensen's opinion, work is more lucrative around Homestead, and he should know since he has worked three winter seasons there:

I worked with green beans and potatoes. Expect to work 80 hours a week, and the work is hard. The pay was $6-7 an hour. Best of all, most farms provide free housing. Of course it's best to have a car. I got my first job on the day I arrived.

The bean season runs from November 1st till April and the potatoes from New Years to the middle of May, so the best time to arrive is October. The farms and packing houses are easy to locate near Homestead along US 1 from Miami. Jan recommends trying F & T Farm (on the road to the Everglades National Park), John Alger Farms on Farm Life Road and Hilson and Son on US 1. Also there is a massive farmers' market on the same highway which employs more than 2,000 people in the season.

The Apple Harvest of Maine

In the early autumn, the local newspaper in south central Maine (around the town of Monmouth) is full of apple picker ads in the 'Help Wanted' columns. The season lasts two months, starting in early September and continuing until the first deep frost near the end of October. Pickers start out at the minimum wage, but graduate to piece work per bushel as soon as their speed reaches a certain level. Rates of pay are standard among orchards, as is the custom of paying a bonus to people who complete the harvest for one grower. Hours are flexible, though people who put in 70 hours a week are preferred. Crews are formed by the orchard foremen according to speed of picking; the French Canadian professional crews are a sight to behold and they earn well over $100 a day right from the beginning.

Once you get a little fitter and master the techniques, apple picking in Maine can be enjoyable, as Roger Brown comments:

Standing on top of an apple tree in the bright sunshine and chatting away to a colleague became a very pleasant way of passing the time. It was good too that the apple-picking season falls during the 'season of mists and mellow fruitfulness'. You get to the top of an apple tree on the top of a hill in Maine and the whole world seems to unroll at your feet. Beyond the white wooden church and steeple of Monmouth, ranges of hills can be seen in the distance creating a rainbow of colours with the bright leaves of the autumnal maples.

VOLUNTARY WORK

The three main workcamp organisations in the US (listed in the chapter *Voluntary Work*) have incoming programmes too. (Prospective volunteers should register through a workcamp organisation in their own country.) For example Volunteers for Peace place about 500 foreign volunteers on 40-50 workcamps in the US. Council accepts around 200 individuals from abroad over the age of 18 to participate in its international voluntary service projects. In the past, volunteers have been placed on environmental projects in Yosemite National Park, the Golden Gate National Seashore and northern Idaho's Kaniksu National Forest, assisted with urban renovation and preservation of historic landmarks in New York and New Jersey, and worked with disabled children and adults on their summer holidays.

Voluntary opportunities in the US range from the intensely urban to the decidedly rural. In the former category, you can build houses in deprived areas throughout the US with Habitat for Humanity (Global Village, 121 Habitat St, Americus, GA 31709). Each summer Winant-Clayton Volunteers place 20 participants in grassroots projects in the USA, mainly in New York, working with HIV/Aids sufferers, patients with mental health problems, inner city youth and the elderly. Volunteers with a British passport are recruited to work for eight weeks from mid or late June followed by two or three weeks of travel. For an application pack send an s.a.e. to WCVA, The Davenant Centre, 179 Whitechapel Road, London E1 1DU (020-7375 0547; www.wcva.dircon.co.uk). If you want a less structured spell of volunteering in New York City, go along to the university soup kitchen at the Church of the Nativity at 44 Second Avenue, by 11am on a Saturday. Volunteers receive a free lunch.

British and French volunteers over 18 can work for eight weeks from early July for several San Francisco organisations including the California Pacific Medical Centre and the AIDS Service Foundation. Applications should be sent by the middle of April to the International Volunteer Program organiser of the *Société Bienfaisance Mutuelle,* 210 Post St, Suite 502, San Francisco, CA (www.frenchfoundation.com). The total fee including airfares from London is £845.

Working outside the big cities is an attractive prospect. For example the US Forest Service organises workcamps to maintain trails, campsites and wildlife throughout the country; volunteers should apply to the individual parks; state-by-state opportunities are posted on the internet at www.volunteeramerica.net/usfs. The Heritage Resource Management department of the US Forest Service operates a volunteer programme to conduct archaeological surveys, record oral histories, etc. The Volunteer Co-ordinator's office is in Modoc National Forest (800 West 12th St, Alturas, CA 96101; 916-233-5811). He sends out application forms, tries to match volunteers with appropriate vacancies and assists with obtaining a J-1 visa. Volunteers/trainees are paid a stipend of about $100 a week in addition to free accommodation.

Archaeological digs which need volunteers are listed in the *Archaeological Fieldwork Opportunities Bulletin* (see *Voluntary* chapter for details). The Forest Service's Volunteer America programme matches volunteers with archaeological and historical preservation projects (800-281-9176).

The General Convention of Sioux YMCAs in South Dakota offers volunteer positions to people who can commit for a year. Volunteers live in rural Native American communities and run the local YMCA Youth Center, working with Lakota children, families and schools. The Y provides housing, a small living stipend and cultural training. Contact the Community Development Director for application details: PO Box 218, Dupree, South Dakota 57623 (605-365-5232; siouxymca@hotmail.com). Summer opportunities also exist at summer camps.

The American Hiking Society collates volunteer opportunities from around the United States to build, maintain and restore foot trails in America's backcountry. No prior trail work experience is necessary, but volunteers should be able to hike at least five miles a day, supply their own backpacking equipment (including tent), pay a $50 registration fee and arrange transport to and from the work site. Food is provided on most projects. For a schedule of projects, go to www.AmericanHiking.org or send an s.a.e. to AHS, PO Box 20160, Washington, DC 20041-2160 (301-565-6704; info@AmericanHiking.org). AHS also publish *Helping Out in the Outdoors,* a directory of volunteer opportunities and internships on America's public lands which costs $16 (US dollars only) including international postage.

The US Fish & Wildlife Service in Hawaii offers 15-20 volunteers the chance to live at one of two very remote island field stations in the northwest Hawaiian archipelago. English-speaking volunteers of all nationalities work on seabird monitoring and alien plant species control for three to six months in exchange for free flights from the US mainland and free living expenses. Programme information is available from the Refuge Operations Specialist, PO Box 50167, Honolulu, HI 96850; 808-541-1201; Dominique_Aycock@fsw.gov.

The Student Conservation Association Inc. (SCA, 689 River Road, PO Box 550, Charlestown, NH 03603-0550; 603-543-1700; internships@sca-inc.org) places anyone 18 or older in conservation and environmental internships in national parks and forests nationwide. Position lengths vary from 12 weeks to 12 months and provide travel expenses, housing, training and a weekly stipend. The SCA website www.sca-inc.org includes a searchable database of open positions as well as an application form.

Carlsbad Caverns National Park has an active volunteer programme and is always looking for new volunteers; details from the Volunteer Co-ordinator, 3225 National Parks Highway, Carlsbad, New Mexico 88220; 505-785-2232; paula_bauer@NPS.gov.

It might also be worth trying the Appalachian Trail Conference (PO Box 807, Harpers Ferry, WV 25425-0807; 304-535-6331; crews@appalachiantrail.org/ www.appalachiantrail.org) which organises work parties to maintain the Appalachian Trail lasting one to six weeks. Volunteers receive food, accommodation and insurance.

CONCLUSION

This chapter has only scratched the surface, but we hope that it has sparked a few new ideas for your trans-American trip. Together with reading Jack Kerouac's *On The Road,* you should be all set. It also helps if you have a cousin or acquaintance living in the US who is willing to guide you through your first few days. As one of our less intrepid correspondents recalls:

> *When we first arrived in the States we went immediately to visit the parents of a friend. I'd never met them before but they made us welcome. A good thing too, because America seemed so strange to me and expensive, that I just wanted to get on the first plane back. I think it was because everything seemed so big and in advance of us. I was used to being in more 'backward' places (i.e. Ghana and Scotland) and America was much more complicated.*

There is no denying that it is preferable to qualify for an Exchange Visitor Programme like BUNAC or Au Pair in America. One of the advantages is that they choose a comprehensive insurance policy for you. If you go on your own, make sure you have purchased enough insurance cover since medical care is astronomically expensive in the US.

You must balance caution with a spirit of adventure, accepting and even revelling in the bizarre. When you learn that it is possible to get a night's lodging in a police cell, at a rescue mission or Salvation Army hostel, you need not necessarily shy away. You might have an experience similar to Benjamin Fry's in Alaska:

> *I stayed in another rescue mission in Anchorage and there witnessed an amazing spectacle: a tearful Indian or perhaps Eskimo confessing his sins in his native language. We were also fed – revolting food but free.*

You may end up in some unlikely situations, but some of them may also lead to a few days of work helping a trucker with his deliveries, joining an impromptu pop group to perform at private parties, gardening on a Californian commune, building solar houses, and so on. If you aren't lucky enough to have the appropriate visa, you should grasp every opportunity to earn a few dollars, taking advantage of offers of genuine hospitality.

If you do conduct a proper on-the-spot job hunt, the two most useful tools you can have are a car and a phone, tools that are synonymous with the American way of life. It also helps to have not only a tidy but conservative appearance. Writing from small-town North Carolina after a stint of working in a pizzeria in Ohio, Peter Stonemann summarises the situation:

> *North America still offers good possibilities of life, but it is not at all the 'dream' that the chauvinistic Yankee propaganda tries to present to the world. Perhaps it was in the past, but certainly it is now extremely difficult to progress here if you do not even have your own motor vehicle. You can only survive, with many poorly paid jobs.*

Even so, you should be able to get some kind of job which will introduce you to the striking cultural differences between Europe and America and which will provide you with some capital with which to explore this amazing country.

Canada

Countries like Canada which are favoured with a high standard of living and a reputation for unlimited job opportunities have traditionally attracted many travellers and emigrants. But, alas, it is not easy to work in Canada, both because of strictly enforced 'Canada-only' immigration policies and high unemployment of about 7% (compared to 8.3% a year ago). However Canadians are hospitable and eager for visitors to like their country. Even the immigration officer who deported one of our contributors expressed regret that the offender had not had a chance to see more of the country.

RED TAPE

British citizens require only a valid passport to enter Canada. Normally on arrival they will be given permission to stay as tourists for six months; incoming tourists will be requested to show that they have sufficient funds, adequate medical insurance and a return ticket or, failing that, some Canadian contacts. Although Canadian Immigration is reputed to be less savage than its American counterpart, many young travellers without much money have been given a rough ride.

To work legally in Canada, you must obtain an Employment Authorization from a Canadian High Commission or Embassy before you leave your home country. The Canadian government offers in the neighbourhood of 17,000 temporary authorisations each year to full-time students to work temporarily in Canada. Participants in the official work exchange must be aged 18-30 years and must have proof that they will be returning to a tertiary level course of study on their return to the UK. The Canadian High Commission in London administers the programme for students of British, Irish, Swedish and Finnish nationality. Other nationalities (like Australian, New Zealand and Dutch) should consult the Canadian embassy locally. The quotas are allocated on the basis of reciprocal agreements between Canada and the partner countries and can fluctuate from year to year.

Interested students should check the website www.canada.org.uk/visa-info or obtain the general leaflet 'Student Temporary Employment in Canada' by sending a large s.a.e. with a £1 stamp and marked 'SGWHP' in the top right-hand corner to the Canadian

High Commission (Immigration Visa Information, 38 Grosvenor St, London W1K 4AA); the premium line Immigration Info number is 09068-616644 (60p per minute) which goes on interminably and does nothing more than read out the written leaflets. Note that anyone with a job fixed up in Quebec must comply with separate and additional Quebec immigration procedures. Processing of all work authorisations normally takes 4-8 weeks if submitted between April and October, 4-6 weeks otherwise.

Students who already have a job offer from a Canadian employer may be eligible for 'Programme A'. They can apply directly to the High Commission in London for an Employment Authorization (reference 1102) which will be valid for a maximum of 12 months and is not transferable to any other job. The other and more flexible possibility is to obtain an unspecified Employment Authorization from BUNAC (see *Special Schemes* below).

Certain special categories of work may be eligible for authorisation, such as nannies who are in great demand but must be qualified (see *Childcare* section below). There is also a category of work permits for voluntary work which takes about a month to process if you have found a placement through a recognised charitable or religious organisation. The authorisation processing fee of C$150 (£65) is not charged for the Student General Working Holiday Program nor for volunteers working for a Canadian charity.

Americans do not require a passport to visit Canada (only proof of US citizenship if requested) but they are not allowed to enter in order to look for work. Like all foreign nationals, they must fix up a job (before arrival) which has been approved by the employer's local Human Resource Centre or HRC (the name for employment offices). The one difference is that they can apply for an Employment Authorization at the port of entry rather than having to apply through a Canadian consulate in the US.

Australians should write to the Canadian Consulate General, Immigration Office, Level 5, Quay West, 111 Harrington St, Sydney, NSW 2000 (fax 02-9364 3099; www.canada.org.au) to request an application form for a working holiday visa which is an open Employment Authorization valid for a year, available to young people (not necessarily students) aged 18-25 who are in Australia at the time of applying. Applicants must prove that they have access to $4,000 (recent bank statements, cash) and have no criminal record. Application forms will be available only after January 1st of each year when the programme opens, and will close as soon as the quota of 4,000 is filled, which is usually in the spring (the date was 12th May in 2000). Processing normally takes 4-8 weeks. Applicants must submit their application before their 26th birthday so people whose birthdays fall in the Australian spring/summer (September to December) should apply when they are 24 at the latest. Anyone with a criminal record (including alcohol-related driving offences) or with dependants is not eligible to apply. The Consulate issues a Letter of Introduction that allows the holder to obtain an open Employment Authorization at the Canadian port of entry within 12 months (non-extendable) of the date of issue. Only one of these letters is issued to a given individual. The Employment Authorisation issued at the port of entry usually has a one-year validity and is a multiple entry visa.

Health insurance regulations differ from province to province for foreign workers. For example in Ontario it is a requirement that you purchase three months of cover (approximately £70) after which your employer should pay. Those arriving to work in Saskatchewan, on the other hand, are immediately covered by free health insurance.

Special Schemes

BUNAC (16 Bowling Green Lane, London EC1R 0QH; 020-7251 3472) offers two programmes: Work Canada for full-time tertiary level students who arrive in Canada between February and September (most depart in summer) and Gap Canada for candidates with a confirmed place at university and who leave in October. Altogether about 1,500 students obtain Employment Authorizations through BUNAC, including finalists with proof that they will return to the UK. This give them the chance to go to Canada for up to a year and take whatever jobs they can find. BUNAC can assist applicants to obtain a Work Authorization in one of three ways: with a definite job offer plus $600 in support funds; with a letter of sponsorship from a Canadian citizen plus support funds of $600, or with support funds only of $1,000. The great majority

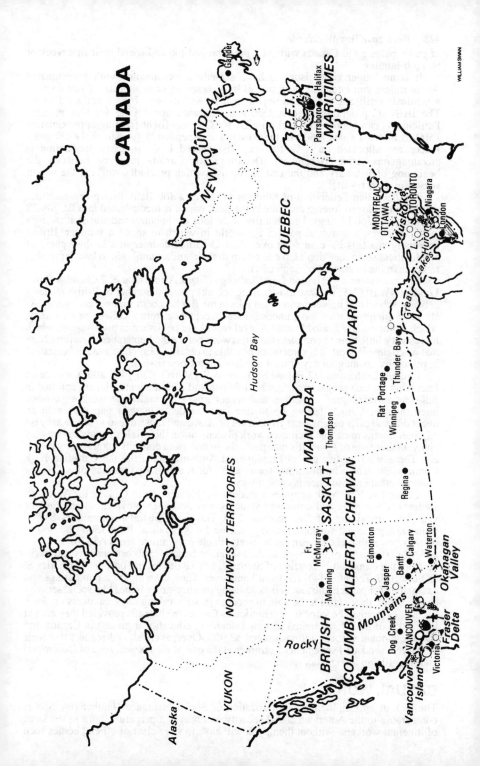

CANADA

WILLIAM SWAN

of participants go to Canada without a pre-arranged job and spend their first week or two job-hunting.

It is no longer compulsory to have a medical examination with a designated doctor unless you intend to work in childcare, teaching or healthcare; if you do need a medical certificate, reckon on paying at least £80 to one of the specified doctors. The BUNAC programme fee is £89, and insurance about £145 for four months. Participants can choose to travel on a BUNAC group flight (costing approximately £500 to the east coast, £600 to the west) or independently (considerably cheaper). Places are allocated on a first come, first served basis so early application is advantageous (from December). Departure for Canada must be between the beginning of February and the end of August (which precludes working the winter season in a ski resort).

The Canadian Federation of Students produces a Job Bank listing organisations that have employed foreign students in the past, which is incorporated into BUNAC's Work Canada Job Listings. The majority of the jobs are in hotels and tourist attractions in the Rockies, a beautiful part of the world in which to spend a summer. British university students have an edge over their Canadian counterparts in this sphere of employment since they don't have to return to their studies until mid to late September rather than the beginning of September.

The placement organisation Gap Challenge (Black Arrow House, 2 Chandos Road, London NW10 6NF; www.world-challenge.co.uk) places a number of British students between school and university in resort jobs in the Rockies both summer and winter. As above, participants must have unconditional acceptance from a college or university, which is not usually available until A level results are published in mid-August, which leaves very little time to complete the paperwork before the September departure. Note that when time is short, it is sometimes possible to obtain an Employment Authorization in person by queuing all day at the Canadian High Commission.

Council Exchanges (52 Poland St, London W1V 4JQ; 020-7478 2007) operate an Internship Canada programme on which British and Irish students who are enrolled in full-time further/higher education and recent graduates undertake work experience internships in Canada lasting up to one year. Students in their gap year with an unconditional offer of a place at HND level or above and those due to graduate are also eligible. Interns must find their own work placements in their field of study before they apply, making use of Council's info pack, the internet and contacts suggested by tutors, etc. Those who qualify get an Employment Authorization from the Canadian High Commission. The administrative fee is £200 for the first two months plus £30 per month thereafter. Insurance is compulsory.

Council in New York operates a student work exchange in Canada for American students. US college and university students may accept employment at any time of year for a maximum of five months. STA Travel in Australia administers SWAP Canada, a packaged working holiday scheme for Australian. Ring 1300 360 960 to book (www.statravel.com.au); the non-refundable programme fee is A$450.

All participants of approved student schemes benefit from orientations and back-up from the Canadian Federation of Students' SWAP offices in Toronto (45 Charles St E, Suite 100, Toronto M4Y 1S2) and Vancouver. They even organise pub outings and excursions for participants, as well as advising on nitty-gritty issues like social security cards, which they claim to be able to process in six working days. Students on work exchanges receive the same tax exemption as Canadian students, provided they earn at least 90% of their total annual income (including educational grants) in Canada and that the amount earned will not exceed $3,000. Overpayers should request that their employers send a T4 statement of earnings at the end of the tax year (end of December) and then file an income tax return.

CASUAL WORK

The lack of an Employment Authorization or Social Insurance Number (the SIN is comparable to the American social security number) is a perpetual thorn in the sides of itinerant workers. Without them, you will have to steer clear of official bodies such as Human Resource Centres, tax offices, etc. and many employers will be unwilling to consider you or, more importantly, pay you.

Ana Maria Güemes from Mexico recommends looking for catering work in the big cities, where so many residents speak with foreign accents that you are taken for a resident if you act like one:

> *It took me a week to find my job as waitress at a restaurant in the Yorkdale Shopping Centre in suburban Toronto, which was displaying a 'Help Wanted' sign. It is important to be confident when looking for a job and talking about previous experience, implying that you have been living in Canada for several years. I put the names of people I hardly knew on the application form as referees (my landlord, my friend's boss) and used a friend's social insurance number changed by a digit. I told them I had just left another restaurant in Toronto, a name I'd chosen at random from the Yellow Pages. I was there for seven months and left with a letter of reference and plenty of money to continue my travels in Europe.*

If you decide to work without proper authorisation, you should be aware that you are breaking a law which is taken seriously in Canada with a very real danger of deportation. If you are working in a job known to hire large numbers of foreigners (e.g. tree-planting and fruit-picking in British Columbia), there is a chance that the area will be raided by immigration control. Raymond Oliver could hardly believe their efficiency: at 10am he gave his B.C. employer a made-up SIN, at noon a phone call came to say it was fake and at 11am the next day an immigration officer arrived to tell him he had to leave the country within a fortnight. If you cannot fund your own departure, you will either be given a 'departure notice' which allows you to travel to the US or be deported and prohibited from returning for a prescribed period. If you are caught and want legal advice, contact the nearest legal aid lawyer whose services are free.

If you have been granted a short stay on arrival on the country, it may be possible to have this extended by crossing over to the States and back again. Raymond Oliver discovered what long memories computers have and wrote of his experiences in 2000:

> *At Vancouver airport, I was kept at Immigration when they noticed that I had been deported in 1992. I had to show them all my money, bank card, etc. and the immigration officer even telephoned the friend I was planning to stay with (even though her sons were at the airport to meet me). I was only given a 17-day visa to cover the length of my holiday. Having said that, I went to Vancouver Island and by ship to Anacortes Island in Washington state. When I came back into Canada at Osoyoos, the immigration officer asked how long I wanted to stay. I could have stayed a year if I could prove I had the funds.*

Prospective employers seldom ask to check the actual SIN card but will certainly ask for the number. Numbers which are issued to foreign workers begin with a 9, though this might prompt an employer to ask to see proof that your status is legitimate. The efficiency of Canadian bureaucracy means that few employers will conveniently forget about your lack of ID. For example a skilled baker from Manchester, who kept telling employers his number was in the post, was dismissed every couple of months when they became suspicious. Obliging employers might be prepared to pay your wages to a workmate who will hand over the cash, so that your name stays out of the books. A variation is to work under a Canadian friend's name and number and ask him or her to cash your pay cheques for you.

Anyone on shaky legal ground should keep a very low profile. It is rumoured that it is not difficult for people without permits to find winter work in ski resorts in the Rockies but not on the slopes. Brigitte Albrech worked as a tree planter in Prince George B.C. using a SIN number given to her by her employer. But because she was German, it was hard to blend in and the authorities somehow heard of her (after she had been working for three months) and sent her a request in writing to leave within six weeks or face a court hearing.

Wages are fairly good in Canada with statutory minimum wages, e.g. $6.85 per hour in Ontario (unchanged for six years; $6.40 for students) and $6-$7 in most of the other provinces except British Columbia where it is $7.60. Most working holiday makers (like most Canadian students) earn the minimum wage, with an average weekly wage of $250-$300 and average accommodation costs of $75+ per week.

Iain Kemble earned well in excess of the average when he got a few days work ferrying buckets of cement to a crew of fence-builders in Alberta. Because this was a government contract (to prevent animals from being killed on the Icefield Parkway between Banff and Jasper), the wage was excellent. Iain concluded that after earning $450 in five days, he must have been the best paid illegal worker in the Banff Youth Hostel.

THE JOB HUNT

The job hunt is tougher in Canada than almost anywhere else; it takes BUNACers a discouraging average of seven days to find a job in Canada. Even Canadian students find it hard to get summer jobs and there will be stiff competition for most kinds of seasonal work. As well as having to cope with the inevitable rejections, remember the weather in summer is often very hot and humid. It will be necessary to look presentable, eager to please, positive and cheerful, even if the responses are negative or the employers rude. Adda Macchich recounts the job hunt that nearly saw her giving up:

> *I decided to settle in Ottawa last February and spent five weeks looking for work, with no luck. I filled out about 50 applications; the answer was invariably 'leave it with me; we'll get back to you' and they never did. You never even get to see the manager. I returned to Canada in June, hoping things had improved as the summer approached. I went to Niagara Falls expecting as many summer jobs as in Cape Cod but was disappointed at the total absence of Help Wanted signs or ads in the local paper, so I returned to Toronto. Spent a whole month on an unsuccessful job hunt, constantly being asked to submit resumés for menial jobs in restaurants and cafés and tramping from one end of town to the other merely to fill out more forms. The only available jobs were those paid on commission, which were advertised everywhere.*

Not too surprisingly Niagara Falls was a dead loss since it has among the highest unemployment rates in the country. Just as Adda had decided it was time to fly back to London she stumbled across a commission-only ice cream vending job which was open to virtually anyone willing to man a stationary or bicycle-powered ice cream unit. At first the money wasn't very good but as the season picked up so did the sales. The most lucrative areas are around the base of the CN Tower, the Skydome and Harbourfront in downtown Toronto. On average, Adda earned between $20 and $60 daily and on good days $100+. The best times are during Caribana, the annual Caribbean festival at the end of July (when she made $200 in a single afternoon) and over the Labour Day weekend at the beginning of September. If interested, ask the vendors for the name and number of their boss. Toronto also has a fleet of rickshaws which employ runners. Matthew Shiel from the University of Swansea did it for the summer and was saving an astonishing C$1,000 a week.

As ever, youth hostel notice boards are recommended for information on jobs. According to Preeti Sharma, staff at the Edmonton Youth Hostel can advise on local work opportunities (10422 91st St; 403-429-0140). Only students with working holiday permits will be allowed to work in hostels. To illustrate the stringency of immigration regulations, even work-for-keep arrangements are difficult to find, as described by the Jericho Beach Youth Hostel in Vancouver (1515 Discovery St, Vancouver, B.C. V6R 4K5; 604-224-3208):

> *Unfortunately, due to Canadian employment regulations, we are unable to have foreign nationals participate in our work exchange programme at the hostel (two hours work in exchange for a free overnight). We do have an employment board at the hostel where we post notices from local companies and individuals offering employment. In addition, the front desk staff are a valuable resource for finding employment in the city.*

In addition to Vancouver, the best cities to look for work are Toronto, Calgary and Edmonton. Jobs for sales staff are advertised wherever you go in Canada. One of the easiest ways to get a job is to apply to branches of European companies like the Body

Shop and Gap. Tanufa Kotecha joined BUNAC's Work Canada programme and quickly learned that Canadian selling techniques are just as aggressive as American ones:

> *I landed a job within a week in Toronto working in a French Canadian clothing store. In my store as soon as a customer walked in, they had to be greeted by a 'sales associate' within 15 seconds! The North American way of selling is pushy and upfront, but it does get results. One must have confidence to sell.*

Almost all shop jobs of this kind pay the minimum wage.

Selling in a shop is too high profile for people without permits, but door-to-door and telephone selling are possible and once again your British accent should work in your favour as it did for Helen Welch in Barrie Ontario when she was hired to persuade people to buy photographic portraits of themselves. This was working well until the last day of May when a freak tornado hit Barrie and the people whom she had been telephoning suddenly didn't have any walls left on which to hang their pictures. So she was forced to move to Toronto in her quest for a roof over her head.

TOURISM

Newspapers are always worth scouring. Ana Güemes got one of her two waitressing jobs from the *Toronto Sun* while Vancouver's papers (the *Vancouver Sun, Province* and *Westender*) and the *Calgary Herald* contain job adverts, especially for dishwashers, waiting and bar staff. Free newspapers like the *Vancouver Courier* are also promising.

The Rocky Mountain resorts of Banff, Jasper, Lake Louise, Sunshine Mountain and Waterton are among the best places to try both summer and winter. Banff seems to absorb the largest number of foreign workers as catering and chamber staff, trail-cutters, etc. It is an expensive town in which to job-hunt but if you are prepared to walk you can find free campsites out of town and up the mountainsides. The huge Banff Springs Hotel alone employs 900 people, as do its sister hotels in the Canadian Pacific group of luxury hotels (Chateau Lake Louise and Jasper Park Lodge). Also try Lake Louise Inn, Inns of Banff Park, Banff International Hotel and Athabasca Hotel in Jasper. The standard wage at all these hotels is $1-$1.50 an hour higher than the provincial minimum wage of $6. During the height of the season there may be very little time off. Between $4 and $7 a day will be taken off for staff accommodation and (in most cases) meals.

One traveller to Western Canada reported:

> *While on holiday in Banff, I met a lot of Australians and Britons staying at the youth hostel. All of them were just on holiday visas, and all of them had found work in the height of the tourist season. I was offered hotel work. There is a lot of work to be had in Canada and men in particular would have no trouble supporting themselves. Canadians are very warm towards foreigners and employers are generally prepared to risk hiring casuals 'black' if they can't get through the red tape. Wages are very good for this type of work.*

Ski Resorts

The main ski resorts in western Canada are Banff/Lake Louise and Whistler/Blackcomb. Ski resorts throughout Canada create a lot of seasonal employment for which Canadian students cannot compete apart from during the Christmas and spring break. Unless you have an employment authorisation, your chances of picking up anything apart from very casual jobs like snow-shovelling and babysitting are minimal. Affordable accommodation is in very short supply in the main ski resorts, as is true worldwide. Most of the accommodation in ski towns is full by October, well in advance of the start of the season. Two reasonably priced places to stay in Whistler are Shoestring Lodge and UBC Lodge. In Banff try Sunshine Village (www.sunshinevillage.com) which has staff accommodation.

James Gillespie from Surrey spent the winter and summer of his gap year working in Whistler. After taking the beautiful train ride from Vancouver, it soon became clear that getting a place to stay would be a major problem. But soon he had a job as a ticket validator which came with a free ski pass and subsidised accommodation:

It was an excellent job and, although sometimes mundane, it was often livened up by violent and abusive skiers trying to get on the lift for free. Going there was the best thing I've ever done and I hope to be living there permanently eventually. I came home with a diary full of experiences, a face full of smiles, a bag full of dirty washing and pockets full of... well nothing actually. I was in debt, but it was worth it.

Jennie Cox from Derbyshire was unsure about what she wanted to do at the end of her degree at Durham University so consequently decided to take a year out so she applied to Gap Challenge in October, attended a two-day selection course in December, completed a skills training course the following July and left for Canada in September. On her return she described her seven months away.

I always wanted to go to Canada and had heard much about the country from friends and family. It's renowned for its friendly people; and Banff, in particular, looked beautiful. I was especially keen to ski and snowboard which influenced my decision. My placement involved housekeeping at Banff Park Lodge and general room cleaning, making beds etc. Overall I had an amazing time in Canada, and I certainly couldn't have asked for a more beautiful placement than the one I had in Banff. To wake up to vast snow-capped mountains each morning was such a luxury, that we had to be careful not to take it for granted. At times, of course, the work could be hard and exhausting, but you had to remind yourself why you were there: young friendly people to meet, lots of places to visit and days up on the slopes snowboarding, topped off by a pint of Canadian lager at night – who could ask for more? I've come back feeling relaxed, happy and refreshed and full of some great memories. Now I just have to find a job.

For jobs with UK tour operators, see addresses for Crystal Holidays, First Choice Ski, Handmade Holidays, Inghams, Skiworld and Thomson Breakaway in the introductory *Tourism* chapter. Venture Abroad (Arc House, 1 Coalhill Lane, Farsley, Leeds LS28 5NA; www.ventureabroad.co.uk) hire reps to guide youth groups in Canada.

Applications for work in Ontario resorts like Blue Mountain near Collingwood are normally considered in November, whereas the deadline is somewhat earlier for work in western resorts since the season starts earlier. Blue Mountain employs up to 700 staff for the season which is running on full steam from Christmas to the March break. If considering ski resorts in Québec like Mount Tremblant, a knowledge of French is necessary. General information about Canadian ski resorts is available on the internet at www.skinetcanada.ca.

Resort contact addresses:

Whistler/Blackcomb, 4545 Blackcomb Way, Whistler, B.C. V0N 1B4 (604-932-3434; kmuller@intrawest.com/ www.whistler-blackcomb.com). Website gives dates of annual recruiting fair; can also apply on-line.

Blue Mountain Resort, RR3, Collingwood, Ontario L9Y 3Z2 (fax 705-444-1751).

Other popular holiday areas (summer more than winter) are the Muskoka District of Ontario centred on the town of Huntsville and the shores of the Great Lakes, particularly Lake Huron. Since most of the holiday job recruitment in Ontario is done through Canadian universities, and the resorts are so widely scattered that asking door to door is impracticable, it is advisable to concentrate your efforts in the west.

University Towns

Living in a university town and becoming involved in the life of a university often leads to a range of casual work opportunities. Almost all Canadian students hold part-time jobs to help fund their education and you may inherit this type of job when they leave university or temporarily while they go away for the vacations. Student Employment Centers may be of use to people with work permits.

Ann Sommerville stayed in Canada for four years altogether, mostly in the industrial city of Hamilton (near Niagara Falls) where McMaster University is located. She pieced together a living from a large variety of casual jobs, including part-time waitressing and washing up, bar work in the campus bar, babysitting and occasional house cleaning (which was easy to get through private advertising), essay typing (especially in December and March as terms draw to an end), and assisting at academic conferences, e.g. working a slide projector, manning a bookstall.

Clinical research is often carried out in university towns by university medical departments and teaching hospitals. The website www.centerwatch.com lists details of current drug trials needing volunteers at the Clinical Research Centre of Montreal General Hospital (514-937-6011; mcti@musica.mcgill.ca), the Queen Elizabeth II Health Sciences Centre in Halifax (902-473-7906; resamh@qe2-hsc.ns.ca), Hill Top Research in Winnipeg (204-453-1835) and others.

Universities can be found in the following Ontario towns: Toronto (two), Hamilton, St. Catharines, Waterloo (two), London, Windsor, Kingston, Peterborough, Ottawa (two), Sudbury and Thunder Bay as well as in the capitals and the biggest cities in all the other provinces.

Tree-Planting

The archetype of the working Canadian is the lumberjack. Nowadays there are fewer jobs for tree-choppers than tree-planters which, in these environmentally-conscious times, is an ideologically sound job to have. In areas which have been logged or burnt, forestry officials are encouraging massive reafforestation and every March planting contractors begin to recruit crews for the season which begins in April. The payment is piece work usually about 10-12 cents per tree though higher when the terrain is steep or uncleared. Rates are best in British Columbia and worst in Ontario. Novices can usually earn $100 a day after a few weeks' practice. In some cases 'rookies' are earning $150 and even $200 a day by the end of the season. A deduction is made for camp expenses, normally about $20 a day. You will need a waterproof tent and work clothes including boots and waterproofs. Many firms do not lend out the equipment, so the cost of shovels and bags (which are expensive) are deducted from your wages. The Tree Planting Webpage is a goldmine of insiders' information with extensive listings of companies and planters' comments on them; see http://web.radiant.net/harihari.

Prince George is an important centre for tree-planting. While travelling in Mexico on annual leave from her job in Germany, Brigitte Albrech met up with a van full of French Canadians who were heading for Prince George to plant trees, and decided to follow them rather than return to her job. She provided the names of three companies: Bugbusters, Folklore and Triple A.

Chris Harrington planted trees and recommends picking up a copy of a magazine called *Screef* in outdoor stores in British Columbia in early March. (The word screef refers to the removal of loose debris with your boot or shovel.) The magazine lists tree-planting companies and gives some job information. But with rising local unemployment, jobs are scarcer than they used to be as Chris discovered when he returned the next year:

> *This time I met many disappointed Canadians who couldn't find work, a situation which is likely to worsen in the future. Without a work visa it's practically impossible. I didn't have one but fortunately had Canadian friends who went to a lot of trouble to help me. Otherwise I would have had to find someone willing to let me use their name and number (the two have to match when fed into a company computer).*

Dates are uncertain due to weather. There is a spring and a summer season with two to four weeks in between. Some B.C. contractors start as early as late March and finish in August, though Chris's job didn't begin until early May. Around Fort Frances and Thunder Bay in Ontario, the season is shorter, late April until the first week of July.

Although Brigitte Albrech agrees that the work is hard and the hours long, she greatly enjoyed the team spirit and solved a few problems she didn't know she had. Chris Harrington paints a fairly negative picture (while concluding that he had a great time):

> *Tree-planting itself consists of a ten-hour day starting about 6am, though overtime is available to masochists. This is awful work, make no mistake. The job is monotonous and weather conditions can be appalling (snow in June!). Coupled with the bugs, this can lead you to question your sanity. One of the worst aspects is 'down time' which occurs regularly between contracts, where*

you will find yourself hanging around expensive motels with no idea when and if you will be working again. How much you earn depends on how well you can motivate yourself. Not easy when you hate the job, it's been raining for a week, you are half way up a near vertical mountain and you've got bags full of trees which you can't find a suitable planting spot for.

Kevin Vincent and his brother both got jobs in the Slocan Valley in B.C. and disagree that tree-planting is one of the most miserable jobs in the world, which may have something to do with the fact that, in his first season, Kev's brother saved thousands of dollars in just two months:

Tree planting is a job which can become a traveller's dream. It is a hard job, but not as hard as people say, no harder than construction work or heavy farm work. The food is great (sometimes outrageous) and camp life is very sociable with people playing music, etc. Whole families with babysitters come along. The money is good, there's no doubt about that. If camping out in Canada's forests and living a real healthy lifestyle for three or four months appeals, plus earning top wages, this is for you.

FRUIT PICKING

British Columbia

The fruit-growing industry of Western Canada takes place in decidedly more congenial surroundings. The beautiful Okanagan Valley of British Columbia is tucked away between two mountain ranges in the interior of British Columbia and supports 26,000 acres of orchards. The Valley stretches north from the American border at Osoyoos for over 200km to Armstrong. Cherries, peaches, plums, pears, apricots, grapes and apples are all grown in the Valley, with a concentration of soft fruits in the south and hard fruits (apples, pears) in the north. All of these must be picked by hand. The harvesting dates vary slightly from area to area, possibly as much as a fortnight or so earlier in Osoyoos than in Armstrong. A useful website is www.island.net/~awpb/emop/harvest2.html entitled Harvest Information and Schedule for Okanagan and Kootenay Regions.

Another valuable source of information is the Casual Labour Co-ordinator working at the Ki-Low-Na Friendship Society in the Okanagan (442 Leon Ave, Kelowna, B.C. V1Y 6J3; 250-763-4905/fax 250-861-5514; www.kfs.bc.ca). Lists of orchardists seeking workers are displayed in this office as requests come in; contact details of local farmers are not given out until there is a vacancy. The Society is a non-profit organisation working with and for Native people but their advice is available to anyone.

The harvests in Kelowna, a town approximately in the centre of the Valley take place at the following times:

Species of Fruit	*Approximate starting date*	*Approximate duration*
cherries	June 25	through July
apricots	mid-July	approx. 3 weeks
Vee peaches	August 5	2 or 3 weeks
Elberta peaches	August 28	"
Red haven peaches	July 20	6 weeks
Prune plums	mid-August	till mid-September
Bartlet pears	August 12	Sep/early Oct
Anjou pears	late September	October
Macintosh apples	early September	3-4 weeks
Spartan apples	late September	"
Newton apples	late October/November	"
Winesap apples	late October	"
Golden delicious apples	September	"
Red delicious apples	"	"
Rome beauty apples	"	"
grapes	September 8	6 weeks

The best source of information on fruit-picking generally is the Agricultural Labour Pool with offices in Penticton and other towns. Of course you have to have legal status to make use of this service. As has been mentioned, immigration raids are frequent and merciless in this area, because it attracts so many illegal workers. Of course students with Employment Authorizations may want to consider trying for a job in the Okanagan, so here is more detailed information about the harvests.

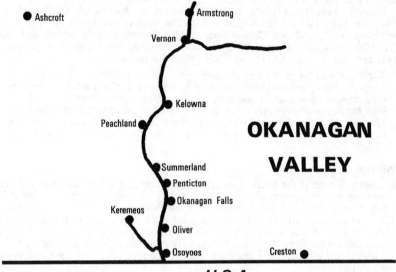

Picking jobs are assigned by the Labour Pool office on a first come first served basis (all things being equal) and so it is important to arrive early in the day. Sometimes 100 hopeful job-seekers have gathered at the door by 7am. When the office is less busy, job-seekers are required to register, giving their name, social insurance number and contact address. Some attempt is made to screen applicants to avoid sending out a picker who has caused trouble elsewhere.

Iain Kemble recommends avoiding the employment office and instead hanging around the local fruit packing shed which all the farmers in the area visit at least once a day and asking for work as they arrive. Professional migrant pickers (many of whom are from Quebec) begin with the cherries in the south of the valley and move up the valley to pick only the peak cherries. Then they come south again to work the apricots in the same way and so on.

Almost all fruit-picking is paid piece work which can be lucrative, if gruelling in temperatures of 35°C. In order to make a lot of money you can't be afraid of heights, though most picking of soft fruit can be done from an 8ft ladder. The rate at present is about $16.50 for half a bin. Inexperienced pickers usually earn between $45 and $55 a day whereas the pros touch $185. The majority of wages are paid directly into a bank account, which is a further difficulty for casual workers without proper papers.

Apples are the Okanagan's most famous export product. There is continuous picking of one variety or another from mid-August to the end of October. Apple-picking can be slow and poorly paid. A basket is worn at the front of the body and this becomes very heavy as it fills up. Experience is not so important for the apple harvest, though if you confess to having none you may be given a job picking up windfalls for the provincial minimum wage of $7.60 (and rising to $8 from November 2001). Especially towards the end of the harvest when all the students have returned to university (approximately mid-September) and the weather is getting colder, the farmers begin to take almost anyone. Although most pickers do not live locally, not many farmers provide accommodation.

If you have trouble finding picking work you can try to get a job processing the fruit, for example at one of the many canneries in the Valley. Some years ago Raymond Oliver found a job at a factory making fruit candy bars in Okanagan Falls (which is where it took them two hours to discover his illegal status).

Berry picking takes place nearer Vancouver in Richmond, Chilliwack and Abbotsford between June and August, though this work is notoriously badly paid. Try contacting the Agricultural Labour Pool at 2337 Townline Road, Abbotsford, B.C. V2T 6G1 (604-855-7281; info@agri-labourpool.com/ www.agri-labourpool.com/ jobseekers/alerts). Raymond Oliver investigated this harvest too:

> *There's plenty of ground crops (strawberries, blackberries, blueberries) around Abbotsford one hour south of Vancouver. Unfortunately there was no accommodation and campsites charge $16 a night. There are pickers' huts but Asian immigrants seem to come in large groups and take them all. The same is true of Aldergrove and Richmond. I was told that if you work hard you can pick 100lb of blueberries a day which would earn you only $33.*

Ontario

The micro-climate in the fertile Niagara region bordering Lake Ontario is excellent for growing peaches, pears, plums, grapes (mostly for wine) and cherries. But it has already been pointed out that Niagara is an employment black spot, and it will be difficult to get a decent job, even though there is no shortage of fruit needing to be picked. To meet farmers, it is a good idea to go to the Saturday farmers' market (around the corner from the employment office on Main Street in Niagara Falls). Paul Donut had a compelling reason to stay in the area because he wanted to stay with a girl he knew:

> *Even here in Niagara I managed to find work. I called around all the local farms listed in the phone book and got a job picking cherries. The pay was dismal as the harvest was poor (most of the time was wasted throwing out the bad ones and being paid only for the baskets we filled with good cherries). However the farm was beautiful, my workmates, all Caribbean, were great fun. The peach harvest was somewhat better and after a couple of months I had enough money to look around for better paying work.*

Paul says he could have found a better-paid job if he had had transport from town to the farm, but since he didn't he had to accept work with the only farmer who would pick him up.

Elsewhere in the province there is a major tomato harvest in south-western Ontario, centred around Chatham and Leamington (pronounced Leemington), which starts in mid-August and lasts for six to eight weeks. Other fruit and vegetable harvests take place around the province, especially in the counties bordering Lake Erie. End-of-season bonuses are commonly paid. Opposite is a chart of harvests.

In addition to the tobacco harvest described below, another seasonal agricultural job which needs to be done on Southern Ontario farms is detassling seed corn. During three or four weeks in July, a large number of people are needed for this work in the Chatham area. Busloads of students are brought in from cities 60 miles away, so if you were on the spot you would have a chance although, as in the tobacco-growing area, local unemployment is high in this county.

Crop	Part of Ontario	Dates of Harvest
Asparagus	Chatham, Aylmer, Tillsonburg, Delhi, Simcoe, Alliston	early May to mid-June
Strawberries	Chatham, Simcoe, St. Catharines, Hamilton, Cobourg, Trenton	early June to mid-July
Cucumbers	Windsor, Leamington, Chatham, Aylmer	mid-June to mid-Aug
Cherries (sweet)	Chatham, Niagara Falls, St. Catharines, Hamilton	early July
Cherries (tart)	Chatham, Simcoe, St. Catharines, Hamilton	late July
Raspberries	St. Catharines, Hamilton, Cobourg	mid-July to mid-Aug
Plums	St. Catharines, Hamilton	Aug/Sept
Peaches	Windsor, Leamington, Chatham, Simcoe, St. Catharines, Hamilton	mid-Aug to end Sept
Tomatoes	Windsor, Leamington, Chatham, Simcoe, Picton	mid-Aug to end Sept
Pears	Leamington, St. Catharines, Hamiton	early Sept to mid-Oct
Apples	Leamington, Simcoe, Hamilton, Owen Sound, Cobourg, Trenton, Picton	early Sept to end Oct
Grapes	Niagara Falls, St. Catharines, Hamilton	mid-Sept to end Oct

The Maritimes

High unemployment in some Maritime areas has driven many locals west in search of employment. However if you are travelling in the Maritime Provinces in August/September, you might try to find paid work picking or 'raking' blueberries in the Nova Scotia towns of Parrsboro, Minudie, Amherst or Pugwash and elsewhere. Earlier in the summer (i.e. mid-June to mid-July), strawberry picking is available. In the autumn you can also look for work picking apples. Head for the Bay of Fundy coast of Nova Scotia around Annapolis Royal, Bridgetown and Middleton. If you're lucky, fruit picking wages will be paid cash-in-hand.

Another seasonal job which you can try for is fish processing as described by Stephen Boss, himself a Nova Scotian:

> *I am financing my round-the-world travels by working in a fish plant during the herring season (mid to late August until the end of September). This job consists of cutting open herring for the roe which is inspected and collected by Japanese technicians to be made into caviare. Cutters make good money. I was successful working for two fisheries in the town of Meteghan.*

The website www.fishroute.net/uscan lists the names but not addresses of fisheries in the Maritime provinces; for contact details, it will be necessary to search the Yellow Pages on-line.

OTHER FARM WORK

If you are interested in working your way from farm to farm and want to meet Canadians, you might consider volunteering for WWOOF-Canada (Willing Workers on Organic Farms). For a membership fee of C$30 (cash) and three international reply coupons, John Vanden Heuvel (RR2, S18, C9, Nelson, B.C. V1L 5P5; 250-354-4417; wwoofcan@uniserve.com) will send a list of more than 400 farms across Canada to prospective volunteers, along with a description of the farms. All volunteers must have valid tourist visas.

Anyone with a background in agriculture might profit by placing an advert in small town newspapers as an enterprising Australian Mark Newton did. While waiting for his job to start at the Biting Fly Institute in Winnipeg, Mark put an advert in the *Stonewall Argus*, a small town north of Winnipeg and fixed up two weeks of work with a pig farmer.

Tobacco

The other harvest in Ontario which has also been traditionally assisted by migrant workers is the tobacco harvest in Southern Ontario. But times are tough for tobacco farmers (due to anti-smoking campaigning) and many have been forced to replant tomatoes. Yet a demand for pickers continues and foreign students have a chance of employment. Until the 2000 season, a travel organisation Canadien National in Paris recruited a group of pickers from Europe, though for this edition they could not be traced and it may be that the exchange programme has been cancelled.

In case students find themselves in southern Ontario in the summer, work commences during the last week of July and lasts until the third or fourth week of September (depending on the first frost) in the area surrounding the city of London, i.e. Tillsonburg, Aylmer, Delhi (pronounced 'Dell-high') and Strathroy. Although the work is not as strenuous as it was before mechanical pickers were introduced, the hours make it a hard job: seven to ten hours a day for six and sometimes seven days a week. Pay will be approximately $70 per kiln or $7 per hour, whichever is higher. A deduction of $2 per meal is made unless the picker remains until the end of the harvest, in which case the deduction is waived. A further 5% of earnings will be lost in contributions. People who wear glasses are warned that condensation can be a problem and to avoid wearing them in the fields if possible.

One tobacco picker, Tim Kelly, describes a typical day of picking:

We would be up at 5.45am every day for breakfast and start work by 6.30. After our one hour lunch break we worked until the kiln was full of leaves, usually around 5pm. Often after supper we were asked to help empty a kiln, which takes another hour of hard work. The picking (known as 'priming') was a very tiring job, and the first few days were by far the worst. Nearly every morning we got soaked from dew off the leaves. During the rest of the day we got bitten by mosquitoes, scratched, bruised, as well as covered in black sticky nicotine tar which accumulates on skin and clothing.

Ontario is not the only place where tobacco is grown in Canada. There are about 80 tobacco farms in the small island province of Prince Edward Island in eastern Canada. While hitching around the region in May, Iain Kemble learned that there had been urgent messages on the radio asking for 800 tobacco planters. He pretended to the lady in the Montague Employment Centre that he had a work permit and was promptly assigned to one of many local farmers of Belgian extraction. He worked in the massive greenhouses from 7am to 8pm bending over a conveyor belt picking out plants at the appropriate stage of maturity. For this back-breaking work, he was paid considerably more than the minimum wage. Good meals and bunkhouse accommodation were provided for about $6 a day. The season lasted about a month until late June. He felt relatively safe from the prying eyes of immigration, but did hear of some Swedish planters who had been raided a few years before.

CHILDCARE

Live-in nannies and mothers' helps are in great demand in Canadian cities. However domestic employment in Canada is governed by a number of carefully formulated and strictly enforced regulations. A detailed leaflet about the 'Live-in Caregiver Program' may be obtained from the Canadian High Commission, though an agency which deals with Canada (such as the Solihull Agency or Childcare International listed in the introductory chapter *Childcare*) will be able to guide you through the various stages of the process. Qualifying nannies must either have six months of training in a related field (teaching, nursing, childcare) or 12 months experience in full-time paid employment as a nanny or mother's help within the previous three years, at least half of which must have been for the same employer. The other main requirement is that the nanny must live with her employers and commit herself to stay for at least one year.

If you are eligible and have found an employer (probably through an agency), you can apply for an Employment Authorization for Canada valid for one year and renewable once. There is a handling fee of C$150/approximately £65 for the permit. (After that it is possible to apply for 'landed residency'.) The procedure for getting an Authorization usually takes three to four months and will include a very strict medical examination by an appointed private doctor who will charge about £80. The Authorization will be valid for one employer, though it can be changed within Canada as long as your subsequent job is as a live-in child-carer.

Working as a nanny or mother's help in Canada has more status attached to it than au pairing in Europe, and the conditions of work reflect this. The federal and provincial governments set out guidelines for hours, time off, holidays, minimum salary and deductions. For example in British Columbia as of November 2000, the gross monthly wage of an overseas sponsored live-in nanny working a standard 44-hour week is $1,337.60. Allowable deductions are $325 for room and board plus various taxes and contributions (some of which may be reclaimable) which leaves a net wage of $775.

A search of the internet will take you to some Canadian agencies though some are more experienced in bringing in nannies from countries like the Philippines and Hong Kong rather than Europe. In all cases, nannies must satisfy the government's Live-in Caregiver requirements. Here is a small selection of agencies:

ABC Nannies Agency, Vancouver B.C. (abcnannies@hotmail.com/ www.abcnannies.8k.com).

Absolute Care Nanny, 1055 Taylor Way, West Vancouver, B.C. V7T 2K2 (604-925-1405; www.absolutecarenanny.com).

International Nannies & Homecare Ltd. 515-119 West Pender St, Vancouver, B.C. V6B 1S5 (604-609-9925; www.internationalnannies.com). Other offices in Ontario and other provinces.

Nannies 4 You, 5515 Duffus St, Unit 46028, Novalea RPO, Halifax, N.S. B3K 5V8 (902-456-0965; jobs@nannies4you.com). Job-seeking nannies must pay a non-refundable application fee of US$50.

Nanny Finders Directory Agency, 204-8055 Anderson Road, Richmond, B.C. V6Y 1S2 (604-272-1622; www.nannyfindersbc.com).

Scotia Personnel, Ltd., 6045 Cherry St, Halifax, N.S. B3H 2K4 (902-422-1455; www.scotia-personnel-ltd.com).

City newspapers are full of ads for nannies and babysitters, especially in August before the school term begins. When one reader replied to nannying adverts in the *Toronto Star*, she found that most were unwilling to employ her without papers. But by persevering she found a nannying and housekeeping job which allowed her to save a considerable amount.

For example, Myriam Nguyen, as resident of France, struck off independently to find a family, with the help of the free Vancouver Courier:

I was really broke but I found out that the Courier was offering a free ad to anyone who would bring three cans of food to be donated to a food bank. Of course it was just a temporary offer but it really svaed my life. Two days later I received the first call and I took the job, though I did get about five other phone calls later. The family was very nice. They asked me whether I wanted to be declared or paid under the table. I chose not to be declared and was paid $7 an hour, and worked 25 hours a week looking after a sweet two year old girl, no housework required. Three months after I started, I moved in with the family which meant I didn't have to pay $300 rent for my basement apartment.

I got my second job after responding to an ad, again in the Vancouver Courier. I was still paid $7 an hour however the duties were much more demanding: two children who bit and screamed at first, and 50% housework including two loads of laundry ever day. I was also offered to clean the three bathrooms but they paid me an extra $40 each time which, I think, is pretty generous. Basically, I am very satisfied with my stay in Vancouver. Childcare jobs are quite easy to find, either through agencies or newspapers. After you get to know some people, you often hear about jobs available.

VOLUNTARY WORK

Some interesting practical community projects are organised by Frontiers Foundation (2615 Danforth Avenue, Suite 203, Toronto, Ontario M4C 1L6; 416-690-3930/fax 416-690-3934; frontiersfoundation@on.aibn.com/ www.frontiersfoundation.org) in low income communities in Canada, which tend to be native communities in isolated northern areas. Some of the projects (known as Operation Beaver) consist of helping the local people to build low-cost well-heated houses or community centres. Others take place on wilderness camps for native children. Project locations have such picturesque names as Dog Creek, Rat Portage and Goose Bay. Whatever the project Frontiers Foundation will pay all food, accommodation, travel and insurance expenses within Canada. A modest living allowance will be paid if you stay beyond the minimum period of 12 weeks (four months for the North West Territories). The accepted volunteer only needs to pay a C$25 application fee, fund a return flight to Toronto and get the appropriate volunteer visa. Send three IRCs for an information pack and application form or download them from their website. The Foundation now has an office out west as well: 9781-127th St, Surrey, B.C. V3V 5J1 (604-585-6646; frontwest@home.com).

The work itself does not occupy all of your time and energies. According to Sarah King, there was time left over to participate in some quintessentially Canadian backwoods activities:

One of the great benefits about being a guest worker was that our activities became a focal point for the community. We played volleyball, helped break in wild horses, watched bears, made wild berry pies and rose-hip jelly, went camping, hunting, fishing and swimming, baked porcupine packed in clay, ate a delicacy of sweet and sour beaver tail, and all took up jogging around a local basketball park.

Another contributor stumbled (or rather strode) across a different way to experience the Canadian bush. Obbe Verwer from Amsterdam spent part of the summer hiking in British Columbia:

After enjoying my visits to a couple of farms listed by WWOOF, I went on by myself to Vancouver Island. I set off to hike through the rainforest along the Clayoquot Valley Witness Trail. When I came to the trailhead, I met the trail boss who was working with a group of volunteers to build boardwalks at both ends of the trails. This was to enable more people to walk part of the trail which is important because this valley has to be saved from clearcut logging. I decided to join them. Actually you are supposed to go through the organising committee to become a volunteer worker but I just pitched my tent and joined on the spot.

All the wood to build the boardwalk had to be carried into the trail, steps, stringers, nails and tools. We worked till 4pm, but it was not strict at all. Sometimes it was pretty hard, but it was fun. The forest impressed me more and more. The big trees, the berries, the mushrooms and the silence in the mist. It was just amazing. It was very satisfying to be helping to save this forest.

The Western Canada Wilderness Committee can be contacted at 341 Water St, Vancouver, B.C. V6B 2K7; 604-683-8220/fax 604-683-8229; info@wildernesscommittee. org). Volunteers should bear in mind that while working in rainforests one is bound to get wet. The WCWC also needs people to work in roadside kiosks, selling T-shirts, etc. for fund-raising. These volunteers should expect a certain amount of hostility from local loggers.

Few international workcamps take place in Canada. One of the few organisations active in the field is in Québec, and the camps they arrange are bilingual French-English and for young people aged 16-25. The co-ordinating organisation is Chantiers Jeunesse, 4545 avenue Pierre-de-Coubertin, CP 1000 Succursale M, Montréal, Québec H1V 3R2 (514-251-8719/1-800-361-2055; www.cj.qc.ca).

Latin America

South America features on the list of the top five destinations among young British travellers at the turn of the century (according to STA and other travel agencies). At one time most Europeans left the continent of South America to the Americans who were so much handier. But that has all changed and many gap year students and others are setting their sights on a trip to the Amazon or the Andes possibly in between a stint of teaching or volunteering. Several gap year agencies have set up South American programmes (like Quest Overseas; see chapter on *Voluntary Work: Gap Year Placements*) and BUNAC has recently introduced a 3-12 month Work Argentina programme for students and recent graduates in conjunction with the national student organisation ASATEJ. Participants (who must have a working knowledge of Spanish) are encouraged to look for work in tourism (ski and beach resorts) and in the capital.

Most Latin American nations do not need unskilled workers from abroad to perform the menial tasks associated with agriculture and industry. For every such job, there are several dozen natives willing to work for a pittance, and gringos (white westerners) will not be considered for such work. However, people who are bilingual in Spanish may find opportunities in the cities, especially bilingual secretaries. Because Britain has few colonial ties with Central and South America, there is a general cultural and economic orientation towards Uncle Sam which means that Americans tend to occupy many jobs rather than Britons. Apart from voluntary opportunities, the main sphere of employment in which foreign travellers have any prospect of gaining acceptance is the teaching of the English language.

TEACHING

Spanning 75 degrees of latitude, the mammoth continent of South America together with the Caribbean islands and the eight countries of Central America, offer a surprising range of teaching opportunities. All but Brazil have a majority of Spanish speakers and, as in Spain itself, there is a great demand for English teaching, from dusty towns on the Yucatan Peninsula of Mexico to Punta Arenas at the southern extremity of the continent, south of the Falkland Islands.

The countries of most interest to the travelling teacher are Mexico, Colombia, Ecuador, Peru, Venezuela, Chile, Argentina and Portuguese-speaking Brazil. Despite high levels of economic and often political uncertainty, demand for English language tuition continues to increase in the various kinds of institution engaged in promoting English, from elite cultural centres supported by the British and American governments to technical centres, from prestigious bilingual secondary schools to agencies which supply private tutors to businessmen. Experience is not always essential to land a teaching job on-the-spot. John Buckley, owner of a printing business in Blackpool, is just one traveller who was surprised at how welcome he was made to feel by a language school (in Brazil) when he had no TEFL training or experience:

> *When I was in Brazil for Christmas and New Year, I thought I would go to the local English school to see what went on, armed with a bunch of roses for the teacher (luckily female) and a little knowledge of Portuguese. Before I knew it, I was teaching English, words, pronunciation, slang and English life in general. This carried on for a few days with the class getting bigger and bigger. I felt like an alien landed from Mars, but what a buzz. I have found my vocation in life and am now looking for a good TEFL training course.*

An interesting volunteer placement scheme is run by Native English, a language school run by a Briton in Cuiabá (Rua Sao Benedito 306, Bairro Lixeira, Cuiabá 78.008-100; steve@terra.com.br) whereby gap year and other students provide English conversation practice and in return are taken on trips around the region to Amazonian villages, national parks, etc.

More detailed information about teaching in Latin America can be found in the 2001 edition of my book *Teaching English Abroad* (£12.95 plus £1.50 postage from Vacation Work, or in libraries).

The Job Hunt

In a land where baseball is a passion and US television enormously popular, American (and also Canadian) job-seekers have a distinct advantage. The whole continent is culturally and economically oriented towards the States and there is often a preference for the American accent and for American teaching materials and course books. On the other hand, many Britons have found themselves highly valued from Colombian universities to language agencies in Santiago. Business English is gaining ground throughout the region and anyone with a business background will have an edge over the competition.

The Central Bureau for International Education & Training arranges for language assistants to work in local secondary schools in a number of Latin American countries for a year. Applicants must be aged 20-30 with at least 'A' level Spanish and preferably a degree in modern languages. Application forms are available from October for a December deadline.

Some US-based organisations arrange for volunteers to teach in South and Central America. The Amity Foundation (10671 Roselle St, Suite 101, San Diego, CA 92121; 619-455-6364; mail@amity.org) has a strong Volunteer Teachers Abroad programme in Argentina in which Americans over the age of 21 with a grasp of conversational Spanish live with a family and teach at a language institute for eight or nine months. Board and lodging are free plus pocket money is paid. Elizabeth Tenney joined the programme and was sent to the small city of Rafaela in the Argentinian Pampas:

> *That city became my second home. I was lucky to find home life so rich and open, ameliorating my fears of being so far from my real family. As much as family life was comforting, my work life was challenging and rewarding. I taught at a small private language institute and spent a lot of time visiting classes and planning English lessons from the kindergarten level to adult classes. My favourite experience was heading my own free-conversation classes for adults in which I was able to get to know my students on a deeper level. The programme ensures enough free time so that you can travel, take classes (I took French, computing and Latin dance) and get involved in community activities.*

But if you are looking for more casual teaching work after arrival, it will be a matter of asking around and knocking on enough doors. There is less competition (although fewer jobs) in the smaller cities, off the beaten track. Try to charm the receptionist, librarian or English language officer at the British Council, Bi-National Center (the American counterpart of the British Council) or any other institute which might have relevant contacts or a useful notice board. Check adverts in the English language press such as Mexico City's *The News*, the *Buenos Aires Herald* or the Caracas *Daily Journal*. English language bookshops are another possible source of teaching leads, for example the English Book Centre in Guayaquil (Ecuador) and El Ateneo in Buenos Aires. Ask in expatriate bars and restaurants, check out any building claiming to be an 'English School' however dubious-looking, and in larger cities try deciphering the telephone directory for schools or agencies which might be able to use your services.

In Lima or Quito visit the South American Explorers (formerly the South American Explorers' Club) clubhouses (addresses in *Travel* chapter) which keep a list of language institutes and are staffed by expats who will be happy to share information with members. At the time of writing they were compiling an extensive volunteer database in order to make information about volunteering opportunities throughout South America available to members. Many of the organisations listed will take on English teachers without a TEFL certification. Membership costs US$40 per year and residents outside the USA pay an additional US$10 for postage. Membership in the UK is administered by Bradt Publications, 41 Nortoft Road, Chalfont St. Peter, Bucks SL9 0LA and in the USA at 126 Indian Creek Road, Ithaca, NY 14850 (607-277 0488/fax 607 277 6122; explorer@samexplo.org/ www.samexplo.org).

The crucial factor in becoming accepted as an English teacher at a locally-run language school may not be your qualifications or your accent as much as your appearance. You must look as neat and well-dressed as teachers are expected to look.

Travellers working their way around the world are more likely to find a few hours of teaching here and there earning $2-4 an hour, and have to patch together hours from various sources in order to make a living. If you have a good education, are carrying all your references and diplomas and are prepared to stay for an academic year, it may be possible to fix up a relatively lucrative contract.

Red Tape

Of course requirements vary from country to country but it is standard for work visas to be available only to teachers on long-term contracts after a vast array of documents has been gathered including notarised copies of teaching qualifications, police clearance, etc. This means that a high percentage of teachers work on tourist visas throughout Latin America. These must be kept up-to-date by applying for an extension from the immigration department or by crossing into and back from a neighbouring country.

Mexico

The enormous demand for English teaching in Mexico has increased with the coming of the North American Free Trade Agreement with the US. Companies of all descriptions provide language classes for their employees during all the waking hours of the week but especially in the early morning and at weekends. Roberta Wedge even managed to persuade a 'sleek head honcho in the state ferry service' that he needed private tuition during the siesta and that busy executives and other interested employees of a local company needed English lessons at the same time of day.

Demand is not confined to the big cities but exists in the remotest towns, at least one of which must remain nameless in order to preserve Roberta Wedge's dreams:

After doing a 'taster' ESL course in Vancouver, I set out for Nicaragua with a bus ticket to San Diego and $500 – no guide book, no travelling companion, no Spanish. On the way I fell in love with a town in Mexico (not for worlds would I reveal its name – I want to keep it in a pristine timewarp so I can hope to return) and decided to stay. I found a job by looking up all the language schools in the phonebook and walking around the city to find them. The problem was that many small businesses were not on the phone. So I kept my eye out for English school signs. I had semi-memorised a little speech in

Spanish, 'I am a Canadian teacher of English. I love your town very much and want to work here. This is my CV...' Within two days I had a job at a one-man school.

Leaving England for the first time, Linda Harrison travelled on a one-way ticket straight from the picturesque Yorkshire town of Kirkbymoorside to the picturesque state of Michoacàn, and suffered severe culture shock. She and a Spanish-speaking friend had pre-arranged jobs at the Culturlingua Language Center (Plaza Jardinadas, Local 24 y 25, Zamora, Michoacàn) which has the advantage of offering its half dozen native speaker teachers accommodation. However it does not offer any pre-service training as Linda found out:

The director told me that I might as well start teaching the day after I arrived. I stumbled into my first class with no experience, qualifications or books. Twelve expectant faces watched while I nervously talked about England. Twelve faces went blank when I mentioned soap operas.

Zamora is an off-the-beaten-track agricultural centre. Culturlingua is always looking for teachers and will consider hiring anyone who is a fluent English speaker and is not painfully shy. The school pays its teachers enough for them to live comfortably and to tour the state of Michoacàn, one of the most beautiful in Mexico.

The city of Monterrey held out no appeal for Paul Donut when he was given the chance to teach there:

A woman on the bus from Monterrey to Mazatlan gave me her phone number and said if I would teach her English, I could stay with her family in Monterrey and she would get me at least two paying students too. But even the prospect of a free bed and meals plus private students couldn't entice me back to a smog-ridden industrial city when I was heading for the Mexican Pacific Coast.

Mexico City is a thousand times more polluted, yet offers the best prospects for language teachers, some of which are advertised in the English language newspaper *The News.* It is also worth checking in the *Mexico City Times* and the *Mexico City Daily Bulletin.* Rupert Baker answered an advert and was invited to attend a disconcertingly informal interview at a restaurant (to which he still wore his tie). He ended up working for six months.

Michael Tunison contacted half a dozen major teaching organisations from the Yellow Pages and was interviewed by Berlitz and Harmon Hall. The starting wage at both schools was the peso equivalent of US$400 per month which seemed typical of the large chains. He later heard of less publicised opportunities to make $700 in institutes specialising in executive language training.

The red tape situation in Mexico is bound to cause headaches. In order to qualify for a work permit, you have to provide a CV in Spanish, notarised TEFL and university certificates which have been certified by a Mexican consulate, a valid tourist visa and a hefty fee. People do teach on tourist visas which will have to be renewed every 90 days either by proving at a local government office that you have enough funds to support yourself or (more inconveniently) by leaving the country and re-crossing the border to get a further 90 days.

A gap-year placement organisation in the UK specialises in Mexico, placing year-out students not only in teaching jobs but environmental and social projects too: Outreach International, Barlett's Farm, Hayes Rd, Compton Dundon, Somerset TQ11 6PF (tel/fax 01458 274957; www.outreachinternational.co.uk).

Bolivia

Even the poorest of Latin American nations offers possibilities to EFL teachers, provided you are prepared to accept a low wage. In contrast to the standard hourly wage of $10-$20 in Europeanised cities like Buenos Aires and Santiago, the wages paid by language schools in La Paz are 10-12 bolivianos ($2). But many travellers prefer Bolivia for cultural reasons, for its colourful social mix.

After finishing university in England and working briefly for a multinational, Ben Yeomans decided that the corporate environment was not for him and that instead he wanted to teach English in Latin America. He chose Bolivia after meeting the director of i-to-i which makes placements in that country:

> *I arrived in La Paz in February of this year and worked at the Pan American English Center, teaching all levels of English. The director is an Englishwoman who receives teachers from i-to-i as well as from individual applications. (She acts as the i-to-i representative and is very helpful.) My working hours varied, but were on average about four hours a day. I also worked as a volunteer for a children's interactive museum using my computer skills. I spoke no Spanish when I went, but now can hold a reasonably intelligent conversation.*
>
> *Bolivia is a great country to be in. It has a huge amount of natural beauty, a very varied geography, interesting and colourful customs and friendly people. I am now in a serious relationship with a Bolivian girl and am planning to stay. My experience of teaching English has shown me that I don't want to continue with this as a career (as I considered once, in a rush of enthusiasm during my TEFL course), so I am quite happy to return to my real profession in computing but in a different environment.*

Judith Twycross received three job offers within a week of arriving in Bolivia's second city Cochabamba. If you have a good standard of education, are carrying all your references and diplomas and are prepared to stay for an academic year, it is possible to fix up a teaching contract. Judith timed her arrival in Cochabamba so as to be a couple of weeks before the beginning of the winter term. With the advantage of a year's teaching experience in Spain and France and a good knowledge of Spanish, she soon found employment:

> *I took with me a letter of introduction and a CV both in Spanish plus a photocopy of my degree certificate. These I photocopied and delivered by hand to the directors of schools and institutes in Cochabamba. I got a list of schools from the Yellow Pages (which you could borrow at a hotel, photocopying kiosk, tourist information office, etc.). I told everyone I met what I was trying to do and received help and advice from hotel managers, taxi drivers and people I stopped on the street to ask for directions.*

The biggest language school in the country is the Centro Boliviano Americano (CBA) which has four locations in La Paz and schools in other cities like Sucre and Santa Cruz. Diana Maisel turned down a job offer here in favour of a more attractive one from the more relaxed Pan American English Center, Avenida 16 de Julio 1490, Edificio Avenida 7° piso, Casilla 5244, La Paz (tel/fax 02-340796). The location is in front of the Monte Campero cinema on the main street El Prado. PAEC have just opened a new branch in Cochabamba (042-97027).

Chile

Unlike the economy of most other South American nations, Chile's economy is flourishing. It has been achieving a remarkable ten percent rate of growth and unemployment is less than 5%. The market for English language teaching is very healthy, although short-term casual teaching is not well paid. Non-contractual work starts at 3,000 pesos per hour, though 4,000 pesos is more common. To find private clients, it may help to advertise. The best results are obtained by putting a small ad in *El Mercurio,* the leading quality daily. Other newspapers such as *La Epoca* and *La Tercera* have classified ads sections which will cost slightly less than *El Mercurio.* The free ads paper is called *El Rastro.* A useful option is to put up a small ad in a supermarket like Almac or Jumbo.

If you want to do more than just a few hours of casual teaching each week, many Institutes will insist that you obtain an official work permit from the *Extranjeria.* These are valid for one year in the first instance and, all being well, can be changed into a *visacion de residencia* which allows an unlimited stay. To get a list of the documents you need in addition to a contract of employment, go to the State *Intendencia,* which includes an *Extranjeria* section, on Moneda in the city centre just west of Plaza de la Constitucion.

The following schools are among the best known language schools in Santiago. Typically these schools offer a newcomer a few hours and will offer them a full timetable only after a probationary three months.

Berlitz, Av Pedro de Valdivia 2005, Providencia, Santiago (02-204 4018). Berlitz has a substantial establishment in Santiago but prefers to interview only candidates who already have a work permit.

British English Centre, Av. Providencia 1308, p.2. Oficina D, Providencia, Santiago (02-496165). Prefer teachers who are fluent in Spanish.

Burford, Avda. Pedro de Valdivia 511, Providencia, Santiago (02-223 9357/274 4603). A small 'agency-type' institute which favours British English.

ELADI Instituto Professional, José M. Infante 927, Providencia, Santiago (02-251 0365).

Fischer English Institute, Cirujano Guzman 49, Providencia, Santiago (02-235 9812/235 6667). Teaches both on and off-site. Offers plenty of structure in planning lessons.

Impact English, Rosa O'Higgins 259, Las Condes, Santiago (02-211 1925/212 5609). Reputed to offer high rates of pay.

Linguatec, Av. Los Leones 439, Providencia, Santiago (02-233 4356). Compulsory one week training course for all accepted teachers which is unpaid but guarantees the offer of some hours of work on completion. Large branch of US-based teaching organisation which considers itself main rival to Berlitz.

Sam Marsalli, Av. Los Leones 1095, Providencia, Santiago (02-231 0652). Hires mainly American and Canadian females.

Tronwell, Apoquindo 4499, 3er Piso, Las Condes, Santiago (02-246 1040).

Wall Street Institute, San Sebastian 2878, Comuna Condes, Santiago (02-332 0330).

Although Diana Maisel had had a disappointing response when she had sent her CV from England to various schools, she had much better results when she arrived in Santiago, helped no doubt by her Cambridge/ELT Certificate. She started gradually with a few hours from several of the above companies and after two months was teaching up to 35 hours a week and saving a lot of money. Meanwhile a friend from the US with no TEFL background failed to persuade any language institute to hire her and so turned to waitressing instead.

Ecuador

Compared to its neighbours, Peru and Colombia, Ecuador represents an oasis of political stability. But in the past two years the country has been experiencing an economic crisis resulting in a radical devaluation of its currency. Still there is a thriving demand for English, particularly American English in the capital Quito and in the picturesque city and cultural centre of Cuenca in the southern Sierra. The majority of teaching is of university students and the business community whose classes are normally scheduled early in the morning (starting at 7am) to avoid the equatorial heat of the day and again in the late afternoon and evening. Many schools are owned and run by expatriates since there are few legal restrictions on foreigners running businesses.

Teaching wages worth $5 or $6 a couple of years ago are now worth only $2 or $3 or even less. But it is still possible to live on these wages since the cost of living is low. Quito is not as large and daunting a city as some other South American capitals and it should be easy to meet longer term expats who can help with advice on teaching. Damaris Carlisle had no trouble finding work when she arrived in Quito because she had the Cambridge Certificate. She ended up working at the South American Explorers Club in Quito (Jorge Washington 311 y Leonidas Plaza, Apartado 17-21-431; tel/fax 02-225228). Here is a brief list of language schools in Ecuador:

Bénédict School of Languages, Edmundo Chiriboga N47-133 y Jorge Paez, Quito (tel/fax 02-432729). Several other branches in Quito.

Centro de Estudios Interamericanos, Casilla 597, Cuenca (07-839003).

Key Language Services, Alpallana 581 y Whymper, Quito (Casilla 17-079770); fax 02-220956.

Nexus School, Jose Peralta 1-19 y 12 de Abril, Cuenca (07-888220).

Technically you shouldn't work on a tourist visa but there is little control. Britons are entitled to a stay of six months on a tourist visa whereas Americans can stay 90 days though both of these can sometimes be extended. A tourist visa cannot be changed into another kind of visa without leaving the country. Many teachers work on a student or cultural visa which is valid for one year.

Peru

The threat of terrorist activities has subsided and Peru is once again a mainstream destination. Lima has many language institutes, especially in the port area of Miraflores, many of which hire and pay a salary to native speakers. James Gratton arrived in Lima looking forward to what had sounded like a dream job. He had contacted the institutes included on the list sent by the Peruvian Embassy in London and was contacted enthusiastically by one (on the strength of a certificate earned from a one-week intensive TEFL training course in London and nine months of living and teaching in Venezuela the year before.) Despite the job not living up to expectations (many of his employer's promises were not honoured), he concluded that the experience could be used as a stepping stone to better opportunities.

Setting up as a freelance tutor in the capital is potentially lucrative. Many company employees have been told by their bosses to learn English within three months or risk demotion, which makes the freelance market very promising. A standard fee is $10 a lesson, though this can be reduced for clients who want to book a whole course. With wages like that and assuming you have found enough clients, it is not difficult to earn over $1,000 a month (in a country where the minimum wage is $70). James Gratton put a cheap advertisement (written in English) in the main daily *El Commercio* and signed up two clients.

Yet Lima is still considered a dangerous city and it may be preferable to consider one of Peru's smaller cities like Arequipa, Nazca or Trujillo. The town of Cusco is a favourite among travellers, many of whom settle down for an extended stay. Among the academies to try are ICPNA on Tullumayo St, Excel on Q'era St and Amauta on Procuradores St near the La Tertulia Café. According to Mónica Boza, a Peruvian traveller who lived in Cusco for five years, wages will be non-existent even if you do find work. She made many friends who had decided to stay in Cusco teaching English, and the best pay they got was an exchange of Spanish lessons. She goes on to say that good places to stay are the districts of San Blas (Saphi St, Ataud St, Carmen Bajo St) and Tahuantinsuyo, a 20-minute walk from the main square, where rooms can be rented for $100 a month, provided the landlords don't treat you like a wealthy gringo and try to cheat you.

Venezuela

Even though the oil boom is fading and rampant inflation is destabilising the economy, there is still a thriving market for English tuition. Proximity to the US and the volume of business which is done with *El Norte* mean a strong preference for American accents and teaching materials.

Nick Branch from St. Albans investigated most of the schools and agencies in Venezuela and worked for several outside Caracas where the pay was considerably less than in the capital:

Merida is very beautiful and a considerably more pleasant place to be than Caracas. The atmosphere and organisation of the institute where I worked were very good. But alas. As with all the English teaching institutes in Merida, the pay is very low. Merida is three times cheaper to live in than Caracas, but the salaries are 5-6 times lower.

Check adverts in Caracas' main English language organ, the *Daily Journal*. Most give only a phone number, but a few addresses are included. English Lab (Apartado Postal 4004, Carmelitas, Caracas 1101; 02-574 2511/573 6120) has a big turnover of staff and gave James Gratton his first job in the city. The best company James worked for was Eduform (Central Polo, Torre 3, Oficina 91, Colinas de Bellomonte, Apto. 69553, Caracas 1050) which specialises in teaching business people. Surprisingly, opportunities for English teachers also exist on the popular resort island of Margarita.

Most people work on a tourist visa which is valid for two months but extendable to six. James Gratton describes the process of getting a work permit as a nightmare:

On no account attempt to get one on your own, since this involves dealing with the DEX, a truly horrific organisation housed in what resembles a prison and with appalling disorganisation. Once they lost 3,000 passports which, it turned out, had been sold on the black market.

A combined work/study contract (internship in American parlance) is the solution available from the Centro Venezolano Americano (Av. José Marti, Edf. CVA, Urbanización Las Mercedes, Apartado 61715 del Este, Caracas 1060-A; 02-993 7911). They employ about 35 interns, normally North American university graduates to work for at least six months earning between 300,000 and 350,000 bolivars per month.

Central America

If you keep your ears open as you travel through Central America, you may come across opportunities to teach English, especially if you are prepared to do so as a volunteer. Salaries on offer may be pitiful but if you find a congenial spot on the 'gringo trail' (for example the lovely old colonial town of Antigua in Guatemala), you may decide to prolong your stay by helping the people you will inevitably meet who want to learn English.

As the wealthiest country in Central America, Costa Rica is sometimes referred to as the Switzerland of the region and there are plenty of private language academies in the capital San José. The school year runs from March 1st to December 1st. Temporary six-month renewable working visas are now issued to teachers working for established employers like the Instituto Britanico (PO Box 8184, San José 1000; 225 0256).

WorldTeach (Center for International Development, Harvard University, 79 John F Kennedy Street, Cambridge, MA 02138; 617-495-5527; www.worldteach.org) is a non-profit organisation that sends fee-paying college graduates to teach English for nine months in Costa Rica and Ecuador. Gap Challenge sends gap year students to Belize (as well as Peru, Ecuador and Costa Rica). Placements generally fall into one of two categories: community service/teaching in the cities or conservation in remote areas. Jessica Crisp from Hertfordshire recently returned from her placement through Gap Challenge in Belize where she taught students in Cristo Rey primary school:

I had wanted to go to a developing country where I could be useful to the community and preferably work with children. I did Spanish A-Level and was keen to use it while I was away. Gap Challenge offered Belize as a country to do a in a house the father Tacio had constructed himself, adobe (mud) and tin. We did have electricity for lights and a telephone and even a television but we had no running water. The bathroom was a large bucket of cold water in a small stone outhouse.

My class consisted of fifteen 8-10 year olds. They were an enthusiastic group with lots of energy which was great for games and acting. I decided to do a Nativity Play with them and channel their energy into something productive. It was a great success and lots of fun. Each weekend my friend and I travelled to a different part of Belize to explore and find out more about the country. I had a wonderful time both teaching and travelling the country and would recommend the experience to anyone who wants to live in a completely different culture and see some beautiful landscapes.

VOLUNTARY WORK

Short-term voluntary work projects are scattered over this vast continent. Many of the opportunities that become widely known are concerned with conservation (treated separately below) and charge a substantial fee. But an approach to almost any environmental, health or childcare non-governmental organisation (NGO becomes ONE in Spanish) might be greeted warmly, especially if the enquiry is made in Spanish. The better funded of these projects might even be able to offer accommodation and expenses.

It is sometimes worth approaching the Embassy of your destination country. At the least they could give you the address of the National Federation of Voluntary

Organisations, assuming there is one. When one traveller enquired at the Anglo-Chilean Society via the Chilean Embassy in London, she was put in touch with an orphanage in Santiago looking for self-funding volunteers. Note that many cultural exchange organisations and Spanish language course providers can advise individuals on voluntary positions and internships.

Development organisations which are active in more than one country in the region include:

AFS Intercultural Education Programmes, Leeming House, Vicar Lane, Leeds LS2 7JF; 0113-242 6136/ www.afs.org. Community service programme lasting 6 months in Brazil, Colombia, Peru and Honduras, for volunteers aged 18-29. Accommodation is arranged with host families. The cost for participating is £2,950.

Alliances Abroad, 702 West Avenue, Austin, Texas 78701 (1-888-6-ABROAD; www.alliancesabroad.com). Sends American students to Ecuador, Mexico, Costa Rica and Guatemala (6 weeks to a year) to live with local families, learn Spanish and do some voluntary work as an English teacher, in a children's home, the tourist industry, etc. Fees range from $2,350 to $6,600.

American Friends Service Committee, 1501 Cherry St, Philadelphia, Pennsylvania 19102-1479, USA (215-241-7295/fax 215-241-7247; hpollock@afsc.org). A Quaker organisation which recruits Spanish-speaking volunteers aged 18-26 to work for seven weeks in the summer mostly on building or teaching projects in Mexico (programme fee $900 plus travel expenses) and Cuba ($750). Mexican partner organisation is SEDEPAC, Apartado Postal 27-054, 06760 Mexico DF (sedepac@laneta.apc.org).

AmeriSpan Unlimited, PO Box 40007, Philadelphia, PA 19106 (800-879-6640; info@amerispan.com). Spanish-language travel organisation that offers unpaid volunteer placements in Costa Rica, Bolivia, Mexico, Guatemala, Ecuador, Argentina and Peru. One-month language programme followed by 1-6 month volunteer placement in health care, education, tourism/marketing or social work. Application and placement fee $350 includes travel insurance.

Amigos de las Americas, 5618 Star Lane, Houston, Texas 77057 (800-231-7796/fax 713-782-9267; www.amigoslink.org). Volunteers, primarily aged 16-21, must meet the language and training requirements in order to spend six to eight weeks between June and August living in rural and semi-urban communities in one of eight Latin American countries (Mexico, Costa Rica, the Dominican Republic, Brazil, Honduras, Nicaragua, Bolivia and Paraguay). The cost is approximately $3,200 including return airfares from the US.

Amizade Volunteer Vacations, 367 S. Graham St, Pittsburgh, PA 15232 (888-973-4443; www.amizade.org). Short-term community service volunteer programmes in Brazil and Bolivia (as well as Nepal and the US). Cost up to $2,600.

Caledonia Language Courses, The Clockhouse, Bonnington Mill, 72 Newhaven Rd, Edinburgh EH6 5QG (0131-621 7721; www.caledonialanguages.co.uk). Spanish language and voluntary work programmes organised in Peru and Costa Rica year round. Community and environmental projects and teaching English, depending on skills and level of language ability.

Casa Alianza, SJO 1039, PO Box 025216, Miami, FL 33102-5216 (volunteer@casa-alianza.org; www.casa-alianza.org). Works with street children in Mexico City, Guatemala City, Tegucigalpa and Managua.

EXIS, Postbox 291, 6400 Sønderborg, Denmark (74 42 97 49/fax 74 42 97 47; info@exis.dk). Volunteer work placements in Guatemala.

Foundation for Sustainable Development, 5547 Mitcham Ct, Springfield, VA 22151 (703-764-0859; fsd@interconnection.org/ www.interconnection.org/fsd). Summer and longer term internships in all areas of development, in Nicaragua and Bolivia (as well as Tanzania and South Africa).

ICADS, Dept. 826, PO Box 025216, Miami, FL 33102-5216) or Apartado 3 Sabanilla, 2070 San José, Costa Rica (506-225 0508; icads@netbox.com). Internships in Costa Rica, Nicaragua and Belize lasting a semester ($7,600) or a summer ($3,400). The well regarded programmes of the Institute for Central American

Development Studies combine study of the Spanish language and development issues with structured internships.

Latin Link STEP Programme, 175 Tower Bridge Road, London SE1 2AB (020-7939 9014; step.uk@latinlink.org/ www.latinlink.org). Self-funded team-based programme working on small-scale building projects in Argentina, Bolivia, Brazil, Ecuador, Mexico and Peru for committed Christians only. Spring projects run from March to July and summer ones July to August/September (7 weeks).

Peace Brigades International, 1a Waterlow Road, London N19 5NJ (020-7281 5370; pbibritain@gn.apc.org). Supplies volunteers to accompany individuals in Mexico, Colombia and Haiti who are in danger of persecution for their politics or religion.

Voluntarios Solidarios/Fellowship of Reconciliation, 2017 Mission St, No. 305, San Francisco, CA 94110 (415-495-6334/forlatam@igc.apc.org). Range of projects in Latin America and the Caribbean, e.g. working with homeless children, run by this interfaith peace organisation.

As you travel throughout the region you are bound to come across various charitable and voluntary organisations running orphanages, environmental projects and so on, some of which may be able to make temporary use of a willing volunteer. A good place in Mexico City to learn about voluntary opportunities throughout Mexico and Central America is the Quaker-run service centre Casa de los Amigos (Ignacio Mariscal 132, Mexico, D.F., 06030; 5705 0521/5705 0646) which provides simple accommodation to people involved in volunteer projects. The Casa's information centre has listings of volunteer opportunities (and other things such as Spanish language courses). Q u a k e r hostels throughout the region are a good potential source of volunteering information.

Other social projects which take on volunteers in Mexico are:

Visions in Action, 2710 Ontario Road NW, Washington, DC 20009 (202-625-7402/ www.visionsinaction.org). 6 or 12 month volunteer positions in Mexico (and Africa) starting in January and July. Volunteers must have a degree or relevant work experience. Positions in human rights, democratisation, journalism, social work, health, environment and research. Costs for EU nationals may be covered by European Voluntary Service funding, otherwise these are $5,500-$6,600.

Mar de Jade, PMB 078-344, 705 Martens Court, Laredo, TX 78041-6010 (postal address); tel/fax 322 21171; www.mardejade.com. Project located on the Pacific coast of Mexico in Chacala, Nayarit, near Puerto Vallarta. Work exchange of 10 hours per week gives you a 10% discount on fees (which are $1,200 a week). Volunteer-study programme includes 3 hours of Spanish tuition daily, 15 hours of community work per week.

Asociacion Cultural Na Bolom, Vicente Guerrero No. 33, San Cristóbal de Las Casas, Chiapas, Mexico 29220; 967-81418/fax 967-85586/e-mail: nabolom@ sclc.ecosur.mx). Volunteers needed for a minimum of three or six months to work in the organic garden, museum, library and as tour guides. Must speak Spanish and be willing to work in this area of political unrest. Accommodation provided in Volunteers' house for 250 pesos per month.

Casa Guatemala is an orphanage and attached backpackers' hostel which relies on travellers to carry out maintenance, cooking, building, organic gardening, teaching the children English, etc. They can use as many as 100 volunteers a year preferably for a minimum of three months. The orphanage office in Guatemala City is at 14th Calle 10-63, Zona 1, 01001 Guatemala (Apdo. Postal 5-75-A; 502-232-5517; casaguatemal@ guate.net/ www.guate.net/casaguatemala), while the orphanage itself is about five hours north of Guatemala City, a short boat ride from the town of Fronteras on the road to the Petén region. The director is Angelina de Galdamez who warns that volunteers should expect a certain amount of hardship. Volunteers must pay a non-refundable fee of $180 however long they intend to stay. UK contact: Pete Brown, 30 Church Road, Upton, Wirral CH49 6JZ; 0151-606 0729.

There are a few famous communes in South America in which passers-by are welcome to stay at free of charge if they join in the work. For example Atlantis on a Colombian mountain is a long-established organic farming community committed to environmental work through its travelling theatre group, the 'Green Theatre of Atlantis'. Write to its sister community in Ireland for details (Atlantis, Burtonport, Co. Donegal).

Conservation

An increasing number of organisations, both indigenous and foreign-sponsored, are involved in environmental projects throughout the continent. Many can be pre-arranged though all charge a fee which may even be equivalent to the price of a holiday. In Ecuador, for example, the Fundacion Planeta Azul (Cuero y Caicedo 1036 y Carvajal, Quito; 02-226732/ planetaazul@earthling.net) supervises a volunteer programme on behalf of the Ecuadorian Ministry of the Environment in 25 mainland national parks and reserves plus the Galapagos National Park. Typically volunteers will be aged 25-35, have a relevant academic background and be willing to pay a registration fee of $100 plus $50 a month expenses. The highest concentration of projects is probably in Costa Rica where the National Parks Authority runs a *Programa de Voluntariado en las Areas Silvestres Protegidas* (ASVO). To be eligible you must be willing to work for at least two months, be able to speak Spanish and provide two letters of recommendation from Costa Ricans or an organisation in your home country. The work may consist of trail maintenance and construction, greeting and informing visitors, research or generally assisting rangers. Details are available from the Director, International Volunteer Program, Servicio de Parques Nacionales, Apdo. 11384-1000, San José; 506-222 50 85/fax 506-223 69 63.

Other specific conservation projects in Costa Rica include:

Artemis Cloudforest Preserve, Apdo 937, 2050 San Pedro, Montes de Oca, Costa Rica (tel/fax 506-253 7243). Volunteers are needed to build trails and plant trees. They must stay for at least a month and pay $175 a week towards expenses.

Caribbean Conservation Corporation (CCC), 4424 NW 13th St, Suite A-1, Gainesville, Florida 32609, USA (800-678-7853; www.cccturtle.org). Runs programmes in Costa Rica using volunteer helpers to monitor and tag leatherback sea turtles, green turtles and neotropical birds. $1,345 for 8 days (turtle programme), $1,645 for 15 days (bird programme).

Casa Rio Blanco Rainforest Reserve, Apdo. 241-7210 Guapiles, Pococi, Costa Rica (tel/fax 506-382-0957). Board and lodging cost $600 a month.

Global Service Corps, 300 Broadway, Suite 28, San Francisco, CA 94133-3312 (www.globalservicecorps.org). Short and longer term conservation and other projects in Costa Rica; fee from $1,800.

i-to-i International Projects, One Cottage Road, Headingley, Leeds LS6 4DD (0113 217 9800; info@i-to-i.com). 1-3 month conservation breaks between March and July in lowland rainforest farms, Indian reserves, Monteverde Cloud Forest, etc. Volunteers pay £595 for up to two months.

Iyok Ami, PO Box 335-2100, Guadalupe, San José, Costa Rica (506-387-2238). Conservation volunteers needed in Talamanca Mountains. Expenses are $500 a month or $150 a week.

Living Among the Giant Grasses, Brian and Patricia Erickson, Apdo. 295-7210, Guapiles, Costa Rica (506-710-6161; brieri99@yahoo.com). Help needed in developing bamboo plantation. Volunteers pay $750 for the first month, $600 thereafter.

El Santuario de la Luz, Cobana de Puntarenas, Costa Rica (fax 506-642-0068; http://roadrunnerreleases.webjump.com). Volunteers needed for building, planting and teaching at this environment awareness centre. Room and board cost $200.

Sea Turtle Restoration Project, PO Box 400, 40 Montezuma Avenue, Forest Knolls, CA 94933 (www.seaturtles.org). 2-week or extended trip to Punta Banco, Costa Rica, for paying volunteers to relocate turtle eggs at night.

Outside Costa Rica, try any of the following organisations which operate in one country (countries are in alphabetical order):

Trekforce Expeditions, 134 Buckingham Palace Road, London SW1W 9SA (020-7828 2275; www.trekforce.org.uk). Expensive conservation and archaeological trips to the rainforests of Belize.

Ecovolunteer Program Brazil, www.br.ecovoluntarios.org

Bospas Forest Farm, c/o Casa Dobronski, Calle Guanhuiltagua N34-457, Quito, Ecuador (02-227777; bospas@hotmail.com). Farm assistants with experience in gardening for fruit farm in subtropical valley in Northwest Ecuador. Monthly charge of $200 for food and accommodation.

Ecotrackers, Backpackers and Volunteer Network based at the Econet Cybercafé, Av. Rio Amazonas, 517 y Roca, Quito, Ecuador; backpackers_volunteer@yahoo.com. They try to match volunteers with local eco-tourist projects.

Fundación Golondrinas Cloudforest Project, c/o Calle Isabel La Católica 1559 (N24-679) y Cristobal Gangotena, Casilla 1211, Suc. 17-21, Quito, Ecuador (02-226602; www.ecuadorexplorer.com/golondrinas). Long and short-term volunteers for project on western slopes of the Andes. Short-term volunteers pay monthly charge of $200-$240 depending on length of stay.

Finca Santa Ines, Apdo. Postal 147, Puerta Parado, 01073 Guatemala (502-634-8145/rosiewood@hotmail.com). Family farm which operates a work-for-keep exchange. Volunteers contribute $40 a week for food and Spanish classes.

G.A.P. Adventures/Eco-Escuela de Espanol, 19 Duncan St, Suite 401, Toronto, Ontario M5H 3H1, Canada (800-465-5600 ext 115; www.gap.ca/can/eco). Combines volunteer opportunities with one-on-one Spanish language instruction in the El Petén region of Guatemala. US$200 per week. US contact for Eco-Escuela is Conservation International, 1919 M Street, Suite 600, Washington, DC 20036 (202-973-2238; ecoescuela@conservation.org).

Coral Cay Conservation Ltd, 154 Clapham Park Road, London SW4 7DE (020-7498 6248; www.coralcay.org). Mount monthly expeditions to Honduras. Fee-paying divers to conduct marine surveys and study reef in the Bay Islands. The cost of participation starts at £650 for two weeks up to £2,550 for 12 weeks, excluding airfares. Non-divers can take scuba course on location for £225.

Utila Iguana Rescue Committee, German-based research and conservation project on the island of Utila off the coast of Honduras (www.utila-iguana.de). Up to 8 self-funding volunteers at a time for 1-3 months. Food costs estimated at $50-$70 a week plus 300 Deutsch Mark charge for lodging.

Pronatura Chiapas, Av. Benito Juarez 11-B, Apartado Postal 219, San Cristóbal de Las Casas, Chiapas, C.P. 29200 Mexico (tel/fax 967-85000; pronaturach@laneta.ape.org). Rainforest conservation, environmental education and sustainable agriculture. Volunteers should speak Spanish.

Nicaragua Solidarity Campaign, 129 Seven Sisters Road, London N7 7QG (020-7272 9619; www.nicaraguasc.org.uk). NSC organises 3-week work and study tours in August to assist agricultural co-operatives and environmental organisations in Nicaragua. The cost is £1,200 which includes air fares to and from Managua and all other expenses.

Organic farming has a large number of proponents in Central America and the US organisation TERN (address in *Agriculture* chapter) can provide a bundle of possible contact addresses of ecological groups, reforestation projects, NGOs, etc. for a fee of $50. Robert Abblett made use of these when he was in Mexico.

OTHER OPPORTUNITIES

Apart from teaching, the only paid work available in Latin America tends to be for bilingual professionals. Council in New York run a working holiday programme in Costa Rica which enables American students who have intermediate level Spanish to look for casual work for up to three months between 1st June and 1st October in hotels, offices and the service industries generally.

Foreign guides are occasionally hired by expatriate or even local tour operators. The Tambopata Jungle Lodge (PO Box 454, Cusco, Peru; tel/fax 084-245695; tplcus@terra.com.pe/ www.tambopatalodge.com) takes on guides for a minimum of six months. They must have formal training in the natural sciences and (preferably) speak Spanish, all of which should be indicated on a CV. The TJL resident naturalist programme, along with other similar and research opportunities in the same area, is facilitated in the UK by the Tambopata Reserve Society (c/o J. Forrest, 64 Belsize Park, London NW3 4EH). Guides for the naturalist programme must be graduate biologists, environmental scientists or geographers over the age of 20. They receive free room and board throughout their stay.

Andrew James was there a few summers ago and reports:

We lived in a jungle camp consisting of wooden lodges a four-hour boat trip up the Tambopata River from Puerto Maldonado. I was one of three English guides who took visitors of all nationalities in groups of about five on dawn walks to explore the rainforest and see the amazing plant life and the occasional animal. I was there for three months and was paid $150 a month for working 20 days a month with the other ten days free to do research, live it up in Puerto Maldonado (a town straight out of the Wild West).

Bilingual secretaries who can produce letters in proper English are in demand from commerce and law firms. Americans should find out if there is a local American Chamber of Commerce (as there is in Caracas) and Britons may do likewise. For example the British-Chilean Chamber of Commerce will supply the names of British companies in Chile. The US-Mexican Chamber of Commerce (1300 Pennsylvania Ave NW, Suite 270, Washington DC 20004-3021; www.usmcoc.org/bvip.html) publishes a list of companies which accept bilingual American students as summer interns.

Translators, particularly of scientific, medical and technical papers tend to be well paid by universities and large industrial concerns. Both types of vacancy are advertised in English language newspapers, which may themselves need proofreaders and editors or know of companies which do. In many large cities there is a sizeable English-speaking expatriate community, predominantly involved in international commerce. The bars and restaurants that they frequent are good job-hunting grounds: not only might you hear about opportunities for temporary work in business, but you could obtain work serving in the establishment itself.

Tourism

Only highly able candidates who have extensive Latin American travel experience and a knowledge of Spanish are hired as overland expedition guides with UK operators like Tucan (1st Floor, 14 Barley Mow Passage, Chiswick, London W4 4PH; 020-8994 2182) and Journey Latin America (12-13 Heathfield Terrace, Chiswick, London W4 4JE; www.journeylatinamerica.co.uk). If you get to know an area well, you may be able to act as a freelance guide though, not surprisingly, this will probably incur the locals' resentment, as Mónica Boza found when she lived in Cusco Peru:

If you have a good knowledge of the trails and want to become an outdoor guide, contact the tour agencies on arrival. But Peruvian guides are very jealous of foreign ones. I have known cases where they called the Migration Service and deportation followed. The adventure tour agencies are mainly along Plateros St like Erick Adventure and Q'ente. ZAS is another one, on the Main Square.

Local opportunities may crop up in one of the many places where tourism is booming. Many expat-style bars and clubs employ foreigners. For example Venezuela's Margarita Island in the Caribbean has dozens of places catering to package holiday makers; try 4th of May Avenue and Santiago Marino Avenue, particularly between June and September and again December to March. In Caracas most foreign establishments are on the wealthy east side of the city in the Palos Grandes/Altamira area. Angie Copley was lucky enough to fix up a nannying job through a UK agency and was flown out to Caracas all expenses paid for a year. She recommends finding out about work by going to British bars like l'Aticos or Weekends. While admitting that Caracas is a stressful place to live (crime, traffic, pollution), she was greatly enjoying the tropical surroundings and the knowledge that the Caribbean coast was just an hour away and the Andes and Amazon a short flight.

Mónica Boza thinks that Cusco is a promising place with clubs like Mama Africa, Ukukus (which has the best bartenders in town), Eco, Up Town and Keros all near the main square. Few corners of the world have escaped the fashion for Irish pubs; in Cusco, try Paddy Flaherty and Rosie O'Gradys on Santa Catalina St.

The Chilean tourist industry also employs the odd gringo. Christine Hauser worked as a waitress in Santiago, though she found that the lack of a work visa was more of a problem than for English teachers since the authorities were wont to raid restaurants looking for illegal workers from other South American countries like Peru. She also landed a summer job at the beach resort of La Serenna 500km north of the capital.

Mexico is another country in which travellers have been approached to work not as waiters or bar staff, but as hosts, entertainers and touts. While travelling in Mexico, Paul Donut was not expecting to work:

I stopped at Creél, a very small town in the Sierra Madre Mountains of north-west Mexico. It is about halfway through the Copper Canyon and looks like a town from a wild west movie. I was very surprised to find about a dozen travellers trying to entice people to stay at a group of small hotels known collectively as Margueritta's. In return for ambushing incoming trains, Margueritta (the owner) gave the travellers a free place to sleep and three excellent meals a day. I had a bit of luck here as I went to stay at a smaller place up the street. While we were on a tour the next day with the Irish manager, I was offered a job as tour guide, guest recruiter, wood cutter and general helper at the pension. I stayed for about a month, in a clean room with free meals and received a commission of $2 for everyone I brought back from the train. I would definitely recommend staying in Creél and going to the hotels for work. You won't make a fortune, but you should be able to stay here for free in return for some light duties.

Anyone who can fix engines, especially on camper vans, should find no trouble earning a living in any touristy area of Mexico. Information on where and when to look for yachts in Mexico which may be needing crew is contained in the chapter *Working a Passage.* You might be able to find day work on boats in some of these harbours before the yachts set sail or perhaps an opportunity to boat-sit as Anne Wakeford did in Puerto Vallarta. She recommends asking boat owners to radio your request for work to their fellow yachtsmen in the morning. She also noticed that there might be work further south helping boats to navigate the locks of the Panama Canal.

Unexpectedly, you can make a tidy profit from collecting bottles and collecting the refunds. According to Bridgid Seymour-East who travelled along the Pacific coast of Mexico, you get back 3-5 pesos for every 660ml bottle of beer costing 10-15 pesos.

The Caribbean

The Caribbean is far too expensive to explore unless you do more than sip rum punch by the beach. A host of Britons, Australians, South Africans, etc. are exchanging their labour, mostly on yachts, in order to see this exotic part of the world.

JOBS AFLOAT

Perhaps the easiest jobs to find are those working on the countless sailboats, charter yachts and cruise ships which ply the Caribbean each winter and spring. From November until May the Caribbean becomes a hive of marine activity. Christmas, since it marks the start of the main tourist season, is a particularly good time to look for work. The main requirement for being hired is an outgoing personality and perseverance in the search more than qualifications or experience. Hours are long and wages are minimal on a charter boat, but most do it for the fun. Board and lodging are always free and in certain jobs tips can be high. It would not be unusual to work for a wage of $50 a month and then earn $700 in tips.

Cruise Ships

For general information about cruise ship work see *Working a Passage.* Contracts are normally for six to nine months and the hours of work are long, often 14 hours a day, seven days a week living aboard the passenger ship with all onboard facilities provided by the ship owner. Most cruise ships active in the Caribbean contract their staff from Florida-based personnel agencies (known as concessionaires), some of which liaise with UK agencies. All workers aboard passenger ships require a C1/D seaman's visa issued by the United States Embassy which is only given through an employer or agency presenting a confirmed letter of appointment.

A long established cruise company which recruits its own staff is Windjammer Barefoot Cruises (Box 190120, Miami Beach, FL 33119-0120; 305-672-6453/www.windjammer.com). The largest cruise line in the world is Royal Caribbean Cruise Lines (RCCL, 1050 Caribbean Way, Miami, FL 33132-2601; 305-539-6000) which has a recorded Job Hotline on 305-530-0471. Similarly Premier Cruise Lines (400 Challenger Road, Cape Canaveral, FL 32920; 407-783-5061) hire some of their staff direct. They specialise in family cruises, so anyone with extensive experience of looking after and amusing children has a chance of being hired.

Charter Yachts

The charter season in the Caribbean is November to May when an experienced deckhand can earn US$400 a week cash-in-hand plus tips. But there will be many weeks when the boat will not be chartered and the wage will fall to around $140-175 while you may have to hang around a boring marina. It is important to stress that a deckhand job is not compatible with a great vacation. It's a tough job with long working hours during which you must never stop smiling. When the guests are snorkelling on the reef, the deckhand will be helping the skipper repair the toilet. While the guests are hiking up a volcano, the deckhand is polishing the winches.

The lack of a work permit can be a definite hindrance in the search for work with a charter company. Immigration authorities are consistently tough throughout the Caribbean. When you leave any boat as a crew you sign off the crew list in immigration where they want to see a ticket not only out of the country but one that connects with a flight to your home country. They also want to see an address where you intend to stay and may ask to see sufficient funds.

Yacht charter companies are unwilling to publicise vacancies, both because they have enough speculative enquiries on the spot and also they are forbidden by their respective island governments from hiring anyone without the proper working papers. However once you are on the spot, it is easier to hear of possibilities, and there are brokers and agents who match up crew with boats. The Danish traveller and sailor Kenneth Dichmann provided the following crew placement agency addresses. They may be able to help people on-the-spot, particularly in late October, who complete an application form and pay the registration fee (usually $20):

Hinckley Yacht Services, PO Box 2242, St. John's, Antigua (268-460-2711/fax 268-460-3740; antyact@candw.ag). $20 registration fee. Att: Jane Midson.

Cassandra's Yacht Services, Nelsons Dockyard, Antigua (809-462-9406/fax 809-462-9450).

Select Crew (Antigua Sails), Rena Night, Nelsons Dockyard, Antigua (809-460-1527/fax 809-460-1489). Must present yourself in person.

CCR St. Martin, Captain Oliver's Marina, St Martin (590-873049). Acts for Sun Yacht Charters between Antigua and St. Martin.

Captain & Crew, Yacht Haven, St. Thomas. Need CV, photo and $20 fee for one year's membership.

Furthermore Kenneth has sent the phone numbers of the largest charter companies in the West Indies. All charter both crewed boats and bareboats.

ATM Yachts, – 800-634-8822.

Sun Yacht Charters – 207-236-9611.

Caribbean Yacht Charters – 800-225-2520. Only bareboats but large staff.

Privilege Charters – 800-262-0308.

Sunsail – one of the largest.

Caribbean Sailing Charters Inc. – 800-824-1331.

Barefoot Yacht Charter – 800-677-3195.

Nautors Swan Charter – 800-356-7926.

Yacht Connections – 800-238-6912. Motor yachts only.

Lynn Jachney Charter – 800-223-2050. Luxury.

Tropic Island Yacht Management Ltd. – 809-494-2450. Luxury.

If you don't get anywhere with the agencies, it will be a case of implementing all the tactics outlined in the *Working a Passage* chapter to commend yourself to skippers, by asking at docks, putting up notices, following up leads learned in bars and so on. One way of breaking into the world of Caribbean yachties is to help with the drudgery of maintaining boats when at anchor. Try to find out when and where boat shows are being held as people are always in a rush to get their boats looking first class. Kenneth was offered a berth in Antigua by a German boat owner in exchange for a little polishing and barnacle scraping for three months but turned it down when the skipper was not willing to pay for food. Instead Kenneth spent a month at the end of the season (May) in Puerto Rico maintaining a boat in exchange for free food and accommodation.

After crewing across the Atlantic Mirjam Koppelaars (from the Netherlands) found that persistence was definitely required when trying to find a crew position in the Caribbean:

> *When our yacht arrived in English Harbour in Antigua, everybody started looking for a job. One got a job on* British Steel *(once sailed by Chay Blyth) due to an affair with the captain; one found a job on a boat we had met in Las Palmas (yes, the sailing world is small); one gave up and flew to the States. I walked to Nicholson Yacht Charters every morning asking for a job, and asked around the docks of English, Falmouth and Catamaran Harbours. This way I found a job for two months as stewardess/deckhand on a 60ft charter yacht.*

Mirjam often earned more in tips than she did in wages. She warns that there were lots of stories of crew not being paid their promised wages, often because of disagreements between owners and captains. From Antigua, Mirjam was offered a job as delivery crew on a yacht headed for Grenada, from where she got a lift with a 36ft trimaran to Isla Margarita in Venezuela. She concludes that her marvellous experiences were all 'part of being in the right place at the right time (and some lucky stars!)'.

JOBS ON LAND

The Work Jamaica programme previously offered by BUNAC has been suspended due to lack of applicants. It might still be worth contacting JOYST (Jamaican Organization for Youth & Student Travel) who was BUNAC's partner. In case BUNAC is able to revive it in future, it is worth including the positive comments of a past participant Andrew Owen:

> *Despite the high cost it is an experience not to be missed. I worked in the kitchens of a large hotel in Montego Bay where I received £10 a week for six days work (9am-4pm). I was provided with three excellent meals a day from the restaurant and my own room 20 yards from the white sand palm beach – PARADISE!*

The choice of job seems to be either in the resorts along the north coast, which offer the advantage of food and accommodation, or in the capital Kingston where the range of jobs tends to be more interesting (e.g. working on the newspaper, radio station, at the Red Stripe Brewery, etc.) but you have to find your own accommodation (many stay in the university halls of residence) and access to Caribbean beaches is not so easy.

The US organisation Alliances Abroad (www.alliancesabroad.com) run a Work & Intern in Jamaica programme.

People find work in night clubs and hotels on other islands. The Cayman Islands are meant to be one of the best places to look for this sort of work, with over 1,500 Americans alone working there. Construction work may also be available on Grand Cayman; ask around at bars. Suzie Keywood from Surrey found work as a bartender at 'Big Daddy's Lounge' in Grand Cayman. Without a 'Gainful Occupation Licence' or work permit (difficult to obtain with hundreds of locals after the same jobs) you should not take for granted that you will be treated fairly. There are plenty of horror stories in circulation concerning maltreatment by employers, such as failure to pay wages and to honour agreements to provide a homeward flight. Keep your beach-scepticism handy, and don't hesitate to cut your losses and run, if you sense you're on to a bad deal.

There are some opportunities for voluntary service. The Bermuda Biological Station for Research Inc. (Ferry Reach, St. George's GE01, Bermuda; 441-297-1880 ext 241/fax 441-297-8143; www.bbsr.edu) accepts students throughout the year to help scientists carry out their research and to do various jobs around the station in exchange for room and board. Volunteer interns from around the world are chosen on the basis of their academic and technical backgrounds. Summer is the peak period (applications must be in by February); otherwise apply at least four months in advance.

In the Bahamas, it might be possible to volunteer on an organic farm on the tiny island of Eleuthera whose owners also run Augusta Sun Produce Co (PO Box N-3823, Nassau; tel/fax 242-327-0066). Volunteers with their own tents are needed to repair the damage done by Hurricanes Gert and Floyd. With the recent upheavals in Cuba, there may be more opportunities in that beleaguered country in the future. The Cuba Solidarity Campaign (c/o Red Rose Club, 129 Seven Sisters Road, London N7 7QG; 020-7263 6452) runs a work/study scheme twice a year in which volunteers undertake agricultural and construction work for three weeks either in July or December/January. No specific skills or qualifications are required but applicants must be able to demonstrate a commitment to solidarity work. The cost of the brigade is approximately £770 which covers the full cost of flights, visas, transfers, accommodation and food. For further information contact the Brigade Co-ordinator (office@cuba-solidarity.org.uk).

The American Friends Service Committee (address above) organises month-long study-work projects in Cuba each July. A list of programmes and organisations in Haiti of interest to potential volunteers is available by e-mail from Bob Belenky (bobelenk@yahoo.com). The organisation Caribbean Volunteer Expeditions publishes a newsletter that might provide leads (CVE, PO Box 388, Corning, NY 14830; 607-962-7846; www.cvexp.org).

Africa

It is difficult to generalise about countries as different from each other as Morocco, Uganda and South Africa; however, the level of casual employment opportunities throughout the continent does not warrant a country-by-country treatment here. The red tape can be truly daunting in emergent Africa, and discouraging both in industrialised Southern Africa and Mediterranean Africa.

While travelling throughout Africa, be prepared for contradictions and aggravations. One traveller recommends carrying an official-looking list of addresses (whether invented or not), particularly of voluntary organisations, to show to suspicious immigration authorities. If you are given a job, you may be able to get a work permit though this is not always necessary.

You must also be prepared to cope with some decidedly uncomfortable conditions, whether you are staying in a cockroach-infested (yet still overpriced) hotel in Cairo while scraping together some money from English teaching; or enjoying the ten-hour truck ride into the Okavango Swamps of Botswana to look for work in the tourist bars and restaurants. As one contributor commented about this journey, 'it's an ordeal guaranteed to make you question whether working your way around some parts of the world is worth it after all.' It certainly wasn't worth it for 19 year old gap year student David Pleydell-Bouverie who in 1999 was working at the remote Matusadona National Park in Zimbabwe, until he was killed by a pride of lions after he failed to zip up his tent.

The African-American Institute (Chanin Building, 380 Lexington Ave, Crn. of 42nd St, New York, NY 10168-4298; 212-949-5666/ aainy@aaionline.org) is a repository of information on opportunities in Africa for employment, teaching, aid projects, etc.

TEACHING

What makes much of Africa different from Latin America and Asia vis-à-vis English teaching is that English is the medium of instruction in state schools in many ex-colonies of Britain including Ghana, Nigeria, Kenya, Zambia, Zimbabwe and Malawi. As in the Indian subcontinent, the majority of English teachers in these countries are locals. Still there is some demand for native speakers in secondary schools, especially in Zimbabwe, Kenya, Ghana and Tanzania.

Africa is not a promising destination for the so-called teacher-traveller. The majority of foreign teachers in Africa are on one or two year volunteer contracts fixed up in their home country while a number of others are placed by recognised gap year organisations in the UK. Missionary societies have played a very dominant role in Africa's modern history, so many teachers are recruited through religious organisations, though even here some of the major organisations like Christians Abroad and Africa Inland Mission (2 Vorley Road, Archway, London N19 5HE; www.aim-eur.org) are being asked to supply far fewer English teachers than previously.

Furthermore, conditions can be very tough and many teachers in rural Africa often find themselves struggling to cope at all. Whether it is the hassle experienced by women teachers in Muslim North Africa or the loneliness of life in a rural West African village, problems proliferate. Anyone who has fixed up a contract should try to gather as much up-to-date information as possible before departure, preferably by talking to people who have just been there. Otherwise local customs can come as a shock, for example finding yourself being bowed to (as Malawians do to anyone in a superior job). A certain amount of deprivation is almost inevitable; for example teachers, especially volunteers, can seldom afford to shop in the pricey expatriate stores and so will have to be content with the local diet, typically a staple cereal such as millet usually made into a kind of stodgy porridge, plus some cooked greens, tinned fish or meat and fruit.

The agency Gap Challenge sent Sarah Johnson from Cardiff to Zanzibar in September to teach English and geography at a rural secondary school:

The expectations which Zanzibari children have from school are worlds away from those of British school children. They expect to spend most of their lessons copying from the blackboard, so will at first be completely nonplussed if asked to think things through by themselves or to use their imagination. I found that the ongoing dilemma for me of teaching in Zanzibar was whether to teach at a low level which the majority of the class would be able to understand, or teach the syllabus to the top one or two students so that they would be able to attempt exam questions, but leaving the rest of the class behind. Teaching was a very interesting and eye-opening experience. I believe that both the Zanzibari teachers and I benefitted from a cultural exchange of ideas and ways of life.

The US State Department (SA 44, Room 304, 301 4th Street, SW, Washington DC 20547; http://exchanges.state.gov/education/engteaching) runs English Language Programs at its Bi-National Centers in a number of African countries, though this operation has been shrinking over the past few years. Normally they hire people who are already resident in the country. If teachers (British as well as American) are prepared to travel to an African capital for an interview, they may well get taken on.

Obviously the British Council in the UK (Teaching Centre Recruitment Unit, 10 Spring Gardens, London SW1A 2BN; 020-7389 4931/ www.britcoun.org/english) places a large number of qualified EFL teachers worldwide and the Peace Corps in the US (Room 803E, 1111 20th St NW, Washington, DC 20526; 1-800-424-8580/ www.peacecorps.gov/volunteer/education/assignments.html) recruits hundreds of volunteer teachers every year. Also the major gap placement agencies, viz. Gap Activity Projects, Gap Challenge (with placements in Tanzania, Malawi and South Africa), Project Trust (Namibia, Egypt, Uganda, Malawi, Botswana, rural Zimbabwe and South Africa) and Students Partnership Worldwide (Tanzania, Zimbabwe, Uganda, Namibia and former South African homelands) are active on the African continent (see chapter *Voluntary Work: Gap Year Placements*). General voluntary agencies like Skillshare Africa, VSO and the Irish agency Concern Worldwide (52-55 Lower Camden St, Dublin 2; www.concern.ie) are also involved in the education field.

Placement Organisations

The following organisations recruit teachers of English as a foreign language and/or student volunteers for schools in Africa. These postings are normally regarded as 'voluntary' since local wages are paid usually along with free housing. In some cases a substantial placement fee must be paid.

Africa & Asia Venture Ltd, 10 Market Place, Devizes, Wilts. SN10 1HT (01380 729009/fax 01380 720060; www.aventure.co.uk). Places British school leavers as assistant teachers in primary and secondary schools in Kenya, Uganda, Tanzania, Zimbabwe, Malawi and Botswana, normally for one term: three months work followed by one month travel including a one-week safari. Programme includes in-country orientation course, insurance and allowance paid during work attachment. The 2001 participation fee is £2,190 plus air fares. Also send volunteers to conservation projects in Kenya.

BUNAC, 16 Bowling Green Lane, London EC1R 0QH (020-7251 3472; www.bunac.org/uk/workghana/index.htm). 9-month placements in Ghana for Britons who have graduated in previous two years in English, modern languages, geography, maths, sciences, accounting or design and technology and who have some classroom experience. Programme fee is about £1,400 including 12-month return flight. BUNAC also run work and travel programme in South Africa lasting 3-12 months (see below).

Daneford Trust, 45-47 Blythe St, London E20 0LL (tel/fax 020-7729 1928; www.danefordtrust.fsnet.co.uk). Youth education charity sends students and school leavers resident in London (only) to Namibia, Zimbabwe, South Africa and Botswana for a minimum of 4 months. Volunteers must raise at least £2,000 towards costs.

Joint Co-operation Trust, 39 Handel Mansions, 94 Wyatt Drive, London SW13 8AH (020-8563 1456; tice@btinternet.com; also 1 Red Lion Lane, Nantwich, Cheshire CW5 5EP (01270 625201; zoe50johnson@yahoo.com). Charity that sends 12-20 British graduates with suitable backgrounds to teach for one year in primary schools in Tanzania (starting August). Interviews are carried out in the UK each spring.

Marlborough Brandt Group, 1A London Road, Marlborough, Wilts. SN8 1PH (tel/fax 01672 514078). Sends a few volunteers annually to teach in the Gambian village of Gunjur for 10 months. Fund-raising target is £3,000.

Right Hand Trust, Gelligason, Llanfair Caereinion, Powys SY21 9HE (tel/fax: 01938 810215; RightHandTrust@compuserve.com). Anglican organisation places school leavers in host parishes in rural parts of Kenya, Uganda, Zimbabwe, Swaziland, Malawi, Gambia and Namibia as volunteer teachers, community workers, etc.

St. David's (Africa) Trust, Beaufort Chambers, Beaufort Road, Crickhowell, Powys NP8 1AA (tel/fax 01873 810665; www.africatrust.gi). 3-4 month placements in Morocco, Ghana and Mali for gap year students to work with needy children.

Sudan Volunteer Programme, 34 Estelle Road, London NW3 2JY (tel/fax 020-7485 8619; davidsvp@aol.com/ www.svp-uk.com). Needs volunteers to teach English in Sudan for about 12 weeks from late November or for 8 weeks from July. Undergraduates and graduates with experience of travelling abroad (preferably in the Middle East) are accepted; TEFL certificate and knowledge of Arabic are not required. Gap year students accepted if they can commit themselves to stay for six months. Volunteers pay for their airfare (about £430) plus UK travel expenses for selection and briefing. Local host institutions pay for insurance and living expenses in Sudan; most are in the Khartoum area.

Teaching & Projects Abroad, Gerrard House, Rustington, West Sussex BN16 1AW (01903 859911; www.teaching-abroad.co.uk). Volunteer teachers work in Ghana, Togo and South Africa. Volunteers are provided with board and accommodation, placement and working arrangements and insurance. No TEFL background required but good spoken English and university entrance qualification. Three-month self-funded packages cost £1,500 for South Africa and £1,600 for Ghana and Togo plus £600-£700 for airfares.

Village Education Project (Kilimanjaro), Mint Cottage, Prospect Road, Sevenoaks, Kent TN13 3UA (01732 459799). Gap year programme which sends about 8 UK students each year to help teach EFL and other subjects in village primary schools in Tanzania for an academic year (8-9 months). Fee is £1,700.

Various US organisations also match volunteers with schools in Africa that need teachers, for example *Amity Volunteer Teachers Abroad* (Amity Institute, 10671 Roselle St, Suite 101, San Diego, CA 92121-1525; 858-455-6364/ www.amity.org) which provides year-long voluntary teaching opportunities in Senegal and Ghana; and *WorldTeach Inc* (Center for International Development, Harvard University, 79 John F Kennedy Street, Cambridge, MA 02138; 617-495-5527; info@worldteach.org), a non-profit organisation that recruits graduates as volunteers to teach English for one year in Namibia and also for six months teaching English to nature guides in South Africa.

Egypt

Respectable and dubious language teaching centres flourish side by side in the streets of Cairo and to a lesser extent Alexandria. Teaching jobs are not hard to come by, especially if you have a Cambridge or Trinity Certificate (and if you are thinking of doing the CELTA course, Cairo is one of the cheapest places to do it). Many parents enrol their children to do intensive language courses in the summer, so this is a good time to look for an opening (assuming you can tolerate the heat).

While the Australian Kate Ferguson was in Egypt, she was handed a leaflet advertising jobs with the International Languages Institute (ILLI) on Talaat Harb Street in central Cairo:

> *I went there to make some initial enquiries and it was not the dodgy exploitative business that I expected. Instead it was quite professional in its appearance. I also got the impression that the Institute was nearly always looking for teachers. The pay was 10 Egyptian pounds an hour. Training, accommodation, medical care and a one-year work permit were all promised free of charge.*

The British Council in Agouza is probably the first place to check for work. The Director of TEFL will give you a form to fill out and then you may be asked to stand in for a practice lesson observed by the usual teacher. (You will be given a lesson beforehand to prepare.) If they think you are suitable they'll take you on which is more likely during the summer. During exam time there is also a need for paid invigilators. The El-Asson School (PO Box 13, Imbaba) out near the Pyramids employs a number of expat teachers.

Dan Boothby has spent time in Cairo, most recently from February 2000, and found it almost alarmingly easy to find work:

> *I taught one-to-one lessons to several people and got about 5 hours a week work and charged £10 an hour. Frankly this was much more than I was worth but if you charge less than the market rate then it is felt that you are an amateur. I taught an isolated and lonely 5 year old, son of the Georgian Consul, where I was more a babysitter than a tutor. I felt so guilty about charging E£50 an hour that I spent an hour trying to get him to learn something. I didn't feel so guilty charging E£55 to tutor the Georgian Ambassador since he probably passed the bill onto his government.*
>
> *I got a lot of students through friends that I made who were teaching at the international schools. The kids at these schools are often in need of extra tuition towards exam times when their parents realise that they've been mucking about all year and are close to failing. The problem is that the kids tend to be very uninterested and so it is difficult to make them concentrate. But I enjoyed one-to-ones. One could build up a large group of students and earn a decent wage but equally teach less hours and have more time – one of the reasons for getting out of England.*

One way of advertising your availability to teach might be to place an advert in the expatriate monthly *Cairo Today* or the fortnightly *Maadi Messenger*. The American University, centrally located at the eastern end of Tahrir Square, is a good place to find work contacts. Also try the notice boards at the Community Services Administration (CSA, Road 21, Maadi, Cairo; csaegypt@intouch.com/ www.csa-egypt.com) where a range of adult education courses for expats is offered. If you do decide to advertise your services as a freelance tutor, it might be a good idea to rent a post office box from a business centre (e.g. the IBA Center in Garden City).

According to Dan Boothby, the best places to meet other expats and find out about work opportunities are Deals Bar and Aubergine Restaurant in Zamalek and Deals 2 near the American University and the BCA (British Community Association) in Mohandiseen where you can only go as the guest of a member. Sunny Supermarket in the leafy prosperous residential district of Zamalek has a good noticeboard for jobs and flat shares. Zamalek along with Heliopolis and Mardi are the best areas to look for private clients, as Ian McArthur found:

> *In Cairo I sought to work as a private English tutor. I made a small poster, written in English and Arabic, with the help of my hotel owner. I drew the framework of a Union Jack at the top, got 100 photocopies and then meticulously coloured in the flags. The investment cost me £3. I put the posters up around Cairo, concentrating on affluent residential and business districts. I ended up teaching several Egyptian businessmen, who were difficult to teach since they hated being told what to do.*

Kenya

Kenya has had a chronic shortage of secondary school teachers for some time, mostly in Western Province. Although legislation has made it harder for unqualified teachers to find jobs, it may still be possible to fix up a teaching job by asking in the villages, preferably before terms begin in September, January and April. Be prepared to produce your CV, diplomas and official-looking references. Basic accommodation and a monthly salary (local rates) may be provided, though not all schools can afford to pay it, especially non-government self-help *Harambee* schools. According to the Kenya High Commission, anyone wishing to travel to Kenya for the purpose of taking up employment must obtain an entry/work permit in advance. This will be issued by the Principal Immigration Officer, Department of Immigration, PO Box 30191, Nairobi, after the employer has filed the application and proved that no Kenyan can do the job.

A UK agency VAE Teachers Kenya sends school-leavers and university graduates on six-month teaching placements from January to poor rural schools in and around Gilgil in the central highlands of Kenya. The cost of £2,780 is all-inclusive. Details are available from Simon Harris, Bell Lane Cottage, Pudleston, Nr. Leominster, Herefordshire HR6 0RE (01568 750329/ harris@vaekenya.co.uk) who spends half the year in Gilgil.

Morocco

English is gaining ground despite Morocco being a Francophone country. Outside the state system there is a continuing demand for native speaker teachers especially in Casablanca and Rabat. Semesters begin in September and January and wages are higher than elsewhere in Africa, typically more than £500 a month. A number of commercial language schools employ native English speakers including the network of seven American Language Centers. The biggest branch in Rabat employs nearly 50 teachers, who must have an arts degree, on a full-time and part-time basis: ALC, 4 Zankat Tanja, Rabat 1000 (07-761269/766121/767103; alcrabat@mtds.com) while the Casablanca branch at 1 Place de la Fraternité (02-275270; alc.casa@casanet.net.ma) employs mainly (but not exclusively) North American graduates with some TEFL certification and experience. A British-oriented school in Casablanca which recruits qualified EFL teachers is the British Centre (3 rue Brahim el Amraoui; british.centre.c@casanet.ma). Another possible employer is EF English First, 20 rue du Marché, Résidence Benomar, Maaris, Casablanca (02-254400) who pay US$720 per month.

TOURISM

Once again travellers' hostels are one of the few providers of casual work in the developing nations of the African continent. It is something that many independent trans-Africa travellers do for the odd week, from Dahab on the Red Sea to the backpackers' haunts of Johannesburg, and is a very nice way to have a break without having to pay for it. While cycling through Africa, Mary Hall stopped at a backpackers' hostel in Malawi where she was even offered a permanent job, but the road called.

Tourism is well established both on the Mediterranean coast of Africa and in the countries of East and Southern Africa where game parks are the major attraction. (Opportunities in South Africa are discussed separately below.) It is possible to find work in hotels and bars in resort areas; try the so-called trendy establishments rather than humble locally-staffed ones. In September 2000 Jane Harris reported from Dahab on the Egyptian coast of the Red Sea that she had seen notices for a waitress at the Tota Restaurant and for an English speaker to work in a travel agency helping to write leaflets in English. Wages were not high but living expenses here are very cheap.

K. McCausland reports on what he found in Morocco one winter:

Agadir is a serious winter hotspot for European tourists and as such there are lots of opportunities in hotels, bars and discos. A little further north on the coast is a beautiful and friendly town called Essaouira. It's the only place where we were offered work and were sorry to have to turn it down. It's rapidly making a name for itself among travellers with a big windsurfing fraternity and a service industry starting to gear up. My girlfriend was offered a job as a receptionist in one of the several new hotels being built. Wages are considerably lower than in Europe, but as the cost of living is extremely low, it's not such a problem.

Purveyors of overpriced carpets in Morocco try to enlist the help of travellers whom they loosely employ to lure high-spending tourists into the shops. You approach a stranger and pretend to want advice on which carpet to buy yourself, and hope that the tourist will follow suit; most 'plants' find that they can't stomach this charade for long.

Anyone with a diver's certificate might be able to find work at Red Sea resorts like Sharm el Sheikh and Hurghada. The British-managed firm Emperor Divers (info.hurghada@emperordivers.com or info.sharm@emperordivers.com) employs diving instructors for at least a year in Egypt. At local dive centres, you can sometimes get free lessons in exchange for filling air tanks for a sub-aqua club. It is possible to be taken on by an Egyptian operator (especially in the high season November to January); however the norm is to be paid no wage and just earn a percentage of the take. Stephen Psallidas confirmed this after spending a month in Egypt over Christmas:

A few people were working in the scuba-diving schools in Dahab including an English guy who had been there three months and had worked his way up from complete novice to Dive Master. In the later stages, he was trained for free as long as he took some novices out diving. Several traveller types were working in the many cafés in Dahab.

The Nile cruise business may offer some possibilities as reported by Ana Güemes several years ago:

In Aswan I met a guy from Texas who had found a job on the cruises that sail between Luxor and Aswan just by offering his services personally. The main reason he was hired as an office aid was that he spoke some French. I was so excited about the possibility of getting this kind of experience that in spite of the temperature being 48°C in the shade and my clothing not the best, I visited some of the cruise offices. Bad business, lack of knowledge of German, difficulty in getting a permit and a strictly male staff were the most common answers I got.

Longer-term possibilities may be available with the overland companies mentioned in the section *Overland Tours* in the chapter *Working a Passage*. For courier work, applicants are required to have first-hand knowledge of travel in Africa or must be willing to train for three months with no guarantee of work. Requirements vary but normally expedition leaders must be at least 23 and be diesel mechanics with a truck or bus licence. Some African specialists are listed here; others can be found on internet sites like www.go-overland.com.

Absolute Africa, 41 Swanscombe Road, Chiswick, London W4 2HL (020-8742 0226; absaf@actual.co.uk).

Acacia Expeditions, Lower Ground Floor, 23A Craven Terrace, London W2 3QH (020-7706 4700; acacia@afrika.demon.co.uk).

Bukima Africa, 15 Bedford Road, Great Barford, Beds. MK44 3JD (01234 871329; www.bukima.com).

Economic Expeditions, 29 Cunnington St, Chiswick, London W4 5ER (020-8995 7707; www.economicexpeditions.com).

Explore Africa, Rose Cottage, Redwick, Caldicot, Monmouthshire NP26 3DE (01633 880224; africaex@aol.com/ www.africaexplored.com).

Oasis Overland, 5 Nicholson's Cottages, Hinton St Mary, Dorset DT10 1NF (01258 471155; info@oasis-overland.co.uk).

Truck Africa, 6 Hurlingham Studios, Ranelagh Gardens, Fulham, London SW6 3PA (020-7731 6142; www.truckafrica.co.uk).

Anyone with skills as a mechanic might be able to find work with an overland company, especially if based along one of the major routes. Suitably connected people might be able to run their own safaris, something Jennifer McKibben observed in Kenya:

> *Some entrepreneurial travellers used to make money by hiring a jeep and taking holidaymakers on mini expeditions. This would either be to places inaccessible by public transport or would undercut the travel agencies on standard trips. They found customers by placing notices in the youth hostel and cheap hotels.*

After working a number of seasons in various capacities in Europe for the tour operator Contiki, Carolyn Edwards toyed with the idea of working further afield. She concentrated her efforts on Acacia since they employ tour guides as well as drivers, whereas many of the others are looking for guides who are also driver/mechanics. At a relaxed and informal interview she was told that she would have to join a training tour for up to 12 weeks before being sent out on her own. The wage offered was £80 a week plus all expenses, apart from flights, injections and visas, though the cost of these would be refunded after two years in the job.

Mountain Treks & Training Ltd (17 Ulley Lane, West Heath, Birmingham B31 3JU; tel/fax 0121-680 3507) run six-week treks in Morocco, Zimbabwe and Namibia for which they need qualified expedition leaders and organisers. Most expeditions take place between June and August. The tour operator Discover Adventure (01722 741123) also needs experienced leaders for mountain bike and trekking holidays in the Atlas Mountains while CycleActive Ltd (Leeming Cottage, Watermillock, Penrith, Cumbria CA11 0JR) has in the past advertised for cyclists to lead tours of Zimbabwe.

In her whole year of volunteer nursing in Uganda, Mary Hall met only one foreigner who had found work on the spot and without a work permit. This woman was asked to manage a tourist lodge in the middle of nowhere and jumped at the chance since it was such a beautiful nowhere.

OPPORTUNITIES IN SOUTH AFRICA

Frightening levels of crime have prompted an enormous brain drain in South Africa. However affirmative action policies mean that it is very difficult for foreigners to land jobs (legally) which could be done by locals. Competition is intense from the formerly disenfranchised black population of South Africa. The openings that do exist are primarily for people with skills and experience, e.g. computer specialists, engineers, electricians and so on.

Check adverts in the Monday edition of the main dailies, the *Cape Times* in Cape Town, and the *Star* and *Citizen* in Johannesburg. The *South African Sunday Times* carries employment ads and is distributed in the UK by A & J Distributors (01628 475197). Roger Blake met travellers working for *Jungle Magazine* in Cape Town and in the music industry. Temporary employment agencies such as Kelly Girl might be willing to register likely candidates whom they are persuaded plan to settle in South Africa. Prospects are generally rosier outside the popular destination of Cape Town.

Red Tape

The government is (understandably) not keen to hand out work permits to Europeans and other nationalities when so many of their own nationals are unemployed. Tony

Forrester found the situation very discouraging in the summer of 1999: 'With affirmative action, it's a nightmare being a white male and looking for a job'. It is worth quoting the Director-General of the Department of Home Affairs, Billy Masetlhe, writing in the *Pretoria Times* in 2000:

Work permits are only granted in instances where South African citizens or permanent residents are not available for appointment or cannot be trained for the position. Employment opportunities are, as a result of the prevailing economic climate in SA, extremely limited and there is at present no special drive or project to attract foreign workers to SA. Even as far as the so-called scarce employment categories are concerned, the position has worsened to the extent where professionally and technically qualified persons are being laid off and are finding it extremely difficult to secure alternative employment.

All that being said, it remains that 23,300 work permits were granted in 1999 (out of 27,300 applications).

Skilled and qualified people can apply to South African embassies for a Work Seeker's Permit (B1-159B) which will allow them to look for work in South Africa for up to three months. One of the requirements is confirmation that you have two interviews lined up; another is that you pay the fee of £55. After a job is found, the foreigner can obtain a work permit from the nearest office of the Department of Home Affairs. Detailed information on the scheme is available from the Consular Section (15 Whitehall, London SW1A 2DD; 020-7451 7299/ www.southafricahouse.com).

An American traveller in Africa J.M. Rapp described the difficulty with work permits that he observed:

The only person I met down there in three months who actually had a work permit was a Canadian girl who got hers to teach ice hockey. I did, however, meet two people who, after turning in a legal application with posted bond for valid professions, were asked to leave the country.

Most people who do casual work have only a three-month tourist visa, which must be renewed before it expires. A 90-day extension can be obtained from the Department of Home Affairs in Johannesburg or Cape Town for a R450 fee. After you have done this a few times, the authorities will become suspicious.

Key tourist places where backpackers work are regularly raided by the Department of Home Affairs, and employers caught employing foreigners without permits are fined heavily (e.g. R40,000) and can be prosecuted under the Aliens Control Act of 1991. Deportations are not uncommon. One UK contributor who was sharing a flat with a Bangladeshi ice cream seller, had his front door nearly broken down by immigration officials who dragged the hapless Bangladeshi off to jail before deporting him two days later. (Our contributor claims that his South African accent was sorely tested that day.)

One solution to the problem is to consider BUNAC's work and travel programme in South Africa. A relatively small number of full-time students and recent graduates under the age of 27 may be eligible for a 12-month working holiday permit. The programme fee is more than £1,000 including return flight to Cape Town, orientation and back up from the South African Students Travel Service. Group departures take place in October (at the beginning of the tourist season), January and July.

One category of foreign worker of which the government approves is sports coach. Specialist programmes exist to encourage this exchange. For example volunteer sports coaches, phys ed teachers, recreation leaders and sports organisers are placed by an organisation called SCORE (Sports Coaches' OutReach, Sports Science Institute of South Africa, 13 Boundary Road, Newlands 7700; or PO Box 13177, Mowbray 7705, Cape Town; 021-689 7395/ score@iafrica.com). The work includes coaching, establishing sports clubs and organising tournaments and festivals in rural or urban settings. Suitable candidates must be interested in hands-on development work and willing to live with a host family. The work period is six months or a year starting in January or July. Participants receive a nominal monthly stipend but pay an administrative fee of $1,200. Several other outreach programmes are based at the Sports Science Institute; check their website www.ssi.uct.ac.za.

After arriving in Cape Town by bicycle, Mary Hall advertised her nursing experience in the newspaper and fixed up a live-in job looking after an elderly man. After two weeks, her employer realised that a local black person could do the same work for a third of the price and Mary got the boot.

Tourism

Cape Town is the tourist capital of South Africa including for backpackers, though jobs are harder to find here than elsewhere. The Backpack Hostel & Africa Travel Centre at 74 New Church St (021-423 5555; www.backpackers.co.za) has been recommended by Brigitte Albrech for its notice board but many others will be able to advise such as Oak Lodge (oaklodge@intekom.co.za). Roger Blake expected to stay in South Africa for three months but ended up spending seven:

There are more than 100 hostels in South Africa, many of which 'employ' backpackers on a casual basis. Within two weeks of arrival I was at a hostel in George on a work-for-keep basis. Through contacts made here I also sold T-shirts at the beach for a small profit and I did a few days at a pizza place for tips only. Then I was offered a job at a hostel in Oudtshoorn (Backpackers Oasis). They gave me free accommodation and 150 rand a week to run the bar and help prepare the ostrich braai (BBQ) that they have every evening. Also I did breakfasts for fellow travellers which was like being self-employed as I bought all the ingredients and kept all the profit. It was a small but worthwhile fortune after six weeks here.

After a non-working trip to Zimbabwe to see the country and renew his visa for South Africa, Roger fixed up another hostel job in Cape Town. He regretted that it didn't work out since it was well paid: 350 rand a week plus 25% commission. For his final couple of weeks in the country he worked for a hostel in Johannesburg. In exchange for touting for custom at the airport he was given free accommodation and three excellent meals a day plus 20 rand per customer. But he found the success-rate discouraging.

Everyone who has looked for a tourist job in Cape Town recommends Seapoint, a beach suburb lined with cafés, ice cream kiosks, snack bars and other places which have high staff turnovers, though wages are low. (Ice cream is also sold from cycle carts; find out whom to contact for work by asking the sellers.) Also try using the door-to-door approach in the flashy Victoria & Albert Waterfront development, Camps Bay and the beaches along the Garden Route. People who can speak more than one language will be especially in demand. Long Street in Cape Town is lined with bars and restaurants where jobs crop up.

The summer season starts around the 10th of December and so the best time to look for restaurant/bar work is the last week of November. It took Mr. Rapp 27 minutes to find a full-time waiting job. He was promoted to head waiter after the Christmas rush, having never waited a table in his life before. The main problem he encountered was trying to exchange the rand he'd earned for hard currency. After hours of chat up and two really nice bottles of wine, he persuaded the girl on the desk of his hostel to exchange dollars for rand.

Bear in mind that these high-profile tourist meccas have been the target of immigration raids. J.M. Rapp noticed that during the busy Christmas season, places on the Waterfront were not hiring people without a permit, though smart places downtown were, e.g. on posh Loop Street; his verdict on this work was 'big money but a hell of a tough racket'. Casual workers might prefer more discreet places. Suburban fast food restaurants such as Spur, Mike's Kitchen and St. Elmo's are often hiring, though the first two are liable to pay only commission. Suburbs to concentrate on are Observatory, Rondebosch, Wynberg and Plumstead. People with suitable backgrounds might aim higher and try a catering agency like the Janine Henderson Agency, 8 Braeside Rd, Kenilworth, Cape Town 7700 (021-761 8036).

Although Johannesburg is frequently described as a 'dump', there are better job possibilities here, for example in the Yeoville area of town where bars, restaurants and travellers' hostels like Rockey Street Backpackers (34 Regent St, Jo'bug 2198; 011-

648-8786/ bacpacrs@icon.co.za) are located. Try also the Backpackers Ritz (39 Caroline St, Brixton; 011-839 2068) which takes on long-term residents at favourable rates. The manager of Rockey Street Backpackers wrote last year:

We would like to confirm that there are several work opportunities for travellers both at our hostel and in the neighbourhood. We are constantly building and improving so we can often offer jobs to electricians, carpenters, plasterers and other artisans, either for free accommodation or a small wage. Also, from time to time we have positions in the bar, kitchen, office and as drivers. Payment is free rent, a weekly wage and a percentage of commissions. In Yeoville itself, there are many bars, restaurants, coffee shops, etc. where travellers can get jobs waiting tables, working on the bar, etc.

Try also the Sandton, Melville and Rosebank areas of Jo'burg where Mr. Rapp says waiters can earn R200 a night.

Resorts along the east coast between Cape Town and Port Elizabeth and even as far as the Ciskei provide employment opportunities, as does the Natal coast especially Durban and Margate. Particularly recommended on the east coast are George, Knysna, Jeffreys Bay, Plettenburg Bay and of course Port Elizabeth. The tourist season lasts from November to March but, as in the cities, December/January is the high season.

According to Iona Dwyer, Tekweini Backpackers in the Morningside area of Durban (168 Ninth St; 031-303 1433) employs foreigners for free rent and a small wage (which soon gets swallowed up in the happy hour at Bonkers, the local pub). If you stay any length of time in one place, you may be asked to act as relief manager or bartender as regularly occurs at Sani-Lodge in the Drakkensberg near Himeville or Sani Top Chalet. The Backpack Hostel mentioned above has a Safari Lodge on the edge of the Kruger Park (tel/fax 051-793 3816).

Gambling is a popular tourist pastime in South Africa, and there is reputed to be a continuous demand for croupiers. Casinos pay well, partly to compensate for the instability of the employment. Sun International is the main casino operator but does not pay cash-in-hand as some do. In the past few years the UK agency Quest (4-6 High St, Eastleigh, Hants. SO50 5LA; 01703 644933) has been recruiting casino staff including croupiers for South Africa.

Work may be available in the boatyards of Cape Town and other places, especially doing the dogsbody jobs of sanding and painting. Activity peaks before the Cape-to-Rio yacht race in the winter.

Selling

Judging from the number of stories of successful selling, South Africa sounds an excellent destination for budding entrepreneurs. It is possible to make a profit by selling anything from hotdogs and chocolates outside discos to Ithuba (lottery) tickets bought in bulk at a discount and sold near post offices or liquor stores. Heideline Brisley (a native South African) offers some tips to travellers willing to consider sales work. She has found opportunities to sell clothes, crafts, jewellery, etc. at a number of coastal resorts between Cape Town and Port Elizabeth and beyond. In Port Elizabeth market stalls remain open throughout the year on weekends, and are open daily during the holidays. Some friends of hers earned R1 per centimetre when they took up hair wrapping on the beachfront here. Another promising place is Grahamstown, 100km inland from Port Elizabeth during the two-week Arts Festival held each year at the end of June.

In Port Elizabeth itself, Heideline offers some specific advice:

One possibility in Cape Town, Port Elizabeth, Durban and Johannesburg is selling roses in restaurants, pubs, clubs, etc. I did this in Port Elizabeth and made between R30 and R120 per night. Tips are frequent as well. Your best bet is to ask a 'rose-girl' for the telephone number of her boss. You could of course buy and prepare the roses yourself; they cost R5 for ten from the African women selling on the street, and you could sell them for R5 each. However, unless you have your own transport, you're probably better off selling for someone who provides a driver and information about which

*places are off-limits. This is a good way of meeting people and making
contact with prospective employers. I got several job offers and ended up
waitressing in a casino.*

Tiring of his job as waiter at a Greek restaurant in Cape Town, Steve answered an
ad (posted up in hostels) for sales people. He was accepted to sell dodgy paintings
door-to-door which he (like so many others who have done this job in various
countries) described as a nightmare. (Perhaps he wouldn't have loathed it so much if
he had earned as much as a couple of Israelis he met who were making R10,000 a
month each.)

He also came across money-making opportunities in the markets of Cape Town:

*I've met several travellers selling arts and crafts items or doing hair-wraps in
Greenmarket Square and St. George's Mall. In the latter you don't even need a
licence; just turn up before 8am and pay R5 for a patch of ground. In the
Greenmarket Square market you have to work for a stall-holder.*

More recently J.M. Rapp also worked in Greenmarket for a few hours each morning
before work at a restaurant, helping to sell jewellery and earning R75 in commission.

Farm Work

The provinces of the Northern Transvaal, the Orange Free State and the Cape are rich
agricultural areas where extra help may be needed at harvest time. The rural economy
of South Africa is dominated by Afrikaaners, though most of them speak at least a little
English. Generally speaking the slog work of fruit and vegetable picking will be done
by local black labourers, but anyone with a background in agriculture might find an
opening, especially if they have contacts.

The towns of Stellenbosch and Paarl to the east and north of Cape Town
respectively are the centres of South Africa's wine industry. Around Stellenbosch
picking begins in late January/early February and lasts for four or five weeks. Further
inland (e.g. around Worcester) it starts a few weeks later, and continues well into
March. If you find a farmer willing to put you up and give you work, the problem of
work permits is unlikely to arise. A mango farming family was advertising on the
internet (www.gapyear.com) for an energetic pair of travellers to help during their busy
season (November 2000 to February 2001) 'ideal for someone looking for adventure
and a crash course in sub-tropical farming'.

Rob Abblett worked briefly at an eco-community near Durban called Absolute
Elsewhere (c/o No. 9, 371 Musgrave Rd, Berea 4001; 031-209 6006). The residents
were happy to accept working visitors from around the word and Rob helped them
clear ground for fire breaks before moving on. Rob is a veteran traveller among
intentional communities and earlier, in Malawi, had exchanged his labour for bed and
board at the Tikondwe Freedom Gardens near Lilongwe (Box 70, Lumbadzi, Malawi),
an organic fruit and vegetable farm which warmly accepted his help with the ground
nut harvest. He was only the sixth foreigner ever to work here and the local villagers
were filled with amusement and amazement to see a white man carrying sacks of
peanuts on his head.

BUSINESS AND INDUSTRY

If you are interested in joining a business in Africa (especially if you have a technical
or managerial skill) you should contact the Commercial Section of the embassy of the
country which interests you for information about job prospects. If you are on the spot,
the expatriate community may be willing to offer advice or even more practical
assistance. Information technology jobs are available in Morocco to people who know
French as well as about computers.

Other work opportunities in Africa include translating business documents from
and into French, German or English, depending on the particular country's position
and trade. You could put an ad in the paper or visit firms. When Jayne Nash travelled
in East Africa, she noticed many temporary employment agencies in Nairobi and
Harare, some with familiar names like Alfred Marks and Brook Street. She reckons

accountants and secretaries would have no trouble finding work.

It is rare to find jobs that are paid through a mediating agency; a possible exception is the limited liability company S & S Human Resources Development (HRDev) in the Ghanaian capital which arranges paid internships with organisations and institutions in Accra, Kumasi, Cape Coast, Tema, Ho and Takordi; details from PO Box TN 1501, Teshie-Nungua Estates, Accra (024-372730; www.hrdevghana.com).

The Black Market

In most countries the black market in currency is not really worthwhile and likely to make you the target of rip-off merchants. You may also encounter a black market in consumer goods such as T-shirts, sneakers and jeans, though it is probably not worth stocking up on these things because people in-the-know (like overland couriers) have this trade sewn up. Keep your ears open for more local opportunities. For example bottled water is three times more expensive in Zanzibar than in Dar es Salaam so you might make a small profit in the water trade (so to speak).

A scam which is common in Cairo and Alexandria is for hostel owners to approach travellers and ask them to go out to the airport to buy duty-free booze. Foreigners can do this and only once, since the purchases are stamped into your passport. The standard payment is just two free nights' stay. Several people have reported that once they arrive at the airport, the hotel owner goes mad and buys hundreds of dollars worth of electrical equipment on the traveller's passport which can cause problems when they leave the country.

Film Extras

Egypt is the capital of the Arab world's film industry, and many of the films require Western extras, often to play drunken, drug-taking, promiscuous degenerates. Be prepared to wear some idiotic, ill-fitting costumes. This pays around E£30-50 (£6-£10) per day, which should cover a few nights' hostel accommodation. Apparently the Cairo film agents tend to hang out in backpackers' haunts such as the Amira and Shams Coffee Shops or hostels in Tawfikia Market. Make enquiries in budget hostels such as the Oxford in Talaat Harb St and the Hotel des Roses. Ex-soldier and Glaswegian Robin Gray was approached on his first night at a hostel. He was taken to the airport for a fruitless four-hour wait for the main actor to show up, but he was paid E£20 for his trouble.

Katherine Berlanny and a friend were approached and asked if they wanted to be extras in a television soap opera. During their one day of employment, they had to play guests at a dinner party which involved some chandelier-swinging on the part of the stars. They could have had more work but had to catch a train to Aswan.

According to Ian McArthur, Western models are also required for TV commercials in Cairo:

Models are normally recruited through the agencies listed in the Yellow Pages (which fortunately has an English language version). A portfolio is an advantage though not essential and a smart outfit is useful if only to create a good impression. I was offered this work at the Hotel Oxford (well-known for its long-term residents) but was told to come back the following day three times in a row, and lost patience. The pay is supposed to be high (£20-25 a day) and can involve several consecutive days shooting, although it tends to be sporadic.

VOLUNTARY WORK

Africa is still very reliant on aid agencies and voluntary assistance. The majority of volunteers in Africa is comprised of trained teachers, doctors, nurses, agricultural and technical specialists who have committed themselves to work with mainstream aid organisations like VSO (317 Putney Bridge Road, London SW15 2PN; 020-8780 7500/ www.vso.org.uk) and Skillshare Africa (126 New Walk, Leicester LE1 7JA; 0116-254 1862; www.skillshare.org) for at least two years. Vacancies in Africa with various charities and aid agencies are posted on the internet, for example on www.volunteerafrica.org, a site provided by Simon Headington who hopes to start a new volunteer sending organisation in 2001/2.

It may be possible to offer your services on a voluntary basis to any hospital, school or mission you come across in your travels, though success is not guaranteed. Travellers who have found themselves in the vicinity of a famine crisis have often expressed shock when their offer of help has been turned down. Passers-by cannot easily be incorporated into ongoing aid projects, but it is always worth asking the local OXFAM, Save the Children Fund or Peace Corps representative.

If you have a useful skill and the addresses of some suitable projects, you are well on the way to fixing something up. Mary Hall had both, so wrote to a mission clinic in Uganda offering her services as a nurse:

> *There wasn't a doctor so the work was very stressful for me. After a couple of weeks I was helping to run the clinic, see and examine patients, prescribe drugs and set up a teaching programme for the unqualified Ugandan nurses. There's an incredible need for any form of medical worker in Africa but especially in Uganda where HIV and AIDS are an increasing problem.*
>
> *We had no running water, intermittent electricity and a lack of such niceties as cheese and chocolate. Obviously adaptability has to be one of the main qualities. Initially I worked on my visitor's visa which wasn't a problem, but when it became apparent that I would be staying for longer, the clinic applied for a work permit for me. Quite an expensive venture (£100) and I think very difficult without a local sponsor. The local bishop wrote a beautiful letter on my behalf, so I got one.*
>
> *A white person is considered to be the be-all and end-all of everyone's problems, and I found it difficult to live with this image. I'd like to say that the novelty of having a white foreigner around wore off but it never did. Stare, stare and stare again, never a moment to yourself. Still it was a fantastic experience. I've learnt an awful lot, and don't think I could ever do nursing in Britain again. My whole idea of Africa and aid in particular has been turned on its head. Idealism at an end.*

This professed disillusionment with aid work has not prevented Mary from pursuing a career in development in Africa and the Middle East. It is worth quoting her more recent job-hunting experiences to illustrate the way that once you work for one aid project, it is easier to move to others:

> *While living in the wilds of Worcestershire I decided that life in England was not for me and got a job in Somaliland, largely as a result of my cycling experience in Africa. Unfortunately the security in Erigavo wasn't so good and we were evacuated after I'd been there for less than two months. It seems that after you have Somalia on your CV the job market opens dramatically so I had a lot of offers including in Rwanda. I'd met the director of International Co-operation for Development in Djibouti when working for Health Unlimited and been very impressed with them. He took a shine to me as I fixed the computer (well, I turned it off and turned it on again and it was fixed - Mrs. Engineer) and when ICD had a job in Hargeisa in Somaliland and another one in Yemen he got them to send me the application forms. It's a bit strange as I'd seen both advertised in the Guardian but hadn't bothered to apply.*

Sending Organisations

BUNAC's Teach in Ghana programme has been mentioned earlier but BUNAC also run a general *Work Ghana* programme. The three to six month community service and development placements start at the end of January or July and are open to Britons who have graduated from university in the previous two years. Work placement is done in Accra by SYTO (Student & Youth Travel Organisation). The work is paid at local rates (e.g. $50 a month) and the overall package is approximately £1,200.

Many other voluntary organisations send volunteers to Africa. Here is a selection of them:

AFS, Arden House, Leeming House, Vicar Lane, Leeds LS2 7JF; 0113-242 6136/ www.afs.org. Community service programme lasting six months in South Africa (and Latin America). Work in S. Centres with disabled children or those in need of remedial teaching. Volunteers contribute £2,950.

EIL, 287 Worcester Road, Malvern, Worcs. WR14 1AB (01684 562577). One of three programmes in Ghana combines 4 week homestay, community work and cultural excursions. Fees are from $1,500 to $2,100 excluding airfares, insurance and admin fee.

Frontier Conservation Expeditions, 77 Leonard St, London EC2A 4QS (020-7613 2422/fax 020-7613 2992; www.frontierprojects.ac.uk). Gives volunteers the opportunity to take part in environmental research and conservation projects in the forests, savanna and marine habitats of Tanzania and Madagascar (and also Vietnam). Frontier projects run in ten-week phases during which volunteer research assistants can make a practical contribution to scientific and other research whilst visiting some of the most remote, beautiful and largely unexplored areas of the world. Each expedition is self-funded and volunteers must make a contribution of £2,450 for 10 weeks, £3,750 for 20 weeks. Detailed information on how to raise funds is provided to prospective volunteers.

Nearly two-thirds of past volunteers have made their careers in international conservation. Clare Ansell enjoyed her time in Tanzania so much that she joined the London office after her expedition:

> *I joined Frontier as a self-funded volunteer and then stayed on for an extra three months as unpaid staff managing a field camp in the Coastal Forests and later returned to work for a time as UK Coordinator in the London office. Frontier offers great opportunities to those who want to make the most of them. I've learned a fantastic amount about the practicalities of the conservation world and personally collected a new species of toad! Scientific training isn't necessary. Interest and determination are what matter.*

Greenforce, 11-15 Betterton Street, Covent Garden, London WC2H 9BP (020-7470 8888/fax 020-7379 0801; greenforce@btinternet.com/ www.greenforce.org). Recruits volunteer researchers to join biodiversity conservation aid projects in Africa (as well as Asia). 10-week stints as fieldwork assistants studying endangered species and habitats. No previous experience needed as training is provided. The cost is £2,350 plus flight.

Health Projects Abroad, PO Box 24, Bakewell, Derbyshire DE45 1ZW. Note that this well-established gap year organisation cancelled its volunteer placement programme in Tanzania in October 2000.

Inter-Cultural Youth Exchange (IYCE), Latin American House, Kingsgate Place, London NW6 4TA (tel/fax 020-7681; admin@icye.co.uk). Makes 6 month placements in South Africa, Togo, Mozambique, Uganda and Nigeria working with children, in environmental work, etc. Enquire about the possibility of being entirely funded by the European Commission (available to EU nationals aged 20-25).

We are grateful to Amelia Cook who, in summer 2000, alerted us to serious problems encountered with Humana-Tvind: 'I came close to enrolling on a Humana project but am extremely grateful I did not.' At the time of going to press, the internet site at www.tvindalert.org.uk warns people that, amongst other dubious practices, volunteers may be placed in dangerous situations in Africa and elsewhere and subjected to psychological pressure. Humana-Tvind was declared a cult *(une secte)* by the French Parliament in 1995 and the British Charity Commission has removed its charity status. This organisation operates under many names worldwide including One World Volunteer Institute and Humana People to People (both in Scandinavia) and the Institute for International Co-operation & Development (USA). Invariably the organisation requires volunteers to pay large upfront fees for training and placement. Further details are available on www.tvindalert.org.uk.

From the US, try any of these placement agencies:

Alliances Abroad, 702 West Ave, Austin, TX 78701 (www.alliancesabroad.com). Volunteer placements in Ghana, Senegal, Benin, South Africa and Mali. Students live with local families from six weeks to 12 months and do some voluntary work, for instance in a children's home or the tourist industry. Fees begin at $2,700.

Cross-Cultural Solutions, 47 Potter Avenue, New Rochelle, NY 10801 (800-380-4777; www.crossculturalsolutions.org). Places volunteers in villages around the town of Ho in the eastern Plains of Ghana to teach English in village schools (among other projects) for short periods. The three-week programme fee of $1,950 covers all expenses while in Ghana but not airfares.

Global Citizens Network/Harambee, 130 N Howell St, St Paul, MN 55104 (651-644-0960; gcn@mtn.org). Teams of paying volunteers are sent to rural villages in Kenya; $1,650 plus airfares.

Global Service Corps, 300 Broadway, Suite 28, San Francisco, CA 94133-3312 (415-788-3666; gsc@earthisland.org). Short and long-term projects in Kenya.

Operation Crossroads Africa Inc, 475 Riverside Drive, Suite 1366, New York, NY 10115-0050 (212-870-2106; www.igc.org/oca). Various seven-week projects from late June in rural Africa; the cost of participation and travel is $3,500. Canadian Crossroads International is at 31 Madison Avenue, Toronto, Ontario M5R 2S2 (www.crossroads-carrefour.ca).

Travelling Seminars Abroad, 1037 Society Hill, Cherry Hill, NJ 08003 (609-424-7630). Students and older volunteers are placed in the village of Bawku in northern Ghana to help build Habitat for Humanity homes, teach in the local schools or do community service. Programme costs roughly $1,200 for three months, $2,000 for six months, plus airfares. Shorter stays possible.

United Children's Fund Inc. PO Box 20341, Boulder, CO 80308-3341 (303-464-0137/888-343-3199/ www.unchildren.org). Volunteers work in rural Ugandan clinics, schools, farms, etc. for short periods or six months. The cost starts at $820 for one week, $1,550 for three weeks up to $6,750 for six months, excluding airfares.

Visions in Action (2710 Ontario Road NW, Washington, DC 20009; 202-625-7402/ www.visionsinaction.org) organises 6 and 12 month volunteer positions in 6 African countries (Burkina Faso, Tanzania, Zimbabwe, Uganda, South Africa and Liberia). Volunteers must have a degree or relevant work experience to fill positions in human rights, journalism, micro-enterprise, social work, health, environment and research.

YMCA Go Global, International YMCA, 71 W 23rd St, Suite 1904, New York, NY 10010 (212-727-8800/fax 212-727-8814; www.ymcanyc.org). Places volunteers for between six weeks and six months in Ghana, Ivory Coast, Mali, Senegal and Gambia to work in education, agriculture and healthcare. The programme fee is $400.

Workcamps

The kind of short-term voluntary work available to unqualified people is generally confined to workcamps which operate in many African countries. Most of the projects have to do with rural development. Normally you have to finance your own travel and pay a not insignificant registration fee to cover food and lodging for the three to six week duration of the camp. Camps are sometimes arranged in winter as well as summer. The work consists of building, installing water supplies, conservation or assisting in homes for disabled or underprivileged children and adults. The national headquarters are often good sources of local information, though not by post.

If you want to arrange a place on an African workcamp before leaving home, you may have to prove to an international organisation that you have enough relevant experience. The listing from VFP (see *Voluntary Work* chapter) for example contains information on workcamps in ten African countries from Niger to Mozambique. The workcamp movement is particularly well developed in North Africa especially Morocco which has a number of regional organisations creating green spaces, building communal facilities, etc. The main language at camps in Morocco is French. Some Moroccan workcamps organisations are:

Les Amis des Chantiers Internationaux de Meknès, PO Box 8, Meknès 50001 (fax 05-517772; acim_b@hotmail.com).

Chantiers Jeunesse Maroc, Maison de Jeunes Ghazia, 31 rue de Liban (BP 1351), Rabat RP 10001.

Chantiers Sociaux Marocains, 4 bis, rue Mohamed El Hansali Kebibal, BP 456, Rabat RP (07-79 13 70).

Twiza Mouvement Association, BP 77 CP 15000, Khemisset (07-55 73 15/ www.multimania.com/twiza3).

French is also the second language of Tunisia, and you may well be the only English speaker on a workcamp organised by the *Association Tunisienne de l'Action Volontaire* (ATAV, Maison du RCD, Boulevard 9 Avril 1938, Tunis, Tunisia; 1-564899 ext 472/fax 1-573065). Some of their projects are concerned with the restoration and maintenance of historical monuments, of which Tunisia has a great many splendid examples.

The Kenya Voluntary Development Association (PO Box 48902, Nairobi; 02-247393/fax 225379) publishes its list of camps in the new year, for example a recent calendar featured an April camp to construct a bridge, a July camp helping at a health centre in the Northern Rift Valley, two camps in August and one in December at a school in Coast Province. If in Nairobi, the KVDA office is on the 1st Floor, Consulate Chambers, Race Course Road. The newly re-formed Uganda Volunteers for Peace & Development (UVPD, Plot 823 Kiwooya House, 2nd Floor, Kibuye-Kategula L.C.I., Entebbe, Uganda; uvpeace@yahoo.co.uk) oversees projects to help disadvantaged children, youth and women. Membership in the association costs 10,000 shillings (less than £4).

To find out about the range of workcamps in Africa, it is a good idea to obtain the international list of projects from a sending organisation (or its website). Sometimes even they find it hard to extract an answer from their counterparts in developing nations, so there is little point in listing them here. If European organisations have to operate on a shoestring, African ones survive on a broken sandal strap and even when international reply coupons are sent, replies are rare. If you decide to try to join a project once you are in an African capital like Maputo, Accra, Harare or Maseru, it should not be hard to track down the co-ordinating office. Ask at the YMCA or in prominent churches.

Grassroots Organisations

Organisations based in Africa actively look for volunteers abroad, though be prepared for problems in communication. The following are listed in alphabetical order by country:

SHUMAS, Strategic Humanitarian Services, PO Box 5047, Nkwen, Bamenda, Northwest Province, Cameroon (237-362682). Development NGO which places volunteers aged 21 or more for 3-6 months in various social and environmental projects in Cameroon including work with rural women and the physically disabled. Volunteers are asked to contribute £350.

Green Fingers, GPO Box 5200, Brikama, Gambia (fax +220 393999). Organisation for Food Self-Sufficiency and Environmental Protection (OFFSEP) is an NGO that has broadened its operations from promoting sustainable agriculture to include education, health and environmental protection. Details from the Director, Baba Gindeh or for Galoya Village (Muslim) in Kombo Central Region, contact Omar Drammeh, Field Operations Manager (fax +220 472277).

CYTOFWEA, Charity Youth Travel Organisation for Working Experience Abroad, PO Box CO 553, Tema, Ghana (022-206427; Nterface@ghana.com). Self-funding volunteers placed in range of development projects.

G-NETT, Global Youth Travel Network, PO Box M542, Kumasi-Ghana (51-26880/ goldlink@ghana.com). Hosts international volunteers for three weeks to six months. Some volunteers assist with the new English syllabus in junior and senior secondary schools.

MIDEP, Mamalteng Integrated Development Programme, PO Box 536, Bolgatanga, UER, Ghana (072-2485. Range of projects aimed at alleviating poverty, and enhancing education, health and the environment. Volunteers stay for a minimum of a month. Fee of £250 covers one-week orientation course and local housing.

Mustard Seed Foundation, PMP No. 8, Trade Fair Center, La-Accra, Ghana (21-778316/fax 21-778316; cttcc.africaonline.com.gh). NGO which is trying to put degraded land to economic use in an impoverished village called Bamboi in

Ghana. Volunteers, preferably with relevant skills, needed for 3-10 months.

WWOOF/FIOH Ghana, c/o Ebenezer Nortey-Mensah, PO Box TF 154, Trade Fair Centre, Accra, Ghana (tel/fax 23321-766825). Runs a varied working abroad programme which includes placing foreign students and teachers in kindergartens, primary schools and a technical school to teach English and other subjects. Volunteer placements last between one and six months and accommodation is provided free. The application fee is US$30 plus 3 IRCs. Farm volunteers are placed on organic and traditional farms in Ghana to help with the maintenance and harvesting of crops like maize and cassava. Volunteers are also needed to work in the bicycle repair workshop and for environmental projects. Volunteers pay between $70 and $190 per month to cover expenses.

Future in Our Hands Kenya, PO Box 4037, Kisumu, Kenya (03-40522; FIOHK@hotmail.com). Volunteers needed for 5 weeks to 6 months. UK link office is FIOH, 48 Churchward Avenue, Swindon, Wilts. SN2 1NH (01793 532353). The movement supports small charities in Africa with funding and volunteers. Ghanaian branch, FIOH Ghana, is also very active (see above).

Nigerian Conservation Foundation (NCF), Lekki Conservation Centre, Km 19, Lagos-Epe Expressway, PO Box 74638, Victoria Island, Lagos, Nigeria (01-264 2498/ info@ncfenvironment.com). Flexible stays for volunteers to become involved with land management, advocacy and fund-raising.

COTN, Care of the Needy, PO Box 2247, Mwanza, Tanzania (0811-218364; cotn@raha.com). Newly formed NGO that helps homeless children and supports rural women. Volunteers needed to work in poor rural people in education and health care and also to work on conservation project ('Rescue Lake Victoria for the Children').

Paul & Delilah Roch Charitable Trust, Box 1120, Makambako, Tanzania (www.SafariTanzania.com). Volunteers needed to help build computer schools in Tanzania for 3, 6 or 12 months (costs $1,000, $1,800 and $3,600 respectively).

WWOOF Togo, c/o Prosper Agbeko, BP 25, Agou Nyogbo, Togo (00228-471036). Places volunteers on organic farms, forest projects, etc. in Togo (no recent confirmation). Send 2 IRCs for information before paying registration fee of $25.

Now that the political situation in Sierra Leone is heading towards stability, voluntary organisations are desperate for voluntary and (especially) monetary help. One such is PASACOFAAS (Pa Santigie Conteh Farmers' Community Development Association, 5a City Road, Wellington, PMB 686, Freetown; pasacofaas 84@hotmail.com) which needs manual and administrative help for its projects in the Bombali District. The director wrote in December 2000 explaining their plight:

> *We want to state that our interest in volunteers is still positive, and in fact has intensified due to an increase in the extent of our activities. The devastation of the entire country caused by the civil war has very much necessitated the services of volunteers in rehabilitating many sectors like agriculture, construction, health, environment, etc. We are sure that by early next year the entire country will be totally free of hostilities and impediments. However, as the war has crippled our economy, our financial sources are very scanty compared to the massive work ahead of us. In this respect we are more interested in volunteers who may be able to influence donor agencies to finance their volunteer roles in our organisation. It is not a condition, but an advantage for both parties.*

Also try CADO (Community Animation & Development Organisation, 1 Ross Road, PMB 1317, Cline town, Freetown; 022-226162/ cado@sierratel.sl). Volunteers of all ages, including gap year students, are urgently needed by CWASRO (Christian Welfare & Social Relief Organization, 39 Soldier St, Freetown; 022-229779/fax 022-224439). The fees for participation are £300/$400 for one month to £975/$1,200 for six months; interested applicants should fax the Project Director, Rudolph Hill.

Throughout Africa there are a great many volunteer workers with VSO, the Peace Corps, Canada's CUSO, etc. in hospitals, schools and agricultural projects who are sometimes willing to put up travellers. Probably the more remote and cut-off the volunteers are, the more welcoming they will be, but be careful not to abuse or presume on this kind of hospitality. Always offer to pay, or go armed with treats.

Foreign embassies might also be in a position to offer useful advice. According to an article in the quarterly magazine *Transitions Abroad* for example the American Embassy in Lusaka, Zambia has a Community Liaison Office who holds information about local charities and aid projects which may need volunteers.

Contacts are a great help here. Your path will be made smoother if you can procure an introduction from a church or family friend. Catherine Young spent a summer trying to set up a play group in a Nigerian village where a friend's father was setting up a medical clinic. But people have succeeded without contacts. One traveller we heard of went to Cape Town Central Library and looked through the 'green directory' which lists hundreds of environmental agencies. He then fixed up some voluntary work on a cheetah reserve near Johannesburg, where he was given free board and lodging but no wages. There is a myriad of plant and wildlife studies being carried out throughout Africa and you might be fortunate enough to become attached to one of these.

An alternative is to pay for experiencing the African wilds: African Conservation Experience (PO Box 58, Teignmouth, Devon TQ14 8XW; tel/fax 01626 879700/ www.afconservex.com) sends people to game and nature reserves in southern Africa (mainly South Africa and Zimbabwe) for between one and three months where they have the chance to assist rangers and wardens and get some first-hand experience of animal and plant conservation. The participation fees are £1,800-£2,135 for a month, £2,275-£2,935 for three months including airfares.

Israel

Most people associate working in Israel with staying on a kibbutz or a moshav. Although there are other working opportunities, including a few in a Palestinian rather than Jewish context, these are by far the most popular ways of having a prolonged visit in Israel, and one which many thousands of international travellers take advantage of every year. Although not everyone enjoys the work they end up doing in Israel (especially if they are there in winter and have been expecting hot sun), most agree that it is an excellent country in which to meet working travellers and (politics permitting) a good place to begin their travels.

Israel is bound to lose its appeal for travellers if the Peace Process continues to unravel and violence escalate. At the time of writing civil war threatens. If the violence continues, it is unlikely that there will be many opportunities in the Palestinian-governed Territories. The Israeli Tourism Ministry has just set up an information line within Israel to answer questions on personal security: 02-675 4906.

The Regulations

Having previously had one of the most lenient immigration policies in the world, the Israel Interior Ministry has been tightening up in recent years. The government is committed to reducing the number of foreign workers (many from Thailand, Korea and Romania) and has had a policy of deporting large numbers of illegal foreigners in order to increase the number of jobs available for Palestinians from the self-rule areas. This also created more job vacancies for travellers, in construction, agriculture and restaurants.

It is obligatory to obtain a B4 Volunteer Visa (at a cost of NIS65/$20) within 15 days of joining a kibbutz, archaeological dig, etc. If you arrange a job after arrival in Israel or through official channels (e.g. the volunteer offices in Tel Aviv), it is fairly straightforward obtaining the visa, but may be difficult if you fix up something informally. If you stay more than three months, you must renew the B4 at a cost of NIS135/$40. Currently only one renewal is permitted, giving a maximum stay in Israel of six months. But the regulations are always changing and, if you want to stay on and your employers are keen, they will probably find a way to get a further extension. Note that when you leave the country, the B4 is cancelled even if it has time to run. If you plan to travel to Egypt or Jordan, you should plan to do it just before your volunteer visa expires.

It is much more difficult to obtain a work permit and virtually impossible for the kind of casual work most travellers do in Israel. People do work on tourist visas which have to be renewed every three months. Some people cross into Egypt and get a new visa on returning. (If you are counting on receiving some wages owed to fund the trip, be warned that wages are often slow to come and you might find yourself trapped with a visa due to expire and no money to make the trip.) Others move onto a moshav and let the volunteer leader get the visa. Be careful not to let your visa expire, especially in Eilat. According to Rupert McDonald, 'people were being chucked out left, right and centre' and police regularly visited places where illegal working travellers gathered. Contrary to what some people believe, a deportation order does not arrive with a free flight ticket.

On arrival, you may be asked to show enough funds to support yourself, which is when a pre-arranged letter of invitation from a kibbutz or moshav organisation can be very handy. All visitors must be prepared for an unpleasant time both entering and leaving the country, with sometimes vicious interrogations, especially if you have been wandering around the country for a long period. Security measures are draconian and luggage may be subjected to painstaking searches by X-ray, chemical analysis, etc. before you are allowed to board a plane. (A copy of a kibbutz certificate and a letter from your home country addressed to you at your kibbutz/moshav will smooth your passage out of the country.)

Note that the website of the Israeli Embassy in London (www.israel-embassy.org.uk) does not include information about the B4 visa though it does have a few listings under the heading 'Educational & Volunteer Programmes'.

KIBBUTZIM and MOSHAVIM

Everyone has some idea of what a kibbutz is: it is a communal society in which all the means of production are owned and shared by the community as a whole. For more than a generation, this idea has appealed to young people from around the world who have flocked to the 250 kibbutzim of Israel to volunteer their services and participate in this utopian community based on equality.

But recent headlines such as 'Kibbutz Kiss of Death' and 'Israel to Privatise Kibbutzim' have alerted the outside world to something that Israelis have known for some time, that the kibbutz movement is in decline or at least changing almost out of recognition. For example the children of kibbutz residents are no longer raised communally and the nuclear family is now the main social unit. Commerce has come to replace idealism as the ruling principle. Twenty-first century pressures mean that some of the founding principles have been abandoned and the economy of kibbutzim has increasingly become based on tourism and light industry rather than agriculture. Some argue that even if the ownership of the land is transferred from the state to the kibbutzim themselves, the spirit of communalism can be retained. Yet the consensus among volunteers is that they would be less inclined to donate their labour to a money-making community. As further evidence of the decline, only one-fifth of the number of foreign volunteers who came in the 1970s arrive in Israel now, i.e. 10,000 instead of 50,000. The director of Project 67, a London and Tel Aviv-based travel company that has specialised in kibbutz placement for 33 years, was quoted in the *Daily Telegraph:* 'We are coming to the end of the whole programme.'

Having said all that, thousands of young foreigners continue to join kibbutzim temporarily and to enjoy the experience. In 2000, the kibbutz movement celebrated the arrival of the 100,000th volunteer since 1967. The vast majority of kibbutzim still accept volunteers and appoint a volunteer co-ordinator. A new edition of the book *Kibbutz Volunteer* by Victoria Pybus (Vacation-Work Publications; £10.99) was published in 2000, providing information about 246 individual kibbutzim as well as lots of practical information about travelling and working in Israel. For an alternative view of kibbutz culture, send an s.a.e. to the London Friends of Palestine (21 Collingham Road, London SW5 0NU) for their leaflet 'The Kibbutz: Who Benefits, Who Suffers?'

If the kibbutz is broadly based on a socialist model, the moshav is on a capitalist model, with members owning their own machinery and houses, though the produce is marketed co-operatively. The kind of experience the volunteer has on a moshav is very different and usually more demanding. Although the term 'volunteer' is used of moshavim, a wage is paid (normally the shekel equivalent of $350-$500 a month) which allows a frugal person to save $100-$200, enough to fund further travels (normally in Egypt) especially if you are prepared to work overtime (usually paid about $3.50 an hour) and if you stay long enough to earn an end-of-season bonus. Paul Bridgland's travelling fund went from 20 agorots (about enough for a box of matches) to $1,000 during the three months he worked on Moshav Pharan.

Arranging a Job in Advance

Two possibilities exist for fixing up a place on a kibbutz or moshav: application may be made through an organisation in your own country or you may wait until you get to Israel. The demand for volunteers fluctuates according to many factors including national politics, the point in the agricultural calendar when you arrive, competition from new Jewish settlers and so on. If you wait until you arrive in Israel, especially in the summer months, there may be a delay before you can be placed, though it has to be said that delays are also possible for people who have gone to the trouble of pre-registering.

There is no doubt that making contact with an organisation in advance will give you a certain peace of mind, especially if you do not have much money. Advance registration is recommended for any traveller who lacks confidence or whose circumstances are unusual such as the determined 56-year old Maureen Dambach-Sinclair who wrote such stroppy letters from her home in South Africa to the Volunteer Center in Tel Aviv about their discrimination on the grounds of age that they eventually gave her a chance. She ended up having a marvellous stay on a kibbutz and was invited back the next year by the volunteer leader.

In Britain the main kibbutz placement organisation is Kibbutz Representatives at 1A Accommodation Road, London NW11 8ED (020-8458 9235/fax 020-8455 7930; enquiries@kibbutz.org.uk/ www.kibbutz.org.il). To register with them you must be between the ages of 18 and 32, be able to stay for a minimum of eight weeks, attend an informal interview in London or Manchester, and provide a signed medical declaration of fitness. Processing takes from three to five weeks (summer is the busiest time). The kibbutz package (which costs from £407) guarantees placement and the B4 visa, and includes flights and transport to the kibbutz. Insurance is compulsory; premiums start at £72. You can either arrange your travel independently and present yourself at the kibbutz office in Tel Aviv, or you can book flights through KR, as an individual or as part of a group. Group participants are met at the airport. Kibbutz Representatives have introduced a Skills Programme which accepts slightly older volunteers (up to 38) who are trained chefs, electricians, lifeguards, engineers, etc. willing to stay for at least three months.

American applicants should contact the Kibbutz Aliya Desk (633 3rd Ave, 21st Floor, New York, NY 10017; 212-318 6130/fax 212-318-6134; kibbutzdsk@aol.com). The requirements are the same as above and the non-refundable registration fee varies with the different programmes. In addition to straight volunteering, there are programmes which involve the study of Hebrew (both for Jews and non-Jews).

Project 67 (10 Hatton Garden, London EC1N 8AH; 020-7831 7626; project67@ aol.com) is a commercial travel company which has specialist kibbutz and moshav programmes. If you book a volunteer placement with them, you are urged to participate in their travel arrangements, though this is not compulsory. Project 67's package costs £250-£280 for kibbutz and moshav placement, which includes an open return flight to Tel Aviv and administration, but not insurance. Occasionally last-minute deals bring the price down. Back-up service is provided by Project Tel Aviv (94

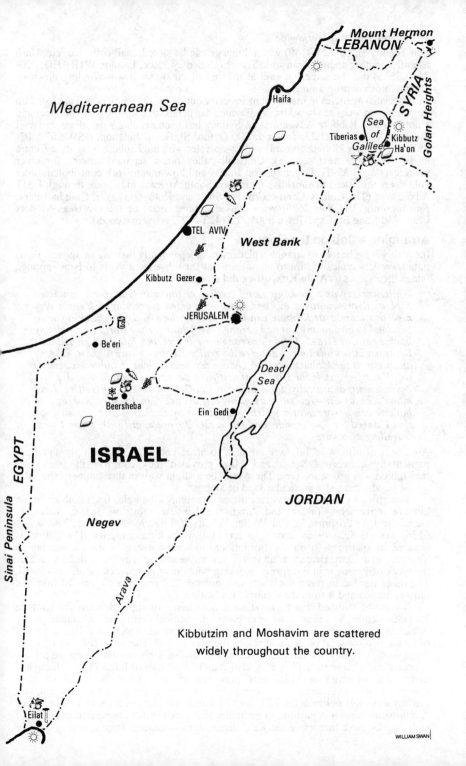

Kibbutzim and Moshavim are scattered
widely throughout the country.

WILLIAM SWAN

Ben Yehuda St; 03-523 0140) where luggage can be stored, mail collected, etc. Until recently, another agency Transonic Travel (10 Sedley Place, London W1R 1HG; 020-7409 3535) did the same but said at the end of 2000 that it was winding down its kibbutz/moshav programme.

Specialist agencies in many countries carry out kibbutz placement. All are listed on the kibbutzim website www.kba.org.il which has details of enlisting as a volunteer and a noticeboard. Kibbutz Adventures in Sydney has been sending Australians to Israel for many years (Level 23, Tower 1, 500 Oxford St, Bondi Junction, NSW 2022; 02-9513 8875/ www.kibbutz.com.au) and co-operates with the Kibbutz Adventure Centre in Tel Aviv (see next section). Unusually, they run a separate scheme for older volunteers aged 35-65. Depending on fitness and how much work contributed, older volunteers are asked to subsidise their stay. South Africans may book through USIT Adventures (The Colony Center, Crn. Jan Smut and Rothgersay Ave, Craighall Park, Johannesburg; 011-880 3635/ www.usit-adventures.co.za) or the Overseas Visitors Club (230 Long St, Cape Town 8001; 021-423 4477/ www.ovc.co.za).

Arranging a Job on the Spot

Inevitably it is cheaper to arrange a placement independently than via an agency. First-time travellers typically turn to an agency but for subsequent visits to Israel arrange things themselves as Allan Kirkpatrick did recently:

While working as a packaging and bottling engineer in Glasgow, I contacted Kibbutz Representatives in London who arranged everything. I spent a very nice two months at Kibbutz Ein-Gedi next to the Dead Sea. Back home to Scotland to give up my flat and arrange everything for my world tour, starting back again in Israel. I didn't arrange my travel and job through Kibbutz Representatives this time. I got a really really cheap one-way flight to Tel Aviv and went to the kibbutz office to choose my next kibbutz. I wanted a kibbutz totally different from Ein-Gedi with its deserts, Dead Sea and dusty environment, and luckily got a place in Ein-Gev on the Sea of Galilee. I did many jobs at Ein-Gev such as gardener, dishwasher, laundry worker and holiday camp worker at a nearby village run by the kibbutz. It was so good that I stayed for four months and met a nice Japanese girl with whom I went travelling afterwards.

A number of offices in Tel Aviv are able to place volunteers who simply show up, particularly between October and May, provided they can pay the necessary registration and insurance fees. There may be a slight wait in the summer especially for those who request a particular kind of kibbutz.

The official volunteer placement office represents kibbutzim from both the main kibbutz movements Takam and Artzi: the Kibbutz Program Center, Volunteer Department, 18 Frishman St, Cnr. 90 Ben Yehuda St, Tel Aviv 61030; 03-527 8874/524 6156; fax 03-523 9966; kpcvol@inter.net.il/ www.kibbutz.org.il). The office is situated in apartment 6 on the third floor, and the opening hours are Sunday to Thursday 8am-2pm. Bear in mind that if you arrive during religious holidays such as the week of Passover in the spring, working hours may be reduced or offices closed. The buses needed to reach the office are: number 222 from the airport, 10 from the railway station and 4 from the Central Bus Station.

It must be stressed that registration is not cheap. To apply through the Kibbutz Program Center, you must take your passport, medical certificate, insurance policy (which must show that your insurer has an Israeli representative), an airline ticket out of Israel, two passport photos and registration fee of $60. This one-off fee covers you throughout your stay, including if you move to another kibbutz (something the private agencies will charge for). They may also want to see proof of funds ($250), though if there is a shortage of volunteers they are unlikely to be strict about this. Comprehensive insurance cover is compulsory, so if your policy is not sufficient, you can buy a suitable policy at the KPC for $55 which provides cover for up to 12 months. A returnable deposit is payable to guarantee that you stay for the minimum period of eight weeks. Note that while the KPC discourages volunteers from applying directly to the kibbutz of their choice, many of the kibbutzim prefer direct contact. Many kibbutzim will want to see a recent HIV test or will arrange for or advise volunteers to have one done.

In addition to the website mentioned above www.kba.org.il, a useful internet resource is the Kibbutz Volunteers Travel Guide maintained by a veteran kibbutz volunteer from Argentina, Marcelo Montagna; www.forum.nu/travel/kibbutz/intro.html. The line taken here is that it is not necessary to pay an agency for placement, and it contains detailed advice on what to do if you don't have enough money to go through the placement offices. It contains a wealth of other information including tips on working elsewhere in Israel and a Volunteer's Forum for posting/answering requests.

There are several private placement offices and agents which you will soon hear about in any of the Tel Aviv hostels. Try to get detailed instructions before setting off to find a certain address, since these offices tend to be hard to locate. Meira's Volunteers for Moshav/Kibbutz is a long-established agency at 73 Ben Yehuda St, Ground Floor, Tel Aviv 63435 (03-523 7369/524 3811; fax 03-524 1604/meiras@netvision.net.il); the entrance to the building is behind the restaurant through the orange terrace and the office is open Sunday to Thursday 9.30am-3.30pm. J. Hains describes this office as 'extremely efficient and friendly' and claims that Meira offers a 'brilliant service'. Meira's is accessible by bus 222 from the airport; ask to be put off at the corner of Hayarkon and Mapu Streets. The charge for insurance here is NIS 250 (New Israeli shekels) plus a NIS200 handling fee, refundable after two months at the moshav.

The Project 67 Tel Aviv office at 94 Ben Yehuda St will place new arrivals if there are vacancies, as there often are in winter. Similarly the Kibbutz Adventure Centre at 66 Ben Yehuda St, Tel Aviv 63432 (tel/fax 03-524 7973) has links with the Australian agency mentioned above but will place all comers. Note that most agencies can make placements on both kibbutzim and moshavim.

The main placement office for moshavim is the Workers' Moshavim Movement at 19 Leonardo da Vinci St in Tel Aviv (03- 696 8335; fax 03-696 0139) which is open Sunday to Thursday 8am-3pm.

When in the past there has been a glut of volunteers, some Britons have reported that they are slower to be placed than other nationalities because of their reputation for hard-drinking yobbishness. Moshav farmers have always been less concerned than the agencies about the nationality of their workers. When Mark Horobin met with a lack of helpfulness in Tel Aviv, he went out into the countryside and approached moshav farmers directly. He says that the ones who had work available were generally willing to sign up new workers for a minimum of three months. It is not too difficult to arrange independently to change from one kibbutz or moshav to another. If you happen to be passing a kibbutz or moshav, it is an accepted practice to walk in and ask the volunteers what your chances are. Make sure you get a letter of recommendation from your last kibbutz to prove that you did not leave under a cloud.

If you are clued up when you visit the agencies, it is possible to request a certain kind of kibbutz or moshav (big or small, politically left or centre, well established or new) and in a certain location, though much depends on the individual volunteer leader and conditions change frequently. The vast majority are located in the fertile lands of central and northern Israel. It is best to be prepared for the climate; for example the north can be cold and rainy in winter, whereas the Jordan Rift Valley can be one of the hottest and driest places in the world.

One possible source of information on kibbutzim and kibbutz placements is the International Communes Desk at Yad Tabenkin Research and Documentation Centre, Ramat-Efal 52960 (fax 03-534 6376; yadtab@inter.net.il).

There are a few hard-to-track-down private farms inland from Eilat which depend on a steady stream of transients for their labour force and which pay good wages. Melon planting begins in early November and lasts till mid-December, while the fruit is picked in the months of March, April and May. At the busiest times, travellers are bussed in from Eilat to pick and pack melons, tomatoes and zucchini.

Life on a Kibbutz
In return for their labour, volunteers receive free room and board and a small amount of pocket money. Most enjoy their stay, and find that some kibbutzim make an effort to welcome volunteers. For example the majority of kibbutzim try to provide occasional organised sightseeing tours for volunteers, sometimes every month. Yet kibbutzim are not the holiday camps which some people expect them to be, based on stories of what they were like ten or 15 years ago. The average working week has increased from 36 to 48 hours, though the pocket money has also increased to about £50 a month. Many kibbutzim give an extra two or three days off per month to allow their volunteers to travel (since travel is difficult on the sabbath when there is no public transport). Hours may be reduced in the hot summer, for example 4am-6am and 7am-10am and extended at busy times. You are entitled to a day off for every six hours of overtime you put in.

Jimmy Hill describes the variety of jobs he did in just two months at a small kibbutz south of Jericho: 'dining hall duties, baby house, chopping date trees, a lot of gardening, working in a vineyard, electrician, turkey chaser and guest house cleaner'. New volunteers are often assigned the undesirable jobs though most volunteer organisers are willing to transfer a dissatisfied volunteer to a different job. Catherine Revell claims that if you are assertive and show willingness to work hard, you can find yourself doing more interesting work; among the jobs she did on three different kibbutzim were kitchen manager, shepherdess and a sculptor's assistant. Increasingly, work is in factories or of an industrial nature, though it is impossible to generalise and interesting options crop up. For example Allan Kirkpatrick from Glasgow spent an enjoyable six weeks at Kibbutz Kfar Blum cleaning a theatre where a classical music festival was taking place. (What made his stay more interesting but less relaxing was that the town of Kiriyat Shemona, 3km away was being bombed by the Lebanese Army at the time, and he spent three days in the bomb shelter.) Another example of how varied a volunteer's work can be found at Kibbutz Yizreel south of Nazareth which has just introduced an English-teaching programme for its growing number of Korean volunteers.

Agricultural jobs are still available at some kibbutzim. One unexpected hazard in the fields is the wildlife. The only job John Mallon was reluctant to do was to carry bunches of bananas since they housed rats and spiders. And although in most respects Deborah Hunter's kibbutz was no Garden of Eden, she recalls several shrieks and hasty descents of the ladder when volunteers encountered snakes in the fruit trees.

Facilities can differ radically from one kibbutz to the next as Kevin Boyd discovered when he moved from a kibbutz 2km from the Gaza Strip fence to another recommended by a woman he had met:

> *My first kibbutz was very poor. Our rooms consisted of two pre-fab concrete huts with very thin plastic walls which meant that there was very little privacy in the rooms. The volunteer leader was unnecessarily harsh and was always throwing people off the kibbutz for being drunk or late for work. After ten days I decided to go to Kibbutz Giniger, one of the oldest and richest in Israel. The people were very nice and welcoming and the accommodation consisted of small houses with their own kitchen and bathroom.*

Although his second kibbutz had a swimming pool, barbecues, volunteers' pub, etc., these were all closed for the winter, and Kevin was made to feel that by arriving in the autumn, he had come just as the party was over. He was told that the best time to join a kibbutz is March, so that you can be well established by the time the hordes arrive in May/June.

Meeting people is the central theme of kibbutz volunteer life and everyone agrees that the social life on kibbutzim is seldom dull. The fact that some kibbutzim administer an HIV test and hand out free condoms reinforces this image. The party atmosphere has prompted some volunteers to conclude that the prejudice against Brits is justified; however Bela Lal is not one of them:

> *In my experience of Kibbutz Afek near Haifa and others I visited, the reputation of Britons is often unfair. Certainly a small number are lager louts*

but the majority respect the kibbutz and its members, thus ensuring that friction is kept to an absolute minimum. It must be said that alcohol fuels many romantic episodes between female volunteers and the few male kibbutzniks who frequent the kibbutz pub on Friday nights, which are usually unwise and prove to be little more than fodder for gossip.

It is difficult to get to know the kibbutzniks, especially if you are there for the minimum stay. If you happen to be around for a Jewish festival, you should be able to join in some of the celebrations. Most kibbutzim still take their volunteers on a trip as a reward for good behaviour and hard work, though not as frequently as they did ten years ago. The kibbutz trip was definitely the highlight for Paul Bridgland:

The kibbutz took us all on a three-day holiday to the south, gave us decent food, free beer and meals out. They were generous. We went sightseeing, snorkelling and hired out boats, one of which ended up being rammed through the side of another at high speed on account of the free beers.

Most of the necessities of life are provided by the kibbutz including stationery, tea, coffee, basic toiletries and cigarettes, though perks differ and have been generally shrinking as wages rise. The non-profit kibbutz shops and bars sell most items cheaply. On both kibbutzim and moshavim, it is a good idea to take along a few personal objects such as posters or a cassette recorder to humanise your life. Other valuable assets are an alarm clock since the working day gets underway as early as 4am to cheat the noonday sun and plenty of mosquito repellent. If you want to get rid of anything when you leave, you may be able to make a profit by selling it.

Julee Wyld from Canada is one of the most recent in a long line of volunteers who have ended up raving about kibbutz life:

I had an incredible experience on the kibbutz, one of the best things I ever did. I adapted well, loved my job (working in the zoo), got along very well with my volunteer leader, made friends from all over the world (many from Europe whom I will visit next month) and even made many kibbutznik friends. I also learned quite a lot of Hebrew, which is exciting to me. The volunteers on my kibbutz (approximately 30) were like family to me. We spent a lot of time together, looked out for each other, took care of each other and these people will be friends for life, something that is very special to me. I consider myself very lucky to have been placed by Project 67 on a very nice kibbutz. I really grew up and changed a lot.

Many volunteers find that the communal lifestyle brings a feeling of relaxation and inner harmony, though after a few months some begin to tire of the menial nature of the work, the boss's attitude and to feel that all that can be gained from the experience has been gained. Kevin Vincent, who stayed on various kibbutzim during his four years in Israel, sums up the experience this way:

Many people love the kibbutz life, a few hate it, but only a handful will disagree that when it comes to a tranquil, easy, relaxed, uncomplicated way of living, a kibbutz is hard to beat. With no money worries, no commitments, no cooking and washing chores and a very short working day, I found the lifestyle therapeutic, a real rest from the normal western rat-race. Add the sporting facilities, the chance to meet people from many different countries and walks of life, it adds up to a very worthwhile experience.

Life on a Moshav

Life is very different on a moshav. As Alison Cooper says, 'getting up at 5am every day, working approximately 75 hours a week for a pittance, and doing your own cooking and washing is bloody hard work.' And there is no wild social life to compensate. On a moshav, you must be prepared for what Vaughan Temby calls the 'usual sweat and tears' kind of hard work. Usually there are few places to spend your money so they are a good place to save.

Moshavim differ as much from each other as kibbutzim do, so while some describe them as 'horrible places, soulless and depressing,' others find themselves working for charming and generous farmers. Sarah Protheroe's job sounds almost Biblical: trimming myrtle for the Jewish harvest festival of Sukkoth, which she thought was infinitely preferable to some of the jobs kibbutz volunteers she met had to do, such as working with battery chickens or in a factory. She also enjoyed the social life on her moshav which included a barbecue each Wednesday and a disco on Fridays, which compensated for the cramped accommodation (nine girls squeezed into a two-bedroom house). Paul Kington found himself working with cows in the Golan region in December, where it was cold and windy and he was the only volunteer. But he wasn't complaining since the work was easy, he had his own heated flat, the people were friendly and he had lots of time to explore some of the best scenery he had very seen. He also had a generous boss who paid him a third more than the going rate plus a bonus. The high season for most moshavim is November to April, so spring is when you are most likely to receive a bonus of up to two months' wages.

A few moshav volunteers live with the *moshavnikit* (moshav farmer) but most are housed in spartanly furnished volunteers' houses where they are responsible for buying and cooking their own food. Some moshav volunteers recommend keeping your wages in the moshav safe including one volunteer who had 500 shekels (the equivalent of 120 hours of labour) stolen from her room. Volunteers often have access only to the moshav shop where prices may be inflated and choice minimal. While staying on a moshav in the Negev, Lowenna Bartlett felt as though she were living in a goldfish bowl, and resented the way the Thai workers loitered and spied on her. After a rape took place on her moshav, she became especially wary.

Alison Cooper describes the problems she encountered with Thais on her moshav in the Arava region:

> *A high percentage of male workers from Thailand are employed on one or two year contracts. The moshav I worked on employed about 100 Thais. Unfortunately the Thais did not mix well with the 50 other volunteers of all nationalities. Women couldn't talk to them without giving them the wrong idea. On a Friday night you had 100 drunken, sexually frustrated Thais on the loose and it wasn't very safe to walk home by yourself.*

TOURISM

The best places for finding work in tourism are Eilat, Tel Aviv, Herzliya (a wealthy resort north of Tel Aviv), and to a lesser extent Haifa and Jerusalem. There is a plethora of cheap hostels around Israel, almost all of which employ two or three travellers to spend a few hours a day cleaning or manning the desk in exchange for a free bed and some meals. If you prove yourself a hard worker, you may be moved to a better job or even paid some pocket money. Heather McCulloch worked for her hostel in Tiberias the main resort on the Sea of Galilee (where it is easy to find restaurant, beach or hotel work):

> *I took the ferry to Israel and almost immediately landed a job in a pension. I worked as a runner/tout before switching to manning reception, which must be the most relaxing job I've ever had. I received free accommodation, one felafal and 20 shekels a day, which was standard for the Tiberias area. Runners/touts received the same but the work was much tougher. Competition was fierce, as was the bus station manager who threatened in hysterical Hebrew to call the police and get everyone deported.*

Julee Wyld did not find her summer job at a water park on the Sea if Galilee nearly as congenial as she had found her kibbutz:

> *My one month there was definitely a learning experience. We worked 12-14 hours a day, seven days a week, some days receiving only one 30-minute break. We spent our days picking up garbage, cleaning toilets and watching the pools and slides. It was the worst job I've ever done, very hard work for only NIS4.80 per hour (equivalent to 80 pence). Crazy. The accommodation and food were included but it was very basic lodgings and the same food three times a day. I really saw Israeli culture and, although I met many nice people,*

many were rude, arrogant, inconsiderate and disrespectful. But I would like to end on a positive note because I did get the chance to meet many other foreign workers.

The Youth Hostel Association of Israel (1 Shezer St, PO Box 6001, Jerusalem 91060; 02-655 8400; www.youth-hostels.org.il) can provide a list of their 32 member hostels around the country which may be in a position to offer free accommodation, meals and pocket money in exchange for six hours of work a day. One private hostel which has been recommended is Achvizland near Rosh Hanikra on the beautiful coast near the Lebanese border. A bed can be earned with three hours of work a day.

Casual work in cafés, restaurants, bars and hotels is also easy to find. As in Greece, these jobs are much easier to get if you're female. The pay is usually low and sometimes non-existent, but you will get free food and drink, and tips. There is no accepted minimum and, as throughout Israel, the price of a day's work has to be negotiated. The places that do pay wages on a monthly basis tend to make pay-day about the tenth of the month, so that is a good time to look for a job because lots of people move on after collecting their wages. Most working travellers also recommend collecting your wages (and paying your own hostel bills) on a daily basis to prevent aggravation later. Also be aware that many travellers have had their money stolen from hostels including one group who lost money entrusted to the hostel 'safe'.

Eilat

Eilat is the main holiday resort on the Gulf of Aqaba, with several large seafront hotels, numerous smaller establishments and more being built all the time. Virtually all aspects of Israeli culture have been killed off, but it is still an established haven for the working traveller despite a general tightening of immigration rules. J. M. Rapp from the US reported that most of the big beach hotels were refusing to hire people without permits, though exceptions were made for clean-cut travellers (mostly couples). The Dolphin Reef were hiring cleaners and for the laundry, and the Princess needed pool staff. It took Mr. Rapp exactly 37 hours to find a job in Eilat helping to remodel the King Solomon's Palace Hotel. After one month he was promoted from carrying 50kg bags as a reward for being one of the few workers to arrive sober for the 11-hour days, 7 days a week. At one point he was earning 1,000 shekels a week.

Inevitably, women work in tourist-related places. Make the rounds of the hotel personnel managers as early in the season as possible. The Tourist Center near the Youth Hostel has lots of bars, restaurants and sandwich bars worth trying. Laura O'Connor describes the range of jobs she did in two months in Eilat:

I had a variety of jobs: sold tickets for a boat cruise and handed out fliers for a restaurant (both for two days), waitressed in a fish restaurant for a week (had to leave as the chef would let me stay in the staff apartment only for sex), worked in Luna Park amusement park and cleaned in my hostel (Fawlty Towers).

The foreign tourist season lasts from late October to March. (When Israelis take their holidays, in high summer when the temperature is in the 40s every day, most workers will be expected to speak Hebrew.) There is such a ready supply of workers desperate for any excuse to stay on that some employers try to get away with murder, as Laura O'Connor describes:

When in November it begins to get cold in the rest of Israel, there is a mass migration to Eilat which is a mega tourist trap. We are our own worst enemy since there are so many travellers looking for jobs that employers can be right bastards.

An additional problem for women is the level of hassle they must endure from male tourists from various countries who are attracted to Eilat on account of its thriving escort business.

The rendezvous point for hopeful workers (mostly men) in Eilat is the dreaded 'Wall' outside what used to be the Peace Café on the edge of town and is now the Good Luck Bar. If you are sitting on the Wall by 6-6.30am, there's a chance of being picked up and given a day's labouring. A spontaneous union system operates whereby any employer offering less than the accepted norm is laughed at. The going hourly rate for café work is about 12-15 shekels while casual construction work pays a little more.

A hostel recommended as a good source of work is Home Hostel just up the hill from the bus station and also Max & Marian's Hostel next door. According to Jane Harris who visited in 2000, the owner of both is a bit of a character and will help residents find work through his network of contacts. Try also the noticeboard at the Underground Pub near the beach which has job notices.

Several travellers warn of the 'Eilat Trap' in which penniless travellers are sometimes caught, unable to extract owed wages from their employer and unable to leave before their visa expires. Like all international resorts, Eilat is expensive, and many people end up sleeping on the beach, where every precaution must be taken to safeguard belongings and also to guard against the plague of mosquitoes. But there are showers, toilets and lockers next to the Underground pub.

Eilat is also an important yachting and diving centre. Vacancies are sometimes posted on the gates to the Marina or on the Marina noticeboard, but work as crew or kitchen staff, cleaners or au pairs is usually found by asking boat to boat. Sarah Jane Smith had the best time of her life in Eilat after she landed a job as a deckhand and hostess on a private charter yacht for scuba divers:

I was taken on cruises lasting between a week and a month to the Red Sea, Gulf of Suez, etc. to some of the best diving spots in the world. I was taught how to scuba dive and also did lots of snorkelling. I saw some of the most amazing sights of my life – the sun rising over Saudi Arabia as the moon sank into Egypt, coral reefs, sharks, dolphins, and so on.

The social life on the marina was better than the kibbutz with hundreds of other travellers working on boats or in Eilat. Every night was a party and I hardly know how I survived it. The only bad thing is the low wages (if you get paid at all) and the hard work. But the harder you work and longer you stay, the better the wages and perks become.

This rosy view of marina work is echoed by Jane Harris who wrote from Dahab in Egypt (September 2000) to describe her experiences on the *Orionia*, the fourth boat at which she asked for work:

The marina is not the place to look for work if you want to save money. You get paid NIS30 per day plus free food and accommodation. But it's great work, cruising on the Red Sea. Our boat takes tourists on four or six hour trips with a stop for swimming, a barbecue and meal on board. To get these jobs we just walked down to the Marina and asked around, and started work the following day. A word of warning: always ask the crew what the skipper is like and how hard the work is. Our skipper was great but lots of them were absolute bastards to work for.

Tel Aviv

Work is just as easy if not easier to find in Tel Aviv as in Eilat. Hundreds of travellers spend some time working in this modern city doing everything from bouncing in clubs to au pairing. There is lots of work in bars, restaurants and beach cafés, especially for women. It is a common practice for cafés not to pay any wages and to expect their staff to exist on tips, which are enough to live on providing the restaurant is sufficiently popular. Try to have a private conversation with the staff before taking a tips-only job.

Many of the dozens of hostels along Hayarkon and elsewhere are good sources of job information or jobs themselves such as a pair of hostels under the same management: No. 1 Hostel at 84 Ben Yehuda St (03-523 7807/fax 03-523 7419) and the Gordon Hostel at 2 Gordon St (03-522 9870). The manager maintains a Work List which job-seekers sign and wait their turn to be matched with a vacancy. Employers phone the hostel daily with offers of jobs in construction, cleaning, dishwashing and gardening. According to Jane Harris who stayed at No. 1 in 2000, the standard hourly rates of pay were NIS15 for dishwashing, NIS15-20 for waiting on tables and construction, and NIS15-18 for cleaning. Another contributor was staying at the No. 1

Hostel when another hostel telephoned asking for a receptionist. This was how she ended up working seven hours a day for two months earning NIS1,600 a month less accommodation. All meals were provided and the atmosphere was very welcoming.

This system is used by other hostels including Momo's Hostel at 28 Ben Yehuda St (03-528 7471; momos28@hotmail.com) to which veteran traveller Jane and her boyfriend moved:

> *Momo's had loads of work coming in, using the same work list system. Pete got work loading and unloading containers, dishwashing and cleaning. I worked for Momo in the hostel. I'd recommend this hostel for work.*

Hostels like this may not be the most luxurious but you are virtually guaranteed work. Another two hostels worth trying are the two Travellers Hostels, one at 47 Ben Yehuda St (03-527 2108) and the other at 122 Allenby St (03-566 0812) which are reputed to have among the cheapest beds in Tel Aviv ($8.50 and $6, respectively). Check the website www.travellers-hostel.co.il or email travhost@inter.net.il for current details. The Kibbutz Program Center recommends several hostels on its website including The Hostel at 48 Hayarkon St (03-516 8989) and Dizengoff Square Hostel at 11 Dizengoff Square (03-522 5184).

It is not difficult to pick up tips on work in Tel Aviv. Try the Leprechaun Pub just off Ben Yehuda St or the Buzz Stop Café on the beachfront, where many working travellers gather for cheap food and conversation. Cafés along the seafront might also be hiring. Tips are high here. This is also a good area for buskers and traders as is Nachalat Binyamin on Tuesday and Friday afternoons.

Jerusalem

Jerusalem is also reported to be a good centre for hotel and bar work, and girls may be offered jobs while wandering round the bazaars. Work is much easier to find in the Jewish rather than the Arab areas, though hostels in the Old City do employ people on a free-bed basis. Buskers and street sellers should head for Ben Yehuda St, the crowded pedestrian precinct in the New City.

Some good sources of information on jobs in Jerusalem are the New Swedish Hostel at 29 David St near Jaffa Gate (02-626 4124), the Tabasco Hostel at 8 Aqabat at-Takiyah centrally located in the markets near the Damascus Gate (02-628 3461), the Palm (02-627 3189) and Fiasel (02-279492), both on Ha-Nevi'im Street in Arab East Jerusalem; the latter two are Christian hostels. You can find dorm beds for as little as 20 shekels. Also check out the notice board in the Goldsmith Building which houses the overseas students union just outside the campus. Jewish travellers might like to follow Amy Ignatow's example and stay at Heritage House in the Old City. You pay no rent provided you can tolerate a constant barrage of orthodox Judaism and the midnight curfew.

The English language *Jerusalem Post* (Jerusalem Post Building, Romena, Jerusalem 91000; fax 02-377646) carries job adverts from managerial positions to English-speaking secretaries, au pairs, etc. Friday is the best day.

Like buskers, sellers of handicrafts report good profits in Jerusalem. In 1998 Amy Ignatow sold smooth stones she had collected from her moshav and decorated with a permanent marker for £3 each. She set herself up in the main square of the Jewish Quarter under a sign that read 'Please Send me to Art School - Buy a Rock'. One man offered her a job painting a sign for his restaurant, so she was pleased with her success.

Home-made jewellery is also popular. David Stokes had mastered macramé (a surprisingly easy skill) and earned his way by selling on the streets of Jerusalem, while Leda Meredith sold woven string bracelets on Ben Yehuda St for 3 shekels each. Also try the evening market around the base of the main bank where it is possible to rent a stand for a modest sum. Some shopkeepers hire English speaking assistants to help them sell their wares to tourists.

One traveller's suggestion for getting an insight into Jewish culture while enjoying a free meal is to visit the Western Wall on Friday evenings where mass worship takes place. Apparently zealous Americans host shabbat dinners and passers-by are sometimes invited into Jewish homes for a meal.

Israel tends to be one of those countries in which penniless travellers end up. Marcelo, author of the Kibbutz Travel Guide website mentioned earlier, describes his experiences in Jerusalem when he was down on his luck:

If you are really desperate, yes, you can beg in the streets. Israeli people are very generous and understanding and, unlike in Europe, begging here works. What I did was I got an Israeli friend to help me write a big sign in Hebrew explaining that I was penniless and needed help to buy a ticket home. With that sign, I sat down on the floor of the underground passage at Jerusalem Central Bus Station, put on a very sad face and waited. I was there three days in a row, eight hours each day, and I collected an average of more than $20 an hour. Yes, about 500 bucks over the three days. I didn't carry on because the objective was to get enough money to fly back to Europe and not to become rich by abusing people's trust. Now this is hard work. Keeping a stone face for so many hours a day requires a lot of concentration, but I was really desperate and I had to do it. People didn't just give me money. A lot of them stopped for a chat as well, many gave me food and all gave me encouragement, so I must say a big thank you to all those who helped me in those times of trouble.

OTHER PAID WORK

Cleaning in private houses throughout Israel can be a lucrative proposition, though it takes time to build up a clientele. Steve Hendry recommends placing advertisements on lamp posts, in shop windows or in the newspaper. You may be able to persuade your hostel to let you use their phone number in the advertisement; otherwise you'll have to rent a flat and install a phone. After persevering at this, Steve was earning well above the average wage in Israel. Religious Jews want to set their house in order for Passover in April and so this is a particularly busy and profitable time for a house cleaner.

The British Council maintains a large presence in Israel and has Teaching Centres in Tel Aviv, Jerusalem and Nazareth, which recruit qualified EFL teachers mainly from the local English-speaking population. The Centre in Palestinian East Jerusalem (Al-Nuzha Building, 2 Abu Obeida Street, POB 19136; 02-627 1131) was closed in 2000 due to the hostilities.

Connect Youth International at the British Council (10 Spring Gardens, London SW1A 2BN; 020-7389 4030/ www.britcoun.org/education/connectyouth) sends young volunteers from England to teach English to teenagers at summer language clubs in northern Israel (as well as Jordan and Macedonia). Volunteers work for five hours in the morning for at least two weeks in July/August. Food, accommodation and insurance are all provided and airfares are subsidised. The deadline for applications is mid-March.

Anyone with secretarial skills may be able to temp though work normally takes quite a while to come along. Manpower in Tel Aviv are reputed to be helpful and do not require a knowledge of Hebrew. They will even arrange work permits for you.

Male visitors may wish to investigate the possibility of donating to a sperm bank; Israeli hospitals are rumoured to pay up to £30.

Many foreign movies and American television programmes are made in Israel, especially around Tel Aviv, Jaffa and Eilat. Several Tel Aviv hostels carry advertisements for film or TV extras. Katherine Berlanny followed up an advert and became a 'crowd artist' in an Agatha Christie movie. Xuela Edwards describes what she found in Eilat where a dodgy US cop show was being filmed:

There were lots of opportunities for work as an extra which pays 50 shekels a day plus a free breakfast. To find this work, you had to turn up at Eva's office, beneath the Neptune Hotel at 4pm and join the crowd. The selection process was pretty humiliating, but endured by everyone in town on the off-chance. New faces may well get work on the first attempt but you can't rely on getting work because they are reluctant to use the same people too often.

Au Pairing

Live-in childcare is absolutely booming and any plausible candidate will have no trouble finding a job. Agencies place a range of nationalities from Colombia to Zimbabwe as well as Europe, America and Australia. Ads appear constantly in papers like the *Jerusalem Post*, though note that many adverts which sound attractive are placed by agencies who, when you ring, say that the advertised job has been taken but they have others on their books. Bianca Tonkin from Cornwall was placed with a wonderful family and offers this piece of advice:

> *There are a lot of jobs here and so you really can pick your job. Once you know that a family wants you, you can afford to lay down the rules yourself regarding hours, money and days off, since it's hard to find an au pair. I must get asked twice a week in my neighbourhood of Ra'anana if I have a friend who wants a job.*

It is a good idea to meet several families if possible and choose the one with whom you feel most comfortable. Hours are long (up to ten a day) but wages are relatively high, averaging $650-$800 a month. You should be prepared to learn how to keep a kosher kitchen.

One agency has been recommended by several readers who have been placed by it. Mrs. Hilma Shmoshkovitz (Au Pair Intermediary, 5 Moholiver, PO Box 91, Rishon le Zion, Tel Aviv; 03-965 9937/ hilma@netvision.net.il) seems to offer an excellent service which includes allowing au pairs a chance to consider different job offers before deciding. The care with which she follows up her au pairs is praised, for example she sends out information before major Jewish festivals to explain what is involved or required and she also sends a reminder to the employing families of their au pairs' birthdays. Many of her satisfied au pairs appreciate that she is a European woman sympathetic to their concerns. After being disappointed by several agencies, Miss Wallace was delighted to find Mrs. Shmoshkovitz:

> *Some of the families here in Israel tend to be very assertive about what they require and expect. Girls I have spoken to say that households can be very hectic and boisterous, and the children given a lot more freedom and so can be difficult to cope with. It is difficult for some girls to stand up to the family in discussions about working conditions, etc. This is why the agent has to be aware of the situation and prepared to deal with it. All of these things are acknowledged and dealt with by Hilma.*

Another long established agency is Au Pair International in a suburb of Tel Aviv (2 Desler St, Bnei Brak 51507; tel 03-619 0423/fax 03-578 5463; www.aupair-international.co.il) run by Mrs. Veronica Grosbard. Nurses are in great demand in Israel to take care of elderly and handicapped people in their homes. Jobs are live-in, the salary is from $750-$900 a month and work permits are available.

The agency Au Pair Israel - Shiluv (76 Ben Yehuda St, Tel Aviv 63433; 03-527 8412) runs an outgoing programme only.

Internships

The Ministry of Foreign Affairs has introduced an Internship in Israel programme to strengthen bonds between young Jewish professionals worldwide with Israel. Candidates must be aged 20-30 and be graduates or be in their third year of higher education. Placements start in October and are in government, public and private institutions consistent with the intern's background. All expenses are covered apart from airfares and a small stipend (not a wage) is paid. For further information consult the Israeli Embassy or Consulate or check the website www.mfa.gov.il/mfa/go.asp?MFAH0egz0.

American students and graduates can participate in a summer internship programme called the Gesher Programme. Enquiries should be directed to the Israeli Forum, 44 Derech Petach Tikva, 66183 Tel Aviv (03-687 8824/if_sarit@netvision.net.il.

VOLUNTARY WORK
The Jewish/Arab village of Neve Shalom/Wahat al-Salaam between Tel Aviv and Jerusalem accepts five or six volunteers to work in the guesthouse, school or gardens attached to the community's School for Peace. In addition to board and lodging, volunteers receive $50 a month pocket money. Details are available from the Volunteer Co-ordinator, 99761 Doar Na Shimshon (02-991 2222; www.nswas.com).

Palestinian Projects
Several organisations can use voluntary assistance for Palestinian projects, though the political situation may put some of these in jeopardy. Unipal (Universities' Trust for Educational Exchange with Palestinians) runs a summer programme of teaching in the West Bank, Gaza and Lebanon. Volunteers teach children aged 12-15 in the refugee camps between mid-July and mid-August. Volunteers must be native English speakers, based in the UK and at least 20 years old. The approximate cost is £380. Applications must be submitted to Unipal (BCM Unipal, London WC1N 3XX; tel/fax 020-7771 7368; www.unipal.org.uk) by the end of February.

Friends of Birzeit University process applications from prospective British, European and North American volunteers of all ages wishing to participate in international summer work camps run by the Palestinian Birzeit University near Ramallah in the West Bank though it was not known if the scheme could continue in the current circumstances. Last year volunteers built the area's first park and planted trees; most work is physical and may take place on refugee camps. The registration fee of approximately £80 covers food, accommodation and trips to other areas of the West Bank and Gaza strip. Volunteers will experience incredible Arab hospitality but must realise that the Israeli military presence can make conditions difficult. Details are available on receipt of an s.a.e with 31p stamp from the Co-ordinator, Friends of Birzeit University, 21 Collingham Road, London SW5 0NU (020-7373 8414/fax 020-7835 2088; fobzu@arab-british.u-net.com).

Jewish Projects
The Friends of Israel Educational Trust (PO Box 7545, London NW2 2QZ; fax 020-7794 0291; foiasg@foiasg.free-online.co.uk) have long run a gap year programme called the Bridge Programme for 12 UK residents a year who are sent to Israeli cities to help on gardening, English teaching and other projects for six months from February. After being chosen at interview, participants' expenses are covered apart from spending money (£600 is recommended).

The organisation Jewish Child's Day (707 High Road, North Finchley, London N12 0BT; 020-88446 8804; www.jewishchildsday.co.uk) publishes a leaflet called Jigsaw which gives information about a summer work scheme for young Jewish volunteers to assist at holiday programmes based in Jerusalem for children with special physical or emotional needs. The cost of participation is £250 plus insurance.

Kishor Village (M.P. Maale Hagalil 252149; Kishor@internet-zahav.net) is a former kibbutz now a sheltered centre for people with mental disabilities. The village accepts foreign volunteers (mainly Danes and Germans at present) to help in the plastics factory, kennels, goat farm and kitchens alongside village members and staff.

For a range of voluntary opportunities in a Jewish context, the Israel Program Center in Philadelphia stores information about many projects. Contact the Community Center of Greater Philadelphia, 401 S. Broad St, Philadelphia, PA 19147, USA (215-545-1451). Similarly, the American Zionist Youth Federation (Israel Action Center, 110 E 59th St, 4th Floor, New York, NY 10022; 212-339-6940) holds details of voluntary programmes.

Christian organisations are also active in Israel. To find out about voluntary opportunities in this context, contact the Christian Information Centre in Jerusalem (PO Box 14308, 91142 Jerusalem; 02-627 2692; cicinfo@cicts.org). It keeps a list of schools and institutes mainly for people with disabilities that take on volunteers.

The privately run Nesher Center runs a Volunteer Placement Service whereby volunteers are placed for between three months and two years in schools and institutes to help needy people. Details available from Ron & Aliza Nesher, PO Box 199, Moshav

Burgeta, 42860 Israel; 09-894-7043/ www.vacationisrael.com/nesherctr.html).
Registration costs $75 and can be done on-line.

Archaeology

Volunteers are needed to do the mundane work of digging and sifting. In the majority
of cases, volunteers must pay a daily fee of $25-$35 to cover food and accommodation
(often on a nearby kibbutz) plus a registration fee (typically $50-$75). Most camps
take place during university holidays between May and September when temperatures
soar. Volunteers must be in good physical condition and able to work long hours in hot
weather. Valid health insurance is required.

Information on volunteering at archaeological digs in Israel is available on the
internet site of the Israel Ministry of Foreign Affairs at
www.mfa.gov.il/mfa/go.asp?MFAH00wk0. The excavation of the ancient port site of
Yavneh Yam carried out by the Department of Classical Studies at Tel Aviv University
(fax 03-640 9457; fischer@ecsg.tau.ac.il) charges volunteers $325 per week for a
minimum of two weeks. But not all digs are so expensive.

Jennifer McKibben, who worked on a kibbutz, in an Eilat hotel and on a dig in the
Negev desert, waxed most enthusiastic about the latter experience:

*Actually the work was often enjoyable but not usually before the sun had risen
(it gets incredibly cold at nights in the desert). It did seem madness at times
when a Land-rover would take a team of us out to an unremarkable spot in the
desert marked only by a wooden peg, and tells us to start digging. I think the
romance of excavations quickly fades once the blisters begin to appear and
that long term camps are suitable only for the initiated or fanatic.*

*However despite the difficulties I really enjoyed the camp. Group relations
were good – there were people of all nationalities – and there was normally a
camp fire going with a couple of musicians. It was wonderful just to spend
time in such a beautiful desert, to go off wandering over footprintless dunes,
over great red hills to look and see no sign of civilisation. More practically, it
was a cheap way to eat well for a couple of weeks, see another area and
extend one's all-too-short stay in Israel.*

Asia

For a continent as vast as Asia, this chapter may seem disproportionately short. That is simply because there are not many kinds of work open to the traveller in developing countries, as has already been noted in the chapters on Africa and Latin America. Third World economies struggle to support their own populations and can rarely accommodate novelty-seeking foreigners. Certainly the kinds of job which travellers get in the developed world (seasonal farm work, tourist resorts, as nannies, etc.) are not available in most of Asia.

The main exception is provided by those countries with a Western style economy, principally Japan, the Hong Kong Special Administrative Region and Singapore. The economic crisis which swamped much of Asia in 1998 has made the situation far more difficult causing the market for experts from western countries to shrink considerably. Japan is reeling at the news that as of 1999 its unemployment rate of 4.4% is the same as that of its great economic rival the United States. The once flourishing currencies of Japan, Korea and Indonesia are now faltering against the dollar, and long-term expats have seen their wages dwindle almost overnight. And yet people with professional skills continue to find work in these countries. There is even an increase in opportunities at a professional level in India, unlike a few years ago when it was very difficult for foreigners, however well qualified, to obtain a work visa.

Having made your fortune in an industrialised country, whether as a graphic designer in Singapore, an English teacher in Japan, a chambermaid in Switzerland or a tomato picker in Australia, you should be able to finance many months of leisurely travel in the inexpensive countries of Asia. In most of Asia it is better to concentrate on travelling for its own sake rather than for the sake of working. The climate is another factor. Although Robert Abblett had carefully planned his trip to India and had the addresses of organic farms where he intended to work, he had not counted on the debilitating heat and decided to enjoy a holiday instead.

However, described below are a number of ways to boost your budget between enjoying the beaches of Turkey and the temples of Thailand.

TEACHING

Although the English language is not a universal passport to employment, it can certainly be put to good use in many Asian countries especially Japan, Taiwan, Korea, Thailand, Vietnam and Turkey. There are thousands of people of all ages eager for tuition in English and native English speakers with a university degree or just a degree of enthusiasm are cashing in. This is also true on the Indian sub-continent but there the educated classes speak fluent English and therefore foreign English speakers are not much in demand. Serious teachers from the UK should always seek the advice of the British Council. Americans should investigate programmes such as Volunteers-in-Asia (Stanford University, PO Box 20266, Stanford, CA 94309, USA; 650-723-3228/fax 650-725-1805; www.volasia.org) which sends volunteer teachers to Indonesia, Laos, Vietnam and China on short (six week) and longer term (1 year) assignments; and Princeton-in-Asia (224 Palmer Hall, Princeton, NJ 08544; pia@phoenix. princeton.edu) with placements in China, Hong Kong, Indonesia, Japan, Korea, Laos, Singapore and Vietnam. The cost of participating starts at about $1,500.

Outside the major cities, paid teaching jobs are rare. If you do end up working for a small locally run school, do not expect to find many teaching materials. You are likely to spend your evenings cutting up magazines and writing stories for the next day's lessons. Off the beaten track, it may be possible to arrange with locals, especially the local teacher, to stay with a family in exchange for conversation lessons. Stuart Tappin travelled around South-East Asia doing this:

> *In Asia I managed to spend a lot of time living with people in return for teaching English. The more remote the towns are from tourist routes the better, for example Bali is no good. I spent a week in Palembang (Sumatra) living with an English teacher and his family. You teach and they give you their (very good) hospitality. I did the same in Thailand. During the three months that I lived in Kanchanaburi (not far west of Bangkok) my only daily expense was a few baht for a newspaper.*

In addition to the information which follows on finding work with language schools in specific countries, it is also worth considering setting up as a private English teacher. Working as a self-employed freelance tutor is more lucrative but hard to set up until you have been settled in one place for a while and have decent premises from which to work. Steven Hendry, a long-time travelling Scot who has taught in Japan and Thailand, describes the steps to take:

> *Be in town for at least a few months and get access to a telephone. Make up a little advertisement (half in English, half the local language) and plaster it all over town as quickly as possible, in universities, colleges, coffee shops, etc.*

More detailed information on teaching English in the countries of Asia is contained in the 2001 edition of *Teaching English Abroad* by Susan Griffith (Vacation-Work Publications, £12.95).

TEACHING IN JAPAN

Teaching English in Japan is one of the classic jobs for working travellers. The demand for language tuition is very strong, and has been reviving again after a bad patch during the Far East economic crisis of the late 1990s. But schools have generally become more selective, and competition for decent jobs can be fierce. It is not uncommon for hopeful teachers to spend several weeks job-hunting in Japan and end up with nothing but a large debt. Julie Fast from the US describes the drastic changes which she has witnessed:

> *When I arrived in Tokyo, there were so many high paying jobs, prospective teachers (experienced or non-experienced) could pick and choose their work. This is no longer the case in Tokyo. I feel I should underline that sentence and write it in capital letters. Things are simply not as they were. When I first started managing a children's English school, I had a hard time finding a good teacher. Now teachers call me looking for work.*

Normally newcomers find it a real struggle to acquire enough teaching hours to make substantial savings possible. To avoid an on-the-ground job-hunt you can try to fix up a job before leaving home with the government's JET programme or with one of the major chains of schools like Nova (described later in this section). Thousands of English schools in Tokyo, Osaka and many other Japanese cities are eager to hire *gaijins* (foreigners) to teach. A great many of these are willing to hire native speakers of English with no teaching qualification, though all expect teachers to have a university degree and preferably some teaching experience. Apart from a few schools (including the most prestigious ones) who advertise and conduct interviews abroad, most schools recruit their teachers within Japan. Because of the way that Japanese society works, using intricate networks of contacts, cold-calling is seldom successful. The most common means of recruitment is by word-of-mouth among expat teachers and by advertising in newspapers, especially the English language *Japan Times* on Mondays, and also *Kansai Time Out* magazine. Note that the Kimi Information Center described below publishes its own newsletter *Kimi Job Opportunities*. In Osaka check out the free English language *Flea Market* and *Japanzine* which are aimed at expats, especially those looking for gaijin houses and internet cafés.

In order to shine over the competition, a number of practical steps should be taken when presenting yourself to a potential employer. These should be taken even more seriously than when trying for teaching work elsewhere in the world, if only because travelling to an interview in Tokyo is a major undertaking, often taking several hours and costing more than £10; so it would be a shame to blow your chances because of a simple oversight.

Dress as impeccably and conservatively as possible, and carry a respectable briefcase. Inside you should have any education certificates you have earned, preferably the originals since schools are catching on that forgery is a widespread practice. (If you apply for a working visa, you must have the original.) Also have a typed resumé which does not err on the side of modesty. Steven Hendry suggests converting 'travelling for two years' to 'studying Asian cultures and languages' and describing a period of unemployment as 'a chance to do some voluntary teaching with racial minorities'. Increasingly prospective employers ask interviewees to teach a demonstration lesson so it is well to arrive prepared for this. Always speak slowly and clearly.

One of the most often recommended places to start the job hunt in Tokyo is the Kimi Information Center (Oscar Building, 8th Floor, 2-42-3 Ikebukuro, Toshima-ku, Tokyo 171-0014; 03-3986 1604/fax 03-3986 3037; www2.dango.ne.jp/kimi) which offers a fax service (315 yen), telephone answering service (3,150 yen/£20 for two months) as well as advising on cheap accommodation and jobs. Private rooms can be rented at nearby Kimi Ryokan - *ryokan* means Japanese-style guest house - for 4,500 yen single, 6,500 yen double. The address is 36-8 2-chome, Ikebukuro, Toshima-ku (03-3971-3766).

Other Tokyo gaijin houses offer dormitory accommodation for about half that price. Try to pick up a list of gaijin houses from the tourist office and look for ones that charge a monthly rather than a nightly rent since these are the ones which attract long-term residents. Because it is so difficult to rent flats, some teachers continue living in gaijin houses after they find work. Try to find a gaijin house favoured by teachers. Among the cheapest is Mickey House (2-15-1 Nakadai Itabashi-ku; Tokyo; 03-3936 8889) whose room charges start at 1,700 yen per night for two people sharing; 10,500 yen for a week and 33,000 yen per month. For a private room the monthly rent is 45,000 yen. Typically rents start at 65,000 yen. In Osaka, Joseph Tame recommends Gamba House in the central Minami district which makes it easy to plug into the network of teachers. The rates are among the best in the city (10,000 yen per week, 30,000 yen per month). While Joseph was staying there he was offered work on several occasions and he claimed virtually everyone else was doing a mixture of English teaching and leafleting.

Red Tape

The key to obtaining a work visa for Japan is to have a Japanese sponsor. This can be a private citizen but most teachers are sponsored by their employers. Not all schools by any means are willing to sponsor their teachers, unless they are persuaded that they are an ongoing proposition. Some schools rely on a stream of Canadians, Australians and New Zealanders on working holiday visas which they must obtain in their home countries (see description of Council's Work and Travel Japan scheme below).

Other nationalities will have to find a sponsor. If your visa is to be processed before arrival, you must have a definite job appointment in Japan. Many Britons and Americans enter with a temporary visitor's stamp (valid for three months), find a job and sponsor and then apply for a work visa. Documents which will help you to find a sponsor are the original or notarised copy of your BA or other degree and résumé. The temporary visitor's stamp can be extended for another 90 days (for example at Kushiro immigration office) for a fee. It is unlikely that someone who has stayed in Japan for six months and then leaves the country will be granted landing permission before a reasonable amount of time has elapsed. Those found to be overstaying their visitor's visa can be deported. Furthermore, employers who are caught employing illegal aliens as well as the foreign workers themselves are subject to huge fines, and both parties risk imprisonment.

Placement from Abroad

If you want to arrange a teaching job in advance, the best bet is the government's JET (Japan Exchange & Teaching) Programme. Anyone with a BA who is under 35 and from the US, UK, Ireland, Canada, Australia or New Zealand (plus a number of other countries) is eligible to apply. In Britain the programme (which accepted 679 teachers this year) is administered by Council Exchanges at 52 Poland Street, London W1V 4JQ (020-7478 2009/fax 020-7734 7322; jetinfo@councilexchanges.org.uk). Non-British applicants should contact the Japanese Embassy in their country of origin for information and application forms. US applicants can obtain details from any of the 16 Consulates of Japan in the US or from the Embassy in Washington (2520 Massachusetts Avenue NW, DC 20008; 1-800-INFOJET/202-939-6772/3; eojjet@erols.com). Applications in Britain are due by early December for one-year placements beginning late July. The annual salary is 3,600,000 yen (equivalent to a very generous £23,000) in addition to a free return air ticket.

A number of the largest language training organisations recruit graduates abroad as well as in Japan. Some chains have been described as factory English schools, where teachers are handed a course book and told not to deviate from the formula. Demand for native speaker teachers is so great that they depend on a steady supply of fresh graduates who want the chance to spend a year in Japan. Often new recruits do not have much say in where they are sent and in their first year may be sent to the least desirable locations. The main employers include:

AEON Inter-Cultural USA, 1960 E Grand Avenue 550, El Segundo, CA 90245 (310-414-1515/fax 310-414-1616; www.aeonet.com). Recruits throughout the US and places 500 native English-speaking teachers in their 270 branch schools in Japan.

ECC Foreign Language Institute, Kanto District Head Office: 5th Floor, San Yamate Building, 7-11-10 Nishi-Shinjuku, Shinjuku-ku, Tokyo 160-0023 (03-5330 1585; www.ecc.co.jp). Other district offices include Chubu: Kanayama Building, 1-16-16 Kanayama, Naka-ku, Nagoya 460-0022 (052-332 6165; ecchr@spice.or.jp); Kinki: 8th Floor, Sumisei Namba Minami Building, 3-19 Motomachi 2 chome, Naniwa-ku, Osaka 556-0016 (066-636 0334; teaching@ecc.co.jp). 320 teachers for 120 schools throughout Japan.

GEOS Corporation, Simpson Tower 2424, 401 Bay Street, Toronto, Ontario M5H 2Y4, Canada (416-777-0109/fax 416-777-0110; geos@istar.ca/ www.geoscareer.com). UK address: GEOS Language Ltd., Compton Park, Compton Place Road, Eastbourne, East Sussex BN21 1EH (01323 739575/fax 01323 739565; london@geos.demon.co.uk). One of Japan's largest English language institutions employing 1,800 teachers for 450 schools, all of whom are hired outside Japan. Recruitment campaigns held in UK, Australia, New Zealand and North America.

Interac Co Ltd. Fujibo Building 2F, 2-10-28 Fujimi, Chiyoda-ku, Tokyo 102 (03-3234 7857/fax 03-3234 6055; www.interac.co.jp/recruit). 280 teachers in 9 branches.

Nova Group, Carrington House, 126/130 Regent Street, London W1R 5FE (020-7734 2727/fax 020-7734 3001; www.nova-group.com). Employ more than 4,000 in nearly 400 Nova schools throughout Japan. Recruitment in North America via Interact Nova Group, 2 Oliver St, Suite 7, Boston, MA 02110, USA (617-542-5027); and 1881 Yonge St, Suite 700, Toronto, Ontario M4S 3C4, Canada (416-481-6000).

TEACHING IN TAIWAN

The hiring policy is virtually universal in Taiwan: all they are looking for is a BA and a pulse. The country remains a magnet for English teachers of all backgrounds since it has managed to escape the Asian economic crisis. Hundreds of private language institutes or *buhsibans* continue to teach young children, cram high school students for university entrance examinations and generally service the seemingly insatiable demand for English conversation and English tuition.

Many well-established language schools are prepared to sponsor foreign teachers for a resident visa, provided the teacher is willing to work for at least a year. Only teachers with a university degree are eligible. Many people arrive on spec to look for work. It is usually easy to find a *buhsiban* willing to hire you but not so easy to find a good one. If possible, try to sit in on one or two classes before signing a contract. (If a school is unwilling to permit this, it doesn't bode well.) The majority of schools pay NT$400-500 (roughly £8 to £9).

Check the Positions Vacant column of the English language *China Post* and the *China News* though work tends to result from personal referrals more than from advertising. Word-of-mouth is even more important in Taiwan than elsewhere because there is no association of recognised language schools and no English language Yellow Pages.

If you want to meet foreigners who are clued up about the current teaching situation, try visiting well-known Taipei hostels such as the Formosa on Chung Shan N Rd, Sec.2, Lane 20, No. 16 3rd Floor (02-2562 2035) which charges about $10 a night for long stays. One of the best notice boards is located in the student lounge on the sixth floor of the Mandarin Training Center of National Taiwan Normal University at 129 Hoping East Road. You might also make useful expat contacts in Taipei at the Community Services Centre, 25 Lane 290 Chung Shan North Rd, Sec. 6, Tien Mu (02-2836 8134) or at the Gateway Community Centre, 7Fl, 248 Chung Shan North Rd, Sec. 6, Tien Mu (02-2833 7444).

One of the few organised recruitment programmes for Taiwan is run by the YMCA (Overseas Service Corps, 101 North Wacker Drive, Chicago, IL 60606; 800-872-9622 ext. 343/fax 312-977-9036) which sends up to 20 North American volunteer teachers to nine localities.

The following language schools hire on a large scale:

ELS International, 6F, No 9, Lane 90, Sung Chiang Road, Taipei (elsjobs@ms54.hinet.net or elsikk@tp.silkera.net/ www.elstaiwan.com). Main branch at 12 Kuling St, Taipei (02-2321 9005/fax 02-2397 2304). ELSI employs more than 300 teachers at 18 schools, mostly in Taipei but also Kaohsiung and Taichung. Minimum starting salary for 25 hours per week is NT$50,000 (approx. US$1,600).

Epact Educational Services – apply@teachtaiwan.com. Recent graduates needed to join Teach in Taiwan programme for a minimum of a year. Details are available on www.teachtaiwan.com.

Hess Educational Organization, 235 Chung Shan Road, Chung Ho City, Sec. 2, No. 419, Chung Ho City, Taipei County (02-3234 6188/fax 02-3234 9488; hesswork@hess.com.tw). Specialise in teaching children including kindergarten age. 250 Native Speaking Teachers (NSTs) in more than 100 branches. Very structured teaching programme and curriculum. Quarterly intake of teachers in September, December, March and June.

Visas

If you are entering Taiwan without a pre-arranged contract you should obtain a 60-day Visitor's Visa before arrival which can be single entry or multiple entry (£25 or £50). Otherwise you will be given permission to stay for just the two weeks (non-extendable) that tourists are granted. Once you find an employer, your employer should apply for a resident visa/card (A.R.C.). To change your status, you will have to leave the country; a round trip to Hong Kong costs at least US$300. Working on a visitor visa is still possible but risky since the regulations are strictly enforced. Without an A.R.C. it will be difficult to exchange any excess earnings into dollars. Detailed information about visas should be requested from the Taiwan overseas office in your country of origin; the Taipei Representative Office in the UK is at 50 Grosvenor Gardens, London SW1W 0EB (020-7396 9152/fax 020-7396 9144).

TEACHING IN KOREA

Although Korea does not immediately come to mind as a likely destination for British TEFLers, it has been long known in North America as a country which can absorb an enormous number of native speaker teachers, including fresh graduates with no TEFL training or experience. South Korea seems to be making a surprisingly rapid recovery from the severe economic difficulties it suffered at the end of the 20th century and English teachers are still in great demand (though wages have gone down because of the sharp decline in the exchange rate).

Hundreds of language institutes (*hogwons*) can be found in Seoul the capital, Pusan (Korea's second city, five hours south of Seoul) and in smaller cities. The majority of these are run as businesses, so that making a profit seems to be what motivates many bosses rather than educating people. Certificates and even degrees are in many cases superfluous. Native-speaker status is normally sufficient to persuade the owner of an institute to hire an English-speaker, though having some letters after your name makes the job hunt easier.

The English Program in Korea (EPIK) is a scheme run by the Ministry of Education, and administered through Korean embassies in the US, Canada, Britain and Australia, to place about 2,000 native speakers in schools and education offices throughout the country. The annual salary offered was 1.6, 1.8 or 2 million won per month (depending on qualifications) plus accommodation, round trip airfare, visa sponsorship and medical insurance. Work starting dates are staggered over the summer with application deadlines falling between January and April. Details of the 2001 programme had not been finalised at the time of writing, so current information should be obtained from the Education Director, Korean Embassy, 60 Buckingham Gate, London SW1E 6AJ (020-7227 5547/fax 020-7227 5503) or from the website epik@cc.knue.ac.kr or contact the office in Korea (82 431 233 4516/7). Americans should contact any of the dozen Korean Consulates in the US. Other nationalities can contact the EPIK office in Korea (Center for In-Service Education, Korea National University of Education, Chongwon, Chungbuk 363-791; 431-230-3943/fax 431-233 6679). Note that EPIK does not attract the praise that the JET Programme does; check Dave Sperling's ESL Café website for details (www.eslcafe.com).

In North America there are brokers and agents who act on behalf of institutes or groups of institutes to recruit teachers. Typically advertisements placed by such intermediaries request only native-speaker fluency and a BA/BSc. Some charge a fee. For example Ko-Am Academy Consulting Inc (14080-D Sullyfield Circle, Chantilly, VA 20151; fax 703-815-3600/ apply@koam.org) recruits year round, as does Better Resource (3700 Wilshire Blvd, Suite 955, Los Angeles, CA 90010; 213-738-1001/ better@wcis.com; www.eslkorea.com). Canadians can apply to Russell Recruiting (3038 West 42nd Ave. Vancouver, BC, Canada V6N 3H2; 604-216-3648/fax 604-267-1539; jimkrussell@hotmail.com), which arranges one year contracts for those with university or college diplomas. Of course there are plenty of agents in Korea, too, like one seen advertising November 2000: email korglen@yahoo.com/ +82-1770 50579.

ELS International/YBM employs 100 native English teachers for English Conversation Centers and other kinds of institute throughout Korea. The central contact address is 649-1 Yeoksam-dong, Kangnam-gu, Seoul 135-081 (02-552-1492/fax 02-501 2478; teach@ybmsisa.co.kr/ www.ybmsisa.com). The recruitment representative in the UK is Judith Howard (jh2@mcmail.com).

William Naquin stresses the importance of arranging the details of a written contract before starting work:

I found my present position in Korea in the classified section of the Seattle Sunday paper. A couple of Korean-Americans in Los Angeles calling themselves 'Better Resource' flew to Seattle two days after receiving my faxed CV. I cannot suggest strongly enough that teachers considering a position negotiated through a US-based broker get everything in writing. My contract was written in exceedingly poor English, and what it failed to stipulate in terms of housing conditions, medical insurance, etc. was only guaranteed orally. It was a mistake on my part to take the broker at his word. Living arrangements here are substandard, with three of us sharing a two-bedroom flat.

William's ability to save $12,000 in one year helped him to tolerate the inconvenience.

One year contracts arranged in advance are often lucrative. They can also be gruelling for those suffering acute culture shock and possibly also contending with an exploitative situation. Discontentment seems to be chronic among English teachers in Korea. So many American teachers have run amok of faulty contracts, that the US Embassy in Seoul issues a handbook offering guidance called 'Teaching English in Korea: Opportunities and Pitfalls' (which can be requested from the American Citizen Services Branch, 82 Sejong Road, Chongro-ku, Seoul, or seen on the internet at http://usembassy.state.gov/seoul/wwwhe8p0.html). The accompanying letter from the American Citizens Services office does not mince words:

Despite contract language promising good salaries, furnished apartments and other amenities, many teachers find they actually receive much less than they were promised; some do not even receive benefits required by Korean law, such as health insurance and severance pay. Teachers' complaints range from simple contract violations, through non-payment of salary for months at a time, to dramatic incidents of severe sexual harassment, intimidation, threats of arrest/deportation and physical assault.

If you wait until you get to Korea, it is usually easy to fix up a job without resorting to an agent, but the visa is more difficult to arrange. Every day there are adverts for teachers in the English language newspapers in Seoul, namely the *Korean Herald* and *Korea Times*. A personal approach to language schools in Seoul or Pusan will usually be rewarded with some early morning and evening work within a week or two. Often new arrivals stay in one of the popular yogwons (hostels) and visit internet cafés to link up with the grapevine and learn about the English teaching scene. The Chongro area of Seoul contains a high concentration of both hostels and language schools and is a suitable area for a door-to-door job search.

Among the biggest language institutes are:

Berlitz Korea, Sungwood Academy Building, 2F, 1316-17 Seocho-Dong, Seocho-Gu, Seoul 137-074 (02-3481 5324/fax 02-3481 3921). About 40 native speakers employed.

Ding Ding Dang English School, 1275-3 Bummel-dong Soosung-gu, Taegu 706-100 (53-782 5200/fax 53-782 6434; dings@thrunet.com). 30-36 classes per week for minimum of one year. Branches in other cities.

English Friends, 733, Bang Hak 3 Dong. Do Bong Ku, Seoul (2-3491 1431/fax 2-3491 1264; www.tefa.net). 25-30 teachers.

Nelson Foreign Language Institute, c/o Mr. Jay S. Wang, North American Office, Nelson FLI, 95 Hess Street South, No. 610, Hamilton, Ontario L8P 3N4, Canada (canlink@bigwave.ca). Hire 20 teachers a month for 60 branches throughout Korea.

TEACHING IN CHINA

Recruitment of teachers for the People's Republic of China is no longer confined to academic institutes in the provinces but is also being carried out by an ever-increasing number of private language institutes. For information about teaching opportunities in the Hong Kong Special Administrative Region, see the section on Hong Kong below.

Opportunities are mushrooming throughout China and many schools and institutes are turning to the internet to fill teaching vacancies. Many English teaching posts in the Chinese provinces remain unfilled, though aid agencies like VSO and Christians Abroad do their utmost to fill vacancies. The requirements for these two-year posts are not stringent and, in return, teachers get free air fares, a local salary and other perks.

Any educated native speaker of English should be able to find a job at a school, college or university in China. As an example, Shanghai has more than 50 schools teaching English. Having a degree and any teaching experience is useful, but not much importance is attached to TEFL qualifications.

If you want a contract fixed up before leaving home, start the application procedure six months or more before your intended departure. Most recruitment is filtered through the Chinese Education Association for International Exchange (CEAIE) in the capital (37 Damucang Hutong, Beijing 100816; 10-664 16582/16583/14933/18220; fax: 10-66416156; ceaieipd@public3.bta.net.cn/ www.ceaie.org) which is a non-governmental organisation with 37 local branches in every province and extensive contacts with institutes of higher education throughout China who wish to invite native speaker teachers.

The task which the Chinese Embassy used to carry out of matching UK applicants with Chinese institutions has been handed over to the Central Bureau for International Education & Training and to Council Exchanges. Details of the application procedure can be obtained from the Chinese Links Officer at the Central Bureau for International Education & Training and also from Council Exchanges. Contact details for the Central Bureau are 10 Spring Gardens, London SW1A 2BN; 020-7389 4431/fax 020-7389 4426); the programme's Development Officer is Dilbahar Tawakkul (dilbahar.tawakkul@britishcouncil.org).

The Central Bureau receives information of posts in China in the new year and sends out this information to universities and interested individuals of any age. The Bureau then screens applications and conducts interviews in March for positions mainly as Foreign Teachers (FTs) but also as Foreign Experts (FEs). The minimum requirement is a university degree though a TEFL certificate and/or teaching experience, preferably abroad, improve your chances of acceptance. Dossiers of successful interviewees are then forwarded to appropriate institutes in China who then communicate directly with the applicant if they are interested in hiring them.

Contracts are for between six months and two years, normally starting in September. Details of the contract are a matter of negotiation between the teacher and the hiring institution. Many applicants will have to choose among offers, as William Hawkes did:

During my last year at university, I obtained a list of Chinese universities and colleges looking to recruit foreign teachers, then faxed my CV and a letter to the ten which suited me most. I received several offers from around China (including a phone call at 3am) and eventually accepted an offer from Qingdao Chemical Institute on the east coast of China. The offer was quite standard: accommodation, unspectacular money... but a friend of mine had taught at this same institute and thoroughly recommended it, so I went and taught English from September to July.

Contracts are for one year in the first instance. Depending on experience and qualifications, teachers are designated either as foreign teachers (FTs) or foreign experts (FEs). The latter usually requires a post-graduate degree and confers much more status as well as a higher salary, a return airfare, holiday pay and other benefits. FTs earn considerably less than what an FE earns, i.e. 1,800-2,400 yuan per month instead of 2,400-3,000 yuan. Most foreign teachers are expected to teach between 12 and 18 hours a week, which sounds a light load until you find yourself with classes of 50 or even 100 students.

Council Exchanges in the UK, US and Australia runs a Teach in China programme for graduates. Placements are in secondary and tertiary institutions throughout China for ten months from August or five months from February. Programme includes compulsory one-week orientation on arrival in Beijing; total programme cost is £625 plus flights. In the UK, the details of Teach in China may be obtained by ringing 020-7478 2018 or by e-mailing TiC@councilexchanges.org.

Another UK-based programme is Project China (01273 775000/fax 08700 523487; scherto@projectchina.org) which works to promote cultural and educational exchanges between China and the UK. 30 native speakers are recruited each year to work at two partner schools in Beijing and one in Shenyang (Northeast China). The Buckland International Education Group (www.bucklandgroup,net) places graduates and undergraduates in various language schools in China.Obviously the highest concentration of English teaching establishments is in Beijing; try for example the Beijing New Bridge Foreign Language School, Chao Yang Qu Yong An Nan Li, Beijing 100022 (01390-117 3737/ www.newbridgeschool.com) which employs 40 graduates to teach.

Some US-based placement programmes to consider are:

Amity Foundation, 71 Han Kou Road, Nanjing, Jiangsu 210008 (86-25-332-4607; wwww.amityfoundation.org). Christian organisation that sends 60-80 people to teach English in China.

China Teaching Program, Western Washington University, Old Main 530A, Bellingham, WA 98225-9047 (360-650-3753/fax 360-650-2847; www.wwu.edu/~ctp). Up to 45 individuals sent to various institutions of higher education and secondary schools throughout China. Compulsory 5-week pre-departure summer training course in TESL, Chinese language and culture for candidates who lack TEFL training or experience, at a cost of $1,200.

Colorado China Council, 4556 Apple Way, Boulder, CO 80301 (303-443-1108/fax 303-443-1107/www.AsiaCouncil.org). 20-35 teachers per year placed at institutes throughout China, including Mongolia.

Global Language Villages, P.O. Box 163, Concordia College, Moorhead, MN 56562 (fax 218-863-7001; www.globallanguages.org). Visiting volunteers spend three weeks teaching in rural Chinese schools. Cost is approximately US$1,795 including travel from the US and full board and lodging. An allowance of about 2000 yuan ($240) will be paid in China.

IEF Education Foundation, US fax 626-965-1675/ mwurmlinger@ief-usa.org. Recruits mainly Americans with at least two years of college education to spend six months teaching English to junior high and high-school aged students in many Chinese cities.

WorldTeach, Centre for International Development, 79 John F Kennedy St, Cambridge, MA 02138; 617-495-5527/800-4-TEACH-O/fax 617-495-1599; info@worldteach.org/ www.worldteach.org. Non-profit organisation which sends volunteers to teach adults for six months in Yantai and runs Shanghai Summer Teaching Program. Volunteers teach small classes of high school students on summer course in Shanghai. Volunteers pay about $4,000 for airfares, orientation, health insurance and field support.~

Travellers in China have been approached and invited to teach English as Rachel Starling discovered:

Whilst travelling extensively in China, I was offered several opportunities to teach English. If you want a place just ask at all the colleges, as it is likely that one school or college will require someone.

With an invitation letter or fax from an official Chinese organisation, you should be able to obtain a long term work visa from the Embassy of the PRC in your country. One of the requirements is a notarised health certificate. The cost of a multi-entry visa for Britons is £60 for six months, £90 for 12.

TEACHING IN THAILAND

Bangkok and other Thai cities are a good bet for the casual teacher. Even in times of economic hardship, Thais do not give up on their English lessons. Yet the economic crash of the late 90s and devaluation of the Thai currency (the baht) preceded the departure of many foreigners, leaving teaching vacancies left, right and centre. Finding a list of language schools to approach on spec should present few difficulties. The best place to start is around Siam Square where numerous schools and the British Council are located or the Yellow Pages which lists dozens of language school addresses.

Another possible source of job vacancies is the English language press, viz. the *Bangkok Post* (with at least five adverts every day) and to a lesser extent the *Nation.* The noisy Khao San Road is lined with expat pubs and budget accommodation (where a room costs B50-80), many with notice boards offering teaching work and populated with other foreigners (known as *farangs*) well acquainted with the possibilities. They will also be able to warn you of the dubious schools which are known to exploit their teachers.

If the Siam Square schools are not short of teachers, which may be the case in the slack season, you will have to try schools further afield. Travelling around this city of six million is so time-consuming and unpleasant that it is important to plot your interview strategy on a city map before making appointments. It may not be necessary to do much research to discover the schools with vacancies. Many of the so-called back street language schools (more likely to be on a main street, above a shop or restaurant) look to the cheap hotels of Banglamphu, the favourite haunt of Western travellers in the northwest of Bangkok. There is such a high turnover of staff at many schools that there are bound to be vacancies somewhere for a new arrival who takes the trouble to present a professional image and can show a convincing CV. As usual, it may be necessary to start with part-time and occasional work with several employers, aiming to build up 20-30 hours in the same area to minimise travelling in the appalling traffic.

Among schools to try after arrival in Bangkok are:

American University Language Centre, 179 Rajadamri Road, Bangkok 10330 (02-252 8170-3). 200 teachers for 4 branches in Bangkok and 11 upcountry, mainly at universities.

British American, Ladprao Soi 58-60, Bangkok (02-539 4866/9; british_american2000@hotmail.com) plus 5 other branches employing 100 altogether.

ECC (Thailand), 430/17-24 Chula Soi 64, Siam Square, Bangkok 10330 (02-253 3312/fax 02-254 2243; jobs@ecc.ac.th/ www.eccthai.com). 500 teachers at 40 branches in Greater Bangkok, 20 elsewhere in Thailand. Prefer TEFL-certified teachers.

Fun Language International, 275 Lee House, 4/F, Thonglor Soi 13, Sukhumvit 55, Bangkok 10110 (02-712 7744-7; engisfun@loxinfo.co.th).

NAVA Language Schools, 34 Paholyothin 7, Phayathai, Bangkok 10400 (02-617 1391; navaoperations@nls.ac.th/). Experience and TESOL certificate not required. Pay of 26,000-29,000 baht per month plus other benefits.

Siam Computer & Language Institute, 471/19 Ratchawithi Road, Rajthewee, Bangkok 10400 (02-247 2345 ext 370-373/fax 02-644 6974; www.siamcom.co.th). Teachers for 35 schools in greater Bangkok and 38 elsewhere in Thailand.

Tourist destinations like Chiang Mai are very attractive to job-hunting teachers and opportunities crop up in branches of the big companies and in smaller schools, as Murray Turner describes:

I am working seven hours a week in Chiang Mai after arriving one week ago. I'm staying at Eagle Guest House (16-18 Chiang Moi, Kao Road Soi 3; tel/fax 053-235387) which is run by Annette who knows everything about language schools (and everything else). I found the job by hiring a bicycle and dutifully doing the rounds of the language schools, several colleges and two kids' schools. I took plenty of passport photos, photocopies of my passport and of my certificate from the one-week TEFL course I'd done.

Anne Kunigagon, the Irish woman married to a Thai whose Eagle Guest House is a great place to find out about the teaching scene in Chiang Mai (mail@eaglehouse.com/ www.eaglehouse.com), wrote at the end of 2000: 'There are still lots of paid and voluntary English teaching posts in Chiang Mai available; the language schools can't get enough'. She sent the following list of possible employers:

AUA, 73 Ratchadamnoen Road, Amphur Muang, Chiang Mai 50200 (tel 053-278 407/fax 053-211 973; aualanna@loxinfo.co.th). Teachers are given training in the AUA way.

British Council, 198 Bumrungraj Road Chiang Mai 50000 (053-242 103). Few vacancies.

Australia Center, 75/1 Moo 14, Tambon Suthep, Amphur Muang, Chiang Mai 50200 (053-276 269/810 552; austcent@loxinfo.co.th).

CEC (Chiang Mai Education Centre), Nimanhaemin Road, Chiang Mai 50200 (053-400 201/ CEC_e20@hotmail.com. Teach adults including business English. Also owns E20 aimed at university students (Sirimangalajan Road, Soi 7, Chiang Mai 50200; 053-895 202).

Nava Language Centre, Nimahnaemin Road, Chiang Mai 50200 (053-400 388-9)

YMCA Language School, 11 Mengrai Rassamee Road, Amphur Muang, Chiang Mai 50200 (053-221 819). Starting place for new arrivals.

Annette's general advice for the job hunt is to dress conservatively and cultivate a reserved manner: 'too many gesticulations and guffawing are not considered polite'. She is developing a volunteer programme called 'Helping Hands Social Projects' by which volunteers teach at a centre for disabled people, school for the blind, etc.

Outside Bangkok and tourist magnets like Chiang Mai and Phuket, there is far less competition from *farangs* for work, particularly in lesser known cities like Nakhon Sawan, Khon Kaen, Udon Thani and Ubon Ratchathani. For a job in a university you will probably have to show a degree or teaching certificate, neither of which will be scrutinised very carefully. The best places are Hat Yai (the booming industrial city in the south) and Songkhla. Hotels are always worth asking, since many hotel workers are very keen to improve their English. If you find a place which suits and you decide to stay for a while, ask the family who runs your guest house about the local teaching opportunities.

Sometimes the happiest and most memorable experiences take place away from the cities and the tourist resorts. Brian Savage returned to England after a second long stint of teaching in Thailand and describes one of the highlights for him:

> *My most rewarding experience was my week teaching English conversation in a rural high school in Loei province in northeast Thailand. These children had rarely seen and had certainly never spoken to a farang before. My work during that week and a subsequent second visit was really appreciated by the pupils. The first visit came about after I was introduced to a teacher at the Chiang Mai school where I was teaching. If travellers get away from Bangkok and the resorts, they too can have experiences such as this, especially in the friendly towns of the north and northeast. A little voluntary teaching can really boost the confidence of students who are usually too poor to pay to study with native speakers.*

In a country where teaching jobs are so easy to come by, there has to be a catch. In Thailand, the wages for *farang* teachers are uniformly low. The basic hourly rate has risen only very slightly over the past six years from B150 to B180 an hour though some decent schools (there are not many) pay B200-250. Company work pays between B250 and B450 depending on location, but the amount of in-company contract work has diminished since the economic crash. The norm is for schools to keep their staff on as part-time freelancers while giving them full-time hours; this is primarily to avoid taxes. Jobs that pay better often involve a lot of travelling, which in Bangkok is so time-consuming that it is necessary to work fewer hours. Most teachers conclude that it is just as lucrative and much less stressful to work at a single institute for the basic wage.

Alternatively, it is possible to work for no money at all. An interesting programme has been introduced by the Youth Hostels Association of Thailand called 'Giving English for Community Service'. Foreign volunteers with some basic English teaching experience spend three to five months teaching English to classes of low-paid members of the community working in tourism. In exchange for teaching up to four hours a day, they receive all living expenses including travel between the provinces in which they work. Details are available from the Hostelling International Thailand International Community Service Programme, Thai YHA, 25/14 Phitsanulok Road, Si Sao Thewet, Dusit, Bangkok 10300 (02-628 7413-5; senesbitt@hotmail.com).

Officially you need a work permit for Thailand, but the authorities normally turn a blind eye to trespassers. You will have to leave the country every three months to renew your visa; most choose Penang Malaysia for this purpose and many have done it four or five times. There is a fine of B100 for every day you overstay your tourist visa. With a letter from your school, you can apply for a non-immigrant visa, which is better for teaching than a tourist visa. It too must be renewed by leaving the country every 90 days for a fee of B500.

TEACHING IN SOUTHEAST ASIA

Indonesia

Most language schools in Indonesia (and Singapore as well) recruit only trained EFL teachers who are willing to stay for at least a year, though there are also many locally-run schools and colleges in Indonesia who are looking for a native speaker but can pay only a bare minimum.

Many of these schools were hit hard by the violence and economic downturn a couple of years ago. Some schools have been really struggling since their clientele, wealthy Chinese students, mostly fled the country. The most stable employment is in the oil company cities but opportunities exist in small towns too. At local schools unused to employing native speaker teachers, teaching materials may be in short supply. One of the problems faced by those who undertake casual work of this kind is that there is usually little chance of obtaining a work permit. It is also difficult for freelance teachers to become legal unless they have a contact who knows people in power.

Travellers have stumbled across friendly little schools up rickety staircases throughout the islands of Indonesia, as the German round-the-world traveller Gerhard Flaig describes:

> *In Yogyakarta you can find language schools listed in the telephone book or you just walk through streets to look for them. Most of them are interested in having new teachers. I got an offering to teach German and also English since my English was better than some of the language school managers. All of them didn't bother about work permits. The wages aren't very high, about 10,000 rupiahs an hour. It is fairly easy to cover the costs of board and lodging since the cost of living is very low.*

Indochina

The demand for English has exploded in Vietnam. Volunteers and teachers are needed in the private and public sector, especially in academic institutes. Demand is strongest in the south where most of the wealth remains. A number of joint venture and independent language schools have been opened in Cambodia and Laos as well as in Vietnam. Whereas the opportunities a few years ago were mainly voluntary and in refugee camps, there is now a booming commercial market supplying English language training. Many joint ventures require varying degrees of professionalism in their native speaker teachers. In the provinces, there is very little competition to meet the demand for English.

Murray Turner described the huge demand for English teachers he encountered in Cambodia a few years back:

> *In Cambodia they are so desperate for English teachers that I met more Dutch, Germans and Scandinavians teaching English than Brits or Yanks. Cambodia is one of the most beautiful South East Asian countries I visited and the people are among the friendliest.*

Wages for casual teachers are about $6 an hour in a country where you can live comfortably on $10 a day. Qualified EFL teachers can earn double that working for an established school like the Australian Centre for Education (PO Box 860, Phnom Penh, Cambodia; fax 023-426608). Tourists are given one-month visas which are non-extendable and in some cases stamped 'Employment Prohibited.' Those who want to work should apply for a business visa at the airport, claiming (for example) to be involved in some export business.

Matthew Williams visited Laos on one of his frequent visa trips from neighbouring Thailand and reported that the hourly rate was higher than in Bangkok (about $7) which goes a long way in a tax-free country where long-stay residents can rent shared houses for $80 per month. University College in the Laotian capital employs 25 teachers with a degree and a TEFL certificate (PO Box 4144, Vientiane, Lao PDR; 021-414873/414052; www.geocities.com/vientianecollege).

HONG KONG

With the birth of the Hong Kong Special Administrative Region (HKSAR) of the People's Republic of China on June 30th, 1997, Britons lost their preferential status. Like all nationalities they must now obtain a work visa prior to arrival if they wish to take up legal employment in Hong Kong. Without a pre-arranged job and a supportive employer, it will be very difficult to work in the former colony. Gone are the days when skilled Britons could find well-paid work in companies with relative ease.

However, it seems that the hundreds of expat bars and restaurants have not been able to attract suitable staff from the local Chinese population and there are reports that once again backpackers are finding work as bartenders and waiting staff, particularly at the Western-style bars in Lan Kwai Fong on Hong Kong Island. Some things hardly change and travellers are still gravitating to the Travellers Hostel in Chung King Mansions (40 Nathan Road, Kowloon) to find out about possibilities.

Regulations

British citizens do not need a visa to visit Hong Kong for up to six months. But if they want to take up employment or join a business, they will have to obtain an appropriate visa for which they will have to persuade the Immigration Department that they possess special skills, experience or knowledge of value to and not readily available in Hong Kong or that they can make a substantial contribution to the economy of Hong Kong.

Applications for an employment visa may be submitted through the applicant's nearest Chinese diplomatic and consular mission, where the visa application forms ID812 can be obtained. Alternatively, the applicant may send in the completed application together with photocopies of supporting documents directly by post to the Immigration Department, Receipts & Despatch Unit, 2/F Immigration Tower, 7 Gloucester Road, Wanchai, Hong Kong (2824 6111; enquiry@immd.gcn.gov.hk/ www.info.gov.hk/immd). The applicant is required to nominate a local sponsor, usually the prospective employer, to vouch for the application. The sponsor will be required to complete and sign a sponsorship form (ID428B) in support of the application. Each case will be considered on its merits. Visitors are not normally allowed to change their status after arrival except in unusual circumstances.

Teaching

The change in the visa situation has of course made it much harder to pick up easy-come easy-go English teaching work. Up until 1997, private language schools were happily hiring Britons with no teaching experience like Jane Harris who was hired without difficulty despite her Scouse accent, and was even paid quite handsomely (HK$230 an hour) for one-to-one teaching. But most employers will now be unwilling to risk the huge fines or threat of jail sentences if caught employing people illegally.

Another factor which has reduced opportunities is that Mandarin Chinese is now competing with English as the language to learn, and is seen as the more politically correct choice by many Cantonese-speaking Hong Kong Chinese. Yet the demand for English teachers remains strong and may increase as many state schools are obliged to switch from using English as the medium of instruction to Chinese. Many parents deplore this change and will want to ensure their children learn English by signing them up for private tuition. It is likely that private language schools will in time get into the habit of obtaining work visas for their teachers, just as happened in Taiwan a decade ago when the regulations changed.

One way round the problem of permits might be to go freelance. Freelancers tend to earn HK$150-$250 an hour, though fees can go as high as HK$400. As always, it is a challenge to find clients. Brett Muir from New Zealand suggests a cunning trick:

> *My recommendation is to hire a paging device (really cheap by the month – major companies have offices in the big subway stations) and write an attractive advertisement for placing in the letter boxes of the ritzy apartment estates in Mid Levels, Jardines, Lookout and Causeway Bay suburbs. Although the gates are locked, the Filipina maids are constantly going in and out, so you just walk in with them to post your photocopied ads. In this way you are always on the phone. Generally it is housewives and businessmen who are looking for conversation practice.*

Another way to attract clients is to put notices up in busy places like the chain of Welcome Supermarkets, though you will have to keep checking that your notices have not been covered up or removed by the store manager who has a weekly clear-out.

A government scheme to recruit qualified English teachers is administered by the Hong Kong Education Department (Expatriate Teacher Exchange, 13F Wu Chung House, 213 Queen's Road East, Wanchai). A programme is in place whereby Christians Abroad (see *Voluntary Work* chapter) supply English teachers (who must have a Christian commitment) to various organisations in Hong Kong.

Other Work

Anyone who is prepared to try to find an employer in Hong Kong willing to sponsor them for a work permit may be interested in the following advice. The job hunt usually starts with the two English daily newspapers, the *Standard* and the *South China Morning Post*, especially the bumper Saturday edition of the latter. Although the majority of adverts require fluent Cantonese, a few may not. Look out also for the free *Hong Kong Magazine*.

Most bars and restaurants will not offer work to people without a visa though as mentioned above there has been a slight softening of the attitude over the past 18 months. Of the many karaoke bars, raucous Australian swilleries, seedy topless joints or olde English pubs which used to hire foreigners on a regular basis, a number have closed and others employ only locals. On the other hand hotel and catering professionals might find legitimate long-term openings. For example the Royal Hong Kong Yacht Club on Kellett Island, Hong Kong has in the past advertised in the UK for an experienced sports club manager. (In the old days the RHKYC and similar exclusive clubs like the USRC on Gascoigne Road in Kowloon, KCC on Austin Road also in Kowloon and the KCC in Causeway Bay, Hong Kong Island were often looking for lifeguards with at least a Bronze Medallion, but it seems unlikely that those opportunities still exist.)

Secretarial and personnel agencies will be interested in you only if they are convinced you intend to stay about two years. Non-Cantonese speakers without visas will have difficulty in securing posts, though a high level of English is valued by many employers. Pay for secretaries varies from HK$8,000 a month at worst to HK$30,000 at best. A good English secretary with shorthand will earn HK$20,000. Hourly rates for temps are HK$55 for typists and HK$80-$90 for shorthand secretaries. Agencies to try are Sara Beattie Appointments for office personnel which in late 2000 moved to the Hennessy Centre (8/F, East Wing, 500 Hennessy Road, Causeway Bay; 2507 9333/fax 2827 0426; sba@sarabeattie.com) and Owens Personnel Consultants Ltd (1201 Double Building, 22 Stanley St, Central; 2845 6220; www.owens.com.hk) whose website lists actual vacancies especially in IT, finance, etc.

Trained nannies may find families willing to hire them though the majority of childcare is done by Filipinas. Babysitters are especially sought after December to February, the busiest time in the Hong Kong social calendar with Christmas and two new years.

Modelling agencies in Hong Kong may be worth seeking out, especially ones which supply fitting models, a vital ingredient in Hong Kong's fashion industry. They get paid about HK$600 an hour for trying on endless brands of shoes and garments. White-skinned, good-looking males and females (Eurasians) are often in demand by image-conscious advertising kings. Try Irene's Model Booking Service Ltd, Flat B, 14/F, Harvard Commercial Building, 105-111 Thomson Road, Wanchai (2891 7667/fax 2838 4840; irene115@netvigator.com) or check the Yellow Pages for agencies like Calcarrie's Ltd (25 Yiu Wa St, Wanchai; 2543 3380).

People who are able to pose comfortably with or without clothes on are needed as models for life drawing classes. The pay is HK$160-$240 per hour. Contact the School of Design, The Hong Kong Polytechnic University (2766 5474).

The environmental pressure group and charity EarthCare (PO Box 11546, Hong Kong; 2578 0434/fax 2578 0522; care@earth.org.hk) recruits 150-200 volunteers each year to work on green campaigns including protection of animals, animal orphanages, vegetarianism, etc. Very simple accommodation can be provided but volunteers must be self-funding. The minimum stay is a fortnight.

Film Extras

The Hong Kong film industry continues to crank out Chinese language movies at a remarkable rate. While the stars are invariably Chinese, *gweilos* (pale-skinned foreigners) are sometimes taken on as extras, often to portray villains, fall guys or amazed onlookers. Once again, enquiries at the Travellers Hostel may prove fruitful.

Carolyn Edwards is one in a long line who was invited to appear in a movie while staying at Chung King Mansions, though from her description it was never going to go to the Cannes Film Festival:

After I'd been there about a week, I was asked if I'd like to be in a movie – wow. The scene took place in a restaurant on Hong Kong Island. Work started at midnight and we worked till 9am. Make-up and costumes came out and I was done up to look like a high class prostitute. For nine hours we had to walk around smiling, drinking imitation Champagne and saying 'cheers'. It seemed to be very amateurish and was quite tiring. We were starving but never fed as promised. When we weren't needed for a scene we slept on the settees. Towards the end, our hair was looking messy and the make-up was all over the place but they still kept shooting. Eventually we were allowed to go and were paid HK$400.

Obviously Carolyn acquitted herself well in her role since she was offered subsequent chances, one of which included a kissing scene and another participating in an aerobics class, but she decided one movie was enough. As usual take a book or pile of post cards for the inevitable long hiatuses between call-ups.

Casual Opportunities

The entrance to the Star Ferry and the corridors of the Mass Transit Railway stations are favourite locations for buskers. Official hassle should be minimal as long as you don't block thoroughfares. Kim Falkingham recommends being able to sing some songs in Chinese. She looks back fondly on one listener who dropped the equivalent of £80 in her cap, but also remembers long days when nobody contributed anything.

Each spring the Sevens rugby tournament draws huge crowds and many temporary bar staff are needed for the long weekend. You get a commission for every jug of beer you sell and can drink as much as you like. Call the headquarters of the major breweries (Fosters, San Miguel, etc.) before the event. People are also hired to sell commemorative shirts and souvenirs on the streets.

For casual opportunities to earn £30 for an hour and a half's work dressed as a clown to entertain at children's parties, see if Mike Abbott Leisure is still around. In the old days he regularly hired itinerants as costume characters to entertain at parties, deliver singing telegrams, etc. The Disney Corporation may provide more regular work for people who like to dress up in costumes since they are planning to build a Disneyland in Hong Kong that will create 35,000 new jobs (and probably take business away from Hong Kong's delightful theme park Ocean World).

ENTERTAINMENT

Many of the opportunities like film extras, busking and modelling described above pertain to other countries in Asia as well as Hong Kong. Here are some scattered suggestions.

Hollywood does not have the world monopoly on film-making. There is an enormous film industry in the Hindi, Chinese and Japanese speaking worlds and it is just possible your services will be required. Foreign travellers lurking around the Salvation Army Red Shield Hostel in Bombay, the Broadlands Guest House in Madras, the main travellers' hotels in Goa, the Banglamphu area of Bangkok, Bencoolen St in Singapore, Malate Pension in Manila, or the 16th floor of the Chung King Mansions in Hong Kong (mentioned above) may be invited by a film agent to become an extra. Vaughan Temby and his two travelling companions spent a day in Bangkok working as film extras for which they were paid 700 baht, though they heard 900 baht is possible. They found this through the Pikanake agency (see *Modelling* below) which is a ten-minute walk from Khao San Road. It can happen anywhere and to anyone. Even the author of this book, while travelling in the Swat Valley of Northern Pakistan, had to disappoint a Pakistani film director also staying at the Heaven Breeze Hotel who wanted her to mount a horse and impersonate a colonel's daughter.

Bombay (now Mumbai) is probably the most promising destination for aspiring 'crowd artists' since every year 700 films are made in 'Bollywood'. The name John B. Francis is famous for acting as an agent and signing up prospective extras; he is a regular visitor to the Salvation Army Hostel (022-284 1824) on the corner of Mereweather Road and Best Street near the Gateway of India and the exclusive Taj Mahal Hotel. If signed up, you must take a rickshaw to the state-run Film City or wherever else in the vast city of Mumbai shooting is taking place. Extras are typically paid 1,000 rupees plus expenses.

Do not ignore other branches of the media such as television and radio. Often there will be English programmes in which you might participate, such as 'English for Today' on NHK, Japan's public broadcasting network. English language publications such as the *Korea Times* and *China Daily* are always worth a try. Aspiring journalists could try writing (but not about youth hostels) for some of the English language glossy business and airline magazines. For example the *Far East Traveller* published in Tokyo (which likens itself to *National Geographic*) pays from 20 cents a word or $45 a photo.

Although not very common, busking can net some worthwhile profits. With a borrowed guitar, David Hughes busked in the subways of Taipei which earned him £10 an hour tax-free. But there was a catch:

Things were fine until strange red graffiti appeared overnight near the spot where I stood. A man who 'represented' some people (gangsters? market traders?) told me to stop, or something might 'happen' to me. By this time we had just enough teaching to keep us afloat so I gladly yielded to his request.

Mimes, guitarists, dancers and musicians should go to Ginza in Tokyo or any Japanese city, especially in the evening. Once a few people gather, the Japanese herd instinct guarantees that the street will become all but impassable. Local taste favours old Beatles and Simon & Garfunkel songs.

Hostessing

The tragic disappearance in Tokyo of the 21-year old British woman Lucie Blackman in the summer of 2000 focussed world attention on the little-understood phenomenon of the 'hostess bar' which was where Lucie was working. Throughout the Far East, but especially in Japan and Singapore, there is an institution quite alien to the West. Hostess bars are patronised by big-spending salarymen who pay large sums for the flirtatious company and flattery of Western women, for titillation but not for sexual favours.

European hostesses in Tokyo tend to work at the more upmarket clubs in Ginza but also in the seedier Roppongi (there are an estimated 10,000 hostess bars in Tokyo alone). They are paid 4,000-5,000 yen (about £30) an hour from 7pm to midnight while earning various commissions on drinks bought by the client. In some establishments, huge bonuses could be earned by accepting an invitation to go on an afternoon date with a client and then bring him back to the club in the evening. It was on just such a date with a new client that Lucie vanished. Until her disappearance from the Casablanca club in Roppongi (which some think had yakuza or gangster connections), hostessing was considered a reasonably safe way to make a lot of money, possibly to clear debts at home or save up for further travels. Hostesses relied on their boss *(mama-san)* to keep troublesome clients in check. If the customer's English was limited, his drink intake excessive and his intentions not of the purest, the hostess knew she might be in for a miserable evening but not a dangerous one. It now seems that hostessing is not as innocuous as many thought. Media reports have uncovered several other cases of hostesses who have disappeared in the past few years.

Modelling

There is a demand for Caucasian faces in the advertising industries of Singapore, Thailand, Japan, etc. Interested people should get some photos taken back home rather than risk being ripped off by agencies which charge you to put together a portfolio and then don't hire you. When you arrive, register with one of the numerous modelling agencies. The daily rate is high (usually around £80), and earnings good if you average more than one or two assignments per week. Jaime Burnell couldn't believe how easy it was:

> When I was in Thailand, I was approached by an American scouting for white/blonde girls to have their photos taken for adverts. White faces sell in Thailand so even me who is not model material usually got paid for one day's work at a rate of 5,000 baht. It was all done very professionally and the photos are kept in a photo library for future use. As long as you don't mind it being used two years later in a soap commercial then go for it. That money let me travel for over two months with some left over. Scouts hang around Khao San Central Bar on the road of the same name.

Try to track down modelling agencies such as Kalcarrie's in Siam Square, Traffic Jam Model Management and the Pikanake Group.

Similar opportunities exist in Japan too. Again, you don't have to be particularly stunning, though obvious tattoos will probably disqualify you since these have connotations of gangster status. There are big agencies in Tokyo and Osaka; otherwise occasional jobs are passed on by word of mouth.

TOURISM

Brett Muir taught scuba in Phuket. Richard Davies funded his stay in expensive Singapore by recruiting travellers for the hostel he was staying at. Working as a croupier in Japan is said to be phenomenally lucrative because of the tips. Thailand affords the best chances as Vaughan Temby discovered:

> We spent a great Christmas on the islands and although we weren't looking for work, we did come across some opportunities. On Koh Samui several bars along Chaweng beach needed staff during the peak season. The huge Reggae's Bar Complex, a little further inland had at least four foreign staff. On Koh Pha'Ngan a friend of mine worked as a DJ and another as a waitress/kitchen helper in the excellent German-style bakery.

Later on Vaughan tried the hotels in Bangkok but was told that they had plenty of local labour and besides he would need a work permit.

Although jobs for foreigners on the popular island of Bali are scarce, you might want to consider extending your stay here as Jennifer and Eric did (which is perhaps more suitable for the *In Extremis* chapter at the end of this book):

> *We've earned several free week stays in 5-star hotels by pretending we were going to buy a timeshare. On crowded streets in tourist resorts, locals are employed to find western tourist couples and offer them a free taxi ride to the complex. One guy that picked us up told us what the qualifications are so we could get our prizes and he a $100 fee. One of the couple has to be over 30 and fully employed; you must have been living together more than three years and your holiday on Bali no longer than four weeks. We pretended we were staying at a more expensive hotel than we actually were. You fill in your ID and agree to listen for 90 minutes to their blah blah (careful, very tricky talk). And you get your prize, whether you buy their timeshare or not. I felt a little nervous though, in my disguise covering tattoos and dreadlocks, but we managed. We got the holiday, parasailing tickets and ugly white T-shirts. A week later we did it again for another company and have collected holidays in India and Aussie. Too bad you have to pay a $50 administration fee but you're still getting a week's stay worth $800.*

Throughout Asia, especially in China, there are many ex-pat run restaurants and hotels. Often these are the most popular places to stay since they are tuned into providing what westerners want. Tim Leffel thinks that it is almost scary how easily they can dominate the market. He goes on to say that anyone who can obtain a long-term visa through local loopholes or by marrying a local, might try to capitalise on this situation.

In a regime which cracks down on gum chewers and maintains urine detectors in lifts, as Singapore does, there is not much future in trying to look for work without a permit, even if there are occasional opportunities for film extras and bar staff. Make enquiries in the many travellers' hostels around Beach Road and Bencoolen Street or visit Holland Village, a favourite hang-out for expats.

Japanese ski resorts provide openings for people with 'a basic understanding of the Japanese language'. Rebecca Barber from Australia spent three months in the ski resort of Imajo, which was fixed up by an employment agency called Auscaddie International (30 Molesworth St, North Melbourne, Victoria 3051; 03-9326 9644/fax 03-9326 9655). Young foreigners were employed to operate the ski lifts, as waitresses, golf caddies and, as in Rebecca's case, in fast food restaurants. Food and accommodation were provided in addition to a good salary. Rebecca's skiing and Japanese improved enormously and she went home with a huge profit – she made A$6,500 in three months and spent little because most things were provided, including transport within Japan.

Another suggestion sent by Rebecca Barber based on a trip to Nepal is to volunteer to assist with one of the multitude of rafting trips which many companies run:

> *When I went on a rafting trip (which are fantastic but expensive by Nepali standards – minimum $200 for ten days), I met a guy who had just done two free trips as 'safety kayaker'. No qualifications were needed apart from being confident of your ability to paddle the river. When in Kathmandu, simply walk into every agency you see and offer to work. You would be unlikely to get full-time or long-term work but as a way of getting a few free trips, living at no expense and getting some great paddling experience, not to mention the chance of future employment, it's ideal.*

VOLUNTARY WORK

Many people who have travelled in Asia are dissatisfied with the role of tourist and would like to find a way of making a contribution. In very many cases this is laudable but naïve. It may be worth quoting Dominique Lapierre, author of *The City of Joy,* the bestseller and later a film which movingly describes life in a Calcutta slum. Although he is talking specifically about India, a similar situation exists in all poor countries:

> *Many of you have offered to go to Calcutta to help. This is most generous but I am afraid not very realistic. Firstly because Indian authorities only give a three-month tourist visa to foreign visitors. This is much too short a period for anyone to achieve anything really useful. Secondly because only very*

specialised help could really be useful. Unless you are a doctor or an experienced paramedic in the fields of leprosy, tropical diseases, malnutrition, bone tuberculosis, polio, rehabilitation of physically handicapped, I think your generous will to help could be more of a burden for the locals in charge than anything else. Moreover, you have to realise that living and working conditions on our various projects are extremely hard for unaccustomed foreigners.

As the director of a project working with forest tribal people in the Bangalore region of India wrote:

As our work is in a remote area with no creature comforts, it is not easy for foreign visitors to stay there and work, and therefore I suggest that you not mention us in your book as it unnecessarily creates false hopes in the minds of your readers.

It must be stressed that Westerners almost invariably have to make a financial contribution to cover food and accommodation as well as their travel and insurance. Some voluntary and travel organisations particularly in the US, can provide a more cosseted introduction to the business of volunteering, in Asia. For example Global Routes (1814 Seventh Street, Suite A, Berkeley, CA 94710, USA; www.globalroutes.org/college.html) offers 12-week voluntary internships to students who teach English in village schools in Thailand and most recently India (Dharmsala) for a fee of $3,950 for the summer and $4,250 at other times (excluding airfares). Placements in India with Cross-Cultural Solutions (47 Potter Avenue, New Rochelle, NY 10801; 800-380-4777) last three weeks and cost $1,950; volunteers join projects in the fields of health care, education or social development in Delhi between September and April. Yet another US organisation is Where There Be Dragons (1-800-982-9203; www.wheretherebedragons.com) which has a summer youth programme in Vietnam among others.

The main difficulty with participating in local voluntary projects (of which there are many) is in fixing anything up ahead of time. And even if you do, the project staff may not know how to utilise the energy of an inexperienced volunteer. Some programmes will seem to western eyes almost completely unstructured, so volunteers should be able to create tasks for themselves.

If you have not travelled widely in the Third World you may not be prepared for the scruffiness and level of disorganisation to be found in some places. If this is potentially alarming, try to find an organisation with an office abroad which can provide briefing materials beforehand.

India & Bangladesh

Several organisations in the UK send volunteers to teach English or undertake other voluntary work in India. For example *Teaching and Projects Abroad* (Gerrard House, Rustington, Sussex BN16 1AW; 01903 859911) arranges short-term teaching and other workplace assignments in Kerala and Tamil Nadu, South India for a fee of £1,700 including flights; *Travellers* (7 Mulberry Close, Ferring, West Sussex BN12 5HY; tel/fax 01903 502595; www.travellersworldwide.com) sends volunteers to teach conversational English (and/or other subjects like music, maths and sport) in India, Nepal and Sri Lanka for £925 excluding flights; *i-to-i International Projects Ltd* (One Cottage Road, Headingley, Leeds LS6 4DD; www.i-to-i.com) sends teaching assistants who have done a TEFL course to various projects in Madurai (India) and Sri Lanka. The fee for a one to three month placement is £1,295 excluding airfares. A technology and management training company in Bangalore which welcomes foreign students as interns is the Reach Institute (reachinstitute@rediffmail.com).

At an opposite extreme from a cushy attachment to a Bangalore computer firm is working for Mother Teresa's *Missionaries of Charity* in Calcutta. It is possible to become a part-time volunteer at Mother Teresa's children's home in Calcutta (Shishu Bhavan, 78 A.J.C. Bose Road), in the Home for Dying Destitutes at Kalighat and other houses run by the Missionaries of Charity in Calcutta and other Indian cities, but no accommodation can be offered. The work may consist of caring for and feeding orphaned children, the sick and dying, mentally or physically disabled adults and children or the elderly. To register, visit the Mother House at 54A A.J.C. Bose Road, Calcutta 700 016. Further information is also available from their London office at 177 Bravington Road, London W9 3AR (020-8960 2644).

Dustie Hickey found her brief time as a volunteer in India so affecting that she returned for an extended stay:

When I was in Calcutta I decided to take a jar of horlicks to the hospital. The nuns were grateful and asked me to come back the following day to play with the children. So I went, taking with me as much paper, crayons and sweets as I could buy from the shop. I spent the morning drawing with them and it was a moving experience. In the afternoon I helped feed the babies. The nuns had their hands full. They invited me to go down to Mother Teresa's home which I did and where I met her. After I'd returned to England, she wrote to me and I plan to return, perhaps to do an arts project with the mentally handicapped. I'd also like to take some of the children to local museums, zoos and gardens if it can be arranged.

As mentioned above, the visa problem can prove a difficult one for people who want to commit themselves to stay longer-term in India. If you do want to attach yourself to a voluntary organisation for more than three months, you should aim to enter India on a student or employment visa (see Indian Embassy website www.hcilondon.org). It is not possible to change a tourist visa to a long stay visa within India.

The *Calcutta Rescue Fund* (PO Box 16163, Clapham, London SW4 7ZT) works with destitute people in Calcutta, running street clinics, schools and training projects in and around Calcutta. For these they recruit volunteer health professionals. Occasionally other self-funding volunteers are recruited for a minimum stay of six weeks. For further information send an A4 SAE to the General Volunteer Co-ordinator at the above address.

Help is most needed during the monsoon. It is possible to slot in after arrival as David Hughes wrote from Calcutta:

While in England we answered an ad for nurses but there is an ongoing need for volunteers in the street clinic where the only skill needed is the ability to communicate in English and read doctors' handwriting (and that's quite a skill). Anyone prepared to give assistance can meet both new and long-stay volunteers at the Khalsa Restaurant (opposite the Salvation Army Red Shield Guest House) between 7.30am and 8am weekday mornings. It's quite hard work (mostly due to the heat) but it can be good fun. You see another side of India.

Another UK-based organisation *Indian Volunteers for Community Service* (12 Eastleigh Avenue, South Harrow, Middlesex HA2 0UF; www.ivcs.org.uk) sends willing volunteers on its DRIVE programme (Discover Rural India for a Valuable Experience). Volunteers start with three weeks at Amarpurkashi Polytechnic in Uttar Pradesh learning about development and then join a hands-on project in the region between September and March. Living expenses are around £30 a week. The India Development Group (IDG, 68 Downlands Road, Purley, Surrey CR8 4JF; 020-8668 3161; www.welcome.to/idg) runs a similar six-month programme in Lucknow for 5-10 volunteers concentrating on appropriate technology to support village life. Yet another organisation with a UK base is Student Action India (c/o HomeNet, Unit 20, 3-38 Dock Street, Leeds LS6 1JF; 07071-225 866; www.gn.apc.org/sai) which can arrange attachments to various Indian NGOs for volunteers to spend the summer or five months from September. A TEFL qualification would be an advantage.

An organisation which places graduates on a voluntary basis in educational institutes in South India is *Jaffe International Education Service* (Kunnuparambil Buildings, Kurichy, Kottayam 686549, India; tel/fax 0481 430470). Volunteers teach for short periods in English medium high schools, hotel management colleges, teacher training centres, vocational institutes and language schools in Kerala State and also at summer schools in various locations in India. As with all projects in India, no wage is paid but you are billeted with a family.

A community service organisation in India which sends self-funding volunteers to projects is the *Joint Assistance Centre (JAC)*, G-17/3 DLF Qutab Enclave, Phase 1, District Gurgaon, Haryana 122002 (0124-635 2141/fax 0124-635 1308; nkjain@jac.unv.ernet.in). The participation cost is $230/£125 for the first month, and $130/£70 for each subsequent month. Andy Green's conclusions about volunteering in India after a stint with JAC are telling:

> *I did two weeks' worth of workcamps and I feel that I was of no help to Indian society whatsoever. Due to differences in climate, food and culture, it is difficult to be productive. I could have paid an Indian a few pounds to do what I did in two weeks. It was however an experience I'll never forget.*

Dakshinayan (c/o Siddharth Sanyal A5/108, Clifton Apartments, Charmwood Village, Surajkund Road, Faridabad 121009; tel/fax 129-525 3114; www.linkindia.com/dax) works with tribal peoples in the hills of Rajamhal and nearby plains. Volunteers join grassroots development projects every month and contribute $5/£3 per day for their food plus a $50/£30 admin fee. In South India, the Center for Co-ordination of Voluntary Works and Research (9 Raja Design Nagar, Desurpattai Road, Gingee Villupuram, 604 202, Tamil Nadu) organises workcamps and longer term projects which volunteers can join for $150 per month plus a non-refundable $50 registration fee.

Many travellers to India stay at monasteries, temples or ashrams, which are communities for meditation, yoga, etc. There may be no official charge or at least a very small one, but it may be assumed that you are a genuine seeker after enlightenment. The *Samanway Ashram* (Bodh-Gaya 824 231, Bihar) has links with various educational and sanitation projects in the state to which it sends volunteers. *Bombay Sarvodaya Friendship Centre* (Friendship Building, Kajupada Pipeline Road, Kurla, Bombay 4000 072; 022-851 3660; daniel@m-net.arbornet.org) is another Gandhian organisation that suggests that foreigners seeking placement in rural areas (preferably long-term) should try to learn some Hindi, be willing to work in difficult and novel situations and have a strong interest in environmental and peace issues and social change.

One of the most famous utopian communities is Auroville near Pondicherry in Tamil Nadu. Volunteers participate in a variety of activities to reclaim land and produce food, and are charged anything from $4 to $15 a day for board and lodging according to their contribution. Information about volunteering is available from *Auroville*, Bharat Nivas, Tamil Nadu 605 101 (0413-622121; entr@auroville.org.in).

Laurence Koe followed up a lead he'd been given and visited a Catholic monastery in a suburb of Mumbai where foreigners were a real oddity. The monks generously gave him their 'deluxe suite' and full board. He tried to repay their hospitality by offering to work but all they wanted was for him to discuss the western way of life with the trainee monks whenever he felt so inclined.

An organisation listed by WWOOF (see *Agriculture*) is a botanical sanctuary in south India which accepts volunteers who are interested in rainforest conservation to help in the garden, kitchen or office and to do maintenance or landscaping. A minimum donation of £7/$10 a day is requested not only to cover food and accommodation costs but to support the sanctuary's work. Details are available from Suprabha Seshan or Wolfgang Theuerkauf at *Gurukula Botanical Sanctuary*, Alattil PO, North Wynad, Kerala 670644.

Environmental organisations are gaining strength in India and interested volunteers might try the *Youth Charitable Organisation* (20/14 Urban Bank St, Post Box No. 3, Yellamanchili 531 055, Vizag. Dt. Andhra Pradesh) which takes on foreign volunteers to work on soil conservation, irrigation and general community development programmes. Volunteers stay two to six months and pay 320 rupees ($7) a day. In the beautiful southern hill station of Kodaikanal, the local school for agriculture and appropriate technology *CLOAAT* has links with projects in the region and runs a new hostel for students interested in global warming and related issues (PO Box 57, Kodaikanal 624 101; 4542-30297; orkrisna@md3.vsnl.net.in). The *Devoted*

Organisation for Reforming Environment or DORE (196-b Khari Bazar, Ranikhet, 263 645 Distt. Almora, Uttar Pradesh; 05966-20458) recruits up to 25 volunteers to help in a range of projects including developing eco-tourism for between one and six months, usually over the summer.

A community organisation in the Himalayan foothills with the charming acronym *ROSE* (Rural Organization on Social Elevation, Social Awareness Centre, PO Kanda, Bageshwar, Uttar Pradesh 263631) can assist volunteers wishing to work with poor villagers, teaching children, carrying out environmental work and organic farming in this village in the Himalayan foothills. Volunteers pay £4 per day for board and lodging. To receive further details send 3 IRCs to the above address. Further details are available in the UK from Cwm Harry Land Trust, Lower Cwm Harry, Tregynon, Powys SY16 3ES (tel/fax 01686 650231). Originally from London, Heather Joiner wrote to say how much she was enjoying her time with ROSE:

> *I am a volunteer who is currently here working in the tiny school. I am also here at ROSE in order to improve my basic Hindi. In the morning we join the primary school children learning basic reading, writing and counting.*

Few opportunities exist in the restricted Himalayan state of Sikkim. One exception is to participate in a programme run by the *Muyal Liang Trust* at the Denjong Padme Cheoling Academy in Pemayangtse at the beginning of a trekking route. Information about placements as volunteers to teach English or other subjects for up to 45 days is available in the UK from Jules Stewart, 53 Blenheim Crescent, London W11 2EG (tel/fax 020-7229 4772; JJulesstewart@cs.com). There is the possibility of teaching for longer periods in neighbouring Darjeeling.

The *Bangladesh Workcamps Association* (289/2 Work Camp Road, North Shahjahanpur, Dhaka 17, Bangladesh; fax 02-956 5506; www.bwca.homepage.com) will try to place you on seven or ten day community development camps between October and February. The participation fee is $20 a day. They publish detailed camp information in English. Applications must be submitted at least by mid-September for autumn camps and by the end of November for January camps, enclosing a non-refundable $25 application fee. BWCA can also accommodate foreign volunteers on a medium-term basis (one to three months or more).

Sri Lanka

Short-term and long-term volunteers and interns can be accommodated at *Lanka Jatika Sarvodaya Shramadana Sangamaya* (98 Rawatawatte Road, Moratuwa, Colombo, Sri Lanka; fax 01-647084/ www.sarvodaya.org) to engage in social, economic and technical development activities in villages; and planning, monitoring and evaluation work at the head office in Colombo.

Samasevaya Sri Lanka (Anuradhapura Road, Talawa N.C.P., Sri Lanka; tel/fax 025-76266) invites volunteers to their rural locations. Volunteers can be used rather loosely for their educational and development programmes, though it is more akin to a cultural exchange. If the volunteer wants to stay past the initial month of their tourist visa, it is sometimes possible to arrange a renewal. The organisation provides simple accommodation in their office complex in Talawa or with local families. They expect a contribution of $3 a day for meals.

As mentioned above *i-to-i* based in Leeds has been sending an increasing number of teachers to Sri Lanka to teach in state schools and orphanages. To join, you must have a TEFL qualification (i-to-i run 20 hour courses for people with no previous training as well as on-line courses) and the ability to cover the training and placement fee of £1,395 as well as insurance and travel costs. Simon Rowland joined the scheme between school in Cambridge and university in York:

> *I am based in a private non-profit making English institute in a town called Binginya. The school, which opened 10 months ago, is run by a local school teacher of English. Additional classes were set up on my arrival for teachers and business people as well as children. The teaching is mostly enjoyable; classes are conducted purely in English except when they occasionally communicate in Sinhala, to my disgust and telling off. They are all willing to*

learn and, I like to think, have mostly improved quite a lot in the three months I've been here. The house I'm living in next to the school is wonderful, as are the meals which are brought to us from another house. The local people are all so friendly and falling over themselves to help me. I'd recommend rural Sri Lanka to anyone and think I've had a unique experience.

Despite reservations about the level of organisational back-up provided in relation to the high cost (for example Simon had no idea where he would be until he arrived in Sri Lanka), he had to conclude that without the UK agency i-to-i, he would never have been able to have the experience.

Interesting internships for people 18-25 are arranged by an organisation in Colombo called Volunteer International Projects (148/1A Kynsey Road, Colombo 7; tel/fax 74-720658; www.volunteerinternational.com). They offer a structured programme in the hospitality industry, business, conservation, teaching and so on. Participants pay between £1,000 and £1,350 for three months (plus travel). A couple of internship placements are available in the Maldive Islands for people fluent in French.

Nepal

Nepal is a promising destination for short-term volunteers and casual English teachers. Richard Davies came away from Kathmandu with the impression that anyone could get a job teaching in Nepal. He had made the acquaintance of an Englishman who had simply walked into the first school and got a job teaching children and adults. He was finding the work very rewarding, but not financially, since he earned less than £10 a month.

People who find voluntary openings in Nepal will be faced with a visa problem. Tourist visas (which can be purchased on arrival for $25 cash) are valid for 30 days whereupon they have to be renewed. This is straightforward for the first three months for a fee of $1 a day. A four-month visa can be applied for at the Immigration Office in Thamel, Kathmandu (01-470650). Normally these will not be granted unless the request is supported by an official organisation like the gap placement agencies which are very active in the country. People who overstay their visas have in the past been fined $4,000 or even put in prison.

Rachel Sedley spent six months in between school and university as a volunteer teacher at the Siddartha School in Kathmandu (arranged through the UK organisation Gap Challenge) and greatly enjoyed the children and the local community, but concludes that 'it seems to me unnecessary to come to Nepal through an organisation, since everyone here is so keen to help.' Rachel's main complaint about her situation was that she was teaching in a private school for privileged children when she had been led to believe that she would be contributing her time and labour to more needy children. While there, she met several people from various schools and orphanages who would love to have English volunteers.

A range of organisations makes it possible for people to teach in a voluntary capacity. No indigenous organisations can afford to bestow largesse on foreigners joining their projects, so westerners who come to teach in a school or a village must be willing to fund themselves. Of course living expenses are very low by western standards, though the fees charged by mediating or gap year organisations like i-to-i (whose new 3-month Teach in Kathmandu programme costs £995 excluding travel) and Africa & Asia Venture, as well as by Nepali agencies (some listed below) can increase the cost significantly. If you want to avoid an agency fee you can make direct contact with schools on arrival. Relevant organisations include:

Cultural Destination Nepal, PO Box 11535, Kathmandu (01-426996/ www.volunteernepal.org.np). Volunteer service work programme. $650 includes language training and homestay plus $50 application fee. Placements last 2-4 months starting February, April, August and October.

Global Action Nepal, Baldwins, Eastlands Lane, Cowfold, West Sussex (01403 864704/ chrissowton@hotmail.com). GAN is a charity which works in the field of education in Nepal, providing dynmamic volunteers to support village teachers in their work and also to improve school environments by building toilets, wells. etc.

Gorkha District & Educational Development Scheme, c/o Joy Leighton, Chairwoman – Fax 01277 841224; joy@leighton.org/ www.nepal.co.uk. Charity is always looking for volunteers to teach English to Nepalese school kids for a minimum of three weeks among other projects.

Grahung Kalika, Southwestern Nepal, Dol Raj Subedi, c/o Mr. Tara Prasad Subedi, P.O. Box 11272, Kathmandu (1-532674/fax 1-527317; mail@multcon. wlink.com.np). Volunteers are needed to improve the English of both pupils and teachers in local schools in Walling, a municipality in the remote Syangja District of western Nepal (260km west of Kathmandu). Volunteers must have an enthusiastic and inventive approach as resources are basic and teaching conditions challenging. Volunteers stay with local families for the duration of their placements (between August and May) and are asked to contribute Rs4,000 (US$60) plus a monthly fee of Rs3000 (US$45) to the host family for food and accommodation.

Insight Nepal, PO Box 489, Pokhara, Kaski, Nepal (insight@mos.com.np/ www.south-asia.com/insight). 3-month placements for all post A-level and high-school graduate native speakers of English starting February, August and October. Non-refundable $30 application fee plus participation fee of $800 ($400 for 4-6 week programme). Full programme includes pre-orientation, placement in a primary or secondary school in Nepal to teach mainly English or in community development projects, a one-week village or trekking excursion and 3 days in Chitwan National Park.

Kathmandu Environmental Education Project, P.O. Box 9178, Thamel, Jyatha, Kathmandu; 01-259567/fax 256615; www.keepnepal.org. KEEP sends volunteers to different trekking villages in Nepal to teach the English language to lodge owners, trekking guides and porters. Volunteers stay with a mountain family. Volunteers must be totally self-funding. Membership fee US$20; logistical support fee US$100.

New International Friendship Club, Post Box 11276, Maharajgunj, Kathmandu, Nepal; (01-427406/fax 429176; fcn@ccsl.com.np). 40 English-speaking university graduates placed in schools or colleges. Volunteer teachers should contribute $150 per month for their keep (unless they become a project expert). Basic Nepalese standard accommodation is provided and Nepali (rice-based) meals.

People's Welfare Committee, GPO 12137, Kathmandu, Nepal (01-412997; jbardewa@wlink.com.np). Volunteer agriculturalists and teachers placed monthly.

RCDP Nepal: Kathmandu Municipality, P.O. Box 14, Kathmandu (1-278305/fax 1-276530; www.rcdpnepal.com). Paying volunteers work on various programmes lasting 2 weeks to 5 months, including teaching English. Volunteers stay with families in villages.

Sermathang Project, 8 Milton Court, Milton Malsor, Northampton NN7 3AX (01604 858225/fax 01604 859323; businesslink1@compuserve.com/ www. yangrima.org). 12-16 volunteers (many in their gap year) are sent each year to teach at the Yangrima High School in the Himalayas. American and Australian volunteers accepted as well as British. £700 contribution to the school's running costs. Start dates in February, April, June and September. New project at Kakani Village School in next village whereby 8 volunteers teach basic English to primary aged pupils.

Voluntary Teaching Nepal: c/o Kamal Aryal, Sangam English Boarding School, Chormara Bazar, Tamsariya V.D.C., Ward No. 7, Nawalparasi District, Lumbini Zone (sangam_school@hotmail.com). Sangam school in Chormara, a village in the Nawalparasi district near Chitwan and the Narayani river, needs volunteer teachers to teach English (and other subjects). Qualifications are not essential but teachers must be able to create their own programme or methodology. Volunteers pay US$30 towards administration costs and US$50 per month to the host family for food and lodging. A registration fee of US$20 is payable in advance with the application form.

VWOP (Voluntary Work Opportunities in Nepal), PO Box 4263, Kathmandu (fax 1-416144; vwop2000@hotmail.com). Willing volunteers looking for a cultural experience can be placed in variety of voluntary posts including teaching English in schools, in remote areas of Nepal. No special qualifications are needed. Volunteers stay with a local family and contribute $50 a month towards their expenses. Registration fee of $20 plus placement fee of $400 must be paid.

Two US organisations of possible interest are:

Educate the Children, PO Box 414, Ithaca, NY 14851-0414 (info@etc-nepal.org/ www.etc-nepal.org). Volunteer positions in Kathmandu area schools for both experienced and new teachers. 3-month teaching internship programme runs from February to May. Small placement fee is charged.

Himalayan Explorers Club, PO Box 3665, Boulder, CO 80307 (888-420-8822; info@hec.org). Volunteer Nepal Himalaya programme in alliance with KEEP in Kathmandu (see above) sends volunteers to a Sherpa village near Lukla in the Everest region to teach English in villages. Volunteers stay with a Sherpa family. Departures are in September and February and programme costs are $150/month (excluding airfares). The HEC also publishes the *Nepal Volunteer Handbook* which includes possibilities for anyone looking to volunteer in Nepal ($20 to Club members).

Eighteen year old Giles Freeman from Australia spent three months in Nepal through Insight Nepal:

I would advise that applicants do have some teaching practice before coming. Classes easily reach 60 or 80 in many schools, making it necessary for the patient teacher to know what they are doing. With no teaching experience, this has proved a little hard, but it's a great challenge. All in all it has been extremely rewarding.

Southeast Asia

The mainstream London-based conservation expedition organisers all run projects in Asia. These expeditions are normally opened to anyone reasonably fit who can raise the cost of joining (typically £2,500-£3,000):

Coral Cay Expeditions, 154 Clapham Park Road, London SW4 7ED (020-7498 6248; www.coralcay.org) recruit paying volunteers, expedition leaders, scuba instructors, etc. for its marine conservation projects in the Philippines and Honduras. Marine expeditions cost from £650 for two weeks to £2,550 for 12 weeks.

Frontier, 77 Leonard St, London EC2A 4QS (020-7613 2422; www.frontierprojects.ac.uk). Places volunteers on 10-week phases on projects in Vietnam (and East Africa). Ian Wingate enjoyed his time in Vietnam so much that he joined the team in the London office after his expedition:

I joined Frontier as a self-funded volunteer and journeyed to the tropical forests of central Vietnam where I conducted biodiversity and socio-economic surveys. Frontier offered me the chance to gain practical conservation experience and the possibility of interesting employment afterwards. I learned a great deal about conservation in Asia and I also found out a lot about myself, my limits, strengths and weaknesses. Scientific experience or qualifications are not necessary. Higher value is placed on interest and determination.

Greenforce, 11-15 Betterton St, Covent Garden, London WC2H 9BP (020-7470 8888; www.greenforce.org). Volunteer researchers are sent to join biodiversity conservation aid projects on land in Asia, e.g. the marine environments of Fiji and Borneo. Projects involve studying endangered species and habitats. The cost is £2,350 plus flights.

Trekforce Expeditions, 34 Buckingham Palace Road, London SW1W 0RE (020-7828 2275; www.trekforce.org.uk). Organise and run conservation projects in the rainforests of Borneo. The expeditions last six weeks and are a combination of jungle training, adventurous trekking in the rainforest and conservation work. Each expedition's project varies and in the past has included work at an orangutan rehabilitation centre and construction of turtle hatching pens in one of the national parks. Help and advice on fundraising are given at introductory weekends and throughout.

Working volunteers are welcomed by Bob Tillotson who has settled in Thailand with his Thai partner Soo. After many years on the road (apparently he used the 1985 edition of this book in Taiwan), he is establishing a sustainable farm in northeast Thailand. Rob Abblett's 12 day stay here was his introduction to third world living and he left feeling exhilarated:

> *My home was a three-sided bamboo hut with mosquito net. When I asked where the toilet was Bob gave me a spade. He likes to give WWOOFers a project which they can accomplish before leaving. Mine was to landscape around one of the sunken ponds on the property, planting, watering and making winding paths. I'm fascinated with alternative technology and I really admired Bob's simple style of living. While I was there he put together a bicycle-powered water pump which would draw water from a well to water his vegetables. 'There must be an easier way' was all I could think whilst the stiff pedals sucked the energy out of my body leaving me drenched in sweat, 'an electric pump, Archimedes screw, another WWOOFer!'*

Bob has written to say that readers who are sympathetic to the aims of his enterprise will be welcomed for a minimum of two weeks though he can accommodate only four volunteers at a time. Interested people (non-smokers) should write to him for an invitation before showing up, enclosing an IRC: Soo and Loong Bob, 268 Thamafaiwan, A. Kaeng Khro, Chaiyaphum 36150, Thailand. Also in the village is another organic farming community run on Buddhist principles: Rainbow House (Barn Sairoong) also accepts volunteers to help with farm work, teach English to the children and learn about Thai culture (PO Box 7, Chaiyaphum 36000).

Most of the activities of NGOs providing educational and other assistance to displaced persons in Thailand are located at the Thai/Burmese border. Occasionally there might be opportunities for volunteers, including English teachers. If in Bangkok, contact the Catholic Office for Emergency Relief & Refugees (COERR), 122-122/1 Soi Naksuwan, Nonsi Road, Chong Nonsi, Yannawa, Bangkok 10120 (fax 2-681 5306; coerr@hotmail.com) which provides services for refugees and poor Thai villagers. One of its projects is to provide English language teachers for a refugee camp called 'Safe Area for Burmese Students' in Maneeloy Village, Pak Tho District, Ratchaburi Province, Thailand.

On the island of Phuket at the other end of Thailand, the Marine Biological Centre is studying and working to conserve marine turtles and runs a project on the island of Phrathong. Prospective volunteers can obtain more details from Chelon, an Italian research group active in the area (Viale val Padana 134B, 00141 Rome; +39-06-812 5301; chelon@tin.it).

Far East

The workcamp organisation in Japan has a reassuring name and acronym: Never-ending International Workcamps Exchange. It is probably not worth writing directly to Nice unless you are already in Japan (2-4-2-701 Shinjuku, Shinjuku-ku, Tokyo 160-0022; nice-do@po.jah.ne.jp/ www.jah.ne.jp/~nice-do) but via one of their corresponding agents such as Concordia or UNA Exchange.

An unusual opportunity is available at a farm in Hokkaido, the most northerly island of the Japanese archipelago, known as Shin-Shizen-Juku (Tsurui, Akan-gun, Hokkaido 085-12; 0154-64 2821), a place well known to the travelling fraternity. The owner Hiroshi Mine welcomes short or long-term international travellers who work in various capacities, especially conducting conversational English lessons in the community or gardening, in exchange for their board and lodging. Those who are prepared to stay for six months can take Japanese lessons and be paid a living allowance and receive a contribution towards their airfare. Australian, New Zealand and American applicants must be aged 20-29 and in possession of a working holiday visa. Others can come on a tourist visa as it is classed as voluntary work which does not require a permit. Mr. Mine organises the English classes, provides transport and some teaching materials. Much depends on the personalities of the other volunteers; whereas some travellers perceive it to be a wonderful opportunity and enjoy a warm atmosphere, others find the place bleak and exploitative. Judging from Joseph Tame's enthusiastic email received December 2000, he falls into the former category:

> Shin Shizen Juku provided a fantastic introduction to Japan. I was there with six other volunteers, all in our twenties. Japanese lessons were given, and the English teaching for local schools, colleges, evening classes, individuals, etc. was very laid back. Even an idiot could do it as it was almost entirely conversation. As it was getting pretty cold in early November, the gardening was quite limited but I can imagine that in the summer there would be loads to do on the huge plot of land. The building we lived in was a large 20-room dilapidated tin shack, but with numerous heaters and a wood burning stove it was quite cosy. The nightlife was great as a local family owned and ran (with the help of a volunteer) a restaurant which would frequently throw parties for us. Then we'd head for our local Onsen or hot springs to soak beside a vast lake of Siberian swans.

The WWOOF contact address in Japan is Glenn and Kiyoko Burns, Akebono 5-Jo, 3-chome 19-17, Teine-ku, Sapporo 006 (fax 011-694 2046/ burns@arabagu.com).

The *Korean International Volunteer Association* organises voluntary placements throughout Korea. Projects include teaching English at an orphanage for at least a month and working in sheltered communities. Details are available from KIVA, 1102 Sekwang B/D, 202 Sejong-ro, Chongro-gu, Seoul 110-050 (02-723 6225; info@kiva.or.kr). Another organisation that may be able to advise is G.V.S., Dae ha B/D 508, 14-11 Youido, Youngdeng Po Gu, Seoul (koreairs@soback.kornet.nm.kr).

The Middle East

The areas of employment to consider are English teaching, nannying or a position in the petro-chemical or construction industries (if you happen to have senior managerial experience). Trained and experienced nannies willing to live a relatively cloistered life should contact the major nanny agencies and check adverts in the *Lady* magazine. Nurses are recruited for Saudi Arabia by agencies in London, though working conditions are said to be much less satisfactory than they were in the past, with stories of wages being paid several months late. There is very little job security, even when you have a signed contract.

Oil wealth during the 1970s meant that many of the countries of the Middle East like Saudi Arabia, Bahrain, Oman and the Gulf states were able to afford to attract professional expatriate workers with superior qualifications and extensive experience. However the price of crude oil has been much lower in the 1990s and these same countries are no longer willing to offer expatriate packages on the same scale. Whereas a professional oil engineer would have at one time been offered a family villa, now the accommodation on offer is more likely to be an apartment. In fact most of these countries have been trying to reduce the number of foreign workers, which is bad news for all the semi-skilled and unskilled workers from the Indian Subcontinent, Philippines, Africa and so on. According to statistics published in *Overseas Jobs Express* newspaper, expatriate workers account for 61% of the work force in Oman, 83% in Kuwait and 91% in the UAE.

The country with the most opportunities for foreigners, both as English teachers and in other capacities, is Turkey. Despite its adherence to Islam, Turkey does not fit comfortably into a chapter on the Middle East; neither does it fit logically into a section on Western Europe (despite its rather hopeless aspirations to join the European Union). But whatever its geographical classification, Turkey is an important country for working travellers.

Countries in the Middle East vary greatly in degree of Islamic restrictiveness. Bahrain and Oman, for example, are favoured by British expatriates for their relatively relaxed atmosphere. Perhaps best of all, the United Arab Emirates are politically stable and can provide a pleasant way of life. Not long after arrival in the UAE, Philip Dray was optimistic that accepting a TEFL contract in Dubai was a good move: first-class accommodation in a luxury apartment complex, cheap shopping, etc.

Despite a fast-expanding EFL market throughout the region, there is seldom room for visiting job-seekers, since a tight hold is kept on tourist visas. It is essential these days to have an MA in TESOL or Applied Linguistics (or at least be enrolled in a distance learning ELT Master's degree) with at least three years of experience, preferably at university level. ELS Language Centers/Middle East comprises 11 Centres in the region which employ 20 full-time teachers and many part-time teachers to teach American English; the regional office is in Abu Dhabi (PO Box 3079, Abu Dhabi, United Arab Emirates; 02-665-1516; elsme@emirates.net.ae/ www.els.com).

Saudi Arabia is a very different destination. Women working in Saudi Arabia sometimes begin to feel that they are treated like prisoners. A further problem for females may be that their western style of dress and behaviour could be misinterpreted as loose by male Muslims and assaults are not unknown. Liberalisation is coming very slowly to the region and it will be a long time before women are allowed to drive cars, let alone function as normal members of Saudi society. If trying to fix up employment directly with a company in the Middle East, try to be sure that you have a watertight contract.

Lebanon is struggling valiantly to recover from its long and painful war, and is looking to a prosperous future in which English will overtake French in popularity, so it may be worth investigating possibilities there. Similar opportunities exist in neighbouring Syria where there's an enthusiastic demand for private tuition in English. The American Language Center (PO Box 20, Damascus; 011-333 7936/fax 011-331 9327) runs American English courses for adults, and anyone with a TEFL background has a chance of getting some part-time hours with them. Occasionally they run their own training programme for EFL teachers and they may also know of individuals who want private tutoring in English. Dan Boothby lived in Syria for a year and found that the best place in Damascua to look for rooms and job advice was Bab Tourma, the Christian quarter of the old city.

Many people consider Yemen to be the most beautiful and interesting of all Middle Eastern states, though the risk of kidnapping discourages many. Mary Hall worked for an aid agency but is familiar with the teaching scene:

There are more and more places teaching English here, the two main ones being YALI (Yemen American Language Institute) and the British Council, both of whom recruit mostly qualified teachers. The others hire any old bod who turns up, not many of whom are qualified TEFL teachers. Unfortunately they don't pay very well. If there is a Yemeni boss, the wages are even less and often not regularly forthcoming. I had a lodger who was teaching at one place for a pittance as the boss took money out of her wages to pay for her lodgings, even after she moved in with me. I think she was getting a couple of dollars an hour. This is something you sort of get used to. It can be very cheap living here, with rent about $50 a month or less if you're not fussy. The six-hour journey to Aden costs just $5. You can get a three month visa if you pay and are HIV-negative.

There is quite a thriving expat community so there are opportunities to pick up work there. Contact details for YALI are P.O. Box 22347, Sana'a (01-416-973/4; yaliroy@y.net.ye/ www.yali.org.ye). Another friend of Mary's (a qualified secretary) found work at the American School (PO Box 16003, Sana'a; 01-417 119; American@y.net.ye). One school which university graduates could try for teaching is the Modern American Language Institute (MALI, PO Box 11727, Sana'a, Yemen; tel/fax 01-241561; MALI1.edu@Y.NET.YE). Unlike most institutes in the Middle East MALI says it is willing to consider enthusiastic and adaptable graduates even if they lack an EFL qualification.

Few international voluntary organisations have programmes in Middle Eastern countries. However Connect Youth International at the British Council (10 Spring Gardens, London SW1A 2BN; 020-7389 4030/ www.britcoun.org/education/ connectyouth) sends young volunteers from England to teach English to teenagers at summer language clubs in Jordan and Macedonian (as well as Israel). Volunteers work for five hours in the morning for at least two weeks in July/August. Food, accommodation and insurance are all provided and airfares are subsidised. The deadline for applications is mid-March.

TURKEY

Teaching English

Turkey's ambition to join the European Union, together with a remarkable expansion in tourism since the 1980s, means that the Turkish middle classes are more eager than ever to learn English. The boom in English is not confined to private language schools *(dershane)* which have continued to mushroom in the three main cities of Istanbul, Ankara and Izmir. There are dozens of private secondary schools *(lises)* and a few universities where English is the medium of instruction.

Turkey is probably a good choice of destination for fledgling teachers of any nationality. Not only are there a great many jobs, but these jobs are often part of a package which includes free accommodation and free air fares (London-Istanbul) on completion of a contract. Virtually all of these employers want to see a university degree and a TEFL Certificate of some kind, preferably the Cambridge (CELTA) or Trinity (TESOL) Certificate.

Unfortunately a high proportion of foreigners who sign teaching contracts do not enjoy their year in Turkey. Bruce Lawson was offered an attractive-sounding job in Istanbul after an interview at a pub in Worthing, but two months later was very disillusioned, and his experiences are not atypical:

> *The contract I signed is a work of fiction that Tolstoy would have been proud of. When we arrived, the director changed our contract, denying us the 15% inflation pay rise in January, leaving us with a fixed lire rate for all nine months, when inflation was running about 170%. We were told that our accommodation would be 20 minutes from the school whereas it is an hour by public transport; we were told that the residence permit would cost £20 but it costs £60; the accommodation is a jerry-built apartment with inadequate heating (and Istanbul in winter is very cold). There are no cooking facilities so you eat out. Most people think Turkey is cheap, but a beer in the good areas is significantly more expensive than in London and you simply can't save on the salary. Private work (which pays up to £10 an hour) is prohibited in your contract, though many people risk it.*

Some in the ELT business are optimistic that the situation is gradually improving, among them a one-time Director of Studies at Antik English (address below):

> *I have worked for approximately four years in Turkey, in Istanbul and in a small remote town in the south. Prospective teachers always hear many horror stories about working in Turkey and to an extent they are well founded. In the past, schools and employers openly abused teachers' rights. But this is definitely changing. There are many good up-and-coming organisations that can be trusted. Teachers should ask around, be careful about contracts and conditions, and not agree to the first job they are offered without checking out the school, its size, reputation, etc.*

This may apply to the established chains, but there are still many dodgy operators and swashbuckling and unscrupulous employers. John Boylan sets out what you should look for when choosing an employer:

> *I worked at four different schools in Istanbul. You'll want a school that's professional (with good resources, support and teacher development), offers a good package (salary, accommodation, holiday entitlement) and has a*

timetable to suit you. Many schools like to boast about how professional they are and ignore their own faults. For example some provide a fake degree to a teacher with no degree, employ teachers without a degree, recruit travellers from youth hostels, fail to pay teachers, gossip about former teachers, and so on.

Although Istanbul is not the capital, it is the commercial, financial and cultural centre of Turkey, so this is where most of the EFL teaching goes on. On the negative side, there may be more competition from other travelling teachers here and also in Izmir than in Ankara or less obvious cities like Mersin and Bursa.

Without a degree and a TEFL certificate it will not be possible for English teachers to get a work permit and virtually impossible to get a residence permit. If working on a tourist visa, you must renew it every three months, either at the immigration office (where you will have to show that you have the means to support yourself; for example having a Turkish friend undertake to support you would help) or more usually by leaving the country and obtaining a fresh tourist visa, which costs £10 in sterling at the point of entry. If you do this too many times the border officials are likely to become suspicious.

Two key recruitment agencies are:

Turkeng Recruitment based in Antalya in southern Turkey (Ayanoglu Mah, 1284 Sok No 8, Varsak, Antalya (242-325 2662; fax 242-326 6778; turkeng@angelfire.com/ www.angelfire.com/biz/turkeng). This agency also has a UK branch at 3 Peck Close, Norwich, NR5 9NF (tel/fax 01603 747042). Turkeng recruits about 50 native-speaker teachers for schools in a variety of towns including Istanbul, Bursa, Izmir and Antalya. An application can be downloaded from their website which can then be submitted with photo, cover letter, full CV and two references. Turkeng interviews by telephone or in person. Most of their contracts are for 9-12 months. Work permits can be obtained both prior to departure and also once in Turkey.

Bosphorus Teacher Placement Service, Maresal Cakmak Cad. Incesu Sk., No. 22/4, B.Evler, Istanbul (tel/fax 212-551 0195/mobile 0 532 463 21 58; bosphorus@e-kolay.net or eslpositions@asia.com). The Recruitment Committee undertakes to find positions for native speakers aged 21-60 with a university degree and teaching certificate (TEFL, TESOL, CELTA, etc.) The typical package on offer includes one-way travel reimbursement, rent-free furnished apartment, free internet access and a salary of $950-$1,250 for teaching 100-120 hours per month. For the 2001 academic year, they claimed to have about 225 vacancies to fill.

Other organisations can place young people on summer camps in Turkey where the emphasis is on teaching English as well as sports. For example the Koparan Summer Camp (Istiklal Cad. No. 34, Bandirma 10200; 0266-714 1414; koparandil@ superonline.com) takes on 40 foreign young people to work from mid-June to the end of August at a purpose built resort on the Sea of Marmara.

For short-term opportunities, the Education Department of the youth travel and exchange organisation *Genctur* (Fahrettin Kerim Gökay Cad., Denizli Apt. 21/1, Kadiköy 81010 Istanbul; 216-347 8484; edu@genctur.com) organises summer camps for children where English, German or French is taught by native speakers who work for seven hours a day in exchange for free board and lodging. Pocket money of $100-$350 is also given according to experience and skills. Applicants must have some experience of working with children.

Among the main indigenous language teaching organisations in Turkey are:

Active English, Atatürk Bulvari 127/701, Selcan Han. Bakanliklar, 06640 Ankara (312-418 7973/418 4975; www.acteng.com).

Antik English & B.M.T., Istanbul Cad., Kirmizi Sebboy Sok. No. 10, Bakirköy, Istanbul (212-570 4847/fax 212-583 7934). 40-50 teachers for this and other Istanbul branches including ones in the Istanbul suburbs of Taksim (antiktaksim@hotmail.com) and Kadikoy.

Best English, Bayindir Sokak No. 53, Kizilay, Ankara (312-417 1819/417 2536; www.bestenglish.com.tr).

Dilko English, Hatboyu Caddesi No. 16, 34720 Bakirköy, Istanbul (212-570 1270; dilko@superonline.com). Branches also in Kadiköy, Besiktas and Saskinbakkal

(Bagdat Caddesi, Kazim Ozalp Sokagi No 15, daire 4, 81070 Saskinbakkal; 216-359 3365). Employs up to 60 teachers.

English Centre, Rumeli Caddesi 92, Zeki Bey Apt. 4, Osmanbey, Istanbul (212-247 0983; www.englishcentre.com). 50+ teachers, mainly British. Has branches in Ankara and Izmir.

Interlang, Istanbul Cad. Halkci Sok., Yalçinlar Han. No. 4, Bakirköy, Istanbul (212-543 5795/fax 212-542 7854). 40 teachers in 3 schools.

Istanbul Language Centre, Yakut Sok. no. 10, Bakirköy, Istanbul (212-571 82 84-94; ilm@ilm.com.tr/ www.ilm.com.tr).40 teachers for 4 branches.

Kent English - Ankara, Mithatpasa Caddesi No. 46 Kat. 3,4,5, 06420 Kizilay, Ankara (312-433 6010; www.kent-english.com). Employ 30+ teachers in Ankara and others in Bolu and Istanbul (Bahariye Arayicibasi Sok No. 4, 81300 Kadiköy; kent@veezy.com).

Childcare

Demand is strong for English-speaking au pairs and also among wealthy Turkish families for professional nannies who have studied childcare and child development. The following agencies make placements in Turkey:

Anglo Nannies London, 20 Beverley Avenue, London SW20 0RL (020-8944 6677; nannies@anglonannies.com/ www.anglonannies.com). Specialises in placing professional English-speaking nannies and teachers in Turkey. Support provided by Istanbul office: Bebek Yolu Sok. No. 25/2, Ebru Apt, Etiler, Istanbul 80630 (212-287 6898/fax 212-265 4340).

Anglo Pair Agency, 40 Wavertree Road, Streatham Hill, London SW2 3SP (020-8674 3605/fax 020-8674 1264; Anglo.Pair@btinternet). Nannies and au pairs (approximately 100) for summer or academic year. Qualified nannies earn £200-£300 a week. Agency has office in Istanbul.

ICEP, 2 Innes Lodge, Iglemere Road, London SE23 2BD (0800-074 6502; london@icep.org.tr). London office of Turkish organisation with offices in Ankara and Istanbul. Au pair in Turkey programme for 3-12 months. Minimum pocket money DM250 a month.

Solihull Au Pair Agency, 1565 Stratford Road, Hall Green, Birmingham B28 9JA (0121-733 6444/fax 0121-733 6555/e-mail: solihull@100s-aupairs.co.uk). Offers live-in jobs for 6-12 months or for the summer. A monetary bonus is usually paid at the end of a contract.

English-speaking nannies are all the rage among the wealthy of Istanbul and to a lesser extent Ankara. The high salaries quoted sound very attractive, though the life of a nanny can be frustrating because of cultural differences. Some nannies have had to get used to having their freedom and independence curtailed, and also the extent to which Turkish children tend to be spoilt and babied. But despite this, many have thoroughly enjoyed their stint in Turkey, including C. Martin who was placed by Anglo Nannies and who commented about some of the cultural differences:

> *Children are often idolised in Turkish famiies and are the centre of attention at family get-togethers. Usually you feel accepted straightaway even if people do not ask you a lot of questions about England. It's best to go with the flow. In Turkish (and all Muslim) culture, kitchen hygiene, child bathing and washing generally are very important. It is important to be flexible and open-minded. But the people are friendly, and working as a nanny in Turkey has been a good experience for me.*

One persistent problem is that it is generally not acceptable for young women to go out alone in the evenings. But Turkish families are normally very generous and allow their live-in child carers to share in family life on equal terms, even in their free time and on holidays.

Tourism

The main Aegean resorts of Marmaris, Kusadasi and Bodrum absorb a large number of foreign travellers as workers. Other places firmly on the travellers' trail like Antalya on the south coast and Goreme in Cappadocia are also promising; Heather McCulloch received three separate job offers in Goreme for the season after her visit, two in hostels and one in a copper shop. Antalya hostels regularly pay travellers $200 a month on top of a bed and one or two meals to man the desk or do other hostel chores. The best time to look is March or early April. Danny Jacobson met lots of foreign workers when he travelled in Turkey this year:

I would say Turkey is a hot spot again. I met loads of travellers working in the south and even in Selcuk. In Fethiye, Oludenez, definitely in Olympos, it was like an Aussie/Kiwi resort complex. There are so many of them working and travelling down there, the Turkish people have started talking English with an Australian accent. I heard the authorities are pretty lenient on giving out permits and that the ones who work casual just leave and come back when the tourist visa runs out. There was one shaved-head tattoo-artist dude working the bar at Oludenez Camping who'd been working casual for years.

As in Athens, Istanbul hostels enlist the help of touts to fill their beds, of whom Roger Blake was one. After a trouble-free seven months in crime-ridden South Africa, he fell victim to a common scam within 48 hours of arriving in Istanbul, leaving him with a travel fund of almost zero:

I found myself a job 'touting' for a new hostel. For this I got my accommodation and not much else (US$1 per person per night and 5% of trips and tours booked by them). I have been here for a month and have earned about 30 million Turkish lire ($80). This is not much considering the early start and long hours. In the mornings I'm at the tram stop; afternoons I go out to the airport and evenings are spent at the bus or train station. Whilst trying to entice potential customers, I was once picked up by the police who gave me a ride in their car. 'Work. Visa. Problem' they chanted. I insisted I had a visa. They drove me to my hostel and let me out, no questions asked.

'Help Wanted' signs can sometimes be seen in the windows of bars, travel agencies, etc. As elsewhere proprietors aim to use native English speakers to attract more customers to buy their souvenirs or stay at their hotels. In the majority of cases, this sort of work finds you once you make known your willingness to undertake such jobs. Roger Blake was given a few opportunities to be a 'lure' for those ever-determined carpet salesmen but declined, despite the earning potential in commissions.

Major Turkish yachting resorts are excellent places to look for work, not just related to boats but in hotels, bars, shops and excursions. (See section on Cyprus for information about Northern Cyprus.) A good time to check harbourside notice boards and to ask captains if they need anyone to clean or repair their boats is in the lead-up to the summer season and the Marmaris Boat Show in May. Laura O'Connor describes what she found in Marmaris:

There's a large British community living there, retired and fed-up Brits who have sold their houses, bought a boat and are whooping it up. There's plenty of work opportunities in the Marina, especially for boat painting and varnishing in April. Also girls can do hostessing on the boats. I was cleaning boats with a friend for enough money to cover my accommodation and evenings in the pub. Just walk around the Marina and ask.

Xuela Edwards also found opportunities in Marmaris but points out the down side:

Affordable accommodation is hard to find and wages are appalling. The Turkish work ethic can be difficult to handle too. Most Turkish businesses stay open from 10am to midnight, and much later for bars and clubs. You might not actually be doing anything but those are the hours. Turks have said to us that the English are strange because they always want to leave as soon as their hours are up and they want a day off. This is alien to the Turkish mentality which regards the office or shop as an extension of the home. Many other travellers we met also found the hanging around element frustrating.

Paying and accepting commissions is the traditional way of doing business and not regarded as ripping off the punter because these commissions are built into the basic price of everything. Therefore it is possible for talented salesmen/women (preferably multilingual) to make good money in Turkey.

Doing a complete season on a yacht can also be lucrative according to Juniper Wilkinson from Canada who was pleased with the C$7,300 she made in just two months, but who warns that tensions on board can become intolerable:

My experience of working on a yacht was one that I am still having nightmares about two months later. My boyfriend and I were very fortunate to get in the same boat while travelling through Turkey. It was a very well known vessel in the yachting world and we were told we were lucky. However the crew of ten - mostly English - were brutal (drugs, depression, etc.) Our hours were long enough (7am-11pm) but having to put up with the behaviour of some of the other staff was degrading. I got off the boat feeling one inch tall.

...and a lot richer. Despite her problems, Juniper says she would do it again but only after checking out the other crew beforehand. She wonders whether a smaller boat might be more conducive to peace of mind, though probably less money. If you can handle long hours, rich demanding guests and the politics of living and working with the same people for the whole four-month season, this is an excellent way to save a lot of money and see the Turkish coast.

Some UK tour operators hire people for Turkey. Sunsail Ltd (The Port House, Port Solent, Portsmouth, Hants. PO6 4TH; 01705 222325) has many openings for skippers, hostesses, mechanics/bosuns, dinghy sailors, cooks, bar staff and nannies to work in the watersports centres at Yedi Buku near Bodrum, Perili near Datca and a club at Marmaris. Applications for the summer season should be submitted by March. Similarly Mark Warner (61-65 Kensington Church St, London W8 4BA; 020-7761 7300) employs seasonal staff for their sailing and watersports holidays and beach club hotels in Turkey. Occasionally resort jobs are advertised on the internet; try www.summerjobs.com or www.overseasjobs.com where jobs as animators, DJs, instructors, etc. at resorts like the Aegean Holiday Village in Bodrum or the Hillside Beach Club in Fethiye may be posted.

Ian McArthur decided it would be an advantage while travelling in Turkey to be musical:

There is a great demand for musicians, particularly guitarists, in places where the 'Marlboro, Levis and Coca Cola generation' predominates. I have travelled around with my friend Vanessa and she has found work playing in bars in Istanbul, Marmaris, Olu Deniz and Patara (near Kas). Marmaris was the goldmine – £30 a night. The problem was that we both hated Marmaris – too many bloody tourists! In Patara she got a job in a bar called the Lazy Frog and played for a place to stay, food and of course beer.

Voluntary Work

The youth travel bureau Genctur (Istiklal Cad. Zambak Sok. 15/5, 80080 Beyoglu, Istanbul; 212-249 2515/fax 212-249 2554; workcamps.in@genctur.com) runs 30 international workcamps for manual and social projects as well as acting as a youth and student travel bureau and co-ordinating summer camps (separate office listed under 'Teaching' above). Recruitment of volunteers for the fortnight long camps takes place through all the major workcamp organisations in the UK and worldwide. Full board and accommodation are provided in return for six hours of work six days per week. Most camps take place in small villages or towns where the traditional way of life persists. An optional three-day orientation takes place in Istanbul before the camps begin for a fee of 100 Deutsch Marks.

On most camps you will have to work reasonably hard in the hot sun (and wear long sleeves and jeans in deference to Muslim customs). Mary Jelliffe recounts her experiences in Turkey:

I applied to UNA (Wales) quite late (in May/June) and heard from Turkey just one week before my camp commenced in August. My workcamp, which consisted of digging an irrigation canal from the nearby hills to the village, took place in Central Anatolia. I was told that our camp was the most easterly, since the majority are in Western Turkey. Conditions in this remote village were fairly primitive. We lived in a half-built school-room sleeping on the floor and sharing the daily duties of collecting water and sweeping out the scorpions from under the sleeping bags. The Turkish volunteers were a great asset to the camp: through them we could have far more contact with the villagers and learn more about Turkish culture in general. In fact I later stayed in Istanbul and Izmir with two of the women volunteers I'd met on the camp.

Conservation projects are run by Ottoman & Ottoman (Gaziosmanpasa Bulvari No. 9, Esen Han Kat: 5/506, 35210 Izmir; 232-445 0599/ ottomanyouth@superonline.com). Volunteers assist university scientists on various wildlife projects like turtle and bird protection in coastal areas. Tented or bungalow accommodation is provided; volunteers must arrange their own travel and be self-catering.

IN EXTREMIS

The best protection against getting into serious difficulties is to have a good insurance policy (see *Introduction*). Some student cards include access to an emergency helpline. For example the Under 26 card (part of a Europe-wide network of youth cards known as Euro 26) includes among its benefits a 'Travel Helpline' telephone number that can answer specific queries and offer advice (legal, financial, etc.) in a crisis abroad. This costs £7 and does not in any way replace the need for insurance. Details from Under 26, 52 Grosvenor Gardens, London SW1W 0AG (020-7823 5363). The counterpart for Americans under 26 is the Council Youth Card (ring 800-GET-AN-ID) which costs $22 a year and provides minimal insurance cover (including medical evacuation).

If you do end up in dire financial straits and for some reason do not have or cannot use a credit card, you should contact someone at home who is in a position to send money.

Transferring Money

If you run out of money abroad, whether through mismanagement, loss or theft, you may contact your bank back home (by telephone, fax or telegram), and ask them to wire money to you. This can only be done through a bank in the town you're in – something you have to arrange with your own bank, so you know where to pick the money up. Money can also be transferred by postal money orders or girocheques to bank accounts abroad. This is most useful when you want to transfer money home to your own bank account; you will need the bank sort code, a cheque card and cheque book. Expect to pay £15-£20 each time.

Western Union, a long-established American company, offers an international money transfer service whereby cash deposited at one branch (by, say, your mum) can be withdrawn by you from any other branch or agency, which your benefactor need not specify. Western Union agents come in all shapes and sizes (e.g. travel agencies, stationers, chemists). Unfortunately it is not well represented outside the developed world. The person sending money to you simply turns up at a Western Union counter, pays in the desired sum plus the fee, which is £8 for up to £25 transferred, £21 for £100-200, £37 for £500 and so on. For an extra £7 your benefactor can do this over the phone with a credit card. In the UK, ring 0800-833833 for further details, a list of outlets and a complete rate schedule.

Thomas Cook, American Express and the Post Office offer a similar service called Moneygram. Cash deposited at one of their foreign exchange counters is available within ten minutes at the named destination or can be collected up to 45 days later. The fee for sending £500 (for example) is £33. Ring 0800 897198 for details. A slightly slower but cheaper system is Thomas Cook's Priority Payment.

Barclaycard holders are entitled to make use of their 24-hour International Rescue service which covers a myriad of disasters including theft of money, tickets and cards, legal problems and medical emergencies. Customers of Barclays can use its Priority International Payment (PIP) to send cash to banks worldwide. The fee is £35 and the sender needs to quote the recipient's passport number.

US citizens can ring the Overseas Citizen Service (202-647-5225), part of the State Department, which can wire cash from someone at home to any US embassy for a fee of $25.

One way of getting money which will not inconvenience the folks back home works best for those who know in advance where they will be when they run out of money. Before setting off, you open an account at a large bank in your destination city, which may have a branch in London. Most won't allow you to open a chequing account so instant overdrafts are not a possibility. But knowing you have a few hundred pounds waiting for you in Sydney, San Francisco or Singapore is a great morale booster.

Embassies & Consulates

Your consulate can help you get in touch with friends and relations if necessary, normally by arranging a reverse charge call. According to the Foreign & Commonwealth Office leaflet *Backpackers and Independent Travellers,* Consulates have the authority to cash a personal cheque to the value of £100 supported by a valid banker's card. But do not pin too much faith in your consulate. When Jane Roberts turned to the British Consulate in Toronto after having all her money stolen, they just preached at her about how she should have thought about all this before she left home.

If you are really desperate and can find no one at home or among your fellow travellers willing to lend you some money, you may ask your consulate to repatriate you by putting you on the first train or airplane heading for your home destination. If they do this your passport will be invalidated until the money is repaid. In fact permission is very rarely granted these days because of the thousands of unpaid debts incurred by indigent travellers; for example there were less than 100 repatriations to the UK in total last year. A British consular official advised us that in the 18 months she worked in India, only two repatriations were approved, despite the queues of desperate people. Deportation is another way of getting home which is best avoided. Although you will be transported at the expense of the government which has decided that you are an undesirable alien, there will be a black mark in your passport for a specified number of years.

The Foreign and Commonwealth Office of the British government makes available travel advice and warnings about potential trouble spots; ring 020-7008 0232/3; fax 020-7008 0155 or check the website www.fco.gov.uk/travel. In September 2000, the government proposed to introduce a new service FCO Direct which would be a 24-hour telephone helpline for use by any Briton who has been robbed, arrested or struck ill. In the US the State Department's Hotline can be reached on 202-647-5225. American citizens may request copies of official Travel Warnings and Public Announcements (the latter cover short term potential dangers to American travellers such as coups or terrorist activity) by writing to the Department of State Office of American Citizens Service, Room 4811, Washington, DC 20520 (www. travel.state.gov/travel_warnings.html).

Legal Problems

Everyone has heard hair-raising stories about conditions in foreign prisons, so think very carefully before engaging in illegal activities. Currently, 2350 Britons are held in foreign prisons, half on drugs charges.If you do have trouble with the law in foreign countries, remain calm and polite, and demand an immediate visit from your Consul. He can at least recommend a local lawyer and interpreter if necessary. Britons should contact Prisoners Abroad (89-93 Fonthill Road, Finsbury Park, London N4 3JH; 020-7561 6820/www.prisonersabroad.org.uk) and Americans should try the International Legal Defence Counsel (1429 Walnut Street, Philadelphia, Pennsylvania 19102; 215-977-9982). Any travellers who would like to visit prisoners should contact these organisations for details, since many prisoners go years without a visit.

Dire Straits

Try not to be too downcast if destitution strikes. Elma Grey had been looking forward to leaving Greece and rejoining her old kibbutz, but she was unexpectedly turned away from the ferry because of her dire shortage of funds. She describes the 'worst down' of her travels:

Back to the Athens hotel where I'd spent the previous evening, feeling utter despair. But I found that other people's problems have an incredible way of bringing out the best in total strangers. Everyone I came into contact with was full of sympathy, advice and practical suggestions regarding possible sources of work. And quite apart from this, the feeling of much needed moral support was probably what got me through the whole thing without my degenerating into a miserable heap. Although I'd never want to feel so stranded and desperate again, in a way it was all worth it just to experience the unique feeling of just how good fellow travellers can be in a crisis.

Several travellers have insisted that when you get down to your last few dollars/pesos/marks, it is much wiser to spend them in a pub buying drinks for the locals who might then offer useful assistance than it is to spend the money on accommodation or food. David Irvine found himself in Tasmania with just $10 in his pocket. He walked into a pub and bet two men $20 each that he could drink a yard of ale, a feat he was fairly confident that he could accomplish.

Less than 24 hours after Ilka Cave from South Africa arrived in Tel Aviv, all her luggage, money and documents were stolen. One of the girls in the hostel suggested that she contact an au pair agency and soon she was living with a nice family and earning a salary. Michel Falardeau wanted to live rent-free in Sydney, so he offered his assistance to a number of charities, one of which gave him a place to live. Mark Horobin was down to his bottom dollar in San Diego and queued up outside the Rescue Mission. Several days later he had signed on as a kitchen helper and stayed for some time.

For information about potential health risks, see the *Introduction*. It is to be hoped that you will avoid the kind of disaster which will require the services of a lawyer, doctor or consul abroad. If you find yourself merely running short of funds, you might be interested in some of the following titbits of information, intended for entertainment as much as for practical advice.

HELP. Look out for churches that conduct services in English: the priest or vicar should be able to give you useful advice and often practical help. But be cautious about accepting help from fringe religious groups – it can be easier to accept shelter from the Moonies or the Children of God than to leave.

You can cast yourself on the mercy of strangers wherever you are. Joe Warnick from the States was glad he'd asked a simple favour in Germany:

I stood on a ramp to the Autobahn as car after car sped by, until darkness surrounded me. I was very thirsty so I approached a nearby home to ask for water. They not only offered me water, but also a place to pitch my tent and a delicious dinner. After a big breakfast the next day, they gave me a ride to a truck stop.

NIGHT SHELTERS. Most large towns and some railway stations in Western Europe and North America have a night shelter run by the Catholic organisation Caritas, the Salvation Army or similar which provides basic but free food and accommodation. They want to help genuine vagrants, not freeloading tourists, so you must appear genuinely impoverished or a potential convert. You can find out where to find these hostels by asking around – any policeman on the night beat should be able to help you. Be warned that many of these organisations are run by religious movements, and you may be expected to show your gratitude by joining in worship.

MONASTERIES & NUNNERIES. Monastic communities often extend hospitality to indigent wayfarers. Sometimes it is freely given but try to be sensitive as to whether or not a small donation is expected.

JAIL. Travellers have on occasion found a free bed for the night by asking at police stations if there are any spare cells. According to US law, all people (including non-citizens) have the right to demand protective custody. You are most likely to be successful (and escape unharmed) in peaceful country towns: the police may have other uses for their cells on a Saturday night in Glasgow or Miami.

SLEEPING OUT. It is illegal to sleep out on private property without the landowner's permission (except in Sweden); most farmers will grant their permission if you ask politely and look trustworthy. In cities try public parks and also railway or coach stations, though you may be asked for an onward ticket. Nicola Hall tries to camp discreetly near a proper campsite so that she can make use of the toilet and shower block. Ian Moody tried to avoid sleeping out on private property in Spain and one night chose a seemingly ideal shelter, a concrete covered ditch. At about 5am he was rudely awakened by a torrent of water which swept away his gear and nearly drowned him. Many people sleep on beaches; beware of early morning visits from the local constabulary and also large vacuum machines. Jonathan Galpin finds a mosquito net invaluable, not only as protection against biting insects but (when doubled over) from falling dew.

SQUATTING. Half-finished buildings usually provide enough shelter for a comfortable, uninterrupted kip. Robin Gray recommends garden huts in large garden centres which are often left open and provide a good night's shelter. Your luggage can be safely stowed in a locker at the station during the day.

FREE MEALS. Hare Krishna have free or heavily subsidised vegetarian restaurants and take-away temples in every major city from Mexico City to Manchester. You may have to endure some minor attempts to convert you. Their food is excellent. Sometimes charities such as the Red Cross give out free food, as David Bamford discovered when he was stranded in Villefranche unable to find a grape-picking job, along with scores of North Africans.

Restaurants may be willing to give you a free meal if you promise to recommend them to a guide book or correct the spelling on their menu (depriving future travellers of the delights of 'miscellaneous pork bowel', 'grilled chicken with swing' and 'vegetable craps'). It may also be possible to do an hour's work in exchange for a meal by going to the back door, possibly at fast food outlets. Some will even give a hand-out if you are brazen enough to request one. When Safra Wightman had no money and no food in Tel Aviv, she offered to give the man at a sandwich stand a ring as security against future payment of two rolls. When she returned with the money to reclaim her ring she could see that the stone had been removed to find out if it was valuable (which it wasn't), so only trade something valueless.

BUFFET RESTAURANTS. In some countries like Sweden, the USA and Australia, reasonable restaurants offer all-you-can-eat buffets. Diners have been known to share their second and third helpings with friends who have merely bought a soft drink.

FREE WINE. You may come across free tastings at the roadside in wine producing areas from California to France (where these tastings are called *dégustations)*. There will sometimes be something to eat – perhaps bread and cheese, or a local speciality.

FACTORY TOURS. Ask tourist offices if there are any food or drink factories nearby that offer free guided tours; these tours normally end with the gift of free samples of whatever is being produced. For example, distilleries in Scotland hand out miniature bottles of whisky, and Kelloggs in North America provide a selection of miniature packets of cereal. Breweries are famous for their hospitality – try Heineken in Amsterdam or Castlemaine XXXX in Brisbane. (Guinness in Dublin charges admission.)

FREE SAMPLES. Look out for demonstrations promoting new foods or gadgets in supermarkets and department stores. This was another of Safra Wightman's survival tips in Israel:

> *In supermarkets it's acceptable to taste the pick'n'mix ranges from dried fruit and nuts to chocolate, sweets, olives, pretzels, etc. On several occasions my boyfriend and I stood for ten minutes 'tasting' then bought two apples on our way out. Everybody including Israelis does the same.*

HAPPY HOURS. To attract customers at off-peak times, bars and pubs sometimes offer free snacks as well as cut-price drinks.

FAIRS AND FESTIVALS. Watch for giveaways at annual fairs and festivals. To take just one example in Italy, there are often free snacks at *sagra* (fairs). For example at *rustida* near Rimini, a payment of 5,000 lire entitles you to an unlimited number of refills of wine.

SCAVENGING FOOD. If you are not too fussy about what you eat you can look for stale or sub-standard food that has been discarded by shops, market stalls or even restaurants. This is especially worth doing around supermarkets in America, where a large quantity of perfectly acceptable food is thrown out after it reaches its 'sell by' date. Fancy resort hotels are also prone to throw out good food on a regular basis. Julian Peachey and many others camping at Eilat dined like kings out of the Club Med skips. While no one he knew suffered any ill effects, the residents of a local 4-star hotel all came down with salmonella.

SELF SERVICE RESTAURANTS. The publisher of this book had an odd experience in a huge New York self-service restaurant. Having eaten his Waldorf salad he went to the water fountain for a drink. On returning to his table to conclude his repast he found a tramp-like character busily wolfing down the much anticipated apple pie: the unwanted guest promptly fled. On leaving the self-service emporium the victim spotted the culprit peering through the plate glass window with several pals, in search of customers who left their tables leaving uneaten remains still on the table.

CASINOS. Large casinos often put on a lavish spread in the staff canteen. Assuming the staff is large and changeable enough, it may be possible to infiltrate it on an occasional basis for a good binge. Paul Edwards has happy memories of the seven cuisines served to staff at the Crown Casino in Melbourne (see Australia chapter). Casinos from Istanbul to Las Vegas are also known to hand round free snacks to punters who may not be required to spend much money.

SOB STORIES. On several occasions David Bamford's account of being mugged was received very sympathetically, once at a police station in Holland where he was fed and a night's free bed and breakfast was arranged. Another penniless student (in Sweden) obtained a police statement that he had been robbed, which he used to wheedle money out of people. Abusing people's kindness is, however, not generally recommended. A well known scam in Greek tourist resorts and elsewhere is for someone claiming to be deaf to sell trinkets or stuffed toys table-to-table in restaurants.

BEGGING. Straightforward begging is normally humiliating, boring, unprofitable and illegal. The best way of achieving results is to make yourself so unbearable that people will pay you to go away – for example, two people impersonating a lunatic and his keeper around the cafés of Paris, would be soon bribed to go away by pleasure-seeking Parisians and tourists.

BEACHCOMBING. Beaches are a good place to look for lost property. After a storm in Greece, Sarah Clifford went beachcombing and found a gold necklace worth £150. A metal detector can be a valuable ally.

CLAIMING DEPOSITS. In Denmark, Sweden, Mexico, France, Spain, Italy, Australia, the US and many other countries you can earn some small change by taking wine, beer and coke bottles or aluminium cans for recycling back to shops for a refund of the deposit. It is best to look for bottles or cans after a beach party, a special event such as a festival or in the dustbins outside holiday villas early in the mornings.

PUBLIC TELEPHONES. In Austria, Spain and many other countries you have to insert money in a telephone before you dial a number, you then have to press a button to get a refund if you are not connected. It is always worth pressing this button when you pass a call box in case someone has forgotten to do this – the banks of telephones in railways stations are particularly recommended.

RECLAIMING PURCHASE TAX. Some large shops in Britain, Denmark, Switzerland, Finland and Italy have special arrangements which allow foreigners to reclaim local purchase tax on goods which they plan to take out of the country. You can profit from this by looking for a local who is considering an expensive and portable purchase such as a video recorder: arrange to buy it for him and reclaim the tax, then split the difference in price. When you buy the recorder you will be given a form to be stamped by the customs when you take it out of the country. Get this stamp, wait for the shift to change, and then re-import the recorder.

BOOKS OF TICKETS. You can buy a *carnet* of ten Metro tickets in Paris at two-thirds the price of buying the tickets singly, then sell the individual tickets to travellers, splitting the difference in cost. You may even get the full face value from busy commuters who don't want to queue for tickets at rush hour. Another trick is to buy group tickets for cable car rides in Switzerland at a substantial discount on the price of buying the tickets individually. For example the journey up Mount Titlis in Engelberg, Switzerland costs twice as much for a single traveller as for a group member ticket. You can then sell these tickets separately to individual travellers at less than the full rate. This has a better chance of success than selling single Metro tickets, since people will want to travel only once.

POSTCARDS. Tourists on beaches and in bars are often happy to pay over the odds for properly pre-stamped postcards and a pen with which to write them.

TRICKS AND SKILLS. If you know that you can drink a yard of ale, juggle four plates or smoke 27 cigars simultaneously, you might find people willing to have a sporting bet with you. For more ideas on this subject see the section on Gambling in *Enterprise*. We have heard of a traveller who erected a sign on the pavements 'Jokes – 25 Cents Each'.

RADIO QUIZZES. British Forces Broadcasting Services (BFBS) hold plenty of competitions and are generous with prizes. Jane Harris entered the daily quiz in Hong Kong and won a HK$400 food and drink voucher for a bar in Wanchai. She recommends tuning in to BFBS elsewhere in the world like Cyprus or wherever British forces are stationed.

WINDSCREEN WASHING. Offering to wash windscreens while cars wait at red lights is by now an old chestnut. A variation heard of in Canada (in the summer presumably) is for women to increase their takings by doing this job topless.

MEDICAL RESEARCH. Teaching hospitals may have research clinics where new drugs and techniques are tested. Many research projects pay their volunteers very well, since in many cases they are funded by large pharmaceutical companies. Check the websites www.gpgp.net or www.centerwatch.com or simply enquire at hospitals and drug companies. A number of medical website addresses are currently seeking volunteers for more than 5,500 drug trials, though some are restricted to guinea pigs with certain conditions like asthma. You might also enquire at university psychology departments, where there may be a need for participants for perception tests, etc. No work permits necessary; only proof of human life.

SELLING BLOOD. Many countries pay blood and plasma donors handsomely, especially the USA and Middle East.

SPERM AND EGG DONATION. In many countries, fertility clinics pay (typically £20) for sperm samples. Usually there is a requirement to have been resident long enough for your blood to be tested. Ian Smith did this in Denmark and was told if his sperm proved amenable to freezing (which it wasn't) he could have donated up to three times a week to a maximum of 30 times. Egg donation is a much more serious business. Private fertility clinics in the US have been offering upwards of $2,500 for donated eggs which involves hormone treatment and surgery.

SELLING RETURN TICKETS. Ask a travel agent if it is possible to get a refund on the return part of your air or train ticket, then travel home by a cheaper method – perhaps by coach, or hitch-hiking.

SELLING BELONGINGS. By the end of your trip many of your belongings may have become expendable. You can try selling them to fellow travellers in hostels, to second-hand shops, or even to passing shoppers if you set yourself up on the edge of a market. Be ruthless about what you do and do not need: you have taken your photos, so you don't need your camera, and you can transfer your belongings from your expensive backpack to a cheaper bag. Be prepared to spend some time haggling.

THE LAST RESORT. Sell this book – but memorise the contents first! Better still, take a couple of spare copies as recommended by Kevin Boyd:

> *I have met so many other travellers who would have sold their mother into slavery for my copy of your book! You should recommend that people take as many copies as they can.*

Peter McGuire sold this book's sister publication *Teaching English Abroad* for 5,000 won (then $6) in Korea to a person who was offered 10,000 won. He made copies of the relevant chapters and doubled his money.

Appendix 1

Travellers' Itineraries

Jane Harris's Escape from Merseyside

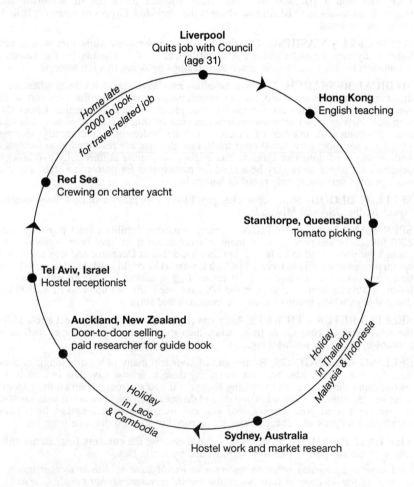

Liverpool
Quits job with Council
(age 31)

Home late 2000 to look for travel-related job

Hong Kong
English teaching

Red Sea
Crewing on charter yacht

Stanthorpe, Queensland
Tomato picking

Tel Aviv, Israel
Hostel receptionist

Auckland, New Zealand
Door-to-door selling,
paid researcher for guide book

Holiday in Thailand, Malaysia & Indonesia

Holiday in Laos & Cambodia

Sydney, Australia
Hostel work and market research

Bridgid Seymour-East's Trip

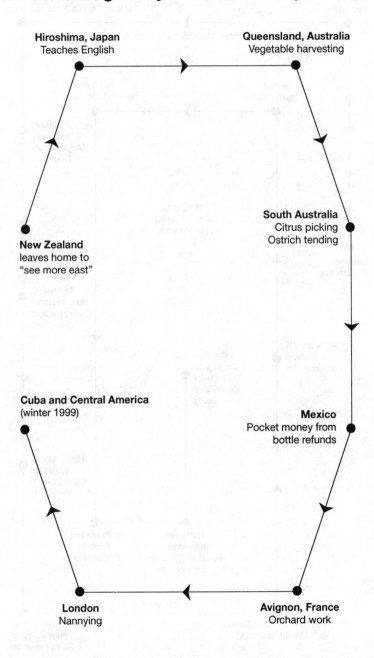

Hiroshima, Japan
Teaches English

Queensland, Australia
Vegetable harvesting

South Australia
Citrus picking
Ostrich tending

New Zealand
leaves home to
"see more east"

Cuba and Central America
(winter 1999)

Mexico
Pocket money from
bottle refunds

London
Nannying

Avignon, France
Orchard work

Robert Abblett's Wanderings

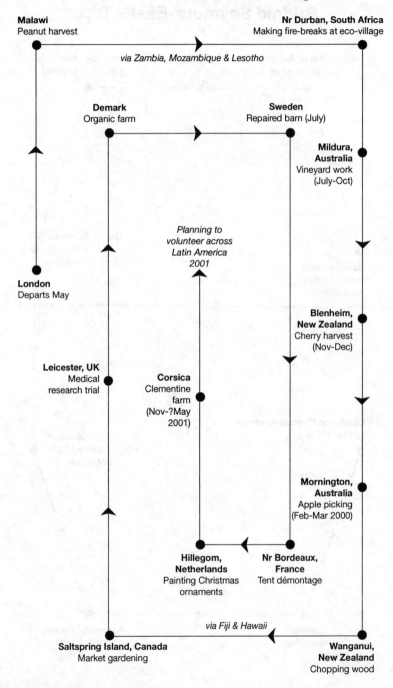

Malawi
Peanut harvest

Nr Durban, South Africa
Making fire-breaks at eco-village

via Zambia, Mozambique & Lesotho

Demark
Organic farm

Sweden
Repaired barn (July)

Mildura, Australia
Vineyard work
(July-Oct)

Planning to volunteer across Latin America 2001

London
Departs May

Blenheim, New Zealand
Cherry harvest
(Nov-Dec)

Leicester, UK
Medical research trial

Corsica
Clementine farm
(Nov-?May 2001)

Mornington, Australia
Apple picking
(Feb-Mar 2000)

Hillegom, Netherlands
Painting Christmas ornaments

Nr Bordeaux, France
Tent démontage

via Fiji & Hawaii

Saltspring Island, Canada
Market gardening

Wanganui, New Zealand
Chopping wood

Tony Forrester's Travels

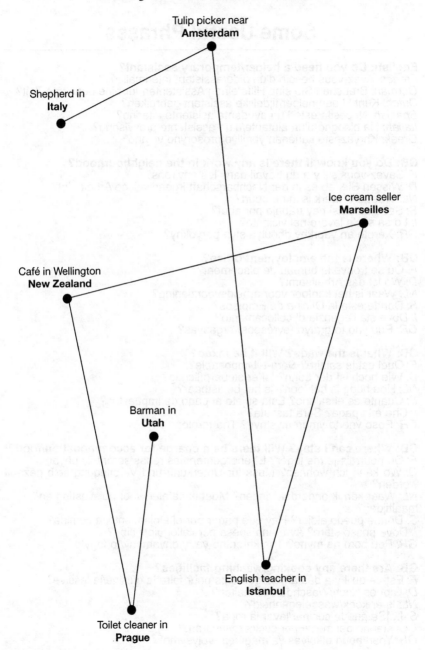

Tulip picker near **Amsterdam**

Shepherd in **Italy**

Ice cream seller **Marseilles**

Café in Wellington **New Zealand**

Barman in **Utah**

English teacher in **Istanbul**

Toilet cleaner in **Prague**

Some Useful Phrases

English: Do you need a helper/temporary assistant?
French: Avez-vous besoin d'un aide/assistant intérimaire?
German: Brauchen Sie eine Hilfe/einen Assistenten für eine begenzte Zeit?
Dutch: Kunt U een helper/tijdelijke assistent gebruiken?
Spanish: Necesita usted un ayudante/asistente interino?
Italian: Ha bisogno d'un aiutante/d'un assistente provvisorio?
Greek: Khryázeste kanénan ypálliyo/prosorynó voythó?

GB: Do you know if there is any work in the neighbourhood?
F: Savez-vous s'il y a du travail dans les environs?
D: Wissen Sie, ob es in der Nachbarschaft irgendwelche Arbeit gibt?
NL: Weet u of werk is in de buurt?
S: Sabe usted si hay trabajo por aquí?
I: Lo sa si c'e lavoro nel vicinato?
GR: Xérete an yaprkhy dhoulyá styn peryokhy?

GB: Where is the employment office?
F: Où se trouve le bureau de placement?
D: Wo ist das Arbeitsamt?
NL: Waar is het kantoor voor arbeidsvoorziening?
S: Donde esta la Oficina de Empleos?
I: Dove sta l'agenzia di collocamento?
GR: Poú yno to grafyo (evréseos) ergasyas?

GB: What is the wage? Will it be taxed?
F: Quel est le salaire? Sera-t-il imposable?
D: Wie hoch ist der Lohn? Ist er steuerpflichtig?
NL: Hoe hoog is het loon? Is het belastbaar?
S: Cuanto es el salario? Esta sujeto al pago de impuestos?
I: Che e la paga? Sara tassata?
GR: Poso yne to ymeromysthyo? Tha forologhiyhy?

GB: Where can I stay? Will there be a charge for accommodation/food?
F: Où pourrais-je me loger? L'hébergement/les repas seront-ils payants?
D: Wo kann ich wohnen? Muss für Unterkunft und Verpflegung selb gezahlt werden?
NL: Waar kan ik onderdak vinden? Moet ik betalen voor huisvesting en maaltijden?
S: Donde puedo alojar? Hay que pagar por el alojamiento/la comida?
I: Dove posso stare? Avra una spesa per l'alloggio/il cibo?
GR: Pou boró na myno? Tha khreothó ya ty dhyamony/to fagytó

GB: Are there any cooking/washing facilities?
F: Est-ce qu'il y a des aménagements pour faire la cuisine/la lessive?
D: Gibt es Koch/Waschgelegenheiten?
NL: Is er kook/wasgelegenheid?
S: [...]Se puede cocinar/lavar la ropa?
I: Ci stanno dei mezzi per cucinare/lavorare?
GR: Ypárkhoun efkolyes ya magyrema/plysymo?

GB: When will the harvest/job begin? How long will it last?
F: Quand commencera la moisson/le travail? Combien de temps dure-t'il?
D: Wann beginnt die Ernte/Arbeit? Wie lange wird sie dauern?
NL: Wanneer begint de oogst/job? Hoe lang zal het werk duren?
S: Cuando comenzara la cosecha/el trabajo? Cuanto durara?
I: Quando incomincia la messe/il lavoro? Per quanto tempo durera?
GR: Poté tharkhysy o theryzmos/y dhoulyá? Póso tha dhyarkésy?

GB: What will be the hours of work?
F: Quelles seront les heures de travail?
D: Wie lange ist die Arbeitszeit?
NL: Wat zijn de werkuren?
S: Cual sera el horario de trabajo
I: Che saranno le ore del lavoro?
GR: Pyéz tha yne y órez ergasyas?

GB: Thank you for your help.
F: Merci de votre aide.
D: Danke für Ihre Hilfe.
NL: Dank U voor Uw hulp.
S: Gracias por su ayuda.
GR: Sas efkharystó ya tyn vóythya sas.

Appendix 3

Currency Conversion Chart

COUNTRY	£1	US$1
Argentina	1.49 peso	1.0 peso
Australia	A$2.70	A$1.86
Austria	22.8 schilling	15.8 schilling
Belgium/Luxembourg	67 franc	46 franc
Brazil	2.67 real	1.85 real
Bulgaria	3.2 lev	2.2 lev
Canada	C$2.17	C$1.50
Chile	811 peso	560 peso
China	12 renminbi	8.3 renminbi
Cyprus	0.89 Cypriot pound	0.60 Cypriot pound
Czech Republic	59 koruna	40 koruna
Denmark	12.1 kroner	8.5 kroner
Ecuador	$1.49	$1.0
Egypt	5.3 Egyptian pound	3.6 Egyptian pound
Finland	9.9 markka	6.8 markka
France	10.9 franc	7.5 franc
Germany	3.2 DM	2.2 DM
Greece	565 drachma	390 drachma
Hong Kong	11.2 HK dollar	7.8 HK dollar
Hungary	436 forint	300 forint
India	69 rupee	46 rupee
Indonesia	12,750 rupiah	8,800 rupiah
Ireland	1.23 punt	0.83 punt
Israel	6.1 shekel	4.1 shekel
Italy	3,220 lira	2,225 lira
Japan	157 yen	108 yen
Kenya	114 shilling	79 shilling
Korea	1,616 won	1,117 won
Malta	0.66 Maltese lira	0.45 Maltese lira
Mexico	13.7 peso	9.5 peso
Morocco	15.9 dirham	11 dirham
Nepal	106 rupee	74 rupee
Netherlands	3.6 guilder	2.5 guilder
New Zealand	NZ$3.31	NZ$2.24
Norway	12.6 krone	9.2 krone
Peru	5 new sol	3.5 new sol
Poland	6.6 zloty	4.5 zloty
Portugal	335 escudo	230 escudo
Russia (market rate)	40.4 rouble	28 rouble
Saudi Arabia	5.4 riyal	3.75 riyal
Singapore	2.5 Singapore dollar	1.75 Singapore dollar
Slovakia	73 koruna	50 koruna
Slovenia	348 tolar	241 tolar
South Africa	11.6 rand	7.8 rand
Spain	276 peseta	191 peseta
Sweden	14.2 krona	9.8 krona
Switzerland	2.5 franc	1.75 franc
Taiwan	45 Taiwan dollar	31 Taiwan dollar
Thailand	61 baht	42 baht
Turkey	970,000 lira	675,000 lira
United Kingdom	1 pound	67 pence
USA	1.49 dollar	–

*Current exchange rates are available on the internet, for example the Universal Currency Converter can be found at www.xe.net/ucc.

Appendix 4

Embassies/Consulates in London and Washington

AUSTRALIA: Australia House, The Strand, London WC2B 4LA. Tel: 020-7379 4334/0891 600333.
1601 Massachusetts Ave NW, Washington DC 20036-2273. Tel: (202) 797-3000/3145; www.austemb.org.
AUSTRIA: 18 Belgrave Mews West, London SW1X 8HU. Tel: 020-7235 3731; www.bmaa.gv.at/embassy/uk.
3524 International Court NW, Washington DC 20008-3035. Tel: (202) 895-6700.
BELGIUM: 103 Eaton Square, London SW1W 9AB. Tel: 020-7470 3700/0891-660255; www.belgium-embassy.co.uk.
3330 Garfield St NW, Washington DC 20008. Tel: (202) 333-6900; www.diplobel.org.
BRAZIL: Consular Section, 6 St. Alban's St, London SW1Y 4SG. Tel: 020-7930 9055; www.brazil.org.uk.
3006 Massachusetts Ave NW, Washington, DC 20008. Tel: (202) 238-2700; www.brasilemb.org.
BULGARIA: 186-188 Queen's Gate, London SW7 5HL (020-7584 9400/0891 171208).
1621 22nd St NW, Washington, DC 20008. Tel: (202) 387-7969; www.bulgaria-embassy.org.
CANADA: 38 Grosvenor St, London W1X 0AA (020-7258 6600). 501 Pennsylvania Ave NW, Washington, DC 20001. Tel: (202) 682-1740; www.cdnemb-washdc.org).
CHILE: 12 Devonshire St, London W1N 2DS. Tel: 020-7580 1023; e-mail: cglonguk@congechileuk.demon.co.uk.
1732 Massachusetts Ave NW, Washington DC 20036. Tel: (202) 785-1746.
CHINA: Visa Section, 31 Portland Place, London W1N 3AG. Tel: 020-7631 1430; www.chinese-embassy.org.uk.
2300 Connecticut Ave NW, Washington DC 200078. Tel: (202) 328-2500; www.china-embassy.org.
COLOMBIA: Suite 14, 140 Park Lane, London W1Y 3DF. Tel: 020-495 4233.
1875 Connecticut Avenue NW, Suite 524, Washington, DC 20008. Tel: (202) 332-7476; www.colombiaemb.org.
CROATIA: 21 Conway Street, London W1P 5HL. Tel: 020-7387 0022.
2343 Massachusetts Ave NW, Washington DC 20008. Tel: (202) 588-5889; www.croatiaemb.org.
CZECH REPUBLIC: 26-30 Kensington Palace Gardens, London W8 4QY. Tel: 020-7243 1115.
3900 Spring of Freedom St NW, Washington DC 20008. Tel: (202) 274-9100; www.czech.cz/washington.
ECUADOR: Flat 3b, 3 Hans Crescent, Knightsbridge, London SW1X 0LS. Tel: 020-7584 8084.
2535 15th St NW, Washington, DC 20009. Tel: (202) 234-7200; www.ecuador.org.
EGYPT: 2 Lowndes St, London SW1X 9ET. Tel: 020-7235 9777; www.egypt-embassy.org.uk.
3521 International Court NW, Washington DC 20008. Tel: (202) 966-6342.
FINLAND: 38 Chesham Place, London SW1X 8HW. Tel: 020-7838 6200; www.finemb.org.
3301 Massachusetts Ave NW, Washington DC 20008. Tel: (202) 298-5800; www.finland.org.
FRANCE: 21 Cromwell Road, London SW7 2EN. Tel: 020-7838 2000; www.ambafrance.org.uk.
4101 Reservoir Road NW, Washington DC 20007. Tel: (202) 944-6200/6215; www.info-france-usa.org.
GERMANY: 23 Belgrave Square, London SW1X 8PZ. Tel: 020-7824 1300/0906-833 1166; www.german-embassy.org.uk.
4645 Reservoir Road NW, Washington DC 20007-1998. Tel: (202) 298-4000; www.germany-info.org.

GREECE: 1A Holland Park, London W11 3TP. Tel: 020-7221 6467.
2221 Massachusetts Ave NW, Washington DC 20008. Tel: (202) 939-5818; www.greekembassy.org.
HUNGARY: 35b Eaton Place, London SW1X 8BY. Tel: 020-7235 2664/09001-171 204; http://dspace.dial.pipex.com/huemblon.
3910 Shoemaker St NW, Washington DC 20008. Tel: (202) 362-6730; www.hungaryemb.org.
INDIA: India House, Aldwych, London WC2B 4NA. Tel: 020-7836 8484; www.hcilondon.org.
2107 Massachusetts Avenue NW, Washington, DC 20008. Tel: (202) 939-7000; www.indianembassy.org.
INDONESIA: 38 Grosvenor Square, London W1X 9AD. Tel: 020-7499 7661; www.indonesia.org.uk.
2020 Massachusetts Ave NW, Washington DC 20036. Tel: (202) 775-5200; http://kbri.org.
ITALY: 38 Eaton Place, London SW1X 8AN. Tel: 020-7235 9371; www.ambitalia.org.uk.
1601 Fuller St NW, Washington DC 20009. Tel: (202) 328-5500; www.italyemb.org.
JAPAN: 101-104 Piccadilly, London W1V 9FN. Tel: 020-7465 6500; www.embjapan.org.uk.
2520 Massachusetts Ave NW, Washington DC 20008. Tel: (202) 939-6700; www.embjapan.org.
KOREA: 60 Buckingham Gate, London SW1E 6AJ. Tel: 020-7227 5505.
2450 Massachusetts Ave NW, Washington, DC 20008. Tel: (202) 939-5600; www.koreaemb.org.
LAOS: 74 Avenue Raymond Poincare, 75116 Paris, France. Tel: 1-45 53 02 98.
2222 S St NW, Washington, DC 20008. Tel: (202) 332-6416/7.
LATVIA: 45 Nottingham Place, London W1M 3FE. Tel: 020-7312 0040.
4325 17th St NW, Washington, DC 20011. Tel: (202) 726-8213; www.latvia-usa.org.
LITHUANIA: 84 Gloucester Place, London W1H 3HN. Tel: 020-7486 6404; www.users.globalnet.co.uk/~lralon.
2622 16th St NW, Washington, DC 20009-4202. Tel: (202) 234-5860; www.ltembassyus.org.
MALAYSIA: 45 Belgrave Square, London SW1X 8QT. Tel: 020-7235 8033.
2401 Massachusetts Ave NW, Washington DC 20008. Tel: (202) 328-2700.
MALTA: Malta House, 36-38 Piccadilly, London W1V 0PQ. Tel: 020-7292 4800.
2017 Connecticut Ave NW, Washington, DC 20008. Tel: (202) 462-3611.
MEXICO: 8 Halkin St, London SW1X 7DW. Tel: 020-7235 6393; www.mexicanconsulate.org.uk.
1911 Pennsylvania Ave NW, Washington, DC 20006. Tel: (202) 728-1600; www.embassyofmexico.org.
MOROCCO: 49 Queen's Gate Gardens, London SW7 5NE. Tel: 020-7581 5001.
1601 21st St NW, Washington DC 20009. Tel: (202) 462-7979.
NETHERLANDS: 38 Hyde Park Gate, London SW7 5DP. Tel: 020-7590 3200/09001-171 217; www.netherlands-embassy.org.uk.
4200 Linnean Ave NW, Washington DC 20008. Tel: (202) 244-5300; www.netherlands-embassy.org.
NEW ZEALAND: New Zealand House, Haymarket, London SW1Y 4TE. Tel: 0906 9100 100 (£1 a minute)
37 Observatory Circle NW, Washington DC 20008. Tel: (202) 328-4800; www.emb.com/nzemb.
PERU: 52 Sloane St, London SW1X 9SP. Tel: 020-7838 9223; http://homepages.which.net/~peru-embassy-uk.
1700 Massachusetts Ave NW, Washington DC 20036. Tel: (202) 833-9860; www.peruemb.org.
POLAND: 73 New Cavendish St, London W1N 4HQ. Tel: 020-7580 0476; www.poland-embassy.org.uk.
2640 16th St NW, Washington, DC 20009. Tel: (202) 234-3800; www.polishworld.com/polemb.
PORTUGAL: Silver City House, 62 Brompton Road, London SW3 1BJ. Tel: 020-7581 8722; www.portembassy.gla.ac.uk.
2125 Kalorama Road NW, Washington DC 20008. Tel: (202) 328-8610; www.portugalemb.org.
ROMANIA: Arundel House, 4 Palace Green, London W8 4QD. Tel: 020-7937 8125.
1607 23rd St NW, Washington, DC 20008. Tel: (202) 328-8610; www.roembus.org.

RUSSIAN FEDERATION: 5 Kensington Palace Gardens, London W8 4QS. Tel: 020-7229 8027; www.russialink.couk.com.
2650 Wisconsin Ave NW, Washington, DC 20007. Tel: (202) 298-5700; www.russianembassy.org.
SAUDI ARABIA: 30 Charles St, London W1X 7PM. Tel: 020-7917 3000; www.saudiembassy.org.uk.
601 New Hampshire Ave NW, Washington DC 20037. Tel: (202) 337-4076; www.saudiembassy.net.
SINGAPORE: 5 Chesham St, London SW1X 8ND. Tel: 020-7245 0273.
3501 International Place NW, Washington, DC 20008. Tel: (202) 537-3100; www.gov.sg/mfa/washington.
SLOVAK REPUBLIC: 25 Kensington Palace Gardens, London W8 4QY. Tel: 020-7243 0803; www.slovakembassy.co.uk
2201 Wisconsin Ave NW, Suite 250, Washington, DC 20007. Tel: (202) 965-5160;www.slovakemb.com.
SLOVENIA: Cavendish Court, 11-15 Wigmore St, London W1H 9LA. Tel: 020-7495 7775; www.embassy-slovenia.org.uk.
1525 New Hampshire Ave NW, Washington, DC 20036. Tel: (202) 667-5363; www.embassy.org/slovenia.
SPAIN: 20 Draycott Place, London SW3 2RZ. Tel: 020-7589 8989.
2375 Pennsylvania Ave NW, Washington, DC 20037. Tel: (202) 452-0100; www.spainemb.org/information.
SUDAN: 3 Cleveland Row, St. James's, London SW1A 1DD. Tel: 020-7839 8080.
2210 Massachusetts Ave NW, Washington DC 20008. Tel: (202) 338-8565; www.sudanembassyus.org.
SWEDEN: 11 Montagu Place, London W1H 2AL. Tel: 020-7724 2101; www.swednet.org.uk/sweden.
1501 M St NW, Washington, DC 20005. Tel: (202) 467-2600; www.swedemb.org.
SWITZERLAND: 16/18 Montagu Place, London W1H 2BQ. Tel: 020-7616 6000/0891-331 313; www.swissembassy.org.uk.
2900 Cathedral Ave NW, Washington DC 20008. Tel: (202) 745-7900; www.swissemb.org.
TAIWAN: Taipei Representative Office, 50 Grosvenor Gardens, London SW1W 0EB. Tel: 020-7396 9152/0891-300 615; www.tro.taiwan.roc.org.uk.
CCNAA/Co-ordination Council for North American Affairs, 4201 Wisconsin Ave NW, Washington DC 20016. Tel: (202) 895-1800.
THAILAND: 29/30 Queen's Gate, London SW7 5JB. Tel: 020-7589 2944.
1024 Wisconsin Ave NW, Suite 401, Washington DC 20007. Tel: (202) 944-3600; www.thaiembdc.org.
TURKEY: Rutland Lodge, Rutland Gardens, London SW7 1BW. Tel: 020-7589 0949/0891-347 348; www.turkconsulate-london.com.
2525 Massachusetts Ave NW, Washington DC 20036. Tel: (202) 659-8200; www.turkey.org/turkey.
UKRAINE: 78 Kensington Park Road, London W11 2PL. Tel: 020-7243 8923/09001 887 749.
3350 M St NW, Washington, DC 20007. Tel: (202) 333-7507; www.ukremb.com.
USA: 5 Upper Grosvenor St, London W1A 2JB (020-7499 6846/0891 200290).
VENEZUELA: 56 Grafton Way, London W1P 5LB. Tel: 020-7387 6727; www.venezlon.demon.co.uk.
1099 30th St NW, Washington, DC 20007. Tel: (202) 342-2214; www.embavenez-us.org.
VIETNAM: 12-14 Victoria Road, London W8. Tel: 020-7937 1912.
1233 20th St NW, Suite 400, Washington, DC 20037. Tel: (202) 861-0737; www.vietnamembassy-usa.org.
ZIMBABWE: 429 Strand, London WC2R 0SA. Tel: 020-7836 7755.
1608 New Hampshire Ave NW, Washington DC 20009. Tel: (202) 332-7100; www.zimweb.com/Embassy/Zimbabwe.

For the names of the relevant personnel in the UK, e.g. the Education Attaché, see *The London Diplomatic List* published frequently by the Foreign & Commonwealth Office and held in most libraries. Check the internet on www.embassyworld.com and www.embassy.org.

Appendix 5

Key Organisations

Agriventure, IAEA, Young Farmers' Club Centre, National Agricultural Centre, Stoneleigh Park, Kenilworth, Warwickshire CV8 2LG (02476 696578/fax 02476 696684; uk@agriventure.com/ www.agriventure.com).

British Council, Information Centre, Bridgewater House, 58 Whitworth St, Manchester M1 6BB (0161-957 7755/fax 0161-957 7762; www.britcoun.org/english). Distributes information pack 'How to Become a Teacher of English as a Foreign Language'.

British Trust for Conservation Volunteers, 36 St. Mary's St, Wallingford, Oxfordshire OX10 0EU (01491 839766/fax 01491 839646; international@btcv.org.uk/ www.btcv.org.uk).

British Universities North America Club (BUNAC), 16 Bowling Green Lane, London EC1R 0QH (020-7251 3472/fax 020-7251 0215; enquiries@bunac.org.uk/ www.bunac.org.uk).

Camp America, 37a Queen's Gate, London SW7 5HR (020-7581 7373/fax 020-7581 7377; enquiries@campamerica.co.uk/ www.campamerica.co.uk).

Central Bureau for International Education & Training, 10 Spring Gardens, London SW1A 2BN (020-7389 4004/fax 020-7389 4426; www.britishcouncil.org/cbiet). Also 3 Bruntsfield Crescent, Edinburgh EH10 4HD (0131-447 8024) and 7 Fountain St, Belfast BT1 5EG (028-9024 8220).

Concordia International Volunteer Projects, Heversham House, 20-22 Boundary Road, Hove, East Sussex BN3 4ET (tel/fax 01273 422218; info@concordia-iye.org.uk/ www.concordia-iye.org.uk).

Council Exchanges, 20th Floor, 633 Third Ave, New York, NY 10017, USA (1-888-COUNCIL; info@councilexchanges.org/ www.councilexchanges.org).

Council Exchanges UK, 52 Poland St, London W1V 4JQ (020-7478 2000/fax 020-7734 7322; info@councilexchanges.org.uk/ www.councilexchanges.org.uk).

GAP Activity Projects (GAP) Ltd, 44 Queen's Road, Reading RG1 4BB (0118-959 4914/fax 0118-957 6634; volunteer@gap.org.uk/ www.gap.org.uk).

InterExchange Inc, 161 Sixth Avenue, New York, NY 10013, USA (212-924-0446/fax 212-924-0575; info@interexchange.org/ www.interexchange.org).

International Association for the Exchange of Students for Technical Experience (IAESTE-UK), 10 Spring Gardens, London SW1A 2BN (020-7389 4774; iaeste@britishcouncil.org/ www.iaeste.org.uk). Counterpart of Association for International Practical Training (AIPT) in the US: 10400 Little Patuxent Parkway, Suite 250, Columbia, MD 21044-3510 (410-997-3068; aipt@aipt.org/ www.aipt.org).

International House, 106 Piccadilly, London W1 9FL (020-7518 6970/1; info@ihlondon.co.uk/ www.ihlondon.com).

International Voluntary Service (IVS), Old Hall, East Bergholt, Colchester, Essex CO7 6TQ (01206 298215/fax 01206 299043; ivsgbn@ivsgbn.demon.co.uk/ www.ivsgbn.demon. co.uk) with branch offices in Northern England (Castlehill House, 21 Otley Road, Leeds LS6 3AA; 0113-230 4600/fax 0113-230 4610) and Scotland (7 Upper Bow, Edinburgh EH1 2JN; 0131-226 6722/fax 0131-226 6723). US branch of Service Civil International: 814 NE 40th St, Seattle, WA 98105 (scitalk@sci-ivs.org/ www.sci-ivs.org).

Jobs in the Alps, 17 High St, Gretton, Northamptonshire NN17 3DE (01536 771150; enquiries@jobs-in-the-alps.com/ www.jobs-in-the-alps.com).

Kibbutz Representatives, 1A Accommodation Road, London NW11 8ED (020-8458 9235/fax 020-8455 7930; enquiries@kibbutz.org.uk/ www.kibbutz.org.il).

Peterson's Guides, 2000 Lenox Drive, Lawrenceville, NJ 08648-4764, USA; www.petersons.com).

STA Travel, 86 Old Brompton Road, London SW7 3LQ plus 250 branches throughout the UK and worldwide (0870 1606070 or 020-7361 6161 for Europe and 020-7361 6262 longhaul; www.statravel.co.uk).

Trailfinders, 194 Kensington High St, London W8 7RG (020-7938 3939 longhaul and 020-7937 5400 for Europe and transatlantic).

usit-Campus, 52 Grosvenor Gardens, London SW1W 0AG (0870 240 1010; www.usitcampus.co.uk). Branches in many other UK cities.

Vacation Work Publications, 9 Park End St, Oxford OX1 1HJ (01865 241978/fax 01865 790885; www.vacationwork.co.uk).

WWOOF UK (Willing Workers on Organic Farms), PO Box 2675, Lewes, Sussex BN7 1RB (www.wwoof.org).

Youth Hostels Association, Trevelyan House, 8 St Stephen's Hill, St. Albans, Herts AL1 2DY (0870 870 8808/fax 01727 844126; customerservices@yha.org.uk/ www.yha.org.uk).

Readers' Comments on the Last Edition

Dan Boothby who tutored English in Cairo: *Work Your Way Around the World was a great book for me when I was 17-20. Even if I didn't get to circle the globe the ideas and encouragement it gave me were very big.*

John Buckley, owner of a printing business in Blackpool: *Having travelled the world since the mid-80s, I never seriously considered working abroad until I bought your book last year ... so when I was in Brazil for Christmas & New Year, I thought I would go to the local English school. Before I knew it I was teaching English. The class got bigger and bigger just because I was there – what a buzz. It was fantastic and I have found my vocation in life! Thanks for the book. If it was not around, this great opportunity and wonderful people would have passed me by.*

Jaime Burnell from Berkshire: *Keep it up. You are a goddess among authors and we'd all be lost without you.*

Tony Forrester (Englishman writing from Utah): *Thanks for such a great book. You inspired me to get away from 9 to 5 drudgery back in 1988 and I've been adventuring ever since. My travels (and labours) have taken me to all five continents and it all started with Work Your Way. I have picked every kind of fruit you can imagine, been a shepherd in Italy, picked tulips from the Dam, taught English in Istanbul, sold ice cream in Wellington and Marseille, cleaned toilets in Prague (not fun!) and been a barman all over.*

Emma Hoare (gap year student before going to Oxford): *I just had to write and thank you. In the local careers advisory centre I was sat down with a pile of leaflets dealing with gap years. Every single one of these dealt with either a structured voluntary course abroad or how to arrange work experience. 'On the road' it wasn't. Then – portentous roll of thunder, sudden bright light – one of the receptionists gave me a book that had just come in. No exaggeration, I promise you. I sat there and read your book until they closed the centre. Then I went straight to Waterstones and bought a copy. Then I went home and wrote to York University declining my place... As you can probably surmise from the gushing tone of this letter, I had an amazing time. I crewed on a yacht, helped with haymaking, went to a sheep-shearers' reunion, did a 12,000ft skydive, saw sperm whales, etc. So thank you. You didn't know me before I went away, and you don't know me now, but I can assure you the transformation is nothing short of miraculous. I hope that one day I'll write a book that is so inspirational and entertaining.*

Amy Ignatow from New York: *Your book is wonderful. It gave me the idea to sell my art on the streets of Jerusalem and look what came of it. I'll write again if Bob and I get married.*

Aaron Lenhart, American volunteer at Simon Community in London: *It is largely due to your book that I am here now and so far it's been a unique and very positive experience, so thank you very much.*

Steve Mardall from Sussex: *Before I leap into some queries, may I first commend you on the book. I find it extremely inspiring, useful and friendly in tone. Inspired by your book, in November I leave for my first round the world trip (aged 31).*

Alena Sestakova (Pilsen, Czech Republic): *I have read your book maybe 100 times.*

Darren Slevin (Irishman writing from northwest Germany where he was working in a tree nursery): *I bought your book in a bookstore in The Hague while working in a bulb factory. It's a brilliant book. I didn't think it was possible to work your way around the world, but after reading your book, I've decided to do it myself. Thank you for the inspiration.*

Julee Wylde from Canada: *I want to say the biggest thank you for all the inspiration. If I needed to blame someone for my travel addiction it would be you! I would like to tell you how much this book means to me, how it has guided me, how I've praised it to so many travellers I've met (I lent it out so many times I really should have charged people – hey another idea) and how it is just an excellent publication.*